LE CORBUSIER, HOMME DE LETTRES

M. Christine Boyer

Princeton Architectural Press

Published by
Princeton Architectural Press
37 East Seventh Street
New York, New York 10003

For a free catalog of books, call 1.800.722.6657.
Visit our website at www.papress.com.

Printed and bound in China
14 13 12 11 4 3 2 1 First edition

Editor: Becca Casbon
Designer: Deb Wood and Bree Anne Apperley

Special thanks to: Sara Bader, Nicola Brower, Janet Behning, Carina Cha, Tom Cho, Penny (Yuen Pik) Chu, Russell Fernandez, Pete Fitzpatrick, Jan Haux, Linda Lee, Laurie Manfra, John Myers, Katharine Myers, Dan Simon, Andrew Stepanian, Jennifer Thompson, Paul Wagner, and Joseph Weston of Princeton Architectural Press
–Kevin C. Lippert, publisher

Library of Congress Cataloging-in-Publication Data

Boyer, M. Christine.
Le Corbusier : homme de lettres / M. Christine Boyer.–1st ed.
p. cm.
Includes index.
ISBN 978-1-56898-973-0 (hc.)
ISBN 978-1-56898-980-8 (pbk.)
1. Le Corbusier, 1887-1965--Criticism and interpretation. 2. Le Corbusier, 1887–1965–Written works. 3. City planning. I. Le Corbusier, 1887–1965. II. Title.
NA1053.J4B69 2010
720.92–dc22
2010004855

CONTENTS

5 .... PREFACE

9 .... LIST OF ILLUSTRATIONS

19 .... CHAPTER 1: Le Corbusier: The Writings of an Architect

49 .... **PART 1:** *Finding a Path that Led to Paris (1907–17)*

51 .... CHAPTER 2: Searching for a Method (1907–1912)

109 .... CHAPTER 3: An Encounter on the Acropolis (1910–1914, 1965)

155 .... CHAPTER 4: The Many Paths to Paris (1910–17)

217 .... **PART 2:** *Life Among the Avant-Garde: L'Esprit Nouveau (1917–25)*

219 .... CHAPTER 5: Forging a Synthesis of Art and Industry: Letters to William Ritter (1917–25)

261 .... CHAPTER 6: A Method for the Arts of Today: Purism, Après le Cubisme, and L'Esprit Nouveau

299 .... CHAPTER 7: The Language of Architecture

375 .... **PART 3:** *To Solve the Equation "Reason = Passion" (1929–40s)*

377 .... CHAPTER 8: Controversy and Poetry, 1929 and Beyond

433 .... CHAPTER 9: Travels to the Americas

487 .... **PART 4:** *The Second Machine Age of the Temps Nouveaux (1930–47)*

489 .... CHAPTER 10: The Janus-Faced Thirties

553 .... CHAPTER 11: Algiers and the Mediterranean Atlas

605 .... CHAPTER 12: Elements of a Secular Faith: Daydreams, Authority, and the View from Above

677 .... EPILOGUE: A Book = A Box of Miracles

687 .... COLOR PLATES

703 .... NOTES

759 .... INDEX

PREFACE M. Christine Boyer

This book on the writings of Le Corbusier began simply enough with a decision taken in 1993 to rewrite an earlier book, *Dreaming the Rational City,* with primary materials drawn from the writings of architects. After visits to the archives of Frank Lloyd Wright, Norman Bel Geddes, and Le Corbusier, it was obvious that these three men wrote copiously about the condition of cities in the twentieth century and about remedies for their improvement. To explore within one volume all of their literary endeavors, how they did things with words, suddenly became an immense task. Thus the project was narrowed to focus on Le Corbusier. The result has been a long journey into Le Corbusier's prolific outpouring of books, articles, interviews, and letters written between 1907 and 1947. His post–World War II literary creativity and treatment of books published and unpublished as artistic artifacts await a separate study.

This book could not have been written without the guidance of numerous scholars who have studied Le Corbusier and his architectural and linguistic expressions. In particular, the writings of Geoffrey H. Baker, H. Allen Brooks, Mary McLeod, and Stanislaus von Moos have been wonderful instructors who have traced out a path before me. Appreciation also goes to the late Lloyd Rodwin not only for helping to select the title of this book, *Le Corbusier, Homme de Lettres,* but for guiding my initial explorations into language and city planning many years ago at MIT.

There are times that this book takes on a biographical nature as Charles-Édouard Jeanneret/Le Corbusier struggled to write, yielding to emotions that surrounded his attempts. Until Jeanneret began to sign his letters as "Le Corbusier" in the mid-1920s, and explainshis reason for doing so, this book retains the prior appellation. Particular attention has been given to letters Jeanneret wrote to two of his mentors:

Charles L'Eplattenier and William Ritter. The first set of letters expresses not only a methodology for looking at art, architecture, and urban form, but contains several metaphors such as the "life of a tree," "a page has turned," "capital accumulated," or the "desert of Paris" that remain important motifs in Le Corbusier's writings across his lifetime. His letters to William Ritter are complicated: many are exercises in creative writing reflecting a fanciful imagination as he learns how to transform thoughts into words; others are journal entries expressing his love of painting and music, and his desire to follow his destiny no matter what obstacles lay in his path. It is noteworthy that his letters to Ritter seldom contain specific references to his architectural and urban projects, but are instead confessions about his state of mind as a traveler, a young educator isolated in La Chaux-de-Fonds, or a combatant reminding his adversaries that "he has gone to the Acropolis." In the pages that follow, when a book has been translated into English, such as Ivan Žaknić's translation of *Voyage d'Orient,* all quotations are taken from the translation, and the English title *Travel to the East* is used in the text. In Jeanneret's/Le Corbusier's outpourings, especially in his letter-writing, a separate problem presented itself: how to synthesize his message and avoid lengthy quotations containing repetitious and extraneous materials that do not focus on his treatment of the language of architecture and urbanism. Paraphrasing, staying as close to the original words used, accompanied with sporadic quotations, was the decision.

Since research for *Le Corbusier, Homme de Lettres* began at the Fondation Le Corbusier during the summer of 1993, the manner of referencing original documents has changed. Materials were originally assembled in boxes containing roughly connected materials. Thus CIAM 4-Athènes-1933 is referenced FLC D2 (4) Doc.1 or Doc. 2. After documents were transformed into computer files, a separate enumeration was created. A letter to William Ritter, for example, is referenced FLC R3-18-274, Paris, 26 May 1913. Some of the letters have been misdated, and wherever possible a correction has been made. It is assumed that the letters assembled are complete, although this assumption is made only to avoid interjecting repetitious commentary about "supposedly the next letter, etc." Finally there is confusion over dates in both secondary and primary material. Different authors attribute different dates to when Le Corbusier arrived in Paris to take up permanent residency, or the date when he met Ritter or Amédée Ozenfant, and so on. The endnotes carry commentary about these disagreements. There is confusion as well in the primary materials: Le Corbusier often references his 1911 trip to the

East as occurring in 1910 in later writings; or he mentions in the 1930s that his research into modern architecture has been in progress for the last ten years, or twenty years, or thirty years, making it unclear what starting date he is referencing; and he mentions that one hundred years of the first machine age has ended, offering contradictory dates for its advent. In this case, 1830–1930 has been selected as the period the first machine age covered.

There have been numerous grants supporting this work from the National Endowment of the Humanities and from Princeton University, enabling lengthy stays in Paris to examine the archives in the Fondation Le Corbusier. Special thanks goes to Stephane Potelle, who not only pointed out relevant material in the archives, but later helped me translate some of Le Corbusier's letters to L'Eplattenier and Ritter; and especially for the many conversations we held about how to interpret the fuller meaning and context of Le Corbusier's words. The initial manuscript was assembled during a year's leave of absence from Princeton University's School of Architecture in 2004–5. During six months of this leave, in the spring of 2005, the Delft School of Design, Technical University Delft offered me a position as a visiting research professor. Delft proved to be a perfect place to write, with sufficient contact with PhD students and colleagues to sustain long days of writing. There is heartfelt appreciation for all the students at Princeton and at Delft, as well as various audiences in conferences from Philadelphia to Vienna, who have heard lectures on materials that form parts of this book. I owe many thanks to Caroline Maniaque Benton, Tim Benton, William Menking, and Joan Ockman for their support.

Especially I must thank Larry Clifford Gilman for his thoughtful and careful editing and the Publication Fund of the Department of Art and Archaeology, Princeton University, for their support.

–New York, November 2009

LIST OF ILLUSTRATIONS

Unless otherwise noted, all publications are by Charles-Édouard Jeanneret/Le Corbusier. Charles-Édouard Jeanneret adopted the pseudonym "Le Corbusier" in 1921 for articles he wrote for the journal *L'Esprit Nouveau*. He continued to use both names well into the 1920s, finally declaring in 1930 that henceforth he would use the name Le Corbusier because he was famous under that name. The name Charles-Édouard would be reserved for his identity card and for the police.

Part 1: Photograph of Charles-Édouard Jeanneret in 1910. FLC L4 (1) 3.
Part 2: Photograph of Le Corbusier (1920–1930). FLC L4 (1) 9.
Part 3: Photograph of Le Corbusier circa 1929. FLC L5 (2) 21.
Part 4: Photograph of Le Corbusier from 1935. FLC L4 (1) 46.

CHAPTER 1:

Figure 1.1: A list of books written by Le Corbusier between 1922–37, reproduced with photographs of their dust jackets above and commentary below. *Oeuvre Complète*, vol. 4 (1939; repr., Zurich: Les Éditions d'Architecture, 1964), 200.
Figure 1.2: Sketches by Jeanneret of Notre Dame from 1908. FLC 1908 B2 (20) 215.
Figure 1.3: Le Corbusier's identity card. FLC R3(13)86.
Figure 1.4: Sketch of a nude reading a book by Le Corbusier, from 1932. Carnet B6 371.
Figure 1.5: Letter from Paul Valèry to Le Corbusier. *The Decorative Arts of Today* (Cambridge, MA: MIT Press, 1987).
Figure 1.6: Sketch of a podium and some of Le Corbusier's scribbling, used to illustrate lectures given in South America in 1929. *Precisions*, trans. Edith Schreiber Aujame (1930; repr., Cambridge, MA: MIT Press, 1991), 19.
Figures 1.7 and 1.8: Two note cards from a lecture given at the Museum of Modern Art in New York City on October 24, 1935. FLC C 3 (17) 8 and FLC C3 (17) 9.
Figures 1.9 and 1.10: Two pages of sketches from *Precisions* (1930) reveal Le Corbusier's annoyance at the academies' rejection of modern architecture and urbanism. *Precisions*, 175 and 177.
Figure 1.11: An ideogram of a book opened to a page inscribed with "doctrine [of] L-C," used to announce books that presented Le Corbusier's evolving doctrine of urbanism. FLC A3-9-6.
Figure 1.12: Signature of ChE Jeanneret, signed on an envelope in 1910.
Figure 1.13: Signature of Le Corbusier, on the bottom of the cover of *The Decorative Arts of Today*.
Figure 1.14: Illustration of a donkey and a raven from a letter written from Chandigarh in 1952 to Siegfried Giedion. *Le Corbusier, Maler Og Arkiteckt* (Copenhagen: Fonden til udgivelse af Arkitekturtidsskrift B, 1995), 21.

CHAPTER 2

Figure 2.1: Seven sketches by Charles-Édouard Jeanneret of details of the Cathedral of Pisa's facade. FLC 5837.
Figure 2.2: Plan and cross section by Charles-Édouard Jeanneret of a monk's cell at the

monastery he called "Chartreuse d'Ema." (Lost original) Jean Petit, *Le Corbusier lui-même* (Geneva: Éditions Rousseau), 43.

Figure 2.3 Watercolor sketch by Charles-Édouard Jeanneret of plan and section of the Moorish Rooms at the Museum of Decorative Art, Vienna, from 1908. FLC 2082.

Figure 2.4: Charles-Édouard Jeanneret photographed in front of a window at 9 rue des Écoles in Paris from May, 1909. FLC L4 (1) 7.

CHAPTER 3

Figure 3.1: Photograph of Charles-Édouard Jeanneret standing at the foot of the Parthenon on the Acropolis, Athens, 1911. FLC L4-19 67.

Figure 3.2: Map drawn by Charles-Édouard Jeanneret of his voyage to the East. *Voyage to the East*, trans. Ivan Žaknić (Cambridge, MA: MIT Press, 1987), 3.

Figure 3.3: Illustration from a letter written by Charles-Édouard Jeanneret to William Ritter on May 2, 1911, while traveling down the Rhine from Mayence (Mainz) to Cologne. Bibliothèque Nationale Suisse, BN Box 357 8.5.1911 16, 1–2.

Figures 3.4 and 3.5: Series of sketches by Charles-Édouard Jeanneret from *Carnets de Voyage d'Orient* (1911), republished in the first volume of Le Corbusier's *Oeuvre Complète.*

Figures 3.6 and 3.7: Charles-Édouard Jeanneret's photographs of Serbian houses, taken on his voyage to the East in 1911. FLC L5 (1) 101 and FLC L5 (1) 112.

Figure 3.8: Charles-Édouard Jeanneret's Cupido 80 camera captured the dress and manners of Balkan women in 1911. FLC L5(1) 12.

Figure 3.9: A panoramic view of Constantinople by Charles-Édouard Jeanneret, from 1911. FLC L4 (19) 197.

Figure 3.10: Charles-Édouard Jeanneret sketched and photographed different cemeteries when he traveled to the East in 1911. FLC L4 (19) 214.

Figure 3.11: The houses of Constantinople in 1911. FLC L4 (19) 44.

Figure 3.12: Series of sketches by Charles-Édouard Jeanneret from *Carnets de Voyage de Orient*, republished in the first volume of Le Corbusier's *Oeuvre Complète.*

Figure 3.13: Charles-Édouard Jeanneret on the Acropolis, Athens, in 1911. FLC L4-19-67.

Figure 3.14: Sketch by Charles-Édouard Jeanneret of the Parthenon, seen through a screen of columns. FLC, *Carnet du Voyage du Orient* no. 3, 115.

Figure 3.15: An undated crayon-and-watercolor sketch by Le Corbusier/Charles-Édouard Jeanneret of the Parthenon's stylobate and the distant horizon. FLC 2850.

CHAPTER 4:

Figure 4.1: With the aid of engineer Max Du Bois, Charles-Édouard Jeanneret planned to patent their scheme for the Dom-ino skeletal house frame in 1915, while in La Chaux-de-Fonds. *Precisions*, 94.

Figure 4.2: Diagram by Charles-Édouard Jeanneret of the arrangement of subjects to be covered in the manuscript. *La Construction des Villes*, reconstructed by Marc E. Albert Emery (Paris: L'Age D'Homme, 1992), 23.

Figure 4.3: Drawing of the Villa Jeanneret-Perret by Charles-Édouard Jeanneret, designed for his parents in La Chaux-de-Fonds in 1912. FLC 30266.

Figure 4.4: Sketch by Charles-Édouard Jeanneret of his writing desk in La Chaux-de-Fonds, circa 1914. FLC, Carnet A1, p. 19.

Figure 4.5: *Persistantes souvenances du Bosphore*, drawn by Charles-Édouard Jeanneret in 1913 at La Chaux-de-Fonds. FLC 4099.
Figure 4.6: *Vin d'Athos*, a watercolor sketch by Charles-Édouard Jeanneret dated February, 1913, while he was at La Chaux-de-Fonds. FLC 4098.
Figure 4.7: Sketch of William Ritter by Charles-Édouard Jeanneret in 1914. FLC, Carnet A1, p. 9.
Figure 4.8: Photograph of the Jeanneret-Perret family in 1914. FLC L4 (16) 44.
Figures 4.9 and 4.10: Sketches by Charles-Édouard Jeanneret for the manuscript of *La Construction des Villes*. FLC B2 (20) 203a and B2 (20) 203b.
Figures 4.11 and 4.12: Title page and thesis of *La Construction des Villes*, title page and 1.

CHAPTER 5

Figure 5.1: Charles-Édouard Jeanneret began to paint daily in 1918, and made numerous sketches, such as this one of nude prostitutes in Paris. FLC, Carnet A3 Paris 1918–1919, p. 190.
Figure 5.2: Amédée Ozenfant and his brother designed the chassis of this Hispano-Suiza sports car. Le Corbusier, *Towards a New Architecture*, trans. Frederick Etchells (1927; facsimile, New York: Praeger Publishers, 1960), 126.
Figure 5.3: Photograph of Amédée Ozenfant–who searched for a more pure form of art, or "Purism"–place and date unknown. FLC L4 (15) 62.
Figure 5.4: The title of the book in this sketch by Charles-Édouard Jeanneret from around 1918 is "La Décadence de l'Art Sacré." FLC, Carnet A3 Paris 1918–1919, p. 184.
Figure 5.5: Photograph of Charles-Édouard Jeanneret in front of the Galerie Thomas, Paris, 1918. FLC 14 (1) 5.
Figure 5.6: Cover of the Purist manifesto *Après le Cubisme* (1918), written by Amédée Ozenfant and Charles-Édouard Jeanneret.
Figure 5.7: Cover of the first issue of the revue *L'Esprit Nouveau* (1920), established by Amédée Ozenfant, Charles-Édouard Jeanneret, and Paul Dermée.

CHAPTER 6

Figure 6.1: "All is spheres and cylinders. Simple forms created constant sensations." *L'Esprit Nouveau* 1 (Oct. 1920).
Figure 6.2: "Eyes which do not see…Steamships." *L'Esprit Nouveau* 8 (Nov. 1923).
Figure 6.3: Voisin advertisement from *L'Esprit Nouveau* 19 (Dec. 1923).
Figure 6.4: Articles of exactitude and efficiency–and thus, purity–exemplified by office equipment. *L'Esprit Nouveau* 23 (May 1924).
Figure 6.5: The editors of *L'Esprit Nouveau* intended the review to be aimed at technically competent specialists or the elites of manufacturing, science, and the arts. *L'Esprit Nouveau* 16 (May 1922).
Figure 6.6: The back cover of *L'Esprit Nouveau* 18 (Nov. 1923) proudly displayed a map of the review's distribution network spreading across five continents.
Figure 6.7: "Le Purisme" proclaimed logic to be an instrument controlling intuition and enabling the artist to proceed with surety. *L'Esprit Nouveau* 4 (Jan. 1921).
Figure 6.8: "Nature et Création." *L'Esprit Nouveau* 19 (Dec. 1923).
Figures 6.9 and 6.10: "Formation de l'optique moderne." *L'Esprit Nouveau* 21 (Mar. 1924).

Figure 6.11: *La Cheminée* (1918), one of the first of Charles-Édouard Jeanneret's oil paintings that he did not destroy. FLC 134.
Figure 6.12: *Still Life with Book, Glass and Pipe* (1918), by Charles-Édouard Jeanneret. FLC 26.

CHAPTER 7

Figure 7.1: A summary of ideas informing Le Corbusier's Purist architecture from the first to the last issue of *L'Esprit Nouveau* (1920–25).
Figure 7.2: "The Engineer's Aesthetic." *Towards a New Architecture*, 15.
Figure 7.3: "Three Reminders to Architects." *L'Esprit Nouveau* 1 (Oct. 1920).
Figure 7.4: "Eyes which do not see III Automobiles." *Towards a New Architecture*, 121.
Figure 7.5: "Architecture or Revolution, a briar pipe." *Towards a New Architecture*, 269.
Figure 7.6: Mass-produced housing with exhibition of Citroen posters. *Towards a New Architecture*, 209.
Figure 7.7: A famous double-page spread from *Towards a New Architecture*, 124–25.
Figure 7.8: The Parthenon compared to the Triple Hydroplane Caproni. *Towards a New Architecture*, 130–31.
Figure 7.9: "40,000 Kilowatt Turbine for Electricity." *Towards a New Architecture*, 249.
Figure 7.10: "The Pack Donkey's Route, the Route of Man." *L'Esprit Nouveau* 17 (June 1922).
Figure 7.11: Le Corbusier likened the profiles of his favorite cities–such as Siena, Rome, Istanbul, and Pera–to that of a beautiful face. *The City of To-morrow*, trans. Frederick Etchells (1925; repr., Cambridge, MA: MIT Press, 1971), 65.
Figure 7.12: "The Barrage." *The City of To-morrow*, 141.
Figure 7.13: "The Contemporary City of 3 Million." *The City of To-morrow*, 172–73.
Figure 7.14: "The Voisin Plan for Paris." *The City of To-morrow*, 278–79.
Figure 7.15 "Iconology, Iconolaters, Iconoclasts." *The Decorative Arts of Today*, 3.
Figure 7.16: "Other Icons The Museums." *The Decorative Arts of Today*, 15.
Figure 7.17: "Plagiarism Folk Culture." *The Decorative Arts of Today*, 27.
Figure 7.18: "The Hour of Architecture." *The Decorative Arts of Today*, 131.
Figure 7.19: Advertisement for *L'Esprit Nouveau* book series. *Almanach d'Architecture Moderne* (Paris: Les Éditions G. Crès et Cie, 1925).
Figure 7.20: Cover of *Almanach D'Architecture Moderne.*
Figure 7.21: The rotunda adjacent to the Pavillon de l'Esprit Nouveau was dedicated to Le Corbusier's "minute and patient" research on urbanism. *Almanach d'Architecture Moderne*, 139.
Figure 7.22: A simple cube of architecture, its openings well-proportioned and its unity regulated, becomes a machine to move you. *Almanach d'Architecture Moderne*, 36.
Figure 7.23: Simple Breton house with flat roof. *Almanach d'Architecture Moderne*, 89.
Figure 7.24: "Soon all the roofs of Paris will be built with gardens."*Almanach d'Architecture Moderne*, 91.
Figure 7.25: Illustration of Innovation's Mikiphone. *Almanach d'Architecture Moderne*, 197.
Figure 7.26: Le Corbusier ends the *Almanac*h with a "brief history of our tribulations" and the ornament (or *cul-de-lampe*) of the publisher, Georges Crès. *Almanach d'Architecture Moderne*, 198.

CHAPTER 8

Figure 8.1: Dust jacket of *Une Maison–Un Palais* (Paris: Les Éditions G. Crès et Cie, 1928).
Figure 8.2: "Normal Plan and Abnormal Plan." *Une Maison–Un Palais*, 7.
Figure 8.3: Arcachon church, painted by Ozenfant, and Brittany house, drawn by Le Corbusier. *Une Maison–Un Palais*, 47.
Figure 8.4: A humble fisherman's hut becomes a house-palace. *The Radiant City* (1935; repr., New York: The Orion Press, 1967), 35.
Figure 8.5: "Delphi, Athens, Rome." *Une Maison–Un Palais*, 15.
Figure 8.6: Rocks in Bretagne and the Alps. *Une Maison–Un Palais*, 23.
Figure 8.7: Steamship on a lake. *Une Maison–Un Palais*, 27.
Figure 8.8: As evidenced over the centuries, "to architecture" is to put in order. *Une Maison–Un Palais*, 41.
Figure 8.9: Following simple, pure traditions, Le Corbusier designed a small house of prestressed concrete projected over a river. *Une Maison–Un Palais*, 55.
Figure 8.10: Villa at Garche. *Une Maison–Un Palais*, 69.
Figure 8.11: Dam in the Alps and Lower Manhattan. *Une Maison–Un Palais*, 81.
Figure 8.12: Rectangular windows allow light to reflect and diffuse across lateral walls. *Une Maison–Un Palais*, 99.
Figure 8.13: A lecture entitled "Technique is the Foundation of Lyricism," delivered in Prague, brought forth praise that Le Corbusier was a poet. *Precisions*, 37.
Figure 8.14: Cover of *Croisade: ou Le Crépuscule des Académies* (Paris: Les Éditions G. Crès et Cie, 1933).
Figure 8.15: Offering a montage of images and texts, Le Corbusier searches for the light of modern times to clear away the debris of the Academies. *Croisade*, 46–47.
Figure 8.16: Athletes place everything in perfect harmony, academicians do not. *Croisade*, 48.
Figure 8.17: Can modern machines of war, needed in life-and-death situations, exit through the gates of the Academy's arsenal? *Croisade*, 50–51.
Figure 8.18: Catastrophes: architecture and train wrecks. *Croisade*, 54–55.
Figure 8.19: Professor Umbdenstock blamed Le Corbusier for mounting a crusade for modern architecture and attracting many acolytes. *Croisade*, 70–71.
Figure 8.20: A reproduction of *Moscophoros*, an archaic Greek statue painted in color by Le Corbusier. *Oeuvre Complète*, vol. 3, 156–57.
Figure 8.21: Le Corbusier sought to forge a unity between primitive and modern art. *Oeuvre Complète*, vol. 3, 156–57.
Figures 8.22 and 8.23: Exhibiting a white blind spot, Le Corbusier speaks for the Algerian native and for the radiant desert. *The Radiant City*, 230–31.

CHAPTER 9

Figure 9.1: One of the note cards Le Corbusier used for lectures, this one explaining "the essential joys" for a talk he gave in 1935 at the Museum of Modern Art in New York City. FLC C3 (17) 10.
Figure 9.2: Le Corbusier, photographed giving a lecture entitled "The relations between architecture and painting" in Zurich, 1938. *Oeuvre Complète*, vol. 3.
Figure 9.3: Dust jacket for *Précisions*.

Figure 9.4: Travel notes from a lecture trip to America in 1935 were published in 1937 as *Quand les Cathédrales étaient blanches: Voyage aux pays de timides* (Paris: Librairie Plon, 1937.

Figure 9.5: This photograph of Le Corbusier, in the cabin of a steamship at a writing desk, may have been taken in December of 1929, during his return voyage from South America to Europe aboard the *Lutétia*. FLC F5 (2) 21.

Figure 9.6: Le Corbusier's sketch of the favela Ascencion in Rio de Janeiro. FLC Carnet B2-287.

Figure 9.7: Sketch of the simple cubes of peasant architecture cascading down the hills of Rio de Janeiro in 1929. FLC Carnet B4-282.

Figure 9.8: Compared to New York, a pathetic paradox, Buenos Aires was a new city on the verge of a great destiny. *Precisions*, 204.

Figure 9.9: Because the Academies refused to allow Paris to change, it was on the edge of a great crisis, according to Le Corbusier. *Precisions*, 177.

Figure 9.10: Self-portrait with Josephine Baker in front of Sugarloaf Mountain in Rio de Janeiro. FLC Carnet B4-239.

Figure 9.11: Le Corbusier frequently sketched musical instruments, and music remained for him a source of secret and lyrical inspiration. FLC Carnet B4-75.

Figure 9.12: Boats, the landscape, and new cities captured Le Corbusier's attention in this view of Montevideo. FLC Carnet B4-237.

Figure 9.13: Donkeys were a favorite subject for commentary and illustration throughout Le Corbusier's lifetime, as in this scene sketched in São Paulo. FLC Carnet B4-59.

Figure 9.14: "Let's Build a Bridge between New York and Paris." Princeton University Library.

Figure 9.15: "Descartes, Is He American?" *The Radiant City*, 127.

Figure 9.16: "Skyscrapers not Big Enough, says Le Corbusier at first sight." FLC B2 (16) 195.

Figures 9.17, 9.18, and 9.19: Sketches of the New York skyline. *Oeuvre Complète*, vol. 3, 16–17.

Figure 9.20: Image of friends around the table in South America, 1929. FLC Carnet B4-25.

CHAPTER 10

Figure 10.1: Cover of *Des Canons, Des Munitions? Merci! Des Logis... S. V. P.* (Paris: Collection de l'équipement de la civilisation machiniste, 1938).

Figure 10.2: Diagram published in *Plans* in June of 1931 that explains that men of authority have the power to choose either to annihilate civilization in war or to equip it for peace. *Des Canons*, 9.

Figure 10.3: "February 6, 1934, in Paris: awakening of cleanliness." *The Radiant City*, 23.

Figure 10.4: "Spanish 'noria,' an age-old method of irrigation." *The Radiant City*, 6.

Figure 10.5: City planning is an art of cultivation: man and nature. *The Radiant City*, 5.

Figure 10.6: Evolution of car design. *The Radiant City*, 32.

Figure 10.7: Small fisherman's hut on a peninsula, described in *Une maison–Un Palais. The Radiant City*, 35.

Figure 10.8: "What About Air War?" *The Radiant City*, 60.

Figure 10.9: On Le Corbusier's trip to South America, he foresaw a radiant city filled with trees and green spaces. *The Radiant City*, 221.

Figure 10.10: If the explosion of urbanism was planned, it would unfold like the bud of a plant. *The Radiant City*, 7.
Figure 10.11: The syndicalist trade union diagram. Le Corbusier, *The Radiant City*, 192.
Figure 10.12: Aerial views taught Le Corbusier that obsolete land divisions made farmlands unfit for machine cultivation. *The Radiant City*, 149.
Figure 10.13: A consequence of the machine age: the city is being invaded by the countryside. It means the death of folk art. *The Radiant City*, 137.
Figure 10.14: Plan for a large statue, never built, that would symbolize the alliance made between the peasant and the steel worker. *Des Canons*, 136.
Figure 10.15: Circulation route of the Pavillon de Temps Nouveaux and vignette of a "circus tent," an inspiration for the Pavillon. *Des Canons*, 13.
Figure 10.16: Children's drawings of the Eiffel Tower decorated the vestibule of the Exposition. *Des Canons*, 29.
Figure 10.17: The Pavillon de Temps Nouveaux was planned to be a three-dimensional book illustrating the Charter of Athens (1933). *Des Canons*, 30.
Figure 10.18: Exhibition panels carried the slogans "The world is not finished" and "It is coming back to life." *Des Canons*, 39.
Figure 10.19: Exhibition panels displaying the history of urbanism and transportation over land, sea, and air routes were assembled by José Luis Sert. *Des Canons*, 42.
Figure 10.20: The Plan of Paris, 1937, panels enclosed a balcony resting area. *Des Canons*, 35.
Figure 10.21: On the first ramp, panels depicted the "sickness" and lugubriousness of contemporary Paris. *Des Canons*, 48.
Figure 10.22: Visualizations of the four functions of the Charter of Athens (1933) were carried out via large paintings of housing, recreation, work, and circulation. *Des Canons*, 83.
Figure 10.23: Le Corbusier designed the panel displaying housing. *Des Canons*, 110.
Figure 10.24: The recreation panel was prepared by Gischia and Mazenot. *Des Canons*, 111.
Figure 10.25: Fernand Léger executed designs for the panel on work. *Des Canons*, 112.
Figure 10.26: The panel for circulation was made by Beauquier. *Des Canons*, 113.
Figure 10.27: Exiting from the displays demonstrating the urbanism of the Temps Nouveaux, the visitor was confronted with a panel of slogans: "The weak and sinister ask us to adbdicate," and the response, "No, the world revives." *Des Canons*, 137.

CHAPTER 11

Figures 11.1 and 11.2: On trips to Algeria in the 1930s, Le Corbusier avidly collected postcards. FLC I5-3-2 and FLC I5-3-83.
Figures 11.3 and 11.4: Le Corbusier illustrated his travel notes from a 1931 trip across Spain, Morocco, and Algeria with sketches of local life and customs. *Plans* 8 (Oct. 1931): 98–99, 102–3.
Figure 11.5: Le Corbusier's initial sketch of Algiers (1931) highlights important elements retained in all of his Obus plans for the city: a government palace, an obelisk on the hill, the seashore, and a Casbah. FLC Carnet B7-463.
Figure 11.6: A second 1931 sketch of Algiers announces the view from Fort l'Empereur. FLC Carnet B7-464.
Figure 11.7: The first plan for Algiers (1931–32): a bombshell, or "Obus," to the people of Algiers. *The Radiant City*, 236.

Figure 11.8: Le Corbusier conquered the sites of Fort l'Empereur with gigantic housing blocks, offering each residential unit terraces, hanging gardens, and wide windows for views over the landscape. *The Radiant City*, 233.

Figure 11.9: In a 1933 letter to the mayor of Algiers, M. Brunel, Le Corbusier sketched a new political grouping of Mediterranean cities laid out like the cardinal points. FLC I1-2-235T.

Figure 11.10: Le Corbusier's final sketches of Algiers as his boat left for Marseilles on July 22, 1934. *The Radiant City*, 260.

Figure 11.11: Photographs from Le Corbusier's 1943 visit to Italy, where he gave several lectures and visited the Fiat factory. *Oeuvre Complète*, vol. 2, 202.

CHAPTER 12

Figure 12.1: The emblem of ASCORAL. *The Home of Man* (London: The Architectural Press, 1948): 117.

Figures 12.2, 12.3, and 12.4: Covers of books written by Le Corbusier between 1938 and 1946, in volume 4 of the *Oeuvre Complète*, 201–3.

Figure 12.5: "Men are ill-lodged; a root cause, a true source of present disquiet." *The Home of Man*, 53.

Figure 12.6: "Architecture, town planning = impeccable biology." *The Home of Man*, 124.

Figure 12.7: The body and architecture are both constructed like an automobile, with a frame, a body, a motor, and organs of feeding and evacuation. *Precisions*, 125.

Figure 12.8: Nature offers a lesson: unity in statue, purity of silhouette, graduated and diverse repetition of all the secondary elements. *The Home of Man*, 123.

Figure 12.9: In modern architecture, a lease can be signed with nature, as in these sketches of Rio de Janeiro. *The Home of Man*, 87.

Figure 12.10: Trees are companions of man; they enter into the lease as well. *The Home of Man*, 97.

Figure 12.11: The Radiant City is a green city, and a pact is signed with nature. *The Home of Man*, 99.

Figure 12.12: Nature teaches the architect many lessons: at the threshold of the house, it is installed as a vigilant guardian. *The Home of Man*, 133.

Figure 12.13: This Janus-faced emblem combines the disaster of Medusa with the freedom of the sun. *The Home of Man*, 156.

Figure 12.14: The cities of France will be reborn, the countryside reoccupied. *The Home of Man*, 75.

Figure 12.15: Le Corbusier was invited in 1935 to provide captions for photographs provided primarily by the Studio publishing house for the book *Aircraft* (London: The Studio Publications, 1935), jacket shown here.

Figure 12.16: This Fairey Long-Range Monoplane attained a record for straight-line flight without refueling in February, 1933. *Aircraft*, number 1, unpaginated.

Figure 12.17: The pleasures of daring, of breaking through present-day stupidities, are illustrated by this American glider in flight. *Aircraft*, number 7, unpaginated.

Figure 12.18: The airplane indicts the cities; they are old, frightening, diseased, finished. *Aircraft*, number 9, unpaginated.

Figure 12.19: The fourth route–the route of the air–joins the existing pattern established by the three former routes of land, water, and rail. *Oeuvre Complète*, vol. 4, 147.

Figure 12.20: A new synthesis is born from the aerial view: linear industrial cities, revitalized farmlands, and small compact, concentric cities. *The Radiant City*, 222.

Figure 12.21: Techniques are no longer regional: books, reviews, and thoughts flash across the world. Materials are distributed by nature, and are, hence, regional. Le Corbusier and ASCORAL, *Concerning Town Planning* (1946; repr., New Haven, CT: Yale University Press, 1948), 97.

Figure 12.22: Le Corbusier wanted to erect new Unités d'Habitation along the crucial meridian of France, on a line stretching form Le Havre to Algiers. Le Corbusier and ASCORAL, *Concerning Town Planning*, 120.

Figures 12.23 and 12.24: Le Corbusier called the architectural concept of airports "two-dimensional architecture." No structure seemed reasonable if juxtaposed against the magnificent aircraft. *Oeuvre Complète*, vol. 4, 199.

Figure 12.25: Once the Second World War was over, Le Corbusier predicted the synthesis of the major arts would be realized in entirely new forms. *New World of Space* (New York: Reynal & Hitchcock, 1948), 103.

EPILOGUE

Figure E.1: Le Corbusier required little for inspiration: a cell with an enclosed garden like a monk's "villa décapotable," open to the sky and the sun; an occasion for solitude and reverie, as sketched in this letter to his family in 1951. FLC R2-2-47 3/6.

Figure E.2: Le Corbusier made a portfolio of 155 lithographs, representing a synthesis of his artworks and his architecture, for *Le Poème de l'Angle Droit* between 1947 and 1953. *Poème de L'Angle Droit* (Paris: Éditions Verve, 1955), cover.

Figure E.3: Ever hopeful that the authorities would accept his plans for Paris, Le Corbusier compiled a personal dialogue with the reader, looking back over the many obstacles his hopes and plans for Paris confronted. *Les Plans Le Corbusier de Paris 1956–1922* (Paris: Éditions de Minuit, 1956), cover.

Figure E.4: "The Magic Box," sketched by Le Corbusier and published in "The Core as the Meeting Place of the Arts." Jacquelin Tyrwhitt, José Luis Sert, and Ernesto N. Rogers, eds., *CIAM 8 The Heart of the City towards the humanization of urban life* (New York, Pellegrini and Cudahy, 1952), 52.

CHAPTER 1
LE CORBUSIER: THE WRITINGS OF AN ARCHITECT

One can raise the definition of architecture to a very high level: MIRROR OF THOUGHT. Architecture is a system of thought.

–LE CORBUSIER, 1925

THE WRITINGS OF AN ARCHITECT

Known for his modern architecture, numbering fewer than sixty buildings, Charles-Édouard Jeanneret/Le Corbusier (1887–1965) also wrote some fifty or so books during his lifetime, hundreds of articles, and thousands of letters. Le Corbusier had a compulsion and a passion to write: lyrically and poetically, rationally and logically, rhetorically and quixotically. His writings reveal a certain randomness of form–travelogues of beloved places visited, lectures recorded and then transcribed, projects in need of defense, catalogues of expositions, and journal articles to sway public opinion. All of his books and articles contain persuasive arguments, calling out to the reader to adopt a new set of tools and a mentality appropriate for a new machine age–they sequentially point to an evolving doctrine of urbanism and offer a permanent record of its formation. [FIGURE 1.1]

Traveling and writing became intermixed activities for Le Corbusier. Travel offered him isolated moments of time, placed apart from his many compelling business affairs; it was valuable time where he could put thoughts to paper, marking his passage through life. He wrote constantly on trains and airplanes, in steamship cabins and hotel rooms. He kept copious diaries, sketchbooks, and travel notebooks, writing over and inserting additions time and again; he maintained lengthy correspondence with his family and his different mentors. Letter-writing was a favored mode of communication. He wrote, for example,

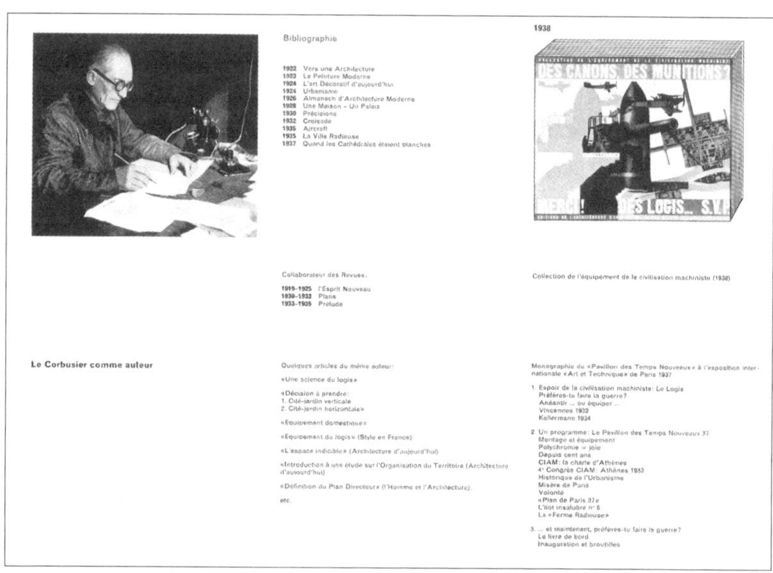

Bibliographie

1922 Vers une Architecture
1923 La Peinture Moderne
1924 L'art Décoratif d'aujourd'hui
1924 Urbanisme
1926 Almanach d'Architecture Moderne
1928 Une Maison – Un Palais
1930 Précisions
1932 Croisade
1935 Aircraft
1935 La Ville Radieuse
1937 Quand les Cathédrales étaient blanches

1938

Collaborateur des Revues:

1919–1925 l'Esprit Nouveau
1930–1933 Plans
1933–1935 Prélude

Collection de l'équipement de la civilisation machiniste (1938)

Le Corbusier comme auteur

Quelques articles du même auteur:

«Une science du logis»

«Décision à prendre:
1. Cité-jardin verticale
2. Cité-jardin horizontale»

«Equipement domestique»

«Equipement du logis» (Style en France)

«L'espace indicible» (Architecture d'aujourd'hui)

«Introduction à une étude sur l'Organisation du Territoire (Architecture d'aujourd'hui)

«Définition du Plan Directeur» (l'Homme et l'Architecture).

etc.

Monographie du «Pavillon des Temps Nouveaux» à l'exposition internationale «Art et Technique» de Paris 1937

1. Espoir de la civilisation machiniste: Le Logis
Préféres-tu faire la guerre?
Anéantir ... ou équiper ...
Vincennes 1932
Kellermann 1934

2. Un programme: Le Pavillon des Temps Nouveaux 37
Montage et équipement
Polychromie = joie
Depuis cent ans
CIAM: la charte d'Athènes
4e Congrès CIAM: Athènes 1933
Historique de l'Urbanisme
Misère de Paris
Volonté
«Plan de Paris 37»
L'îlot insalubre n° 6
La «Ferme Radieuse»

3. ... et maintenant, préféres-tu faire la guerre?
Le livre de bord
Inauguration et broutilles

FIGURE I.I: One of four pages in volume four of the *Oeuvre Complète* illustrating books written by Le Corbusier/ Charles-Édouard Jeanneret, alone or in collaboration with others, from 1938–46. This page describes Le Corbusier as author, giving a list of his books and a few articles written from 1922–37. The illustration of recent books begins with *Des Canons, Des Munitions? Merci! Des Logis...S. V.P.* (1938), a monograph written for the Pavillon des Temps Nouveaux at the Exposition Internationale des Arts et Techniques dans la Vie Moderne, Paris, in 1937.

hundreds of letters to the Swiss art critic, novelist, and painter William Ritter (1867–1955) between 1910 and1925, confessional outpourings of his emotional state of mind and the evolution of his thoughts. These letters were also experiments in narrative description and literary phrasing until he eventually arrived at a more staccato and telegraphic style of writing, quick to read and to the point.

How to account for the neglect by architectural historians to consider the proliferation of manifestos, books, articles, and letters from such an important architect of the twentieth century? Preference has been given to Le Corbusier's heroic period of modern architecture from the 1920s, or his poetic constructions from the 1950s. Only recently has a biography of the architect been written by an impartial narrator, and up until now only infrequent use of his copious letter writing has been made.[1] [FIGURES I.2 AND I.3, p. 687]

When Le Corbusier became a naturalized citizen in 1930 at the age of forty-three, his French identity card labeled his profession *homme de lettres* (man of letters). He did not call himself an architect or painter. While it can be argued he made no claim to the title of "architect"–being self-taught and distrustful of all schools of architecture–there were no restrictions placed on the use of this title in France until 1940.[2] To be a "man of letters," an intellectual, was perhaps a persona he affected in order to mask that he was indeed self-taught, but it was also an attempt to engage in the life of the mind, to stress the importance of writing and lecturing as creative activities, to wrangle over general principles and points of an argument.

Writing for Le Corbusier, as he often confessed, no matter how difficult, was an expression of his intimate thoughts, his innermost emotions, and he learned as a young man that it was a way to escape from a deep depression that hung over his head. While confined to his hometown La Chaux-de-Fonds after his trip to Turkey and Greece in 1911, he would read aloud to his brother and circle of friends his earliest travel writings and those he had written on Mount Athos and Athens; he would send pages of this manuscript to Ritter for comment and criticism, rewriting and perfecting his phrasing where advised. He began to keep a journal, sometimes in epistolary form, experiments in writing that he also sent to Ritter for comment and supposed correction.

Throughout his life, Le Corbusier kept up his interest in writing, the play and constructions of the mind. To be involved with the battle over words, positions advocated, was part of being an intellectual engaged with reforming modern society. He wanted to write poetry for modern times, to be lyrical and affect the emotions, as well as to offer rational displays of an orderly mind. He liked to think of himself as a poet of relationships, an inventor of neologisms, who enjoyed word plays such as "Dom-Ino" or utilized projective analogies such as *machine à vivre* (machine for living) or *machine à emouvoir* (machine to move you emotionally). He was also concerned with the ability to use language with the same precision, rapidity, and effectiveness as optical instruments. How to do things with words: persuade, convince, or tell stories that entertain? He often described his arguments as moves in a game, a metaphor for the manner in which he deployed ideas, advanced his points, or defended his position–always traveling toward an objective, moving along an axis or a line of fire.

Le Corbusier's books are seldom read in their entirety; there is a tendency to skim over their pages, quoting here and there in support of what may be a reader's predetermined position on modern architecture. His bountiful journal writings and numerous letters inscribe his reactions to everyday life, emotional struggles, and intimate thoughts of loneliness and unfulfilled achievements, yet they have been largely ignored. How does the reader come to terms with Le Corbusier's knowledge and love of cities, history, food, and travel? He would make it known that the architecture of an era is recognizable through its structural language, how the elements of wall, pillar, door, window, and materials form a unity, a harmonious whole. This is true of Le Corbusier's written language as well–he was an artisan constructing a method to analyze contemporary times, calling out to the reader to use his words as tools, to think with them, to take them up again and again in the battle for modern architecture and urbanism. His words exist in order to influence later generations.

Reflecting back over his experiences as an architect-urbanist in 1956, Le Corbusier told a story about a Brazilian woman who visited his atelier in Paris, bringing greetings from a group of modern architects in Rio de Janeiro. She told him that when no evident solution to an architectural-urban problem appeared among the architects, one of them would say "Go look in the book the father (*le père*) made!"[3] The "book" meant the five volumes of Le Corbusier's *Oeuvre Complète* and the "father" was Le Corbusier. He remarked: "This gentle small word touches me intimately."[4]

He believed that books, houses, urban plans, drawings, and paintings were similar manifestations of a mechanized society. But alongside his recognized love of the machine, technological achievement, and Cartesian logic, Le Corbusier was also a romanticist–responding to projected feelings and emotions radiating from objects and the landscape. There is always a poetic side to his language–of space and time, of universal harmony, of physical unity. He was fascinated with natural objects: pebbles, sun-bleached bones, bits of rope, leaves, trees of all kinds and shapes. He looked backward, over a lifetime of personal struggles, or in search of architectural precedents and the origin of urban problems.

As much as he forged ahead into brave new worlds, it is often overlooked that Le Corbusier was an ardent student of the past, trying to resolve the antithesis between tradition and innovation. It has been suggested that the map he drew of his voyage to the East (1911)–on which he marked visited sites and lands with an "I" for industrial production, efficiency, and economy; an "F" for folklore and tradition; and a "C" for classical culture–can be used as a template for how he organized his experiences of life.[5] Succinctly writing in *Precisions*, he claimed "I am considered a revolutionary.... I have had only one teacher: the past; only one education: the study of the past... museums, travels, folk art... pure works.... It is in the past that I found my lessons of history, of the reasons for being of things. Every event and every object is 'in relationship to.'"[6] Thus it is argued that the fifty or so books Le Corbusier wrote and assembled, as well as the outpouring of letters, notebooks, and articles he committed to pen and paper, should be treated as literary endeavors worthy of analysis in their own right. They should be considered "in relationship to" his architecture and artistic expressions.

LEAVING TRACES BEHIND

Le Corbusier finished his final piece of writing, a little book entitled *Mise au Point* (*Bringing into Focus*), in July 1965, a month before he died swimming in the Mediterranean Sea on the twenty-seventh of August. He opened the text in the following manner:

> Nothing is transmissible but thought. Over the years a man gradually acquires, through his struggles, his work, his inner combat, a certain capital, his own individual and personal conquest. But all the passionate questions of the individual, all that capital, that experience so dearly paid for, will disappear. The law of life: death. Nature shuts off all activity by death. Thought alone, the fruit of labor, is transmissible.[7]

Le Corbusier is paraphrasing a thought previously written in *When the Cathedrals Were White* (1937). At that time he was concerned about "conceptions" that became distorted and were swallowed up in guns and bayonets as soon as a frontier turned into a line of demarcation, setting off explosions and assuring that war would inevitably follow.[8] Everything is consequently

> artificially organized against the very precepts of nature; nature ends a life, an admirable activity, by death; and nothing is transmissible except the nobility of the fruit of work: thought. Everything else disappears: the immense attainment of an individual during his lifetime. Everything dissolves, everything has to be begun again by each individual person: struggle, effort within one's self, individual, passionate, and yet disinterested conquest. That is the law of life: death.[9]

What does the reiterated metaphor "law of life: death" mean but his attempt at the end of his life, when personal struggles overwhelmed, or when war and annihilation threatened, to transmit thought through words, no matter how limited or inaccurate they might be? It is a gesture to leave behind an immortal trace of the experiences he had witnessed in life.

Thought flows from one place to another; life experiences shape both the how and the why of that thought.[10] From the time of his youthful travels to Paris in 1908, Le Corbusier was aware of the trajectory of life, deploying repetitively the expression "a page has turned," fearful that he had yet to achieve the greatness he believed was his destiny. As his many references to the "law of the meander" reveal, he knew that life, the process of thought and of writing, has a goal, moving toward a target, with force and a certain momentum. But obstacles cause life, thought, writing to get stuck: eddies form, movement zigzags from side to side, building up tension and resistances, eroding the banks of a river, causing meanders to form. Then suddenly pressure accumulates, causing the river to break through the meanders, to flow once again straight toward its final resolution and fulfillment. Life, thought, and writing are governed by a spirit of inquiry that travels along a trajectory until reaching their goal. Such was Le Corbusier's belief instilled in his writing and experienced in life.

TO BE A "MAN OF LETTERS"

Why did Le Corbusier label his profession "homme de lettres," placing himself within the French intellectual and literary tradition rather than the tradition of French architecture? Homme de lettres was a term already out of date in 1930, when Le Corbusier used it on his identity card, having been replaced with the word "intellectual," a label first used against the defenders of Alfred Dreyfus in 1900. Did the dated terminology conjure up images of being a prophet of modern times, carrying forward the banner of revolution forged in the 1870s, using words as tools to persuade and convince?

When compared to the literature of modernity, there is a standard complaint about Le Corbusier's modern architecture. If one searches the photographs of his architecture, so this argument goes, it is impossible to find one remnant or memory of the unmodern.[11] A quotation seized at random from his writings offers proof. When Le Corbusier wrote about the garden city of Pessac, for example, he claimed "Here you have an example of modern town planning, where the relics of bygone days, the Swiss chalet and the like, have been relegated to the past. The mind, once it can be freed from romantic associations, will be eager to find a satisfactory solution of the problem [of housing]."[12] It is clear from this point of view that Le Corbusier was on the forward-moving conveyor belt of time, putting a brave new world on display, proclaiming only one narrative–that of modernity, the spirit of the time, a new time (i.e., *esprit nouveau* or *temps nouveau*).

In juxtaposition, the literary narrators of modernity tend to act as a counterweight to Le Corbusier, writing in despair over the forward thrust of time, wanting to halt the movement, to dwell in its eddies and turns. These writers mourn the memory of a lost time when the world appeared unbroken, before the ruins of progress kept piling up at their feet. Marcel Proust is exemplary in this position, as is Walter Benjamin. Trying to understand the tumult of events, they focus on the wealth of reality, the details of everyday life. They carefully follow Paul Valéry's reflexive dictum that "A work of art should always teach us that we had not seen what we see."[13]

Le Corbusier on the other hand builds a house like a machine, creating rooms devoid of traces of everyday life. In this account, the writer of modernity and the modern architect face each other across a gaping and irreconcilable void. But things are not that simple, as the conundrum of Le Corbusier's stated profession, homme de lettres, indicates. Indeed author Paul Valéry's didactic, corrective spirit informed Le Corbusier's early position, as his famous chapter "Eyes which do not See" in *Vers une Architecture* (*Towards a New Architecture*) reveals. Le Corbusier was exploiting Valéry's claim that most people see with their intellects more than they do with their eyes; they direct their acts of seeing "out there" rather than understanding the manner in which they see, perceive, form meanings, and act. Valéry noted:

> They perceive with the dictionary rather than with the retina; and they approach objects so blindly, they have such a vague notion of the difficulties and pleasures of vision, that they have invented beautiful views. Of the rest they are unaware.[14]

A person who sees is a person who understands both the "what" and "how" of perception. For Valéry, and for Le Corbusier, who an individual is, what one thinks, is inseparable from what one does–who is as important as what. And a book resembles a person: it bears witness to dreams and faults, it reveals the workings of the mind. Valéry would write about the material form of a book in 1945:

> A book is a singular object, an open and shut thing which changes its nature completely in that simple act. I open it: it speaks. I close it and it becomes a thing to be looked at. Thus more than anything else in the world, it resembles a man. At first approach, a man is his form and color; next his voice strikes us, and finally his voice is transformed into a mind that mingles with our own.[15]

A book is both a work of art, held reverentially in the hands and admired sensuously, and it is also an assembly of expressions of the mind, revealing struggles and mysteries along the trajectory of life. [FIGURE I.4, p. 687]

Le Corbusier often pointed out the influence "men of letters" had on him, placing his own writing in relationship to those who preceded him. He received a letter of admiration from Valéry for his 1925 book *L'Art decorative d'aujourd'hui* (*The Decorative Arts of Today*); this letter was published as the frontispiece of subsequent editions. Valéry called this book "admirable," noting there were coincidental points of view in both literature and philosophy. Buildings, however, are seen by themselves and impose their presence on observers, whereas what is written depends on the reader's expectations and habits, and thus writers must always refer to the past. "One cannot even make a start with the experience of purity except by bringing in the scattered examples of it to be found in the past."[16] [FIGURE I.5]

At least in his imagination, Le Corbusier kept company with men of letters. He sent Romain Rolland one of his books, probably *Precisions* or the first volume of *Oeuvre Complète*, and received a note of thanks in 1930. Rolland believed Le Corbusier brought a breath of fresh air into the century's preoccupations. Already an admirer of his houses on piloti drinking in light, and his cities of cement and crystal bathing in lawns of green, he was anxious about only one thing. Le Corbusier proposed the same architectural form for all countries. Rolland disliked such uniform treatment of the elements composing a place, the elimination of nature's variety, and worried that Le Corbusier's uniform proposals would produce boredom and weaken individual fortitude.[17]

Homme de lettres is the profession Le Corbusier gave himself in 1930, accepting as his duty to contribute to the cultural atmosphere of the twentieth century, to write and speak with inspiration, to move along the miraculous and terrifying trajectory of modern life. In his last recorded interview, in May 1965, given to Hugues Desalle, he was asked

40, rue de Villejust – XVIe

Sir,

I have only one word to say about your book, and it's a word I seldom use: admirable.*

And I write it with some embarrassment. My thoughts are at one with yours on most of the subjects you touch on. It is too easy for me to approve my own feelings.

I may add that in literature, and even in philosophy, there are now analogous or coincidental points of view. But in these fields for insuperable reasons (too long to set out) one has to 'mesh' with the past. Buildings are seen by themselves and impose their presence on the observer, whereas what is written requires from the reader a willingness and good will, which depend on his expectations, and his expectations depend on his habits, etc. One cannot even make a start with the experience of purity except by bringing in the scattered examples of it to be found in the past.

Believe me, sir, I hold your work in especial regard, and I am doing my best to make it known.

With all my thanks and fellow-feeling,

(Signed) Paul Valéry

**L'Art décoratif d'aujourd'hui* (1925, *Collection de L'Esprit Nouveau*) published by Editions G. Crès, Paris.

FIGURE I.5: **Le Corbusier often referred to notes and praise he received from men of letters, such as this undated letter from Paul Valéry, inserted into the frontispiece of subsequent editions of *The Decorative Arts of Today*.**

"how he placed himself [in relation] to Greek architecture," and offered the following reply:

> On one occasion, a man told me, "You've learned neither Greek nor Latin, you'll never be able to write."...And it turned out later that, not being able to build certain things, I could drawn them; but not being able to explain them entirely in drawing, especially when it came to urbanism, I had to explain them, so I wrote. One day Paul Valéry told me...I wrote like an angel....He wrote it to me or he told me....I don't know how the situation came about, but anyway I knew Paul Valéry–he said to me, "You write wonderfully"; while everybody else was telling me, "You have no style, to have a style you have to have a twisted style."[18]

Language and writing seem strange insertions in Le Corbusier's response to a question about Greek architecture, but they are potent indicators of his overpowering desire to communicate, of links between writing and his emotional states. Obviously the supportive words of Valéry brought a degree of recognition and satisfaction, ones that he referenced in various struggles.[19] Le Corbusier's response, however, returns us to the issue of being an homme de lettres, a man who, having studied Greek and Latin, especially their grammatical structure, "knew his letters" as the Greeks say, and therefore achieved the accolades of literary recognition and social acceptance. A man of letters is a public intellectual who exhibits excellence in more than one area: writing essays, critical articles, revolutionary pamphlets, even novels and poetry.

Is it coincidental that Le Corbusier called himself an "homme de lettres" in 1930, a year after the appearance of his first public writings in defense of modern architecture, his first attempts to retaliate with "j'accuse"?[20] During this time, French art critics writing in the press stung him with their barbs, noting he was not a native citizen of France, not a patriot. He was instead a Bolshevik, as his trips to Moscow, which began in 1929, proved; he was a traitor to the architects and builders of France, as his nude white architecture demonstrated. He had been severely criticized in 1928 and 1929 by the art critics Alexandre de Senger and François Fosca, but especially by Camille Mauclair, an "indefatigable polygraph" of more than one hundred books, including novels, poetry, music, travelogues, and every type of criticism and critical theory. Unfortunately this well-known man of letters disliked Le Corbusier's "machines for living," calling them nude hygienic boxes with no soul and thinking his manifestoes of *L'Esprit Nouveau* misguided.[21]

Hence the persona of homme de lettres might be a protective shield, warding off criticism leveled not only at him personally but at his architecture and even more so at his paintings and writings. Le Corbusier revealed how deeply he was wounded by repeating in many different books and lectures his own belief that the series of fifteen articles written by Mauclair for the conservative newspaper *Le Figaro* were called into existence by professional organizations of carpenters, stonemasons, and manufacturers of tile and slate roofing and paid for by the Chamber of Commerce.[22] Mauclair's words were supposed to vanquish modern architecture, suppress the use of modern construction materials, and block the trajectory toward a *temps nouveaux* (new time). Collected into a book format in 1933 with the title *L'Architecture va-t-elle mourir?* (*Is Architecture about to die?*), Le Corbusier wondered on whose side the "real crazies" stood.[23] He never forgave this critic, and so we find him in the final interview of his life still worried about being accepted as a man devoted to literary or scholarly pursuits, engaged in issues of controversy and conflict for the betterment of mankind.

THE WRITER AS GRAPHIC DESIGNER

Concerned about the visual impact of his books, Le Corbusier was meticulous about the design of the page layouts, the selection of typefaces, the shapes of the books, the rhetorical impact of his ideas, and the promotional materials. For example, he sent William Ritter a copy of the first volume of *Oeuvre Complète* in 1930 and explained:

> I wrote to the editor Girsberger, Kirchgasse Zurich, to send you the book which he published on my work of architecture 1910–1930. It is a grand album carefully made. You will find there my first steps on a route that seems to me to be enlarging more each day. The book ought to appear simultaneously in Paris. But one still dawdles there over the unaccustomed format, which I already imposed on Zurich. Because I think that it is the only one that allows the proper reproduction of plans and sections and all the stuff of our trade.[24]

For the first time he signs his letter to Ritter "Le Corbusier," and then adds "You understand it: it is necessary to bow down before M. Le Corbu. Ch. É. Jeanneret is a reference for the police administrator. It is necessary to sign logically. And that is how one changes names without suspecting it."[25]

Ritter was not pleased with the format of the book, which he allowed may have been expedient for displaying architectural drawings but extremely impractical to take notes from and to hold in one's hands in order to read. And while he may have addressed his letter of thanks to his friend "Corbu," since evidently Le Corbusier existed, he asked permission to remain faithful to Charles-Édouard Jeanneret.[26]

Le Corbusier became interested in graphic design during his trip to Germany in 1910, where he witnessed firsthand the brilliant reforms in book-making and typography the Werkbund had accomplished and how books were artfully displayed in shop windows and in advertisements. He was aware that a new communications network lay behind Germany's revolution in the decorative arts—a network that extended from the design of cardboard boxes and advertising posters, to new alphabets and page formats, exhibition materials for congresses, and the pages of illustrated periodicals. Le Corbusier would eventually extend the word "architecture" to cover "the art of typography as it is used in the making of newspapers, periodicals and books."[27]

Obviously influenced by Le Corbusier's statement that a "house is a machine for living," Valéry in 1927 called a book a "machine for reading" (*machine á lire*).[28] He noted there were two virtues of a book. It is to be read from word to word and line to line, a linear progression that provokes a chain of mental reactions in the reader. But the page is also an image to be seen, allowing an immediate and simultaneous look to run over the page, visualizing the arrangement of images and words. The text read and the text seen are two distinct processes–attention to one excludes the other.

Le Corbusier mixes these genres: to look at images, to read texts. He was not only a "man of letters" but a man of the media utilizing every means of expression to make known his work, to express his opinions publicly, to record his experience of modern times—manifestos, expositions, radio, and later television talks, interviews in the press, and cinema. In the 1930s as Le Corbusier struggled to make a synthesis of all of the arts, he wrote about the prevalence of images such as photographs and the cinema, which over the last fifty years had replaced tasks once reserved for the painter. Images from illustrated magazines and the newspapers now opened up contemporary consciousness, extended understanding, and filled minds with natural splendors both small and large.[29] Many of Le Corbusier's illustrations allow the force of the image to dramatize his words, short-circuiting the slow process of verbal description.

Writing projected his ideas and thoughts beyond actual realization, allowing his developing doctrine to be tested in front of a larger audience. Before committing his thoughts to writing, however, Le Corbusier first developed his ideas in lectures, which he began to give in 1924. Illustrations inserted into subsequent books often resembled the chalk figures he drew on the blackboard of a lecture hall, or they were diagrams drawn on large sheets of paper unfurled as he outlined his interpretive schemes in colored chalk, then reproduced in black and white.[30] [FIGURES I.6 TO I.10] His lectures were improvised from a series of note cards; he first outlined the plan and then, drawing images on the blackboard or sheets of paper, he ordered his thoughts as ideas surged form his head. He believed his lectures enabled his thoughts to become precise, rendering them clear and extending his thought. Commenting in 1951 on his lecturing style, he noted,

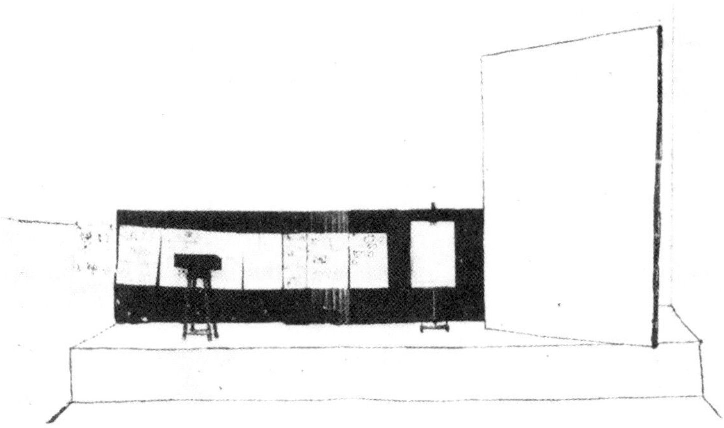

FIGURE I.6: During his lectures, Le Corbusier improvised drawings around spoken words. This sketch of a podium and some of his scribbling is used to illustrate lectures given in South America in 1929.

> And when one draws around words, one draws with useful words, one creates something. And all my theory–my introspection and my retrospection on the phenomenon of architecture and urbanism–comes from these improvised and illustrated lectures. And so what is characteristic is that the ideas ended up by creating a doctrine–architecture and urbanism make a whole–and so this thesis of architecture and urbanism has now become accepted world-wide, professed everywhere, practiced everywhere, and one does "Corbu" in the entire world. It is perhaps highly regrettable, but it is like that.[31]

After developing his ideas in lectures, Le Corbusier still had to commit his words to paper. The ten lectures on architecture and urbanism delivered to a Buenos Aires audience in 1929, for example, were transferred to written form during his return voyage from South America. Spoken and drawn in an improvisational manner, he now had to arrange on paper what he called "the frightening steps of logic" required.[32] He had placed before his South American audiences twenty-five years of research, which had jelled into a system. Now it was necessary to obtain a general verdict on this series of related facts that made up his doctrine. He remarked on the word "doctrine," and the fact that he had often been called doctrinaire. But he was clear: a doctrine means a set of concepts leading closely from one to another in accordance with the laws of logic.[33] The test of this doctrine would come only after it had been read and assembled in the minds of his readers.

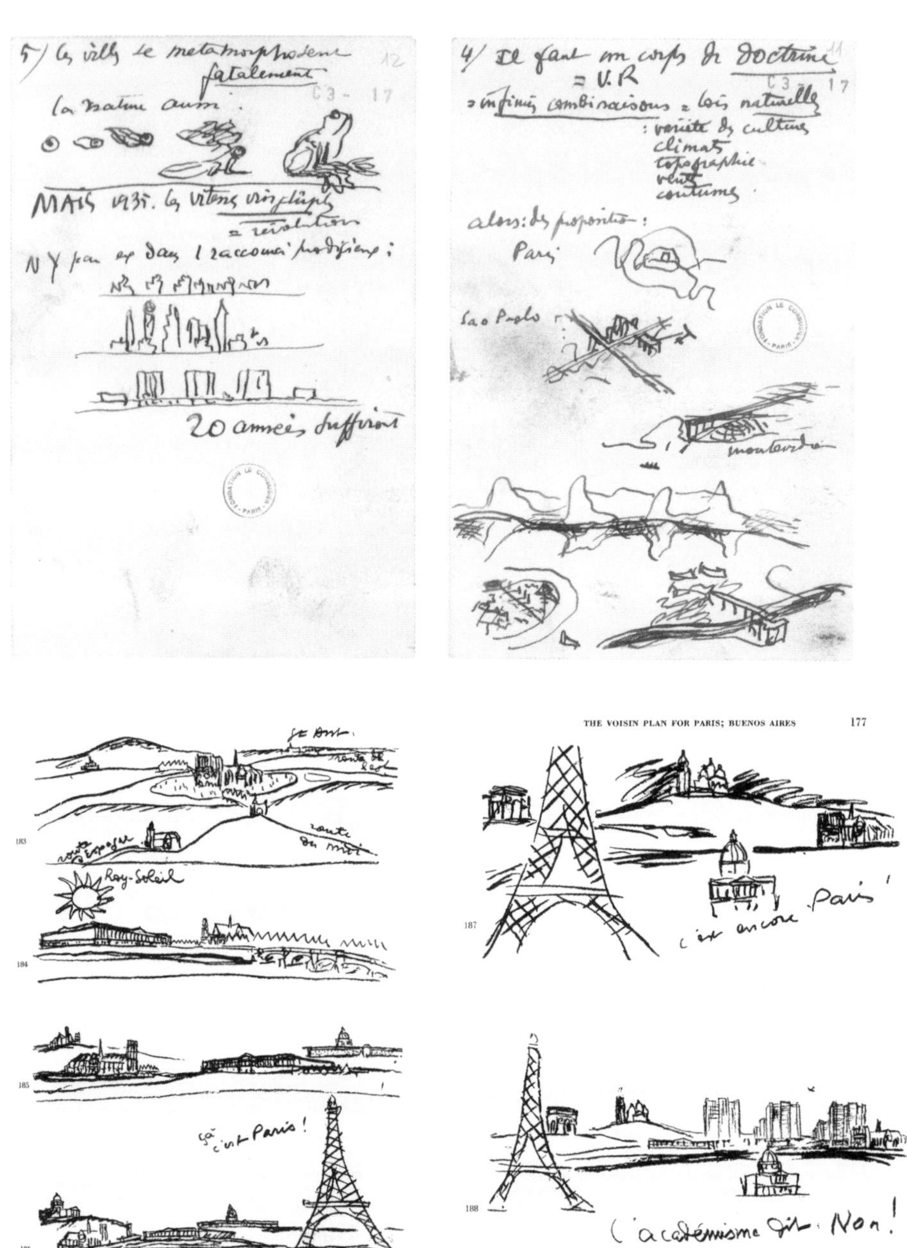

183 St Denis // route de l'est/road east // route d'Espagne/road to Spain // route du midi/road south // **184** Roy-Soleil/Sun King // **186** ça c'est Paris!/this is Paris

187 c'est encore Paris!/it is still Paris // **188** l'académisme dit Non!/academism says No!

FIGURES I.7 AND I.8: Le Corbusier relied on small note cards to organize his lectures. These two cards are from a lecture given at the Museum of Modern Art in New York City on October 24, 1935. FIGURES I.9 AND I.10: Two pages of sketches from *Precisions* (1930) reveal Le Corbusier's annoyance at the academies' rejection of modern architecture and urbanism.

The lectures in *Precisions* appear among the material that Le Corbusier would refer to in 1948 as the "points of doctrine," constructed across a series of books written in the 1930s and 1940s. In *Precisions,* Le Corbusier claims in the introduction that his doctrine involved many questions of "how" and "why." In pursuit of answers to these questions, he developed over the years a "daring response," unusual, staggering, and even revolutionary. The doctrine can be discovered, he explained in 1948, if the reader weaves together diverse texts and images from *Precisions* (*Précisions*, 1930), *The Home of Man* (*Maison des Hommes*, 1941), *L'Urbanisme des Trois Établissements* (1945), *Concerning Town Planning* (*Propos d'urbanisme*, 1946), and *Looking at City Planning* (*Manière de penser l'urbanisme*, 1946).[34] [FIGURE I.II, p. 688]

It is well known that after 1927 Le Corbusier dedicated the morning hours until one in the afternoon to painting before turning his attention to architecture; but time for writing must also be accounted for in his daily routine. After returning to La Chaux-de-Fonds in the fall of 1911 Le Corbusier began to devote mornings to writing, a practice he may have partially continued throughout his life.[35] In the 1930s, Le Corbusier began to utilize a pictogram of an open book as the potential cover for books under preparation, as if the reader had stopped to contemplate the ideas appearing on the page and developing into a doctrine. How words are arranged on the page, how typographic formats make reading more efficient, how images and texts interact–all are acts that engaged Le Corbusier in the construction of his books.

CONSTRUCTING A BIBLIOGRAPHY

How many books, articles, and letters did Le Corbusier write? The answer is still unknown, for architectural historians have paid little attention to his writings and urban theories, holding more securely to the analysis of his oeuvre as a modern architect. As a result, there is no definitive bibliographic list of Le Corbusier's written materials. H. Allen Brooks has counted 4,261 letters written to 950 people that exist in the archives of Le Corbusier.[36] Le Corbusier was careful to preserve as many letters as possible. Always attentive to his legacy, or to protect his intimate thoughts, he admonished his brother Albert for destroying some letters his parents had forwarded to him. All were worthy of safekeeping. Of the surviving early letters, there are 682 written to his parents and brother. William Ritter received 246, and his wife, Yvonne Gallis, 144. The early letters in particular provide poignant accounts of the struggling artist's emotional states and evolving set of ideas as he moved toward what he believed was his "destiny."

There are different lists of books that Le Corbusier compiled: one, for example, published in volume 4 of the *Oeuvre Complète* (1947), consists of some of the books he wrote from 1922–47 and is reproduced with photographs of the dust jackets and a short commentary on those written after 1937. Le Corbusier drew up another list in *Les Plans de Paris* (1960) consisting of forty-five titles: the first appeared in 1912, the last in 1960. In both lists he was selective of the books he included, and neither of these lists includes his copious journal articles or notebooks, much less his letter writing. There are also incomplete lists drawn up by Darlene Brady in *Le Corbusier, An Annotated Bibliography* (1985) and another list presented in *Le Corbusier, une encyclopédie* (1987).[37, 38]

As for the number of books and how to divide them into periods of time–there is disagreement here as well. Marie-Brigitte Preteux, for example, counts the number of Le Corbusier's books to be fifty-three, noting that all but three concern architecture and urbanism. She divides the list into six different time periods: before 1920 he wrote two books; 1921–29 he wrote six; 1930–39 he wrote twelve; 1939–45 he wrote eight; 1950–65 he wrote sixteen; after 1965 there were three books published posthumously.[39] Catherine de Smet uses World War II to divide a list of thirty-five books into three time periods: 1912–39, 1940–46, 1947–60. She counts fifteen books written over twenty-nine years before the war, nine books written during the six years of war, and eleven books after the war, written over fourteen years.[40] The writings of Le Corbusier under consideration here were written between 1907–47; they are examined for his thoughts on urbanism, which he claims jelled into a doctrine by 1948. They do not focus on his more artistic and poetical writings after World War II, explained in brief in the Epilogue.

What's in a name? As has been noted above, at the time of his naturalization, Le Corbusier changed the name he signed in his letter to Ritter from Charles-Édouard Jeanneret to Le Corbusier, reserving the former name for the police and his identity card. Supposedly Amédée Ozenfant told Jeanneret in 1920, "To purify architecture that is your role!" Subsequently when he wrote on architecture in the pages of their jointly edited magazine *L'Esprit Nouveau,* Jeanneret took the pen name of Le Corbusier, transforming Lecorbésier, the name of the father of his grandmother, into a new meaning: the raven-archer.[41] He often called himself "Le Corbu," the raven, and signed his paintings and letters with the sign of this bird. [FIGURES I.12, AND I.13]

FIGURES I.12 AND I.13: Until sometime in the mid-1920s, Le Corbusier/Charles-Édouard Jeanneret signed his letters as "ChE Jeanneret." He started to use the pseudonym Le Corbusier in 1921, for articles appearing in *L'Esprit Nouveau*. The top signature appears on an envelope written in 1910, the bottom on the cover of *The Decorative Arts of Today*.

The raven-archer suggests other associations as well: *arche* signifies the medieval sign for the transverse arm of the cross of crucifixion, or it references the summer and winter eclipse of the sun. As "archer" it may also refer to the ancient Greeks, who transposed an everyday instrument of use, the stringed bow, into a lyre, the instrument of musical harmony.[42] Thus Pythagoras, who made the connection between sound and numbers, may be another self-portrait.[43] Le Corbusier was extremely close to his mother, who was a music teacher, and to his older brother, Albert, who played the violin as a young man. Albert subsequently turned to the study of the Dalcroze method of rhythmic dancing and composition. Le Corbusier would retain a lifelong love of music, rhythm, and harmonious compositions.[44] Stringed instruments were the perfect object types, aiming for harmony; they contained analogous mathematical curves with deep resonance, responding in waves of sound to emotions and sensibilities deep within us.[45]

In a letter written to Sigfried Giedion from Chandigarh in the 1950s, Le Corbusier called himself a donkey, not a genius, as some have done. He included a drawing entitled "Paraphrase on the entry into Jerusalem," placing on the line of the foreground the Parthenon, then the Leaning Tower of Pisa, and in the future, the Villa Savoy, all favorite symbols of the architect. In the foreground of this drawing, a little below the horizon line, he places a standing raven with a donkey on his back. Underneath the design he wrote "Does the genius carry a donkey or is the donkey carrying the genius?" for this is the walk of the honored transposed into the walk of the crucified.[46] [FIGURE I.14, p. 688] Jeanneret/Le Corbusier developed a distinctive way of seeing things, as this drawing reveals: a strong sense of inherited and controlling models from the past seen from a distance and given an ironic twist. Such twists or turns are reminiscent of the manner in which he inverts the story of the donkey path, which he admired in his earliest study of "The Construction of Cities," but disliked in the final book, entitled *Urbanisme* (*The City of To-morrow*).

It remains an open question whether Jeanneret's self-image was that of a painter, misunderstood and crucified by the critics while his pseudo-self, the architect, was avidly admired and called a genius. Which persona is doing the carrying, the donkey or the raven?[47] The answer remains elusive in part because Le Corbusier was sensitive to all criticism, whether aimed at his painting, architecture, or writing. Thus his writings have to be read on several different levels in the manner his pseudonyms provide: Jeanneret, Le Corbusier, Le Corbu, LC, or Corbu.[48] The shifting identities only add to the difficulty in discerning exactly what role writing held in the imagination of the architect.

Mary Patricia Sekler notes an important 1926 text written by Le Corbusier in which he describes the splitting of his names and his identity, even though it does not answer the question about why he wrote so persistently, so copiously:

> Le Corbusier is a pseudonym. Le Corbusier only does architecture. He pursues ideas independent of interest, he does not have the right to compromise himself through deceit, through convenience. It is a being free from the weight of the flesh. He must never (but will he succeed) degrade himself.
>
> Ch. Édouard Jeanneret is a man of flesh and blood, who has had all the exhilarating and heart-breaking experiences of an eventful life. Jeanneret Ch. E. paints pictures because, even though he is not a painter, he has always been interested in painting and because he has always painted himself... a "Sunday painter."[49]

THE LANGUAGE OF ARCHITECTURE AND THE ARCHITECTURE OF LANGUAGE

Le Corbusier developed an early understanding that architecture was a mental structure developed out of language and mathematics–it was not like a language, a commonly used metaphor, but actually structured or modeled in Le Corbusier's mind as a language. With Cartesian clarity he wrote "The pursuit of a scientific solution leads to the classification of the diverse elements of a problem."[50] Writing for Le Corbusier was a tool of thought, working out "elements of doctrine" as a scientist might do in a laboratory, making and verifying discoveries, then unifying these elements into a system of thought. He claimed in September of 1920,

> To write a little puts ideas clearly, engages, compromises, constrains one to follow the strength of its theory. It is necessary to reflect constantly, all the time, at each pretext to be sensible. To be sensible, is to be conscious, the contrary to that which one attributes to sensibility. To write and to make the step of a giant and to cross clearly the underground forces of one's instincts and sensations.[51]

The argument developed in this book focuses on how Le Corbusier developed his concept of the language of architecture not as a metaphor, but as a deeply structured analogical model linking together different levels of thought on architecture, urbanism, decorative arts, and painting. He was interested in the concrete workings of this system of thought, and would argue that architecture is a system of relationships extending from the house to the palace, a unity achieved outside of decorative embellishments, a pure system that evolves from the times and the place.[52]

The compositional elements–or determinants–of Le Corbusier's architectural language were the five points of modern architecture–piloti, roof garden, free plan, horizontal window, free facade–which gave rise to an unlimited number of lyrical expressions.[53] Ordered by mathematical relationships of proportion, equilibrium, or harmony, these elements produce a purity of expression, an elegant solution, or a coherent thought. Such statements touched the eye that sees, the heart that beats, and the brain that registers. The theoretical composition of five points contains extensions and corollaries–they develop into the house:city relationship, extending from a "unité d'habitation" to a "radiant city," composed by the "tracé régulateur," then the "modulor," offering a solution for peace and a reason for living.

It was not only a matter of defining the elements of a new architectural language but of expressing a spiritual intuition beyond that which the machine or science could state.

Sometime in the 1920s or early 1930s, Le Corbusier made an accounting of the marvels and discoveries of the world–those acquired and those lost because science and rational thought have discovered many marvelous things and explorers have crossed the two poles:

> There are no longer unknown lands to discover, there are no longer any landscapes that we ignore, now all is measured with instruments: the infinitely grand, the infinitely small. One knows. Objectivity is the queen; one makes of it a new goddess. The time has arrived of incontestable realities.[54]
>
> Mystery, dreams, supposed grandeur, poetry are confined to one's interior, to personal appreciation–truly creative fact, truly individual. Poetry is stronger here, bursting forth more than ever, compensator for the various explorations made by science. The "how" takes the place of the "why"; from a situation confronting exterior events, we pass to a situation confronting interior events. It is the case of the isolated self; it is the creation of a universe for itself. It is the gesture of individual creation, of personal judgment, of intervention which gives to each a conscience. To act and not to submit: definition of individual liberty. We are masters of our freedom through the faculty of our mind to be interested in appreciating innumerable exterior facts.[55]

Le Corbusier's *Almanach d'Architecture Moderne,* planned to be the twenty-ninth issue of the journal *L'Esprit Nouveau* (1925), is an eclectic arrangement of essays written by Le Corbusier; it ignores any contribution Amédée Ozenfant might have made. In part a catalogue for the Pavillon de l'Esprit Nouveau, it also includes excerpts from his travel journal to Constantinople (present-day Istanbul) and Athens in 1911 and a lecture offered on modern architecture. Most importantly it is a clarification of the elements that will crystallize by 1927 into the language of modern architecture, or the five points of architecture.

In an introductory page of the *Almanach,* Le Corbusier raises the definition of architecture to a very high plane. He calls it a "Mirror of Thought. Architecture is a system to think with."[56] And later, he adds, when the epoch has harmonized the play of technique, comfort, and spiritual aspirations, "then an architecture can be formulated and become the expressive verb of a milieu."[57]

He begins to lay out the elements of this language, taking a simple house, a box, for his laboratory experiment.[58] The house, he argues, has two ends: it is a "machine for living" (*machine à habiter*), that is, a machine to aid by its exactitude, to satisfy needs and comfort, and it is a "machine to move you emotionally" (*machine à emouvoir*), a place of meditation, where beauty resides and brings calm to the spirit. Thus the house should be designed to answer both rational and emotional needs. It is attached to every gesture, like the snail to his shell, and should be designed to this measure.

The box, this cube called a house, affects us emotionally through what we see. "My eyes transmit to my senses the spectacle that is offered to them."[59] Broken and incoherent lines upset, continuous lines, rhythmically ordered and smoothly proportioned, please. Arranged into geometric forms, this simple box of architecture becomes a *machine à emouvoir.*[60] He accords the word "simple" high honor and gives it great significance–it is the result of economy, exactitude, precision of intention. "Great art is simple, grand things are simple."[61] But it is a simplicity that results from complexity, from a source of richness: "The concentration, the crystallization, of a multitude of thoughts and means."[62]

Le Corbusier's crystallized words are few, making architectural discourse clear and precise: "house:city," "architecture:urbanism," "nature," "the sun as dictator," "trees and stones that speak," "precision," "purity" and "order," "equilibrium" and "harmony," "tool," "standard," "economy," "utility," "efficiency," "the elegant solution," "radiant." These words–and others–are thinking-tools, or "force-words," used to understand and reason about modern experience, and they form the base of his numerous narratives.

The language of architecture that Le Corbusier sought not only contained the five points but reduced itself to five verbs:

> "To classify," both biological and aesthetic phenomenon, "to dimension" taking into account the logic of functions and considerations of site, "to circulate"–a modern word that meant "everything"–"to compose" with light, and "to proportion" geometrically, in order to provoke sensations...a series of sensations is like the melody in music, Erik Satie used to say: the melody is the idea, harmony (in music) is the means, the tool, the presentation of the idea.[63]

Like a botanist, Le Corbusier traveled the world in search of ideas, classified them into hierarchies, associated them with other ideas, hoping they would "transmute" into a system, a "doctrine." He would reiterate in 1945 as World War II drew to an end and thoughts of reconstruction loomed ahead:

> We have still to learn the language that we have to speak. Gone are the metopes, pediments, tympana and even modern capitals. There will be different things, since the form of the sheltered domain is new. It is built otherwise than before and our technical civilization will express its own sensibilities. With what violence, with what eloquence and with what prodigious invention over a span of 40 years, has cubism already budded and flourished.[64]

THE LITERARY MILIEU OF PARIS

Trying to unravel the conundrum of why Le Corbusier labeled his profession homme de lettres, one must recall the literary milieu of Paris and the effect it had on the young Charles-Édouard Jeanneret during his frequent trips to the city between 1908 and 1917 and after he moved there permanently in 1917. Paris was the international center of artistic and literary experimentation in the early twentieth century, and it pulled Le Corbusier toward it like a magnet. In this milieu he quickly understood that discourse was essential to promote the artistic avant-garde, to aid in negotiations with art dealers and gallery owners, to generate public opinion receptive to the new art, and he was certainly aware of critical reviews of exhibitions published in mass-circulation newspapers and "little reviews," in explanatory program notes and exhibition catalogues.

When the high-spirited Jean Cocteau, together with the dress designer Paul Iribe, published the short-lived *Le Mot* between November 1914 and March 1915, they hoped it would be the mouthpiece of common sense, equilibrium, and intellectual order to offset the disasters and trepidations of war.[65] Another new publication was *L'Élan*, the first issue appearing in April 1915. Amédée Ozenfant, its founder-editor, used Henri Bergson's suspect concept of *élan vital* (vital impetus), a term creating all manner of confusion and disorder before the war, but he tempered the word by clarifying that *élan*, rather than meaning riotous energy, was now an expression of French finesse, a patriotic and optimistic word expressing France's courage and will to succeed.[66] It was a luxurious journal for wartime, printed with several different inks on colored paper or paper painted in colors.[67] The announcement for forthcoming issues proclaimed that "We hope that our friends on the front will thus have the proof that we think of them…Our desire is to prove to foreigners that France, even on the front, forgets neither art nor thought."[68] For the brief year of its existence, *L'Élan* refused to print any realistic portrayals of the battlefront, proclaiming that one ought to love life, not the hideous theater of war.[69]

Guillaume de Kostrowitsky (1880–1918), calling himself Apollinaire in reference to Apollo, the god of the sun, was the optimistic animator around whom younger writers and artists flocked in wartime Paris.[70] An innovative poet, art critic, publisher, and prankster with a ferocious enthusiasm for life, his youthful admirers hoped he would reveal the laws of an *esprit nouveau* (new spirit) since war had destroyed the old. The journal *SIC (Sons, Idées, Couleurs)* offered its inaugural edition in January 1916. Under the editorial direction of Pierre Albert-Birot, a protégée of Apollinaire, this little magazine was dedicated to following his example by aiming "To love life and to tell you so; to live it and to invite you to do the same."[71] Birot even accepted Apollinaire's suggestion that the horrors of war could be a positive and liberating force.[72] In March 1917, another journal, *Nord-Sud*, run by Paul Dermée and Pierre Reverdy, struck a similar note, claiming they too would follow just as enthusiastically the new path that Apollinaire had traced and the new horizons that he had seen.[73] Rather than stress the conflict of war that appeared to some Parisians to be a world apart, they dedicated themselves to expressing "the living art of today."[74]

During the war, Apollinaire began to define the outlines of this esprit nouveau. In the program notes for the controversial ballet *La Parade*, a collaborative effort of Cocteau, Picasso, Eric Satie, and Diaghilev, he wrote that such gestures were

> The point of departure for a series of manifestations of the "esprit nouveau"...which will undoubtedly seduce the elite and which promises to imbue both art and social habits from top to bottom with universal joyousness, for common sense demands that they should at least reach the same level as scientific and industrial progress.[75]

Le Corbusier may have attended this performance, Ozenfant apparently did; both were influenced by its intent.[76]

Another sounding gong for esprit nouveau stressed France's Mediterranean and classical roots. Having already drawn an alliance between nationalism and classicism, in the preface to a catalogue of French artists exhibited in Norway in 1916, Apollinaire believed

> Intelligent and open, France continues, even during the war, the civilizing mission that Greece and Rome have transmitted to it, naturally as the nation the most ingenious, the most sensitive, the most measured.[77]

Esprit nouveau was thus a concept intertwined with the renaissance of France's cultural inheritance presumed to be Greek, Latin, and Mediterranean.[78]

In a lecture entitled "L'Esprit nouveau et les poètes" ("The New Spirit and the Poets") given in November 1917 and published on the first of December 1918, in *Mercure de France*, Apollinaire clarified,

> The "esprit nouveau" which is making itself heard strives above all to inherit from the classics sound good sense, a sure critical spirit, perspectives on the universe and the soul of man, and the sense of duty which lays bare our feelings and limits or rather contains their manifestations.[79]

In this lecture, Apollinaire called on poets to explore new fields and to pay attention to new technologies if they were to survive in the twentieth century. Their progress depended on copying the experimental manner of scientists. Poets must make use of new discoveries within the subconscious and confront spatial changes that the era of the telephone, the radio, and aviation had brought. They must borrow techniques from the cinema and the phonograph, look both to the future yet be attentive to the everyday, and offer eye-opening shocks and great guffaws of laughter.[80] Just as the newspaper juxtaposed on a single sheet the most diverse matter from faraway places, so the poet must present the past-present-future all at once.[81] And just as the phonograph brought sounds from the entire world to everyone's ears, so the words of the poet must resonate with these same tones. He must exploit as well the new book of images that the cinema presented, and utilize the rhetorical strategies of advertising that reached out from every city wall to entice the eye.

Perhaps the most important contribution of Apollinaire's esprit nouveau was to draw attention to modern means of communication, such as advertisements, posters, cinema, the telephone, the phonograph, daily newspapers, and the airplane, and to stress the need for artistic and literary experimentation in the manner of laboratory scientists. In this lecture, Apollinaire also proclaimed:

> The "esprit nouveau" is above all the enemy of aestheticism, of formulae, and of cultism. It attacks no school whatever, for it does not wish to be a school, but rather one of the great currents of literature encompassing all schools since symbolism and naturalism. It fights for the reestablishment of the spirit of initiative, for the clear understanding of its time, and for the opening of new vistas on the exterior and interior universes which are not inferior to those which scientists of all categories discover every day and from which they extract endless marvels.[82]

Weakened by a head wound received in the trenches on the seventeenth of March, 1916, Apollinaire died on the ninth of November, 1918, during the influenza epidemic. His death was a total shock to the Parisian avant-garde, occurring just as the Armistice was about to be signed. Beyond anyone else, Apollinaire had been able to draw something life-enhancing from the chaos and devastation of war. He had outlined a road to the future, but now he was gone.[83] He understood that war taught a dualistic mode of vision, which the poet of an esprit nouveau must incorporate. Such a poet was a visionary looking into the future, drawing on the richness of past traditions but thrilling over the potential of tomorrow.[84] Apollinaire, grasping this new vision, set the tone for postwar cultural expressions: calling for a return to order, duty, and morality while simultaneously illuminating the path to the future and revitalizing the present. It now fell to others to carry forward the banner for this esprit nouveau.

THE POSTWAR RETOUR À L'ORDRE

Architecture and solid constructions were paradigmatic postwar clichés. The important Exposition de la Cité Reconstituée set the tone for reconstruction when it was organized in 1916 by the Association Generale des Hygienistes et Techniciens Municipaux. In the first two years of war, the northeast regions of France had been devastated: hundreds of towns and villages were occupied by the Germans and hundreds of thousands of homes destroyed. The exposition called on architecture–as the most collective, least individualistic of the arts–to direct the esprit nouveau of reconstruction, for architecture, after all, was the art of peace, of stability, and the mother of all the arts.

How could writers and artists dare to create, think, or philosophize after the ferocity of war? How could the work of mourning and the act of remembering be reconciled so one could begin anew? Responses were varied, but the war would remain until the 1930s an indispensable grid on which the avant-garde would be reconstructed and the future of France rebuilt. As an antidote to German influence and as a major rallying point during the war, the French had claimed that their culture was the only pure, universal, and objective one. The appeal to classicism, so masterfully employed in support of the war, would continue to lead the *retour à l'ordre* after the war, a phrase coined in 1919.[85] It represented a new classicism of profound and internal renovation aspiring, in the words of Raymond Lefebvre, to be "A classicism of revolt for order, the classicism of human unity, that which shows an eternal progress toward the universal and permanent, the true classicism that lives in us."[86] Both a regenerative force and a metaphor for the alienation of the individual deprived of collective society and strong religious experiences, this new classicism called for a general regrouping of artists, and the creation of collective works subordinating individualistic expressions to the whole.[87]

Drawing contrasts between France and Germany, making transpositions between different media, proselytizing for an esprit nouveau and the return to order, pursuing adventures in new technological fields, calling for a synthesis of all of the arts and pursuing collaborative endeavors, expressing a love for the Mediterranean: these were among the many influences swirling around the artistic and literary avant-garde in Paris before and after World War I. These currents swept up the young Charles-Édouard Jeanneret in their eddies and would remain lifelong influences.

L'ESPRIT NOUVEAU

After meeting Ozenfant in 1917, and devoting himself to his method of painting in 1918, Le Corbusier and Ozenfant write a manifesto entitled *Après le Cubisme* (1919). By 1920 the two, joined by Paul Dermée, began to edit the review *L'Esprit Nouveau*, dedicated to the memory of Apollinaire. Ozenfant and Jeanneret followed Apollinaire's lessons rigorously, albeit cathartically. Their doctrine of "Purism" was a cleansing effort, a purification of all emotional sentiments and a strenuous mastery over inner compulsions. They placed on the same level painting, architecture, and all aesthetic expressions, acts of construction ruled rigorously by universal and invariant laws. These rules and their elements gave rise to the language of architecture and to the claims that painting is "architectured," that it is constructed like a language.[88]

In an article published in *Création Revue d'Art* (1921), Ozenfant and Jeanneret write about the synthesis of art and architecture and the language they both speak. It is through material forms, through their proportions, and through the relationships of their elements and their organization into a unity that the brain is prepared to comprehend the special state of mathematical nature in painting and in architecture. One of the highest delectations of the human mind–or so the two believed–is to perceive order; to perceive order in nature and to understand the proper participation of man in this ordering of things. A work of art is the masterpiece of this human ordering.

In order to transmit a specific emotion or an exact thought, they write, it is essential to utilize material elements as precisely as well defined words of a verbal language. A Purist word follows the laws of composition internal to the work of art; it conjugates these words, conserving their universal meanings. If a Purist work of art is readable, it is because it utilizes intelligible words.[89] In their analogical reasoning, verbal language through rigorous selection and continuous evolution prevails over all other forms of artistic expression: those of design, sculpture, music, rhythm, dance, folklore, and other means of communicating ideas and thoughts. Architecture and all the arts have become "pure creations of the mind," distilled to their essential elements and reduced to syntactic and logical rules just as language is structured.[90] And yet, in spite of this purification, there remains a poetics emanating from material objects: they move the spectator, they act on the mind, they "radiate" outwards through established relationships and proportions. From these early lessons, two intertwined themes remain in Le Corbusier's creative work throughout his lifetime: one registering rational abstraction, the other emotional sensations. They reduce to the oft-quoted analogy that a house is a "machine for living," and the less frequent repetition that a house is a "machine to move one emotionally."

Writing, painting, and architecture are drawn into an ensemble through the functional expressions of the machine. Machines bring together means and ends in the most efficient and elegant manner. The relationships among the parts and the systemic organization of the whole are the important things. The "spirit of the machine," a spirit of construction and synthesis engendered by pure conception, was a motto used to guide the editors of *L'Esprit Nouveau*.[91] The machine established proportions and utilized new materials. It revealed the style of the times, not in items produced, but in the process of production itself. This spirit of construction was needed to create a poem, to execute a painting, to build a bridge, to plan a city. The aim of *L'Esprit Nouveau* was to affirm the existence of this constructive spirit in contemporary works and to show that it also operated in major works of the past. Working toward a synthesis of diverse activities, past, present, and future, was working toward the future of an esprit nouveau. It was to follow the path Apollinaire had illuminated.

CONCLUSION

There are many reasons examined in this book for why Le Corbusier wrote: to construct a language of modern architecture and urbanism; to convince, persuade, and educate his followers that this was the route toward tomorrow; to defend his position and overcome the many obstacles set in his path and so retain hope against all hope that he would eventually achieve something of grandeur and magnitude. Writing also gave witness to Le Corbusier's existence, to the joy of creativity, making a synthesis of all the arts that animated his life. But the main reason why Le Corbusier wrote may actually be quite simple, and requires little explanation: unable to put all of his thoughts about urbanism into drawings and visual images, yet compelled to explain them, he was forced to write. To repeat a quote taken from his last interview in May 1965, given to Desalle, we find the claim:

> And it turned out later that, not being able to build certain things, I could draw them; but not being able to explain them entirely in drawing, especially when it came to urbanism, I had to explain them, so I wrote.[92]

The books, articles, and letters examined in this book cover the writings of Le Corbusier from 1907–47; texts written between the ages of twenty and sixty. They explore the method he selects to develop "elements of a doctrine" put into service throughout the world when peace returned in 1947. This examination does not cover the books Le Corbusier wrote after World War II, a time when his writings take on a more repetitive form, inserting already written texts into new arrangements, creating artistic constructions out of this self-reflexive assemblage, or writing to defend or describe particular buildings under attack.[93] The intention in this book is to trace out the development of Le Corbusier's pledge to develop an urban theory appropriate to the temps nouveaux. It is not an apologia for his urban plans, which have been severely criticized by generations of observers shocked over impossible schemes such as the Voisin Plan for Paris or Obus plans for Algiers, nor does it answer those who blame Le Corbusier's Unité d'habitation for social problems that abound in apartment ensembles on the periphery of Paris or in urban sites around the world.

This book is instead an exploration of the "evolution" of Le Corbusier's ideas on urbanism, how he developed "elements of a doctrine," and how he elaborated his concepts and ideas. What were the key influences in his self-education as a young architect? How did he come to an early adoption of Cartesian logic and list-making, giving rise to a consistent practice throughout his lifetime? How did he intertwine this penchant for order, precision, and proportion with a love for the organic processes of nature, deploying basic metaphors of rocks, trees, and meandering rivers across his writings? How did he balance the equation he created between rationality and poetry?

It is Le Corbusier's compulsion to explain his theories of urbanism by utilizing words with specific force, and the emotions and imaginations that envelop his pledge to put these thoughts down on paper that open the territory before us for exploration. The question remains unfathomable and extremely personal: What was Le Corbusier's need to write that produced such a torrent of words?

PART 1
Finding a Path that Led to Paris (1907–17)

CHAPTER 2 SEARCHING FOR A METHOD (1907–1912)

> *To create at 20 years and to dare to continue to want to create: aberration, error, stupendous blindness—unprecedented pride. To want to sing when one does not yet have lungs! In what ignorance of one's being must one be plunged?*
>
> —CHARLES-ÉDOUARD JEANNERET, 1908

I. TRAVELS TO ITALY, 1907

On September 3, 1907, a month before his twentieth birthday, Charles-Édouard Jeanneret left La Chaux-de-Fonds for a two-month trip to Italy, Budapest, Vienna, and Paris.[1] Except for occasional visits, he would not return home until 1911, following his voyage to Constantinople. During these travels he wrote many letters, journaled, and filled sketchbooks with notes and drawings. These are important not only for reconstructing his travels but for tracing the development of his style, his rhetorical modes, and his self-education.

In letters written to his first mentor, Charles L'Eplattenier at the École d'Art, Jeanneret searches for grounds on which to base his method of analysis.[2] He appears to learn more from museums and books than from technical experts or formal classes. He is full of doubts, not yet sure what occupation he should follow: painting, the decorative arts, architecture, or urbanism? Or can he forge a new synthesis of all? As he gathers knowledge, he teaches himself how to translate it into writing, experimenting with ways of describing what he sees, with various points of view and sensibilities. Travel, as it will throughout his life, supplies him with food for thought and with valuable spare time to put pen to paper. He uses time on trains to keep up an extensive correspondence, seclusion on steamships to assemble notes into a book. Rides in an airplane provide moments of revelation, quickly jotted down.[3]

Charles Jencks calls Le Corbusier's style of writing confessional.[4] He (Le Corbusier) is extremely opinionated, struggling in solitude with his ego, and this style allowed him to personalize history and to become the most influential architectural writer of the twentieth century. But Jencks fails to take the rhetorical nature of Le Corbusier's writings into account or to study his mode of argumentation, his challenges and defenses. Furthermore, Jencks considers Le Corbusier's ability to switch swiftly between opposites a paradoxical dualism that marked his character until the end of his life. On the contrary, I argue in this book that this dualism was a mode of argumentation that asked the reader to take one side, then the other, and to weigh the pros and cons–a self-contained dialectic, not a mere character tic but a mode of argumentation that moves the reader toward a decision.

As his copious letter writing reveals, to take a tour through his letters is to discover that to write something down also affected how Jeanneret classified, reasoned, and remembered. Writing allows principles of thought to be clearly stated, categories to be carefully defined, logical arguments proved or refuted. That is how Descartes described his discourse of logical inquiry, and it is a lesson Jeanneret exploited to the fullest. Writing enables items to be arranged in lists, their order rearranged according to different criteria, and their location used as a visual prompt for memory recall. It forces the creation of categories, hierarchically arranged classes, and comparative analysis of items. As we shall come to understand, Jeanneret was an avid list-maker all of his life, eventually exploiting this technique of argumentation into a visual pattern that could be scanned by the eye. Simple two-by-two tables set up binary oppositions and contrasts, enabling analogies to be made and contradictions to be examined. In this manner knowledge advances.[5]

His opening letter to L'Eplattenier (Florence, September 19) explains that he had waited to write until his ideas were a little ordered (*un peu ordonnées*). He then sets up a play of positions, first saying that one often admires a work of art too soon, at the beginning, or overlooks what one ought to admire. At the same time, he is amazed that after so short an apprenticeship at the École d'Art he can discern artistic merit quickly and correctly. And, he says, he has a method for resolving the problem of judging too quickly: he writes his impressions of the moment daily in a notebook, then rereads and corrects these first ideas, remembering and judging more precisely. He is thus able to order and "classify" his strongest impressions, offering a list of the six strongest.[6] While he appreciates the lessons that L'Eplattenier has given him, which have taken him this far, still he confesses that he is not yet "cultivated" enough to make definitive judgments. Indeed, he travels to escape his ignorance of the parameters that structure a rigorous practice of interpreting, judging, and comparing images from art, architecture, and urban sites.[7]

In his journals, Jeanneret recorded his thoughts on art, cities, and local customs and colors. Along with his sketchbooks, these would form a self-reflective archive to be turned to again and again in later years. Writing long letters to L'Eplattenier (and later to William Ritter, his second mentor), often including extracts from his journals and sketchbooks and asking for advice, would be another means by which he strengthened both his critical eye and his writing style.[8] In his letters and sketchbooks, and later in his published books, he practiced writing over writing–inserting passages from notebooks into letters and scribbling over drawings. His tenses change and his voice shifts from personal to formal, emotional to analytical, as he tries to narrow the gap between perception of aesthetic forms, their interpretation, and their translation into words. He developed a method of describing what he saw, what he liked, and what he did not, a staccato verbal rhythm measuring out both his written thoughts and his journeys.

This opening letter to L'Eplattenier, in which he outlines his method for interpreting works of art, includes his first impressions of Pisa, a place he was always to love. There he joins his schoolmate and traveling companion Léon Perrin.[9] Sitting on the grass, before the Piazza del Duomo at three o'clock on a sunny afternoon, he is struck by his first contact with the Piazza as by "a great marvel." He wishes to sharpen his critical judgment and discern categories into which he can sort visual impressions, but is aware that this endeavor cannot be separated from the painter's rapport with an architectural scene or an urbanistic setting. And a new problem confronts him: how does one transfer experiences based on emotional and visual perceptions into words? How does one speak of colors with precision? [FIGURE 2.1, p. 689]

He spent four days on the Piazza, slipping away for only a few hours to visit the Civic Museum. He had never seen anything like the Duomo's facade–yet he plays the devil's advocate and deprecates its artistic value–for, he says, he expects (as he has been taught) that the ducal place (Doge's Palace) will, when he sees it, deliver an aesthetic blow like that of a sharp bludgeon (*le coup d'assomoir définitif*). Yet he also believes he will never regain the calm he felt when seated on the

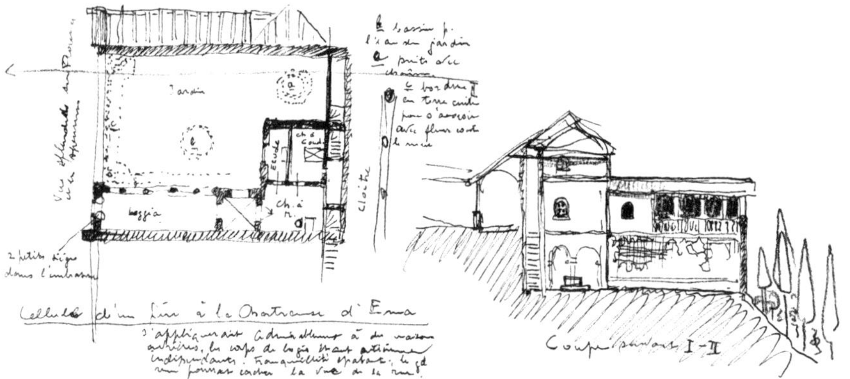

FIGURE 2.2: **Plan and cross section by Charles-Édouard Jeanneret of a monk's cell at the monastery he called "Chartreuse d'Ema." The sketch refers to visits he made in 1907 and 1911, but is undated.**

grass before the Duomo at six o'clock in the evening, with the world far away and the building erected before him.

He has recorded one moment in his notebook so it will not be forgotten. As if he was looking at a series of Impressionist paintings, he employs a rich array of color words: there are yellows of every hue, white and ivory and dark patina, all set against an extraordinary ultramarine. Where the Baptistery projects its shadow, there is a vibration of rich yellows, of red-inlaid and blue-black marbles. An hour later, the sky behind him turns orange and mauve while green doors stand before him, marbles in flat sienna and columns of rose white. He returns on Saturday morning: this time the facade is in shadow, its colors displaying a new subtlety. Yesterday evening, the facade was an allegro of gold and deep ultramarine; in the morning, the blue-black marbles are indistinct, as if seen through a fog.

After four days in Pisa, Jeanneret travels to Florence. Calling Florence a perfect city (*une ville trop complète*), he admits he sees it as a tourist, not as a specialist. He does not see why he should sketch an old palace like the Palazzo Vecchio, for he cannot understand its mystery: "It surprises you, it has such jolly touches in its brutal facade, so much force in its bell tower, with a color so warm and robust."[10] It is a problem of categorization, for the Palazzo does not fit any model he knows. He turns abruptly to the paintings he has seen: Giotto, Orcagna, Raphael, Titian, Botticelli.[11] One afternoon he visits a nearby monastery that he calls *la Chartreuse d'Ema*: "I would like to live all my life in what they call their cells. It is a solution, a unique pattern for workers' housing–a kind of terrestrial paradise."[12] [FIGURE 2.2] But he returns to study the

Palazzo Vecchio–the small fountain, the ornamental shields of the old Florentine families, the courtyard of the Bargello.

Two days later, he wrote to L'Eplattenier for clarification. "The city appears to me *not rich* in architecture, isn't that true? Or are my eyes blinded by Pisa? As I said to you the Palazzo Vecchio is a great marvel, but it is difficult to study, it has an abtruse power, isn't that true?" And again he turns to art for solace before interjecting, "Or am I mistaken and ought I...to draw the Palazzi of the city? A word from you on this subject will be of great use."[13] Nor is this his last letter about troublesome Florence, for he writes from Venice on October 28 that in Venice he finds again the emotions of Florence.[14]

H. Allen Brooks thinks that Jeanneret's inability to understand the architecture of Florence is proof that he had yet to acquire the concerns of an architect–mass, volume, space, materials, construction, plans, urban spaces–and saw two-dimensionally, as a decorator, not three-dimensionally, as an architect. He also points out that Jeanneret is already expressing his belief that the key to architecture is to be found in painting, as Le Corbusier wrote in 1958: "The secret of my quest must be sought in my painting."[15] Charles Jencks refers to this visit to Florence as the "first test" of Jeanneret's "dialectical frame of mind," in which he tests his own impressions against those of his master, of Ruskin, even of Baedeker. Yet Le Corbusier fails this test, says Jencks, for he sees nothing to admire architecturally in Florence and even doubts his own impressions.[16]

In any case, Venice was not pleasing enough for a prolonged stay. It rained for five days, causing many bothersome moments of forced idleness, giving a sense of great inertia. Crayons were not used; paper remained white. Yet there was, of course, much that Jeanneret admired in Venice: the Doge's Palace and Saint Mark's Square, for example. He was even present at a veritable apotheosis: a dramatic sky covered in black clouds, asphyxiating in a yellow fog with the sun shining brilliantly on the side of the Basilica di Santa Maria della Salute–the sea, the sky, the houses making an immense torch seen through the rain or his tears. With all this ecstatic scenery to absorb, it was merely by chance that the young travelers paid two brief, unprofitable visits to the International Exposition of Painting before it closed. "It is just to say that a trip of two months across Italy renders you...a collector of useless ecstasies."[17]

Returning to his impressions of Florence, he recounts an image grasped while leaving the city. The train made a detour that allowed him to see repeatedly the enormous cupola of Brunelleschi. To see it from the piazza, where one had to constantly dance from leg to leg, avoiding vehicles of all sorts—even a funeral—and then to see it from the outskirts, as the travelers of the Middle Ages would have when they arrived at the summit of a hill, and suddenly a monster of stone, a hill larger than those surrounding the town, would arise—these were completely different things.[18]

II. VIENNA SOJOURN, 1907–8

Leaving Venice on November 7, Perrin and Jeanneret moved on to Budapest, where they stayed for three days. Jeanneret coolly reports that after seeing in this city both huge, ugly architecture and terrible, frozen modern art, all designed without any vital principle, how useful Italy had been. The two move quickly on to Vienna, but here Jeanneret is shocked at first by the "modern villas." He is later able to admire their materials, but notes that their construction is masked and falsified. While Perrin remains optimistic before this great unknown (of secessionist art and architecture), Jeanneret is a little alarmed or frightened.[19] Within a few weeks, he comments as an aside that Perrin had found comfortable rooms with a bourgeois landlady as sweet as the honey of Hymettos and was thus conserved in sugar, while his lodgings on the other hand were hell and he was kept in vinegar.[20]

The purpose of this trip to Vienna was to study contemporary architecture. Jeanneret was expected to attend art or architectural school and find employment in an architectural office. He had little success at either, yet had plenty of work designing the villas Stotzer and Jacquemet in La Chaux-de-Fonds.

A letter written jointly with Perrin to L'Eplattenier in early January 1908 speaks of plans to leave Vienna and go to Dresden, as L'Eplattenier had apparently advised, at the end of January or as soon as Jeanneret completed the designs for the villas. Naively, they ask for guidebooks on Dresden: it is, they say, impossible to judge what architectural office Jeanneret should enter and to discover the forty or thirty modern villas among the three hundred thousand villas in the city. If only they had some informative books and the addresses of good modern schools, then valuable time would not be wasted as it had already been in Vienna. What guidance L'Eplattenier was able to give them is not known.[21]

In Jeanneret's part of the letter, he says he is more convinced than ever of his weakness in modeling and believes it necessary to acquire a solid knowledge of form. It would be easy to adapt this knowledge to architecture later. He chides L'Eplattenier for forgetting his students' ignorance of human and even animal forms. L'Eplattenier had acquired such knowledge in his own youth in Paris, but "we" go forward as blind men, struggling against ignorance.[22] Jeanneret has decided to continue his architectural practice for half of each day. He admits that he will probably rarely need to draw figures, but if he wants to succeed in architecture he must learn the basics.[23] Apparently this letter is one of self-justification, for at the end of December, while in Vienna, Jeanneret had already begun to study with the sculptor Karl Stemolak. Yet he is not yet able to admit this to L'Eplattenier.

He reports that he works furiously on the designs for the Villa Stotzer and struggles against discouragement. He feels that an enormous ditch separates him from the truth, although there are moments when, completely absorbed in his work, he achieves some satisfaction. Yet he understands with cruel clarity the extent of his ineptitude. He asks for comments, for he has done all that he is able to do on his own.[24] Such swings between elation and despair, inspiration and blockage, were to continue for years, until he settled on a method of analysis and composition in painting, architecture, and writing.

At the end of February, after nearly four months in Vienna, he writes a twenty-four-page letter to L'Eplattenier.[25] For the first time, he manages to describe some of the cityscape. In the overall grayness of cement, he notes, modern structures such as the Postal Savings Bank, the Steinhof church and colony, the Academy of Commerce by the Deiningers, and a smattering of villas (all designed by Otto Wagner) occasionally stand out. These are interesting, sometimes even sincere works, but unfortunately they can scarcely move imbeciles (like himself) who have found St. Mark's or San Michele beautiful. Wagner attracts and hypnotizes many young architects, but Jeanneret thinks he designs false facades, suppresses the posts and coursings around windows, and despises any recourse to nature (*l'appel de la nature*).

Jeanneret labels Wagner's influence the "German movement" and characterizes that movement as the pursuit of extreme originality with no interest in construction, logic, or beauty. Here, for the first time, he sets ideological contrasts in play, comparing Germany and its "innovations" to what he calls the "Latin movement" in France, exemplified by La Chaux-de-Fonds and other efforts inspired by the great works of the past. He opposes the German movement and argues, utilizing for the first time an organic analogy that he will use repeatedly for the rest of his life, that the logic underlying the Latin movement is the logic of life: life, which moves from seed to roots, then to stem and leaves, arriving finally at the flower.

Having sketched these contrasts between Germany and France, Jeanneret concludes that "we" (he and L'Eplattenier) must recognize that they have been gravely mistaken. Although he lost four months in Vienna, he gained in *certainty*, a surety that he swears will continue. Why, he asks rhetorically, did he leave his master and travel at all? He answers: In the beginning, in Italy, to be baptized in Beauty and to take possession of the measuring stick of masterpieces that would guide him in the future. In Germany, supposedly to learn the technique of his art. But he was not as fluent in German as he had thought, which worked against him. He could not enter any of the schools. Even if he could enter the Technischeschule, all courses would be in German, so he would understand little. Besides, he admits, the subject matter itself would be difficult, since he has no head for mathematics. He was thus left to educate himself, but in what manner?

School was not feasible. Nor was he eager to stay in Vienna for the four or five years required to learn a language and complete a degree. Perhaps he could train by working in an architectural office. But, he admits, he would constantly be finding fault with the ideas of his boss, presumably a member of the German movement. There was only one option: self-education through sheer attentiveness. He must counsel himself at every moment, listening and overhearing conversations, jotting everything down in his notebook, on guard from morning to night. Through self-education, he would gain sufficient knowledge to pass an examination to gain the equivalent of a diploma, and therefore, some self assurance.[26]

He recapitulates his framing formula: the streets of Vienna have taught him nothing, and he fears it would be the same in Dresden. Yet he has learned something from Vienna, and it is this: *before judging, look deeply and compare.* Applying this principle to the German movement, he finds that Wagner and his school are sincere, executing works of taste most of the time. But looking in depth, he finds them embryonic, their productions swollen either with the old style or a complete lack of proportion.

Having compared the Germans and the Latins, Jeanneret comes to the point: he ought to learn his trade in a place where he is not an ignoramus. Since he is enraged at every step in Vienna, he will never work arduously at his technique there, and hence, never build.

To learn everything about the technique of building, he must enter an office for some hours each day. And he must also adhere to that application of nature that L'Eplattenier had taught his students. (Here his logic wavers as he notes that his brother Albert had received a major blow to his career in Berlin; he wants to avoid a similar situation.[27]) Moreover, he wishes to be among friends of his own age. Only in Paris can he accomplish all these things, and so it is to Paris that he and Perrin will go within the month. (Perrin's contribution to the logic of this decision is not described.) Jeanneret concludes:

> It is decided, it is irrevocable, we have seen and judged. If you blame us, my good dear master, ah well, excuse me, but it is yourself you blame because of your teachings that have led us here.
>
> Revolt, you say! Yes, but it is an injurious word that will not be said because we are certain that you agree.[28]

Evidently L'Eplattenier was, as Jeanneret anticipated, chagrined that his students were not following his advice to go to Dresden, because Jeanneret complains in the next letter that L'Eplattenier treats them as if they were ten-year-olds. They did not understand why he wanted to keep them from continuing their education in Paris. Certainly there had been rewards in Vienna: Jeanneret had gained much from studying with Stemolak (misspelled Steinolak), and, since submitting the plans for the two villas, he had spent every Sunday roaming the city, studying "modern" houses. But he reverses these gains by revealing a "secret": all the so-called modernity of Germany that enchants us is made in reality of brick plastered to appear as stone. This dishonest hoax is obvious once he looks at a structure in the photographs he took, for there all the details of construction are visible.[29] Nevertheless he confesses (in an odd aside that will reveal its full import only in the future) that it is the Germans, not the French, who led him back to the Parthenon.[30] He reiterates: it is "technique" that he lacks, and he cannot learn it in Germany because of the language problem.

He continues the reasons why he should go to Paris two days later in another letter.[31] Which was better, to attain (supposedly in a city L'Eplattenier would select) one or two years of theory before entering practice or, as suggested several paragraphs later, to practice in Paris, and if he had time left over, to follow theory in the École Polytechnique Supérieur? He sums up: Having received a strictly artistic education, his knowledge was built on a void because he has not the slightest notion of "technique." That holds him back at every step, and upsets him when he executes architectural compositions, because he has to venture into the unknown where he does not allow himself the least bit of fantasy or daring. On the other hand, if he enters into a great office where one is designing important buildings, he will not profit from it because all the technical aspects would be discussed in language he does not know.

In these argumentative letters to L'Eplattenier, Jeanneret seems always in a hurry. His search for "modern" villas cannot have taken more than two weekends, if that much; he wants to gain technical expertise now, not later; and it is time to earn money, for he complains it has been a year and a half since he had done so (nevertheless, there had been deposits in his bank account during this period from the villas he helped design in La Chaux-de-Fonds). Above all he wants to surpass as quickly as possible his present stage of design, restricted to indigenous houses and villas.

He returns to the question: should he study technical matters now or later, when he might understand them better? There are two answers: either to go to Paris, where there are schools of construction, and simultaneously to work in an office five or six hours each day, *or* to go to Zurich (as a substitute for Dresden) and study with one of L'Eplattenier's colleagues. Here he slips in another point: his artistic education was accomplished primarily by visiting museums, and Paris held an invaluable assemblage of museums. In Paris, Notre Dame would be his master in artistic matters, but in Zurich there would be nothing to compare.[32]

Jeanneret writes to his parents on February 28 that L'Eplattenier does not approve of his and Perrin's plan to go to Paris. Nevertheless, he believes, "There is a decision in the air: Burn what you have adored, and adore what you have burned!"[33] This is a phrase he will repeat as his estrangement from his beloved mentor and fellow students in La Chaux-de-Fonds eventually grows larger. A few days later, he writes to L'Eplattenier that it is time to make a decision.[34] He again compares Germany and France, but admits that he is indifferent to whether taste and art come from Germany or France, for only museums and nature are important to him, nothing else. He remarks on the Moorish room in the Museum of Decorative Arts, which has more to say about plan, light, beauty, and the rules of art than any school whatsoever. [FIGURE 2.3, P. 689] The same thing could be said for the museum's fifteenth-century Gothic furniture. He reiterates that it is "technique" that matters—con-

FIGURE 2.4: Charles-Édouard Jeanneret photographed in front of a window at 9 rue des Écoles in Paris from May 1909: In the distance, over the rooftops, Notre Dame can be glimpsed.

struction methods, materials, and structure. Taste, style, and simplicity: all that is to be acquired with age. "A writer," Jeanneret says, applying a linguistic analogy that he will develop more fully at a later time,

> can be worthy of this name only when he knows his alphabet, when his syntax allows him to make phrases that hold together. He takes a style, amplitude, grandeur, only on the day when his mind becomes untangled from the traces of construction... and is no longer occupied solely with art, being sure then that his thoughts will be expressed in a language that readers can understand.[35]

Jeanneret concludes: going to Paris appears to be the sole logical route. L'Eplattenier asserts that he could accomplish all he wishes in Germany, but Jeanneret feels the better solution is to reside in a French city, take courses as a day scholar, and work five or six hours daily in a big office. In this way he could learn theory and check it each day in practice. And in Paris, moreover, one works by the hour in offices, allowing one to attend school part-time. It is a matter of urgency for L'Eplattenier to decide whether he agrees that he should go to Paris.[36] [FIGURE 2.4]

III. PARIS SOJOURN, 1908–9

It appears from the gap in the letters to take Jeanneret four months to write to L'Eplattenier after arriving in Paris in late March 1908.[37] Perhaps he assumes that L'Eplattenier is angry with him for not following his advice, and so postpones writing. Another reason for this delay may be that he is as ill prepared for Paris as he was for Vienna and does not want to confess it.[38] A third may be his increasing self-doubt as to whether he has the necessary training to obtain an apprenticeship in architecture. Though he has been involved in the design of three villas by the age of twenty, he begins to consider these works superficial, dominated by figural ornamentation and sculptural form–errors attributable to L'Eplattenier's instruction. He must praise yet negate his mentor's advice, transcend his teaching, begin again on a higher plane, i.e., burn what he has adored while adoring what he has burned. He has come to Paris to sharpen his skills and to learn mathematics, structures, and materials; he does so by his own method of self-instruction, namely studying in the Bibliothèque, reading, and sketching.

Eventually–just prior to July 3, 1908, when he presumably writes his first letter from Paris to L'Eplattenier–he finds part-time work with Auguste and Gustave Perret. He has found a new mentor and is free to follow his own course of study in the afternoons.[39]

The first two letters to L'Eplattenier from Paris are the most important, for they underline a tendency seen in his earlier letters: he has a penchant for Cartesian rationalism, for drawing up lists, making categorical organizations and logical deductions. He has demonstrated this analytical ability in his attempts to persuade L'Eplattenier that he should go to Paris. He finds it is a noble game to play with comparisons, oppositions, and contrasts–setting each end of an argument against the middle. In Vienna he was acutely aware of his need for what he called "technique," but like Descartes, his self-education is primarily a dialogue with himself as he struggles to uncover the deceptions in the knowledge he has received. He hankers after an ideal to guide him, a method of architectural imagination that will be heavily reliant on discursive form. Like Descartes, he feels compelled to write, not only to tell of his struggles and scrupulous self-criticism, but to examine his method of thought and analyze his judgments by making lists of comparisons and deductions.[40] Lists will become a favorite method of Le Corbusier's to size up a situation, to draw comparisons between points, to arrive at a decision. He desires conceptual clarity, a mode of pure reason to direct his vision. And to enable him to pursue this ideal that will prepare him for action, he seeks solitude. His letters to L'Eplattenier from Paris are thus remarkable not only for openly disgreeing with his mentor and fellow students but for containing the beginnings of his autobiographical discourse. He is polite, but senses there are errors in L'Eplattenier's teaching that require him, Jeanneret, to go back and fill in the holes. He borrows styles of writing and argumentation from others, as he will often do, apparently experimenting with a new amalgam, trying to rid himself of parasitic ideas while being torn by self-doubt and depression. Throughout, his intellect cannot be separated from his keen visual sensibility and his yearning to draw, to create, to surpass what he can so far understand and put into practice.

He confronts the task of repudiation head-on, becoming a devil's advocate against his own cherished beliefs. He writes that he feels himself an "outlaw" due to the excellent education he has received from L'Eplattenier, which has caused him to need an ideal, one far beyond his abilities, so that each day brings suffering and disillusionment, each day his hand and his thoughts betray him.

Most difficult appears to be the choice of an occupation.[41] He mixes the metaphor of battle with that of capital acquired through hard work–metaphors he will often repeat in later writings. The problem, he says, is how to dispose of his capital along the major lines of battle so it can be used at the right moment. It is necessary to have at his disposal different kinds of information, all well-placed in order for their synthesis to produce the desired work. But if one attacks these forms of understanding out of order, then there comes a time when one realizes that behind the lines one has neglected something, and one is completely stopped; one must fall back, yet simultaneously hold the conquered place. Jeanneret's self-education thus causes him to march backward into battle. For though he has practiced architecture, he has not been much concerned with mathematics or any form of technical knowledge, which are difficult to achieve on his own.

He tries to set a rational program for himself that will enable him to systematically learn the tricks of his trade. Each day he sets himself a task. Often he is surprised to be thrilled over a mathematical problem, even carried away by it. Aside from pure mathematics, he is reading Viollet-le-Duc's ten-volume *Dictionnaire raisonné de l'architecture française du XIe au XVe siècle.* He finds him to be wise, logical, clear, and precise:[42]

> I have Viollet-le-Duc and I have Notre Dame which I use as my laboratory table so to speak. In this marvelous building I verify the statements of Viollet-le-Duc and I make some small personal observations. It is here also that I make some drawing sessions "after the antique" (!) and I assure you that these "sessions" are not the bright moments of the day. I have a profound disgust of myself. No, frankly, I am terrified to prove each day my incapacity to hold a crayon: I do not feel the form, I can not turn the form: and am desperate from it.[43]

Again he blames his education, which does not allow him to dare to model a sphere or any other geometric design. His mind has been petrified with forms of self-conceit and duplicity. If he had been taught about the assemblage of geometric forms and how they admit shadow and light, about logic, reason, and deduction, then after seven years of art school he would know how to design. But it is only Paris that enables him "to see beyond where he is."[44]

After five months, at the end of November, he writes his second Paris letter to L'Eplattenier.[45] He had contemplated a visit home, but feels that Paris has changed him, and needs to warn his mentor of the new person he has become so there will be no misunderstandings: "Perhaps you were not wrong to make of me something other than an engraver, because I feel strong."[46] Now that he knows where he is going, he can make the effort with victorious enthusiasm. Enclosed within the solitude of his own thoughts, with all that Paris inspires in him, he must discipline himself, follow a harsh regime of work:

> Paris the immense city–of ideas–where one loses oneself, if one is not severe with oneself and without pity. Everything is there, for the one who wants to love–(love of the divine spirit which is in us, and which perhaps is our [guiding] spirit, if we invite it to this noble task).... Paris is death for dreamers, the smarting whip at each minute, for some minds that want to work (it provides work).... Only if I had a little more time to think and to learn! Real life, cruel, devours time.[47]

Time is measured, the hours are passing, the pages of life turn, never to be recaptured–these will become oft-repeated motifs throughout Jeanneret's writing. He is always in a hurry, there are too many things to occupy his life, he must discipline the use of his time if he is to achieve some greatness before the hour sounds. He then explains that his "concept is set" (*mon concept s'établit*)—that is, the mental idea that allows him to organize his perceptions is formed, and though he will not talk of it directly, he will begin to explain the ideas on which it is based. He is filled with enthusiasm, prodded forward by the feeling that he can achieve his ideal. "I have before me 40 years to attain what I outline on my not yet clearly defined horizon."[48]

He knows that a cruel struggle is threatening with those whom he loves, and he feels they should meet him halfway lest they not be able to go forward together.

> Oh, how I ardently wish that my friends, our comrades, would discard the small life with its daily satisfactions and burn that which they hold most dear, believing that these cherished things were good—[in order that] they feel how low they were aiming and how little they *were thinking*.[49]

Jeanneret admits that his concept of the art of building is rough, because up to this point that was all he could achieve. Vienna dealt a blow to his idea that architecture was constructed out of purely sculptural forms; in Paris, he feels the immense void within himself, and tells himself, "Poor thing! You still do not know anything, and, unfortunately, you do not know *what* you do not know."[50] He lists several practicing architects whom he has asked for advice, including the Perrets, all of whom said to him, "You know enough about architecture."

> But my spirit revolted and I went to consult the ancients. I chose the most zealous fighters, those whom we, we of the twentieth century, are ready to resemble: the Romanesque era. And for 3 months I studied Romanesque architecture, in the evening at the Bibliothèque. And I went to Notre Dame and I [audited] the end of the Gothic course of [Lucien] Magne, at the Beaux-Arts...I suspected by studying the Romanesque that architecture was not the eurhythmic affair of forms, but what else? I still did not know exactly. And I studied mechanics, then statics; oh all that took place during the entire summer. How many times was I mistaken, and today, with anger, I am aware of the chasms over which is formed my science of modern architecture.

> With rage and joy, because I know finally what is good, I study the forces of matter. It is arduous, but it is beautiful, these mathematics, so logical, so perfect![51]

He continues his studies, auditing Magne's course on the Italian Renaissance and Boennelwald's on Roman-Gothic architecture. In the workshops of the Perrets, he sees constructions in concrete (*le béton*) and understands the revolutionary forms it demands.

Having listed all of his achievements in Paris, Jeanneret is finally able to write to L'Eplattenier the phrase that he has repeated two times already,

> These eight months in Paris cry out to me: logic, truth, honesty, away with dreams of the past arts. Eyes high, go forward!...Paris says to me: "Burn what you have loved, and love what you have burned."[52]

He names his fellow students—Grasset, Sauvage, Jourdain, Paquet and others—calling them all "Liars...because you do not know what is architecture...liars, yes, and more, cowards":

> The architect ought to be a man with a logical mind, an enemy, because suspicious of it, of the love of the sculptural effect, a man of science and of the heart, an artist and a learned man.[53]

After a brief sortie into the architecture, religion, and materials of the past, he speaks of the future, of "the art of tomorrow":

> This art will exist. Because humanity has changed its manner of living, its way of thinking. The program is new....One can speak of the art of the future, because this new structure, it is iron, and this iron is a new material. The dawn of this art becomes dazzling because out of iron, a material subject to destruction, one has made reinforced concrete [béton armé], an unprecedented creation.[54]

Having justified his year of travel and self-education, and with a degree of self-righteousness, he turns to criticize L'Eplattenier, who expects his students, all young men twenty years old, to meet responsibilities too advanced for their age. Because L'Eplattenier has achieved his own inner strength, he believes he sees the same strength in his students, but they have yet to acquire this strength through study, travel, and solitude, as Jeanneret is struggling to do. Pushing Jeanneret's comrades to become architects too soon makes them arrogant:

> Arrogance remains at the bottom of their everyday life....They are tied to their premature concept. They have hardly had sadness, hardly had difficulties: without difficulties one cannot make art: art is the cry of a living heart....One does not build on sand....Your soldiers are ghosts. When the struggle is here, you will remain alone. Because your soldiers are ghosts, since they do not know that they exist–why they exist–how they exist. Your soldiers have never thought. The art of tomorrow will be the art of thought.[55]

Then again the refrain "The Concept high and forward!" and the complaint that only L'Eplattenier is able to see into the future–his students see only by luck, and will sooner or later fail.

What appears to be criticism of L'Eplattenier can be read as Jeanneret's justification of his own lifestyle and path of self-education, as well as his growing awareness that the principles of modern art lie elsewhere than in the lessons that L'Eplattenier offers. As if to lessen the sting of his criticism, Jeanneret resorts to a parable of a tree, another image that he will repeat in various forms throughout his life. Wanting to soften what appears to be an angry rejection of the path carefully prepared for him by L'Eplattenier, he writes:

> Just as a tree on an arid rock took 20 years to sink its roots generously says, "I have struggled–let my offspring reap the harvest" and allows some seeds to fall on some patches of soil which line the rock....The rock is warmed by the sun, the seed bursts, it pushes forth its small roots with such vivacity! What joy in order to point its small leaves toward the sky! But the sun heats the rock, the plant looks around it with agony; it becomes dizzy with the intense heat; it wants to throw its roots toward its great protector [parent tree]. But the tree has taken it 20 years to sink–with struggle–its roots across the cracks in the rock....With anguish, the seedling accuses the tree that created it–It curses it and dies. It dies of not having lived–by itself.

> That is what I see in the country. In my agony. I say: to create at 20 years and to dare to continue to want to create: aberration, error, stupendous blindness–unprecedented pride. To want to sing when one does not yet have lungs! In what ignorance of one's being must one be plunged?
>
> The parable of the tree makes me afraid....for the tree prepared for suffering.[56]

Having thus lashed out at his mentor, he begins again to worry that he will have to flee from the suffocation of his old comrades, as already he has fled from two or three others. He must struggle against their ignorance, for he now assumes that they know nothing. He fears they will injure him, apply brakes to his quest to see higher and go farther. He wants something more out of life than the group around L'Eplattenier can offer, and he is not above taking pride in his Spartan existence, and the discipline and moral commitment he has achieved while in Paris.

> They do not know what Art is: intense love of oneself: one seeks for it in retreat and solitude, this divine "self" perhaps the earthly self if one forces it–through struggle–to become it....It is in solitude that one struggles with oneself, that one is chastised and that one is whipped. It is necessary that friends from below [in La Chaux-de-Fonds] look for solitude....Where? How?[57]

After his visit home at the end of 1908, Jeanneret returns to Paris and works for the Perrets for almost a year, until November 9, 1909. During this stay, he writes only a few postcards to L'Eplattenier. To his parents he writes that he begins to learn "methodically," that his interior life is disciplined and all sentimental stories finished. Yet he also writes of romantic love and of his impressions of the great Romain Rolland's lecture and of springtime in Paris.[58] After leaving the Perrets, he plans to remain in Paris until Christmas vacation, going to museums, reading, and enjoying the life of the city. He tells his parents that he will not stay in La Chaux-de-Fonds very long.[59]

Discarding these plans, and in spite of his severe criticism of his École d'Art comrades and his belief that L'Eplattenier's teachings are built on sand, Jeanneret suddenly returns to La Chaux-de-Fonds in early December and joins that band of devotees gathered together under L'Eplattenier's direction, which would be called *Ateliers d'art réunis* (workshops of combined art), formally organized on March 15, 1910. L'Eplattenier envisioned this group as the continuation of his *Cours Supérieur* (advanced course) at the École d'Art, a workshop in which his former students could be employed.[60] The subjects were once again the decorative arts (e.g., sculpture, mosaics, mural painting, and metalwork) and remained distant from the rationalism that Jeanneret had begun to espouse while in Paris.[61] Jeanneret does not stay long. He takes up his travels again in April 1910, this time going to Germany, where he will remain, except for vacations, until May 1911, when he departs for the East.

His German sojourn, traced in detail below, entails an ambitious program of travel, study, and writing. He intends to survey the new art of "urbanism" subscribed to by German municipalities and to write a book entitled *Étude sur la construction des villes* (*Study of the Construction of Cities*). While in Germany, he is commissioned by the École d'Art to write a small booklet entitled *Étude sur le mouvement d'art décoratif en Allemagne* (*Study of the Movement of the Decorative Arts in Germany*), from 1912. Both of these projects are instigated by L'Eplattenier to widen his student's education. Not only would Jeanneret study how the decorative arts were taught in Germany and how their products were marketed–knowledge that would help L'Eplattenier strengthen his concept of the Nouvelle Section within the École d'Art–but he would strengthen his architectural and urban exposure so that he might one day take up a teaching post in La Chaux-de-Fonds.[62]

Due, however, to Jeanneret's hostility to the so-called German movement in the arts, as well as to mounting anxieties over his lack of a professional diploma and to feelings of estrangement from both his *Ateliers d'art réunis* comrades and L'Eplattenier, the German interlude encompasses moments of turbulence and empty depression. He suffers a severe writer's block on his *Études*, if not in his letter writing. While he would write repeatedly to L'Eplattenier that the brochure for the *Étude* was almost finished, there is no evidence that this was ever actually the case. On the contrary, he apparently made little progress on his book projects.

IV. GERMAN SOJOURN, 1910–11

Some architectural historians consider Jeanneret's twelve-month stay in Germany from 1910–11 to be the most formative period of his self-education.[63] Brooks, for example, claims that no period during Le Corbusier's formative years was as important as this time in Germany:

he learned proportions following the *tracés régulateurs*, Spartan classical forms and geometric shapes advocated by the Werkbund; white became his color of choice; and he found his ideal, a synthesis of French artistic genius and German organizational abilities. Especially important are the four months between November and April, when he worked for Peter Behrens, learned proportion, conscious style, and the correct use of materials, and came to admire clear geometric forms, the application of regulating lines, and machine processes of precision and purity. Supposedly he was a convinced Medievalist when he arrived in Germany in mid-April, but he departed a year later in May a devoted Classicist. Although he was already convinced that modern architecture was an intellectual procedure, and that *béton armé* was a revolutionary new material that would transform life, his "evolution" was not yet complete. This transformation, it has been argued, was painful, and Jeanneret was psychologically tormented throughout the change. Other insults were added on top of these difficulties: it took Behrens seven months to offer him employment, and he never gave Jeanneret the special attention he thought he deserved or craved, nor was Behrens the model father figure he so emphatically desired. Due to these insults it is assumed that Jeanneret repressed any debt in his self-formation that he owed either to the contribution of Behrens or to the importance of German principles of urbanism.[64] The argument developed here, however, considers influence to be a two-way street, and in spite of the torture and depression he endured, Jeanneret finally found the ideal he had been seeking throughout his travels, a product of his interminable comparisons between the lessons he drew from Germany and those obtained one year before in France. He has already admitted that Germany, not France, taught him to look to the Parthenon, yet he makes a clear distinction between the higher arts of France compared with the baser artistic inclinations of Germany. He would eventually combine within himself both the ideal of French artistic genius and the promise of German industrial creativity, an integration of individualistic artistic expression with logical processes of thought.[65]

His exposure to a wide range of new experiences, and their impact on his development and self-education, cannot be denied. An avid self-analyzer, he already had a method by which he could record his reactions, tempering and overturning opinions he made at first sight. As he had done ever since his travels to Italy, he kept a notebook of his reflections and prejudgments, in order to reread them, correct them, and sharpen their aim—even overwriting them at a much later date. Except for summer vacation, he remained in Germany seven long months before entering Behrens's office on November 1, 1910. During the first spring of his visit, he resided in Munich, making study trips to different cities in order to visit exhibitions and schools of decorative arts or analyze their urban composition, and of course, to visit museums, attend conferences, go to concerts, and immerse himself in the ebb and flow of everyday life along city streets. He conducted research for the *Étude sur la construction des villes* in various libraries and cities, and by June of 1910 he began to make visits to various schools and workshops for the commissioned work on *Étude sur le mouvement d'art décoratif en Allemagne*. He keeps up a lengthy correspondence with L'Eplattenier and fills at least five different sketchbooks with notes and drawings.

Among the important lessons Jeanneret learned in Germany was the conviction that the future of modern architecture was in its definition as an urban art. But what did that mean? On one hand, he concludes, it involves knowing the appropriate rules and material expression of good city design, and how to apply them so that the public understood their intent. Yet there is much more, because a full concept of "urbanism" is steeped in many ancillary elements. What made Munich, Berlin, or Stuttgart such vital centers in his mind, and what was the persuasive–discursive, even polemic–role of the architect in the new cultural economy of the metropolis? Could an artist intent on originality and autonomy of expression remain blind to the social context, to discursive entanglements with tradition, everyday life, and commerce in metropolitan centers? Tentative answers to these questions can be found in Jeanneret's first two writing projects, which overlap in time and are intermeshed conceptually. Both are intimately tied to Jeanneret's developing awareness of "urbanism"–not just reliance on Camillo Sitte's proposals outlined in *The Art of Building Cities*–but urbanism in the full-blown sense of the word. He had come to Germany to study this new art, but he never untangles it from innovations made in the decorative arts. Perhaps one of the reasons he had trouble completing his study on the construction of cities is that much of what he initially wanted to say about cities is published in *Étude sur le mouvement d'art décoratif en Allemagne* (1912), and the rest, he discovers in 1915, had already been said.

In many different ways, Jeanneret's letters to L'Eplattenier and his notebooks from *Les Voyages d'Allemagne* are a discourse not only on the progress of his two writing projects, but on his evolving definition of urbanism beyond the meaning of good city form and the role it demanded of the artist-architect. And of course, these writings reveal much about his personality, since this trip, like all of his voyages, is a defining experience. Six days after arriving in Munich he writes his first letter to L'Eplattenier, opening on a sour note, hoping to purge himself of some bile acquired in the last "105" minutes. Getting rid of such negative feelings is a prompt to write. Never before had he seen such a worthless city as Munich, especially in the matter of food. He finally found a restaurant after twenty-five minutes of travel, then a forty minute wait, only to be offered a poor cutlet, and then another twenty minutes' delay to pay the bill, and that double what it was worth! His colleague Octave Matthey suffered the same indignation, but apparently had a better disposition to accept it. Apart from these initial difficulties, he has seen a multitude of pretty girls, adding in the same line that he has stopped wearing the bandage over his left eye because it has no effect and he has decided this time he would really learn German. It is as if food is the entryway to the sensations, desires, even anxieties that travel unleashes, for his first letter to his parents also contains comments that Munich is a city of "domestic gastronomy" and its restaurants closed on Sunday nights, so how was he to become more robust?[66]

In his letter to L'Eplattenier, he continues to describe his first impressions of Munich–and admits that he has not yet discovered its beauties. On his way there, however, he had been enchanted by Karlsruhe, then Stuttgart, and felt that German art was making great progress over what he had seen in Vienna the year before; but not in Munich, unless it be the university and a church designed by Theodor Fischer, the one architect he could praise. Except for seeing a school, church, and house in Stuttgart and the Garnissonkirche in Ulm, all designed by Fischer, he would have continued to ignore that architect's name. But he was impressed with the "architectonics" of these projects because they were built in prestressed concrete (*béton armé*) and in concrete blocks (*blocages de béton*), revealing a robust appearance, not the morbidity or dryness of other contemporary works. However, finding that most German architects resided in Berlin and not in Munich, Jeanneret declares his plan of attack has altered a bit. Above all, he wants to work for three or four months with an architect (if possible one that is building in prestressed concrete) in order to learn more German and to spare himself one or more holes in his training (*tuyaux*). In this respect, Fischer has caught his eye, and he has presented his portfolio to him and hopes for the best. Fischer, it appears, was impressed with

Jeanneret's design work, which included architectural projects and studies of nature, and he commented favorably on the originality of his rendering, how he drew inspiration from the surrounding countryside (*pays ambiant*) and not just a single flower or tree.

Jeanneret asks L'Eplattenier if he would once again give him the address of William Ritter, because except for his friend Octave, they are quite alone in Munich.[67] He begins to report on the scenes of Munich: there is a superb store filled with all sorts of stuff such as embroideries, pots, statues, furniture, things from India, from Greece–a mixture of peasant works and modern products, the former the more beautiful. But all of these objects, while they gave him great pleasure, make him anxiously aware that La Chaux-de-Fonds was backward, poorly organized, and her products very small and quite "Gothic." He was struck by the discipline and organization of the Germans that enabled all sorts of talent to shine forth. And then he returns to the framework that opened his remarks: he comments on his looks, that he would like to be a bit fatter and grow a mustache and then the patch over his left eye might look more appealing. And he thinks often of Paris because of its cuisine, especially good butter, whereas in Munich one eats only because one is hungry and the cuisine, when it is thrown together, is watery. This is a style of composition that Jeanneret will often use in his writings: a frame that opens and ends or contains what appears in the middle to be an assemblage of notes.

He closes on a different register: he will add a page of resumé–"The first idea of the small work of which we have spoken: you can return it to me, adding in the margins corrections and compliments."[68] Such an oblique reference to the purpose of his trip was necessary evidently because Jeanneret's parents had not been told why he was going to Germany, and they would have been upset to know that this trip, like the others, was a study trip, not one in which he was gainfully employed. Nevertheless, not wanting to waste time, he asks L'Eplattenier to show this letter to his parents and so save him the bother of having to write the same news twice.[69]

A short while later he writes again to L'Eplattenier that he has found interesting material in the library where he goes to work everyday, but he is obliged to translate the articles, and while he is learning German in this manner, his progress is terribly slow.[70] Meanwhile he has found that most authors quote from Sitte's book *The Art of Building Cities,* making it a monument on which the architecture of German cities has been reformed, and so he will borrow from these same citations. Thus important questions will be resolved by quoting the master himself, and he will avoid the lengthy time it takes to express himself in writing. He thinks that instead of using examples of monuments from cities Sitte had selected, it would be politic of him to draw on the beauties that Swiss cities offer. The question then becomes how to procure useful documentation of these cities. For example, with respect to La Chaux-de-Fonds he needs one or two plans from before the fire (May 5, 1794) and some views that ought to be found in the historical museum or in the city archives. He believes it would help their cause to make a visual comparison between the traditional city and that of today. And he needs similar materials for the other cities he will compare–having these set before his eyes, he can order his ideas and advance with surety. Can L'Eplattenier help him obtain the necessary images so he can continue his work? He is full of enthusiasm because he has the presentiment that this comparative method of visual imagery will be very useful and will allow him to get beyond the boredom of laying out the pages of the brochure. Nevertheless pursuing this *étude de l'art de bâtir les villes* can hardly do him harm!

As for the other things that push him onward in Germany (i.e., being employed in an architect's office), he would like to conclude them as soon as possible. But he has not yet decided his plan of attack, in Munich or elsewhere, and has searched in the *Deutsche Kunst* and other journals of art for an outline of the most advantageous route to travel. He has found that Munich is not the center of architecture, and nothing holds his admiration there. However he must be resigned, although it is difficult, for he has met no one of interest and so it will be until he does. On top of these problems, the weather does nothing but rain! Meanwhile L'Eplattenier has been to Paris, and Jeanneret wonders how he has found it and if there is anything new. Jeanneret allows that he is learning excellent lessons from the things he has seen in Germany: there is beauty to be found in the surrounding ensemble that counts, a lesson he draws from Sitte, and this beauty is related to proportion and the vigor of the overall plan. As well, there is the value of contrasts: in the use of strong materials, in offsetting simplicity with richness judicially introduced. And then he repeats his request for help in gathering and sending him materials.[71]

In the middle of May, Jeanneret divulges he is having trouble obtaining the book on cities written by Sitte. While it is everywhere quoted, evidently it is out of print and thus he feels without this small book he has "his beak in the water."[72] Could L'Eplattenier send him his own copy? He is writing the preface to "our" brochure and finds that the plan is well organized and the conclusions will produce themselves. All in all it will be an amazing work! But he had gone to Fischer's office in the morning and has failed completely to obtain a job. He has a complaint, one that he has said before and will continue to repeat in other letters: everywhere in Germany he is well received, but in the end all the places are occupied and all the doors are shut. Fortunately there is his writing task, which for the moment is a palliative of sorts. His father has written to him of L'Eplattenier's triumph (over winning the competition for a monument, *Hommage à la République*), and he hopes that his mentor will not become too proud with the multitude of praises that surround him. Perrin has also told him about the preparatory courses at the École d'Art.[73]

By the beginning of June, he claims to have finished most of the brochure, although it has been difficult to write in French. The material is dense, and it will possibly spark greater interest beyond the architects of La Chaux-de-Fonds.[74] In any event, he has benefited from this study. But now he really has need of Sitte's book, for no library seems to be able to produce it. Once again he begs for L'Eplattenier to send him his copy. He is eager to return to La Chaux-de-Fonds for the opening of L'Eplattenier's monument in July. By that time the brochure will be finished, and they can review and modify it together, before sending it out to print. Then he comments that he has been introduced in Munich to an exceptionally modern milieu (no doubt referring to his introduction to and reception by Ritter) and has met all the brave and resolved men, but he cannot find a position in an architect's office. It will be extremely difficult, since the Germans seem to be protectionists–and this even slows him down in his objective to become proficient in German. "This brochure is a fortunate affair for me, it allows me to find my way to the side of all the nervous tension and demoralizing delays."[75]

Within a few days, on the seventh of June, he writes again that he is planning to take a vacation now that he has finished writing his "pauvre texte," and all the illustrations have been assembled. But he needs advice on how to represent them on a page, and should he make studied drawings or rapid sketches, and which is more congruent with his "eternal" prose? Tomorrow or the next day he plans to go to Berlin to see an exhibition on housing that will close by the middle of June. But he is not sure and asks for advice on the special things he should see in that city, and requests a reply by the next mail. While he knows this trip to Berlin will be important, and he might travel in the company of Ritter, he doubts it will be valuable at this point of his journey because his German is still very rudimentary. It might be worthwhile, however, to meet one or two architects. He claims that all his efforts at the moment are concentrated on learning German, and for some time he has been taking four hours of conversation each day.[76]

In spite of this indecision, he leaves abruptly for Berlin the very next day and stays for two weeks. He attends some of the sessions of the third annual Deutscher Werkbund discussing "materials and style" and the effect they have on the design of cities. He takes an organized tour on June 10 to see Peter Behrens's recently designed AEG (Allegemeine Elektrizitäts Gesellschaft) buildings, and is shown many of the products Behrens designed after being appointed artistic director in 1907. The following day he attends the Städtebau Ausstellung, where he sees examples of Sitte's influence on town planning, and a few days later he goes to the Grosse Berlin exhibition, where competition plans for the expansion of Berlin are displayed. He also visits the Cement-und-Kalk-Industrie Ausstellung, organized by Behrens, an exhibition that also focused on the issue of "materials and style," and he toured several garden cities outside of Berlin.[77] Certainly this trip was more important than Jeanneret had imagined it would be: within a few short days he has been exposed to a wealth of ideas on "urbanism" and modern architecture, which caused him to enthusiastically write many pages in his notebook about the relationship between architecture and city planning.

Most importantly, especially for someone who grew up in an industrial town of watchmakers, Behrens's designs and the AEG shock him thoroughly, for they reveal completely new processes at work.[78] In his *Sketchbook* he notes that the beauty of the electric lamps and other articles he was shown result from their proportions, being simple objects with forms appropriate to their use. But he was most impressed by the number of workers in the factory: six thousand men and women, another eight thousand in the machine hall, comprising thirty-six thousand altogether. And he immediately develops absolute admiration for the engineering and administrative genius of this colossal combine, for they seem to have found a balance between the workers' needs and the machines' demands. Nevertheless he notes: "Soon the human arm will be entirely useless," for he had witnessed several machines accomplishing automatically a variety of operations but supervised by only one man. Even more amazing was the fact that each electrical product required a great number of steps and tiring tasks such as riveting and welding, all accomplished by machines. The worker had only to prepare the piece of work and set it up at the end. And while he found the facade of the Turbine Hall to be "full of character," he returns to comment on its immense interior, the colossal size of the pieces produced, and how they were maneuvered. And he mentions another detail: it was impossible for so many workers to enter or leave the hall all together, so there was an ingenious system of time cards and clocks that printed the time of entrance and exit on a card inserted by each worker. At the end of the week when the card was full, all they had to do was add up their hours of work. With great efficiency this simple machine controlled all the exits and entrances of all thirty-six thousand workers. Jeanneret was impressed by the scale of the operations, as well as the innovative time clock.[79]

Two days after returning to Munich, Jeanneret writes to L'Eplattenier that his trip to Berlin was very fruitful, and when he has the time he will send him a clean copy of all of his notes. But he is disappointed to learn that the inauguration of L'Eplattenier's monument has been postponed until September 4, for he was looking forward to working with L'Eplattenier in July in order to polish the brochure on cities. Now he has four weeks ahead of him with nothing to do, and he does not want to spend all the time on vacation. In spite of this perplexing change of plans, he has outlined a clear program for the following winter and spring. He has been to see Peter Behrens, Hermann Muthesius, and the interior designer Bruno Paul when he was in Berlin, and he hopes that he can make a training course with Behrens or Paul and one more with Hermann Jansen, the prize winner of the competition for "Grosse Berlin." But he comments: "Can you imagine that no one wants to believe that I am an architect, and they all attribute to me just the qualities of a painter?"[80] Even though he swears to them that he knows his trade, he has only a Parisian certificate in his pocket, and so his protests make little difference. Thus he returns to his writing projects: he is beginning to work on the decorative arts, having visited the school at Weimar on his return from Berlin, but unfortunately the director Henry van de Velde was not there. Nevertheless he jokingly refers to his work on cities: saying all it takes is one prince or king to offer the money and automatically there will be results. Having seen many wonderful examples of the new manner of building cities in

Berlin, how materials and architectural style must relate to the urban ensemble, he is certain of the principles that must be put in place before cities can be reformed aesthetically.[81]

Jeanneret writes to his parents that he visited ten or twelve different cities (on his return from Berlin) and confesses that it was time he revealed to them the purpose of his travels over the last two months. He is glad that he has not been able to find work in an architectural office, because what he has seen and studied have brought a marvelous new orientation to his work. It was not a "colossal work" as his father would say, but merely a study of the art of building cities. "This study will end with a vigorous critique of the means used in La Chaux-de-Fonds and has for its aim to transform all of those mistakes. This study will be published in a brochure, of which the importance goes beyond my expectation. This was for me a passionate question and I hope a lot in its direct results. It will be signed by L'Eplattenier and me and will have interest not exclusively local."[82] The task has been extremely difficult but is now almost ready. The problem, however, is that it is written in very poor French, and he needs the calm of the countryside to improve its style. He confesses that he agreed with L'Eplatteneir to keep this "study" a secret until the work was done, because they did not want the enemy to prepare defenses against their attack. They have very big dreams for the future, so grand in fact that they have trouble finding the exact words to describe them, and so did not want to divulge their thoughts before they were ready. "What to say about that which is done; that which is future belongs to no one, not even those who foresee."[83] He ends his letter trying to tell his parents not to worry about the well-being of their two sons. "In a period where all is chaos, where all which is banal, is prone, where all that which is a rising strength is contested, I estimate that those who do not want to follow raised battle flags, have good heads."[84]

Within a few days Jeanneret is back at work on his German–by answering a bulletin board request for conversational practice, he meets a new friend, August Klipstein, a student of the history of art.[85,86] Meanwhile he continues his writing projects–this time complaining that his idea of using Swiss cities is useless because the visual materials he has been sent are so bad.[87] Anyway there is no point of sending more illustrations, for he has finished the work and only needs to review it with L'Eplattenier. Other than visits with Ritter, a comment that Octave Matthey is turning toward things Persian, and that he, Jeanneret, is obsessed with Spain, having a friend (Klipstein) who has been there and able to evoke its lively ambience, there is no other news to report.[88] By the twenty-first of July he goes on a hiking trip in the Tyrol with Octave and then returns to La Chaux-de-Fonds, where he spends a month's vacation with his family in the countryside. Having helped prepare festive celebrations for the inauguration of L'Eplattenier's monument, he returns to Munich on September 17, not waiting to hear L'Eplattenier deliver his paper "L'esthétique des villes" at the Union des Villes Suisses.[89] This is a strange omission, because preparation for that conference paper was one of the reasons Jeanneret was sent to Germany in the first place, but he is worried over his unsettled plans for the winter, and this caused him to leave abruptly.

Finally it is time to spell out his troubles to L'Eplattenier. He writes on the first of October that it is always the same song–once he is outside the door there comes a flood of ideas. So he would love to recount a small thing or two. He is concerned that a work of art only fills the masses with enthusiasm when everything conspires to make it a thing of beauty. The people do not seem to want this beauty–but in spite of themselves are gripped by the force of an ensemble. That is why Jeanneret is astonished to see the fury of so many people who did not like, even hate, L'Eplattenier's monument. Yet on reflection, Jeanneret begins to understand why. Most people have lost the instinctive tradition of beauty, and need a dose of eclecticism in order to like it. Therefore the problem of our time is not the failure to know but the lack of power to give our creations of art an ensemble, or an ambiance of beauty.[90]

Following the lessons he has learned while in Germany, he contends that the future of artists depends on making contact with the people, because artists are trying to reform civic art. In order to realize this reform, it is necessary for the people to agree, and this will happened when we know how to draw inspiration out of them, or at least impose some of it on them. Thus Jeanneret has been thinking about a new project L'Eplattenier has received for a commemorative monument for a local patriot, Numa Droz. Jeanneret does not like the site that L'Eplattenier has selected for his monument, and he dares to correct his mentor and test out his own new ideas about an "ensemble" and the communicative aspects of civic art. He recalls examples of obelisks glimpsed during his travels: in Karslineplatz it took the shape of a factory chimney in the overall silhouette of the streets; and the depressing example of the Place de la Concorde, where the pedestal killed the obelisk. "The obelisk in Rome ought to be stupid; but the two obelisks in Luxor, continue to be grandiose. Because they gave their surface to the facades, and the facades conferred on them the character of being an obelisk–it is necessary to think of the two volumes, of the ensemble."[91]

Octave has asked ironically: why present this enormous block of bronze to the liberation of a small revolution made one day by a few watchmakers? What would he make for the great Revolution of 1789? Having offered the opinion of this joker, Jeanneret dared to admit that he too has been a bit frightened by the twenty meters of granite composed over the poor memory of Numa Droz. L'Eplattenier wants to construct a work of civic art, to make something for one of the men who belonged to a pantheon of great men from the region. But Jeanneret wonders whether the commissioners would allow him, for the same cost, to make a temple in place of a bust. Since Jeanneret would like to give this pantheon a form that has an ambience, so that each person coming in contact with its architectural harmony and power would be moved, he has taken up his old idea of renovating the incoherent railroad plaza and transforming it into a more worthy entrance to town. But he does not have the exact measurement of heights and volumes, so he can offer L'Eplattenier only an intention of what he plans. Considering that he has been studying the works of Camillo Sitte, his scheme is rather surprising: he places the monument on a central axis leading from the center of the railroad station, adjacent to a small kiosk (E), thus ignoring Sitte's advice that a monument must never be placed in the middle of a square, but to its side or along a wall. The three bays of the railway facade and bays of the post office (two darkened structures) are lined with arcades of boutiques, and opposite the post office is a national bank (A) or some other administration building with its ground floor raised above the level of the square. In this manner the railway tracks would be hidden from view. All these structures would be made of yellow stone, or at least a stucco of yellow tone, as the dictates of neoclassicism demand. From this plaza one then enters into a smaller square bordered with smaller structures (B) and two small houses (C), all modified in color and perhaps also in their roofs. Trees would be planted to screen the post office, and so this small place (ECBA) will be given an ensemble, and its materials coordinated with that of the station and its two fountains.[92]

There is nothing spectacular about this renovation plan, except that it reveals a greater interest in classicism than in the ideas of Sitte. Jeanneret appears to be idling away his time waiting to hear from Behrens and fiddling with some of the lessons his library searches and the Werkbund have taught him. He adds comments on his writing projects, about good and bad photographs, and further research done on parks and cemeteries, but he has difficulty with bridges and would like some help. And he would like to have some aphorisms from L'Eplattenier on Swiss architecture. It was necessary to hide the horror of present-day La Chaux-de-Fonds yet reveal the beauty of its ancestral heritage, and consequently make the citizens hope for civic improvement. Then he makes a final comment: "Behrens must respond one of these days. I am full of anxiety: because it is so easy for these Molochs to tell you: 'come back in two years!'"[93] He remains perplexed why he finds the doors closed everywhere, at a time when work for winter should already be set. But there is, he admits, a world to explore in the libraries even limited to his own small profession. He makes a note to buy many of the books that interest him, for they will be indispensable in furthering his work.[94]

A letter to his parents is more open about his anxieties: he has returned to Munich but is sick with fever and diarrhea, and thinks he may have cholera.[95] He is awaiting a response from Behrens, who told him he would decide by the first days of October. He fears the worst yet has no other plan for the future. He must attend to his German, at least to achieve a reading ability, because it is essential to know the literature relevant for his trade. He is anxious about the road ahead, and while he remembers all the pleasant times in La Chaux-de-Fonds, warmed by the happy ambience of the sun, by which he means the idealist L'Eplattenier, a life without a goal is killing. Life must have a goal, and not be an arrow lanced toward death. Before dying one must know how to play, to acquire joy from a soul that needs to be loved, a flower that speaks of harmony. He must be able to see beyond realities, a dream full of nature that recharges the heart.[96]

Finally Jeanneret can wait no longer. He goes to Berlin on October 17 in order to see Behrens. The great man is not there, and so he is forced to wait four whole days to achieve an audience. Immediately afterwards he travels to Dresden, where his brother Albert has just moved in order to study with the Eurhythmic master Émile Jaques Dalcroze, and visits the garden city of Hellerau. On the twenty-fifth, he receives word that he has been accepted in the atelier of Behrens.[97] Then on the twenty-eighth of October he writes a postcard from Potsdam, announcing that he knows L'Eplattenier is angry with him, thinking him too indifferent, but his mentor must understand that he has spent a difficult month and has only just received his mail. Perhaps L'Eplattenier already knows that Behrens has offered him work and that he will be moving to a garden city, Neu-Babelsberg, five minutes outside of Potsdam and a twenty-five minute train ride from Berlin. He remarks on a strange coincidence: he left Perret's office on November 2 the year before, and he will enter Behrens's on November 1. He is jubilant over this exciting year, certainly worth more than one spent in school, where they pretend to create architects![98]

All does not go well while Jeanneret is working a full-time job in Behrens's office. After a week of employment, he writes a long twenty-four-page letter to L'Eplattenier on November 8, admitting in the beginning that for several weeks he has had no satisfaction with himself–a total loss of serenity and joy that prevents him from being effusive in letter writing. It is only by putting aside such scruples that he takes up his pen, for he fears words written in black on white when he has lost contact with himself, when he floats and follows the flow of a current that pleases no one. Moreover, he is very isolated and cut off from news. He finds the suburb of Neu-Babelsberg deserted–not even an automobile in sight. His companions tolerate him during the working day, but he finds himself to be incredibly naive. Dedicating this evening to writing L'Eplattenier, however, enables his spirits to improve.

He follows this melancholic view with a small allegory: he knows that his mentor prefers the optimistic pine tree, pushing all of its branches upwards, to the weeping willow, more mature in experiences of life, drawing joy from its own skepticism, a tree that sees in the mirror of water only a fugitive image. He mentions that Octave immerses himself in dreams of going to Bruges "along the canals of the dead city...drifting, floating," but finds that reality is hardly the sister of dreaming, and concludes by saying: "No, Constantinople, Stamboul, I will not see you!"[99] Apparently Octave, in spite of his tendency toward morbidity, has gained Jeanneret's admiration, and he explains that he will become one of our "hommes de la 'vraie Vie'"[100] He appreciates Octave's innate philosophy of life: when others try to stop you, full of bile, he says "Little fish in the water, bird fly away!"[101]

Continuing the letter, he shifts to the third person, and comments that if he writes laconically to L'Eplattenier the struggler, it is because today he is the opposite of a fighter even though he knows that these pages of confession will not please his mentor. He recognizes that L'Eplattenier has given him strength that will somehow enable him to turn the weakness of these past days into something beneficial, but he has a need to confess. Instead of eliciting L'Eplattenier's anger and scorn, he hopes his mentor will find in this "fine and morbidly prepared meal, a morsel of good bread of affection."[102] It is this affection that unites all of L'Eplattenier's students–young artists gifted with a valuable inspiration–and makes them look calmly toward him, their master. Then Jeanneret comments on letters written by another student, Hagen, and how he admires his healthy naivety, courage, and idealism. He is a fine example of how L'Eplattenier has removed from each of his students that fatal flaw of becoming a "chic type." Hagen writes that L'Eplattenier wants him to study in Lucerne or Germany but Jeanneret warns–no doubt reflecting his own experience–that Hagen should not be isolated, especially in a German city. He needs the solid companionship of a group, and at most his isolation must be only of a short duration. Furthermore Hagen has few linguistic abilities: French escapes him more than it does Jeanneret, and to learn German is a problematic story! Look at what Ritter refers to as his own "cretinisant": after fifteen years of residence in a German country, he still is far from fluent in the language.[103]

Jeanneret continues the letter the next evening, shifting registers: his last letter written to his family has upset them, and he is angry over his inapt hands and his maladroit pen. If every day one cannot make the most out of one's triumphs, it is because there is a law of life, and it is very normal that he should taste here and there some bitter fruits. He closes by asking L'Eplattenier about his work on the granite figure he is carving of Numa Droz. Finally he confesses at the end of this long letter that he is obliged to stop the chit-chat and give L'Eplattenier advice about a remarkable book that appears as if it had been written "especially for you." There has been nothing better–or so Ritter believes–since Ruskin. The book, *Les Entretiens de la Ville du Rouet: essais dialogues sur les arts plastiques en Suisse romande*, written by Alexandre Cingria-Valneyre (1908), has not been a popular success, but nevertheless, Jeanneret advises, it carries important lessons even for L'Eplattenier.[104]

While there is no direct mention of Behrens in this lugubrious letter, or how difficult Jeanneret found his new taskmaster to be, letters that Jeanneret wrote to Ritter and to his parents reveal that throughout the autumn and winter he was extremely lonely and in a black hole of depression.[105] He was too tired from his long days at work to find his usual solace in writing–either keeping up his correspondence or on his two different *Études*. He was, however, reading Cingria-Valneyre, and so thoughts naturally drifted to his homeland, to the time when he would return to work with the small band of colleagues around L'Eplattenier. Now that he thinks fondly of them, as the letter above clearly reveals, and he admits he was mistaken two years earlier when he wrote his scathing letter to L'Eplattenier calling his comrades ignorant, even liars, proclaiming that he must put them behind him. Lonely and without friends in Neu-Babelsberg, he longs for the warm embrace of their friendship. Once he returns to the fold, he and his comrades will take up the cause of the "la vraie Vie" and forge a new "Jura style." On the final page of the Cingria-Valneyre book, Jeanneret wrote: "Finished reading 22nd of November 1910 at Neu-Babelsberg…in a year, at Rome, I will reread it, and, in my sketches, lay the foundations for my own Jura, Neuchâtelois discipline."[106] He writes to his parents,

> And I am obsessed by a vision: of beautiful straight lines, but of svelte and classic relationships; infinity of clarity in the harmonies, of the intense sun and layering of a purity to make you shake with ecstasy, a dry and nude plane, but some blue Apennins. And then some cypress. Rome![107]

He spends Christmas holidays with his brother Albert in Dresden, meeting the architect Heinrich Tessenow, who had just been chosen to design Dalcroze's Festival Hall in Hellerau. But within a few weeks of this vacation, he writes a forty-eight-page letter to L'Eplattenier, apologetic for the time that has passed since he last wrote, but feels all contact has been cut.[108] He denies, of course, that he is estranged from L'Eplattenier, for he professes the affection they feel for each other cannot be altered, but it is otherwise with the band of students around him. He senses their feelings toward him have weakened, while he to the contrary, due to his miserable isolation, is led to think of them very often, daily almost, as his future comrades of struggle and joy. Because everything that he does in Germany–each deduction made, the entire purpose of his trip–fatally turns his thoughts to the future, he now believes that his place is to be with his mentor and his comrades. When he gives L'Eplattenier the reasons for why he should return, he expects his mentor will be astonished to find that these thoughts are daily mixed with traces of sadness, regret, and disillusionment caused by the situation in which he finds himself.

He procrastinates, not specifying the reasons until the second half of the letter when he finally divulges that he is eager to put his stupefying new ideas into practice, to teach about the educational reforms he has learned in Germany–but he feels, as he did in Paris, that he has grown apart from his comrades, that they do not share his ideals or his desire to create a regional architecture based on workshops and crafts organization. Far from recanting his previous critique, he now suspects the gap may have grown wider, and he finally admits it may also include L'Eplattenier, whom Jeanneret increasingly dares to criticize in spite of his many denials to the contrary. All these mounting anxieties place him in a very black mood that cannot solely be attributed to the tyrant Behrens nor to Jeanneret's transformation into an ardent classicist, as had been claimed.

In order to clarify the feelings that wash over him intermittently like gray waves, fog or passing clouds, he is obliged to divulge that he carries an accusation that contradicts all positive feelings. This accusation is simple: his friends, his comrades, ignore him. They may protest this accusation, but Jeanneret has already felt the rupture during the past summer–and this cut extends to a very wide group, including Octave, Perrin, even Hagen. Perhaps this mixture of feelings–longing for his friends mixed with estrangement–is the result of being outside the sentiments of "la vraie Vie" because his circumstances no longer allow him to practice that life, and thus he has been led, more than ever, to want to renew contacts with his comrades. But they rebuff him, and he is proud. He often writes postcards to tell them he thinks of them, but considering that they are less busy than he, and that he is the one who is cut off, he cannot write long letters. Can you believe, except for a few services they have asked of him, Jeanneret has never received a word from the "Ateliers"? He retorts: "Memory retreats from where one offers it a resting place; affection from where one calls it."[109]

Having written these lines, they now fill him with fear. He reminds L'Eplattenier that he only wanted him to see the dark clouds and fogs that pass. Then he turns to comment that in his last card, L'Eplattenier seemed to be disappointed that Jeanneret had not spoken more objectively about his work, ideas, and projects, being content to express himself only with vague albeit real feelings, which upset him so deeply at the beginning of his stay in Neu-Babelsberg. But Jeanneret reports that he has overcome all these disagreeable and irrelevant elements, and is now prepared for action and in a state of mind to accomplish it. Yet having already dirtied a number of pages with his "egoisms," he would like to say something else.

He has had the occasion several times to write L'Eplattenier some brusque and pointed words on his monument to the Republique. Ought he to confess that he does not have the same high regard for it that he had at first glance? This is a fault of his character: he was occupied with inherent mistakes concerning the subject of the commemorative monument (although he had attributed these thoughts to Octave, the ironical joker) rather than with the qualities through which it would inspire admiration. Now he is disappointed to see that L'Eplattenier is the creator of a work that is denied the beauty of perfection. Here again is a fog that passes, which he cannot define precisely. What bothers Jeanneret is that L'Eplattenier is not up to date: he fails to know the new tendencies expressed by those admirable "constructors" in painting who build on the ruins sown by the Impressionists. For the first time he lays down his famous aphorism:

> They evolve *to create volumes which play* under light in rhythms based on geometry, joy of form in the end returned for a feast of the eyes and that condones the battle that Rodin won and which was a Waterloo for him.[110]

And he inserts that this artistic movement is "like a Phoenix that is burned but reborn under a new form younger and more radiant." It is difficult to consider that Jeanneret's choice of words is a mere coincidence: he wrote two years earlier in his prior criticism of his comrades and mentor that "he must burn what he loves, and love what he burns," and now refers for the first time to clear geometric forms and Rodin's frozen moments of movement. They are called on as witness to the fact that something better will rise from the ashes of defeat. And once again he uses the metaphor of battle, albeit this time it is a major threshold, a Waterloo.

He continues this line of argument. This artistic expression, like all the thought that is contemporaneous, comes from Paris, the city that some call tired. But Paris will shine again one day, and arrogant Germany will be in the shadows. Then Jeanneret tells L'Eplattenier not to worry, he is not wandering from the subject matter but striving to be clear. Did his mentor know that the study of the modern movement in Germany has led him into a bewilderment that grows deeper every day? He plans to describe exactly what he has seen, but the enormities of the subject matter will tempt L'Eplattenier not to take him seriously. Thus he makes a proposition: L'Eplattenier should spend fifteen days in Germany–especially while Jeanneret is in Berlin before the first of April–because it is absolutely necessary that he see things for himself. Jeanneret would be able to show him some serious holes in his thought. It is not recorded whether L'Eplattenier visited Berlin or not, but this is the first mention of April 1–the day Jeanneret will stop working for Behrens.

Finally Jeanneret arrives at the heart of the letter and begins a resumé of what his *Étude sur le mouvement d'art décoratif en Allemagne* might include. Knowing it presents an ambivalent position, he nevertheless puts it forward because it contains some lessons he is eager to put into practice in La Chaux-de-Fonds. He makes a list of the positive and negative things he has learned in Germany. On the side of Germany he finds an admirable organizing ability and a deductive spirit, but its creative genius is mediocre and obliged to capitulate before stronger people. He declares: "France subjugates Germany. And Germany yields."[111] Pride born of German's economic victories is matched by arrogance in the aesthetic domain, allowing sightless artists to blind the nation. This will eventually cause Germany to fall before a new god, that of the Latin genius. The struggle between the Latins and the Germans was foreseen, Jeanneret argues, fifty years ago by Joseph Arthur de Gobineau, who theorized about racial inequality. Gobineau's fundamental axiom rested on the belief that the white race was more gifted than the yellow, red, or black; he stubbornly searched among the colossal mélange of races for the oasis where the privileged race took shelter from unworthy contamination. Jeanneret misinterprets Gobineau's conclusions for his own purposes thinking that Gobineau discovered this oasis to be in Greece, in Etruria, in ancient China, and in certain parts of India. To the contrary, Gobineau actually believed that modern Greeks were thoroughly "blackened" and did not descend from the ancients.[112]

Nevertheless, Jeanneret continues his confused story of the contest between nations in which the weakest one succumbs. France was a mixture of races, but Germany and the rest of Europe were totally contaminated with elements of yellow. Gobineau showed that a fatal flaw for all progress lay in turning away from the oasis of purity (i.e., Greece). Thus in 1850, when France, bathed in "bourgeoisism," heard the first cries of the Impressionists' revolt, she covered them over with the turgidity of style emanating from the satisfactions of an exhausted race.

Today there is a similar state–already it undermines, in an underhanded but powerful manner. The reality is that Germany became formidable, thanks to an extraordinarily favorable state of things, putting into full use its qualities of race, determination, and discipline. The scientific spirit of Germany triumphed and opened the way for the classical ideal of the first empire. But again the French crowd affected the German horde, and its bourgeoisism entered there too, leaving only the knowledgeable elite to follow the routes toward classicism. It was a rare genius like the architect Karl Friedrich Schinkel who could express concretely in splendid buildings "this scientific appetite for things Hellenic."[113] In an apparent contradiction to this appraisal yet in support of his ideological position, Jeanneret shifts back to the contest between nations. While all of Europe slept, only France was busy at work. "Courbet, Manet and their followers were the great devastators: like diggers they slowly undermined the building at its base and provoked a real storm."[114]

After 1870, Germany triumphed economically. Its patriotism was whipped on by pride, while its cooperative organization (*organisation en conferation*) enhanced development. Art became one of the stones of its economic edifice. In effect, the arts that triumphed in Germany were the utilitarian ones, so that its architecture actually derived from the industrial arts. Abstraction, intuition, and metaphysics were nowhere to be found in her fine arts, hence painting and sculpture were stupid in Germany and always behind the times, or blindly sought protection by borrowing from the modern movement in Paris. "This is the extraordinary thing. France only operates through revolution, it ignores in its mass the good fruits that it possesses, and Germany, more open through its industrial development to every innovation, Germany *shows France, that France has some geniuses!*"[115] Then Jeanneret inserts a note that while much is lamentable in the German decorative arts, there are changes to be found that shock, changes expressive of proportion and unity. These are seeds of the art of tomorrow, already sown in the simplicity, joy, and health expressed in the rhythmic work of Dalcroze, which contradicts the exacerbated tendencies of Strauss. "Because already in these hysterical forms is the new germ which will be the expression of tomorrow."[116]

Jeanneret turns to explore the field of German architecture and the decorative arts. "There are two things to consider: *Revolt*– then the creation of a New Code."[117] But revolt (the movement called "Art Nouveau" in the 1890s), which came from Belgium, then moved to France, and finally arrived in Germany, was not important at all.

It was the code that bore fruit: a code that rested on the proportions and rhythms of classicism, a code that spells out the conditions of cooperating on an ensemble. German minds were turned toward a new source that came from Vienna—not actually based on rationality or intuition, but imbibing in the desire to satisfy the parvenus Jewish financiers' artistic tastes, which leaned toward Egypt and Assyria. "Germany was secessionist like a bloating paper put in contact with a bottle of ink, absorbing it all."[118] In France a reaction set in, but in Germany perseverance, formidable and unbelievable progress, produced little by little a conformance of taste, which slowly turned toward a critical study of classicism. With terrible rapidity, 1900 unveiled research in all directions, and wanderings too. Yet 1900 revealed an evolution leading toward an unguarded door, and for some decades preparing the return of the empire and moving forward from there. Still, Germany, looking for future inspiration, will find her master to be the French. And France, having finally stopped both its antagonism toward Germany and its open display of economic inferiority, begins to stir and recover as well.

"Do you think [Jeanneret asks L'Eplattenier] that the exposition in Brussels and Munich's manifestation at the Salon d'Automne were not a big slap in the face, under which things begin to break up and change?"[119] France owes Germany a major debt for this abrupt awakening ("une fameuse chandelle")! Jeanneret is referring to the 1910 Brussels International Exhibition of April–November 1910, where the German exhibitions were favorably reviewed, and to the 1910 Salon d'Automne, in which Munich workshops subsidized by the German emperor decided not only to exhibit individual objects but to coordinate them into a single well-designed ensemble organized solely for the purpose of exhibition. Thus a unified plan, organized in advance, was accepted by each contributor, knowing that it required the designer to coordinate each object with the whole ensemble. It was the creation of this "ensemble" that Jeanneret found to be so remarkable, even revolutionary.[120]

In comparison, Jeanneret had little to say about architecture in contemporary Germany. He recognized Behrens, Bruno Paul, Messel, and Schmitz—Olbrich was expelled by these men—to be the peaks of the classical movement, but Messel literally copied the Petit Trianon in Versailles and the Parthenon, while Behrens was inspired only by the Doric and the Empire. In Behrens's office, Jeanneret was forced to copy classical profiles traced from either Schinkel's work or from the Acropolis, or from furniture photographed from the Napoleonic

Empire. Meanwhile Bruno Paul in the last three years affirms his eclectic faith: at first "Bieder Meyer," then the Empire, today Louis XVI.

Jeanneret pauses for a moment to ask again: "Do you believe me?" and then continues to account for the things he has seen. He remembers that it is Stauffifer who had torn away his own impure addiction to the Middle Ages and revealed to him admirable styles, things that Jeanneret had already divined during his stay in Paris. He inserts a memory for proof:

> I will always remember that morning full of spring flowers of the white Chestnut trees and the dwarf lilacs, when arose ["déploya"] before my eyes the colossal and unexpected spectacle of Versailles. This was the moment when my dark mythologies collapsed and then radiated classical clarity.[121]

But he admits it was a long time before he got rid of all the meanness that made him see art as very small and dark. And now here he is, full of enthusiasm for Greece, for Italy, and only a small interest remains for the arts that once made him so sad, the Gothic of the north, the Russian barbarians, and the German tormentors.

> This is my evolution. I have before my eyes and often look at the sixty interiors of Versailles, of Compiègne, of Fontainebleau. What lessons to learn from them! I have also a splendid book of Doric, Ionian, Corinthian, of that Roman art made of colossal vaults and huge plain walls.
>
> And for some months, my ideas have been set. I will not go to America, nor to Belgium. But I will remain here until I know the language, shortening perhaps my stay with Behrens in order to go to Hellerau to build with Tessenow the Institute Jaques Dalcroze, following the proposition that was made to me. Then I will make a study trip in Germany, and following I will go to collect my thoughts. Where? To Rome.
>
> Then, afterwards, if you still want me.[122]

This confession to L'Eplattenier of his "happy aesthetic evolution" is the only thing that enables Jeanneret to remain in Germany and continue his nomadic life without a home–an essentially exhausting life that was sometimes depressing. But the feeling of his immense weakness sustains him, admonishing him to be patient and continue to struggle. His conception of art is still developing, and he is still too weak to attain it–yet the ideal he has been pursuing since the early days in Paris has finally found substance in classicism.

> At Behrens, the shock has been brutal. Can you figure, that having frolicked in all sorts of flowery fields, and having explored them, I am obliged to forget them! I arrived at Behrens' nearly oblivious to what was a style, totally ignoring the art of moldings and their proportions. I assure you that it was hardly easy. And it is, moreover, from proportions that harmonious form is born.[123]

Jeanneret could not recount everything he had discovered in Germany, but he concedes that opposed to the bizarre inventions of the foolish and the baroque, severe Behrens exercises rhythm and subtle proportions of which Jeanneret had been ignorant.

> I had and still have infinite pain. Add to that, a tyrannical, brutal, hand of iron, the struggles in an office where all the great works are made, an office peopled by 23 blacks who tremble, believe me, under the gray humor of this colossal.[124]

Turning back to his account of the astonishing things he had seen while in Germany, he tries to be clear that these retrograde tendencies of the modern movement–whatever their logic, given the novelty of the problems posed and the new materials utilized–produce works that with few exceptions are marked by a new breeze. He closes with his opening refrain: the things he has told L'Eplattenier about his friends ought to be taken as very delicate matters. They are sensations extremely vague albeit real. Thus his mentor can understand that Jeanneret was surprised not to hear anything from his comrades–the Ateliers d'Arts Réunis–whom he expects to rejoin as soon as possible–no news about work, no incidental report from those whom he calls his friends, enemies, and critics.[125]

THE BATTLE BETWEEN GERMANY AND FRANCE

When *Étude sur le mouvement d'art décoratif* was published in 1912, becoming Jeanneret's first printed book, its language had been smoothed out by his mother and the argument between Germany and France somewhat clarified.[126] Now it is Germany that is clearly revolutionary, not France, although only momentarily, because Germany does not have an aesthetic legacy to maintain this superiority for long. Like most of his other writings, Jeanneret opens and closes on a refrain–in this case it is the cultural war between France and Germany. In between this framework he inserts long descriptions and positive evaluations of Germany's modernity in architecture, urbanism, and the decorative arts. He is less racist than he had been in his 1911 letter to L'Eplattenier when he sent him a resumé of the book, and he is not as keen an advocate of classical forms as he seems to have become in his letter-writing. Instead his *Étude* is written expressly for administrators and aesthetic reformers in La Chaux-de-Fonds, where 450 copies were distributed for free. But his message appears to be aimed as well at France. While Jeanneret holds France to be the arbiter of taste and inventiveness in the fields of painting, sculpture, and other fine arts, Germany has become a model that France must emulate and absorb if she is to win the cultural war between nations. In consequence, his *Étude* comprises an explanation of the many magnificent German innovations in the broad field of the decorative arts, including the establishment of cooperative workshops and arts-and-crafts associations, the reform of professional education, the awareness of publicity and the use of the press, and the development of the concept of "urbanism" as applied to German cities. These are reforms that Jeanneret will continue to stress over the next three decades–only modifying his appraisal of garden cities.

In France, new market conditions led by mechanization and industrial production had by the early twentieth century created a crisis in the decorative arts. Yet Germany had solved these same problems by uniting manufacturers, designers, and craftsmen into an array of cooperative associations, and this enabled the nation to become a major competitor for international markets. Thus markets in France were inundated with utilitarian, practical everyday products produced in Germany. A press campaign against "Made in Germany" products erupted in France by the end of 1911, becoming most virulent in the spring of 1912 until it ended a year later.[127] Yet Jeanneret would maintain in the *Étude* that "c'est Allemande" is no longer a pejorative phrase. His description of the AEG works, which he first saw in 1910, expressed a fascination with the giganticness of the equipment, the administrative reforms, and the sound mechanical execution of products–all the result of technical perfection and practical training promoted by the German Werkbund. He retained this enthusiasm for modern industrial processes, and throughout the *Étude* outlined the many new challenges it presented to the artist-architect, challenges that led him to constantly expand his definition of the "decorative arts" until it included the entire aesthetic and visual milieu of modern life, including the streets of the city.

Jeanneret is mesmerized by new aesthetic modes of experiencing the city, and although he maintains the garden city will eventually make the city redundant, he cannot shake his fascination with the full array of experiences that cities present. In the *Étude* he offers vignettes gleaned from his strolls along city streets, witnessing new displays in shop windows and department stores designed for a spectator's pleasure. He attends many theatrical and musical performances that enhance city life; in fact he finds that music and rhythmical movement express the most advanced seeds of modern art–for it is movement, change, and innovation that have taken possession of the modern spirit. In his diagnosis of contemporary times, he is particularly attentive to the artist's role in marketing products and the use of publicity. He is aware that a new communications network lay behind Germany's revolution in the decorative arts–a network that extended from the design of cardboard boxes and advertising posters, new alphabets and page formats, to congresses, expositions, and illustrated periodicals.

Most of Jeanneret's comments on everyday life in the modern metropolis have gone unattended, perhaps because the *Étude* was aimed primarily at educational reformers.[128] In laying stress on the need for collaboration, Jeanneret may have been influenced by the French sculptor, furniture maker, and educational reformer Rupert Carabin, who was "stupefied" by what he saw at the Munich exposition of 1908. His report to the Parisian government was widely discussed in the press during Jeanneret's first stay in Paris. Drawing attention to the decorative ensemble of the rooms he saw, Carabin noted that simple and well-designed objects executed expressly for the purpose of exhibition were simultaneously available in shops in German cities, and even the work done by apprentices worthy of display. What a shock to find all of these aesthetic and educational innovations were executed by Germans, but not by the French! It is Carabin who likened the dangerous challenge of Germany to the battle of Sedan and the defeat of the French in 1870. "The Sedan of commerce, [he wrote in his 1908 report] with which we have been threatened for so many years, is now no longer to be feared, it is a *fait accompli* and we must play our part."[129] Carabin's many reforms involved the development of professional apprenticeship programs decentralized throughout France, with educational programs based on practical training–innovations Jeanneret already sees implemented across Germany.

It is not known when Jeanneret met Carabin: the first mention of his name is in 1913, when he wrote Ritter that through Carabin he was trying to have the *Étude* republished in France. Probably he met him on his first stay in Paris.[130] Jeanneret circulated at least fifty copies of the *Étude* in France at the time of its original printing, and the work itself was intended to play on France's anxiety by describing precisely how Germany had achieved such revolutionary success in the industrial and decorative arts. He opens and closes his study by reviving national rivalries, returning to the fatal year of 1870, when Germany triumphed and the bourgeoisie took notice. As economic prosperity spread throughout Germany, a rare moment in the arts was born–Berlin expanded, Munich was renovated, and Stuttgart improved! Berlin was the center of this new spirit in the practical arts and inscribed it in stone: the Reichstag, the Dome, the Monument of Guillaume, and the Victory Column were all symbols of its new power. Yet Berlin totally ignored the idealistic preoccupations emanating from protesting painters in Paris. It created its state, its industry, its commerce, its army, but gave nothing to the concerns of painting or the fine arts and continued to absorb whatever flowed its way from Paris. Thus German superiority would eventually decline in spite of its sudden and apparent success in the applied arts. Somewhat ambivalently Jeanneret adds: "These facts certainly force the two countries to face each other; Germany revolutionized, France evolutionized. It is an accidental fact in Germany, that today leads to a disproportion between the very minimal roots and an overlarge flower."[131]

Germany was victorious by surprise in 1870. She was stupefied, then enchanted, next proud, finally arrogant, and it is this arrogance that Jeanneret feels will blind her in the future. She organized into a new power and proved it through fantastic constructions of boats of war, barracks, formidable arsenals, and gigantic palaces. Since its revolution was entirely an economic and practical one, it did not touch the fine arts. But it called on artists (Jeanneret utilizes this term to stress the fact that the architects he praises were initially artists, and perhaps to underscore the collaboration of all the arts that formed the essence of this German revolution) to solve utilitarian and modern problems. So were erected public buildings, schools, administrative offices, factories with colonies of workers, railroad stations, market halls, slaughterhouses, convention halls, theaters, music halls, and garden cities. The problems posed were well solved: strong, practical, and active. And they trumpeted their success through effective publicity, mounting expositions of all sorts, transforming their journals of art into organizations that sponsored conferences and competitions. They even turned to address social issues, which they said could be resolved through art, through harmony. They broke down the walls of the ivory towers that in France kept artists from responding to the general needs of the masses.[132]

Germany was revolutionary: her arts became applied and men sworn to art left their isolation and turned to concentrate on architecture. Peter Behrens, the former painter from Munich and Darmstadt, became director of the section of architecture in Dusseldorf, then artistic advisor to the AEG. Bruno Paul, an illustrator, was named director of the School of Berlin, with its focus on architecture and the decorative arts, and the same could be said of the painter Bernard Pankok and his directorship of Stuttgart, and so on goes Jeanneret's list. Since Germany is many different countries within one nation–Prussia, Bavaria, Wurtemberg, Saxony, and so on–there is no universal style, and hence each school takes on the different characteristics of its region. But amidst this decentralization of power, the German state played an active role in the domain of the applied arts: one had only to recall the German expositions beginning with Turin in 1902 and ending with the Paris Salon d'Automne of 1910. France has done nothing comparable, and prefers to be ridiculed. What gives Germany this power? What machinery drives this stupefying organism? What lessons does it teach for reform in the applied arts? In order to answer these questions, Jeanneret had been sent to Germany to see for himself.[133]

In the conclusion of the *Étude*, Jeanneret returns to the refrain that while Germany has triumphed, she begins to express weakness in the immense terrain that she alone has been exploiting. Art is not her driving force, and she looks to France for inspiration. German's industry, her practical experience, however, is privileged among all nations, and hence the expression "c'est allemande" no longer retains its pejorative sense. Having been slapped in the face by Germany, will France leave behind her lethargy in the domain of the applied arts? The marvels of Germany in the industrial arts ought to be known. In this hour of international agreement, information ought to penetrate barriers.

> Germany is a book of practice. If Paris is the threshold of Art, Germany remains the great workshop of production. Experiences

> have been made there, struggles have become effective there; the erected building [*la bâtisse*] and rooms, with their fabled walls, recount the triumph of order and of tenacity.[134]

THE INDUSTRIAL ARTS

In between these sections on national rivalry–where Jeanneret praises Germany's strengths, achievements, and power even though he allows that France will be triumphant in the end–is inserted a three-part review of a number of German initiatives in the industrial arts. Here he is in awe–describing in detail the impressive educational reforms that link artists to industrialists, the precise area in which France is most threatened. He turns first to examine expositions and conferences, beginning with the Werkbund. Founded in 1907 in Munich, this organization's sole purpose was to link artists with industrial and manufacturing enterprises, and to develop a plan to elevate technique and taste through education and publicity. The Werkbund held a yearly congress where admission was by invitation, the choice of members being very important. The Werkbund developed traveling expositions, publications, conferences, and even a Museum of Art in Commerce and Industry. And their efforts included accomplishments in Austria and Holland as well.[135]

Next Jeanneret reviews the German Museum of Commercial and Industrial Art–a traveling display that stressed the importance of the image in contemporary times. It selected for its first project the reform of printing, next the poster, then paper and small containers. In one of their expositions in Berlin, called "Art at the service of the Merchant," Jeanneret saw packages of chocolates designed by Joseph Hoffman, cigar boxes, letter paper and envelops, postcards, and posters, all created by decorative artists. Another exhibit, erected during a hairdressers' conference, took the theme of women's toilettes from Egyptian times to the present and suggested designs for contemporary objects such as perfume bottles, powder boxes, brushes, and jewelry.[136]

He turns his attention to Munich, noting that when artists failed to find a market for their work, they formed a bureau under one director, offering free advice to manufacturers on a variety of artistic questions. Through these collaborative efforts the Germans began to make products full of taste. Munich is a city known for art and initiative–and recently it created a huge exposition (Ausstellung München) opened during the tourist season from spring to fall. It instituted theatrical events and special musical weeks, and exhibited many collaborative efforts of artists and merchants: reformed theater sets, charming modern restaurants, posters, prospectuses, and books. In the summer of 1910, it held a competition for the decoration of store windows along the major shopping street: an artist and a given store worked together on a display in shops of silk, confectionaries, patisseries, bookshops, restaurants.[137]

Among the many expositions that Jeanneret describes, he focuses in detail on two expositions in Berlin because of their avant-garde nature. These are the two expositions that he attended on his first trip to Berlin in 1910.[138] The Exposition of German City-Building (Die Allgemeine Städtebau Ausstellung) presented the problem of cities in theoretical terms. He judged the German efforts in this field to be uniquely reformist; compared to the Americans who followed the exploitative practices of their building constructors; and the French who were retarded and perpetuated mediocre traditions. Intent on reform, the Germans reorganized many of their planning bureaus and showed tendencies toward progressive new plans. Noteworthy were regulatory reforms involving the location and layout of cemeteries, and projects executed by renowned architects such as Behrens and Schumacher, who built chapels and crematories, grouped tombs in ensembles, and designed sepulchers.

The pretext for this exposition had been the competition for a new town plan to control the metropolitan extension of Berlin. Jeanneret found these designs, exhibited in the hall of honor, to be enormous, impressive, and beautiful. He exclaimed:

> One feels oneself face to face with men capable of confronting whatever problem. Berlin wanted to be not only practical and hygienic, but also beautiful and there was in the discreteness of this competition, which will last for several years, a little of the Florentine pride, which had led to be erected the cupola of Ste Marie des Fleurs.[139]

On the other hand, the exposition was aimed at professional men, and most of the spectators paid little attention to those mysterious graphics called a town plan. Jeanneret, on the other hand was so impressed by the display that he dedicated several days of profitable study, and notes that he would eventually describe these lessons in his forthcoming work on the construction of cities.[140]

The second exposition was that of the clay-chalk-cement industry (Cement-und-Kalk-Industrie Ausstellung) organized by Behrens, and here again lessons were decisive. One visit would dispel any doubt that new materials–more practical, economical, hygienic, fireproof, and also beautiful in a rational manner–had radically transformed architectural form. In turn these new materials had completely overturned practices in the building trades thought for years to be immutable. Now a new freedom was flowing, and new concepts along modern lines developing. In the Werkbund meeting accompanying the exposition, everyone spoke of marching toward the future. One speaker asked the following question: "Does the artistic imagination guide the material, or is it the material which dictates the form of art?" His answer stressed that architects should not create forms and give them to the engineer to express, but ought to know intimately the materials with which they worked, in order to give them an adequate form and functional use.[141]

ART IN THE SERVICE OF COMMERCE AND REAL ESTATE SPECULATION

The second part of Jeanneret's study concentrated on two themes: art in the service of commerce and art in the service of real estate speculation.[142] For the first study, he visited various successful workshops throughout Germany and was impressed by the cooperative effort among artists. He noted the admirable displays in their shops, as well as their locations at strategic points of the city in the luxury districts and along arteries frequented by tourists. With no obligation to buy, a spectator could enter the ground floor to find thousands of bibelots, jewelry, ivories, stuffs of all sorts–all arranged with excellent taste. Richly edited and illustrated catalogues were spread out on tables for the spectator's perusal. There were model rooms designed by one artist on display at different locations throughout the city where a spectator could move from a salon, to a dining room, bedroom, reception room, as if some rich landlord had honored him with a visit to his hotel. The guiding conception was unitary, the effect irresistible, although Jeanneret allowed not to Parisians who dislike the Germans, and remained skeptical as to the tasteful effects. But what is offered to the eyes is in some way the German soul, and if the French do not admire it–Jeanneret advised–they can at least be impressed by the undeniable harmony of the ensemble. Every item carries the same desire to realize relationships, proportions, and comfort; and this desire is a basic element in the German revolution of the decorative arts.[143]

He visits factories of furniture and tapestry in Munich and Hellerau and studies their innovative training centers, built around three-year apprenticeship programs. Ten apprentices were allotted to one master, and from the beginning students were taught to make useful and sellable items, advancing over time toward more complex products, each intended for sale. Above all the factories that Jeanneret visited rose the important AEG works, producing all kinds of electrical machines and appliances. Its forward-looking director exploited the new direction modern architecture was taking and repressed the terrible practice of ornamenting metal in both household items and machines. A committee searched for a man who knew how to realize simple and proportional forms utilizing the plastic capacities of new materials. They chose Peter Behrens and named him art director in 1907. He designed the factory halls as an integral architectural creation–they were austere and appropriate expressions, in the midst of which the machines constituted grave and impressive notes. All of the products, like lamps, electric fans, and household utensils, were offered not only for modern comfort but were presented in a modern, almost impersonal style. Behrens had designed all of their forms, not allowing one visible item of either the building or the industrial products to pass without his review. This authoritarian imposition of "art" might have created a lamentable event, but fortunately the committee selected a man for the occasion. Now his Turbine Hall is called the "Kathedrale der Arbeit," and he has also designed a colony of workers' housing, sheltering some 150,000 souls, who depend on the AEG for their bread.

> Behrens is the powerful, profound, grave genius, thoroughly hallucinated by domination, who brings together the work and the times and thus [displays] the contemporary German spirit.[144]

There are modern reforms in printing and bookmaking that captured Jeanneret's attention. Germany is a country of bookstores, but it fell behind the times, never realizing the reforms preached in England by Ruskin and realized by William Morris. But here again Behrens and other artists were called to the front: designing a new alphabet inspired by a return to good Latin tradition. Now most of the books printed in Germany utilize this type. There were similar reforms in the design of the page, in the fabrication of papers, and in bindings. Ordered by the state, Behrens gave a daily course for three weeks in 1909 on how to renovate the design of placards, posters, and calling cards. Since that time, certain bookstores in Germany offer a seductive look that would be impossible to encounter in Paris.

Not only bookstores, but department stores in France have also fallen behind the art of display developed in Germany. These great emporiums are really miniature worlds where one can find everything, and they know how to open their doors to a great engulfing crowd and how to display beautiful materials. They teach the client how to dress for seduction, comfort, luxury, and beauty. Attentive to the desires of a gawker (*badaud*), the department store provides him with physical impressions and sensual contact in order to intoxicate and tempt. Jeanneret is impressed by these new techniques exhibited by the modern merchant, and finds their display windows in such astonishing taste that they stop the crowd pressing ever forward. Their doors become portals to a new world: of elevators, of professional salesmen who never press a client to buy an item. In order for the client not to suffocate as if in an Oriental bazaar, this fantastic display is inundated with light, given an order, a rhythm, and a feeling for color. In order to exploit all the decorative resources inherent in the merchandise, it is necessary to display tact, taste, and a certain chicness–words Jeanneret uses to define this new art of presentation. "It is an art entirely new, young by some years. It developed with thundering rapidity."[145]

Now the word "decoration" designates this art and "decorator" the man or woman occupied with window displays. Germany has established high schools of the decorative arts where problems given to students are practical exercises: table decorations, festival decorations for a house or for streets, decorative arrangements for pavilions of display and entire expositions. Students learn how to draw plans, elevations, and the architectonic details of decorations; they study color, scenic lighting, and how styles relate to luminous projections. Other courses follow the painting of posters, the design of fabrics, and the general considerations of interior design and how to display isolated pieces in shops, museums, and expositions.[146]

The last section of this review focuses on art in the service of real estate speculation–or the construction of garden cities.[147] To travel to the city for work and enjoyment yet to live in the country, Jeanneret notes, has become common practice not just for the aristocratic classes but for the middle classes and in some cases for the working classes as well. Consequently a new type of real estate speculation develops, requiring a new organization: that of the garden city. While this novelty originated in England, it is a practice that has a unique set of characteristics in each application. In Germany, there is a desire to create a beautiful and harmonious ensemble, a democratizing gesture that takes the idea of a private hotel and presents it–at least in appearance and comfort–to the masses. Thus building societies offer small charming towns in proximity to great cities, composed of villas or structures with the appearance of villas. Sometimes the style of these garden cities is modern, designed by Fischer, Behrens, or Paul, as in the example of garden cities surrounding Berlin. They have cast off their old clothes for the new, and Jeanneret rather ambivalently praises the blow they deliver as not being hideous, the material used only less good than the best, hence the results are rentable and mark a progress of sorts.[148]

Considering the formidable extension of Berlin, to which the competition of Grosse Berlin gave evidence, Jeanneret understood that speculators were buying up all the most favorable land outside the center of cities. They created societies whose aim was none other than the construction of garden colonies independent of the state and lying along lines already drawn by the railways. In the heart of these colonies, they located the railway station, off which streets radiated in all directions. And they tied the colony to the city with one hundred to two hundred trains every day, a communication network so excellently organized that one could visit the most remote colonies often because these trains were faster than those to suburbs linked by ordinary tramways.

The uniqueness of these garden cities–at least for Jeanneret–lay in the fact that their aesthetic reform was based on a complete "renaissance of taste" and provided inhabitation conceived by artists in the latest style. Each prospectus advertising a garden-city writes of beauty, harmony, good taste, and novelty. It puts on display the artist (i.e., architect) in charge of overseeing the construction, organizing competitions or selecting other well-known artists to design parts of the plan. All of this is done to ensure that monetary returns will be maximized. Expositions such as the City-Building Exposition (Städtebau Ausstellung) were intended to showcase these "revolutionary tendencies."[149] Plans revealed streets designed as park avenues and curved to utilize the terrain in the best manner, stations conveniently placed, and leafy open spaces jealously guarded. All of the houses were designed by Muthesius, Paul, Behrens, or another among their talented group.

If a visitor coming from Berlin would walk on a summer evening or in springtime through one of these garden colonies, he would be struck with the sense of what it was like to live amidst beneficial calm. A healthy life is produced by streets designed as places of rest for the eyes.[150] Jeanneret believed that in ten years, when the impact of the countryside on family life is measured in full, this visitor would regard the garden cities as admirable places in comparison to the incomplete joys of big city life, so dramatically marked with dissonance. Eventually the visitor would recognize the big city as an error, a persistent mass impossible to sustain. In its place, he would feel the greater need for a culture more domestic or family-oriented.

> And looking around him, he would conceive what the first great festivals announce for the future where, in the most favorable circumstances, it is allowed for a genius to be revealed, some artists to make a work of art almost completely unified: the cycles of music, the cycles of theater.
>
> What is it that I dream of in saying that? These things, I have felt them in all the city-gardens, in Munich, Hagen, Stuttgart, Berlin. I felt it almost as a reality some months later at Hellerau near to Dresden.
>
> It was an effect more astonishing than elsewhere.[151]

Jeanneret describes at great length this garden city, where his brother was living and studying with Dalcroze.[152] Hellerau was uniquely designed by the greatest artists of Germany: Tessenow, Muthesius, Riemerschmied, Ballie-Scott (England), Theodor Fischer, Bestelmeyer, and so on. The residents were at first the workers from the factory of the Deutsche Werkstätte für Handwerkskunst, then others, no matter whom. Two societies were in control of the development. Gartenstadt-Hellerau was the directing organization that acquired the large tract of land and allowed speculators to build under its regulatory control and along principles set down by the Werkbund. This society sold land to a second organization, the Baugesellschaft-Hellerau, which built workers' housing designed by one of the famous architects mentioned above. These two societies realized a profit of 4 percent, and whatever surpassed that was returned for the improvement of the ensemble. Workers rented their houses as a right of possession for thirty years, extending the lease if they desired. But if their conduct was judged offensive, they could be dismissed. Each worker was in turn part of a governing body. If they wanted to raise or lower their rent, or create some modification to the plan, that was a decision they made in their general assembly.

Thus Jeanneret concluded Hellerau was a collective manifestation: it took capital, heretofore allocated to private profit, and returned it to those who produced it.

Hellerau, moreover, had the ambition to become an educational center, and this is what attracted Dalcroze to build his Eurhythmic Society there. This great institute (designed by Tessenow) assembled students and teachers from all over Europe. But, Jeanneret remarked, even better is the fact that each student born in Hellerau would be educated by this institute. Having visited Hellerau many times, he confessed that he saw realized–or almost–the ideas that the expositions of Berlin merely suggested. Every summer, festivals of rhythmical music were given in the new theater, located in the most eminent position of the town plan. Thus Hellerau became the "director's seat" of ideas and values embodied in the Werkbund. It gave witness that contributions of artists to real estate activity could give birth to the most elevated expressions.

POPULARIZATION OF THE ARTS IN THE PUBLIC DOMAIN

Since concepts of artistic creation are pervasive throughout Germany, municipal officials cannot remain indifferent.[153] From sanctuaries of routine, they have little by little become progressive actors. And once again Jeanneret gives examples, beginning with the lessons he learned from viewing the Berlin Exposition on "La Construction des villes." He reiterates: Munich and Berlin, having reacted against the American method of gridded street plans, have instead reformed their planning bureaus and inaugurated new processes. In opposition to extension plans made by some anonymous bureaucrat, they have substituted plans designed by a responsible artist of their own choice. This is only the first step in an immense task, and some municipalities have gone further. Cities like Ulm, for example, have tried to suppress real estate speculation by buying up almost all the suburban land of the city, freezing its price at an assessed value, and so reserving the area for a workers' garden city to be developed in the future.

Municipalities tend to have their preferred architects, and a quick survey reveals they are almost universally resistant to modern ideals and hold a monopoly on bad taste. But some cities like Munich reach beyond this level and are honored by a university inaugurated in 1910 and built by Bestelmeyer. It was certainly an ideal monument, marking a new stage in municipal architecture. Its beauty was allied with comfort, its austere grand lines dominate, and the students learn, in spite of themselves and by infusion, the taste for a tranquil and beneficial beauty. There are other great examples of universities giving witness to the potential of modernism: the University of Iéna, built by Theodor Fischer, reveals complete harmony with its small city and the hills that surround and dominate it, while the new university in Berlin under construction (the Tilleuls) is another witness to the violent duel between the progressives and the reactionaries.

Artist-architects are involved with administrative buildings as well: in Dresden, for example, there is a new Hotel-de-Ville and the celebrated slaughterhouses (architect Erlwein); in Hamburg there is a popular park (in construction, Fritz Schumacher); in Berlin, the imposing streets of West Berlin, where the trams run in green parkways bordered with flowers between allées of trees; in Stuttgart, the reconstruction of an old quarter; in Munich, the four new cemeteries, celebrated everywhere (architect Grassel), modern market sheds (architect Bertsch), and the list could continue. Architects have explored new terrains as well: railway stations, of which Hamburg offers the most striking type (also Fischer in Stuttgart and Munich, and Ludwig Hoffman in Berlin), and projects for the subway (the Metropolitain of Berlin). And there is also the management of forests with taste and the matter of pruning trees and arranging them along the avenues in harmonious groupings.

Little by little in Germany, Jeanneret summarizes, art rules over official constructions, and extends to the conservation of ancient works as well. Munich restores its old churches in a very remarkable manner, manifesting a very modern spirit and not being timidly archaeological. And the cities of Frankfurt, Cologne, and Dresden have hired a young photographer, Mademoiselle Suzanne Hoffmann-Darmstadt, to publish a set of postcards showing the most remarkable but unknown works of these cities. "This is the sort of publicity without gossiping [*caquetage*] that all cities ought to use if they want to strengthen their artistic patrimony under the vise of real estate speculators."[154]

It was deemed appropriate to end this survey of architectural expressions in the public domain with a summary of the manifesto of the Werkbund, since its principles ruled over all of these new artistic endeavors, principles to which Jeanneret thoroughly subscribes.[155] Knowing that construction, whether public or private, was linked directly to the applied arts, the Werkbund took the occasion of having its manifesto published in August 1908 by the royal authorities of Prussia. Thus Jeanneret professed that a national economy guided by art and technique is no hindrance to the manifestation of art. Many times in the last decades there has been proof to the contrary that too much money was at the disposition of the architect! Paradoxically one can add "the more the decor is rich, the less the effect marks progress for art."[156]

The artistic impression of a commercial edifice, for example, does not lie in the exterior décor, which is only an affair of style, but rests in the expression of grand forms born from the program, the technical requirements, and the needs of the epoch. Thus the artist-architect ought to possess all the knowledge relative to modern progress: he must know new materials and how their use is related to comfort, utility, and economy. Jeanneret repeats: since the artist-architect with the least means attains the degree of beauty the most pure, he must have a deep understanding of all the different branches of the building industry, their materials, their use, their manipulations, and their prices.

The great obstacle to the implementation of these capacities, however, lies with the bureaucrats who apply routine answers to new problems. This system excels in covering up the mistakes or inactions of each employee, allowing impersonal officials to wield authority over decisions. The situation is aggravated by administrative centralization that throws up obstacles to any personal initiative. The heads of the public works department, even if they are excellent administrators, are in general profane in the field of construction, and are neither artists nor technicians. Therefore a new authority is needed to consider these matters, and that is why the Werkbund requests that every important public construction be offered only to architects in order to avoid any impersonal control over design work. It requests further that the author of a public works project be given full responsibility over it, and that this responsibility be announced publicly. In order for the dispensation of state revenues not to work against the artistic constructor, power must not be given to someone who may know how to economize, but understands nothing about "the art of building."

Since a building is an organism whose structure makes its diverse parts come alive, it should impress the viewer through its simplicity and strength, and the harmony of its masses and contours more than through costly materials and the multiplicity of exterior ornamentation. Patrons of architecture should search to save on superfluous decor, but never on the artist. Because restraint in design allows more money to be allocated for necessary items, and because collaboration is required for this effort, one artist must be responsible for the whole.

This responsibility will guarantee that all forces be concentrated in the creation of a most perfect work with the most restrained application of means.[157]

EDUCATION

There were thousands of repercussions throughout Germany evoked by the Werkbund's manifesto. Rather than list them all, it was sufficient to repeat the refrain cited at the opening of Jeanneret's *Étude*: the Germans are conscious of their "artistic physiognomy," and through the harmonious efforts of artists and tradespeople have tried to put this into practice, enabling each worker to gravitate to the sphere that is proper to his talents. The lessons to be drawn were many: there were academies of Beaux-Arts in almost every key location within each province. There were new schools of industrial arts, schools for interior architecture and architecture, and all of these new schools redirected the torrent of young energies that up to now had been developed only in the Hochschulen. Jeanneret proceeds to list the characteristics of the different schools he visited in Munich, Weimar, Hamburg, Dusseldorf, Berlin, Dresden, and Hanau (Hanover).[158] He concludes:

> A school remains a school, and the work of students seldom goes beyond imitation more or less well understood of the thought of the master. Thus everything comes down to the value of the master and this is what makes the German schools of today so interesting. It is evident that students exposed to the influence of Fischer, Van de Velde, Hoffmann, Behrens, Paul, Kreis, or Pankok, might sometimes develop into personalities, but in all cases, they will become at least most of the time good workers.[159]

Again his appraisal is laudatory: there is a new pedagogical principle at work in Germany, where a school no longer is a prison but *a place of student research*, and where the student is treated as if he were a man, given both freedom and responsibility.

Jeanneret would retain the lesson of these German reforms in education, in public awareness, and in expert control over design issues long into his maturity. He was greatly impressed by the Werkbund as a new authority to conceive of and implement needed reforms. It placed men of elite training, mostly artists turned architects, in control of the directorship of new schools, convinced they must work collaboratively with industrialists, government officials, merchants, real estate speculators, artisans, and students. The kernel of this philosophy lay not only in the many expositions, workshops, and apprenticeship programs created, but in practical examples, such as those Jeanneret witnessed firsthand in the AEG works. And newly designed garden cities, under the control of the same group of artist-architects, seemed at first glance to offer solutions to the great social issue of workers' housing and the wasteful expansion of cities, yet constituted educational and cultural attractions of their own. Reform in the decorative arts extended from the smallest bibelot in a shop window to the largest plan of a city.

Another extremely valuable lesson retained from Germany throughout his lifetime was Jeanneret's enthusiastic awareness that publicity lay at the core of the Werkbund's success. Again he saw the best artists being utilized in the design of publications, posters, advertisements, typefaces, book designs, and in the presentation of merchandise from packaging to model showrooms. Images in publications, in catalogues, and in prospectuses were essential ingredients of this new commercial art, publicizing successful reforms and elevating the taste of the public. The comparison of good and bad images, and images reflecting stages in a city's development, were rhetorical tools he would cleverly exploit.

Design guidelines–or what Jeanneret refers to as codes–were also new procedures to ensure the unity of the ensemble in civic design, interior architecture, and exposition displays. The ambient or radiant effect of nature, colors, the landscape, and the site, already components of his artwork, were strengthened by his new awareness of the well-composed ensemble. He became a staunch advocate of purity and simplicity in the honest treatment of materials, and of the application of straight lines and simplified forms. His interest in prestressed concrete, in smooth surfaces devoid of decorative ornamentation and abstract geometrical forms, as well as in new building techniques and new materials, grew even stronger. And he was on the verge of pronouncing, *avant la lettre*, "Ornamentation is a Crime"! Abandoning the morbidity of his "gothic" obsession, he accepted the classical purity of the Doric witnessed in the gigantic AEG factory, the Dalcroze Institute at Hellerau, or the tracings of the Acropolis he had been required to execute. And of course, all of his "happy evolution" must also be read against his desire to travel to the East, to seek popular art forms outside the norms of his educational training, and to witness for himself the white marbles lying on the ground with the blue sea below and the sky above.

CHAPTER 3
AN ENCOUNTER ON THE ACROPOLIS (1910–1914, 1965)

Yet why must I, like so many others, name the Parthenon the undeniable Master, as it looms up from its stone base, and yield, even with anger, to its supremacy?

–LE CORBUSIER, 1914

THE "REVERSED" GRAND TOUR

The aristocratic ritual of the Grand Tour, which by the end of the seventeenth century had become a must for young men of the educated elites of northern Europe, was a trip across the Alps and through upper and central Italy, ostensibly devoted to studying monuments and landscapes and culminating with a prolonged stay in Rome.[1] The Grand Tour was an ascent to lofty regions both literal and figurative: the physical heights of the mountains and the cultural heights of Italy. It was also a journey of contrasts and comparison: lands of rainy weather and of sunny weather, wealth and poverty, past and present, progress and backwardness. And as the illustrated travel accounts, or *Voyages Picturesques*, of the eighteenth century advised, any trip to exotic climes was enhanced if some danger was also experienced.

Although the Grand Tour was no longer mandatory by the early twentieth century, Charles-Édouard Jeanneret made a similar journey in 1911. His Grand Tour, however, has been called "reversed": instead of going to Rome, he went to Constantinople and Athens. He experienced a series of contrasts paralleling those of the traditional Grand Tour, traveling through the plains of eastern Europe to the heights of Mount Athos and the Acropolis. In doing so, he also passed from being a painter to being an architect. [FIGURE 3.1]

FIGURE 3.1: Photograph of Charles-Édouard Jeanneret standing at the foot of the Parthenon on the Acropolis, Athens, 1911

He published a number of travel articles from this trip as letters in the periodical *La Feuille d'Avis de La Chaux-de-Fonds* in 1911 and added a roughly equal number when he tried unsuccessfully to publish the articles as a book in 1914. All were eventually assembled into a small, square book entitled *Voyage d'Orient* (*Journey to the East*), published posthumously in 1966. Six weeks before he drowned while swimming in the Mediterranean on August 27, 1965, Le Corbusier read the proofs for *Voyage d'Orient* and added the following note to the last chapter: "Completed at Naples on October 10, 1911, by Charles-Édouard Jeanneret. Reread on July 17, 1965, 24 Nungesser et Coli, by Le Corbusier."[2] Thus he juxtaposed 1911 with 1965, the naive, young Charles-Éduoard Jeanneret with the wiser, self-constructed Le Corbusier.[3]

Vladimir Propp has suggested that in all stories, the central character starts by missing something, whether they know it or not. They set off in quest of what is missing, and in the tests of the resulting journey the hero is transformed. In keeping with this view, the hero in this story, Jeanneret, ends up in a different place from where he begins;

he solves the enigma, achieves the quest. But the voyage is full of tension and surprises.

In 1929, in the introduction to volume I of *Oeuvre Complète*, Le Corbusier said that

> Though I have to admit that my hands are soiled by the scourings of past centuries, I prefer washing them to having to cut them off. Besides, the centuries have not soiled our hands. Far from it they have filled them.[4]

Perhaps his 1965 encounter with his own past, in reviewing *Voyage d'Orient,* can be seen as a chronological reversed tour, backward across a lifetime, and as a recapitulation of his own youthful recourse to the mythological schemes and moods of the shared, historical past. As the youthful architect was enriched by the historical past, so the mature architect was enriched by his personal past–the emotional, poetical, and irrational instincts that had molded him as an architect. The scourings of past decades had not soiled his hands. Far from it; they had filled them.

DISCOVERY AND INVENTION

In *Le Corbusier's Formative Years*, H. Allen Brooks claims that the 1911 voyage of self-discovery remained a vivid experience in Jeanneret's mind, a trope mentioned in every one of his future books, because during it his ideals received their final shape. He returned mature and whole from this rite of passage, Brooks argues, his past integrated with his present.

But Jeanneret was only twenty-three at the time; he still had much to learn, invert, and invent. Even Brooks believes that Jeanneret was basically a provincial until after his famous encounter with Ozenfant in 1917–18.[5] On this latter view, Jeanneret remained a naif throughout his trip, not clearly aware of the political tensions racking the Balkans. These tensions would erupt in the first Balkan War in 1912, which pitted Greece, Montenegro, Bulgaria, and Serbia against a weakened Ottoman Empire. In any case, care must thus be taken when deciding what Jeanneret really discovered on his tour.

One school of thought views Jeanneret's accounts of the tour as auto-fictional. According to this account, Jeanneret turns himself by main narrative force into a self-educated architect and a self-created man, one of the spiritual elite whom he so admired.[6] For example, Brooks believes that Jeanneret's account of a "sudden conversion to classicism" at the foot of the Acropolis in 1911 was invented to suppress the great debt he owed to Peter Behrens and other German influences during his painful evolution. Perhaps Brooks's use of "sudden conversion" refers to Jeanneret's obsession with the Acropolis and all things Greek, expressed in his many letters written to William Ritter during the time he felt confined to La Chaux-de-Fonds after his return from the East. Before then, Jeanneret openly admitted that it was Germany rather than France that had led him to the Parthenon, although, he said, he was influenced by Cingria-Valneyre rather than Behrens to accept white cubic architecture as his ideal, since Behrens's classicism amounted to copying Schinkel's drawings or the Parthenon's ornaments.[7] And during his travels to the East he would admit to L'Eplattenier that his time in Germany had direct repercussions on his architectural and urban conceptions.[8] The lines of influence, intention, and invention in Jeanneret's self-representations can sometimes be difficult to untangle.

The German issue is particularly complex. After his reversed Grand Tour, Jeanneret continued work on two writing projects that examined the German and French struggle for supremacy in architecture and the decorative arts (as described in the previous chapter). Although he was secure in his belief that the dominant aesthetic influence radiated from France, there was much he continued to admire about the Germans up to the outbreak of World War I. Furthermore, he still placed his hope on his *Étude sur le mouvement d'art décoratf en Allemagne* (1912) as a key that might open for him a career in France; he was not above using it to gain appointment to certain French governmental commissions as late as 1918.

Certainly, he did not look fondly on the time he spent in Germany: he was extremely isolated there, experiencing the pain of rejection from his companions in La Chaux-de-Fonds, convinced he had evolved beyond their immature stage, stung by their indifference. Yet there is no question of outright suppression or denial by Jeanneret of all German influences at this point in his development. Under the tutelage of Ritter he began to try his hand at novelistic prose and genre-writing, to capture in words and drawings the sense of time and space he received from Constantinople, Athens, and Rome. And he longed to transcend the narrow confines of bourgeois existence, to rebel against his duty to write descriptive prose and factual accounts concerning the art of constructing cities, to immerse himself in the sense of an elsewhere beyond the normal.

In 1914, he sought to make a book out of his notes for *Voyage d'Orient,* which, in spite of all attempts, had been only half-published in *La Feuille d'Avis.* The articles and manuscripts that comprise Jeanneret's "Voyage to the East" can be divided into three parts.[9] The first part is a series of letters written about his impressions as he traveled from Germany down the Danube to Turkey and his stay in Constantinople. These are the twenty articles published in the daily *La Feuille d'Avis de La Chaux-de-Fonds* between the twentieth of July and the twenty-fifth of November, 1911.[10] The second part consists of observations about everyday life in Constantinople. Jeanneret writes lyrically about donkeys and women, cafés and bazaars, the picturesque qualities of the city, the sea, the boats, and a disastrous fire in Constantinople, before he is forced to tear himself away from a place that he has come to love. These essays conclude with a piece on "The West" written in Pompeii and Naples the eighth and the tenth of October. None of these articles that constitute the second part were previously published.[11] The third part of the book consists of two chapters written in 1914 in La Chaux-de-Fonds, a chapter on Mount Athos and a chapter on the Parthenon.[12]

These latter two chapters are written from a retrospective viewpoint. No doubt aware of wartime propaganda stressing France's Mediterranean roots and of the fact that Turkey was allied with Germany, Jeanneret's stress on the influence of Greece may have been as much a marketing gesture as an act of auto-fictional revisionism. Nevertheless, we must still ask what place Constantinople and Athens take in Jeanneret's narrative development. What desires and fears, what ideals of purity and romance underwrite his defense of folklore and primitive man? And why does he eventually elevate the Parthenon to such lofty heights over his beloved Constantinople?

WHERE IS THE ORIENT ON THE MAP OF EUROPE?

As already noted, the primary goal of Jeanneret's reversed tour was Constantinople, not Rome. He stayed there fifty-one days, and most of his 1911 articles concern his journey through the Balkans and his experiences in the city. From the unpublished accounts of his travel companion August Klipstein, it appears the two wanted to see Constantinople, the city of Islam, because they hoped to find there an art devoid of narrative content, an abstract art without figuration.[13] [FIGURE 3.2]

Not that Jeanneret had anything against Rome per se. During his difficult time in Berlin and Munich in 1910–11, Jeanneret longed to take a soothing voyage of escape to Rome, where he could study both

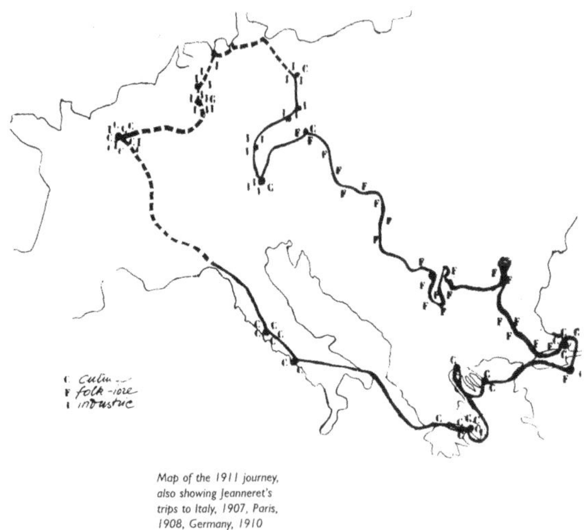

FIGURE 3.2: **No longer a requirement for the educated elite of northern Europe, the Grand Tour still left its impression on the map Charles-Édouard Jeanneret drew of his voyage to the East. He labeled all of the European sites with "I" for Industry; most of the Balkan places and Constantinople were marked with "F" for Folklore; and Greece and Italy were labeled with "C" for culture.**

folk art and the origins of classical art. Influenced by Alexandre Cingria-Vaneyre's *Les Entretiens de la villa du Rouet: essais dialogues sur les arts plastiques en Suisse romande* (1908), Jeanneret believed that the people of the Suisse-Romande–as Cingria-Vaneyre described them–were a unique people who had preserved their Greco-Latin roots. In valleys cut off from the rest of the world by mountain ranges, traces of a classical heritage could still be found in their popular arts. The Suisse-Romande lineage of geometric design, with its regular and calm features, Cingria-Vaneyre suggested, must be re-inserted into the region's architectural language if the latter was to attain new vigor. This book heightened Jeanneret's resolve to learn the lessons of Rome, even though Cingria-Vaneyre was actually recommending Greece and the area around Constantinople as the landscapes to study.

In a January 1911 letter to L'Eplattenier (already cited in Chapter 2) and again in a May 8 letter, Jeanneret writes about his "evolution." Not only has he rid himself of his morbid taste for the Gothic, but he is full of enthusiasm for the arts of Italy and Greece. He remembers lessons he absorbed from his study of Versailles, Fontainebleau, and a splendid book filled with images of the Doric, Ionian, and Corinthian orders and the colossal vaults and large plain walls of Rome.[14] In May he announces "scandalous news": he will depart in three weeks for the Orient, Constantinople, and probably Greece, returning through Rome.[15] The past four years of student life are finally over, with all their troubles; to climax this experience he has before him eight months of freedom, enthusiasm, and youthfulness, which he will put to good use.[16] While he admits that he has kept this decision a secret since January, he only did so, he says, until he was certain of his new direction.

He asks L'Eplattenier's advice on several points. First, he wants to write and publish an account of his trip, but wonders which journal would be receptive. Not *Le National,* too politically conservative; *La Sentinelle* is better, but L'Eplattenier might think that this would compromise his own reviews there. Last he mentions *La Feuille d'Avis*, which is politically neutral but does not pay. The second item on which he wants advice is more alarming. His studies in Germany have completely impoverished him, and of the nine hundred to one thousand francs he should have received via his father only three hundred have been sent. He assumes that seven hundred francs are still owed him; these ought to be sent right away, for he will need them on the trip. He asks l'Eplattenier to reply (and presumably send the money) by the next mail.[17]

In Berlin, he receives a letter from L'Eplattenier, who is indeed alarmed at his proposed trip to the Orient and assumes that it will cause Jeanneret to postpone writing his study on German cities.[18] Jeanneret responds that he cannot remain rooted to the ground in Germany under the pretext that he must write. Anyway, the trip to Germany has proved to him that the key is to know Berlin and Munich in depth, which he already does. Meanwhile, he says, his parents have lent him money for the trip, so L'Eplattenier need not worry about his request for funds. As for sending L'Eplattenier the *Étude* right away, that seems too complex a matter to explain. "To write is very difficult for me if I am to do it with care."[19] He was not given a deadline for the *Étude*, but judges that everything can be completed when he returns from his voyage. He is thankful that l'Eplattenier will sound out Georges Dubois about writing for *La Feuille d'Avis*, perhaps even about getting paid. If Dubois prefers, Jeanneret can write him immediately to give him a feeling of how he will work.

Meanwhile, he has visited the villa Osthaus, Van de Velde's latest work, and is even more convinced that his ideas concerning the "radiating" influence of the Parisian spirit on German art are correct. He will detail this influence in the *Étude*.

By this time, Jeanneret had met his second mentor, Ritter, also a friend of Cingria-Vaneyre. An enthusiastic adventurer who traveled throughout the Balkans, Ritter published a romantic novel of peasant life in Slovakia, *L'Entêtement Slovaque* (*Slavic Infatuation*, 1910). His account of simple Slavic houses that seemed to spring naturally from the soil apparently spoke to Jeanneret's interest in the "exotic" East.[20] This interest was not an unusual one; in 1910 the East, or Orient, was still an essentially empty place on the European mental map, one of the last refuges of the exotic elsewhere. Whatever the West was, the East, in the Western imagination, was its reverse. The West was an enlightened land of rationality, democracy, industry, and high culture; the East was a quasi-mythological region of marvels and mysteries, despots, economic stagnation, and, as Jeanneret marked on his map in 1914, folklore.[21] It was this vision of a world beyond the realm of European progress that Jeanneret longed to experience.

He had also met his lifelong friend Klipstein, who was interested in studying the influence of Byzantine icons on El Greco, on whom he was writing a doctoral dissertation.[22] The two young men decide to travel together to the East by the Balkan route.

Jeanneret writes to Ritter on March 1, 1911, that after five months of gray, penitential hours working nonstop in Behrens's office, the arrival of spring bring him new joy. Ritter has taught him the attraction of classical, "Latin" light in which the sky is blue, the sea beneath one's feet is blue, and the rocks are gold, evoking the image of a classical monument crowned by nude women in full clarity (the word for light, *lumière*, is crossed out and the word for clarity, *clarté*, substituted). His mind is open to the classical spirit, he says; his dreams obstinately carry him to those lands.

He discloses that an opportunity will soon present itself: he prepares a splendid voyage. It was Ritter who made dear to him the land of Slovakia, the plains of Hungary, the countries of Bulgaria and Romania. Now Jeanneret wants to cross by foot a corner of Bohemia, to see Vienna again, and this time to admire it, to go down the Danube by boat, and to arrive at the Golden Horn, at the foot of the minarets of St. Sophia–and there to achieve absolute ecstasy, if he is not an imbecile, and allow his soul to "quiver ineffably" (*tressaillir ineffablement*) before the immortal marbles. Yet, he writes to Ritter, L'Eplattenier will think he is not prepared for such a momentous trip and his father will think it is time to work. He plans to travel with his friend Klipstein, whom he notes is the antipode to himself: a studious art historian who is writing a dissertation on El Greco, his head full of former voyages to Spain, Morocco, France, and Italy.

He begs Ritter to tell him more about the East and to tell him what to read so he can begin his initiation. Just mentioning the words *des portes de Fer* (Iron Gates) on the Danube thrills him with fantastic visions of somber and barbarian hordes. And "Constantinople!"–it could not be more fairy-like than the magical paintings by Signac he had seen in Munich, bathed in an atmosphere of color and light. He asks for the correct citation of Ernest Renan's "The Prayer on the Acropolis," which of course should be on his list of grand initiators.[23]

In early May, on a trip down the Rhine from Mayence (Mainz) to Cologne, Jeanneret writes another letter to Ritter.[24] Anticipating the style of his travel accounts of the Orient, he practices lyrical and fictional narration and places pencil sketches in the midst of his writing. [FIGURE 3.3, p. 690] Fascinated with colors, he begins by describing the river water in the morning as a beautiful dirty gray; the mountains, through which the river cuts a gorge, pass from green to the hour of blue after sunrise. Then it is midday and all is ocher. He writes of beautiful groupings of villages along the Rhine, noting that their enclosing walls trace parallels along the river. Factories rise up, sullying the sky with their black smoke, quickly followed by another scene of green cypress trees.

He announces that the voyage to the East is settled: he and Klipstein will leave from Dresden by the end of the month. Traveling straight to Constantinople, they will hardly have time to study the countries they cross, but he remembers how enthusiastically Ritter has spoken of Slovakia, also his drawings of the countryside and the village festivals. He asks Ritter to indicate the most characteristic route from Prague to Vienna or, even better, from Dresden to Prague: "I know you don't like that one does things superficially. However be indulgent and send them to me!"[25]

He will, he promises, send Ritter letters during the voyage. His scribbling will form a review of all the things that impress him, just as this letter describes the voyage down the Rhine. Colors, architecture, and nature will form the basis of his reports.

But, he complains, his linguistic faculties seem frozen. He remains staring at the blank page before writing even straightforward statements and making the easiest conjugations. Ritter can judge for himself, for this letter is full of mistakes. Before his stay in Germany, his French was impeccable, even if he had not yet achieved his own style; now he is humiliated: "All this indicates that it was essential for me to leave these Germans as quickly as possible and to return to Latin countries. You find me in a crisis of gothophobism."[26] He finds Nuremberg and the cities of the Rhine disgusting and congested, without open space. Modern life, he moralizes, cannot exist in such places of restraint. Only Cologne is different: there he climbs the cathedral's dome and stays there an hour, listening to the Mass, his eyes taking in the view from this major and unitary vertical.[27]

Klipstein and Jeanneret depart on May 25, 1911, for a five-month trip through the Balkans to Constantinople, Mount Athos, and Athens before returning separately through Italy. Jeanneret would remark from time to time in his letters that Klipstein was, far from being a sympathetic travel companion, too egocentric to become an intimate friend. For Jeanneret, the trip is meant largely as an escape into a fairy-tale world before taking up the burden of professional duties. All during the voyage, and in spite of his literary efforts, he keeps up a serious correspondence with L'Eplattenier about his return to La Chaux-de-Fonds and his appointment as a master teacher. He had to be nominated and his credentials put in order, otherwise he must enter as a plain worker and become a teacher at a later date.[28] He receives word while in Constantinople that he has been appointed *maître d'école*; he accepts the appointment with trepidation and a degree of humor. He writes to L'Eplattenier that upon receiving the news he looked at himself in the mirror to see if he had the head of an employee (*la tête de l'emploi*) and panicked because he did not have a mustache. More seriously, he is frightened by the name "school of decorative arts" and fears the teachings will not be modern. Since his travels to Germany he has formed a definite dislike for all schools–but if the school is led by L'Eplattenier, of course it must be different.[29]

Jeanneret sails from Patras for Brindisi on the fifth of October, then travels to Rome and Naples before returning to Switzerland in early November to take up his post. From his comments to Ritter, it seems that he longed to surrender himself to the rapturous East, to extend himself to experiences beyond self-control and discipline. But this desire for the forbidden would be accompanied at times with fear, containment, and dark moods. The Eastern trip would thus not be without emotional difficulties. Jeanneret would suffer both rapturous surrender and a sense of threat from an invasive alien power, and would in the end make a crucial distinction between Constantinople and Athens, elevating the rationality of the latter over the sensuous mystery of the former.

LEARNING TO WRITE

We do not know how much Jeanneret revised his youthful travelogues before the manuscript was given to a typist in 1914 and sent to Ritter for critique. It is difficult to reconstruct the order in which the unpublished materials were written due to their numerous flashbacks and insertions. Thanks to L'Eplattenier, the first half of his travel notes as mentioned above were published as serialized articles in *La Feuille d'Avis* between June and November of 1911. But Jeanneret remains unaware of this, for he writes L'Eplattenier on August 4, 1911, that his "poor articles" do not proceed, and he has heard nothing from the publisher of *La Feuille d'Avis*. He confesses that in spite of the battles that L'Eplattenier wages for him, apparently he has made a mess of things.[30]

There will be several occasions when Jeanneret complains of writer's block. Yet after returning to La Chaux-de-Fonds, he will spend numerous evenings over the next several years reading aloud to others or rereading to himself his articles and notes on the East. They alone seem to give him solace during difficult times, and the East will remain emblematic to him of escape and enchantment.

In *Le Corbusier: The Creative Search*, Geoffrey Baker suggests that the Eastern articles

> underscore Jeanneret's desire to penetrate the very heart of a culture; he records the interconnected activities that comprise the complex web of the city [Constantinople], commenting on behavior patterns, atmospheric effects, work habits, recreational pastimes and even disasters. It was within this rich and elaborate context that he perceived architecture, seeing it as being immersed in an endlessly varied myriad of life and emotions. In consequence he strove to uncover the exclusive uniqueness of every place, describing how its special character receives architectural expression.[31]

Many architectural historians, unfortunately, pay selective attention to Jeanneret's writings and rhetorical style, placing emphasis on the architectural and urban references and overlooking the atmospherics Baker cites. They tend to quote from his writings in a scattershot way, without analyzing the development of ideas from one book to another, and seem confused by Jeanneret's mode of reasoning, which blends supposedly incompatible themes such as folk art and classical art, the primitive and the technological. And they do not recognize that Jeanneret deliberately undertook his Eastern voyage as a painter and artist, opening himself to the sensuous influence of pottery and local fabrics. He conceived of himself as going to the East not primarily to see architectural structures, but patterns, colors–the bright pinks, ochers, and azures of the Balkans and the gold and bronze tones, the reds and blacks and dark greens, of the Byzantine icons. He was interested not so much in analyzing Eastern architecture as in soaking up the atmospheric context of that architecture: he was fascinated by the handmade curves of Syrian pots and the feminine wiles of women in veils. Only in 1914, back in La Chaux-de-Fonds–at the time he inserts his Greek recollections into the text–does he envision himself primarily as an architect or builder.

At the end of the *Voyage d'Orient*, Le Corbusier adds an epilogue in the form of a confession taken from his 1911 notes. This reads, in part, as follows:

> These notes are lifeless; the beauties I have seen always break down under my pen; there were murderous repetitions. [The writing] would bore me and torment me for hours, disheartening hours of vexation, of despair.... During my hours of gold, ivory, and crystal, there were flaws, stains, and cracks–because of these notes that I so wanted to write! I didn't know my own language, I have never studied it! I can still hear the tol-de-rol of the four or five adjectives I know.[32]

Even so, his trip to the East allowed Jeanneret to experiment with being a creative writer. Writing both obsessed and distressed him; he felt compelled to write, but here, as in architecture, he felt that his lack of formal training made him ineffective. He seems to have suffered from writer's block: something inhibited him from revealing his deepest motives.[33] Jeanneret may actually have learned how to turn his depression and anguish to his own advantage, for they seemed to fuel his desire to write a torrent of words. This was especially the case with the Eastern essays, which were more autobiographical and so tied to his sense of isolation and self-absorption.[34]

At the time of the Eastern voyage, Jeanneret had been struggling for a year and a half with writing two commissioned reports, *Étude sur le mouvement d'art décoratif* (1912) and the never-published *Étude sur l'urbanisation.* He promised L'Eplattenier that the outline and pamphlet for both were nearly completed, so his travels would not seriously interrupt their progress; there is, however, no evidence that these studies—whatever outline and pamphlet meant—were then anywhere near completion.

Jeanneret's Eastern travel memoirs were his testing ground as a writer of poetic realism rather than—as his two *Études* were so painfully requiring him to be—a mere chronicler of urban places and interpreter of events in the decorative arts. They contain a mélange of writing styles. He borrowed from Camillo Sitte a method of writing in sharp contrasts, juxtaposing places that he dislikes with those that he likes and setting up a repetitive drumbeat of death and life. He tried, as Baker notes, to emulate Taine's use of word-pictures to frame the life of a city, its local customs and vernacular architecture. A more important model was the flowery picture-writing of Ritter's *L'Entêtement Slovaque* (1910), which he admired.[35] Ritter's colorful depictions of peasant life, handcrafts, simple houses, and landscape settings deeply affected Jeanneret's approach to the East.[36] Most important of all was the Oriental oeuvre of the fin-de-siècle Turkophile, travel-writer, and novelist Pierre Loti, especially *Aziyadé* (1879) and *La Mort de Philae* (1909), both of which Jeanneret read while in Constantinople.[37]

Loti was the *nom de plume* of Julien Viaud, a French naval officer and diplomat. As Viaud's alter ego, Loti immersed himself in what he aestheticized as the sensuous, theatrical East, especially Turkey, adopting the local dress, habits, and language. His writings blurred fact and fiction, presenting an intricate tapestry of autobiography, travel lessons, and journal notes. His tone was nostalgic as he mourned the loss of the "authentic" East, replaced by mimicry of the West. A champion of the Ottoman cause, he deplored the "Great Game" of those Europeans intent on dividing the world, including the remains of the Ottoman Empire, into subjugated colonies.[38]

Jeanneret seems to have cast himself as a sort of Loti double, completely absorbed in the intoxicating charm of the perfumed East. Or perhaps Loti merely matched the disposition he had already adopted before leaving Germany. When he began his journey it was his express wish to see the white vertical columns of Grecian marble in their ruinous form lying parallel to the horizontal lines of the sea, but this dream would be greatly embellished by romantic Eastern apparitions. Mask-wearing, which erects a distance between one's inner and outer selves, seems to have allowed a certain melancholic distance to appear in his writings. This element may also have led at times to his writing block.

Whether Jeanneret's interest in foreignness and cultural difference issued in what amounts to a factual travel account or a fantasy adventure, and no matter how many insertions and corrections were subsequently made, there remains a linear aspect to this (as to all) travel writing: a sequence of places is visited. The text describes a kind of cartography, a space structured by language into an origin, a destination, and stops in between. The "voyage" is the line linking the visited sites. The reader is simultaneously invited to visualize a scheme or map and to crystallize the descriptions of places into particular images. The text thus articulates two kinds of space: an overall one ruled by the linearity of writing, and another in which one repeatedly extrapolates from the written word to the individual object or place. A movement back and forth occurs between a space that is traveled through and a space schematized into an assemblage of forms–an orthogonal map and a bird's-eye perspectival view.[39]

Edward Said, in his now-famous *Orientalism* (1978), argued that "The Orient was almost a European invention, and had been since antiquity, a place of romance, exotic beings, haunting memories and landscapes, remarkable experiences."[40] Jeanneret's Orientalizing, however, is a matter not merely of distancing, of "othering"–though it is that–but of grappling with something unknown, something outside himself. It is exploration as well as projection. His travel writing is a record of how he encounters this Other and how what is typical of a people–their culture, way of life, and environment–is turned into written discourse by the traveler.[41] Perhaps this is another reason why Le Corbusier was so fond of *Voyage d'Orient*, the opening of a life-time discourse on method, plots, and plans. The double nature of his travel writing–schematic space plus image-populated space–can be seen as prevailing throughout a long lifetime of literary production, the "map" aspect of the early form corresponding to his ongoing concern about the way space is organized and the "images" aspect corresponding to his specific architectural designs and urban plans.

LEARNING TO SEE

Jeanneret was learning not only to write, but to see–to acquire knowledge through observing appearances and recording impressions in words, drawings, watercolors, and photographs.[42] He bought a new camera, a Cupido 80, especially for the trip, and exposed hundreds of nine-by-twelve-centimeter glass plates, many of which survive.[43] This German-made camera, adept at capturing long shots, was his constant companion. He writes L'Eplattenier that he is ecstatic about the miracle of photography, calling the camera "a brave objective eye unaccountably precise!"[44] Yet his painterly eye was also at work. He made quick fragmentary sketches, stopping suddenly to record direct impressions. He drew in bold black outlines and made watercolors in bright splashes of color. He filled more than six sketchbooks with all kinds of material, including over six hundred pages of scribbled notes. To this activity must be added the postcards and letters to L'Eplattenier, Ritter, parents, and friends. He was in a rush to seize the moment, to capture it visually and in words that synthesized, condensed, and translated his feelings.

During the first leg of the trip, voyaging down the Danube, he complains to Ritter that there is no time to write, although every day he records copious notes. Nor is he able to sketch, for he sees only a few things that enthuse him. Moreover, they are always short of time, for at each stop they search for paintings by El Greco and run after vases in shut-away places. Yet he contradictorily says toward the end of this letter that everything on this river excites curiosity, admiration, and contemplation.

They will, he continues, soon leave Belgrade and travel by horse over the mountains. He thinks he has a bit of religious masochism, which makes him suspect his happiness and turn toward melancholy and depression. He concludes by drawing what he says is his first sketch of the Danube: a simple sectional cut of sky above, water below, and in between, a line for the land.[45]

Upon arriving in Constantinople, he complains that all trades fail him: his watercolors do not go well, and he wonders if the city is a mirage. He and Klipstein are in a strange state of mind and constantly ask one another if they have gone crazy. Probably the *sacré tabac* (assumed to be hashish) they are smoking plays tricks on them. But every morning he continues to write in his journal, though it is a "poor, sad work." He is waiting for a revelation.[46]

Jeanneret experienced both the trip and the East itself as fugitive interludes in which he sought refuge from the shadow of the teaching and writing responsibilities that would eventually engulf him. His aim was to capture temporal slices of space in time, whether in paintings, photographs, or words, directing the gaze to insignificant details, close-up distillations of the everyday. He used his discerning eye to travel through space, across a landscape, focusing close or pulling away to enclose the spectator within his panoramic gaze. Light, reflections, colors, and tones texture his panoramic views. The landscape through which he travels becomes a melodic flow of fantastical images, in which the following refrain repeats itself: climb the heights of a plateau, mountain, or village, take a long look toward the horizon, then pan across the plains below; descend, travel horizontally, repeat. He utilizes the horizon to stage his pictures, he says, bringing all lines of the work into unity.[47]

The Greek word *horizein* means "to limit." Jeanneret's continual reference to the horizon, beginning with that simple horizontal line in his sketch of the Danube, is a paradoxical gesture in which space appears both infinite yet enclosed, endlessly open yet framed. Moreover, this spatial gesture corresponds to a complex affective condition. He forges toward the horizon in quest of adventure, but begins to understand, as the journey proceeds, that he is on a nostalgic journey toward a past that cannot be reached. A horizon is not an object that can be attained. In the course of his travels he would gradually become aware that the mystic Orient once to be found beyond the confines of "civilization"–he did not question that it *had* existed–was lost to the twentieth century. His travel notes are constantly interrupted by rude intrusions from the modern world. He recognized that he could at best capture only fugitive afterimages like his photographic plates, glimpses of a past quite distinct from the degraded reality of the present. His journal offers snapshots of yesterday to readers of today and tomorrow: it is directed toward a future he cannot avoid, yet from which he flees and a past that no longer exists. Thus his tone is mixed, his voice often melancholy, and his approach confused: death, blackness, and dark violet wash over the scenery he depicts in words and images. [FIGURES 3.4 AND 3.5]

TRAVEL WRITING

Jeanneret opens *Journey to the East* with a series of reminiscences or flashbacks to his journey's point of origin, then projects forward toward his goal, setting up a conceptual map that the reader will follow from north to south. Like Pierre Loti, whom he references in his correspondence, he will describe the Orient as if it were a fantastic and hallucinatory stage set, a Turkish box full of scenic surprises and colorful decor, fashioned out of clichés and stereotypes. And he will retain memories of Turkish wooden architecture seen along the Bosporus and white cubic houses of the Balkans and Greece, eventually absorbing these into his language of architecture (the box raised in the air on piloti, long horizontal windows, and a free facade). He will also call a house a box of miracles, to be filled with marvelous things.[48]

Les pages suivantes contiennent des croquis, impressions de voyages de Le Corbusier

CROQUIS DE VOYAGES ET ETUDES

Orient

FIGURES 3.4 AND 3.5: **Series of sketches by Charles-Édouard Jeanneret from *Carnets de Voyage de Orient* (1911), republished in volume one of Le Corbusier's *Oeuvre Complète* (1964)**

But he begins with the industrial cities of Germania, "Eyesores... slashed by black factory chimneys and blotched by leprous filthy and stinking fumes."[49] The once-romantic German towns can no longer enchant him, for "the foul taste of gable and tower builders had left the junk-heap effects of a ruffian."[50] He flees from these visual stenches and from the people of the north, seeking the intoxicating light of the sun, the blue of the sea, and the white walls of the temples of the south. Yes, he says, he was young and made rash judgments, and yes, his eyes are myopic, but he was also a keen observer, and in spite of the skeptics who taunted him, he believed that travel would sharpen his senses and enable him to make wise distinctions.

Jeanneret confesses to L'Eplattenier in a letter written from Belgrade on June 9 that they have spent all their allotted money on Serbian shawls and pottery.[51] To afford more purchases, they have placed themselves on rations. Klipstein complained about missing his beer and beefsteak, but Jeanneret was ecstatic over splendid hours along the Danube and the search for exquisite pots and shawls. The only problem was how to transport their buys in their baggage, and how much it would cost if they shipped them home. In the next chapter, "Letter to Friends," the one he calls a "ceramicological" epistle, he recalls Serbian pottery in joyful, even erotic tones. To touch the

> generous belly of a vase, to caress its slender neck, and then to explore the subtleties of its contours. To thrust your hands into the deepest part of your pockets and, with your eyes half-closed, to give way slowly to the intoxication of the fantastic glazes, the burst of yellows, the velvet tone of the blues; to be involved in the animated fight between brutal black masses and victorious white elements.[52]

Another theme often to be repeated follows, this one juxtaposing the simple mind of the southern peasant with the educated intelligence of the industrialized north–to the romantic advantage of the former. Here Jeanneret gives full expression to Orientalist tropes. The artist peasant's craft was a creation of "aesthetic sensuality," while the commercial arts imported from the north were humiliating. Jeanneret takes distance from himself, and by using an impersonal pronoun he makes an excuse: "We had to flee from the invading and dirty 'Europeanization' to the tranquil refuges where–abating, and soon to be submerged–the great popular tradition survives."[53]

Folk art, he proclaimed, was a universal art; it would outlive the highest brand of civilization. "It remains a norm, a sort of measure whose standard is man's ancestor–the savage, if you will."[54] These men of the south, who know nothing of reason, have an instinctive appreciation for the "organic line," an innate sense of how to correlate the useful with the beautiful.[55] Their simple minds never wander farther than the neighboring grocer, yet their fingers unconsciously obey deeply structured rules. Simple, sensuous forms are generated, like those found in Mycenae. There is tradition here, nothing discarded in the quest for the new, "in contrast to those forms of a disturbing fantasy, or a stupefying imbecility, conceived by who knows whom in the unknown corners of large modern factories."[56] In the end, "We others from the center of civilization, are [the] savages."[57] Le Corbusier will often repeat this trope in later years: who are the real savages, the primitive or the civilized, the South or the North, the Americans or the Europeans? He develops a special love for "simple" objects and people, for they are productive of a sense of distance from all he dislikes.

The text of "Letter to Friends" follows the flow down the Danube, a black line in "interminable flight" plunging through vague terrain, countries Jeanneret knows nothing about, giving rise to sounds and rhythms of music he has never heard. Icons of modernity make an appearance in silhouetted form, not all negative: the steamship and its captain, which he will come to avidly admire. He cannot sleep during this night on the Danube, and so sat on the deck wrapped in his coat, before a coffin draped in black.

> This symphony of blacks and whites beneath the moon, and on this glistening mirror, all this nautical apparatus painted with brilliant whites, the gaping jaws of the ventilators, the black banks of the river, the somber coffin appearing as a giant muted smudge, the moving silhouette of the captain surveying his bridge up there, and the sole whisper of the two pilots on the poop deck, and suddenly, rudely, and deliberately punctuating the path, the somber clang of the bell on the top deck each time a small light shone out of the water–a night light from one of those little windmills asleep on the river of which I will speak to you again–but this coffin, disquieting as it is with its two dark wreaths, would reveal to me again and again this conspiracy of silence and the horizontality of outlines–all this flooded the heart with a great calmness, troubled but

FIGURES 3.6 AND 3. 7: Charles-Édouard Jeanneret's photographs of Serbian houses, taken on his voyage to the East in 1911

> occasionally by an aroused shudder or by taking heed of welled-up tears.[58]

Jeanneret will soon slip into the mirage of the Orient, where blacks and whites yield to the full array of a language of colors. He takes on a clear identity as the steamship slips toward the East. Approaching the captain "I explained my wishes, saying I was a painter and was looking for a country that had retained its integral character."[59] From time to time, Jeanneret would recall that he was supposed to be an architect–as L'Eplattenier had prescribed–and at these points he inserts into the text panoramic shots of cubic shapes and geometric forms against close-up shots of interior courtyards. [FIGURES 3.6 AND 3.7] But his writing soon drifts toward the folk arts and peasant ways. "In watching out for Charybdis, I run into Scylla!"[60]

An Eastern language of flowers ("signs of thought," as they are called) awaits the traveler on this route: the yellow acacia, flower of the graveyard and symbol of sorrows and regrets; the fragrant white lily of purity; the red rose of passion; the green vine of hope.[61] In this garden of paradise, Jeanneret juxtaposes pure abstract grids and geometric forms against the natural lines of flowers and vines, comparing these to the floral patterns and abstract designs of Persian ceramics.[62]

> They are marvelous, these [Hungarian] villages of the great plain....The streets belong to the plain, entirely straight, very broad, and uniform, cut at right angles, punctuated throughout by little balls of dwarfish acacias....Each house has its own courtyard....Beauty, joy, serenity gather here....The trellis assembled from latticework casts a green shadow, its white

> arcades bring comfort, and the three great whitewashed walls, which are repainted each spring, make a screen as decorative as the background of Persian ceramics. The women are most beautiful; the men clean-looking. They dress themselves with art... the people contrasted and harmonized with the enormous white walls and with the flowerbeds of courtyards which make here and there a strangely successful complement to the distinguished appearance of the streets.[63]

He sends Ritter much the same description. The straight line dominates the villages, underscored by an infinite repetition of small balls of acacias. Everything seems concentrated in courtyards: comfort, beauty, and joy.

The next chapter in *Voyage d'Orient* offers a flashback to Vienna, a city he does not like. He pities the poor people of Vienna, many without work, and despises the idle rich, who amuse themselves frivolously. The city's festival of flowers is perfumed and morbid, its women depraved–inflamed by their desires–and its men always dressed in black, like a second violinist in this orchestra of colors.[64] Vienna is a "kaleidoscopic cinema where dance the most dizzying combinations of colors. It is, quite simply, chic Vienna enjoying herself, while poor Vienna watches the show."[65]

And so he must flee to the East, down the Danube. The next chapter begins with an explanation: it is better to take a boat than the Orient Express, for the railroad is symbolic of the degradation of the West, a linear projectile of steel and fire plunging toward the East to contaminate its essence. At least, so Jeanneret saw it. Few railroad lines actually crossed the Ottoman Empire in 1911. Paved roads were another rarity, and the number of automobiles fewer than one hundred. For the most part, travel was by horseback, mules, donkeys, and camels, or else along canals and rivers by boat.[66]

Jeanneret struggles, he tells his readers, with how to write about this two-week trip down the Danube to Vác, and of his first encounter with the East, which enthralls yet crushes him. He fears he creates only childish, imprecise impressions. What's more, he complains at the end of the Danube chapter, his writing was mutilated by an editor and a pair of scissors.[67]

As he struggles with his prose in this section on the Danube, his writing changes tenses and images. He flashes back to a Berlin cemetery, and then forward to bloody battles between the north and the south.

"Again in my imagination I was going down the river in the direction pointed by the bows. Belgrade lay at its elbow, the magic door to the East. Then came the tragic echoes of the march from Kazan, bleeding from worldly combat. The Iron Gates where the cohorts of Trajan raised their eagle banners....Confused, I followed these vicissitudes which were to be my own."[68] Melancholic strains of death continually arise: the calm of the cemetery, the cries of battle, the invasion of the north.

His writing flows on: nothing to see, he reports, but the horizontal line where water and sky merge together, punctured here and there by sharp architectural forms. Suddenly Pressburg makes an appearance, the cube of its fortress raised high on a mountain[69] This vision floats away, then Estergon emerges, "A cube and a dome supported by many columns. From afar, each of them hints at some marvel. A cube animated by a wonderful rhythm, and which the rising mountains present like an offering on this altar that they themselves make for it."[70]

Despite Jeanneret's fulminations against railroads, he and Klipstein travel from Vác to Budapest by train, a forewarning (as he says) that industry has invaded this terrain and that Jeanneret will not like the city. He finds it, in fact, "a leprous sore on the body of a goddess," an image he will repeat years later when writing about Buenos Aires and Algiers.[71] From the citadel, one gets a panoramic view of the damage:

> The Danube encircles the mountains, condensing them into a powerful body that faces the boundless expanses of the plain. But over this plain there spreads a dull black smoke into which the network of streets disappears. Eight hundred thousand inhabitants have rushed here in the last fifty years.[72]

He is shocked by the discordant styles of the public buildings that line the river banks. Order is suddenly restored in a focused close-up seized from the citadel:

> Ancient huts appear like a blossoming among acacias. These simple dwellings are united by walls behind which trees shoot up. These dwellings spring up naturally on this undulating ground. We spend hours on this peaceful hill watching Taban, invaded by the night, light up with the quiet little lights of evening gatherings. There was a great calm. Suddenly there arose...a sad change. It was a saxophone or an English horn....What a strange and grandiose melody in the still landscape![73]

And then the refrain: the same sectional drawing he had sent to Ritter from Coblenz reappears in words. "All things meet again within a horizontal line, over which they accumulate and into which they merge. It's like, in geometry, a plane seen through a horizontal section."[74]

The line of travel flows on through Belgrade and Bucharest to Tûnovo in Bulgaria, the gateway to Turkey. He does not like Belgrade; it is dishonest, dirty, and disorganized. He withdraws from the first person to the more distant-sounding "we": "We had imagined a door to the East, swarming with colorful life, populated by flashing and bedizened horsemen wearing plumes and lacquered boots!"[75] He escapes to the Serbian countryside, where the roadways are fragrant with chamomile, and the "endless fields of corn form an expansive, indolent, and weary arabesque on the purplish-black of the farmland."[76]

His account moves on to a chapter describing Bucharest. It is a city that bedazzles him. He finds its women splendid, recalling seductive visions of fashionable Paris. But it is really the beautiful gypsies, the *tziganes*, that captivate and torment him the most. Dressed in lemon yellows, dirty greens, and rotting purples, they fill the city with a lingering fragrance from the lilies they sell in the streets. The call of that city is so strong it makes Jeanneret's blood pound and his brain explode.[77]

A chapter on Tûnovo follows. It is built on a high plateau, filled with scrubbed and whitewashed houses decorated with flowers, a perfect backdrop for the joyful colors and smiles worn by their inhabitants. At sunset he climbed its huge rock, where tumultuous houses were crimped along tortuous paths. From those dry heights, where only chamomile bloomed, he could see the plain stretched out below. The unattainable horizon beckons.

> The sun has set right there, and all the way down it bleeds into a great horizontal line: it must be the Danube over there. On the other side, in a semicircle, the Balkans froth and swell at this hour so exquisitely blue. A frieze of light cobalt marks this highest mountain where the Shipka winds its way, the gateway to Turkey which we shall enter on horseback in a few days.[78]

Tûnovo is a picturesque and clean town, for its inhabitants

> take care of their dwellings with a solicitude that, to us, would appear exaggerated. They want them to be clean, gay, and comfortable: they adorn them with flowers. They dress in

FIGURE 3.8: Charles-Édouard Jeanneret's Cupido 80 camera captured the dress and manners of Balkan women in 1911.

> embroidered clothing whose flamboyant colors tell of their joy of life. Their dishware is florid and artistic, and rugs, woven by the women following age-old tradition, cover floors that are scrupulously maintained. And each spring, the house that one loves receives its new coat: sparkling white, it smiles the whole summer through foliage and flowers that owe to it their dazzle.[79] [FIGURE 3.8]

Nevertheless, he found the Balkans disappointing–they should have afforded some dangerous adventures, yet he was nearing his goal without mishap. His begins the long chapter "On Turkish Soil" and soon finds more exciting tableaux to describe: the Turkish town of Adrianopolis appears full of nobility with its splendid mosques.

> The scenery could have been painted by Decamps. The good man really struck the right note: a storm-blackened sky against which a mountain rises up in light ocher: the trees converge to a hard, opaque shadow, and the clouds make grim patches on the ground. It is a setting for battles.[80]

Jeanneret now becomes an enthusiastic tourist, for there are new customs to see and different foods to taste. Wide-eyed, he absorbs new scenes as they open before him: cafés where men smoke the *narghile*, the strangely shaved heads of Turkish men, and the little donkeys, always overburdened, who go up and down the streets. He loves these small beasts, plodding along, for they seem to represent the humorous juxtapositions that for him stereotype the East. They will remain a beloved motif:

> It is amusing to see how these lazy old buggers load them down, with bundles of freshly cut grass so crookedly stacked that they tumble to the ground, bringing with them an entire patch of fragrant prairie grass, or with enormous baskets filled with tomatoes, onions and garlic. This whole bundle–the donkey, the Turk, the straw or the tomatoes, and all–is so wide that it often fills the entire street.[81]

There are new foods to be devoured and new table manners to be studied. A local restaurant has an entire wall of windows, against which are the ovens, whose aroma spreads over the street below. On a marble slab inside the café, tomatoes, cucumbers, beans, cantaloupes, and watermelon are laid out.

> We are served a very heavy noodle soup with lemon, then some little stuffed squash, and some barely cooked rice sautéed in oil. As a rule the Turks eat no meat. Limiting themselves to a vegetarian diet, they don't need knives; hence the table knife is unknown. To this very rich menu they always add a few cups of fruit juices, cherry, pear, apple, or grape, which they drink with a spoon; wine is condemned by Mohammed. The aristocratic Turks of the old regime use only their fingers and a piece of bread to eat with; they handle it with great finesse.[82]

However, at a dinner at the home of a bourgeois merchant, the talk turns to "progress." This displeases Jeanneret, and he makes fun of the scene. The evening ends with music played on a mandolin and a guitar. Asked whether he prefers serious or frivolous music, the waltz or the madrigal, Jeanneret is unable to state his preference.

> They seemed displeased, and, after tuning their instruments and shuffling around innumerable musical scores for more than an hour, they spent two minutes playing a piece for me that depicted a call for retreat in a military barracks–that is,

FIGURE 3.9: A panoramic view of Constantinople by Charles-Édouard Jeanneret, from 1911

> the sound of the trumpet and then drums that fade away little by little in the distance.[83]

Disenchantment is beginning to set in: the rhythmic flow of likes and dislikes has ended in a bugle call to withdraw. The prelude to his voyage has ended and the major theme is about to begin.

He arrives finally at his destination, to worship Constantinople, a city he already believes is beautiful. [FIGURE 3.9] He begins to read some of Loti's books and repeats some of his motifs. But first, to mark his entrance and the beginning of the chapter "Constantinople," he describes the view from his balcony, with cypress trees in the foreground, the silhouette of the Golden Horn beyond, the minarets and cupolas of the mosques puncturing the sky, and when there is a moon, the sea tying the minarets together with a shimmering thread. But he also wants reality to puncture this dream: the hour is full of madness, he is surrounded in suffocating fragrances, the sky is a pool of fire as in an icon, the night trickles with gold, his imagination wanders, but something is not right. Is it déjà vu, or the exhausted copying of a cliché? His suspended judgment and the use of another's expressions are accompanied by another shift to "we." The sunsets that bathe the city in golden light are an Oriental illusion–he wants them to be removed so that the city can be seen in pure light, bright colors. He finds the color yellow to be menacing, turning it into a symbol of the dark, drugged aspect of the "Orient" that drinking too much mastic, or reading too much Loti, engenders. He wants

> to sit upon her Golden Horn all white, as raw as chalk, and I want light to screech on the surface of domes which swell the heap of milk cubes, and minarets should thrust upwards, and the sky must be blue. Then we would be free of all this depraved yellow, this cursed gold. Under the bright light, I want a city all white, but the green cypresses must be there to punctuate it. And the blue of the sea shall reflect the blue of the sky.[84]

He sends a postcard to L'Eplattenier the day after his arrival, confessing that he is happy to have finally arrived in Constantinople in spite of having received at first "a bizarre impression." He is now eager to remain in Constantinople, for he has need of placing "my small person and my impressions" on a stable base.[85]

His heart is heavy, however, for reality appears to be worse than the mirage. Constantinople is an enormous city of disarray and disorder, not the primitive landscape he had sought. It is better to return to the illusion and the *trompe-l'oeil.*[86]

The reader may wonder whether Jeanneret is here mimicking Loti, who was likewise upset by the modernization of Constantinople during his own visit in August 1910, and by the oppressive spectacle of the fires of 1911 that destroyed more than ten thousand houses. In any case, for both men, obsession engenders fear as well as empathy; their passion for the "Orient" is born on a somber note, mixing love with death.[87] Although Jeanneret mentions Loti several times in this manuscript, aware that Loti helped save the mosque at Broussa, or that only Loti understood the unfathomable mysteries of Turkish women, the exact borrowings from the books Jeanneret was reading while in Constantinople can only be assumed. The parallels, however, are striking.

Imperially corrupt Byzantium has died, Jeanneret says, and its spirit cannot be roused from the stones that remain. Here again, as in the Serbian fields, is Loti's vanishing East, with its morbid terrain of tombs and cemeteries. Yellow pervades the view, as it would in the pages of an aging photographic album, melancholic and mournful. Jeanneret's color-words reflect his inner emotions: yellow, gold, and black for him represent overwhelming melancholy, morbidity, and death. The mythical Orient of his dreams no longer exists. For three full weeks he remains disenchanted by what he sees before him, until one day he asks himself why is he so stupid to be so morose instead of being enthralled over the image the three parts of the city compose. He cries out, "Pera, Stamboul, Scutari: a trinity...there is something sacred about it."[88]

Now he will triumph over adversity and enter the tableau in quest of the fantastic and hallucinating, fully aware, as was Loti, that their imagined Constantinople is already past when it is present, is alive only as it disappears. There are, after all, more tombs than houses.

> Sweet Death has its altars everywhere and unites all hearts with the same serenity and the same hope. Yet Scutari resolutely takes refuge in the mystery of her cypresses, where thousands upon thousands of neglected tombs are covered with moss, and she leaves Pera and Stamboul facing each other beyond the Bosporus, on European soil.
>
> Pera, perched on a mountain, overlooks Stamboul on her hills and covets her. The Golden Horn between them crouches dull and formless. But two bridges unite them, one almost abandoned, the other shaking with feverish vitality. To bring them together even more, there are also hundreds of rowboats furtively spaced between fully inflated sailboats and the massive hulls of huge steamers whose harsh blasts are accompanied by dense black smoke, always blown toward Stamboul—because of the Bosporus—where it flicks its dirty tongue at the naive whiteness of the poor mosques.[89]

The harsh, heartless European town centers on the tower of Pera, north of the Golden Horn. Jeanneret colors it purple, the color of dried blood. And yet there are mysterious houses there, propped up like dominoes:

> Wooden houses with large spread-out roofs warm their purple colors amidst fresh greenery and within enclosures whose mystery delights me [original manuscript has ravishes and torments, not delights]. Although they group themselves quite harmoniously around all these summits formed by really enormous mosques, a poisoned atmosphere hangs over Pera, under an unrelenting light. Stone houses scale up within, thrusting upward like upright dominoes, offering two sections of white walls riddled with windows and then two-adjoining walls the color of dried blood. Nothing softens the severity of this height. There are no trees, for they would take too much space.[90]

Stamboul (Jeanneret favors the archaic form of the name), the old Turkish town, is in contrast a labyrinth of streets, all comings

FIGURE 3.10: Charles-Édouard Jeanneret sketched and photographed different cemeteries when he traveled to the East in 1911.

and goings; like Babel it blends Greek, Armenian, Hebrew, and Arabic. Stamboul is the Queen of the Orient, bedecked in jewels—and prostituted by trade. He colors it violet, again using the spectrum's last visible color. The houses hang

> against the side of this great hill like a suspended carpet of violet wool blended with tints of emerald; the mosques on the crests are its prestigious fasteners. Here there are only two types of architecture: the big flattened roofs covered with worn tiles and the bulbs of the mosques with minarets shooting up. They are linked to each other by cemeteries.[91] [FIGURE 3.10]

These cemeteries are an echo of a Stamboul that has disappeared. Following Loti, Jeanneret sees Stamboul submerged in tombs—though he will later recall his sojourn there as the best time of his own existence. They

> extend right into the courtyards of houses...come right onto the streets, settle under the foliage and rival the big turbes in which the sultans lie within the walled enclosures of the mosques; and blue thistles bloom all over this soil....The life of the Turk passes from the mosque to the cemetery by way of the café where he smokes in silence.[92]

In a letter written to L'Eplattenier almost two weeks after his arrival, Jeanneret opens on a note of bile: he wanted to capture in watercolors the calm of the cemeteries, and so ventured out to what he hoped would be an isolated location, but the police made him leave because he had no permit. He had experienced the same rude expulsion several times.[93] Having relieved his annoyance over losing valuable time, he proclaims of Constantinople that in "all cases, it is other than what one imagines."[94]

He is in a very bad mood, he says, and puts his letter writing aside for the day. When he resumes, he picks up his description of the infinity of cemeteries–their closeness to the houses, their placement inside courtyards. Sometimes a thousand of them will be erected on an arid plateau without a blade of grass, sometimes cypress trees have been planted–the thought of these beautiful places enables him to suppress his black humor. "It is not easy to love Constantinople: it is necessary to work a lot."[95]

He is preoccupied with this city that he wanted to love but cannot, and mentions that he learned to see Stamboul through the paintings of Signac.

> I believe there is an hour when it is "orientalized" [*s'orientalisé*], or if you want, when it has a little of that fairylike quality which compose all our dreams: it is 3 or 4 o'clock in the morning at sunrise when Stamboul is in fog. It is then that the imagination can work.[96]

He turns his attention to the mosques, expecting them to appear as he had seen them in photographs of old Stamboul, solemn in their majestic coats of whitewash, containing no shadows, nothing hidden from view. At a glance he would understand the great cube from which spring four gigantic transverse arches, holding aloft a crown, a sparkling dome with thousands of tiny windows. He writes in a chapter devoted to "the Mosques" in *Voyage d'Orient*,

> An elementary geometry orders these masses: the square, the cube, the sphere. In plan it is a rectangular complex with a single axis. The orientation of the axis of every mosque on Moslem soil toward the black stone of the Kaaba is an awe-inspiring symbol of the unity of the faith.[97]

But something jars one's view of these bold constructions, these simple forms in white: they are not white, in fact, but have recently been painted, ornamented. Once again, Jeanneret has recourse to describing the old, ideal Stamboul seen in black-and-white photographs or imagined from guidebook descriptions. In the same letter to L'Eplattenier cited above, written two weeks after his arrival, he writes:

> The interior of Saint Sophia leads me voluntarily to blasphemy... the dogs are dead and the cypress cut. The Golden Horn is blue! The Greek cuisine excellent, a little heavy and the mosques in general of bad architecture. The cemetery of 'Eyoub, a dream. That of Santori too dusty.[98]

He complains the Turks had never developed a national spirit of building, which allows them to construct whatever they want. The concept of domestic architecture does not exist with them, at least not as he had seen it in Hungary, Bulgaria, or Romania.[99] Feeling, as he says, isolated from his comrades, who are gathered around L'Eplattenier, Jeanneret turns to discuss their love affairs. Here he makes a passing reference to Turkish women, saying that their bizarre clothing is both ugly and ridiculous (an opinion he will soon correct, as described below).

The rest of the letter discusses his new position as school master. He wonders who else has been elected, because he has received little news, and describes his loyalty to L'Eplattenier, as well as his hopes and fears for the new school. He suspects jokingly that L'Eplattenier will challenge him, even muzzle him like a dog every Monday before work begins.[100]

In his next postcard to L'Eplattenier, however, Jeanneret admits that finally he has been conquered by Constantinople, and has learned to enjoy this love affair.[101] This change is also reflected in *Voyage d'Orient*. In the chapter "She's and He's," he spells out his worship of the young women and little donkeys of Stamboul–a quixotic juxtaposition of incongruent exotica. The donkeys had won him over from the first moment, for he always begins with simple things. But the women he hated for the first three weeks, all that time in which his heart was heavy with failed expectations. Yet Loti had taught him how to delve into the ineffable, so one day he found these women

> ravishing despite and also because of that second skirt flung over their heads, that makes an impenetrable veil. You will find

> real coquettes underneath. I bet you…that almost all of them are young, adorable, with ivory cheeks a little full and with the innocent eyes of gazelles–delicious! After all, these veils conceal a penetrable mystery. It seems to me that there are thousands of them who wish to display their beauty, and devilish as they are, they know how to get around all the codes.[102]

At about this time he also wrote a postcard to Madame l'Eplattenier containing the following lines:

> Here one does not touch lightly upon the subject of women. But just yesterday…a young Turkish girl, so exquisite I'd say (though it makes me bite my tongue), one á la Loti, spoke to me. Then all the walls caved in, and here I am sending greetings to all women–friendly, adoring, loving, ecstatic, and who knows![103]

Thus, in addressing the subject of the women of Stamboul, Jeanneret gathers together all the Lotian clichés. For Loti, Stamboul and Oriental women were in a sense identical. They represented the Turkish mystique and could be used to gain insight and entry into the Orient. Jeanneret's Oriental women, like Loti's, are innocent primitives, craving male domination and more or less willing for sexual encounters–or so he hints. Their unlimited sensuousness is heightened by their willing, even eager submission to what Jeanneret now calls a despotic, perhaps wise, custom. Disillusioned to some extent with Constantinople itself, he realizes that he can finally approach the impenetrable Orient via the beauty of its veiled women.[104] He recounts a chance meeting with one of these young gazelles:

> It would be superfluous for me to tell you that she was young and exquisite and that during our entire conversation I admired her through her veil. But those to whom I wrote some banal cards that evening knew that I had talked to a divine little thing and that, for a long time to come, I would remain stupefied.[105]

There are other experiences to recount in a subsequent chapter, such as the Turkish bazaar with its detestable souvenirs and its ingenious fake *anticas*, which opens like Ali Baba's cave in the "Open Sesame" story:

FIGURE 3.11: The houses of Constantinople, which he carefully photographed in 1911, left a lasting impression on Charles-Édouard Jeanneret.

> One discovers and dislodges from beneath the piles of coarse earth the most sumptuous nuggets of the East, from the Islam of Europe to as far as the jungles, brought here piece by piece across the sands, mountains, and brush by the solemn caravans.[106]

[FIGURE 3.11]

A chapter on "Two Fantasies, One Reality" follows, describing walks at twilight, when "The night becomes black and clear. Gold and black, supreme elegance, supreme power!"[107] There are fogs that crush down, hiding everything from sight, slowly giving rise to colors; they change as quickly as his emotions. On the water, masts, lines, and sails of the boats slip by and disappear in the fog, while high on the hills mosques rise up and are lost in the clouds. He no longer detests this gold, these colors, and now describes almost hallucinatory visions:

> I turned around. In a chalky blue and frothy coral whirl was the Genoese Tower–a fantastic sight. It leans and rests upon a shoulder of tall houses spiked with chimney stacks. It is cylindrical, without a single window, and is capped by a projecting crown, closed, obtuse, and hard like a piece of machinery. The whole gigantic and somber apparatus looked like a tragic battleship. I thought I heard the wail of a siren, and I had a presentiment of something ominous, for I was a little beside myself.... A large pink cloud swept the apparition away. It returned and once more

> disappeared. Finally, the red disk of the sun asserted itself. It hurled terrible darts, it pierced the clouds, it triumphed. The mosques blanched, and Stamboul appeared, while the Genoese Tower straddled Pera, unyielding, red at the tip of its shoulder in shadow. When the last vaporous layers were lifted, I thought I had been dreaming.[108]

Finally, it is time to depart, and Jeanneret's lament is contained in a lengthy chapter, "A Jumble of Recollections and Regrets." He has come to love this city of the East, enveloped, despite its disappointments, in clouds (sometimes literal) of mystery and enchantment. After a twenty-four-hour quarantine at the mouth of the Black Sea, his ship passes Constantinople one last time. Melancholy strikes him:

> The light was behind Stamboul, giving it a monolithic appearance.... The mist of light upon the sea was dissolving into this great back lighting that extended as far as Mihriak outlined against a sky annihilated with brightness. I don't believe I shall ever again see such *Unity!*[109]

There is a melancholic flashback to the strange spectacle of a building fire witnessed by Jeanneret on the twenty-fourth of July–cafés were crowded, idlers stood gawking, street vendors sold lemonade and ice-cream–another scenographic Lotian image appears. For fires puncture the harmony of Loti's stories, interrupting the dream and eradicating the past. In *Aziyadé,* for example, he used the motif of fire as catharsis: it woke him from his Turkish idyll, allowing him to regain his lost equilibrium and leave Stamboul before being entrapped.[110] So too, the fire in Jeanneret's *Voyage* is a tableau of Oriental golds and blacks devouring his dream *of A Thousand and One Nights*, and is the book's finest spectacle. It is the fire, leaving nine thousand houses in ashes, that finally offers him the grandeur and magic of the Orient in all its golden splendor, which he now fully accepts. But it is also diabolical, destroying what Jeanneret has allowed to penetrate into his inner self, for he is about to depart from Stamboul.

> It seems like an intermission at a theater where a great, extraordinary spectacle is performed, but whose audience is blasé because they know it all and nothing more can interest them. For Stamboul has been burning like this for centuries.[111]

> Against [the fire-lit sky], the minarets and domes of Bayazit are outlined in a splendid unity, incomparably majestic, carved out of solid gold. At times, one can see in the glazing panorama and beneath the immense cloud of golden smoke, other minarets as white as overheated iron. Whirlwinds of glowing embers, dancing diabolically, fly off to carry the devastation hundreds of meters away.[112]

> [Klipstein and I] discuss the fantasy created by domes and minarets. We find at last the part of Constantinople of grandeur and magic we had dreamed of. A breath of imperial Byzantine madness is mixed up with a fatalistic and cynical sensuality. If one goes from one viewpoint to another, it's to get a better view of the contrast between the black disc of a dome outlined against a brocade of fire and the solemnity of an obelisk. We circle before the joyous shower of sparks, searching for a favorable viewpoint as if in front of a painting.... It is an exaltation of joy. What utter joy![113]

Yet as the fire subsides, ecstasy gives way to grief:

> There we stand before this spectacle that is beyond understanding and leaves us stupid, overcome by a great melancholy. Looking anguished at the thrashings of this enraged dragon, we repeat over and over: It's horrible, it's horrible![114]

And then there are only recollections and regrets.

> It's over, and yet I haven't said a thing! Not even a word about Turkish life–a word! It would take a book. Our meager seven weeks did not suffice to give us a glance of it.[115]

He returns to the reasons why he undertook this journey: to study folk art and to find the sources of classical art, which are paradoxically intermixed. He confirms this intermixing through a series of recollections. He remembers the corpse in a Greek Orthodox funeral procession in Pera. It shocked and repulsed him, but our aim is to live well and harmoniously, he says, not to be concerned with looking good at one's departure. He continues, after this apparent irrelevance, to discuss the question of what sources and strengths folk ("peasant") art draws upon:

> Peasant art proceeds from the art of the city. It belongs to it as one of its by-products. It is a cross-breed, but still beautiful, with interesting characteristics and, in any case, showing powerful strength. Primitive art [on the other hand] is a precursor. Fortunately the peasant remains a real primitive man when he creates. Still he has his bad taste, his pride, and his laziness. That is why he steals from the city its style and its language, but he will reinterpret them unconsciously and with naiveté! It is an innate strength that bursts out in spite of and almost against itself. This is very strange but it brings about artworks full of awkwardness and barbarism which appeal to our sophisticated tastes. Look at the peasant houses on the Rumanian plain: they have a dazzling and astounding brilliance; the stucco is white, the base an intense blue; the corners are painted or shaped, representing pilasters; the pillars that border the windows and pediments are painted a strong blue, sometimes set off by a glorious yellow. These are classical architectural elements, but they are all used incorrectly because there is no base under the columns and no entablature above them. The capital (the flower, the ornament) is its aim, and an end in itself. Because, even if the vocabulary has been that of the city (because of a pathological inclination toward "bourgeoisism"), the soul, the aspirations, and the hand are those of a primitive man. It is painted with gusto on a spring day, to last a whole year and to provide the peasant with a festive setting and a gay and colorful shelter. He *wants to feel decent and like a king in his palace.* Thus the primitive man wraps himself in bright colors and creates beauty around him.[116]

> But the city should not return to the country; it would be as though one were to give to the symptoms the disease itself as a cure. The city must follow its own course and be reborn on its own.[117]

There follows a series of comparisons of the life that is dying in the East and the life that is exhausted in the West. As usual with Jeanneret, there is also a swing to the other side, to global optimism:

> Purification is a vital necessity, and as we avoid death by the simple desire to live, we shall return–yes, to the health that

> belongs to this epoch, a health appropriate to our contingencies, and then from there to beauty. Throughout the world, we are *recovering*; the scales are falling from our eyes. The infectious germ will be opposed by a youthful, vigorous, joyous germ born of the need "to conquer or to die."[118]

Yet personal ambivalence haunts his epistolary writing at this time. Is he a painter in words and colors, or an architect of simple forms and a reformer of contemporary taste? Before returning to La Chaux-de-Fonds, he sends two postcards to L'Eplattenier, one from Pisa and one from Rome. He is anxious about his return, and blurts out "What is it that you want from me...? I do not know at all what I am to do at La Chaux-de-Fonds, I am waiting for you to explain it to me!"[119] A sense of transition is on him:

> I am tolling the bells of my youth. In a month, ahead, it will have been finished. Another man, another life, difficult horizons, a route between walls. Believe that I am often sad because of it, and the joy of return is mixed with deep melancholy. I have in my soul, black and white; I jump from the darkness into the light, and that makes something tragic and bitter remain with me.[120] [FIGURE 3.12]

ENCOUNTERS WITH MOUNT ATHOS AND THE ACROPOLIS

Jeanneret did not publish any articles about Mount Athos or Athens in 1911. It is not until 1914, back in La Chaux-de-Fonds, that he writes the two chapters "Recollections of Mount Athos" and "The Parthenon."[121] By the time he does so, Turkey is the recognized ally of Germany and enemy of France, and World War I is about to begin. Interest in the Balkans and Greece is at a peak, and Jeanneret hopes this will generate new interest in his travel writings. In these two chapters he drops some of his Lotian style, moving from a language of colors to that of pure architectural forms.

He opens his recollections of Mount Athos by describing a series of misperceptions that need to be corrected: our intellectual pursuits are misguided by a hodgepodge of antiquated ideas, we are misfocused, we are petrified by having looked too long behind us. We need to be purified in order to take up the task of the present! Does he draw these messages from his memories of Mount Athos? We cannot be sure, for his writing once again begins to wander as if in a dream. It is clear,

FIGURE 3.12: **A series of sketches by Charles-Édouard Jeanneret from *Carnets de Voyage de Orient*, republished in the first volume of Le Corbusier's *Oeuvre Complète* (1964)**

however, that he is no longer primarily a painter, as it seemed in earlier chapters of *Voyage*, but an architect–and an architect he will remain. He has solved the enigma at the heart of his personal narrative, and has crossed over the liminal border into maturity. Approaching Mount Athos, he begins to describes the landscape in architectural terms: once again the unattainable horizon dominates his account:

> I think that the flatness of the horizon, particularly at noon when it imposes its uniformity on everything about it, provides for each one of us a measure of the most humanly possible perception of the absolute. In the radiant heat of the afternoon, suddenly there appears the pyramid of Athos![122]

As an architect, he now searches for primary elements and structured forms, for clear pure lines and volumes in space. He is searching for those few primitive forms that will generate an infinite number of architectural expressions.

> The obsession for symbols that lies deep inside me is like a yearning for a language limited to only a few words. My vocation may be the reason for this: the organization of stone and timber, of volumes, of solids and voids, has given me, perhaps, a too general understanding of the vertical and the horizontal, and of the sense of length, depth, and height as well.[123]

They took mules up the steep slopes, he recalls. The monastery rose before them. "It was the porch of an ancient fortress, together with smooth bare walls, on top of which perched cellular dwellings high up in the sky with their galleries open to the sea."[124] In spite of–or perhaps because of–the fact that women are forbidden to penetrate the sanctity of Mount Athos, Jeanneret's memories of the site merge the exotic with the erotic.

> The night was conducive to any emotional contemplation made languid by the warm, moist air, saturated with sea salt, honey, and fruit; it was also conducive, beneath the suspended, protective pergola, to the fulfillment of kisses, to wine-filled and amorous raptures.[125]

There are disturbing anachronisms in "this land with the most Dionysian of suns and the most elegiac of nights... dedicated only to the dejected, the poor, or the distressed"; while fifty dirty monks, perhaps with leprosy, beg for alms.[126] Having never earned a fig in their life, they arouse his indignation.[127] Yet the languorous Byzantine spirit, belonging to another age, still spread its aura over the site. Why was there not a more resolute architecture in this place of solitude, with its frugal meals? But once again he doubts his ability to record on paper "the impression that the patches of earth, the perpendicularity of the red rocks, the expanse of the sea have stirred in the depths of my soul, without opening to them the light of day!"[128] In this Delphic world, Jeanneret senses the uproar of a sea in delirium. Is it the wine, his intestinal attacks, his loneliness, or a foreboding of catastrophe?

> At the sharply pointed peak of the pyramid of Athos, we experienced all around us a slight estrangement, and if, to get our bearings, we looked down into crevices cushioned with light and formed by the buttresses raised out of the sea, the utterly unknown image of a profile of land would appear detached, as

> if in ether. For the sea, sparkling with a white glitter, evades the searching eye and hollows out this strange void, which we perceive in a kind of waking nightmare, when fixing for ourselves a point of reference, we venture to imagine our world as it revolves in its atmosphere, tracing its path in infinite space. Thus, from the summit of the pyramid of Athos, a shadow was cast upon the sea all around us, except in the isthmus at the west, as if a body had fallen into this luminous immensity.[129]

And then the recognition: "As for me, pushed to action by the demanding conviction of a builder who dreams of uniting steel with concrete in strong rhythms, I am happy to know that once upon a time a Zeus of bronze once stood upon this hill." Visions from epic times still affect him; he knows that Byzantium is as empty as an echoless chasm, yet it still moves him.[130] Why this strange attraction? Is it because the church of Athos provides a concise model?

> The powerful unity of its language is so sober that it confers on this impression [its clearly articulated plan and section] the purity of a diamond. Hard and solid, it is the crystallization of a Hellenic clarity, mysteriously combined with indefinable Asiatic evocations.[131]

Inevitable dualisms, he says, still haunt him. He has spent hours examining the crypts enshrined in morbid gold, when a shame suddenly overcomes him:

> Unless you are a builder, you, the visitor who passes beneath the vaults of temples, cannot conceive the anguish of standing before these imperious verdicts in stone. We live in an age so lacking in scrupulous craftsmen, and heaven mercifully spares us from encounters with our predecessors: they would look down upon us with dismayed astonishment; then they would hurl down their wrath upon us and put us to flight. The ever present memory of their labor fills me with a gnawing anxiety and makes me dread each regulation according to which today, [based] on our drawings, the works of architecture are built.[132]

In this state of agonized consciousness of modern inadequacy, Jeanneret moves on toward Athens.

His encounter with Athens begins with a combination of pleasure and frustration. He writes to Ritter that he is bathing nude in the classical waters of Salamis, at an hour when cobalt blue spreads across the folds of the mountains and the rising waves of the sea. But he is in quarantine, on an island, and the Acropolis is not even in sight: when they arrived, their clothes were taken to be fumigated, and they were told to stay in quarantine for four days–what an insult! "And the Parthenon is there, so close!"[133] This letter is full of fanciful and imaginary descriptions of Mount Olympus where Jupiter reigns, and of the agonizing pilgrimage to the Sacred Mountain of Athos. The latter was only a ghost of what it once must have been–not beautiful, merely interesting. But, he says,

> I am full of hope for the Acropolis. I see from this island those arid mountains made of brown stone, the blue sea, but above all an unknown extraordinary light that links without melting the difference in value, mountains to sky–and I know that the columns and the entablature and their ivory marble will be a soul in this landscape, a sacred meaning [the word of God]. I am foolishly happy.[134]

There are other marvels to report: he stares for hours at two Greek women that come to the beach. Nothing more beautiful will appear at Delphi in the caryatides of the treasury–Maillol, in copying their thick, fat arms and legs, merely transformed them into clay. Jeanneret has purchased his own archaic clay statue, composed of sausage-like forms and rings of clay, which he calls his Maillol. He has collected many treasures during this trip and professes to be financially ruined, but "I am certainly happy, and I often dream of my treasures which have left for home."[135]

Although he spent three weeks in Athens, he makes little mention of the city itself, claiming he spent every day on the Parthenon, drawing, painting, photographing, touching the stones, and contemplating their meaning. [FIGURE 3.13] He draws in his notebook the temples of the Acropolis seen through a curtain of upright columns, cubes on their platforms that reach out to draw the surrounding landscape into the view.[136] [FIGURE 3.14, p. 690]

The Acropolis he describes as a theatrical spectacle:

FIGURE 3.13: Charles-Édouard Jeanneret on the Acropolis, Athens, in 1911

> The Acropolis–this rock–rises alone in the heart of an enclosed frame. Slightly to the left beyond Piraeus, where vapors rise from the sea, one senses that the open sea is just beyond and that flotillas enter there. Hymettus and Pentelicus, two very high mountain ranges, like two wide adjoining screens, are located behind us, orienting our sight in the opposite direction, toward the estuary of stone and sand, the Piraeus.[137]

The monochrome of the place is overwhelming: the uniformly red landscape, the marble of the temples, as red as terra-cotta or the color of bronze.

> The entablature of a cruel rigidity crushes and terrorizes. The feeling of a superhuman fatality seizes you. The Parthenon, a terrible machine, grinds and dominates; seen from as far as a four-hour walk and one hour by boat, alone it is a sovereign cube facing the sea.... After weeks of being crushed by this brutal site, I wished for a storm to come and drown in its floods and swirls the biting bronze of the temple.... When the storm did come, I saw through the large drops of rain the hill becoming suddenly white and the temple sparkling like a diadem against the ink-black Hymettus and the Pentelicus ravaged by downpours![138]

In a flashback, he returns to the voyage to Athens from Mount Athos, reiterating how calming the sight of the Acropolis is from afar—nothing shocking, nothing dramatic, strangely ambiguous, unreal! The ship nears Athens:

> Very far away in the center of the harbor, at the bosom of some hills forming an arch, a strange rock stands out, flat at the top and secured on its right by a yellow cube. The Parthenon and the Acropolis! But we cannot believe it; we don't give it a thought. We are bewildered; the ship does not enter the harbor but continues on its course.[139]

After the four days of quarantine, he recalls, he was finally allowed to enter the city. Yet he could not yet approach the overwhelming, cyclopean rock with its fabulous cube, and refers to it abstractly:

> I made up a thousand excuses not to climb "up there" right away....I drank coffee all afternoon absorbed in reading the voluminous five-week-old mail picked up at the post office.[140]

The sheer artistic weight or centrality of the Acropolis remains a puzzle to him:

> To see the Acropolis is a dream one treasures without even dreaming to realize it. I don't really know why this hill harbors the essence of artistic thought....Why this architecture and no other? I can well accept that according to logic, everything here is resolved in accordance with an unsurpassable formula, but why is it the taste—or rather the heart that guides people and dictates their beliefs despite their tendency to ignore it at times—why is it still drawn to the Acropolis, to the foot of the temples?[141]
> [FIGURE 3.15, p. 691]

By 1914, the Parthenon and Acropolis have achieved their full measure of influence over the architect. Yet in a flashback from 1914 to 1911, as he recalls sitting at a sidewalk café in Athens, he can express the Parthenon's impact only through an imagery of death and loathing:

> Every hour it grows more deadly up there. The first shock was the strongest. Admiration, adoration, and then annihilation....

> I don't like going there any more. When I see it from afar it is like a corpse. The feeling of compassion is over. It is a prophetic art from which one cannot escape. As insentient as an immense and unalterable truth. But when I come upon a drawing of Stamboul in my sketch book, it warms my heart![142]

Jeanneret's "up there" of the Acropolis can be read as a trope for high art, all the inheritance of Greek civilization, and the suppression of folk art, which was lowly yet lovely. In 1914 he draws a map of his voyage on which he marks its highlights C (culture), F (folklore), or I (industry). Most of the Balkans and Constantinople are marked with F, Athens with a C. "Up there" is also where something obscure, frightening, colored in tones of shocking red, scorched his spirit. There had been months of escape into lyrical poetry, an uncontrollable flowing of words in the language of colors, and the organic flowering of nature's sinuous lines, but "up there," he was face to face with this simple cube on its platform, a cruel, crushing rationality, a hard exactness. It shocked him to his core. He wrote,

> Painstaking hours spent in the revealing light of the Acropolis. Perilous hours, provoking heartrending doubt in the strength of our strength, in the art of our art.[143]

Constantinople would represent for Le Corbusier a confession of love: the dense accumulation of life and dilapidated buildings, of people and their resignation to take life as it comes. This aesthetic of primitivism, which he projected onto the city, was juxtaposed against the clarity and purity that the Parthenon imposed. The struggle between Constantinople and Athens was finished only in 1914, at which time the Parthenon won out: from then on, the power of that monument becomes an obsession and a generating ideal for the perfection of his craft.[144] It spoke to him in truthful words; it demanded a moral commitment that he too, as an architect, must create works that were pure, truthful statements, never straying from a path of purity, luminosity, and harmony. It was a hard, crushing commitment, from which he must not deviate. His love of Constantinople, for folklore, for the simple peasant, for landscapes and nature would remain to punctuate his thoughts on this journey toward an architecture that spoke to modern times.

RETURN TO LA CHAUX-DE-FONDS

On a train to Pisa, on November 1, only a few days from home, Jeanneret writes a long letter to Ritter. It is a death-obsessed document. He opens, "The last day of a condemned man"[145] He recalls a funeral scene from four years before–grave diggers, golden cross, torches, women cupping candles in their hands. After remarking that he expects to find a spiritual and eloquent statement about architecture in Pisa, he continues with death:

> All is in ruins or collapsed in Italy. For me Italy is a cemetery where the dogmas that were my religion are rotting in the soil. Is it possible, such a mass murder? In four years, I have made a terrible effort. I am full of the Orient, of unity and of power. My gaze is horizontal and I do not see the insects at my feet. I feel myself brutal. Italy had made me be a blasphemer.[146]

He inserts a long passage that is prescient of the city plans he will design in the 1920s, which are discussed further in Chapter 4.[147] But, he continues, the presentment of death holds him in its clutches.

In this document Jeanneret seems caught between futures of constraint or freedom, of taking up his duty or following his destiny, of an insupportable reality or a surrealistic dream. In spite of his many references to death, he claims that he accepts his future. L'Eplattenier will receive him in a few days and, Jeanneret says, will find him to be a good worker, capable of applying himself to hard labor for some years to come. Yet he still needs to confess to Ritter, and allow unconscious feelings to rise to the surface. Referring to the group of comrades surrounding L'Eplattenier, he pronounces:

> We will make Art!
> A stupid idea! It is no longer necessary to make Art, but only to enter tangentially into the body of our time, to dissolve into it until one becomes invisible. When we all have disappeared, the stone will become a grand block. It will remain for us then, some Coliseums, some Baths, an Acropolis, some Mosques, and the mountains of Jura, will be a setting for these [works] as beautiful as the sea [has been for those other great works.] Some youths will pass by a long time afterwards, their passions aroused.[148]

At the end of this letter he returns to his depression, claiming that he would be lying if he put some pink into his dark life, as if he were still writing about the fogs of Stamboul. He is in mourning, unconsciously resigned, without thought because it would be too much for him.

And so, in a deep depression, Jeanneret returned to La Chaux-de-Fonds. The next few years were to be extremely difficult. He felt smothered and confined in the small town, and sought an escape route to Paris. His only moments of solace appear to have arisen from his continued need to write down his experiences, thoughts, and imaginations and send them to Ritter for comment–and from occasionally rereading his own travel writings from the East.

CHAPTER 4
THE MANY PATHS TO PARIS (1910–17)

To create as in commerce, a demand: a city has the architect it merits.

—ATTRIBUTED TO WILLIAM RITTER

I. THE CONSTRUCTION OF CITIES

The word *urbanisme* (urbanism) appears in the French language for the first time around 1910, the same year that Jeanneret began his one-year study tour to Germany to inquire about this new field.[1] L'Eplattenier proposed that he and Jeanneret coauthor a book that summarizes the principles of urbanism and critically analyze the planning of La Chaux-de-Fonds. This small, Swiss industrial town had made administrative but not architectural innovations toward progress and economic risk-taking. In the eyes of L'Eplattenier and Jeanneret, it showed neither sense nor taste in its architecture or layout. It could learn, they believed, from Germany, where art and industry were forging a new, joint path through urbanism.

The primary industry of La Chaux-de-Fonds had long been clock-making. By 1900 it had 60 percent of the world's timepiece business, but mounting pressure from mechanization and competition by other countries threatened its dominance in the early twentieth century.[2] To meet these challenges, its businesses were centralizing and mechanizing. Jeanneret's own father, Édouard Jeanneret-Perret, was a timepiece manufacturer struggling to uphold the tradition of handcrafted parts. However, the rising relative cost of handcrafted specialized parts was making them too expensive for cost-minded customers, and Jeanneret-Perret was forced to close his workshop in 1918.[3] Since the struggle between craftsmanship and mechanization had been debated in La Chaux-de-Fonds since the onset of the industrial revolution, we can view Jeanneret's personal goal in Germany as finding a new equilibrium between artist and machine, art and industry.

This preoccupation deepened as he surveyed the results of the German Werkbund in 1910–11 (see Chapter 2) and struggled to conceive of useful roles for architects and artists in modern times.

Precision was another of Jeanneret's lifelong interests. Here the pocket-watch (invented in the 1500s) played a role, for its large-scale manufacture encouraged the creation of strict job schedules and precisely aligned instruments. The watch industry was thus a major force behind the development of the factory system in the late eighteenth century.[4] Jeanneret, steeped in this tradition, made more remarks after his first visit to Peter Behrens's AEG Turbine factory in 1910 about assembly-line production and the use of an innovative time clock to manage the entrances and exits of workers than he did on the building's architecture.

L'Eplattenier and Jeanneret surmised that it was time to apply the same spirit of innovative reform to the architectural order of the city. L'Eplattenier intended to present a paper on "L'Ésthetique des villes" ("Aesthetics of Cities") at the general assembly of the Union des Villes Suisses at La Chaux-de-Fonds, September 24–25, 1910, and advised Jeanneret to go to Germany to distill the aesthetic principles on which various examples of the new "urbanism" were based; with this information in hand, they would coauthor a booklet expounding the new ideas.

In 1902 L'Eplattenier had already read Camillo Sitte's 1889 book *Der Städtebau nach seinen künstlerischen Grundsätzens* (*City Planning According to Artistic Principles*) in Camille Martin's French translation, *L'Art de bâtir les villes* (*The Art of Building Cities*).[5] He became an ardent follower of Sitte based on this distorted and embellished translation. Martin transformed Sitte's rambling message into an ordered method, so L'Eplattenier and Jeanneret expected that the principles of urbanism could be codified into a set of rules for how to build cities artistically–though this was never Sitte's intent. Moreover, Martin often advocated principles opposed to those of Sitte, even fabricating a chapter on the picturesque superiority of curved and crooked streets over straight. Consequently, L'Eplattenier and Jeanneret's booklet would place emphasis on streets and their picturesque irregularities. Martin also took the liberty of emphasizing only medieval architecture, being preoccupied with the restoration of medieval structures at the time he translated the book; consequently he blurred Sitte's major lesson that cities grow organically over many centuries, and hence include a medley of different architectural forms up to and including those of the present. And wherever he could, Martin substituted French and Belgian examples for Sitte's German and Austrian ones.[6] His reworking of Sitte's intent left its mark on Jeanneret and L'Eplattenier's future study, a work that became increasingly problematic until it was abandoned in 1917.

In an article written in early 1910, "Renouveau d'art" ("Renewal of Art"), L'Eplattenier manifested the influence of Martin's interpretation by pointing out that La Chaux-de-Fonds's monotonous, rectilinear street pattern did not conform to the terrain. In addition, the overlapping effects of numerous now-defunct city plans meant that houses had been designed in idiosyncratic architectural forms, while contemporary developers of massive new housing blocks repeated to infinity banal rectilinear forms.[7] L'Eplattenier was convinced that cities must be planned with an eye to beauty and that regulatory laws should control both land development and the preservation of historic structures. Journalists and educators should be taught to campaign actively for the beautification of cities, and young artists and artisans should be trained to become future leaders in this municipal crusade. These leaders must also be familiar with the latest scientific advancements in order to find in them a style for the future.[8]

Jeanneret consented to return to Germany on a quest for the principles of urbanism, and (once again) embarked with little advance preparation. This time he was confounded by not having a sound understanding of what actually constituted "urbanism." He left for Munich in mid-April 1910, although why that city was selected remains obscure. After two months he received a letter from L'Eplattenier, written on behalf of the Commission de l'École d'Art, which spelled out a broad mandate for additional study: "You must write a report on everything concerning professional teaching, the organization of the crafts, and the creation, manufacture and sale of artistic products; you can add notes on everything germane to art in the city and in architecture—in short, on everything that might foster the development of art and beauty here at home."[9] Jeanneret was thus simultaneously engaged in two intertwined writing projects, neither with a fixed deadline: an École d'Art–commissioned report on the applied arts in German schools and a coauthored booklet based on his survey of "urbanism." Material for both would be gleaned from visits to libraries, exhibitions, conferences, and urban sites undertaken intermittently between his arrival and May 1911, when he left for the Orient (see Chapter 3). In his letters he often referred to the two studies as one project, the *Étude.*

Only over time, in fact, would these two reports become perfectly distinct projects.

Eventually, in 1912, hoping to popularize reforms in the decorative arts throughout Switzerland, l'École d'Art would publish Jeanneret's *Étude sur le mouvement d'art décoratif en Allemagne.* But his study on "urbanism" floundered and took different directions, never achieving publication.

Jeanneret went to Germany in mid-April; on June 2, 1910, he claimed in a postcard to L'Eplattenier that he had almost completed the brochure *Étude sur l'urbanisation.*[10] Now all that remained was for L'Eplattenier to revise the full draft. At about this time he received his commission from l'École d'Art. These projects were clearly a burden: he had written to L'Eplattenier, probably in May, that although these were the years of enthusiastic work, sometimes it was sheer drudgery to acquire all the baggage necessary for the future. Everywhere, he said, he saw exciting manifestations of modern art that he had never dreamt were possible, but the writing of the brochure was punishment. Perhaps it would be ready in two weeks–maybe publication would be possible by September or October–but he remains evasive as to the precise date.[11]

Meanwhile, in the previous month or so, Jeanneret had met (almost certainly for the first time) his second mentor, twenty years his senior, the art critic, painter, novelist, and musician William Ritter, who would transform his life.[12] Ritter would become Jeanneret's intimate confidant, advising him on writing and encouraging his artistic development. He was worldlier than L'Eplattenier, having traveled widely, and was conversant on a wide range of contemporary issues. He would remain the only mentor whom Jeanneret never broke with or criticized extensively. Their new friendship was no doubt one reason why Jeanneret began to pull away from L'Eplattenier and had difficulty completing their coauthored work.

As discussed in Chapter Two, Jeanneret's concepts of "urbanism" and the decorative arts were completely intertwined, both in early developmental chronology and materials studied. Yet his report *Étude sur le mouvement d'art décoratif* would be published in 1912, while he set aside the *Étude sur l'urbanisation* and did not pick it up again until June 1915. At that time he wrote to his friend Max Du Bois that since the war had destroyed so many towns, houses, and farms in northeastern France and Belgium–which would require rebuilding–it was time to publish the work.[13] By then, his interest in city construction had

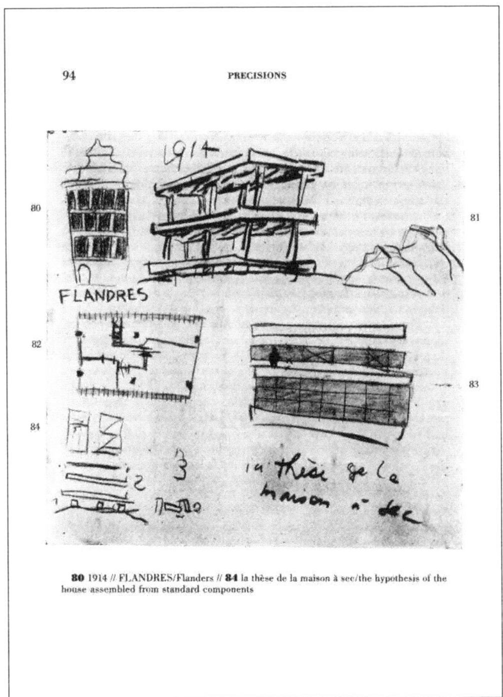
94 PRECISIONS

80 1914 // FLANDRES/Flanders // **84** la thèse de la maison à sec/the hypothesis of the house assembled from standard components

FIGURE 4.1: **With the aid of engineer Max Du Bois, Charles-Édouard Jeanneret planned to patent their scheme for the Dom-Ino skeletal house frame in 1915, while in La Chaux-de-Fonds.**

begun to mesh with the development and promotion of his "Dom-ino" scheme, also conceived for reconstruction efforts, leading him eventually to conclude that the solutions for housing and urbanism were one and the same. Jeanneret called his system for rapid production of low-cost housing in reinforced concrete Dom-ino because the plan for the floor slabs and pillars resembled a number four or six domino piece. Supposedly, local unskilled workers could fill in the skeletal frame by erecting walls from rubble, and could install doors and windows of their own design. [FIGURE 4.1]

In 1915, though he was eager to publish the material he had already written on city construction, he scribbled on one of its pages that his theory of urbanism was probably useless. The work needed to be strengthened and given a new orientation. So, from July 28 to September 16 he studied in the Bibliothèque Nationale in Paris. That summer he began yet another work, an illustrated album entitled *France ou Allemagne* (*France or Germany*), a fresh exposition of ideas he had already espoused. He finally produced a manuscript for *Étude sur l'urbanisation* in 1915 or 1916, then titled *La Construction des Villes*.[14]

Within a year, even that manuscript appeared to him to be completely passé; it would eventually be rewritten and seriously revised as a series of essays for *L'Esprit Nouveau* in 1924 and collected in book form in 1925 as *Urbanisme* (published in English as *The City of To-morrow*).

Jeanneret, being more of a humanist than Sitte, did not want to limit his concept of urbanism to aesthetic problems of central cities. He was also interested in rehabilitating workers' housing along aesthetic lines.[15] As his *Étude sur le mouvement d'art décoratif* reveals, he was fascinated by the garden city of Hellerau, calling it a collectivist manifestation because it solved the great social issue of housing. There is also an earlier encounter with collectivized housing, expressed in a letter to his parents from Florence in 1907.[16] After visiting the Carthusian monastery d'Ema, he wrote: "I went yesterday, to the Chartreuse [the Carthusian monastery], I found the solution for a unique type of workers' housing.... Oh those monks, what contentment!"[17]

He spends the afternoon at the Chartreuse de Galluzzo, where H. Allen Brooks, among many others, claims he underwent a profound architectural illumination. The design of this monastery formed the basis for his immeuble-villas of 1922, the Pavillon de l'Esprit Nouveau of 1925, and numerous proposals for Unités d'Habitations (his housing blocks). Most architectural historians believe that it was a complete revelation to Jeanneret that individuality and community life could not only coexist but could even strengthen each other. In the *Modulor,* writing of himself in the third person, Le Corbusier speaks of this formative experience, claiming that "His studies were complex and far reaching: basic measures of urbanism ('Ville Contemporaine de trois millions d'habitants,' 1922), determinations of the cellular unit (capacity of dwellings), the mesh of communications (network of roads and transport lines): in reality, a process of fundamental architectural organization that he had already experienced once, fifteen years earlier, at the Charterhouse of Ema in Tuscany (individual freedom and collective organization)."[18]

Brooks also argues that the origin of Jeanneret's architectural promenade can be found in the bridgelike walkway that linked together each monk's modest house of several rooms with its fireplace, cellar, attic, terrace, and small private garden. Living in isolation, with their meals brought to them each day, the monks were immersed in pleasant surroundings that enhanced contemplation and reflection. On Sundays and Feast days they broke their isolation, speaking to each other during services, meals, and long strolls in the countryside. This became Le

Corbusier's lifelong ideal of the good life—contemplative isolation with communitarian sharing. He returned to the Chartreuse monastery only once, on his return from the East in October 1911.

While in Munich studying the problems of "urbanism," Jeanneret published his first article, "Art et Utilité Publique" ("Art and Public Utility"), in *L'Abeille* (La Chaux-de-Fonds, 15 May 1910). It was a summary of his early thoughts on urbanism.[19] He begins by proclaiming that the great issue of the day is the art of building cities—as L'Eplattenier would have agreed—but goes further, declaring that "art" must also become social, not divorced from everyday life. Only then, he says, will it be lively and moving, not static or dead. He praises the old city of Stuttgart for having shown that art and everyday life could work together. Everything in that small city obeyed the order of an ensemble, so that seventy-two individual houses appeared to be the work of a single architect. This idea was achieved by the union of art and utility, working collaboratively toward an ideal. Stuttgart had listened to the rules prescribed by Camillo Sitte (and, unbeknownst to Jeanneret, by Sitte's translator, Martin): its streets were curved, its squares enclosed, its facades oriented toward the sun, its sidewalks wide and arcaded. One man conceived the plan and directed it, but the credit must go to the Society for the Well-Being of the Working Classes (a philanthropic association) for having chosen this man: for he selected in turn all the other collaborators and forged their individual endeavors into a unity. In closing, Jeanneret advises those who remain doubters to stop between trains when passing through Stuttgart and allow their eyes to see "the material realization of a poet's dream."[20]

As described in Chapter Two, in Germany Jeanneret assiduously observed developments in the decorative arts, architecture, and urbanism, visiting many expositions and museums and establishing personal contacts. Many lines of influence marked his "evolution" (as he himself described his changes during this period): He followed the Werkbund's attempts to fuse art, commerce, and industry; learned the value of the ensemble, whether of buildings or furniture; and came to understand that individualistic aesthetic expressions could be coordinated with social needs. While attending the annual Deutscher Werkbund and the Allgemeine Städtbau Ausstellung in Berlin in June 1910, he heard Theodor Fischer speak about the artistic utilization of new materials, noting, for example, that reinforced concrete, while it might be practical, economical, fireproof, and hygienic, only became interesting when architects considered it as a form of art. Karl Ernst Osthaus spoke on

"Material and Style," initiating Jeanneret to theoretical discussions on the relationship between utilitarian forms and artistic expressions, as well as the need for architects to collaborate with engineers. Osthaus believed that architects are obliged to obtain in-depth knowledge of materials and building techniques in order to develop a modern style in which the logic of forms correlates with specific functions. It was after viewing images of garden cities at the Grosse Berlin Ausstellung that Jeanneret exclaimed he would henceforth dedicate himself to the problem of constructing cities.[21]

During the spring of 1910, he continues to reformulate the outline of his booklet on cities. He writes to Ritter from Berlin on June 21 that he has just gone to the expositions mentioned above, understands that garden cities were by now a general movement in England, Germany, Austria, Sweden, Holland and Belgium, and believes they are worthy of further study. Vienna may have been developing in concentric circles (no doubt a reference to the 1893 extension plans of Otto Wagner, of which L'Eplattenier approved and Jeanneret did not), but Berlin has adopted a radiating street pattern, allowing its surrounding forests to penetrate almost to the core of the city. He adds that most German cities had begun to reform their cemeteries with respect to both location and design.[22]

Spending the summer in La Chaux-de-Fonds studying the construction of cities, Jeanneret explains to Ritter before returning to Germany in September that although he wants to finish this work, he has trouble expressing himself in French. He complains: "I wait, but nothing happens on the page." In contrast to this blockage, his "black misery," he has read two books by Ritter and praises his writing as poetic and powerful, especially in *L'Entêtement Slovaque.* On a more personal note, he says that he is overwhelmed by the way Ritter receives him, allowing him, a mere student of life, to draw close to him. He calls La Chaux-de-Fonds a "leprous spot" (*tache lepreuse*), a term Ritter had used for the thick incoherence of that small city. Yet he finds there is a breeze of artistic idealism coming from the region's old eighteenth-century farms, which gives him hope.[23]

In spite of complaints and excuses, he appears to have achieved an outline for *La Construction des Villes* during the summer of 1910 and to have revised it during the autumn. He divided the work into two parts, a thesis and a critical analysis of La Chaux-de-Fonds.[24] The thesis contained three chapters. One was on the general principles of "urbanism"; a second on the building blocks of cities, such as lots, streets,

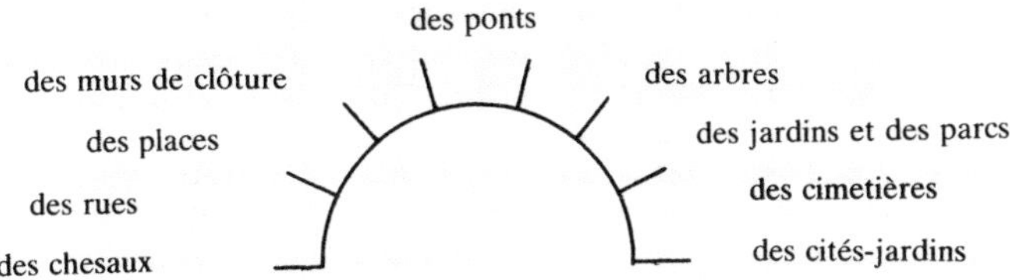

FIGURE 4.2: At the center of this page from *La Construction des Villes* (1910) is a diagram by Charles-Édouard Jeanneret of the arrangement of subjects to be covered in an unpublished manuscript.

places, and enclosing walls; and a third on implementation. During this period he was studying up on new subjects suggested by L'Eplattenier, including bridges, trees, gardens and parks, cemeteries, and garden cities. While he claimed that the study of bridges was giving him trouble, this part of the work seems to have a logical structure in which bridges hold a central place. As visualized in his diagram, this construction places types of city spaces on one side of an arch and moves over the arch via bridges to the embellishments of nature on the other side. His subjects are grouped in successive pairs–lots + streets, streets + places, places + enclosing walls–then juxtaposed on the opposite side of the arch to pairs of trees + gardens/parks, gardens/parks + cemeteries, cemeteries + garden cities. While this construction gives some indication of Jeanneret's penchant for logical processes of thought, besides exploiting his love of symmetry and dualistic pairs, it would have been difficult to sustain within the linear treatment of a book, and may also have added to his delay in producing a manuscript. [FIGURE 4.2]

Back in Munich by mid-September, he works alone on *La Construction des Villes,* trying to answer questions that L'Eplattenier had raised. He also waits to hear from Behrens, and finally decides impetuously to go to Berlin to find out for himself if he will be employed or not. He writes to Ritter from Berlin on October 14 that each hour of every day tests his patience; the situation is unbearable, since Behrens gives him no sign of life![25] Finally he writes at the end of October, seven months after arriving in Germany, that he will enter Behrens's office on the first of November. His life is about to take a new turn–of course he will have to put aside his writing projects–but he is elated to join the band of thirty young men assembled around the architect in Neu-Babelsberg, twenty-five minutes from Berlin by express train.[26]

After two months of working with the great architect, however, Jeanneret expresses something other than elation in another letter to Ritter.[27] First, the work leaves him indifferent. Second, he judges men harshly who love glory. Third, Behrens has become a victim of his own success; he wants a lot of money, so he accepts too many projects and inevitably loses control over the work. Jeanneret loves Behrens as a man, but in order to preserve his admiration, he must consider that such a tyrant is sick. An architect should be above all a thinker. Because architecture is made out of abstract relations and subtle rhythms, it is disastrous if an architect exercises an intrusive hand (*main habile*). Anyway, Jeanneret explains, since no one style appears to reign in this culture, he will ignore the taskmasters of the profession and continue his bizarre self-education "outside of the law." He would have preferred to work with Tessenow, designing the new institute and theater for Jaques Dalcroze in the garden city of Hellerau near Dresden, where his brother Albert was now studying eurhythmics, but apparently he was not offered either the job or enough money to allow him to quit Behrens's office.

He blames Ritter for telling him that it was stupid (*crétinisant*) to learn German, for Jeanneret has found himself in the sad position of forgetting his French yet ignorant of all other languages. He is sorry to be such a complainer, but confesses that he has never experienced such a lamentable period. It was only good fortune that has guided him toward the stewardship of Ritter and saved him from a disastrous fate.[28]

Brooks believes that it is because Behrens initially ignored all of Jeanneret's attempts to meet for the first seven months of his trip to Germany that Jeanneret "rarely said a kind word about either Behrens or Berlin and gradually his dislike embraced most things German–irrespective of how much he was favorably influenced by them."[29] Although he worked in Behrens's office only five months, his "debt was so great, indeed so profound, that Le Corbusier thought it best that it should be left unknown."[30] In addition, Brooks notes, during the brief time Jeanneret worked for Behrens he underwent a painful conversion to classicism, perhaps a major reason for his depression. Jeanneret adopted a Spartan type of classicism: pure geometric shapes under clear light. At the same time he accepts that "white"–i.e., the unadorned material surface–is the only proper color for buildings, he also realizes that standardization and industrialization are the key to the future of architecture.[31] While I have debated some of Brooks claims about

Jeanneret's sudden conversion in earlier chapters, it is clear that he was developing in a different direction from his master. All these lessons learned in Germany stand in direct contrast to the teachings of Sitte, and to the ideas that L'Eplattenier espoused, and hence were the cause of a great deal of consternation.

II. LETTERS OF CONFESSION

Jeanneret's voyage to the East in 1911 required him to put aside both of his writing projects until his return. By then his struggles with L'Eplattenierand La Chaux-de-Fonds in general had begun to cause trouble, no doubt delaying further the coauthored *La Construction des Villes*. Jeanneret confided to Ritter in a letter written in Greece on September 10, 1911, that it was only to him that he still wrote, exaggerating that even L'Eplattenier is neglected.[32] There is so much to write about, and at the close of each day he is painfully aware that the days and the trip are too short. "And you are the only one to whom I would love to recount so many things because you understand me and excuse my sillinesses [*niaiseries*]."[33] He knows that his decision to travel to Asia was far from foolish, for he has, he says, placed his foot on profound lands and would go even further, to Jerusalem or Cairo. But he has fallen sick, so decides to forego that adventure until such time as he could travel with "A true friend. Because during this trip I at times experienced emptiness caused by the absence of someone who understood me."[34]

Jeanneret did correspond with L'Eplattenier whenever he needed money, letters of introduction, or news from home. L'Eplattenier for his part appears to have been incredibly patient with these many requests, and dutifully answered as soon as he could. No matter what the sense of estrangement may have been, Jeanneret nevertheless remarked at the end of his letter to Ritter, mentioned above, that he was happy to return to work with L'Eplattenier, who was his great teacher and friend. Perhaps as a way of excusing this duplicity, he likens himself to a lectern, with its feet seeking support here and there. He desires fixed points, stability and serenity, in order to achieve what he believes is his destiny. He apologizes for "having stranded himself on a sentimental beach. It is a rest, which is sometimes not bad."[35]

The letters that Jeanneret writes to Ritter during the five years following his trip to the East, when he is confined to La Chaux-de-Fonds (1911–17), reflect his desperate search for a path to Paris, for it is from this city alone that a fresh European culture is radiating.

These are letters of confession about his innermost feelings, including deep depression and a yearning for greatness, accepting that as his destiny. Writing seems to assuage his pain. These letters are also places of experimentation in descriptive and narrative technique. Ritter is after all *un homme de lettres*, and Jeanneret desires to play with the magical substance of language until his own sentences and words contain the same richness of spirit as Ritter's. Can his thoughts and emotions be put on paper effectively? Can he find figurative language to describe his feelings about architecture and urban places, the moral and intellectual obligations of an architect in modern times? What are the precise elements and the correct syntax of the "language of architecture"? Already he has developed some effective expressions in letters to L'Eplattenier, phrases and analogies (e.g., "volumes under clear light") that will form a permanent part of his writing stock. He has developed the metaphorical use of trees and defined architecture as an intellectual process. In his 1911–17 letters to Ritter he will fill out his grammar of architecture with terms such as *unité*, destiny, geometry, equilibrium, simplicity, utility, hygiene, and modernism. As he gathers self-confidence, even arrogance, his style becomes more staccato and he uses more imperatives and declarative pronouncements. Over time, as he forges his writing into a didactic tool (*machine à ecrire*), his drive to confide in Ritter wanes.

His next letter (1 November 1911) to Ritter after that from Greece is somber and funereal: "Regarding death, I am full of it inside me."[36] His Eastern voyage draws to an end, and he approaches La Chaux-de-Fonds. He inserts a discussion about architecture and urbanism that reveals in its dreamlike quality thoughts that will become immortalized in his urban plans of the 1920s, but that are quite at variance with ideas he will express in *Étude sur le mouvement d'art décoratif en Allemagne* and in his notes for *La Construction des Villes*. He knows that over the last four years he has made a "terrible effort. I have absorbed knowledge in the East, about unity and power."[37] All the ornamental concerns that used to delight him now seem to frighten him; he rhapsodizes instead over pure forms.

> I stutter over elementary geometry with the eagerness of one day having knowledge and being able to construct. In their feverish course [on a color wheel] red, blue, and yellow have become white. I am crazy over the color white, of the cube, the sphere, the cylinder, the pyramid of the disc all a single [color] and great

> empty void. Prisms rise up, balanced, with rhythm, they begin to advance...They have only some white sky above them, they rest on a base of polished marble, a monolith that no color stipples.[38]

He describes rooms of black and intense red, a golden Buddha, great walls unified in white, and an imagined city of bold, simple forms:

> Down straight roads with windows like a checkerboard on the facades. No ornament. A single color, a single material for the entire city. Some autos roll by, some airplanes overhead without anyone paying them attention. There will be streets on the roofs, in the midst of flowers and trees. One will mount them on great staircases and one will pass over bridges. Then one will descend. To descend well made stairs with the air of an emperor filling one's heart.
>
> Here and there will be a temple, a cylinder, a half-sphere, a cube, a polyhedron. And empty spaces in which to breathe.[39]

Suddenly he shifts to contrasting subjects: sex, debauchery, love, marriage, the obligation to have a wife and family, and the meaning of life. He declares himself to be already dead–that is, immured in La Chaux-de-Fonds–and is resigned to return to work with his comrades, with high hopes that they will accomplish remarkable things.

Perhaps this letter is merely an experiment in fictional narration. It has a dreamlike organization, combining strenuous detachment and emptying with an exultant vision of future cities. Even so, he is revealing mental images that will become recurrent themes. It appears that he has been studying geometry seriously (he makes references to *n*-dimensional space); moreover, this city of his dreams cannot be seen all at once, for only with movement do its volumes rise up, recede, and return:

> At midday the light reduces the cubes to a surface; in the evening the arc of the sky rises up from the forms. In the morning they are materialized with shadow and light, clear as a working drawing. One perceives their bottom, top, and sides. Night is more than ever white and black.[40]

When the sun is at the meridian a cube is reduced to a surface, following Henri Poincaré's coupure of a volume cut by a plane; at night the surface is black and white, like a checkerboard. This space, which lies in Jeanneret's imagination, can achieve the analytic precision of a working drawing or simultaneously be filled with arbitrary constructions, hypercubes whose top, sides, and bottom are seen all at once.

Most importantly, this urban vision is categorically opposed to the bucolic milieu of the garden cities and the psychological comfort of the enclosed square that Sitte advocated. And while it may only be a daydream, it makes the outline for the *La Construction des Villes* even more troublesome. Jeanneret had been exposed to new ideas in Munich, Berlin, and the East and had undergone a self-confessed "happy evolution"; now he wants to create something great, something classical, something beyond the constraints of regionalism and decorative ornamentation. But this places him in constant struggle with the opinions on architecture, urbanism, and the decorative arts that L'Eplattenier, his comrades, and even his earlier self espoused. His funereal state of mind forewarns that he will experience confinement within both l'École d'Art and La Chaux-de-Fonds.

Arriving home, he writes to Ritter that things are very black and horizons are pushed up against one's nose. He needs to love the work he does, and thinks fondly of his time in Germany, shedding some tears over Munich, even Behrens. At least in Germany there is architecture that counts! An editor, a family friend, has agreed to publish a pamphlet of some of Jeanneret's articles from Constantinople. He will send Ritter the manuscript, and asks whether he should accept this proposal.[41]

His next letter to Ritter is also mixed: he has found a room in a grange, which he shares with two friends. Within these immense white walls he can forget the horrible town and its sad people. But, he says, "I feel myself a stranger here, and I cannot put it in my head that it will be forever."[42] He writes again a few days later, apologizing for his bad mood, and continues to describe his new retreat: a former convent with an immense kitchen as black as a grotto. From its window he sees horizons up close, repeating "horizons up against the nose!" The fog is dense and the rain icy cold.[43] He begins to complain about L'Eplattenier. He is a man of remarkable energy and astonishing intelligence, but Jeanneret accuses him of being insensitive to the works of modern times, the music, literature, and painting, all radiating from

Paris. In spite of his immense talent L'Eplattenier remains a simple activist, ready for conquest–he loves Roman history, Napoleon I, and Carnegie–but ignorant of more refined things.

Yet Jeanneret has work to do. He finds that he is to be the designer of one villa, and perhaps another. Rather enigmatically, he inserts "And my narrations?" (i.e., the pieces comprising *Voyage to the East*) before confessing that to speak of them is always to speak about his intimate self.[44] He has learned that there is some delay in printing the manuscript. His next letter asks whether Ritter has received the manuscript and the sketches included. He will send the map of the trip when he has drawn it. Again he mentions his black mood. Yet, he says, after two-and-a-half months of depression, he has decided to make an about-face and go to the end of the road.[45] Apparently, he has decided to focus on achieving something significant in La Chaux-de-Fonds, and forgets for a while plans of escape.

The first few months at La Chaux-de-Fonds are filled with exhausting days. He sets up his architectural office in close association with Les Ateliers d'Art Réunis and begins to design a house for his parents, which he calls affectionately "la petite maison" ("the small house") or "la maison blanche" ("the white house"). [FIGURE 4.3, p. 691] In January he begins to teach in the Nouvelle Section of l'École d'Art. He is also completing his *Étude sur le mouvement d'art décoratif en Allemagne*, which he submits to l'École d'art on February 1, 1912, and in that same month he receives a commission for the Villa Favre-Jacot.[46] Yet neither all this activity nor his resolutions of making an about-face seem to cheer him up. On a train to Zurich, on March 5, he takes up his pen to write Ritter: by the end of the month he says, he begins work on two villas, which makes him blue with fright. He tries to find the cause for his malady. Can he blame Turkey? It cannot be denied that seven months of song after five years of arduous study have made his soul something other than a watchmaker working twelve hours in his shop. What a disaster–it cannot be helped, but he has changed![47]

He reproaches Ritter for his advice to make people remember that he, Jeanneret, has gone to the Acropolis. Apparently this has not helped, and he finds himself full of anguish over future combats. He is fearful that he may not have within himself the faith required for builders of temples. He marches along a slowly ascending line that is punishing because Switzerland is not an open country; it has limited horizons. He feels isolated, alone. He is constantly asking why, what is the reason behind things. Basically, one lives to work, to earn money, and to satisfy one's pride and decency as a man. But one dreams of the Acropolis and of returning there.

Should one work for one's own betterment or for the good of everyone; should one be egotistical or altruistic? To be a supportive member of a group means to be a small number in a large mass, to be avant-garde is to place oneself all alone on a pedestal—but someone must be the Pope! He describes a memory from Paris: he was sitting in a corner of the Louvre where it opens onto the Tuileries, reading some pages of Maeterlinke on justice. That is when he understood that every act in life is capital accumulated; it allows one to do something greater at a later date. Life presents images, slowly as if in a magic lantern. Their acceptance is marked with a plus sign, their delay or refusal with a minus. And because someone else makes the calculations, and due to his own unhealthy curiosity, Jeanneret is sick with uncertainty.[48]

He spends the spring in gloomy turbulence, always asking "why" and complaining that his friends—Octave, Perret, and others—are fleeing from La Chaux-de-Fonds. Sometimes, he says, he is so depressed that he does not even feel like writing to Ritter.[49] By June, he tells Ritter he is "worried about your silence" and attributes his depression partly to this cause.[50] He has waited week after week for a letter or a visit, but nothing happens. He dreams about Venice, Ravenna, and Paris as soothing compensation; everything in his surroundings remains either static or indifferent.[51]

Another cause for his depression is revealed in a letter written on August 24, 1912—conflict with L'Eplattenier. The corrections of others make him rebel. It is necessary to throw a lot of things away, especially some people whom he thought loved him, and who believed they loved him. It had been a play of masks, but now the masks must be taken off. Everything is obscure, macabre, likened to a sad Christian cemetery, as opposed to Muslim cemeteries in Constantinople, which he admired. "It was necessary to break with L'Eplattenier. To defame, to make crumble. To tear up, to uproot—to reject."[52] It is a great deliverance, filled with enormous sadness, with the sense that he has been stuck in a stagnating bog. After ten months of suffering it is a rude awakening![53]

Now, Jeanneret says, that he has a strong presentiment of modernity, it strengthens him. But there is always the cadaver of last year to be buried if one is to proceed. Because he has listened with a cowardly ear to instructions, there are some anachronisms in the houses he built this year. He had made something unsuitable, and this threw him into an abyss of depression. Suddenly he sees the blackness of his state; and suddenly he can see white. Music, he wrote, is the great promoter of joy; the hour of combat is always announced by music, and he listens attentively. From the bottom of a black hole, looking upwards, one can perceive the scherzo forces in motion. He makes a list: at twelve he climbed the Alps, at fourteen he was near Florence, at twenty-two he was in Paris, at twenty-four he went down the great river to stand at the foot of the minarets and under the frightening machine of the Parthenon.[54] He asks Ritter: What is to happen? What to keep and what to use in this hour of flight where he finds no help?[55]

Later that autumn, he sends Ritter a copy of a form letter that he is circulating: it explains that he was seeking a French publisher for *Étude sur le mouvement d'art décoratif en Allemagne* and wonders whether, if the recipient judges the work to be sound, he will write a line or two in support of the work, and would he point him to an editor who might take charge of it.[56] No French publisher was ever found for the book, although parts were published in the French journal *L'Art de France* in April and May 1914. *L'Art de France* was launched in 1913 "to work to maintain French taste and the genius of the national tradition" in the decorative arts. Its more immediate aim was "to insure by all possible means the success of French Art in the Exposition of 1916" (finally mounted in 1925 under the title Exposition Internationale des Arts Décoratifs et Industriels Modernes).[57] Jeanneret felt these were goals he had endorsed in 1912, and he hoped that his *Étude* might be an entry point into this Parisian dialogue if only it were republished. Still, there remained the issue of his endorsement of German superiority in the industrial arts; by 1914 he was anxious that he might, because of it, be labeled a German sympathizer, and wrote to the editor of *L'Art de France* asserting his "Latin" nationality by birth and in all matters of taste.[58]

The day after he sent him the copy of the form letter described above, Jeanneret wrote to Ritter again, this time revealing a deeper sorrow: a young man, one of the few intelligent friends Jeanneret had discovered, had killed himself in front of the entire town in an airplane accident. Already the mourners were citing it as an act of God, but Jeanneret criticized those "who do nothing but stand still and place themselves beneath the pillars of the Protestant church, they do not kill themselves in an airplane or in anything else."[59] He also notes the death of Ritter's own father and the story Ritter wrote about the same

FIGURE 4.4: Sketch by Charles-Édouard Jeanneret of his writing desk in La Chaux-de-Fonds, circa 1914

time "The Second Pilgrimage to the Tomb of Mahler." He admires the manner in which Ritter's emotions enter into his language, and so into the reader.

He is eager to see Ritter again and he asks him to please comment about his *Étude,* because no one has made any comments at all. Should he re-edit it, and how? He speaks again of his Eastern articles, which he nicknames Bibi-la-Douleur (Bibi-the-mournful). Here, too, there appears to have been complete silence from others.[60] [FIGURE 4.4]

Within a week, he sends a postcard stating that the articles on Constantinople have been sent: he finds this cycle of tellings to be the best. Certain phrases bother him less than they did when he wrote them originally, and some are even evocative of the place. Perhaps now that he sees the words formed in silence within his head, printed on paper, and read aloud to his brother (and now on their way to Ritter for comment), he can be proud of this work while admitting failure in those writings already published. Of the four hundred copies of his *Étude* distributed in La Chaux-de-Fonds, not a single word has yet, he thinks, been spoken. How he dislikes the provinces![61]

In the next letter, written in part on the train to Bern, he writes that his life is in constant agitation, like small waves in a frog pond. Uncertainty keeps him from making decisions about his future. He lives only for the moment, which seems to engulf him. Writing again a few days later, he says he is pleased with the house he has designed for his parents. The main room is white, the countryside blue, and the soil itself blue, royal blue. He begins to write a complex narrative fantasy built on his memories of the Danube, battles, the Slovak mountains, the hill of the cemetery. He fears that Western civilization is coming, and the East, homeland and generator of all poetry, will no longer have an empire:

> The skyscraper will triumph, Pathé, and the phonograph, and German glass trinkets, and beer and Kirsch and bordellos and the police, and firemen, and international laws, and straight streets, and protestant churches, and men of affairs and German construction societies.[62]

He swears he will return to Stamboul and go to Spain, to Morocco, and feel the hot wind called the Sirocco. In spite of all these dreams of escape, he notes that walking in the pine forests with his mother above their "white house" moves him deeply. After seeing the world, experiencing the multitudes of people–yellows, blacks, reds, and whites–at a time when the spirit is free to cross over space, it alights on the altar of one's wonderful homeland: the canton of Jura.[63]

Finally, Ritter replies: he has read Jeanneret's travel tales with enthusiasm. Jeanneret sends him a postcard of thanks for encouraging him to write and to paint. Jubilantly, he proclaims that the last year of overwhelming tasks has not crushed him, but made him stronger for the struggle toward his ideal. He will send more stories about the East and make more sketches of Andrianapolis, Athos, and the Acropolis.[64]

He takes two trips to Paris in November and December, but makes no mention of these to Ritter. He writes instead in a postcard at the beginning of 1913 that he has great joy in seeing his mother happy in the white walls of their new house. He describes it in colors of freshness: white, rose, and lemon yellow. The Jura, which he now regards with absolute defiance, he colors in somber tones, ocher and green-black. He has no tears for the place.[65]

In the middle of the month he begins to write about Paris. It is calling to him, embracing him with rhythm and happiness. Paris is a vital center where once again the arts will be resurgent. Architecture, too, will eventually triumph, although there is little evidence at the present of such a conquest–still, he has faith! He admits that even though he has been molded by German art and written about it, he draws no spiritual satisfaction from it.[66] It is France that appeals to him, and where he longs to be.

Jeanneret has begun at this time to correspond with his old schoolmate Max Du Bois, whom he had met again in 1909 in La Chaux-de-Fonds. Du Bois had just completed an engineering degree in Zurich and was working for Professor E. Mörsch, a specialist in reinforced concrete. Du Bois eventually settled in Paris, establishing his own firm, SABA (Société d'Application de Béton Armé), to promote the use of reinforced concrete (*béton armé*) in industrial buildings.[67] He has published his own translation of Mörsch's book on reinforced concrete, *Le Béton Armé,* and gave Jeanneret a copy. Jeanneret writes to Du Bois on January 17, 1913, hoping that Du Bois will be interested in collaboration. He is convinced the future of architecture lies not just in modeling itself after the industrial arts, but also in inserting industrial building processes into every stage of the design work. If the architect and engineer collaborate–the lesson he has learned in Germany–then progress in housing might be achieved.[68]

Meanwhile, there are more letters of confession to Ritter. Jeanneret remains, he says, in a dark hole; he sends Ritter photographs of his parent's house that he feels betray him because they show its many mistakes.[69] Yet his architectural and artistic obsessions seem ever stronger:

> Some memories [of his voyage to the East] erect themselves as judges, decadent and intense seductions, motives, ordering him to paint. The sap of life, and presence, perhaps morbid, of things loved, impose themselves under the form of women to paint; nude or clothed; masturbation of a bachelor.[70]

> Architecture becomes imperatively Greek [Attica]. Far from all Gothicism. Monochrome and rectilinear: no, cubic. Cubism masters the rhythms of the builder, the rhythms of the sculptor, the rhythms of the painter that deeply agitates the surface in order to subtly restore the very profound to the very prominent, to the same flat plane.[71] [FIGURES 4.5 AND 4.6, p. 692]

He is having trouble in La Chaux-de-Fonds: some are angry with him because he no longer appears to be a local. Yet his tastes are simple; all he desires of life is a house in which to relax in, some wine, clean women, and music, surrounded with colors and flowers, spheres and prisms. His thoughts are inevitably called toward France, toward the land on which the sun sets. "France, which spreads out before us, modulated land full of soft mists and supple slopes leading toward the *center.* The sun sets, under the form of a *circle,* over Paris, toward Paris which is the centre, the middle of the circle."[72] Paris has become his new symbol and France his new obsession–but where will he find the road that leads there?

Le Corbusier would recall in his "Confessions" of 1925 that it was after the completion of his *Étude* that "I succumbed to the irresistible attraction of the Mediterranean. And it was high time, after ten years' work (published in all the reviews) on German decorative art and architecture."[73] And his new idea of architecture was formed:

> Architecture is the magnificent play of forms under light. Architecture is a coherent construct of the mind. Architecture has nothing to do with decoration. Architecture is in the great buildings, the difficult and high-flown works bequeathed by time, but *it is also in the smallest hovel,* in an enclosure-wall, in everything, sublime or modest, which contains sufficient geometry to establish a mathematical relationship.[74]

These recollections, however, are a retrospective composition by Le Corbusier after he had been transformed once again by his third mentor, Amédée Ozenfant, and by Purist ideals. But what they establish, however, is that Greece and classical architecture became an *idée fixe* that he would return to across a lifetime.

In 1913, he was still struggling with depression and seeking a path toward an ideal, be it Greece or the Mediterranean–especially Paris. But escape he must! Aware that France was considering various educational reforms in the decorative arts, he hoped his *Étude* might open a door there. On its strength, he might be invited to be a consultant or to join an architectural partnership. And his *La Construction des Villes* held many lessons drawn from German urbanism, which he believed the French should hear, so there lay another opportunity–once it was finished. New building materials were beginning to occupy his mind–here too there might be a way, perhaps through a partnership with Du Bois. But he had yet to make an amalgam of the decorative and industrial arts, housing and urbanism. That would occur at the

FIGURE 4.7: During World War I, Charles-Édouard Jeanneret would often go for walks with William Ritter, his mentor from Landeron, Switzerland, sketched here by Jeanneret in 1914.

end of the year, when he understood that the future of architecture and of the decorative arts lay in the creation of a comfortable home for modern times.

In May he asks Ritter for advice about his duty to his parents. They are fifty, he twenty-five. He feels that a generation gap separates them, yet he does not know how to leave for Adrianopolis, Paris, or Chicago. Too much money has been spent on the house he designed for them, and he begins to fear it was a great mistake. The socialist commune is in control, and there will be nothing to build in 1913 (in fact, local building activity did not revive until 1916). Should he abandon his parents or remain? He must break the chains that bind him to this hateful town and its miserable people. At twenty-five, he believes, a man is in movement; at thirty, he stops and looks around, tests the soil; at forty, he selects his place and puts down roots. But in La Chaux-de-Fonds nothing moves, all is stagnant.[75]

By the end of the month, however, he reports that he is more optimistic. He is helping to set up an association in Switzerland like the Werkbund, with its bylaws based on his paraphrase in *L'Étude sur le mouvement d'art décoratif* of the Werkbund's manifesto of 1908. He is referring to a thirty-member Suisse Romande league, L'Oeuvre, with a publication of the same name, which had recently been established.[76] (The Suisse Romande lies in the Western, French-speaking part of Switzerland.) This achievement lifts his spirits, and he hopes he will get beyond his depression. He requires contact with great works, active involvement, not spectatorship–and it worries him that he is frittering away valuable time. There is wonderful news, however: his former patrons, the Perrets, have triumphed–they have executed a work that will make them famous–nothing even in Berlin or Munich surpasses it.[77] Jeanneret is referring here to the Théâtre des Champs-Elysées, which had just been inaugurated. It must have thrilled him that "the elite of the Parisian worlds of high society, politics, finance, theater, literature and the arts" attended its gala opening.[78]

At the end of September he mentions that he has written a "popular" article on the Swiss house for the illustrated periodical *L'Almanach helvétique* and needs good views of those "adorable houses" at Coudre and Hauterive to accompany them.[79] (Although Ritter resided in Munich, he was originally from the Neuchâtel region of Switzerland and kept a house in Landeron. During summer vacations, Jeanneret and Ritter often walked together through the region–some of the best hours of his life, Jeanneret said.) [FIGURE 4.7] Jeanneret remembers that Ritter has some albums of photographs of regional architecture, and trusts that he can use some of these images. He would especially like to have shots of windows and facades.[80]

As usual, Jeanneret is arrogant at the start of a new project, but a few months later admits that he knew nothing about this topic, did only a morning of research in the Berne library before writing the article. Besides, he had been pressured into making it "popular," so it was hopelessly naive and compromised. He admitted that he was still very much influenced by Cingria-Valneyre, whom he first read in 1909, but evidently had forgotten his message while writing this article.[81] He would go even further next year and denounce any attempt to define a regional style of architecture. If commanded to

> make a house that would be *Swiss*; or...one from Geneva, for example, or from Neuchâtel, from La Chaux-de-Fonds!...I would decline the offer....No, I would continue to be faithful to what I admire whatever that is, to be open to influences, from wherever they come: because I have never heard proclaimed, emanating from any ambient milieu, an ensemble of dogmatic laws.[82]

FIGURE 4.8: Photograph of the Jeanneret-Perret family in 1914: father Georges Édouard (top left), son Albert (top right), Charles-Édouard (bottom left), and mother Marie (bottom right)

During the fall of 1913 he makes several trips to Paris to buy furniture for the interiors he is designing for local patrons, to whom he ascribes little knowledge or taste.[83] After one trip, he writes to Ritter that he has executed one interior design well, so others in La Chaux-de-Fonds have offered him similar work and he expects there will be more.

Since September, he writes in the same letter, he has been reading Ritter's new book *Edmond de Pury* (on the painter of that name) and it greatly impresses him.[84] He writes about "the law of equilibrium" that corrects all things, and admits that his own "cubism" has now been internalized, and its plastic realization primary, enabling him to regard *Pury* with admiration and comprehension.[85] He has also begun to read Gabriele D'Annunzio's *Le Feu,* and these two works press him to admit an idea he has held for some time: "I have fear of marriage, considering it as a great void into which things fall, the bad before the good."[86] Instead of the relationship with his cousin Marguerite that his family seemed to be pushing on him, he wants a love where the body and heart both find a place of enchantment, a heroic terrain where love is the beginning and not the end. Since he is only at the threshold of what he believes he can accomplish, full of great hopes of what will come, he wants to be free to achieve such things. Only then will he understand what it is to "be called a man"![87] [FIGURE 4.8]

His Parisian experiences in the fall of 1913 lifted his spirits. During his visit in November, he saw Perret and was thrilled by "two hours of enchantment in an atmosphere of the avant-garde and its wonderfully serene strength."[88] He also spent an evening in the company of the poet Charles Vildrac, the author of *Livre d'amour.* These, he tells Ritter, are "people who construct their life, accomplish these functions in the best and most sincere manner possible, and repudiate the storm of Catholic mysticism with a head held high, a pure heart and an honest life: a tranquil force in the river [of life]." He mentions several reviews such as *L'Occident, La Nouvelle Revue Française,* and *Les Cahiers d'Aujourd'hui,* and singles out the decor of the Théâtre du Vieux Colombier, which had opened fifteen days before his writing with a robust if somewhat juvenile manifesto.[89]

While rather obscure in its references, this letter is full of significance. It is clear that Jeanneret wants to go to Paris to live in the atmosphere of the avant-garde, for only there, he believes, will he be able to achieve the greatness of his "destiny." He is suffocating in the conservative atmosphere of La Chaux-de-Fonds, he knows that marriage would be a trap, and his work is confined to the decorative arts and patrons for whom he has little respect, but he is the only son at home, and his duty to his parents weighs on him. While in Paris, he reads Adolf Loos's essays "L'architecture et le style moderne" and "Ornement et crime" in *Les Cahiers d'Aujourd'hui.*[90] This anarchist-oriented journal of art and literature, organized by Vildrac and others in 1912, mounted a strong crusade against ornamentation and superficial decoration in the applied arts.[91] Jeanneret, too, was leaning toward simple, well-made forms, a direct, sober "cubism" devoid of superficial decoration, although these forms were opposed to both the taste of his Swiss clients and the French interior decorator's impulse to focus on a piece of furniture as an object in itself and not part of an ensemble. Yet he was increasingly disinclined to submit either to the poor taste of his clients or to the rule of the ensemble that Germany taught, for his avant-garde posturing was on the rise. Further, as he now understood from reading Loos, a modern style had nothing to do with nationalism, either French or German. This confusing position begins to contradict his message in the *Étude des arts décoratifs.*

Jeanneret's ambivalence returns: what should he use as a model, from whom should he draw inspiration? Cingria-Vaneyre had held the white cubic forms of Greece suitable for a regional Suisse Romande architecture, but Jeanneret feared that he would never attain the great heights of architecture if confined to such a backward place. There were German artists who taught a broad concept of the decorative arts that included modern industrial techniques, but he is leaning toward the Parisian avant-garde, where things German were increasingly suspect. Although he often mentions painters who became architects later in their lives, from Palladio to Behrens, he does not yet see the path that ties his own painting to architecture.[92] Interior decoration of whatever philosophy says nothing about the construction of cities, which is beginning to be one of his passions. Finally there is the sophistication of Perret, who combined neoclassical forms with new building materials and techniques. Which mentor should he follow? Which path might take him to Paris?

A letter written to Ritter in December 1913 (and interrupted at least twenty times, according to internal marks, once for a three-day trip to Paris) is another full of confession. He admits an inconsolable discontent. He refuses to remain in La Chaux-de-Fonds. Even animals leave their home when the time has come. He is ready, healthy, and free to accomplish his work; his parents, on the other hand, want to see him with a wife and children, to be settled–never to leave La Chaux-de-Fonds. He is seized with nostalgia for travel, and if the work order for which he waits comes soon, he will go to Rome for Christmas, sure that he can pay back the cost of such a trip. He complains that his parents keep a careful eye on him–thinking, for example, that if he stays out late he is with prostitutes. While he knows that this espionage is affectionate, it still makes his life insupportable.[93]

He will, he says, go to Paris to see the Salon d'Automne and swear at Metziner and Picasso for shocking him with their audacious violations of the rules of painting. But with Vildrac he knows he will see some really beautiful paintings and know that there is art in Paris.[94]

Resuming the letter after returning from Paris, he reports seeing forty interiors on display at the Salon d'Automne. "I noted that visitors were enchanted...The triumph of modern ideas is no longer a myth." Still the problem remains: how to provide a suitable home for the times (*l'habitat conforme*), and from whom should he draw inspiration? No evident answers were offered by the salon, poisoned by pretension. He allows that there are one or two personalities he can admire, but suddenly shifts focus as if to underscore his ambivalence over who they might be: "My admiration goes without reserve to engineers who construct phenomenal bridges, who work for what is useful, the strong, and the pure." He hopes that artists can aspire to be like engineers–useful and serious, not parasitic.[95]

In simplicity and utility there is much to be praised, but he cannot apply these in his home town. He tries to discern what an architect ought to teach his clients. So important is this matter that he has decided to write yet another article on architecture and try to publish it in a Parisian review.[96] He has discovered another source of inspiration: the design theory advocated by the decorative-artist-turned-interior-designer Francis Jourdain. (A cofounder of *Les Cahiers d'Aujourd'hui,* it is probably Jourdain who suggested the journal publish translations of Loos's two essays in 1912 and 1913.) Furthermore, although he does not mention Jourdain's name in this connection, it is his minimalist set designs that Jeanneret admired at the Théâtre du Vieux-Colombier. He had also seen two of Jourdain's interiors–a bedroom ensemble and a salon-dining room–on display at the Salon d'Automne of 1913, and admired them. Either sensing something new in the decorative arts or being overtly instrumental, he writes a letter to Jourdain on December 21 seeking an audience in order to clarify whether Jourdain's principles of design might be able to guide him.[97]

In this letter, he confesses to be very "troubled by the problem of interior decoration. I would have liked to dispel my uneasiness, to find in the diverse manifestations of Parisian artists a direction...I expected a lot and I was delighted at first, then rather worn out and disconcerted...However, I returned with one durable impression: that of your work in the Salon d'Automne."[98] Jourdain's rooms contained simply constructed furniture devoid of ornamentation and without reference to national traditions; this interested but troubled Jeanneret, contradicting his nationalistic message in *Étude.*

At the end of January 1914, he writes to Ritter with enthusiasm, uncharacteristically declaring he is "totally satisfied and totally grateful."[99] He must speak of Athens and Delphi, what joy! And forget the miserable readers of *Feuille d'Avis*! How grateful he is for Ritter's advice! Such jubilation may have derived from Ritter's approval of his new work on the "Mount Athos" and "Athens" chapters. His agonizing writer's block seems to have dissipated. His better spirits may also have stemmed from the article on architecture that he had just begun to write. "Le Renouveau dans l'Architecture" ("Renewal in Architecture") would be published in the second issue of *L'Oeuvre* (1914).[100] His idea of the role of the architect in society was becoming clearer, and his mode of argumentation sharper and more emphatic; this, too, may have relieved his relentless frustration over his inability to express himself in narrative prose. Also noteworthy is his choice of title, recalling but departing from L'Eplattenier's 1910 "Le Renouveau de l'Art." His conflict with L'Eplattenier was allowing him to substitute architecture for art, unlocking his creativity.

In this article, he argues in a mode that he had often deployed in letters to L'Eplattenier: after examining a series of bipolar positions, resolution is sought on a higher level. He also deploys a telegraphic and didactic style of writing at variance with the flowing romantic descriptions he wrote in imitation of Ritter and Loti. And here he is not only repeating lessons he learned from Germany and Loos, but taking new positions that he will reiterate again and again in the years of Purism.[101] He is asking the reader, as he will many times in his lifetime, to take a position, and to debate with him for or against modernism or regionalism, architecture or engineering, utility or beauty, purity or ornamentation. These are not incompatible positions in a dualistic philosophy, but polar opposites, or considerations on a line of argumentation that the mind can take on any number of positions. The pairs are arranged in order to seek a resolution, not force a choice. He uses symmetry and equilibrium like an acrobat on a tightrope (one of his own oft-used metaphors)–each point must be kept in balance.[102]

He opens by declaring it necessary to ask why new architecture so often is in discord with its surroundings. It is the intruder, and so creates dissonance. Would it be possible to avoid this by creating a regional architecture? This problematic pairing, in which modernism appears to be the aggressor and regionalism the defender, both opens and closes the essay–with a partial resolution. There he says that new architecture, pure and sincere, will eventually make its influence felt in the city. As for regional architecture, it is too soon to take a definitive position, for regionalism is not an a priori determination, but an intuition acquired over time. It arises from understanding the local milieu, and it is necessary to know how to wait for its arrival!

Between these endpoints, he takes a position on another pair of considerations: the use of new materials and the question of an appropriate aesthetics. Implicitly his arguments link architecture and the city. He writes telegraphically: the problems of housing are modified, the manner of building transformed, but concepts of art remain static and regressive. So a divorce occurs between the requirements imposed by progress and the effects of a *retardataire* aesthetics.

He compares Mansart's Dome of Les Invalides and Perret's Théâtre des Champs-Elysées, both in Paris. Here the transformation in building techniques is apparent. Architecture can no longer wear masks. Perret's architecture reveals that it is built of reinforced concrete, and not of massive stones.

Progress, Jeanneret argues, always imposes itself, is conquering, brutal. For proof he cites the "American city plan" of the eighteenth century. Wherever circumstances allowed, on flat terrain, built all at once, new towns arose following this scheme. They confronted aesthetics with the imperative word "useful" (*le verbe impératif de l'Utile*). The apparent contradiction between utility and beauty is a challenge that must be accounted for. The clinching argument follows: new and subversive forms of architecture satisfy, without dissimulation, new needs. The Romans had need of water, so they built the aqueduct; the people wanted games, so the Colosseum was built. The refrain returns: mankind innately desires to progress. But for years, architects have been a shriveled-up race (*race ratatinée*), so today's heroes are the engineers. Thus architecture (remaining the domain of artists) does not follow the path of progress but keeps to a sterile eclecticism. For the last half century it has remained on the margins of progress, irresponsibly staying aside from society.

He returns to the question of new materials and aesthetics. The error in most new architecture resides not internally but externally, not inside the house but on its facade. All houses–from the smallest hut to the largest palace–should be constructed according to the latest technical discoveries, but the architect continues to create cornices and ornaments, which often have no use at all. Why does this farce continue? Because architects learn in schools to trace over without end ornaments, and ornaments, and still more ornaments. Why have we become savages after twenty centuries of culture, again inscribing tattoos? (Here he is clearly echoing Loos, who said in "Ornament and Crime," "The Papuan tattoos his skin, his boat, his oar, in short, everything that is within his reach. He is no criminal. The modern man who tattoos himself is a criminal or a degenerate."[103]) Le Corbusier continues: "Haven't we become sufficiently civilized to play with beautiful proportions, with the beauty of nude material, 'with a form simply and rationally adapted to function'?"[104] It is not decoration that counts. Jeanneret reaches for the supreme example: take away the friezes and ornaments from the Parthenon and still the Parthenon thrills. And look at Pompeii, its houses stripped of ornamentation by lava: how to explain the enthusiasm that grabs you when you pass from room to room and then into the garden? How sad that the architect is absorbed in fabricating ornaments. One must suppress these affectations, clear everything away–then the city will recapture a unity. Then modern architecture will become the law of the city.

Returning to the issue of modernity versus tradition, Jeanneret closes the essay with an unattributed quotation from Adolf Loos's "L'Architecture et le style moderne" (1910):

> A lake in the Alps. The blue sky, green water, all is peaceful and pure. The mountains and the clouds are reflected in the lake, as are the houses, farms and chapels, which do not resemble works made by man, but look as if they have come from God's own workshop, just like the mountains and the trees, the clouds and the blue sky.[105]

III. THE OUTBREAK OF WAR

While Jeanneret was exploring paths to Paris, all was not well with the Nouvelle Section that L'Eplattenier had established within l'École d'Art, where Jeanneret had been teaching since January of 1912. The intent of the new section was to draw art and industry together in greater collaboration, but this erupted into a debate within the École itself, a debate that Jeanneret exploited to his own advantage, as explained below. L'Eplattenier was forced to resign from l'École d'Art on March 18, 1914, and Jeanneret was supposed to leave by April 30, although he managed to hang on for another month. L'Eplattenier's resentment over Jeanneret's role in this debacle was so great that he refused to speak to him, or even acknowledge his presence, until early 1916.[106] Jeanneret, however, defended his actions to Ritter at the end of March, claiming he was waiting for an opportune time to air all the dirty linen in public.[107]

He had worked during January and February on a competition for a bank in the canton of Neuchâtel but was eliminated in the first round. Nevertheless, he professes–and here is another reason for his better spirits–his project was the only one out of seventy-two that advocated a new line, affirming "that architecture was *an art*, it is about art."[108] Thus his design stood out against all the superficial treatments. Yet he is still seized by unhealthy hesitation, sometimes paralyzed, because "in each volume, detail, and ensemble, the possibility is there of making a Parthenon, or at least something perfectly beautiful. Thus impotency grips you and you contract."[109]

Meanwhile, he continues working on his "Athos" chapter and rereads Ritter's *Pury* with great joy. He sends a postcard to Ritter on April 11 with remarks about working relentlessly on his chapter, stealing small quarter-hours in the evening during these tumultuous times. When he has finished and he is calm, he will read Ritter's *D'Autrefois*. Having already skimmed a few pages, he judges the work will inspire him.[110]

Although the Nouvelle Section was forced to close, Jeanneret believed he tried to save it by writing a forty-five-page booklet in its defense, *Un mouvement d'art à La Chaux-de-Fonds, à propos de la Nouvelle Section de l'École d'art.* He hoped to make known to an international audience not only the origin and success of the educational reforms the Nouvelle Section advocated, but why some teachers opposed and eventually destroyed the section. He devoted a chapter of fourteen pages to responses elicited from six internationally recognized experts, all men he had met during his travels, who evaluated the reforms proposed. In a March 6 form letter to Peter Behrens, Rupert Carabin, Theodor Fischer, Eugène Grasset, Karl Ernst Osthaus, and Alfred Roller, he explained that the Ancienne Section of l'École d'Art had ignored the message Jeanneret had preached in his *Étude,* and so failed to understand initiatives taken by the Germans to promote the arts and industry.[111] He wrote not a word about L'Eplattenier's leadership in this reform, and why he would be forced to resign within a few days.

The publication of Jeanneret's booklet on April 2 was too late to save L'Eplattenier and his group, but Jeanneret was not above ulterior motives, the cause of L'Eplattenier's animosity. By calling on members of the Werkbund (Behrens, Fischer, and Osthaus), his appeal presented to Parisian educational reformers (e.g., Carabin and Grasset) the lessons he had absorbed from Germany, not L'Eplattenier, and that he believed the French must assimilate. Not surprisingly, one of the French champions of collaborative efforts, Emmanuel de Thubert, editor of *L'Art de France,* would republish fifty pages of Jeanneret's *Étude* that same April and May. Interested only in the reasons for Germany's success in the decorative arts, Thubert eliminated Jeanneret's portrayal of the triumphant French spirit dominating all of the arts. Because Thubert believed there were further lessons that France might learn from Germany, he asked Jeanneret to be a foreign correspondent for the magazine, and as his first assignment to review the German Werkbund when it met in Cologne on July 3–5.[112]

Thus the spring of 1914 was consumed with frantic activity in writing, painting, interior design, and waging war against the conservative faction of l'École d'Art. On the first of May, Jeanneret writes to Ritter, describing the turmoil of the last few months and everyone's treachery in spite of the fact that he works only for what he thinks is correct, neither a critic nor a flatterer. He is profitably engaged as an interior designer, but here too he complains that while he struggles against the prejudice, routine, and bad taste of his clients, still they destroy his work when they take possession of it! He knows he should not throw pearls before swine but he feels his simple honest efforts have been wasted–and this includes his efforts at l'École de l'Art and involves his comrades as well. He asks Ritter to look at how his thinking has gradually been "deformed" over the last two and a half years: he came home in 1911 a socialist, but their leader assassinated the Nouvelle Section, and therefore made him doubt his own beliefs and opened a great void.[113] All of this had occurred because he had been profoundly touched by one man (L'Eplattenier). On top of this, his comrades in the *Ateliers d'art réunis* all marry or abandon themselves little by little to baser instincts. He feels overwhelmed with feelings and oppressions he has carried within himself for a long time, but turning inward he "remains like an upright column–in meditation."[114]

And he is surrounded by nature, which is opening up after a long winter's rest. And because fog makes one concentrate on things close at hand, he sees his father leaning on the balustrade in the upper garden of the "white house," spreading an astonishing feeling over every thing below: white wall, wooden arbor, propped-up house (*maison accotée*), and dominant forest. Ritter has not seen the Jeanneret-Perret villa, which is mangled by irreparable defects, yet some parts are lively and animated. It is a strange house due to what Jeanneret calls the anachronism of its site; perched high on a hill, the view from the balustrade reminds one of the sea, which beckons the gaze from afar.[115]

Ten days before leaving to cover the German Werkbund, he announces he has finished writing "Athos"–"a laborious undertaking." "It is strange. A reproach always held me back, which I constantly had to surmount: it seems to me that in writing I exit from my competences and play the ridiculous role of a music lover."[116] He has read Ritter's *D'Autrefois* and is full of respect and admiration. He thinks of the cinema, and how it invents all sorts of magical things, while a novel, in contrast, can poetically evoke life, allowing it to resonate in one's thoughts.[117]

During his trip to Cologne on the way to the Werkbund, he stops in Nancy. In a June 28 letter, he explains that primary forms will always be the strongest and greatest means of architectural expression. The day before, when he visited the Cathedral of Strasbourg, he was reminded that seven or eight years before he had realized on entering its vaulted dome that it was a powerful, serene, and honest construction. In order to be an architect, he confesses, it is necessary to get to the basic root of the problem and let the plant develop as a tree. Nancy is a very pretty city, even admirable, but it seems to speak the language of a weakened courtesan, and its family links to medieval intelligence are questionable. The Strasbourg cathedral, on the other hand, is among the best he knows, and he places it side by side with the Greek temple, allowing Gothic and Classical forms to become equivalent in his developing language of architecture. It affects him, for it stands as witness to a belief and speaks in a unanimous voice, while contemporary man hesitates and is uprooted each hour by so many vile banalities. What can an architect do today who has soul and wants to be symphonic? "We do not have the harmony of our alphabet. Thus the architect is a being without a house, the dregs of society which one doesn't need"[118] All these concerns, Jeanneret interjects, are interrupted by the news-hawker on the street below his window announcing the assassination of Archduke Franz Ferdinand in Sarajevo that very day, on June 28, 1914.

He turns back to speak of an "eternal balance." The nave of Strasbourg brings back his love of the Gothic–which he had sworn off after returning from the East and from Paris. But what his whims and fogs had hidden, has returned–or better yet "re-presented" itself. Then he speaks of the hot Sunday afternoon, of the bordellos of architecture, of simplicity that must exist somewhere, and he cries out, "I wish so much that painting and our arts would be pure. So simple and stripped of all story, place, age, hour. Just a strong expression of life. Vases, domes, tabernacles and small glories brightened by sunlight one by one."[119]

The "eternal balance" that Jeanneret sought was out of the question as World War I quickly unfurled. He writes to Ritter at the end of August. His pen is heavy and disobedient. For thirty intense days he has thought of Ritter but not had the courage to write. Everything is turbulent. No one knows anything, everyone hears contradictory news or lies. He worries over Ritter's whereabouts: is he alone in his house, and what does he think of this war? Ritter might be in the worst of situations–that has compelled Jeanneret to write. Could he be of some help? He has money and would gladly send some, if only to repay a few of the many personal debts he owes. And now Louvain is destroyed! There is no reply to his letter, so Jeanneret writes to Ritter's sisters–what has happened to Ritter? In this imbecilic and atrocious hour, he says, he fears the worst and begs for reassurance.[120]

Like most expatriates, shortly after the outbreak of World War I Ritter had returned to his homeland. He settled in Landeron, a town in the Neuchâtel region. Jeanneret eventually located him there, and during the war visited him often. They would paint, go for mountain hikes, and have endless conversations, cementing the most intimate period of their relationship. Jeanneret increasingly comments on the use of the telephone: annoying in his office or useful to contact Ritter. Yet he keeps up a lively written correspondence with Ritter, continuing to experiment with style.[121]

On September 22, Jeanneret's letter to Ritter is full of pain–the Cathedral of Reims has been destroyed! He had to re-look at images of that vessel of glory to fully hate this dastardly act. And he swears that he suffers in the body of an architect, for his recent visit to Strasbourg has enabled him to feel the pain of this unimaginable deed. How can this marvelous fruit of the soul of Europe be struck to the earth by a pig with the name of Guillaume or Kronsprinz! Everything collapses before the criminals and so many worthy men are going to die. One is afraid to read the newspapers. But he will visit Ritter soon and they will climb the mountains and look toward France. He has pressing work in his office, but admits that he would prefer to carry a pickax and gather round the cathedral, "to piously raise up the ruins." (The cathedral was restored after the war.)[122]

Jeanneret goes to Berne at the beginning of October to see the Werkbundausstellung, which he called a splendid national effort. There are, he reports to Ritter, many exhibitioners, and they present a serious, conscious effort of remarkable clarity. His enthusiasm for these displays stems from the tendencies they revealed of things he had witnessed the past July in Lyon, where he attended the International Town Planning Exhibition on "La Cité Moderne" and viewed some of the architecture of Tony Garnier. What admiration he held for Swiss mechanics, statisticians, merchants, and industrialists! And he protests that the term "fatal," with which one qualifies the declaration of war, is a capitulation of the spirit. Nothing is fatal, except for the miserable nationalist education and the revengers and counter-revengers of the military who make each act and word a subject of defiance and hatred. The artificial atrocity of this heinous struggle will be unmasked and the world will soon return to normal everyday life.[123]

Meanwhile, and in spite of the war, Jeanneret is busy with work on some houses and preparations for the future. But what will that be, for the future appears to be erected on "mud"? He wonders whether the civic spirit now consists of taking hold of industry, which has died everywhere, and making it live again. But can he support a civic ideal erected on the ruins of others?[124]

These rather cryptic remarks probably refer to two projects that Jeanneret was developing at the end of 1914 in collaboration with Max Du Bois. Because he tends to write to Ritter only about artistic concerns or to confess his innermost thoughts, he does not reveal these new plans, which he hopes may offer a route to Paris. After the outbreak of war, Du Bois had returned to Switzerland, and the two friends picked up their discussion of *béton armé* where they had left it the previous year.

The first collaborative project with Du Bois was the Domino housing scheme, for which Jeanneret's earliest drawings are dated December 3, 1914. The proposal was intended to aid in reconstructing damaged regions of France and Belgium; perhaps Jeanneret's conscience gripped him, for in this case he intended to profit from the ruin of others. The second project was a competition entry for the Pont Butin over the Rhône River near Geneva, announced that same December. Du Bois, back in Paris by the beginning of the year, was expected do all the necessary technical calculations in order to meet the entry deadline of February 22.[125]

On December 9, Jeanneret writes Ritter that he has an imminent rendezvous with a person from Paris–again not revealing Du Bois's identity.[126] On January 9, he writes that his head is broken from overwork and too many New Year celebrations. Without divulging specifics, he complains "I industrialize and commercialize"[127]–which produces heartbreak, nausea, and disgust in his work.[128] The next month he writes that he is jealous of Ritter, who must be skiing and enjoying himself while Jeanneret is suffering. As has been noted several times, Jeanneret often tries to alleviate his pain by turning to descriptive writing. As if lyrical passages can ease his exacting technical tasks, he waxes eloquent on a landscape of orchards, basking in descriptive phrases that depict a painting. He is pressed with work, making exact lines with the use of a ruler, but would rather be running through the fields and woods in order to experience this dream of the orchards of winter; brush in his hand to scratch their outlines on paper, and shaping there in ivory or in sugar what he lyrically calls "the equivalent purities of Tuscan mysticisms."[129]

The next month brings another war tragedy and reminds him of his beloved Stamboul: Armies of the French-English alliance have tried to take the Dardanelles straits, which lie between the Balkans and Anatolia, but were stopped because of the mines. "A good cause, but an atrocious end! Poor, dear Stamboul...probably my first bereavement.[130] Only the music of Ernest Chausson (playing as he writes) and the thought of victory fill him with joy.

On returning from Geneva in April, where he has presented "his bridge, in the manner of Caracalla," he writes a letter to Ritter, as he has done several times while traveling.[131] He describes how the rectilinear city of Geneva appeals to him—this, he feels, is the chosen place of all Suisse Romande. "The train rolls on...I am plunged toward Zurich, a Teutonic capital, and the mood within me accords with the miserable sadness etched by the rain beating against the windowpanes and the crudeness of village after village."[132] He is on his way to Soleure for a wedding and will enclose a sketch of the town in the letter. Soleure reveals the strength of the French—with an Italian basilica on its acropolis, marvelous French palaces, and the immortal name of the French military architect Vauban attached to its walls.[133]

More than two weeks later, near the end of April, he writes that La Chaux-de-Fonds is still gripped by winter. His bizarre occupation, interior decoration, requires that he always be in his office to answer every question, for he cannot trust his employees. As if it were a random project, he encloses an image of the bridge he has designed with Du Bois in February, stating that it is the first of his works with which he is satisfied.[134]

In his next letter, he announces that he must go to the Côte d'Azur (on the Mediterranean) for his business with "Belgium"—a rather obscure way of mentioning the Dom-ino project to Ritter. He has, he relates, been invited to visit Auguste Perret, whose advice he seeks.[135] He will, as usual, take his sketchbooks and journal and send Ritter copious notes.

IV. A MEDITERRANEAN INTERLUDE

Soon after returning from his visit he sends the first of these exercises, a series of dreamlike ideas called "First Steps in a Dwelling." A peristyle with squared columns, a paved floor with white walls, pilasters, an altar, a sarcophagus constitute the vestibule. He describes in detail the white walls and decorative ornamentation, windows, and vaulted ceiling of the large living room.[136]

The next day he sends a thirty-page letter comprising the journal he kept during his trip to the Côte d'Azur, on which (from May 27 through June 5) he passed through Geneva, Lyon, and Marseilles.[137] He was in a land attended by grief and rage, alongside enthusiasms both crazy and stupendous. From the window of the train he watches the countryside unroll, anchored by the majestic Rhône. He was traveling with an exquisite young girl entrusted to his safety–when "I saw her for the first time, and for the first time perhaps also, found–I, the loner, and heretofore with little knowledge of women–a profoundness, a tranquility, a richness of impressions."[138] Since the train schedule was not well organized, they shared a cold supper together in Lausanne before they departed again.

Having left behind La Chaux-de-Fonds, his office, and the interiors he was designing, Jeanneret began to daydream about former trips through Italy and, inevitably, the East. "But at 11 o'clock, on the platform of Lausanne, I felt the cruelty of the present times: a woman, call her a fiancée in order not to say lover, was returning to Geneva" after having accompanied her man thus far.[139] The couple were glued together, their faces united and moistened with the girl's tears. The mother of the mobilized boy watched, knowing that the last moment was reserved for her. The train left, and the young girl now sitting next to Jeanneret cried softly all the way to Geneva.[140]

He lists the names of small stations where the train stops. He looks at the people, ponders their silence, the pleasantness of the men called up for military service; sees them mount the train alone, without an embrace, without anyone. It upsets him.[141] He takes a rose that someone is selling to raise money for the wounded, and hides within his train compartment. The day before yesterday, he was writing about his desire for action–but here he is shy, feeling useless, daring only to look from the corner of his eye at the young French trench fighters (*les poilus*) who are returning "there"...and the train rolls on.

He is appalled at the contradictions of sorrow mixed with joy. There are uniforms of different colors to describe, the changing countryside as the train moves south, war stories overheard. "The first bayonet. Formidable instrument at the end of the barrel. Long, black, admirably assembled."[142] He calls the afternoon express from Lyon to Marseilles "the train of women in mourning. There are some in black crepe in every compartment."[143] The normality of the streets in Lyon makes Jeanneret lash out at himself for always being a man of pathos, of sensations and emotions without relief. The train of mourning has gotten on his nerves. His body is gripped with fatigue; yet the calm, the passivity of everyone, touches him emotionally. "Because finally, [the reality is] this country is at war, and for 9 months I have [only] imagined it in its horrors."[144]

As the journey continues Jeanneret's writing turns to a stream of consciousness: soldiers, officers, a few wounded, soldiers on parade mix with indifference, even boredom on their faces. And always the question for him: what does this Swiss think about the war? His response: "Nothing until now."[145] The landscape of the Rhône takes on a southern appearance; "It is the house that concentrates, typifies, expresses the feeling of this landscape."[146] Its clay materials and surfaces dried by the sun are typical–yet it is constantly raining. He traces the red line on the map in the corridor of the train as they pass through Arles, Avignon, Orange. This is it, classical lands! They pass by houses of stone, the first olive trees, cypresses, a sky full of melting colors, Van Gogh more than Cezanne. The color tones change: gray walls, pink earth, gray olive trees, radiant pink and blue flowers, steel gray sky, emerald green, not much black or red. The entire plain is planted: wheat fields, vineyards, groves of fruit trees, vegetables in geometric outlines. If one lived in France, one changed one's work: no longer in the factory or the field, but the gatherer of the Boche (Germans).

He has arrived at his destination and begins to write without the use of verbs, drawing out long lists of color tones, such as those in a bouquet of anemones–pale mauve, white, red, violet, pink. The geraniums? They disgust him with their crazy verbosity. His writing table? Full of enormous roses. The air already hot, the landscape arid mountain, dotted with oak trees, junipers, wild roses. "La Chaux-de-Fonds"–literally, "the deep hole"–"Here the word takes on its meaning."[147]

He wishes to write about Marseilles and how it disturbed his tranquil promenade, but he must first write a few words on Auguste Perret. He is always absolutely calm, with a clear attitude and a head held high, his face not aggressive but welcoming, happy, dreaming, or nostalgic; flat and round, the nose chiseled by Michelangelo, beard like a necklace outlining his face from ear to ear. Cheeks of a cherub and a hat with ribbons complete the picture. "The phrase short and concise, the thought always in action.... This man has disciplined language."[148]

They talk about cubism. Perret is a cubist, and Jeanneret admits that he agrees with him. Unfortunately the word is rather stupid and says very little. But Ritter would not accept cubism, Jeanneret says, and would ask: "And tell me, Jeanneret, that Titian would never have drawn an exact perspective today after Daguerre."[149] Yet not a word of theory is spoken with Perret. Jeanneret thinks one must reflect, feel, especially if one works in the fields of poetry and emotions. Always he feels the meagerness of his acts when he takes out a piece of paper and tries to make something beyond the things that Ritter knows; "I wish for the day of release and clear vision."[150]

Finally Jeanneret describes Marseilles. He begins by inserting into his letter copies of the text of postcards he wrote to Perret and to the Swiss painters Paul Théo Robert and Louis de Meuron. The staccato language is similar yet different, and evidently important enough to include as writing exercises. To Perret, in part: "A city of life, crowded with life, masks, battleships, tides, shells and fishes of unimaginable scales. City of fortresses and city of peoples."[151] To Paul Théo Robert: "Black women, dreadnought, flotillas, scaly fish in the jewels of a goddess, shells, crowd of masks, Chinese, Gourkas [*sic*], and Kamerat [*sic*]! Empire and Alexander the Great in the facades.... All the sculpture, all the ancient gestures. Frescos, cameos, and Italian opera. Bronzes. Beyond the fortresses, the sea and the islands."[152] And to Louis de Meuron: "Lilies, roses, passion flowers in the gardens, mimosa on the trellis; the eucalyptus in the gardens, pine trees along the edge of the sea, cypresses near the houses, oak cork trees on the mountains."[153]

Jeanneret follows the postcards with a single long phrase of three pages, a flow of words without stop.[154] At the end of this inundation of words he states simply: "The phrase is long, as the impressions are intensively multiple."[155] Then another torrent of words follows, punctuated with sentences describing Marseilles at sunset and the life of the port as the evening meal draws near. Fog begins to roll in, closing down this theatrical scene.

It is time to return to La Chaux-de-Fonds, so Jeanneret begins to write about the entrance to Geneva and the foothills of the Alps and the shiver they provoked.[156] Traveling through Switzerland, he writes of pastel colors, a blurred painting, as if someone was trying to erase all the scenes he recalls from the south: "Returned to my country[,] I reminded myself that everywhere a terrible war was being waged."[157]

V. REWORKING LA CONSTRUCTION DES VILLES

After sending these writing exercises to Ritter, Jeanneret returns to business affairs. He writes to Du Bois about their Dom-ino scheme: Perret found it "very good," even suggesting the idea might be appropriate for factories, schools, and public buildings. Jeanneret now understands that the simple Dom-ino structure could be extended in length by linking it together, also stacked into two-story apartments. "The moment seems judicious to me to publish my study, which is already written, on *La Construction des Villes*. I could come to Paris immediately to find a publisher."[158] Ten days later he sends a postcard to Ritter explaining that he must go to Paris for three weeks to find some images and some catalogues, and to pursue his research in the Bibliothèque Nationale–not a word about Dom-ino.[159]

Although Jeanneret could confide in Ritter the most intimate details about his struggle with writing and his elation over painting and architectural forms, he seems not to have wanted to involve him with prosaic commercial endeavors. He sends Ritter (17 July 1914) an illustration of his hand raised over a paper, holding an implement for engraving, and explains briefly how to achieve the best results with this tool. He mentions in this letter that he is seized once again with enthusiasm for his work, but says nothing about what this entails.[160]

Jeanneret leaves for Paris on July 28. He remains there for six weeks, returning on September 13.[161] He sends only a few postcards to Ritter during this trip, remarking near the end of August, as he had remarked before, that the great city tells us that we are alone, each with his own idea, yet the desire to express ideas makes one establish relationships. Though he feels alone in the city, nevertheless he draws consolation from his belief that a man alone is a very rich marvel. Paris still pleases him, though it suffers from the war. "But the city, all cities, prove that we live by conventions; the convention of a sojourn so completely imbecilic and old."[162] Once again, although he does not say so explicitly, he is finding the manuscript of *La Construction des Villes* troubling and his visit to Paris perhaps a waste of time. We may wonder: do the "conventions" that city dwellers live by cause his writer's block, or do his emotional ties to Paris produce the conflict, or is there some other reason?

When he becomes disillusioned with one writing project, Jeanneret inevitably begins another. Also, with the war headed toward its second year and no end in sight, it was time to prove once and for all the artistic superiority of France over Germany, utilizing his comparative method for propagandistic ends.[163] The immediate trigger for this new project is an article by Léon Daudet entitled "L'Art Boche" ("German Art") from the March 1915 *Nouvelliste.* A noted conservative, Daudet attacked Perret's Théâtre des Champs-Elysées for being influenced by German architectural forms. Jeanneret, who greatly admired this design, suggested that Perret collect information to prove that German architectural forms were derivative of French neoclassical forms, not the other way around. In the end, it is Jeanneret who comes to Perret's defense, sketching a plan for a new book with the working title *France ou Allemagne.* He feels it is time that he clarified his own position about German design, ambivalently expressed in *Étude sur le mouvement d'art décoratif en Allemagne.*[164]

He explains in his Paris sketchbook of 1915 that this work will be composed of photographs arranged on each page in three rows and two or three columns. Building on his comparative method but using photographs, he will take the best of contemporary French decorative art–paintings, interior designs, architecture, and objects, including weaponry, automobiles, and airplanes–and prove the superiority of French over German expressions. To these he will add a small text that details only "names, dates and method employed." He expects to finance the scheme through what is now called product placement, that is, by requesting that "The authors [of the illustrated works] and stores [that sell these works] share the expenses." This was logical, he concluded, because the images in his book would be excellent advertisements for the products depicted–the French ones, that is.[165] In developing ideas for this book he draws on his *Étude,* only adding visual material. But even here he was not entirely novel, for he had already noted in *Étude* that the contemporary period was saturated with visual imagery, and while in Munich he had intended to make a slide lecture with images of modern architecture and design.

Setting up pictures in a comparative matrix would circumvent the torturous task of writing. And he would add a historical dimension by returning to 1870, as he had in *Étude,* when the French were humiliated by the Germans. He would show the flowering of French taste in the fine arts during the subsequent decades and the relegation by the Germans of art to industrial production. As in the *Étude,*

FIGURES 4.9 AND 4.10: **Sketches by Charles-Édouard Jeanneret for the manuscript of *La Construction des Villes*, drawn while in the Bibliothèque Nationale de Paris in 1915**

1900 would be the moment when the Germans awoke and began to organize for war–first in the international marketplace, then in the field. He would reiterate France's failure to decentralize apprenticeship training and refusal to base that training on experience. He would point out that Germany had reorganized its schools and apprenticeship programs after 1900 into new schools, associations, and expositions, all sponsored by the state. The book would be

> an album that should be the synthesis of all the activity of the two peoples during this historic period. The arts are the image of the people.... Let this publication be a mirror in which one sees oneself and measures one's rival.... The verdict will be clear.[166]

To get the illustrations he needs, he turns to Carabin and Perret. Carabin responds on December 11, 1915, that he will send him an account of French design beginning with the Exposition Universelle of 1878 and ending with that of 1900. Jeanneret should supplement this by reading magazines, newspapers, and books from the period. Apparently Jeanneret took Carabin's advice seriously. He began intensive library research in La Chaux-de-Fonds, concentrating primarily on the creation of a wide-ranging list of illustrations. Perret responded on January 17, 1916, with a list of French architectural monuments of

LA CONSTRUCTION DES VILLES

Esquisse de 1910 page 31
Textes de 1910 abandonnés en 1915 page 36
Textes de 1910 conservés en 1915 page 69
Résumé de 1915 page 161

ESQUISSE DE 1910

THESE [1]

La question considérée à un point de vue élargi, exprimant le rêve de l'homme de vivre en société *afin d'en obtenir une amélioration de son sort.*

1) Les hommes se groupent dans le but d'en retirer des avantages.
2) Les faibles de corps [2] ne seront plus dès lors destinés à périr ; ils payent leur tribut à leur façon.
3) Conséquence : création d'une réglementation, des lois.
4) Dès lors, sécurité, et ses conséquences : plaisirs, aspiration à l'idéal.
5) Telle est la ville idéale, *qui fut*, quelques fois déjà.
6) Mais les abus surviennent. [3] Plèbe, aristocratie : crises. Puis XIXe siècle et [4] industrialisme à outrance ; crise sociale. Déséquilibre actuel [5].
7) D'où sort un immense désir de mieux : les nobles idées dites utopiques.
8) Ne pas conclure du désarroi actuel pour déclarer tout effort inutile, au contraire.
9) Le XXe siècle annonce la puissance des institutions communes. Chacun sera un membre actif, participant de la vie publique, puis de la vie intellectuelle.
10) D'où un élargissement considérable à effectuer tout ce que nous faisons maintenant.
11) Il en [6] découlera : une ville politique, une ville intellectuelle. Halles pour réunion. Maisons du peuple. Salle de spectacle. Promenades et quartiers de beauté à l'usage de chacun. Nouvelle conception des écoles : Beauté et contact plus grand avec la nature.
12) Car il faudra l'Education.
13) Conclusion : Respect de la [7] patrie, atténuation des motifs de haine. Elévation générale du sentiment moral.

1. Nous regroupons les éléments d'un sommaire présentant chaque partie en quelques lignes et les éléments d'un développement schématique du propos
2. *de corps* adj. ult.
3. suppr. *Crises*
4. nous ajoutons *et*
5. esquisse *d'où s...*
6. nous écrivons *Il en* au lieu de *D'où*
7. nous ajoutons *de la*

FIGURES 4.11 AND 4.12: **Title page and thesis of the manuscript *La Construction des Villes*, by Charles-Édouard Jeanneret**

the nineteenth century, essential examples of what he assumed was Jeanneret's major argument: that in France new materials and building techniques led to the development of new architectural forms. Perret's list included all well-known iron and glass structures, such as Labrouste's reading room in the Bibliothèque Nationale, Baltard's Halles Centrales, Dutert and Contamin's Galerie des Machines at the Exposition Universelle of 1889, and Perret's own revolutionary Théâtre des Champs-Elysées.[167]

During the summer of 1915, Jeanneret was also researching *La Construction des Villes* in the Bibliothèque Nationale. [FIGURES 4.9 AND 4.10] The notebooks recording that research consist of sketches and enumerations of engravings and plans, what amounts to a list of images: plans, silhouettes, and bird's-eye views of cities and of details to clarify particular points.[168] There is no particular order: Bruges and Nuremberg, gardens from around the world, Rome and its environs, classical sites, the Champs Elysées, the Place Vendôme, Venice, more gardens, the Carthusian monastery d'Ema with its gardens, Pompeii and Pisa, the Patte Plan of Paris, Versailles, Rouen, Peking...There is a long section of illustrations from Camillo Sitte, garden cities and linear cities, and finally, the Acropolis. [FIGURES 4.11 AND 4.12]

In 1915, while he still believed the war would soon end, he produced a promotional brochure, or *précis*, for *La Construction des Villes*.[169]

It includes the following line, used earlier when praising Strasbourg and garden cities, but now attributed to William Ritter: "To create, as in commerce, a demand, a city has the architect it merits (W.R.)."[170] In other words, if a city is to be commercially successful, then it must hire an architect of merit to arrange its general appeal as the developers of garden cities in Germany had. It is the ensemble under the control of one architect that reappears as essential in Jeanneret's thought. He reveals his debt to both Sitte and L'Eplattenier for their belief in the role of art in the beautification of cities, but he shows new orientations as well: he is concerned with modern materials, the role of the engineer, the issues of utility and hygiene. He does not propose to offer new rules or technical advice, but to create a "demand" for "urbanism" by awakening the public to ask new questions and pose new answers. Because Jeanneret believes that architecture is an intellectual activity, he will, he says, work on the reader's mind until collaborative efforts result and new ideas are accepted. A good government, he argues, supports new ideas and a bad one refuses them.[171]

His mode of argumentation, he says, is simple: he will study examples from the past until he understands their causes and effects. He uses a series of telegraphic expressions: "The task: the power of Art. The city being the field of action, to make it become the field of emotions....The arousal of feelings through forms, colors, sounds; the arousal of feeling in the city."[172] In this new writing style, more telegraphic, simplified, and argumentative–heavily influenced by that of Adolph Loos–he makes his final escape from the laborious task of writing descriptive prose. On January 19, 1916, he would confess to Ritter that "I like more and more this style of writing through suggestions, agile and sharply indicated."[173] This new style places emphasis on the verb, rather than the adjective: it stresses construction and action, making the flowery phrases of his 1910 draft material for *La Construction des Villes* obsolete, demanding that they be stripped of superficialities and masks until the basic structure of thought is laid bare. This exemplifies Jeanneret's increasing use of the mask metaphor. He had used it in 1912, announcing his need to break with L'Eplattenier; in 1914, in speaking of his new line of architecture; and again in 1914, in praising Perret's Théâtre des Champs-Elysées in his article "Le Renouveau dans l'Architecture." To rip away masks was to lay bare a structure, whether of an argument, work of art, or personal relationship.

There were other troubles with the *La Construction des Villes* manuscript besides floweriness. L'Eplattenier's primary idea in the construction of cities was beauty. But beginning in 1910, Jeanneret saw there was another element, equally if not more important: utility.[174] An ardent follower of Sitte, L'Eplattenier would have argued that utility degraded pure art and served only commercial ends; Sitte assigned "space" pejoratively to the engineer and the hygienist. But having broken with L'Eplattenier in early 1914, Jeanneret could now openly admire the engineer and the hygienist. Indeed, as already seen, in writing to Ritter he increasingly praises the engineer. Sitte and L'Eplattenier maintained that the struggle between the aesthetic and the practical was irresolvable, but in his 1915 brochure Jeanneret advocates for a new unity to be forged out of art and utility.[175]

His trip to Constantinople in 1911 had been one rupture in his study of cities, his disagreements with L'Eplattenier a second, and the outbreak of World War I a third.[176] Nevertheless, by 1915 he was trying to publish both *La Construction des Villes* and *Voyage d'Orient*, and was counting on a wide audience for both. The demolition of the northeast regions of France had made the reconstruction of cities imperative and prompted the Dom-ino scheme.

Developing a new plan for *La Construction des Villes,* Jeanneret judges that much of his original thesis is useless. Germany, which had inspired it, is now an enemy. He drops the critical analysis of La Chaux-de-Fonds, which had been L'Eplattenier's idea anyway. The section on cemeteries is eliminated; he enlarges the section on implementing plans. He proclaimed to Ritter on November 17, 1912, that he believed contemporary cities were nothing but publicity campaigns: "The skyscraper, Pathé [producers and distributors of cinema], the phonograph will triumph...and men of affairs and the German societies of construction."[177] Thus garden cities can no longer be considered an antidote to the commercialization of urban space or to real-estate speculation based on "American street plans," and the section on garden cities, although not entirely dropped, is inserted into another section dedicated to trees, gardens, and parks.[178]

Yet, as reconstituted by Marc Emery, the manuscript of 1915 retains much material from 1910, and so remains an ambiguous work.[179] The material it retains—even extensive reference to Camillo Sitte—reflects Jeanneret's developing, sometimes contradictory thoughts on urbanism, encyclopedic inclusiveness of historical material, and growing awareness of how the city's form affects the vision of spectators.[180] He is still applying lessons learned in Germany about the unity of the ensemble that subordinates all individual expressions to the whole, and is still enamored of Sitte's analysis of winding streets and blind squares, but is also thrilled with the straight line and right angle, and comments on these two—the picturesque and the sparely Euclidean—often appear contradictory.

He divides the 1915 manuscript of *La Construction des Villes* into three parts, reviewed in some detail below. First, general considerations; second, a lengthy analysis of the constituent elements of the city, supported by historical materials; and third, implementation procedures. In the latter he discusses his interests in engineering and modern machinery, which point toward the city of tomorrow.

PART 1: GENERAL CONSIDERATIONS[181]

Like its brochure, this work is dedicated to "the authorities"—government officials—as well as to architects. It is they who must develop harmonious ensembles, enabling the city to eradicate incoherence. In this introduction, he narrows his message to the tracer of city plans (who is interchangeably the geometer, engineer, or architect), for it is his responsibility to offer citizens the joy of living in a well-made city.[182] He calls on the architect, engineer, painter, sculptor, and poet to collaborate, and likens the tracer of plans, applying rhythms, forms, and colors, to a musician with his notes or a painter with his palette.

The plan of the city is a work of art with an ideal, and shares in the same laws that govern the other arts: those of fitness, equilibrium, and variety. In the city, the tracer of plans must do a lot with a little, knowing that all is relative and depends on making a perfect adaptation to the given context. Borrowing from Loos without attribution, Jeanneret utilizes the example of clothing: "Considering that a man richly dressed will only appear such surrounded by companions soberly dressed, [the city planner] will know the value of contrasts."[183]

PART 2: THE CONSTITUTIVE ELEMENTS OF THE CITY[184]

This part of the book is divided into five subsections: (1) introduction, (2) division of land into blocks and lots, (3) streets, (4) places, and (5) walls of enclosure.

1. INTRODUCTION[185]

Jeanneret lists the constituent elements of the city.[186] Cities must reconsider the urbanism of the nineteenth century and redirect their development according to more rational means. The nineteenth century based the problem of the city on grandeur and beauty, but also discovered the necessity of hygiene. It developed regulatory controls, the distribution of drinkable water, street cleaning, and so forth–yet the twentieth-century planner has fallen behind in hygiene. He must solve the problem of smoke and smells from factories and railroads; the circulation of streetcars, vehicles, and bicycles; the use of wind, sun, trees, and water to produce places of tranquility and repose. To master these diverse elements, it is necessary to make them concur in a useful and beautiful end.

He summarizes: the first task for the tracer of plans is to choose districts worthy of housing, those good for factories, those needed for grand commercial arteries and for the business center. He must reduce the incompatibilities between them and focus on the important but generally misunderstood problem of circulation. (Implicitly, he has divided land uses of the city into the four functions of housing, industry, commerce, and transportation that will become staples of CIAM's [Congrès Internationaux d'Architecture Moderne, or International Congresses of Modern Architecture] functional city of 1933). One must research the shortest routes for vehicles and for pedestrians, enabling the two networks to intersect without harm, all the while facilitating rapid commercial transactions. Points of orientation are also necessary: public buildings distributed according to their services, their forms expressive of their aims, become perfect landmarks. Then the plan of extension must be considered, its major lines of development protected by law. Such a regulatory plan is the result of the complex science called "La Construction des Villes," which studies the division of land, streets, places, monuments, walls of enclosure, bridges, trees, gardens, parks, and cemeteries, which the subsequent study examines in detail.

2. DIVISION OF LAND INTO BLOCKS AND LOTS[187]

When land is divided into blocks and lots as the city expands, the planner ought to be guided by a few simple rules. He should reject acute angles, because they yield only hideous and meager surfaces on which to build. Obtuse angles are better, except they leave acute angles in opposite lots. Hence the right angle is the best solution for lots: it determines reciprocity among the contiguous parts and creates the most favorable intersections of streets.

3. STREETS[188]

Jeanneret calls this the most important chapter because streets endow a city with charm or ugliness. As we move through the streets of a city, we find cause for enthusiasm and dreams, or a heaviness that makes that city detestable. He cites some lines from Sitte, who values irregular terrain. Architects object because regularized parcels are the easiest to develop. But if they know the elementary rules of the art of making plans, it is often on irregular ground that the most interesting solutions are created, because there the architect must use all his wits: he cannot merely draw parallel lines in a machinelike manner. This passage contradicts Jeanneret's claim in the previous subsection that the right angle is ideal, and begins to make the manuscript an ambiguous work. He appears to be unable to shed his obsession with curved and picturesque streets, absorbed from L'Eplattenier's teachings and from reading Camille Martin's translation of Sitte.

The street belongs to everyone, Jeanneret asserts. From this right of the street stems the obligation to develop specific organs adapted to diverse needs. "It is a question of making the roads practical, especially for beasts of labor charged to carry heavy burdens, and to avoid for men fatigue and boredom."[189] Flat designs must be avoided; the planner must become a geometer of three-dimensional space.

Commercial streets should be spacious, allowing for traffic flows, yet at points should become containers of intense activity. Streets that pedestrians use should be straight, connected by subtle intermediary capillary flows. Such considerations produce Jeanneret's first rule: "The width and slope of streets can–ought–to vary and…a system of streets all of the same width is appalling."[190] Taking an example from sixteenth-century Anvers, he remarks that

> the question here was not to divide the ground into a mosaic recalling a game of checkers, but one considered streets, the city being a living organism, as large arteries: the main points being united through main streets, [and] innumerable small commercial canals, lanes, bridges and covered passages establish the shortest and most natural, communications between all the points.[191]

He next considers the issue of boredom and advises that the planner must play with optical illusions. Changing impressions and surprises are the best palliative for fatigue. He examines streets short, wide, convex, or concave; side streets; parallel streets. He provides diagrams that he refers to in a repetitive fashion. Finally he concludes that nonparallel, well-proportioned, curved streets

> give the richest impression in varied aspects: finally the eye will have something on which to rest, and therefore, seeing this, will become interested in the architectural motifs of facades: instead of being in a street as if in a desert, where the eye grasps nothing if it is not the obsessive flight of four lines to a point on the horizon placed on a surface without limit, the traveler will experience a comfortable feeling of finding himself entering a vast chamber with changing tapestries.[192]

He recalls the roads that peasants trace in order to come to town, a memory from Florence. Utility alone is the peasants' guide. Their best roads follow the slope and consider the climate, effort expended, and maximum speed. They are never drawn by utilizing a taut string. Their line of mounting is subtle, always making a decorative effect in the countryside, forming intimate relationships with hills and valleys. The tracer of plans for the city ought to follow such lines, allowing the city to express that it too is a natural creation.[193]

Throughout his analysis of street form, Jeanneret makes reference both to Sitte and to Marc-Antoine Laugier, the seventeenth-century city designer who taught that accidents vary the picture and that relations and oppositions, regularity and variety, must be part of the plan. Jeanneret argues that perfectly aligned streets are planned by uninspired architects, who allow cold uniformity to prevail because they have not followed Laugier's maxim: "Grand order in the details, but confusion, fracas, tumult in the ensemble."[194] Laugier's actual claim was somewhat at variance: "It is therefore no small matter to draw a plan for a town in such a way that the splendor of the whole is divided into an infinite number of beautiful, entirely different details so that one hardly ever meets the same objects again, and, wandering from one end to the other, comes in every quarter across something new, unique, startling, so that there is order and yet a sort of confusion, and everything is in alignment without being monotonous, and a multitude of regular parts brings about a certain impression of irregularity and disorder which suits great cities so well."[195]

Jeanneret comments that he has not offered a set of techniques that constitute a method. He has offered advice and sometimes rules, but this is not an explicit method, because the lay of the land must always guide the geometer. He must dream of its future construction and envision its ruin if future builders do not follow his ideal–thus he must impose laws to guide its development.[196]

He admits that he is often reproached for returning to the picturesque and not staying with the modern progressive layout of cities, but retorts that one can just buy a copy of the journal *Städtebau*, the official advocate for Sitte's art of building cities, and review in its pages what modern plans of city development are all about. One will come to understand

> that the life of man in the city is not a theory, but a reality lived everyday, and that man...cannot be treated as an abstract element in an algebraic equation; that his dreams can not be enclosed in a design of elementary geometry.[197]

Therefore, Jeanneret believes the checkerboard city will gradually disappear and administrative concepts will be transformed. It is only then that the straight street will take up its rights:

> The straight line, the most noble line in Nature, but justly the most rare! The solemn columns of a forest of pines; the horizontal of the sea; the grandeur of the immense plain![198]

The straight line is grand and beautiful when it is the exception and when it is closed at its end by a glorious structure. He offers as an example the Champs-Elysées crowned by the Arc de Triomphe, or the Parisian boulevards of Napoleon III. Since the second law of beauty requires the feeling of embodiment or enclosure, the straight line must not plunge forward to infinity–its length must be reduced and its extremities enclosed. Small cities ought to renounce the monumental street, and everywhere geometers ought to use the straight line modestly.[199]

4. PLACES[200]

Camillo Sitte, at least as translated by Camille Martin in *L'Art de bâtir les villes,* called for the reconstitution of what he called the "irregular" places that stem from medieval times. Jeanneret believes that Sitte's book ought to be required reading for city administrators, but since its French translation is out of print, he proposes to review the laws Sitte–

in fact, Sitte and Martin–established based on principles of aesthetics and utilitarian requirements. He lists three main categories that must be considered in the construction of places: first, the tranquil places in the midst of the network of streets; second, the thing of beauty; and third, the crossroads, or collecting point of several streets.[201]

He devotes pages to this analysis of tranquility, wondering, to begin with, why there are no longer public places like the forum of antiquity, the commons of the Middle Ages, or the cathedral square. Why is intellectual and political life today confined to journals and newspapers? Why can the factory worker only hope to recuperate from the day's work at home, but not in public spaces of the city? And why have the few open places of the twentieth-century city been allocated to the automobile?[202] He turns to Sitte for advice.

The indispensable principle that creates a beautiful place is that of embodiment: something graspable by the eye. "A long straight street not enclosed, is a non-existent volume for the eye, by consequence inexpressive."[203] Unity must be created by later additions to these open-air rooms, the enclosed streets; they must respect what has preceded them, not be thrown together like universal expositions.[204] He prefers the intimate cathedral square in Ravenna to monumental places such as St. Mark's in Venice, the Signoria of Florence, or the Palio in Sienna.

Public spaces, whether intimate or grandiose, delicate or colossal, must also engender emotions in the spectator–they must be a thing of beauty.[205] Here Jeanneret comments on the emotional effects of materials, comparing the Frauenkirche in Munich and St. Mark's Square in Venice: one city, wanting to manifest its power, erected a rude, red-brick cathedral with a huge, ninety-seven-meter wall that crushes the spectator; the other, hoping to enclose its power in a glorious crown, built a fairyland of gold and marble, dazzling the entire world with its glory.

During the Middle Ages, the same spatial principle that marked the Frauenkirche, that of affirming grandeur and dominance, became generalized throughout Europe. It required that the space at the foot of a cathedral be much smaller than the breadth of its facade, allowing it to overpower the place. Spectators arriving at these facades were suddenly confronted with massive structures that added to the emotional effects of their beauty. Understanding nothing of these spatial laws, the nineteenth century set about disengaging the cathedrals of Europe from their abutting structures. Notre Dame de Paris and (a slightly different case, discussed by Jeanneret in detail) the cathedral of Ulm were profaned by those who demolished the small, surrounding structures from which they obtained their grandeur, and left them wallowing in open space.[206]

If a cathedral survives the devastations of these disengagers, another threat comes from the architect-archaeologists.[207] We think we can wake up the soul of past ages with materials and workers from the twentieth century. But these are works, as Ruskin taught, belong to all of humanity; they should be protected from the architect-archaeologist as much as from neglect. Ignoring this, Ulm was degraded and Notre Dame de Paris devastated.

All cities have places of glory where the arts come together; here, too, Jeanneret draws from Sitte.[208] As in a domestic interior, there are two sorts of rooms in the city: an intimate room where one lives, and a grand reception room where one parades. The intimate room will be filled with irregularities, revealing a variety of tastes and desires, while the grand reception room should be marked with a unity and clarity that only geometry can confer. Each object of luxury that is placed in this public room plays the role of an ornament, one that relates to all the objects surrounding it, but, being the most precious, must carry the spirit of place. An ornament is made of "forms playing in beautiful volumes under the caresses of light"; its use of materials pleases the heart.[209]

A monument is an ornament for a grand public space. Jeanneret lists a few rules offered by Sitte that govern the ideal placement of a monument in a public space. It ought never to conflict with the circulation of vehicles or pedestrians, yet should be placed so that a spectator can admire all of its sides. Jeanneret takes a long tour through a variety of cities, from Berne, Florence, Venice, Nuremberg, Salzburg, Pompeii, and Rome before concluding that "*The center of the place was always free* and all the monuments are grouped along its edges."[210]

Sitte makes an exception for places of absolutism created by royal decree that celebrate the cult of the individual.[211] What makes places such as the Place Vendôme or the court of the Louvre exceptional is that they were built all at once. Hence they carry the power of centralization, for "L'État, c'est moi"; they speak the lines of a simple geometry expressive of *unité*.

5. WALLS OF ENCLOSURE[212]

Walls hold a special place in Jeanneret's urban poetics, and he dedicates several pages to their treatment. Utilitarian preoccupations have caused this simplest means of construction to be forgotten. The wall of enclosure is capable of "evoking the most varied sentiments": it is capable of beauty, even splendor. But today, enclosing walls are too thick.[213] Neighbors use too complicated means, or disparate materials such as dry brick, artificial stone, or iron grilles. In the eighteenth century, one knew how to make tranquil and simple walls. High walls of masonry make the street charming and offer the eye, wanting always to rest on surfaces, a sense of cohesion.

> A wall is beautiful, not only because of its material beauty, but also for the impressions that it evokes. It speaks of comfort, it speaks of delicateness; it speaks of power and of brutality... and sometimes it holds back mysteries.[214]

PART 3: MEANS OF IMPLEMENTATION[215]

In the third and last section of the manuscript, Jeanneret draws together the "simplistic aphorisms" of art and utility, the realms of the ideal and the real. There are, he begins, two factors that make cities ugly: prejudice against art and misconstrued procedures of construction. Art and economy have most often been treated as incompatible, as have art and hygiene or art and utility.

But art needs utility in order to be grand. For good collaboration, however, one must differentiate among types of beauty. Some structures are beautiful even though they have no pretension of being artistic, for their construction is perfectly congruent with their purpose. A factory, for instance, is made of vast supports of granite that carry its open interior, its means having been adjusted to its ends. There are added accessories, such as chimneys and pylons, and all of this can be arranged in beautiful proportions, making the factory beautiful. We admire the beauty of locomotives or airplanes, dynamos or race cars, because we read their anatomy clear and simple. What is true of the factory is true also of the aqueduct, bridge, or reservoir:

> Aqueducts and reservoirs are capable of beauty because their cubic volume, the materials out of which they are built, in brief their organism, requires equilibrium, repetition, strength, simplicity, so many essentially architectonic factors.[216]

Jeanneret shifts to the question of drafting technique. The engineer (the tracer of plans) ought to express in clear images the reality of the territory under his control. In most cadastre offices the city is represented by simple traces that locate the forests, grand routes, and houses on paper, but the contour lines are in such a light color that they often describe absolutely nothing at all. This almost-blank paper allows the geometer with his square and compass to trace out streets in straight lines that slice through contours.[217] German cities have introduced radical reforms in tracing out plans for their suburban extensions, including contour lines and site specifications.

The present, Jeanneret believes, is more favorable for the construction of cities than any past time. Finally the game of chance has been discredited: though it may have created some picturesque beauties, it has also spoiled many a city. But since artistic tradition is presently dead, confusion reigns.

> The cruel reality is the absence of a logical program which consists of projecting into the future, of discerning through calculation the future needs of the collectivity. The duty of directors is to prepare the site where the realities of tomorrow will be born.[218]

In Germany, and sometimes in England, the process of the construction of cities has been taken out of the hands of unprepared and irresponsible administrators and placed in the hands of architects who are artists.[219] These men have to imagine the future of a city, to discern the steps required to move forward, and to satisfy the contemporary spirit with modern conceptions. They require awareness of the lessons of past works, the artistic feeling of a painter, and the three-dimensional power of a sculptor. And their work entails constant sacrifice, for they know they will never see their life's work completed.

Jeanneret concludes his manuscript as follows:

> The rationale for the development of cities ought to be placed within *living, responsible* hands. It ought to finally leave the administrative sewer where everything is *anonymous*, dead, sterile. The future of a city is too lively a question to be resolved by a dead organism.[220]

La Construction des Villes was never finished or published. While performing his research in the Bibliothèque Nationale in the summer of 1915, Jeanneret uncovers the work of late-nineteenth-century urbanists such as Patrick Geddes, Theodore Mawson, Raymond Unwin, and Joseph Stübben, as well that of the more contemporary authors Marcel Poëte and Eugene Hénard.[221] It now seems to him that he has nothing to add to this already extensive discourse on "urbanism." As for his visual project, *France ou Allemagne*, the nationalistic book of comparative photographs, he finds he has been upstaged by Geddes, who has already promoted the use of visual-comparative materials in studying urban development.[222]

His ideas about the didactic nature of images would also be eclipsed by the exposition "La Cité reconstituée" (May and June 1916), organized by the Musée Sociale, which focused on the work of Geddes.[223] Jeanneret thought to display a mock-up of his Dom-ino project at this exhibition, but Perret advised that it was not an appropriate venue. It was a reconstitution of material from the "Cities and Town Planning Exhibition" in Belgium, which had been destroyed with the onslaught of World War I, and comprised a vast, chronologically arranged collection of engravings, watercolors, perspectives, photographs, drawings, and plans concerning the construction of cities. All of this outpouring of comparative and visual material was arranged so that the viewer could diagnose the problems of urban development.

Not only did the exhibition's methods anticipate Jeanneret's, but its intentions did as well: it sought to win public support so that postwar reconstruction could proceed efficiently, based on rational town plans and industrialized building techniques. To this end the exhibition held several design competitions, including a design for an industrial village in the north of France and for the reconstruction of villages in Belgium.[224] Jeanneret found that the Musée Sociale, a group of social reformers, had been an advocate since 1908 for the rational planning of French cities, and had drafted legislation to implement their goals. They considered the planning of cities and questions of hygiene, open space, and comfort to be of prime importance to the physical and moral development of the French. In advance of Jeanneret, they had already turned to the lessons of Germany. However, they had also looked at Belgium, where a subtle sense of art and utility had been combined in the renovation of towns. Hygiene and beauty, transportation planning and real estate speculation, and plans for suburban extensions and workers' quarters were all principles of urban planning identified by the Musée Sociale.[225] *La Construction des Villes* was clearly not going to be as revolutionary as Jeanneret had believed, and thus would not provide the hoped-for road to Paris. It is not surprising that in 1916

Jeanneret gives up on *La Construction des Villes, France ou Allemagne*, and Dom-ino, which were all conceptually linked.

VI. THE DOM-INO PROJECT

While Jeanneret was in Paris during the summer of 1915, restructuring *La Construction des Villes* and conjuring up ideas for *France ou Allemagne*, he began to fill his sketchbook, Carnet 1: 1914–1918, with notes and drawings for the Dom-ino project. Intensive development of the scheme seems to have taken place from August to December.[226] Hoping to find a model for peasant housing, Jeanneret studied–as his sketchbooks recount–a work produced by the Musée Sociale and organized by the statistician Alfred de Foville. *L'Enquête sur les Conditions de l'Habitation en France, Les Maison Types* (*Inquiry into the Conditions of Housing in France, House Types*, 1894) was a social, economic, and cultural investigation into the defining characteristics of a universal "house-type," that of the French peasant. Social engineers, under the umbrella of the Musée Sociale, thought that if one controlled all spatial aspects of peasant housing–social, economic, and technical–then the behavior of the inhabitants would be improved as well.[227]

The weather is beautiful the autumn after Jeanneret's return from Paris, and he writes to Ritter suggesting that he, the historiographer of Slovakia, must come to Sague in order to draw the admirable architecture of the region, its windows, village corners, and colors.[228] It is not known if Ritter made the trip to study vernacular architecture. On October 13 he casually mentions he has "forgotten" to tell Ritter about Max Du Bois, an engineer in Paris, and Lambelet, whose father was a director of a cement factory in Beaumont sur Oise.[229] Speaking as if these were new acquaintances, Jeanneret explains only that Du Bois is the founder of the Societé Béton Armé (SABA) and that he might be interested in working with him.[230]

Jeanneret has already sent Du Bois detailed Dom-ino structural drawings for comment. But the Balkan invasion on October 3–11 has dashed his hopes that war would soon be over so reconstruction could begin.[231] In the meantime, he works on a promotional sales brochure, ever hopeful that some means of escape from La Chaux-de-Fonds will materialize. As if to warn Ritter that he plans to flee, without specifying how, on November 2 he sends him a copy of a letter he has just received from a disgruntled subcontractor who complains that all Jeanneret has done for four years is to defend the interest of the subcontractor's clients as if they were his (Jeanneret's) clients. Jeanneret executes whatever he believes to be his (aesthetic) duty, and this has cost this merchant dearly. So he will no longer do business with Jeanneret. He only wants to be banal, no longer driven crazy by Jeanneret's demanding arguments.[232]

Jeanneret asks Ritter how he should judge this incident, which is typical, he says, of many others. He notes that his mother has come to the conclusion: "You can no longer remain in La Chaux-de-Fonds, you are unpopular."[233] Her list of infringements includes his swaggering manner of dress, collection of articles from the East, l'École d'Art affair, and the protests of his subcontractors.

He is waiting for some news from Paris about "cement" (i.e., though he does not say so specifically, word from Du Bois), but nothing comes. He will write to inquire what is happening. He comments cryptically that he chooses to say no more on the matter. He reports that he is working on his writing from ten to twelve each night and has placed on his working desk, cleared from the daily activity, his third small "feuillet de lettres" (his manuscript of *Voyage to the East*).[234]

A friend has shown him the *Grand Revue* of October 1915, in which a M. Storet (with whom he has corresponded) admiringly quotes long passages from Jeanneret's *L'Étude*. Yet Jeanneret wonders: what is happening with those in Paris, why no response from Du Bois about the necessary calculations on the Dom-ino scheme? [235]

On December 8 he asks Ritter to speak seriously about the typewritten brochure he has recently received. It is an urgent matter, and he will come if Ritter sends word. He swears that he wants to quit reinforced concrete and just attend to pastel drawings, but he is looking for a subject, because to draw in pastels one must have a subject![236] Even as he writes to Ritter of his preference for painting and writing, he has been developing a sales brochure to promote the Dom-ino project–and sends him the published brochure in November. Meanwhile he is pestering Du Bois to complete the necessary engineering work and to obtain a patent for the Dom-ino idea. And he continues to develop design specifications for Dom-ino, writing Du Bois in mid-October that the idea can be applied to large-scaled villas at no greater cost than that of workers' housing, and that the idea can be used for urban designs as well. He is so pleased with the order that arises from using standardized units such as windows, doors, slabs, and posts that he exclaims: "Order, rhythm, and unity reign in our invention."[237]

Du Bois files the application for the Dom-ino's patent on January 11, 1916.[238] Yet Jeanneret continues to write Ritter only about painting and writing. He admits that he likes more and more the style of writing by suggestions, agile and incisive indications written in a telegraphic style. This is what he finds in Ritter's writing on the small village in the Marais. Plain, simple, words in a line delivered with speed–these are becoming touchstones in Jeanneret's own writing and have already made his manuscript for *La Construction des Villes* problematic.

In the middle of February he writes in jubilation: some good angels have just placed in his hand a yellow envelope with a clean draft just typed of his "souvenirs" of Athos and the Acropolis. He allows himself to drown in this dream of the Orient–but he no longer seeks to write "a student's notebook," but "the book of a student who wanted to believe in his master." (This is an oblique reference to L'Eplattenier, who had finally spoken to him after two years of silence).[239]

On March 20 he writes that he had just sent off a letter to Paris concerning the Cité Reconstituée exposition, where he proposes to construct on the Jeu de Paume one of "our" Dom-ino houses. Given the geopolitics of the war and ever-hopeful that his scheme will see the light of day, he remarks that Poland and Sicily are now the cardinal points of the map that may direct his future, for they too may need his Dom-ino scheme. Beyond that he sees nothing happening, because La Chaux-de-Fonds is without hope. He has just passed some dreary weeks making a design for a competition but not finding the resources to ply his trade, hence every effort comes to nothing. There are only eight days left to complete everything for this competition, so he must work all the nights. It will be a project in "the Swiss style" with a grand roof and windows divided into bays (*à meneaux*) with small panes of glass.[240]

Two days later he thanks Ritter for his comforting words and writes that he is still desolate–not only in terms of the competition project that is supposed to be made in the Swiss style but also regarding his inability to make a good plan for his life. He confesses that he abandons himself to these sad things... his mother often says to him that he is no good... and a kindly friend of his father's tells him that he has an "irascible character." He agrees. He exhausts himself by imposing a strict order on all that he does, perhaps an unreasonable request.

But he feels his trade calls for it. Moreover, he has never been able to do any work with "the smile of Joconda."[241]

During most of the spring of 1916, Jeanneret fails to visit Ritter, explaining in letters that he is sick at heart. As for his work, he writes, he has reached an impasse: to please people is to profit from the sordid affair and to sacrifice himself for money. To do what one feels should be done displeases everyone (apparently a reference to the disgruntled subcontractors).[242] On July 4 he announces that he has new work, the Scala *cinéma variété*, but the client is a "hyena" without much money who plays a lot of dirty tricks. Jeanneret is losing sleep over it and finds the work scarcely inviting.[243] The next month, he has yet another assignment: a small villa (the Villa Schwob).[244]

For relief he writes to Ritter, asking rhetorically how long Europe has been enraptured with the Bosporus–for this mythical place is still full of life for him. He has been reading Ritter's work on the painter Carrachi, and it has made him think of the Bosporus. One can travel along the western bank of that water, he comments, and say that Asia is over there! This dream of the East still captures his fascination. How he would like to depart for unknown riverbanks! He confesses that he is on the edge of destruction; physically and mentally tired. But Ritter's Carrachi offers him companionship. And one evening he reads for some hours with Albert and friends some of his own pages on the Danube and Stamboul. That old manuscript still has life in it! When one is exhausted, to read and to draw–these are the good things in life.[245]

In the middle of September, he complains that work has left him no time to write or read since July 1. He is a slave to numbers and lines–mostly numbers, though as for the lines, he scarcely has time to trace them as they occur, without reflection. That distresses him. He finally has the opportunity to realize the goal of designing a villa the way he wants to, but his clients already have the masons on-site, who begin to dig the foundations before Jeanneret has finished his design.

He writes about wanting to publish his *France ou Allemagne*, but not before Ritter publishes his *Petite Ville dans le Marais*. Nevertheless, the mock-up (*maquette*) leaves tomorrow for Paris, where his ex-patron Perret and his friend Sebastien Voirol have made arrangements for editors to review it. As for the small *dominos en béton armé*, he comments, it is a matter of setting up a "Society" in Paris. For this reason he will leave for Paris on October 15. Now it appears that Italy too will have need of rebuilders, in which case his Dom-ino scheme will stretch from La Chaux-de-Fonds to all corners of the world: Paris, the North, Sicily, and Lombardy.

> All this in order in the end to cast in durable stones an idea put down again and again on ephemeral paper: thus it is not sufficient for a man to invent, it is necessary that he feel its realization, the feet, body, the "reality."[246]

Once again Jeanneret is being more instrumental than he admits to Ritter, for he had actively sought Perret's aid in finding a publisher for his *France ou Allemagne* in France during the summer of 1916.

On September 29, Perret responds that he has discussed the project with Voirol, who feels that Jeanneret should expect not to be paid for such a work at the beginning, but to eventually receive a percentage from its sales. Perret had an alternative solution: "My friend Ozenfant of *L'Élan* (which is going to reappear), could take charge of the printing at a low cost; in this way we would be completely free."[247] Amédée Ozenfant was at that time also an editor of the government Service de la Propagande, publishing pamphlets and booklets at government expense, and Perret noted in his letter that perhaps La Propagande might be interested in *France ou Allemagne*.[248]

From Paris, in October, Jeanneret writes to Ritter that soldiers are absolutely magnificent; marked by a virile beauty, resembling steel. "The city disagreeable everywhere it is not magnificent."[249] He continues to write about the atmosphere of war in the next letter, saying that he finds it impossible to grasp. He goes to the cinema and sees some 550 soldiers in action: they are fabulous, but it is only film. "And as one speaks with so much casualness, there is suddenly a phrase from a woman in mourning which hits you in the back: *one compares.*"[250]

He visits Perret's apartments, and from the terrace at Passy sees a small, splendid, and eternal city. This suspended garden, nine floors above the ground, is like a Jules Verne novel realized. Many things in this apartment are there in order to seduce, to impress, to make one believe in possibilities. Behrens and Hoffman cannot compete with this: they seem shortsighted in comparison, merely men of some talent.

> However the architect ought to be more than that: he is the prophet with his table of Law: he is the man who will see further than the musician, because his materials are heavier and it is necessary to make stronger foundations in order to raise and attach the architraves to the columns.[251]

He has come to the realization that the war has only just begun. They tell him "he ought not to be, he cannot be neutral!"[252]

> We have omitted in our dull morning risings, in our not so grand daily work, in our little proud sleeping place, we have omitted the moral point of view. We pass to the side of the thing, we discuss to the side of the question.... But tomorrow I will be in Switzerland and will take part in the agonizing questions of "potatoes" [i.e., the exacting questions his clients raise].[253]

In Jeanneret's next letter, on November 10, he writes succinctly that he has returned home and is working hard. Next month he will begin a shuttle between Paris and La Chaux-de-Fonds, until finally he settles in Paris. By January 26, having just returned from Paris, he writes that he has only ten days to wrap up so many affairs in La Chaux-de-Fonds. He is leaving for Paris![254] And on February 8 he sends Ritter his Paris address. The road that leads to Paris has at last been taken.[255]

Yet the very next day he writes, as usual, that he is imprisoned by hard work. And he seeks comfort, as usual, in his memories of the East, sending Ritter a drawing of Constantinople. On the back he explains that the purpose of his sketch, like that of his prose, is to show why Constantinople is so beautiful:

> A hojah swims on the waves and some little boats follow the wind in their sails. We put some cypress trees in the garden of the hojah, whose walls are stained orange and the woods daubed with somber ochre.[256]

PART 2
Life Among the Avant-Garde: L'Esprit Nouveau (1917–25)

CHAPTER 5
FORGING A SYNTHESIS OF ART AND INDUSTRY: LETTERS TO WILLIAM RITTER (1917–25)

[Ozenfant] said to me, "Jeanneret, it is necessary to paint." With the firmest tone, with the force of a friend. There is only freedom in painting. Can you ever make a work of freedom in architecture, can architecture achieve a strong expression of the freedom of art, an expression that moves in a good direction, all the effort of a man, all his passion, his strength, his entire life? No! Thus it is necessary to paint.

–LE CORBUSIER

Paris is so provincial!

–LE CORBUSIER

None of Charles-Édouard Jeanneret's writing projects turned out to be the path that led to Paris, although they did help introduce him to various intellectual and official circles. Instead, he made the leap when his friend Max Du Bois arranged for him to work in the Bureau d'Architecture of the Société d'Applications du Béton Armé (SABA, Society of Applications of Prestressed Concrete). Here he was to offer architectural advice and supervise construction of buildings, dams, bridges, and concrete transmission poles. Du Bois and Jeanneret also created the Société d'Entreprise Industrielle et d'Études (SEIE, Society of Industrial Enterprise and Studies), which researched the uses of reinforced concrete, constructed industrial buildings, and operated a brick factory in a suburb, Alfortville, near Paris.

Jeanneret finally moved to Paris in late January or early February 1917, at the age of twenty-nine, and settled at 20 rue Jacob.[1] He arrived just when the Parisian avant-garde was regaining its prewar strength, and discovered suddenly that painting was the central passion of his life. Despite this newfound clarity, his letters to Ritter are ambivalent. On the one hand, they express his enthusiasm for being a man of affairs: exploring ways to apply reinforced concrete, directing his own brick factory, and, as the war draws to an end, becoming involved with city planning and reconstruction. On the other, he is increasingly absorbed in the world of art, often painting after leaving the SABA office, working until the wee hours. He would eventually attribute his loss of the sight in one of his eyes to these efforts, although he had earlier trouble with his eyes, as we have seen in Chapter 2.

This struggle to honor art and industry at the same time appears to both animate and torment him. He becomes acutely aware of his generation's need, especially after the war, to be "constructors," involved with practical matters of industrial development and reconstruction, but also desires to express himself artistically and admires the rigor of Ozenfant's aesthetic theories of "Purism" (allegiance to which might, incidentally, place him in the midst of the Parisian avant-garde). He remains enthralled by both worlds. Will he be a painter or an industrialist? Or can he forge a synthesis?[2]

Although part of avant-garde Paris, his letters to Ritter express isolation. He appears to be becoming as puritanical and strict as the aesthetic Purism he begins to adopt. Ritter does not appear to be supportive of Jeanneret's new direction in either art or writing. Jeanneret continues to send him his journal in installments, but his entries have become somewhat tedious–short and repetitive. His belief that he can do great things is dogged until 1925 or so by the fear that he will never achieve his "destiny." His need to confess seems inexhaustible as he swings between elation and despair. It does not help that Ritter believes Jeanneret's avant-garde efforts are not as revolutionary as Jeanneret imagines; his proclamation that "all has been said, all has been done" (i.e., before, by others) comes as a heavy blow to Jeanneret and may have been the final reason for him to stop writing his letters of confession.[3] He never cuts this friendship entirely, but in 1921, at the age of thirty-three, he is sure of his own, independent way: there is a new "duel" to fight with those who "command or control today."[4] It will be four and a half long years before he actually achieves control of his creative impulses and veering emotions and begins to push the world around him in a new direction. By that time his confidence is high, and his writings are appearing frequently in print, narrating the world of tomorrow into existence for a wide public.[5]

THE BOREDOM OF WARTIME PARIS

Shortly after his arrival, Jeanneret writes Ritter of the strange boredom of wartime Paris, musing on how concern about oneself diverts one's thoughts from the front. (In an aside, he apologizes for his preoccupation with business affairs.) The Latin Quarter is sad; not like a cadaver, but like a fantastic vest bought for some odd reason and worn once that remains in the closet as a troubling witness, staring out at you. Even the prostitutes are far from enticing, although he includes a drawing of one on a train whom he found appealing. He would like to paint four or five of these so-called "jaguars," paintings that would be full of color. [FIGURE 5.1, p. 693]

Paris is quiet but full of assurance: terror of the sort that preceded the battle of the Marne no longer soaks up one's strength. War rules but is not too bad, except for some gunfire in the distance. Nevertheless, it gives rise to much complaining, and all the great leaps of energy that marked the beginning of the war have contracted. He would like to be a soldier–not to be heroic, but because the equipment is so alluring. The officer has set the style by the cut of his jacket. But all the cafés of Paris have such dirty windows, and he feels the need for comfort.

> One is snared by an overwhelming desire to create beautiful images: reality becomes prosaic. I would like to see this evening in the fog the skyscrapers of New York. Paris is so provincial!... To surrender oneself to passionate adventures. And wisely on Monday to restore everything to normality.[6]

He is impatient as ever about his work: each day, he complains, a page falls from the calendar that one had been told about when one was twenty. Nevertheless, he continues to paint, to pursue a dialogue with himself, and to think about Ritter.

One warm Saturday at the end of May, he sends Ritter a postcard from Chartres. A long letter follows the next day. This cathedral is symbolic, he exclaims: its stones speak of tragic heroism, of man's titanic effort to express his own damnation. Its courses are like unachieved thunder, a clamor that no one listens to. How far away those centuries seem![7] He wonders what it would be like if one day all (personal) hope were extinguished by the passage of time: "one counts when one is thirty that there are some things that one has not done; a page has turned, a page not filled."[8]

He is restless about love, life, work, and pleasure. War has put an unwelcome damper on his ambition. He is driven to paint, in this land of painters, sometimes until after eleven at night. He reads, in the calm of his old deserted house, some verses or prose: gripping and strong, soft and nostalgic. And one is aware of being careful of what one says, of selecting the correct word. But this constant preoccupation with oneself means that life passes on the streets without him. He would like to live a good full life, like all those brave boys and confident girls who fill the boulevards every Saturday night, but "one cannot give one's body to these easy girls.... Instead of throwing semen into this public bucket...one would want to caress them softly. One would certainly be mocked!"[9]

Yet Paris feeds him, and he interprets what he sees in his own special manner. The stones of its palaces, embankments, bridges, great Gothic churches, and the Roman church of Saint-Sulpice "sing to you of the time of the individual–his epoch, his ideas, styles, and hates. The Individual. It is there in stone; it was detested; but the centuries have made friends with it."[10] Compared to what he mistakenly thinks is an individual endeavor, not a corporate effort, the present is grotesque: men are assembled into packs set against each other. He would like to find a way to escape, to let time pass and to wait.

He says he vaguely remembers a letter he wrote to Ritter from Pisa, after his voyage to the East and Rome, before entering the Gothard tunnel and receiving the kiss of L'Eplattenier. Apparently still feeling pangs of guilt, he repeats that he has finally broken the strings of attachment to his former mentor, although many of his comrades have not. His life has moved on: "One does not sow seeds that do not develop."[11] Everything will improve when the war ends.

Jeanneret expresses his gratitude to Ritter and Ritter's companion, Janko Czeda–models for those who know how to see. Lessons are to be learned from their commitment, works, and labor. For those whom they have touched, the lesson will remain. He speaks of hope:

> Days of clarity will come, although this clarity may only be within oneself. It remains until the last hour, joy of hopes to shine one day, when normality returns [after the war]. The

> cathedral of Chartres touched me with the effect of the most terrible struggle. Do not say that the Gothic is serenity. It is a poignant and titanic battle...Chartres is a life of willful forces and obsessive optimism, of tight fists and set jaws.[12]

Yet Jeanneret also continues his complaints: Paris is without music, unless one counts the frantic tic-tac of typewriters in his office or the rings of the telephone. There are pianos in many apartments, but only noise comes from them, never melodies. He is irritated in this wartime city and can find few distractions. "Will I always be in eternal instability?"[13]

> Is it necessary to wait...hands crossed over one's belly as God would want? Experience has taught me that vigilance, faith are necessary, never to deny the initiative of the explorer. Therefore we eternally make an act of effort...and we keep on the horizon, very far in the Midi, an outcropping of white rock, a roof of roman tiles, and a palm tree, some eucalyptus, some mimosas.[14]

Perplexed as to why, Jeanneret feels that he already has some adversaries in Paris. He already has twenty or so associates, both good and bad, so he is no longer completely unknown; but he remarks that it "is necessary to read some works about America, in order to have the sense of space, of refreshing air."[15]

He wonders, is there always a conflict between the admiration of magnificent things of the past and feelings of life and power, of purity and passion, in things of tomorrow? "I live this paradox of adoring the unknown and of constantly locking myself up in the old dust of things."[16] There was a time when Ritter answered his questions, when the scales fell from his eyes. He arranges all Ritter's letters on the corner of his table as if they were a manuscript. Ritter often gave him courage, but he is no longer answering Jeanneret's letters, and Jeanneret wonders why.

Another note of anxiety, a personal one: he glimpsed in the metro a woman he might have loved, the second time in some months.

> You wish for me a great passion. Thank you. A woman beside the immense pleasures of the heart is only a stupid apéritif.

> I prefer the bordello: animal-like and the water closet...I do not dissociate love from storm and danger. I seek something other than a curving mouth and some eyes.[17]

In his next letter he writes about the tension between industry and art. In his industrial enterprise, he must search tirelessly like a committed traveler on an unknown road. Always the same problem: to establish the opportunity, to inspire confidence, to execute what one is allowed to do–then, perhaps, success will follow. It is also difficult to work in his elected field, art, be it writing or painting. He mentions Perret, the master who taught him to love pure and simple architecture like the Parthenon, but adds in a somewhat melancholy tone that if one day Jeanneret is defeated by some unknown fatality and abandons that magnificent structure, he would like it to be remembered that he once believed in it. He has written it all down in an article and hopes for Ritter's comments. (In February 1908, in a letter to L'Eplattenier, Jeanneret had attributed his understanding of the Parthenon to lessons learned while traveling in Germany. Now, under wartime censorship in France, he downplays German influences whenever it is strategically convenient.)[18]

As if mention of the Parthenon was a trigger to dream of other things, he begins to write about painting–about Delacroix's depictions of the Orient, about the vendors' carts full of summer opulence, tomatoes, lemons, bananas, peaches, and yellow and violet plums, the splendors from Persia. One dreams of Chinese junks and *caiques* (Greek fishing boats) on the waves of the Orient, of ports overwhelmed by the sun, and the ambiance of women behind curtains overlooking the port, in the depths of obscure rooms. "One constantly dreams and desires; one must paint all these dreams."[19]

Jeanneret returns to La Chaux-de-Fonds to supervise his projects there but feels rejected and criticized, even finds himself labeled "anti-Semitic" and an "intellectual." Tomorrow he will be thirty years old; at this advanced age he has experienced what it is like to mix art and Industry, but he has decided to turn toward the Latin concept (France) and leave the Werkbund to the Boche (Germans), and so hopes to finally attain a little harmony.[20]

He will not, however, ever be able to completely separate art and industry, France and Germany. He may conceive of France as the place where he can reach fulfillment as an artist, but it is industry and the lessons he has learned in Germany that speak to him of the future. In the years to come he will continue to write about this ambivalence until, by 1925, he has achieved a resolution and a degree of security.

Returning to Paris, he sends Ritter a postcard of Nevers cathedral. The terrible war continues; he wonders when it will be possible to live again! Yet he confesses himself strengthened, even purified by these trying times, and holds his "star"–his ambition, his belief in his destiny–always before him.

THE WRITTEN ACCOUNT OF A "MAN FROM THE JURA [JURASSIEN] IN PARIS"

At the end of January 1918, he sends Ritter a long letter. Apologetic for not writing for so long, he encloses the journal he has been keeping since October 16. It is written in brief lines, as if he had been in daily conversation with Ritter, and opens with the remark that he makes bricks in a workshop filled with robust machines.

> The scene magnificent. Enormous gasometers, 4 formidable chimneys [of the electric company]...All of this suburb is very Napoleon I...the bureaucrat, the *lawyer,* the functionary, the architect...will be rubbed out one day, finally! I will make beautiful engravings of my factory and I will be able to talk of my "stocks" and "my sales" like a rice or coal merchant.[21]

Two days later, October 18, he journals that he is leafing through his stash of five hundred illustrations of cities that he collected in the Bibliothèque Nationale in 1915 for his intended book on the "Construction of Cities." He is jubilant: an entire world is in these old prints. If only Ritter were there to share his joy.

He does not journal for a week, being ill. But, he now writes, he is still thinking of Rome, of Michelangelo, of the tragic life, of enforced work, of an implacable destiny. His painting, moreover, is always at least ten times less than what he wants. His writing as well: he wants to fill the page, but inevitably there is white paper left over. In his next entry, November 10, he continues to complain about his inept painting, also that there are too many antique merchants, tailors, dress designers, and art dealers in Paris. His office lies in the heart of all this richness, and each day he sees Monets, Cézannes, and magnificent furniture. He becomes saturated with such marvels, and thus his evenings are wasted, without any results in his painting.

Within a few days, he turns to talk about his new SABA project, the construction of an enormous refrigerated slaughterhouse in Toulouse. Even though he is distressed and isolated in this city of luxury, especially after the death of Rodin, the great innovator, he finds the problem of a modern slaughterhouse to be magnificent, a generator of real architecture originating in America, in Chicago.[22] The slaughterhouse job is a competition, not a commission, and he doubts he will win, as his heart is not in the job and his gestures are tentative.

On December 2 he writes about the poetry of the suburb of Alfortville, where his brick factory is, and begins to describe its life:

> I entertained yesterday my driver and his father at a bistro in a corner of the factory. I had great pleasure with these honest and intelligent men. Alfortville will perhaps give me great joy; I feel alive among modern things, in the midst of the labor of arms and machines, in the flow of the river that rolls by.[23]

But he is sad in his Paris office, for he feels uncertain about every question concerning interior design. A few days later, he comments that the responsibilities of his brick factory are heavy. But he hopes it will be successful one day, and remarks that he has really matured over the last two years, and is able to give his brick business all the attention it deserves.[24]

In late 1917 and early 1918, he is consumed with business affairs. By the end of December he finishes the design for the slaughterhouse. He writes in his journal that he believes he has made a work of architecture, "Certainly my first work with the breadth of intelligence."[25] It is a victory for SABA, even though the engineers actually wished him ill; but the workers, who were all enthusiastic, convinced them it was a good piece of work. He is absorbed in Taylorism,[26] "The horrible and ineluctable life of tomorrow."[27] Though upset by it, even indignant about it, he addresses himself to Taylor: "You guide this labor toward a useful end, you who know how to appreciate the beyond [*au-delà*, i.e., the future, of efficiently managed industry and administrations]."[28]

He comments that artists judge the war differently from bankers, but the future is hardly secure. He liquidates his affairs in La Chaux-de-Fonds, is just able to pay everyone with no money left over. Hopefully the slaughterhouse will succeed and he will receive a considerable sum, so the New Year opens full of promise.[29]

In his January 24 entry he writes that the days are full of joy and sadness mixed together. He mentions for the first time the name of Amédée Ozenfant, a new friend whom he lunched with the previous day. The date of their actual meeting remains uncertain, although it was probably November 4, 1917. Jeanneret announces triumphantly:

> Yesterday lunch with Amédée Ozenfant; some doors are opened on the beautiful Paris of the future. Finally a contemporary, one of my age; one who is respected a lot. His painting is that of a mystic in the sumptuous manner of the most beautiful paint, smothered and polished as if with a burnishing tool. Cubism bears its fruits; the absolute and true form of beauty; an impeccable technique and a material form supportive of all noble ideas.[30]

Whatever the date of their first meeting, the link between Ozenfant and Jeanneret was fortuitous. A year or two older, Ozenfant was more sophisticated than the still-unformed Jeanneret and was immersed in a variety of artistic and literary circles. His father had been a builder, one of the first to experiment with the formulas of François Hennebique, the (reputed) inventor of reinforced concrete. He wanted his son to become an architect, but instead Ozenfant studied painting under Jacques-Emile Blanche. Far from ignorant of industrial design, however, Ozenfant and his brother designed the Hispano-Suiza sports car, which made a sensation at the Salon de l'Automobile of 1911. Reviewed in the magazine *Omnia* in September 1912, it was praised for its strikingly simple geometric forms and its clear and precise outlines. Its entire form had been conditioned by its function: to maximize the speed at which the vehicle penetrated space.[31]

Ozenfant was the founder-editor of the review *L'Élan*, which made a brief appearance in 1915. Inspired by the Ballets Russes, he would be among the participants of the shocking benefit performance of "La Parade" in 1917. The spectacle nearly caused an uproar when Picasso's cubist scenery was revealed, when Satie's dance-hall melodies were heard, when Cocteau's story unfolded. In the third year of war, the audience was not amused. The press reiterated: the escapade that tried to make the audience laugh in the midst of war was treasonous, baring scandalous German influences, and demonstrating far-from-patriotic behavior. Ozenfant was however an excellent guide to the Parisian avant-garde, one who shared interests to those Jeanneret was

254 TOWARDS A NEW ARCHITECTURE

"AMERICA"

A Racing Car of 250 h.p., capable of over 160 m.p.h.

and likely to endure. That is the story of ten ages of work organized within the family unit; and the story too of every past age up to the middle of the nineteenth century.

But let us observe to-day the mechanism of the family. Industry has brought us to the mass-produced article; machinery is at work in close collaboration with man; the right man for the right job is coldly selected; labourers, workmen, foremen, engineers, managers, administrators—each in his proper place; and the man who is made of the right stuff to be a manager will not long remain a workman; the higher places are open to all. Specialization ties man to his machine; an absolute precision is demanded of every worker, for the article passed on to the next man cannot be snatched back in order to be corrected and fitted; it must be exact in order that

FIGURE 5.2: Amédée Ozenfant and his brother designed the chassis of this Hispano-Suiza sports car, featured in *Towards a New Architecture*, in 1911.

FIGURE 5.3: Photograph of Amédée Ozenfant—who searched for a more pure form of art, or "Purism"—place and date unknown

just beginning to express. Soon the two would join forces to formulate an aesthetic for modern times. [FIGURES 5.2 AND 5.3]

Most scholars assume that Perret introduced the two men, hoping that Ozenfant would publish Jeanneret's *France ou Allemagne*. However, the context where they met–a meeting of Art et Liberté–has seldom been explored.[32] This group of progressive artists, architects, musicians, and writers was formed in 1916 with the express intent of protecting Auguste Perret and the fashion designer Paul Poiret from attackers–such as Léon Daudet–who attributed German influences to their work and called them unpatriotic. This group intended, as did Jeanneret in *France ou Allemagne*, to establish the rational, constructive, and synthetic nature of French classicism as a base on which French modernism would rise. It was a perfect milieu for Jeanneret: having felt suffocated in La Chaux-de-Fonds, he was eager to utilize his talents in the propaganda war against Germany and craved to absorb the lessons swirling around the modern artists of Paris, even those whom, like Picasso, he did not quite understand.

Meanwhile, the war continues, and Jeanneret writes his second daily journal (eventually sent to Ritter at the end of March 1918). He notes on January 31 that the Gothas–a type of biplane bomber first deployed by Germany in 1916–had bombed Paris the night before, and people had been massacred.[33] Nervousness has settled over the city, a sense of gravity and fear, for the planes would certainly return.

> I assisted, yesterday, at the Pont des Arts, during the bombardment. I understood nothing about it. There were about fifty people on the bridge to listen to the roar of the cannon, the explosion of enormous noises close by, to see the glow of fires. There were bombs at hundred meters from us; one did not know what bombs were [before this]. Fog and moonlight, smoke, searchlights, and fatigue enveloped their minds, it was morning that one understood the disasters.[34]

All calm and resolute enough: but that evening, alone in his office, he believed he would crack. Calm soon returned, and he could write that if ever he did break down, then he must protest against this low and cynical life that had attracted him.

> It is necessary to imagine the soul of a life that one would want to have. It is necessary to make it superior, to see only higher.

> And to be detached, to be turned away from everything that has nothing to do with realizing something superior; and there is only the abstract that will survive and it is necessary that one suffers.[35]

He shifts to news of his slaughterhouse: of the nine contestants, only two remain, and he is certain he will win because the other scheme costs twice as much as his. "Mine is a personal creation, it is alive, it is an organism. The others lost because they were incompetent or based on insufficient research."[36] In spite of his confidence, he does not win the competition.

Entry March 4: He is alone, his days filled, as usual, with intense work. He loves the "laboratory" that is Paris.[37] He is painting women with curls of blond hair, paintings his friends Max Du Bois and Barthelemey Rey find idiotic. Jeanneret believes, however, that Ozenfant will soon set him straight with respect to painting. Although romantically lonely, he believes that his days reveal many eventful signs and that his "star" holds steady.

Within a week, on March 14, he journals shocking news: his friend Rey has been killed by a Gothas as he ran to help in a raid. "I saw yesterday the effects of the last raid. For the futurists a new form of expression: enormous shock, explosion, and the dead strewn with flowers."[38] At the first sight of these raids, wisdom takes charge and you go down into the underground or into a cinema. "Those pigs the Boches!"[39]

He begins to describe Ozenfant. He can write on the Metro; he is a painter with faith in all the "ists" and "isms"; he works on a portrait for three months. In his office, crudely lit by electricity, he sets up his American music stand, his card indexes, his telephone, and his box of paints and his easel, grouping everything around a stuffed armchair. During working hours he runs a couture shop where all the grand courtesans come. At midnight he takes the Metro home. He inherited a considerable fortune, but only last year he was swindled out of it, forcing him to work. [40] Meanwhile "One lies in wait for a raid, they are on the alert. And I hardly feel like going to sleep."[41]

Jeanneret sends Ritter this second journal but complains on March 23 about keeping his journal, which Ritter suggested he do for him and Janko. It requires Jeanneret to think of them every day, yet he believes they will not be content with what he writes.[42] He lives in constant turmoil, is fragmented by the everyday tedium of his business affairs, yet must keep his dream above the morass. He sees some interesting things, but they leave him indifferent because his heart is not in the writing. "I am not a spectator, not a chronicler, but an activist. To write, it is to revive the past, what it was by the hour."[43]

Obviously his need to write, to rid himself of a sense of isolation and boredom, even fear, has apparently not elicited sufficient response from Ritter. Jeanneret says he is troubled by Ritter's long silence, explaining it as part of the exile from his former home in Munich that Ritter must suffer. When there is a chapter of sadness, everything becomes gloomy and the bad spreads everywhere. Ritter has been given a great soul in order not to fall into nonsense and pieces. He will be rewarded after the war, and Jeanneret hopes to read his works that are born of it, which are sure to be dense, each page offering something on which to meditate.

As for Jeanneret's own life: everything he does is in quest of money–although he does not have a lust for money. He hopes that he will earn money in order to show Anatole (Schwob), Meyer, and Spellman that he too can be strong and successful. As for art and ideas: he loves and practices them ten times more than in La Chaux-de-Fonds. He designs and paints, between eleven o'clock and midnight. His work goes well–though the citron yellow is surprising in the morning.[44]

In mid-June he sends Ritter his journal pages from May 6 to June 13. He says that although they have not met for the last ten months (the time during which he has been sending Ritter his journals), he thinks of Ritter's intense happiness and his immense sadness. His idealism, his great faith in spite of everything, his courage and confidence–all these memories of Ritter guide Jeanneret with a soft hand. As for his own small lamp of faith, it shines always to his advantage. Paris allows him to have heart and feeling for things and life.

His reports in his journal for May 12 is as follows:

> My thoughts about art are raised toward material expression: a form, a line always esoteric. My attempts are deformed, deceptive. All my imagination is at work. I want clarity, a clearness, which only tolerates a pure crayon, rhythmic discipline, and moderation of color. And I paint some orgies. My women have a bestial lasciviousness, thick, in rut. And I stop myself from touching a nude woman, for her back, breasts, mouth are of an adorable material, are like a dream that I will spoil with my rude fingers. My excess of feeling remains mostly outside of the bed

> and sadly I have a more intimate joy to thrust my tongue into a large fresh rose.[45]

His courage deepens when about to begin a work of art: "To throw in a compressed twenty minutes, his cry onto paper, violent spots of red ochre and blue, it was an intoxicating promise of a possible talent that will ask only for time to be expressed."[46]

Within himself, he says, the decision has already been made. His instinct is to remain at home, fleeing from all futile comrades. Or if he goes toward the attraction of the boulevards, where all the women are, it is to find an expression of the most ideal mathematics of his dream of beauty.

His entry for May 22 is full of the beauty that spreads over wartime Paris: the soft voluptuous robe of a bride, flowers, birds, sirens, bombardments. The spring weather is so pleasant that it makes everyone smile, yet it is sad to think of the soldiers, millions of them under the treacherous gas and the cannon. Though the world is crazy, full of hatred and fury, so much sunlight ought to lift the hearts of men of battle. He writes also that he has new work in his factory. He is often ashamed of the success that has come to him. He comments that he has finished with lascivious paintings and is devoted to more Catholic tastes.[47]

Guilt about L'Eplattenier still haunts him. It was his first mentor's dream to make each of his students strong. He still believes he was a loyal, even enthusiastic supporter, and is sorry for the complete break between them due to their differing ideas. Evidently L'Eplattenier does not want to renew acquaintance, while Jeanneret believes he is ready. But the sirens wail, their magical and opulent noise spreading over the city; cannon, trumpets, and the night cover over these thoughts. There is the sound of cannons far away; the Boche aircraft approach, and within five minutes will be here with their dirty, idiotic bombs.[48]

In early June, Jeanneret's diary is awash with bouquets of flowers from the Midi (the regions of the south of France). They are

> my ostensible witnesses, my living friends, my companions of voluptuous hopes, my animator of bad thoughts: roses always my flower that I kiss; tulips that I question and insult…they [tulips] always speak to me of gambling houses or bordellos.[49]

He remembers the wonderful bouquets that his mother made (interjecting at this point that his endless descriptions of flowers covers over the noise of faraway cannons, where the horde is unleashed in a drunken and lusty rut). They ravished him, their freshness astonished him, his artistic soul took inspiration from them.

Ten days later his journal entry is all business: he had visited a colleague whose machines work better than his. On the second of August, he writes another letter, sending what he now calls his "idiotic journal" from June 27 to July 28, which will enable Ritter to read the "barometric situation" of the last five weeks as experienced by a "man from the Jura [Jurassien] in Paris." These are days of forced idleness because of a labor strike in his factory. Hoping, he says, to forestall criticism of his painting, he tries to explain the new direction his artistic work has taken. In comparison to the work of Ritter, who designs landscapes and makes geological studies, Jeanneret designs bottles of Medoc, coffee pots, and pipes. Moreover his palette has been reduced to four colors: red ocher, yellow, blue ultramarine, and black. He begins to taste success as he approaches a method. Soon he will paint in oils, and in three or four years maybe he will demonstrate something and exhibit his work in public.[50]

His journal entry for June 27 mentions that Ozenfant has just arrived from Bordeaux, where he has been for some months escaping the bombs over Paris. They spent almost the entire two days he remained in the city together.

> He said to me, "Jeanneret, it is necessary to paint." With the firmest tone, with the force of a friend. There is only freedom in painting. Can you ever make a work of freedom in architecture, can architecture achieve a strong expression of the freedom of art, an expression that moves in a *good direction*, all the effort of a man, all his passion, his strength, his entire life? No! Thus it is necessary to paint.[51]

But Jeanneret asks, "Will I have the courage?" Ozenfant said "It is necessary," adding his voice to those who over the last five years have said "You will do well, one day."[52] Ozenfant represents a discipline of steel. "Everything in life shows me the only force possible [is] of discipline, of order, of clarity."[53]

But two days later there is a surprising entry. Just when Jeanneret has decided to dedicate himself to painting, it has been proposed that Du Bois, Bornand, and Jeanneret take charge of the direction of SABA.

On July 4, he comments that it is (American) Independence Day and describes how "the American troops, by the thousands, march on the Place de la Concorde."[54] They have come from afar to die for God or some equivalent; the huge crowd was stupefied, and slowly won over. The blue horizon of the Ile de France spread itself over the black and white of the crowd, the soldiers covered with flowers, and their bayonets encircled in garlands. The crowd of women, in the end softened by this strange brown and massive vision, cried out "The soldiers, our soldiers!" Their trumpets blasted out, an airplane made loops above the obelisk of Luxor. "All over the country there is an immense enthusiasm and confidence....These troops broad of shoulder like some machines were here to give Hindenburg the poignant terrors of a nightmare.[55] These people have heart. The others, the Boche, have too much reason, and no comprehension of life, which is about joy and the sun.

Jeanneret repeats: "Ozenfant said to me: 'Jeanneret, it is necessary to paint.'"[56] Years pass, and five years from now, it will be necessary to have taken a position, yes or no, with regard to art, and to have achieved something. Four days later, in early July, he is in despair–the situation at the bank is no good, the brick factory in Alfortville flounders. All work is stopped until he receives some advice.[57]

On July 22, he writes he was required to show his designs of architecture–his slaughterhouses, his Dom-ino scheme, and his Villa Schwob–to a group of Swiss authorities. All of these projects were on crumbled and ripped paper, which caused him a good deal of distress. Instead of his new life as a painter, his old life as an architect continues. He unrolled his old papers, and was accorded a lot of praise. Evidently, the review committee was surprised that he was so accomplished, for within a week, the Swiss had given him money.[58]

On July 26 he writes he has met Ford, son of the famous American, and reveals his lifelong insecurity about being self-educated as an architect.

> He asked me "you are an architect with a diploma from the government?" "No Monsieur, I detest the École des Beaux-Arts"; "Excuse me, but I know that you are an architect, with a diploma from the French government."[59]

"SO YOU NOW MAKE PAINTINGS."

On September 3, Jeanneret complains that he sent Ritter a good dozen pages of his journal on August 2 but has not heard a word about them. He will leave for Bordeaux in ten days to visit Ozenfant–his life has reached a pinnacle after so much bad luck.[60] Soon, in a postcard from Bordeaux, he describes the city as pompous and at least two centuries behind the times. If he was not so tired, he says, he would write in a happier mood. Finally he can see good horizons in his life, and he will soon cease describing himself as a character in a Balzac novel.[61]

Back in Paris by October 1, he writes triumphantly:

> The curve of my destiny has inflected toward painting. This last year of solitude had led me through some experiences of which the subconscious effect...lead promptly to a decision. Decision made, realization also but still incomplete. In fact, I design every day now from 1 a.m. to 5. In hiding, unknown to the world. The fact of having the brick factory, the architectural office, and of being named a short while ago as delegated administrator of la Société des Applications de l'Everite with vast offices on the Boulevard Malesherbe, implies the chopping up of my days, and...when I am at my painting, I am somewhere else. I keep [the fact of painting] an absolute secret, it would be a scandal if anyone knew that daily I am entertaining the muses.[62]
>
> [FIGURE 5.4, p. 693]

Both Ozenfant and his "star" have led him to this decision: to paint. It was Ozenfant who told him to work at his painting. Ozenfant has the most lucid mind that Jeanneret has ever met:

> He is the master that I have searched for such a long time.... Two years older than me, he has had a life which allies itself with mine. He only wants to see in me an equal, only a comrade as developed and as advanced, but one in which the means of expression have not yet found their directives. Thus he teaches me the trade and I am, it appears, a good student.[63]

Furthermore, Ozenfant, already known among modern painters, having "reviewed" the work of Picasso and Apollinaire, wants Jeanneret to mount an exposition, just the two of them in a new gallery (the Galerie Grégoire). Jeanneret has therefore dedicated himself to the task:

he must show work of the most rigorous discipline, for theory must be evidenced in examples. The date of the exposition has been settled: November 15, although at the time of writing, Jeanneret admits, he has only one design ready! He explains to Ritter that this is not going to be an ordinary exhibition of some paintings.

> We proceed according to a doctrine. And this doctrine, which allies us intimately, which gives us such confidence as it is based on strength, obliges us to publish it in order to explain the tendency of our work. It will appear anonymously as a publication of the Galerie Grégoire, in order to shine a light ahead of us.[64]

It has not been for naught, Jeanneret believes, that the two have lived lives intensely "modern," both appreciating the grandeur and destiny of good modern work, its intelligent conduct, its formidable, grand calm to come. They have searched, not far from cubism, for an expression appropriate to this view.

> And we have considered the great works of the past, created out of slow and concentrated work, with judgment always present, passing through the laboratory researches of the last years, in order to join together in a modern view the same works of industry, born of so much labor, order, will, ingenuity, and clairvoyance.[65]

The first volume of their doctrine, *Après le Cubisme* (and as it turned out, the last in their series of "Commentaries on Art and Modern Life" ["Commentaires sur l'Art et la Vie Moderne"]), will introduce the exposition and contain ten to fifteen photographic illustrations. Jeanneret explains that the rubric "Modern Life" allows them to treat subjects of their own selection. Thus the second volume will study the question, "What is architecture of the time?" or "something analogous with an interview of Loucher or of Citroen. The third volume: 'the techniques of painting.'"[66]

Jeanneret expresses his concern that Ritter will laugh at him, mocking his attempts. So he affirms that he and Ozenfant understand the facts of industry, its serious purpose, and they will resist all the easy buffooneries–too subtle and lazy–emanating from Apollinaire and his crowd.

Then Jeanneret returns to the (unmentioned) task at hand: treating Ritter as an instrument in his new endeavors. Having explained their manifesto, he now asks for help. They want to republish it in a widely read journal, preferably *Mercure de France*, but its publisher, Alfred Vallette, will reject them if they contact him directly. It would be better if Ritter could introduce Jeanneret (reintroduce him, actually). Their booklet will appear on November 15, so its republication in *Mercure* would have to be sometime after that date. In conclusion–as is his custom when making a poignant request for aid–Jeanneret draws up a resumé of the case. First: Does Ritter think he can introduce him to Vallette, who already knows Ozenfant, publisher of the review *L'Élan* in 1915–16? Jeanneret calls this the best review made up to that time, and believes that Ritter will receive Ozenfant enthusiastically as would Vallette. He has kept a collection of *L'Élan* in order to show to him. Second: Could Ritter name other personalities who might be interested in these "Commentaries on Art and Modern Life"?

Jeanneret ends by mentioning again his thrill that the door is now opened on his future. And he reminds Ritter, "You know well that you are at the base of this evolution. Therefore are you not content?"[67] Jeanneret closes on a refrain: "An aim higher than ever to attain and now no longer a spectator, but an actor."[68]

A few days later, on October 4, Jeanneret sends Ritter his journal for the period from August 7 until September 5, 1918. This contains his daily comments up to the time he leaves Paris for Bordeaux to work with Ozenfant, and fills in some of the details about how his second "evolution," the decision to give up architecture for painting, was achieved.[69] On August 7, he writes that if it were not for Ozenfant, he would have drowned in Paris. His friend Goudouin, who is a cubist and fills his paintings with the most violent visions of life, has the soul of a great architect and piles up prisms into monumental images; he also appeals to Jeanneret. Ozenfant in the calm of the laboratory, Goudouin in the full maelstrom of life: these two painters set Jeanneret's defense of his timid body against his daring spirit. This, he claims, is his crucifixion.[70]

The next day he writes in his journal from the Romanesque town of Doué-La-Fontaine, where he has gone to contract some work with the American army. How he admires the rectilinear and disciplined arrangement of houses, recalling the grandeur of Caesar. Jeanneret the architect can understand this place, and feel how idiotic many of his earlier, artificial studies have been.

> Oh, L'Eplattenier, your houses which required pinewood to become stone, with...ornamental details. Pig, go. It has all to me the same commonness.[71]

No matter how many hours he works, with little reward, he will remember this Romanesque town, its rectitude among the cypress trees carrying the lesson of how to build well, in well-matched blocks, straight and regular without cornices or small decorations. He compares this image to that of the lively American soldiers, their necks like bulls, their thighs matching columns, the beautiful complexion of their faces. They have another stature from that of the Europeans; they are built better.[72]

Jeanneret returns to Paris, but writes on August 21 that he is still in a sad stupor. He remains in a state of revolt yet does nothing. His friend, Jean Pierre de Montmollin, on the other hand, has decided to join the Legion and will experience the ultimate splendor of battles, and will die. It makes Jeanneret even sadder, struck by his own cowardice and meaninglessness. He does not act; he only assists those who do. Like gangrene, he is tied to a life of the second order.[73] Every hour proves his deficiency in matters of bravery and daring. "Never have I been so conscious of my faults, so disarmed and weak."[74]

The next day, August 22, Jeanneret returns to his business affairs. He might become the administrative delegate of a society that is forming, which should make him rich and powerful. But he is so upset about the prospect that he leaves the office in the afternoon and goes to the cinema, where the random and fantastic adventures of an American film thoroughly distract him. When he exits the theater, it is the hour of women on the boulevards, women of summer, with their adorable, pointed, and dancing breasts, with their rosy faces as in a painted work–but all this only increases his irritation.

> I do not have a sou in my pocket. I live daily with fifty thousand francs of merchandise at Alfortville, and fifty thousand francs of debts. And these women, it would be so sweet to fondle them; these imbecilic women so beautiful. I am without a sou, and my factory is closed but the benefactor appeared three weeks ago to give me the strongest and best machine that exists, I will triple the output of bricks. I live in hope this will solve everything... I have such a crazy need of working at design, new torture of the

> inquisition, how to design? How to place the mind in the necessary repose in order to conceive a living work?[75]

He knows that Ozenfant, still in Bordeaux, waits for him to bring the design work he has achieved (for "Commentaries on Art and Modern Life"). But this very day, in the midst of all this turmoil, someone has proposed to put at his disposal within five months an entire factory to manufacture furniture after the war. Moreover, his slaughterhouse design finally enters a phase in which it may be realized. And the philanthropic organization "Renaissance des Cités" has charged him and Goudouin to make plans for the reconstruction of devastated towns in the northeast of France, besides summoning him to put together a conference on the construction of factory towns.

One part of him wants to be a head of industry, to become almost a mechanic, and he knows he has already achieved considerable ground in this field. To refuse or to accept?

> But I am only thirty, and I smile at the sun; I lead a double life which is false and bad, and I will not choose. I do not have the strength. I will do everything and it will run on.[76]

Ten days later, September 2, he writes that for the last few Sundays he has been painting austere, monochromatic still lives: bottles, books, prisms. He is pleased with some of these compositions: having achieved a degree of order and truthfulness, in durable colors.

> Seduced by a landscape, an urban site in colored light, I reveal them as an organism coming from the earth, set up in prisms, animated by the play of shadow and light...they dirty my canvas. My still lives [on the other hand] sometimes attain the spirit of noblesse. Or otherwise, failure, they are inept.[77]

He notes that he leaves that week for Bordeaux, where Ozenfant will teach him how to paint in oils. As for his paradoxical affairs–the brick factory, the new machinery, the architectural office, the Société des Applications de l'Everite (Society of Application of Everite)–he has at least three banks that offer him money, yet he does not know how he will pay for the trip to Bordeaux, and he is clothed in rags. He paints on Sunday bottles full of water (not wine, which he cannot afford). But he sees "liberation." He has also been asked to make plans for the reconstruction of Salonica, and his first report has already left for Athens.[78]

He recalls being under the authority of L'Eplattenier, when his comrades at the Atelier d'Art Réunis were occupied with designs inspired by "the culture of pine trees," referring to the practice of making decorative patterns based on pine trees. And he arrived from Paris as the Messiah, the Devil incarnate, and they abused him, calling him "steamship" and also "Eternit" ("The Everlasting"), the latter name because he abolished tile roofs, made woodwork with cement and whitewash, and preached Ripolin (the name of a white paint company) against the Moorish arabesque. Eternit was a Swiss company that fabricated slabs and posts in prestressed concrete, as well as roofing materials, under the slogan "Eternity for France, her colonies and protectorates," or, more briefly, "Useful for Eternity" ("Usines Eternit").

But now his fortunes have turned, and the mocking Eternit has brought unexpected luck. Jeanneret begins a play on the words "Eternit" and "Everite," for evidently a banker has misunderstood his vocation, thinking he worked for Eternit, but in the end in spite of this mistake offers the dumbfounded Jeanneret the opportunity to be the administrator of his new Société d'Everite. He promises after the war is over an astonishing amount of activity: the rebuilding of innumerable houses, furniture design, tourist hotels on the front. Then along come the hungry wolves, his friends Du Bois and Bornand, and immediately they find a way to pilfer a part of these affairs and demand that Jeanneret share with them some of his riches to be gained in the future. He reveals a dislike for cooperative business adventures, preferring independent action instead, a lifetime flaw even when cooperation was required.

Among all the activities that seem to spill over Jeanneret as the war draws to its end, his old *L'Étude sur le Mouvement d'Art Décoratif* shines forth. This work still has a fabulous vitality, he says, and because of the lessons it taught he has received work from the Ministry of the Interior, the Renaissance des Cités, Salonica, Ford, the furniture factory, and the Société de l'Everite itself. While he may no longer advocate some of the ideas it sets forth, he is not averse to using it to gain access to official circles.[79] Since the defense of French decorative arts was a motive behind plans for the Exposition Internationale des Arts Décoratifs, Jeanneret's contacts in these circles may have helped to assure that he be among the exhibitors when the exposition finally took place in 1925. Yet the Minister of the Interior, Louis Bonnier, who invited Jeanneret to give three lectures on the decorative arts and to propose educational reforms to the Ministry of the Interior in 1918, nevertheless in his role as director of architecture parks and gardens for the exposition tried in 1924 to prevent the realization of Jeanneret's Pavillon de l'Esprit Nouveau.

In his journal, Jeanneret turns from his business affairs to explain to Ritter, one more time, the direction that Ozenfant is taking in art. Only last year Ozenfant wrote an article on cubism, calling it passé. Cubism was just the ground level, but there was a new movement toward greater naturalism that would undermine it. Having prophesized such a shift, Ozenfant wants to demonstrate it in the works he proposes to exhibit. Because he expects that a lot of noise will be made by this exposition, he wants Jeanneret to exhibit his paintings as well. Jeanneret is flabbergasted–having thought that God had wanted him to make bricks, not art.

There are other things to discuss as well: for one, the Americans, who have conquered opinion and the hearts of everyone. They are truly amazing, a revelation.

> Have these people found the true life (*la vraie vie*)? I am ready to believe it.... These people are honest, strong, talk straight, and have the candid eyes of grand virgins. So the hens [French women] deflower them. And we others are the fried fish of the Seine.[80]

Paris is returning to calm–no more air raids and bombs. Now the war of communication begins. Optimism renders one egotistical, beastly, even dirty.

On September 5, he writes that he leaves for Bordeaux the next day. After ten years, ten years of constant work from which he has nearly cracked, he finally is going on vacation. Tomorrow he will travel toward the sea, toward rest and wonderful ideas, toward Ozenfant, who waits for him.[81]

His next extant letter to Ritter is written on November 20. The book *Après le Cubisme*, first of the "Commentaries on Art and Modern Life," has gone to press. "It achieves a small historic event in the world of painters."[82] Then he explains that due to the armistice, his and Ozenfant's exposition has been postponed. Most Parisians

FIGURE 5.5: Photograph of Charles-Édouard Jeanneret in front of the Galerie Thomas, Paris, 1918: The first exhibition of Purist paintings by Amédée Ozenfant and Charles-Édouard Jeanneret took place in a fashion atelier, renamed Galerie Thomas for the occasion.

have gone on an eight-day spree, but not Jeanneret and Ozenfant, who surround themselves with the most serious type of people. The other evening Auguste Perret, Jeanneret's former employer and advisor since 1909, came to visit, making him very nervous. What would this great architect think of his turn toward painting? He wonders as well what Ritter thinks of the influence of Ozenfant on Jeanneret. He had sent him the series of *L'Élan* a month ago, but there has been not a word.

For the past eight weeks Jeanneret has been leading a new life, dense, without a minute lost: "A man can do a lot if he wants to use his time."[83] Finally, "A word about Auguste Perret, he absolutely embarrassed and disarmed me: 'So you now make paintings.' I was completely babbling, stuttering."[84]

LIFE AMONG THE AVANT-GARDE

On December 19, writing from St. Nazaire, where he has moved his studio in order to work with Ozenfant, Jeanneret describes the last three months of work: he has allocated every evening from eight to midnight to designing, painting, and writing for the exposition and the book. "My designs are as formal as engravings on copper plate, without one weakness."[85] Some of his paintings take weeks to accomplish, they are so thoroughly studied and executed. Two are in oil, following the strictest of rules, full of paint and as smooth as an Ingres (although not as good).[86]

Finally, he writes, he has found his place in Paris, almost at the top of the ladder of the avant-garde; he is the business administrator of two large operations and is extremely clear in his ideas.

> Our generation begins; it is (dedicated to) action...I have put order in my ideas of art, almost in my life. I still flounder in my business affairs, for that is not categorized. But 1919 will do it. Then I will be more of a man and more ample in my work.[87]

The exposition with Ozenfant (to open December 21), plus the book *Après le Cubisme*, place him in a very advanced position among artists. But a quick aside:

> I saw the immense steamships, the movement of the port, the buoy, the cow-boys, the Americans who depart. Victory is in everything, in the disarray as well. The future is obscure. Some huge internationalist movements are striking out all over the world.[88]

He invites Ritter to their exposition of paintings at the Galerie Thomas. [FIGURE 5.5] For this first of several "Commentaries on Art and Modern Life," the announcement declares, "the task is to define the spirit of our epoch."[89] It continues:

> We live in a magnificent time, a little compromised, often misunderstood, little recognized, even misrecognized...Thanks to the scientific and industrial spirit, acting in intimate collaboration, some works of impressing breadth have been realized, some constructions of an "esprit nouveau" have been erected everywhere, bridges, factories, dams, etc....carrying within them the visible germs of a development, supporting a clear, refreshing, general beauty. Already some machines, because of their very number, give us a new gratification, a new factor in the concept of modern art.
>
> Artists remain outside of modern life.[90]

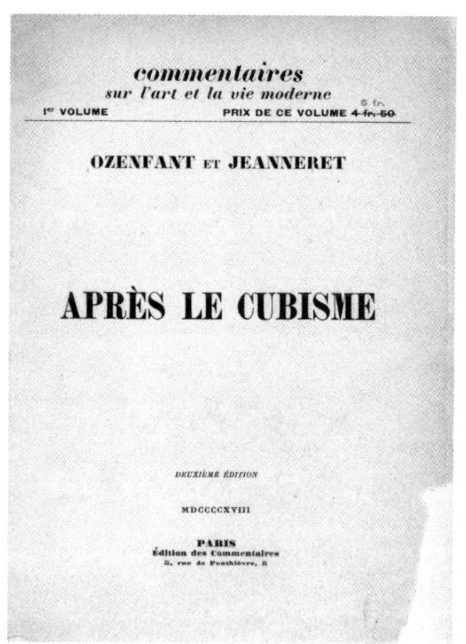

FIGURE 5.6: Cover of the Purist manifesto *Après le Cubisme* (1918), written by Amédée Ozenfant and Charles-Édouard Jeanneret

Cubism has betrayed the movement toward modern times. Thus art, the only thing that counts today, is not of the times. This first volume of the "Commentaries" will define the cure. "Purism," is about:

> A healthy art, hostile to all obscurities...while recognizing the interesting but artificial sensibility of cubism, withdraws from impressionism and naturism, and considers that laws are not constraints but "invariants," unfailing guides to obtain a static, clear, lucid, organic, general, serious, controlled, concentrated, clearly conceived and strikingly executed art.[91]

The volume *Après le Cubisme*, about a hundred pages long, will (the announcement says) be illustrated with ten photographs of works by Purist painters. It is to be the first of a series of volumes on modern life. The announcement is signed simply "The Editors."[92] [FIGURE 5.6]

On January 20, 1919, Jeanneret sends Ritter not only *Après le Cubisme* but also his journal for October 21 to January 1. He complains about Ritter's silence, wondering what has happened to him, and apologizes that he himself has been unable to write due to fatigue caused by preparing for the Purist exposition. It was a great success, and was even filmed as a documentary (he uses the word *actualité*, the name of the short documentary films produced by the Lumière Brothers between 1895–97) and projected at Gaumont's. He mentions bumping into Vallette, the editor of *Mercure*, in the streets, who claimed to have been waiting for an article from Jeanneret for at least three years, but admitted that he did not like Jeanneret's housing scheme with flat roofs. Now that the war was over, there were so many houses to be rebuilt in Picardie, the Somme, and Champagne that it would be a frightening event (Vallette said) if they all were replaced with flat roofs.

> I replied to him, "not at all, this village will be as beautiful as a machine." He rebounded, "You think so?" "Certainly, it is not a slip of the tongue; a village beautiful as a machine." He was disconcerted, groaned, recognized that "it was defensible" and that I was right, but that it was frightening. "Ah, it is not lost, your word, a village beautiful as a machine, a village beautiful as a...!" I authorized him to make of it an incendiary bomb, "It will be put as the epigraph of your article." We parted very good friends.... He sees with terror the imprint of modern life, and delights more in a life that is dying.[93]

Before closing, Jeanneret remembers a remark of Ritter's—that he, Jeanneret, had forgotten the joys of the heart, being preoccupied with constructing. He replies that the heart goes into construction. The fact is that since Jeanneret has been in Paris, he has made a "decisive evolution": his ideal, his goal has become clear. He judges that heart, altruism, and affections are all mixed up in this goal.[94]

In his journal for October 21 (included in the portion enclosed with this letter), he writes that work on *Après Le Cubisme* is almost finished. He has been working late in an intimate collaboration with Ozenfant. "I believe that we say there some strong and wise things."[95] The exposition is planned for November 15 (eventually postponed to December 21), yet he has only two works that are ready.

> I begin to realize, and to realize art, with the taste which made me love so much the factories. I aim at a durable art. My brick factory even participates there, my contacts with business, with the men who operate, with my machines. I really see before me. I found in Ozenfant a good revealer. We will work usefully, with courage and simplicity in harmony with that which we love around us.[96]

Two days later, October 23, 1918, the war is over. The Boches, he writes, have been routed. All of a sudden Paris is lit up. At the crossroads of the great streets, the electric lights have been stripped of their blue coverings. One sees day in Paris after months of black night, thick, dangerous darkness. There will be no more raids. But there is the "grippe"–since one does not call the Influenza by name. The third chapter of *Après* was polished yesterday, the collaboration intense. They drink cognac, chamomile, and linden tea–and smoke–to ward off the grippe. He has even suggested a new "Commentary" about "Linden Tea and Chamomile."[97]

Entry November 7: Jeanneret comments that the armistice is signed (with Austria on November 3, with Germany November 11).[98] Paris is struck silent, unconscious of a formidable, frightening victory that one never dared dream of. The exposition is planned for the next week: for six weeks Jeanneret has gone to bed somewhere between midnight and four in the morning. The book has been printed; no one knows about it yet, and so it will create quite a stir.[99] On November 10, a day when Paris is celebrating its victory, they mail to members of the avant-garde in Montparnasse the prospectus for the first volume of "Commentaries," declaring war on cubism. One hour later, they learn that Apollinaire had died, the supporter of cubism to whom their barbs were directed. His death is regrettable: the loss of a strong adversary, one of the few strong men among so many followers.[100]

He made that week his first painting in oil (one of the two referred to in the letter mailed with this journal section to Ritter). It will appear in the exposition and in the book.

By November 12, armistice with Germany having been signed the day before, Paris is celebrating: crowds flood the boulevards. "The Americans lead the bacchanal, hurling, dancing, and making absurd noises: [the jazz] of the blacks."[101] The French are mere spectators, generously allowing joyfulness to those who have won the war: the Tommies (British), the soldiers, and Clemenceau.

Jeanneret does not write another entry in the journal until January 1, 1920. There has been considerable confusion in his life–he wants to embrace everything, to touch all the poles of life, to be passionately involved with art and industry. New Year's day is the time to calculate, it is a threshold to cross.

> Everywhere maximum effort. Everywhere ardor. To love everything. Why not?...How I want to act everywhere....In art, I see

> clearly. Hence I gasp for breath and believe in everything. I am crazily fatigued.... Life is so very beautiful.[102]

He sends this journal to Ritter on January 20. There is a break of several months in his letter writing.[103] On April 10, he writes that he feels somewhat ashamed about his own cheerfulness. Evidently Ritter has expressed extreme pessimism about the future, refusing to make any plans, while Jeanneret is full of *joie de vivre.* He writes that he is making new plans every day, moving with constant courage and renewal of confidence. Instead of his former insecurity and self-doubt, he has made a definite choice in art and in thought. He is economical with both his time and his sympathies. While his business affairs still occupy part of each day, he reserves every evening and Sunday for painting.

> I decided to logically erect my life and I think to be able to soon realize my vocation to paint; soon, in two years, in one year perhaps. Around this decision, I organize all the rest. And I no longer run after the nightingale.... I no longer make architecture, from which art is banished for a long time: I make organization, administration, negotiation.[104]

All of these business considerations, in which he expects to have grand success, are only to allow him the freedom to pursue art. Above all he wants to be able to show results: money, paintings. "My situation in Paris is *determined.* I exist for art, even beyond my actual means. In one year it will be necessary to pay back the credit that has been accorded to me."[105]

He includes a page from his journal, written on December 29, 1918. Here he writes that although people are tired of cubism, they have found *Après le Cubisme* to be not of their taste. Behind the pseudonyms in the press, one recognizes colleagues. He claims that these things are indifferent to him–his only aspiration is to achieve something in painting with which he can be content. He closes by saying that for the last three weeks he has been completely absorbed in his business affairs: slaughterhouses, spas and vacation villages, interior decoration and mechanics. He has been delegated administrator of the Société d'Entreprise Industrielle et d'Études. "Here this journal stops for the moment–it no longer appeals to me; I work."[106]

A COMPULSION TO AIM EVEN HIGHER

Starting in early 1919 Jeanneret ceases to write in his journal, although he still occasionally writes letters to Ritter. On June 1, he writes that he has escaped the bitterness and sadness of last year. Now more than ever, he is inspired by serious research. In contradiction to Ritter, who believes that theory ought to follow the work, Jeanneret finds that theory imposes itself on the work, making it strong and demonstrative. This manifesto, moreover, involves everything that he does–the precepts by which he lives, practices his art, conducts his business affairs. This manifesto has placed a straight bar across his life. "A rule does not stand in the way, art like all creations proceeds by rules. These rules are sublime in their rectitude and their coordinated mechanism."[107]

Everywhere normality returns to Paris: theaters are full, cinemas and dance palaces open, jazz bands agitate, bistros are frequented. Today was the first eight-hour workday; some workers left at 4:30. Jeanneret wonders what they will do with their leisure time and the thirty francs they have earned. Meanwhile his double life continues: working during the day and painting during the evenings.

Business affairs take Jeanneret to Lyons, Clearmont, Bordeaux, Perigeux, and Toulouse. In July, he sends a short note describing how he sketches in trains, cafés, and slaughterhouses.[108] At the end of August he returns to La Chaux-de-Fonds for a few days to help his parents move. Due to the postwar depression and the increasing industrialization of the watch-making industry, his father's business has failed; the house that Jeanneret designed for his parents has had to be sold. He is distressed that after two years time, he and Ritter were unable to meet while he was in the area, but is happy to relate that his parents have found the most perfect house to rent–pretty, clear, and Purist. He knows Ritter is skeptical about Purism, but it is a doctrine formulated in order to guide the work.[109]

Jeanneret returns to Paris without seeing Ritter; he has been too occupied with liquidating his father's business, dealing with lawyers and notary publics, and signing documents in Bern. He did review from top to bottom the Villa Anatole Schwob; he had not realized the maturity, healthiness, and rigor this work had achieved. "This house situated in Paris would have gained me ten years, and perhaps held me to the ways of architecture."[110]

He is, he writes to Ritter, still crushed with responsibilities. He is chagrined that as for news of Ritter, he has only some brief reports about his writings on Venice and Slovakia.[111]

Jeanneret is aware that Ritter is susceptible neither to Purism nor the new direction in which Ozenfant is leading him. This is clear from his next letter, written October 13, in which he remarks that he will come to visit without Ozenfant. He asks Ritter to allow him to achieve the same friendship with Ozenfant that he has with Ritter. He believes that Ritter, even though he has declared war against his new friend, will change his opinion, for Ozenfant has been Jeanneret's companion for more than a year. And Ritter knows what that means to Jeanneret.[112]

> But I know very well that we are actually, you and me, in conflict over ideas. Doctrinaire, I have certainly become, sectarian, autocrat, but not the pope, because I have not looked for followers. I beg you only to give me credit of three to four years; I have fixed ideas, which I work to realize. You have known me nervous and upset, brusque, and quick and under pressure. While I am still the same, I am already a lot less nervous because now I have given a direction to my work...Our disagreement is only on the surface, to the contrary of those reigning between my comrades of la Chaux and me, disagreement in depth, on bases, on everything.[113]

He does not write again until December 9. It has, he writes, been a difficult year. Each second of the day is held in suspension by the hope of succeeding in business; the rest is dedicated to painting. Painting has established his destiny, and the direction has been set.[114] The year 1919 has brought considerable success to his business. He will leave the Société after orienting it toward a good destiny. He began with a check of ten thousand francs, and two years later, he has more than one million. (This refers to the Société d'Entreprise Industrielle et d'Études [SEIE], created in 1917) Perhaps Ritter can understand why he no longer is able to write. How he has aged, even taken on the appearance of an old man; indifferent to others, with a steel grip on himself! "I have become pompous [*un pompier*]–I do not believe it–but one who comprehends what the Parthenon represents."[115]

Architecture made him fearful of whatever is easy to achieve. He thinks that perhaps in ten years time he, as a painter, will make true houses, no longer asked to make houses like all the others. He has been cleansed of the dust of architecture. Now he perceives that the Villa Anatole Schwob, seen before with great satisfaction, is only tentative. There are better works to do, less banal.

Jeanneret was to hew to this view of painting as preparatory to or facilitative of architecture throughout his life. None of Jeanneret's paintings were ever accompanied by a verbal explanation, yet he would always maintain that it was through painting that he arrived at architecture, and that the key to understanding his architecture lay in his paintings, where his basic principles of design–form, color, and composition–found expression.[116] Many years later he wrote, "The secret of my quest must be sought in my painting."[117]

He now turns to write about *Après le Cubisme*. From it, he says, there will follow "work that has more precision, clarity, security, and unity. That will be for the exposition at the Galerie Druet in January 1921, at which date it will be necessary to achieve a high point."[118]

Once again he describes his hard life: he reads nothing and sees no one. There is so much to think about, to decide, to obtain, so difficult to struggle to defend oneself and to succeed.

> One is confronted with one's life, work, goals, without relief; the days are very short, the fatigue very heavy, and there are wounds in the heart, a bitterness has infiltrated it. With past joys, present sadness, in the end every animal with his suffering. What good is talking. I paint.[119]

He paints all day every Sunday, and finds that his art is becoming more precise–but he still needs more hours in the day to dedicate to it. He stops writing this letter, interrupted by the rudeness of a friend who pays him an unwelcome visit.[120]

Jeanneret's correspondence with Ritter is interrupted until March 14, 1920, during which time Jeanneret, Ozenfant, and Paul Dermée begin to plan a new journal. Writing in March, Jeanneret says he believes the interruption is probably his fault. He knows that Ritter has returned to Munich, but he does not know anything else. He has been completely absorbed in his business affairs: but his joys are not there, nor his reason for living. He lives totally in painting. His life has become so abnormal that he fears it may destroy his health. Every evening until midnight, Saturday after the middle of the day, and the entire Sunday he paints or designs. He has set before himself a difficult task: January 21 will be the date of a great exhibition at the Galerie Druet. He and Ozenfant must be successful, for a misfire would be disastrous. This task takes up whatever time and energy he has left after the demands of business are met. He has locked the door and lives like a monk, a puzzle to and forgotten by the entire horde of comrades and friends. He writes to no one.

He closes the letter by reminding Ritter what close friends they had been and still are. Even if they are apart and do not write each other very often, still, Ritter (to whom Jeanneret seems to attribute telepathic powers) must be aware of Jeanneret's thoughts even from a distance.[121]

In June, Jeanneret writes that his line of fire now comes from Paris, not from the small town of La Chaux-de-Fonds. His ambition, following a new beat, has pushed him toward accomplishing an excessive amount of work. He believes he will succeed and finds himself, on all sides, surrounded with important people in his work as well as his art. His life has a program, although the days have only twenty-four hours, and he must sleep at least seven.

> I must do everything outside of the ten hour of business affairs: to think, to act, to write, to paint, and even to take care of this small heart always crushed and bruised by other pains. When the program is grand and ruled as ours, it sets up a hierarchy of rights over time. It would be untenable, and one would break down physically and morally from it, if it would last all of life.[122]

He works every moment that he has for the exposition at the Galerie Druet. For more than a year he has not taken even half a day for a promenade or a small relaxation.

Deciding not to detail his plans for this exposition, because he fears not being able to achieve them, he says he nevertheless will be honest with Ritter. He is no longer making sketches, because he has dedicated himself to more serious works: he executes some paintings that are like extensions of his Villa Schwob (*la prolonguement de ma villa Schwob*) and is proud of his work. His attention is fixed on the Parthenon and on Michelangelo, yet he remains modest and a plodder.

> A painted work is as total as architecture. It is only because I have rediscovered and *sensed* this truth that I consented to paint and hence my entire being is occupied there. An art without weakness.[123]

Contact with intellectuals and those who speak of art are useless to him, and he remains indifferent to their opinions. He is upset only by his own judgment, because it is always severe and demanding.

He has stopped writing, even to his parents. His brother Albert, who by this time has also moved to Paris, takes care of that. He knows that Ritter understands him.

In July he writes that he has completed five paintings and has ten more to do for the exhibition at the Galerie Druet, scheduled for January 1921. He and Ozenfant are thinking of buying a hut and locating it some twenty-five minutes from Paris, to which he can commute by automobile and where he can paint. His days are a series of disjointed bits, with no time to lose, but he is very happy and balanced.[124]

Except for a postcard in August, Jeanneret does not write Ritter again until January 30, a week after the opening of their exhibition at the Galerie Druet and three months after the publication of the first issue of *L'Esprit Nouveau,* on which there has yet to be a word written to Ritter.[125] He says that he feels the need to build bridges with all those with whom he has become estranged over the last nine months of disciplined isolation. It was a formidable task to prepare for the exhibition, but their book *Après le Cubisme* declared an aesthetic, and it was necessary to put it into action. "The public reacts: praise or indignation. We have thought to be very wise, and we are treated as crazy. For the most part the impression is good."[126]

For the first time he mentions *L'Esprit Nouveau,* announcing that it goes well. It represents a lot of work, but they have wanted to generate some clarity in this troubled time. At the same time, Jeanneret has pursued his business affairs and has been engaged in many different places. He earned a fortune that would have allowed him to leave this difficult and non-gratifying life. But then the economic crisis arrived, and in a few weeks he was ruined. "From that [the threat of bankruptcy], I will gain liberty for myself, and the occupations for which I am made."[127]

After years of silence, preparation, he is in the line of fire and it is necessary to work.

> This is why I did not write. I have through my diverse activities, raised all my friends against me. The trouble of my business affairs crashes down with all the others, and cost me the harshness of those who up to now flattered me in order that I earn

> money for them. So much for them, I am not touched. I exit from all this, solid and more skillful.[128]

Now he fears, since he has heard nothing from Ritter, that he too is raised against him. He reminds Ritter that he was the first to want him to paint. He thinks that Ritter would understand his painting; he takes as much care in painting as in architecture or business, and the result is apparent. "My paintings are now mature works, controlled, well done, and solidly constructed."[129]

He keeps in memory Ritter and Janko, in Landeron–they taught him about art.

> To say it truthfully I believe that we have conceived an art, resulting from actual tendencies and opening a possible road toward the destinies of an epoch that sets more and more its shape.[130]

Now that the exposition has been accomplished, it is necessary to set another date and to achieve something even greater. He hopes that Ritter will forget the hole that Jeanneret has made in their relationship, and write to him.[131]

"ALL HAS BEEN SAID, ALL HAS BEEN DONE."[132]

On March 11, 1921, Jeanneret writes to Ritter on the letterhead of *L'Esprit Nouveau: Revue Internationale d'esthétique*, 95 rue de Seine. In addition, he sends the four copies of the journal that have appeared to date. [FIGURE 5.7, p. 694]

Over the last several years, Jeanneret has often repeated that he cares little about what others think of his painting, or writing, or financial position. Now he says this again, saying that he believes Ritter knows that his character is too strong to be injured by criticism. The claim has become so repetitive that one is led to believe the inverse: it is a shield raised to defend self-esteem. Introspective and ambitious, he has harnessed his depression to serve creative impulse. Yet he remains vulnerable when he reveals his thoughts in words or paint.

He explains to Ritter that *L'Esprit Nouveau*, which he and Ozenfant founded, was initially directed by one whom they have now fired. Its tendencies and opinions will be given an "axis" (manifesto), to appear in Number 5 and be completed in Number 6 of the review. He asks Ritter not to get upset at what he sees, but to have faith.

This is a review of the new generation, which begins to express itself with strength. This tendency can be found for the most part among painters, men of action, engineers, and economists. "Period of healthy courage and clarity, the twilight of impressionism, of symbolism, of what was aside from action."[133]

> You did not like our booklet *Après le Cubisme*. That is too bad, because what I think was there [is] what gave me my aesthetic...I believe that you will reread it with another spirit....You have a lot of fear for collaboration, collaborative work. [But that] is the reason for our [Jeanneret and Ozenfant's] success. A moral force and an indefatigable force of action, because while one relays [the information], the other works. A collaboration as intimate as that with Ozenfant can only be because of existing points of contact, strong and healthy...Outrageous lyricism is not about being an architect; I have always understood my trade in the true meaning. An architect is a controlled lyricist.[134]

Their paintings are certainly not for everyone: yet that does not concern him. He is sure if Ritter were present that after a few skirmishes, the two would arrive at an understanding.

He will send him the review on a regular basis. The review comes from another epoch, with other cares, heavy anxieties, a difficult and serious time, full of rationality. "The young people of today are serious. There is no other way. The times of Apollinaire are far away. That was cubism."[135]

In closing this letter, which is a reply to one sent by Ritter a month before, he remarks that he is grateful for their friendship. "I can not forget that you were the first to have pulled me away as much from the Pope of la Chaux [L'Eplattenier] as from a stupid trade that I would have had in building houses for whom?...But I no longer want to write anything about that. It is impossible for me and outside my way of life. You remain the only one to whom I write."[136]

Two weeks later he writes again. Jeanneret has need of support, for he has arrived at a "tragic point in his business affairs." The economic crisis has swept him up (along with his industrial activities in SEIE), and his days are dedicated to dry and difficult tasks concerning banks, shares of capital, and the hordes (a mass of critics). This time he will be drowned. How difficult it is to declare bankruptcy! Everyone tells him it is forbidden, there are already too many bankrupts, they will destroy the country. Yet he reports that to maintain "a healthy and tranquil morale...is easy for me"; "We make a great war and small enemies do not reach us."[137]

He thinks of Ritter, now residing in Aix-en-Provence, a countryside that Ritter loves so much. Jeanneret thinks of escaping this summer to Rome, when all is finished. A final note: by tomorrow Ritter will have received the first six issues of *L'Esprit Nouveau.*[138]

By July 30, once again troubled, Jeanneret writes that he has closed the door on the SEIE, gaining 150,000 francs for the society and memories of a sterile struggle.

> Therefore it is painting now. The morning remains dedicated to directing the Review. Your "all has been said, all has been done" [in art and architecture] could not have been a heavier blow. You know well that I am not at all in agreement....I am at an age when a creative precision is manifested. I take no interest in "what ought to be my life"; it is necessary that it be fruitful. One has attained the required stripes and that is why henceforth I will be in competition with those who command today. That's a good duel!...The young Le Corbusier bears fruit that I was not expecting so soon. One asks me for houses. I am conflicted about it because I desired a year's rest.[139]

This is the first time he has mentioned the name Le Corbusier to Ritter, and of course he complains about architectural commissions because they conflict with his plans to become a painter.

In fifteen days, he says, he leaves for Rome to relax. He stops writing because he no longer likes to tell so many stories about things. He hopes Ritter will send a word from time to time to mark his own stopping places.[140]

There is a gap of nearly one year in the extant letters–the next is written on April 7, 1922. At that time, apparently, Ritter was trying to decide whether to move to Paris or to Prague. Jeanneret says he is not eager to see his old friend in Paris. As is his usual manner when trying to win a point, he lists the reasons why Paris is not a good idea. First there is a housing shortage. Second, he is afraid that Ritter would be greatly disillusioned in Paris; *Mercure* is no longer up to date; the *N.R.F* (*La Nouvelle Revue Française*) is the publication of a small group that has turned in on itself. Third, the theater, ballets, concerts, and expositions now all belong to the younger generation, and Ritter will not like them.

Finally, Ritter would experience heartbreaks and indignations because he would find the Parisians not serious enough.[141]

Jeanneret is attentive to every move of the new postwar generation, with its spirit of affirmation and desire to act, its call for a return to order, its hoped-for progress toward the universal and permanent.[142] He uses all this ammunition to persuade Ritter that he would not find Paris inviting. He compares Ritter to himself and Ozenfant. Ritter's compass points south, theirs north (perhaps meaning that Ritter is guided by a southern star full of romance and sentiment, while Jeanneret and Ozenfant follow the north star of rationality and purity). For another, they are of different generations. The new movement of rationalism scoffs at things once deemed to be sacred. There is great moral health in Paris, but it despises "sentiment." In Paris, ideas, intelligence, are all the rage; this perturbs the art world and upsets defining notions.

> The atmosphere is bitter and hard, quarrels, blind jealousies, meanness, short-sightedness. One is fabulously isolated, each in his own island.... The atrocious economic crisis acts with grave consequences for intellectuals. Intellectuals die from hunger.[143]

In contrast to his intimate knowledge of Paris, Jeanneret admits he does not know Prague, another city Ritter was considering, so he cannot offer advice. He does know, however, that there are some enthusiastic young people there. It is still a place of goodwill, while in Paris everything seems to have been done and one accepts only small changes. Jeanneret turns Ritter's own criticism "All has been said, all has done" against his potential decision to move to Paris.

He repeats that he has lost the use of one eye. It makes everything more complicated.

> For the rest, I never see anyone, outside the review, where I see too many people.... I write no one. You are my unique correspondent. My days desperately filled; 16 hours. Painting, Review, business affairs... Lost all my money, cleaned out. Painting does not sell. "Le Corbusier," new incarnation seems to work; brilliant perspectives, freedom for art as much as possible.... In architecture, complete success: I am the only one of my category. Success of esteem, the press, etc. in Paris, for a stranger. All that is hardly important. Each day I am faced with a work to settle, with upsets, etc.... At 35 it is the age where one gives you credit,

> but the age where it is also necessary to produce.... Non-creators, fall, more or less quickly.[144]

This is how he forges a synthesis of art and industry: Le Corbusier, the name of the architect; Charles-Édouard Jeanneret, the name of a painter. Mary Patricia Sekler notes an important 1926 text written by Le Corbusier in which he describes the splitting of his names and his identity.

> Le Corbusier is a pseudonym. Le Corbusier only does architecture. He pursues ideas independent of interest; he does not have the right to compromise himself through deceit, through convenience. It is a being free from the weight of the flesh. He must never (but will he succeed) degrade himself.
>
> Ch. Édouard Jeanneret is a man of flesh and blood, who has had all the exhilarating and heart-breaking experiences of an eventful life. Jeanneret Ch. E. paints pictures because, even though he is not a painter, he has always been interested in painting and because he has always painted himself... a "Sunday painter."[145]

In his letter examined above, he speaks for a moment about Ritter, who has once again been uprooted and searches for a new place of rest, but he quickly turns back to himself:

> I live in some white and empty rooms, with nothing on the walls, and nothing as furniture. How practical and agreeable it is... In less than two months will appear... my book "Architecture et Rèvolution" collection of Corbusier articles in [*L'Esprit Nouveau*]. I will send it to you. You will see there my ideas on architecture reminding you that at school at 20 years old one nicknamed me "Paquebot" ["Steamship"].
>
> "All has been said, All has been done, there is not even a new transgression." It is you who wrote me that last year. Yes and no. Not for sins, not for painting: admit this curve [he draws a spiral, a combination of repetition and change].[146]

Two months later, he writes about changes planned for *L'Esprit Nouveau*. It will be shortened from one hundred to fifty pages and will no longer try to define the new spirit of the times. Each year there will also be larger volumes, of three hundred pages or so, a greater development of subjects already considered by various collaborators, but in a denser manner. There is also to be a narrowing of themes. "Henceforth, a magazine more direct, faster, more readable. Our readers are not the usual readers of a review; the speed factor intervenes."[147]

He has been able to extricate himself from his business affairs. Now his telephone rings less and architecture seems to have picked up. He has completed the designs for a factory at Auteuil, but it lacks the "shock" of the "new."

> 5 years of pause [in being an architect] makes me a good architect; I have totally lost the memory of "motif" and I compose like an old gentleman.
>
> That which I have equally lost is the art of writing a letter. A white piece of paper makes me apprehensive. One no longer knows how to raise a question without being able to follow it up, and this would lead further away; and I have acquired the fear of beautifully written epistles, finding myself more secure with my paintings and my houses.[148]

Jeanneret apparently writes only once or twice over the next two and a half years. Finally, on February 24, 1925, he writes on a very large piece of paper, calling it the "paper of an urbanist." The New Year is always good for making accounts (though he is a bit late), so he begins his list: after ten long years of painful activity he has passed the Cape of Storms and has become a very happy fellow, leading an ideal life,

> Very simply dedicated to things that I love: to paint, to make architecture, to write. 16 hours of maniacal work, never a Sunday, never a visit; in excellent mood, gay as a lark, more optimistic than ever, stubborn as a mule, and always aimed toward the same end. My mother always said to me "You will never lose the north [star]." Say it: my efforts are useful; they find an echo, very loudly...they achieve success.[149]

He wants Ritter to understand that in the middle of all this struggle he always remembers the Sundays spent with Ritter in Landeron, how important Ritter has been for him. "Wasn't it you who were the support that enabled me to make the jump from La Chaux, and to leave forever a country that makes me angry when I think about it?"[150] All the same, he trembles at the thought of meeting Ritter, and wonders what he would think of him now. He has become antisocial. Ritter might like his architecture, but his paintings would distress him. He would believe that Jeanneret has abdicated and locked himself away in a dry formula.

> I would try to persuade you that it [a painting that took months to achieve] contains all the power and passion, of impatience for former things so summarily done. I am happy to make a painting, which is for me the most *difficult* game, the most torturing of all that I have undertaken up to here. Architecture is for me a game [that is easier].[151]

He goes on to say that he is not earning much money and doesn't care, though money would allow him some vacation and an occasion to visit Ritter.

> Nothing like that on the horizon for the moment: bitter life, precipitous, furiously filled, in the modest situation of a monk in a white room, [opening] on a garden. Le Corbusier is not Peter Behrens, the one who had a lackey who watched him eat.[152]

CHAPTER 6
A METHOD FOR THE ARTS OF TODAY: PURISM, APRÈS LE CUBISME, AND L'ESPRIT NOUVEAU

> *The life of the mind is an incomparable lyric universe, a complete drama lacking neither adventure, passion, suffering... nor comedy... This world of thought, where one can discern the thought of thought and which extends from the mysterious center of consciousness, to the luminous expanse where the madness of clarity is awakened, is as varied, as moving, as surprising... as admirable in itself as the world of affective experience dominated only by instinct.*
>
> —PAUL VALÉRY, 1937

I. PURISM IN OUTLINE

In September 1918, Amédée Ozenfant and Charles-Édouard Jeanneret met in Bordeaux, where Ozenfant had fled in March to escape the bombardment of Paris. The outline of the history of their first collaborative effort, the Purist manifesto booklet *Après le Cubisme,* prepared to accompany an exhibition of their own paintings, has been traced through Jeanneret's correspondence and journals in the previous chapter.

Ozenfant had earlier coined the word "Purism" in his "Notes sur le Cubisme" in the last issue of his review *L'Élan* (1916). Purism was, according to Ozenfant, to be an approach to the arts based on universal and permanent ideas rather than vacillating or fashionable ones.[1] After cubism, art and its methods must be in tune with the precise and constructive spirit of modernity, as exemplified by the machine and by industrial techniques. Purism would be "a turn of mind, a way of feeling, an attitude vis à vis contemporary life"; its art would follow the laws of its own material forms, even as science followed the laws of nature.[2] And it would be just as experimental and innovative. Moreover, Ozenfant asserted, cubism was a specialized precursor or subset of Purism. In "Notes," he wrote that

> Cubism has assured itself an important place in the history of the plastic arts because it has already partly realized its purist aim of purging the plastic language of extraneous terms, just as Marllamé attempted to do for verbal language.
>
> Cubism Is a Movement Of Purism.[3]

Cubism, having achieved a poetics stripped of description and representation, had entered into crisis. Its precepts were copied by ignorant painters who reduced them to the decorative and the formulaic. Such followers of the fashionable forgot that the value of cubism stemmed not from the absence of representation but from the optical relations it set up within the forms and materials it deployed. Whatever could be salvaged from its initial directions must be utilized to create a new method, an art appropriate for modern times: Purism. This was the basic position to which Ozenfant converted Jeanneret.

The two men co-signed *Après le Cubisme* in November 1918 and pursued similar themes across the pages of their review *L'Esprit Nouveau* from 1920 to 1925.[4] The machine was their favored metaphor; their method a reflective questioning of thought itself; language their special focus; writing (assisted by photography) their propaganda tool.

Purism was not greatly innovative. It drew chauvinistically on the *esprit nouveau* of French wartime propaganda and was immersed in the general postwar *retour à l'ordre* (return to order), an attempt to discipline and clarify aesthetic expression by basing it on geometric and classical forms. Ozenfant and Jeanneret were thus not the only artists in Paris who sought principles by which to cleanse art of its prewar frenzies and to rationalize it in accordance with the rigor, precision, and efficiency of modern science and industrial mechanics.

II. THE ROOTS OF PURISM: POINCARÉ AND VALÉRY

In their desire to develop an art conforming to the principles of modern science, Ozenfant and Jeanneret wrestled again and again with a central issue of early-twentieth-century thought: the quest for a rigorous scientific account of the mind. In this endeavor they were influenced by the spirit if not the letter of the writings of Paul Valéry, who was in turn influenced by philosopher-mathematician Henri Poincaré. There was direct influence from Poincaré on Purism as well, as Ozenfant attended his lectures at the Sorbonne.

Poincaré taught that mathematics was a bridge linking art and science, the ideal and the real. Mathematics in the early twentieth century was advancing in two opposing directions: one toward philosophy, the other toward physics. In the first type of thought, mathematics reflected on itself and on the workings of the human mind by withdrawing from the exterior world; the other demanded that the mathematical sciences be concerned with external reality.

Correspondingly, Poincaré said, there were two kinds of minds: one preoccupied with logic, proceeding step by step toward proof, leaving nothing to chance, and the other based on intuition, discovering new territories to explore. The first type of thinkers he called analysts, the second geometers. Progress in reasoning, he advised, requires both: "It is by logic that we prove, it is by intuition that we discover."[5]

Poincaré noted that scientists seek elegance: they condense much thought into small books containing a few equations, but these equations can be applied to thousands of possible situations. Economy of thought and effort thus lies at the base of intellectual beauty. Form is what is important, enabling transformation from a single theory to other, isomorphic groups of problems.[6] This is elegance. Likewise, he wrote, in architecture "the buildings we admire are those in which the architect has succeeded in proportioning the means to the end, in which the columns seem to carry the burdens imposed on them lightly and without effort, like the graceful caryatids of the Erechtheum."[7]

Purism sought a kindred elegance. This required a method, and Ozenfant understood from Poincaré that the creation of a viable method involves the careful selection of facts and the arrangement of these facts in an intuitive order. These two steps reflected the two complementary modes of thought, logical and intuitive. That is, the mind must detect similarities hidden beneath apparent discrepancies, and follow those facts to a law or to an illuminating analogy with other facts.[8] Ozenfant, utilizing Poincaré's terminology, called such underlying facts "constants" or "invariants."

Poincaré's emphasis on the uncovering of occult or hidden significance was definitely on Ozenfant and Jeanneret's minds, as shown by their use of the following quotation from Poincaré in *Après le Cubisme* (without attribution):

> If the Greeks triumphed over the barbarians, and if Europe, heir of the thought of the Greeks, dominates the world, it is due to the fact that the savages loved garish colours and the blatant noise of the drum, which appealed to their senses, while the Greeks loved the intellectual beauty hidden behind sensible beauty, and that it is this beauty which gives certainty and strength to the intelligence.[9]

Ozenfant and Jeanneret also had recourse, especially in evolving Purism beyond *Après le Cubisme*, to the ideas of writer and philosopher Paul Valéry. Valéry published his first letter on the arts, "La crise de l'esprit," ["The crisis of spirit"] in *L'Atheneum* in 1919. In place of the disorder of modern art, he proposed continuity and respect for tradition. Architecture, the supreme art, the mother of painting and sculpture, should reject novelty, strangeness, and shock, which had heretofore epitomized modern art. Its aspects of solidity, rigor, and permanence were drawn from the laws of geometry, a discipline invented by the Greeks. The architect, infused with the soul of geometry and pure reason, defined for Valéry the prototypical modern man.[10] Ozenfant and Jeanneret had already responded to the pull of this *esprit de géometrie*, making rather ad hoc statements defending architecture as an intellectual and poetic activity; it was Valéry who tied architecture most directly to the aesthetic of modern times and gave clarity to Ozenfant and Jeanneret's tentative treatment.

Valéry referenced architecture as the model for a modern method of the arts in his Socratic dialogue *Eupalinos* (1921). From Poincaré he received the idea that the bridge between art and science lay in the universal language of mathematics. Valéry argued that the mental structures of mathematics ought, in fact, to be explicitly the basis for architectural "style." He develops his argument using an analogy to music: an architect should work with geometric forms as a composer works with musical sounds, both being abstract disciplines controlled by exact rules that express a mathematical order. Valéry also endowed his ideal philosopher-architect with a moral responsibility to construct rhythmic and orderly forms, searching for the ideal beyond movements and styles. An architect, he advised, should obey three principles:

utility exercised by the body, beauty tied to the soul, and solidity destined to resist the attractions of time.[11]

Valéry claimed that most people see with their intellects more than they do with their eyes. They form visual images (or mental models) in the mind, and it is between these images that the analogical faculty is exercised.

> Something whitish, cubical, erect, its planes broken by the sparkle of glass, is immediately a house for them—the House!—a complex idea, a combination of abstract qualities. If they change position, the movement of the rows of windows, the translation of surfaces which continuously alters their sensuous perceptions, all this escapes them, for their concept remains the same. They perceive with the dictionary rather than with the retina; and they approach objects so blindly, they have such a vague notion of the difficulties and pleasures of vision, that they have invented *beautiful views*. Of the rest they are unaware.[12]

Valery's didactic, corrective spirit—"A work of art should always teach us we had not seen what we see"—was basic to Purism as preached by Ozenfant and Jeanneret.[13] They also followed Valéry's *Eupalinos* in addressing the pages of *L'Esprit Nouveau* to the organizational elite, that is, to architects and those who were the heads of railroad companies, construction firms, and governmental offices.[14]

III. THE ORGANS OF PURISM: APRÈS LE CUBISME AND L'ESPRIT NOUVEAU

APRÈS LE CUBISME

In November 1918, in the same week that Apollinaire died and the end of World War I was declared, Ozenfant and Jeanneret finished the manifesto *Après le Cubisme* (*After Cubism*). It was essentially an elaboration of Ozenfant's 1917 "Notes sur le Cubisme," but Jeanneret added remarks on numbers, proportions, and modern machines. Publication was intended to coincide with an exhibition of their paintings starting November 10, but due to the Armistice both exhibition and publication were postponed until the latter half of December.[15] The pamphlet was publicized as the first in a series of "Commentaries sur l'Art et la Vie Moderne" ("Commentaries on Art and Modern Life"), the second volume of which would be "Vers une Architecture." This was announced in *Après le Cubisme* as already being in print, though in fact it had not yet been written (it did not appear until 1923). There were to be six other titles in the series, but only "L'Art décoratif d'aujourd'hui" and "Le Nombre et la Plastique"; were ever published, the former in 1925 and the latter in 1948, when it appeared as *Le Modulor.*

The war had been devastating, but, as the opening lines of their manifesto optimistically state, it encouraged Ozenfant and Jeanneret to seek a new beginning:

> The War over, everything organizes, everything is clarified and purified; factories rise, already nothing remains as it was before the War: the great Competition has tested everything and everyone, it has gotten rid of aging methods and imposed in their place others that the struggle has proven their betters.[16]

The major elements of Purism were laid out in the following pages. Basically and persistently, Jeanneret and Ozenfant favored a machine analogy for both nature and art:

> If observed carefully or sensed seriously, however, nature resembles not a fairyland without plan but a machine. Laws allow us to consider that nature acts like a machine. This very complicated machine produces a very complex fabric, but one woven to a geometric pattern. Physical and mathematical geometry define the laws of force that are effectively its organizing axes.
> This machine acts in accordance with laws so rigorous that, despite its infinite complexity, the most rigorous measurement cannot produce evidence of the slightest variation in what its produces: Invariability.[17]

The machine was intimately related to science–was, in fact, the physical expression of science, much as art is the physical expression of aesthetics. It was therefore Ozenfant's and Jeanneret's wish to prove that art and science were modeled on similar thought processes. Both depend on number, both seek to express natural laws based on constants or (appropriating Poincaré's terminology) "invariants." They argued in *Après le Cubisme* that the

> supposition that Science and Art are necessarily incompatible is unfounded. Both aim to put the universe into equations...

> Only their techniques differ.... Science advances only by dint of rigor. Today's spirit is a tendency toward rigor, toward precision, toward the best utilization of forces and materials, with the least waste, in sum a tendency toward purity. This is also the definition of Art.[18]

In seeking to erect a purely formal foundation on which aesthetics might rest, Purism subscribed to the belief that a unique and universal "mathematics" existed in the external world as the ultimate "truth." Mathematics is about essences; it abstracts from things of the world, erasing all that is contingent until it arrives at what is constant and invariant.[19] Hence in the art of Purism, conception and composition must express this invariance. "Generality is what is invariable in form, what is permanent, what endures.... Purist art should perceive, retain, and express what is invariable."[20]

Accordingly, Jeanneret and Ozenfant thought that art should utilize invariant, quasi-mathematical, machine-pure forms that established a visual order, forms that resounded within the mind, responding to primordial needs and sensations. This would be the firm base on which postwar reconstruction could stand:

> Now order and purity illuminate and orient life; this orientation will make the life of tomorrow a profoundly different life from that of yesterday. The latter was troubled, uncertain of its path, but this one that is beginning sees it lucid and clear.[21]

To obscure or romanticize the lucid form of the machine was, from this point of view, a sort of perversion. During the war, for example, Ozenfant saw camouflaged boats like so many floating cubist paintings in the port of Bordeaux. Their magnificent structures were completely transformed by the camouflage markings, the natural lines of their construction, even their three dimensional volumes, broken up by a bewildering pattern of shapes and colorings. He found the result artistically intolerable. Transmission of meaning was disrupted, reality and illusion were deliberately confused. Perhaps this dislike of communicative distortion motivated him to seek instead a lucid reading of the structural order underlying a work of art.[22] Contemporary artists believe they are in touch with modern times because they paint modern objects such as ocean liners, railway cars, and metro lines in romantic and picturesque terms, but their facile admiration of ships defaced by camouflage reveals the poverty of their thought:

> They completely miss the point. The structure of an ocean liner has an organic beauty; it leaves them indifferent; but let the war make camouflaged ships necessary, and all of a sudden these vessels become the unhoped-for theme of the "renewal of the subject" and the "originality of vision"! Poor magnificent ships, marvelous in their balanced structure and ample architecture, gleaming and crisp beneath their clear varnish, they are admired for their camouflage, misshapen, ludicrous, blending into the ambient landscape, unrecognizable...This is not a step forward, it is merely a mode of naturalism or impressionism under cubist camouflage.[23]

In contrast, the subject matter of a Purist painting will probably be simple; it is necessary to rule out "artistic" and decorative subjects, as well as subjects that are decorated, which is to say camouflaged. The subject can be humble: it often will be, since, for example, a bottle whose form is now ubiquitous, banal for the indifferent observer, harbors within it, and for that very reason, a high degree of generality. The subject might be a tree, if this tree is not exceptionally individuated. It might be a landscape chosen for the beauty of its volumes and not for its picturesque effect or color produced by accidental causes.[24]

L'ESPRIT NOUVEAU

Ozenfant appears to have suggested to Jeanneret that they launch an international review to promote Purism.[25] Their interests, however, were never restricted to Purism in the sense of aesthetics. Instead they took up the sweeping challenge of Apollinaire and Valéry: to construct a new mode of thinking and acting that would enable a new modern man and a new modern society.[26] Their review carried the banner *L'Esprit Nouveau* in memory of Apollinaire, who had drawn their attention to the innovative means of communication in the early twentieth century, and how these changes ought to affect writing, poetry, and all of the arts. The Dadaist poet and essayist Paul Dermée, who would join them in launching this new review, was an ardent follower of Apollinaire and had already published two of his own works by his own publishing house *"Esprit Nouveau."* The choice of title was hardly unique, however, having been used as a rallying cry throughout the war, and in general as an expression of "being of one's time."

In December 1919, Ozenfant traveled to Geneva, Bern, Zurich, Basel, and Strasbourg to research possible printers. By February 25, 1920, Ozenfant, Jeanneret, and Dermée had signed two different contracts: one public and one secret. These documents established a commercial company both to publish an international review of art and to create an anonymous society for the publication of lengthier *Éditions de L'Esprit Nouveau.* Dermée was named director of the review and charged with conducting all external relations both nationally and internationally, collecting materials and comments from all collaborators, establishing an archive of illustrations, and responsibility (in agreement with the other two directors) for final editing. Jeanneret was the general manager, overseeing all financial arrangements and payments and carrying out whatever negotiations were necessary to advertise and promote the review. Ozenfant was responsible for the layout, choice of typography and paper, and the supervision of printing.[27] In general, literary questions were delegated to Dermée, whose profession was listed on the contract as *homme de lettres*, while Ozenfant was an *artiste peintre* and Jeanneret an *architecte*, the latter two to be involved with questions on the plastic arts. A council of five members would offer administrative, marketing, and intellectual advice, although the overall ideological direction of the review was to be controlled by Dermée, Ozenfant, and Jeanneret. It remains unclear if any others were ever in fact involved.[28] Apparently Jeanneret held a greater number of shares in the company, and would eventually gain strategic control over the journal's direction when differences began to emerge.[29]

Several more months passed before *L'Esprit Nouveau* was more than an idea. Having already contacted several international collaborators, Dermée had to explain to them that the journal was postponed, and that the first issue would not appear yet. On May 5, 1920, Theo van Doesburg replied to Dermée's request for collaboration, noting that he was glad to offer support for a review in France that shared the same aims as *de Stijl* in Holland. The latter journal, founded in 1917, had been called Bolshevik by many Dutch literary and artistic reviewers because it was committed to overthrowing the artistic tastes of the petite bourgeoisie and anything else that was perceived as blocking the way to the esprit nouveau. As van Doesburg wrote, *de Stijl* was primarily dedicated to expressions in painting and architecture, with a few contributions on music and philosophy. But he and its other producers were very concerned that a (broader) avant-garde literature did not exist in Holland, so he suggested that *L'Esprit Nouveau* might like to republish the manifesto against contemporary literature that *de Stijl* had published in its April 1920 edition and thus strengthen its cause. He was also concerned about the method of payment for articles, whether there would be illustrations, and who the other contributors would be.[30]

Dermée replied in August that he would mention the *de Stijl* movement in the pages of *L'Esprit Nouveau* and publish its manifesto, but that the review had been postponed until October. He also stated that *L'Esprit Nouveau* planned to be a monthly publication of about 120 pages, abundantly illustrated and with plenty of space for international reports.[31]

On September 10, 1920, the three directors discussed plans for the first issue. There was to be one article in each of seven aesthetic categories: general, literary, the plastic arts, music, the new arts (e.g., cinema and the circus), French and foreign reviews, and book publishing. Jeanneret made a financial report on the number of subscriptions, and it was decided that he should contact the Société de Publicité to see if they would help secure advertisements for *L'Esprit Nouveau*. Ozenfant discussed technical issues, including typefaces and how photographs might be displayed. They agreed upon a list of pairs of artists (mainly French) or art categories whose work would be presented in the first six issues, one pair per issue, namely Picasso and Seurat, Cézanne and Lipschitz, el Greco and Le Fresnaye, Ingres and Léger, primitive art and Gris, Mexican art and Derain. It was also decided that along with a photograph of each artist, a short biography and small summary in italics would preface each article. Concerned with publicizing the new review, Ozenfant and Jeanneret were scheduled to present at the next meeting a scheme to attract industrialists and businessmen, while Dermée would do the same for art dealers.[32] [FIGURE 6.1]

The first issue opened with a declaration: "There is a new spirit. It is a spirit of construction and of synthesis guided by a clear conception."[33] This was followed by the statement that *L'Esprit Nouveau* would cover experimental aesthetics: it was not to be a review in the ordinary sense of the word, examining and describing artists' oeuvres or exhibitions, but would provide commentary on the intentions of the artist, following the same spirit that animated all scientific research. Art, physics, physiology all follow laws, the text proclaimed, and these laws cannot be deduced from principles already known in advance but

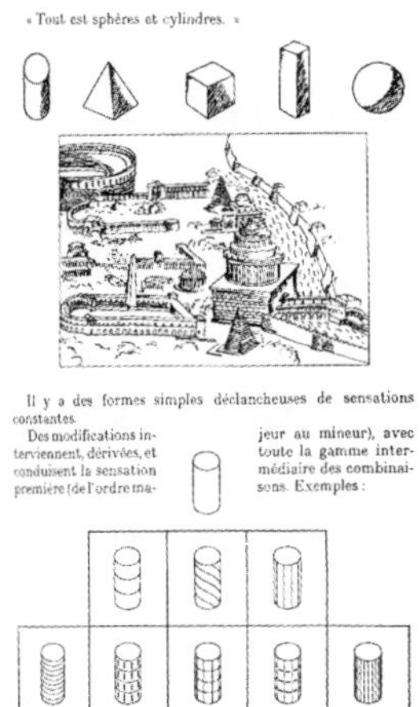
« Tout est sphères et cylindres. »

Il y a des formes simples déclancheuses de sensations constantes.

Des modifications interviennent, dérivées, et conduisent la sensation première (de l'ordre majeur au mineur), avec toute la gamme intermédiaire des combinaisons. Exemples :

FIGURE 6.1: Page from *L'Esprit Nouveau* 1 (Oct. 1920): "All is spheres and cylinders. Simple forms created constant sensations." According to the journal's authors, these forms were the base on which Roman architecture was built.

must result from experimentation and intuition. Following this analogy of aesthetics and physical science, Purism aimed to ground art in a rigorous system of thought. It considered a painting to be an exercise or a "testing-out" of ideas until over time these achieved order and precision. Theory preceded experimentation, and was sharpened and corrected in practice. They declared the basic philosophy of *L'Esprit Nouveau* to be as follows:

> Neither artists nor workers sufficiently take into account [that] it is in general production that the style of an epoch is found, and not, as so many believe, in some productions with ornamental aims, simple encrustations on a structure which, all alone, engendered the styles. The shell is not the style Louis XIV, the lotus is not Egyptian art, etc.
>
> The airplane and the limousine are pure creations which completely characterize the spirit, the style of our times. Contemporary Arts ought equally to proceed from it.[34]

L'Esprit Nouveau published twenty-eight issues between October 1920 and January 1925. The twenty-ninth issue, devoted entirely to architecture, did not appear until sometime later in 1925. Entitled *Almanach d'architecture moderne*, printed in book form, and authored solely by Jeanneret (signing as Le Corbusier), it was really a catalogue for the Pavillon de l'Esprit Nouveau.[35]

From its inception, *L'Esprit Nouveau* was no ordinary journal. During the postwar literary outpouring it was the only journal to be edited by two visual artists and the first to place literature, the plastic arts, music, and science on the same level. As Valéry had hoped, or so Ozenfant and Jeanneret naively proclaimed, a new amalgam of art and science was about to be forged, an epoch of precision where logical thought and principles would rule, where the mind and the senses would resonate together. Far from being revolutionary, however, the encyclopedic pages of *L'Esprit Nouveau* entertained many of the ideas fashionable in Paris during the first two decades of the twentieth century. For one, they reflected the popular writings of Poincaré and Valéry. For another, they exhibited the renewed influence of Seurat and Ingres on painting; the widespread fascination with new modes of transport such as steamships, trains, automobiles, and airplanes; the music of Eric Satie and the Group of Six; the new appeal of sports and the circus, the cinema, ragtime, and jazz; plus the flow of images coming from America with its skyscrapers, grain silos, and factories.

Like *Après le Cubisme*, *L'Esprit Nouveau* was a product of the war, though the devastation of war never appeared in its pages. Ozenfant and Jeanneret, along with other contributors to the magazine, were steeped in the nationalistic and propagandistic jargon of wartime and postwar France. War had, as they saw it, strengthened France. Drawing on the security and clarity that images of classical antiquity provided, the country had mounted a major offensive against the German invaders. Reason and clarity triumphed! This argument was deployed again and again as Ozenfant and Jeanneret defined the new postwar order required (they said) by machine civilization. Certain key words rang out repeatedly across the pages of *L'Esprit Nouveau*: hierarchy, clarity, austerity, measure, precision, equilibrium, universalism, and collectivity.[36]

Most editorials were anonymous, and in an effort to suggest the existence of a variety of contributors Ozenfant and Jeanneret adopted several pseudonyms, which leads to confusion over how to attribute authorship. They reserved their proper names for articles they wrote together during the first two years of the review, when they were actively extending the method and doctrine of Purism.[37] Otherwise Ozenfant would sign his pieces as Saugnier, de Fayet, Dr. Saint-Quentin, or Vauvrecy, while Jeanneret wrote as Paul Boulard, also Vauvrecy, or–a name that he invented for this purpose–Le Corbusier. When he wrote on architecture, the byline was Le Corbusier-Saugnier, making it unclear to this day how much Ozenfant contributed to these articles, which were collected and published as *Vers une Architecture* in 1923. Jeanneret dropped "Saugnier" in the work's second edition, yet dedicated the book to Ozenfant. By the time of the third edition in 1924, he had eliminated even the dedication, bearing witness to his increasing disagreement with and independence from Ozenfant.[38]

On the masthead, Ozenfant and Jeanneret do not appear as editors until the major reorganization following issue 17 (of June 1922). After a hiatus of a year and four months, the eighteenth issue finally appeared in November 1923. There were, in fact, three distinct periods of *L'Esprit Nouveau.*[39] The first were the three issues when Dermée was editor-in-chief and aesthetics and literature were the journal's primary focus. His somewhat independent direction, and his interest in psychology and how it influenced aesthetic creativity, created confusion and dissension, so he was dismissed.

The second period extended from the time Dermée was expelled until the break of 1922–23. This second period, during which both Jeanneret and Ozenfant were actively involved in directing the review, contains all of the articles that would be published as *Vers une Architecture*; the use of overlapping pseudonyms in this period creates the issue of attribution. The third period was 1923–1925, when Jeanneret, now more frequently referring to himself as Le Corbusier, was in firm control of the review. [FIGURES 6.2, 6.3, AND 6.4]

In the third period, the journal's look was restylized. Despite Ozenfant and Jeanneret's numerous disclaimers of admiration for a machine aesthetic, the formal changes made to *L'Esprit Nouveau* were supposed to mimic the new machine style. In fact, the pages of the review did not so much resemble the machine as extol it. Technical installation details of a Roneo door or Or'mo office furniture were used with greater frequency in advertisements and articles, while medical illustrations and statistical graphs underscored their ideal of order, precision, perfection. Typography was apparently deployed to reflect the idea that each part should be shaped to its function: bizarre, somewhat arcane typography was adopted for majuscules and editorials, setting them apart so they could be readily grasped. In short, the machine was held up in words and images as admirable, functional, complete in itself. For example, a piece on the Fiat factory at Turin called it

> one of the most impressive spectacles of industry.... Here is the solution of the problem well posed. Here is what the work of

Paquebot « FLANDRE », Cie Transatlantique, construit par les Chantiers et Ateliers de St-Nazaire.

DES YEUX
QUI NE VOIENT PAS...

★

Les Paquebots

PAR

LE CORBUSIER-SAUGNIER

« Il y a un esprit nouveau : c'est un esprit de construction et de synthèse guidé par une conception claire.

Quoi qu'on en pense, il anime aujourd'hui la plus grande partie de l'activité humaine.

UNE GRANDE ÉPOQUE VIENT DE COMMENCER

Programme de l' « Esprit Nouveau », N° 1, Octobre 1920

« Nul ne nie aujourd'hui l'esthétique qui se dégage des créations de l'industrie moderne. De plus en plus, les constructions, les machines s'établissent avec des proportions, des jeux de volumes et de matières tels que beaucoup d'entre elles sont de véritables œuvres d'art, car elles comportent le nombre, c'est à dire l'ordre. Or les individus d'élite qui composent le monde de l'industrie et des affaires et qui vivent, par conséquent, dans cette atmosphère virile où se créent des œuvres indéniablement belles, se figurent être fort éloignés de toute activité esthétique. Ils ont tort, *car ils sont parmi les plus actifs créateurs de l'esthétique contemporaine.* Ni les artistes, ni les industriels ne s'en rendent compte. C'est dans la production générale que se trouve le style d'une époque et non pas, comme on le croit trop, dans quelques productions à fins ornementales, simples superfétations sur une structure qui, à elle seule, a

L'ESPRIT NOUVEAU

1925

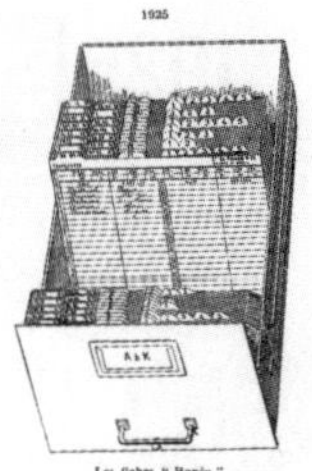

Les fiches " Ronéo "

∴

Lorsqu'un facteur de notre équation technico-cérébro-sentimentale a démesurément poussé, survient une crise, les rapports sont détraqués, les rapports entre notre entité cérébro-sentimentale et les choses de notre usage, extérieures à nous et que nous continuons à produire sous une forme routinière ou alors en anticipant et en réaction contre un état de choses admis. La notion de cause à effet s'affaisse. Nous sommes saisis d'inquiétude parce que nous ne sommes plus

Les tiroirs roulent doucement sur des galets (Ronéo)

BESOINS TYPES

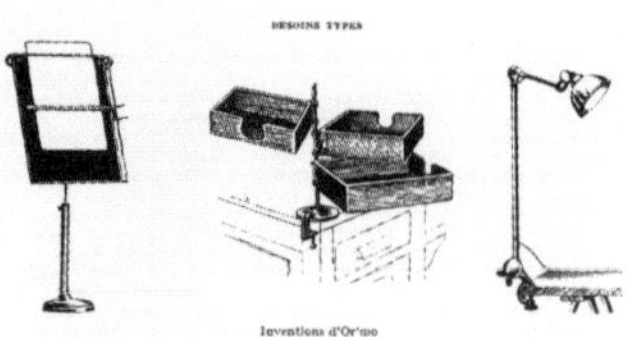

Inventions d'Or'mo

adaptés; nous nous révoltons contre un asservissement obligé à des choses *anormales*, qu'elles soient rétrogrades ou qu'elles soient par trop anticipées.

La boussole nous sauvera du détraquement; la boussole en l'occurrence, c'est nous-même : un homme, une constante, à vrai dire, le point fixe qui est le seul objet de notre sollicitude. Il faut donc s'attacher à retrouver toujours *l'échelle humaine*, la fonction humaine.

Puisqu'aujourd'hui sévit la crise, il n'est pas de plus urgente besogne que de nous efforcer à une réadaptation à nos fonctions, dans tous les domaines. Suspendre quelques instants notre attention captée par les labeurs habituels et songer *au pourquoi*, réfléchir, soupeser, décider. Et répondre *au pourquoi*, avec ingénuité, innocence, candeur. Autant dire, se débarrasser des habitudes acquises, déposer dans les coffres de sa banque, au troisième sous-sol, derrière une porte d'acier, son capital de souvenirs et, laissant là toute la poétique du passé, formuler des désirs terre à terre.

Comment on classe habituellement les plans.

Comment on les classe mieux (Ronéo).

La recherche du mieux conduit à des renversements de conception.

FIGURE 6.2: Purism was a pedagogical reform that taught a new way of thinking and seeing. This page of *L'Esprit Nouveau* 8 (Nov. 1923) states, "Eyes which do not see...Steamships." FIGURE 6.3: This Voisin advertisement from *L'Esprit Nouveau* 19 (Dec. 1923) was probably designed by Amédée Ozenfant free of charge, in the hopes that Voisin would increase its contributions to the review.

FIGURE 6.4: In *L'Esprit Nouveau* 23 (May 1924), articles of exactitude and efficiency–and thus, purity–were exemplified by office equipment such as card indexes, file cabinets, and desk lamps manufactured by Roneo and Or'mo.

> each can be if it is well organized. The factory of clarity, the production rigorously controlled, the economy of time and money.[40]

Another typical example is an article on the "Formation of the Modern Optic" accompanied by a photograph of the nocturnal lights of Times Square, a photo of the drawer of a card catalogue, and a comparison of a typewritten page to a handwritten one.[41] As these cases and quotations illustrate, in the third period a more telegraphic style of writing and text/image juxtapositions was codified. Short precise sentences, repetition of key phrases and words, were extolled as an effective manner to convey ideas.

All but one of the articles Ozenfant and Jeanneret wrote together on modern painting and published in *L'Esprit Nouveau* were subsequently republished as *La Peinture Moderne* in 1925.[42] During the third period of the review, Jeanneret–now definitely morphing into Le Corbusier–also wrote two articles of his own for each issue, one on urbanism and one on the decorative arts. These were collected in two volumes as *Urbanisme* (1925), published in English under the title *The City of To-morrow and its Planning*" (1929), and *L'Art Décoratif d'aujourd-hui* (1925), published in English under the title *The Decorative Art of Today* (1987).

As his business enterprise SEIE (Société d'Entreprises Industrielles et d'Études) weakened in the monetary crisis of 1919, finally closing in 1921, Jeanneret not only began his architectural partnership with his cousin Pierre Jeanneret in 1922, but also developed his Citrohan housing project and planned his urban scheme for la Ville Contemporaine. Preparing for his participation in the Exposition Internationale des Arts Décoratifs in 1925, he utilized the review to publicize his attack on traditional aesthetic forms and to promote the name of "Le Corbusier." His obsession with painting lessened as he shifted to focus once again on architectural and urban preoccupations, and as he sharpened his tools of combat to wield against the decorative arts. In this multipart attack, the pages of the review reveal a concept of modernity in which the equipment of the house must be rationalized and traditional furniture replaced; objects of use must be stripped of all ornamentation and their pure and simple forms revealed, modern materials must be used, and traditional architectural constructions and regionalisms surpassed. Simultaneously, Le Corbusier (as we may now call him) began work on the design of four villas for the well-to-do bourgeoisie in the suburbs of Paris: L'Atelier Ozenfant (1923–4);

the double villa at d'Auteuil (Villa La Roche), destined for his brother Albert Jeanneret and Raoul La Roche (1923–25); and l'Ateliers Lipchitz and Miestchaninoff (1923–25). He also embarks on plans for the housing estate of Pessac (1925–28). Le Corbusier's modern aesthetic is worked out through frequent discussion in the pages of *L'Esprit Nouveau*: cubes of white raised on pilotis, walls punctuated with horizontal strips of industrial windows or *la fenêtre en longuer*, flat roofs, and roof gardens—although its codification into five points of modern architecture would not appear until the end of the 1920s.[43]

By August 1924, Ozenfant and Le Corbusier were diverging in style and interests. At that time Le Corbusier complained to Ozenfant, "You no longer collaborate on *L'E.N*; it upsets me, even makes me indignant. If you won't write essential things that you feel, then why are we doing *L'E.N.?*"[44] A few days later Ozenfant replied,

> I realize that our writing together is becoming difficult, not that our ideas conflict, but because even though we hold them in common, they seek expression in different modes and languages; you are more direct, I am inclined to philosophy; all in all, however hard it is to write them, the articles on painting are good; I think that those on art deco [written by Jeanneret alone] would have benefited from our collaboration, in any case that would have been more fair to me. I agree that from now on—except for the book in process—it would be easier for us both to write on our own.[45]

A year later, the collaboration was officially dissolved. On July 25, 1925, Ozenfant—no doubt angered by Le Corbusier's failure to involve him in plans for the Pavillon de l'Esprit Nouveau at the Exposition Internationale des Arts Décoratifs of 1925—sent a letter to the Société des Éditions de l'Esprit Nouveau (which had a grand total of two members, Ozenfant and Le Corbusier) declaring his resignation as administrator of the Société and codirector of the review.[46] Le Corbusier responded four days later that although he could not accept Ozenfant's resignation, both the review and the collaboration were finished.[47] The last issue of *L'Esprit Nouveau* had already been published in January 1925.

IV. L'ESPRIT NOUVEAU: TARGETING THE ELITES

Ozenfant and Jeanneret believed that artists and architects could no longer stand to the side of the major forces shaping industrial society. They must be active constructors of a new society. A new scientific mentality had been born with the machine, a new spirit or *esprit nouveau* that encompassed a planning mentality. Questions abounded: What revolutions had the machine effected? What were the laws that governed these changes? What knowledge of society, economics, politics, law, medicine, production processes, and consumption needs must be known in order to project the future and chart the direction in which society must move? How to use this information to create a new man who both accepted and promoted a new society? And to which political and scientific leaders could the avant-garde of that new society turn? To gather the necessary information from capable men and from societal processes, to arrange this data into functional explanations that inputs to their effects or outputs, to know how to select wisely between alternative directions, and to project a pathway toward the future–all of this would define a scientific planning mentality. It would involve not only the creation of a new epistemology and a new consciousness, but also the structural reform of society, of laws, of the economy.[48] It was for this purpose, more than for the promotion of Purism as such, that Dermée, Ozenfant, and Jeanneret established *L'Esprit Nouveau* and received the monetary backing of some members of the corporate elite.

Ozenfant and Jeanneret believed that the state alone could not change society; they were enamored instead with the power of the industrial elite to understand and shape the processes of collectivized production and mass consumption, so it was to these elites that they turned their attention. The slogan on the back cover of the magazine confirmed straightforwardly that "*L'Esprit Nouveau* is the magazine of the elite."[49]

Intended to be the great connector of people who think, *L'Esprit Nouveau* was encyclopedic and internationalist, gathering together the materials of a general theory of knowledge, an epistemology to match the spirit of the times, then placing these materials in the hands of technically competent specialists. If architects or artists were not to be marginalized, they must learn how to discern the laws and the direction of the forward movement of machine society. And they must know how to communicate, to exchange information with industrial and governmental leaders who were in charge of directing societal change, those already responsible for great industrial

L'ESPRIT NOUVEAU

est le

MAGAZINE

des

ÉLITES

FIGURE 6.5: The editors of *L'Esprit Nouveau* intended the review to be aimed at technically competent specialists and the elites of manufacturing, science, and the arts.

innovations, collectivized production, and mass consumption. If these elites were not taught to accept new ideas in the architectural, urban, and decorative arts, then necessary reforms in these realms would never be implemented.[50] In the issue of November 1921 (double number, 11–12), Ozenfant and Jeanneret reiterated their intention that *L'Esprit Nouveau* be the great disseminator of ideas among the elites.[51] [FIGURE 6.5]

The technocratic orientation of *L'Esprit Nouveau* is not surprising; the need to appeal to technocracy was one of the lessons that Poincaré and Valéry had taught and was not far from thoughts Jeanneret had expressed in his *Étude sur le mouvement de l'art décoratif.* Ozenfant and Jeanneret considered collaborating with a review entitled *La Producteur* in 1920 because it advocated a Saint-Simonian view of a society governed by directors of administrations. Jeanneret could properly call himself an industrialist, having established a small enterprise (SEIE) shortly after his arrival in Paris in 1917, and he still had a small brick-making factory in operation in 1919. During this period, as his letters to Ritter reveal (see Chapter 5), he studied *The Principles of Scientific Management* (1911) by American engineer F. W. Taylor; he applied some of Taylor's efficiency techniques to a slaughterhouse he planned while working with SABA (Société d'Application du Béton Armé). Translated into French in 1912, Taylor's book influenced French industrialists reconfiguring wartime production into a postwar

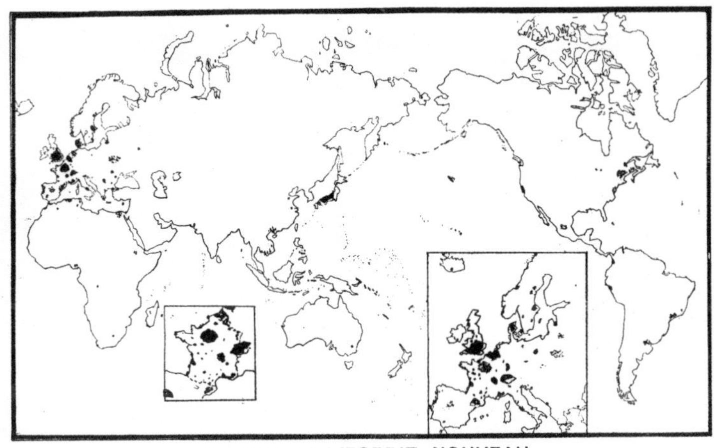

FIGURE 6.6: The back cover of *L'Esprit Nouveau* 18 (Nov. 1923) proudly displayed a map of the review's distribution network, spreading across five continents.

economy of reconstruction; Ozenfant and Jeanneret advocated it in *Après le Cubisme.* Thus one aim of *L'Esprit Nouveau* was to teach the principles of efficiency in many areas of work, principles that spoke directly to industrialists and elites. The second industrial revolution of the early twentieth century was based on new industries and new management techniques; the industrialists and elites who guided this revolution formed the very basis for the esprit nouveau and were responsible for transforming society through the widespread application of electricity, the chemical industries, new construction techniques (especially reinforced concrete), and the automobile and aeronautical industries.

[FIGURE 6.6]

Perhaps in pursuit of his officially assigned responsibility to market the review to industrialists and financers, in 1920 Le Corbusier wrote a text (never published) on *L'Esprit Nouveau* that echoes many of these themes.[52] In it, he begins by drawing on his earlier comparison of Germany and France, claiming that the intellectual movement in Germany is dedicated to subjective, metaphysical, and romantic Expressionism, while in France ideas are oriented entirely toward concrete problems and based on research into the primordial conditions of art. The French esprit nouveau is thus a positive and material movement based on rationality, clarity, and intelligence–and *L'Esprit Nouveau* is the mouthpiece of this new spirit. Its subtitle is correspondingly ambitious: *Revue Internationale Illustrée de l'Activité Contemporaine, Arts, Lettres, Sciences, Sociologie* (*Illustrated International Review of Contemporary Activity in the Arts, Letters, Sciences, and Sociology*). "International," Le Corbusier writes,

> because it wants to link the elites of all peoples, the elites who bring something constructive to the times. Arts, Literature, Sciences, Sociology, because this is the highest manifestation of the mind, because for too long the arts have been too far from the sciences, because the leaders in these various groups have been ignored for a long time; for too long they have worked in isolation, and for too long been despised.[53]

Science has advanced to such a degree that it has forged a completely new society and given birth to a new mode of thought. This mode of thought is being expressed through practical works, carrying the mark of a clear mind. "It is a spirit of construction and of synthesis guided by a clear conception. The development of ideas and multiple production [of goods] are the daily proof of this."[54]

Although society is being organized according to this new spirit, the arts and letters have, Le Corbusier wrote, only just left their revolutionary period, which had been a mere prelude to the new age. They have yet to realize that construction is the base not only of industrial activities but of all the arts. All art is construction, no matter what kind of genius is expressed; it must be based on the rule of constants (what Ozenfant called invariants) extracted from the physical world.

> In the single field of the engineer, problems are resolved each day that are entirely guided by the requirements of a practical and scientific order, which, unconsciously, affect aesthetics, proceed from aesthetics, and add to aesthetics. Already this activity covers the continent with gigantic works, bridges, machines, boats, airplanes, representing superior products for the patrimony of humanity bringing with them, not only the impressive aspects of their technical triumph but a style which is precisely the style of the epoch, a grandeur which is not only of a mechanical and scientific nature, but which has something proportioned, beautiful, a grandeur that one can call Roman.
>
> Such activity is found equally in the sociological and economic domain where a similar grandeur, similar interests

> at play, similar social demands are formulated, and a singular unitary spirit clarifies and leads to a solution.
>
> Arts, themselves, exiting from a brutal revelation, are moved toward a rational construction, and, feeling the grandeur that surrounds them, are searching for a worthy expression.[55]

In their November 1921 pitch for more subscribers, Ozenfant and Jeanneret noted that the intellectual effort of the modern era has made possible a marvelously fecund elite, but one that has not yet found its place in either society or government. Elite workers, constrained by a degree of specialization unheard of in earlier times, now formed part of this intellectual effort. Therefore the aim of *L'Esprit Nouveau* was to follow all the different manifestations of intellectual work in philosophy, science, sociology, literature, and the arts. Intellectuals must be interested in seeing that the needs of all men are satisfied–both materially and intellectually. The elites need encyclopedic knowledge in this new era; their work will perish otherwise.

Having introduced for the first time a negative tone, they continue in this vein. Such, then, was the aim of *L'Esprit Nouveau*: to enable various elites–scientific, artistic, industrial, or administrative–to understand the general mechanisms that are "killing" the world.[56] These elites must be taught what they do not see with their eyes, they must be shown how to remove procedures, thoughts, perceptions that inhibit them from adopting the new spirit of the machine age.

V. IMAGERY IN L'ESPRIT NOUVEAU

In *L'Esprit*, the images used to illustrate texts were deliberately taken from catalogues of companies whose advertising helped finance the review, including Omega, Innovation, Hermès, Peugeot, and Voisin. Since Ozenfant and Jeanneret spurned "style," the merely aesthetic, these text-image juxtapositions were graphically banal compared to experiments with the materiality of language in other publications. Investigations into the effects created by shifting typefaces, rearranging cutouts and frames, and playing with colored backgrounds were kept to a minimum in conformity with Purism's dictates of clarity, sobriety, and functionalism.[57]

Much has been made out of the financial backing of *L'Esprit* by companies whose advertisements repetitively adorned its pages.[58] Less has been said of the obsession with order and the notions of classification that arose from the repetitive appearance. Advertisements of filing cabinets manufactured by Roneo, office furniture produced by Or'mo, suitcases and trunks from Innovation–repeated issue after issue, often in the same position and order–became metaphors for the typological simplification that Purism extolled.[59] Advertisements of filing cabinets and wardrobes were perfect metaphors for the simple, invariant types and standardized forms produced by the law of order, economy, and efficiency. The point was not lost on the opponents of Purism: Henri Bergson used the drawer metaphor in *Thought and Movement* (1922) to denounce the "dry rationalism" to which Ozenfant and Jeanneret adhered. His student Bachelard repeated the metaphor in *Poetics of Space*, claiming that "concepts are drawers in which knowledge may be classified; they are also ready-made garments which do away with the individuality of knowledge that has been experienced."[60]

L'Esprit Nouveau utilized every opportunity to extol the image of "dry rationality." Between 1923 and 1925 (the third period of *L'Esprit Nouveau*), Le Corbusier wrote copy for at least twelve advertisements for Innovation. This company held a patent on a system for hanging rather than folding clothes in a trunk, and the advertisement text Le Corbusier wrote declared it was "the most scientifically studied and the most solidly constructed trunk that has ever existed."[61] He placed one of his ads for Innovation opposite a page on which an ad for his forthcoming book *Vers une architecture* appeared. Beneath the image of a set of drawers he wrote, "We have devoted ourselves to the search for perfection, driven by a motivation analogous to that which achieved the construction of the automobile and the ocean liner." Such analogical associations based on the juxtaposition of different images would soon become a stock in trade of Le Corbusier's thinking. A similar advertisement appeared in issue 22. Le Corbusier's copy explained: "In order to conceive and to construct well the mechanics of a house, it is necessary to recognize the gestures which are customary for us and which are repeated every day. *To these gestures, there is a response,* to these needs which are a question, a request, an answer is required."[62]

In other ad copy for *Innovation*, Le Corbusier wrote as follows:

> Architecture
> It is necessary to construct in series in order to be housed.
> If one does not construct in series and if one perpetuates in
> Architecture functions that have nothing in common with
> the uses of modern life, one will not be able to be housed.

> The average apartment persists in having nothing that corresponds with our most legitimate needs; the entire apartment remains such that no furniture serving more than one purpose can be accommodated. To construct in series is to achieve an acceptable price. It is thus to confront the plan of the apartment; it is to determine the givens of the plan, it is to begin the indispensable reorganization of the domestic economy. When one constructs in series one establishes a model. To establish a model susceptible of execution in series, is to come close to a definitive solution: [a] standard, economy, maximum refinement.[63]

Photography, being a mechanical and technical operation, might be thought to have epitomized the art of the engineer, yet the pages of *Esprit Nouveau* never showcased photography as such: rather, photographic or drawn images were presented as expressions of precision and clarity in other objects.[64] First came large images of structures expressive of the traits of order and precision, such as American grain silos and factories.[65] To these were added images of the airplane, steamship, and automobile. By 1922 the typewriter, typed page, and printed page were emblematic of "a new clarity and precision," generators of "an internal elegance," "a new morality, the morality of The Good Job." Within two more years an entire array of small manufactured goods from pipes to purses had been portrayed, simple mass-produced type-objects satisfying man's fundamental needs.[66] "The rows of shops each thrust on us the innumerable products of modern industry, all characterized by that imperative precision which is the inescapable consequence of mechanism; objects of all kinds which are presented to us in impeccably good order."[67]

Ozenfant and Jeanneret searched these ideas for models, for ways to generalize their Purist ideals. By disavowing the machine aesthetic, they meant they were not interested in simply making everything look mechanical, copying the precise look of the machine, the shiny steel surface of the ball bearing, or the style of the steamship, with its exposed pipes, lacquered surfaces, portholes, and funnels. They focused instead on the clarity of monumental shapes, the purity of their shining surfaces, the sober geometry of rounded volumes and tubular forms. These, rather than formal analysis, were tools that aided perception. Yet some readers, if not the editors, of *L'Esprit Nouveau* and other journals espousing the same aesthetic did turn the picturesque nature of these images into a machine aesthetic.[68] From industrial

LE PURISME

INTRODUCTION : La logique, le facteur humain, les points fixes.
L'ŒUVRE D'ART : Son but, hiérarchie, ordre.
SYSTÈME : Sensations primaires, sensations secondaires, art ornemental, art symbolique, le thème-objet, la sélection naturelle, la sélection mécanique, choix du thème-objet, l'élément puriste.
LA CONCEPTION.
LA COMPOSITION : Choix de la surface, lieux géométriques, tracés régulateurs, modules, valeurs, la couleur.
LA SENSIBILITÉ.
LE PURISME.

INTRODUCTION

LA LOGIQUE, dérivée des constantes humaines, sans laquelle rien n'est humain, est un instrument de contrôle et, pour celui qui sait inventer, un guide de découverte ; elle contrôle, rectifie la marche parfois fantasque de l'intuition et permet d'aller de l'avant avec sûreté.

C'est le guide qui, tantôt précède l'explorateur et tantôt le suit ; mais sans l'intuition elle est un stérile engin ; nourrie par l'intuition, elle permet de « danser dans les chaînes ».

Rien ne vaut qui ne soit général, rien ne vaut qui ne soit transmissible. Nous avons tenté d'établir une esthétique rationnelle, donc humaine.

On ne peut construire sans points fixes. Aussi avons-nous cherché dans un premier article (1) à en déterminer quelques-uns.

(1) « *SUR LA PLASTIQUE* », Esprit Nouveau, nº 1, 15 octobre 1920.

FIGURE 6.7: In *L'Esprit Nouveau* 4 (Jan. 1921) "Le Purisme" proclaimed logic to be an instrument controlling intuition and enabling the artist to proceed with surety.

architecture–steamships, airplanes, and the automobile to porthole windows, spiral staircases, tubular railings, door handles, funnels, and air vents, the brilliant surfaces of lacquer and metal, a minimum of clutter, simple and practical sanitary facilities, and visible electrical wiring–they created an international iconography of modernism. That that iconography was not what its avant-garde had intended did not prevent the outcome.

VI. ESSAYS BY OZENFANT AND JEANNERET IN L'ESPRIT NOUVEAU

Ozenfant and Jeanneret published in the pages of their review many ideas derived from early-twentieth-century aesthetics, psychology, sociology, anthropology, and linguistics. Authors such as Sorbonne professor of "aesthetics and artistic science" Victor Basch, psychologist Jules Lallemand, sociologist Charles Lalo, art critic Maurice Raynal, medical doctor Pierre Winter, and Jeanneret's brother Albert Jeanneret contributed important essays on the aesthetics of science and art (Basch), the importance of normative aesthetics (Lallemand), aesthetics and sex (Lalo), Ozenfant and Jeanneret's second exhibition of paintings (1921, reviewed by Raynal), sports (Winter), music and rhythm (Albert Jeanneret), and more. However, for brevity's sake I shall concentrate on a selection of pieces dealing with basic issues of Purism that were coauthored by Ozenfant and Jeanneret themselves. Since these pieces were published under a joint byline, there is no way to distinguish which ideas, exactly, came from which writer; however, both were clearly willing to endorse all the basic ideas in all the essays. [FIGURE 6.7]

"LE PURISME"

Early in the course of their journal, Jeanneret and Ozenfant took care to restate the fundamentals of their new isms as they saw them at that time, using a linguistic analogy that would recur repeatedly in later writings:

> The Purist element issuing from the purification of standard forms is not a copy, but a creation whose end is to materialize the object in all its generality and its invariability. Purist elements are thus comparable to words of carefully defined meaning; Purist syntax is the application of constructive and modular means; it is the application of the laws which control pictorial space.... Purism strives for an art free of conventions which will utilize plastic constants and address itself above all to the universal properties of the senses and the mind.[69]

Applying the laws of geometry would make a work of art readable and transmissible. This emphasis on geometry would be reiterated by Ozenfant in 1922: "Let us make geometry a science of the Spirit, a corrector of the excesses of intemperate sensibility but let us not replace the mysticism of sensibility with the mysticism of the golden section or of the triangle.... [as Newton pronounced] 'Physics, beware of Metaphysics.'"[70] In his memoirs he stated that classical values of measure and harmony were uniquely French because

> We are geometers but we understand geometry in our own way, which is not the way the entire world understands it. In our great parks, like Versailles, reason is, of course, dominant but its ascendancy is that of the orchestra conductor and not of a tyrant. Our great gardeners knew the secret of giving a certain amount of freedom to what Spinoza termed "native" nature.[71]

In "Le Purisme," Ozenfant and Jeanneret go on to speak of the existence of a "hierarchy" of "aesthetic sensations":

> The highest level of this hierarchy seems to us to be that special state of a mathematical sort to which we are raised, for example, by the clear perception of a great general law (the state of mathematical lyricism, one might say); it is superior to the brute pleasure of the senses; the senses are involved, however, because being in this state is as if in a state of beatitude.
>
> The goal of art is not simple pleasure, rather it partakes of the *nature of happiness*... But there is no art worth having without this excitement of an intellectual order, of a mathematical order; architecture is that art which up until now has most strongly induced the states of this category. The reason is that everything in architecture is expressed by order and economy.[72]

Purism strikes out at cubism because it deserted the cause of pure art and turned abstraction into something decorative, making form, color, and composition arbitrary and fantastical. In *Après le Cubisme* they had likened its aesthetic to those of a good ornamental carpet or to the pleasures of life that result from a Brillat-Savarin cuisine. Such efforts could not produce an art of today.[73] Instead, "Purism" must enact a mental hygiene of rigor and clarity. "The tool is ready: using the raw elements, we must construct works that make the intellect respond; it is this response that matters."[74]

"AESTHETICS AND PURISM"

In drawing up a fresh summarization of their position in the fifteenth issue of *L'Esprit Nouveau* (February 1922), Ozenfant and Jeanneret relied both on theories already advocated in their earlier pieces "Sur la Plastique" (in the first issue) and "Le Purisme,"[75] and on the input of friendly critics such as Maurice Raynal, whose review of their 1921 paintings had appeared in the seventh issue of *L'Esprit.*[76]

Philosophy, they write, has helped them understand the field of aesthetics and explore the question of what constitutes beauty. Most assume beauty is whatever gives pleasure. But not all paintings give everyone pleasure. Some admire the Parthenon, others do not; some like to be caressed, others do not. But no one appears to be *indifferent* in front of the Parthenon, and that is important. The Parthenon elicits sensations with intrinsic qualities that are universal; and these stem not from beauty but from form. Thus, a European or a savage, when shown a ball, shares the same sensations inherent in the form. They may associate it with different ideas, but their feelings are constant or universal:

Painting is thus a "Machine To Move One Emotionally."[77] Sensations, moreover, are received directly by the eye. Thus the quality of a work of art lies in the nature of its conception and the exactness of its transmission. Take a straight line: the eye is forced into a movement of continuity and calm. But a broken line causes the eye to change direction, to modify its course, sets up a cadence and irregularity. Or consider color: red wakes you up, blue instills serenity. These are standards, they produce the same sensations in all spectators. Thus simple forms of geometry, because of the lucid reactions they provoke in the spectator, offer the most universal language and established the foundation on which the Purist aesthetic was built.[78]

All systems of ideas need an appropriate system of expression. The present may have its mode of feeling, but not yet a language in which to express it. It will find one only if it looks to geometry and pure expressions of thought.[79]

A work of art, the authors continue, arises from a natural need for order; man is compelled to create due to this need for order. Utilizing an image that Le Corbusier will often repeat, they tell the reader to look at a table after a meal. Once hunger has been satisfied, a man often aligns all the crumbs of bread. He did not do this before he ate, but only afterwards, out of a need for order that dominates him. Observing the figures he has created out of crumbs, he feels pleasure, for to create order is the most elevated human need. Its expression is the cause of art.[80]

Since the highest sense of order the mind can achieve is in mathematics, this perception they call "mathematical lyricism." It is a sensation far superior to the brute pleasure of the senses. The mind creates a system out of abstract signs in both geometry and language. These systems render symbols intelligible and communicable. A work of art is analogous to geometry and language; thus, it too must create a system that communicates meaning while acting physiologically on the senses. If the creator of a work of art wants to put the spectator in a certain state, then he must use means that produce certain effects. It is not sufficient to merely copy from nature forms that move him. He must employ a Purist syntax and apply universal laws that generate pictorial space.

The use of primary elements, the choice of object-types led by the desire for unity and order, the selection of rules of syntax that order pictorial space–together, these enable Purism to endow its art with universal properties that affect both the mind and the senses.[81]

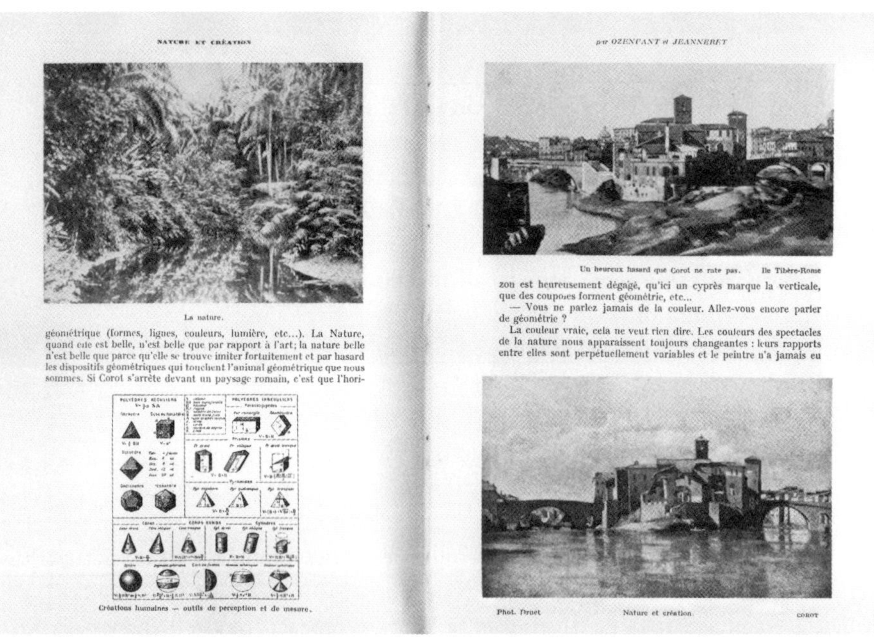

NATURE ET CRÉATION

La nature.

géométrique (formes, lignes, couleurs, lumière, etc...). La Nature, quand elle est belle, n'est belle que par rapport à l'art; la nature belle n'est belle que parce qu'elle se trouve imiter fortuitement et par hasard les dispositifs géométriques qui touchent l'animal géométrique que nous sommes. Si Corot s'arrête devant un paysage romain, c'est que l'hori-

Créations humaines — outils de perception et de mesure.

par OZENFANT et JEANNERET

Un heureux hasard que Corot ne rate pas. Ile Tibère-Rome

zon est heureusement dégagé, qu'ici un cyprès marque la verticale, que des coupoles forment géométrie, etc...

— Vous ne parlez jamais de la couleur. Allez-vous encore parler de géométrie ?

La couleur vraie, cela ne veut rien dire. Les couleurs des spectacles de la nature nous apparaissent toujours changeantes : leurs rapports entre elles sont perpétuellement variables et le peintre n'a jamais eu

Phot. Druet Nature et création. COROT

FIGURE 6.8: "Nature et Création": Utilizing a matrix of images that enabled side-by-side comparisons in *L'Esprit Nouveau* 19 (Dec. 1923), Amédée Ozenfant and Charles-Édouard Jeanneret denigrated images drawn from fanciful nature and praised those regulated by rules of geometry.

"L'ANGLE DROIT"

Ozenfant and Jeanneret continued to clarify a method for Purism during the third period of the review, when their style of writing became more telegraphic, juxtaposing shorter sections in quick succession and utilizing more photographs and images. For example, in "L'Angle Droit" ("The Right Angle"), opposite a page where two paintings are juxtaposed–one by Meissonnier "speaking falsely" and one by Mondrian that "speaks the truth"–their argument follows a staccato beat:

> A qualified work of art is one in which the emotive property is universal and durable...It is in the past that one will find the axial laws of a work of art...Experience acquired through the analysis of the past offers a certain security to the judgment of actual works; the permanency of our organism allows, in effect, to establish certain laws of permanency applicable to art of all times.[82]

> One can argue that the law of gravity rules all objects and beings of the earth, man as well as the objects he creates. Instinct protests against instability, even the appearance of instability upset him. (Leaning Tower of Pisa.) Art can not go against this interior need of our nature.[83]

A basic law of nature is gravity, visibly defined as the vertical applied to the horizontal plane.

> The horizontal and the vertical determine two right angles; among the infinity of possible angles, the right angle is typical, the right angle is one of the symbols of perfection. In fact, man works on the right angle.
>
> That explains and justifies the orthogonal spirit. It is the origin of human activity and it is the necessary condition for the most transcendent of his works of art.[84]

Since the orthogonal is a sign of permanence, the oblique must be a sign of the unstable or variable. The mistake of Expressionism was to allow the oblique to express dynamism or instability. It became a witness of unsettled minds. Before Expressionism was Impressionism, admiration of the instantaneous photograph. It banished the general and the essential to the benefit of the accidental, the fugitive, and the fragmentary. This established a false base on which Futurism could rise. All three art movements, Ozenfant and Jeanneret write–Impressionism, Expressionism, Futurism–failed to achieve a method; they denied all that was durable and humane. Then the cubist revolution took place and the orthogonal began to regain its destiny as an incontestable fact.[85]

"NATURE ET CRÉATION"

Ozenfant and Jeanneret often argued that nature was a disruptive agent in the process that purified thought, one that led the artist to depict picturesque and romantic scenes. [FIGURE 6.8] Yet nature could also be utilized analogically to reflect the vitality of the mind. In "Nature & Creation," they asked rhetorically if they experienced an emotion before a setting sun.[86] Yes, they answered, if it is truly beautiful or sublime. Then why don't they paint such generous abundance that nature has bestowed on man? "Pardon us, art is not the butler charged with reminding Monsieur of both small and great emotional experiences, or a Cook's guide of beautiful voyages. Nature provokes emotions, certainly! Art to the contrary is the moment when man ought to take account of himself."[87] Nature is exterior to man; it is the outside milieu in which he lives. Joys, however, resides inside him, they arise from the satisfaction of constants in his sensibility and mind. Nature is beautiful only when by chance it has a geometrical disposition. If Corot stopped before a Roman countryside, it is because the horizon was apparent, a cypress marked the vertical, and these created geometry in his mind.

Bringing their argument to a close, Ozenfant and Jeanneret discuss the spectacle of colors that nature provides and the impossibility of an artist capturing the myriad of tones as they constantly vary. They compare art to music; piano music provides an admirable example. It is controlled by a necessary and sufficient choice of sounds. Without this limit it could only make translatable a small amount of sounds. But on the piano one can play Bach, Puccini, Beethoven, or Satie. It has a schematic and systematic method, but the music produced makes us laugh, cry, or dance. A weak painter thinks only of multiplying nuances of colors and shapes. An untalented writer is like a dictionary-maker who thinks only of multiplying words without killing any. The number of words in the standard and authoritative dictionary of the French language, *Petit Larive et Fleury,* is over 73,000. Have you ever seen a piano that offers so many sounds? A dictionary needs to be created with forms, colors, and words that will be necessary and sufficient; only then will artists achieve a method that will make them as happy as musicians.

"DESTINÉE DE LA PEINTURE"

In comparing art to music, Ozenfant and Jeanneret rely on a model of language. To follow this analogy, however, entails more than mere competence in knowing how the rules apply or comprehending the syntactical relationships of the basic elements, as the authors have outlined. It also implies that the user of this language must know how to perform, how to communicate, and how to move the audience, as evidenced in the domain of music and the dictum "a painting is a machine to move you." Looking ahead at the future of painting, Ozenfant and Jeanneret begin to sketch the nature of performance that includes a lesson on practice and responsibility. In "Destinées de la Peinture" ("Destinies of Painting"), they resort to a lesson in the history of art to clarify their story.[88] All civilizations prior to the nineteenth century, they recount, were pre-mechanical, with only rudimentary techniques.

They nevertheless had to meet the most practical requirements of defense, of land improvement, of creating cities and towns, of inventing metal. It was the latter–the invention of a new material–that allowed civilization to develop and mature. Eventually, a new material, steel, enabled the machine age to evolve and to revolutionize society. A new spirit arose that broke with centuries of inertia and provoked the greatest perturbation of all times. It overthrew the conditions of work, brutally suppressing former hierarchies. It developed cities to such an extent that they began to threaten the basic unit of the social order–the family. The future of this machine civilization depends on what it will do with this new material. Will it adopt economical mechanisms, utilize energy more effectively, and so produce freedom and liberate higher ambitions? Techniques of this new era are still at a rudimentary stage; everything remains more or less in the state that nature gave it, and engineers are still called artisans (i.e., as opposed to *artists*).[89]

But suddenly the authors become melancholic. It is the word "artisan" that caused their depression, interrupted their train of thought. The word brings forth memories of the stifling Cluny Museum or the somber galleries of the Museum of the Decorative Arts. These collections of so-called "art" block the path of artistic expression as it moves toward pure and true ends.

After this rupture–actually, they say, a warning–the authors return to their argument, noting that artisans of former times were also not considered to be artists, and their tools were rudimentary as well. Hence the products they produced never ended up in museums but were listed as merely useful items. Art was reserved for the satisfaction of superior needs, those of the mind as well as emotions. Those arts that knew how to speak, to communicate with the spectator, were at the service of priests, magistrates, tapestry-makers, journalists, generals, schoolmasters, image-makers, and photographers. The priest, for example, asked the painter and sculptor to put in public places sermons and images that would speak to the people. The prince showed his glory in flattering effigies, the journalist was pleased to recall the many diverse facts of daily life, and above all the photographer satisfied the crowd's taste for imitation. Art, in spite of the many services demanded of it, always aspired to satisfy poetical needs. It was understood by the elite that art should aspire to the higher levels of the mind.

Contemporary times need an art that will enrich our emotions through our minds. It is a matter of attaining what Bach, Bergson, and Einstein have achieved in their respective fields. There should be a similar aim for the art of today, the perfect coordination of the senses and feelings. Since it is understood that man is both a sensual and cerebral being, a work of art can no longer produce sensations that are not cerebral, merely pretty colored forms telling small and large stories. Modern man longs for the security of higher ideals, such as those religion once gave him. But now he is filled with doubt, and an agonizing void erupts around him. The more the machine invades life, the more man has the need to fill the space that religion used to fill. Art must fill this void, leading to new heights as it has done before in works achieved by the Egyptians, Phidias, Ictinos, Mozart, and Bach.

"FORMATION DE L'OPTIQUE MODERNE"

In this essay, Ozenfant and Jeanneret remind their readers it is important not to lose sight of the fact that the emotional power of a work of art stems from optical phenomena.[90] For example, prehistoric art touches us without need of explanation. We do not know its origins or the reason for its existence, but the sensations it produces are universal. Even though the exterior world has changed dramatically since primitive times, the fundamentals of our optical laws have not shifted. Modern times have merely modified the functional intensity and speed of life; technology has penetrated and extended all modes of existence. We now tolerate all types of spectacles heretofore unknown, especially the predominance of images and new ranges of colors. Modern times have produced an education for both the eye and the ear. A peasant arriving in Paris is immediately assailed by a multiplicity and intensity of noises, suddenly surrounded with a cacophony of images that he must register with a speed to which he has not been trained. Civilization today is entirely urban. It thus requires that those who think and create must submit to innumerable elements, constituting an absolutely new enveloping milieu. Adapting to this new urban environment, they create new tools that answer new needs. [FIGURES 6.9 AND 6.10]

The spectacle of the street has been transformed as well. Boutiques are now set up in quick succession, one after another, imposing on the spectator innumerable and precise objects, all produced by the machine. Here is where geometry lends a hand to commerce: it offers its power of attraction, its ability to condense needs and desires into a single image. Even fruits, vegetables, chickens, and lambs are ordered in neat rows and perfect pyramids. So convincing is the resulting order that it excites our appetites and makes us jubilant. The power

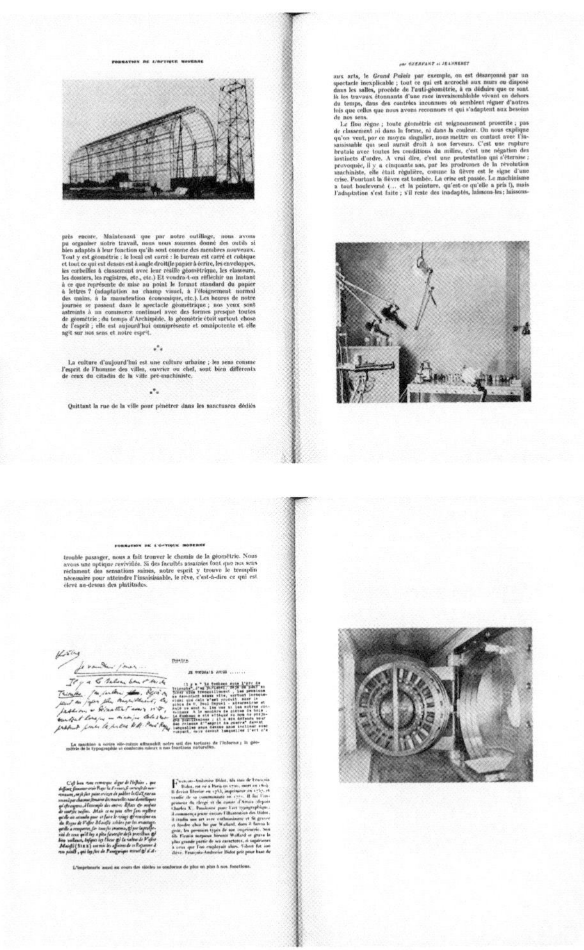

FORMATION DE L'OPTIQUE MODERNE

près encore. Maintenant que par notre outillage, nous avons pu organiser notre travail, nous nous sommes donné des outils si bien adaptés à leur fonction qu'ils sont comme des membres nouveaux. Tout y est géométrie ; le local est carré ; le bureau est carré et cubique et tout ce qui est dessus est à angle droit (le papier à écrire, les enveloppes, les corbeilles à classement avec leur résille géométrique, les classeurs, les dossiers, les registres, etc., etc.) Et voudra-t-on réfléchir un instant à ce que représente de mise au point le format standard du papier à lettres ? (adaptation au champ visuel, à l'éloignement normal des mains, à la manutention économique, etc.). Les heures de notre journée se passent dans le spectacle géométrique ; nos yeux sont astreints à un commerce continuel avec des formes presque toutes de géométrie ; du temps d'Archimède, la géométrie était surtout chose de l'esprit ; elle est aujourd'hui omniprésente et omnipotente et elle agit sur nos sens et notre esprit.

⁂

La culture d'aujourd'hui est une culture urbaine ; les sens comme l'esprit de l'homme des villes, ouvrier ou chef, sont bien différents de ceux du citadin de la ville pré-machiniste.

⁂

Quittant la rue de la ville pour pénétrer dans les sanctuares dédiés

par OZENFANT et JEANNERET

aux arts, le *Grand Palais* par exemple, on est désarçonné par un spectacle inexplicable ; tout ce qui est accroché aux murs ou disposé dans les salles, procède de l'anti-géométrie, à en déduire que ce sont là les travaux étonnants d'une race invraisemblable vivant en dehors du temps, dans des contrées inconnues où semblent régner d'autres lois que celles que nous avons reconnues et qui s'adaptent aux besoins de nos sens.

Le flou règne ; toute géométrie est soigneusement proscrite ; pas de classement ni dans la forme, ni dans la couleur. On nous explique qu'on veut, par ce moyen singulier, nous mettre en contact avec l'insaisissable qui seul aurait droit à nos ferveurs. C'est une rupture brutale avec toutes les conditions du milieu, c'est une négation des instincts d'ordre. A vrai dire, c'est une protestation qui s'éternise ; provoquée, il y a cinquante ans, par les prodromes de la révolution machiniste, elle était régulière, comme la fièvre est le signe d'une crise. Pourtant la fièvre est tombée. La crise est passée. Le machinisme a tout bouleversé (… et la peinture, qu'est-ce qu'elle a pris !), mais l'adaptation s'est faite ; s'il reste des inadaptés, laissons-les ; laissons-

FORMATION DE L'OPTIQUE MODERNE

trouble passager, nous a fait trouver le chemin de la géométrie. Nous avons une optique revivifiée. Si des facultés assainies font que nos sens réclament des sensations saines, notre esprit y trouve le tremplin nécessaire pour atteindre l'insaisissable, le rêve, c'est-à-dire ce qui est élevé au-dessus des platitudes.

La machine à écrire elle-même affranchit notre œil des tortures de l'[illegible] ; la géométrie de la typographie se conforme mieux à nos fonctions naturelles.

L'imprimerie aussi au cours des siècles se conforme de plus en plus à nos fonctions.

FIGURES 6.9 AND 6.10: **"Formation de l'optique moderne": According to Amédée Ozenfant and Charles-Édouard Jeanneret in *L'Esprit Nouveau* 21 (Mar. 1924), the hours of the day were spent within a geometrical spectacle–the skeletal framework of hangers and towers or laboratory equipment, for example, shaped the visual experience of the modern world. [Figure 6.9] Other examples of the modern functional optic could be found in the precision of a well-typed page or the polished, exact gears of a bank vault. [Figure 6.10]**

of geometry lies in this ordering; these urban still lives cause us to turn our backs on the rotting beef of Rembrandt.

These spectacles of geometry are determined by the same mind that established the cadastral ordering of a city's streets, the square houses with nearly uniform windows, the rows of parallel sidewalks, the alignment of trees, the regular punctuation of street lamps, the lines of tramways, and the impeccable mosaics of pavement. Everything is divided into quarters by geometry. Even if we look up at the sky cut out by street walls, it gives us in a precise outline the tracing of an urban geometry. Entering into the house in order to work, the sensation is even more ordered, because the tools that organize our work are so well adapted to their functions that they appear to be new prosthetic devices. All is geometry: the rooms are squared, the desk is squared and cubic, and every thing on top of it is at right angles–the writing paper, the envelopes, the registers, and so on. Even the standard format of writing paper has now been adapted to the visual field, to the normal reach of the arms, to an economical manipulation. All the hours of our working days are spent within this geometrical spectacle, forcing our eyes to interact constantly with forms that are always geometrical. Today geometry is omnipresent and omnipotent; it acts directly on the senses and the mind.

This geometrical spectacle affects culture as well. Since it is an urban culture, the mind of the man of the cities, worker or boss, is different from that of the citizen of pre-industrial towns. Yet the moment one leaves the street and moves into the sanctuaries dedicated to art, the Grand Palais for example, one is confronted with an inexplicable spectacle: everything is arranged anti-geometrically. One is convinced these are the astonishing works of a race that lives outside of time, in unknown countries where other laws rule than the geometrical ones we have adapted to the needs of our senses. In this strange place fog reigns, nothing is classified either in form or color. Through this strange method, it is explained, the spectator is put in contact with the indefinable. Fifty years ago, the machine overturned everything; unfortunately there are those who do not adapt, and must be ignored.

Ozenfant and Jeanneret are convinced that a new, imperative era has arrived that has enabled man to take a giant step toward the future. Modern man has found that he is a geometrical animal. His spirit is geometrical, and his senses and eyes are trained more than ever through geometrical clarity. Man has achieved an exacting mathematical mind, yet the individual often lives in a fog and is ill-adapted to modern times. Art has always held the function of creating entire systems out of objects, hence the antidote to this chaotic state is not disarticulation and fog, but the entire reorganization of life. Today we intend to put our house in order, our brain in order, our painting in order, the entire milieu in order, until their appearance soothes our eye and erases the mistakes of a troubled passage. Once the road of geometry has been found, it gives birth to a modern lens, so that our minds find the necessary springboard to attain the unreachable, the dream that rises beyond mere platitudes.

VI. L'ESPRIT NOUVEAU: CONTEXT AND CRITICISM

Architects were quick to adopt the *esprit de géometrie* that Valéry so clearly established as a rallying cry for postwar artistic expressions, and soon developed a movement around this banner. Their advocacy may have been ideologically motivated as well. During postwar reconstruction and throughout the 1920s, architects were marginalized, no matter how much they were called the grand "constructors," no matter how often architecture was hailed as the mother of all the arts. Even though there was great need in France to produce housing destroyed or not built during the war, architecture remained in a state of crisis. Between 1914 and 1925, accelerating construction costs and rent controls conspired to keep housing activity to a minimum. In Paris, for example, the number of housing units built in 1925 did not exceed the number built in 1913 despite accelerated population growth. Where housing was constructed, moreover, architects were not necessarily called upon to design the work; many self-designed units were erected during this same period of time.

Furthermore, an astringent conservatism in architectural taste was standard in the academies, which were in control of the design of all public building projects and monuments. In domestic architecture, a similarly conservative taste argued that regional vernacular styles promised greater moral and social stability, that they lay at the heart of French identity.[91] A major advocate of regionalism in the 1920s was Gustave Umbdenstock, a professor of architecture at the École Polytechnique and chef d'atelier at the École des Beaux-Arts. He argued that the "home" was a vital link in the process of social control, and directly attacked the ideas espoused by Ozenfant and Jeanneret in *L'Esprit Nouveau*. In his *Cours d'architecture professé à L'École Polytechnique*, published in 1930, Umbdenstock claimed that the roof of either a humble or bourgeois abode symbolized "family"; it was a healthy and moral symbol, and should not be suppressed. Mischaracterizing Ozenfant and Jeanneret's work, Umbdenstock argued that to make a tabula rasa of tradition, to deny what was vital to the national health and social order and impose instead a dreary and crushing architecture, not only made no sense but was destructive to common beliefs.

Those who rallied round the *retour à l'ordre* and *esprit de géometrie* accepted Valéry's challenge that architecture contained a social and moral mission. Geometry meant "modern" architecture, not traditional forms. It saved money by eliminating ornamentation. It was an intellectually purified ideal. Based on the right angle and the regulating trace, as Purism proposed, it would give architects a role as the innovators in housing and urbanism.

VII. THE ARTIST AS PURIST

As this chapter has shown, Jeanneret's ideas about architecture and art were thoroughly interpenetrating during the period in which he and Ozenfant were promulgating their philosophy of Purism. In "Le Purisme" Ozenfant and Jeanneret had written "We have decided the necessity of an 'architectured' painting."[92] The adjective "architectured" is the moment when all the forms find their principle of coherence, their exact and purified relationships, their mathematical ordering. Thus painting attempts "to satisfy the senses and the mind at the same time." Its elements are "like words of a language" creating "a symphony of sensations in the spectator."[93] It is moreover via painting that the language of architecture will develop.

This may be part of what Jeanneret meant when he said in later years, "Look at my paintings to understand my architecture." Le Corbusier would call his early oil painting *La Cheminée* an emanation of the landscapes of Greece: space and light. It was a key to understanding his approach to plastic art: "Mass in space. Space." [94] After an early phase of research and development under Ozenfant's tutelage, Jeanneret's paintings eventually achieved the appearance of geometric constructions, as if they had been measured and composed with precision instruments–as, indeed, they practically had been.

As Jeanneret's letters to Ritter indicate, through the summer of 1918 he was still preoccupied with watercolors of landscapes, prostitutes, and nudes. He did not begin to paint in oils until November, shortly before his and Ozenfant's exposition at the Galerie Thomas was scheduled. There is some debate over what oil paintings Jeanneret exhibited at the Galerie Thomas. Perhaps the first oil painting he did not destroy, and thus allowed to be shown, was *La Cheminée*, mentioned above. Often referred to as the "Acropolis" the composition places two books and a small cube at eye-level on the marble mantel of a fireplace as if they were masses in space arranged in perfect harmony, as the volumes on the Acropolis had been placed. This composition reflected

Jeanneret's obsession at that time with Greece and the Parthenon. Or, he might have included the rather bland *Still-Life with Book, Glass and Pipe.* The ideas behind this painting display a preference for the life of the mind, as symbolized by the book opened to pages showing Ionian capitals, as well as the tabula rasa on which a new age would rise.[95] It coincides exactly with the premises of Purism, so it too would have been appropriate for this first exhibition.[96] Both works reveal Jeanneret's developing relationship between painting and architecture: works based on pure simple forms, straight unbroken lines, clear contours, orchestrating expressions of unity. [FIGURES 6.11 AND 6.12, p. 695]

Although he never described the methods he imposed on himself in any of his letters to Ritter, referring only to the fact that he was painting with a rigorous procedure requiring a painstakingly long period of time to compose and then construct a work of art, Jeanneret struggled at this time to instantiate Purist ideals in his own painting. His hints to Ritter were clarified in *Après le Cubisme* and, later, in *L'Esprit Nouveau.* The horizontal line of the Earth and the orthogonal stance of man, the cosmic axis and the right angle, were Purist symbols of perfection, the basis on which harmony was to be constructed.[97] The Cartesian geometric grid, *le tracé régulateur*, was an instrument and armature, correcting excessive emotions and ensuring rational control over the intuitive process of composition. As they wrote in *L'Esprit Nouveau* in 1920, "The preparatory diagram procures satisfaction of a spiritual kind which leads to a search for ingenious and harmonious juxtapositions. It invests the work with eurhythmy."[98]

Ozenfant and Jeanneret had a second exhibition of their paintings, all still lifes, at the Galerie Druet in 1921 (January 22 to February 5). Their work was not well received by the critics, causing Jeanneret henceforth to withdraw his paintings from public review. They did however print a positive review of the exposition by the art critique Maurice Raynal in the seventh issue of *L'Esprit Nouveau* (April 1921).[99] Raynal believed these two artists had the audacity to remind all artists that art is an ensemble of methods and means through which an object is realized. They sought a deductive method on which to base their art: one that stems first from the mind and second from feelings. In order to reconstruct their world, they make a tabula rasa of all that education and the contingencies of life have taught them. Having done so, they rediscover art as if it was a new America.

They are purists who believe that beauty and truth are capable of perfection, and they argue that an egg is an egg, or a sphere is a sphere.

Hence the basic elements of their art consist of the sphere, cube, cylinder, and polygon, drawn by using the straight line, the point, the triangle, and the circumference. There are mathematical universals to be discovered at the base of all of the plastic arts. Their works of art are demonstrations of this research into the invariant, their method of geometry a call to order ("un rappel à l'ordre"). Hence they produce rather cerebral works of art, not destined to ornament walls as decorative art. They resemble instead words, stripped of all the charms of adjectives, but words linked through relationships considered to be laws.

VIII. CONCLUSIONS

Guided by their belief in the latest scientific and technical endeavors, as their manifesto *Après le Cubisme* proclaimed, Ozenfant and Jeanneret hoped to uncover the qualities of mathematics and physics that would elicit a new aesthetics appropriate to the twentieth century. They looked for new standards in industrial models, in everyday manufactured items, in peasant art. They searched for new rules of machine production, new processes of planning the future, new principles of aesthetic reform. Modern art, they believed, made an appeal to the mind; it spoke a new abstract language. It appeared that only scientists, technicians, and social engineers understood these new codes and were equipped to be the true creators of the logical and abstract languages of modern art. If Apollinaire intended to forge a new lyrical poetry out of the new technologies of communication, hoping to avoid the marginalization of poets in modern life, then Ozenfant and Jeanneret wanted to create a poetics of esprit nouveau with their new readings of "economy," "exactitude," and "precision," and so demarginalize artists and intellectuals.[100]

Art can no longer be isolated from contemporary activity. One law above all rules modern life: the law of economy, the perfect adaptation of the means to the end. Means-end analysis follows the law of nature: the law of selection, which classifies genres, develops them, makes them precise, and leads them toward the development of a type. All inventions follow this law: innovations are only useful when they attain a degree of condensation, when all that is superficial has been eliminated. This is the lesson that Poincaré had taught and that Ozenfant had first absorbed: that an aspect of science is to effect economy of thought in the same manner that a machine effects economy of effort; the importance of a fact is measured by the return it gives, by the amount of thought it economizes.[101] Art must do likewise.

CHAPTER 7: THE LANGUAGE OF ARCHITECTURE

> *To write a little puts ideas clearly, engages, compromises, constrains us to follow the strength of its theory. It is necessary to reflect constantly, all the time, at each pretext to be sensible. To be sensible, is to be conscious, the contrary to that which one attributes to sensibility. To write and to make the step of a giant and to cross clearly the underground forces of his instincts and sensations.*
>
> –LE CORBUSIER, 1920

I. INTRODUCTION

The early 1920s were the years of Le Corbusier's first maturity as a writer, a time when he published prolifically, mostly essays in *L'Esprit Nouveau*. Along with some new material, those essays reappeared in a series of volumes from 1923 to 1925, three in 1925 alone. After that year came a hiatus; his next major work did not appear until 1929.

In these major writings of the twenties, Le Corbusier defined for himself a distinctive style of architectural discourse, a telegraphic, aphoristic language about architecture. Using that language, he sought to state, investigate, and purify a "language of architecture," a communicative system of architectural forms having its own parts of speech and grammatical rules, a tangible speech in which modern life itself might be stated, investigated, and purified. [FIGURE 7.1]

II. VERS UNE ARCHITECTURE (1923)

> *The Plan proceeds from within to without; the exterior is the result of an interior....If there come into play intentions which do not speak the language of architecture, you arrive at the illusion of plans, you transgress the rules of the Plan through an error in conception, or through a leaning toward empty show.*
>
> –LE CORBUSIER, *TOWARDS A NEW ARCHITECTURE*

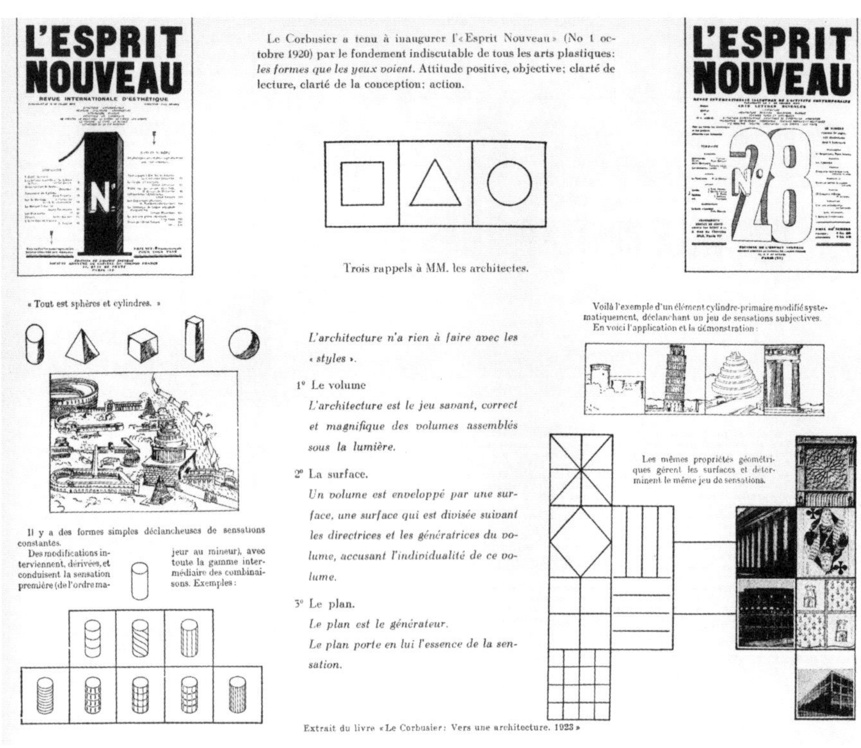

FIGURE 7.1: A summary of ideas informing Le Corbusier's Purist architecture from the first to the last issue of *L'Esprit Nouveau* (1920–25)

"The language of architecture"—and what might that be? Language about architecture, or architecture as language? For Le Corbusier, it meant both, and with similar principles in play, for in both written and architectural compositions, signs must combine harmoniously in order to communicate.

But how deep does the metaphor go? Can verbal and architectural constructs attain an equal status, utilizing similar processes of conception and composition? Are they structured in a similar manner? Can architecture, in particular, an abstract discipline based on relations between numbers, reveal (like the best language) the actual workings of the mind, as Paul Valéry hoped?

Valéry defined the book as a machine for reading (*machine à lire*, 1926), Ozenfant the painting as a machine for emotions (*machine à émouvoir*, 1921), and Le Corbusier the house as a machine for living (*machine à vivre*, 1921).[1] In all three cases, the metaphor depends for its strength on the fact that books, paintings, and buildings all operate in a sequential manner on their users to yield specific effects. Ideally, at least for these thinkers, they do so by bringing together means and ends in the most efficient manner possible: a page constructs a clear expression, a painting is ruled by pure lines and forms, a simple unornamented house provides for basic needs and comforts. On this view, the relationships among the parts and the systemic organization of the whole–the machine design–becomes the focus of writing, art, and architecture.

The machine metaphor assumed that the mind itself is a mechanical material, subject to reliable manipulation by a variety of "machines." This is typical of the rhetoric of modernism, which tended to assume that all truth could be measured and mapped in a formal, scientific manner. But modernism's discourse was also haunted by a sense of emptiness, of blank spaces of ineffable immateriality that could not be articulated. For modernism, rhetoric was thus both a persuasive didactic tool and a device for discriminating among perceptions, clarifying concepts, refining awareness, diminishing the territory of the inarticulable. To correctly state a problem in a formal system ruled by axioms, theorems, and proofs was an attempt to fill in the void where words failed, over the horizon of the expressible and effable. The ineffable or inexpressible can be seen, on these terms, as an asymptotic limit to rational thought and language. Somewhere near that unattainable asymptote, pure poetry and the language of pure forms begin to merge.

The heart of *Vers une Architecture* (*Towards an Architecture*, altered to *Towards a New Architecture* in the English translation) is Le Corbusier's attempt to take rational expression toward that elusive line, to create texts, machines of language, that can serve as adequate tools to investigate the "language of architecture," architecture *as* a language, architecture as a compositional, communicative art. His method of argumentation, and the style and layout of the entire book, address the problem of how to write/design/construct ideas and forms that communicate their meaning in a clear and precise manner. In it, borrowing from Adolf Loos, he states one of his famous aphorisms: "The plan proceeds from within to without; the exterior [is] the result of an interior."[2] Since both books and buildings are "machines," this statement should be as applicable to this book as to any of Le Corbusier's buildings–and it is. This is a book shaped from within by its grammar, the language of its forms, its rhetorical gestures. Le Corbusier opens with a synopsis of his themes; these are reiterated at the opening of each chapter, a series of telegraphic messages reinforced through continuous repetition.

At the core of the book, he constructs the metaphor of the "language of architecture" and of the musical and geometrical patterns it simulates. The elements of this architectural language are light, shape, walls, and space. Its grammar utilizes only these elements, classifying them with respect to their human aims. If an architect does not obey this grammar, he will not speak the language of architecture correctly: he will build fanciful illusions based on errors of conception. He will formulate meaningless expressions.

Vers une Architecture is Le Corbusier's first book devoted to architecture. It is a collection of essays, all but one written between October 1920 and May 1922, all but one previously printed in *L'Esprit Nouveau*, and all originally published under the name of Le Corbusier-Saugnier, the joint pseudonym used by Jeanneret and Ozenfant on collaborations.[3] Ozenfant was probably responsible for its use of photographs of American grain silos and of his own design for a Hispano-Suiza automobile chassis. Since he was a dedicated race-car driver, perhaps the many references to speed records, and the design and assembly of racing cars, can be attributed to him.[4] Since it was Jeanneret's specific task to apply the principles of Purism to the language of architecture in *L'Esprit Nouveau*, Le Corbusier is generally credited with the sole authorship of *Vers une Architecture*. However, detailed attribution remains problematic.

In this section, I present a selective précis of *Vers une Architecture* with an eye to tracing Le Corbusier's rhetorical methods and philosophy of architecture's "language"–his language *about* architecture and his language *of* architecture. The book's three-part structure is notable, a chronological and thematic layer cake: After a telegraphic opening synopsis of his themes ("Argument"), there is a group of chapters concerned with housing written in 1921, then three concerned explicitly with "the language of architecture" written in 1922, then another chapter on housing written in 1921, and a final chapter, also on housing, written in 1923.

FIRST PART: CONSTRUCTING A MANUAL FOR HOUSING

Bearing in mind Le Corbusier's enthusiasm for mathematics, it is notable that the word "argument" bears a mathematical meaning (value operated on by a function) as well as a traditional literary one (statement of what is to come).Thus the reader of *Vers une Architecture* learns from the "Argument" what the elements are that form the grammar of the house: plane walls, simple geometric volumes, openings through which light

FIGURE 7.2: Engineers can teach architects about mathematical calculations and the feeling of harmony.

can pass. They also know that the language of architecture must produce lyrical expressions. Now, in Chapter 1, "The Engineer's Aesthetic and Architecture," they are introduced to Le Corbusier's analogy, "The house is a machine for living in," which dominates this first part of the book. [FIGURE 7.2]

Maria Lucia Cannarozzo has argued that "machine for living" is a metaphor, not an analogy.[5] The point is nontrivial. Metaphor reverberates on many different levels, taking the reader in different directions, while analogy insists on resemblance, precision, specific correspondence.[6] Cannarozzo argues that the metaphor "machine for living" allows Le Corbusier to apply Taylorism and biology to architecture–separating functions, redefining them, and reordering them according to a new synergy. She also argues that the "machine for living" metaphor dominates *Vers une Architecture,* condensing many different analogies appearing in different chapters. It allows the writer to speak of the future, hence the title of the book. It produces a contradictory play between the mechanical and the classical that begs for a resolution, an equilibrium that takes something from the old and acquires something of the new; it focuses attention on the function of machines, and thus condenses into a house-tool, house-city, house-region.[7]

However, I use the term "analogy" deliberately while recognizing that Le Corbusier's figures of speech also reverberate on different levels at once. Le Corbusier is deploying lessons learned from reading Henri Poincaré on the application of mathematical analogies; he is aware of mathematical functions, and his machine-figure contains a functional argument. Employing carefully selected terms, Le Corbusier applies with precision the analogy of the machine not only to the shell of the house but to its equipment and furniture, as well as to the planning of cities and regions.

Poincaré advised the historian, physicist, and mathematician to make a selection of facts; they must not wander randomly amid the chaos of the world. "The only facts worthy of our attention are those which introduce order into this complexity and so make it accessible to us...unite elements long since known, but till then scattered and seemingly foreign to each other."[8] The goal of science is to effect economy of thought, just as a machine effects economy of effort: "When language has been well chosen," Poincaré advised, "one is astonished to find that all demonstrations made for a known object apply immediately to many new objects; nothing requires to be changed, not even the terms, since the names have become the same."[9] Both Le Corbusier and Poincaré are, then, looking for generalizable patterns that make facts intelligible. Such economy of thought is the point of all Corbusier's "An *x* is a machine for *y*" analogies–a steamship is a machine for transport, an airplane is a machine for flying in, a motor car is a machine for moving in, a chair is a machine for sitting in, a house is a machine for living in.

This first section on housing is a resumé of what will follow and is contained in the four chapters: "The Engineer's Aesthetic and Architecture,"[10] "Three Reminders to Architects,"[11] "Regulating Lines,"[12] and "Eyes which do not See."[13] All deal explicitly with the problem of the house and its furnishings.

Le Corbusier prefaces his discourse with an evolutionary history of tools and machines. He begins with the first tool (he says) that man ever made: a simple house. Man's tools are thrown onto the scrapheap as soon as they are out of date, but never has this been the case with the house. Civilization may evolve, religions fall, but the cult of the house has remained static for centuries. That is the reason why our houses disgust us, why we frequent restaurants and night clubs instead. If we remain within our gloomy homes we are demoralized, imprisoned like wretched animals.[14]

Engineers, being neither architects nor decorators, fabricate useful tools; they do not build houses or design moth-eaten boudoirs. "Our engineers are healthy and virile, active and useful, balanced and happy in their work. Our architects are disillusioned and unemployed, boastful and peevish."[15] It is the fault of the schools of architecture: they are hothouses where flowers are forced, where unclean orchids are cultivated. Yet architecture is to be found in small items like the telephone and in large structures such as the exceptionally perfect Parthenon; it could as well be in the houses that make the street, and the streets that make the town.[16]

Architects must begin at the beginning. They must use those elements that affect our senses and reward the desire of our eyes by their delicacy or brutality, their serenity or riot. They must deploy forms that our eyes see clearly and our minds can measure.[17] The rationality of the machine has transformed our external world, but the house has not been adapted either to this new perspective or to the new social life it effects.[18] "We"–that is, right-thinking architects like Le Corbusier–"claim, in the name of the steamship, of the airplane, and of the motor-car, the right to health, logic, daring, harmony, perfection."[19]

Le Corbusier interjects several refrains that will be repeated throughout this book. The first is that "Architecture has nothing to do with the various 'styles.'"[20] "The 'styles,'" as he will say in the argument for "Eyes which do not See," "are a lie." He adds that those styles "Are to architecture what a feather is on a woman's head; it is something pretty, though not always, and never anything more."[21] This denigration of feminine decoration is another recurrent theme of the book, and will be revisited later.

trois rappels à
MM. LES ARCHITECTES

L'architecture n'a rien à voir avec les « styles ».

Les Louis XV, XVI, XIV ou le Gothique, sont à l'architecture ce qu'est une plume sur la tête d'une femme ; c'est parfois joli, mais pas toujours et rien de plus.

L'architecture a des destinées plus graves ; susceptible de sublimité elle touche les instincts les plus brutaux par son objectivité ; elle sollicite les facultés les plus élevées, par son abstraction même. L'abstraction architecturale a cela de particulier et de magnifique que se racinant dans le fait brutal, elle le spiritualise, parce que le fait brutal n'est pas autre chose que la matérialisation, le symbole de l'idée possible. Le fait brutal n'est passible d'idées que par l'ordre qu'on y projette. Les émotions que suscite l'architecture émanent de conditions physiques inéluctables, irréfutables, oubliées aujourd'hui.

FIGURE 7.3: Le Corbusier constantly reminded architects that architecture was the play of pure forms under light: cubes, cones, spheres, cylinders, and pyramids, as in American grain elevators or factories.

Architecture, in contrast, is an abstraction rooted in naked facts, irrefutable facts forgotten today. So the second refrain carries the reminder: "Mass and surface are the elements by which architecture manifests itself. Mass and surface are determined by the plan. The plan is the generator."[22] In this oft-repeated refrain, Le Corbusier is taking a geometry lesson from Poincaré, who taught that a straight line is a point that has been displaced in space. It is a matter of extending a way of seeing, projecting one form onto another. If the line, in turn, is displaced, moved along any line but itself, it engenders a surface plane of two dimensions–corresponding to a plan (i.e., on paper). If this surface is displaced along a line orthogonal to itself, a volume or cube of three dimensions is the result.[23]

The first of the three "reminders to architects" is centered on "mass." It begins with oft-repeated phrases:

> Architecture is the masterly, correct and magnificent play of masses brought together in light. Our eyes are made to see forms in light; light and shade reveal these forms; cubes, cones, spheres, cylinders or pyramids are the great primary forms which light reveals to advantage; the image of these is distinct and tangible within us and without ambiguity. It is for that reason that these are *beautiful forms, the most beautiful forms* [24] [FIGURE 7.3]

To back up his argument he looks at history: "Egyptian, Greek or Roman architecture is an architecture of prisms, cubes and cylinders, pyramids or spheres: the Pyramids, the Temple of Luxor, the Parthenon, the Colosseum, Hadrian's Villa."[25] The architects of today cannot conceive of primary masses because they are not taught to do so at school.[26] The engineers of today, however, do use primary masses or elements, following rules that control their organization, and so create works that ring in unison with the universal order. "Thus we have the American grain elevators and factories," of which illustrations are provided, "the magnificent First-Fruits of the new age. *The American engineers overwhelm with their calculations out expiring architecture.*"[27]

The second "reminder" is addressed to "surface," the way that surfaces clothe primary masses:

> Surfaces, pitted by holes in accordance with the necessities of their destined use, should borrow the generating and accusing lines of these simple forms. These accusing lines are in practice

> the chessboard or grill–American factories. But this geometry is a source of terror.[28]

That is, as the "Argument" puts it, "Architects to-day are afraid of the geometrical constituents of surfaces."[29]

The third reminder concerns the Plan. The Plan will soon be revived when the problem of cities is addressed. Remember that the plan of the Acropolis is full of variations and changes of level, its masses asymmetrically arranged, the whole massive, elastic, sharp and dominating; it is excellent, but "Modern life demands, and is waiting for, a new kind of plan, both for the house and the city."[30]

A good plan, he reminds the architect, is a matter of vision, of what will enable the eye to transmit "to the brain co-ordinated sensations" so that the mind can derive "from these satisfactions of a high order."[31]

> A plan calls for the most active imagination. It calls for the most severe discipline also. The plan is what determines everything; it is the decisive moment. A plan is not a pretty thing to be drawn, like a Madonna face; it is an austere abstraction.[32]

Le Corbusier turns to explore two specific plans of which he approves, a scheme by Tony Garnier for the Cité Industrielle and Auguste Perret's conceptualization of a City of Towers. In contradiction to Garnier's plans for an industrial city de novo, Le Corbusier finds that industrial districts of present-day cities are noble quarters where geometry reigns in the interiors, but dirt infects their exterior surroundings, and incoherence runs riot as their development spreads throughout the town in a dangerous and costly manner. They are thus on the exterior devoid of a plan. As for the City of Towers, it is time that new needs of "modern business" allow the American skyscrapers, enormous constructions sixty stories high, to be located at certain collecting points in the plan of the city. Assembling all the necessary services that economize on time and effort, they also generate peace of mind: from the fourteenth floor of the skyscraper all is calm with the purest air, while at their foot stretch parks and trees. When such a city of towers is created, then there will be architecture worthy of the times!

A new era is coming, but not without turmoil–and the key to it all is the Plan:

> In architecture the old bases of construction are dead. We shall not rediscover the truths of architecture until new bases have established a logical ground for every architectural manifestation. A period of 20 years is beginning which will be occupied in creating these bases. A period of great problems, a period of analysis, of experiment, a period also of great aesthetic confusion, a period in which a new aesthetic will be elaborated.
> We must study the *plan*, the key of this evolution.[33]

The next chapter, "Regulating Lines," continues Le Corbusier's evolutionary account of the history of housing. It begins with a story about a primitive man who stops his chariot, cuts down a few trees, levels the earth, opens a road, drives stakes into the ground to steady his tent, and surrounds the whole with palisades in which he opens a door. He does the same for a small shelter or sanctuary for his gods. When the archaeologists arrive many years later and uncover these works, they find not only that everything has been ruled by right angles, straight axes, the rectangle, circle, and square, but everything has been generated by elementary mathematical calculation. This man, who was primitive only with respect to the resources at hand, *regulated* his work:

> For all these things–axes, circles, right angles–are geometrical truths, and give results that our eye can measure and recognize; whereas otherwise there would be only chance, irregularity and capriciousness. Geometry is the language of man.[34]

Forgotten today is the fact that great architecture stems from the beginnings of humanity:

> Architecture is the first manifestation of man creating his own universe, creating it in the image of nature, submitting to the laws of nature, the laws which govern our own nature, our universe. The laws of gravity, of statics and of dynamics, impose themselves by a *reductio ad absurdum*: everything must hold together or it will collapse.[35]

In the third chapter, Le Corbusier takes up the task of reforming "Eyes which do not See." He particularly addresses the elite men of organization and industry, not architects or ordinary readers. He begins with a refrain to be repeated three times, at the beginning of each

DELAGE. FRONT-WHEEL BRAKE

This precision, this cleanness in execution go further back than our re-born mechanical sense. Phidias felt in this way: the entablature of the Parthenon is a witness. So did the Egyptians when they polished the Pyramids. This at a time when Euclid and Pythagoras dictated to their contemporaries.

EYES WHICH DO NOT SEE

III

AUTOMOBILES

FIGURE 7.4: **If the chassis of an automobile could be standardized and perfected over time, so too could architecture.**

lesson–one on ocean liners, one on airplanes, and one on automobiles–a refrain first presented in the opening issue of *L'Esprit Nouveau*: "There is a new spirit: it is a spirit of construction and of synthesis guided by a clear conception."[36] [FIGURE 7.4]

The first lesson compares the decorative artist to an engineer using the example of steamships. The decorative arts are likened to "the straw which drowning men are said to clutch in a storm," that storm being the new spirit that the machine has aroused.[37] Unknown to the world, daring and masterful engineers have conceived and constructed steamships as gigantic palaces and thrown them on the seas to float.[38] But architects, stifled by custom, continue to construct houses with thick walls, small windows, wretched roofs, to decorate the surfaces of facades and fill drawing rooms with outmoded furniture. Le Corbusier introduces his alternative view, which would revive architecture:

> A house is a machine for living in.[39]
> Our modern life, when we are active and about (leaving out the moments when we fly to gruel and aspirin) has created its own objects: its costumes, its fountain pen, its eversharp pencil, its typewriter, its telephone, its admirable office furniture, its plate-glass and its "Innovation" trunks, the safety razor and the briar pipe, the bowler hat and the limousine, the steamship and the airplane.

268 TOWARDS A NEW ARCHITECTURE

old architectural code, with its mass of rules and regulations evolved during four thousand years, is no longer of any interest ; it no longer concerns us : all the values have been revised ; there has been revolution in the conception of what Architecture is.

Disturbed by the reactions which play upon him from every quarter, the man of to-day is conscious, on the one hand, of a new world which is forming itself regularly, logically and clearly, which produces in a straightforward way things which are useful and usable, and on the other hand he finds himself, to his surprise, living in an old and hostile environment. This framework is his lodging ; his town, his street, his house or his flat rise up against him useless, hinder him from following the same path in his leisure that he pursues in his work, hinder him from following in his leisure the organic development of his existence, which is to create a family and to live, like every animal on this earth and like all men of all ages, an organized family life. In this way society is helping forward the destruction of the family, while she sees with terror that this will be her ruin.

There reigns a great disagreement between the modern state of mind, which is an admonition to us, and the stifling accumulation of age-long detritus.

The problem is one of adaptation, in which the realities of our life are in question.

Society is filled with a violent desire for something which it may obtain or may not. Everything lies in that : everything

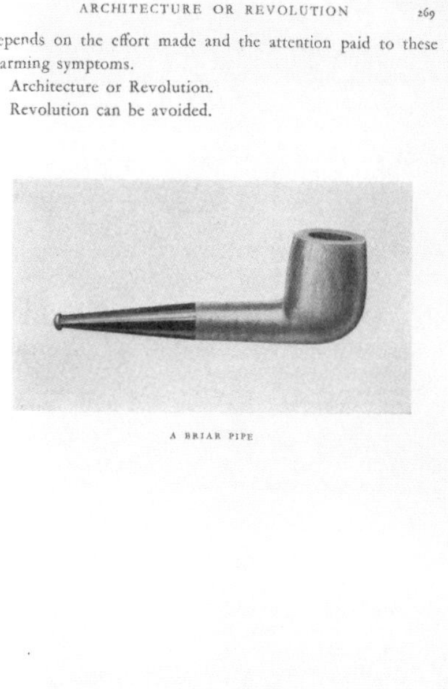

ARCHITECTURE OR REVOLUTION 269

depends on the effort made and the attention paid to these alarming symptoms.

Architecture or Revolution.

Revolution can be avoided.

A BRIAR PIPE

FIGURE 7.5: Among the modern objects brought to perfection was the briar pipe, a standard against which architecture could be compared.

> Our epoch is fixing its own style day by day. It is there under our eyes.
>
> Eyes which do not see.[40]

Machines are bringing a new sense of order to work and to leisure. [FIGURE 7.5] After characteristic digressions on the need to plan whole cities and for art (which is "in its essence arrogant"[41]) to address the technocratic elite, he sings the praises of the steamship:

> If we forget for a moment that a steamship is a machine for transport and look at it with a fresh eye, we shall feel that we are facing an important manifestation of temerity, of discipline, of a beauty that is calm, vital and strong.[42]

A serious architect will look at the steamship and find in it his freedom from the slavery of past traditions that restrict conceptions of the house. He will find the problem clearly stated and the solution a step forward: "The steamship is the first stage in the realization of a world organized according to the new spirit."[43]

The second of the three lessons in the "Eyes which Do Not See" chapter concerns the airplane, opening (as all the chapters do) by repeating the dicta already given in the opening argument:

> The airplane is the product of close selection.
> The lesson of the airplane lies in the logic which
> governed the statement of the problem and its realization.
> The problem of the house has not yet been stated.
> Nevertheless there do exist standards for the
> dwelling house.
> Machinery contains in itself the factor of economy, which makes
> for selection.
> The house is a machine for living in.[44]

Architects should understand how the modern airplane, a product of the Great War, was invented:

> The War was an insatiable "client," never satisfied, always demanding better. The orders were to succeed at all costs and death followed a mistake remorselessly. We may then affirm that the airplane mobilized invention, intelligence and daring: *imagination* and *cold reason*.[45]

But unfortunately there has been no salutary war as a client for architecture, demanding clarity and innovation of thought. Even in the north of France, devastated by the war, reconstruction failed to produce a modern architecture because the concept of a dwelling was missing. While engineers applied themselves to building dams, bridges, steamships, mines, and railways, architects fell asleep.

> The airplane shows us that a problem well stated finds its solution. To wish to fly like a bird is to state the problem badly, and Ader's "Bat" never left the ground.[46] To invent a flying machine having in mind nothing alien to pure mechanics, that is to say, to search for a means of suspension in the air and a means of propulsion, was to put the problem properly: in less than ten years the whole world could fly.[47]

How then to state the problem of housing correctly? What are the necessary and sufficient conditions to be addressed? The standards

MASS-PRODUCTION
HOUSES

FIGURE 7.6: Steamships, airplanes, and automobiles had standards of mass production that moved toward perfection. They taught architects what might happen if housing developed a standard and encouraged its perfection.

FIGURE 7.7: This famous double-page spread from *Towards a New Architecture* exemplifies Le Corbusier's comparative method: a four-by-four matrix of images to be compared, each perfecting their standards of production over time.

124 TOWARDS A NEW ARCHITECTURE

PAESTUM, 600–550 B.C.

When once a standard is established, competition comes at once and violently into play. It is a fight; in order to win you must do better than your rival *in every minute point*, in

HUMBER, 1907

AUTOMOBILES 125

THE PARTHENON, 447–434 B.C.

the run of the whole thing and in all the details. Thus we get the study of minute points pushed to its limits. Progress.

A standard is necessary for order in human effort.

DELAGE, "GRAND-SPORT," 1921

are simple: a house is a shelter against weather, thieves, and the inquisitive. A room needs a surface to walk on, a bed to sleep on, a table to work at, bins in which to store things. The number of necessary rooms is few: one each for cooking, eating, working, washing, and sleeping. There is no need for the furnishings of the decorative arts, for mirrored wardrobes and gilded commodes, damasked wallpapers and draped windows. Instead, use manufactured products: built-in cabinetry with numerous drawers to hold your clothes like an Innovation trunk, or to store your dishes, books, and paintings so that space is uncluttered and the walls are clear. Fundamentals: chairs are for sitting in, electricity for giving light, windows for admitting light and to see outside, pictures to be looked at–and a house for living in.[48] [FIGURE 7.6]

A manual for the dwelling must be printed and distributed to all mothers of families. For architects the manual will dictate the location of the bathroom, its glazed wall, a balcony for sunning, adjacent dressing room; it will advise bare walls for the bedroom, living room, and dining room; space-saving furniture will be built in to avoid clutter.[49]

The final lesson for "Eyes which do not See" approaches the problem of housing by studying the manner in which an automobile chassis was standardized and perfected. It opens with the logical refrain:

> We must aim at fixing of standards in order to face the problem of perfection.
> The Parthenon is a product of selection applied to a standard.
> Architecture operates in accordance with standards.
> Standards are a matter of logic, analysis and minute study; they are based on a problem which has been well "stated."
> A standard is definitely established by experiment.[50]

This is followed by a famous two-by-two grid of four images, namely, the temple at Paestum (600–550 B.C.), the Humber automobile (1907), the Parthenon (447–434 B.C.), and the Delage Grand-Sport automobile (1921). [FIGURE 7.7] If we read across the rows of this two-by-two square, by comparing temple to temple and auto to auto, then each standard or type evolves to its perfection, from Paestum to Parthenon or Humber to Delage. Reading down the columns, comparing temples to autos, reiterates the lesson: the temple is a type that derives from a standard perfected over time through selection until it arrives at its perfected

FIGURE 7.8: The Parthenon has reached perfection, while the steamship, airplane, and automobile are still evolving. This is the challenge to those who design housing–it too can be perfected once its standard has been selected.

type–the Parthenon–just as the automobile will perfect its standard in time and achieve a perfected type. It is left to apply the analogy to housing, to find its standard and its perfected type. [FIGURE 7.8]

Now Le Corbusier begins an elaborate argument about the production of standards, weaving his argument in and out of universal needs and standardized products, spiritual order and standards of emotions. The first motor-cars were constructed along the traditional lines of a slow-moving horse carriage. Their forms had nothing to do with the laws that govern solid bodies propelled through space at high speed. By studying these laws, however, a standard was soon achieved and then varied according to need: the mass in front for sports cars requiring speed, the bulk at the back for touring cars demanding comfort.[51]

This is how culture evolves, through selection: rejecting, pruning, cleansing, until the clear and naked essentials emerge. There are important lessons to be learned from looking side-by-side at the Parthenon and the motor-car: they involve selection in two different fields, only one of which (temple-building) has reached its perfected climax. It remains to apply the model of competition by which the automobile evolves to the challenge of the house.[52]

Le Corbusier reminds the reader that it is equally important to apply selective standards to furniture, to forget about the precious "piece" with its charm. A chair is a machine for sitting in and should, implicitly, not be decorated more than any other pure machine. Le Corbusier reminds the reader of what Loos had taught:

> Decoration is a sensorial and elementary order, as is colour, and is suited to simple races, peasants and savages. Harmony and proportion incite the intellectual faculties and arrest the man of culture.[53]

In architecture the measure of "harmony and proportion" rests both on the plan of the house and on its furniture. Both must achieve their standards. As for beauty, it can only reside in applications of elementary forms (sphere, cube, sphere, cylinder, and cone) that speak to the mind.[54]

In closing this third and final "lesson for architects," Le Corbusier once again returns to the Parthenon, this time as a hopeful reminder of the perfection man can achieve when he applies himself to a problem well stated. The perfection of the Parthenon is beyond the understanding of contemporary man; the sensations it evokes can be compared only with those generated by huge and impressive machines. He repeats the refrain from the opening of this "lesson": "But we must first of all aim at the setting of standards in order to face the problem of perfection."[55]

SECOND PART: THE LANGUAGE OF ARCHITECTURE

A major theme of Le Corbusier's, the relationship of architecture to language, is carried by the second section of *Vers une Architecture*, "Architecture," composed of three chapters: "The Lesson of Rome," "The Illusion of Plans," and "Pure Creation of the Mind."

This three-chapter section is introduced by "The Lesson of Rome." Here Le Corbusier begins by arguing that language and architecture are similar tools, both constructed out of simple elements, following structural laws, and having an infinite number of poetical meanings. In making this argument he is exploiting the limits of his writing tool, his language about architecture, working out how to effectively structure his message, move the reader, teach.

Moreover, language and images elaborate what architecture cannot say (in the language of built forms), but only emotes. A repeated chorus reminds the reader that engineers create practical, even ingenious constructions of stone, wood, and concrete, but only when the heart is touched does art enter in: as Le Corbusier also says, "Architecture goes beyond utilitarian needs."[56] Then eyes behold thought expressed by means of shapes revealed in clear light. These shapes are the elemental units that the grammar of architecture will arrange. And there must be semantics as well, in order for this language to achieve lyrical or poetical expression. So, Le Corbusier continues, emotions are aroused when the relationships between shapes reflect a mathematical creation of the mind, and only then do they correctly speak the language of architecture.[57]

"The Lesson of Rome," first of the language-of-architecture chapters occupying the central position in *Vers une Architecture*, is a discourse on history.[58] Le Corbusier applies Loos's paradoxical method of argumentation, constantly juxtaposing examples from the past against those of the present. He demands that the reader live in two worlds at the same time, feeling the crisis of modernity in the contrast between antiquity and modernity, classical and mechanical, tradition and innovation. Following Loos, he argues that modern society has borrowed its techniques of thinking and feeling, constructing and teaching, from the Romans. Modern culture is therefore not in balance. To achieve unity in all the arts, the moderns must learn from the Greeks.[59]

To draw in the reader, Le Corbusier offers the intriguing claim that Rome is picturesque, a bazaar–but compared to the Greeks, the Romans had bad taste. Ancient Rome had no plan, and Renaissance Rome, worse, exhibited pompous outbursts in all corners of the city. The modern Rome of Victor Emmanuel continues this tradition of huddling all things together.[60]

On the positive side, the business of ancient Rome was to conquer the world, and it did so in "the spirit of order." A paradox: Rome within (i.e., within its walls) is without a plan, but Hadrian's Villa, outside of Rome, had a plan. It was the first example in the West of space planning on a grand scale. Modern man has failed to employ the Roman power of organization–for that is the lesson that should have been retained! The word "Roman" *means* "Unity of operation, a clear aim in view, classification of the various parts."[61] The Roman mind effects architecture: simple masses with immense surfaces adorned by the mere repetition of simple geometrical forms such as cupolas, cylinders, rectangular prisms, and pyramids. Everything speaks of elementary geometry. This is the first lesson of Rome: how to construct. Later ages forgot their simple language of architecture.

Pompeii is more appealing than Rome due to its rectangular plan, even though its builders preferred the ornate Corinthian order to the unadorned Doric (both Greek in origin). Another contact with Greece occurred when the Greeks came to Rome to build the tiny Byzantine church of Saint Maria in Cosmedin. Here again are displayed "The unassailable power of proportion, sovereign eloquence of relationships,"the mathematical precision through which perfection is approached.[62] Le Corbusier claims that the same powerful, positive forms and walls of rough lime plaster, painted entirely white, can be found in modern barns and aircraft hangars. Again the refrain is repeated: "Architecture is nothing but ordered arrangement, noble prisms, seen in light."[63] The Greeks created an architecture that deployed quantities, numbers, relationships, measures, and rhythms. Such an architecture, based on mathematics, speaks to the mind. Yet the Greeks allowed the ineffable to speak as well:

> In the balanced silence of S. Maria in Cosmedin there stand out the sloping handrail of a pulpit and the inclined stone book-rest of an ambo in a conjunction as silent as a gesture of assent. These two quiet oblique lines which are fused in the perfect movement of a spiritual mechanics–this is the pure and simple beauty that architecture can give.[64]

This is the second lesson of Rome: the presence of a "spiritual mechanics."

After discussing St. Peter's as a gigantic geometry spoiled by barbarian hands, Le Corbusier closes his argument by inverting the order of words used in the opening: Rome is a bazaar, but a picturesque one. It fell asleep after Michelangelo. Our modern taste judges Rome severely: "The lesson of Rome is for wise men, for those who know and can appreciate, who can resist and verify. Rome is the damnation of the half-educated. To send architectural students to Rome is to cripple them for life."[65]

Now Le Corbusier is ready to prove his point that the language of architecture must balance its interior structure of elements with the exterior relations of its forms. The second chapter of this central section of *Vers une Architecture*, "The Illusion of Plans," opens with the dictum, "The Plan proceeds from within to without," a refrain that will be repeated four times within the chapter and is the heart of its argument. It is joined to a clarification–"The exterior is the result of an interior"[66]–variations of which are repeated five times in this chapter, culminating in the paradoxical claim that "The *exterior* is always an *interior*."[67]

Critical, he says, of all aims that do not clearly and distinctly speak the language of architecture, Le Corbusier will deal only with things that the eye can appreciate, simple diagrams and undeniable truths. Only ordered ideas exhibiting precise intentions are communicable.[68] A plan is like a table of contents, condensing many ideas like a crystal or geometrical figure. The École des Beaux-Arts reduced the plan to recipes and tricks, producing star-patterns on paper, but in reality a plan "Is a plan of battle....Without a good plan nothing exists, all is frail and cannot endure, all is poor even under the clutter of the richest decoration."[69] This is the "vital fact," and allows the main line of argumentation to be introduced: "A plan proceeds *from within to without*."[70] In an aside he offers his demonstration: within architecture the plan concerns the architectural elements of the interior–that seems apparent, but he will prove that without, in the arrangement of building to site, "The *exterior* is always an *interior*."[71]

The title of the next subsection repeats the point: "A Plan Proceeds from Within to Without." An intriguing example is offered: a building is like a soap bubble, its "exterior the result of an interior."[72] A more developed argument follows involving the mosques of Asia Minor. The reader is directed on a promenade from the exterior street, through a little doorway, into a small vestibule of the Green Mosque at Broussa, into the noble white-marble interior filled with light, where the eye perceives on each side smaller spaces in subdued light and, turning around, still smaller ones in shade. A cluster of ideas creates a rhythm of movement in light and volume, in scale and measure–an aim or intention that "tells you what it set out to tell you," nothing more, nothing less.[73] In the Green Mosque, as in Santa Sophia and the Suleiman Mosque in Stamboul, "The exterior results from the interior."[74] A second example: the small Casa del Noce at Pompeii. From the street to the little vestibule, from the shade in the columned atrium to the far end where brilliant light from the garden spreads through the peristyle, the interior makes a large space. Suddenly, the vision contracts, like the lens in a camera, as the eye perceives the tablium erected between the two: then "you are conscious of Architecture."[75]

The interior elements that comprise the architectural language of the Casa del Noce are few and simple: vertical walls, the horizontal slab of the floor, holes for the passage of light. Architecture is meant to make the spectator gay, serene, even sad, and does so with the play of light and shadow. Light falls between walls that reflect it, or the impression of light is extended outside through peristyles and pillars.[76]

Yet the problem of proportion remains, to be tackled in the next subsection, "Arrangement." It appears that Le Corbusier is utilizing the method of Descartes, the straight line of argumentation, the classification of intentions with clearly stated ends. The "axis"–a Cartesian trope–is perhaps the first human expression, as the toddler moves or man strives in the tempest of his life, the means of every human act, the regulator of architecture, "A line of direction leading to an end."[77] It is rational, purposive, and directed–not like the lines of the schools of architecture, which are plural, crossing each other in star shapes leading to the undefined, to nowhere without end. Axes cannot be seen from a bird's-eye view, as in plans on a drawing-board, but only from the ground, by a beholder standing upright and looking straight in front of him. He adduces his famous lesson on axes, borrowed from Choisy: "The axis of the Acropolis runs from the Piraeus to Pentelicus, from the sea to the mountain. The Propylaea are at right angles to the axis, in the distance on the horizon–the sea."[78] The lesson of the plan of the Acropolis is that it places to the right of this axis and to the left the entrances to the Parthenon and the Erechtheum: "Architectural buildings should not all be placed upon axes, for this would be like so many people all talking at once."[79]

There follow lessons from the Forum of Pompeii and the House of the Tragic Poet, and support gathered from Camillo Sitte, all the time repeating the refrain: arrangement is the grading of aims, the classification of intentions. The reader is now amply prepared for the title of the next subsection: "The Exterior Is Always an Interior."[80]

The schools imagine that the eye of the spectator stays fixed on the center of gravity determined by the axes. But the eye absorbs more than is intended. The eye is always on the move, the spectator turning right and left, interested in everything–the gravity of the whole site, and its entire surroundings. Intelligence measures and anticipates cubic volumes both near and far, low and high, the geometrical disposition of forms, and the densities of material. The elements of the site also speak the language of architecture: walls, light, and space. These create in the spectator the effects of sadness, gaiety, or serenity. "Our compositions must be formed of these elements."[81] Using again the example of the Acropolis, he explains that the temples all turn toward each other, creating an enclosure that the eye embraces.

Finally, a reminder that there is "Transgression" (the title of the next subsection of the chapter on "The Illusion of Plans"). Transgressions occur where the architect has *not* followed the rule "A plan proceeds from within to without."[82] The marring of Michelangelo's design for St. Peter's at Rome is noted again, and Versailles is offered as evidence that bird's-eye views and star patterns transgress the truths of architecture. These deceptions inspired the plan of Karlsruhe, presenting absolute proof that the star exists only on paper.[83] The conclusion follows: architecture must deal with plans that the eye can judge, indulging in big aims without vanity and avoiding the errors of paper plans.

The third and final chapter of the central section of *Vers une Architecture*, "Pure Creation of the Mind," focuses on the artist, who composes profiles and contours as pure creations of the mind.[84] The reader is reminded that architecture is composed like a language.

The argument of this chapter is carried through a series of text/image juxtapositions, a form of literary montage Le Corbusier first experimented with in the pages of *L'Esprit Nouveau*. These photographs are taken from the 1914 album of Frédéric Boissonnas, *Le Parthénon: histoire, l'architecture et la sculpture*.[85]

The first two photographs (of the Parthenon and the internal portico of the Propylaea, gateway to the Acropolis) are placed on a left-hand page. The caption of the first reminds the reader that Greeks united the temples of the Acropolis and the landscape into a single composition: "On every point of the horizon, the thought is single."[86] A quick shift to the present: we moderns will "talk" Doric when everything accidental in art is sacrificed and man reaches the highest level of the mind, that of absolute austerity. The caption under the Propylaea photo restates the theme: "The plastic scheme is expressed in unity."[87] Opposite these two photos, on the right-hand page, is a single image of the Propylaea. The caption reminds the reader that emotion arises from relationships between architectural elements, from things in harmony with the site, and from the unity of an idea that spans from materials to the contour–like those we experience when looking at a beautiful face.

The second set of photographs presents the Propylaea on the left, the Erechtheum on the right. The refrain "Emotion is born of unity of aim" is followed by an amplification of the intention: to achieve in marble a pure, clarified, austere composition in which nothing more can be sacrificed, when the triumphal moment arrives and one is confronted with "Closely knit and violent elements, sounding clear and tragic like brazen trumpets."[88]

The emotions that the images evoke in Le Corbusier are passed through words to the reader. The architecture of forms is likened to poetical expressions. The text–interspersed between these photographs–runs for four or five pages, comparing the emotions aroused by the Parthenon to the vibration of an internal sounding board that vibrates in harmony with the exterior forms. Thus the reader is presented with another analogy for architecture: music, with its deeply structured rules and unique notational system, whose rhythms and sound patterns move us without the need for symbolic reference. When a chord is struck within man, his axis is touched. This is the axis on which man is organized in accord with nature and on which all objects of nature are based. The laws of physics, science, and mathematics proceed from the single intention that lies behind this axis. Le Corbusier shifts to contemporary times: if everyday objects appear as objects of nature it is because they are also based on this same axis. This is the definition of harmony: accord with the axis that lies in man and within the laws of the universe.

A work of art, Le Corbusier repeats, must have unity of aim. If we see clearly, then we can read, learn, and feel the harmony within us. A clear statement, "pure creation of the mind," gives a living unity or character to the work (e.g., the moldings on the Propylaea or the annulets on the Parthenon).[89] But why are proportion, harmony, rhythm understood in contemporary works of art such as painting and music, but not in architecture, which has been demoted to utilitarian functions? Boudoirs, water closets, radiators, ferro-concrete vaults, or pointed arches are constructions, but they are not architecture.[90]

Next, after so many images of the Acropolis, the reader is rudely confronted with an ugly image of a plaster cast of the Beaux-Arts. The image has the effect of jarring the reader into awareness that architecture is not mere construction, but a plastic art seen and measured by the eyes.

As if presenting an autobiographical aside, Le Corbusier admits that the architect must know construction as a thinker knows his grammar–it is a technique more complex than writing or designing. He must learn this grammar well, but he should not vegetate there, for the architect must also express himself lyrically. Soon after comes the much-repeated refrain that Le Corbusier first utilized in 1911:

> Architecture is the skillful, accurate and magnificent play of masses seen in light; and contours are also and exclusively the skillful, accurate and magnificent play of volumes seen in light.[91]

Greece and the Parthenon mark the culmination of pure creations of the mind because they brought the development of profile and contour into perfection. They were a personal invention of the great sculptor Phidias, who molded light and shade into the infallible and severe geometry of contours, the pure outline of profiles. They ravish minds, touch the axis of harmony: no religious dogma, no symbolic forms, no naturalistic representation, just pure forms in precise relationships.[92]

A MATTER OF HOUSING: ARCHITECTURE OR REVOLUTION

Vers une Architecture now descends from its three-chapter climb up the Acropolis to speak again of housing, of the modern city seething, as it were, at the feet of the Greeks' supreme achievement. Two chapters handle this recursion to practical tasks. The first spells out the urgent need for "Mass-Production Houses." Until the problem of the house is addressed, the equilibrium of society is in danger of being upset. "Architecture has for its first duty, in this period of renewal, that of bringing about a revision of values, a revision of the constituent elements of the house."[93] It must do so by creating a new spirit for constructing and living in mass-produced houses, a new way of thinking about such houses in architects and common men, until the house-machine has been achieved.

The ostensible reason for this urgency lay in the expected passage of the Loucheur law in the early 1920s, authorizing the construction of half a million new dwellings throughout France. Architects were scarcely prepared to meet the demand. The situation, Le Corbusier thought, demanded they return to the beginning: creating new workshops and training technical experts who could conceive of and execute standardized units, and apply these to the creation of mass-produced housing. Industry had already produced "new materials," first steps toward industrializing the building of houses: "Cements and limes, steel girders, sanitary fittings, insulating materials, piping, ironmongery, water-proofing compositions." But when these products were introduced, they involved enormous labor costs and produced only partial solutions. Thus natural products such as wood and stone soon returned to replace artificial materials. Other areas demanded reform, such as the provision of modern systems of water, lighting, or heating, effectively installed inside cavity walls instead of on top of traditional thick walls made of stone. In addition, roofs no longer needed to be pitched in order to throw off water; heavy window armatures no longer needed to deprive the interior of light; these and other changes were altering the conception of what a house entailed.[94]

> In the next twenty years, big industry will have co-ordinated its standardized materials.... Financial and social organization,

> using concerted and forceful methods, will be able to solve the housing question, and the yards will be on a huge scale, run and exploited like government offices. Dwellings, urban and suburban, will be enormous and square built and no longer dismal congeries; they will incorporate the principles of mass-production and of large-scale industrialization.[95]

Inevitably, Le Corbusier believed, buildings built "to measure" would soon cease to exist. A house "will be a tool as the motor-car is becoming a tool."[96] The house-tool will be a democratic tool, healthy, morally sound, a beautiful poem. Big industry is ready to collaborate, the suburban railways and financial organizations will be involved, and the schools of architecture will be transformed.

> We are dealing with an urgent problem of our epoch, nay more, with the problem of our epoch. The balance of society comes down to a question of building. We conclude with these justifiable alternatives: *Architecture* or *Revolution*.[97]

This phrase, "Architecture or Revolution," is also the title and theme of the last chapter, the only one written expressly to accompany the 1923 republication of this set of essays from *L'Esprit Nouveau*. It repeats lessons already delivered in earlier chapters but deployed once again to persuade the reader that the necessary reforms of the house-tool are close at hand. It juxtaposes the millstone of past achievements against the present record of magnificent innovations. The tone of emergency is heightened, and the argumentative nature of the work accentuated: architecture is in crisis because the decorative arts, the schools of architecture, the fears and tastes of ordinary men hold it back and do not allow it to employ modern tools, procedures, and materials, whether in the design of the simplest item of equipment or the plan of the most complex town. [FIGURE 7.9]

"Architecture or Revolution" is the antithesis that increases in stridency and accelerates its pace across the pages of this last chapter. Such antithetical proclamations or pairings were (and remain) a standard technique of propaganda and publicity, and were cleverly deployed by Loos. The dramatic alternatives, "architecture or revolution," mirror each other on several different levels, and also link *Vers une Architecture* to the forthcoming *Urbanisme* (*The City of To-morrow*).

ARCHITECTURE
OR
REVOLUTION

FIGURE 7.9: Architects have a choice: to design functional housing or let the masses revolt.

In the final chapter of *Vers une Architecture*, the reader is bombarded with the word "revolution" and its cognates: first in the chapter title, then twelve times within eighteen pages (not counting its reappearance at the top of every right-hand page). New problems have been resolved by new tools: mass production has revolutionized the methods and scale of architecture, the new materials of steel and concrete have overturned the old codes and the "styles" of the past. But new needs, produced in the wake of these changes, have gone unmet, causing society to oscillate dangerously. There is social unrest, for neither the artisan nor the intellectual has a shelter that answers his needs. Thus, revolution threatens.

Le Corbusier begins with a historical review to show that the tools man has created to answer his needs have evolved only slowly until suddenly, in the present era, they have been dramatically transformed. Tools of the past were in man's hands, but now they are beyond his grasp, and he is confused. He feels he is slave to a frantic state in which he experiences neither freedom, comfort, nor amelioration. To pass through this crisis he must achieve a state of mind that understands that things have actually improved.[98]

In the past, man "lived like a snail in its shell, in a lodging made exactly to his measure; there was nothing to induce him to modify this state of things, which was indeed harmonious enough."[99] His society was stable and endured. Today, men create mass-produced articles using machines. Absolute precision is required, as each worker repetitively produces one tiny unit that automatically fits into the assembled whole. He sees the end result of his labor only when the finished piece passes, "In its bright and shiny purity, into the factory yard to be placed in a delivery-van…and this will fill him with a legitimate pride."[100] The factory operates on three different time shifts, not on an eight-hour day. Yet no one has thought how the worker can make healthy use of his free time. His lodging is hideous and his mind not educated to use hours of liberty. Thus the inevitable result: "Architecture or demoralization–demoralization and revolution."[101]

After underlining that the modern workman's needs are not met, Le Corbusier argues that neither are the needs of the intellectuals met, those men who design bridges, ships, and airplanes, who create motors and turbines, who direct industries, organize goods in the shop, finance huge undertakings, and who write articles in the press about the marvels of modern industry and about labor in crisis.

> These people have their eyes fixed on the display of goods in the great shops that man has made for himself. The modern age is spread before them, sparkling and radiant–on the far side of the barrier. In their homes…they find their uncleanly old snail-shell and they can not think of having a family.…These people, too, claim their rights to a machine for living in, which shall be in all simplicity a human thing.[102]

Both the worker and the intellectual utilize the most brilliant and effective tools of the day but are prohibited from using them to provide a better shell for themselves. Nothing is more discouraging, irritating, and consequently–"Architecture or Revolution." The barrier that blocks the radical transformation of the house and town is the principle of private property, which aims to maintain the status quo. Every other endeavor in modern society is subject to the "rough warfare of competition," but not the landlord, who is king. Even here things are beginning to change, and soon it may be possible to achieve a comprehensive building program and avoid revolution.[103]

In essence, Le Corbusier argues that only a revolution in architecture can prevent a violent social revolution. There are new materials, inventions, formulas that create a "revolution in methods of construction."[104] Old "styles" can no longer clothe architecture except as "parasites": "all the values have been revised; there has been revolution in the conception of what Architecture is."[105] He concludes as follows:

> Society is filled with a violent desire for something which it may obtain or may not. Everything lies in that: everything depends on the effort made and the attention paid to these alarming symptoms.
>
> Architecture or Revolution.
>
> Revolution can be avoided.[106]

VERS UNE ARCHITECTURE: CRITICAL ASSESSMENT

Reyner Banham has said that *Vers une Architecture* is one of the most widely read and least understood of all architectural writings of the twentieth century, yet it has little to do with architecture.[107] The book consists of "rhapsodical essays" assembled side by side with no underlying connection nor argument. Banham infers that its chapters can be read separately without doing violence to the whole. He also considers that Le Corbusier's rhetoric, in which he places antithetical images side by side in Loos's manner, generates ambiguous meanings. For example, his compound concept house:machine sometimes treats the house as a utilitarian tool and a product of "mere" engineering, sometimes as a beautiful object to be revered, sometimes as something spiritual, ineffable. And while Le Corbusier insists that architecture has nothing to do with "styles," still, Banham points out, he remains a prisoner to both form and style. No matter what Le Corbusier professes to the contrary, a machine aesthetic is prescribed by the mechanical objects listed and imaged throughout the book: grain silos, steamships, automobiles, airplanes, machine parts.[108]

Banham deconstructs *Vers une Architecture* into two themes: an academic or classical one and a mechanistic one. The text's classical references, in which the Parthenon is emblematic, consist of two blocks of essays: those that demonstrate a preference for architecture of elementary geometrical forms whose mass and surface are generated by "the plan," and those that express how art and architecture embody spiritual ideals. The mechanistic essays, inserted before and after the classical ones, preach the lessons of the machine, praise the engineer, and develop the famous metaphor "A house is a machine for living in." In this juxtaposition, Banham argues, machine design mediates between the abstract rules of architectural design and the guiding paradigm of the Parthenon. He takes as exemplary of this crossplay of intentions Le Corbusier's famous double-page spread juxtaposing images of Greek temples against those of automobiles. And in spite of Le Corbusier's emphasis on the process of design, Banham maintained, he never defines the set of design rules that would generate volumes assembled under pure light. Nor does he consider that technique, not just the plan, generates form. Thus his thought is flawed, and he remains captive to the primacy of form and to meditations on style.

Geoffrey Baker takes a more traditional approach, arguing that Le Corbusier's oeuvre has two parts: a set of inadequate theoretical proposals and a series of buildings in which his architectural skills are put on display.[109] The theoretical proposals remain suspect, especially as they were developed in *Vers une Architecture.* Baker's analysis of the book organizes it into three main sections: a theory of architectural composition, a Purist theory of how standards evolve, and an application of that theory to how modern life should be lived. The latter, Baker claims, is the most flawed section. Le Corbusier's "evolutionary" theory is simplistic, excluding many forces that influence the development of artifacts. Baker does not agree that the same evolutionary laws can be applied to a bistro glass and a house. "In fact, the limitations of [Le Corbusier's] theory become fully exposed when applied to the dwelling and, beyond that, the city. In any assessment of his work we have to separate out these two areas and review them in a way that acknowledges his theoretical deficiencies."[110]

I have argued to the contrary that *Vers une Architecture* has everything to do with the reform of the modern house, which will lead toward the reform of the city. The order of chapters is important, not arbitrary. Le Corbusier wraps his central argument on the language of architecture and the architecture of language, with sections that begin with the problems of how to state precisely the problem of the house so that it will find a solution, and ends with a section on how to avoid revolution by industrializing the production of the house-tool and thus answering the needs of modern man. Language remains his central concern: to persuade, to move, to illustrate the necessary architectural reforms. To construct a book, a painting, a house, a city is to follow the formal rules of syntax and apply the semantics of poetry so they communicate lucidly and precisely to the reader or the viewer. The purity of these formal constructions reveals their intention, factual knowledge, memory of traditions, innovations, the force their implementation demands. The visual-verbal imagery explodes under the reader's eyes, as these montages are intended to be seen all at once. Le Corbusier's writings call out to us to see things anew, persuading us to adopt a new order of things, pushing us toward an architectural revolution.[111]

In the articles comprising *Vers une Architecture* Le Corbusier was asking how architects might design machines for living like the engineer designed machines for traveling on water, flying through air, or driving on land. How were order and classification reiterated by ordinary tools of everyday use? He was not interested in copying the style of modern machines, as Banham criticized. The lessons of Le Corbusier's analogies lay in the logic of construction, in the process of production that generated forms, and not in their surface style or in their overt meaning. As far as suggesting design rules, Banham overlooked the simple elements of a structural logic that Le Corbusier was hinting at: the five points of architecture that would become the elements of his language of architecture, as we shall see below.

Finally, *Vers une Architecture* points directly at the next book on the Le Corbusier shelf, *Urbanisme* (English title: *The City of To-morrow*). The last sentences of *Vers une Architecture* declare an alarming tension and the hope of a solution: "Architecture or Revolution. Revolution can be avoided"–if, we understand by that point, we literally re-form the modern world in accordance with the dicta of Purist architecture.[112] The ending of *Urbanisme* is strikingly similar: Le Corbusier repeats the "architecture or revolution" in the final sentences of *Urbanisme,* and proposes the same solution–a fully sane architecture. "Architecture versus revolution. Things are not revolutionized by making revolutions. The real revolution lies in the solution of existing problems."[113] In the following section, we shall see how Le Corbusier revisited the architecture-versus-revolution theme of *Vers une Architecture* with an expanded discourse on urbanism rescued and improved from his earlier, faltering steps in the never-finished *Étude sur la construction des villes.*

III. LE CORBUSIER'S DREAM OF A RATIONAL CITY: URBANISME (1923–25)

Charles-Édouard Jeanneret began working on the manuscript entitled *Étude sur la construction des villes* in 1910. Studying in the Bibliothèque Nationale in Paris in the summer of 1915, he learned that his chosen subject, urbanism, was a complex problem that had engendered considerable study since the 1870s. Apparently doubting whether he had anything original to say on the subject, he abandoned the project in 1916. Yet his interest in cities never waned, and in the pages of *L'Esprit*

Nouveau he attempted to extend the doctrine of Purism to the order of the city, often recycling materials originally assembled for the *Étude*.

Early in the 1920s, Le Corbusier developed his scheme of the generating plan and applied it not just to architectural forms but also to streets and towns. He designed the Ville Contemporaine as a model for the Salon d'Automne 1922 and made frequent reference to the problem of planning cities in *Vers une Architecture*. During the third period of *L'Esprit Nouveau* (1923–25), when all but one of the articles republished in 1925 as *Urbanisme* were written, he embellished his discourse on urbanism and on the threat of revolution posed by uncontrolled urban development.[114]

In *Urbanisme*, much as in *Vers une Architecture*, a keystone or core chapter is prefaced and followed by supportive material. The core chapter of *Urbanisme* is Chapter 7, "The Great City Today," which appears in the middle of Part One. It is prefaced by theoretical chapters discussing binary oppositions that need to be resolved before the language of architecture can be applied to the city and revolution avoided, and followed by chapters studying effects arising from the Great City that are themselves revolutionary.

Part One, "General Considerations," consists of ten essays appearing in the same order as they were first published in *L'Esprit Nouveau*. All but the first, "The Pack Donkey's Way and Man's Way," appeared in the review between November 1923 and January 1925–the period when Le Corbusier was firmly in control of editorial policy and was experimenting with text/image juxtapositions and a telegraphic or staccato style of writing. Only one of the articles was written under the pseudonym Le Corbusier-Saugnier.[115] Part Two, "Laboratory Work: An Inquiry into Theory," contains the description of "A Contemporary City for 3 Million."[116] Part Three, "A Concrete Case," applies this theory to the Voisin Plan for Paris.[117]

ANTITHESES MUST BE RESOLVED.

The section opens with a first antithesis: the way of the donkey and the way of man. This argument inverts Le Corbusier's earlier discussions on the sinuous line of the donkey path, which he had formerly advocated.[118]

Man, being rational, walks in a straight line; he has a goal and knows where he is going. The donkey meanders along, zigzags to ease his climb or to gain some shade. Man is governed by rational

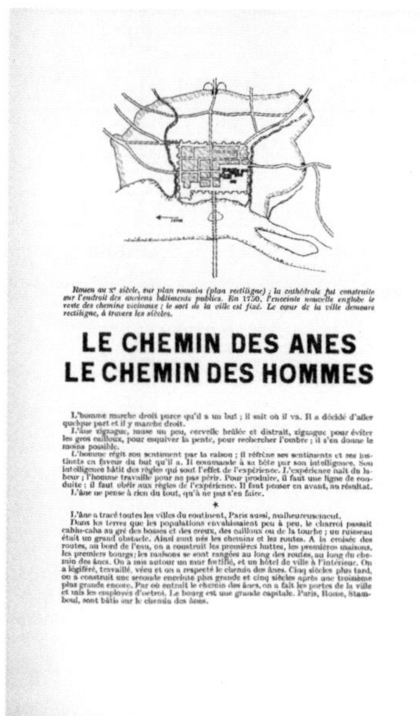

Rouen au Xe siècle, sur plan romain (plan rectiligne) ; la cathédrale fut construite sur l'endroit des anciens bâtiments publics. En 1750, l'enceinte nouvelle englobe le reste des chemins vicinaux ; le sort de la ville est fixé. Le cœur de la ville demeure rectiligne, à travers les siècles.

LE CHEMIN DES ANES
LE CHEMIN DES HOMMES

L'homme marche droit parce qu'il a un but ; il sait où il va. Il a décidé d'aller quelque part et il y marche droit.

L'âne zigzague, muse un peu, cervelle brûlée et distrait, zigzague pour éviter les gros cailloux, pour esquiver la pente, pour rechercher l'ombre ; il s'en donne le moins possible.

L'homme régit son sentiment par la raison ; il refrène ses sentiments et ses instincts en faveur du but qu'il a. Il commande à sa bête par son intelligence. Son intelligence bâtit des règles qui sont l'effet de l'expérience. L'expérience naît du labeur ; l'homme travaille pour ne pas périr. Pour produire, il faut une ligne de conduite ; il faut obéir aux règles de l'expérience. Il faut penser en avant, au résultat.

L'âne ne pense à rien du tout, qu'à ne pas s'en faire.

*

L'âne a tracé toutes les villes du continent, Paris aussi, malheureusement.

Dans les terres que les populations envahissaient peu à peu, le charroi passait cahin-caha au gré des bosses et des creux, des cailloux ou de la tourbe ; un ruisseau était un grand obstacle. Ainsi sont nés les chemins et les routes. A la croisée des routes, au bord de l'eau, on a construit les premières huttes, les premières maisons, les premiers bourgs ; les maisons se sont rangées au long des routes, au long du chemin des ânes. On a mis autour un mur fortifié, et un hôtel de ville à l'intérieur. On a légiféré, travaillé, vécu et on a respecté le chemin des ânes. Cinq siècles plus tard, on a construit une seconde enceinte plus grande et cinq siècles après une troisième plus grande encore. Par où entrait le chemin des ânes, on a fait les portes de la ville et mis les employés d'octroi. Le bourg est une grande capitale. Paris, Rome, Stamboul, sont bâtis sur le chemin des ânes.

FIGURE 7.10: Donkeys meander, following a zigzag route. Man, being rational, walks in a straight line.

feelings; he formulates laws, and considers the result in advance. The donkey thinks of nothing except what will save him trouble. Yet he is responsible for the form of every city in Europe: Paris, Rome, and even Stamboul.[119] These cities have no arteries, only capillaries, so growth brings sickness; their survival necessitates a surgical operation. [FIGURE 7.10]

"The Pack-Donkey's Way has been made into a religion!"[120]

Camillo Sitte's book was responsible: he glorified the curved line and the beautiful towns of the Middle Ages. In the age of motorcars, however, a city must live by the straight line. It is paralyzed by the curving line. "We must have courage to view the rectilinear cities of American with admiration."[121]

Having established the superiority of the straight line, Le Corbusier advances his theories about "Order" in the following chapter.[122] Addressed to newspaper critics who like infinite variety, the curved line, and twisted, distorted objects, and who impose these stupidities on others, Le Corbusier's argument sets up an antithesis between nature and geometry. Since the house, the street, and the city are points to which human energy is directed, they should be ordered.

Otherwise they thwart us. Man reasons, he practices order, and his toil is dictated by the straight line and the right angle; Nature is all confusion and the accidental, full of surface appearances. Man makes things that contrast with nature; the closer these things are to ideas that he formulates in his mind, the less they resemble the body, and the closer they come to pure geometry. Thus, "A violin or a chair, things which come into close contact with the body, are of a less pure geometry; but a town is pure geometry."[123]

The art critics do not like the "crystal" that Le Corbusier is trying to establish, so once again he calls on history for support:

> The prehistoric lake village; the savage's hut; the Egyptian house and temple; Babylon, the legend of which is a synonym for magnificence; Pekin, that highly cultivated Chinese town; all these demonstrate, on the one hand, the right angle and the straight line which inevitably enter into every human act.[124]

Only the turmoil of the last one hundred years has destroyed the geometrical order of the Great City.

The third chapter, "Sensibility Comes into Play," discusses emotional sensibilities of equilibrium or disequilibrium.[125] Le Corbusier applies his evolutionary argument to the development of Western culture, which he believes "shines so crystal clear." Culture is not absorbed from textbooks or pillaged treasures, but requires centuries of effort to evolve.[126] Therefore, Man never copies or steals another's sensibility. Le Corbusier turns to the example of the craftsmen of the North, who began with copying what they saw in Rome: the Pantheon. By the year 1000, they were discouraged and thought the end of the world was near. But by 1300, the cathedral had been born out of classical culture, not stealing but ingesting and digesting this culture until a completely new sensibility evolved. The evolutionary road continues; now modern man searches to reach a further stage. This road demands a hierarchy of sensibilities and leads toward geometry and the classical. "Equilibrium means calm, a mastery of the means at our disposal, clear vision, order, the satisfaction of the mind, scale and proportion."[127] Disequilibrium, in contrast, means conflict, disquietude, difficulties not resolved, a state of bondage, and questioning.

> Where the orthogonal is supreme, there we can read the height of civilization. Cities can be seen emerging from the jumble of the

> streets, striving towards straight lines, and taking them as far as possible. When man begins to draw straight lines he bears witness that he has gained control of himself and that he has reached a condition of order. Culture is an orthogonal state of mind.[128]

The spirits of geometry, exactitude, and order form the strategic base, projecting this journey toward progress and the beautiful. The reactionary forces feel the power of this forward movement as it gives birth to new forms and new feelings, throwing the old machine out of gear.

Having described the highest equilibrium achieved by the straight line and the right angle, the orthogonal state of mind, Le Corbusier offers an antithesis in the next chapter, "Permanence"–that between reason and passion. He offers a fact: "Immense industrial undertakings do not need great men." He compares the engineers with their equations, ruled papers, slide rules, and fateful figures to raindrops that fill a bucket drop by drop, in contrast to a great torrent that washes everything away.[129] "The point is that the products of reason must be most carefully differentiated from the products of passion."[130] Real passion, icy cold or burning hot, inspires man to behave in ways that are not those of reason–it speaks of emotion, which guides man's destiny.[131]

Le Corbusier advances a hypothesis borrowed from Poincaré: the greatest works of art, those that move us, are born of a conjunction combining both passion and reason.[132] Emotions guide man's destiny:

> The immense undertakings of humanity become more and more elaborated, more and more audacious and of a temerity that might well bring down the anger of the gods.[133]

> The engineer is a pearl of a man and like a pearl on a string he knows his two neighbors, he knows only cause and effect. The poet, however, sees the entire necklace of pearls; he combines reason and passion.[134]

Now Le Corbusier can return to the issue of cities and revolution. Industrial achievements and their tools have created a revolution; they have upset the equilibrium, destroyed standards and age-old classifications. Conflict occurs between the poet and the engineer, but it is the poet's foresight, not the engineer's, that can imagine the city on a new scale. A city's business is to make itself permanent; this depends

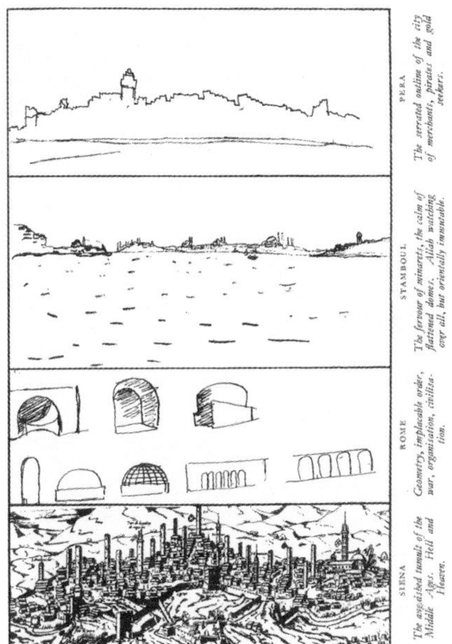

FIGURE 7.11: **Le Corbusier likened the profiles of his favorite cities—such as Siena, Rome, Stamboul (Istanbul), and Pera—to that of a beautiful face.**

on more than mere calculation. "And it is only Architecture which can give all the things which go beyond calculation."[135] [FIGURE 7.11]

The tropes of permanence and passion reappear in the next two chapters, both entitled "Classification and Choice."[136] We must throw out everything that does not bring joy, everything that creates despair, especially the despair of cities. Now an objective survey of facts is needed. Most important of all facts are the soul of the city, its poetry, which holds the secret of our happiness.[137] City planning, concerned with what produces happiness or creates misery, denounces the egotistical gratifications that have been responsible for creating great cities. He compares Stamboul to New York, two cities that inspire antithetical feelings of comfort or discomfort. Stamboul is a terrestrial paradise, the eye sees its pure forms, the mind achieves serenity and joy; New York is like the Alps, a tempest or battle, exciting but upsetting. It may stimulate our practical achievements, but it wounds our sense of happiness.

> Whenever the line is broken, jolted, irregular and constructed without rhythm or the form is over-acute or bristling, our senses are painfully and grievously affected. Our spirits suffer as a result of this confusion and harshness, this lack of "good manners," and the word "barbarous" comes at once to the mind. But when

> the line is continuous and regular, and the forms are full and rounded without a break, and governed by a clear guiding rule, then the senses are solaced, the mind is ravished, liberated, lifted out of chaos and flooded with light. Then...we are happy.[138]

A city can overwhelm with its broken lines; one has only to go north and see the spires of the cathedrals, which Le Corbusier claims are symbols of the agony of the flesh, dramas of the spirit, hell and purgatory. Our eye is stimulated by rotations and changes of scenery, but it quickly tires of repetitions; it is like the palate, which enjoys the variety of a well-arranged meal.[139] Yet he never forgets Descartes's lesson that behind the eye stands the mind, soothed by certain forms when it understands the relationships that brought them together.

The mixed forms of the city bear witness to all the antitheses Le Corbusier can raise. Before there is resolution, however, the eye is battered into submission by the junk of dead and bygone styles. "A decision must be arrived at in regard to the prohibition of certain injurious forms and the encouragement of stimulating forms."[140]

The next chapter, also titled "Classification and Choice," repeats the refrain that an architect's duty is to create things that go beyond calculation, but adds a variation:

> The city is a whirlpool, yet it is nonetheless a body with definitely placed organs, and it has a shape. The character, nature and structures of this body can be understood.[141]

We need to submit the city, the line of its evolution and the path of its development, to scientific investigation. "Statistics, graphs, are the *a, b, c,* and so on of an equation whose *x* and *y* can be calculated in advanced with a certain approximation." They endow the architect with essential foresight.[142] With foresight of the development of the city, the architect must center his focus on its details, the individual residential cells, that constitute the whole city. There must be unity in the detail, in order for the mind to consider the noble composition of the whole.[143]

Again Le Corbusier appeals to history: Abbé Laugier's advice to Louis XIV. He adds that in Turkey, Italy, Bavaria, Hungary, Serbia, and Switzerland, before the nineteenth century, men's houses were boxes, modified very little with the passage of time. "There was a universal standard and complete uniformity in detail."[144] It calmed the mind.

> To put it shortly: if the builder's yard is to be industrialized, it must pass from an anachronistic construction of single dwellings [made] "to the requirements of clients," to the construction of whole streets, indeed of whole districts.[145]

This will be achieved by the design of a proper cell. If the housing cell is standardized and mass-produced, its repetitive use will create a tranquil framework and lead forward to great architectural schemes. "*Town planning demands uniformity in detail and a sense of movement in the general layout.*"[146]

Moreover—perhaps a surprise for readers who have heard Le Corbusier eulogize the beauty and purity of the machine over and over again—we must plant trees; they help emotional and spiritual well-being and bring peace to the mind. The gigantic city of tomorrow will rise up out of green open spaces: it will have unity in detail. After so many antitheses, battles, and oppositions, both man and nature will be in accord.[147]

A MATTER OF LIFE OR DEATH

The Great City, which Le Corbusier claimed was fifty years old in the 1920s, had exploded in size without anyone foreseeing such an event. Adjusting to the new conditions, industrial and commercial life also achieved an overwhelming scale. And yet the city, based on an outmoded framework, presented a crisis that must be resolved: order or disorder, life or death. A Darwinian figure, survival of the fittest, is invoked:

> Such cities as do not adapt themselves quickly to the new conditions of modern life, will be stifled and will perish. Other and better adapted cities will take their place.[148]

The skeleton of the original city paralyzes new growth, and this in turn stifles the life of the nation: "The great city determines everything: war, peace and toil. Great cities are the spiritual workshops in which the work of the world is done."[149] Fashion, styles, ideas, and technical methods all come from great cities. They determine the demand and means of execution for all material goods; they set their quality, price, quantity, and destination. Only if the city is reordered will the whole country be renewed. And it is the architect, Le Corbusier believed, who must make a scientific investigation into the causes of the development of the city and determine its guiding principles.[150] If the architect does not act soon, disaster threatens the individual, the city, and eventually the nation. Architecture or revolution.

The speed of city growth has been cataclysmic. Consequently, "Man lives in a perpetual state of instability, insecurity, fatigue and accumulating delusions. Our physical and nervous organization is brutalized and battered by this torrent."[151]

Again a pseudo-Darwinian claim: The law of survival is at work, operating with a brutal force on the survival of men squeezed into urban centers.

> The great city, with its throbbing and its tumult, crushes the weak and raises the strong.... And these great cities challenge one another, for the mad urge for supremacy is the very law of evolution itself.[152]

When cities struggle forward following policies of chance, disorder, drift, or idleness, their death will surely be the end result. But when they strive toward order and respond to the appeal of geometry that speaks directly to the mind–as Purism teaches–they create a "crystallization of pure forms." Implicitly, such cities will be stronger, prevail, and survive.

Men venerate the excellent examples of cities from the past, but have done nothing so far to avoid inevitable disaster:

> Our preoccupation with the past has given us the soul of an undertaker's nature. And for all responses to the splendid and overwhelming impact of this new age we take on the air of some old gentleman pottering about among his old engravings, who, completely taken aback, says, "Go away, I am *much* too busy!"[153]

Such inaction allows confusion to remain at the original heart of most cities, producing a life-threatening situation. In the age of the machine, death knocks at the door of such cities. Comparing the automobile and the city, Le Corbusier summarizes "the first problem of city planning":

> Alas, we have become like the rusty engine of some out-of-date motor-car; the chassis, the body, the seats (the peripheries of our cities) can carry on still, but the motor (the center) is *seized*! This

> means complete breakdown. *The centres of the great cities are like an engine which is seized.*[154]

Le Corbusier analyzes the problem of the center in terms of access. Until the nineteenth century, the city was entered through the gates of its fortifying walls, and its streets led into the center. Today the railway station is the gate of the town; it lies within the center while the boundaries are stifling zones. "*The centres of our towns are in a state of mortal sickness, their boundaries are gnawed at as though by vermin.*"[155] Thus the second problem of city planning arises: how to create free zones for development in the heart and on the periphery of cities.

Le Corbusier's solution: pull the centers down and completely rebuild them. Likewise, abolish the wretched suburban belts and relocate them further out in the countryside. Turn these peripheral sites into protected and open zones. If we ignore the problem of the center, it is as if we "concentrate on an athlete's muscles and blind ourselves to the fact that his heart was weak and his life in danger."[156]

STUDY THE EFFECTS OF THE GREAT CITY!

The chapters following "The Great City" focus on its effects. The chapter on "Statistics" begins by amplifying a point already alleged in the previous chapter: statistics reveal the past and foreshadow the future.[157]

> Statistics give us an exact picture of our present state and also of former states; connecting them with a line so expressive that the past speaks clearly to us, so that by following the development of the curve we are enabled to penetrate into the future and make those truths our own which otherwise we could only have guessed at. Thus the poet pursues his way through a number of vital truths which are indispensable to the sure performance of the work that lies before us.[158]

Following Poincaré's distinction between the analyzer and geometer, Le Corbusier agrees that the work of a statistician is one of analysis, not invention; he is incapable of conceiving any idea that is clear or open, bold or inspired. Statistics arose out of the challenge of complicated machinery–making it imperative that someone be aware in advance of minute changes in operations, and thus forestall breakdown and collapse. The statistician is by nature respectful and timid, and every proposal for change is resisted. But, Le Corbusier insists, "We must destroy, to mend. Be remorseless."[159]

What do statistics reveal? Violent population growth, the expansion of suburbs, the super-saturation of the center, districts where tuberculosis is rampant. Statistics are merciless things. They prove that new factors have upset the course of events and that slight modifications are absurd. "The great city of to-day as it exists in actuality is an absurdity." It wears out millions of people, dooms the surrounding countryside to decay.[160]

The next chapter, also on the effects of the Great City, is "Newspaper Cuttings and Catchwords."[161] It is prefaced by a personal ad: "Young man, 29, with serious intentions, no friends, desires to make the acquaintance of a really nice shop-girl with a view to marriage. Great capacity for devotion. Write J. R."[162] Thus the newspapers record the fact that the great city is a dumping ground for unresolved problems. They recount traffic congestion, accidents and deaths, trees dying, the housing question, loneliness and alienation.

> Newspapers give us the curve registered by that seismograph the world; their news paragraphs emphasize the daily drama which is being enacted all around us, and the workings of science, history, economics, and politics.[163]

Again Le Corbusier levels his aim at the art critics whose articles appear in newspapers, swaying the public to reject his proposals for alleviating the crisis of the cities. These critics call his ideas utopian and revolutionary; they blind the public with the use of warn-out phrases and catchwords against the new spirit, which is beginning to change the course of events. Their criticisms against the terrible uniformity of mass-produced housing, the dreadful speed of the traffic proposed, the loss of individuality Le Corbusier's schemes would engender; they despise his plans as the result of applying too much science, being too mechanical.[164]

Le Corbusier retorts at the beginning of the next chapter, "Our Technical Equipment": "What gives our dreams their daring is that they can be realized."[165] He offers a detailed telling of an international collaboration that industrial production has forged, the construction of a magnificent dam high in the Alps.[166] [FIGURE 7.12] He paints the scene: The whole valley hums with the sound of well-oiled pulleys on steel cables carrying buckets of material for miles across the valley to the

FIGURE 7.12: Le Corbusier often praised the collaborative and innovative effort witnessed in great engineering feats, such as the building of a dam.

heights of the pass and the glacier. The containers are dumped and loaded automatically, the materials mixed and shoveled automatically in exact proportions. By careful timing, one cable comes down while the other goes up, like a series of suspension bridges against the pure blue sky. The work produced is more exact than a man could do with his two hands. "It may seem absurd, but one's mind goes back to the Giants building Valhalla."[167]

> At the foot of the barrage is a sort of cowboy camp–the huts in which the workers eat and sleep are perfectly built and equipped, all standardized and comfortable and as clean as a hospital.[168]

The example of the dam provides evidence of future potentialities; it presents dazzling horizons to the eye. It teaches that the law of physics, the use of the slide rule and equations, will henceforth lie at the base of all human achievements, and that a scrupulous director must oversee the entire operation in every one of its mechanical parts. "Human toil to be successful must be carried out under a condition of *order*, and only this will bring a great undertaking to success."[169] Moreover, this project foreshadows an internationalist future. The cable bobbins are made in

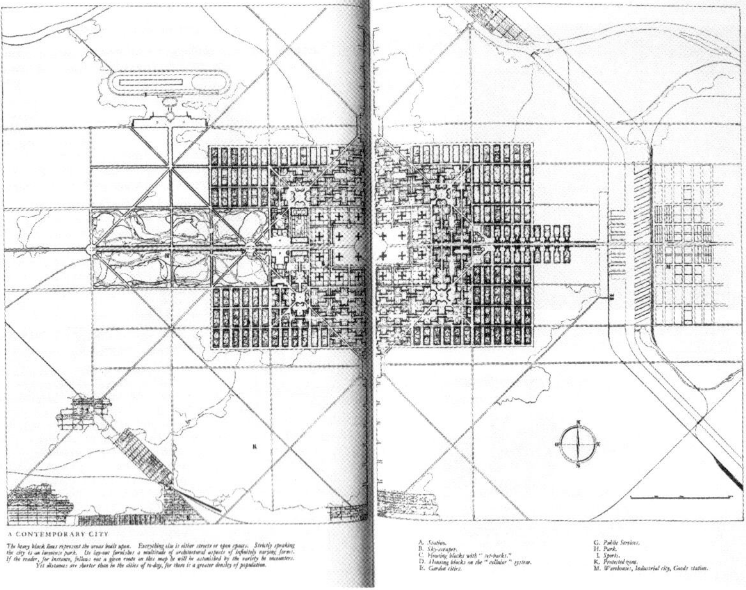

FIGURE 7.13: **Le Corbusier developed a plan for a city of three million people in order to illustrate his dream of a rational city.**

France, the railway engines in Leipzig, the toboggan runs in the United States, the electrical machines in Switzerland: here is the whole world in collaboration.[170]

But with the city, the situation is not quite the same as the creation of such a magnificent dam; the city demands something more.

> It is a question of soul, of something which we have at heart; something which is no longer international nor multiple, but individual and cannot be added to by others; something which is *in man* and the power of which dies with him. It is a question of *Art*.[171]

And Le Corbusier repeats: "What gives our dreams their daring is that they can be realized."[172]

To prove his argument that the vital thing in the city is to have an idea, a concept, and a program, he offers examples of two great city planners from history. Louis XIV built the Place Vendôme, one of "the purest jewels in the world's treasury," with picks and shovels against a network of over-crowded alleys: "An idea was needed, well thought out, clearly presented."[173] Haussmann did the same. His equipment was also only the shovel, the pick, the wagon, and the wheelbarrow, but he too had an idea, a concept, a plan.[174]

DEMONSTRATION PROJECT: THE CONTEMPORARY CITY

Now Le Corbusier is prepared to offer the reader his own dreams of a rational city. The second part of *Urbanisme* is entitled "Laboratory Work: An Inquiry into Theory" and discusses Le Corbusier's scheme for "The Contemporary City of 3 million inhabitants" that he drew up for the Salon d'Automne in 1922. [FIGURE 7.13] Two chapters follow this demonstration, "The Working Day" and "The Hours of Repose."[175] Here the four functions of the city that every architect must consider are outlined: housing, transportation, work, recreation. These claims will be clarified and strengthened after the formation of the Congrès International d'Architecture Moderne (CIAM) in 1928.

As Le Corbusier's reader already knows, a plan must be a work of technical analysis and architectural synthesis. It must contain two kinds of arguments: human ones–which are fundamental and stem from the mind, the heart, and intuition–and historical, statistical, and analytical ones–which allow the planner to master the environment and to project into the future. Yet contemporary authorities put forward feeble reforms

> In a sort of frantic haste in order, as it were, to hold a wild beast at bay. That *beast* is the great city. It is infinitely more powerful than all these devices. And it is just beginning to wake.[176]

Le Corbusier develops his principles of town planning, a skeletal system as a standard type applicable to any city, any place. The basic principles have already been described in earlier chapters: decongest the town center and augment its density; increase the speed at which traffic circulates; develop more open space and parks.

Now it is a matter of embellishing the theory. Le Corbusier calls on geometry to support his plan. The principles of Purism are reiterated and the lessons of mass-production applied.

> The result of a true geometrical lay-out is *repetition*.... The result of repetition is a *standard*, the perfect form (i.e. the creation of standard types). A geometrical lay-out means that mathematics play their part. There is no first-rate human production but has geometry at its base. It is of the very essence of Architecture.

> To introduce uniformity into the building of the city we must *industrialize building.*[177]

The architect who loves irregular sites, not geometrical ones, is a twisted creature; he applies all of his creative abilities to getting around these irregularities. Architects who produce such things do so only to please other architects.[178]

The next chapter, "The Working Day," begins with the dictum that "A city made for speed is made for success."[179] The skyscraper contains a whole city district, it "remains a noble instrument" but verticalized. New York is wrong, an absurdity, it condenses too much.[180] A skyscraper offers sublime views; as the horizon spreads out before him, man's thoughts take on a more comprehensive cast, and his spirit is roused to vital activity.

Skyscrapers contain the brains of the city; they concentrate all the apparatus for abolishing time and space, such as telephones, cables, and wireless; also banks, business offices, and control of industry, finance, commerce, and the various specializations. The railway station, as the gate to the city, is located in their midst, and all around lies vast open space. "This is the ideal city."[181]

In the chapter, "The Hours of Repose," Le Corbusier returns to themes he had developed in his *Étude sur la construction des villes*– the organization of residential quarters with grounds for games and sports at the door of all dwellings, and garden cities with small agricultural plots where residents become small producers. Now he inverts his advice on roads, straight or curved. He advocates the straight road with its good sense of purpose for working districts as well as for housing. Winding roads in housing create inevitable disorder:

> The eye can not see the curve as originally drawn on the plan, and each individual facade has its own restless importance: such housing schemes give one the impression of a field of battle or of the after-effects of an explosion.[182]

If the surrounding countryside is picturesque or filled with trees and grass, then the curved street is fully justified as a road for strolling or a walk winding through garden cities. But he warns, the curved street is essentially picturesque, a pleasure that soon becomes boring if too frequently applied.[183]

Residential cells must be grouped together in the center of the city. Yet every man dreams of a detached house, and fears that grouping his cell with others will limit his freedom. On the contrary: "It is possible by a logically conceived ordering of these cells to attain freedom through order."[184]

> We must arrive at the "house-machine," which must be both practical and emotionally satisfying and designed for a succession of tenants. The idea of the "old house" disappears, and with it local architecture, etc., for labour will shift about as needed, and must be ready to move *bag and baggage*.... Standardized houses with standardized furniture.[185]

It is important to design houses that present a pleasing silhouette against the sky. In most towns the silhouette appears as a painful gash, a ragged and tumultuous line with jutting broken forms. In contrast, the profile of housing built in reinforced concrete, seen against the sky, becomes a pure line. Such clear-cut shapes in turn must be offset with the rounded forms of foliage, the arabesque of branches. Nature provides the mediating factor in the urban scene: a tree modifies a scene that is too vast, its casual forms contrast with the built rigid forms. In tightening up the urban landscape it is also important to find units of measurement based on the human scale, the size of the human body. If there is no common measure, then the huge buildings will crush the spectator.[186]

Here Le Corbusier digresses extensively into the dynamics of progress, culminating in the assertion that the evolutionary law of existence is simple: nothing stands still or goes backwards. We must produce or die, go forward or be destroyed. Such is the definition of life.

> Our world, like a charnel-house, is strewn with the detritus of dead epochs. The great task incumbent on us is that of making a proper environment for our existence, and clearing away from our cities the dead bones that putrefy them. We must construct cities for to-day.[187]

DEMONSTRATION PROJECT: THE VOISIN PLAN

The third part of *The City of To-morrow* applies the theories of Le Corbusier to a case study, the Voisin Plan for the center of Paris.

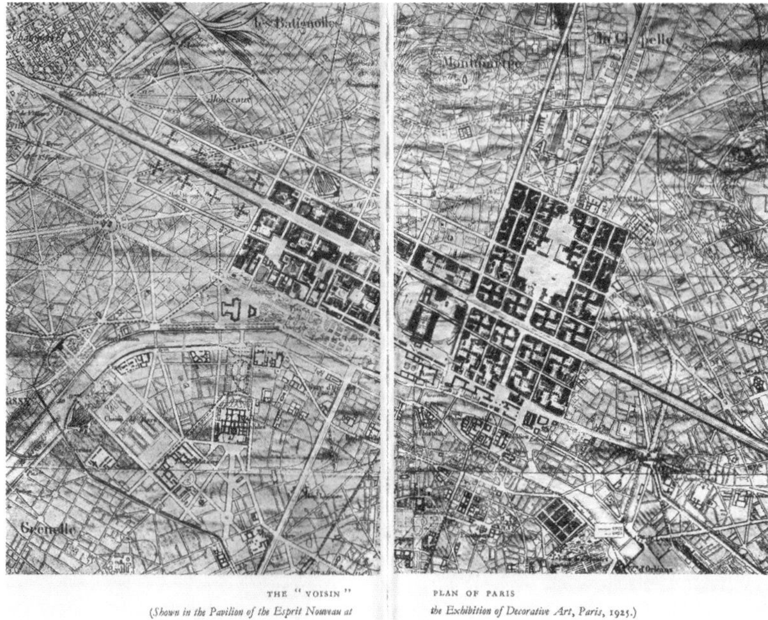

FIGURE 7.14: Plans to modernize Paris were opposed by the academies, so Le Corbusier offered his Voisin Plan as compensation.

His first chapter in this section, "Physic or Surgery," introduces the conceit that Paris is sick, strangled by cancer, its heart and lungs mortally seized. The knife is inevitable, a matter of demolition and reconstruction.[188] [FIGURE 7.14]

For the past twenty-five years, the Committee for the Preservation of Old Paris has been hard at work. Le Corbusier believes we should look ahead, not behind. He repeats his attack on art critics who bandy about words such as "Fatherland," "ancestor worship," or "the ideal," and when it is a matter of demolishing rotten old houses full of tuberculosis they shout out, "What about the iron-work, the beautiful old wrought-iron work?" Yet these same worshippers of the past live in modern houses with lifts or in small houses hidden in deep gardens.[189]

No, surgery must be applied to the center of Paris as it was in the days of Richelieu and Haussmann. Their work still provides Paris with its vital organs, arteries where motor traffic circulates, parks as lungs where Parisians go to breathe; they saved Paris.[190]

> Now that we have the motor-car, the airplane, and the railway, would it not seem a sort of mental cowardice to go on being satisfied with the sumptuous but decayed heritage of the past?[191]

The next chapter, "The Centre of Paris," presents the Voisin Plan as displayed in the Pavillon de l'Esprit Nouveau at the Exhibition of the Decorative Arts in 1925.[192] Le Corbusier is not, he says, offering a final solution for the center of Paris, only attempting to raise the level of discussion and to provide alternative standards and principles by which to assess the problem. He offers his scheme in opposition to the medley of small reforms with which Parisians constantly delude themselves.[193] Since the business center of Paris cannot be displaced, there must be a frontal attack on its most diseased quarters, those with the narrowest, most congested streets. Its center must be transformed, or transmuted, into the most splendid system of communication. Then our new "city rises vertical to the sky, open to light and air, clear and radiant and sparkling."[194]

All the junk will be cleaned off. In its place immense crystals of glass will appear, six hundred feet tall. For the pavilion, Le Corbusier painted a huge panorama (some sixty or eighty square yards) depicting contemporary Paris from Notre Dame to the Étoile. Behind it rose the new city, not the wild spires of Manhattan but silhouettes of pure forms. The Invalides, the Tuileries, the Place de la Concorde, the Champ de Mars, and the Étoile remain, juxtaposed to the new business city–because they too had followed the traditional and normal laws of progress.[195] Le Corbusier makes an important aside:

> In these days the past has lost something of its fragrance, for its enforced mingling with the life of to-day have set it in a false environment. My dream is to see the Place de la Concorde empty once more silent and lonely, and the Champs-Elysées a quiet place to walk in. The "Voisin" scheme would isolate the whole of the ancient city and bring back peace and calm from Saint-Gervais to the Étoile.[196]

The final chapter, "Finance and Realization," briefly discusses the problem of implementation: who will finance the demolition and rebuilding the plan entails?[197] Haussmann filled the Emperor's coffers with gold by improving the value of real estate. Le Corbusier's scheme will improve the business district of the city, offering an opportunity for international capital to invest in the center of Paris. Such internationalization will have an additional benefit: it will ensure that Paris will not be destroyed in the future by long-range guns, as the Germans tried during the Great War.[198] They will have too much invested in it.

Le Corbusier concludes his sweeping thesis on urbanism by modestly claiming to be a technician. He has studied the smallest cell and the consequences of its collective grouping; he has analyzed how a city develops; he has found a formula that establishes the rules on which modern city planning must rest.[199] He returns to the theme of revolution or equilibrium, couched in quasi-Darwinian terms:

> My scheme is brutal, because town existence and life itself are brutal: life is pitiless, it must defend itself, hemmed in as it is on all sides by death. To overcome death, constant activity is necessary.[200]

Le Corbusier says that he is not a provocateur overthrowing the government or capitalism, as the Russian revolutionaries are. He is merely offering a technical work with the clear understanding that "Things are not revolutionized by making revolution. The real Revolution lies in the solution of existing problems."[201]

IV. L'ART DÉCORATIF D'AUJOURD'HUI (1925)[202]

> *Is clothing–at least in its affiliation with the feminine toilette–a decorative art? It is, without a doubt, and the most venerable, that which leads all the others.*
>
> –HENRI COUSZOT, 1925

In the early twentieth century, women's clothing, indeed fashion in all cultural departments, was integral not only to French modernity and the economy, but to the life of Paris. The city was constantly on display; the windows of its many luxury boutiques and department stores were expressly designed to lure women to consume. The 1925 Exposition Internationale des Arts Décoratifs gave a high profile to the fashionable woman by locating a double row of luxury shops, each facade designed by a different architect, at the center of the Exposition on the rue des Boutiques along the Pont Alexandre III. At nighttime, this street of shops turned into a spectacle of colored lights and water displays.[203]

Le Corbusier took exception to the feminization thus evidenced, mounting a biting critique across the pages of *L'Art Décoratif d'aujourd-hui* (*The Decorative Arts of Today*).[204] This book has been called the most shocking of the four in the *L'Esprit Nouveau* series, an iconoclastic polemic attacking the entire history of the decorative arts. It has also been summarily dismissed, as when Banham labeled it as having "only local interest."[205] More than the other three, *L'Art Décoratif d'aujourd-hui* is written in an aphoristic mode that borrows the style developed by Peter Altenberg, Karl Krauss, and Adolf Loos in turn-of-the-century Vienna, and is worthy of close analysis of how Le Corbusier deployed this tool.[206]

Le Corbusier read two of Loos's essays–the celebrated "Ornament and Crime" essay of 1908 and "Architecture" of 1910–shortly after their translation into French in *Les Cahiers d'Aujourd'hui* in 1912 and 1913.[207] "Ornament and Crime" was so important to Ozenfant and Jeanneret that even in a badly translated version, they reprinted it in the second issue of *L'Esprit Nouveau* (1920).[208]

Loos's intent was to modernize Vienna by reforming the practice of its badly educated craftsmen, who ornamented in a costly and elaborate manner all the material artifacts of everyday use, food, clothing, and architecture; Le Corbusier sought to adapt Loos's manner of argumentation, his lively improvisations and paradoxical juxtapositions, to mount a similar reform of the decorative arts as put forth in the 1925 Exposition. Taking his cue from Loos on the importance of writing in the public sphere and the extension of architecture to many different realms of human activity, Le Corbusier wrote as follows in *L'Art Décoratif d'aujourd-hui*:

> Architecture is in the smallest things and extends to everything man makes: the apotheosis of the decorative arts in the year 1925 thus marks, admittedly by a paradox, the awakening of the architectural movement of the machine age.... What would be lamentable, in the face of a phenomenon so vast and at the same time touching our hearts so closely as individuals and as a society, would be to see huge amounts of money directed by the State into organizing the glorification of the floral hatbox: the building of immense and ostentatious exhibition halls to enshrine in "sublime" surroundings the escapade of a flower-bud swanning from an umbrella handle to the back of an easy chair.[209]

Perhaps it is Loos who taught Le Corbusier to utilize a conversational tone in his writings and structure his arguments in a nonlinear, paradoxical, richly interwoven manner. Their choice of subject matter was similar as well, for Le Corbusier will deploy many of Loos's arguments in defense of his own position. Loos considered objects of everyday life–food, utensils, clothing, and furniture–to be worthy of critique and reform. To critique and reform them, he structured his written thoughts in a paradoxical and circular manner, training his readers to view things from different perspectives. Following Loos, Le Corbusier seeks to strip his own writing style, the act of covering blank pages with linguistic signs, of false coverings until the unadulterated self or truth appears in all its honesty and nudity. Clothing becomes his master trope for false coverings and superficial spectacles. Good style is a matter of creating a pure language through words that cannot be distorted.[210]

A REVOLUTION IN THE DECORATIVE ARTS [FIGURE 7.15]

Consistent with Le Corbusier's practice in the other *L'Esprit Nouveau* volumes, the introduction to the *Decorative Arts* provides a resume of themes repeated as the leitmotif of each chapter. They set up a montage of contrasting ideas, an interdependent whole in which each theme takes on value only in association with all the others. They are bound together by a pre-existing pattern of meaning already generated by Loos's associative texts. Confessing his multiple debts to Loos, Le Corbusier begins the book proper with a chapter on "Iconology, Iconolaters and Iconoclasts" and the following strange admission: "The past is not infallible. There were ugly things as well as beautiful." With ironic ambivalence he praises the jury members of the decorative arts, who believe that objects of use should be decorated, creating an atmosphere of comfort to counteract the emptiness the machine has wrought. Then he protests and applauds the machine instead, for it has transformed objects of use into willing slaves. "We sit on them, work on them, make use of them, use them up; when used up, we replace them."[211] To Loos's anti-ornamental stance, Le Corbusier has added the machine that is capable of stripping bare every item of use. Far from being victimized, the machine now offers man an alternative future: the ability to master his interior and exterior worlds.

L'Art Décoratif d'aujourd-hui opens with the following vignette, composed like a verbal Purist painting:

An ostrich.

ICONOLOGY
ICONOLATERS
ICONOCLASTS

ICONOLOGY

Coaches are on the move along the highways of Europe. Escorts with pistols in their saddle-holsters, etc.

FIGURE 7.15 **Following the precedent set by Adolf Loos, Le Corbusier offered an iconoclastic polemic attacking the entire history of the decorative arts.**

> Lenin is seated at the Rotonde on a cane chair; he has paid twenty centimes for his coffee, with a tip of one sou. He has drunk out of a small white porcelain cup. He is wearing a bowler hat and a smooth white collar. He has been writing for several hours on sheets of typing papers. His inkpot is smooth and round, made from bottle glass.
>
> He is teaching himself to govern one hundred million people.[212]

The round shapes of a bowler hat, white collar, inkpot, bottle glass, and white porcelain cup–simple practical items of everyday use–appear simply, precisely. The image can also be read as a self-portrait of Le Corbusier, who has set himself up as a sort of Lenin opposite in his discourse on "revolution or architecture." Thus *L'Art Décoratif d'aujourd-hui* begins on a revolutionary, or at least counter-revolutionary, note that recalls themes developed in *Vers une Architecture* and *Urbanisme*: one creates a revolution by revolutionizing *things*. But strangely, one does that, at least in part, by writing books. Lenin as writer gives witness to the power of the word to transform acts; the architect, as Le Corbusier explains, reformer and revolutionary in his own terrain, also takes up the challenge to educate the masses in order to rid them of their desire for useless ornamentation in the decorative arts.

Maison Pirsoul.

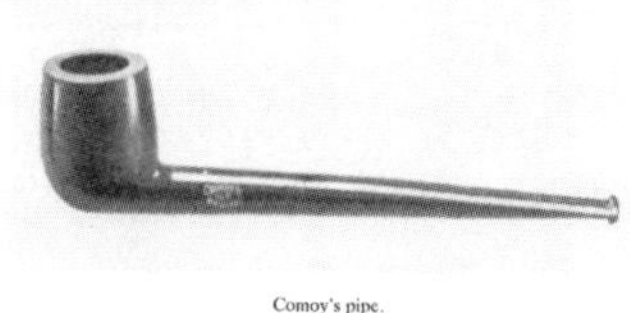

Comoy's pipe.

OTHER ICONS
THE MUSEUMS

There are good museums, and bad. Then there are those with the good and bad together. But the museum is a sacred entity which debars judgement.

PLAGIARISM
FOLK CULTURE

To be idle, void of ideas, to have a bric-à-brac mind, to be one of the crowd, the *bourgeois*-king of today, and quite openly to *despoil*, without pretence or verbal disguise, a neighbouring race engaged like its fathers and ancestors

FIGURE 7.16: In a contemporary museum of art, Le Corbusier would install useful objects, such as an electric lightbulb and modern bathroom fixtures. FIGURE 7.17: Folk culture from the past, Le Corbusier professed, was a source of distraction enabling artists to avoid the need to create.

In his verbal vignette, Le Corbusier gives Lenin the appearance of a well-dressed English gentleman who displays a degree of moral certainty. So dressed, Lenin is prepared to rationalize modern life and balance his exterior and interior life. Throughout *L'Art Décoratif d'aujourd-hui,* Le Corbusier refers only to masculine forms of dress, and those revolutions that make men masters of their domestic interiors and public facades.[213] He mentions the realm of "ladies' joy" only once, while denigrating the industrialist who achieves commercial success by stuffing every department store with ornamented luxuries.[214] Although Le Corbusier does not expressly attack the feminization of the city of light inscribed by the 1925 Exposition Internationale des Arts Décoratifs, fashion is important to his vision of modernity. He transforms Loos's admiration of the man in the blue apron into praise for the railway engineer's plain black attire; rather than explicitly denigrate the *femme moderne* as a passionate consumer, he exalts the naked man with his simple tools that allow him freedom to think about art.[215]

Antiquarians, professors, museums, publishers, and art critics, just as Loos had proclaimed, are to blame for titillating and intoxicating the public with dazzling diamonds, pure gold, marble, and mirrors.

They have turned decoration into a religion that the masses accept as an opiate (which point Le Corbusier makes with a nod to Lenin). A paradoxical twist: we admire artifacts from the past and from primitive cultures because they are "the work of the tamed savage who is still alive in us." But culture progresses in a different direction toward the interior life of the soul, which is why Loos preached about finding equilibrium between exterior and interior life and where Le Corbusier's reforms come back in, for equilibrium cannot be found within the decorative arts of 1925.[216]

The second chapter discusses the difference between good and bad museums, another Loosian trope. A true museum, Le Corbusier opines, should offer a complete picture of the past, the reason why things were created and how they might be improved. But the objects in today's museum are exceptional: "They are not a fundamental component of human life like bread, drink, religion, orthography." They are poison and opiates, and cannot educate the masses.[217] A true museum would give some indication of the present century. [FIGURE 7.16] It would contain machine-made objects of utility that vary only in their finish and quality, such as a plain jacket, a bowler hat, a well-made shoe, an electric lightbulb, a radiator, a tablecloth of fine white linen, drinking glasses, bottles of various shapes, bentwood chairs, a bathroom, Innovation suitcases, Roneo filing cabinets, fine leather armchairs.[218]

There are ethnographic museums too. Here Le Corbusier again borrows from Loos. The colonialist, with the approval of the general public, brings back from exotic places items that belonged to royalty or to a deity but ignores the calabash, a utensil of everyday use. Educators in their books and schools misrepresent the original purpose of these exceptional pieces and prod their students to compete with them until they stuff everyday lives with showpieces of little use. "The naked man does not wear an embroidered waistcoat; so the saying goes"; he wants to think, to develop tools and objects of use.[219] Only after he is fed, clothed, and housed will he attend to what is noble and best. Subtly, Le Corbusier has here introduced his main subject, the house, by first introducing the metaphor of the museum and the necessary reform of interior furnishings, for his argument goes from inside to out–as he has proclaimed architecture itself must proceed. [FIGURE 7.17]

Le Corbusier moves on to examine the problem of folk culture, past and present. He calls Argentine tangos, Louisiana jazz, Breton wardrobes so many plagiarisms designed as diversions to fill empty holes leftover after work is done and to compensate for the rigors of a regimented life. "The cinema, the café, the theatre, the stadium, the club, the 'five o'clock,' suppers, dance halls, domestic wireless"–so much background noise means that modern man is never alone with himself. He cannot bring order to his interior life![220]

Lest one think that Le Corbusier is dismissive of all folk arts, he emphasizes that there are important lessons to be learned from past cultures, those that produced objects expressing an idea, revealing how something is worked on and perfected over time:

> At the *Cuadro Famenco* of the Diaghilev Ballet eight Spaniards dance and sing; forty negroes of the *Syncopated Orchestra* gesticulate and fill one with nostalgia.
>
> Throughout, all is clean, concise, brief, economical, intense, essential...A line has been etched; I see it and I remember.[221]

Yet Le Corbusier repeats that progress is inevitable, it cannot be stopped, even in the lands of folklore that he loves so much–the Balkans and Stamboul. Regrets are useless. An international style is rising, frontiers are falling, and regional characteristics being abandoned.

The message is repeated, echoed, redoubled. "Gilding is fading out...we appear to be working toward the establishment of a simple and economic human scale."[222] The hierarchical system of labor imposed by the decorative arts is failing; now teamwork counts. In an odd juxtaposition, but one that brings two important themes into the foreground, housing and truth, Le Corbusier proclaims that the modern era democratizes when working-class housing and the bathroom enter everyday speech. He makes his first reference to Diogenes, iconic searcher for honesty and radical advocate of streamlined living: "Diogenes is not so far away."[223]

Now another paradox from Loos is deployed. If Loos's generic aristocrat allows ornamentation to survive, it is because he focuses on achievements in other areas. So Le Corbusier will accept that diversions such as dance-halls and nudity in the music halls serve legitimate needs. In the inevitable march of progress they are "purgative, because we are waiting for this completely new society to organize itself."[224] But he will not be so tolerant with the decorative arts of 1925 and of those who make furniture only with wood and ignore the new materials of steel and aluminum. The important achievements of the day are not from them, but are the products of laboratories.[225]

Le Corbusier once again takes up the theme of revolution–industrial, social, and moral. "The industrialist thought to himself: 'Let us smother our junk with decoration: decoration hides all manner of flaws and blemishes.' Camouflage is sanctified."[226] While "his clothing tended to become a plain black, or mottled; [and] the bowler hat appeared on the horizon," still the industrialist produced junk, hiding all faults and imperfections underneath a decorated surface.[227] Stuffed with these commercial triumphs, department stores became luxurious realms of "'ladies' joy!'"–Le Corbusier's first and only mention of "ladies" in this book.[228]

Meanwhile, the railway engineer, commerce, calculation, and the struggle for precision call the industrialist's frills into question. This same railroad enters the peasant's land, bringing baubles and trinkets in its wake. Folk culture is forgotten, except in the cities where committees are formed for its preservation and where art lovers invented the mystique of the handcrafts. "Later the cinema would finish off the work of the railways. The peasant on the Danube has chosen. Folk culture no longer exists, only ornaments on mass-produced junk. Everywhere!"[229]

Thus the revolt, and the need to repeat Loos's dictums over and over again! All objects to which ornamentation is applied must be replaced with items designed at a human scale to mesh with human needs. And since the whole machine of man's anatomy can be defined by his structure, why shouldn't his needs, which are merely a means of supplementing his natural capacities, prosthetic devices that extend his hands, arms, or legs, be addressed by designing a type-object?

> Thus the cupped hands of Narcissus led us to invent the bottle; the barrel of Diogenes, already a notable improvement on our natural protective organs (our skin and scalp), gave us the primordial cell of the house; filing cabinets and copy-letters make good the inadequacies of our memory; wardrobes and sideboards are the containers in which we put away the auxiliary limbs that guarantee us against cold or heat, hunger or thirst, etc.... Decorative art becomes orthopaedic.[230]

And in the machine age, the decorative arts are transformed into the arts of the engineer; they provide type-objects that answer type-needs, including chairs to sit on, tables to work on, electric lights to see by, typewriters and filing cabinets to transfer and store one's thoughts. This leads to architecture, in which the problems of purification, simplification, and precision must be addressed before poetry can come into existence.[231] From Le Corbusier's pen, the word "poetry" does not mean "verse," which has clearly not waited for a pure architecture to come into being, but the quality of ineffable freedom, liberated creativity, and direct experience that he believes will be the rewards achieved by applying Purist principles to all forms of architecture.

Having developed his ideas about tools, type-objects, and the decorative arts, Le Corbusier reiterates for emphasis, secure that his reader can follow his logic. He paraphrases Loos's paradox: "*Modern decorative art is not decorated*....The paradox lies not in reality, but in the words....This is the paradox: why should chairs, bottles, baskets, shoes, which are all object of utility, all *tools*, be called *decorative art*?"[232] And: "It seems justified to affirm: *the more cultivated a people becomes, the more decoration disappears*. (Surely it was Loos who put it so neatly.)"[233] The fact is that the decorative arts of today are items of use produced by engineers. These are the objects he repetitively lists and prescribes as fitting assemblages for modern interiors, worthy to be in the collections of museums of modern design.

Now Le Corbusier preaches the lesson of the machine with an almost religious fervor–indeed, explicitly connecting machine shapes to the sacred. There is nothing in nature, he says, that competes with the pure perfection of even the humblest machine. It is a pure relationship of cause and effect; a precise geometry of shining disks, spheres, and cylinders of polished steel; its joy is brutal and overwhelming. "Our hand reaches out to it....Our senses are moved at the same time as our heart recalls from its stock of memories the disks and spheres of the gods of Egypt and the Congo....Geometry and gods sit side by side."[234] Confronted with such modern gods, it is easy to proclaim, as did Loos: "Decorative art can no longer exist any more than can the 'styles' themselves."[235]

Having established continuity with the past, Le Corbusier can now develop another theme. The course of the soul of man flows between two river banks: fear of the unknown and the serenity that knowledge provides. Folk cultures are born of fear, the Parthenon from a revelation of exact and perfectly balanced knowledge.

> The shepherd who shapes his staff and carves into it an annulet of flowers and stars, a snake, or a lamb; the Papuan who inscribes on his paddle the figure of an albatross and a surging wave; they are both making an act of devotion toward nature. The practice

> of their art has amassed the experience of generations and their candid works have thus passed beyond the level of superficial observation to that of true re-creation. Integration.[236]

But decorative arts applied merely to surfaces have nothing to do with either fear or serenity.

In the twentieth century, science dissects the world before our eyes, offering us stunning and disturbing photographs and emotive diagrams, graphs, and tables. It introduces us to the mathematical basis of the cosmos and increases our serenity. "We now approach the mystery of nature scientifically, and far from exhausting it, we find it becomes more profound for every advance in our knowledge."[237] The loss of folk culture leaves a void, but architecture extending from the smallest item to the largest house creates an atmosphere receptive to the inner life of the soul. "The hour of architecture sounds"[238]:

> Diogenes, throwing away his bowl, had said "This child shows me that I still have something I can do without."
>
> To identify the superfluous and throw it away.
>
> The superfluous is something that serves no purpose.
>
> Everything which moves us serves a purpose.
>
> Everything that obstructs is surplus to needs. What is not superfluous? The essential.
>
> One moment, here come the sophists: "everything serves a purpose, everything moves us."
>
> Answer: "There are only twenty-four hours in a day."
>
> That is indisputable, unchangeable, the constant. That is the arbiter of everything. You cannot be moved by everything: you don't have time for it. You have to choose.[239]

Far from repressing sensitivity, as the critics proclaim, critical awareness becomes more active, and does not allow futile objects of the decorative arts to be easily tolerated. They steal time and absorb too much space in daily life, they are criminal and degenerate. Le Corbusier applies Loos's attitude of moral rectitude: "I claim the right to be harsh with these superfluous, inessential objects."[240] They have no reason to exist. To cleanse the world of the unessential and superfluous is the entire project of *L'Art Décoratif d'aujourd-hui*. Yet the reader must be warned:

The *Dixmude*.

THE HOUR OF ARCHITECTURE

Now that the decorative arts are in decline, justice demands recognition for the service records of several generations of active, enthusiastic, disinterested people.

FIGURE 7.18: **Whitewash, proportion, comfort, and calm were evidence of the Esprit Nouveau in architecture.**

> The sense of truth has no formula. You can't get it at the chemist's. This sense of truth is the force of a man. Diogenes replied to Alexander the Great: "Get out of my light!"...I have the right to say that to objects and to ideas, which are no more than lackeys. Each of us is a master: "Get out of my light."[241]

Le Corbusier arrives at his final refrain, the essential revolution that his other two books also urge: the reform of the house. Referring to the so-called style of the decorative arts of 1925, he proclaims, "Many think against a background of black. But the task of our century, so strenuous, so full of danger, so violent, so victorious seem to demand of us that we think against a background of white."[242] [FIGURE 7.18]

He goes on: Loos taught that to love purity is a moral act, and preached that reform of the house extends from the interior to the exterior. He wrote of whitewashed houses existing wherever culture remained in balance. Le Corbusier comes later in the twentieth century, after the virus of the decorative arts, with its wallpaper, gilt porcelain, tin "brassware," and cast-iron decoration, even Pathé-Ciné and Pathé-Phono, has destroyed the tradition of whitewash. To arrive at a new equilibrium, to be master of one's inner and outer soul, it is necessary to apply the Law of Ripolin–a coat of fresh white paint! (Ripolin was then, and remains today, a French brand of paint. White Ripolin was often used to paint interior walls.)

> Once you have put Ripolin on your walls you will *be master of yourself.* And you will want to be precise, to be accurate, to think clearly. You will rearrange your house, which your work has disturbed.[243]

> If the house is all white, the outline of things stands out from it without any possibility of mistake: their volume shows clearly; their colour is distinct. The whitewash is absolute, everything stands out from it and is recorded absolutely, black on white; it is honest and dependable.
>
> Put on anything dishonest or in bad taste—it hits you in the eye. It is rather like an X-ray of beauty. It is a court of assize in permanent session. It is the eye of truth.[244]

Then, one last time, Le Corbusier attacks the decorative arts of 1925, deploying all the Orientalist tropes he can drum up. The time has finished when men

> Can lounge on ottomans and divans among orchids in the scented atmosphere of a seraglio and behave like so many ornamental animals or humming-birds in impeccable evening dress, pinned through the trunk like a collection of butterflies to the swathes of gold, lacquer or brocade on our wall-paneling and hangings.[245]

V. ALMANACH D'ARCHITECTURE MODERNE (1925)[246]

An advertisement in Le Corbusier's 1925 *Almanach d'Architecture Moderne* displays the covers of four books in the *L'Esprit Nouveau* series, all containing articles published in the review from 1920 to 1925. Each book in the series is not meant to stand alone but, devoted to the separate fields of architecture, urbanism, decorative arts, and modern painting, each would raise questions to which the others respond. [FIGURE 7.19, p. 696]

The first row of the two-by-two matrix shows the covers of two books written by Le Corbusier and already reviewed in this chapter, *Vers une Architecture* and *Urbanisme.* The second row contains Le Corbusier's *L'Art Décoratif d'aujourd'hui,* discussed above, and Ozenfant and Jeanneret's *La Peinture Moderne*. The cover of *Vers une Architecture* gives a perspectival view of the promenade on the steamship *Aquitania*. This photograph has the appearance of a truncated pyramid, the well-known illusion allowing a two-dimensional representation of linear recession into three-dimensional space.[247] Thus, a two-dimensional perspectival view mediates the representation of architectural form, and is an apt metaphor to announce a book on the trials and tribulations of modern architecture. The truncated pyramid transposes two different visual orders, two irreconcilable opposites, and thus becomes a résumé of what its book aspires to be: a machine for examining the antitheses and paradoxes that modern architecture must confront and transcend.[248]

The cover of *Urbanisme* outlines the straight routes of the 1860s plan by Haussmann, superimposed on the meandering paths of medieval Paris. Here again is a résumé of the book behind the cover, a series of opposites and their resolutions: chaos/order, winding roads/right angles, architecture/urbanism. If we read these two images in sequence, that is, across the top row of the two-by-two matrix, we see a contrast and comparison of an architectural and an urban image. We are presented with the antithesis of traditional and innovative architectural forms, the resolution of which will be achieved by adopting a new form for the city.

The first entry of the second row is an image of the cover of Le Corbusier's *L'Art Décoratif d'aujourd-hui*, an aerial view of the Eiffel Tower juxtaposed against the serpentine park at its base (both designed by engineers for the Universal Exposition of 1867). The camera lens offered the nineteenth century new perspectives and exceptional sights, teaching the eye to see in new ways; this view of the Eiffel Tower reveals a spiral metallic shape projecting skyward toward the camera lens that is juxtaposed against the serpentine outline of Alphand's park. The purpose of the image is to remind the reader of the revolutionary forces that must be released in order to erase the puerile decorative arts glorified at the 1925 Exposition Internationale des Arts Décoratifs. As Le Corbusier will reiterate in the pages that follow, the time of the decorative arts is over, replaced by an era when a geometric or mathematical order controls all architectural forms, from the smallest pot of cream to the largest structures.

This third image is juxtaposed against the cover of *La Peintre Moderne*, which contains the articles of *L'Esprit Nouveau* written by Ozenfant and Jeanneret to clarify their doctrine of "Purism."

This image was first used to illustrate the article "Sur la Plastique" in the first issue of *L'Esprit Nouveau.*[249] Itself a two-by-two matrix, it presents a top row of two mages, a painting by Monet and a sculpture by Rodin, considered "bad" because they are out of date and do not recognize *la physique de la plastique* (bodily manifestation of the material). In the lower row are two other images, a painting by Seurat *(Can-Can)* and a Greek statue of a woman. Each of these "good" images carries within them some invariants of geometry as key to their composition, and offer proof that man's need for order is universal and constant. Reading across the second row, we are offered a vision of the decorative arts reformed by the precepts of Purism.

If the images of the book covers are read down the page, then the new architecture toward which we are traveling is juxtaposed against the decorative arts that also need to be reformed, even as the modern city and modern painting will be reordered by the universal constants of geometrical forms.

By juxtaposing all these images, however they are to be scanned, Le Corbusier seeks to link them into a system of thought or language of architecture. Ferdinand de Saussure proclaimed in the early decades of the twentieth century that language is a system of signs expressing ideas.[250] The structure of relations among words, syntax, concepts, metaphors, thoughts, processes, and procedures is the linguist's focus. In his search to link architecture, urbanism, the decorative arts, and painting, Le Corbusier utilizes this structural model of language not as a metaphorical borrowing, but as a conceptual correlation. He is interested in the concrete workings of a system of thought–architecture and its corollary arts. In the introductory pages of the *Almanach,* he defines architecture in structural terms: It is a "*Mirror of thought.* Architecture is a system to think with."[251] When our epoch has harmonized the play of technique, comfort, and spiritual aspirations, "Then an architecture can be formulated and become the expressive verb of a milieu."[252]

The *Almanach,* originally planned as the twenty-ninth issue of *L'Esprit Nouveau,* was to focus on architecture. But the problem of the decorative arts arose, and the issue of how they related to architecture and urbanism had to be resolved. Perhaps this is why Le Corbusier used the title *Almanach d'Architecture Moderne* for this eclectic arrangement of essays. It is in part a catalogue for the Pavillon de l'Esprit Nouveau but also includes excerpts from Le Corbusier's travel journal to Istanbul and Athens in 1910, a series of lectures offered on modern architecture,

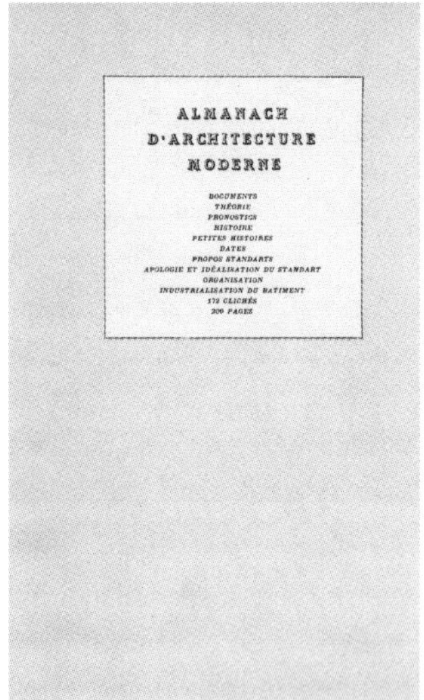
ALMANACH
D'ARCHITECTURE
MODERNE

DOCUMENTS
THÉORIE
PRONOSTICS
HISTOIRE
PETITES HISTOIRES
DATES
PROPOS STANDARTS
APOLOGIE ET IDÉALISATION DU STANDART
ORGANISATION
INDUSTRIALISATION DU BATIMENT
172 CLICHÉS
200 PAGES

FIGURE 7.20: **The *Almanach d'Architecture Moderne* is part catalog for the Pavillon de l'Esprit Nouveau, part eclectic array of essays and lectures.**

and elements that will crystallize by 1928 into a system, the five points of architecture. [FIGURE 7.20]

In a 1929 article, Le Corbusier outlined the tribulations experienced during the construction of the Pavillon de l'Esprit Nouveau, and how these led to his decision to publish the *Almanach,* in part as a catalogue for the pavilion.[253] Le Corbusier emphasizes how he constructed the pavilion without having the promise of money or even the permission to do so. In the end, the site on which it was erected was entirely hidden, invisible to anyone who passed along the Cours la Reine–thus, many visitors failed to discover it at all, and so he decided to publish the *Almanach.*[254]

Opening the *Almanach,* Le Corbusier speaks directly to the reader, announcing this work as the golden book of the Pavillon de l'Esprit Nouveau for the Exposition Internationale des Arts Décoratifs in 1925, the culmination of a theoretical movement now five years old.[255] Speaking of the four books whose covers form the advertisement discussed above, he says that they "were the theory of which the Pavilion ought to be the materialization."[256] Designed in two parts, the pavilion contained an exact replica of a machine for living attached to a vast rotunda exhibiting the grand diorama of the city for three million developed in 1922 and the large diorama for the Plan Voisin (described in the pages of *Urbanisme*). [FIGURE 7.21] The cellular unit could be combined into an apartment block and extended to the city. For it,

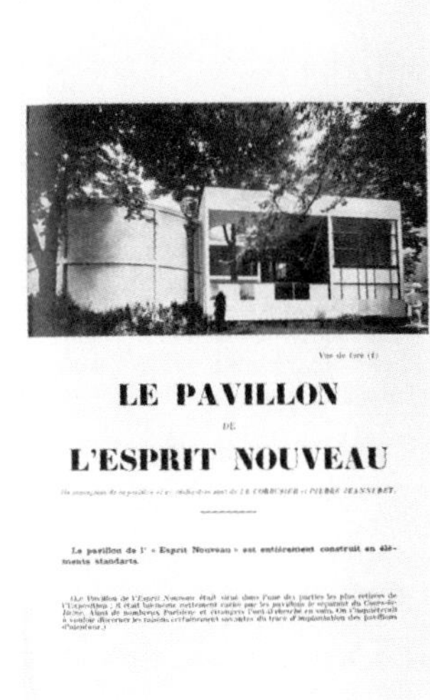

LE PAVILLON

DE

L'ESPRIT NOUVEAU

Le pavillon de l' « Esprit Nouveau » est entièrement construit en éléments standarts.

FIGURE 7.21: The rotunda adjacent to the Pavillon de l'Esprit Nouveau was dedicated to Le Corbusier's "minute and patient" research on urbanism.

Le Corbusier designed doors, windows, and cabinetry that he imagined could be standardized and fabricated as tools of the house.

The critics, specifically those in charge of the exposition of 1925, were indignant over Le Corbusier's proposals. They did not like standardized housing units, nor mass-produced furniture, nor the idea that everyone would be forced to live according to the same regiment, work in identical offices, and find their recreational hours controlled as well. They pitied the poor resident of Le Corbusier's future housing, required to think constantly about the functional utility of every item in daily use. These critics proclaimed that they preferred to be inspired by the nostalgia of disorder.[257]

Le Corbusier's responded to these protestations. These "men of 1870" could not imagine that a city composed of great geometrical forms would offer constantly shifting spectacles, not uniform views. Such a city would play with space, with near and far perspectival views, with height and depth, presenting a combinatory arrangement of architectural forms beautiful in all their variety. As far as standardized housing and furniture were concerned, there was nothing unique about his proposal; every age created its standard types and repeated them over and over. Now it was merely a matter of creating standards responsive to modern needs.

One must transform awful uniformity into a constantly renewed diversity if one wants to speak of urbanism. If one looks at the suburbs and interior streets of cities (e.g., Vienna, Berlin, London), one will find everywhere such uniformity, sad effect of a lack of organization! If Le Corbusier is in the end to be blamed for the unpardonable crime of being led astray by the logic of science and the machine, then he accepts responsibility, for he does not want to live in the nostalgia of disorder nor in a past that is now defunct.

He returns to the theme of language:

> If I [have] analyzed word for word the bibliographic article of *L'Architecte* [written by the "men of 1870"], it is because I find there a successful example of innumerable clichés...by means of which one is tied to a defunct past and by means of which one wants to stifle opinion about the young manifestations of a new spirit. This article...summarizes in a professional publication and under a professional pen, the multiple indignations that the L'Esprit Nouveau Pavilion suffered during the summer and that made me aware of the barbs of journals....Words are so powerful! One does a lot with words.[258]

"L'ESPRIT NOUVEAU IN ARCHITECTURE"

First off in his *Almanach* of diverse articles, after the introductory material, is a lecture Le Corbusier gave in 1924, "L'Esprit Nouveau en Architecture."[259] He describes a series of glass slides that accompanied his lecture and that he arranged into an argument as he spoke. These are images drawn from everyday life that Le Corbusier assumes offer shocking contrasts and perturb normal assumptions. For example, an image of the steamship *Paris* reveals astonishingly superb work–the ship itself–at complete odds with the decoration of its salon. The grand lines of the ship are the work of engineers, the interior that of so-called decorators. There are other images, such as those of bank vaults–works of such precision they are almost beautiful, and yet the banker, in absolute discord, will place in his bank a Louis XIII table with enormous turned legs and feet.[260] Something is obviously wrong with the decorative arts of today!

Le Corbusier recounts a small story about a visit he made to the Alps with a poet friend.[261] They stopped to observe a group of engineers constructing a huge dam–the same dam discussed in greater detail in *Urbanisme*, as reviewed above–but when they exclaimed their enthusiasm to the workmen and claimed that cities could be radically transformed by such logical and practical works, they were laughed at and called barbarians for neglecting to consider aesthetics. These engineers, trained to conceive works of pure calculation, remained incapable of imagining the consequences of similar activity extended to other domains. That is why it is essential to reform values, to realize that a new life, a new spirit, and the creations of a machine society are radically opposed to old habits, traditions, and ways of life. On the line of historical development, there is always a point of inflection where a certain culture is transformed and passes into a completely different one. Think of the medieval period succeeding that of the Romans. Between 1000 and 1200 there were turbulent times, after which everything was radically modified by new modes of thought. The Roman city, composed of pure geometry and simple prisms where the horizontal line dominated, was radically transformed by the vertical appearance of church spires and the pitched roofs of houses.

Today, prestressed concrete creates works of pure geometry, allowing architectural proportions–"which are the language of architecture"–to be expressed in a perfectly orthogonal manner.[262] Through prestressed concrete, the present era moves toward an orthogonal system and a pure geometry beyond that which any other period has been able to achieve.

In 1920, Le Corbusier explains, when Ozenfant, Dermée, and Le Corbusier established the review *L'Esprit Nouveau*, they wanted to put into place a constructive program based on the machine, thinking it to be a new phenomenon. By 1925, however, these ideas were more or less acceptable, no longer revolutionary. *L'Esprit Nouveau* taught the lesson of the machine: the law of economy and geometry. It proved that man only lives through geometry: it is his language, he is revealed through the order he creates.[263] The first thing a man does is to establish the orthogonal before him, to put everything in order, and to see clearly. He measures space by three orthogonal axes; a principle so innate that we forget the protests of the nineteenth century, the reaction set against the rule of order and the machine.[264]

Valéry affirmed in *Eupalinos* how determining geometric order has been in aesthetics and architecture. He was able to say things about architecture that professionals cannot because their lyre is not tuned accordingly. Valéry presents the following dialogue between Socrates and Phèdre:

> "If I tell you to take a piece of crayon or chalk," says Socrates, "and draw on the wall, what would you design? What would be your initial gesture?" And Phèdre, taking a chalk, tracing on the wall, responded: "It appears to me that I traced a line of smoke; it goes, returns, buckles, turns back upon itself and gives me the image of a whim without goal, without beginning, without end, without any meaning other than the liberty of my gesture in the movement of my arm."

Le Corbusier's remark is that

> If one had asked me to trace something on the wall, it seems to me that I would have traced a cross, which is made of four right angles, which is a perfection carrying in itself something divine and which at the same time...those four right angles make two axes, coordinates through which I can represent space and measure it.[265]

Modern man, Le Corbusier continues, has acquired this law of geometry, and he is surrounded with pure and clear forms, standardized products of the machine. Still the public protests against this machine, making society lose precious time over what is inevitable. Take, for example, a house for an ordinary man, which has been revolutionized completely by the engineer and the architect. The house must achieve two goals: it must be a *machine á habiter*, an efficient tool in the speed and exactitude of its operations, a tool that satisfies its inhabitant's physical needs. But the house must also be a place for meditation, where beauty exists that brings calm to the spirit. The engineer oversees the practical functions of the house; as for beauty, that is the domain of the architect.[266]

The house, Le Corbusier believes, is an anthropocentric matter, attached to our gestures as the shell is to the snail. It should be made to our measure. Here, too, a total reform of architectural values is needed. The architect must study the doors and windows of a house, for a house is a box merely opened by cuts in its walls. The houses of Pompeii had great openings in their walls for the passage of light, bays onto gardens and doors for the entry of men; in France, climate and life are different, making holes in the wall more difficult. Windows became small openings determined by the height of a story. Today, prestressed concrete has overturned all of this, and the *fenêtre en longeur*–horizontal window–becomes superior to any window of any height because it allows light to flow onto all of the lateral walls. The primordial architectural sensation is that of light.

Until 1900, when one spoke of a house one spoke of walls and a roof. Walls were for defense and used to carry floorboards; they became thick in order to be solid. This has been obviated by modern materials. Now the walls can be as thin as paper and the solidity of the house will not suffer. If once the inclined roof was needed to evacuate water, now Portland cement allows flat roofs with terraces. This new type of construction admits the beauty of geometry, of the orthogonal. Lines that are broken are painful, ones that are continuous pleasurable: a system of incoherent lines affects us negatively, whereas rhythmic lines put us in balance and satisfy us. They offer a spiritual point of view, for they carry perfection within them. Thanks to the machine, we can now coexist with these pure forms of geometry.[267]

It is also necessary, Le Corbusier continues, to resolve the problem of the architectural whole: that of harmony and proportion, or the deployment of the *tracés régulateurs* (regulating lines). Since emotional factors in architecture stem from that which the eye sees, namely surfaces, forms, and lines, the architect must invent relations, rhythms, and proportions that animate the emotions. One begins with a cube: that is the first and strongest sensation. A window is cut, a door opened, and immediately relationships between spaces are created. Mathematics is at work. One introduces unity by organizing the diverse elements, employing regulating lines. It is a matter of finding the law of geometry that rules and determines a composition and into which one introduces

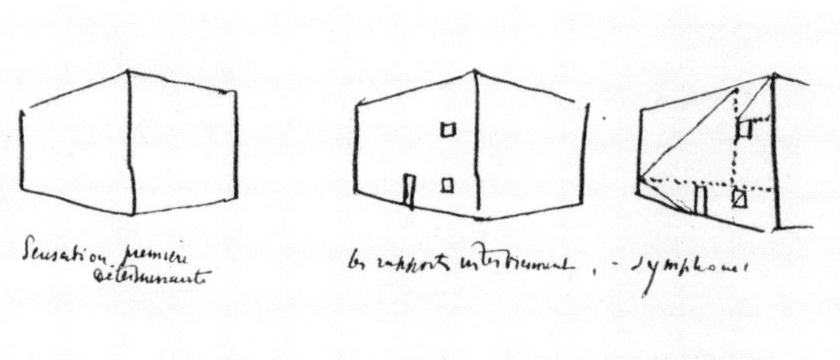

FIGURE 7.22: A simple cube of architecture, its openings well-proportioned and its unity regulated, becomes a machine to move you.

some displacements, some alignments, until a perfect harmony governs the whole.[268] [FIGURE 7.22]

Now Le Corbusier derides the cornice: a sentimental element, a paradox designed not by an architect but by a builder. It is expensive and upsetting because it is wasteful. To suppress the cornice has revolutionary and aesthetic consequences. Economy demands the simple: it has effected a revolution, but still the cornice remains, even on skyscrapers. It must be suppressed! Great art is simple, great things are simple. The simple synthesizes the complex; it is a concentration, a crystallization of a multitude of thoughts.

Le Corbusier proclaims that it is the spirit of geometry that determines architectural destinies, and urbanism, which is banging on the door of the future, is traced out geometrically. It is a matter of totally transforming existing cities–Paris, London, Berlin, Moscow, Rome: "The only possible guide will be the spirit of geometry."[269]

A TURNING

Following the discussion of the new spirit in modern architecture that outlines what will become known as the five points of modern architecture, Le Corbusier inserts a chapter on mosques, followed by a chapter on the Acropolis, the first written during and the second after his travels to the East in 1910. Then he includes an essay written in 1924 on "A turning."

At the time of this writing, Le Corbusier thought the Exposition Internationale des Arts Décoratifs in 1925 would represent a major turning of events.[270] Finally, after twenty years of experimentation and struggle, he believed the spirit of the new time would triumph, new scientific and mechanical ideas would prevail, and a completely new architecture would become the "expressive verb" controlling many milieus. The modern aesthetic had indeed been formulated and put into practice; the debate clarified little by little through experimentation, and most seemed to agree with the direction this aesthetic was going. Regionalism had finally been buried by truly universal aspirations that stemmed from a human base, an immense achievement produced by a new technology and based on a new humanism.

In this turn of events, the field in which modern architecture will be applied defines a new problem. It is no longer a matter of the house or the palace, but of urbanism. Urbanism composes with elements that it groups: streets, districts, central business districts, garden cities, industrial cities. Each of these groupings ought to be formed by perfected elements that are well-adapted to their use. Urbanism imposes standards; the standard is the serial unit; this is the modern process of production that leads to lower prices and quality. However, the process of construction still remains outside the production by serial units because it rests in the hands of architects. Now a turning point arrives: it is recognized that without serial production, nothing useful can be produced. When asked what he is searching for in his consideration of series, Le Corbusier replies: a door and a window. Architects, on the other hand, search for multiple forms that change with each individual expression. Here lies both the difference and the turning point toward modern architecture.

The refrain is repeated: most agree with the direction in which contemporary aesthetics is going. Yet if modern architecture remains tied to the decorative arts then it dies, because the decorative arts die. "It dies because it has nothing to do with *the true; it is crushed by the useful object.*"[271] Materials, machines, and tools must be used with precision if contemporary architecture is to rise. But we are prevented from achieving such perfection because industry is not trained in construction techniques. All the elements that comprise a building have not been standardized. The vital cells of architecture, as well as its elements, such as doors, windows, and all interior arrangements, must become the object of the architect's attention.

Before the issue of urbanism can be raised, a perfect cell has to be prepared that can be reproduced in quantity. Industry has the machines, engineers have the technical ability, so when architects focus on the task of the cellular unit they will find perfection through standardization. Then the urbanist will not be stopped by an anachronistic and unusable unit, and the aestheticians will have at their disposal exactitude, which is the key to rigorous relations, which make proportion...and Parthenons.[272]

FOLKLORE

The article "Construire en Série" ("To Construct in Series") follows, in which Le Corbusier asserts that if one can satisfy many by creating a standardized object, then one is assured that human constants have been satisfied. He likens this achievement to folklore, which has existed over the centuries in a form that reflects universal sentiments felt by mankind.[273] Lasting architecture, he believes, embodies the spirit of a cycle. It introduces a model, a system that becomes a type. This type, over a long period, becomes perfected until it becomes a standard and

FIGURE 7.23: This simple Breton house with a flat roof reveals a new standard, constructed in reinforced concrete. FIGURE 7.24: Roof gardens, horizontal windows, flat roofs, and reinforced concrete are elements of Le Corbusier's language of architecture, affecting the entire city.

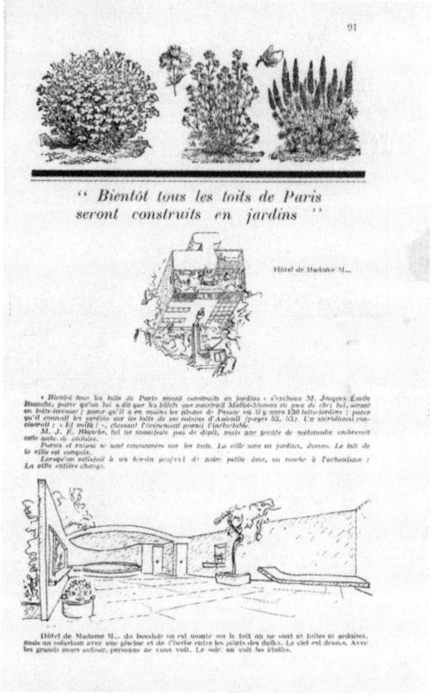

91

" Bientôt tous les toits de Paris seront construits en jardins "

Hôtel de Madame M...

stops developing. It involves the plan, section, and elements of a house. In this manner, regional architecture is elaborated. It considers local climate, customs, territorial enclosures, boundaries, and frontiers.

Le Corbusier continues this discussion of folklore in the next article, "Un Standart Meurt Un Standart Nait" ("A Standard dies a Standard is born"). [274] He approves of vernacular buildings, true human works such those that as exist in Brittany, Provence, the Gironde, the Jura, or Tuscany. They have evolved over time into a standard.

But new construction techniques can suddenly overturn attitudes based on ancestral regionalism, and a tidal wave can follow that transforms all the accustomed objects and house plans.

He gives the example of a simple Breton house: established some centuries before, it became a standardized type and has not changed. Its alignments are exact, like the sun and the wind off the ocean. Its pediment (*fronton*) obeys with precision an obscure but felt aesthetic as invariable as the letter "a." It appears in the countryside like a hard crystal; a thing of geometry that signals the work of man and cheers him from afar. It is as clear as any rallying sign, this sign of the Breton countryside.

But the railroad brought tile to Brittany, and replaced this house's thatch roof. Its gable wall, built over the centuries for thatch, received the tile badly; at its joint with the wall, water infiltrated. A sly person introduced the gutter, projecting well beyond the wall. More infiltration occurred, more water intruded. Tile roofs destroyed the silhouette of the Breton roof, and the Breton facade disappeared in village after village. In ten years, any sign of Breton will be gone.

Other changes are introduced. Every evening, a fine and subtle Italian dances passionately to the music of a mechanical piano in the new salon of a Breton country inn. He is a mason, the one who came one day to build in prestressed concrete this new room of the inn. He has made a flat terrace where one climbs to see the sea and an outside staircase that leads up to it, and has molded in cement a balustrade of a rough type. Prestressed concrete has arrived, and it will resist the waters of the sea. [FIGURE 7.23]

Le Corbusier points out the moral: the railroads have linked the countryside with the city. Perfection emanates from the city. Today the standard is set in the city. "Soon all the roofs of Paris will be constructed with roof gardens."[275] Poetry and reason will meet on the rooftops when the city is immersed in gardens above and below. Since the roof of the city is conquered, the entire city changes its appearance as well. [FIGURE 7.24]

INNOVATION

The Esprit Nouveau Pavilion was not meant to be realized with the traditional means that exposition structures employ: plaster, wire mesh, and stucco. Instead it demonstrated industrialized processes in the construction of its floors, walls, skeletal structure, tiles, paints, and metal tubing. In researching industrial production, Le Corbusier recognized the important role that items manufactured under the name Innovation had played in his own thoughts, and so to end this *Almanach* he offers it praise in an article entitled "Procèdès et Matériaux Nouveaux" ("New Procedures and Materials").[276] He congratulates this company of engineers for creating many useful items, and for guiding his own attempts to create object types that respond to different need types. Most particularly, Innovation over the years had been able to avoid the road that furniture-makers, carpenters, and glass-makers always took, a road blocked by the presence of so many "styles" of the sort evidenced in the Exposition of 1925. By examining technical procedures and deriving important new lessons from these analyses, Innovation produced objects with a new kind of beauty, the first manifestation of the machine-age spirit.

To underscore his point, Le Corbusier examines a folding pocket phonograph patented in 1924, the Mikiphone.[277] A mere four and a half inches (ten centimeters) in diameter and less than two inches (four centimeters) in depth, it was small enough to fit into a pants pocket. He was reminded that the same year a musician friend of his bought a gramophone at great expense, of huge size and with enormous feet. Dismantling it in order to clean it, Le Corbusier discovered some pieces of cast iron, weighing kilos. Having absolutely no use, this weight was added simply in order to be able to sell the phonograph as a piece of expensive furniture. This is how the commercial spirit rules over the decorative arts. In contrast, the Mikiphone is made by the watch-makers of Geneva. Everything changes when the precision of watch-makers rules. Yet it is scarcely necessary to report that this tiny phonograph would have been rejected by the jury that controlled the Exposition Internationale des Arts Décoratifs in 1925.[278] [FIGURE 7.25]

CONCLUSION

How then are the four books, published by Georges Crès as the *Collection of the Esprit Nouveau*, concerned with the "language of architecture," whether in the sense of architecture as language or the language about architecture? [FIGURE 7.26] In an article concerning the integration of the arts published in *Création Revue d'Art* (1921), Ozenfant and Jeanneret elaborate on their analogy that art including architecture is a language.[279] In order to transmit a specific emotion or an exact thought, they explain, it is essential to utilize material elements as precisely as well-defined words of a verbal language. A Purist word follows the laws of composition internal to the work of art, it conjugates these words,

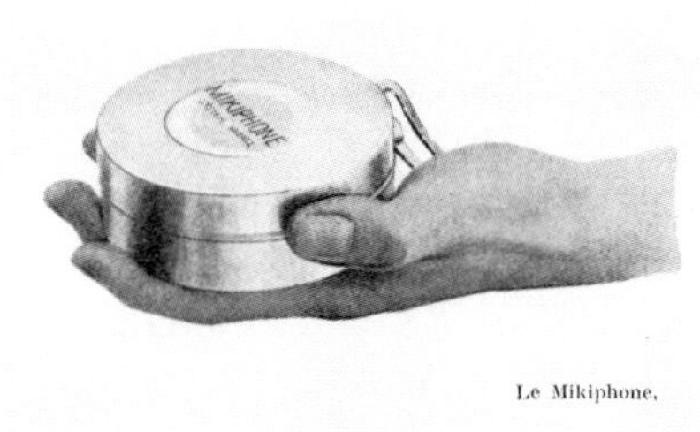

198 HISTOIRE BRÈVE

HISTOIRE BRÈVE DE NOS TRIBULATIONS

Nous avions rédigé pour cet Almanach l'*Histoire brève de nos tribulations*.

Elle n'avait d'autre but que de faire pardonner la précarité d'exécution de notre pavillon, le retard apporté à son achèvement. Nous étions, sans un sou et la direction des services d'architecture de l'Exposition nous avait interdit de réaliser notre programme.

Alors, cette histoire brève devenait longue, longue bien que concise, parce que nos avatars furent innombrables, sans fin. Il n'y eut pas de répit, jamais, durant une année.

Cet Almanach ne contiendra pas l'*Histoire brève de nos tribulations* parce que trop d'amertume se dégage malgré nous, des faits et que cette histoire concise et exacte d'événements notés quotidiennement, serait comme une vengeance.

Il est déplacé de raconter ses malheurs quand on a le bonheur de pouvoir les oublier.

. . . .

Voici pour terminer banalement, un cul-de-lampe de l'Imprimerie Darantière à Dijon où s'impriment cet Almanach et aussi la Revue de l'Esprit Nouveau.

FIGURE 7.25: Le Corbusier praised the efficiency and convenience of Innovations's small phonograph, the Mikiphone, yet noted it would have been rejected by the jury who judged the decorative arts. FIGURE 7.26: Le Corbusier ends the *Almanach* with a "brief history of our tribulations" and the ornament (or *cul-de-lampe*) of the publisher, Georges Crès. Crès had been brave enough to publish the *Almanach* and the four *Esprit Nouveau* volumes.

conserving their universal meanings. If a Purist work of art is readable, it is because it utilizes intelligible words. In their reasoning, verbal language through rigorous selection and continuous evolution prevails over all other forms of language: those of architecture, the decorative arts, painting, sculpture, music, rhythm, dance, folklore, and all other means of communicating ideas and thoughts.

Ozenfant supposedly told Le Corbusier in 1920, "To purify architecture that is your role!" The vocabulary of this new architecture, being tested in both projects and writing, constitutes the five points of architecture (piloti, roof gardens, free plan, rectangular windows, free facade) structured according to a poetry of relationships.[280] These elements and this syntax in the hands of a talented architect will generate a form of writing that is both readable and moving (a machine to move you). Such a system creates an architectural thought clarified without words or sounds. Through volumes seen under pure light and in precise and harmonious relationships, it reveals a thought transmitted to eyes, then the brain.

The language of Purism is also intertwined with the act of writing about architecture: in the form of the well-typed page, in the format of the four books of Esprit Nouveau, in typographic manifestations, in theoretical clarifications. Writing for Le Corbusier was a tool of thought; working out "elements of his doctrine" as a scientist might do in a laboratory, making and verifying discoveries, then unifying these elements into a system of thought. He claimed in September of 1920:

> To write a little puts ideas clearly, engages, compromises, constrains us to follow the strength of its theory. It is necessary to reflect constantly, all the time, at each pretext to be sensible. To be sensible, is to be conscious, the contrary to that which one attributes to sensibility. To write and to make the step of a giant and to cross clearly the underground forces of his instincts and sensations.[281]

The contaminations of architecture and writing continue. As Le Corbusier claims, the Pavillon de l'Esprit Nouveau is a demonstration of one of the cells of a great building that will adorn the streets of Paris in the near future. It is a materialization of theories that appeared in the review and in the four books of the Esprit Nouveau.[282] The pavilion consists of two parts: the first on the right representing in exact dimensions a mock-up of the cell of habitation, an example of the machine of living where reason and the heart can be satisfied. This cell becomes a house-type, good for the city or the country. Urbanism assembles many of these cells, organizes them, allows for hanging gardens, modifies the streets, the lots, putting sport at the foot of the house, creating the type "immeubles-villas." It introduces a new module into the city, a new order of grandeur.

Adjacent to the mock-up of the cell is the second part of the pavilion: a vast rotunda sheltering two huge dioramas of the Ville Contemporaine and the Plan Voisin. These two vast paintings–each ninety or one hundred square meters, Le Corbusier wrote–explain, comment, make viable a number of theoretical aspects of urbanism.[283] Every wall is covered with propagandistic imagery, didactic texts, individual pages from *L'Esprit Nouveau* plastered on the entrance wall of the "urbanism stand," colossal polychrome letters, "EN," stamped on the lateral facade of the pavilion.[284]

Le Corbusier exploits all the means available to make known his work, to develop his ideas, to convince elite administrators, workers, sometimes the general public, of the path to the future. Writing becomes a tool of combat. There were many incensed by the message that *Esprit Nouveau* promulgated and the architectural projects Le Corbusier demonstrated. The aesthetic sensibility of these critics was upset by phenomena they could perceive, but whose position they could not support. An impassioned combat arose around Le Corbusier and his ideas; it was a battle waged over the future of a culture and civilization.[285] As a result, the writings of Le Corbusier begin to defend the cause of modern architecture, protecting through writing ideas and projects under attack, as the *Almanach* offers evidence of.

As we have seen, in 1924 Le Corbusier gives a lecture at the Sorbonne on "L'Esprit Nouveau and Architecture." This is the beginning of an active program of public events, as Le Corbusier is asked to give many lectures in different countries expounding on his ideas of architecture and urbanism.[286] These lectures, he explains in the late 1930s, help make his ideas precise and clear, and extend his field of thought. He develops an improvisational manner of speaking: from notes, he lays out his plan. Utilizing colored crayons that organize his thoughts, he sketches out his theory on long sheets of paper, two meters by one and a half meters. In the midst of this improvisation the correct words come to his mind, the precise ideas, and the exact conclusions. He collects these lecture notes and drawings, turning them into chapters in subsequent books, as he does with the 1924 Sorbonne lecture placed in the *Almanach*.

Le Corbusier develops a technique of writing that will continue throughout his lifetime, recycling and transposing material from journal articles collected subsequently into book format, inserting sections of a book into later books, utilizing material appropriated from catalogues and magazines. Catherine de Smet thinks this practice offers Le Corbusier time to experiment before codifying his ideas into a larger, more permanent format of a book.[287] I consider Le Corbusier's four books of the Esprit Nouveau collection to be laboratory notebooks, theoretical projects that test elements contributing to his doctrine of architecture, urbanism, the decorative arts, and painting. He often uses verbs, such as to study, to research, to examine, to reveal; he calls on the reader to open one's eyes, to learn the lessons, to remember; he teaches how to classify, to put in order, to reform. He wants to deploy language with the same precision (rapidity and effectiveness) as optical instruments. Thus his study of the language of architecture occurs on two different levels: the abstract, system-defined elements of a science and the more material configurations of great buildings bequeathed by time, small hovels surrounded by enclosure walls, "Everything, sublime or modest, which contains sufficient geometry to establish a mathematical relationship."[288]

PART 3
To Solve the Equation "Reason = Passion" (1929–40s)

CHAPTER 8 CONTROVERSY AND POETRY, 1929 AND BEYOND

Do poetry, beauty, and harmony enter into the life of modern men and women; or must we consider its scope as being confined to the mechanical performances of the mechanical functions postulated by "the machine for living in"? To me the quest of harmony seems the noblest of human passions.

–LE CORBUSIER, 1929

I. CONTROVERSY

FIRST DEFENSE OF MODERN ARCHITECTURE: *A HOUSE–A PALACE*

On May 5, 1927, a jury met to select a winner of the international design competition for the Palace of the League of Nations to be built in Geneva. The nine members were indecisive, selecting three groups of nine winners each. Among the nine winners in the first group was the submission of Le Corbusier and Pierre Jeanneret, but also the academic projects of Camille Lefèvre, Giuseppe Vago, Henri-Paul Nénot, and Carlo Broggi. Since only the project of Le Corbusier and Pierre Jeanneret fulfilled the stated programmatic needs and budget, these two architects considered themselves the rightful winners of the competition. However, the radical modernism of their design triggered an extraordinary series of maneuvers to have it discredited. By September, the first breach in the competition's terms was committed: the jury raised the budget, enabling some academic projects to compete with Le Corbusier and Jeanneret's solution. Protests erupted in the international press and, as a result, five disinterested diplomats were charged by the League of Nations to review the projects and to designate a winner following a strict mandate, considering both cost and function.

On December 27, 1927, a second breach of terms occurred. The five ambassadors passed over the submitted projects to choose instead one architect, Nénot, president of the Salon des Artistes Française and architect of the Sorbonne, to be joined by the three other academicians, namely Broggi (Italian), Vago (Italian-Hungarian), and Lefèvre (French). This new team was asked to submit a completely new design for the project.

Upon hearing of this decision, Nénot told the newspaper *Les Annales* that the barbarians had been stopped. Without naming Le Corbusier and Jeanneret, he bragged that those who are anti-architecture, who deny all the beautiful epochs of history, had been suppressed.[1] A renewed battle in the international press soon followed, with many commentators championing the Le Corbusier and Jeanneret design as the rightful winner, the only solution that came in under (original) budget, and the only clear demonstration of modern architecture. Le Corbusier and Jeanneret instructed their lawyer to send a letter to the president of the League of Nations protesting the jury's action. On March 5, however, the League confirmed the ambassadors' decision.

From the controversy's inception in 1927 and on into 1929, modern architects raised a storm of protest. They claimed the competition had been rigged from the beginning, that it had always been about nationalism, not architecture. The projects had not even been publicly viewed–in fact, were rolled up and in storage. Christian Zervos, editor of the *Cahiers d'Art*, made an appeal to the public, whom he claimed wanted a new spirit, a spirit for modern times. In his article "Qui Bâtira le Palais des Nations?" ("Who Will Build the Palace of Nations?" 1927) published in the *Cahiers d'Art*, he said that the League must be a model for the future, and ought to have a worthy house, one emblematic of modern times.[2] Haussmann, Louis XIV, Jules II, and the cathedral builders all rejected the past, breaking with tradition to create something completely new. It is not possible to build the colossal nonsense of Nénot, architect of the Sorbonne, or of Vago, who designs postage stamps. Le Corbusier and Jeanneret's project, on the other hand, is a manifestation of a new European cultural elite.[3]

Entering the fray in his own defense, Le Corbusier writes a small book entitled *Une Maison–Un Palais* (*A House–A Palace*, 1928), a clever arrangement of text-image juxtapositions that serves as a catalogue of the defeated League of Nations project. [FIGURE 8.I, p. 697] Le Corbusier opens by telling the reader they are imaginary listeners to a conference where images have been inserted at appropriate moments.[4] He continues by introducing the refrain "a house, a palace," and announces that after composing a work of architecture answering all the needs of comfort, the mind finds itself on a higher plane, a plane beyond utilitarian needs, a plane where lyrical powers reside that move the spirit and bring joy.[5] "This elevated intention becomes for us, today, a definition of architecture."[6] Le Corbusier thus defines his book from the outset not as a bleak utilitarian tract but as a venture into the poetics of architecture, which arise from but transcend mundane needs of the day.

Architecture no longer derives from the tortures of the academies, blinded by the prejudices of the pre-machinist era; it is the product of the spirit of the times. Yet the young, Le Corbusier claims, wishing to escape the cadaverous effusions of the schools, think that architecture is only utilitarian, concerned strictly with needs, having nothing to do with emotions. They are mistaken, he says: architecture must answer both utilitarian needs and "serve the god within us."[7]

Hence "a house, a palace," a single product. A house is meant to shelter, but it must also address our sensibility. Joy is found in harmony, when quantities are placed in precise relationships, when the language of geometry is spoken.

Anticipating the complaint that geometry is dry, the exact opposite of poetry, Le Corbusier asks the reader to visualize a bridge, to consider why it moves us, why it is a poetical statement. In the midst of the incoherence of nature and cities, it is a place of geometry, a place where mathematics rules. The bridge as an act of will, a thing of optimism, is a clear and unambiguous thing–and it brings joy.[8]

So architecture concerns both utility and passion, as do objects such as the airplane, submarine, dirigible, racecar, and boat, for which we feel pride and affection.[9] Though architecture also involves bidets, central heating, and the "machine for living in," it must always understand that its focus is man, who has both a head and a heart and lives to act.[10]

Le Corbusier turns to what he calls the heart of the issue, the great social problem: the house. It must break with ancestral traditions that restrain it from answering the needs of today. Here he shifts his mode of discourse from straight text to text-image comparisons: the image on the right-hand page of the open book will, he says, constitute the evidence of his argument, the text on the left the proof (i.e., the logic). He begins by drawing a square, which he says is proof of action because it contains an interior force. It can be the plan of a house. Next he draws an irregular polygon, and calls it an event without

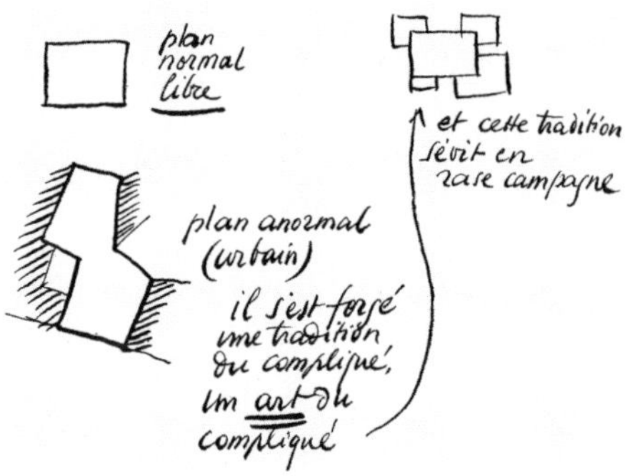

FIGURE 8.2: **If a square rules the plan of a house, there is order and calm, while an irregular polygon is without control.** FIGURE 8.3: **Simple peasant houses attract Le Corbusier's praise—they can become palaces in his mind.**

control. It produces an abnormal plan for a house, and everything in it is likewise abnormal. The polygon is, however, the current image of a city: everything in it is abnormal, deformed, complicated, and arbitrary. Then he offers a third image, a disorderly set of rectangles, and proclaims: "[This] shows us why a house has stopped being a palace."[11] [FIGURE 8.2]

The text-image discourse that follows is an interweaving of three different arguments. He has to first convince the reader that today, a house is no longer a palace. This is intermixed with a second proof (as he calls it) that a house can be a palace. He must then show that a palace, too, is a machine for living in. In conclusion, both the house and the palace combine utility and passion.

The first two proofs will involve discussion of a traditional fisherman's hut, an image of which he juxtaposes with one of his and Jeanneret's designs for the Palais des Nations on the dust jacket. We know from his earlier writings that Le Corbusier's evolutionary history of architecture begins with primitive man, who sets out his hut in geometrical form, finding instinctively through his innate sense of order the regulating trace that generates the plan of the whole.

ARCHITECTURE AS PLANT, HOUSE AS PALACE

Le Corbusier likens architecture to a plant with deep roots, a metaphor he will develop further. Because man is occupied in his daily life with thousands of small affairs, when a new event takes place he thinks it

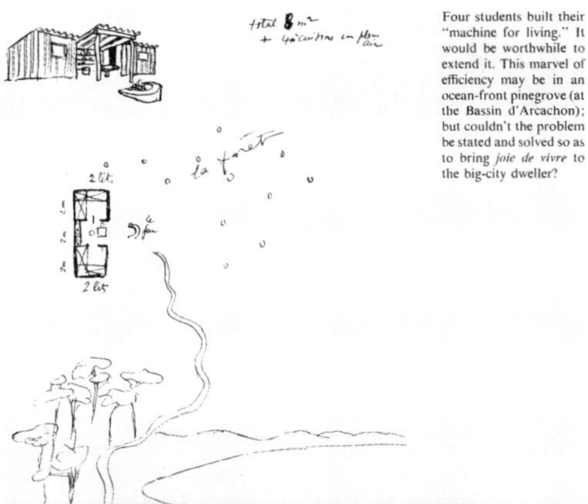

FIGURE 8.4: **Making a synthesis of the heart and the mind, this humble fisherman's hut becomes a house-palace.**

is spontaneous, even incongruous or random. Yet, Le Corbusier maintains, in architecture there is little spontaneity, and nothing is capricious. Architecture arises from a long and arduous process: "types develop over time with profound reasons for their existence, reserves of architecture; investigate them attentively. It is through them that we will make palaces of our houses."[12] [FIGURE 8.3]

Le Corbusier begins his rather complex proof that a house is a palace and a palace a house by looking at rural life, where he finds a seeming paradox: amidst all the tumult the machine age has wrought since the Great War, the normal conditions of the countryside still allow a house to rise in humility and simplicity. An example: in the Bay of Arcachon on the Atlantic coast lies a tongue of land isolated from the world. Here the fishermen are only tenants; they do not want to build houses out of stone on land that they do not own. They live here only "temporarily."[13] This affects the manner in which they build their houses: they make a shelter, nothing more. They are not encumbered by pretensions of history, culture, or the taste of the day: they build a shelter with the poor material they find lying around. They make it with their own hands, with no professional knowledge. Yet they are attentive to the least gesture, wanting to attain the maximum with the minimum. In order to place each thing, they turn around like a cat in a room searching for a particular place; they weigh it in their hands, they calculate unconsciously, and they find the point of equilibrium, the center of gravity. "And in this harmonious cadence, intuition suggests and rationality reasons. They give in to a bout of very decent, natural lyricism, a lyricism entirely human!"[14] The fisherman becomes a poet. [FIGURE 8.4]

The man begins with one room, a shelter from the harsh sunlight. He locates his well for water. From the first evening he makes a bench—a plank riven in two and fixed in the sand, well placed, where he sits when at home. He constructs a place for washing, an oven as in Knossos or Mycenae; he plants a fig tree that gives a dense shade. Each of these things is a monument: the bench, place of washing, oven, and fig tree.[15] Having raised the contentious (as he puts it) word "monument," Le Corbusier asks the reader directly to close their eyes, to evoke the architecture of history, and "think architecture"—then, with open eyes, with eyes that have just come from reviewing the pages of an architectural history book, to look again at the villages of the fishermen.[16] All the elements that make up the great monuments of architecture can be found in the simple fisherman's house: the facades, the entrances, and the other elements disposed in such a manner as to ennoble the ensemble. They constitute a total truth—each part born of another, each depending on the other. Nothing is rejected; everything is used, though not overworked or repeated. It is a totally efficient organization. These simple fishermen's houses are isolated in the pine forest or grouped in hamlets along the shore, but all have a common human measure: a human scale based on the foot, the shoulder, and the head.[17] One day it occurred to him: "But these houses are palaces!"[18]

Now his argument moves simply and directly (he says), as if he were mimicking the steps that produced the simple and pure fisherman's house, applying them to the construction of a palace. One defines a palace as a house if it strikes through the dignity of its appearance. Dignity is a dominant attitude emanating from decency; it is dominant because all of its elements stem from the order of monuments. A monument is that which assembles pure forms according to a law of harmony, and harmony results from a perfect agreement between cause and effect. The cause is a matter of housing: comfort; and a question of structure: the construction. The effect is jubilation on seeing the spectacle of such a wise and elegant play of the mind.[19]

Today, prestressed concrete has replaced the wood from the pine forest, the machine for living substitutes for the rustic program, and the aspirations of cultivated men take the place of the primary lyricism of the fisherman. As a consequence, none of these huts will remain, and new propositions will arise based on different programs. Modern man, however, can attain the same spirit of architecture as did the simple fisherman if he knows how to realize a harmonious order of the elements, and to make of his house a palace.[20]

He summarizes to drive the point home, returning to his opening metaphor of a plant. When architecture has developed into a system, a reserve remains in its seed. This seed is the potential of architecture, and the reserve will eventually flourish into a lyrical flower. Thus the house can always become a palace. It lies in the hands of the architect to manipulate this reserve, just as it had laid in the hands of the simple fisherman.[21]

ARCHITECTURE AS ORGANISM

But what do the hands of the architect hold, and how can he exploit these reserves to achieve the potential of a house-palace? He must first attend to a few simple propositions, which also preface the story of the fisherman's hut. They involve intentions, geometry, nature, and eloquence. Le Corbusier directs these propositions to the younger generation of architects, who resist these lessons and do not wish to see with the eyes in their heads. He begins with "intentions" of architecture that project beyond those of brute sensation. The mind likes to contemplate the play of intentions offered by a work of art, trying to grasp their meaning. Since art is subtle, it can generate an infinite number of perceptions. Thus the mind contemplating a great architectural work constantly discovers new intentions. Yet the light changes, seasons pass, and the young do not see what the old see. The old have a soul that predisposes them to things that arouse their passion.[22]

The power of nature constantly battles with man, destroys his work, makes no exceptions. Man studies the apparent chaos of nature in search of order and meaning lest he perish, tries to dominate her yet calls her "mother earth."

Then Le Corbusier suddenly shifts his argument from art and nature to the "implacable order" of geometry: "The only language that we know how to speak is geometry, and we have inserted it into nature because all is only chaos without and order within, an implacable order."[23] Our creative power stems from geometry. Using the terms of this useful language, we have raised the most sacred thing of all: beauty. And it has allowed the expression of other human conceptions that stem from the mind: nobility, grandeur, and majesty.[24]

Having mentioned nature and the divine language of geometry, Le Corbusier presents a photograph of the valley of Delphi, followed by three drawings, two of which were made during his 1911 trip to the East. [FIGURE 8.5] The first is a simple sketch of three platforms of stone, standing as "violent and pure witnesses" over the valley and Gulf of

FIGURE 8.5: Geometry rules over the Valley of Delphi and dominates the plain of Athens, while in Rome there are symptoms of decadence.

Corinth. They speak of the sublime on a magnificent site where nature and temples combine.[25] The second sketch is of the Acropolis in Athens seen from afar, perched high on its plateau. He notes the same geometry is the base on which temples and palaces are built; it is expressive of the will to power that all priests and tyrants understand. "Geometry: clarity of mind and mysterious infinity of combinations."[26]

Beneath the sketch of the Acropolis is one of the Fabricius bridge in Rome. Le Corbusier calls the latter a clear symptom of decadence, the distended crystal where intense relationships crack. Measure–the sign of the mind, the word of dignity–no longer exists in this work. The three sublime platforms of Delphi are crushed under decorative and disorderly abundance.[27] We hear the wildness (*dévergondage*) of the "enfants terribles," the younger generation of architects, who dream of attaining great works but refuse to pass slowly through the necessary stages required to achieve such heights. Instead they present cadavers deprived of the source of life. In this way, the Americans build cities, and people witness Versailles without understanding.[28]

He turns to the machine, which now imposes the most crushing rhythm and intense geometry on modern man. This is a new stage of history, gripping man with new emotions of purity, rigor, and precision–a stage inconceivable before yesterday. After war (World War I), for those who knew how to see and to feel, the vital line of continuity with the past was broken. An explosive force of "constructivism"

FIGURE 8.6: **Stones standing upright in nature grip the spectator's heart and mind.** FIGURE 8.7: **Nature, when in equilibrium and harmony, produces a moving concert.**

occurred. And the young, who come and go with their voracious optimistic appetites, established a "style" based on this vague word without beginning or end. It contains too much; it defines neither an aesthetic nor a category of human production.

There is no tool to measure or to appreciate contemporary works. All we have is a tuning fork within us, a tool of harmony that vibrates in the presence of justly tuned works.[29] The eye only measures what it can see.

> Suddenly, one is stopped, seized, measuring, appreciating: a geometrical phenomenon is erected under one's eyes: a rock standing upright as witness, the indubitable horizontal of the sea, or the meander of waves. And through the magic of associative communication, one finds oneself in the land of dreams.[30]
>
> [FIGURES 8.6 AND 8.7]

Reveries, dreams, and memories of voyages keep haunting Le Corbusier's text, establishing the manner in which he inserts lessons drawn from the past yet addressed to the young. He remarks that the perception of dazzling works of synthesis most often appears during fortunate moments of a voyage when the traveler comes upon a work of nature and of man, and finds the two works to resonate in harmony. These moments create the ineffable hours of life.[31]

He returns to the themes of utility and passion, to the young and their masters. He reminds the younger generation that the history of progress is a matter of work, and that of culture a matter of a spiritual architecture (of ordering); both are the result of a passionate research into harmony. "A tool is only useful or functional when harmony rules between the organs of man." When they enter into an ensemble and constitute an "organism," something viable, alive, and moving, only then do emotions intervene–stemming from the passions of man.[32]

He repeats that the meaning of architecture is to put things in order. Culture oscillates between tormented lines of a provisionary powerlessness and the shining crystallization of a master.[33] In the French Renaissance, the masterful writings of Vitruvius were first translated by Jean Goujon. Then architects had before their eyes the "Doric" style, re-establishing the orthogonal in their minds, and suddenly there was full light and freedom in their designs.[34] Vitruvius was inspired by the Parthenon, by the power of its light. It called forth the exactitude of geometry, unadorned as Diogenes, but like him, dressed eloquently and subtly.[35]

In contemporary times, the geometry of steel can be eloquent like the clothes of Diogenes. This word "eloquence" irritates the younger generation, but in the end, they too must learn that true joy lies in the quality of the play, in its finesse and nuance, and that in this truth, history renews itself without end.[36] Otherwise everything becomes a dull "system," a vulgarization erected by adoring students.

In closing, he explains that the word "organism" has helped him describe the fusion of two different intentions that must work in harmony: that of the functional and the emotional. A rule of functional coordination is manifested in objects he calls organisms: steamships or race cars, bridges or dams. It is a label of praise when attached to the works of man, and endows them with a capacity of being alive and viable, not static or dead.[37]

Le Corbusier ends his discourse on organisms with an example: he shows a plan and section, then announces that these are images of neither an Egyptian temple nor a Roman house. They are the plan and section for wine vats made of prestressed concrete. It is a simple design that struggles against the resistances of nature (the pressure of the liquid) while its feet elevate the vats above the ground, allowing for the circulation of air necessary for making wine. Yet the work raises within the spectator all the joys of architecture.[38] Whether it is a matter of a house, palace, temple–or these simple vats–at the base is a clear and living organism.[39]

THE RESERVES OF ARCHITECTURE

Now he is ready to return to his argument that a house is a palace and a palace a house. He calls on history to witness that across the ages and under all kinds of climates, the house of man has been given a type. Even in the primitive house, man does not know how to act without geometry. He is exact; there is not a piece of wood or ligature that does not have a precise function.

Below a simple hut, he places an image of man during archaic times, when nature struggled against him. His house is straight and rectangular, each piece revealing the power of architecture. One day, he will contemplate this rustic tool that answers his needs, and his spirit will be carried aloft on the wings of lyricism. Then the brutal fact becomes the materialization of higher intentions, and on the Acropolis, the temple of the goddess will rise. When things are still obscure, man thinks about events that dominate him, and he constructs a cyclopean work, a surrounding wall within which he ardently practices religious rites. He mind establishes agonizing relationships between the altars, tables of sacrifice, and the great stones.[40] Le Corbusier shows a drawing of Stonehenge: these great dolmens and menhirs give evidence across the ages that architecture means to put things in order.[41] [FIGURE 8.8]

Again Le Corbusier reiterates his message: in the ordering gesture, primitive architecture reveals a reserve from which all the elements of great architecture–the Parthenon, the prestigious splendors of Babylon and Nineveh–stem. All the elements are there, at the disposition of a lyrical inventor; it requires only the imagination of a creative artist to cultivate this seed, to make it blossom, to make it shine as a work of splendor, the round and firm fruit of high thought. It is merely necessary that the spirit of a creative man understands and is gripped by the powers at his discretion.[42]

Le Corbusier returns to the problem of proving that a house is a palace and vice versa. The problem is that nothing remains of a palace; the academies have sullied the meaning of the word. Their palaces are no more than the image of lewd pretensions, robbed of a healthy spirit and a pure soul. He becomes angry when he thinks of the Palace of the League of Nations and the competition he lost; his competitors' work was nothing but a stew of hanged meat where maggots have swarmed. Stomachs of men of the machine age cannot digest food so close to putrefaction. The academies put a lie to all the works that afflict the heart of the great city, where even the healthy institutions of modern life such as banks, offices, and assembly halls are covered with

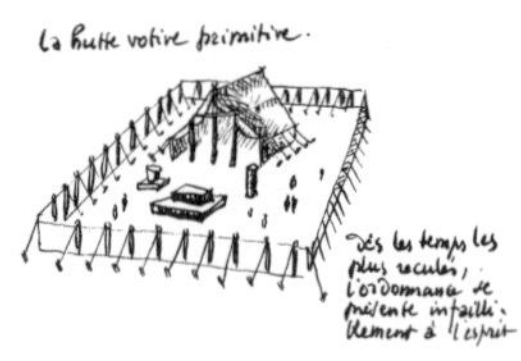

FIGURE 8.8: **As evidenced over the centuries, "to architecture" is to put in order.**

useless masks of stone. Here is the vilest state of humankind, where the false and the pretentious reign. In such a state a house cannot become a palace.[43]

The following pages contain an exposition of villas designed by Le Corbusier and Pierre Jeanneret, accompanied by photographs of their demonstration project at Stuttgart. The text explains there is a new modern architecture that contrasts with the tradition of its forebears because it is conceived in the spirit of the machine age that attends to and realizes comfort. He outlines the five points of this architecture: 1/ flat roofs on which one plants a garden, where reception is placed closer to the roof garden and not at the ground level; 2/ the house raised into the air on pilotis, far from the ground and much healthier. Light is everywhere, because prestressed concrete allows for 3/ a free plan, 4/ an open facade, and 5/ horizontal windows that almost touch the lateral walls of the room, turning them into reflectors. The attentive, observant mind has taken the new material of prestressed concrete and moved it toward the noblest destiny of architecture. Guided by a new spirit, it has turned the house into a palace.[44] [FIGURES 8.9 AND 8.10]

Le Corbusier notes that it remains for him to prove not only that the house is a palace, but that the palace is a house, and turns to the "house" he designed for the administration of the League of Nations. In this next proof, he says, he will rely on the eye of man: a man standing upright who regards with his eyes, who looks at images.[45]

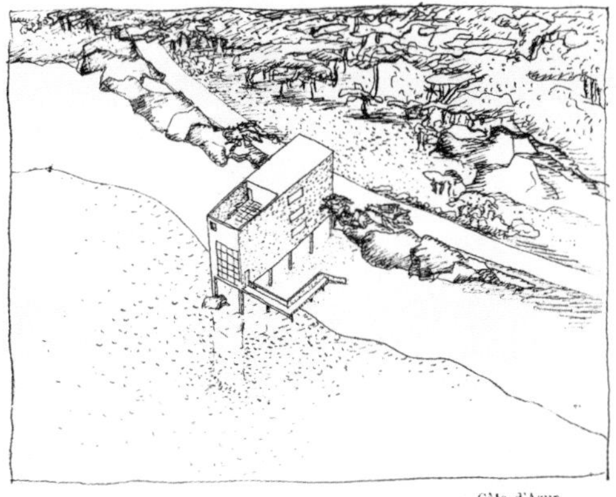

FIGURE 8.9: **Following simple, pure traditions, Le Corbusier designed a small house of prestressed concrete projected over a river.** FIGURE 8.10: **The house-type possesses an architectural potential; it can achieve the dignity of a palace.**

He selects an image to begin his demonstration: the preliminary construction of a dam in the Alps. This is a colossal collaboration of ingenuity and boldness, where gigantic machines have placed in the hands of man means beyond anything history has imagined.[46] To this "frontispiece," Le Corbusier adds another image, one of lower Manhattan. The reader can grasp with his eyes that like the dam, the gigantic city is also the result of calculations based on statistics. [FIGURE 8.11] Now the evidence of the modern dam in the Alps begins to have meaning, for the truth is that cities are breaking up; they are inundated by innumerable new organs of modern life that cause their death at an accelerating speed. The struggle is hopeless between the scanty framework of old cities and the torrent of new life pressing down upon them. The forces need to be dammed up! Le Corbusier turns to examine the new framework he plans to impose on this crowded terrain: the contemporary city for three million. The plan proves that modern man can make of the house a palace, and through the principle of unity that operates under the sign of the times, the palace itself will be a house.[47] The joys of architecture

> are in the wise, correct and magnificent play of forms under light. They are in the relation of cause and effect that reveals the intention, which unveils the play of the mind, which shows without ambiguity the rules of the game.[48]

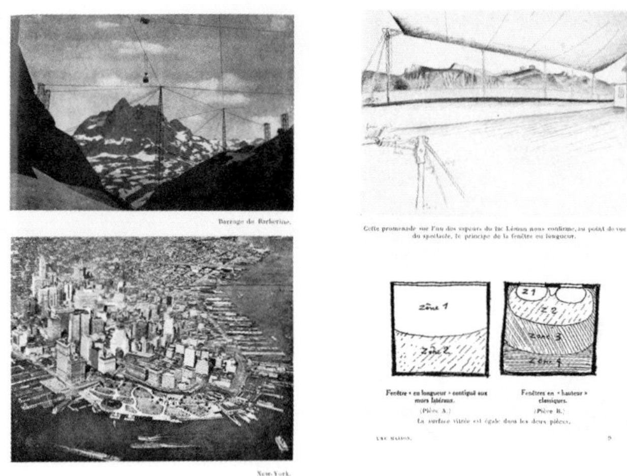

FIGURE 8.11: The construction of a great dam in the Alps and the gigantic city of New York are both products of mathematical calculation. FIGURE 8.12: Rectangular windows allow light to reflect and diffuse across lateral walls.

They exist in simple things, in the apparent, which is like a crystal hard and glittering that admits no compromise. "Such clarity and purity, are they not signs of modern times? And are they not also the sign of the new institutions which, at Geneva, ought to respond to the hope of new societies?"[49]

Now Le Corbusier turns to the designs that he and Pierre Jeanneret executed for the Palace of the League of Nations.[50] First he describes the magnificent site along the shores of Lake Geneva as it opens on the horizon toward the Jura Mountains to the east. Although academicians claim that a "palace," to be worthy of its name, must have an infrastructure like a fortress, Le Corbusier does not agree that strength lies in cyclopean walls. It lies rather in the extent of the sky above and through the impeccable and unique horizontal line the site allows.[51] Palaces of the past such as Versailles, the Doge's Palace, even the Vatican are academic formulas that have nothing to do with the present program, which concerns administration. In offices one works on sheets of paper, one reads or writes, thus this "palace" requires a number of rooms, each supplied with a desk, some chairs, and one or more tables for typewriters. Today is the age of paper, which has replaced the spoken word. To write and to read requires sufficient and regular light. The best solution requires rectangular windows that stretch across the wall, allowing light to diffuse on lateral walls.[52] [FIGURE 8.12]

Moreover, the grand assembly room, meant to seat twenty-six hundred people, is a room to discuss proclamations about world peace and world war made by people from the four corners of the Earth, all speaking different languages and demanding to be heard, and must be an organ of hearing and visibility. He recalls that not a word was heard if he wandered away from the guide in the Pantheon, at Saint-Sulpice or Notre Dame, and in similar monumental spaces. Thus in Geneva, only disaster would follow if the great assembly room was constructed according to the canons of the academy.[53]

Visibility is another problem in the assembly room. Each person ought to be able to see clearly, no matter where they sit. There must also be a room for journalists, with perfect visibility and good acoustics.[54] There are further problems of lighting, circulation, heating, and ventilation–technical problems that Le Corbusier and Jeanneret answered efficiently and effectively.[55] Their solution created an aesthetic, a matter of putting things in order based on both mathematical relationships and the creative power of the architect. "Smiling, clear and beautiful: we have said that this was the real program of architecture."[56]

Returning to his theme of the young architects who reject all definitions of the word "eloquence," Le Corbusier remarks that they erroneously believe that to act in purity is to limit oneself to the severe study of useful functions. But there is a hole built right in the middle of their logic; they forget that every human act is a kind of movement. Elements born from analysis are grasped through a rhythm, which ties them together, assembles them, composes them, and orders them. This act emanates from a will, and this will is an unconscious imperative. It concerns a particular conception within each individual. It is not simply a matter of cause and effect, but of being animated by passion as well. An individual's work is none other than the product of both an incontestable reason and an ineluctable passion.[57]

He concludes: his Palace of the League of Nations is based on a new aesthetic far beyond the formulas of the academies. It offers "a lyricism of lines, a poetics of ordering, an act of devotion with respect to nature."[58] It is designed by an honest man (another reference to Diogenes), the cost being exactly that of the credit allocated, not triple or quadruple. Such an aesthetic is not a manifestation of academicism but of an ethic, of an individual.

> At the origin, underneath, within, in the depth, there is something intangible, pure, truthful, an unalienable thing, ineffable: an individual passion.[59]

IN DEFENSE OF ARCHITECTURE

In 1929 Le Corbusier's masterpiece, the Villa Savoye, was under construction; the lectures from his 1928 trip to South America, *Précisions sur un état present de l'architecture et de l'urbanisme,* had just been published; and the first volume of the *Oeuvre Complète* was about to be issued. These two books, as Le Corbusier himself argued, have complementary styles of exposition, the former outlining the theory of a new architecture and urbanism, the latter showing how the theory was applied in projects.[60] Having spent the first half of the 1920s honing the method of Purism as it applied to architecture and city planning, the decorative arts, and painting, in these two books Le Corbusier would begin to elaborate this doctrine into a wider belief system that would stir the world through the movement of modern architecture. Significantly, the Congrès Internationaux d'Architecture Moderne (CIAM), which summoned a select group of architects to defend the cause of modern architecture after Le Corbusier had won but then lost the League of Nations competition, had just completed its first meeting at La Sarraz in the summer of 1928. The same year, Sigfried Giedion published his *Bauen in Frankreich* (1928) and Le Corbusier his *Une Maison–Un Palais* (1928).

1929 also marks the first time that Le Corbusier defended himself in the press, directly answering criticisms aimed at him by his fellow architects. This work, entitled "Défense de l'architecture" and written in epistolary form on his way to and from Moscow in 1929, was intended as a response to Karel Teige, who published an article titled "Mundaneum" in the Czechoslovakian journal *Stavba* (April 1929) denouncing Le Corbusier's drift toward historicism and formalism and calling him a traitor to the cause of modern architecture. Although "Défense de l'architecture" was not published in France until 1933, Le Corbusier took the opportunity to open a dialogue with Teige concerning conceptual and methodological issues in modern architecture. He also commented in general on the trend toward "objectivity" then rallying under the banner of "Neue Sachlichkeit" ("New Objectivity"), which was beginning to attract many young advocates. Le Corbusier's open letter concerned the art of discourse: both the language of architecture and the language of words through which men address ideas to each other. It is a theme reiterating the important message of *Vers une Architecture* about the language of architecture and the architecture of language (examined in Chapter 7). All meaning resonates from relationships between the architectural elements: they speak directly to the eyes without need of words, they constitute the poetics of architecture.

Teige was a devoted follower of Le Corbusier's "machine for living in," a delegate to the first CIAM congress, and a promoter of modern architecture in his native Czechoslovakia. But he questioned Le Corbusier's use of regulating lines and the golden section, and was dismayed by Le Corbusier's 1928 site plan and buildings for a Society of Nations.[61] How, he asks rhetorically in *Stavba*, could Le Corbusier suddenly reveal a project expressive of such monstrous monumentality? Had the episode surrounding Le Corbusier's other project for the Palace of the League of Nations (1926–28) been for naught? Teige was particularly distraught by Le Corbusier's new design for a museum of knowledge, the Mundaneum, in the form of a spiral.[62] He found it a purely symbolic monument reminiscent of the archaic ziggurats of Babylon or the stepped pyramids of Mesoamerica. "How can modern architecture resemble an American 'antiquity'? Where do the roots of the non-modern and archaic character of Le Corbusier's Mundaneum lie? What is the origin of this error and delusion?"[63] Teige believed Le Corbusier's plans for the international city and the Mundaneum had no rationale, and would never be built.[64]

He reminded Le Corbusier that modern architecture addresses the real needs of everyday life in contemporary society. It rejects abstract metaphysical speculations, and instead develops pragmatic designs for factories, bridges, offices, railway stations, workers' housing, schools, and hospitals. It does not offer designs for churches, palaces, castles, triumphal arches, festival halls, or tombs. "The only aim and scope of modern architecture is the scientific solution of exact tasks of rational construction."[65] Le Corbusier, in his project for the Mundaneum, made an error of "monumentality." He had made the same mistake in *Une Maison–Un Palais,* revealing the danger of thinking that architecture is an "art" taking into consideration such vague attributes as "dignity," "harmony," and "architectural potential."[66] The machine age "has no time for 'art' and monumental architecture," which leads to nothing but mere "composition"–a word Teige used to summarize all the architectural faults of Le Corbusier's Mundaneum.[67] Teige called upon Le Corbusier to "return to the solid reality of the starting point demonstrated so precisely by the motto the 'house is a machine for living in,' and from there, once again to work toward a scientific, technical, industrial architecture."[68]

Le Corbusier was stung by these accusations. Replying in "Défense de l'architecture," he asserts that "Neue Sachlichkeit" has created "a loss of clarity" and a desire to go back to the beginning to clear up the distortion–all well and good, but he reminds Teige that *L'Esprit Nouveau* in 1921 also went back to zero, and did so not in order to remain there but to begin again on a stable base. Teige should have addressed his criticisms to Nénot, not to Le Corbusier, "Because I believe I know the meaning of words in architecture and because your arguments, which (objectively speaking) having the same interest as my own as expressed in *L'Esprit Nouveau,* in my books and works, obviously find in me a convert....You indulge in a very fashionable game...you speak in a way that contradicts your thought and suggests the opposite of what you really are: a poet."[69]

Le Corbusier is critical because, he says, Teige mystifies by romancing the machine, while others intend to control public discussion with police measures and to march under the popular slogan "The machine age has abolished art."[70] On the contrary, Le Corbusier has a free and expressive spirit, and believes that architecture has everything to do with art. He pulls out his evolutionary argument about the creation of tools, competition, and progress, a forward thrust that pressures man to create something better and above all not to remain with the status quo. He reminds Teige that the "elegant solution" of the mathematician and engineer is an exclusively aesthetic notion.

Then Le Corbusier takes another aim at Teige's accusation that the word "composition" is the opposite of "architecture." He refers to an argument he made in *Une Maison–Un Palais* and also across the pages of *L'Esprit Nouveau* that architecture lies all around modern man, from the smallest item such as a pen or a telephone to the largest thing such as a battleship or the conduct of war. "Architecture is a phenomenon of creation which follows an order. Whoever talks of ordering talks of composing. A composition is the essence of human genius, it is there that man is architect and there indeed is the precise meaning of the word 'architecture.' Composition is thus not the problem; the word does not belong solely to the Academies. If the product is impure, it is the fault neither of the word nor of the function that it expresses."[71]

In this battle over words, Le Corbusier claims Sachlichkeit implies "incompleteness," which is none other than a mathematical concept of openness, or indeterminacy. There is something lacking in the hard life it advocates. He asks a rhetorical question: what keeps men from revolution, from destroying everything and starving to death amidst the ruins? The answer lies in tools that answer his needs, allow him to compete, save him time, and, as ordering devices of daily activity, endow him "with the capacity to think and dream about things."[72] That essential motive of thinking and dreaming enables man to create, to conceive an idea; it is his "reserve" that facilitates resistance and fills him with pride.

Now Le Corbusier turns to the heart of the debate: Teige's accusation of sheer formalism. He reiterates his famous refrain about visual forms, revealed under pure light for eyes that perceive "the masterly, correct and magnificent play generated by the plan and section."[73] He shifts the level of the argument, moving from objects that exist within the house, to the way things are put together, are "composed," out of walls and slabs. To emphasize his point, he uses a strange form of the verb "the way they have been 'architectured.'"[74] He warns Teige not to confuse the army with the battle, the architect's trade with the plumber's! The house or palace is a machine for living in, an assembly of useful equipment; having posed the problem, now it is a matter of its resolution. "It is there that the spirit takes delight. It is there that the shocking sensations arise, that matters of proportion emerge, that their inevitable influence operates on us, and that emotion bursts forth."[75]

History has filled our hands with useful items and established a new moral order of honesty and purity. Here Le Corbusier calls on Diogenes–that man in search of honesty who threw away his bowl because the hollow of his hands was sufficient to hold his meal. Le Corbusier notes that Teige and the advocates of Sachlichkeit would destroy Diogenes's bowl as well if it were not useful. But a new game is being played in the resolution of an architectural problem. Thus the paradox: there is no architecture without a problem well posed, yet there is architecture the moment man pursues a creative end, opens up the unlimited field of quality, and searches for the "purest," most "elegant" solution. But don't confuse this with the primary postulate of Sachlichkeit, which declares only "that which is useful is beautiful"! Beauty and utility are independent functions. Because waste is foolish and useless, it displeases us, but that does not make the useful beautiful.[76] Architects must equip a nation with that which is "necessary and sufficient," but architecture does not stop there. It can go further and deal with quality and with emotions.[77]

Le Corbusier now answers Teige's criticisms of the Mundaneum point by point. He begins with an autobiographical account of the last fifteen years of his architectural practice, which allows him to declare himself on the side of "architectural lyricism."[78] Only the year before, he gave a lecture in Prague entitled "Technique is the Foundation of Lyricism." In red and blue pastels he drew three plates, one above another. [FIGURE 8.13] The lowest contained construction techniques, new materials, chemistry, and physics. The middle plate held sociology, everyday needs, and contemporary building programs. The highest plate included economy, Taylorization, and standardization. But above these plates a horizontal line was drawn, on which rested a pipe, its smoke curling into the sky in an indeterminate form, and a bird flying freely about in the air higher still, higher than human thought can soar. The same technical, sociological, and economic elements that enable lyricism to fly above the ground as the poets allow determined Le Corbusier's Mundaneum.[79] It is worth noting, at this point, the goals and structure of the Mundaneum. Le Corbusier's problem was how to synchronize the works of man into what he called an "instantaneous visualization." A huge chain of knowledge arising from traditional objects, souvenirs, archaeological digs, documents, histories, illustrations, scientific experiments, and much more began with prehistoric times and accumulated as it evolved toward the future. Le Corbusier's solution was divided into three naves, one each for the objects, their time, and their place; these naves, arranged in a helix, were entered from the top, where the prehistoric age was displayed. As the spectator descended the helix, the diorama of the ages became vaster and more precise, the naves expanding. The structure was never built, although the design would reappear in later schemes.

Le Corbusier continues his defense: the Mundaneum (also referenced as the Sacrarium) is not a contradictory expression for a city of modern science, because all science is based on knowledge of the past. The Mundaneum is designed to show how ideas, not objects, have moved men forward along the path of progress. It calls for the display of man's work from across time and space through images, graphics, and statistics, scenographically arranged to reveal the cultural context, the physical environment, and the epoch from which it sprang.[80]

Le Corbusier agrees with Teige's claim that only contemporary needs pose programs, needs for facilities such as factories and railway stations, not churches or palaces. As for the pyramidal form of the Mundaneum and the use of the golden section, he justifies their usage

TECHNIQUES ARE THE VERY BASIS OF POETRY 37

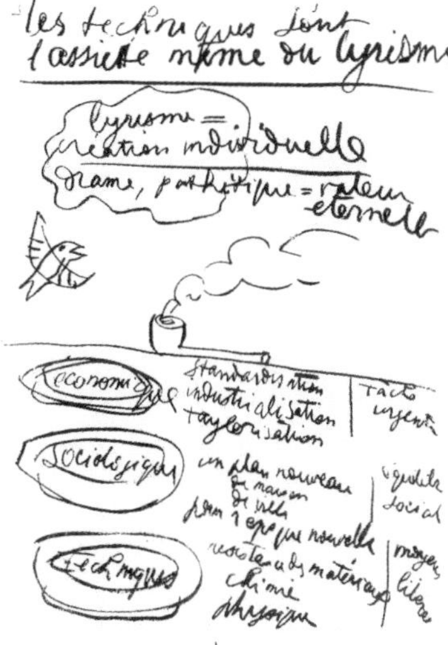

1

les techniques sont l'assiette même du lyrisme/techniques are the very basis of poetry // lyrisme = création individuelle/poetry = individual creation // drame, pathétique = valeur éternelle/drama, pathos = eternal values // économique/economics // standardisation, industrialisation, taylorisation/standardization, mass production, efficiency // tâche urgente/urgent task // sociologique/sociology // un plan nouveau de maison, de ville, pour l époque nouvelle/a new plan for the home, the city, for a new period // équilibre social/social peace // techniques/technique // résistance des matériaux, chimie, physique/strength of materials, chemistry, physics // moyens libérants/means of liberation

FIGURE 8.13: A lecture entitled "Technique is the Foundation of Lyricism," delivered in Prague, brought forth praise that Le Corbusier was a poet.

as architectural "purifiers," rendering the composition precise and clear. They are Le Corbusier's elected method of regulating forms, just as Teige's method is the slide rule.

He turns to explain the aerial views of the project, which Teige called "puerile waste."[81] The view from the airplane gives evidence: "It is clarity itself, an impeccable reading."[82] As for the pyramid, he needed to resolve the problem of how to reveal the history of human creation as it continuously evolved and accumulated over time, and so he allocated space that unfolds as a spiral in a tripartite nave so that object, place, and time could be arranged side by side.[83] And then the ultimate proof, "The dictionary of architecture . . . the cube, the sphere, the cylinder, the pyramid, and the cone, are our only uniquely architectural words."[84]

Le Corbusier resolved the problem of the Mundaneum by enabling the spectator to climb the ramp to the top of the pyramid, to cast an eye over the intertwining of nature and geometry, taking in the force of the magnificent four views over each quadrant of the site, while shedding the preoccupations of daily life, "the press of his pants or his digestion," allowing his mind to expand to the horizon. At the top, the spectator enters the hall of prehistory and begins his descent, following the steps of mankind forward as he descends toward the future and greater perfection. Le Corbusier's myth of progress seems total, the very definition of "history" a credo he now states at monumental scale in the language of pure architectural forms. The building itself is an instructional allegory progressing toward the future.

In conclusion, Le Corbusier thanks Teige for this opportunity to enter a contemporary architectural debate. He uses the personal pronoun to address his concern and vulnerability,

> That the words I have used in these present notes will be exploited to launch accusations against me, will be put in quotation marks by academics here and by avant-gardists there.[85]

In a letter to Teige of August 4, 1929, Le Corbusier mentions that he is writing his "Defense of architecture," but does not enclose the manuscript. He nevertheless notes points in his defense that elicit a response from Teige in September. He requests that Le Corbusier send him the essay as soon as possible, and speaks repeatedly of his esteem for the work of Le Corbusier and his profound admiration of the man himself. Yet he also points out that his dislike of the *tracé régulateur* has absolutely nothing to do with "Neue Sachlichkeit," and furthermore that he is not interested in the "style of the day." He is ardent about defending the cause of architecture as a science, and continues to believe that abstract sculptures such as the Arc de Triomphe or Obelisque are not architecture. He does allow, however, that a scientific work could be beautiful and poetical, but believes this is due to its absolute perfection and not its aesthetic form. He repeats: architecture is not a construction, not an art, but an organism, a living being that functions, and it is within its functioning that poetry might lie. He discusses the possibility of publishing Le Corbusier's "Defense," to be accompanied by Teige's original complaint and subsequent response. He was eager to receive Le Corbusier's "Defense," which he had not yet read. Although Le Corbusier is traveling in South America, he manages to send Teige the manuscript of his "Defense" through diplomatic channels. Teige receives it on October 9, and writes the next day about plans to publish the thirty-page epistle, Teige's response to it, and Le Corbusier's response to that.[86]

DUELING WITH THE ACADEMIES

Le Corbusier finds himself in an in-between place. On one side, he is being attacked by the academics, who hate him as a functionalist barbarian, and for the arrogance his rational logic reveals, and on the other side, he is attacked by ultra-Purists who have taken his word literally about the glories of the machine and now accuse *him* of being too concerned with mere appearances–doing unto him as he had done unto the academics. Never receptive to criticism from any direction, Le Corbusier mounts defenses on all sides, trying to achieve an equilibrium between art and the machine, a coherence between lyrical and rational expression. He seeks to make the language of architecture an autonomous artistic expression, liberating it from all symbolic attributes and stylistic considerations, while on the other hand he believes this language contains poetic and subjective intuitions radiating from the landscape, nature, vernacular forms, compositional relationships, and harmonious proportions. As much as he tries to insert poetry into the language of architecture, it falls either on deaf ears or does not resonate with those out of tune. Le Corbusier continues to be blamed for both his functional rationalism and for abandoning the cause of modern architecture. Not dissuaded by any of these attacks, he continues his pursuit of a synthesis of artistic and functional expressions.

His turn to primitive objects, organic forms, and simple craftsmen–praising or utilizing them as motifs in his writings, paintings, and architecture of the late 1920s and 1930s–can be seen as a way to shield himself against attacks coming from conservative critics, who believed his advocacy of "nude" white architecture was detrimental to the nation and denatured the spirit of the family as the bastion of French identity. His fascination with these forms and materials also drew inspiration from his many trips in 1928 and the early 1930s to the Atlantic coast of Le Piquey and the Bassin d'Arcachon near Bordeaux. Primitive artifacts simplified by centuries of selection had already been placed in the interior of the 1925 Pavillon de l'Esprit Nouveau as perfect accompaniments to industrial products. So this turn was really a strengthening of attitudes already expressed.

In addition Le Corbusier often describes how a spectator's senses, when confronted with optical phenomena, give rise to aesthetic emotions. The origin of such emotions radiating from a site or an object stems from his experience on the Acropolis in 1911. He believes the Parthenon is a work of art radiating vectors into the landscape, its harsh poetry making a deep emotional impact on him, never to be erased. It is there, where the temples drew the landscape into their fold, that man's ability to judge harmony and beauty arose. An internalized "sounding board" resonated vibrantly in accord with nature and with man's creations.

Over the next several years, having lost the competition for the Palace of the League of Nations to academicism in 1927, Le Corbusier mounts an ongoing defense against state authorities, cynical and ignorant political officials, and the polemics of cultural critics. In the introduction to the second volume of the *Oeuvre Complète 1929–1934* (1935), he speaks of the many accusations brought against him during those years:

> No arguments were spared; we were accused of denying the fatherland, the family, art and nature. We were pictured as creatures without souls. We were cried down as materialists, because we made technical researches, based on natural needs and directed to satisfy social requirements.[87]

Just as the final judgment of the jury in the League of Nations competition was being deliberated, in 1927, M. von Senger published a series of articles in a small newspaper, *La Suisse Libérale*. Collecting these into a book, he distributed it for free to all the municipalities, cantons, and federal offices in Switzerland, raising considerable hostility against Le Corbusier's proposal. Two years later, Senger was praised by the cultural critic Camille Mauclair in the conservative newspaper *Le Figaro* for "saving Fatherland, Nation, Beauty and Art, and whatever else was wanting."[88] This small match resulted in the flaming 1933 publication of a series of 15 *Le Figaro* articles written 1929–33 by Mauclair and compiled into a book *L'architecture va-t-elle mourir?* (*Is Architecture going to die?*). Mauclair called Le Corbusier "the high priest of concrete nudism," his "machine to live in" fit for a garage but not for a home; he was in addition profoundly anti-human and anti-French.[89] By 1933, Mauclair's debate had escalated, proclaiming that modern architecture–because it was an international style–was communist. A house is a tool like an automobile; this meant as far as Mauclair was concerned that man was enslaved to a machine, hence a communist. This message of modern architecture moreover had spread all over the Bolshevist world via the pages of *L'Esprit Nouveau* and the activities of members of CIAM.[90]

Mauclair praised regional architecture, not the leveling uniformity of modern architecture, and called for the protection of craftsmen in the battle against their increasing unemployment and threatened destitution. He wrote: "I love French stone, its glorious past, the corporative soul of its artisans."[91] Many decades later, when reflecting back over his accomplishments and the many obstacles placed in his path, Le Corbusier recalled the time he complained to Mauclair about his attacks and the many slanderous lies he made in 1933. The critic apparently responded, "What could I do? I have never met you, never seen any of your constructions, never read one of your books."[92]

Gustave Umbdenstock, professor of architectural history at the École des Beaux-Arts, was another virulent critic of modern architecture, particularly Le Corbusier's modern villas, constructed of prestressed concrete devoid of ornamentation. Umbdenstock's voluminous *Cours d'architecture* (*Course in Architecture*) of 1930 contained a lengthy section on the regional architecture of France, promoting it as a social stabilizer and a buffer against Germanic and Bolshevik influences.[93] He argued that the "home" was a vital link in the process of social control. The roof, moreover, on either a humble or bourgeois abode, symbolized "family." It was a healthy and moral symbol, and should not be suppressed. To make a tabula rasa of tradition, to deny what was vital to the national health and social order and impose instead a dreary and crushingly uniform architecture, made no sense to Umbdenstock.[94] He had been made honorary president of the Association des Architectes Anciens Combattants (AAAC, the Association of Veteran Architects) in 1930, and in such a role became the spokesman for architectural nationalism.

Umbdenstock's lecture "La Défense des métiers de main des artistes et des artisans français" ("Defense of handcrafts of artists and artisans"), given at the Salle Wagram on March 14, 1932, was sponsored by the Chamber of Commerce. As a direct response, Le Corbusier published *Croisade: ou le Crépuscule des Académies* (*Crusade: or the Twilight of the Academies*, 1933) and printed a transposed rendition of Umbdenstock's talk. [FIGURE 8.14, p. 697] It is through this text that we can recall some of the debate.[95] Umbdenstock proclaimed that France was blessed with the best craftsmen, excellent stone, and wonderful wood; there was no need to challenge the superiority of such handwork, nor to utilize concrete or modern materials. He offered five points in the "defense" of the crafts, perhaps a direct response to Le Corbusier's five points of modern architecture recently defined. First, the nudity of modern architecture compromises the vital force of the French race and puts the nation in danger. Second, French workers in the building trades are aware of the dangers of mechanization, standardization, and serial production, and fear that their privileges will be lost and unemployment and lower wages will inevitably result. Third, for some illogical reason, Umbdenstock believed that banishing the use of materials extracted from the earth and replacing them with metallic materials and prestressed concrete would result in "dangerous domination." Fourth, all architects will be replaced by rational technicians and engineers who have no interest in the subtle sentiments of beauty. Fifth, young students of architecture feel this threat emanating from modern architects, whom they have read about or heard in lectures. While these kings of modernity may reign in other countries, they are undesirable in France, especially new immigrants lacking the privilege of being a native. (Le Corbusier became a naturalized French citizen in 1930, so this is a not-so-veiled comment on his foreignness.)

Le Corbusier believes these attacks against modern architecture were launched by money. Called into existence by the Chamber of Commerce, or professional organizations of carpenters, stonemasons, manufacturers of tiles and roof slating, they struck out against industrialization and machine processes: the cause, they believed, of economic depression. Moreover, the Loucheur Law, passed in 1928, promised lucrative subsidies to those producing housing for the working class, but it left a loophole. Into this hole rushed the octopus arms of large corporations, creating housing estates for the working class. The lust for money was evident: building shoddily, these developers created a wake of rotting suburbs in their trail.[96]

Le Corbusier offered a rebuttal. Mauclair was the first to make the charge that behind the wall of prestressed concrete stood a wall of money that required Le Corbusier to promote this material.[97] Of course, Le Corbusier denied this, and felt a reply was needed to many other false accusations this critic had made, not just that about money, but other charges that Umbdenstock had made as well. He has often been called a vile foreigner–or worse even, a German–and is glad to provide the information that he is a naturalized citizen of France born in La Chaux-de-Fonds, a town settled by Frenchmen around 1350. In this Swiss town he grew up surrounded by simple, pure architecture derived from the traditions of France, and he is still to this day devoted to such architectural simplicity.

After centuries of political turmoil, these French emigrants developed in the eighteenth century a prodigious industry–the manufacture of precision watches. A watch of the eighteenth century not only told the time of day, but the phase of the moon, the solstices and equinoxes, and the birthday of the king and the queen. Rabelais, Rousseau, Voltaire, even Kropotkin and Lenin visited to admire the town's libraries and workshops. They understood that the revolution of 1848 succeeded in La Chaux-de-Fonds, giving its people liberty, ingenuity, a stubborn character. Le Corbusier is glad to expound on the spirit that surrounded him as a youth, one that instilled in him an invincible attraction for the Mediterranean, an inflexible love for pure forms in space, and complete freedom in thought, purism, even idealism.

Next, the "dirty business" of money. In 1920, he explains, one of the editors of *Le Figaro* told him that not one of the lines of the newspaper was written free of charge, but contained only issues that concerned the Chamber of Commerce. The shoe is really on the other foot, for it is Mauclair who is promoting moneyed interests–while Le Corbusier has never accepted a sou for his promotion of prestressed concrete.

Le Corbusier considers another of their criticisms: that his principles of freedom and architectural purity will produce, in the midst of the depression, yet more unemployment. Umbdenstock calls this "nudism" a disaster that brings unemployment to certain industries: those which make tiles for roofs, cabinet-making, wood carving, glass-making, decorating, antique dealing. When the "nudist" style is over, he fears, and all the old craftsmen have gone to their graves with their trade secrets intact, the young will have no masters, and the trades will have died from starvation.[98] Never addressing unemployment directly, Le Corbusier replies that outside of academic circles, architecture depends on truthful types, i.e., men belonging to trades of the twentieth century. They open a new cycle of civilization based on new materials and they create a spiritual equilibrium. And so life continues.[99]

At this point in his career, in the early 1930s, Le Corbusier has had his fill of attacks on his ideas and his architecture. He has reached maturity and is anxious to build, but he is defeated in competitions and kept from implementing his plans again and again. He fears that the daily press poisons public opinion again him.[100] He is well aware that it is through books, journal articles, and magazines that universal thought is spread, and it will be to the press that he confines his defense of modern architecture and his response to Mauclair and Umbdenstock.[101] By the time he returns from the CIAM conference in Athens in August 1933, his small book *Croisade, ou le Crépuscule des Académies* is in the bookstores. This defense of modern art and architecture against the claims of money and authority was originally written for the *Travaux Nord-Africains* and addressed to Umbdenstock, whose attack on Le Corbusier had been published by the same journal.

The controversy between Le Corbusier and Umbdenstock had begun some time before. Le Corbusier was invited to a conference organized by "Les Amis d'Alger" (Friends of Algiers) in March of 1931. In March 1932, Umbdenstock delivered his lecture "La Défense des métiers de main" ("Defense of handcrafts"), where he talks about "Art et Patrie" ("Art and Nation"), explicitly attacking the points made by Le Corbusier in Algiers on "Architecture Revolution accomplished though modern techniques" and the "Radiant City." Le Corbusier replied in *Croisade* by proclaiming that a campaign against modern art was being waged in the press in the name of *la patrie*. Certain building industries, fearing modern techniques and materials, were financing this campaign. The leader, Le Corbusier said, was Umbdenstock, architect and professor at the École des Beaux-Arts in Paris and honorary president of AAAC.[102] This small booklet, finished on June 15, 1932, would thus be a duel between honesty and deception, moderns and ancients, young and old.

Algiers, Le Corbusier begins, is in crisis: its expanding population is squeezed between the cliffs and the sea, its circulation of goods, people, and cars is strangled by narrow, winding roads and inadequate services. Has Umbdenstock's crusade come to Algerians in their hour of need?

Le Corbusier explains that Umbdenstock's course on modern architecture uses examples drawn from the past, but they are only a verbal gargling, a gurgling of the dictionary (*un gargarisme verbal, un glouglou du dictionnaire*). Rather, the past presents persuasive lessons of revolutionary movement that offer much food for thought. A professor ought to be able to discern the false from the true, so Umbdenstock should teach his students about the continuous line of development that spread its light over the French nation.

> It is the capture of Constantinople by the Turks, in 1453, and the flight of Byzantine scholars, which suddenly allowed Hellenic light to flow over the gothic world: a singular exceptional hour when the gothic structure was dressed in antique clothing! It is the administration, the centralization, the management of royalty which pushed the architect, under Louis XIV, toward showy and striking attire...opening perilously a fissure between structural conditions and those of ornament. It is in 1932 that a mechanical and scientific world rises up with unprecedented violence, proposes and imposes entirely unprecedented constructions and achieves a new social contract based on material and spiritual expression.[103]

The men who raid the history books, however, do not think of la patrie, but only of money. They are more attentive to officials and juries than to their drafting boards.[104]

Having discredited the academicians, Le Corbusier suggests that students go instead to the factories and the ateliers to find men who act and decide, who take pride in their work when it matches the rhythm of the machine. These seldom think that la patrie is involved; if Le Corbusier has mentioned la patrie so many times, a word generally reserved for political campaigns, it is because Umbdenstock uses it so much in his own attack.

Le Corbusier has been moved by the honest house, "a machine to live in." Machines reject all parasitical organs, allowing only those elements that operate and that in turn operate on our bodies and sensibilities. He has studied how man built an honest house, how he made a "naked" architecture–a pejorative term when used by Umbdenstock. This is a major point in their debate. To build a simple house is not a matter of legislating that all facades be masonry ones, fifty centimeters thick and dug deep into the ground, as Umbdenstock advocates. It is a matter of housing the brave men of the twentieth century and constructing cities for contemporary times.[105]

Students understand this "nude" architecture based on pure geometric forms and built by modern men, and no longer want to design in the style prescribed by the schools. That is why Umbdenstock speaks continually of la patrie (i.e., appeals to nationalism to drum up support for a position lacking intrinsic merit).[106] Yet Le Corbusier believes that history offers an alternative connection between architecture and la patrie. France is the country of architecture, in which an uninterrupted line leads from Romanesque to Gothic, Renaissance, Classical, and on to the iron and prestressed concrete of the nineteenth century. Instead of fearing the international movement of modern architecture and blocking its development, Umbdenstock should reveal to his students this impeccable continuous line of architectural events.[107]

Le Corbusier selects for praise technicians from the École Polytechnique. They give to technical work a unity, polish, and grace that all creations of nature manifest. At his control table, the technician grasps the levers of command: he directs energies and currents, he innovates and invents. He will construct the infinite network of roads, expressways, ports, factories, manufactories, automobiles, airplanes, cities, towns, and farms across the country. Light shines out from the heights of the École Polytechnique.[108]

Le Corbusier, because he was trained to be an artisan in the wonderful cleansing flood of around 1900 in La Chaux-de-Fonds, still retains his love of a well-crafted work. He will stop his car to gaze upon it, even in the midst of a hurried day. But he does not like to glance at the pastries of the Grand and Small Palais or the Gare d'Orsay. And if he wants to look at art, he does not go to the Salon des Artistes Françaises or the Nationale, but to an exposition of Cezanne, Matisse, or Derain, of Picasso, Braque, or Léger; there he finds the spirit that guides the nation toward its future.[109]

He is full of praise for the slow-motion camera that allows things to bloom again and again before one's eyes. With the objective eye of the lens and the watchmaker's machinery, events once veiled in mystery now reveal tightly enclosed buds that begin to twist with passion, frenetically agitating toward the light. Does Umbdenstock ever wonder what might be enclosed in the bud of calculation? At the end of the eighteenth century, a revolution took place that thrust everything along the path of mathematics. It gave birth to the machine, and machines begat other machines. Man changed the age-old nature of his relationship with his environment. A new springtime breaks out; due to the machine a new social contract is slowly set up. That is the object of Le Corbusier's own crusade: to put this new world in order. It is the task of the École des Beaux-Arts and especially of the École Polytechnique to prophesize, to project beams of light ahead; but it is the task of the architect and urbanist to act.[110]

In the light of the new springtime that shines on the world, Umbdenstock's lecture sounds like a screeching (*cottacs*) noise in a heroic symphony. His message is wrong: trades do not die. Only the feet of Louis XV chairs perish, or should have 175 years ago.[111] It is the schools that killed the trades: they deceive students by teaching them to be parasites, to be abject copiers of outmoded traditions and handcrafted work, to make paper architecture with a peacock's feather. The academy pulls on the brake, sounds the alarm, and counsels prudence; it speaks grandiloquently but falsely.[112]

Le Corbusier points out that the best handicraft trades lie far from the directives of the academies, in the chassis of an automobile, the fuselage of an airplane. The academies continue the traditions of the nineteenth century, despite the sunrise of modern times, the return to zero, loyalty to the new materials of steel and prestressed concrete, the rigor of mathematics, and the decency of a social revolution. Now a devil has raised a new crusade in defense of handcrafts and French artists and artisans. It is an affair of money![113] The pyramid of power still links the state and the government to the academies, the conservators of dead things. Not content with being conservators, the academies intervene to dictate and guide. They dispense medals, prizes, and diplomas. Fortunately, another sunrise will come tomorrow.

Le Corbusier ends by repeating lines from Umbdenstock's own arguments: "All the life of man represents only stages of constant perfection…neither shoddy work, the precarious, or the provisional will arrive at the top rank of…impeccable execution."[114] Le Corbusier agrees wholeheartedly, and calls on all the efforts of modern times to act as his witnesses: the engine of the airplane, the splendor of a steamship, electric lights, the machine room of a hydroelectric factory, the form of the zeppelin, women's fashion after the war, Costes crossing the Atlantic, the Van Nelle factory of Rotterdam, even the honest modest works of the laboratory (i.e., Le Corbusier's own designs), which have been the pretext for Umbdenstock's outburst. That is why the professor proclaimed "In all times, events stronger than men have brought forth some wills whose role is to preach about crusades. The crowd flocked to hear these fortifying words, thanks to which a new faith blossomed under the beautiful light from dreams of a regenerated humanity."[115] Le Corbusier thanks Umbdenstock for saying these words, which actually form his own faith, and sends condolences to the professor who so thoughtlessly commits suicide.

FIGURE 8.15: Offering a montage of images and texts, Le Corbusier searches for the light of modern times to clear away the debris of the academies. FIGURE 8.16: Athletes place everything in perfect harmony, academicians do not. FIGURE 8.17: Can modern machines of war, needed in life-and-death situations, exit through the gates of the academy's arsenal?

Le Corbusier and the younger generation that he believes is on his side ask Umbdenstock to inscribe on the facade of all new buildings the following slogan: "DISASTER TO THOSE WHO, IN ERROR, LOOK BEHIND."[116]

Le Corbusier turns to address the young through a series of photomontages taken from the weekly illustrated periodicals *VU* and *VOILÀ*, under which appear written messages in mimicry of a silent film with inter-titles. [FIGURE 8.15]

He begins with a refrain–"Leaning on the railing of the gallery"–that he will repeat four more times, each time shifting his argument to another register. Le Corbusier reiterates his own conviction: architecture must put everything in harmony. Everything rests on relationships. The photomontage that follows reveals confusion: juxtaposed against a Beaux-arts drawing of the interior of an ornamented palace is a photograph of the interior of a railway engineer's control room, the train following tracks that cross a steel bridge. Next is a sketch placing a Beaux-Arts sports stadium against snapshots of athletic figures seized at the moment of pole vaulting and diving. Renditions of the Beaux-Arts Arsenal appear opposite photographs of turntables, airplane propellers, and a zeppelin. "Everything relates."[117] [FIGURES 8.16 AND 8.17]

The refrain is repeated, and he explains, "It is just in the smallest things, in the most modest houses of men, that melody can be inserted."[118] The following images stress contemporary confusion. Designs by Umbdenstock for the exterior and interior of the Bank of Algeria are seen against a photograph of musicians and a catalogue of incredibly ornamented clocks. More images of the Bank of Algeria follow, then a photograph of a train wreck. The text reminds the reader that money, finance, the bank, and the state live in a world of stone and gold. There are train wrecks and also architectural catastrophes: three photographs of a modern Siedlungen follow. This is why he begs students to "look more often to the Parthenon!"[119] [FIGURE 8.18]

The refrain again, a third time, accompanied by a photograph of a group of students eating together. Outside the École, students discuss architectural issues passionately. They understand that a house gives pleasure or sadness, and they sense strange reactions spreading everywhere. The route they seek toward the spirit of the time is blocked by Hitler, by the authorities in the USSR, in Italy, in Switzerland, by the academies in France, by municipal councils, even by the League of Nations! They know that to please they must be conservative, that to displease is to innovate. How can they choose?

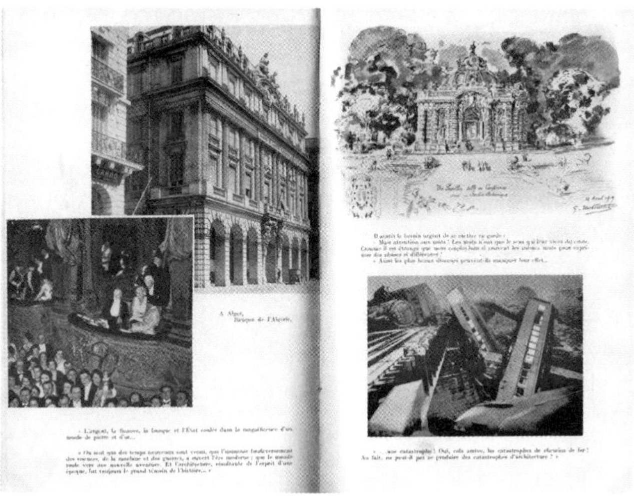

FIGURE 8.18: Catastrophes: architecture and train wrecks

Photographs of exacting details of the Parthenon follow. The past can offer shelter; to the neophyte architect Greek art offers a language that is brief, striking, and admissible. More lessons can be grasped in the great cathedrals of France. Underneath two photographs of the carvings from the facade of Vézeley, Le Corbusier raises a salute to their carvers–but he asks students to deny that men who carved the stone on the Gare d'Orsay and certain cinemas after 1925 be considered their brothers.

The fourth repetition of the refrain ("Leaning on the railing of the gallery") is accompanied by a photograph of a small stone house in Provence designed by Le Corbusier and Jeanneret.[120] For twenty-five years, Le Corbusier says, he has struggled against everything that was not true, loyal, pure, clear, and firm. Ever since he spent a month on the Acropolis at the age of twenty-three, the lies of the academies have not deterred him. From then on he understood that besides solving rationally posed problems, he could offer delight, grace, proportion, harmony, and joy. After that, the problems of urbanism opened before him, allowing him to offer the joy of living to millions in spite of all the town councilors' objections. He learned that architecture was never about "design." In fact, design is its enemy. Architecture concerns interior biology, materials, and lyricism.

Underneath three photographs of the roof garden of the Bestiqui apartment on the seventh floor above the Champs-Élysées,

FIGURE 8.19: **Professor Umbdenstock blamed Le Corbusier for mounting a crusade for modern architecture and attracting many acolytes.**

Le Corbusier explains that prestressed concrete has offered marvelous promenades, enchanting places that can replace all the old roofs of tile and slate. Here too are the stones of France, but in slabs, not in blocks. On these rooftops one can devote oneself to the monuments of Paris: the Arc de Triomphe, the Eiffel Tower, and more.

The caption for two plans from the Radiant City continues the theme of liberating openness: the ground is freed for automobile circulation, allowing the city to become green, for sports to be at the foot of houses, for a gigantic park to spread throughout. The glass facades of the houses open wide on this expanse of green and onto the infinity of the sky.

Le Corbusier's plans of the Palais des Soviets in Moscow follow, describing how this organism of extreme complexity–a biology–was achieved. Yet ultimately the government of the USSR preferred a project from the Italian Renaissance.

One more photograph follows: Le Corbusier's plan for Algiers, which, he explains, erases all distinctions between lower and upper classes, allowing everyone to attain an optimal house.

The final and fifth repetition of the refrain occurs beneath a photograph of Le Corbusier delivering a lecture before a large crowd and one of Umbdenstock with his arm raised in a gesture that mimics an image of crusaders lecturing to statues of the prophets.[121] [FIGURE 8.19]

Le Corbusier closes his quixotic set of photomontages with a small poem, almost a prayer. He has for once literally united poetry and controversy.

> How depressing and disparaging these discussions.
> The polemic is sterile.
> Words! Oh words, treacherous or vague words, veritable
> prisms of crystal which following the position of the light,
> project blue, red, yellow or indigo, green or violet.
> Noise of trifling quibbles [*chipotes*], gnashing
> of disputes.
> Weariness. Ambiguity. Uncertainty.
> Architect, speak less and show your work.
> Clear discourse of work.
> Loyalty
> Truth
> Object of debate
> Proof.[122]

Yet he has not quite concluded his *Croisade,* because he adds an epilogue dated several months later, November 1932. This closes with a section entitled "Assurance" ("Certitude"). In it, he preaches the poetics of architecture with rhapsodic fervor: how architectural considerations are overwhelmed by impassioned generalizations about history, human nature, and emotion. He recalls a scene that came to him while standing on the Acropolis: a pathetic discourse came forth, almost a cry, violent, sharp, slicing, and decisive–the marbles of the temple carried a human voice! [123] When a house is finished, everything resolved, built, and paid for, and the sun penetrates through the openings, while water and heat circulate in the arteries of this living body, all of a sudden,

> From the depths of this being a silence is hollowed out. We tremble at the voice that rises little by little, that discusses, recounts, sings, and describes the human epic: it talks about essential feelings which dominate our gestures, our works, our mistakes, our course of action in the daily struggle–these are acts of the soul which form the base of our existence: events through which we suffer, cry, pray and call out in joy.[124]

The works that accompany our life are the provocateurs of these emotions, this human voice; they allow us to suffer the immense noise raised up in opposition against us.

> If a destiny is tied to the Acropolis of Athens, it is to keep in the hollow of the mountains of Pentilicus and Hymettus, the sound of the human voice and the validation of the gestures of men.... The varied inflections of this voice indicate to the heart, to eyes, to touch, works of merit standing erect in the countryside, towns and cities.[125]

In the name of the Acropolis, many noble items such as the wall, the horizontal line, the bridge, the airplane, the dam, the autostrada, take on significance, become monumental. These constructions contain something that moves man, a deep emotive power that goes beyond utility. His days are enriched, and he has the courage to live.

The academies invoke the Acropolis of Athens, which they have never seen. They weave a veil of deceit, money, vanity, insensitivity. As a result, the people of the North, the first ones to work on the machinist adventure, were seized with a devastating rage: they sought a complete laundering of these lies that became almost a religion of negation, of the void, of exactness, of nothingness. It was a mental attitude (i.e., of Sachlichkeit) with moralistic intentions that allowed them to create a few works of contemporary architecture. But after these rigorous efforts, it is necessary to admit the people of the Mediterranean, where the sun cleans and purifies better than the fogs of the north, where the sun denudes the blocks of stone, stripping them of morality, leaving behind only proportion. From Athens to Alicante, the modern architect must listen to the Acropolis, allow all materials to obey their internal law.

II. THE POETICS OF ARCHITECTURE: "A MACHINE TO BE MOVED BY"

As we have already seen, Le Corbusier never saw himself only as a mechanic, a dry solver of dry problems. His mature concept of the architect's role blended the mechanic with the plastic artist, humanist revolutionary, social reformer, Pythagorean geometer, and poet. On occasion he was not, as quoted before, beyond dipping into actual verse. Architecture was for him not merely a civil engineering specialty, the reply made by materials and cost constraints to mundane needs without regard for the aspirations of the human inhabitants, but a form of high art. His many discourses on the formal language of architecture and the verbal language about architecture, discussed in Chapter 7, were informed by these concerns. His controversial writings in defense of architecture were also based on his poetics. And a further class of writings now to be examined begins to outline a distinct poetics—that of ineffable space—and points toward the synthesis of the arts.

VERB AND MACHINE

The most important machines for Le Corbusier were those that facilitated travel: train, automobile, steamship, airplane. With accelerating speed they propelled men and life forwards toward a new future. He made rhetorical use of this machine image not merely as a symbol of progress, but as an expression of mathematics and geometry, precision and efficiency. The machine, an artifact planned and created by man, had metaphysical significance: it was a model of man's ability to project, calculate, and trace a path toward the future. It informed a functionalist critique of inefficiency, useless consumption, the market economy, the great city, and the academies.[126]

How could he get language to perform with the same precision, speed, and effectiveness? He had already asserted in his *Almanach* (1925) that "one can raise the definition of architecture to a very high level: MIRROR OF THOUGHT. Architecture is a system of thought."[127] In "Architecture of the Machine Epoch" (1926), he elaborates the argument first developed in *Almanach* and continued in his various defenses of modern architecture, reviewed above.[128] He begins by looking up the meaning of "architecture" and "art" in two different dictionaries, *Larousse* and *Littré*. *Larousse* defines architecture as "the art of constructing and decorating buildings according to determined rules" and art as "the application of knowledge in the realization of a conception." *Littré*, on the other hand defines architecture as "the art of constructing buildings" and art as "the manner of making something according to a certain method or procedure," giving "alchemy" as a synonym.[129]

Le Corbusier compounds these four definitions. A hybrid *Larousse-Littré* would define "architecture-art" as "to construct and ornament buildings according to certain methods or procedures," or "to construct buildings by applying useful knowledge to the realization of a conception." Thus, he concludes, two antagonistic conceptions of "architecture" as an art exist side by side. Those who follow tradition would like the first hybrid, and those who believe a change is needed would prefer the second.[130]

These two compounds reflect two different poles of architecture: on one hand, to construct buildings (the technical domain), and on the other, to embellish them, render them glorious and pleasing (the domain of feeling). Yet, he maintains, these dual domains are indivisible.

Whatever man does, he does with passion, but his acts are guided by reason toward a useful goal. Le Corbusier has, he says, proven that "The house is a tool: domain of pure technicity," but he also argues that sentiment is present, sometimes exuberant, allowing the house to "say 'I exist', to radiate....With this passage from one aim to another, from the function to serve to the function to radiate, is situated architecture."[131] Le Corbusier is utilizing the verb "to radiate," *irradier*, in a specific manner. He finds there is a radiant presence in a work of art that instills itself in the language of architecture and affects the thoughts and emotions of the spectator.[132] Remember that he has also utilized this verb in the *Almanach*, where he noted that in the Esprit Nouveau pavilion

> We want[ed] to create an architectural site made of materials, light, proportions in which can live comfortably works of high emotive potential, some dense and strong works from which radiates thought or emotion. We detach[ed] from the wall sculpture and painting and let them alone act with the radium they can contain.[133]

As argued in this collection of articles, mostly written during the 1930s, Le Corbusier is working toward a synthesis in which both architecture and art will "radiate," and like radium, affect the "emotions." He has previously explained in the *Almanach* that the house has two aims. It is first a *machine to live in*. But it is also a place for meditation, a place where beauty exists and brings calm to the spirit. "Everything that concerns practical ends of the house, the engineer provides; for that which concerns meditation, the spirit of beauty, the order which rules (and will be the support of beauty), that will be architecture."[134]

Yet the sad truth is that the house as a tool suitable for the new machine age is completely lacking. The architect has to begin from scratch: walls are no longer needed to support floors, pilotis can raise the house in the air above the ground, a roof is no longer required. But in order for the new house to link up with feelings, the architect also must start from scratch, "to put in equilibrium the equation reason = passion."[135]

Still, Le Corbusier has to describe how passion intervenes to conduct "the work to its useful destination: 'to radiate.'"[136] Over the ages, some pure systems of arrangement have been capable of provoking emotion, systems that "spread their effect from the house to the temple."[137] A "harmonious play of forms... [is] imprinted on fabricated objects and on the conduct of thought: this unity is a style."[138] Such pure forms or proportions constitute the language of architecture; they express themselves in surfaces, forms, and lines that the eye can see. "Here is the real architectural invention: relations, rhythms, proportions, conditions of emotion, a machine to be moved by."[139] But the work must be polished: a perfect unity introduced, where the diverse elements are ruled by the regulating trace or line. The result is a work of great simplicity: "the crystallization of a multitude of thoughts and means."[140] This simplicity exercises a precision of intentions and a rigor of absolute reasoning, supported by proportion, and provoking "this joy of mathematical order."[141]

In an unpublished article from 1927, he continues this discussion about architecture and the "mathematical domain" by referring to the decorative arts, which since 1925 have, he says, evolved toward forms where geometry reigns.[142] But he fears that in this domain where the fashionable is so quickly exhausted, these geometrical forms may constitute just another style. The machine has fomented a total revolution and forged a spirit that appreciates pure geometrical expressions, but he needs to pursue this geometric spirit deeper, to reach more fundamental laws that underlie every proportional system. He turns for support to *L'Esthetique des Proportions dans la Nature et dans les Arts* (*The Aesthetics of Proportions in Nature and in the Arts)*, a book written by Matila Ghyka in 1927 that offers the reader the elegant play of algebra based on the principle of harmony. Nature, plants, the human body, the movement of stars, and many other things

> constantly encounter and are matched up against some precise formulas which are formulas producing the greatest output.... The "divine proportion" appears... in arithmetic, in geometry, in natural objects and in paintings, architecture of the great ages (Egyptians, Greeks, Gothic, Renaissance, French Classicism, etc.).[143]

In these great works, everything is based on proportions and "radiates" light: our judgment and emotions are born from these determined and measured relationships.

In an unpublished manuscript, Le Corbusier returns to review Ghyka's book in 1934, upon its republication.[144] By this time he has been severely criticized by Teige and others for his dependency on regulating lines and the golden section, and for proposing that architecture is an art. Once again, therefore, he garners support from Ghyka. Ghyka, he says, has given four hundred pages of regulating traces, a crystallization of mathematical thought across the ages.

POETICS OF SPACE

Throughout the 1930s, Le Corbusier searches for a more spontaneous unfolding of simultaneous effects radiating from an object, building, or landscape. He listens to voices and sounds emanating from a site, echoing from afar (as he once recalled "listening" to the Parthenon). He sought unpremeditated creations that would "radiate" intense feelings from the work of art to the spectator through mathematical proportions, the system of relations within the language of architecture, or the resonance an object established with its surrounding environment. He is open to the poetic inspiration of natural objects, rough materials, and bold colors, and utilizes biomorphic forms in his architectural projects and works of art. He notes the energy and spirit that emanate from children's drawings and primitive artifacts. Averring his appreciation for the primeval and "authentic" quality of what he called "folkloric art," he draws renewed inspiration from the premodern cultures of the Mediterranean and from the peasants of France.

In a brief statement in *Prélude* (December 1933) attributed to Le Corbusier, he writes that he is amazed by a "basic set of tools" he has seen during a visit to the Louvre. These objects, produced by Egyptians, Chaldeans, Cypriots, Cretans, and Mycenaeans, are witnesses to the springtime of the Mediterranean culture. He is thrilled that he, a man of the twentieth century, has been placed in immediate contact with his "brothers" across so much time and distance. Graphic signs painted on vases, the cuts traced by tools in clay or bronze, established an eloquent discourse.[145] Yet, he pondered, what is happening to language in modern times?

At the start of the human adventure there were innumerable and shapeless languages; even today, he remarked, the USSR has fifty-eight. But eventually cultures became organized, transportation

1935. Exposition d'art dit «Primitif»
de Louis Carré, dans l'appartement de Le Corbusier.

Plein, vide, lumière, matières: une tapisserie de Léger, une statue de Laurens

Un bronze du Bénin, un galet de granit de Bretagne, un marbre grec

La *technique des groupements* est en quelque sorte une manifestation de la sensibilité moderne dans la considération du passé, de l'exotisme ou du présent. Reconnaitre les «séries», créer à travers temps et espace des «unités», rendre palpitante la vue des choses où l'homme a inscrit sa présence. Ces quelques photos proviennent de l'exposition dite «d'Art primitif», organisée par Louis Carré, partiellemen dans l'atelier de L-C en 1935

Possibilités d'exposition du «Musée sous façades»

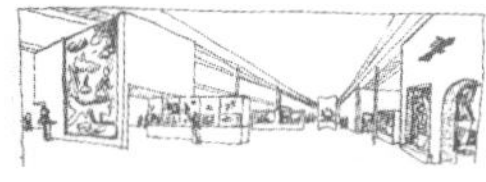

FIGURE 8.20: **A reproduction of *Moscophoros*, an archaic Greek statue painted in color by Le Corbusier, held a prominent place in the exhibition of the Arts of the Primitives.** FIGURE 8.21: **Le Corbusier sought to forge a unity between primitive and modern art.**

established, idioms of speech assembled into families and groups. Latin gave thought a universal tool. Yet Le Corbusier is ambivalent about whether this is progress or not. Standard French has been imposed in all the schools, and he predicts within twenty years different patois throughout France will be eradicated. Local idioms of expression are disappearing under the effect of all the routes of transportation. Although a national tool is created, one unique language, this may have uncertain effects on local cultures.

In July 1935, Le Corbusier hosted an exhibition organized by Louis Carré on "Les Arts des Primitifs" ("The Arts of the Primitives"), an eclectic arrangement of objects including Peruvian ceramics, bronze sculpture from West Africa, a polychrome cast of the archaic Moscophoros, a Greek female torso in marble, and even a rounded granite boulder from Brittany. [FIGURES 8.20 AND 8.21] These were displayed alongside a figurative painting by Le Corbusier (the *Parqueses d'huîtres*), a tapestry by Léger, and a plaster sculpture by Laurens.[146] A month before the exhibition opened, Le Corbusier wrote a short piece entitled "Les Arts dits Primitifs dans La Maison d'Aujourd'hui" ("The Arts Called Primitive in the House of Today"), in which he boldly proclaimed that the "works of the spirit do not grow old" because they are animated and united by an energy operating in time across periods, cycles, and series. "The contemporary is established in the depths of the ages."[147]

Modern architecture appears to be contemporary with works from earlier epochs because it and they are animated by the same truth, raw force, and energy that ring out across the ages. "The arts called primitive express the ages of action. In 1935, action dominates."[148]

A few months after the exhibition, in September, Le Corbusier published another short piece, "Le Lyrisme des objets naturels" ("The Lyricism of Natural Objects"). He harks back to directives given for the Exposition Internationale des Arts Décoratifs in 1925 that restricted all objects displayed to those created by artisans or artists. That is why Le Corbusier equipped the Esprit Nouveau pavilion with industrial products, almost all of which existed commercially, placing these alongside a few artworks by painters and sculptors whom he respected.[149] Objects of modern industry such as a ball bearing, an airplane model used in aeronautical trials, or geographical maps were all objects that he believed were linked to deep subjective experiences. He explained:

> The door was open on natural elements and it is at this moment that I began to collect pebbles, seen in the fields or on the

> road, some morsels of wood in the forest, some pinecones and particularly along the seashore, moving residue, that each tide throws out: some shells with the harmony of ancient Greece, some columns of seaweed, some flotsam rounded by the waves and having yielded to the effect of an implacable law. One day, I discovered some butcher bones (humble knuckle bone or shoulder blade, sectioned by the saw of the butcher and washed and whitened by the sea). And I found myself the possessor of a collection of moving elements because they are the manifestation of grand natural events of true laws.[150]

Le Corbusier contended that these objects have nothing to do with the decorative arts but are "incontestable facts" (*faits indiscutables*). He calls himself a lyrical poet, one who knows how to look and to find. Consequently he surrounds himself "little by little with these witnesses that cohabitate so well with works of art, and that are judges against all that is artificial, fickle of spirit, a hoax, or a foolish act."[151] Le Corbusier calls his modest treasures "my P.C." (my private collection).[152]

FOLK-LORES AND MATERIALS THAT SPEAK

In a 1937 article, Le Corbusier takes up the theme of the "'true,' the single support of architecture."[153] He repeats a definition of architecture that he often makes: "It is to construct a shelter."[154] The snail-shell and the creature that inhabits it take on the same image, but architecture requires clarity and directive thought to achieve such transparency. Across the ages, the "architecture of folk-lore" achieved purity. Shelter became a biological type, fulfilling its task. Yet there is more to the story:

> Something was born: a spiritual being. It existed in all parts of the work, in each minute of the enterprise. And thus one could claim: show me your house, and I will tell you who you are." Folk-lores have no need of explications: they speak, they are speaking machines.[155]

During the course of the nineteenth century, he argues, schools arose, far from land on which one built, far from materials to be used, and far from the great transformations taking place within the heart of man. Consequently cities were covered with "dirty things; a monstrous flowering of works without soul!"[156] But the land and materials must be listened to: the desert speaks, the stone speaks, even the trees speak.

Thus in 1937, a paradoxical article by Le Corbusier appears about "the stone: *friend of man*."[157] By this time, he says, modern architecture, with its framework of iron and prestressed concrete, has definitely killed the facade of stone. Yet he confesses that some materials turn him into a poet, bringing him great joy. He calls out a trinity:

> Stone, whitewash, wood, are friends of man. They have an eternal presence around us. They are fundamental products of apparent nature: rocky crags and trees–materials of diverse utility, close to the hand, which we are forever accustomed to: stone, whitewash, wood. The hand extends to touch them, to caress them–instinctive gesture of familiar affection. The stone, whitewash, wood, friend of man, in spite of the innumerable afflux and sometimes seduction of the new materials of modern chemistry.[158]

Yet a crime is often perpetrated against stone: some stonemasons polish the surface of a stone wall, rendering it entirely smooth, closing its pores. "One says that he has *killed the stone*."[159]

Le Corbusier asks rhetorically: Has he become an advocate of handwork in this era of machine civilization? The issue is complex. There is no longer any need to build in stone, even if stone enthralls us. Thus the question must be posed in a different manner: "Do not assassinate stone, but reveal its splendor. All stones possess their own proper nature. It is not necessary to make it uniform–by brutalizing it–the living skin of stone."[160]

Then Le Corbusier allows the stone to speak for itself: "Stone speaks through the wall, the profile, the molding, the base, and the statue."[161] It creates many different walls, with many beautiful textures.

He turns to speak of the profile of stone: where the cut of the stone reveals the life of the work. "*The cut of the stone!* What a beautiful word. To cut the stone with a chisel and hammer in the hand, what a beautiful gesture! It is worthy of some poignant terms."[162]

> A profile is as individual as a profile of man or woman. One sees admirable profiles exiting from the chisel of humble workers in towns and countryside. One saw in Athens, on the Acropolis,

> thirty years ago, the intense profile of the Parthenon; the columns and pieces of the architrave were still on the ground, laid there by the powder explosion that in earlier times fell the Temple.[163]

Modern science has discharged stone of its old duty to carry weight. Just as the automobile has put the horse to pasture, now stones sleep in fields, waiting to be awakened. "We wake it up? Never to deprive us again of sunlight, of light, of the extended view that we have conquered. But we wake it up in order that it once again is near us, in contact with our hands, the old faithful friend."[164]

Next, in 1939, Le Corbusier turns again to folklore, in an article entitled "La Maison Individuelle" ("The Individual House"). Here he proclaims that there is nothing more beautiful to study than these pages of human history (i.e., folklore), full of the strictest truth.[165]

> One does not enter upon folk-lore from the exterior; it is by studying it under the double prism of utility always conjugated with the passion of comfort that it is necessary to look for the secret of its lesson. And it is necessary, each time, to be situated within the conditions of their birth; the place, climate, culture, the technical means, the materials. Certain of these factors remain...local, and cannot be considered under other latitudes. Others have advanced considerably, even immensely so what was made before cannot be remade today. Otherwise, it would be lying (that is very much in fashion, however).[166]

Folklore is never far from regionalism, and Le Corbusier turns to look at the natural elements of sun, altitude, quality of air, and the like. "Autochthonous materials, or imported materials, new technology: it is difficult to fix some laws for regionalism. It is a question of deference, of conquest and of creative power."[167] The housing that Le Corbusier proposes will be individualized, supporting the life of a family. It will be regionalist, with materials and values conforming to the milieu, and they will constitute folklore when everything is so well put (*mise au point*) that a veritable new biology appears.

THE DESERT

In the spring of 1933, Le Corbusier flew over the M'Zab with the pilot Louis Durafour. He made sketches of Arab houses and villages, seen

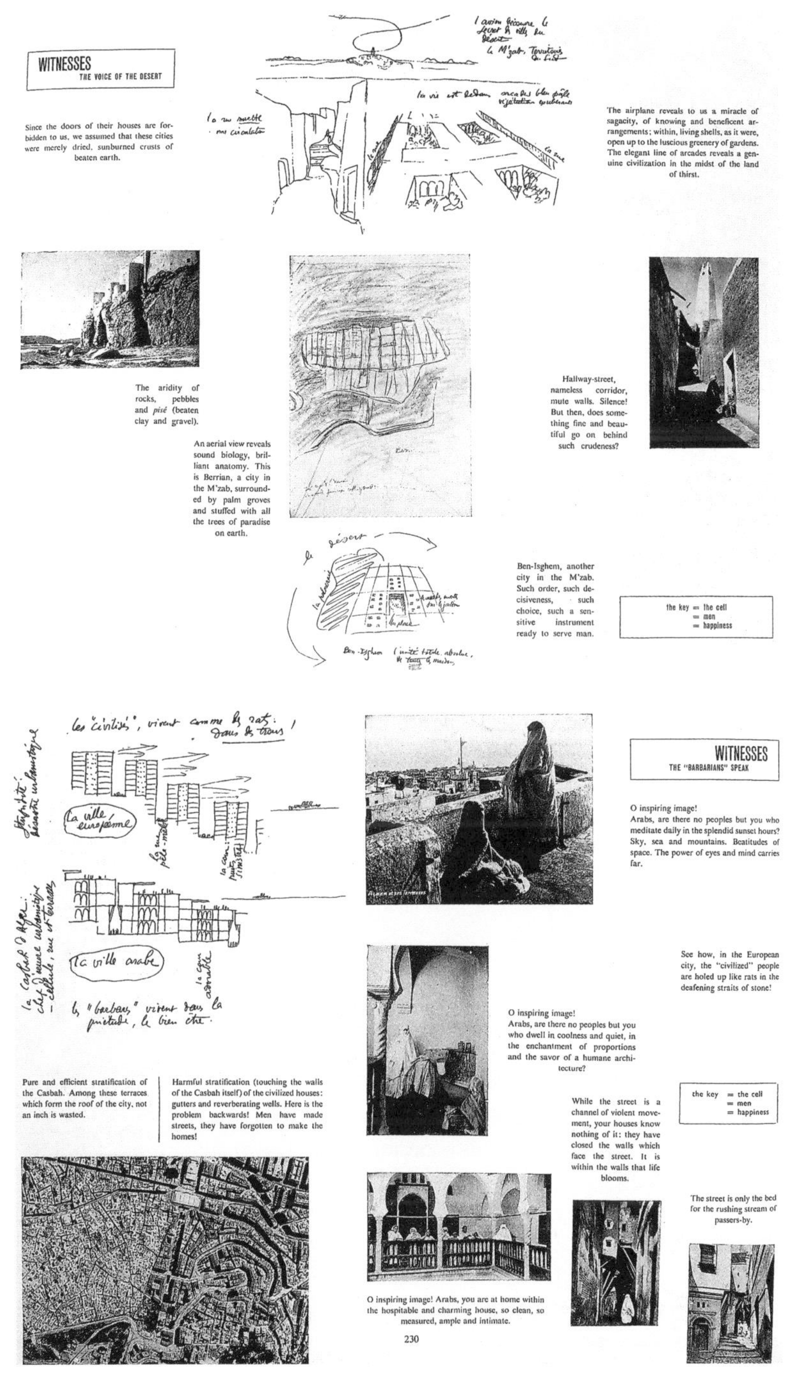

WITNESSES
THE VOICE OF THE DESERT

Since the doors of their houses are forbidden to us, we assumed that these cities were merely dried, sunburned crusts of beaten earth.

The airplane reveals to us a miracle of sagacity, of knowing and beneficent arrangements; within, living shells, as it were, open up to the luscious greenery of gardens. The elegant line of arcades reveals a genuine civilization in the midst of the land of thirst.

The aridity of rocks, pebbles and *pisé* (beaten clay and gravel).

An aerial view reveals sound biology, brilliant anatomy. This is Berrian, a city in the M'zab, surrounded by palm groves and stuffed with all the trees of paradise on earth.

Hallway-street, nameless corridor, mute walls. Silence! But then, does something fine and beautiful go on behind such crudeness?

Ben-Isghem, another city in the M'zab. Such order, such decisiveness, such choice, such a sensitive instrument ready to serve man.

the key = the cell
= men
= happiness

WITNESSES
THE "BARBARIANS" SPEAK

O inspiring image!
Arabs, are there no peoples but you who meditate daily in the splendid sunset hours? Sky, sea and mountains. Beatitudes of space. The power of eyes and mind carries far.

See how, in the European city, the "civilized" people are holed up like rats in the deafening straits of stone!

O inspiring image!
Arabs, are there no peoples but you who dwell in coolness and quiet, in the enchantment of proportions and the savor of a humane architecture?

Pure and efficient stratification of the Casbah. Among these terraces which form the roof of the city, not an inch is wasted.

Harmful stratification (touching the walls of the Casbah itself) of the civilized houses: gutters and reverberating wells. Here is the problem backwards! Men have made streets, they have forgotten to make the homes!

While the street is a channel of violent movement, your houses know nothing of it: they have closed the walls which face the street. It is within the walls that life blooms.

the key = the cell
= men
= happiness

The street is only the bed for the rushing stream of passers-by.

O inspiring image! Arabs, you are at home within the hospitable and charming house, so clean, so measured, ample and intimate.

230

FIGURES 8.22 AND 8.23: **Exhibiting a white blind spot, Le Corbusier speaks for the Algerian native and for the radiant desert.**

from the air and then on the ground. He describes this trip in 1935 in *La Ville Radieuse* (*The Radiant City*), usurping the voices of Arab, desert, and oasis for his own. [FIGURES 8.22 AND 8.23] He sees, he says, from a double perspective, a too-close-up view of the Arab and a too-far-away image of the European. His blurry sight enables him to draw comparisons between what he conceives to be an uncontaminated and enduring native culture exempt from the corrosive effects of European decadence. His comparisons of timeless Arab and modern European, of static and mobile, of silence and noise, reveal a desire to recover an elsewhere lost in the process of European modernization. This is an attempt to defuse the threat of homogenization that modernization and development inevitably engender. The same attempt is embodied in all gestures that constitute Le Corbusier's poetics of architecture. If Le Corbusier's projects for Algiers were military projectiles fired on a recalcitrant colony, intended to strike through the apparent chaos of reality with geometric surety, then his poetics of space worked in the reverse direction, allowing the visions of Algeria to penetrate his eye in both lyrical and painterly terms.[168]

Perhaps Le Corbusier has read Mauclair's *Les Couleurs du Maroc,* a book of impressions, daydreams, and confessions written during Mauclair's travels through Morocco in 1933. Mauclair, the conservative art critic of *Le Figaro* whom Le Corbusier criticized in his own defense, was an ardent opponent of Le Corbusier's architecture and urbanism, and assured his readers that his own book was not a book on urbanism–such as those Le Corbusier wrote. Instead, he was searching for a "new world," an "enigmatic race," turning his back on the hideous "machines for living," nude and hygienic boxes with no soul, that irritated him in Paris.[169]

Le Corbusier assembles in the pages of *The Radiant City* a montage of words, photographs, and sketches. He begins his spatial poetics with "WITNESSES The 'Barbarians' speak."[170] He repeats three times next to three different photographs "Oh inspiring image!" and writes: "Arabs, are there no peoples but you who meditate daily in the splendid sunset hours? Sky, sea and mountains. Beatitudes of space. The power of eyes and mind carries far." Opposed to this quiet realm of poetic contemplation where the "ineffable" resides, are European cities where

> the "civilized" people are holed up like rats in the deafening straits of stone!...The airplane reveals to us a miracle of sagacity, of knowing and beneficent arrangements, within living shells, as

> it were, open up to the luscious greenery of gardens. The elegant line of arcades reveals a genuine civilization in the midst of the land of thirst.[171]

Absent from this poetic space, not even mentioned, is the fate of "civilized" man, who is not at home in his degraded house, encumbered with stuff and an illogical plan. From other writings, we know that Le Corbusier's housing reforms during the 1930s had the explicit goal of making the resident feel at home in his shell the minute he entered his doorway.

Here, however, by a natural regional process,

> The layout of these houses has made them well-filled shells. No opening to the outside; all walls are party-walls. But within: a poem!...Whereas everything seemed to go against man: desert, stoniness, sun's infernal blaze, suddenly the most lilting melody is heard: architecture and paradisiacal verdure, streaming waters, coolness, flowers and fruit: palm trees, orange groves, apricot and pomegranate trees, green shadow and starry nights to worship, filtered through the date palms.[172]

Le Corbusier pulls out all the clichéd images: songs of the desert, the fragrance of flowers, the coolness of gardens, and starry nights. The Mediterranean climate and sites have captured his imagination ever since his voyage to the East in 1911, and effect innumerable recitations.

THE LESSON OF THE GONDOLA

Another landmark in the ongoing development of Le Corbusier's poetics of architecture was his visit to Venice in July 1934, to participate in a conference on "Les arts contemporains et la réalité" (Contemporary arts and reality) organized by the Institute Internatiónal de Coopération Intellectuelle.[173] He was asked during the conference to comment on the relationship between high art and popular art in contemporary times, and responded by speaking poetically about the lesson of the gondola, a lesson that told of the ideal unity of art and everyday life.[174] It is also a story about three necessary factors in city planning: transport, housing, and civic consciousness.

In the 1941 publication of this story, he begins by examining the history of the popular arts. In the Middle Ages and Renaissance, when peasants were obliged to visit the city or château, they had no training to understand the spirit of what they saw, the rule and subtle proportion of the major works of architecture. Nevertheless, they did experience joy from such encounters. So they pilfered from what they saw, making a collection of superficial and unrelated elements, out of proportion and deprived of proper harmony. They reconstituted these stolen elements in their own work, developing over time "a variety of period pieces of considerable charm, even admirable in their own way."[175]

Now the first cycle of the machine age is over, one hundred years have passed (i.e., 1830–1930), and, Le Corbusier believes, there will be a renaissance for all mankind in the second cycle of the machine age, the temps nouveaux. This will take place through objects of daily use, what he has elsewhere call the "equipment" of machine society. To clarify, he turns to the example set by Venice. Since it was a city built on water, the first requirement was to solve the practical problem of transportation. It did so by naturally developing the most "perfect equipment": the gondola. He calls the gondola a "biological entity," a permanent type. But here he shifts registers to remind the reader he is speaking about the interpenetration of "white civilization" by "primitive art," "negro" art of the tropics or desert. The "primitive arts," Le Corbusier proclaims, including the gondola, serve a useful purpose. "They have reconditioned our eyes; a return to the outlook of primitive art has made it possible for us now to appraise all around us (the gondolas themselves, the landing stages) with a fresh and seeing eye."[176] Intending to shock, Le Corbusier pronounces the gondola as moving as great statuary.

To confirm his position, he commands the reader: look at the rowlock for the oar, the position of the gondolier, the alarming angle of the gondola itself, all permanently on the verge of capsizing–in order to go straight! Here lies beauty of an entirely *mechanical* origin, the outcome of physics and dynamics. Look at the many little bridges, "like jewel cases ready to receive their content: a gondola and a gondolier standing upright. There is an established unity."[177] Look at the streets of Venice: streets without the menace of wheeled traffic! Nothing is out of proportion, everything is perfectly combined, the steps, the small houses, the water, the gondola–a perfected system.[178] Moreover, the gondola

> is a *standardized* object–indeed much more "standardized" than an automobile. The gondola has not changed for centuries and by that very fact has achieved something of the perfection revealed in Greek temples.[179]

SYNTHESIS OF THE ARTS

By the mid 1930s, Le Corbusier was well on his way toward a synthesis of the arts, expressed in his writings as a theory of "ineffable space" (*espace indicible*). In 1935, with an article published in the journal *La Bête Noir* titled "Sainte Alliance des Arts majeurs ou le Grand Art en Gésine" ("Holy Alliance of the major Arts or the Grand Art coming into Being"), he argues that architecture is an entirely plastic event supportive of a total lyricism. "An entire thought can perhaps be expressed through architecture alone."[180]

"The work of art is a conscience which opens its door on something that is not in the house, but in its own landscape externalizing itself in all directions outside of architecture, profound, to the faraway."[181] In other words, the work of architecture, as a formal expression, always provides a lyrical escape.

In his attempt to synthesize the arts, Le Corbusier asserts that wall murals and architectural polychromy have space-creating potential: their visual intensity opens space toward something "indicible" ("inexpressible," or "ineffable,"), which he relates to the "fourth dimension," the immensity of space extending itself in all directions. Vibrations (metaphorical) from site or object are helpful in moving Le Corbusier beyond abstract reasoning and systematic thinking. It is a matter of opening the viewer to emotional experiences gathered from the vectors of "radiation" coming from site, nature, or object, and allowing these to penetrate the eye and the heart.

He continues to write about art and architecture, opening toward the "ineffable" in "La querelle du réalisme." ("The quarrel over realism").[182] This paper, delivered at the Maison de la Culture in 1936, was intended as a rebuttal to Louis Aragon, who had expressed sympathy with social realism. Le Corbusier believes instead that a page has turned on the temps nouveaux, requiring both art and architecture to begin over again from the position of zero. Ever since the cubist revolution, which was thrown like "a shell to the end of its trajectory," there could be no turning aside.[183] Now it is a matter of "synthesis" of the arts,

> Where the pure and renovating spirit of modern times will be expressed through organisms having a mathematical interior, consisting of exact and inalienable places where the work of art will shine out with all its strength in exact agreement with the potential forces of the architectural work.[184]

Le Corbusier admits that architecture responds to the needs of humans with no requirement for the presence of art. Nevertheless, in starting again from zero, architecture reorganizes its skeleton and its flesh, creating a veritable symphony in the manner it allows light to play on its walls. This opens it up to the arts. Its mathematical forms and measured proportions engender a lyricism of beautiful works. Thus, Le Corbusier allows, he is prepared to accept talented artists in certain selected spots as long as the architect retains control. Architecture should either be left bare, without art, or together the architect and artist must put into play geometry, symbols, "anthropocentric powers," pushing these expressions to the limits of clarity.

In both of the articles just mentioned, Le Corbusier speaks of revolutionary forces transforming modern consciousness and opening a new route to modern times. He believes, as he says in "Holy Alliance," that

> the photo, the cinema, the everyday press, the magazine, made in [the last] fifty years an invasion into the field of contemporary consciousness, they opened all, extended, quartered, pierced, and filled our understanding with a multitude of natural splendors: nature and macrocosms and microcosm. What information![185]

Contemporary life has been inundated with images replacing tasks once reserved for the painter. They have brought new conceptual understanding into ontological givens. An era of construction has arrived; a new life begins with a new consciousness of the world, where the great factors in play are the sun, nature, and the cultivation of the body and the mind.

Nor was the dream of an all-encompassing synthesis a passing fad for Le Corbusier. Nine years after "Holy Alliance" in 1944, he writes an article for an issue of *Architecture d'Aujourd'hui* again dedicated to the synthesis of the arts. In a version published in 1946 he inserts into this piece a new discussion of "Architecture and the Mathematical Spirit," and utilizes some of its paragraphs in *New World of Space* (1948). He begins all three versions with the following sentences:

> To take possession of space is the first gesture of living beings, of men and beasts, of plants and clouds, fundamental manifestation of equilibrium and duration. The first proof of existence is to occupy space.[186]

He then considers architecture, sculpture, and painting, and how they affect their surroundings. He begins, of course, with the Parthenon, and the "vibrations, cries or shouts...and arrows darting away [from it] like rays, as if forced by an explosion; the near and distant site is shaken by them, affected, dominated or caressed." The environment reacts:

> All the ambiance comes to bear on the place where a work of art is...it imposes...its profoundness or its projections, its hard or soft densities, its violences or its softnesses. A phenomenon of concordance is present, exact as mathematics, true manifestation of plastic acoustics; thus one is allowed to speak of one of the orders of phenomena [which are] the most subtle conveyor of joy (music) or oppression [*le tintamarre*].[187]

He relates this radiating or "ineffable space" (*espace indicible*) to the fourth dimension of which the cubists spoke, and that Le Corbusier, as an artist, has also observed over the years. This dimension belongs to the proportions given to a work of art, and is contained within an artist's intentions. Every successful work of art holds a mass of intentions. "Thus a boundless depth opens up, effaces the walls, drives away contingent presences, *accomplishes the miracle of ineffable space.*"[188]

Le Corbusier cuts short "this insatiable dialectic of words" to focus on some of his own experiments. He is beginning to reflect on his own past, to draw a continuous line uniting his early laboratory works with later experiments. He begins with the small house he built for his parents in 1923. It occupied a minuscule site surrounded by a wall on the shore of a lake. In this wall he made a single opening, and placed within it a vertical column made of a simple pipe. The land was very small; one had enclosed it willingly in some walls lacking horizons; one let the luminous extent of the water on the lake and the intensely engraved lines of the mountains appear only in the precise place of this opening, a view through the sublime crossing of the right angle, man's measuring tool. Next he refers to houses he constructed when he was seventeen years old–they were decorated from top to bottom–and the white, nude cube he designed when he was twenty-four. In both cases he knew the design spoke an incoherent language, was devoid of a mathematical rule, a regulator to control the chaos of its arrangement. It was necessary to make a mathematical intervention. There follows another remembrance: when he was apprenticed to be an engraver of watches, decorating them with figures drawn from nature. One day he discovered a law of nature, that of the tree and its smallest branch:

> The oldest branch, the first to leave from the soil, proposes an accumulating series, probably incontestable.
> The entire tree is a pure mathematical function.[189]

More stories from his youth: he remembers retrieving from a cook of an alpine farm the hoofs of a goat that he started to ornament with his penknife. He became fascinated with the way the bone was assembled, and how the ligaments and muscles were articulated and attached. Years later, after he had arrived at what became known as the five points of architecture, he made a comparison. The goat jumps from rock to rock, and all of his powerful body falls on four small supports; so too a house falls on its pilotis. "The hoof of the goat and the piloti of prestressed concrete make a mathematical statement in the work, creating some intensely equilibrated ensembles, agile and intelligent."[190] He moves on to discuss his Cartesian skyscrapers and the brise-soleil (the window sun-shield) for his housing on the heights of Fort l'Empereur in Algiers, and he concludes that it is imperative to enter into concordance with site, sun, and topography.

> That is what it means "to situate" something; to harmonize the human work and the environment, to offer to the mind of man some rules of nature. To make sound, to make consonant, to produce a consonance. To make harmony rule. To accomplish, if one can do it, the miracle of "ineffable space."[191]

CONCLUSION

Le Corbusier was on the defensive: he was neither the dry rationalist without a heart his critics believed him to be nor a stark mathematician without a spirit that some of his admirers required him to be. He was continually on the edge—controversial yet admired. He had sought since his youth to forge a synthesis between art and utility, art and industry, art and the machine, and then in the early 1920s to draw into closer relationship architecture, city planning, and all of the arts. Now in the late 1920s and 1930s, he begins to rework the calm, quiet tenets of Purism, adding research into poetry and creating a more personal, passionate approach. He is even willing to accept cubism as the revolutionary force behind the production of modern art. He has achieved fame as an architect, but not as a painter, and does not have another public exhibition of his paintings until 1938.[192] Thus his defense may not only be to quell his many architectural critics but to strengthen the position of his painting, and the murals he begins to paint in 1935, sheltering them under the strength of his acclaim as an architect by making a synthesis of all of his creative work.

Ozenfant had told him in 1918: "There is only freedom in painting....Can architecture achieve a strong expression of the freedom of art, an expression that moves *in a good direction*, all the effort of a man, all his passion, his strength, his entire life?"[193] Le Corbusier would finally reply in 1962

> I had the idea...to explain through facts, that a man animated by visual abilities was very naturally capable of practicing arts which were not at all separated by frontiers: urbanism and architecture (indivisible sciences), painting, sculpture. And having dedicated his life since the age of fifteen to these researches, that is to say during sixty years, there is no feeling of "touche-a-tou" but, very simply, to be a free man.[194]

The words "synthesis," "alliance," and "unité" become more frequent in his 1930s writings; as do acoustical metaphors such as "sounding board," "resonance," "harmony," and "vibration." The verb "to radiate" takes on its various forms: radiant, radiating, radium. They give to architecture and simple objects a human quality, animating not only their milieu, but speaking directly to their creators and observers. They contain a spiritual energy both concentrated within and projected outwards. Le Corbusier locates this creative spirit in the spontaneity of primitive arts, in rustic environments, and begins to fill his artworks with gentle curves, nude bodies, shells, ropes, and bones. Spontaneity, unparallel freedom of expression, unity of place and object engender his poetic spirit.

Yet the Purist poet of proportional relationships will not give up on mathematical order as he searches to fill out the points in his doctrine, drawing architecture and urbanism into a unité. He becomes a poet of the right angle. It is a tool with which he takes possession of space. Nature being horizontal, man vertical, together they form a right angle, a balance, an equilibrium–so needed in the chaos of the 1930s. Reality is more than ever in need of mathematical ordering, ineffable space a matter of mathematical rigor. With this tool of the right angle Le Corbusier mounts the road toward unité–honesty, rectitude, clarity, correctness–the social reformer of a new time to come.[195]

CHAPTER 9
TRAVELS TO THE AMERICAS

Cliché as intellectual (and linguistic) ornament.
—*Karl Kraus*

I. INTRODUCTION: CONTROVERSY AND ESCAPE

THE CRITICS

In 1929, Le Corbusier was under scathing attack by Karel Teige and other hard-line functionalists for having allegedly abandoned the cause of modern architecture. At the same time, he was being criticized in the international press for advocating a revolutionary crusade in the name of machine worship and sterile reason. Particularly painful were the denunciations by Swiss critics, who turned public opinion against his projects for Geneva. Alexandre de Senger, for example, wrote in the winter of 1928 that Le Corbusier was a neo-Jacobean, frightened by the artistic works accumulated with love over the centuries and refusing to have his architectural work contaminated by known facts or realities. "Le Corbusier," de Senger wrote, "complains 'the moon is not round, the rainbow is a fragment, and the play of veins in the marble unsettling, inhuman.' Le Corbusier has written 'nothing in nature attains to the pure perfection of the machine.'"[1]

Another critic, François Fosca, maintained that it was absurd to claim that a telephone, typewriter, or gramophone offered aesthetic pleasure, that a gas meter or a sewing machine were beautiful. Through his love of the steamship, automobile, locomotive, phonograph, and cinema, Le Corbusier betrayed a secret dissatisfaction with life in Europe, an unacknowledged desire for escape. This state of mind revealed an appetite for adventure and travel—in short, for exoticism. All the machines that Le Corbusier thrilled most over could transport him quickly to exotic realms or else bring the exotic to him. "Exoticism is the attraction of that which is faraway, different, and poorly known. It is born of a disaffection with that which surrounds us, and is familiar

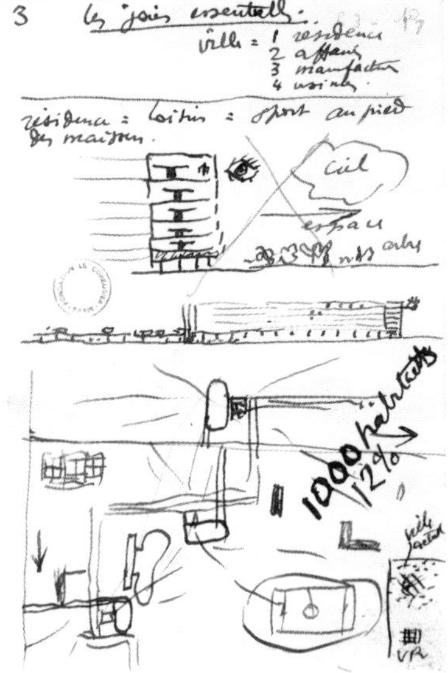

FIGURE 9.1: One of the note cards Le Corbusier used for lectures, this one explaining "the essential joys" for a talk he gave in 1935 at the Museum of Modern Art in New York City. FIGURE 9.2: Le Corbusier, photographed giving a lecture entitled "The relations between architecture and painting" in Zurich, 1938

to us; it proceeds from a latent or sworn romanticism. It is the idea that elsewhere, and not here, will bring happiness."[2]

Le Corbusier, Fosca contended, makes an idol of the machine, and so imitates

> the savage, who falls on knees before the first gramophone that he hears, and venerates it as a god. It recalls equally the *nouveau riche* who employs a *valet de chambre* and a chauffeur, but who, in the depths of his soul, fears them. The true modern man, the truly civilized, uses machines, but he keeps from making them into divinities.[3]

Le Corbusier, moreover, this "man who is occupied with architecture and the decorative arts in a word, is totally lacking an indispensable quality, an aesthetic sensibility."[4] That is why Le Corbusier always has in his mouth the word "austerity." Since he can neither feel nor comprehend art, he hates all aesthetic sensuality.[5]

Given this harshly critical atmosphere, it is no wonder that in 1929, at the age of forty-one, Le Corbusier left for his first trip to the Americas. He had already sent his "Defense of Architecture" to Karel Teige in August and announced he would leave for Buenos Aires on September 5.[6]

A few years later, in October 1935, while suffering setbacks over his project for the Exposition Internationale des Arts et Techniques of 1937 and blockage of a number of his city plans, Le Corbusier accepted an invitation for a lecture tour of the United States sponsored by the Museum of Modern Art (MoMA), to be combined with an exhibition of his models, plans, and large photogravures.[7] The forty-eight-year-old architect gave at least twenty lectures in just over a month (October 24 to November 27) in fifteen venues from Maine to Illinois.[8] [FIGURES 9.1 AND 9.2]

This was Le Corbusier's first visit to the United States. He expected to find its cities less sick than those of Europe, but found instead the same impasse: authorities lacked nerve, allowing property owners and money to bar the route and force millions to live amid the great waste of cities that he likened to tombs.[9] Worse, many in America thought mechanization had caused the Depression, and thought it was necessary to turn back. Le Corbusier believed to the contrary that the second machine age had begun, a new page had been turned, and America's duty and honor was to continue to blaze a path to the future. He saw a country that was young, its people naive but full of energy, and he assumed they would eventually achieve equilibrium.[10]

It is natural to compare the trips of 1929 and 1935. Both were lecture tours, both presented opportunities to secure architectural and planning commissions, both resulted in books. Aboard the *Lutétia*, on his way back to Europe from South America in December 1929, Le Corbusier gathered together the substance of his ten lectures delivered in South America, including many drawings he executed during his talks, and published the collection in the subsequent year as *Précisions sur un état présent de l'architecture et de l'urbanisme*.[11] [FIGURE 9.3, p. 697] He also assembled notes from his 1935 trip into a book, *Quand les Cathédrales étaient blanches: voyage aux pays de timides* (*When the Cathedrals Were White: A Voyage to the Country of the Timid People*). [FIGURE 9.4] The latter is a more poetic arrangement, not a collection of lectures, and reveals both his delight and despair over what he personally believed was the United States' lost opportunity to plan cities and build skyscrapers on the rational principles of modern times.[12] Yet he was also enchanted by the experience of exploring the United States firsthand and carrying on a love affair with Marguerite Tjader Harris, which may have influenced the manner in which he cast what he saw.[13]

Both trips, in various ways, were escapes into exotic realms—suggestively echoing, in some respects, Fosca's charge that Le Corbusier

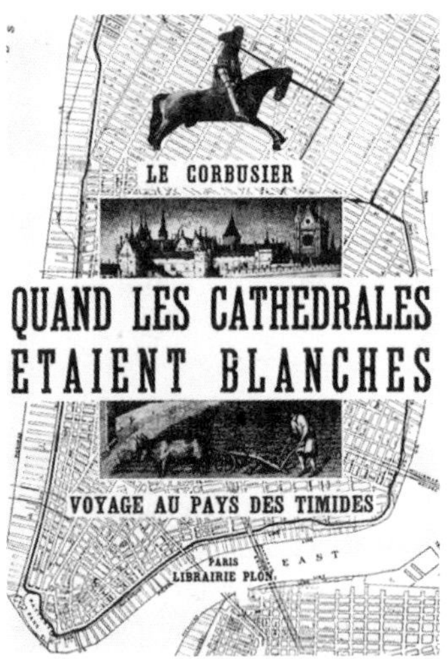

FIGURE 9.4: Travel notes from a lecture trip to America in 1935 were published in 1937 as *Quand les Cathédrales étaient blanches: Voyage aux pays de timides.*

seeks escape, adores the exotic, is possessed by "the idea that elsewhere, and not here, will bring happiness." Both books, as geographically structured travelogues, draw repeated contrasts between America and Europe, civilized and primitive, narrating stories based half on illusion, half on reality. They cannot be mistaken for dry factual narratives. Indeed, they illustrate the point that every construction of another place or culture is also by definition a construction of self, necessarily based on a series of oppositions between here-there, us-them. These journals explore what Mary Louise Pratt has called a "contact perspective," one that "emphasizes how subjects are constituted in and by their relations to each other. It treats the relations among...travelers and 'travelees,' not in terms of separateness or apartheid, but in terms of copresence, interaction, interlocking understandings and practices, often within radically asymmetrical relations of power."[14]

These two travels to the fabled West have also to be compared to Le Corbusier's earlier trip to the mystic Orient in 1911. In all three cases, the destination is transfigured in writings through a complex, ambiguous system of romantic distortions shot through with bolts of modernist clarity. In the Oriental writings, Le Corbusier was a young man longing for new adventures; he was open to the transformations that travel might engender. In travels to the West, however, he is a reformer with a message to bring to these timid people; he is bent on transforming their lands, educating them, offering his eminently superior French brain to cool and channel their brawling brawn. He has shifted from object of study to subject for his studies, from submissive acolyte to eager reformer. Yet he self-consciously returns to the "primitive" lands of the East, for they are never far from his mind as he explores the lands of the West. He had recently included several pages of sketches from the East in the opening pages of the first volume of his *Oeuvre Complète* (1930), perhaps because that trip developed no knowledge nor prescribed any action, and indeed represented an escape from the modern adoration of the machine. His writings and sketches of the East were attempts to evoke the spirit of faraway places, steeped in fantastic visions and poetic impressions. The writings of the West are in addition immersed in the rhetoric of instrumental control and knowledge. Like his earlier travel to exotic lands, Le Corbusier is escaping from alienating forces in his own culture, even his own obsession with the machine, but he finds the peoples of the West to be tainted as well with their own sicknesses. Le Corbusier is the doctor who knows best, who will perform therapeutic miracles with reason and delight.

II. PRECISIONS

ADVENTURE STORIES

Blaise Cendrars, who started writing stories, real and imaginary, about Brazil's fifteen-meter-long serpents, frightening crocodiles, and dangerous rivers in 1924, urged Le Corbusier to go to South America to see the continent for himself.[15] In his introduction to *Precisions,* Le Corbusier describes his experience in terms of just such feverish adventure tales, only complicated by the elusiveness of such adventures in real life:[16]

> Everything I write [about South America] corresponds to the books, to the stories of our childhood: the rain forest, the pampa....There are jaguars: our companion shot at one eight days ago, but we don't see any! We go to a stalking shelter built in bamboo and branches in the heart of the forest; after fifteen minutes: nothing. Why would the animals come here just where we are waiting with a gun? At night we hear the parrots calling wildly they are green like the leaves; one doesn't see them. There are enormous snakes; here are some photos of them; last month a man on the plantation was killed; we don't see any. The pond is full of crocodiles; they're at the bottom. Here on the trail are the tracks of the deer, the boar. Here on the trail a tatou was run over.[17]

The emphasis is repeatedly on what is *not* seen–what is contrary to cliché expectations. As we shall see below, *Precisions* is a book both dominated by cliché and (as above) sardonically aware of cliché. It is also, of course, a book about architecture, being a collection of ten public talks on that subject. Le Corbusier says that he placed before his South American audiences his twenty-five years of research, which had jelled into a system. He believes

> it is useful to submit to a general verdict this series of related facts which make up a doctrine. The word doctrine does not frighten me at all. I have often been called dogmatic. A doctrine means a set of concepts leading closely from one to another in accordance with the laws of logic.[18]

The lectures in *Precisions* thus present some of what Le Corbusier would refer to in 1946 as the "points de doctrine," constructed across a series of books written in the 1930s and 1940s. In *Precisions,* Le Corbusier says his doctrine involved many questions of how and why. In pursuit of answers to these questions, he had developed over the years a "*daring response,* unusual, staggering, revolutionary. For the facts of the problem, the reasons for the 'how' and the 'why' are much more upsetting today than one may think."[19] And for Le Corbusier the quest for this "how" and "why" is architecturally of the essence: if he were ever to teach architecture, he told his South American audience, he would instill in his students

> a sharp sense of verification, of free will, of the "how" and the "why"... [and] to cultivate this sense tirelessly, till old age even. This verification I should want on the very objective plane of facts. But facts are mobile, changing, especially in our time. I should teach them to despise formulas. I should say to them: *proportion is all.*[20]

He would also ask his students to write: to undertake a difficult task, the comparative analysis of the existence of cities. He would want his students to understand "that before drawing, one must always know 'what it is about', 'what it is for,' 'to do what.' Excellent practice for fashioning one's judgment."[21] And his students must study material objects, like a restaurant car of a railway, or a steamship. They must draw up plans and sections, and show how these objects work, function, and operate.

And they must above all "open their eyes" and learn to see when they walk along the streets of their cities, by looking at magazines and albums of architecture coming from Europe, by going behind fanciful facades to find where honest objects lie.[22]

In this chapter, these two sets of travel-writings will be examined for the manner they trace out a zone of contact as important to Le Corbusier as to the reader. He draws a number of concepts into the constellation, tools he uses to alter the arrangement, to move the Americans forward toward the second machine era of the *temps nouveaux*. The reader, however, should keep in mind that Le Corbusier's preoccupation was the provision of housing and the development of rational city plans for everyone, everywhere. He puts it plainly in *Precisions:* "A word in passing. I shall never speak of anything but the homes of mankind. It is a problem of homes for mankind, is it not? I have always refused to study houses for the noble inhabitants of Parnassus."[23]

THE CULINARY ART OF ARCHITECTURE AND THE EDUCATION OF DESIRE

Food is an insistently recurrent trope in both *Precisions* and *When the Cathedrals Were White.* Le Corbusier is aware that the operations of a culinary system are like a language—they state many things about a society, a culture. As he says in *Cathedrals,*

> Through a long tradition of cooking, through, the wise design of meals, through the effect of wine, man's good companion, the Frenchman has learned how to eat and how to act at table. Meals are still among the good moments of life.... French people talk when they are eating; conversation is a sign of culture. Business matters are forgotten; men and women enjoy their taste for companionship.... [But] American restaurants are devoid of conversation.[24]

Why are food and eating so peculiarly preeminent in the system of signs that Le Corbusier puts forward in these two books? What does that preeminence accomplish?

The role of food or the culinary sign has been called a transignifier: it not only plays on a double or multiple register in order to dissimulate or compensate for a lack or an excess in the general order of a culture, but it also enables jumps or slides between orders or terms that appear to be disconnected.[25] Food reveals the tensions and transactions of exchange between various spheres: edible and inedible, bodily needs and desires, chefs and heads of state. In *Food for Thought,* Louis Marin maintains that all cookery involves a theological, ideological, political, and economic operation by means of which an edible foodstuff is transformed into a sign/body that is eaten. In the Christian Eucharist, the transformation is double and total: Logos (Word) becomes bread absolutely, bread becomes body absolutely, both are eaten so that eater and eaten can become each other absolutely. The Word is received into the mouth: God speaks Himself, is eaten by the believer; the believer in turn utters praises. Sacred feasts in other religions put in play similarly profound relationships between the divine, the tangible, the spoken: edible and the eater, thing and body, what is shown and its sign, need and desire.[26]

"Food for thought" is not the substitution of rational clarity for desire, mind for body. It is, rather, a matter of enlisting the mind in the maintenance of arousal, in the creation of desire. The origin of desire is often sight–or sight partly frustrated by concealment, recalling Le Corbusier's treatment of the elusive exotic, the jaguars "we don't see"–and begins with praise articulated through language. Language, food, and the erotic are inextricable, not only as signs but anatomically: the tongue is an organ not only of taste but of speech and sex. Le Corbusier, in employing his tongue to speak to his audiences, to offer him his own Logos, and in speaking so much of food, seeks to inform and educate desire and the judgment of desire, "taste," while amplifying it. Taste is an art of discernment, as applicable to aesthetic judgment as it is to food. "Taste" has metaphoric and metonymic properties, as in a taste for pain (synaesethetic), a man of poor taste (metonymic), taste as appetite or desire (extension), a taste for life (metaphoric). There is taste of and taste for: "of" referring to knowledge or recognition, "for" to the appreciation of different sensations. To speak of desire is to speak with authority, to educate about the destabilizing forces of desire for food, drink, sex, or power.[27]

Le Corbusier meant to teach his hearers and, later, his readers how to desire the visions he spreads before their eyes. Both of his American travelogues, 1929 and 1935, are food for thought, transignifiers, and rhetorical events that instruct and popularize ideas that Le Corbusier is formulating into a delectable "doctrine" of architecture and urbanism. They are intended to trigger the appetite of imagination and prompt the desire to take in the words he presents: particularly in

Precisions, he is a chef who spreads dishes before the reader's eyes, even as he must teach them–even force them–to desire what he offers:

> You [i.e., one in Le Corbusier's position as lecturer in South America] are facing a numerous and hostile audience. By hostile I mean to say that it is in the position of a diner whom one wants to make eat chicken without chewing it. New ideas after new ideas are thrown at him; his means of absorption are overwhelmed. So you have to give him food he can swallow, that is, to show him clear, indisputable, even crushing systems.... When you are facing an audience whom you have little by little attracted into the imaginary regions outlined by your charcoal, you must express, *enlighten, formulate.*[28]

Le Corbusier positions himself as the quintessential European, wiser, more knowledgeable, brimming with ideas that he wants to substitute for the inadequacies and impairments that prevail in the Americas. His mission is, in part, to *enlighten* by presenting *clear, indisputable, even crushing systems.* His travelogues, the sites where he makes his pursuit of this mission verbally visible to the reader, are always written with the center in Europe: they describe adventures into the unknown margins, adventures that are hopefully full of surprises and mysteries, but they are always travels in time, backward to younger countries and forward to the future. Europe, especially France, home of gastronomy *par excellence,* of educated taste in every sense of the word, remains in the present.

Of course, food does not exhaust the metaphoric complexity of these works, which he organizes using a series of signs that enable his discourse to shift in several directions in a play of resemblance and difference–between Europe and the Americas, male and female, young and old, rich and poor, black and white. Later in this chapter, I shall examine the ways in which tropes, clichés, and assumptions about blackness, femininity, and clothing also come into play; but first, a bigger bite of Le Corbusier's use of food as transignifier in *Precisions.*

In the "American Prologue" to *Precisions,* written in December 1929 during his return voyage to Europe aboard the *Lutétia,* Le Corbusier notes that from the airplane, flying over South America, he had seen sights that were cosmic. [FIGURE 9.5] Yet he starts this aerial account with ordinary things–culinary things.

FIGURE 9.5: **This photograph of Le Corbusier, in the cabin of a steamship at a writing desk, may have been taken in December of 1929, during his return voyage from South America to Europe aboard the *Lutétia*.**

> The earth is like a poached egg, it is a liquid spherical mass contained in a wrinkled skin.... some of the folds of the wrinkles are broken, that is the reason for those daring outlines of rock that give us an idea of the sublime. Like the poached egg, the earth is saturated with water on its surface; this is constantly in the process of evaporating and condensing. From a plane you can see on the plains of Uruguay the clouds that will sadden a home, or assure abundant crops, or rot grapevines; or that encounter of clouds which results in lightning and thunder, feared as if gods.[29]

Le Corbusier vacillates between negative and positive poles, between poverty and abundance. He continues with his story: the sun rises, bursting forth from the edge of the horizon, climbing into the sky with amazing speed, yet sadly marking the transience of life and the irreparable loss of time. All that dies decays, yet decay is life:

> Here, the poached egg inclines us to melancholy, even to despair; I believe the "poached egg" is neurasthenic. Let your poached egg rot, or, if you are short of time, remember the appearance of your mother's jams; formerly, pots of jam covered with a paper

> soaked in alcohol or in milk. And a few months later, a frightful mold had grown on the paper. The rain forest, the exuberant vegetation of the meanders, are the molds on our earth.[30]
>
> The earth is not a uniform green; it has all the veinings of rotting bodies–you, trees, all of you, seen from the sky, seem nothing but mold. And you Earth, Earth so desperately damp; you are nothing but mold! And your water, in vapor or in liquid, manipulated by such a faraway star, brings you, all at the same time, joy or melancholy, abundance or misery.[31]

Shortly after the global poached-egg metaphor, Le Corbusier writes about the simple houses of people composed out of "love," which therefore speak of desire. He asks the reader to

> watch one day, not in a luxury restaurant where the arbitrary interference of waiters and wine-waiters destroys my poem, but in an ordinary small restaurant, two or three customers who are having coffee and talking. The table is still covered with glasses, with bottles, with plates, with the bottle of oil, the saltshaker, pepper mill, napkins, napkin rings, etc. Look at the inevitable order that relates these objects to each other; they have all been used, they have been grasped in the hand of one or the other of the diners; the distances that separate them are the measure of life. It is an organized mathematical composition; there isn't a false point, a hiatus, a deceit. If there were a moviemaker there not hallucinated by Hollywood, filming this still life, in a "close-up," we should have *a testimonial to pure harmony*. . . . I find again in what I call the houses of men these inevitable arrangements. I have already explained these ideas in *A House, A Palace*.[32]

The good house thus arises from the harmonious disorders of shared life lived authentically, just as the unselfconscious sharing of food produces harmonious disorder, a Purist still life. In this "poem" of a shared meal with simple people in a popular place, Le Corbusier shifts registers to explain that he too composes with love, that the modern world of technology and truthful houses of men are his privileged sites. It is a matter of being able to discern between the primitive and the civilized, the truthful and the deceitful, the cultivated and the corrupted: luxury restaurants versus ordinary small restaurants, Hollywood distortions versus clear seeing. The taste must be educated.

Next he darts aside to the matter of race, linking the unspoiled, well-eaten meal of the ordinary small restaurant to the truthful houses of Rio de Janeiro's blacks, whose qualities Le Corbusier's educated European eye sees "with perfect understanding":

> But important Brazilian personages are furious to learn that in Rio I had climbed the hills inhabited by the blacks: "It is a shame for us, civilized persons." I explained serenely that, first of all, I found these blacks basically good: good-hearted. Then, beautiful, magnificent. Then, their carelessness, the limits they had learned to impose on their needs, their capacity for dreaming, their candidness resulted in their houses being always admirably sited, the windows opening astonishingly on magnificent spaces, the smallness of their rooms largely adequate. I thought of the low-cost housing in our Europe poisoned by the princes of the Renaissance, the popes, or by Mr. Nénot, and my eternal conclusions after so many countries visited in over twenty years, becomes more certain every day: it is the concept of life that we must change; it is the concept of happiness that must be made clear. That is the reform, the rest is only a consequence: "The Blacks will kill you in those awful neighborhoods; they are extremely dangerous, they are savages; there are two or three murders per week!" I answered, "Why do you want them to kill me, who look at them with perfect understanding? My eyes, my smile protect me, don't worry."[33] [FIGURES 9.6 AND 9.7, p. 697]

The parallel with his Oriental journey many years before is explicit:

> And I remembered that back in 1910 [sic 1911] the people of Pera said to me of the Turks of Stamboul: "You're crazy to go there at night; they'll kill you, they're roughs." But the houses of Pera, their banks, their trades, their customs houses, their European protectorates, the ambiguous nature of their architecture showed me the real site of evil thoughts.[34]

Le Corbusier returns to his culinary figure:

> We are at the saturation of Brillat-Savarin [French gastronome, 1755–1826)]: cooking for diplomatic lunches and dinners, wearing dinner jackets or tails (in the style of the generals of the Grande Armée). We take leeks, asparagus, potatoes, beef, butter, spices, fruit; and using a science that has filled whole books, we denature everything and reduce everything to the same taste. The only result is that with the wine and the smelly cheeses, one has filled stomachs enough so they lose some intellectual control. And then they talk business: war, alliances, customs, taxes, innumerable speculations are treated. Like snakes they digest the uncountable dangerous schemes of a world that really no longer exists.[35]

The "baldachins of red plush and golden ribbons of the academic palaces of Geneva" are comparable to the recipes of Brillat-Savarin, while his own schemes for the Palace of Nations provided a nourishing meal because he was concerned with the welfare of humanity. Gastronomic displays of sophistication are indigestible and produce only waste. He asks the reader:

> What do you make of diplomacy: and "the culinary art of architecture"?[36]

> Tell me if the taste of the cooking of the big international hotels, cooking with that Brillat-Savarin sauce and the indigestion due to the goose liver paste with truffles, doesn't throw up in you when facing these jaundices of the Salon des Artists Français?
>
> Tell me if you find Brillat-Savarin in the porches of Chartres or Vézelay? They are from before the academies, are they not? And in the Indian masks of the museum of Rio?[37]

It is, then, the science of cooking–architectural and gastronomical–with its historical treatises and rules, that has over-manipulated, over-thought, and over-designed both food and buildings until they result in so much richness they must be purged, vomited up. By utilizing the culinary sign, Le Corbusier has been able to introduce and shift between different registers, unifying the dissonant topics around which his discourse will unfurl. It is from water, the egg, and mold that life is generated: but it is a poached egg (i.e., cooked, and therefore denatured or civilized) that appears neurasthenic, prone to decay.

Man has tampered with nature's purest form–the egg–upset its balance, and destroyed its harmony. Yet amidst this melancholy there are joys, for the egg and the mold promise new life. This potential must be nurtured and guided to fulfillment. There is hope: for there was architecture before there were architects, primitive masks like those of Rio before there were works of art–all offer spiritual food that nourishes. [FIGURE 9.8]

Soon another reference to food occurs, and a particularly strange one. It begins innocently enough with the fact that for the Argentines, Paris is a mirage, an unattainable dream that orchestrates their life, even though he is ready to admit that South Americans want to write their own history, "a spiritual fabrication that is like a doctrine, a description of oneself, a self-definition. History doesn't exist, it is made up."[38] The youth of São Paulo explain to him "we are 'cannibals,'" meaning not savagery or gluttony but an esoteric rite, a communion with the best forces that come together in this land of immigrants and mix with legendary feats of native warriors. If one eats the body of one's ancestors, then one becomes those ancestors–or so Le Corbusier reasons. He slips into a fictional narration:

> The meal was very light; we were a hundred or five hundred eating the flesh of one captured warrior. This warrior was brave, we assimilated his qualities; and more so, this warrior had in turn eaten of the flesh of one's tribe. Thus, in eating him one assimilated the very flesh of one's ancestors.
>
> The youth of São Paulo, calling themselves cannibals, wanted to express in this way their opposition to an international dissoluteness, by proclaiming heroic principles whose memory is still present.[39]

Yet Le Corbusier immediately labels the South Americans "timid" (a word that will recur in the subtitle of *When the Cathedrals Were White*) and the Parisians "brave" because the former are cowed, their energies dissipated before the enormity of the land and their tasks, while Parisians concentrate their energy, become daring and achieve great heights. He repeats a refrain from his own youth:

> Paris is without mercy; a pitiless battlefield. It is a place of championships or of gladiators. We face and kill each other. Paris is paved with cadavers. Paris is a synod of cannibals, who establish the dogma of the moment. Paris selects.[40] [FIGURE 9.9]

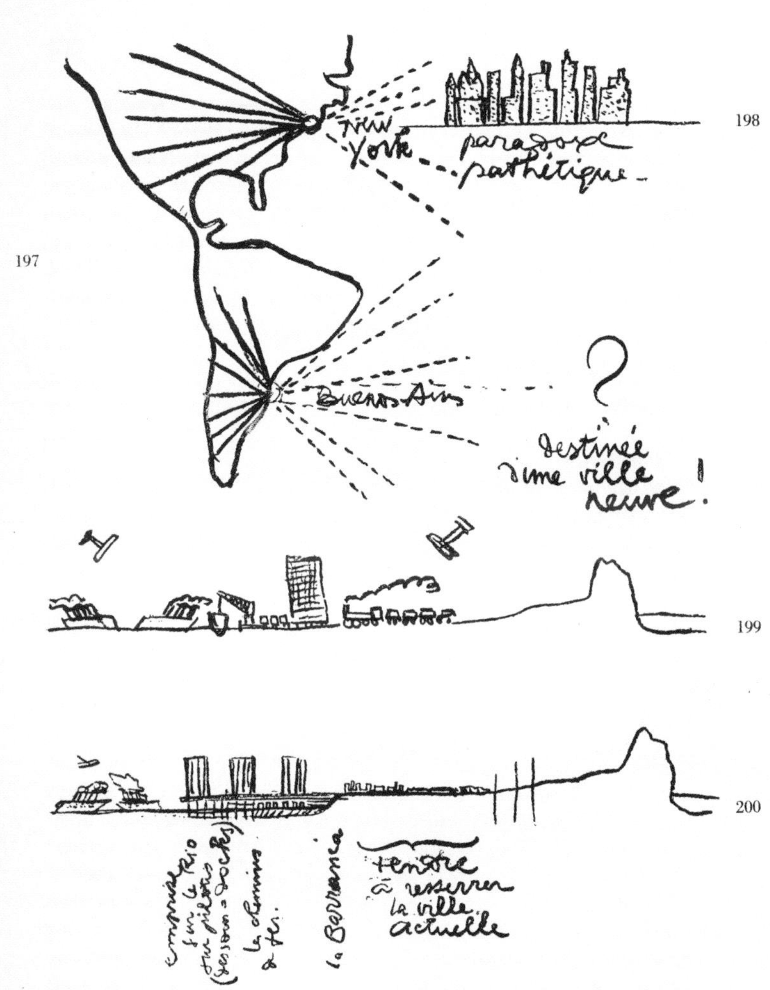

197, 198 New York // paradoxe pathétique/pitiful paradox // Buenos Aires // ?destinée d'une ville neuve!/destiny of a new city // **200** emprise sur le Rio sur pilotis (dessous = docks) le chemin de fer/extension on the Rio on pilotis (below = docks) the railway // la Barranca/the Barranca // tendre à resserrer la ville actuelle/try to contract the present city

FIGURE 9.8: **Compared to New York, a pathetic paradox, Buenos Aires was a new city on the verge of a great destiny.**

FIGURE 9.9: Because the academies refuse to allow Paris to change, it was on the edge of a great crisis, according to Le Corbusier.

Le Corbusier reiterates this narrative about his own role in South America by wrapping it in a story about cannibals and gladiators, timidity and bravery. He is offering ideas that come from "the guiding lighthouse" of France to the margins of the world, the antipodes.[41] There is a play going on here between how the South Americans will look at an object, the representation of their cities as plans drawn and envisioned by Le Corbusier, and how that object will affect them if substituted for their own. What if the body of ideas, as violent as any battle between gladiators, is not of their own construction but his? He is, of course, the brave warrior on whom the "cannibals" are invited to dine, risking rejection and intimidation if they do not savor and ingest the enticing meal he both is and offers. But his anxiety is not that great since he believes South Americans have devoured the flesh of many ancestors no matter their origin.

III. BLACKNESS, HOT JAZZ, CLOTHING, DEATH

Desire's onset is generally upon sight, at the moment one's eyes first see a thing, a place, a person. The compulsion to see the desired object again is often likened to thirst, hunger, or lust. Language articulates desire, augmenting it with praise. To educate about desire–Le Corbusier's mission in South America–implies that the sophisticated voyeur will impart to the naive, youthful child the ability to achieve self-control over the destabilizing forces of desire (for food, drink, sex, or power). To educate woman, in particular, about desire is to prescribe her proper place within the patriarchal household.[42]

Yet from the blacks, with their simple goodness, and from women, controlled by their emotions, the sophisticate, the man, the white man, needs something. He cannot be fully alive without restoring something in himself, fortifying his blood, with the help of the noble savage and the feeling woman. At least, such are the assumptions that have sometimes been made by European cultured thinkers.

In the late 1920s, "negrophilia" swept through Paris, a *culte de nègre* embracing a strange mixture of American jazz, African tribal masks, and voodoo dances and rituals. No one epitomized–and exploited–this projection of "primitive" spiritualism better than Josephine Baker, who rose to immediate fame when the Revue Nègre opened in Paris in 1925. Just nineteen years old, Baker achieved instant fame as reviewers struggled to describe the contradictions she embodied. One wrote,

> Her lips were painted black, her skin was the colour of a banana, her short hair was stuck down on to her head and gleamed dully like caviar, her voice was shrill, her body moved in a perceptual trembling and twisting. She grimaced, she tied herself in knots, she limped, she did the splits and finally she left the stage on all fours with her legs stiff and her bottom higher than her head, like a giraffe in old age. Was she horrible, delicious, black, white? She moved so quickly nobody could decide...Her finale was a barbaric dance...a triumph of lewdness, a return to prehistoric morality.[43]

While Parisians celebrated Baker's blackness, believing that her *danse sauvage* and primitive sensuality–dancing bare-breasted with a string of bananas or conch shells strung about her waist, her gyrations and rhythmic motions–were authentic expressions of the primitive sexuality that black bodies supposedly contained. She was, in actuality, a meticulous creator of her dramatic personae, and became a millionaire in four years by deliberately manipulating notions of black savagery and feminine artifice. She pushed the limits by parodying jungle themes: men in white suits and pith helmets "plundered" women from the sub-Sahara on stage, while black men wore loincloths and beat tom-toms under a palm tree. She exploited the essentialist notion that black bodies were liberated from constraints and unaware of the sexual repression that bourgeois society apparently suffered. Baker was a self-constructed queen: she walked leopards on the streets of Paris, wore tiaras and jewels, and adorned herself in leopard skins. These performances communicated that this "unrepressed savage," like a female Tarzan-figure, had tamed herself, had transcended the bestial, and in turn was able to tame both beasts of prey and natural forces.

Soon after Le Corbusier's discussion of food, examined in the preceding section, he turns to Baker, whom he had met on the steamship *Giulio Cesare* on the voyage from Buenos Aires to São Paulo and contacted again at several points on this South American trip. They sailed back to France together on the steamship *Lutétia,* during which time Le Corbusier assembled the notes of his lectures into *Precisions*.[44]

[FIGURE 9.11, p. 698]

Le Corbusier expresses passion for the popular arts and the simple tunes of the blacks, which transcend the ordinary and usher in the pulse and rhythm of modern times. [FIGURE 9.10, p. 698] Yet he cannot refrain from describing Baker, and black people generally, in childlike and animalistic terms, repeating all the primitive stereotypes about jazz and negritude that informed Parisians in the 1920s.

> In her steamship cabin, she picks up a little guitar–a child's toy–that someone gave her and sings all the blacks' songs: "I'm a little blackbird looking for a white bird; I want a little nest for the two of us..." or "You're the wings of the angel who came, you're the sails of my boat, I can't do without you; you're, etc., etc.; you're the weave of the cloth and I put all you are in the cloth, I roll it up and take it away; I can't do without you."
>
> In the North American music invented by the blacks, there is an invincible stock of "contemporary" poetry. You search for its bases: the tom-tom of Chad shaking the folk music of the Bavarian mountains or of Scotland, Basque songs, etc. Clergymen visiting Uncle Tom's cabin. Thus today in the extraordinary melting pot of the USA where everything is of the new twentieth century, and where the timidity of big clumsy boys has till now paralyzed the expression of a contemporary poetry, you have the simple naive black who has made this music that pours all over the world....I see in this music the basis of a style capable of being the expression of the feelings of a new time. We must realize that it contains the most profound human traditions: Africa, Europe, America. I feel in it an energy capable of wearing away the methods of the academic conservatories of Brillat-Savarin, as the architectural techniques dating from the Neolithic through Haussmann and broken off cleanly by Eiffel or Considère are now being worn away.[45]

There must be a primitive world as an ante-type of Europe: societies of expression, not abstraction, that Europeans can inhabit no matter how briefly. Le Corbusier's list of hyperboles evoking the historical roots of jazz strain credibility, their excess intended to rip away the roadblocks erected by Europeans and the "timid big boys" of the United States and allow for a free-flowing, revitalizing contact with simple, naive sources of black spirituality. At least, this is how Le Corbusier imagines the Americas. Yet he does so more complexly than many who ran after the *culte de nègre*: he plays a game of mirrors, of illusions and inversions emerging out of his desire to embody seemingly contradictory registers of the poetic and the rational, or, as he had earlier stated, to solve the equation of reason and passion. Does he turn to music because it does not speak, is not explanatory, yet possesses a power at once inaccessible, unutterable, and significant in its revitalizing effects?

Jazz becomes the backdrop for his desired transformations, and as backdrop it allows him to keep the experience of blacks mute and unexplored. In his comprehension of jazz, Le Corbusier never ventures far from descriptions offered in the pages of *L'Esprit Nouveau.* Darious Milhaud, for example, had written that when jazz arrived in 1918 from New York, Parisians were shocked by the sounds and instruments, which were almost never grouped together: they believed that the syncopated rhythm, with its stress on the downbeat, replicated the pounding of the heart and the circulation of blood. Although this was mechanized music, as precise as a machine, and shockingly new, it nevertheless had very old roots; it evolved from the blacks of America, combing Negro spirituals as one source, religious songs of the slaves as another.[46] Albert Jeanneret, Le Corbusier's brother, also wrote about the binary rhythms of ragtime, how they acted on the body, how the ancients and primitives were preoccupied with such rhythms. Once the music stopped, he said, there was an immediate emptiness that remained unsatisfied until the melody was played again and again.[47] Rhythm lies at the base of life and of all the arts, and that is why jazz has such a great effect. In modern life, Jeanneret believed, the body must regain the suggestive power of action; it must achieve a harmonization between the body and the mind similar to the precision expressed by the machine. It is necessary to train the body to realize musical rhythms in the tempo and harmony of gestures and movements, assembling these measures into phrases, and phrases into scores. Abstraction and precision arise from the laws and relations of measure (musical meter).[48]

Le Corbusier will offer similar thoughts on the revitalizing and unifying power of blackness, mediated through the mechanical perfection of jazz, in *When the Cathedrals Were White:*

> Negro music has touched America because it is the melody of the soul joined with the rhythm of the machine. It is in two-part time: tears in the heart; movement of the legs, torso, arms and head. The music of an era of construction: innovating. It floods the body and the heart; it floods the USA and it floods the world. Hence, everything in our auditory habits change. Psycho-physiologically it is so powerful, so irresistible that it has torn us from the passivity of listening and has made us dance

> or gesticulate, participate. It has opened the cycle of sound of modern times, turned the pages on the conservatories. New cadences, new cries, unknown groups of sounds, an exuberance, a flood, a vertiginous intensity.... Launched by the Negroes, it is American music, containing the past and the present, Africa and pre-machine age, Europe and contemporary America.[49]

In *When the Cathedrals Were White*, however, Le Corbusier opines that the implacable exactitude and staggering precision of "hot jazz" must be listened to amidst the clamor of skyscrapers and the roaring of subways. Its improvisations, in which one sound quickly replaces another, are compared to the piercing sirens reverberating off city walls, the kidnappings and gang wars, the machine guns, the speed and cruelty that disturb the night of New York. Nothing like it has ever been heard in Europe; you have to go to America to see and hear it for yourself. In *Cathedrals,* Le Corbusier also describes his fascination with tap dancers, "as mechanical as a sewing machine," and imagines "the old rhythmic instinct of the virgin African forest has learned the lesson of the machine and that in America the rigor of exactitude is a pleasure. Idea of a masterpiece: exactitude."[50] "Savagery is constantly present" in such performances, Africa not far removed with its "tom-toms, massacres, and the complete destruction of villages or tribes. Is it possible that such memories could survive through a century of being uprooted? It would seem that only butchery and agony could call forth such cries, gasp, roars."[51]

In the midst of this rapturous narration on American jazz, Le Corbusier suddenly inserts a memory from North Africa, for his thoughts are never far from that trip as well.

> When I flew over the Atlas Mountains in a plane, I realized their formation–through erosion, geological dramas, the action of winds–was completely independent of our moral anxieties; man is in a kind of cyclone; he builds solid houses to protect and shelter his heart. Outside, nature is nothing but indifference, even terror. The clouds come from far away, go far away, calm or broken up; sometimes the sky is blue. By itself the grand sport of the sky affects our hearts. Duality appears in the contrast between the unfathomable march of the elements and our precise, careful calculations, as sublime as they are puerile, established in the heart of the tumult.[52]

American jazz has understood this lesson:

> It is the equivalent of a beautiful turbine running in the midst of human conversations. Hot jazz.
>
> Jazz, like skyscrapers, is an event and not a deliberately conceived creation. They represent the forces of today. The jazz is more advanced than the architecture.... Manhattan is hot jazz in stone and steel.[53]

These thoughts about jazz are juxtaposed with comments about the failures of conservatories in Europe, of the music that escapes the comprehension and ears of professional musicians even though the world is filled via the phonograph

> with new music: that of the machines and that of folklore. Sensibility is liberated; it is filled up by moving revelations. They are the foundations of cathedrals of sound which are already rising.[54]

Yet Le Corbusier cannot refrain from inserting that in America's hot jazz he finds "mathematical France, precise, exact; I find in it the masses of Paris, a society worthy of interest, so measured, precise, and supple in its thoughts. A controlled sensuality, a severe ethics."[55]

CLOTHES MAKE THE MAN

Interestingly, Le Corbusier praises not only the hot jazz of American blacks and the plaintive primitive authenticity of Josephine Baker for having "opened the cycle of sound of modern times, turned the pages on the conservatories," having introduced "new cadences, new cries, unknown groups of sounds, an exuberance, a flood, a vertiginous intensity" that liberates the European mind from being control without sensuality, stone and steel without heat, except for the example set by feminine clothing. The women of France, as well as the jazz musicians and dancers of America, have shown the way forward to the desired fusion of machine-beauty with humanness. Once again, tropes of pompous artificiality (recalling the absurd clothing of the generals of the Grande Armée) and shipboard formality are contrasted to the relaxed, the practical, the authentic.

In *When the Cathedrals Were White* Le Corbusier mentions to the purser of the *Normandie*, the steamship on which he sailed to the

United States in 1935, that there is need to reform the ship's etiquette and activities. Instead of spending a dissipating week of entertainment, where passengers dressed and acted as if they were still at the Place de l'Opera, the ship ought to be a place of repose, of study and preparation; he would prefer, instead of costumed events, to dress in sports clothes and spend his time in the library.[56] While the stewards might dress in vermilion in keeping with the pomp of the ship, all the male passengers dressed as if they were attending a country funeral. "It is a curious end-result of civilization that men, who used to wear ostrich plumes on their heads, rose, white, and royal blue, a vesture of brocades or shimmering silk, should no longer know how to do anything but thrust their hands into the pockets of black trousers."[57]

It is therefore necessary that men's clothing be reformed, although Le Corbusier allowed this would be as difficult as changing the ethics and institutions of society. Clothing is more than a mere covering:

> Costume is the expression of a civilization. Costume reveals the most fundamental feelings; through it we show our dignity, our distinction, our frivolity, or our basic ambitions. Though standardized, masculine dress does not escape individual decision. But it is no longer suitable. From what persists, we have proof that the machine age revolution has not reached maturity.[58]

Early in *Precisions*, to begin his lecture on the need to reform the equipment of housing, Le Corbusier has inserted a story about women's fashion. Women have achieved reform in their clothing because they understood that to follow fashion was to deny themselves important new roles in modern life. They wanted to participate in sports, to take on jobs and earn a living, to drive cars, take a metro or bus:

> So women cut their hair and their skirts and their sleeves. They went off bareheaded, arms naked, legs free. And get dressed in five minutes. And they are beautiful; they lure us with the charm of their graces of which the designers have accepted taking advantage.
>
> The courage, the liveliness, the spirit of invention with which women have operated the revolution in clothing are a miracle of modern times. Thank you!

But men, Le Corbusier continued, are a sad case. They still wear starched collars, dress as if they are generals in an army, and wear suits with inadequate pockets, unable to carry the things needed during the day. Women have thrown out "etiquette" born at the court and "good manners" as taught in the convents. They were bored with laws prescribing what they must wear, how they must sit, move about, and even work. They gained new leisure time, an hour of relaxation in which to think.

If Le Corbusier's travels to the "new world" were partially an escape from the "carrion beetles"–his critics in the European press–then perhaps his focus on clothing and its proper fit takes on another meaning as well. Clothing describes not only the spectacle of urban life, but symbolizes in addition the act of covering the blank white page with linguistic signs. A writer's style becomes his clothing, it is his appearance in the world where he is constantly on display, being observed and judged.[59] In this case Le Corbusier is not only reverting to Loos's advice to adopt suitable clothing for modern times, as well as his own concerns, since as a youth he was never well-dressed, but is also making a judgment of how well his ideas were "suited" for an American audience. He wants to be wooed, to be open to their receptivity and to respond in kind, but he is as ever extremely sensitive to criticism, especially in the press. He is a mature adult seeking professional acclaim; he cannot merely be open to impressions but must be the seducer as well. For such a performance he must be accordingly dressed.

THE BLACKNESS OF DEATH

In *Precisions*, the first lecture that Le Corbusier offers a South American audience is devoted to how "to free oneself from academic thinking." He believes that "conventions, customs are words of surrender!"[60] They are constraints imposed by the academies, and it is necessary to turn one's

> back on charnel houses, a violent dawn [has begun].
> Why evoke charnel houses? Because the emanations of innumerable dead things assail our nostrils.... It is academism that is thus clutching the vital parts of the social body.[61]

In *When the Cathedrals Were White*, death again invades, only now it is not imported from the academies of the Old World; it arises from deep flaws in the brash projects of the New. A funereal sadness prevails in the United States: in the Americans' taste for Surrealism, in their black polished-stone entrances to skyscrapers, in the pink and black lobbies of moving-picture palaces, in the wax manikins in shop windows of Fifth Avenue, which evoke Greek tragedy. The violent life of Americans swings tragically between two poles: youthfulness, pride, and power versus uncertainty, inferiority complexes, and funereal sadness.[62] "This country, which as yet is familiar only with technical maturity, faces the future uneasily."[63]

Melancholy pervades and a funereal spirit reigns because Americans know that the scale of their enterprises has not been "the product of elegant, supple, complex mathematics–of proportion–but that of exaggerated dimensions and the heaping up of opulent materials."[64] They have not been able to make all their black and gold come alive. That is the reason for their inner sadness, that is why they have invented astonishing types who swim against swollen currents of colossal dimensions: Charlie Chaplin, Buster Keaton, Laurel and Hardy. Disproportion "is the rule in the USA: an abyss opens up before sensitive persons at every step. In reality, it is less amusing than in the movies. It is a serious matter, pathetic, unsettling."[65]

"I AM HAPPY."

All of Le Corbusier's discourse about the primitive, the sexual and racial other, blackness, death, and anxieties took place in 1929 and 1935 amidst an outpouring of apocalyptic studies decrying the end of Europe, the demise of western civilization, and the return of barbarism and chaos.[66] Somewhere in the world there had to be an antidote to a European civilization deemed deficient and moribund, over-refined and spiritually exhausted; somehow there had to be a way to stabilize the disruptive forces threatening moral and social disorder, lest all collapse into nonsense and madness. Le Corbusier's great hope was that he would find this in South America and the United States.

I suggest that his attitude toward the savage, the black, and the female was a form of modified conventionality. These were the binary opposites of Europe; they offered spiritual, emotional, and sensual release from the brute forces of technology and the market, which threatened ever-greater instrumentalization, mechanization, and commodification. The primitive, like music, lay beyond explanation, in a realm devoid of cause and effect, in the land of the unutterable and unpredictable. It could regenerate the West. Perhaps this is why Le Corbusier's trip to South America was such a happy one.

> The tourist is tireless in his praise, his enthusiasm is reborn at every corner; the city [of Rio de Janeiro] seems to be made for his pleasure. People wear light-colored clothes, they are hospitable; I am greeted with open arms; I am happy; I am in an auto, a motorboat, in a plane. I swim in front of my hotel; I go back to my room by elevator in a bathrobe, at 30 meters above the sea; I stroll about on foot at night; I have friends at every minute of the day, almost till sunrise; at seven in the morning, I am in the water; the night was a spectacle watching crowds in the streets meant for sailors, stupefying, containing innumerable different passions and polite complaisances, scowling or dramatic; there is not, for the tourist, as in continental cities an hour of the night when everything stops, when one goes to bed because there is really nothing more to see; the sea and the sky are always there, and it isn't dark; the beaches spread out bordered with quays and paved avenues; the harbor is full of all sorts of lights.[67]
>
> [FIGURES 9.12 AND 9.13, p. 699]

By 1935, however, he found it necessary to affirm that Western European man represented the most perfect and highest form of civilized humanity.[68] Though the importance of jazz was still tremendous, the need for rejuvenation was de-emphasized. At least an illusionary coherence had to be created, a possible future envisioned that countered the senseless anarchy of material abundance, lacking the internal order and hierarchy that the United States so obviously presented.

It has been claimed that the relationship between these perceived crises of Western civilization and the rhetoric of modernism can be understood in relation to death.[69] There was on one hand a crisis of abundance: the telephone, airplane, radio, electrical power, plastics, skyscrapers, the sprawling wasteful metropolis–all promised an endless supply of material objects. Yet absence reigned in the midst of plenty. The voice was here, but the living speaker was somewhere else, at the other end of the line, connected to us only by an incomprehensible technological network. A sense of impending death inhabited modernity: the past ticking away, the irrevocable dread of mortality. Le Corbusier's talk of funereal American gloom has already been noted. Elsewhere in *Cathedrals* he describes his visit to Radio City in New York to broadcast his talk over fifty stations the third day after his arrival in New York. There was a clock constantly ticking out the time. "I pointed out to my companion, Fernand Léger, 'Notice the needle that goes around so fast: it marks the seconds and nothing else. The clock beside it marks the hours. Small matter! The hours will return tomorrow. But the dial with the secondhand is something cosmic, it is time itself, which never returns. That red needle is material evidence of the movement of worlds.'"[70]

Oswald Spengler wrote in *The Decline of the West* (1919), "It is something beyond comprehension, this transformation of future into past, and thus time, in its contrast with space, has always a queer, baffling, oppressive ambiguity from which no serious man can wholly protect himself."[71] He characterized the rhetoric of modernism as "world-fear," which "runs through the form-language of every true artwork, every inward philosophy, every important deed.... Only the spiritually dead man of the autumnal cities...is able to evade it by setting up a secretless 'scientific world-view' between himself and the alien."[72] Modernity construed its history as everywhere traversed by discontinuity and rupture, absence and otherness, emptiness and blackness.[73] This lack of a future connected to a past, of an assured awareness of continuity and the power of tradition, marks modernism. The themes of death, the fears of mortality hide the deeper awareness of the end of history, of the reification of experience, of the mass of material objects devoid of value.[74] At this point we might recall Fosca's accusation that Le Corbusier resembled a *nouveau riche* who is surrounded by servants–i.e., wondrous machines–yet "in the depths of his soul, fears them." While damning Le Corbusier, Fosca was implicitly noting his awareness of the negative side of technological society.

IV. UNITED STATES: SALVIFIC CATASTROPHE

In a footnote at the very outset of the preface to *Cathedrals*, written in June of 1936, Le Corbusier declares that *Cathedrals* "is the fruit of fifteen years of work; it is dense; it is like a cellar filled with every kind of food. I have been reproached for it. Even today I am unable to preside over a polite drawing room where etiquette is queen."[75] Again, the contrast between the authentic and the over-refined. Le Corbusier is making no apologies. He is not going to follow the rules of polite discourse: he is down in the cellar cooking up a new infrastructure, and he intends to upset the reader. He repeats from *Precisions* the scene of a table after a meal has been completed–but this time the emphasis is on waste, leftovers to be eliminated:[76]

> I am going to show through the USA, taken as an example, that the times are new, but that its living quarters are uninhabitable. The table has not been cleared after dinner; the remains of a banquet have been allowed to lie in disorder after the departure of the guests: cold sauces, picked bones, wine spots, crumbs, and dirty silver scattered about.[77]

Thus he opens both *Precisions* and *Cathedrals* with food and a meal, but plays the figure differently each time. In both cases his ultimate concern, of course, is the equipping of society with adequate housing and masterful city plans.

Louis Marin has described the art of cooking as one of the languages of human culture by which cultures constitute themselves through differences and mutual oppositions.[78] Thus, rather than seeing the technological and financial superiority of the United States, especially New York, as a menace and challenge to Europe, Le Corbusier's constant comparisons retain France, especially Paris, as the center of distinction. Indeed, the centrality of Europe, France, and Paris have if anything increased since *Precisions*.

A recipe is a type of list: it includes not only a list of ingredients but also a list of rules to guide action. Together, these two lists entail a plan of action: a shopping list for the ingredients and a list of procedures to follow in preparing a dish intended for human consumption. Among the oldest lists are recipes for medicines, lists of instructions designed to relieve the ills of mankind.[79] Le Corbusier sets out his own recipe across the pages of *When the Cathedrals Were White*, following these with prescriptions of how to put these ingredients to use. Repetition not only allows him to draw up a list of comparisons, but allows him to convey the superabundance of American production through the accumulation of images.

"Yes, the cathedrals were white, completely white, dazzling and young," the book opens, "and not black, dirty, old."[80] And once again, in the present, things will be "young, fresh, new. Today also the world is beginning again."[81] Yet Manhattan is not simply the new beginning: it is a catastrophe. On one hand (Europe, cathedrals), there is the debris of the past; on the other (America, Manhattan), disorder and uncertainty caused by too-rapid development, too much change and instability, producing great waste. Thus the conceit that gives the book its title:

> The cathedrals belong to France, and Manhattan is American. What a good opportunity to consider this fresh twenty-year-old city against the background of one's awareness of the skyscrapers of God. This new place in the world, New York examined by a heart full of the sap of the Middle Ages. Middle Ages? That is where we are today: the world to be put in order, to be put in order on piles of debris, as was done once before on the debris of antiquity, when the cathedrals were white.[82]

Le Corbusier had already announced at the end of *Precisions* that he would travel to Manhattan in 1930, although he was

> afraid to face that field of hard labor, the land of selection in the violence of business, the hallucinating sites of out-and-out production....The USA is a Hercules, whose heart, it seems to me, is still timid and hesitant. We in Paris are drawers of essence, the creators of racing motors, the fanatics of pure equilibrium.[83]

After finally having traveled to the United States in 1935, he has not modified his position. Europeans are still older, wiser, full of the knowledge and expertise that will guide the youthful exuberance and uncertainty of the new world toward maturity, equilibrium, and measure. It is worthwhile, Le Corbusier proclaims, to take a trip to America to see reality, to understand that a page of history has turned.[84] There are things and places you have to see for yourself: elevators that work, doors that open and close automatically, Rockefeller Center, the George Washington Bridge, the dazzling lights of Broadway. Drawings will not suffice, neither will photography, nor literary evocations, "it is necessary *to have seen*."[85]

After his preface to *Cathedrals*, Le Corbusier sets the stage with a series of "Atmospheres." First, a chapter on the "Greatness of Things" fills out a list of what Europe represented "when the cathedrals were white."[86] Europe was organized into crafts, utilizing new techniques and creating an unexpected system of forms;[87] "wherever the white race was" it developed an international language, spreading ideas, culture, style, and "love of art, disinterestedness, joy of living in creating."[88] "White, limpid, joyous, clean, clear, and without hesitations, the new world was opening up like a flower among the ruins."[89] That is the image Le Corbusier wants the reader to retain: an image devoid of uncertainty, eyes turned from the past to look at the future, filled with the joy of new beginnings. A new beginning has opened again, and of course there will be a role in the *temps nouveaux* for the expert planner: "Eyes that see, persons with knowledge, they must be allowed to construct the new world."[90]

He drives his message home with repetition: "when the cathedrals were white," they were expressions of a "liberated spirit," for there were no academies to control thought. Everywhere art was direct and raw, witty and erotic, fearful and natural.[91] The people invented a French tongue, new words, a new language, and consequently, a new society. They sought the laws of harmony and turned their backs on the antique.[92] Paris became "the torch of the world." "The cathedrals were white, thought was clear, spirit was alive, the spectacle clean."[93]

After opening on this optimistic note, Le Corbusier turns to look with melancholy at the reality of the present, in a chapter entitled "Decadence of the Spirit."[94] He takes the same approach as in his by-then-famous book *Towards a New Architecture,* accumulating a series of aperçus as a résumé of arguments, his cellar storehouse of food to which he will return. Everywhere in the present he finds a failure of spirit, not as in the Middle Ages "when the cathedrals were white"; now money rules, architects look backward, they fear new methods and impose regulations. Yet he ends his "atmospheres" on a positive note: greatness lies with intentions, not in the mere size or scale of things. "When the cathedrals were white, the whole universe was raised up by an immense faith in the energy, the future, and the harmonious creation of a civilization."[95]

Having placed these travel writings under "the sign of the white cathedrals," Le Corbusier is prepared to open his book on the United States.[96] As any traveler must, he presents his credentials: he is an investigator of cities around the world who has revealed thousands of times his "dream" of opening the door on the future.[97] In his travels, he is constantly on the lookout for builders who reveal the same "tension, energy, tenacity and fidelity to a great idea" as did the masons who built the cathedrals.[98] This tension and energy are exampled by Buenos Aires, Moscow, Barcelona, Rome, and Algiers, but it is New York that captures his imagination. "I cannot forget New York, a vertical city, now that I have had the happiness of seeing it there, raised up in the sky."[99] His arrival at the city is a transcendent experience: when the *Normandie* stopped at quarantine, or so Le Corbusier told his audience a few days after his arrival in New York, he saw rising up in the morning fog "a fantastic almost mystic city and thought here is the temple of the

FIGURE 9.14: Giving a lecture at Princeton University on December 4, 1935, Le Corbusier illustrated his belief that Paris could learn from New York, and New York from Paris, if only a bridge were built. FIGURE 9.15: The skyscrapers of Manhattan were a challenge hurled at the Eiffel Tower and Notre Dame de Paris. Perhaps Descartes had been an American, for he seemed to understand its gridded pattern of streets.

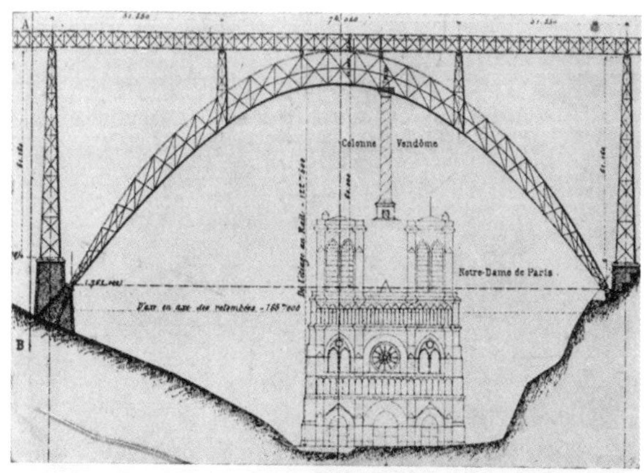

7. IS DESCARTES AMERICAN?

new world!"[100] The boat advanced and the apparition was transformed into an image of brutality and of unforgettable savagery (*inouie*). "This brutality and savagery do not displease me. It is thus that great enterprises begin: by strength."[101] Because America is in permanent evolution, animated by a unique potential found nowhere else in the world, it is capable, Le Corbusier feels, of being the first to realize its destiny and accept his gift, the "Radiant City."

> The world is undergoing one of the great metamorphoses of history. The collective and the individual collide instead of combining. Is a synthesis possible? Yes, in a program on a *human scale* and guided by *human wisdom*.[102]

Approaching the middle of the book, Le Corbusier begins a comparison, "France-America." "Let's work together," he urges. "Let's throw a bridge across the Atlantic."[103] [FIGURES 9.14 AND 9.15] The French "would enter into the spirit of the city quite readily, and we would speak to Americans not of 'our traditional, historic, and exquisite taste'"–the dead concerns of the academicians–"but of the things which trouble them and the things to which they aspire: wise conceptions of life. And, also, our celebrated 'measure' would not be an eternal restriction, but an active thing: 'You are strong, but we have reflected.'"[104]

He soon resumes this theme of salvific collaboration in a section at the center of the book entitled "Crescendo."[105] Here he again describes arriving in New York, seeing the "mystic city" for the first time. He is excited, he says, because he finds an architectural spirit in America, manifest in everything from skyscrapers to clothes, objects to interior decoration.[106] Not so in France, where restraint holds back, artists are pilloried, and the old cling to their accumulated treasures. "When the cathedrals were white, spirit was triumphant. But today the cathedrals of France are black and the spirit is bruised. The works of the new civilization are coming together in a symphonic crescendo. The guiding spirit is faltering. The young act, *but they do not know*."[107] New York ("the young") has gotten ahead of itself and cannot control its exuberance: "It is a titanic effort of organization and discipline in the midst of chaos...it is a kind of snorting monster, bursting with health, sprawled out at ease."[108] And this is where the wiser, older spiritual strength of the French comes to the fore: it must liberate itself from repression and guide the world, as it has done for two thousand years.[109]

> In this situation Cartesian reason could diagnose and suggest. I have a persistent feeling that France and America could exchange a solid handshake and do each other an infinite amount of good.[110]

He follows with a section critical of the École des Beaux-Arts in Paris, suggesting a position advocated by the neo-syndicalists for educational reforms in France.

> When the cathedrals were white, there were no governmental diplomas; the crafts (and architecture) were practiced regionally in terms of local resources of raw materials, climates, customs. Controls were worked out in the midst of jobs to be done, through corporation. Those corporations were not "Institutes." Small groups of foremen and masters supported by the respectful esteem of their comrades, passed judgment on the technical qualities of the young. It was a living procedure, on a human scale.[111]

Later, he returns to the theme of etiquette and respectability that holds France back, that determines that all remarks are refined, her great reserve of knowledge hidden under a veil of patina. He prefers instead to be raw, open, with the freedom to speak his mind, lessons he draws from the youthful exuberance of United States:

> When the cathedrals were white, the stone was raw from the blows of the axe or the chisel, the edges sharp, the features clean, the faces hard. Everything was new, discovery and creation; and stone after stone a civilization was growing. People were happy; they acted.... There were no Paris salons filled with literary talk, there was no.... Chicago Register.[112]

Transformation will happen, he says, when individuals reform their consciousness, and after considerable self-examination and inner reflection they in turn change the consciousness of the collectivity. That will occur only if some are daring risk-takers, ignoring what is polite and acceptable etiquette.

The book closes:

> A new age has begun. A new Middle Age. Through the blood and suffering of battles, we must observe the flawless unfolding of the creative work. The interior, the fabric, the nave of the cathedrals was purity itself, but the outside was organized like an army in battle, as hirsute as an army.[113]

LOVE AT FIRST SIGHT

Cathedrals, written in the spring of 1936, came at the end of a long list of books about New York written by other authors, most of which described the United States as a menace to the world. The list extends from J. Villani, *Paris, New York, Paris* (1928); C. Cazamian, *L'humour de New-York* (1929); F. Debat, *New York: images mouvantes* (1930); G. Duhamel, *Scènes de la vie future* (1930); Paul Morand, *New York* (1930); and J. Renand, *New York flamboie* (1931).[114] Instead of fearing New York, Le Corbusier sought to express his absolute fascination with speed and efficiency that had built this mountain of stone, to hold it out to the world as an exemplar of courage.

An important influence on his interpretation of New York was an essay by his companion Fernand Léger, published in *Cahiers d'Art* in 1931.[115] Léger opens by calling New York "the most colossal spectacle in the world, especially the spectacle of the city seen at night from the heights of a skyscraper." It is a "radical vision":

> I adore this overloaded spectacle, all that unrestrained vitality, the virulence that is there, even in mistakes. It's very young.[116]

> Destroy New York–it will be rebuilt completely differently.... What a magnificent job for an artillery barrage....The Americans would be the first to applaud, and then what would you see? A little later a new town could be built. Can you guess how? I'll give you the answer in thousands! In glass, in glass!...A transparent, translucent New York, with blue, yellow, and red floors! An unprecedented fairyland, the light unleashed by Edison streaming through all that and pulverizing the buildings.[117]
>
> [FIGURE 9.16]

For Le Corbusier, New York was literally love at first sight–even if not exactly a jejune or straightforward love. At least three times in *When the Cathedrals Were White*, he writes about the moment he first saw the skyline of Manhattan. The repetition itself underscores the

Finds American Skyscrapers 'Much Too Small'

Herald Tribune photo—Acme

Charles Edouard Le Corbusier, the famous French architect, with a model of his Villa Savoye, which he recently designed

Skyscrapers Not Big Enough, Says LeCorbusier at First Sight

French Architect, Here to Preach His Vision of 'Town of Happy Light,' Thinks They Should Be Huge and a Lot Farther Apart

FIGURE 9.16: The *New York Herald Tribune,* October 22, 1935, repeated Le Corbusier's proclamation: New York's skyscrapers are not big enough!

importance of first sight, making room for the hyperbole he deploys. And he admits: "I was in a mood for joking when I landed in America!"[118] At the beginning of the book he inserts a section from the radio talk he delivered the third day after his arrival on the *Normandie*, already quoted:

> Monday morning, when my ship stopped at Quarantine, I saw a fantastic, almost mystic city rising up in the mist. But the ship moves forward and the apparition is transformed into an image of incredible brutality and savagery. Here is certainly the most prominent manifestation of the power of modern times. This brutality and this savagery do not displease me. It is thus that great enterprises begin: by strength.[119]

In the pivotal "Crescendo" section, he writes again about his arrival, but now registers disappointment with both Manhattan and Paris:

> We saw the mystic city of the new world appear far away, rising up from Manhattan. It passed before us at close range: a spectacle of brutality and savagery. In contrast to our hopes the skyscrapers were not made of glass, but of tiara-crowned masses of stone. They carry up a thousand feet in the sky, a completely new and prodigious architectural event; with one stroke Europe is thrust aside, with its dimensions sophistically set by the resolutions of town councilors and "the force of our traditions."[120]

And finally, near the end of the book, he is again exuberant, in an extract from an article intended for *The American Architecture*:

> From Quarantine, the town appeared to me, in the morning haze, like the promised city–distant, azure and mother-of-pearl, with its spires thrust up toward the city. This is the Land of the New Times and this is its fantastic and mystic city: the temple of the New World!...I exclaimed to myself: "What brutality and what savagery!" But so much explosive force here in the hard geometry of disordered prisms did not displease me. Coming from France at the flat end of 1935, I had confidence.[121]

Prominent is the insistently recurrent dynamic of desire, (American) darkness, (French, or at least Le Corbusierian) clarity, the arrival of the confident savant, uniquely equipped to solve the "equation of reason and passion." It plays out in 1935 much as in 1929: the leap of desire at first sight, the insistent tropes of brutality, savagery, and primitive spirituality, the contrast of authentic (albeit unshaped) transcendence to "flat" France, Cartesian France. New York is not only hot jazz in stone and steel; it is Josephine Baker in stone and steel–or she is New York in flesh and blood–or both. It is also a passage that ties together his memory of his first sight of Athens in 1911, when his boat passed by the savage rock with its jewel, the Parthenon, and proceeded to quarantine. He was restrained for several days from going "up there," to pay his respects to the horrendous temple that would resonate its awesome truth to the end of his life. And it is reminiscent as well of his first sight of Constantinople, which was met with disappointment and equivocation, before he opened himself to its seductions. [FIGURES 9.17, 9.18, AND 9.19]

FIGURES 9.17, 9.18, AND 9.19: Sketches of the New York skyline from the Hudson River, during arrival and departure

V. "NEW YORK IS A CATASTROPHE."

Le Corbusier's follows his enamored arrival in New York with a dramatic, superficially contradictory announcement: what he saw was a catastrophe. There is, of course, no contradiction. It is precisely because the New World energy of New York is unshaped, brutal, that it needs its colonist-lover, Le Corbusier, to tame, shape, and civilize it (even as he needs to be rejuvenated by its primitive energy). Constantly comparing both New York and the United States to a young athlete too strong for his own good, an adolescent not yet in control of his body, or an acrobat who must achieve equilibrium or fail, Le Corbusier is able to create a role for the wisdom, knowledge, and ideas that flow from Europe.

> New York....is a catastrophe with which a too hasty destiny has overwhelmed courageous and confident people, though a beautiful and worthy catastrophe. Nothing is lost. Faced with difficulties, New York falters. Still streaming with sweat from its exertions, wiping off its forehead, it sees what it has done and suddenly realizes: "Well, we didn't get it done properly. Let's

> start over again!" New York has such courage and enthusiasm that everything can be begun again, sent back to the building yard and made into something still greater, something mastered! These people are not on the point of going to sleep. In reality, the city is hardly more than twenty years old, that is the city which I am talking about, the city which is vertical and on the scale of the new times.[122]

He compares this to the achievements of France and its *mission civilatrice* in Morocco. France sent its army to build both a network of roads and charming villages, but this only caused the Arab to raise his eyebrows in doubt and to hold out his hand for help. Unable to find a teacher or guide, the Arab refused to respect France with any conviction.[123] The message is poignantly clear: France must be wiser when applying its reserve of knowledge and deploying its mission to civilize in the New World.

"New York is an event of worldwide importance." Twenty years ago, Europeans would not accept this, but now they admit that

> New York, strong, proud of itself, in prosperity or in depression is like an open hand above our heads. An open hand which tries to knead the substance of today. New York has a style, has style, is mature enough to have acquired style. There are not just ragged things there; there is quality....The people, the shops, the products, the architecture, have achieved a character which is grand, intense, and healthy. It is full of life; they are places of robust life. The Place de l'Opéra in Paris is no longer anything but a relic.[124]

It is impossible to know the city or the United States as a whole, for they both are too large, but from an airplane a traveler like Le Corbusier can understand more clearly the enormity of this urban agglomeration. "You get the idea of catastrophe, urban catastrophe–harassed life of men, women, and children; the sections in which human wastes stagnate."[125] There is, in addition, another even more fascinating, ethereally beautiful catastrophe, "the fairy catastrophe: Manhattan, a city of skyscrapers, a vertical city."[126] The airplane view, which was also so revelatory to Le Corbusier in South America, allows him to see Manhattan as a fish swimming in the Hudson and East rivers with its backbone along Fifth Avenue and its lateral bones the side streets:[127]

> The fins along the two flanks represent the most perfect disposition of forms for a mercantile port. When you see it from a plane you think: Manhattan is a type-area for a modern city; the range of banks sheltered from the sea has the purity of a theorem.[128]

This purity, however, is not unstained:

> But now look at it on foot, along the avenue which skirts the river; the docks and ships form the teeth of a comb as far as you can see. The arrangement is clear, logical, perfect; nevertheless, it is hideous, badly done, and incongruous; the eye and the spirit are saddened. What could have been a communal enterprise, ordered in a serene and monumental unity, what could have been an endless jewel case for those marvels: liners or freighters—everything lacks order, everything has been badly constructed in the worst parts and even in the best ones. It was done by rapacious money-grubbers. This fringe along the water, around the whole periphery of Manhattan, is nothing but dirty scum.[129]

It is necessary to make a fresh start, to reconstruct the docks for loading and unloading, to build an elevated highway along the waterfront, to plan "a necklace of useful architecture around the city."[130] Within this ring, for the present, skyscrapers thrust upwards toward the sky, producing "an architectural accident." Proportion is violated:

> Imagine a man undergoing a mysterious disturbance of his organic life: the torso remains normal, but his legs become ten to twenty times too long. Thus the torso of normal houses set in normal plots of ground has suddenly been raised up on an unexpected support. They have become lost in an abstract tangle of calculations.... the result has been catastrophe.[131]

A hundred times he thought: "New York is a catastrophe, and fifty times: it is a beautiful catastrophe."[132]

Yet on a cold, clear night, on a rooftop balcony overlooking the city, New York is

> a Milky Way come down to earth; you are in it. Each window, each person, is a light in the sky. At the same time a perspective is established by the arrangement of the thousand lights of each

> skyscraper; it forms itself more in your mind than in the darkness perforated by illimitable fires. The stars are part of it also—the real stars—but sparkling quietly in the distance. Splendor, scintillation, promise, proof, act of faith, etc. Feeling comes into play; the action of the heart is released; crescendo, allegro, fortissimo. We are charged with feeling, we are intoxicated; legs strengthened, chest expanded, eager for action, we are filled with a great confidence.... Everything is there, and it is real.[133]

But he gives the wheel yet another spin: even amidst such beauty, he must label Manhattan a "fairy catastrophe." He explains that upon seeing an album of photos of New York entitled *The Magical City* displayed in the windows of Scribners, he began to argue within himself whether it was true or not, finally deciding to replace it with *The Fairy Catastrophe.*

> That is the phrase that expresses my emotion and rings within me in the stormy debate which has not stopped tormenting me for fifty days: hate and love.
>
> For me the fairy catastrophe is the lever of hope.[134]

Thus he is able to write fantastic fairy stories about acrobats and giants, cowboys and gladiators, in order to describe the skyscrapers of New York and the American problem of unrestrained exuberance. Yet the most captivating allusion is to the cluster of jewels on a queen's tiara that the nocturnal festival spreads out.

> No one can imagine it who has not seen it. It is a titanic mineral display, a prismatic stratification shot through with an infinite number of lights, from top to bottom, in depth, in a violent silhouette like a fever chart beside a sick bed. A diamond, incalculable diamonds.[135]

THE GREAT WASTE

New York is not alone in either its grandeur or its catastrophic messiness. Throughout *Cathedrals*, Le Corbusier repeats the refrain of "the great waste" of American cities, sprawled out across great regions into suburbs and garden cities or crowded densely into the great wastelands of slums. It is a criticism that can be applied to European cities as well, but is more apparent in the United States.[136] He repetitively writes about a whole people rushing to and fro in eternal and sterile movement, eradicating nature as they push into the suburbs, spreading transportation networks, building water, gas, electricity, and telephone systems at great expense. He calls Grand Central a "magic station" but nevertheless a "tumor of the great American waste," for it is the head of the gigantic expanse of Connecticut suburbs.[137] He admires Ford for producing an inexpensive and mass-produced automobile, but it has led to an abuse of speed, travel, and standardization.

In the first century of the machine age (1830 to 1930, approximately, in Le Corbusier's reckoning), cities were built for money, not for men. They are an illness, a cancer, a great waste, and they have cut the family in two.[138] Men spend their entire day in the city, where "it's advertising and competition–a battle," while women are at home alone for twelve hours of the day. "How are such different voltages to go together in unity? They are not in harmony....I have the feeling that in general these men and women, in spite of all their good will, have difficulty in communicating with each other....Every day there is a kind of distance between them, a trench....Thus the 'great waste' is paid for in a cruel way."[139] As we see below, this does not exhaust Le Corbusier's views on American sexuality.

Because the American businessman commutes long hours by train, he fills the wasted time by inventing monumental newspapers composed of multiple sections–another great waste.[140] Le Corbusier has a grudge against American newspapers–filled with advertisements, pictorial supplements, and stories about gangsters, they even rearrange the truth. As a city planner he understands the "weight of the modern paper, then, is a direct function of urban discomfort."[141] He is ambivalent about American advertising, whether or not it is a cancer, but believes it both a product and producer of great waste.[142] Its origin lies, he believes, in the great size of the country, necessitating extraordinary means to inform the population that this product exists, and that an antidote is available, and so a battle ensues. Page after page of newspapers are filled with extravagant claims for food or aids to digestion.

> It was hardly worth while to free the Negroes in the 1860s, since there are dreadful new hidden chains which fetter life to the point of breaking the family cell: American hard work, their effervescence, the fabulous machinery of skyscrapers, telephones, the press, all of that is used to produce wind and to chain men to a hard destiny.[143]

If Le Corbusier were in charge, he would forbid advertising that lacks interest and charm. Huge posters erected alongside the highway, with their images of cellophaned food and exuberantly healthy young men and women, create too many mirrored reflections or reduplications. "M. Ingres, raising his finger, said to his students: 'Gentlemen, reflections are unworthy of great art.'"[144] In contrast, Paris has enjoyed posters since 1890, but they are remarkable frescoes full of wit and plasticity.

> But on the other hand I cannot pass by the luminous advertising on Broadway. Everyone has heard about that incandescent path cutting diagonally across Manhattan in which the mob of idlers and patrons of motion pictures, burlesque shows and theaters moves. Electricity reigns, but it is dynamic here, exploding, moving, sparkling, with lights turning white, blue, red, green, yellow. The things behind it are disappointing. These close-range constellations, this Milky Way in which you are carried along, lead to objects of enjoyment which are often mediocre. So much the worse for advertising! There remains a nocturnal festival characteristic of modern times. I remember that the light filled our hearts, and that the intense, powerful color excited us and gave us pleasure. And on Broadway, divided by feelings of melancholy and lively gaiety, I wander along in a hopeless search for an intelligent burlesque show in which the nude white bodies of beautiful women will spring up in witty flashes under the paradisiacal illumination of the spotlights.[145]

LOVES AND HATES

Le Corbusier's love affair with New York and America is almost stereotypically stormy. He wants to declare "I am an American," yet from the moment he saw the vertical city of New York projected violently into the sky, it was a scene he both hated and loved.[146] He is offended at this blow to human hope and the diminution of life it entails; every day for two months, his heart is torn between hate and love for this new world; hours of despair spent over the violence of the city, hours of enthusiasm over its fairy splendor.[147] He could praise its infrastructure–the Holland Tunnel, the Pulaski Skyway, the George Washington Bridge, Grand Central station, even Central Park–and yet struggled to establish balance between hopelessness and hope.[148]

> The American is a Janus: one face absorbed by the anxieties of adolescence, looking toward the troubles of his consciousness; the other face as solid as an Olympic victor's, looking toward an old world which at certain moments he believes he can dominate.[149]

Upon his return to Paris, he realizes he had pushed it aside while listening to the clamor of the United States. He experienced hate and love in New York; now he feels shame and delight in Paris. It is not grand in scale, not built in the workyard of modern times, but nevertheless has harmony in the smallest details and in the grand ensemble. Manhattan holds no threat to Paris, for lying dormant within his beloved Paris there is a "sense of proportion which will master the new tasks and establish itself in the city in new and triumphant prisms."[150] Paris is a metonym for that European "sense of proportion," that corrected taste, which Le Corbusier believes will educate the appetite, tame and free the savage energies of the new lands as it will reorganize the old.

Comparisons continue: like the appetites associated with food and eroticism, Le Corbusier's urbanism thrives on repeated rhythms of approach and withdrawal, deferral and satisfaction, refusal and acceptance. He admires the efficient installations in New York skyscrapers: their banks of elevators, restaurants, bars, showrooms, barber shops, dry-goods store, and post offices. And he thrills over the office equipment, from telephones to telegraphs, radios to pneumatic tubes. Compared to this, business offices in Paris are mediocre, even wretched and miserable. "Already in New York Rockefeller Center affirms to the world the dignity of the new times by its useful and noble halls, just as the skyscraper of Howe and Lescaze does in Philadelphia."[151]

Another reversal: Europe is afraid of building tall structures, fearing what will happen if they lose contact with the ground. Yet Le Corbusier waxes enthusiastic over the feeling of space that skyscrapers allow. Not only do elevators work, and with speed deliver you to great heights, but his

> myopic eyes easily, even very clearly, grasp the activities in the street–people, cars in movement. In offices on the sixty-fifth floor (about five hundred and eight-five feet), this feeling of security persists. There is joined to it a joyous and exalting sensation of space, extent, freedom, which I had always imagined, and

> which I enjoy here to the fullest degree. There is no feeling of dizziness.[152]

INFERIORITY COMPLEXES AND AMERICAN SEXUALITY

Amid these oscillating comparisons, Le Corbusier frequently restates his belief that Americans may be serious improvisers, even tenacious about their ideas, but have yet to taste the joys of thought: thought turned into a line of conduct, thought achieved in maturity.[153] He believes they suffer from "inferiority complexes." They have imposed great discipline on their individual morality, but this "inner discipline clashes painfully with the voracity of their gigantic collective enterprise." And again, the central armature or guiding thesis of Le Corbusier's treatment of the Americas: "In Europe—we have been trained in thinking for a long time. We have humanized the foundations of man's condition. In this matter we are the strongest."[154]

Inferiority, distorted sexuality, and morbidity are all, as Le Corbusier represents them, symptomatic of America's maladjusted, imbalanced urbanism. The city shapes sexuality, sexuality goes up on display in the city (recall Le Corbusier's "hopeless search for an intelligent burlesque show" on the streets of New York), and sexuality determines the invisible architecture of intimate relationships, what Le Corbusier calls "the key of everything: the family."[155] Therefore the alert observer, he whose taste is good, whose desire is educated, who has been "trained in thinking for a long time," can diagnose an entire society from the street, from the window of a hotel room or the observatory deck of a skyscraper. He remarks on the girls of Vassar, whom he finds devoted to studying the black paintings of Caravaggio and the even more funereal works of the Surrealists. These strange unveilings allow Le Corbusier, he says, to diagnose the American soul: Americans are obsessed with inferiority complexes and gripped by a funereal spirit.[156] The appeal of Caravaggio "reveals…a complex disturbance and the anxieties of sexual life."[157] Suddenly Le Corbusier can explain why the grandeur of skyscrapers appears in this land of timid people, why suburbs spread horizontally across the land with no rationality:

> In its gigantomachy American city planning betrays a timidity which is a hazard at the very moment when it would be desirable to react and act rightly; it is the result of a lack of equilibrium, of unbalance, and it carries with it rather serious disturbances of the core of the social cell—the key of everything: the family.[158]

Le Corbusier moves on to comment about a costume ball that he attended, the Quartz Ball in New York. He finds that the American male, when pulled away from work that devours him, "talks freely about his inferiority complex"–driven by his awareness of the thinking, appraising European mind with which he is confronted:

> Each time I am embarrassed by that gesture of humility; I see an erect Manhattan, the drives of Chicago, Ford in Detroit, and so many clear signs of youthful power. They seem to see a flash of steel in our glance and, behind our foreheads, a well-oiled chain of tests, appraisals, judgments. Certainly we reflect, we weigh, we try to see where things are going.[159]

It all goes back to sex: because of the great waste of American cities, where men spend long hours at work and women live isolated lives in the suburbs, the American woman had developed into a dominating and magnificent type that must be worshipped like a fetish. The two sexes have lost complete contact with each other. That, for Le Corbusier, seems to explain why Americans adore little blondes in the movies, have invented the "vamp" (a woman who openly exploits men using her sexuality), and why magnificent wax manikins in the shop windows of Fifth Avenue

> make women masters, with conquering smiles. Square shoulders, incisive features, sharp coiffure...The manikins in the windows have the heads of Delphic goddesses. Green, lamp-black, red hair. Antique-like heads, here one as if from a tragedy, there one like a Caryatid, Athenas from the Acropolis Museum. Polychromy. When polychromy appears it means that life is breaking out.
>
> Next door I note the funereal entrances of the Empire State Building.[160]

Le Corbusier knows that this dominating type is an ideal, but he believes American women do have the need to be adored and turned into fetishes because they (like the men) suffer from inferiority complexes. "Consequence: idols on pedestals, fervor–magnificent wax manikins."[161] In the tragedy of the great American waste, the contrasts are epic: Americans may be champions in business, but not in life.[162]

VI. ANALYSIS, COMPARISON, CONCLUSIONS

Madge Bacon claims that both *Precisions* and *Cathedrals* are "vigorously didactic and indulgently polemical."[163] *Cathedrals*, she points out, builds on themes introduced in *Precisions*. Both books reveal increasing interest in the vernacular and regional; both are anti-academy, pro-authority, and for the power of the state, offering design strategies based on aesthetics, poetry, and mechanization to solve social problems. Both extend CIAM discussions (1928–33), although *Precisions* is less concerned with social and political issues. Yet *Cathedrals* reveals evolution in Le Corbusier's thinking about the new cultures of the Americas. More specifically, Bacon argues, Le Corbusier's "bittersweet" account of his trip to the United States, an assemblage of ambivalent impressions, is the result of arriving in America armed with a number of stereotypical assumptions about its culture and society drawn from the pre–World War I ideology of *américanisme*. He arrived believing that America would be a model modern culture and a catalyst for change, but reality crushed his expectations, left him distraught. In addition, the trip produced no new commissions.

Moreover, Bacon places a different emphasis on Le Corbusier's comparison between New York and Paris than made here:

> Even though he frequently alluded to distinctions between New York City and Paris, he did not pose them in that antinomic relationship. Rather, his intention was to find common ground between them to advance his Radiant City. Yet he still used the polemical methods of his European counterparts. He pitted America's decadence, a consequence of capitalism, against its virtues and possibilities for redemption precisely because it was the youngest and freest of countries.[164]

I suggest, however, that Le Corbusier drew sharp comparisons intentionally between New York and Paris, feeling secure about his adopted homeland. He apparently experienced the same shock on first sight of Constantinople (1911), Algiers (1931), and New York (1935), for none of these cities matched those of his imagination. The shock made him most vulnerable, desiring a return to common ground before opening his heart to newer and deeper impressions, allowing the site to become a source of creation and invention. While he may have been dismayed by the reckless economy that produced the Great Depression, he was far from crushed by his firsthand experience of this marvelous city on the banks of two rivers. As in Algiers, he crowns the city with a sparkling tiara, stimulating his eye to create new forms.

Remember that Le Corbusier was the master chef, spreading enticing dishes before his audience. He knew his food for thought was not a normal affair, that his audience must be coaxed to sample his dishes, But he was secure that his cuisine had been prepared by careful thought, proportioned and balanced. It is to educate the taste and desires of the young in the New World that he has come bringing the gift of his knowledge carefully prepared over decades. Yet his first contact was not devoid of influence on the architect-planner in search of commissions; he found the physical infrastructure, the mechanical devices of skyscrapers, up to his expectations, and was totally enamored by the nocturnal festival of light the city produced–its titillating tiara. Yet Paris is always the winner in his comparisons, and the Parisian–more mature, wiser, knowledgeable–retains his title of conqueror-educator-civilizer.

NEO-SYNDICALISM, REGIONALISM, FOLKLORE

Precisions and *Cathedrals* must be viewed against Le Corbusier's involvement with the neo-syndicalist publications *Plans* and *Prélude,* and with the "spirit of the thirties," which he so obviously embraced. This spirit, which young intellectuals expressed in a variety of new publications was one of revolt: refusing politics, being neither left nor right.[165] The neo-syndicalists wanted to reform men of authority and governmental institutions, educate youth to be constructive, promote world peace, and plan the economy.[166] Interested in speaking to a younger generation that appeared more appreciative of his work than the academies and other authorities, Le Corbusier assumes the "young"–including South America and the United States–need guidance from those with experience and expertise–the role, as we have seen, that he consistently assumes for himself. He is not only an adventurer who travels to exotic realms in search of new experiences, but an architectural and planning expert with a constructive message to sell. This is the transformation that he has undergone since his youthful pilgrimages to Constantinople and Greece.

In an article written in August of 1935, "L'autorité devant les tâches contemporaines" ("Authority before contemporary tasks"), Le Corbusier says he believes that authority, when faced with contemporary issues, needs clairvoyance. He understands that the world is troubled, disorderly, that its equilibrium has been broken by the Depression, so that the future appeared unsupportable. Consequently the authorities–those in power, be they captains of industry or men in government–must be taught to see clearly, become agile, and live in the movement of time. This recalls his dedication, twenty years earlier, of *La Construction des Villes* to "the authorities"–government officials and architects (see Chapter 4). Le Corbusier's cultural top-downism, in which the role of Europe (especially France, especially Paris) is to educate the taste of the callow peoples, is thus paralleled by institutional top-downism: he does not seek to create a mass movement directly, to transform the desires of the *demos* that can then be implemented through bottom-up institutions, but to convert the decision-makers, the authorities, that relatively tiny elite that already holds power. This elitism is also evidenced in the dedication of *L'Esprit Nouveau* to the elite men in control of corporations and government administrations, and to the authorities who could implement wise city plans.

When an event is absolutely transforming, overturning the established equilibrium, then revolution must enter into the very body of authority as well, or so Le Corbusier argued. Only such acts usher in something absolutely new.[167] In *Precisions,* Le Corbusier was content to offer his advice through a series of lectures, developing astonishing plans once he had left. But in the United States the situation was more severe. He was impressed with the manner American businessmen made clear decisions, acting quickly and sincerely in matters concerning their enterprises, but he could not understand why they lacked a "directive line" in public affairs, where decisions were made slowly and with great uncertainty. The European knew better and was stronger.

Yet Le Corbusier cannot be written off as just another pith-helmeted cultural imperialist. On the contrary, as we have seen in our discussion of *L'Art Décoratif d'aujourd-hui* (*The Decorative Arts of Today,* 1925) in Chapter 7, he frets over the breakup of regional cultures and folklores under the pressures of industrialization, modern transport, and modern communications. From at least 1925 onward, his writings, published and unpublished, show a deeper, more nuanced interest in such cultures and folklores, be they of France, Algeria, Greece, South America, or the United States. Recall, too, that in "La Maison Individuelle" ("The Individual House," 1939, discussed in Chapter 8), he fused folklore and regionalism with the qualities of the ideal house. During this period of the 1930s he begins his study of the synthesis of arts and augments his private collection of objects. There are new experiments with photomurals and aggressive color schemes. And he

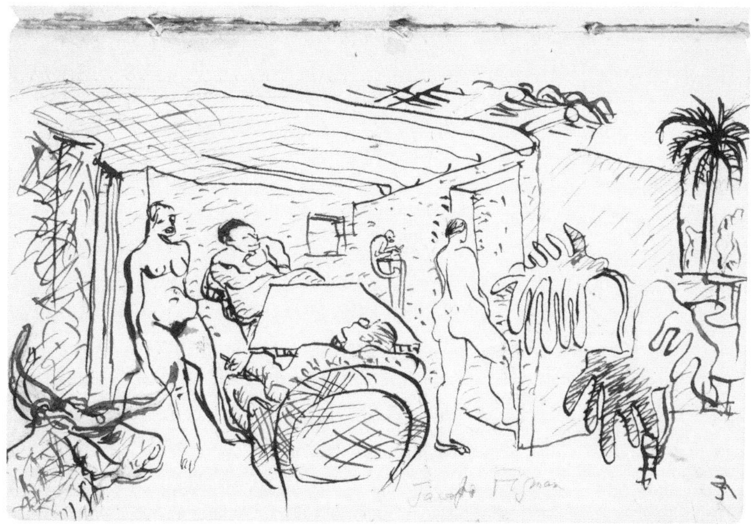

FIGURE 9.20: Le Corbusier enjoyed himself on his travels to South America, as this witty sketch depicts—a primitive hut, male companionship, and nude females in a tropical climate (1929).

is increasingly ambivalent about the influence of modern means of transport and whether they will eradicate local patois, customs, and folklores.

In an unpublished anecdote from his 1929 trip to South America he tells a witty tale about a lunch given in his honor at the Copacabana.[168] In the middle of the round table was a vase of orchids, and he remarked on the loveliness of the flowers. A host replied they were indeed beautiful, rare, and extremely costly because they came from England. Le Corbusier was astonished: to be in the tropics where orchids grow on tree trunks in nearby forests, and yet it was believed necessary to import these flowers from a land filled with fogs and greenery! Nor was that the end of the surprises, because suddenly someone exclaimed "M. Le Corbusier, here is a taste that you have never had in your life" The sommelier approached the table and presented a bottle of wine for Le Corbusier's examination. He read the label and was flabbergasted to see "Neuchâtel," a wine that he had tasted during twenty years of his youth. "Allow me, I said, to take five of these orchids for Josephine Baker who stays at the same hotel. I traveled with her since Buenos-Aires. We are excellent friends!"[169] [FIGURE 9.20]

This is an anecdote full of unresolved contradictions. He is at a table eating, like the table that opened the pages of *Precisions*, but there is no mention of the inherent need to order the debris, nor the desire and fulfillment that food elicits. He avoids mentioning that he, the urbanist, would clear away the clutter of life arising from patterns of need and fulfillment. Instead he is critical of his hosts importing of European flowers and wine, even though this evidence of "European taste" is the same educated taste he wants his American audience to accept in order to tame their bestial and youthful energy and accept his proposals of change. And even more contradictory is his gesture to offer some of these hothouse flowers to Josephine Baker. Perhaps he is ironically gesturing toward her own posturing of royalty, as artificial as those of his South American hosts. There is a deep contradiction in the heart of this anecdote: how can the European/French/Parisian genius impose his ideas on boisterous young cultures without homogenizing those cultures, or reducing them to an adored "provincial status"?

It is clear that Le Corbusier is looking for cultural authority over his host countries, but the exercise of that power produces contradictory effects. He adores the machine, but also the ethnographically particular. Thus he holds an ambivalent feeling for modern modes of transportation, producing cultural homogenization he abhors. A lament on the early stages of what we now call globalization made it into the pages of *Precisions*:

> Came the telegraph, the telephone, steamships, airplanes, the radio, and now television. A word said in Paris is with you in a fraction of a second! The long intercontinental transfers that were based on an annual rhythm now obey hourly schedules. Crowds of emigrants cross the seas, new states are born, made of a mixture of all races and peoples: the USA or your country. One generation is enough for this lightning alchemy. Airplanes go everywhere; their eagle eyes have searched the deserts and penetrated the rain forest. Hastening interpenetration, the railway, the telephone unceasingly run the country into the city, the city into the country.[170]

As a result of this "interpenetration," regional cultures have been erased, and a sense of homogenization created instead. Through multiple communication devices, you can know, hear, and see all landscapes and songs of the world. Knowledge of the world has expanded exponentially, but simultaneously it eradicates all mystery:

> You have seen the blocks of ice of the North Pole close up.
> And the locomotive has brought you the suits of London and the fashions of Paris. You [i.e., the South Americans] are wearing bowlers![171]

Le Corbusier's interest in ethnography was influenced by his friendship with Georges Henri Rivière, who entered the museological scene in 1928 with an exposition of pre-Columbian art at the Musée des Arts Décoratifs and soon became an assistant to Paul Revit, director of the Musée d'Ethnographie.[172] Between 1928 and 1935, Revit and Rivière made twenty-five expeditions to Africa accompanied by an array of ethnographers, apprentices, and photographers. They adopted Marcel Mauss's advice, suggesting that a box of preserves represents a society better than beads, no matter how beautiful, or stamps, no matter how rare. Their aim was the presentation of a civilization in its totality: not just artistic productions, but everyday objects and techniques, tools, industries, food preparation, customs, finery, costumes, ritual objects, and legal rules. Le Corbusier's travel writings reflect their doctrine that ordinary, everyday objects and events tell more about a culture than artifacts of high artistic pretension.

Le Corbusier was sufficiently interested in Rivière's plans for reorganizing the Musée d'Ethnographie to write a letter to Rivet on October 7, 1935, expressing his desire to collaborate in the project.[173] He explained that it was not a matter of architectural work, but a question of the *mise en scène* of works of art to be seen from different points of view. While Rivet might be involved with scientific classifications, Le Corbusier was more interested in the material aspects of objects, and believed he had the aesthetic competence and correct love of works of art to be able to create the proper atmosphere for each of the objects on display. He was sure that he could create a presentation that would astonish and ravish the spectator. Rivet replied in December that the plans for the Musée d'Ethnographie ought to be based solely on a scientific classification of objects, and that this extended as well to their presentation to the public; while he was sure that Le Corbusier could give to the objects an incomparable "atmosphere," nevertheless the intent of the museum directors was more austere. They held no other desire than to modestly evoke the reality surrounding these objects.[174]

Le Corbusier's South American travel writings can be read as inquiries into the lyrical materiality of objects and the magical *mise en scène* of cities, such as the rocks and bays of Rio de Janeiro that fired Le Corbusier with enthusiasm, or the soil of São Paulo, red as embers, or the transparent blue sky that hung over Buenos Aires with its myriad of stars. Yet he alleged in 1929 that this lyrical enthusiasm had nothing to do with South America itself, but with his own state of mind, his happiness and pleasure, while voyaging across the continent.[175]

Traces of his pen and pencil, an imprint of his imagination leaving marks on the map–these travel writings are attempts to make the sites he visited, the objects he studies, the events he experiences, "visible" to the reader–a feast for the eyes, food for thought. He blends the documentary with the visionary, deploys frequent hyperbole, and allows the repetition of clichés to offer stability as he travels about.[176] Change, evolution, transmutation, and transformation are, after all, his favored clichés; they are what he expects of the New World and form the moving backdrop of everything he sees. Yet the jaguars are elusive, and there are no neat beginnings or endings to his travel writings, nor are his points of view unified into linear narrations. They belong to that curious class of writings that exist to vex the reader, to elicit and educate desire–that is, appetite–by provoking and destabilizing rather than tabulating and fact-mongering. Its tables are, by intention, the gracefully cluttered surfaces of a commonplace restaurant where life is authentic.

And no matter where Le Corbusier travels, it is a question of offering the people of the *temps nouveaux*, the second machine era, housing that meets their needs and answers the great wastage of cities. Having returned from the United States, he tells his Parisian audience in a radio talk that America had established two significant coefficients: they have halved the selling price of an automobile since World War I, but the construction index has risen two and a half times higher, thus five times higher than the automobile index. Urbanism has escaped being industrialized, and this evasion has made the purchase price of a house so costly that no one is interested in constructing housing. "A house became a type of myth."[177] But if the house were constructed in factories where machines are produced, if it was considered to be a consumer item like an automobile, not an object of vanity, then its cost index would fall from five to one. Efficiency of industrial production would enable housing to be a benefit to the entire society and make rational cities, villages, and farms the norm, not a dream. In consequence, as a bonus, it would solve the economic crisis of the Depression.[178]

This is Le Corbusier's fundamental message in both sets of travel writings: that the Americas offer a "lever" of stimulation, of hope, of fruitful deeds;[179] that the energy, innovative spirit, exuberance of the "new world" must be tamed and educated to achieve the wisdom of maturity and knowledge of Europe; that contact with the "primitive," ingestion of its strength and consumption of its vitality, a cultural cannibalism of the noble foe, will restore whatever crisis of spirit Europeans may suffer:

> That France, because it [is] artistic and Cartesian, is a guiding lighthouse everywhere....that the USA is the great motor of the modern world, that....a sublime order will be the result of assimilations and...greatness will be a lever for yet unknown poetry–that the cities of the world, and in particular the cities of the countries known as "old," could become not the museums of a beauty that was revolutionary in its time, but irresistible generators of mass enthusiasms, of collective actions, of common joy, of pride, and consequently of widespread human happiness.[180]

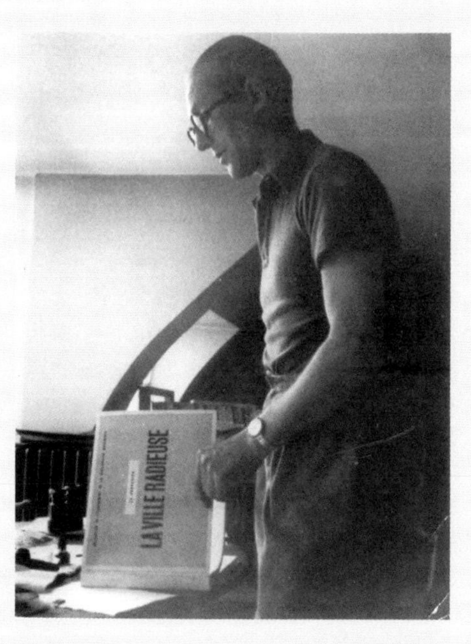
LA VILLE RADIEUSE

PART 4
The Second Machine Age of the Temps Nouveaux (1930–47)

CHAPTER 10
THE JANUS-FACED THIRTIES

What we have created leads us where we do not know, do not want to go.... The world has never had less of an idea of where it is going.

—PAUL VALÉRY, 1932

I. THE SPIRIT OF THE THIRTIES

Although France was not hit by economic depression until 1931, the collapse of the American stock market in October 1929 set the intellectual milieu of Paris in flux. New journals edited by young intellectuals poured out between 1929 and 1932. Deploying similar vocabulary and ideas, these questioned the decadence and agony of France, indeed of the world, and set out to establish a new order.[1] *Esprit*, edited by Emmanuel Mounier; *Combat* and *L'Homme nouveau*, under the editorial control of Jean-Pierre Maxence; *L'ordre nouveau*, by Robert Aron and Arnaud Dandieu; and *Plans*, by Philippe Lamour, were a few of these new journals. Although leaning in different ideological directions, they expressed a common "spirit of the thirties." A participant of the movement, Denis de Rougement, spoke in December 1932 of "a common cause of the young French":

> It seems that the solidarity of peril creates among us a unity that neither teachers nor doctrines could have done, a unity of refusal in the face of the disheartening misery of an epoch when all that an individual can love and desire is cut off from its living origins, stained, denatured, inverted, diminished. Some groups, such as *Ordre nouveau, Combat, Esprit, Plans, Réaction*, proclaim a rupture, and still more through their constructive actions will perhaps reveal, in their diversity, the first lines of a new French revolution.[2]

These new reviews refused to accept the society in which they lived: the political game, parliamentary life, political parties. The state was suspect and capitalism the cause of economic crisis, yet Fascism and Bolshevism seemed no better. There was a total crisis of civilization, a crisis of spirit and will, of economic misery and pauperization, which required a complete rupture with the status quo, a new cultural revolution. They sought a third way, a future modern, humane, and free of the centralized state. Production would be subservient to consumption, and the State subordinated to man in his natural groups or communes. The word *plan* became one of the most stylish words of the early 1930s, followed by *order, spirit, humanism, surpassing, revolution*, and *renaissance*.

The rise of both international Fascism and Communism was as important as economic depression in the formation of the "spirit of the thirties." The young intellectuals shared a fundamental position: "neither left nor right" for politics, "neither Moscow nor Washington" as an economic model.[3] These editors, all in their early twenties in 1930, were a different generation from those who had fought in World War I; they were pacifists, and wanted nothing to do with the myopic politics of the old combatants or the honor and glory they reaped. And they wanted to act–not just to think and to write about the problems of humanity. Studying the experience of the left and right abroad, they hoped to adapt these positions to the conditions of France. France needed a new mission, one worthy of the revolution of 1789. They spoke of alternative directions, of rejuvenation, renewal, renovation, and the discovery of new ways to transcend crisis and disorder.

Le Corbusier was older than this younger generation–forty-three years old in 1930–yet he spoke the same language of humanism, revolution, and unity, and also hewed to "neither left nor right." Perhaps he even adhered to the "spirit of the thirties" longer than the others because it bolstered his own belief in an alternative future, a *temps nouveaux*, or second machine age, such as he believed had begun in 1930. Searching in that troubled decade for a solution to the great problems of the century, he was certain that urbanism was a key element in the solution.

Thus we find Le Corbusier, during the first half of the 1930s, on the editorial boards of several periodicals, suggesting ways to overcome the deadlock of the capitalist crisis of overproduction and underconsumption, and respond to both Fascism and Communism.[4]

Between January of 1931 and April of 1932, Le Corbusier published sixteen articles in the review *Plans*, which was published by Jeanne Walter with Philippe Lamour as editor-in-chief and an editorial board composed of Le Corbusier, the Sorelian Hubert Lagardelle, the businessman Françoise de Pierrefeu, and the surgeon Pierre Winter.[5] This "group of six," as they called themselves, oversaw *Plans* from January 1931 to September 1932. Each issue of about one hundred pages contained an editorial position paper entitled "La Ligne Générale" ("The General Line") followed by three sections, the first containing articles by the editorial board, the second commentary on the arts and reviews of cultural events, especially cinema, and the third essays portraying economic, political, and scientific "facts." Printed on expensive paper with photographs, *Plans* looked for evidence of progress toward a new order from sports to machinery, housing to culture. Its slogan proclaimed: "Against war it is necessary to construct Europe. *Plans* wants institutions of a modern world, a constructive youth, organized peace, rational economy."[6] Many of the articles that Le Corbusier wrote for *Plans* would be republished as chapters of *The Radiant City* in 1935.[7]

Le Corbusier next joined the editorial board of *Prélude: organe mensuel du comité central d'action régionaliste et syndicaliste* (Lagardelle, Pierrefeu, and Winter) in the publication of sixteen issues from January 15, 1933, to July/August 1936.[8] *Prélude* appeared in newsprint and was a brief eight pages. Its message, displayed in bold slogans, aphorisms, and brief directives, was professedly aimed at men of authority, those responsible for solving society's manifold crises. Of the thirteen articles Le Corbusier wrote for this periodical between 1933 and 1934, seven would also form chapters of *The Radiant City*. In addition, the "group of six" joined Pierre Ganivet in the publication of *L'Homme Réel: Revue du syndicalisme et de l'humanisme* beginning in December 1933. Essays written by Le Corbusier for this review would be reissued in the first section of *The Radiant City*.

Although *L'Homme Réel* was, like most of the other new reviews, politically neutral in the early 1930s, after February 1934, when bloody riots broke out in Paris between the right and left, it became increasingly difficult for anyone to remain apolitical. The editorial policy of *L'Homme Réel* began to move toward the left, against Fascism and in support of the Spanish anarchists. On September 21, 1934, Le Corbusier wrote to Pierre Ganivet requesting that his name no longer be associated with the journal.[9]

For the other journals it also became necessary to choose the right or the left, for or against Fascism, remilitarization of the Rhine, sanctions imposed on Mussolini, war in Ethiopia, civil war in Spain. In the second half of the 1930s, movement quickened toward the catastrophe of war, and the "spirit of the thirties" began to dissolve. One by one the new reviews, forced to become politically engaged, chose separate ideological paths.[10]

NEO-SYNDICALISM

Le Corbusier's neo-syndicalist sympathies belong primarily to this period of collaboration on *Plans* and *Prèlude* between 1930 and 1934, yet influence his ideas well into the 1940s. The doctrine of neo-syndicalism, which the two journals advocated, can be described as a complex political gesture moving awkwardly in different directions at once but generally discontent with anarchy and disequilibrium in the economic world, the drift of liberal democracy, and the lack of discipline and strong authority in public affairs. It was open to alignment with more right-wing policies, yet followed the "spirit of the thirties" in advocating "neither Left nor Right." Editorials and other articles by the editorial board in *Plans* reveal the complex of issues that concerned the neo-syndicalists and their relationship with ideas that Le Corbusier espoused.

In their first editorial, "Ligne Générale" ("General Line"), they proclaim that their review "has a necessity, an aim, a plan."[11] They propose the creation of a new humane civilization, a rational material order, answering questions arising in the wake of the industrial revolution. Faced with worldwide depression and social unrest, the editors find man bereft of directives to enable him to see clearly what had to be done. Thus it is their intent to objectively study the theoretical origins of the collective economy in the USSR, the doctrine espoused in Italy, and the pragmatic evolution of the United States, searching for a route out of the economic, political, and spiritual malaise. It is the aim of the review "to order the social view, to organize the activity of man, to give him a healthy body in a logical city."[12]

In the next article, Philippe Lamour blames the contemporary world crisis on a clash of civilizations. The older civilization established its base on the autonomy of the individual, on rights protected by Roman law, on the simple exchange of a domestic economy. The other, a collective civilization, grew out of machine society, the factory, and the industrial order, and required solidarity among men and the creation of instruments of universal exchange.[13] Since the artificial maintenance of individualistic institutions provided neither economic security nor order, Lamour proclaimed that a "revolution" was necessary. The isolated citizen could no longer be considered to be the fundamental unit of a collective and interdependent society. Only man as a member of an organized social group was able to express feelings of solidarity and fuse into a common culture. These groups or syndicates formed the base of society from which the new order would grow.[14]

Economic anarchy would be replaced by a federal and syndical order where the absolute right of private property would be subordinated to its use, and man would be given rational functional tools in the city, housing, and health, and new moral values to liberate his personality. "The tendency towards unity, universality is the supreme ethic."[15]

In his own article "Invitation to Action," appearing in the same first issue of *Plans,* Le Corbusier argues that architecture and city planning can provide the essential functions modern man requires.[16] But architecture cannot help society if it does not have a program. "Cities are made by planning, and architecture can do nothing without such plans."[17] Yet modern cities exist merely as paper plans, because governmental authorities refuse to carry them into action. Le Corbusier reiterates his well-formed position: houses needed throughout Europe could be built inside the factories that now lie idle; if houses were prefabricated and mass-produced, they would be affordable, and meet the immense consumer demand for adequate housing and domestic equipment. Industry must apply the same attention as it had already given to the automobile, the ocean liner, and the airplane.[18] Le Corbusier returns to his metaphor of the disorder left after a meal:

> But our minds, already learning to cope with the new dimensions ahead, have already freed themselves, have already torn themselves away from the table cluttered with the remains of a centuries-old meal: those rotting cities, those infinitely subdivided fields, that incoherent distribution of population, that morality now becoming as fragile as a bubble. Our minds are insisting on a clean tablecloth.[19]

The second issue's "Ligne Générale" outlines two contradictory conceptions of the word "peace," rival conceptions that are keeping the world in disarray.[20] One group, considered the winners of World

War I, thought of peace as imposing humiliation and reparations on the defeated through the Treaty of Versailles (1919). The other group wanted the treaty revised, and perpetual peace installed as a result. Because Germany had invaded France four times in the past one hundred years, France was hypnotized by the question of security. It sought to punish the Germans with heavy reparations. This obsession enabled France to ignore the mounting anarchy of inflation, famine, and poverty in the countries of Eastern Europe along the Danube, caused by the grain crisis. *Plans* believed it was necessary to revise the treaties and give birth to a new idea of "Europe" because England was decadent, Germany was desperately wondering whether its next revolution would follow Communism or Hitlerism, Italy was federalizing all its malcontent areas, and the United States was a capitalist failure with more than ten million unemployed.

PEACE, WAR, PLANNING

Le Corbusier took up the banner for peace as espoused by *Plans*, claiming that architecture and urbanism are actions that come from the heart; they establish peace because they are neutral and enthusiastic procedures. Peace, Le Corbusier argued, is none other than construction.[21] When war is declared it is a macabre irony: capital, handwork, primary materials, transport, discipline all are aligned in an immense, inhuman, and fantastic effort. It is worthy of admiration, until one realizes that "It is DESTRUCTION." Yet the same ability to mobilize land, people, production, and to realize a plan could be made for the sake of building a new world. "Stock of tools: command and army, machines and circulation, discipline? EXACTLY THE SAME AS THAT TO MAKE WAR!"[22]

In the final part of *The Radiant City*, completed in March 1935, he revisits this theme. There, as has been his longtime practice, he argues in terms of polar opposites: war or peace, wasting or planning, destruction or construction. He asks the reader to take positions with him, to argue for and against the extremes until one side has been transformed into the other. Waste is a "snickering and drunken tyrant....Waste is strangling us, bewitching us, bogging us down, sucking us dry of all our substance."[23] It is up to Authority to stop this insane race toward chaos, to adopt a plan that kills waste. A plan is revolutionary; it must become reality in the cities, villages, and farms.

When one makes plans, one lives a life of peace that comes from struggle, from doing battle, from daring. Peace is constructive, but

> *War* is a stampede of uprooted human hordes, hordes of individual men helplessly caught up in a rushing torrent. They are called together and harangued; they are offered an antidote to their flagrant despair: action, plunder, conquest, It is a way of giving them hope (and a way of creating armies; of turning those men into cannon fodder).[24]

Once war is declared then production begins, everything is on the move, and men are fed. But this mad, satanic dance is destructive.[25] There must be, instead, a call to arms for organization; mobilization of the land, the people, and production, action, and conquest to make the plan a reality. The same action, equipment, and discipline are required for peace as for making war. The choice is simple: to be constructive instead of destructive.[26]

Le Corbusier devotes to this thesis part of his *Des Canons, Des Munitions? Merci! Des Logis... S.V.P.*[27] [FIGURE 10.1, p. 700] Throughout his many travels across the world, Le Corbusier says, he has noted the same condition: "Man lost his habitation."[28] Housing is the key to every problem. It allows one to work, to stretch oneself, to raise one's arms, to be cooled or warmed, to rest, to meditate, to excite the eyes and balance the sensibilities, to live from the sap (vigor) of affection and friendship. "The problem of housing primes all the others. To work, to circulate, are only incidences. Housing is the key."[29] To create housing, therefore, should be the major preoccupation of any society–or would society rather make war, and spend its money on cannons and munitions? Le Corbusier's reply is emphatic: it is preferable to mobilize the same prodigious forces for the construction of housing. War will have "*no reason for existing*...will find no one available if modern society is occupied with realizing the very condition of its vitality: to create huts" (*créer le gîte*).[30] The construction of housing requires the same courage, strength, and struggle as war, but regenerates rather than destroys. [FIGURE 10.2]

Le Corbusier has, he says, gone to the authorities; he knows they have the law in their hands, so they can elaborate and transform these laws. If they choose, they can make society rich. They can establish the regulations of land, determine the manner in which it is used and what it will contain. They can suddenly achieve immense economy, and repel the great waste of urban agglomerations. The authorities are the fathers of society, they are its "planners." "BUT NO! The [artillery] shell is everywhere in the world. Propaganda is made through the press and the cinema: 'CANNONS, MUNITIONS!'"[31] Absolute folly!

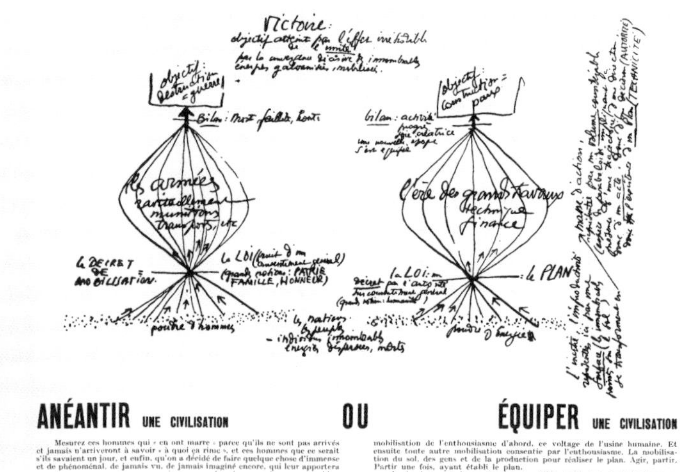

FIGURE 10.2: Le Corbusier inserts a diagram published in *Plans* in June of 1931 that explains that men of authority have the power to choose either to annihilate civilization in war or to equip it for peace. He would choose the road to peace.

Le Corbusier was thus well aware in the 1930s of the potential for another war. He often wrote about the difference between destructive and constructive forces, and repeats over and again that the technology involved in the production of weapons could be diverted to housing. Increasingly he uses the word *love*, love for one's fellow men as a requirement if one is to redirect aggressive instincts toward peace and restore the essential joys of life to all mankind. He calls on the authorities, again and again, to be wise shepherds and to deploy their powers rationally in the creation of laws and plans that can divert the forces of industry, land, money, and material away from war into the production of housing.

World War I had been devastating, the number of casualties beyond belief as mass-produced firepower, aerial bombardments, and lethal gases mowed men down. Disillusionment and despair lingered across Europe for two decades. War no longer appeared, to many, to be a legitimate tool; there was hope that the League of Nations would secure the rule of law throughout all lands. The realization of such a world order required, as Le Corbusier saw it, an alternative approach: a new civic consciousness, a positive political vision, a plan for peace. But these conflicted with geopolitics based on the sovereignty of individual states. Tolerance of difference, mutual respect, love of humanity were required. Here Le Corbusier was ever alert to the potential of the new routes of travel, which overcame distances, eradicating boundaries and–he hoped, as did many–drawing the world together in unity. To the extent that love of mankind and belief in the joys of living could be established, they might lessen the power of conflicting groups. CIAM was an island of civility: its cosmopolitan, international reach brought together men from many different countries intent on promoting modern architecture and urbanism in order to relieve the suffering of mankind.

Yet Le Corbusier believed that the planner-architect should be a technician, not involved with political issues nor invading the terrain of authority. For example, in August of 1933 during CIAM IV, just five months after Hitler had been appointed interim chancellor in Germany, a year after local National Socialists had dissolved what they called the "Jewish-Marxist" Bauhaus in Dessau, and a few months after the Bauhaus, having moved to Berlin, was finally closed (April 12, 1933), some members were hoping that CIAM would protest the censorship of modern architects and the "Neues Bauen" throughout Germany. Yet Le Corbusier neutralized all political involvement, opening the Congress with the following claim: "This is a congress of technicians...The problems of architecture and aesthetics, of architecture and politics are not of general interest to the group and it would be absolutely dangerous if they were to be discussed."[32]

Throughout the 1930s, Le Corbusier's politics swing back and forth. In *The Radiant City*, for example, a caption underneath a photograph of right-wing extremists–whose demonstration in Paris

FIGURE 10.3: The opportunist in Le Corbusier saw urban riots as one way of cleansing the city and enabling its renovation.

on February 6, 1934, resulted in fifteen dead and fifteen hundred wounded—calls this uprising "the awakening of cleanliness."[33] [FIGURE 10.3] Yet elsewhere Le Corbusier refers to the leftist Popular Front's rise to power, which this same riot helped to create, as "the young and clean authority."[34] He maintained his posture of neutrality throughout the 1930s, of being "neither Left nor Right," and offered his plans for different cities from Algiers to Paris as neutral documents, proud that he was never paid for his efforts. Although Le Corbusier's position in the 1930s is read in the context of neo-syndicalism, he may not have been as committed to its doctrine as he found it convenient to pour his own wine into these new skins, that is, hoisting his sail to any wind coming from the right or the left that would move his plans for architecture and urbanism forward.

TO CONCEIVE FIRST, CONSTRUCT LATER

To construct, to build a new world, galvanized the "spirit of the thirties," but it required a plan. In March 1932, in a letter to the editorial board of *Plans*, Le Corbusier clarified his position on the board. The intent of the journal, he said, was to establish plans for contemporary society and to explain the institutional and cultural obstacles preventing their implementation.[35] The editorial group understood that the most important problem facing France was planning the entire "equipment" of the country, with its necessary corollary, the modernization of the countryside. His first schemes for Algiers offered a solution containing "something overwhelming and of truth, of health and magnificence," but would the French and Algerian authorities have the courage to put his plans into action, given that his schemes, like those advocated by *Plans*, questioned fundamental elements of society: its institutions, authority, and property relations?[36] He was gripped with enthusiasm and hoped to go there within a few weeks to defend his schemes. And then "we shall see!"

In 1933, he wrote an article entitled "To conceive first, to construct later." The phrase inverts and extends a postulate proclaimed by Auguste Perret ten years earlier, when he instructed young architects "to construct."[37] Architecture, Le Corbusier says, is stopped, choked, and plunged into crisis because it has constructed too much without having conceived enough. Thus today it is necessary to conceive, to plan, to think ahead. Architects must formulate programs to give men of the machine era all the necessary elements for a happy life based on individual liberty established through collective participation. His slogan "first conceive, then construct" evokes an architectural struggle against "routines and lies, and conflicts of doctrines"[38]–a veritable revolution:

> Past, present, future: fifty years of architecture representing an evolution so violent of events and of thought that such evolution becomes, in truth, a revolution.[39]

In this revolution, an entirely new machine society has replaced a pre-machine one, breaking down traditions. The battle has been against the academies–those fearful archeologists, flatterers of the lazy, pessimists without courage. It is a classic Le Corbusier repetitious rant against his old foes: The academies have suffocated lively forces, they falsely declare they support the nation, lying that they are the spirit of "*la patrie*." Yet no matter how many barricades they erect, they cannot stop the course of revolutionary and progressive events.

> Academy, Authorities, Schools, Diplomas and entertainer of vanities through the masquerade of defrocked princes and kings. In the middle of the 19th and 20th centuries, in the midst of the prodigious explosion of machinery, of science, of new techniques, of new procedures, they cry "retreat." Having done so, they torment and caricature materials and trades: pretentious and liars, they affirm against all evidence: "We are the preservers of the trades"; winking before works overloaded with beautiful or ugly decoration from other times, they add: "–some beautiful trades."[40]

Eventually the barricades they raised were destroyed, and the young went out to find "the new," namely "the harmonious expression of needs of today." The power of the academies was over, merely a matter of funerals. But too much money stood behind their "golden flag" so the necessary cleansing was far from instantaneous or complete–though there had been some explosions of enthusiasm in the generations of 1900, of 1910, after World War I, and now again of 1933. Nineteen hundred returned to "healthy materials." In 1910, prestressed concrete made its entry into architecture, introducing the first freedoms, offering new plastic elements capable of determining a new aesthetic. The Russian revolution struck. In the city, day by day, the industrial revolution announced its effects. Automobiles were unfurled along the streets and new speed animated humanity. Time no longer had the same measure. Society was transformed.

One no longer speaks of "facade," but of the plan of the city. Parts of the production process are Taylorized; economic restructuring occurs where handwork costs more than material. And yet there is catastrophe in this revolution. The countryside is deserted, while the ranks of the cities swell. "Man left his snail shell forever. This migration evokes the worst calamities of history. From now on it is a question of urbanism."[41] It is a matter of attacking the "eternal inviolability of property," of envisioning methods to mobilize the land for the sake of public well-being. Yet nothing is simple or clear. As one world is disposed of and a new one born, conflicts remain to be resolved.

Le Corbusier turns his attention to international events. He sees Germany equipping herself, covering its land with new houses. Yet they present only a mask of modernity, for the ruling solution in Germany is the multiplication of garden cities, which allows the authorities to keep the mass of workers inert and immobile. The Germans understand neither prestressed concrete nor the architecture of iron, the two elements that offer a solution to an ancient debate over how "to carry the house and how to light it; to construct a wall of solid support and how to weaken it by piercing some windows."[42]

Le Corbusier turns to announce his latest synthetic program, "Air-Sound-Light." These are the elements he will use to construct the new snail shell for the man of the modern machine age:

> It is on the measure of 24 hours that we will organize the healthy and harmonious day of the machinist man. We can establish the timetable of this day; a timetable on which are inserted the useful hours of work and those of indispensable rest; where intervenes the acts of the collective participants and the silences of the free individual disposition.
>
> It will be necessary to assign exact places for these diverse activities. Architecture will answer the needs of the body and those of the mind.[43]

And again, the emphasis on the centrality of planning, of forethought and political authority, strong enough to reshape society, rewrite the laws, yet subservient to the true "dictator," the plan:

> It is necessary today, to *conceive.*
> To conceive and direct; that is to assign some aims.
> It is necessary today, *to make plans.*

> These plans are they only pieces of paper, utopian dreams, some manifestations without import? Certainly not! These plans are the great task of today. They analyze present conditions; they synthesize choices that must be made; they enounce decisions to take, they point out the obstacles.
> Plans are the torch bearers.
> And if the authority owes that it is not possible by legislative means to realize plans, it is necessary to make new regulations.
> And if the authority does not have men who have the moral force of entrepreneurs, it is necessary to change these men.
> Plans are the truth of modern times. They are the dictators. All the means are ready to begin the work.
> It is necessary to conceive.
> To conceive, to decide, to be organized, to act, to direct the era of great works.
> To conceive first.
> Then to construct.[44]

THE TIME HAS COME FOR ACTION!

Plans and *action* were bywords of the neo-syndicalists, and certainly, as we have already seen, of Le Corbusier. In April 1930 he wrote to Oswaldo Costa in São Paulo, speaking about ideas he had developed for Rio de Janeiro during his South American voyage the previous fall.[45] He states that a grand machine era has begun, and cities all over the world have arrived at the hour when they must adopt a plan. The time has come for action! When he returned from South America in December 1929, he says, he found a syndicate of banks studying his plans for Paris. He is hopeful that fermentation sets in even in Paris, that everyone cringing under the rule of the old was finally prepared to act, and that outside of Europe, in young countries like Brazil unconstrained by the past, they would accept their "destiny" and adopt brave new plans for the modern machine era. He pointed to the example of Moscow: it works, acts, and becomes the leader of the contemporary stage of worldwide evolution. Contrary to what most Europeans think, Moscow reveals that it is full of intelligence, faith, ardor, grandeur, and action.

A few months later, he wrote again to Costa, eager to hear whether South America will offer him the occasion to execute a "grand work" of urbanism, allowing him to put the last decade of research into practice. He is full of strength, he writes, bubbling over with ideas, and surrounded with a group of young workers in his atelier eager to carry out his orders, though he is aware that his friend Agache was already developing schemes for Rio, so his own involvement there is a delicate issue. He pointed out that he was "of an age [forty-three years old] when it is necessary to produce. You others of Brazil give me that occasion." Moscow had also offered him the possibility to reconstruct that city. He made a report of seventy pages and twenty-one designs with excellent propositions, and planned to publish all of these innovative schemes in a book entitled *Réponse à Moscou* (*Reply to Moscow*).[46] Within a few months he relabeled these schemes *La Ville Radieuse* (*The Radiant City*)–"An epithet that says everything."[47] This was the germ of the project that would eventually include so much of his essay writing of the early thirties, and to which we now turn.

II. THE WELL-PLANTED TREE: THE RADIANT CITY

La Ville Radieuse (*The Radiant City*: *Elements of a Doctrine of Urbanism to Be Used as the Basis of Our Machine-age Civilization*) is compiled from publications written between 1931 and 1934, with a conclusion added in 1935, and hence is composed of distinct, often conflicting layers of material.[48] It is cryptic, replete with oblique references, and is exasperatingly repetitive. Inspired in part by Le Corbusier's three trips to Russia between October 1928 and March 1930 as well as his voyages to South America, Spain, and Algeria between 1929 and 1933, this collection reflects his participation in the ostensibly apolitical but practically conservative, even reactionary, neo-syndicalist publications *Plans* and *Prélude.* It heralds a new era–the temps nouveaux–based upon the conjunction of architecture and planning.[49]

During the 1930s, economic crisis brought the building industry to a standstill, fomenting revolutionary discussions throughout the world. Le Corbusier filled the rupture of those years with the development of some twenty different city plans based on his ideas of what a Radiant City might be. He claimed he was nonpartisan, a disinterested spirit who offered his plans as a gesture of freedom, neither left nor right. It was not a matter of class conflict and revolution, because the revolution of modern architecture and housing had been accomplished. Le Corbusier was now concerned with action, requiring the development and implementation of plans.

The introductory chapter of *The Radiant City* is, in Le Corbusier's style, a résumé of what the book will contain. He offers the work, he says, as a guidebook to a solution of a revolutionary situation, proclaiming, consistent with his planning emphasis in the 1930s, that

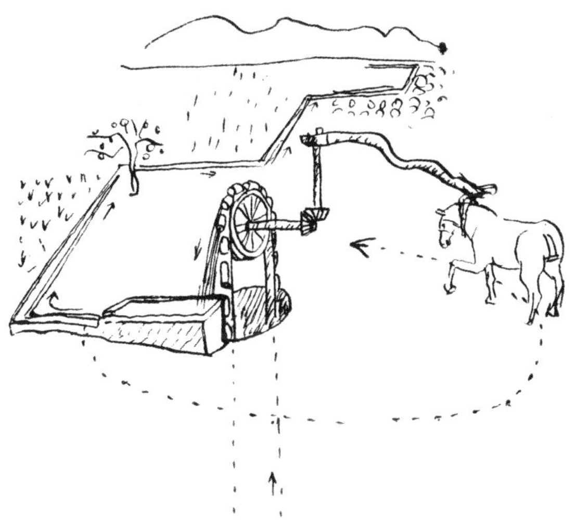

FIGURE 10.4: In the difficult years of the 1930s, Le Corbusier took refuge in the wisdom of men who worked to produce their food, such as farmers and fishermen.

"the plan must rule." This might be called revolutionary, hence destructive, but on the contrary, it is based on a constructive principle steeped in the courageous belief that a new civilization dedicated to action and great achievements is dawning. "Modern society is throwing off its rags and preparing to move into a new home: the radiant city."[50]

Two magnets pull him forward: man and nature. He is pleased with "primitive men" such as farmers and fishermen, who put their tools to use and work to produce food that makes their existence possible; who know how to enjoy the pleasures of work, the family, and the community. From these simple men in their basic homes, with their primary tools, the architect-planner can learn his trade. [FIGURE 10.4]

Le Corbusier turns his back on the empty shell of the city, on its refuse and scum, and its useless exchange of uncertain communications. He moves instead to places where "order is coming out of the endless dialogue between man and nature, out of the struggle for life, out of the enjoyment of leisure under the open sky, in the passing of seasons, the song of the sea."[51] His unit of measure will be man, using the "basic binomial" of man plus nature to determine a range of spatial relations. The guideline he will follow is the one nature lays down. Each year with the cycle of seasons, she cleans up and throws out, while man continues to "crouch in a pool of dead things…ruled by a system that is like a dead branch fallen from the tree of life."[52]

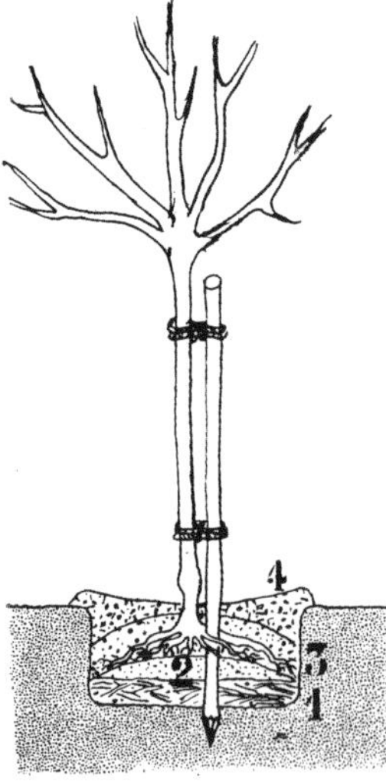

FIGURE 10.5: **City planning is an art of cultivation: man and nature.**

"The tree of life"–this is no throwaway phrase, but the ruling sign of the entire book. The tree is a rich metaphor, one that Le Corbusier used in his youth to describe the teachings of L'Eplattenier (see Chapter 2) and now deploys throughout *The Radiant City*, sometimes explicitly, often implicitly.[53] He will also exploit the metaphor as he further develops his "elements of a doctrine" throughout the 1930s and 1940s. The opening lines of *The Radiant City* explain how to plant a young sapling, with a rod for straightening its growth. It is an image exemplary of the disciplinary techniques he intends to impose on the city. [FIGURE 10.5]

> To plant a tree well:
> 1. good earth and basic manure
> 2. a covering of fine soil
> 3. very fine vegetable earth
> 4. subsoil and fertilizer.[54]

The tree metaphor takes on new poignancy in the 1930s in several of Le Corbusier's writings. It is a perfect vehicle to dramatize the shift in his concepts and thoughts from the mechanical laws of Purism toward symbols of organic creation, entailing a modified modernism attentive to the climate, topography, and materials of a given region. Nature becomes his new authority, the sun a dictator just as the leaves turn toward it. He is eager for action, to plan and to construct, and finds that a tree not only follows the laws of nature, but those of mathematics as well. The tree epitomizes the radiant city, a green city. Yet he likens it to a technical city plan that "expresses a whole fruit with its skin, its seeds; it can only blossom, some day, into a normal plant, the roots at the bottom and the flower at the top–and not vice versa…but when it is finished the plan will nevertheless emerge in its totality."[55] The tree is an

> image of complete construction. A delightful spectacle…the most fantastic, yet perfectly ordered arabesque, a mathematically measured play of branches multiplied each spring by a new life-giving hand. Leaves with finely placed nerves. A cover over us between earth and sky. A friendly screen close to our eyes. A pleasant measure interposed between our hearts and eyes and the eventual.[56]

In this introductory chapter of *The Radiant City*, after proclaiming that absolute individual freedom is the cornerstone of his urbanism and invoking the authority of nature, which never allows land to lie fallow and unproductive–nature is always productive, an uninterrupted movement–he turns to a story from his motor trip to Algiers in the summer of 1929, when he traveled through Spain along the most beautiful modern freeway.

> It cuts right across land that has been under the plow for centuries. Unlike the cities and railroads, which give a false impression of everything, this road leads one directly into the soul of Spain. So far that road has caused no trouble to anyone.[57]

Yet it bothers Le Corbusier because of what it projects, for in the shop windows of every small town and village he sees an invasion of light fixtures, supposedly handcrafted. Compositions of colored glass and beaten brass, they are produced by the thousands in factories. This type of progress has "destroyed the only people in the world who live in a state of noble serenity–of inner life. (The Mediterranean coast, Barcelona, Tarragona, Valencia, Alicante, Murcia, Almeria, Malaga.)"[58] Like nature, Spain was fortunate enough to follow the cycle of seasons–and her road represents the spring that follows a dormant winter in which she avoided the winds of mechanical change. Will this freeway become the carrier of machine-age refuse, or will it mark out a clear line of conduct?

Since this introductory chapter is ostensibly about revolution, Le Corbusier turns to consider whether Paris has delivered on the revolutionary promise of liberty, equality, and fraternity. Can the city guarantee liberty when it has worshiped since 1919 a new religion founded on making money? Does it offer equality when it has denied the realization of Le Corbusier's dream of a modern classless city, envisioned since 1925, that would eradicate the slums between the Place des Vosges and the Stock Exchange?

As for fraternity, he has offered Algiers a plan to break the deadlock caused by its rapid population expansion. His radiant city will make Algiers the capital of North Africa and secure her potential in the Western economy. But the bankers who give orders have rejected his schemes: they have denied the people a share in the basic joys of the sky, the sea, and the mountains. They say the time is not ripe for fraternal considerations, and Le Corbusier should stop rocking the boat!

In conclusion, Le Corbusier makes his final appeal to the conscience of humanity. The Depression has proven that the old civilization based on the measure of money, the big deal, and shady transactions is collapsing.[59] Money made the horizon and the sky insignificant; it postponed physical fitness and the improvement of one's body to another day. "All that is needed is that this capacity," the capacity for discipline and teamwork, "should not serve the cause of rape or cruelty–war and looting–but be directed toward initiative, construction and the very real need for beauty."[60] Such is the meaning of the word "radiant" (*radieuse*): the fulfillment of basic simple pleasures.

MODERN TECHNIQUES

Following the introduction, in the second section of the book, Le Corbusier opens his discourse on the planning of cities, regions, and the nation with the claim that all inventions of the last one hundred years (1830–1930) have produced a revolutionary situation requiring a revolutionary solution. And to make a revolution there must be a doctrine.[61]

The subject he wants to discuss is the problem of city planning. He understands that the dwelling changes its form slowly, for it must struggle against passive forces of preservation that offer man a sense of security. It is transformed only when new customs appear, and these occur only when the world itself has been radically upset. Yet man is a discoverer and an inventor, even when this disturbs old habits, entails chaos, and brings disorder. He constantly confronts two states in opposition, the active life and the passive life, and wants to achieve equilibrium.[62]

A battle issues from this confrontation, one in which the future of architecture and the life of the world is at stake. He gathers documents, he says, offers a proof. He begins with the struggle between the ancients and moderns over the Palace of the League of Nations affair. This upset modern architects and gave rise to the spontaneous formation of the International Congress for Modern Architecture (CIAM). His first document of support is thus the preparatory program for CIAM, a rallying point that brought forty-two delegates from different countries together for the first time in 1928. He backs up this document with a letter praising such international action written by Paul Otlet, the founder and director of the Musée Mondial in Brussels. These foundational texts offer proof that a threshold has been crossed.

For a battle, there must be a plan of action. "A plan serves to show where one can go, to state what one wishes to do, to prove *that one can begin to fight.*"[63] The second CIAM meeting was dedicated to "the minimum house," and Le Corbusier and Pierre Jeanneret presented their program, their plan. Again there is opposition. The dwelling place is a biological event, its envelope a static system. These two distinct orders–one living, the other moribund–confront each other. Traditional methods of building have reached an impasse and created a worldwide housing crisis. "Man today is an animal deprived of its lair: he can only mope."

There are infinitely flexible traditional methods of construction: the lake house, the Gothic wooden house, the Swiss chalet, the Russian *isba*, the Indochinese straw hut, the Japanese tea house.[64] With tradition on his side, he advances the proposition that the solution for a standardized, industrialized, Taylorized house exists if architects clearly differentiate between two unrelated functions: the system of circulation and the structural system. "The running of a home consists of precise functions in a regular order," their logic biological, not geometrical.[65] The architect must understand that the facade is a provider of light; the partitions are membranes, while the floors are carried by posts. Thus the structure of a house has a free and independent framework enabling an open plan of circulation. [FIGURE 10.6]

With such a program, customs made sacred by tradition can be abandoned. But abandoning some customs, he argues, does not require

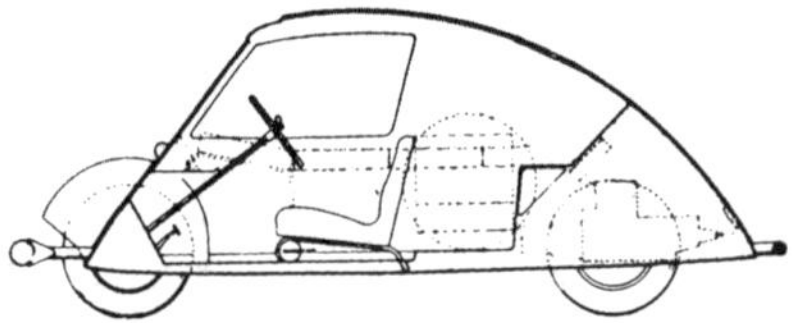

In 1928, Le Corbusier and Pierre Jeanneret conceived this car and called it the "Maximum Car." In 1935 the Société des Ingénieurs Automobiles held a contest for the "Minimum Car." The Société wished to present our "Maximum Car" in a supplement to its album.

. . . .

Cars have been made and driven since then, and no one has ever called attention to the "Maximum Car" of Le Corbusier and Pierre Jeanneret.

FIGURE 10.6: **If the automobile could evolve, why couldn't the design of housing evolve as well?**

that all traditions be erased. It is necessary to look in two different directions at once: toward folklore and toward science.

> We will learn more from the savages, from men close to nature whom the Academies have not touched; but above all, we will have to seal new pacts in the scientific world (especially with physics and chemistry) and in that of large scale contemporary production.[66]

Le Corbusier brings forth other documents. The next is from the third CIAM meeting, which focused on the rational division of building lots and the question of low, medium, or tall building.[67] His argument in support of tall buildings and open space begins with two contradictory conceptions of the city that also confront each other and necessitate a choice: the horizontal dispersion of garden cities and the concentrated vertical cities of tall buildings. The garden city leads to individualism, but also to an enslaved and sterile isolation. It is destructive of collective forces and annihilates collective will. By increasing the amount of time lost in discomfort and travel, it constitutes an attack on freedom. [FIGURE 10.7]

FIGURE 10.7: **If the small fisherman's hut on a peninsula brought pleasure to its inhabitants, why couldn't a similar cell be designed for those who resided in cities?**

Le Corbusier's argument for tall buildings rallies round the elevator, "the keystone of all modern urbanization." It is a crime to make anyone, rich or poor, walk up more than three flights of stairs. Moreover, elevator buildings reorganize the way building lots are divided and the number of streets required, and dictate the layout of the ground plan. He touches on harmony: how to adjust the height of a dwelling to human dimensions.[68] "A height which is pleasing, first of all, to our human gestures: the height of a lair: clearly a biological function. Then the useful height, which determines the volume of air to be taken into our lungs and the quantity of light streaming in through the facades."[69] Here too a revolutionary situation prevails.

Le Corbusier once again modulates a reference to revolution by turning at once to history, considering simple timber houses constructed in medieval times. He has determined that most of these houses adopted a natural height of 2.2 meters.

> Examples remain to bear witness: the chalets of Bavaria or Tyrol; Swiss or Scandinavian chalets; Gothic or Renaissance wooden houses in Rouen, Strasbourg, Zurich, Toggenbourge; the Russian isba, etc.[70]

That is the reason Le Corbusier selected this natural height for his own "villa-buildings": the Citrohan house, the Ozenfant house, the La Roche villa, and the Esprit Nouveau cell.

He found more proof in 1933 while traveling through the Cycladic islands during CIAM IV:

> Here the profound life of past millennia has remained intact; the wheel does not yet exist. Perhaps it never will exist, the topography is so rough. We discover the eternal houses, living houses, houses of today which go far back in history and whose plan and section are exactly what we have been thinking of for a decade. Here in the bosom of human measure, here in Greece, on this soil redolent of decency, intimacy, well being, of what is rational forever guided by the joy of living, we find *measurements on a human scale.*[71]

Moreover, 2.2 meters is the height given to all living space aboard an ocean liner, whether a cabin or a luxury suite. He examines a majestic site in Vézelay, on a tip of land jutting out from a hollow of a valley, on which stands a Romanesque basilica. On either side of the street leading up to it are houses as old as time, whose windows open onto distant horizons. The director of *L'Architecture Vivante,* Jean Badovici, bought several of these crumbling abodes with oak-beamed ceilings and modernized them. The height between stories is 2.2 meters. He connected two stories together, turning them into a modern living unit and filling them with the instruments of modernity. A few men gather there: Le Corbusier, Christian Zervos, Fernand Léger, and Matila Ghyka.

> We are in a lair for men. On our shoulders are ceilings that suit us. Our eyes find varied and contrasted prospects; our steps have a lively movement. Everything is minute, but everything is big. It is a jewel-box on the human scale. It is a place of well-being, of calm and diversity, of measure and proportion, of thoroughly human dimensions. Harmony. All of us unanimous in recognizing and proclaiming this.[72]

On the other hand, the minimum house spreading throughout Germany, Poland, and Russia is not a place to live but a cage. In its place we need the maximum living room, with a glass wall taking up one entire side of the home. Within this cube, "exact respiration" can

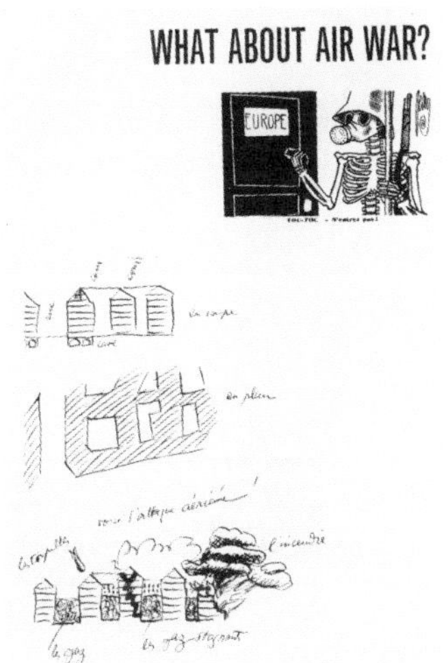

FIGURE 10.8: The newspapers declare that not one city will be spared in the next war, but all will be razed to the ground.

be introduced, and artificial electric light allowed to flood the bathroom and kitchen.[73] The word "artificial" upsets sensitive souls, but it has at its root "art": the best way of doing something. "And in this way, man, through his creations, brought himself into harmony with the perfections, the constants of nature."[74]

Le Corbusier returns to the troubling word: building houses requires sites that are "artificialized"–the natural ground reserved for one function alone, to carry the weight of the structure. He has deployed artificial means on difficult sites where topography baffles every initiative, such as Algiers, Stockholm, Montevideo, São Paulo, Rio de Janeiro, Zurich. Man has been making artificial sites from the beginning of time–Le Corbusier merely intends to carry this tradition further by increasing the number of these artificial sites, now superimposed and equipped in order to bring "basic pleasures" to all the city's inhabitants. He offers "artificial garden cities" stacked up vertically: "And instantly, the events of urban life are organized: traffic problems are solved; 'communal services' eliminate waste and bring the urgently needed benefits of emancipation to the running of each home."[75]

He ends this section on "Modern Techniques," with a final but alarming document, "What about Air War?"[76] [FIGURE 10.8] Poison gas factories are building up huge stocks, and in the next war, not one city will be spared. They will all succumb to fire, collapse, and death by gas. Political leaders told the people in 1914 that the war would be over in three months, the devastated areas rebuilt so that in the spring of 1915, the sun would shine on brand new towns and cities. The war lasted five years, followed by fifteen years of panic, crises, disasters, and despair.

> Like a sinister apotheosis, [this discussion of air war] crowns these chapters devoted to *Modern Techniques*. The evocation of its frightful reality thrusts us dramatically into MODERN TIMES...the obscenity and infamy of war must become the pretext for rallying enterprising souls and overthrowing secular customs, and be the herald of the Radiant City."[77]

THE TREE OF KNOWLEDGE

One of the articles that Le Corbusier published first in *Prélude* and republished in *The Radiant City* was a response to H. G. Wells, who had made an appeal for the appointment of Professors of Prediction, men capable of pointing the way to the future. This offered Le Corbusier an opportunity to expound on his theories of education, which he called "a perilous subject."[78] While the sciences have made progress, the arts have foundered. Le Corbusier does not believe in schools meant to inculcate imagination; in fact all of them should be closed down. If there are to be schools, they must teach only subjects that are exact and based on verification–the complete opposite of prediction. Like Descartes before him, Le Corbusier distrusts teachers, for they uproot a student from the school of doubts provided by life. Teachers develop a hard core of certainties that they feel obliged to pass on to their students. If they were to predict the future, Le Corbusier fears, they would soon become pontiffs with ignorant followers.

Mistrustful of teachers, Le Corbusier is however voracious for lessons. Like a tree that blossoms, these emerge spontaneously from the works of man engaged with life. He believes that the tree of life is the only worthwhile teacher–but to read its lessons one must be immersed in life, be one of its inventors.[79] [FIGURE 10.9]

As an architect, Le Corbusier is drawn toward the joys of discovery but understands only the present; he is not a man who predicts the future. The authorities who labeled his 1922 Ville Contemporaine "the city of the future" were wrong; since they live in the past and off the past, they could not recognize that he was concerned only with contemporary events. They call modern art "revolutionary" when it is an honest and licit expression of the age.

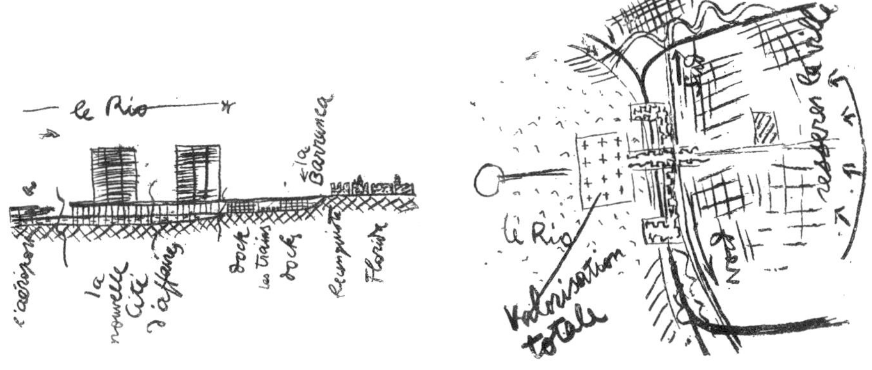

FIGURE 10.9: "Energy ideas" sprang up during Le Corbusier's trip to South America: He foresaw a radiant city filled with trees and green spaces.

Le Corbusier reiterates: in order to seize the solution as it rushes by, it is not necessary to be a professor, but a worker at a specific task–an inventor. Truly fruitful lessons come from making plans, not talking about them, endlessly predicting the future.

THE TREE OF LIFE

In the third section of the book, entitled "The New Age," Le Corbusier lays out what will become the core of his developing doctrine.[80] He tells a story about a day filled with the variety of nature's play. Sun and water, dew and vapor, clouds and rays of sun, lightning and thunder–all compose a pastoral symphony across twenty-four hours of the day. "This prodigious spectacle has been produced by the interplay of two elements, one male, one female: sun and water."[81]

To the unperceptive eye it appears that the foliage crowning the tree stands motionless and quiescent around its trunk. But slow-motion film reveals that each one of these leaves is an eye hypnotized by the sun, continually turning to look at "the great solitary traveler who passes from East to West across our sky once every day always in the face. It is the sun that governs us."[82] On the movie screen, man can see billions of leaves, which form the complex existence of hedgerows or great forests, contracting, twisting, and contorting in obedience to the commands of the sun. These billions of leaves proclaim the law of the earth: "The sun is our dictator."

Le Corbusier shifts to another level to explain the importance of the sun and water to man's well-being and equilibrium. The airplane flies over estuaries, along great rivers, and high above the savannah. It provides a new way of looking: the aerial view. Now the eye can discern the characteristics of various regions of the world and gauge their diversity. The different "characters" of nature the eye thus observes become guides to human creations. "The music of our constructions–and by music I mean the poetic emanations they create–will be produced by the interplay of the characters we have created."[83]

The airplane allows the eye to perceive immense deltas, the reed beds of atolls, the slender groups of palm trees in the savannahs, and the material growth of virgin forests. It reveals the movement of water in the subsoil and the patterned progression of green veins across the yellow plain. Water flows according to the law of gravity. A rivulet meets another rivulet, and width is added: that is simple arithmetic. Widths are added to form a great river. The river flows toward the sea, reaches a delta where its powerful flow is subdivided, an invariable process again following the laws of simple arithmetic, before it flows gently through the estuary and out into the open sea. From the airplane the eye can observe, however, where water flowing smoothly toward the sea meets an obstacle, a rock. This causes a meander to be formed, a tiny break in the flow. Erosion begins as water is forced to eat away at the opposite bank of the flow, causing it to crumble. Forced back to the opposite side, the same erosion takes place lower down on the stream. The water deserts the straight line of gravity and begins to zigzag. Its flow to the sea has been obstructed by an abnormality, and a meander is formed.

In terms of human achievements this is a demoralizing influence–everything sinks into silt, civilizations disappear, and great works are engulfed, unless a sudden and miraculous energy breaks through. But nature cannot stop before such obstacles; she finds a solution.

> *When the time comes, the meander is dispensed with*; the river breaks through and returns to a straight course once more. Though, even so, this new route will still be encumbered for a long while with parasites, with evil vapors, with fevers and rotting decadence.
>
> And so it is also in architecture and city planning; in sociology and economics; in politics.[84]

Flying across the wild stretches of South America, on his way back to Buenos Aires, he observed the settler's farms, then the hamlets, villages, small towns, and finally the capital city.[85] His reactions were guided by a visible framework: all South American towns since the conquest have been based on the *cuadra* (square) with sides 110 meters in length. It is a simple geometrical unit suited to control and exploitation, determined by the length of a man's stride and the distance he is able to see. Suddenly the aerial view revealed an appalling disease, the wasting of an organism, and the lack of vigilance draining away the vital energy of the land–the immense scab of Buenos Aires. Where nature would have provided the requisite structure of viscera, lungs, bones, and limbs, human heedlessness has allowed a primary, organic form of life to exceed the dimensions of its cellular structure.[86]

Le Corbusier's narrative eventually returns to the human relationship to nature.

> On the one hand, nature: a cone opening away from us towards infinity. Its point transfixes us; its contents are always flowing into us.
>
> On the other hand, another cone, also opening away towards infinity: human creation.
>
> Between the two cones where their points meet stands man. Man the perceiver and man the revealer: the focal point.[87]

Man must struggle with nature in order to survive, yet he is a product of nature and must adhere to its laws. "Nature is wholly mathematical in substance, but our eyes perceive it as a series of chaotic spectacles (for the most part)."[88] Man projects the laws of nature as a manifestation of his human spirit into geometry. In this artificial universe he can live in harmony; if he abandons it, he is doomed to suffering and shocks.

FIGURE 10.10: **If the explosion of urbanism was planned, it would unfold like the bud of a plant.**

There are, in particular, simple laws of nature that man must follow in the design of cities, or else produce ineffective solutions. Take for example the idea of "deurbanization" that was formulated in Moscow in 1930. Given the symbol of a man in a thatched hut or log cabin beneath a pine tree, it stood the laws of nature on their head. Man is born to live in groups, to collaborate, not to dwell as hermits in the woods. In Germany during the 1920s, when architects in search of sunlight for their houses arranged them in wearisome parallels and ill-balanced silhouettes, these starved forms were another example of ineffective creation inverting the laws of nature.

But when a minister of Louis XV sowed pine trees on the Gascony sand dunes in order to stop the inundation of whole villages from sand blown in by the Atlantic winds, he achieved his goal immediately and provided the region a means of subsistence in the timber and resin industry. This idea was an effective creation. And when the Dutch a thousand years ago decided to turn land lying below the level of the sea into a productive and habitable region, they harnessed the wind and the sea into a coherent system of dykes, canals, and windmills. This prodigious conception, an effective creation, gave birth to a new country of lush farmlands and inestimable wealth.

Inspired by the laws of nature, the effective solutions of the Radiant City guarantee everyone the world's basic pleasures: sun in the house, sky through windowpanes, trees to look at. The basic materials of city planning are sun, sky, trees, steel, and cement, in that order of importance. The metaphor of a tree keeps reappearing as Le Corbusier examines from different angles the binomial of man and nature. A cabin beneath the pine tree becomes a deadly image of asocial man, the well-planted trees of Gascony an image of prudent man, the pinecone offers the promise of regeneration, the treelike naturalness of the radiant city a balm for the eyes. The tree bears witness to the passage of time and never stops changing its shape beneath a play of light and shadow, in the motion of the breeze, as the weather changes from season to season. It becomes a metaphoric vessel for Le Corbusier's developing doctrine. [FIGURE 10.10]

THE LIFE OF A TREE

Le Corbusier often repeats across the pages of *The Radiant City* the following message about the life of man: The spirit animating the law of nature is mathematical; the play of numbers projects its effect throughout space and time. The law of nature prescribes the 24-hour cycle of the earth, the 365 days of the solar year, the 30-day rhythm of the month. These are the units by which man's undertakings are measured.

> The life of man is an alternating thing: action, then cessation of action, *once every day*...victorious politician or tattered hobo, *all* men must sleep, always, every day of their lives! *The 24 hours of the solar cycle* constitute the measuring rod of all human activities: they are what give our lives their scale and their perspective.[89]

Articles reproduced from *Plans* appear in the fourth section of the book, which is entitled the "Radiant City." They continue the demonstration of this fundamental law of nature. [90] The twenty-four-hour cycle of the sun is in control (recall that it is the trees' "dictator"). It is the yardstick and rhythm of human life, the unit to which all distance, dimension, and distribution must conform.[91] The Earth carries every variation of climate and topography; its axis is tilted so we have four seasons with their amazing events: seedtime, growth, harvest, rest, health, joy, melancholy, sadness. "Law and unity are the product of diversity, of movement, of life, held together by a great mathematical axis running through them."[92]

But what if the daily balance sheet of body and mind, action and repose, reveals a deficit every evening? Death is victorious. What if the balance sheet shows a surplus? Then there is new life: light and joy! We need a vision so that our eyes can follow the trajectory of a well-balanced equation. Our goal is to rid ourselves of the objects that destroy present day life. Everywhere the plans, the graphs, the prototypes already exist.

Opponents will say the task is too vast.[93] They must be reminded that for five years a major war was waged: millions of men were mobilized and fed, cannons and dreadnoughts were constructed, the aviation industry created, typhoons unleashed by bombs and shells. Miracles of transportation were performed.

Yet any reform set on paper, drawn with right angles, is accused of being American. They argue the straight line is German and the curve is French. That is patriotism gone mad! In 1922, Le Corbusier created a new scale for the Contemporary City, but was worried lest its vast open spaces be filled with boredom and emptiness.[94] After eight years he understood that the true functions of the machine age were comfort and personal liberty within a collective organization. We work in order to live, and machines are able to work for us and lead to our liberation. But new needs arose, innumerable and unjustifiable desires, so that now we live in order to work. If authority imposes a regulation banning idiotic merchandise and preventing waste, then we can begin again to work in order to live.[95]

THE BATTLE OF TREES

The fifth section of the book contains articles written for *Prélude;* one of which is entitled "Bolshoi...or the notion of Bigness."[96] During a trip to Moscow in 1928, Le Corbusier listened to a speech given by the president of the Centrosoyus in which he heard the word "bolshoi" repeated several times.[97] Asking the interpreter what the word meant, he was told all modern architecture must be big in size and proportions; it must appear under the sign "Big, bolshoi." But what does the word really mean, Le Corbusier continued. "Big" was the answer. So "Bolshevism" means that everything and every theory must be as big as possible, examined in depth, the whole envisioned. Up to that point, the newspapers had taught Le Corbusier that Bolshevik meant a man with a red beard and a knife between his teeth.[98]

Le Corbusier brings the sign of the Bolshoi back to Paris. He has long admired the Pont Neuf. It was built by Androuet Du Cerceau in 1550 in the Renaissance style at a time when Paris was all Gothic, when no other impulse was allowed expression, but Du Cerceau took a prodigious step into the future: he not only built a masterful stone bridge over the Seine, he threw a bridge of greatness over three centuries, during which Paris had been marking time and not acting. Du Cerceau was able to create for the king what was needed: a work of material and spiritual bigness. To look at the bridge, to ponder the effort of carpenters and masons, and to admire the king who took possession of his new white, luminous bridge, swelling with its lyrical majesty in the Gothic city, is to be aware of the value to any city of a truly big thought.

> Thirteen years after the Great War and Big Bertha,[99] after the Atlantic had been crossed by air, after a hundred years in the machine age, an architect, with the full approval of the city authorities and as a *gesture of respect to history,* has just finished a project on the Left Bank end of the Pont Neuf executed in the style of Du Cerceau. [Le Corbusier is referring to the new apartment buildings at the end of the Rue Dauphine] That, you see, is the attitude they take to life! History says: *"Enterprise, belief and action."* But what do they proclaim? Retreat, abdication, treachery...and lies.[100]

He draws another example from the city of Berne, where there are three or four arcaded streets lined with admirable town houses. It was necessary to redevelop these houses into tourist shops. The authorities decided to look backwards: they required that the facade of each house be rebuilt in new stone exactly as in the past. Tourists flood to the city, eager to swallow this lesson in fake history. In contrast–

> Bolshoi! Bigness of mind, and mustered on every side, all the forces of good and the assurance of a *joy in life* to replace the present snickering, treacherous, fallacious joy of *hoping to possess*![101]

Throughout this story from Russia, Le Corbusier says he holds a recurrent image in mind:

> A plant or a tree, growing in good earth in the sunlight, unencumbered by any obstacles; good, solid, abundant roots; a fine trunk; noble branches; beautiful leaves, radiant flowers and fine fruits; grace of bearing, a supple and easy stance; a harmonious spectacle; a fine plant, a noble tree.[102]

Man, too, is a product of nature, and his works can grow and rise like a gigantic tree. This occurs but rarely, however, because his spiritual plants are not grown in good earth and are trammeled underneath by heedless feet. Only disinterested spirits know how to plant a seed and tend it without being troubled by customs, criticism, or impatience, or by a thirst for fame and praise. Instead they calmly follow a conventional path and produce works that bear normal fruit.[103] If one constructs according to a farsighted plan, one is treated as a utopian, a dangerous enemy of the established order; works of negation and destruction, on the other hand, always find takers.

Trees fight against each other in a life and death struggle; so too do men. Le Corbusier tells a story about the war that people say will break out between the USSR and China. A banker told him there would be two results from this war: it would produce a great need for guns, munitions, canned food, vehicles, and equipment that would save capitalism, revive the economy, and it put the USSR out of the competition between states for supremacy because an entire generation would be exhausted by war. The banker assured Le Corbusier that Krupp and Creusot were already making preparations, that big financiers had been

THE PYRAMID OF NATURAL HIERARCHIES

What is the specific characteristic of authority? That it is always recognized, appraised, and measured, according to its results. But who is to be judge? Units able to pass such judgments must be formed from those manifesting a capacity for that particular task.

All men work, practice a trade. All men are capable of making judgments about things concerning their own trades.

Men's trades must therefore form the foundation for our edifice of authority and power, for our hierarchy of responsibility. It is in the hearts of those trades that the eternal and fruitful struggle of creative effort versus academic sterility will be fought out.

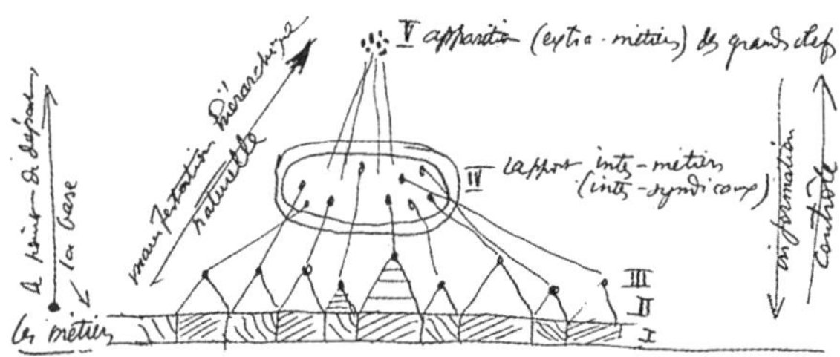

The diagram above may therefore be taken to express the various trades of society, one beside the other, forming the great foundation of society's labor (I).

From the heart of each trade will rise the pyramid of natural hierarchies (II) (this may entail the most violent struggles; but the conflict will never exceed its proper limits and spread outside the official decision-making groups).

The activities of the various trades should be simultaneous; that is the first step in a planned economy. On the next level, the qualified deputations of each trade (III) meet at an inter-union conference (IV) where the main problems of economic interdependence are hammered out and a state of balance achieved.

FIGURE 10.11: **Men of trade form the foundation upon which authority and power are based: the Syndicalist trade union diagram is shown here.**

working out plans for months. Even though Russia had yet to declare war, the banker believed that money placed in the right hands would produce the projected results.[104]

Le Corbusier is stupefied, he says, with admiration for this gigantic plan that only a few men have organized. They have been able to turn the sick world upside down, providing everyone with bread and hope. This is what it means to make a plan, and it must mean "Bolshoi" as well! "Satan could not do better."[105]

Why do these men not understand that instead of making munitions, they could reconstruct the entire world? Le Corbusier replies: the mass of men cannot understand that correct city planning is a linear conception taking years to reveal its effects; they want bread now. To realize the Radiant City means a complete political reorganization. The mass of men are intent instead on delivering a stab in the back to the only country that is attempting essential reforms (the USSR).

This is what to govern, to think big means. "Blood, mourning and shame. Such is their plan."[106] But Le Corbusier is obstinate: he will continue to draw up plans under the only true sign, that of harmony. And he will continue to make them as big as possible!

In a *Prélude* article on "Truth from Diagrams" (Part 5 of *The Radiant City*), Le Corbusier presents a drawing that he claims is characteristic of authority in a state of balance. At the bottom are trade units, each performing particular tasks. It is at this level, he explains, that the battle between creative effort and academic sterility will be fought. From the heart of each trade group rises a pyramid of natural hierarchies entailing violent struggles, but none reaching beyond its proper limits. On the next level qualified deputies meet in an inter-union conference where problems of economic interdependence are resolved and a state of balance is achieved. This leaves the top authority at liberty to concentrate on the country's higher purposes: the direction and purpose of civilization.[107] [FIGURE 10.11]

Political administration requires the notion of a boundary, a territorial definition that demarcates a frontier to be supervised. Yet the telegraph, the airplane, and the camera have made the concept of frontier obsolete. A frontier, Le Corbusier explains, is built up in stages: the family, then the tribe, and later the region. A centripetal center of attraction emerges, and another one elsewhere, and in between these two fields of attraction a frontier occurs. Order moves in a centrifugal manner: from the center to the periphery. When two regions conflict with each other, the normal void at the frontier is filled, and the two rise up in arms. That is why the frontier of dissension threatens today.[108]

This unnatural situation is the result of wars, rape, violence, the machine age, and new forms of transportation, creating disorder and economic chaos in their wake. No one was prepared for the conflicts that suddenly arose. That is why Le Corbusier calls for the nation to be reorganized both economically and spiritually. New regional administrative centers will engender new social aggregations, what he calls "natural regions" determined by climate, topography, geography, and race.

Communication infrastructure–railroads, ships, and planes, mails, telegraphs, and radio–also have to be reorganized until they work together in harmony. Le Corbusier wonders if it is possible to conceive of a new world unity. He commands the reader to open the atlas, to consider the world as a whole, and to base one's thinking on the cosmic reality that controls everything–the sun. The map of the world reveals that the machine age civilization is restricted to areas where the sun is neither too hot nor excessively cold.[109] The true line of trade should be longitudinally based, not latitudinal. The latter causes territories to get in each other's way, compete with each other, and ignore all that space to the north and south. Le Corbusier would reorganize political frontiers, leaving open areas near territorial boundaries. He naively assumes this would protect the world from national conflicts and international wars.[110]

A LUMP OF COAL IN A BRAZIER

In articles appearing in *Plans,* Le Corbusier reiterated his fear that cities were reaching their limits, building on top of themselves and forming towering cliffs. The streets, the basic organ of the city, were noisy and dangerous, forcing automobiles to crawl along at slow speeds and pedestrians to zigzag from side to side. Office buildings were dark and noisy, the air of residential buildings tainted with dust and soot. How can anyone live without serenity, relaxation, joy, or freedom?

> The man in the city is a lump of coal in a brazier; he is being burned up simple for the energy he produces. Then he fades and crumbles away. Every year, fresh contingents flood in from the country to replace those who have been burned out.[111]

A reaction sets in: the railroad whisks the laborer, the clerk, the shopgirl out of the city. Like an exploding shell, the city reaches as far out as the eye can see. One day out of seven, these suburban dwellers are allowed to relax in their little houses surrounded by greenery. But they remain isolated and alone because their friends live on the opposite side of town, in another suburb.

> Suburbs are broken, dislocated limbs! The city has been torn apart and scattered in meaningless fragments across the countryside.... Suburban life is a despicable delusion entertained by a society stricken with blindness.[112]

A great adventure lies before us. Americans rushed ahead into the machine age; like true pioneers they have had the courage to improvise, but they did not foresee the consequences, and today are trapped in so many dead-end streets. America's gigantic lesson is a negative one. Russia and Italy are building new regimes. We must somehow learn

FIGURE 10.12: Aerial views taught Le Corbusier that obsolete land divisions made farmlands unfit for machine cultivation.

how to gauge these events, to evaluate and judge. Only then can we invent, decide, and act.

Increasingly in the 1930s, Le Corbusier modulates his machine metaphor with organic associations. The tree metaphor has been stressed, but the city is also likened to a body, with head, heart, lungs, and feet. The suburbs are limbs torn off from a trunk expanded grotesquely out of shape. "All architectural products, all city neighborhoods or cities ought to be *organisms.* This word immediately conveys a notion of character, of balance, of harmony, of symmetry."[113] He tells of a large farm in the Alps where pigs are fattened inside boxes just the size for a fat, grown pig. The pig grows inside this box until it is fully grown, then is taken to the butcher for slaughter on a stretcher because it cannot walk on its own stunted legs. Such are present-day architectural and planning projects: "Compressed and deformed by the relentless interference of so many factors entirely foreign to the problem–by stupidities."[114]

In Russia, a new economy requires the construction of new buildings: factories and dams, agricultural settlements, industrial cities, residential districts, office buildings, conference halls, clubs, stadiums, railroad stations, and airports. The building regulations have been entirely rethought. There is a theory and a plan. Each time, the function has been clearly delineated before architects begin to design an organism to fulfill the function.[115] In the West, inadequate sites have led to orthopedic architecture; in the USSR, architects have freedom in their plans.[116] We must undertake a wholesale reorganization of land tenure in the country and the cities. [FIGURE 10.12]

If you are one of the city's parasites, you will live like a sick dog and you will be burned up as a lump of coal in the furnace. The parasites must return to the land, find some fruitful form of activity. But let us not accept the illusory solution of garden cities!

> The city must pull itself together, contract, become human again...as a result of a simple and joyful reorganization founded on the 24-hour solar cycle that is our unalterable destiny.[117]

We must purge our cities, "put our house in order."[118] The cities, villages, and farms of France are all obsolete and falling down. Their remains may give witness to the virile and dignified life that once was lived there, but they have no use in modern life. "We are living in an antique shop; we could be living in the area of present-day realities."[119] We must make the decision: purge the old city, build the Radiant Green City.

The list continues of the things that need to be reformed. Le Corbusier concludes, hammering relentlessly on his great point: there is no respite, no solution to the problems of the city, because there is no plan.[120] We must recognize that the despot everyone is waiting for is not a man, it is a plan.

The lessons of history teach that "an old city must always be replaced by a new and that a new city must have *a biological organization that conforms to the necessities of the machine in which we are living*!"[121] Private land tenure invested with private rights is an obstacle to the Radiant City; jurists must find a way to resolve this antagonism and provide the authorities with the means to perform their duties. The certainty remains: an old city must be replaced by a new one.

THE TREE OF (CIVIC) LIFE

In an article on "The spectacle of modern life" written for *Prélude* (appearing in Part 5 of *The Radiant City*), Le Corbusier further discusses the political reforms that are required for this new age. Most men, he begins, work for money, only a few for quality. Yet working for money stimulates only a few of man's talents, leaving most inactive.[122] It even encourages defects in character. Thus labor needs to be reorganized if its fruits are to be redistributed in a beneficial manner.

There is, moreover, a need for (of course) a plan, for rules of the game, and for discipline. Even children demand rules for their games. Rules enable man to achieve harmony with the forces that have been unleashed upon the world, allowing him to work efficiently.

> By efficiently, I mean so that everyone receives a merited share of their benefits. And by merited share, I mean the right to eat, the right to expect a serene end to a life that has been filled with fruitful labors, and the right to know the reasons for all the daily actions we are obliged to perform.[123]

He turns to Holland for an example.[124] Le Corbusier had recently visited a magnificent factory in Rotterdam where he discovered that all connotations of despair had been removed from the word "proletarian" and replaced with an enlightened spirit of collective action. The factory rises from the banks of a canal alongside the railroad tracks, two parallel lines glistening in the grass. On the horizon, across the flat meadows, rise derricks from the harbor outlining bold profiles in the sky. The road into the factory is smooth, bordered with brown-tiled sidewalks. The glass and metal facades of the factory buildings rise high against the sky. All is serenity, everything open to the outside, inside a poem of light, immaculate lyricism built in an atmosphere of honesty. Everyone can see the manager in his glass box, and he can view the horizon and the life of the great port. In the glass refectory everyone eats together. Everyone is neat and clean, healthy and strong. There is no proletariat here, but a graded hierarchy with a voluntary respect for order and kindliness. The mechanics have all become gentlemen! Everyone participated in the design of its program during the five years it was being planned.[125]

The day he visited this factory, Le Corbusier proclaims, was one of the most beautiful days of his life.[126]

The next day he met the director of the East Indies Airline at the Amsterdam airport. Only those who have experienced flying high over virgin jungle, estuaries, mountain chains, and unexploded stretches of territory can understand the emotions he felt when he gazed on the vast mural map of Europe, Africa, and Asia, marked with

FIGURE 10.13: A consequence of the machine age: the city is being invaded by the countryside. It means the death of folk art.

red and blue lines representing eight different routes that were flown by this airline. He shuddered with excitement as he realized that airplanes were at that very moment flying along those lines, but each at a different (local) time of day.

He points up the contrast, the rapid progress: back in 1909, he stuck his head out of the window of his Paris apartment to see Comte de Lambert flying over the city. That evening Paris was mad with joy. To arrive at such collective action from individual flights to the airline routes crisscrossing the world, personal participation must be experienced at every step of the way.[127]

THE RADIANT FARM AND THE TWENTY-FOUR HOURS

Farms, Le Corbusier argued in the seventh part of *The Radiant City*, labeled "Rural Reorganization," "are the folkloric expression of a region. I have a complete respect for folklore. The study of folklore, on ceaseless travels, has been fundamental to my education."[128]

Yet the peasantry was a source of political tension between the wars. Half to a third of the population of France remained farmers on small, unproductive plots. They were increasingly bitter as commodity prices declined, taxes rose, and their representation in public affairs remained minimal. Nevertheless, in 1935 France spent nearly half as much again on wheat subsidies as it did on national defense, because it hoped that the countryside would enable the nation to withstand the depression ransacking the economy.[129]

In the early 1930s, Le Corbusier, echoing neo-syndicalist ideas, began to develop plans for the reconstruction of the countryside, seen as the opposite pole to the city.[130] In "Reply to the Peasants" (appearing in Part 7 of *The Radiant City*), he argued that the "country is the other city of to-morrow....The highway is our means of salvation. By means of the highway we can win back our country regions, all our country regions. And it is also by means of the highway that these country regions will be linked together."[131,132] And earlier in the *The Radiant City*, he says: "The concept of *city planning* must be applied not only to the great cities but also to the towns, to the countryside, to the country in its entirety."[133]

The money civilization had extended its grip to the peasant and turned his life into a barren wasteland, forcing him off the land and into the city. Thus, one of the noblest tasks of the present was the reconstruction of the countryside. This called for plans for both the city and the countryside based on one value alone, that of man.

It meant replacing the cruel civilization based on money with another one based on harmony and cooperation. [FIGURE 10.13]

There is a duty, or so Le Corbusier proclaimed, to turn our thoughts to the peasant, to make him into a brother and not an underprivileged enemy. But first there must be rural reorganization and redistribution of the land. France must face the fact that her topography, regional winds, water sources, and sunlight make tending the soil a precise and varied business that requires constant initiative, invention, wisdom, and attention. It must not turn agriculture into some form of monopoly organization, but nurture its diverse and particular products. Le Corbusier thought the variety of soil types and climates were more suitable to "garden" cultivation than to large-scale farming. It led toward a modern equation made up of two variables: the family farm at the center of a land allotment system and the cooperative village as the heart of the peasant community.[134]

Norbert Bézard, an agricultural laborer from the Sarthe region and a member of the *Prélude* group, asked Le Corbusier to do for the countryside what he had done for the city: produce plans for a Radiant Farm and a Radiant Village.[135] After years of research, Le Corbusier concluded that cities were bulging with human detritus that should not remain there, but must be returned to the countryside.[136] Yet his travels also caused him to conclude that the farms and villages were rotten with age and crumbling away. Compared to the city dweller, the peasant on his farm lived a wretched existence.

> From the airplane, I look down on infinitely subdivided, incongruously shaped plots of land. The more modern machinery develops, the more the land is chopped up into tiny holdings that render the miraculous promise of that machinery useless. The result is waste, inefficiency, individual scrabbling.[137]

> Yet the city as well as the farm were organic entities: they are products of human creativity. A farm...is a thing that resembles the products of *nature*...a kind of geometrical plant that is as intimately tied to the landscape as a tree or a hill, yet as expressive of our human presence as a piece of furniture or a machine.[138]

The peasant must be offered the same technical and spiritual revolutions of modern times as the city worker, until the farm becomes a modern tool. A body of mechanical and architectural equipment must surround the peasant's every action, equipment that is "as impeccably efficient as the machinery that propels and sustains the aviator when his craft sweeps him up into the sky."[139]

Consequently, the peasant can no longer be treated as a "clodhopper." He reads newspapers; he is informed and educated by the radio; he is in contact with the city through buses, the railroad, and books. His work dictates that he be in constant cooperation with others, so certain machines can be owned collectively and at everyone's disposal. There can be cooperative repair shops, a cooperative store, and a cooperative silo. These will safeguard him from the grip of financial speculators, moneylenders, and crooks.[140]

Le Corbusier, with Bézard's help, spent six months penetrating the "secrets" of rural life. Everything was classified and ordered, and drawn in plan and section. A model was built as a prototype of the modern farm.[141] He organized the Radiant Farm around the family unit. "Family" implies a house: it must be hygienic, flooded with light, a piece of equipment kept in good shape, as an automobile or a tractor is maintained.[142] Raised on piloti to avoid the damp, it was located on a site outside the farmyard so that it commands both the farm and the road leading to it. In one direction it looks over the farmyard, in another, the orchard, in a third, the flower garden, and in the fourth, it oversees the road leading to the village. In warm weather, the family gathers under the house between the piloti to eat, drink, read, or see the sunset. During the day women do the washing there. In cold weather the traditional kitchen sitting-room becomes the center of life: commandeered by the women during the day, by the men when they are relaxing. Since the farmhouse is to be heated by modern equipment, there is no need for the open hearth. All modern equipment is there—radios and phonographs, bedrooms for the parents, the children; two bathrooms with showers, one for women, the other for men.[143]

The farmyard has a concrete floor, free from standing water. The equipment shed holds a tractor, plough, weeder, dung-spreader, sower, roller, hay-mower, reaper and binder, tedder, hay-turner, potato-planter, and potato-digger, in addition to a two-wheeler, a hay cart, an automobile, and a van. There is a separate a workshop for the maintenance of all this machinery. On the other side of the farmyard are the animal sheds, whose layout is also rationalized. Beyond the sheds lies the barn, where crops are stored and a corner reserved for the care of sick animals. A railing runs across the barn's ceiling with hooks along its rollers for moving heavy goods.[144] Le Corbusier believed he had thought of everything that would make the Radiant Farm.

Like the farm, the plan of the cooperative village was a function of transportation, storage needs, and merchandise-handling problems, and required a horizontal site. The first building is the communal silo for storage of products, designed for the loading and unloading of trucks. A section of road leads to the smith, the garage, the repair shop, the gas station, and the communal machinery store. Another leads to the cooperative supply buildings: dairy, bakery, grocery, fish counter, butcher's counter, deep freeze, hardware, haberdashery, cobbler, whatever the farmer might need. Here is where collectively bought goods are retailed to the peasants, keeping their prices in check. At one end of the village is a post office, a school, and a communal apartment house for the inhabitants of the village.[145] At the other is the village hall, containing the mayor's office and the labor unions. Nearby stands the club, with its library, auditorium, and sports grounds. Such is the Radiant Village.[146]

Having reformed the countryside, there was one more issue that Le Corbusier had to address: cultivation of the mind and body during leisure. He repeatedly used (e.g., in "Truth from Diagrams") a circular diagram representing the twenty-four-hour solar cycle, sunrise to sunset. In the pre-machine age, he argued, each day revolved in an uninterrupted progress from cause to effect. Men's hands and minds worked together in permanent collaboration.[147] Man was active, responsible, creative, and participating. Then came a revolution: work was snatched out of men's hands and entrusted to machines. A new hierarchy formed, with those at the top having the most intense involvement, those at the bottom having the least. In most industries a vast pit of boredom was dug all around the worker, turning him into a proletarian. This uselessness had to be inverted, the laborer given back responsibility and allowed to participate. Such was the syndicalist program.[148]

The disc representative of the twenty-four-hour cycle of the machine-age civilization had a new sector of time added to it in the 1930s: that of leisure. To man's productive day must be added maintenance of the body, cultivation of the mind; time for handicrafts, competitive sports, and family life. Then the word "proletarian" will disappear, and man's day will be truly productive.[149]

The vague notion of "leisure time" must be transformed into a "disciplined function," for the machine age has developed new tools to enhance leisure time.[150] Now an agricultural or industrial worker has a radio; he can listen to Beethoven or Stravinsky, important lectures, orations of heads of state. The movie house assails him once a week with ostentatious lessons in luxury living and comfort. The book, the newspaper, and the magazine have transformed his world. There are only two limits to the fantastic meal being set on the world's table: one is the twenty-four-hour cycle of the sun, and the other is the economic crisis that occurs when the world can no longer consume what it produces. We must learn, Le Corbusier advised, to master this machine![151]

III. THE 1937 EXHIBITION AND THE TEMPS NOUVEAUX

The early thirties culminated in 1935 with *The Radiant City,* but from 1932 to 1937 Le Corbusier was also preoccupied by–and repeatedly frustrated in his hopes for–the Exposition Internationale des Arts et Techniques dans la Vie Moderne, planned for 1937.

As the 1930s unfurled, the specter of war grew and countries began to rearm. Workers grew increasingly restless, ready to unite in protest, while economic depression continued to hold the West in its grip. Italy invaded Ethiopia in 1935, Germany remilitarized the Rhine in 1936, and Franco began his battle against the Spanish Republic the same year. The master plan for the Exposition reflected these political tensions, undergoing at least twenty different revisions between 1932 and 1937 and contradicting Le Corbusier's belief that a plan, a neutral document, could stand outside of the political fray. When the Popular Front came to power on June 5, 1936, this loose and fragile coalition of leftists had a brief twelve months to build all the structures for the Exposition. The government hoped that the Exposition would reveal "the feeling of national cohesion," but this was not to be. The Popular Front was itself out of power by June 22, 1937, before all the exhibitions at the Exposition had been completed.

The Exposition of 1937 was a symbolically important event for the Popular Front. It placed on review the machine as the agent of leisure and liberation, and created a cultural laboratory to judge the success or failure of its governmental rule.[152] The Popular Front wanted to send a message to the world about a newfound harmony between industry and labor; it had, in fact, already passed legislation within the first few months of its existence raising wages, establishing procedures for collective bargaining, and granting workers a forty-hour workweek and two weeks of paid vacation per year. It had also created social insurance measures, child labor laws, and free primary-school education.[153] For the Exposition, it erected the Palais de la Solidarité to showcase labor unions, an ideal factory displaying the many improvements of daily life that machine production provided. "Solidarity" meant, for the Popular Front, intervention by the state on behalf of the needs of the working class.[154]

Yet preparations for the Exposition were, as already mentioned, fractious. A wave of spontaneous labor strikes began in May 1936, threatening the stability of the Popular Front and impeding construction of the Exposition, which itself became a place of hostilities between industrialists and labor. Labor unions wanted to preserve, under the worsening conditions of the Depression, whatever pyrrhic victories they had recently achieved; industrialists claimed that the Confédération Generale des Travailleurs and the Communist Party were working around the clock to sabotage the Exposition. The trade unions were furious when companies refused to hire more workers, accusing some contractors of withholding necessary building materials as a protest against the Popular Front and others of refusing to pay overtime or of hiring cheaper labor from the provinces.[155] Planned to open on May 1 (International Labor Day), inaugurating a six-month celebration of labor, the Exposition was delayed three weeks, and many exhibitions remained unfinished until deep into the summer.[156]

It was also hoped that the Exposition would manifest cooperation among nations. But at the southern entrance to the Trocadero, in the largest section of the Exposition dedicated to foreign exhibits, the pavilions of the Soviet Union and Nazi Germany faced off. In sheer size, the Russian palace surpassed all the other displays, crowned with Vera Mukhina's monumental sculpture of a young man and woman stepping forward into the future, their arms interlocked, the hammer and sickle raised on high. Opposite stood the neoclassical German pavilion designed by Albert Speer, with its group of statues, an aggressive arrangement of three nude figures suggestive of Aryan-Greek archetypes. The pillars of the pavilion drew the spectator's gaze upwards toward the display of the eagle and its swastika.[157]

A DEMONSTRATION PROJECT: "UNITÉ D'HABITATION"

The "contemporary perturbation"–as Le Corbusier called the turmoil of the 1930s–stemmed, he said, from the simple matter of housing.[158] Civilization suffered from not being lodged, from not having industry address the issue. Therefore, Le Corbusier spoke to a CIAM group in London in May 1934 of his plan to create a "working model" of his vision of housing, titled "Unité d'Habitation" (Unit of Habitation), to be installed as part of the 1937 Exhibition. This ambitious, complex piece would, he intended, remain after the fair as a permanent establishment.

The site proposed for this experimentation was the belvedere and promenade on the Bastion Kellerman, which had originally been constructed as part of the fortifications of Paris by Napoleon III. Le Corbusier grouped a series of dwellings commanding a magnificent view to the east of the Cité Universitaire, sufficient in number to provide all the necessary common services, including hospital facilities, sporting and sunning installations, and a network of roads for automobile circulation. This model would constitute a "demonstration" of all his research. In order to give a broader context to this work, Le Corbusier transferred the entire project into the hands of CIAM, which at its CIRPAC (executive body of CIAM, or Comité International pour la Résolution des Problèmes de l'Architecture Contemporaine [International Committee for the Resolution of Problems of Contemporary Architecture]) meeting in London, May 1934, designated a committee of direction to stand behind the French CIAM group as they prepared material for the Exposition.[159]

There were still several years to go. The issue of housing throughout France was an urgent problem, and Le Corbusier felt the time for theorizing was over. In early 1935, in an unpublished essay, he labeled the issue *l'urbanisme totale*.[160] Forget about transforming furniture, the decorative forms of useful objects, constructing jolly garden suburbs and comfortable private hotels! These ameliorative attempts irritated him, he said, for they were "only details, derivative fragments." Instead, it was urgent to convince society to undertake a new adventure: the material realization of the second era of machine civilization. This meant an entire renewal of the country and the economy, resulting in the production of useful objects of consumption, which he equates to housing in cities, towns, and villages.

In the midst of the Depression, still hoping that the hour of great works had been sounded, Le Corbusier pondered the role authority should play in society in an essay published in *Architecture d'Aujourd'hui* in September 1935.[161] Some men, he says, those reputed to know how to assure the most regular steps, are placed at the head of certain functions. Thus authority becomes a static regulator and holds everything in equilibrium: techniques, labor, salaries, even ethical values. Yet one of these factors, that of scientific technique, has escaped the status quo and transformed the very facts of life, breaking the equilibrium and allowing conflict to erupt. Society now becomes divided between those who look behind, grasping for security and certitude, and those who look ahead, attracted by the unknown and the sparkling promise of the future. In this troubled moment it is necessary for authority to see clearly, to be agile and able to bend. Thus, revolution enters into the body of authority and the hour of "clairvoyants" arrives.

Le Corbusier introduces the subject of the Exposition of 1937. He labels Edmond Labbé, the authority placed in charge of preparations, one of these clairvoyants. Until 1934, the Exposition had been called the Exposition Internationale des Arts Décoratifs, repeating the error of 1925 and placing elite artisans of the luxury trades in control. They were completely indifferent to the mass of unemployed and destitute tradesmen that the Depression had created. But finally, Labbé was selected to be the general commissioner, and he chose a new title for the exposition, Arts et Techniques. The hour of clairvoyance arrives and the flower of happiness opens!

Le Corbusier reminds the reader that in 1925 he wrote about "architecture or revolution." "Revolution" commonly means to smash everything and to place oneself on the top of the debris, but "architecture" signifies "to put in order," to conceive, organize, and build. After long years of research and investigation, Le Corbusier can once again declare "revolution *and* architecture." Architects are revolutionaries with the aim of making the temps nouveaux develop and thrive; they are the new authority to be entrusted with the direction of society. Their research stretches across social, psychological, and biological phenomena, across economic and political facts. They are patient and strong, curious and supple, constantly reexamining origins, sowing seeds, and caring to make an entire tree grow straight and tall (Le Corbusier is here reusing the master metaphor of *The Radiant City*). This tree represents for Le Corbusier a continuous and harmonious cycle without rupture, season after season, year after year. The architect–"the man of authority with this tree"–will make forests grow. The architect will fix what is to be done and how to undertake it; he will bear evidence to the spirit of the times.[162]

In France, there is a place where this spirit can be illuminated. It is the École Polytechnique, where great leaders of all grand enterprises are trained. The light of architecture of the temps nouveaux throws a beacon ahead, it lights the way to the future. Le Corbusier does not speak to the dictatorship of the École des Beaux-Arts, obsessed with their limited meaning of architecture, but to the great "harmonizers" who throw a light on plans, who will be the authority at the foot of the wall.

FIGURE 10.14: Le Corbusier planned to erect a large statue of painted wood in front of a display of agrarian reforms that would symbolize the alliance made between the peasant and the steel worker—collaborating to build metallic constructions for farms and villages. This, like so many other ideas for the Pavillon de Temps Nouveaux, was defeated for lack of money.

PAVILLON DES TEMPS NOUVEAUX

Des Canons, Des Munitions? Merci! Les Logis... S.V.P, whose role in Le Corbusier's rhetoric of war and peace was explored earlier, is both a collection of various articles and project descriptions that demonstrate his ideals for the Radiant City and Radiant Farm as well as a catalogue describing the Pavillon des Temps Nouveaux (Pavilion of the New Times, intermittently called the Pavillon des Temps Modernes) that Le Corbusier's atelier designed under the guidance of CIAM for the Exposition of 1937.

Le Corbusier opens *Des Canons, Des Munitions* with a description of Jean Epstein's recent documentary being shown in Paris under the auspices of the Fédération du Bâtiment (Building Federation).[163] *Les Bâtisseurs* revolves around a story from the Middle Ages, when everyone and everything were united in order to build the cathedral of Chartres. Afterwards the world fell into a hole of brutality and failure of conscience. Six hundred years followed, during which the gap between cause and effect grew wider, all rational sense was lost, and unity was pulverized. Then, in the nineteenth century, a new cycle of discoveries began and new links between cause and effect were felt, so that even though there were difficult times, full of fracas and dismay, underneath was a unanimous march toward a new unity. So too in the 1930s: "Unity, that is adequate enough to allow us, in the immense tumult, to be able to seize today by the hand. And to make evident, in doing so, the reason for our lives."[164] This was the purpose behind the Pavillon des Temps Nouveaux. The reference to the builder of cathedrals allowed him to link *Des Canons, Des Munitions* (1937) to *When the Cathedrals Were White* (1935).

Le Corbusier had many difficulties securing sufficient credit to build any one of the seven successive proposals he designed for the Exposition, beginning with his earliest plans in 1932. He summarizes these struggles in the catalogue portion of *Des Canons, Des Munitions.* Before doing so, however, he has to set the record straight–it should be understood that the development of modern techniques and machines effected changes in the arts and daily life, not vice versa. [FIGURE 10.14] But the Exposition inverted this argument, introducing a few technical objects or technical allusions into its many displays of art, hence "Arts et Techniques." The result is a puerile game of decorative amusements, a gesture of reform from the outside in rather than the inside out, and so far merely imitates the disastrous Exposition des Arts Décoratifs of 1925. On the contrary, Le Corbusier argued, it is necessary to accept the existence of wholesome and natural techniques, and to realize that art is their flourishing effect.

If one takes the mass of men by the hand to see how they are made in body and mind, if one goes into their houses to see how they sleep, eat, create a family, raise their children, to understand what they talk about, their work and concerns, their small corner of blue sky that gives them hope, then one would be stupefied to see the mean manner in which they are housed: on dark narrow streets, in cramped city districts. In this new civilization full of mechanical and mathematical rigor, why do the mass of men stagnate in such a dung heap? The fox in the forest, the bird in the trees, the fish in the water, they too struggle every moment to survive, but at least the fox has the forest, the bird the leaves, the fish its streams, rivers, and oceans. Man has lost contact with the sun, the sky, and the trees–he vegetates in a state that is against nature. That is why the problem of urbanism is that of the hut (*gîte*).

Le Corbusier returns to his opening theme, cinema, for he accepts that the Exposition is after all a matter of entertainment, no matter how didactic the Pavillon des Temps Nouveaux may be. There are movies that dare, from time to time, to reveal this "joyless street"–the great misfortune of the times. (Le Corbusier is referring to the 1932 silent film by G. W. Pabst, *The Joyless Street*, which had been criticized for revealing the destitution of housing and living conditions throughout Germany.) But not Hollywood, of course, where goddesses and gods carry the sun of artifice within their bruised hearts: one does not want to pay a franc to be enlisted in that morass.

Since World War I, housing with light, space, and greenery has been born; it breaks through here and there, sporadically and exceptionally.[165] Le Corbusier repeats the refrain about the nameless street without joy–a "savage mark"–always dark, narrow, suffocating, walled in with houses and jammed with the torrent of automobiles. In this description he repeats "savage mark" three times, and adds the complaint that modern work now separates the hands from the head, allowing only a few to become creators.[166] The rest are required to spend their joyless days coming and going to work along dreadful streets. At the end of the street is a door, a courtyard, a staircase, another door, and a room where one is huddled and surrounded with a "leprous morale." And always under the window appears the joyless street.

All the necessary techniques exist: steel, cement, glass, air conditioning, soundproofing, the common sharing of domestic services, and the separation of pedestrians from automobiles. These have already accomplished an architectural revolution, and entail the solution of urbanization as well. They bring sun, space, and trees into each housing unit and create the Radiant City. In "radiant housing," the men will feel a just relationship between cause and effect, between labor and his recompense, between the technique and the art of the temps nouveaux.

In May and June 1936, Louis Aragon organized three roundtable debates among different artists at the Maison de la Culture (House of Culture) on the question of "realism" in art. These debates became known as "La Querelle du Réalisme" ("Argument over Realism"), and two of them were published in *Commune* (1936). The sympathies of most left-leaning intellectuals lay with a Soviet-style social realism rather than with non-objective painting derived from cubism. Aragon, as director of the Maison de la Culture under the sponsorship of the French Communist Party, had already offered a series of lectures in 1935 with the title "Pour un Réalisme Socialiste" ("For a Socialist Realism"). He called for artists to be engaged in social and political reality. In the transformation of this reality, artists should strive toward a more accessible art with topical subjects capable of engaging a wider audience.[167] In the context of 1936, when the Popular Front had just been elected to power, this meant giving art back to the people.

Of course Le Corbusier did not agree, nor was he interested in "realism" as such. In his talk at the Maison de la Culture entitled "Destin de la peinture" ("Destiny of Painting"), he proclaimed that all representational or documentary functions once the province of painting have been replaced by photography, the cinema, and illustrated magazines. He held a separate definition of realism, if one must use the word: it was a matter of meeting the needs of the country in terms of housing and equipment, and was no longer an artistic idiom. He was interested instead in the synthesis of the arts, albeit one in which the architect retained control over all of the other arts.[168]

In the same month, on the fifteenth of June, Le Corbusier wrote a text or address describing the Pavillon des Temps Modernes as "un palais de l'urbanisme" (a palace of urbanism). It was a text also carrying the names of Pierre Jeanneret, CIAM Groupe France, and the architects of the Maison de la Culture to whom it was addressed. Le Corbusier was critical of the meager manner in which modern techniques had been deployed by society. The technical progress of the machine was used exclusively for the benefit of a few privileged people and to the detriment of the majority.[169] The mass of people were excluded from the benefits of new techniques in the building industries; they were forced to live in slums that killed their children, work in factories that poisoned their health, and pay exorbitant prices for services such as gas, electricity, water, and transportation, money that should have been spent in feeding their children. They lacked kindergartens, community clinics, sports arenas, and sanitariums. Yet the privileged few benefited from the work these same laborers did. Society, Le Corbusier argued, camouflages this inequity, placing responsibility on the machine as the cause of the workers' misery, claiming they are not yet sufficiently civilized to benefit from a comfortable home. It was the intent of the Pavillon des Temps Modernes to destroy this ideology by showing how machines can assure the worker's well-being.

This text's overtly leftist position reflects the fact that it also carries the name of Pierre Jeanneret, a sympathizer with the left as well the left-leaning Maison de la Culture. But it also represents Le Corbusier's political maneuverings: the Popular Front had just come to power, and he needed to win their support if his plans for the Exposition were to be executed. Thus his "palais de l'urbanisme" would have, he says, a double aim: to be a permanent installation after the Exposition was over as well as a demonstration for "the people" of a program to eradicate their misery. Consequently, he suggests that the architects of the Maison de la Culture would be the liaison between his own collaborators and the Exposition officials. He makes a political gesture by calling on the leftist sympathizers of the Maison de la Culture under the direction of Aragon for help in raising the funds he needs to execute his plans and spread his message.[170]

Since the early 1930s, Le Corbusier had been called upon to defend himself against accusations that he only designed villas for the rich, that his interest in creating efficient business districts only benefited capitalists, that he had no sympathies for the plight of the workers. On the contrary, Le Corbusier argues in 1931, the plight of the workers is why he finally decided, after considerable research, that a human cell of fourteen square meters per inhabitant was the basic unit on which all of his calculations for housing should be based.[171]

In *The Radiant City* he explains that this module was developed while considering plans for Moscow in 1930. Based on confused thinking, however, the USSR has decided to "deurbanize," because the city as such was assumed to be a capitalist tool. "The present craze for words seems to have got out of hand. Yesterday, I received a letter from Germany on the subject of *Anticapitalist Architecture*! This is mere folly! Semantic floundering!"[172] Milioutin, the People's Commissar, published a book denouncing Le Corbusier's Voisin Plan for renewing Paris as capitalist, for a business center must be capitalist, yet Le Corbusier's Centrosoyus building (Palace of Light Industry), an administrative center for Soviet cooperatives, was sited next door to the Gostorck, the Foreign Trade Center, and surrounded with vast office buildings for the administration of industries and business affairs. So even the Russians are building a business center, and a business center by definition must be capitalist!

Le Corbusier was, he goes on, accused at the 1931 special CIAM meeting in Berlin of building only for the rich—even though at that time he showed forty meters of plans for the Radiant City and he had already built workers' housing in Pessac (1923–26). Denied a water connection by the authorities, these apartment blocks stood empty for six long years. What seems even more outrageous to Le Corbusier is that Milioutin, the People's Commissar, lives in a model apartment building in Moscow, "designed by Ghinsbourg [*sic*]" according to plans derived from Le Corbusier's apartment villas published in 1922.[173] So why must he continually be called upon to defend himself against accusations that he is a bourgeois capitalist? Le Corbusier admits he builds houses for the rich, but he has been researching the problem of housing and city planning since 1914. His concern has always been man, neither rich nor poor.[174]

Le Corbusier has also been criticized, he says, for using the word *palais* when he wrote *Une Maison—Un Palais* (1928). Yet in outlining the program for the Pavillon des Temps Modernes he again utilizes this controversial term: "Un palais de l'urbanisme." The program he envisioned for this palais was a visual polemic in three parts. First, it will display a set of comparative tableaux, a visual demonstration of technical progress from the beginning of the machine age to the present, plus a record of the history of Expositions and how these have marked the progress of technology. Second, other comparative tableaux will present the benefits achieved in architecture, housing, and urbanism following the proclamations of CIAM. Links will be made to trade groups showing how they have developed freely and creatively. Third, the palais will contain a documentary resumé of the misery of life found throughout France, with a clear demonstration of the differences between classes. It will deliver its message with precision, and proclaim as its standard bearer that the people are the army in a political struggle for a better life.

In an essay published in *The March of Times* in 1936, Le Corbusier describes the history of universal expositions. He focuses on how earlier expositions visually displayed the progress of the machine over the last one hundred years.[175] Until the middle of the nineteenth century, he argued, the age of the mechanic (the manual laborer) prevailed, but then a new age arrived, the age of the machine, offering a new anatomy of bone and muscle, extending the arm of man. An extra-human force captured and domesticated the power of seas, lightning, rivers, making them usable. At first only engineers and heads of industry profited from these innovations, but in the latter half of the century, the great international expositions revealed to the masses the promise these machines held for their own betterment. In gigantic halls, immense crowds were witness to the benefits this new collaboration between man and machine engendered. But the promised abundance could not be delivered because the benefits were deregulated, badly distributed, and without a rational plan.

The man-machine collaboration had nevertheless opened a miraculous door on the unknown: research penetrated the secrets of the natural world, while chemistry, physics, and biology explored the laws of life. Religion rose up to fight against this new devil of science. In spite of progress, man was molested, and his vital needs forgotten. Scientists and men of money took advantage of this situation; mixed up with the devil, they could not be stopped; they allowed the machine to dominate and crush the worker. Man fell into despair, with violence as the inevitable result.

Le Corbusier breaks away from his historical account to declare that the program of the temps nouveaux must be the celebration of life, to show how the machine can be used to serve the needs of man. Consequently, the theme of the Exposition of 1937 must place man in the center, everything directed toward one aim: his simple happiness. Hence, Le Corbusier reiterates, the Pavillon des Temps Nouveaux will be a manifesto dedicated to housing, a notion inseparable from urbanism. It shall take as its two themes leisure, or the provision of the essential joys of living, and the realization of housing by industrial production.

About the same time as these two essays were written, Le Corbusier was interviewed for *1937, Notre Revue.* Asked about his proposals for the Exposition, he explained that as early as 1932, when people first began to discuss the possibility of an Exposition in Paris, he proposed that it be renamed "1937–International Exposition de l'Habitation."[176] And he published this thesis in a small booklet of sixteen pages, complete with a number of plans and designs. As he conceived the Exposition, it would focus on housing, its equipment, the arrangement of land uses, the requirements for light, air, and silence, the provision of public services, the recuperation of physical and nervous energy, child-raising needs, and so on. But far from imposing his ideas on all the other exhibitors, Le Corbusier would provide in his own manner "one element of a district of housing"–the Pavillon.[177] He shows the interviewer a photograph of a model "unité d'habitation," a housing group distilling his ideas of the Radiant City.

STYMIED AMBITIONS

Le Corbusier's favored site was on the edge of the Bois de Vincennes, the park at the eastern end of the great axis crossing Paris. This demonstration project would provide a stage for displaying the equipment needed for domestic life. After the Exposition, it was his intention that the interior wooden display frames needed for the exposition would be dismantled, but the building would be transformed into a permanent housing project. No official response was ever given to his proposal, however, as official plans for the Exposition began to flounder.

In 1934, when the Chamber of Commerce picked up the idea of an Exposition again, Le Corbusier submitted a modified version of the same proposal. This time the city responded, allowing Le Corbusier to select a site on the Bastion Kellerman for his modified "unité d'habitation" for four thousand, but reducing considerably the amount of money allocated for the project.[178] After nineteen months of work, it was suddenly pointed out to Le Corbusier that he had signed a contract requiring demolition of his demonstration project after the Exposition closed; a clause in small print had been inserted precisely to prevent its permanent installation. Obviously this forced Le Corbusier to abandon any idea of creating a permanent demonstration project for his Unité d'Habitation.

To get a fresh breath of air from these malicious attacks, Le Corbusier departed for North America (see Chapter 9). While in New York, he received a letter from Edmond Labbé, commissioner general of the Exposition, offering him a site near the Porte d'Italie. This time Le Corbusier proposed a model museum of knowledge in the shape of a square spiral. Intended to represent all cities and regions of France, its form would allow each locality to build outwards over time as their needs required from an elementary square cell, fourteen meters on each side. But once again the necessary credit was denied.

At the end of 1936, a brief four months before the opening of the Exposition, Le Corbusier was finally offered sufficient credit allowing him to erect the Pavillon des Temps Nouveaux: a fifteen-thousand-square-meter cube of cables and yellow-toned canvas, a kind of circus tent, sited at Porte Maillot.[179] This annex of the Exposition on the western periphery of Paris also contained the Centre Rural, where a model farm, village, and country fair were the major displays. Unexpectedly, this juxtaposition allowed the Pavillon des Temps Nouveaux to take advantage of demonstrating reforms proposed in the Radiant City that extended to the countryside as well.[180]

"Regionalism" was the key organizing theme promoted by Labbé, the secretary general of the Exposition. In two sections of the Exposition, the Regional Center on the left bank of the Seine and the Rural Center in the annex at the Porte Maillot, visitors were introduced to the diversity of regional cultures in France. These two exhibitions, however, gave quite different views of rural society. In the regional center, seventeen regions were represented by twenty-seven buildings grouped around a plaza as in an open-air museum. Each architectural structure was built in the "typical" style of its region. There were many who were critical of this commercialization of folklore, fearing that it offered not only decor for the comic-opera, but models for suburban dream houses as well. It spread the wrong message–that everything was well in the provinces of France. On the other hand, the Rural Center, reflecting plans that Le Corbusier had already developed for the Radiant Farm, contained a model village for the future rather than an idyllic tableau of the peasantry. Its displays were intended to link traditional forms of rural life to modern equipment: prototypes for a mayor's office, a model farm, a house for agricultural workers, a post office, a cooperative store, and a house of culture with a cinema, meeting rooms, and a restaurant. In place of a church as the major symbol of village unity, a grain silo was erected.

PHOTOMURALS

Given limited funds, short time, and an out-of-the-way site, Le Corbusier required an innovative approach. He proclaimed that "instead of printing a book," that is, the model community he had intended, "I will print the table of contents. That is how we will make the 'Pavillon des Temps Nouveaux.'"[181] The approach would be education rather than demonstration. It was important, Le Corbusier argued, to educate both the authorities and the public about the issue of housing, to fully develop and express the knowledge of housing (*savoir habiter*).

The Pavilion was assembled as a book, the visitor expected to be a reader–literally, in part–who would stop, study, and ponder messages about the most austere and serious problems of urbanism placed squarely on review. [FIGURE 10.15] The visitor would be bombarded by blown-up graphics and brilliant colors meant to shock.[182] The interior of the Pavillon des Temps Nouveaux also took on populist overtones, dedicated to the people, consistent with Le Corbusier's desire to get on the good side of the Popular Front (in power during the design of

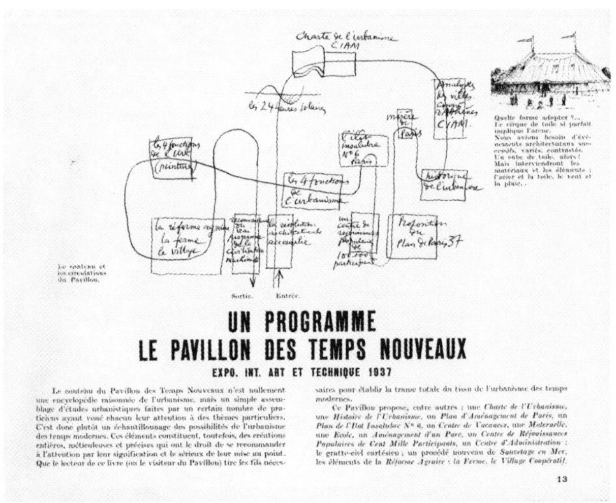

Quelle forme adopter ?...
Le cirque de toile si parfait implique l'arène.
Nous avions besoin d'événements architecturaux successifs, variés, contrastés.
Un cube de toile, alors!
Mais interviendront les matériaux et les éléments : l'acier et la toile, le vent et la pluie...

Le contenu et les circulations du Pavillon.

Sortie. Entrée.

UN PROGRAMME
LE PAVILLON DES TEMPS NOUVEAUX
EXPO. INT. ART ET TECHNIQUE 1937

Le contenu du Pavillon des Temps Nouveaux n'est nullement une encyclopédie raisonnée de l'urbanisme, mais un simple assemblage d'études urbanistiques faites par un certain nombre de praticiens ayant voué chacun leur attention à des thèmes particuliers. C'est donc plutôt un échantillonnage des possibilités de l'urbanisme des temps modernes. Ces éléments constituent, toutefois, des créations entières, méticuleuses et précises qui ont le droit de se recommander à l'attention par leur signification et le sérieux de leur mise au point. Que le lecteur de ce livre (ou le visiteur du Pavillon) tire les fils nécessaires pour établir la trame totale du tissu de l'urbanisme des temps modernes.

Ce Pavillon propose, entre autres : une *Charte de l'Urbanisme*, une *Histoire de l'Urbanisme*, un *Plan d'Aménagement de Paris*, un *Plan de l'Ilot Insalubre N° 6*, un *Centre de Vacances*, une *Maternelle*, une *Ecole*, un *Aménagement d'un Parc*, un *Centre de Réjouissances Populaires de Cent Mille Participants*, un *Centre d'Administration* : le gratte-ciel cartésien ; un procédé nouveau de *Sauvetage en Mer*, les éléments de la *Réforme Agraire* : la *Ferme*, le *Village Coopératif*.

13

FIGURE 10.15: Circulation route of the Pavillon des Temps Nouveaux and vignette of a "circus tent," an inspiration for the Pavillon

the pavilion). Most of its walls bore enlarged photographs of written proclamations, hand-painted graphics, slogans, and aphorisms covering hundreds of meters of standardized panels, dividing the interior of the pavilion into sections. Huge photomurals or photomontages on the History of Cities, the Spirit of Paris, the Misery of Paris, and four large panels portraying the four functions of CIAM–Housing, Work, Transportation, and Recreation–were also on display.

These photomontages, primarily pedagogical tools, offered documentary evidence, delivered forcefully in a cinematic sequence or narrative line intended to keep a viewer's interest.[183] In a talk delivered in Rome in October 1936, discussing the relationship of painting and sculpture to architecture, Le Corbusier spoke briefly of the only occasion on which a wall might legitimately be decorated with figurative images–essentially, in pedagogical installations such as the Pavillon des Temps Nouveaux:

> There are sometimes very precise occasions that enter into architecture: when it is necessary publicly to demonstrate, to prove, to reveal, to instruct; here is the wall in photo-montages.... All can be told, shown, built in sensational apparitions of the world, of the immense unknown world.[184]

As initially conceived, the pavilion was to have covered all of the regions of France, but in the end the tent was too small and time too short, and so the focus was limited to Paris. The square tent was brightly colored inside and out. Space was divided by green, blue, and red partitions: gray flooring and canvas of an aggressive yellow added their own effects. This was in keeping with the view that Le Corbusier expressed in *Les Canons*, namely that color "represents an immense architectural power the use of which is lost today, after the century of academicism that we have just crossed."[185] The pavilion's colors were meant to be shocking, modulated throughout by panels of writing also on diversely colored backgrounds in addition to the huge photomurals in black and white. Le Corbusier intended this "full orchestration" of color to sustain the visitor's curiosity while they examined and studied the austere conditions of cities and countryside.[186]

The presentation of documents followed a cinematic line that took the spectator through various sites and up two different levels of ramps, across translucent platforms through which light fell to the floor below. The visitor promenaded alongside of, below, above,

Double niche dans le vestibule, décorée de quatre Tour Eiffel, peintures d'enfants (agrandies). Exécution : Simon et H. Rein.

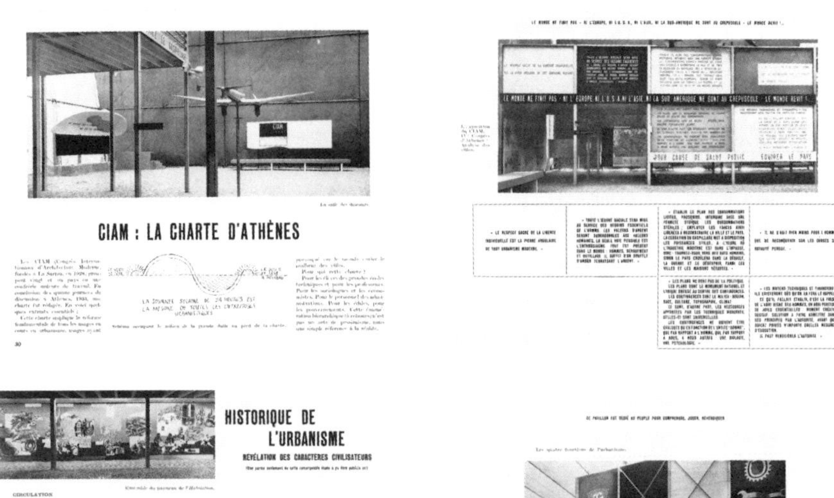

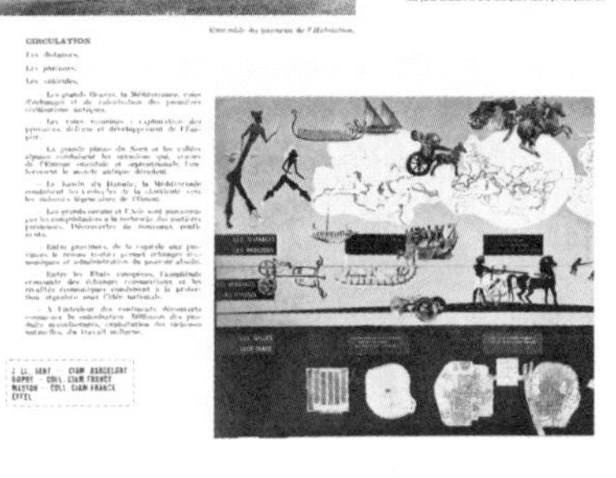

FIGURE 10.16: Children's drawings of the Eiffel Tower decorated the vestibule of the Exposition, executed by Raoul Simon, a house- and sign-painter from Vézelay, and H. Rein. FIGURE 10.17: The Pavillon de Temps Nouveaux was planned to be a three-dimensional book illustrating the Charter of Athens (1933). FIGURE 10.18: Exhibition panels carried the slogans "The world is not finished" and "It is coming back to life." FIGURE 10.19: Exhibition panels displaying the history of urbanism and transportation over land, sea, and air routes were assembled by José Luis Sert. FIGURE 10.20: The Plan of Paris, 1937, panels enclosed a balcony resting area. FIGURE 10.21: On the first ramp, panels depicted the "sickness" and lugubriousness of contemporary Paris.

through, and behind a bewildering variety of visual materials. The first section documented the architectural revolution that had already been achieved.[187] It was important to show that a new era of solidarity had begun, and that all the marvelous inventions of the machine age would henceforth be applied to the satisfaction of human needs.[188] To this end, the slogans assembled on the panels throughout the pavilion were written by men dedicated to reform: for example, those of the trades, the *Prélude* group, and the group from *La Grande Relève*.[189] And while most of the pavilion consisted of architectural surfaces, panels, and painted scenes–nothing that reminded Le Corbusier of the decorative arts–there were a few sculptural items that showed how architecture and the arts were linked to each other: a model of an airplane lent by the Minister of Aeronautics, or a suspended sculpture by Henri Laurens. Le Corbusier had hoped to display the bronze propeller from the *Normandie* and some agricultural machines, but these displays were too heavy, and the time too short for assembly.[190] [FIGURE 10.16]

On the wall opposite the entryway, the visitor advanced toward the second section of the promenade, the Charter of Urbanism drawn up by CIAM, and then viewed a sampling of documents that had been presented and discussed at the fourth CIAM congress, which took place in Athens in 1933. The Charter, born of this congress's study and debate of urban problems in thirty-three cities of Europe, Asia, Africa, and America, required that equilibrium be established between man and his natural surroundings. It was important that students and professors of the great technical schools understand this message; hence the CIAM display was given a major place opposite the entry to the pavilion.[191] [FIGURES 10.17 AND 10.18]

The third section depicted the history of urbanism. One then moved up the first ramp and viewed the lugubrious misery of Paris.[192] The saddest aspect of this sordid affair, as Le Corbusier said in *Des Canons, Des Munitions* lay in the fact that Paris had abandoned its historic line, its courageous march toward the grand, the clear, and the beautiful.[193] For the last fifty years, the suburbs had been allowed to strangle and sully the bravery of Paris. Authorities permitted only meager improvements within its center and mummified the rest. Paris was dying.[194] [FIGURES 10.19, 10.20, AND 10.21]

The route of the exhibition next takes the spectator through three different sections on design: the 1937 Plan for Paris; the "ilôt insalubre No. 6" (the unsanitary block No. 6) in Paris, and a popular leisure center for one hundred thousand people.

In *Des Canons, Des Munitions* Le Corbusier elaborates on the cell of habitation, and the individual-collective "binomial," which rules society. If one of these terms is missing, he states, then society will be intolerably inhumane, the individual absolutely isolated, and the delicate steps needed to achieve peace unattainable.[195] Through urbanism, however, these two terms can be harmonized, brought into balance.

He returns to the organic metaphor he utilized in *The Radiant City,* comparing the benefits of modern urban planning to that of an expanding fruit tree: an impeccable organization of roots, trunk, and leaves with innumerable flowering branches, a joyous thing. "A flower: housing. The fruit: a social cell–the family–living in the joy of physical and spiritual health."[196] Thus urbanism moves continuously back and forth between the individual and the collective, from the cell of habitation to the city, from the individual flower to the whole tree. This is how Le Corbusier introduces his idea of the unité d'habitation: each structure will contain around 2,700 people. Grouped together, two or three of these unités become a new social organization. They are in turn attached to other unités of revitalization, culture, health, education, or clubs. The isolated individual is transformed into a collective being, and the world achieves a new unity.[197]

The open plan, reform of private property relations, and a new modular dimension for the housing cell were all part of Le Corbusier's demonstration project for the unité d'habitation, which was shown in graphic form in the Pavillon des Temps Nouveaux instead of as the hoped-for built-to-scale model. Moreover, as Le Corbusier explains in *Des Canons, Des Munitions* after considerable research he had come to the conclusion that 2.2 meters was the ideal dimension for a man standing upright, his arm raised. This became the module for the interior ceiling height of a human habitation. This measure, or "modulor," rules over the sectional proportions of housing, and causes a veritable architectural revolution. Housing subsequently turns into a series of small cells that can be stacked on one another and aligned along an interior street. Each small house has sun, space, and greenery before it. With the open plan that the construction allows, the interiors of this cell flexibly respond to the different desires of its inhabitants–and they are full of colors: white, rose, blue, whatever is desired.[198]

The next section of the pavilion that the visitor goes through is on the highest platform, originally planned to be a place to rest, read, and contemplate but endowed, in the event, with four large and overwhelming photomurals. Each expressed one of the four functions

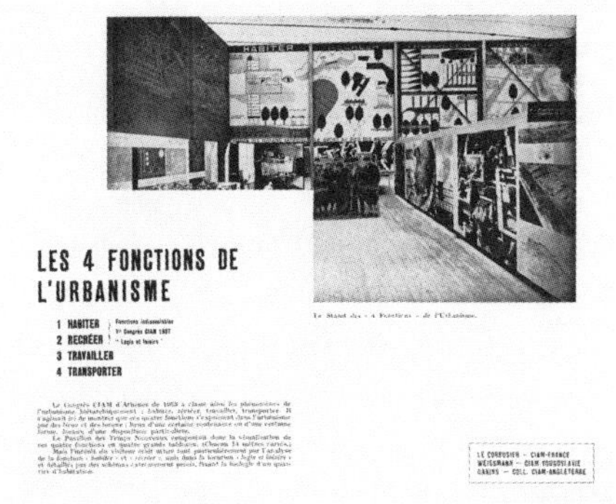

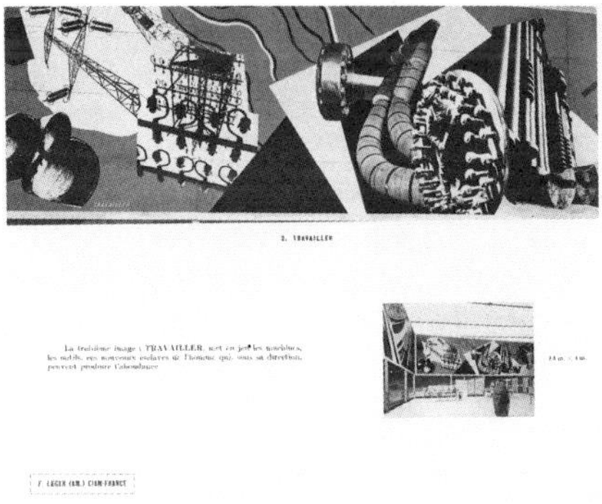

HABITER
LES 4 FONCTIONS DE L'URBANISME
1 HABITER
2 RECRÉER
3 TRAVAILLER
4 TRANSPORTER

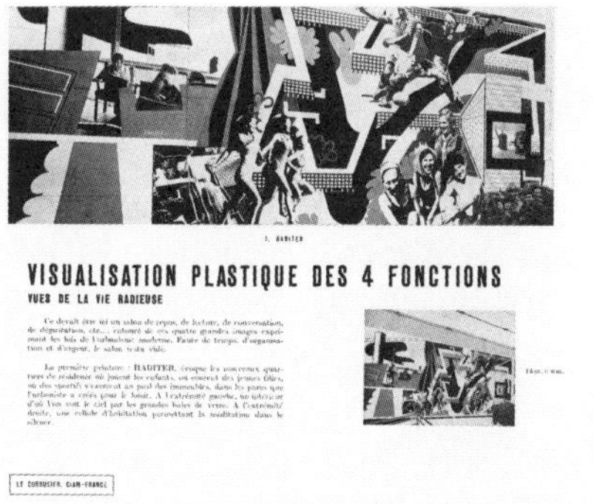

VISUALISATION PLASTIQUE DES 4 FONCTIONS
VUES DE LA VIE RADIEUSE

GISCHIA ET MAZENOT

BEAUQUIER

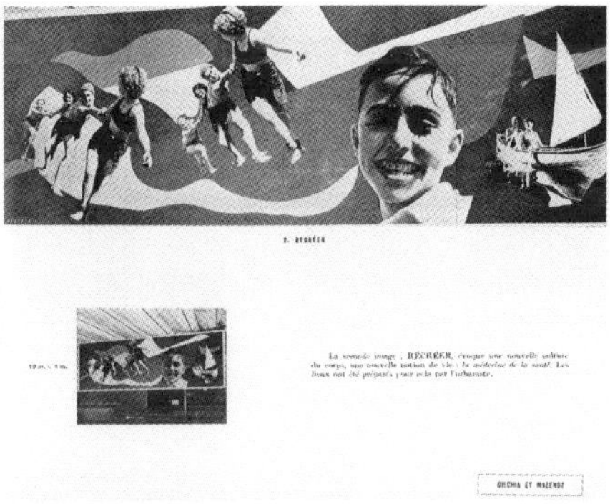

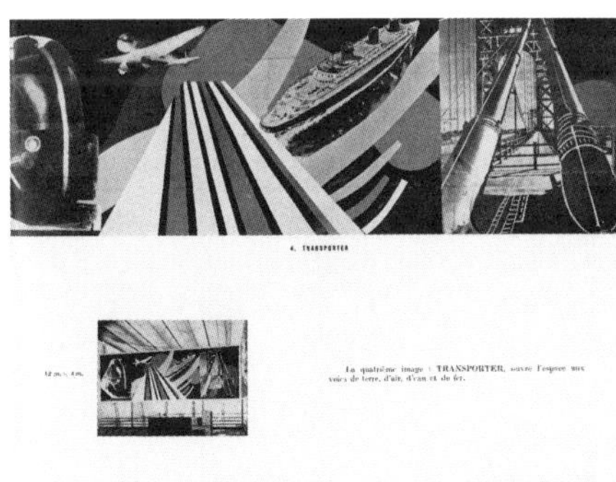

FIGURE 10.22: Visualizations of the four functions of the Charter of Athens (1933) were carried out via large paintings of housing, recreation, work, and circulation. FIGURE 10.23: Le Corbusier designed the panel displaying housing. FIGURE 10.24: The recreation panel was prepared by Gischia and Mazenot. FIGURE 10.25: Fernand Léger executed designs for the panel on work. FIGURE 10.26: The panel for circulation was made by Beauquier.

CIAM had spelled out as the laws of modern urbanism: housing, recreation, work, and transportation. The first mural, on housing, executed by Le Corbusier, depicted a new residential district of unités, juxtaposed with images of young girls active in various sports activities in parks at the foot of each building. In the upper-left corner, an interior shot revealed a glimpse of the sky seen through huge panes of glass.[199] The second image, on recreation, prepared by Gischia and Mazenot, placed special emphasis on the exercise of the body.[200] The third image, executed by Fernand Léger, depicted work: an assemblage of machine parts, tools, and cranes.[201] The fourth, carried out by Beauquier, depicted travel along land, rail, water, and air. [FIGURES 10.22–10.26]

The spectator then moves down the ramps to consider the Radiant Farm and Cooperative Village. Here the message first proposed in *The Radiant City* is repeated: the peasant works the land with tools that are exact and rigorous for his task. He lives in harmony with nature and observes its laws. He needs to be given modern tools for his farm and village, and be allowed to have a modern way of life.[202] Each regional plan must be designed to support specialized regional production, which is a function of its geographical situation, climate, ethnography, soil, and subsoil.[203] As the visitor exits the pavilion, one more set of graphic displays appears, headed by the following slogan: "The world is restored!"[204] [FIGURE 10.27] Le Corbusier wrote in *Des Canons, Des Munitions* that pessimists have proclaimed the end of the world, but those who attend to its general biology see it coming back to life. They ask only that all production be directed toward the support of man, so that he is nourished, dressed, housed, and given recreational facilities. Everything boils down to housing. "It is therefore a question of the lair: the true lair of man of the machine civilization. This lair does not yet exist."[205] The final panels therefore display what the effects would be if the world set itself the task of housing mankind, if anarchy were replaced by organization, if buildings were an industrial product. Everything would change. Architects, instead of building palaces, houses to rent, churches, or villas, would find work in providing for the four routes of land, rail, water, and air. Finally, imagine if all the effort and money consecrated to the fabrication of guns and shells, to tanks and airplanes, were devoted instead to the production of housing! Then the machine society would be equipped with an immense power: tools, administration, and cooperation. "Solidarity on the plan of life."[206]

LE MONDE REVIT...

Le monde revit ! telle est la phrase qui apparaît aux yeux du visiteur du Pavillon à sa sortie des démonstrations de l'urbanisme des temps nouveaux. Il faut savoir s'éloigner des misères contingentes, s'élever assez au-dessus des événements locaux pour acquérir cette vue spéciale — cette vue d'oiseau — d'en haut, *qui fait saisir la* DIRECTION *des masses en mouvement.*

Les pessimistes, les faibles, les peureux veulent invoquer une proche fin du monde et nous conduire à l'abdication.

Nous répondons, forts de la biologie générale des événements du monde : « Non, le monde revit ».

137

FIGURE 10.27: Exiting from the displays demonstrating the urbanism of the Temps Nouveaux, the visitor was confronted with a panel of slogans: "The weak and sinister ask us to adbdicate," and the response, "No, the world revives."

CHAPTER 11 ALGIERS AND THE MEDITERRANEAN ATLAS

> *The adventure of man is a continuous oscillation between his irresistible desire to become an intelligent animal and his insatiable desire to remain a confused god. His victory is to be both, in the highest degree, but neither exclusively.*
>
> –ÉLIE FAURE, 1930

I. THE REWRITING OF ALGIERS

Le Corbusier's preferred projects in the Janus-faced 1930s were his plans for Paris and Algiers. The exceptional quality of the Algiers site, its dynamic population, and the culture, climate, materials, and colors of the meridian captured his imagination and allowed the expression of neo-syndicalist idioms. After initial visits to the city in 1931, he designed six different plans for the city from 1932 to 1942. Once again his personality was linked to the Mediterranean as a source of deep lyrical expression. He confessed in *When the Cathedrals Were White* (1937) that

> in the course of years, I have felt myself become more and more a man of everywhere with, nevertheless, one strong root: the Mediterranean, queen of forms under the play of light; I am dominated by the imperatives of harmony, beauty, plasticity.[1]

Yet "the Mediterranean" concealed what has been called a "white blind spot," a site where Le Corbusier promulgated a discourse of racial and colonial denial.[2]

His approach to Algeria was essentially visual: he drew sketches and made exhibition drawings, collected maps, charts, postcards, and photographs, participated in cinema projects and built models, all appended by writings, both poetic and descriptive. These formed the raw materials of his cartographic discourse, a veritable atlas structured by narratives about the Mediterranean axis, Algiers's role as the head of Africa, and the *mission civilatrice* (civilizing mission) of France. His cartographic moves were essentially linear: climbing a hill to gain a vantage point over the city and acquire information, then sketching these observations as his eye took symbolic possession of the city before committing an account of what lay before his eyes and under his feet to words. Only after such exploratory probes did he chart his course, map the city, and manage its space.[3] These cartographic views, assumptions, and stories constitute his attempt to rewrite Algiers.

WHITE BLIND SPOTS

Most French citizens in the 1920s and 1930s saw the colonized world through the cinema, international expositions, and illustrated press. These visual representations of the French colonies were basically imaginary: for example, few feature-length films with colonial themes were shot on location in the 1920s, most being filmed on sets built in Parisian studios. These narratives helped persuade the French that they were beneficent bearers of civilization to the colonized.[4] Films of Morocco and Algeria tended to focus on military feats: men called "pacifiers" (*colons*, or settlers) who persuaded natives, sometimes through sheer charm, to side with France. They also exploited the supposed incompatibility of the French and Arab civilizations.[5]

The headquarters of the Foreign Legion–born the same day as the French invaded Algeria, March 10, 1830–were in Algeria, at Sidi Bel Abbès near the Saharan-Moroccan border. Due to unemployment and poverty in France, its ranks swelled to thirty-three thousand during the Depression, years when it was needed to control mounting Algerian unrest.[6] Also, films portraying Legion men hardened by discipline and atoning for their sins in heroic adventures reached their peak of popularity during the 1930s. Stereotypical depictions of active, adventurous French men, their virility manifest, offered an antidote to–or at least anodyne for–the stalemate of economic depression.

There were travelogues as well, portraying life in the colonies as beautiful and calm, and films of French explorers on African expeditions crossing the Sahara by car or airplane.[7] Collectively, these films were instruments of imperialism, carrying a double message of dominance and dependence. They normalized the exploitative practices of European settlers and the Army while legitimizing the subordination of "natives." As David Slavin states in *Colonial Cinema and Imperial France*,

1919–1939, "Willful amnesia, selective recognition, male fantasies, and white blind spots distorted French vision and produced a full-blown politics of denial."[8]

In Algeria, white blind spots rendered the racial sphere completely invisible and immune to analysis. It allowed Algerian settler society, composed of *pieds-noirs* working classes (Algerian-born Frenchmen), a flotsam of impoverished immigrants from the south of France, Spain, Sicily, or Malta, plus wealthy settlers and colonial administrators, to consolidate their position of racial superiority and cultural dominance over the indigenous Algerians. Little opposition was raised in France, and no government policy was successful in breaking with the colonial system. White male dominance over "natives" and women was rendered invisible by blind spots that occluded strident protests of the indigenous elites increasingly frustrated with colonial rule.[9] And they occluded as well a powerful Islamic revivalist movement, which utilized the veil, the mosque, Arabic, and traditional customs as tools of resistance against Western colonization and cultural homogenization.[10]

Le Corbusier's schemes for Algiers were positioned within this politics of denial. He did not perceive, or if he perceived did not challenge, the white blind spots engendered by colonial power, the politics of race and difference, and his own spatial poetics of the primitive and the authentic. His six urban plans for Algiers must also be read against the conservative policies of the neo-syndicalist journals *Plans* and *Prélude* and his own eventual collaboration with the Vichy government in 1941–42. He never understood that his call for action by colonial government reinforced racial superiority and protected the privileges of the ruling elite. Rather, he assumed that indigenous Algerians had been assimilated, given the rights of citizenship, and treated with equality, either ignoring or remaining ignorant of their protests and resistance movements, believing them happy and content, always greeting the conqueror with a charming smile. He never sought their support nor spoke to them directly. Indigenous Algerians are the silent voice behind his writings and urban schemes: he does not allow them to speak, but presumes to speak for them.

In particular, Le Corbusier accepted Algeria as a natural extension of France to the south: the hopeful land of virile activity, Grands Travaux (Great Works), and modernization. He saw a new Latin race and a Mediterranean Federation allied north, south, east, and west, as a bulwark against Germany and Italy. His loyalty to the *mission civilatrice* enabled him to rhetorically configure his schemes toward Algiers (with remarkable insensitivity) as artillery bombardments, labeling each plan by 1935 an *obus*, or exploding shell.[11] Le Corbusier's white blind spots allowed him to escape into an imaginary poetics of space.

During his visits to Algiers in the 1930s, he collected photographic postcards from kiosks in the government square, supposedly typical scenes and types of Algerians, many of them women, adding mythic strength to his imaginary Algeria. [FIGURES II.1 AND II.2] Emphasizing the timelessness and backwardness of North African Arabs, these photographs of half-naked women and picturesque daily routines were ubiquitous tourist items. A quick glance through Le Corbusier's collection reveals many scenes of the Casbah, views over the stepped terraces of the houses toward the sea, a man carrying water in its narrow streets, ordinary domestic activities such as smoking cigarettes or preparing food.[12] These are intermixed with bare-breasted young women from the South, weaving or belly dancing, camels in the Sahara, nomadic tents, and oasis markets. In *The Colonial Harem,* Malek Alloula has claimed that such photographic postcards, whose golden age was from 1900 to 1930, and which often depict veiled women or women in exotic poses, define "the practice of a right of (over)sight that the colonizer arrogates to himself and that is the bearer of multiform violence."[13] Mingling pornographic views with everyday scenes and ordinary tasks naturalized these women in poses and dresses conforming to Western fantasies of picturesque life. They normalized acts of penetration to remove the veil, enter the harem, and conquer private interiors, and consequently perpetuated the myth that North Africa had both land and women to exploit. Conflating the allure of Muslim women with that of the land legitimated French domination over both.

Some have seen a break with the rules of Purism that Le Corbusier's sketches and drawings of Algiers represent, a turn to organic nature, animals, and humans.[14] Whether this constitutes a rupture rather than a reflection of lifelong interests in folklore and nature is, however, debatable. It certainly represents his involvement in national debates over regional architecture as a place-based architecture responding to climate, topography, and raw materials, and depending on non-mechanized labor and a close relationship with the land. In these debates, led by critics such as Camille Mauclair and Gustave Umbdenstock, it was an issue of protecting French identity against intrusions of modern architecture, or specifically, Le Corbusier's dry

FIGURES II.1 AND II.2: On trips to Algeria in the 1930s, Le Corbusier avidly collected postcards.

geometries and nude white architecture. Le Corbusier for his part wants architects to learn from both past and present models, but only those demonstrating innovation, transformation, and spirit, not those reflecting retrograde copying and slavish plagiarizing. His association with the neo-syndicalist journals *Plans* and *Prélude* added to his own deepening sense of regionalism, and on his trips to Algeria he found good examples drawn from the past to moderate his modernism.[15]

On his first visit, Le Corbusier crossed the Casbah by foot in the company of the French Algerian Pierre-André Emery, an early collaborator in his atelier who had returned to Algiers in November 1926. One day, when Emery was otherwise occupied, he asked his apprentice Jean de Maisonseul, later director of the Musée National des Beaux-Arts d'Alger, to accompany Le Corbusier on his explorations. Maisonseul recounted many years later that they entered houses, supposedly forbidden to tourists, Le Corbusier with sketchbook in hand, having observed a woman–usually large-breasted–whose image he wished to capture on paper. He apparently filled three sketchbooks with his measurements of dwelling interiors and many drawings of nude women executed in color crayons. Later, he stated that these sketchbooks were stolen from his atelier once he returned to Paris.[16]

Le Corbusier saw Algiers in gendered terms, comparing the form of the city to a female body.[17] His conflation of Arab women and the city as unveiled, exploitable, and unable to resist his penetrating male gaze was, paradoxically, a classic white blind spot. The colonist held the Muslim woman inferior to man, yet she was the entry point for control over Eastern culture.

IMAGINARY GEOGRAPHY

Algeria held a special place in the imaginary geography of the French. It was a poetic substitution for "the Orient" after France lost control of Egypt and Sudan in the late 1890s, and was also figured as a southward extension of France after emigrants displaced from Alsace-Lorraine in 1871 relocated there. Its archaeological sites were reminders that it had once been both the ancient breadbasket of Rome and a Christian terrain belonging to the West. Viewing media coverage of the popular *croisières*–automobile expeditions into the desert–many viewers could assume that to penetrate and exploit the Sahara was France's natural right.[18] These expeditions helped to map out and develop opportunities for economic exploitation, including Algeria as a major importer of French automobiles.

Albert Sarraut, Minister of Colonies in several interwar cabinets, twice governor-general of Indochina (1911–14 and 1916–19), and an ardent colonial, argued in the 1920s that it was "absolutely indispensable, that a methodical...propaganda by word and visual image, journal, conference, film and exposition be activated in our land among adults and children."[19] He was aware of the threat to empire of public apathy in France as well as of sedition in the colonies. France must learn that Asia and Africa were not abstract and distant lands, but vital to the well-being of the mother country. They must recognize that exploitation of these lands was a guarantee of prosperity in the homeland, and would thus support French investments, private and public, that would carry civilization to backward regions, spreading roads, canals, and telegraph and telephone networks throughout the empire.[20] Only an active policy of information (propaganda) would enable sufficient investments to counter the threat of communism in the colonies, dampen German attempts to discredit France's colonial administration, and contain Italian aggression in Libya and Abyssinia.[21]

Some eight hundred thousand Frenchmen visited Algeria around the time of the opening of the Algerian Centennial in May 1930, a jubilant and insensitive celebration of the original French invasion and possession of Algeria in 1830. The French even staged a reenactment of the original 1830 invasion of Algeria, with soldiers wearing nineteenth-century regalia.

THE TECHNOLOGY OF EMPIRE

For a hundred years, Algeria had been an important economic asset to France: wine, wheat, livestock, cotton, sugar, and other products from the land, along with tools and small metal objects, were major exports to France, and Algeria in turn was expected to develop a healthy consumer market for French products and to attract lucrative foreign investments. When economic depression hit France in 1931, the first reaction was to impose protective tariffs on foreign imports. Overseas infrastructural investments were stopped as well. As a result the bottom dropped out of the price of Algerian goods–especially wine–and development projects stalled. French banks refused to extend credit to natives, enabling wealthy colonials to accumulate native farmlands at extremely low prices. Already pushed off the land as fields were transferred to wine production in the 1920s, farm labor was mechanized, and the agrarian sector was commercialized, Berbers and Kabyles drifted toward Algiers, overcrowding the Casbah and erecting on its outskirts the first *bidonvilles*, so called for the metal gas containers (*bidons*) used for construction material.[22] The plight of the Algerian was, however, smack in the middle of the white blind spot in Le Corbusier's rewriting of Algiers.[23]

ASSIMILATION OR ASSOCIATION OR EMANCIPATION

The *mission civilatrice* was accepted by the colonials as a sacred trust and assumed as a natural right. The natives in the colonies were apprentice Frenchmen; they must learn to think, act, and speak like the French. But assimilation as a mission was on shaky ground by the 1930s, stumbling over the issue of citizenship. Muslim elites and Algerian veterans of wars were demanding the rights of French citizens: representation in Parliament, equal pay for equal work, development of educational institutions, an Arabic-language press, and more. The more Algerians protested, the more fiercely their requests were resisted. Algeria in the 1930s was at loggerheads: growing bitterness among Algerians as the "rights of man" were withheld meeting head-on with growing stubbornness among French colonialists justifying their refusals on grounds of racial and technical superiority.

Since Algerians far outnumbered the French, if they were properly educated and given the rights of citizenship, it was feared they would soon become the managers and usurp the privileges of colonization. Thus entrance to schools was tightly controlled: in 1930 the total number of Algerian high school attendees numbered a mere 776. Fewer than 100 Algerians were certified as teachers of higher education, and as late as 1939, a mere 89 Algerians attended the local university.[24]

II. LE CORBUSIER'S PROJECTILES

FIRST TRIP TO ALGERIA

While Le Corbusier developed his plans for Algiers in the 1930s, the nation was split between nationalist and colonialist sentiments. The Muslim elite demanded political representation, while colonial administrators, the army, and the French colonialists resisted. Le Corbusier needed the support of all three of these latter forces if his plans for Algiers were to be implemented. He also appealed to groups that could see his schemes as a unique vehicle for modernization and an alternative to proposals backed by the state. Les Amis d'Alger (Friends of Algiers) was one such group, promoting modern architecture as a substitute to the widespread acceptance of vernacular "Mediterranean" style or neoclassical forms. Association de l'Urbanisme Algérois (the Algerian Urbanism Association) was another.

Rodolphe Rey, president of the Association de l'Urbanisme Algérois, invited Le Corbusier to a conference convened in Algiers by Les Amis d'Alger. Reconstruction of the derelict Marine quarter had been an issue for some time, and it was hoped this would present an occasion for the display of modern architecture. Le Corbusier was to give two talks, one for the public and another for specialists, as he had done in South America. The first (public) lecture on March 17, 1931, entitled "La Révolution architecturale accomplie par les techniques modernes" (Architectural Revolution accomplished through modern techniques), contained many of the same ideas developed in his Buenos Aires conferences of 1929. The second, "La Ville Radieuse," developed his theoretical projects of 1929–30.

Meandering across the city in the first days after his arrival, Le Corbusier jotted down impressions in his sketchbook. Upon returning to Paris, he proposed to study the issue further and offer a "proposition" for the future development of Algiers.

> Here, the urbanistic problem is very clear. You have a magnificent site, one of the most beautiful in the world. But the city by expanding, steals each day from its inhabitants a little of the beauty with which nature has favored it. It is choked, so much that in order "to see" Algiers, it is necessary today to leave Algiers. Intolerable paradox. This beauty of Algiers can and ought to be protected.[25]

Le Corbusier's first impressions of Algeria were published in the *Journal Général Travaux Publics et Bâtiments* in June 1931 in an essay entitled "Louanges à l'Algérie"("Praises to Algeria").[26] Le Corbusier found in the East an antidote to things that drove him to rage in the West, marking those comparisons with the deficiencies in his homeland that travel always engenders.[27] Struck by the dynamism of Algiers, he deployed all of the staples of Orientalist literature, from pirates to the smell of orange blossoms on soft night breezes. Algiers is

> head of the colonies of Africa, spirit of the Algerian-born settlers (colons)....The difference with Paris is this: there is no restrictive

> "but" which brakes all initiatives on the secular soil of Paris, there is faith, the force of desire to go forward... and also the pathetic need as here to exit from an inexplicable urbanistic situation.[28]

Le Corbusier from the start makes Algiers express the opposite of what he does not like about Europe. He begins the moment his boat enters the port: in "Louanges à l'Algérie," he says he could see on a shoulder of land an immense building of prestressed concrete being erected. It was the new government palace of Algeria, designed by the architect Jacques Guiauchain, with construction by the Perret Brothers. He is thrilled to find a government able to decide to build a "modern" structure to house its own operations. But, of course, there will be disappointments to register as well, for the rest of Algiers, spreading out before his eyes toward infinity, strikes him as a bricolage of insignificant structures erected by "expatriate Latins" from the Piedmont. Algiers has been built on top of donkey paths, which, of course, Le Corbusier dislikes. He complains that to go by foot from the port (Casino) below to the Saint George (his hotel) above takes more than an hour, following the serpentine twists of Rue Michelet. From his hotel to the end of the city it is three quarters of an hour, from the casino to the west of the city another hour. In this first act of surveying, he has drawn the four cardinal points on his imaginary map. And he is vexed! "Three hours to cross a city that has just been born, it is long!" Add to this the number of automobiles circulating in the city and clearly this new city is already in crisis![29]

But it is spring, and the gardens soon seize Le Corbusier's attention. Once in a while, too, from the bends in the Rue Michelet, a spectacular sight is achieved: sea, Casbah, hills of beautiful trees, and gardens full of palm trees, with the perfume from orange trees wafting on the air. "It is then that the spirit is gripped by the Muslim."[30] There are stories to recount as well, about Corsairs and pirates on the sea and about Arab architecture, the most mathematical ever known. He is ready, he says, to open himself to the exotic, to be seduced by ordinary details of everyday life, and by fantasies of love and enchantment. He begins with simple things:

> The Arab house is measured by the length of a stride, the height of the shoulder. In the quarter... all the small negotiations of love and of dance take place on some patios and small rooms, all dimensioned by the calm measure of the foot, and the heights of

> everything are estimated by a head carried on shoulders: column the height of a shoulder, and above, passage for the head. In Arab architecture one walks.[31]

He returns to his imaginary story about Corsairs: their city was the Casbah. These men were pirates on the sea, and when they returned, they moored their boats, mounted the Casbah, and found their wives. They stayed some weeks or some months before leaving again. Le Corbusier is so taken with his story that he immediately proclaims: "It is necessary to save the Casbah, historic city, today stuffed with a poor population. The Algerian government must maintain this anchor attached to the history of the Arab nation. It is necessary to regulate the Casbah."[32]

He returns to his story, remembering that the French conquered this capital of pirates in 1830. And so, one hundred years later, the city is the capital of Algeria, a French country, its colonization accepted with a smile. It appears to Le Corbusier that everywhere in the countryside, the mountains of Kabylie, the coastline of vineyards, the oasis of the desert, a smile is naturally on the face of each: "One does not hate his conquering."[33] The Muslim Algerian retains his culture, mountains, oases, costume, dignity. "It appears that one has protected the Arab dignity and that there is no hate, but only friendship."[34]

Le Corbusier is confused by the duality the country represents. He cannot stop drawing comparisons with the West, its industry, and politics of colonization, yet he is enthralled by his imaginary East. He speaks of Roman ruins, then of Arab sights, as if to compensate: the ploughed fields of Kabylie, and the Arab oasis. But he soon returns to the sight of "mountains, bays, olive trees, and vineyards around the Roman ruins, the entire countryside plunges you into Rome. Rome coping with barbarians, Rome having vanquished the same countryside, sea and mountain"–not unlike France.[35] Crossing the plains, mounting the plateau, passing over the Kabylie by a route of zigzags and narrow passes, he remarks that "this landscape seems eternally old, browned under the sun; Africa, Africa."[36]

SECOND TRIP TO ALGERIA

Le Corbusier returns to Algeria in August 1931, this time accompanied by his cousin Pierre Jeanneret and his friend Fernand Léger on a twenty-six-day motor expedition. They journey in a Voisin 14 CV automobile across Spain, Morocco, Algeria, and into the territories of the south, toward the oasis of Ghardaia and other towns of the M'Zab. Le Corbusier writes to his wife Yvonne that the Sirocco (the hot wind off the Sahara) had been blowing while they were in Morocco, and the heat burning hot, how he loves such intense heat! He remarks also on the extraordinary order that Marshal Hubert Lyautey was able to impose on Moroccan cities during his regime, an order infinitely better than anything to be found in France. From Algiers he writes again: they are preparing to leave for the desert and to return to the north, following a single vertical line drawn from Biskra in the south to Algiers, then Marseilles and Paris. This vertical axis or meridian will remain emblematic in Le Corbusier's cartographic account, one he uses repeatedly to link Paris and Algiers in subsequent years.

He publishes his account, illustrated with sketches, in *Plans* the following October.[37] An opening note mentions that this trip, taken without preparation or program, is really an "adventure" to find an "elsewhere." Le Corbusier calls this an immense and passionate risk to pretend that it could be done, because modern times have disciplined all the seas and the lands, and soon there will no longer be any "adventures" left, at least not according to the old meaning of the word.[38] In this travel account, Le Corbusier says that he wants to establish a greater acquaintance with the customs and historical roots of the Mediterranean people, for this is a period of time when folklore and regionalism recur in his thought. He is looking for a style of life that will enhance the stultifying ways of the north and become a personal source of enrichment. He will examine the ways geography affects the construction of houses and cities. He will also express themes congruent with his political stance on neo-syndicalism; but nowhere will he be critical of colonization. It remains an emphatic white blind spot. [FIGURES II.3 AND II.4]

He begins by remarking on the trip across Spain along a new national highway, the same account repeated as an opener in *The Radiant City* (see Chapter 10 of this book). The route is modern, yet it has deranged neither the Spanish soul nor culture. He still finds simple whitewashed houses, constructed with the same set of rules as has been used over the millennia; the work of the land is meticulous, not done to make money but to realize a normal way of life. Le Corbusier draws a comparison: the misadventure of the North is evident–it brings about defeat. "But how the Latins play out their destiny in their turn: *clarity*. We have need of clarity!"[39] He returns to the theme of the road

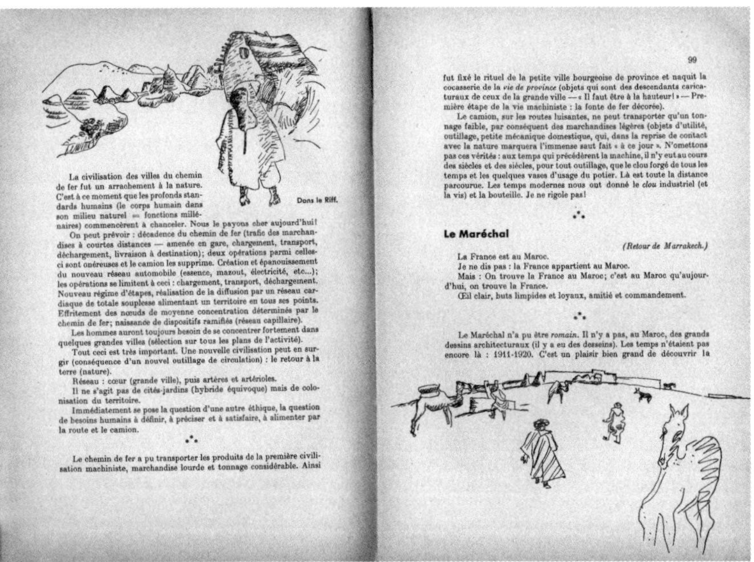

La civilisation des villes du chemin de fer fut un arrachement à la nature. C'est à ce moment que les profonds standards humains (le corps humain dans son milieu naturel = fonctions millénaires) commencèrent à chanceler. Nous le payons cher aujourd'hui!

Dans le Riff.

On peut prévoir : décadence du chemin de fer (trafic des marchandises à courtes distances — amenée en gare, chargement, transport, déchargement, livraison à destination); deux opérations parmi celles-ci sont onéreuses et le camion les supprime. Création et épanouissement du nouveau réseau automobile (essence, mazout, électricité, etc...); les opérations se limitent à ceci : chargement, transport, déchargement. Nouveau régime d'étapes, réalisation de la diffusion par un réseau cardiaque de totale souplesse alimentant un territoire en tous ses points. Effritement des nœuds de moyenne concentration déterminés par le chemin de fer; naissance de dispositifs ramifiés (réseau capillaire).

Les hommes auront toujours besoin de se concentrer fortement dans quelques grandes villes (sélection sur tous les plans de l'activité).

Tout ceci est très important. Une nouvelle civilisation peut en surgir (conséquence d'un nouvel outillage de circulation) : le retour à la terre (nature).

Réseau : cœur (grande ville), puis artères et artérioles.

Il ne s'agit pas de cités-jardins (hybride équivoque) mais de colonisation du territoire.

Immédiatement se pose la question d'une autre éthique, la question de besoins humains à définir, à préciser et à satisfaire, à alimenter par la route et le camion.

⁂

Le chemin de fer a pu transporter les produits de la première civilisation machiniste, marchandise lourde et tonnage considérable. Ainsi

99

fut fixé le rituel de la petite ville bourgeoise de province et naquit la cocasserie de la *vie de province* (objets qui sont des descendants caricaturaux de ceux de la grande ville — « Il faut être à la hauteur! » — Première étape de la vie machiniste : la fonte de fer décorée).

Le camion, sur les routes luisantes, ne peut transporter qu'un tonnage faible, par conséquent des marchandises légères (objets d'utilité, outillage, petite mécanique domestique, qui, dans la reprise de contact avec la nature marquera l'immense saut fait « à ce jour ». N'omettons pas ces vérités : aux temps qui précédèrent la machine, il n'y eut au cours des siècles et des siècles, pour tout outillage, que le clou forgé de tous les temps et les quelques vases d'usage du potier. Là est toute la distance parcourue. Les temps modernes nous out donné le *clou* industriel (et la vis) et la bouteille. Je ne rigole pas!

⁂

Le Maréchal

(Retour de Marrakech.)

La France est au Maroc.

Je ne dis pas : la France appartient au Maroc.

Mais : On trouve la France au Maroc; c'est au Maroc qu'aujourd'hui, on trouve la France.

Œil clair, buts limpides et loyaux, amitié et commandement.

⁂

Le Maréchal n'a pu être *romain*. Il n'y a pas, au Maroc, des grands dessins architecturaux (il y a eu des desseins). Les temps n'étaient pas encore là : 1911-1920. C'est un plaisir bien grand de découvrir la

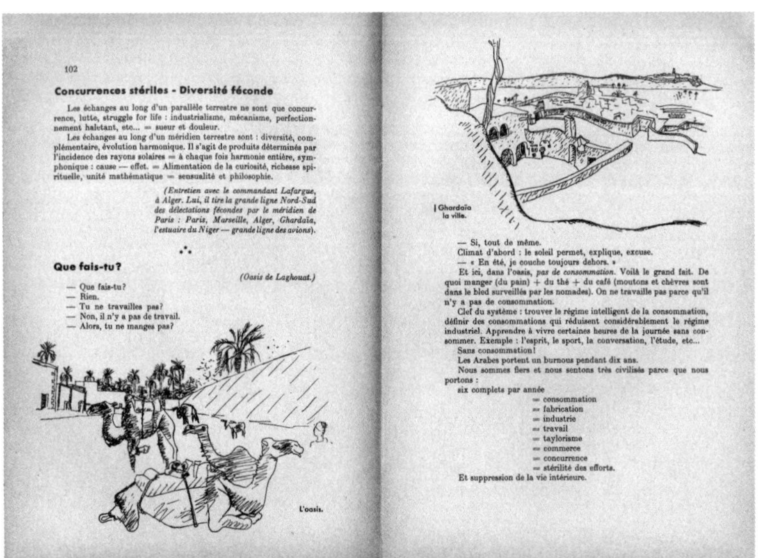

102

Concurrences stériles - Diversité féconde

Les échanges au long d'un parallèle terrestre ne sont que concurrence, lutte, struggle for life : industrialisme, mécanisme, perfectionnement haletant, etc... = sueur et douleur.

Les échanges au long d'un méridien terrestre sont : diversité, complémentaire, évolution harmonique. Il s'agit de produits déterminés par l'incidence des rayons solaires = à chaque fois harmonie entière, symphonique : cause — effet. = Alimentation de la curiosité, richesse spirituelle, unité mathématique = sensualité et philosophie.

(Entretien avec le commandant Lafargue, à Alger. Lui, il tire la grande ligne Nord-Sud des délectations fécondes par le méridien de Paris : Paris, Marseille, Alger, Ghardaïa, l'estuaire du Niger — grande ligne des avions).

⁂

Que fais-tu?

(Oasis de Laghouat.)

— Que fais-tu?
— Rien.
— Tu ne travailles pas?
— Non, il n'y a pas de travail.
— Alors, tu ne manges pas?

L'oasis.

Ghardaïa la ville.

— Si, tout de même.

Climat d'abord : le soleil permet, explique, excuse.

— « En été, je couche toujours dehors. »

Et ici, dans l'oasis, *pas de consommation*. Voilà le grand fait. De quoi manger (du pain) + du thé + du café (moutons et chèvres sont dans le bled surveillés par les nomades). On ne travaille pas parce qu'il n'y a pas de consommation.

Clef du système : trouver le régime intelligent de la consommation, définir des consommations qui réduisent considérablement le régime industriel. Apprendre à vivre certaines heures de la journée sans consommer. Exemple : l'esprit, le sport, la conversation, l'étude, etc...

Sans consommation!

Les Arabes portent un burnous pendant dix ans.

Nous sommes fiers et nous sentons très civilisés parce que nous portons :

six complets par année
= consommation
= fabrication
= industrie
= travail
= taylorisme
= commerce
= concurrence
= stérilité des efforts.

Et suppression de la vie intérieure.

FIGURES II.3 AND II.4: Le Corbusier illustrated his travel notes from a 1931 trip across Spain, Morocco, and Algeria with sketches of local life and customs.

of the South that will make Spain live: and he likens it to blood that circulates, a metaphor he will continue to deploy.

Le Corbusier draws a line on his cartographic map somewhere between Algeria and Malaga, marking the separation of waters, the Mediterranean from the Atlantic. As a consequence, cultures, social regimes, architecture, and customs follow a fated connection as water flows. "It is LIFE which leads, it is movement which projects forward, it is circulation which supplies the rapid, effective, economic vehicle–a stream, a river, a flood, a torrent, a tunnel under the mountain."[40]

In Ceuta, Spanish Morocco, having left the route, one finds piles of coal on the quays of the port. The railroad belonged to the civilization of coal. It produced the urban economy, concentrating workers in cities, and established a brutal regime out of sync with the pace of the horse and of man. Cities were an "uprooting of nature." From then on, human standards ("the human body in its natural milieu = thousand year old functions") began to falter.[41] One can project the decadence brought by the railroad, and now by the light truck with its automobile routes. The effect creates "the diffusion through a cardiac network of total suppleness, supplying a territory in all of its points," but he fears it will bring destruction in its wake.[42]

A new tool of circulation, the auto route, may however bring about "a return to the land (nature)."[43] "Network: heart (the big city), then arteries and small arteries. It is not a matter of garden cities (ambiguous hybrid) but the colonization of territory."[44] If the railroad transported weighty merchandise and heavy loads, it also developed the small bourgeois cities of the provinces and gave birth to the caricature of "provincial life." He believes, mistakenly and optimistically, that the truck on its gleaming new routes can carry only lighter loads, it will bring only useful everyday items, effecting only positive transformations. Thus it will not damage the purity and virginity of these regions, only relieve the boredom of isolation and the need for false pretences.

These statements about the effect of modern means of circulation form a prelude to Le Corbusier's travel adventure in the South: he has prepared the reader to compare civilizations (North/South), to think of returning to the land and nature, of folklore and regionalism, that the new tool of the route facilitates. He has also readied the reader to accept colonization by the French as a natural fact of economic development. He moves across Morocco, applauding the results of Lyautey's rule: "One finds France is in Morocco; it is in Morocco that today one finds France. Clear vision, transparent and loyal aims, friendship and authority."[45] Lyautey has conquered Morocco through "charm and honesty." Completely confused in his blindness, Le Corbusier cites one example: at Marrakech, when Lyautey's army was about to enter into bloody conflict with the troops of the Sultan, he sent a town crier into the streets to explain that some objects buzzing in the sky would fly over the city, friendly not bellicose objects. No one should be afraid.[46] But of course, they were afraid of these airplanes, and the bellicose French.

Next is the city of Fez, "magnificent and noble." He outlines three basic but admirable elements that compose the city. The first is the "human cell," the effect of building a house from within to without. It is

> economical, exact, working with the dimension of human limbs, gestures, occupations...and is the same reason for the city, basic biological element, well constructed in itself, it establishes the stock unit and is multiplied. And the ensemble serves the cell. *Man is comfortable in the city and at home*; comfortable.[47]

The second element to be praised is the Medina (the Arab city), compressed into "a compact molecular state" yet protected by the burning sun from rotting and disease. In the Medina, everything is useful. One can find whatever one wants delivered quickly due to its concentrated form. And the moment one leaves its gates, one plunges into "the splendor of pure nature."

The third remarkable element is the "grand architectural play" to be seen in the Palace of the Sultan, with its courtyards and gardens, its rooms and sparkling tiles. Here the mind is absorbed with researching the moves and hoaxes that mathematics and geometry pose to each other.

This description of Fez is followed with comments on sterile competitions and prolific diversity: once again comparing the North to the South. In the South, goods are produced by the rays of the sun, creating a symphonic harmony of cause and effect. "Nourishment for curiosity, spiritual richness, mathematical unité = sensuality and philosophy."[48] Visiting the commandant of Algiers, he sees him draw "a large North-South line of prolific delights through the meridian of Paris: Paris, Marseilles, Alger, Ghardaia, the estuary of the Niger–the grand line of airplanes."[49]

Moving along this meridian line, Le Corbusier is enamored by the Oasis of Laghouat and the simple life of the Arab. He asks a man what he does, and finds the answer is nothing; he does not work because there is no work. Le Corbusier assumes he must be hungry, before realizing that climate says everything: "the sun permits, explains, excuses."[50] There is no need to consume in the oasis. That is the lesson the South teaches the North: an intelligent management of consumption that will reduce the immense size of the industrial order now lying prostrate and in depression.

> To learn to live certain hours of the day without consuming.
> Example: mind, sport, conversation, study, etc.
> Arabs wear their burnoose for ten years. We are proud and we feel very civilized because we wear: six complete suits per year.[51]

The oasis, he says, home to about forty thousand inhabitants, is a giant collective work traced out over years. It was constructed by a people, the Mozabites, who fled more than a thousand years before from religious persecution into the remotest regions of the desert, and to this day they still display utmost discipline. This has enabled them to control commerce in all Arab cities throughout the Mediterranean region. Le Corbusier calls the oasis of these Mozabites "paradise," and notes that cities without the greenery of the Arabs of the desert are a disgrace. "As elsewhere, it is necessary to appreciate the grandeur of the simple life of the nomads."[52]

Le Corbusier introduces a jarring divergence. Once, all work in the oasis was motivated by the necessity of immediate consumption. No thought was given to money until, with the new truck route bringing them everyday items to consume, they learned to earn money in order to buy whatever they wanted. Artificial consumption soon followed. The route introduced a new vision of life in the desert: to earn money no matter when or how. This is the vision that leads to the full catastrophe of the Depression.

He underscores the tragedy of the route. A good apéritif of *anis* or grenadine is sold at the Hôtel du Sud in Ghardaia for a franc; it is served with ice and a carafe of pure water drawn from a nearby spring. "*One franc*" (very cheap).[53] There are also imported bottles of beer that cost five francs, far cheaper than in Paris. These drinks represent "all the modern phenomenon of production, the transport industry: railways, steamships, trucks, same infrastructure of the machinist life."

And, more, the "*de-regionalization* of tastes, of foods, and of customs."[54] The locals learn to drink imported beer and iced apéritifs, abandoning "the adorable green mint tea boiling hot" that used to combat their thirst. "The Arab mint tea is *also* a paradise in countries of thirst; I say, *also*. But I do not feel like renouncing the miracle of my ice cold beer. Thus, we are here in full conflict!"[55]

But why shouldn't the iron pot replace the earthenware pot? Things are not so simple: for the Arab has developed a taste for new pleasures. The cinema tells the Arab of the oasis, not only how to use the iron pot but much more–now gramophones absurdly turn an Argentine tango, a musical manifestation of the modern soul.

The journey has upset Le Corbusier because there are disappointments and ambiguities imposed on his dream, with its screen full of white blind spots. Still, the dream taught him a most important lesson. It requires collective effort to make the desert blossom, in contrast to individualistic European ways. Returning to Marseilles on the steamship, he lists a number of restraints willingly accepted by the passengers. They and the sailors, the service workers, the mechanics all function in the small space of the boat. Because space is limited, everyone accepts a rigid classification. On land they would protest that the government interferes:

> Make a program: present some technical projects, fix the conditions in which each ought to play his part: immediately you will see rise up in mass: protestations, rights of man, sacred liberty, sublime meaning of the individual; petitions, delegations, deputies, Parliament, the collapse of the cabinet.... Make them accept. The aim being before the eyes of each, order, cohesion, action, trust, force become the fated and prolific consequence of a discipline freely consented to. We envision modern times: make a program, yes, make a program! Establish technical plans for the organization of contemporary society.[56]

Only a few sketches remain of Le Corbusier's initial perceptions of Algiers, those made in the summer of 1931. The first offers a view from the bridge of a steamship, a horizontal sweep of the city locating the Government Palace, the seashore, and the Casbah.[57] The second respects the view of the city, leaving it untouched.[58] These initial views, however, record the visual concepts behind all of Le Corbusier's Algerian redesigns and rewritings over the next ten years. [FIGURES II.5 AND II.6, p. 700]

"DEATH OF THE STREET" AND OBUS A

Before beginning to work in earnest on plans for Algiers, Le Corbusier republished his views on "Death of the Street" in the December 1931 issue of Camille Lopez's review *Chantiers Nord-Africains,* published in Algiers. Originally written for the Salon de l'Auto of 1930, this essay is a eulogy to the French automobile industry and displays the way that Le Corbusier links housing to the problem of circulation.[59] Perhaps he thought it would interest the Algerians because they were the biggest importers of automobiles, and were beginning to suffer all the problems of the automobile age.

The contemporary city suffers, he says, from two basic problems: streets no longer work and good homes need to be provided for everyone. To avoid revolution, it is necessary to take a clean sheet of paper and begin work on calculations, diagrams, and the realities of life. Speeds must be classified so that "biological speed" never comes in contact with vehicular speeds and high-speed vehicles never cross the path of slow-moving objects.

In early 1932, with ideas about routes, highways, and housing circulating in his mind, and filled with inspiration from his spring and summer travels, Le Corbusier begins to work out the plan for Algiers that will eventually be known as Obus A.[60] Le Corbusier had been asked by Les Amis d'Alger to join in the debate over what direction the future development of the city should take. Under the leadership of an energetic mayor, Charles Brunel, elected in 1925, the city had been discussing modernization plans for a few years. Les Amis d'Alger were particularly interested in renovation plans for the Marine District, alleviating its unsanitary and congested condition and transforming it into a business district. Algeria had experienced rapid economic growth up to 1930, so the future looked prosperous, and an efficient business district was much needed. They feared, however, that official plans were retrograde, based on nineteenth-century ideas without any consideration for automobile traffic or relieving congestion in overpopulated districts. Nor were these architect-planners aware of the advances modern architecture had made. They turn to Le Corbusier for help. After his first visit, Le Corbusier believes he has found in Algiers a municipal government more adventuresome than those in France, one with the authority and will to implement his schemes. He wants not only to shock his audience with audacious plans, ones they will never forget, but to prove his professionalism by inserting his schemes–all voluntarily made–into those for which funds have already been allocated. He will need, however, collaborators to carry out his ideas.[61]

He writes to the city architect of Hussein-Dey, Henri Ponsich, at the beginning of February 1932 to say that he has begun work in earnest on schemes for the redevelopment of the city. But a disaster has befallen him: his sketchbook filled with notes and drawings from his earlier visits to Algiers has been stolen from his atelier. Can Ponsich recount for him the important landmarks to jog his memory, especially those of Hussein-Dey? In spite of the loss of valuable material, he is optimistic that he will accomplish something of grandeur.[62]

Ten days later he writes again that the urban plans for Algiers advance, but now he requests some photographs from the sea in front of the Casbah and the Casino and from various land points looking toward the Casbah. He is hopeful that his plans will be ready by the middle of March. He mentions speaking with the film director Pierre Chenal, who is interested in filming the most notable aspects of Le Corbusier's project–but he needs Ponsich's collaborative help.[63]

The following week, another letter claims the project is "magnificent." It is urgent that Ponsich tell him the amount of money allocated for the development so he can adjust his scheme accordingly, for he desires to make his plans as realistic as possible. He will make models, painted white. Again he mentions that he continues to discuss with Chenal a film of Algiers, but he is waiting for Ponsich's reply.[64]

In March 1932 he writes to Rodolphe Rey, president of Les Amis d'Alger, proclaiming that his project expresses "the great directing lines" that bring a "dazzling" solution of modern times to the urban crisis of Algiers:

> It is a great act of faith. I delude myself with the idea that Algerians with their civic mindedness and their activity will be able to realize such a thing.... I am very smitten by my project.[65]

In fifteen more days, he writes, his study for Algiers will be finished. It will follow the directives of the 1930 guidelines but include some of his own special interests. He offers Algiers an ideal arrangement for housing, the creation of useful terrains for the expansion of population, a solution to its circulation problem, and the classification of urban elements, plus respect for the past and the reconstitution of the historical axis of the city, considering topography, geography, winds, sun, and relationships with the hinterland.[66] He is eager to come to Algiers and present the project himself.

His next letter to Ponsich, of April 9, states that the work is finished, and asks why he has received no response to his offer to come to Algiers to show off his scheme, which he offers gratuitously to the city. He is busy with plans to travel to Moscow and Rome, so it is imperative that his schedule be organized. He notes that the film is ready to be made without delay but needs to have fixed dates and appointments.[67]

Now he begins to get a bit anxious. Almost a month later he complains again. After working for four months almost nonstop on his plans for Algiers, he still has received not a word from the men of the city. He is filled with "the disagreeable feeling that when everything will be finished, Algiers will have signed with Prost or Rotival!" (Le Corbusier is making reference to a preliminary Regional Plan, actually awarded, in the event, in December 1932, to Henri Prost, who was then working on the Regional Plan of Paris, and to the engineer-urbanist Maurice Rotival.)[68]

He describes this first Algiers plan, Obus A, in *The Radiant City* in the following terms: "My project (a first step in coming to grips with so vast a problem), was a projectile project, intended to determine the line of fire."[69] He referred to his plans as an *obus*, an exploding shell, much in the manner he described the liberation that the cubist painters fomented twenty years earlier.[70] [FIGURE II.7] In a similar gesture of liberation, his plans for Algiers will be a bombardment. The municipal authorities had already decided in their 1930 plan to demolish the Quartier de la Marine, offering an unencumbered site in the heart of the city for development, and had proposed that blocks of housing replace overcrowded slums in the area. Le Corbusier urged, "Here you must build a business city, the 'City' of Algiers like the 'City' of London, and here you must create highways, both seafront and perpendicular ones, to constitute the vital axes of Algiers."[71]

Le Corbusier was obsessed with the lay of the land around the city: the inaccessible terrain of Fort l'Empereur had to be conquered, the magnificent views toward the sea or the mountains must be preserved. He studied military relief maps and aerial photographs, drew sketches, and made copious notes, writing lyrically about the spirit of place. There were precedents on the site, images from the existing city that mirrored his own compositions. He describes these in *The Radiant City*: the Arcades des Anglais, constructed around 1850 and sheltering a population of fishermen ever since, had the biggest boulevard

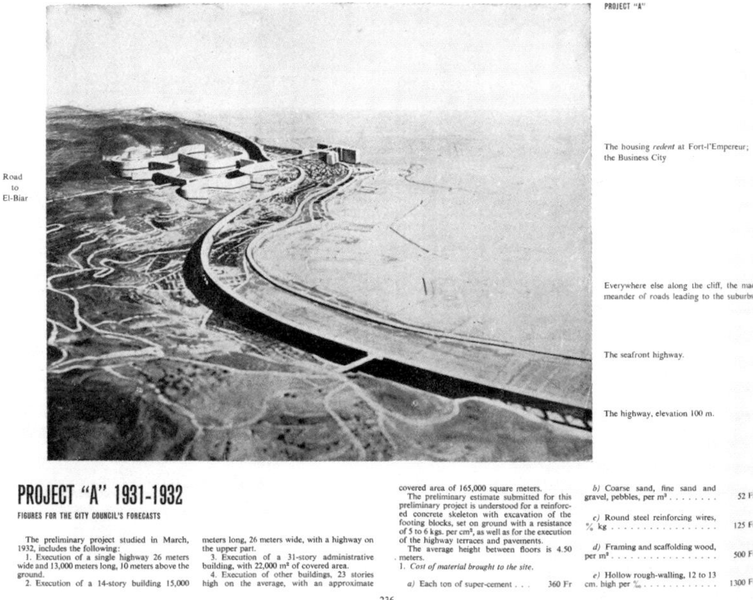

PROJECT "A"

Road to El-Biar

The housing *redent* at Fort-l'Empereur; the Business City

Everywhere else along the cliff, the mad meander of roads leading to the suburbs.

The seafront highway.

The highway, elevation 100 m.

PROJECT "A" 1931-1932

FIGURES FOR THE CITY COUNCIL'S FORECASTS

The preliminary project studied in March, 1932, includes the following:

1. Execution of a single highway 26 meters wide and 13,000 meters long, 10 meters above the ground.
2. Execution of a 14-story building 15,000 meters long, 26 meters wide, with a highway on the upper part.
3. Execution of a 31-story administrative building, with 22,000 m² of covered area.
4. Execution of other buildings, 23 stories high on the average, with an approximate covered area of 165,000 square meters.

The preliminary estimate submitted for this preliminary project is understood for a reinforced concrete skeleton with excavation of the footing blocks, set on ground with a resistance of 5 to 6 kgs. per cm², as well as for the execution of the highway terraces and pavements.

The average height between floors is 4.50 meters.

1. *Cost of material brought to the site.*

a) Each ton of super-cement . . . 360 Fr

b) Coarse sand, fine sand and gravel, pebbles, per m³ . . . . 52 Fr

c) Round steel reinforcing wires, % kg . . . . 125 Fr

d) Framing and scaffolding wood, per m³ . . . . 500 Fr

e) Hollow rough-walling, 12 to 13 cm. high per ‰ . . . . 1300 Fr

236

FIGURE II.7: **The first plan for Algiers (1931–32): a bombshell, or "Obus," to the people of Algiers**

of Algiers running overhead;[72] an elevator near the business city lifted cars from the lower port to a higher boulevard.[73] His plans marked "the reconstitution of the historic axis of Algiers," that which he had seen the commandant draw from Paris to Ghardaia and beyond.[74] Le Corbusier's approach was eminently pictorial: the Casbah intact but cleaned up, the boulevard winding its way along the sea, the hill, and the obelisk of Fort l'Empereur, the Admiralty Point, the surrounding countryside–all mobilized as elements of his scheme.[75]

Le Corbusier located his business center on land cleared by the city, which displaced its historic center but kept the Arab quarter separate from the European district. He preserved two mosques in the Arab City, surrounding them with massive green lawns, and kept the Arab Palace on Bastion 23 before the Marine, allowing it to remain a "like a tie pin before the city."[76] He also protected the Casbah, "the Arab city which contains some masterpieces and a trace [of small streets] worthy of being known... emptied of 60 or 100 of its packed-together constructions, it becomes a prodigious historic document!"[77] Two skyscrapers (thirty-one stories and twenty-three stories) fronting the sea were connected to the elite housing by a *passerelle* rising from the lower port, which gained the summit of Fort l'Empereur without damaging the

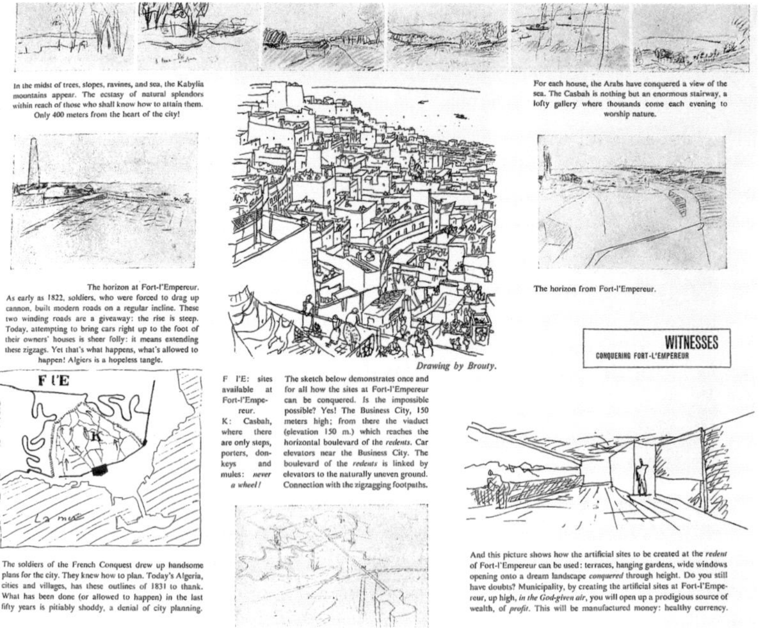

In the midst of trees, slopes, ravines, and sea, the Kabylia mountains appear. The ecstasy of natural splendors within reach of those who shall know how to attain them. Only 400 meters from the heart of the city!

The horizon at Fort-l'Empereur.
As early as 1822, soldiers, who were forced to drag up cannon, built modern roads on a regular incline. These two winding roads are a giveaway: the rise is steep. Today, attempting to bring cars right up to the foot of their owners' houses is sheer folly: it means extending these zigzags. Yet that's what happens, what's allowed to happen! Algiers is a hopeless tangle.

Drawing by Brouty.

For each house, the Arabs have conquered a view of the sea. The Casbah is nothing but an enormous stairway, a lofty gallery where thousands come each evening to worship nature.

The horizon from Fort-l'Empereur.

WITNESSES
CONQUERING FORT-L'EMPEREUR

F l'E: sites available at Fort-l'Empereur.
K: Casbah, where there are only steps, porters, donkeys and mules: *never a wheel!*

The sketch below demonstrates once and for all how the sites at Fort-l'Empereur can be conquered. Is the impossible possible? Yes! The Business City, 150 meters high; from there the viaduct (elevation 150 m.) which reaches the horizontal boulevard of the *redents*. Car elevators near the Business City. The boulevard of the *redents* is linked by elevators to the naturally uneven ground. Connection with the zigzagging footpaths.

The soldiers of the French Conquest drew up handsome plans for the city. They knew how to plan. Today's Algeria, cities and villages, has these outlines of 1831 to thank. What has been done (or allowed to happen) in the last fifty years is pitiably shoddy, a denial of city planning.

And this picture shows how the artificial sites to be created at the *redent* of Fort-l'Empereur can be used: terraces, hanging gardens, wide windows opening onto a dream landscape *conquered* through height. Do you still have doubts? Municipality, by creating the artificial sites at Fort-l'Empereur, up high, *in the God-given air*, you will open up a prodigious source of wealth, of *profit*. This will be manufactured money: healthy currency.

FIGURE II.8: Le Corbusier conquered the sites of Fort l'Empereur with gigantic housing blocks, offering each residential unit terraces, hanging gardens, and wide windows for views of the landscape.

Casbah.[78] The Casbah's architectural character, its indigenous restaurants, bars, clubs, and any ingredient essential for the tourist industry, already protected as a historic preserve by municipal legislation, was also saved in Le Corbusier's scheme.

On the slopes of Fort l'Empereur he located five or six rectangular curving *redents*, assembled into a unit by the *passerelle*, allowing the exploitation of otherwise inaccessible and undeveloped slopes. He focused attention on the views from Fort l'Empereur, reserving this section for the provision of housing for the elite. Each apartment in the redent opened onto the view of the sea or the interior countryside.

> And this picture shows how the artificial sites to be created at the *redent* of Fort l'Empereur can be used: terraces, hanging gardens, wide windows opening onto a dream landscape *conquered* through height![79] [FIGURE II.8]

> Does there exist in any city in the world, a system of roads and mains as perfect as this? As economical, as easy to reach?...

> In this plan, on the inaccessible land of Fort-l'Empereur we see that the principles fundamental to the layout of the Moorish dwelling have been reinstated: the contrast of various heights, the patio opening on to a garden surrounded by high walls, the view of the sea. Now *that* is good regionalism![80]

Running at right angles to the passerelle and touching the Casbah at its highest point, a giant viaduct followed the topography along the coastline, stretching out for more than twenty-eight kilometers. Underneath fifteen kilometers of this roadway, Le Corbusier suspended two-story "cubes of habitation" in sufficient number to absorb population increases among the workers of the port for years to come. These cubes offered different types of cells for different sizes of family and opened onto an interior street four meters in width.[81]

In June 1932, the Mayor of Algiers, Charles Brunel, called on Le Corbusier at his Parisian atelier.[82] It was a troubling visit. The mayor wanted to leave quickly, saying merely, "Your ideas are for 100 years from now!"[83] A few months after this visit, Le Corbusier writes to his friend Ernest Mercier as follows:[84]

> I have a heart blown up by a vast and foolish enterprise. I made for Algiers some plans of urbanism which are true and magical. I offer them gratuitously to the city of Algiers. Because they are magical, one turns away from me in fright: the mayor, the bank. One goes to make an atrocious thing in Algiers: burying the city in the lowest design.[85]

OBUS B (FALL 1932–FEBRUARY 1933)[86]

Having launched his projectile and been summarily rebuffed, Le Corbusier realizes he has to organize public opinion if his scheme is to be accepted by the mayor, and he is to be officially asked to draw up a regional plan. He must make a new plan of attack by forming a group of technicians to sway public opinion and completely disqualify any other plan. He will seek the cooperation of Camille Lopez, editor of *Chantiers Nord-Africains,* and of Edmond Brua, editor-in-chief of the weekly *Travaux Nord-Africains.* He will also publicize his plans in Paris with the aid of Jean Badovici, who would publish his Obus scheme in the fall of 1932 in *L'Architecture Vivante.* Le Corbusier's own collaboration on the editorial boards of *Plans* and *Prélude* would also help to publicize his views.

Brua thinks the time is favorable, and the era of grand works more likely to happen in Algeria than in France, because France needs to make Algeria the bastion of its North African empire. Thus Brua suggests that Le Corbusier, in order to secure local public opinion with respect to modernization, develop a questionnaire. With the aid of Mercier, Le Corbusier develops different sets of questions. These were a polemic for his own theoretical schemes, not a fact-finding tool, and the surveys may never have been performed. Some questions were: "Algiers, will it become the Capital of North Africa?" and "This expansion of Algiers, will it be realized in a delay of 20 years, from 1932 to 1953?"[87]

In subsequent letters to Ponsich, Le Corbusier is hopeful that his model, plans, large photographs, and lecture would play an important part in the upcoming Exposition d'Urbanisme et d'Architecture, to be held in Algiers in 1933. Aware that the banks were the financiers of Algiers, he was eager, he said, for them to take note of his schemes. He sent along a copy of *Architecture Vivante*, which had just published the review of his proposals, and asked if Ponsich, one of the organizers of the exposition, could guarantee that his large scheme (more than twenty meters long) would be given the place of honor. He wants public opinion in Algiers to be struck by the magnificent documents he has assembled.[88]

At the end of December 1932, Le Corbusier learns from the Algerian press that Prost and Rotival have been officially appointed to create the study for a Regional Plan.[89] His worst fears indeed have been realized. He writes to Brua:

> The last number of *Travaux Nord-Africains* brought me a New Year's gift: the nomination of Prost and Rotival for the Plan of Algiers!...Rotival had made an agreement with me in order to realize our plans....Rotival played a "trick" on me....He admits my ideas, he copies them, he uses them. Therefore there is no opposition to the thesis. I conclude from this: a/ Prost wants only to be a distant advisor, b/ Rotival will have the upper hand, c/ between Prost and me, there are some differences of doctrine but not between Rotival and me. Therefore I will very well be able to work in common with Rotival and with Prost by ricochet.[90]

THIRD VISIT TO ALGERIA

Le Corbusier makes a third visit to Algiers in February 1933 for the Exposition d'Urbanisme et d'Architecture, a seven-day affair opening on the seventeenth and closing on the twenty-third. Organized by a group of architects sympathetic to modern architecture and the proclamations of CIAM (Les Amis d'Alger, Société des Architectes Modernes de Paris, Le Groupe Algérien, and the Chambre Syndicale d'Algérie des Architectes Diplômés), this exposition attempts to sway public opinion toward modern architecture and urbanism, to act as a rallying point for a new conception of the city and a vehicle for progressive modernization.[91] In preparation for this exposition, and due to the mayor's rejection of his first scheme, Le Corbusier begins in the fall of 1932 to transform his Obus plans. He focuses on the business district, leaving the viaduct housing along the bay to be built at a future date. His skyscraper scheme appears in the form of an "H" linked to the passerelle at a height of 158 meters. Where the junction with the viaduct might have been, at one hundred meters, he adds a loggia of three levels, forming an immense window opening onto the sea. He conceives of his scheme in more realistic stages, focusing for the present on drawing the Marine District and Fort l'Empereur together. Yet this suppression of the dorsal spine of his Obus A scheme, that is, the viaduct housing tying the entire city together from the suburbs of Saint Eugène to those at Hussein-Dey, left the problems of circulation and the provision of adequate housing for the poor unresolved. It creates an imbalance in the overall scheme, with only the one-hundred-meter-high skyscraper intended as a counter to the massive developments on Fort l'Empereur.

At the exposition, Le Corbusier presents his models, photographs, and plans of Obus A and the softer, gentler scheme of Obus B.[92] Gaston Martin, reviewing in 1933 the talk that Le Corbusier delivered at the exposition, called him a great enthusiast for everything that lives: animals, plants, even clouds.[93] He loves and understands nature. But looking at his schemes for Algiers, Martin noted that Le Corbusier chose to group all business activity of the city in the Marine District along the seafront, in order not to lose time in commercial transactions. This would be the vital node of the future African metropolis and the crossroads of two grand routes of communication: one along the coastline and the other from Fort l'Empereur. This was a grand scheme, but impossible to implement, though Le Corbusier would disagree. Yet Martin praised Le Corbusier's plan as well: Le Corbusier allowed the sun, air, light, and the direction of the dominant winds to determine the form of his city.

Toward the end of his talk, Le Corbusier was so taken with enthusiasm that he drew the outlines of Marseilles and Istanbul, seen from afar. He believed it was the equilibrium achieved by the masses composing their different profiles that made each so beautiful. Then he turned to draw the face of Algiers, a radiant city, seen from the sea. This too, he promised, could be beautiful, as pure and complete as the other two profiles. One sees the green hills coming down from Fort l'Empereur to touch the sea, and on the highest of these hills a brilliant jewel of a thousand lights: this is the center of residences for future (elite) Algerians, immense houses where glass, the material of modern construction, sparkles under clear blue sky. Martin allowed that Le Corbusier's enthusiasm was infectious, and that frenetic applause ended his conference. "But there are always some malcontents, and one was able to see, in the galleries, three persons who did not stop showing their distain for urbanism....But just as water cannot wet the feathers of the goose, the clearest ideas can have no hold on circumvolutions in the brains of certain retrograde minds."[94]

It is difficult to understand why Le Corbusier continued to revise his plans for Algiers. He had been rejected by Brunel; Prost and Rotival had received official approval to develop a regional plan; yet in spite of this opposition Le Corbusier continued to improve his Obus plans. Holding Prost as his enemy in an opposing camp, Le Corbusier was no doubt convinced that he was needed in Algiers, that this enterprising city was the battleground for the cause of modern architecture. In his letter to Brua of December 1932, he writes,

> I do not ask for money. I have offered gratuitously my plan to the mayor...I see through my intervention the occasion to bring to Algiers regulatory laws that will allow the realization of modern architecture. It requires for that the presence of an architect such as me...it is you who have said [it requires] a poet.[95]

On the last day of this third visit, on March 17, 1933, Le Corbusier takes an airplane flight toward the M'Zab with the pilot Louis Durafour. He has his sketchbook on his knees, ready to draw and jot down his impressions. Lessons learned from this flight will be reproduced in *Aircraft* and repeated in *Sur les 4 Routes* (*The Four Routes*).[96] The bird's-eye view from the airplane reveals everything to him, enables him to understand the densely packed cellular structure of Arab villages, the rhythmic alignment of their houses surrounded with walls, punctured here and there by a minaret or lush green palm trees. He arrives at a new consideration of the human dimensions of a radiant city, and perhaps this too influences him to remodel his plans for Algiers.[97]

OBUS C (LATE 1933–EARLY 1934)[98]

Le Corbusier had already written to Brunel on March 8, 1933, that he was going to rethink the business center, the highways, the seafront, as well as the design of automobile garages, marinas, the railroad station, and the housing *redents* on Fort l'Empereur. "Everywhere life circles intensely. I would like to understand the questions posed, the reasons, the causes."[99] He will establish exact numbers, and strengthen his scheme with technical materials already drawn up by qualified engineers and statisticians. And he will also submit a plan for preserving the Casbah. As an enticement, to pique the mayor's interest, Le Corbusier was going to suggest to CIAM and to CIRPAC that the Congress for 1934 be held in Algiers.

On July 27, 1933, Le Corbusier again writes to Brunel. He has, he says, never stopped thinking about the city's problems.[100] He includes sheets of designs, sketches made from Fort l'Empereur, and studies concerning the Marine District. He is on his way to a CIAM congress in Athens, and explains to the mayor that this group will make a diagnostic of the condition of twenty-one great cities of the world. Le Corbusier mentions the Congress will consider a request for convening the 1934 CIAM Congress in Algiers. And he is proud to announce that he is having success with his urban plans for Anvers and Stockholm, although the results of competitions are always slow to be revealed. Then, almost as an aside, he inserts the remark:

> You will see appearing little by little this sign which ought to interest you:
>
> [FIGURE II.9]
>
> Paris, Barcelona, Algiers, Rome, a new economy locked up in a rich dimension.[101]

He repeats this cartographic symbol in a December 1933 letter that was later reprinted in *The Radiant City*.[102] This time he addresses the mayor directly:

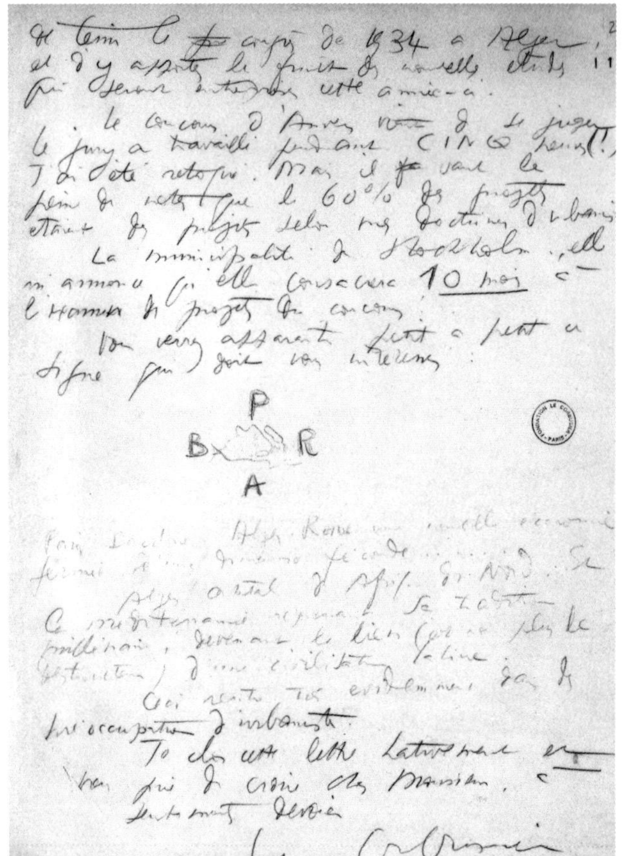

FIGURE II.9: **In a 1933 letter to the mayor of Algiers, M. Brunel, Le Corbusier sketched a new political grouping of Mediterranean cities laid out like the cardinal points: a north-south axis from Paris to Algiers, and an east-west one from Rome to Barcelona.**

New groupings, and regroupings, new units of importance must come into being which will give the world an arrangement that is less arbitrary and less dangerous. The Mediterranean will form the link of one of these groupings, whose creation is imminent. Races, tongues, a culture reaching back a thousand years–truly whole. An impartial research group has already, this year, though the organ *Prélude*, shown the principle of one of these new units. It is summed up in four letters, laid out like the cardinal points:

Paris, Barcelona, Rome, Algiers. A unit extending from north to south along a meridian, running the entire gamut of climates, embracing every need, every resource.

> Algiers ceases to be a colonial city; Algiers becomes the head of the African continent, a capital city. This means that a great task awaits her, but a magnificent future too. This means that the hour of city planning should strike in Algiers.[103]

The myth of a Mediterranean union, drawing both sides of the inland sea together, was a reassuring argument relying on geography and stressing so-called natural features of climate, landscape, and shared cultural history.[104] The famous square that Le Corbusier referred to proposed that Algiers become one of the endpoints of an axis of power: Paris and Algiers, crossed with that of Barcelona and Rome. Le Corbusier saw this quadrilateral as a natural alliance that would guarantee European presence in North Africa and secure its colonial rights over Algeria.[105] While Algeria might be a meeting place of two cultures, it was the European civilization, with its technical organization and financial powers, that remained in control. Algiers was thus a stabilizing force in his cartographic imagination, buffeted from the South by an uncivilized hinterland and from the East by increasing unrest.

The Municipal Council of Algiers never examined Corbusier's various plans, although Brunel finally responded to his many inquiries on April 16, 1934, thanking him for volunteering his work and for the dedication he had shown the city of Algiers. Nevertheless, Brunel said, the Council had already made a decision on the reconstruction of the Marine District, and was not going to rethink a judgment that had the approval of both the Superior Authority and the French government.[106]

But Le Corbusier was not to be dissuaded by these pleasantries, for he now was convinced that public opinion in Algiers supported his scheme even though municipal authorities opposed him.[107] It was necessary once again to wage a vigorous battle through the press. Jean Pierre Cotereau, a professor at the École Polytechnique and friend of Le Corbusier, authored a series of nine articles between May and July 1934 in *Journal Général, Travaux Publics et Bâtiment.* Nor was it enough that Cotereau praise the plans of Le Corbusier; he also added his own concerns over political unrest and explained in detail the true destiny of Algiers. Le Corbusier also wrote to Jean Pierre Faure, an engineer in Algiers, for help in publicizing Obus C. Faure would write a series of articles in defense of Le Corbusier's schemes in *Travaux Nord-Africains* beginning in October 1934.[108] There would also be publication of Obus C in *Architecture d'Aujourd'hui* and *Architecture Vivante.* And material in

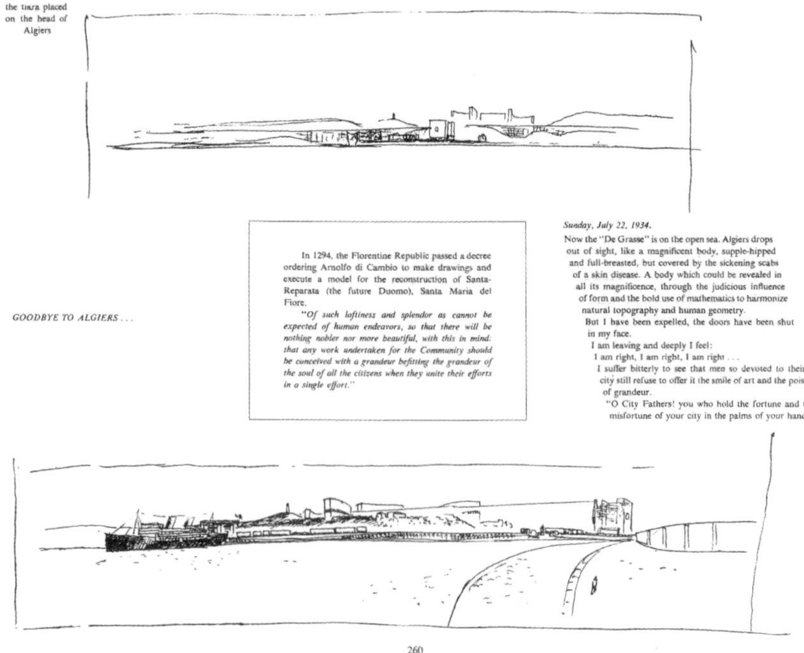

the tiara placed on the head of Algiers

GOODBYE TO ALGIERS . . .

In 1294, the Florentine Republic passed a decree ordering Arnolfo di Cambio to make drawings and execute a model for the reconstruction of Santa-Reparata (the future Duomo), Santa Maria del Fiore.

"Of such loftiness and splendor as cannot be expected of human endeavors, so that there will be nothing nobler nor more beautiful, with this in mind: that any work undertaken for the Community should be conceived with a grandeur befitting the grandeur of the soul of all the citizens when they unite their efforts in a single effort."

Sunday, July 22, 1934.

Now the "De Grasse" is on the open sea. Algiers drops out of sight, like a magnificent body, supple-hipped and full-breasted, but covered by the sickening scabs of a skin disease. A body which could be revealed in all its magnificence, through the judicious influence of form and the bold use of mathematics to harmonize natural topography and human geometry.

But I have been expelled, the doors have been shut in my face.

I am leaving and deeply I feel:

I am right, I am right, I am right . . .

I suffer bitterly to see that men so devoted to their city still refuse to offer it the smile of art and the poise of grandeur.

"O City Fathers! you who hold the fortune and the misfortune of your city in the palms of your hands!"

260

FIGURE II.10: **Disheartened after being rejected by the authorities of Algiers, whose natural topography he had harmonized with human geography, Le Corbusier drew these final sketches of the city as his boat left for Marseilles on July 22, 1934.**

The Radiant City, largely compiled between 1933–34 and finally published in 1935, would add to the publicity push. But all of this effort was in vain. Official opinion never changed, and by the end of 1934, Le Corbusier had said goodbye to Algiers, reproducing his sad farewell in *The Radiant City*: [FIGURE II.10]

> Now the "De Grasse" is on the open sea. Algiers drops out of sight, like a magnificent body, supple-hipped and full-breasted, but covered by the sickening scabs of a skin disease. A body which could be revealed in all its magnificence, through the judicious influence of form and the bold use of mathematics to harmonize natural topography and human geometry.
>
> But I have been expelled, the doors have been shut in my face.
>
> I am leaving and deeply I feel:
> I am right, I am right, I am right.[109]

During the time (1934–36) that Obus C was circulating in the press, at expositions, and through letters, across Algeria there were Muslim demonstrations, strikes, and boycotts of European merchants in protest of colonization and economic depression. These expressions of outrage were met with harsh repression. Reflecting a hardened political line, Mayor Brunel was replaced in 1935 by Augustin Rozis, a right-wing and anti-Semitic politician.[110]

Despite his definitive defeat in 1933–34, Le Corbusier did not let the subject of Algeria rest, though plans for Algiers took a backseat as he was preoccupied with many other projects and travels. A governmental decree in 1935 made it possible to establish regional projects in the colonies with more permanent planning bodies, replacing the provisional regional plans developed by Prost and Rotival between 1933 and 1935. In 1936, perhaps encouraged by this development, Le Corbusier writes another poetic treatise on Algiers, "En Alger, Des Logis Radieux" (In Algiers, Radiant Housing").[111] Everything in Algiers remains, he says, in confusion, forcing into retreat money, honor, civic works, even production. The government of France has washed its hands of the Le Corbusier affair, allowing local rivalries to annihilate his schemes. As a result Algiers is denied the destiny that geography has bestowed on it, and will not become the head of North Africa.

He had offered Algiers a modern infrastructure, a joyous, optimistic, and constructive work that satisfies the needs of the present and those of tomorrow. But academicians cry out in alarm. Calling on *l'esprit-France*, they do not understand the splendid poetry of the times, and thus deny the appearance of modern architecture. But architecture, Le Corbusier continues, is made not of "beautiful picturesque silhouettes" or "beautifully constructed decors" or "great thick walls" rooting the nation in the soil of the fatherland. Architecture is about shelter and transportation, static events and mobile displacements. The duty of an architect is to first provide shelter for the family, then community structures, administrative and civic buildings, and shelters for transportation on land, rail, water, and air. "The elegant discourse of architecture" is composed of simple elements of walls, spaces, volumes, materials, and colors. They support the essential joys–sun, space, and trees–and their benefits are promised to everyone, not just a privileged few. If the critics would only allow its destiny to be fulfilled: "In Algiers, some radiant housing!"[112]

> If one sees clearly, everything is possible. Yet incredibly,
> In this admirable site where the sun is king, where the sea spreads out ineffably, where the mountains of Kabylie outline the far horizon, where the Atlas mountains make in the blue of the distance a grand backdrop wall for the desert–in this exceptional symphonic landscape man, through conformity to his scholarly routines, through stupidity of academic teachings, destroys, step after step, the very elements of this lyrical nature.[113]

The city of Algiers would be completely transformed by the scale of his intervention, yet he maintains his plans are a communitarian enterprise, one offered for the public's well-being. Architecture of modern times demands a vast new scale; the time has come for grandeur and unanimity. [114] That is why for the last five years, in spite of retrograde administrators, sarcasm, and shaking heads, Le Corbusier has proposed a "great work" for Algiers. The young already hope for such things, believing in the spirit that blows in the wind. They expect that soon, Algiers will build radiant housing for all. Facile in slipping between lyrical strains and rational schemes, Le Corbusier adds that, of course, it will be necessary to pass some laws and establish an exact and virile authority.

A moment of optimism about political tensions in Algeria appeared in 1936, when Léon Blum and the Popular Front came to power in France. The Blum government promised a more conciliatory treatment of the colonies. Under such changed political conditions, various factions of Muslim opposition came together in a coalition and adopted in the summer of 1936 an official program called the Charter of Demands of the Muslim Algerian People. This called for widespread reforms: rescinding all laws of exception, offering universal suffrage and parliamentary representation, and providing compulsory free education, health legislation, and unemployment compensation, among other concerns. The Blum government responded positively but vaguely with an open-ended commitment to these demands. Meanwhile political demonstrations continued, and the question of Algerian national independence was raised for the first time on Algerian soil. Those who supported assimilation, association, or emancipation splintered into separate groups during the winter of 1936–37. Fearful that Muslims were making headway under Blum, the Federation of Mayors went on strike in 1938, burying all legislative reforms of the Blum government in parliamentary maneuvers.

FINAL SCHEMES FOR ALGIERS

Perhaps the publication of this mournful 1936 essay on Algiers was occasioned by one more opportunity for Le Corbusier to present Obus C to the public, namely through L'Exposition de la Cité Moderne (Exposition of the Modern City), organized by Les Amis d'Alger in April 1936. Its proclaimed purpose was to define a modern city and to present a program by which Algiers could become an exemplar. It was a decidedly colonial affair, however, ignoring Muslim Algerians' political concerns as it continued to promote economic development and the interests of France.

Emery, now Le Corbusier's Algerian spokesman, expressed hope that a truly collective Mediterranean architecture, responsive to climate and site yet French in spirit, utilizing modern techniques, would become the symbol for economic and colonial expansion. He regretted that Morocco, Spain, Italy, and Greece, even Syria and Palestine, had sent no materials to exhibit at the exposition, because they would have lent credibility and full expression to his concept of a collective Mediterranean modernity, one that might pull together Algerians and Europeans intent on modernization. A poster for the exposition juxtaposed elements of Le Corbusier's Obus housing schemes with a Doric column, suggesting a path by which the classical past became the modern, but without mentioning traditional Muslim culture. Given this context, Le Corbusier's Obus C was not surprisingly given a prominent position at the exposition and was much discussed in the local press as a model for modernizing the city. A diorama three meters long of Algiers seen at night, initially built for the Salon de la Lumière in Paris, was the centerpiece of his display.[115]

Algiers was far from the only project on Le Corbusier's mind during 1934–36. He was still controversial politically, offering his services to Mussolini and proposing plans for Addis Ababa after the Ethiopian campaign of 1935–36. In the fall of 1935, he finally made his much-postponed trip to the United States, focusing on writing *When the Cathedrals Were White* in the spring of 1936 and returning to Rio de Janeiro in July of 1936. Throughout these years he continued to reformulate different proposals for the Pavillon des Temps Nouveaux at the Exposition Internationale des Arts et Techniques (Paris, 1937). That same year, two years after the 1935 French decree replacing the provisional regional plans developed by Prost and Rotiva, a Permanent Committee for the Regional Plan of Algiers was established by decree of the French government on November 6, 1937.[116] Le Corbusier was appointed to this forty-five-member committee in December, and began to initiate more pragmatic approaches to his schemes for Algiers.

Obus D was worked out in 1938 in collaboration with Algiers's chief engineer, Pierre Renaud, a member of the Committee for a Regional Plan. It reduced Le Corbusier's heroic schemes to a single three-pronged skyscraper (Y-shaped in cross-section) dominating the seafront. Obus E (1939) introduced another skyscraper scheme, with a brise-soleil vaguely referring to Muslim decorative window screens. Le Corbusier's last Algiers plan, the Final Plan Directeur (1941–42), was developed while Le Corbusier was collaborating with the Vichy government. He expected, as a member of Vichy's Study Commission for Questions Relating to Housing and Building, that his schemes for Algiers would finally be authorized. This, of course, was not to be, and shortly after the Americans landed in North Africa on November 8, 1942, Le Corbusier abandoned all efforts to modernize Algiers.

The Plan Directeur is described shortly before Le Corbusier makes his last trip to Algiers in the essay "Palms et Horizons sur Alger" ("Palms and Horizons of Algiers"), which appears in the magazine *Fontaine* in May 1942. France, he proclaims, has been brought to its knees and suffers the consequence of a strange defeat, not because of its capitulation to Hitler's demands, but due to what he calls "the great upset" of the end of the first machine era. Instead of innovative ideas, old concerns dominate, money controls, mediocrity reigns. He uses the word "poetry," he says, as an antidote to this stale situation; it comprises the forces of enthusiasm that organize the economy and master the social. Cities are sick because poetry has abandoned them. Architecture and architects, even the engineer, have fallen into a very low state. "So much hideousness has therefore soiled Algiers as it has soiled Paris."[117]

After thirty years of obstinate perseverance and patient research, Le Corbusier once more offers the administrators of Algiers a new proposition: a "plan directeur" (master plan) for the city and its region.

> The word is new, the thing is new.... joy being reintroduced in the primordial cell, the family, and civic space, product of enthusiasm, of confidence and of faith, being written into communitarian works, giving to enterprises strength, irresistible power, standing the sparkling city upright against the complete failures of the times.[118]

He equates this *plan directeur* with poetry, the missing ingredient in contemporary cities. It is not an abstract thing, but built on the reality of North Africa.

> This sun, this space of sky and sea, this greenery have surrounded the acts of Salambo, of Scipion, of Hannibal as of Ker-Eddin, the Barbary Pirate. The sea, the chain of Atlas and the mountains of Kabyle, unfurl their magnificent blues. The earth is red. The vegetation is of palm-trees, eucalyptus, gum trees, cork-trees, olive trees and Barbary fig trees. From the lowest plain to the confines of the sky, this symphony never wearies.[119]

He still calls the Casbah, built by the Turks, a "masterpiece of architecture and urbanism" and compares it favorably to the town of the European colonists. Over the last fifty years, they have built a new city out of little box houses, opening onto burning streets and petrifying the desert with masses of broken stone. They crowd inhabitants together between two walls stuffed with local furniture, and the views out of their windows are onto other walls. Yet all around them lies the "sweetness of nature," completely ignored.

Le Corbusier recalls his first adventures in Algiers, strolling through the uproar of the streets of the old city, mounting from the sea straight upwards, following the line of the largest slope of the cliffs until he reached the culminating point of Fort l'Empereur. Algerians, for the most part, do no come here; they have never seen this amazing view. It was precisely here on these magnificent heights that Le Corbusier unfurled his urban schemes for tomorrow.

To Le Corbusier's consternation, the city council talks about building a metro to quickly transport people far away onto small plots of land. They intend to house still others in small boxes at the foot of the Casbah on land recovered by demolishing hovels. What a misadventure, what loss of poetry threatens the city! Le Corbusier would have located a park filled with high palm trees from the desert in the Marine District, spreading a tapestry of green at the foot of the city.

One more time, Le Corbusier explains: Algiers lies on the meridian of Paris. On this line lies the capital of French Africa, facing the sea and looking toward Europe.[120] Yet at this very moment there are preparations afoot to kill the destiny of Algiers, a destiny written in history, in geography, in topography.[121]

Thirty years of research on cities have given Le Corbusier a certainty that Algiers is a "land of possible miracles."[122] Thus, he goes on to say, he arrived in the springtime of 1942 to speak to the governor, the prefect, the mayor–to those responsible for the management of the city, the region, of Africa–and to tell them one more time of his vision for Algiers. He addresses the managers of Algiers directly: it is men like you who, through initiatives and responsibilities, will conduct the city toward Olympus.

> Everything is in your hands: the destiny of 500,000 inhabitants of this present and future Algiers, the wonder of this French Africa of which the head–the capital–will be made joyous by your orders, the recognition of the mother-country [i.e., France] because you will have acted at the moment when others are satisfied to expedite some current business, and the astonishment of the world before this phoenix of France which, yet again, and in full compassion, is reborn form the ashes.[123]

III. MEDITERRANEAN GEOGRAPHY LESSONS

We already know that the Mediterranean entered the imagination of Le Corbusier as "pure forms assembled under clear light," a phrase he repeated from the time of his first voyage to the East in 1911. We know how he juxtaposed the North and South and drew on the meridian axis that flowed from Paris to Algiers as a source of inspiration, and we are also aware of his confession, made in *When the Cathedrals Were White* (1937), that even though he was a world traveler he still felt the pull of one strong root, that of the Mediterranean.[124] But we have yet to explore the full meaning and use of the adjective "Mediterranean" in the geographical theories of the neo-syndicalists, and in the cartographic texts of Le Corbusier during the 1930s.

The Mediterranean is, by and large, imaginary, other than as a body of water: it is a particularly fertile representation, changing its meaning with place and time.[125] Geographers of the eighteenth century, for example, interested in the relationships between nature and society, portrayed the Mediterranean as an object of study transcending borders and frontiers. "Climate" was for them a tool by which regions could be delineated. The burning sun, the dry air, the rocky lands, the blue sea, the olive tree, and the grapevine determined, albeit impressionistically, a geographical unit connecting the northern and southern sides of the inland sea. They engendered, on this view, the genius of a civilization.

By the end of the nineteenth century, the anarchist geographer Élisée Reclus had extended this definition to the historic, economic, and cultural space of the Mediterranean. He originated the idea that people's "identification" arose from a certain regional space, constituting in this case a Mediterranean people. A crossroads not only of three continental masses (Europe, Africa, and Asia), but of three races (Aryans, Berbers, and Semites), the Mediterranean becomes the central axis of civilization, uniting North and South, East and West. France, Reclus wrote, "historically became the place where the races of the north were united with the south, where the Mediterranean civilization came to intersect with elements of Celtic and German culture."[126]

Reclus thought the best social structure was a decentralized state, a federation formed by associations of producers and groups freely choosing to associate together. These natural groupings governed themselves from below, in contrast to the hierarchical and exploitative practices of the centralized state and of capitalism. He found evidence of embryonic anarchist associations in the south of France and throughout the Mediterranean region. These groups, Reclus believed, could still feel the call of the Greek agora and the central squares of the Italian towns, those places that allowed a liberated conscious to discuss and debate communal affairs freely and openly.[127]

The more the Mediterranean was posed as the creative root of identity, both individual and collective, the more issues concerning the romantic mystery of its "unity" and the specification of its "Latin roots" were raised.[128] The Mediterranean imaginary became a spiritual barrier that Europeans could erect against dangers emanating from the Germanic culture or from modernization. It spoke of equilibrium, measure, harmony, of happiness, lyricism, and spiritual joy set against brutality, discord, and tragedy.

Another writer steeped in the mystery of the Mediterranean, though on his own idiosyncratic terms, was Albert Camus. In a lecture on February 8, 1937, in the Maison de Culture of Algiers, he questioned how to define "the new Mediterranean culture" (*la nouvelle culture méditerranéenne*).[129] He did not want to speak of a "nationalism of the sun," of past traditions based on a period of decadence like the Roman Empire. "The Mediterranean that surrounds us is to the contrary a living country, full of games and smiles."[130] He opposed the poetic power of this Mediterranean culture to the abstract ideologies emanating from Europe that alienate man from contact with his everyday world. The "Mediterranean" spoke of man, of his life, of courtyards and cypress, of the Doric, of Spain, and of truth being assassinated as he spoke. Still, it was an evasive concept. "The Mediterranean is...this smell or this perfume that is useless to express: we feel it always with our skin."[131] It is diffuse and turbulent, like the Arab quarters or the ports of Genoa or Tunisia.

In 1938, with a few friends, Camus published the journal *Rivages: Revue de Culture Méditerranéenne.* They sought, they said, to keep alive things from the Mediterranean that gave them joy.[132] "At a time when a taste for doctrines would want to separate us from the world," Camus wrote,

> It is not bad that some young men, in a young country, proclaim their attachment to a few perishable and essential possessions which give meaning to our life: the sea, the sun, and women in the light. They are the things of a living culture, the remainder being the dead civilization that we repudiate.[133]

The potential of the Mediterranean to evoke an intangible ideal, the "ineffable spirit" of its land, climate, and culture, was harnessed by the neo-syndicalists in the 1930s. They borrowed from Reclus the notion of a Mediterranean federation, one of three European regions that would install peace and harmony throughout the world.

THE SPIRIT OF GREECE IN LES TEMPS NOUVEAUX

The choice of Athens as the location for the fourth CIAM conference in 1933 offered Le Corbusier his second and final voyage to Greece. Aboard the *Patris II*, chartered by the members of the congress, he sailed from Marseilles to Athens and back on July 29 and August 13, 1933. Although the congress officially began in Athens, the days spent on the ship were filled with debates about the urban crisis affecting thirty-three different cities.[134] Upon arrival in Athens, the CIAM delegates found the Acropolis illuminated in their honor, and an official government welcome was arranged for the first and second evenings. On the evening of August 3, a reception took place in the courtyard of the neoclassical buildings of the École Polytechnique. Le Corbusier was expected to deliver a technical speech on illumination, acoustics, and air-conditioning entitled "Air-Sound-Light" at nine o'clock, but when the hour arrived he was nowhere to be seen. About a quarter to ten he arrived, disheveled. He later explained to a few colleagues that he had been completely absorbed by a visit to the Acropolis and had lost track of time.[135]

By the summer of 1933, Le Corbusier's plans for Moscow and Algiers had been rejected. He was aware that many CIAM delegates were also hostile to his approach, and may even have been supportive of the diatribes against him by Professor Umbdenstock and the journalists Mauclair and Saugier. (For an account of these attacks, see Chapter 8.) Perhaps to sway his opposition, Le Corbusier unleashed an enthusiastic tribute to the Acropolis and the continuity that existed between classical and modern art. Or perhaps he lavished so much attention on Greece to compensate for his tardiness. Recalling the Acropolis and his sudden awakening to its crushing truth in 1911 was also a way to link the architecture of antiquity to his present battle over ideas.

In his talk, Le Corbusier calls on the Acropolis to legitimize his architecture and urbanism, for the truth that it revealed to him in 1911 had been his standard bearer across all the intervening years.[136] It represented a moral order that he believed was absent from the troubled 1930s. Its implacable truth enabled him to oppose all those who stood for the status quo, who resisted change and looked behind them, holding onto the past. He opens with the following words:

> Twenty-three years ago I came to Athens; I remained 21 days on the Acropolis working without stop and nourishing myself by this admirable spectacle. What have I been able to do during those 21 days? I ask that of myself.... I left, crushed by the superhuman aspect of things of the Acropolis. Crushed by a truth which is neither smiling, nor light, but which is strong, which is one, which is implacable.... I have tried to act and to create a harmonious and humane work. I have done it with the Acropolis in my depths, in my guts. My work was honest, loyal, obstinate, sincere.[137]

Then he swings his argument to attack the academies, who lie. Le Corbusier believes that the Acropolis and the modern reveal the same attitude, strength, and purity–both are revolutionary forms, both moved toward the perfection of standardized forms. He is making reference, however, not to the Acropolis of neoclassical beauty, but to the balance the Acropolis realized between the spirit of rationality and that of lyricism, to a site that achieved equilibrium between mathematical rigor and the radiating sensuousness of its surrounding landscape. He continues his introduction:

> When I returned to the West and I wanted to follow the teachings of the schools, I saw that they lied in the name of the Acropolis.... It is the Acropolis that made of me a rebel. This certainty remained with me: "Remember the Parthenon pure, correct, intense, effective, violent, of this clamor thrown into a landscape of grace and of terror. Strength and purity."[138]

He calls on the Acropolis to support the popular arts, arts that breathe life into the dull and whitened forms of neoclassical art. The same harmonic relationships, the same mathematical rigor, are felt like an invincible command in popular art as in the greatest works of art. He recalls that with some friends–Fernand Léger, Christian Zervos, Matila Ghyka, and his brother Albert–he visited the port of Pireaus that morning. The group stopped before some boats (*le cabotage*, coasting vessels):

> These boats are painted in the strongest colors. The color, an expression of life! It is not the Greek spirit under its insipid and monochrome form that we saw there, it is the color in all its bursting power: blood, azure, sun–red, blue, yellow–life in its manifestation the most intense.
>
> In these boats of Pireaus which are painted as those two thousand years ago, we have found again the tradition of the Acropolis...strong, strict, exact and intense, sensual. The Greek spirit lives on in the sign of the master; mathematical rigor and law of numbers bringing us harmony.[139]

Thus, as Le Corbusier had proposed in *Vers une Architecture*, the Acropolis and its buildings belonged more to modern times than to antiquity: they are not a standard of beauty but a moral standard, a reason to become a revolutionary. He concludes his introduction by stating that

> in order to finish with the Acropolis, in the name of this harmony, it is necessary in the whole world, without failure and with a valiant soul, to harmonize. This word in truth expresses the reason of being of the present times.
>
> In the name of the Acropolis, a forceful harmony, conquering, without weakness, without failure. To make of oneself a brazen soul. Such is the admonition of the Acropolis! We pass on to modern times.[140]

He then proceeds to the technical aspects of his talk. Once more, however, in the conclusion, he calls on his fellow CIAM members to seek the solution that will bring into equilibrium all the technical forces of the new machine civilization; to understand that it is no longer a matter of architecture *or* revolution but architecture *and* urbanism. He wants them to also remember the lessons of the past, to gather the universal elements that remain constant for all time, and to achieve the new architecture and urbanism with the same spirit that built the Acropolis. "My dear comrades of the congress, we run toward adventure, the beautiful adventure! Architecture and Urbanism."[141]

It was not only the Acropolis and the forms of fishing boats painted in brilliant colors that enthralled Le Corbusier; he was also moved by the modest houses from the Aegean islands that he discovered–or so he professed later, in *The Radiant City*–for the first time.[142] These were true products of the Mediterranean culture, like those he saw in Algeria, statements of clarity and purity that resonated with the landscape, the climate, and the light. He wrote in *The Radiant City* as follows:

> Here the profound life of past millennia has remained intact; the wheel does not yet exist. Perhaps it never will exist, the topography is so rough. We discover the eternal houses, living houses, houses of today which go far back in history and whose plan and section are exactly what we have been thinking of for a decade. Here in the bosom of human measure, here in Greece, on this soil redolent of decency, intimacy, well being, of what is rational forever guided by the joy of living, we find *measurements on a human scale.*[143]

Le Corbusier was not alone in these opinions, though his lyric intensity may have been unusual. At the opening session of CIAM 4, the dean of the architectural faculty of the École Polytechnique, Anastase Orlandos, welcomed the group of modern architects, telling them that they would be struck by the spectacle of peasant houses on Greek islands, their simple white geometric forms, planar surfaces devoid of ornamentation, and logical lines. These *naïf* houses, built two or three hundred years before, reveal the same principles that this group of modern architects are trying to make the "civilized world" understand. Modern architecture, he argued, found its aesthetic roots on Greek soil in traditional and natural forms.[144]

VOYAGE TO GREECE

Between 1934 and 1939, Le Corbusier wrote three short articles on Greece that reveal his continued sensitivity to the Mediterranean spirit.[145] All three appeared in *Le Voyage en Grèce*, a tourist publication issued in Paris by the shipping company Neptos under the direction of Héracles Ioannides. Its artistic director, Eístratios Eleftheriades (Tériade), selected to write essays those artists he was interested in, among them Le Corbusier.[146] In the first article, "Point du Départ" ("Point of Departure"), Le Corbusier is still listening (he writes) to the call of Greece that sounds out the true, the pure, and the strong. He repeats his belief that the Parthenon made him a revolutionary in 1911, and from that moment forward he knew that the academies lied. Yet he is able to praise the West for all its accomplishments:

> It established the dictionary, the syntax and the discourse of a refined culture–But, in this last period, the beatings of our heart have been oppressed by thick layers of traditions.[147]

Thus, life has been forgotten–all its intensities, ardor, violence, and laughter ignored. Yet underneath this blockage, Le Corbusier believes the essential forces of a new machine civilization are rising. While the machine may dominate man, reducing him to a banal byproduct, still the "modern era" can save itself by acting wisely, by choosing a true destiny: "to act, to wrestle with the immense events of nature, to command them…I know that Greece will give us the *humane* conclusion, the humane line which pierces and disperses the disarray."[148]

In the second essay on Greece, published in 1936, Le Corbusier writes about the popular painter Théophilos. He calls him an "authentic" Greek, full of clarity, exempt from artifice. He is a character from the old Greece that can still be found outside of commercial and industrial cities.[149] Le Corbusier calls the landscape of Greece "blond and Apollonian in the ravishing sunlight. True. Splendidly radiantly, ingenuously, naturally true."[150] Théophilos crossed this landscape, painting walls and signs for cafés; his work was a spontaneous reaction to the laws of nature, to mathematical sensations. Le Corbusier believes that nature tells us about her laws, reassures us, and radiates harmony within us. "Objects are mediums. Thus Théophilos is a medium. Through him we are carried straight into the nature of Greece."[151] Without such mediums carrying messages from our eyes to our brains, which are racked by tumults, "we would not see those things which are facts, stripped of the arbitrary, exact, moving, natural."[152]

In May 1939, Le Corbusier writes his third essay on Greece. It concerns the human scale of things, superimposing several thoughts from earlier writings.[153] This time he opens by referring to the "Dionysian" light of Greece that suddenly, within seconds, can be inundated with black storms. Greece is a land of extremes, of constant confrontations of human nature with nature itself, constant evaluations of human values and human scales.

> Thus the house that shelters from such extreme reactions is naturally lacking in embellishments or flourishes.... A being occupied with normal daily work is scarcely inclined to such puerile diversions; but he sings and dances, he whitewashes his house, inside and out, the day before each Sunday in certain places, or for grand yearly festivals; he eats olives, bread and honey; he dresses in white wool.... He takes hold simply and actively with his hands and his heart.... This housing is always, being perpetuated, unchanged, living, a correct human reflection.[154]

Le Corbusier confesses that he is not an archaeologist, able to define the regional differences between these simple houses; but he felt pushed toward the East as a young man, to the lands where "he *saw architecture*."[155] He was not able in 1911 to view the houses of the Greek islands, but saw these for the first time twenty-two years later, in 1933. Between these two voyages to Greece, however, he came to understand "that the Mediterranean is the inexhaustible reservoir of useful teachings for our wisdom."[156]

The purpose of the life still perpetuated by the Greeks in their villages, houses, and customs is to affirm the "human scale." The architect who has seen these simple island houses of Greece cannot abide the mountains of artifice that surround him in the West.

> The rites, the bad habits installed without previous examination in our thoughts; these manual and intellectual deformations which falsify, from their birth, our inventions, our creations, our enterprises, overloading them with mummies, cadavers or parasites; this amnesia of measure which makes us disproportion the very large or very small, all mixed up, far from all human scale.[157]

These are anti-human acts of disharmony, of war, money, ill-fated urbanism, and architecture, all taking place in the first era of machine civilization. But looking at simple Greek villages and their houses, the lesson of harmony reappears, giving to all of man's works, thoughts, and knowledge a certain order: harmony at the human scale. "We have to find again the living conditions of our acts; then our houses and cities will express them."[158]

LATIN WEST, MEDITERRANEAN EAST

Camus claimed that one approaches the Mediterranean from the East, not from the Latin West, yet Le Corbusier and the neo-syndicalists drew inspiration from the Latin Mediterranean, its language, and its culture. In the 1930s, their concept of these roots encouraged them to look to Italy and to the works of Mussolini for support.

In the spring of 1933, an article by Le Corbusier entitled "Rome" appeared in *Prélude.*[159] He is all in praise of the discipline, order, and purity that marked the concept of Rome. This simple word expresses, he says, a precise concept, revealing a "conscious strength." A series of similes follows: "Rome is like round, like full, like whole, like central, eminently geometrical, simple and essential."[160] The Rome that Le Corbusier is referencing is that of antiquity, not that of Mussolini, for he follows this string of metaphors with the statement that Rome remains a living fact, the work of the people after two thousand years.[161]

Le Corbusier is aware that in the 1930s, the power of this word is contradictory because a failure of spirit holds men in the grips of economic depression. It is also a sign of insolence and pretension, because the word "Rome" simultaneously signifies "hearts of bronze." Thus the word is paradoxical: it signifies individual conscience and a Christian duty to "love one another," yet simultaneously represents the center of an empire and strict command.

But the mere thought of antique "Rome" sets Le Corbusier's heart beating, because of its simple geometric forms and organizing logic that haunt all (subsequent) human creations. He recounts a history lesson from schoolbooks: Roman legions conquered the Barbarians. They laid down stone-paved roads that remain all over Europe still to this day. These Roman roads drove straight across the essential features of a given countryside. In the natural center they put down a sentry post from which the whole terrain was controlled. Military engineers always accompanied the Roman legions, geometrician-architects who built cities of order, prodigious collaborations between nature and geometry.

These cities and the Roman camps were classified, hierarchicalized, dignified. Everything following straight lines: the norm of action.[162]

For public spectacles the Romans built circuses, where vast crowds formed a living, thrilling group. Down from the mountains, bringing cool water, a line of aqueducts stretched across the countryside. They built great baths and stadiums, because Romans took care of their bodies. "They conceived, they classified, they reduced everything to order: Rome meant enterprise."[163] The Republic was the object of their care, the public good the reason for their city, participation a way of life. "They were lucid, strong, simple and geometrical. They created cities that worked like machines: machines of which the product was action."[164] These are the lessons of destiny that Le Corbusier thinks are relevant to modern times. In the midst of Depression and a failure of spirit, lucid thought, commanding words, and clear actions are desperately needed.

Later in the spring of 1933, in an article published in *Prélude* just before he went to Athens for CIAM 4, "Esprit Grec–Esprit Latin, Esprit Greco-Latin" (really a collection of anecdotes), Le Corbusier makes a comparison between the (ancient) Greek spirit and the Latin, and of both to contemporary times. He is wary, he says, of making dry classifications, he who always puts things in order, makes lists, and admires the efficiency of card indexes and filing cabinets. Now he warns that classifications are arbitrary (an index card placed in one file cabinet and not another) and mutilate continuity. In spite of this danger, however, he knows that in order to work, to decide, and to act, he must classify and determine directions. Thus he contrasts the Greek and Latin spirit, finding the one to balance the other as opposites until a new synthesis is forged.

It is a matter of finding spiritual direction in the dark times of the 1930s. He believes that our acts stem not from rational thought but from "a sentimental or spiritual imperative which illuminates our horizon, outlines a fatal orbit and conducts us implacably like the sun."[165] Both the Greek and Latin spirit are under the sign of the same Mediterranean sun and its light, yet he is wary of such a comparison and adduces the images of a "watershed" like "a verdict of destiny" that sets up regimes that may share an origin yet go toward opposite ends.[166]

His own awakening to such a conflict took place one evening as he stood gazing at the illuminated Place de la Concorde in Paris, looking around at the Obelisk and the two Palaces, architectural monuments meant to be seen with light pouring down on them from the sky, turning them into gracious and charming architectural events. But in the night, seeing them illuminated from below, he began to understand that there were two faces, light and shadow: one full of smiles and serenity, the other of alarming might and implacable mathematics.

Another story follows, about the sun that rises to the east of the Rhine, about the light that comes from Germany. From 1870 to 1914, this light shone on architecture and condemned the face of the city from the Rhine almost to Moscow. Only the USSR appeared with clear and true aims, for it had a plan for the future, an expression of modern times. But it put a stop to this truth, this clarity and purity, in 1933, and turned instead to consult the ancients, who said, "It is necessary to go to Athens and to Rome."[167] In Rome, Mussolini reconstructs Italy, but fails to give it a dazzling modern face. "Pastiche and parody!"

> Rome copies Rome... Moscow copied Athens and Rome: frightening anachronism, fatigued academism, defection, desertion on the line of fire, abdication, fatal unconscious, tragic renouncement.[168]

Le Corbusier calls on the Acropolis, the Greek spirit, and the heroic men who traced the profile of the Parthenon. They knew extraordinary economy, and plunged mankind into "a violent perfection, provoking, galvanizing, beyond habitual habits and practices."[169] This Greek spirit knows about exactness of action, the lyricism of forms, of mathematical rigor as a law of the world.

He then explains that although modern techniques are international and universal, they offer each region the opportunity to express its own spirit. Each region has only to hold up its ideal and put it into play. But this means to act completely, from the top to the bottom, with truthfulness, clarity, and purity. The Latin spirit is caressed by the wing of the Graces: a soft sun, and soft light falling on harmonious solutions. It does not necessarily get to the depth of the question, calling on one's responsibility, like the Greek spirit. The latter is heroic and implacable. "It grips man not in some retrospective and spectacular attitudes, but at the moment, in the full intensity of present time and present things."[170]

Le Corbusier sees around him a world in complete disarray: the English lost in their past, the Germans out of control. Only in lands around the Mediterranean, he feels, can a decision still be made to act with humankind in mind. That choice brings renewal, and through this renewal, the machine becomes the workshop of human enterprise, where a modern conscience rules. This is what he calls the Greek-Latin spirit: harmony ruling over all that is made and done. "Economy and action; force and a smile."[171]

This discourse reveals that Le Corbusier was conflicted about "Rome." The Latin spirit of ancient times called for action; that Le Corbusier could support. Yet he was wary of the neoclassical tendencies that Mussolini was unveiling–and yet again, he remained ambivalent, for Mussolini held the power of authority to put modern plans into action.

This interest in courting the favor of persons with top-down power had been explicit ever since Ozenfant and Le Corbusier (still writing as Jeanneret) had dedicated their magazine *L'Esprit Nouveau* to the organizational elite (see Chapter 6). It was also in evidence in March 1932, when he wrote to Guido Fiorini, an architect and member of the Roman section of MIAR (Mouvement Italien pour l'Architecture Rationnelle) regarding a proposed visit to Rome. At the time, Le Corbusier was completing his first project for Algiers. He was, he told Fiorini, scheduled to leave on the twenty-third for Barcelona, and expected to go to Moscow on his return and to Algiers in mid-May, and suggested his visit to Rome could be either before or after his trip to Algiers.[172] He was eager to give two talks in Rome, not about aesthetic issues of modern architecture, but addressing himself to men of authority in government or big industry. The first talk would focus on the architectural revolution accomplished by modern techniques, and how industry in the 1930s kept architects from "building"; the second lecture would reveal how modern architecture supported urbanism, and how urbanism depended on "authority."[173]

Evidently Fiorini was not successful in arranging the proposed visit. Le Corbusier writes to him again in August 1932, after his return from Barcelona.[174] He is jubilant about his great success in that city, and announces the hour of the Latin countries sounds, and the second cycle of the machine epoch will be dominated "by Latin grace." He had just finished his plans for Algiers, which he thinks will create a veritable revolution, and while he may have some defenders, he is aware that the effort necessary to implement his scheme will of necessity be great.

It is not until June of 1934 that he actually goes to Rome and subsequently to Venice, where he participates in the Congrès de l'Art et la Réalité (July 25–28), organized by the Institut de Cooperation Intellectuel de la Société des Nations.[175] Mussolini, in his *Discourse to Architects*, delivered on June 10, 1934, seemed to take a clear position in favor of modern architecture, pronouncing it a rational, functional expression of modern times. Having already confessed his faith that great works would be accomplished in the Mediterranean region, Le Corbusier must have been pleased to find a state authority seemingly supportive of his own opinions about expertise and planning. Italy, he now enthused, would be the country to show the rest of Europe what collaborative efforts between an architect-urbanist and a governmental authority might actually achieve.[176]

He was very interested in a proposed new town to be built at Pontinia. He wrote to Fiorini on July 3, 1934, proposing that the two collaborate on the design and suggesting that Pietro Maria Bardi, an Italian delegate to CIAM 4 and coeditor with Bontempelli of *Quadrante*, might also like to help.[177] Le Corbusier had already discussed schemes for Pontinia in *The Radiant City*. Formerly subjected to malaria and death, the Pontine region had been drained, linked to a transportation system, and transformed into fertile farmland. Two villages had already been built there: Littoria, which Le Corbusier called a wretched little town of the garden-city type, and Sabaudia, designed by a team of young architects on a choice site, which he labeled a "dream of pastoral life." There was to be a third village, Pontinia, which Le Corbusier believed should be expressive of the modern age and based on the principles of the Radiant Farm.[178]

On July 13 he also writes to Magnelli, director of the typewriter manufacturer Olivetti, concerning the planned development of a factory and village complex in the Piedmont for the Olivetti Corporation. His letter refers to an architectural competition for the site, which he admits is "a lamentable adventure for serious men. They can sometimes allow an unknown to triumph, which is very good," but when it comes to execution, quality control, and cost effectiveness, these things belong in the domain of professional experience. He understands that for the sake of publicity, Olivetti has had to follow the procedures of an Italian competition, and the winners would have to be Italians. However, Le Corbusier proposes that he be charged with the design of the new plans that would actually be used, since there was no requirement to implement the winning scheme. He called this proposal a "practical method": it left the door open for an unknown local genius to shine, yet allowed collaboration with an expert, namely Le Corbusier. He asks

Magnelli, "What do you think?" and adds a postscript that he would be in Algeria July 14–21 and Venice July 25–28. He is hopeful that he will receive a reply by that time.[179]

He writes another letter, this one to Bardi on August 7, 1934. He is disappointed not to have seen him personally while in Venice, a city that Le Corbusier claims is "one of the most admirable things that one can see and one of the greatest lessons of urbanism and civicism that one can dream of."[180] He had read the thirteenth volume of *Quadrante* (May 1934), almost all of which was dedicated to Le Corbusier's work, but needed to correct some errors. First of all, he does not make political statements, and has not affirmed the opinions of Antonio Sant'Elia. But he was even more annoyed at the photograph of himself in a Fiat Balilla that appeared in the magazine. Fiat gained a lot of free publicity, and while Le Corbusier is willing to lend himself to such acts, the issue of free publicity weighs on him. He asks Bardi if he will intervene on his behalf and suggest to Fiat "that the least they could do is to offer Le Corbusier a Balilla that he would use with pleasure."[181] In addition, and just as annoying, Le Corbusier had heard that Fiat was spreading rumors he had toured Italy with Bardi in a Balilla. Apparently free publicity was no joking matter, for the letter continues to mention that the Balilla (that he hoped Fiat would give him) would replace an old Peugeot that is used by his atelier and that is about to fall apart. [FIGURE II.II]

There is one final question Le Corbusier wants to address to Bardi, whom he now praises as one of the most subtle Italians, with a good sense of reality. He asks him if his trip to Rome had represented "a gentle gesture on my part" and would Bardi confirm if "the word" that Le Corbusier had pronounced in Italy had made any effect–would it lead to his future involvement through commissions and interventions? He reminds Bardi this is not a national affair, not a matter of rivalry, but a universal issue of placing technical expertise to use in a country where the young had enormous goodwill but not yet the necessary experience.[182]

Nothing came of these offers to collaborate, so Le Corbusier wrote again to Fiorini at the end of November 1934, mentioning again his interest in all these Italian affairs.[183] He sends him the second volume of his *Oeuvre Complète*, and dedicates another to Mussolini because he wanted the Italians to be aware of his work. He is eager for them to consider his schemes for the Radiant Village and Farm in the Sarthe as potential plans for Pontinia. He claims that he admires the turn of events

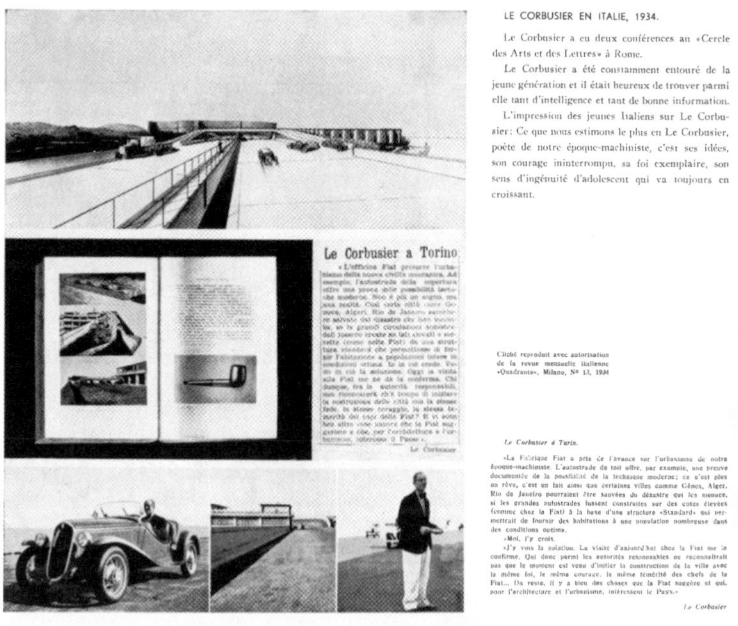

LE CORBUSIER EN ITALIE, 1934.

Le Corbusier a eu deux conférences au «Cercle des Arts et des Lettres» à Rome.

Le Corbusier a été constamment entouré de la jeune génération et il était heureux de trouver parmi elle tant d'intelligence et tant de bonne information.

L'impression des jeunes Italiens sur Le Corbusier: Ce que nous estimons le plus en Le Corbusier, poète de notre époque-machiniste, c'est ses idées, son courage ininterrompu, sa foi exemplaire, son sens d'ingénuité d'adolescent qui va toujours en croissant.

Le Corbusier a Torino

Cliché reproduit avec autorisation de la revue mensuelle italienne «Quadrante», Milano, Nº 13, 1934

Le Corbusier à Turin.

«La Fabrique Fiat a pris de l'avance sur l'urbanisme de notre époque-machiniste. L'autostrade du toit offre, par exemple, une preuve documentée de la possibilité de la technique moderne; ce n'est plus un rêve, c'est un fait ainsi que certaines villes comme Gênes, Alger, Rio de Janeiro pourraient être sauvées du désastre qui les menace, si les grandes autostrades fussent construites sur des cotes élevées (comme chez la Fiat) à la base d'une structure «Standard» qui permettrait de fournir des habitations à une population nombreuse dans des conditions optima.

»Moi, j'y crois.

»J'y vois la solution. La visite d'aujourd'hui chez la Fiat me le confirme. Qui donc parmi les autorités responsables ne reconnaîtrait pas que le moment est venu d'initier la construction de la ville avec la même foi, le même courage, la même témérité des chefs de la Fiat... Du reste, il y a bien des choses que la Fiat suggère et qui, pour l'architecture et l'urbanisme, intéressent le Pays.»

Le Corbusier

FIGURE II.II: **A collection of photographs from Le Corbusier's 1943 visit to Italy, where he gave several lectures and visited the Fiat factory: He believed the automobile testing grounds on the roof of the car factory offered proof that cities like Algiers and Rio de Janeiro could be saved from disaster.**

in Rome: the Romans have lit the lantern of Diogenes, who sought a man capable of commandeering the city. In Italy, as in the USSR, the problem of direction, of planning the future, has been resolved, while in France everything remains to be done. He also mentions that he is still interested in the Olivetti affair, and thinks a small committee of intelligent architects should gather to discuss its development.

Le Corbusier will intervene in the sixth Volta Congress (Rome) in October 1936, with an essay, "Peinture, Sculpture et architecture rationalist" ("Painting, Sculpture and Rationalist architecture"). His increasing involvement with Fascist Italy does not go unnoticed by members of CIAM. During his Volta talk, Le Corbusier announces that he has just received a letter from the secretary general of CIAM, Sigfried Giedion, expressing his fears that by association Le Corbusier's name will be misused by the Fascist empire, and he is in danger of placing himself in the camp of the enemies of modern architecture.[184] Apparently Le Corbusier paid no attention to such chiding.

THE LATIN HOUR HAS STRUCK

During the 1930s, Le Corbusier and the neo-regionalists restructured Europe into what they considered natural geographical and economic units, positioning the Paris-Algiers, Rome-Barcelona axes within a Mediterranean bloc. The Latin hour had, they proclaimed, struck: in the Mediterranean region grand works would be built. The Mediterranean sun acted like a visual magnet for Le Corbusier's theories; it warmed his body and enlivened his eye. In his mind, he dotted the slopes of Algiers with brilliant sparkling jewels and filled them with hanging gardens. The blue of the sky, the green of the trees, and the red of the earth played on his lyrical mood. The Mediterranean sea, sun, and sky offered up for contemplation the simple cubic houses of the Aegean and the crushing marbles of the Acropolis, the collective life of the oases, the simple Muslim with no need to consume useless objects. The horizon of the sea stretching toward infinity instilled a simple geometry of straight lines and planes on which he could rest his notions of the absolute and the ephemeral, the immutable and the finite. This spiritual bond with nature was the antithesis of his cartographic will to master, to dominate, to penetrate the site.

Open the atlas, he commanded, read the facts of geography, races, climate, topography, and begin to think of the cosmic reality that controls all things–the sun.[185] The sun became his symbol of Janus-faced power in the 1930s, both a cruel dominator and a warm embracer, a destroying light giving rise to shadows and obscurity, instilling passivity or action, bringing death or nourishment. This violent opposition between light and darkness–both embraced–reflected his ambiguous politics as well. Being "neither left nor right" helped him maintain his white blind spots long after the political context demanded partisanship. It allowed him to locate the true, the beautiful, the pure in the Mediterranean, yet to offer sketch plans for Addis Ababa after Italy invaded Ethiopia in 1935–36; and in November 1939, after Italy occupied Albania and the Italian-German alliance had been formed, he solicited the commission for the French pavilion at the E42 Exposition in Rome.[186]

This Janus-faced sun reflects his own tragic self-contradiction: his attempt to be "neither left nor right" in order to bring radiant living to the common man. But this amoral stance turns in practice into his alliance with whoever happened to grab the reins of power. It is a contradictory stance that he assumed erroneously from an early stage, believing autocratic authority necessary to effect change.

Though dreaming of a better life for the people, he is nevertheless profoundly undemocratic in his thinking, only appealing to popular opinion in outright propaganda of the crudest type, like the "surveys" that may or may not have been administered in Algeria. His solar cult, his idealization of the "crushing weight" of marble or light, complemented his worship of authority. It becomes almost a Tutankhamen or Louis XIV complex: sun worship allied with monarchy or authoritarianism in the service of sun-baked architectural projects on a grand scale. This is the tragic self-contradiction of a power-worshipping would-be reformer–the paradox of imposing liberation from above, by Fascist decree if necessary.

He would write in 1941 that he is a technician and not an administrator. The latter must not abuse his powers–he must assemble, align everything within a framework of time and space, but not aspire to omnipotence. Whereas the technician is subtle, flexible, resourceful, "moving his rifle from one shoulder to the other as easily as he changes his shirt, capable of forging to the right so as not to get blocked on the left; he is like water [as in the meander], fluid, but impossible to stem, he will always find a way, always arrive where he wishes to go, he is ingenuity incarnate. And he is open to wise suggestions. But the pencil must be left in his hand."[187]

CHAPTER 12 ELEMENTS OF A SECULAR FAITH: DAYDREAMS, AUTHORITY, AND THE VIEW FROM ABOVE

> *Immense hopes were laid down on paper, blind certainties darted forth from the plan. A new society appeared, giving up then regrouping itself, leaving behind secular attitudes and perceiving some modes of a new life, rejecting some words of order and formulating an ethic expressive, one time again, of realities of the human soul.*
>
> –LE CORBUSIER, 1939

I. POET AS DAYDREAMER, URBANIST AS POET

Freud compared the writer to a child at play who creates an imaginary world in which things are arranged to be more pleasing than reality.[1] When the child grows up, he or she finds a substitute for his or her earlier fantasies in daydreams, cherished as a most intimate possession. Freud noted that every fantasy or daydream fits into the changing impressions of life. It carries a date-stamp, and hovers between three periods of time. There is some present event (date one) powerful enough to rouse an intense desire, enabling the dreamer to wander back to the memory of an earlier experience (date two), when this wish may have been fulfilled, even if only in the imagination, and then to create a new situation that secures fulfillment of the wish in the (imagined) future (date three). Past, present, and future are threaded together on the string of this wish running through them.

Writers of romances and novels, Freud says, place a hero at the center of their stories. The reader follows this hero through dangerous adventures in the hope that all troubles and pitfalls will be transcended, and safety finally achieved. For a moment the reader is released from reality, as if in a daydream, enjoying the sense that he or she, too, is an invulnerable hero who can accomplish unbelievable feats. Through a series of transitions, then, Freud traces all imaginative productions back to simple daydreams and wishes. Daydreamers, however, carefully hide their egotistical wishes, lest others be repelled or shocked by them, while a writer exposes them to public view. The writer must therefore utilize all his or her poetical skills to please and overcome the estrangement that exposure to fantasies normally entails.

Can a creative writer–one who dreams of the future of cities and housing, say–also be compared to a daydreamer? Le Corbusier certainly saw himself in the role of a hero, an embattled protagonist with many obstacles to overcome. His dream of himself as the Hero of Les Temps Nouveaux perhaps carries the date-stamp of 1922, when he presented his schemes for the Contemporary City for Three Million; or of 1911, when he first wrote down his daydream of a future city on his return voyage from the East and sent the daydream to William Ritter for comment; or of that night in October 1928, in a poor sort of house in Prague where he stopped with others to have a drink, when the poet Nesvald, radiant and strong (as Le Corbusier would tell the tale in 1939), cried out "Le Corbusier is a poet!" and all glasses were raised in honor of poetry. That night, Le Corbusier said in 1939, he received a profound recompense for all his struggles.

Le Corbusier loved to see himself as a poet, and his discourse is phrased in poetical terms–evocative, spell-casting, illogical, emotive. He is pleased to call himself a poet, and takes umbrage when the word is cast against him. Yet he saw his heroic tactics as borrowed from Descartes: to go in a direct line from one place to the next without getting lost, out of the morass of mental battle and confusion.

In an article of 1939, "L'Urbanisme et le Lyrisme des Temps Nouveaux" ("Urbanism and the Poetry of the New Times"), Le Corbusier defends his poetic diction in an imaginary conversation with those who accuse him of renouncing his crusade for the rational and useful, instead expressing his ideas in lyrical and poetic terms.[2] He begins by noting that works of utility are surpassed everyday by better ones; the equipment of every country is made and then unmade. Such is the evolution of the works of mankind; one civilization disappears as a new one makes its appearance. When honor is bestowed on a man or a thing, however, it raises a

> feeling of gratitude, admiration, enthusiastic devotion, cry of emotion. And one no longer talks of utility but of love; function is not considered, but attitude.... It is a question of poetry. And that which resides in human enterprises is not that which is useful, but that which moves one.[3]

Le Corbusier looks back over the past twenty years to what he calls his first line on architecture: "Architecture is the wise, correct and magnificent play of forms under the light (*L'Esprit Nouveau*, 1, 1919)."[4] From that time onward a debate unfurled. "Have the gods, perhaps, directed my hand from the beginning of this task?"[5] If he has been able to follow a path since 1922, the year he designed the contemporary city for three million inhabitants, a path that carried him forward into "virgin lands for the temps nouveaux, can the reader imagine that such an effort could be nourished by reasons of utility alone?"[6] Le Corbusier is willing to depart freely from his conceit of the Cartesian straight line of victory, and to utilize a variety of rhetorical figures, moving the reader in a bewildering variety of directions, so much the better for impact. He asks rhetorically, how was it possible to change direction constantly, zigzag to overcome obstacles as a river meanders, yet continue to have faith and believe

> in order to raise oneself above innumerable defeats, battles each time lost, in order to incite oneself to begin again tomorrow? It is a great list of important checks.... Immense hopes were laid down on paper, blind certainties darted forth from the plan. A new society appeared, giving up then regrouping itself, leaving behind secular attitudes and perceiving some modes of a new life, rejecting some words of order and formulating an ethic expressive, one time again, of realities of the human soul.[7]

In such "adventures" or "games," something grand has to intervene: "spirit, the flowering of man.... When the heart is attached to action, when emotion spreads over the course: beauty, splendor, harmony. Poetry."[8] Every plan that Le Corbusier made was, he says, nourished by his firm belief in poetry, even though one day he was denounced–"This rationalist is a poet!"–in an effort to crush him, while others complained of rationalism, functionalism, impenitent Jacobinism, and implacable reasoning. But deep within himself, he knew that another motive activated him. As a touchstone, he kept in memory that night in Prague, already mentioned, where the poet Nesvald cried out "Le Corbusier is a poet!" and all glasses were raised to poetry.

When a society breaks with the tradition of its housing and begins to create new forms, there shine forth the first rays of a new conscience. Once valued shelter is rejected, accepted points of view and usages are abandoned. A new point of view has arrived.

> A point of view is the effect of a climb or a decline, of a displacement to left or to right, of an approach to or a retreat from a thing considered. The thing considered is the well-being of man. Can the well-being of man have been lost from sight? It seems to me yes, in these times. Can it be reconsidered? It seems to me yes, in this present time. Is it a question of utility? Yes, but of grand utility–not accessory or localized, fragmented, but a grand and true utility. Everything is reconsidered, and the problem linked to the great human axes. I think that a great mutation is operating [in 1939], that some migrations are imminent, that cities are to be made and remade, in a word that the occupation of the Earth will be put in question, one time again.[9]

Authority, preoccupied with explosive events, has not yet had time to understand the breadth of this mutation; it is not prepared for its new tasks.

> Authority shares in the catastrophe, it dirties itself there, it is used up there, and it is exhausted there. One day, the page will be turned and the new texts will describe the new adventure, one day the door will be opened, the light will be there, in front, inundating the immense plane of this new activity of men.... It requires, for this concern, a dose of unlimited faith, and a serene optimism, long and patient perseverance.[10]

If men will not reconstruct their cities, then Le Corbusier fears there will be revolts (his "architecture or revolution" theme). If the ownership of land is not reformulated, and cities continue to expand while the fields of the countryside are emptied, then the result will be perilous. There is hope, however, and no matter how many times he has gone down to defeat, as the indefatigable knight, the hero of his daydreams, he is ready for a new battle. "Another point of view is prepared."[11]

One must address these issues to the young, to teach them about nature, modern tools, and the human heart. It is certainly about "the poetical order that it is necessary to speak to them. Poetry, again, one day, will live."[12]

ALWAYS READY FOR A NEW BATTLE

In 1946, Le Corbusier writes of how to teach urbanism to architects. The task of reconstruction, at long last, is about to begin. Yet no one teaches urbanism at the École des Beaux-Arts, and only historical urbanism is taught at the Institut d'Urbanisme at the Université de Paris, and most of the information they spread is incorrect.[13] Urbanism has two different definitions: if taken from the side, it is an art of geometry in two dimensions, a work on paper that locates streets and sets out blocks and lots for building. If taken from the front, however, urbanism is the art of organizing space. Yet the verb "to reconstruct" bothers Le Corbusier: to reconstruct inclines one to imitate the things destroyed, to reconstitute their former states. To *construct* opens up space before man, illuminates the spirit, promises an extraordinary tomorrow.

Furthermore, professionals must be taught about the work of constructing, must be trained to become the great harmonizers of the future. They must work in laboratories where details of construction are developed, then assemble in congresses to discuss these things, to explain their discoveries, to raise questions about the unknown. They must draw on their own memories, read specialized reviews and books. The press must be used, the radio, whatever spreads information, until ministers, professionals, and citizens draw up some postulates, affirm some rules, define a doctrine. This becomes a science, and this science of urbanism can be professed.[14]

Here Le Corbusier exposes to the light of criticism a few of his deeply held fantasies, though they so often had met with the repulsion Freud says is the fate of exposed daydreams: his urban schemes, especially from 1939–46, were rejected by the authorities and academies as the fanciful outpourings of an avant-garde theoretician, sheer "poetry" irrelevant to the problems facing the nation.

Le Corbusier was correct about the need for reform: on the threshold of World War II, Paris had at least twenty-two thousand houses that were more than one hundred years old, one out of five houses in the city had no running water, and only 15 percent of the population had a bathroom. Throughout France, at least five hundred thousand lived three or four people to a room.[15] Yet urbanism as a field of study was so recent that Jean Royer could say in a conference on urbanism and reconstruction in 1943 that the French Academy had only recently inscribed the word in its dictionary.[16] Le Corbusier was also correct that the academies were not prepared for the new tasks facing the nation. Since little architecture had been constructed throughout France in the 1930s, there were few architects who actually had practical experience, and this was restricted to prestigious structures and private houses. The professors of the École des Beaux-Arts were scarcely equipped to address matters of housing, infrastructure, and urbanism.[17]

Intervening realities disturbed Le Corbusier's daydream of harmony and the temps nouveaux. In 1935, Hitler renounced all restrictions on armaments imposed on Germany by the Treaty of Versailles, and began the next year to move troops into the Rhineland. A buffer zone no longer existed between France and its arch-enemy, forcing France to retaliate and arm for war. By March of 1938, Germany entered Austria: now its axis of power stretched from the Baltic and North Seas to the Mediterranean. With Vienna and the Danube under its control, Germany had access to Budapest, Belgrade, and the Black Sea as well. Making clear its policy of expansion, the next year Germany invaded Poland on September 1, 1939. Two days later, France and England declared war, followed by Canada, Australia, New Zealand, India, and South Africa. In May of 1940, Germany invaded France, and by July the Battle of Britain was imminent.[18] The map of the world was clearly being restructured, a fact that did not escape the geographical imagination of Le Corbusier.

Le Corbusier's heroic daydream was undaunted by the staggering realities of the run-up to World War II. It is with a mixture of naivety, abstract coolness, and blatant opportunism that Le Corbusier absorbs into his daydreams these steps toward war. In an unpublished article written in December 1938 he considers what he euphemistically refers to as "the problem of immense migrations of Jews."[19] As the Jewish people were "chased" from countries under Hitler's occupation, they were forced to migrate, and formed for Le Corbusier what he opportunistically labels the "avant-garde of great transformations."[20] This forces the issue: it now becomes necessary to raise the question everywhere, in every society, of how men are to be assembled and redistributed on the land.

He, as an urbanist, is the man for the job! He feels morally inclined to express through material works the state of a culture or civilization and to pay attention to certain "realities." Thus, he argues coolly, the Jewish population, suddenly placed in acute and dramatic circumstances, offers society an important and urgent opportunity. He repeats: thousands of Jews are "chased" from Germany and Austria; millions more will be "chased" from Poland and Romania. Where are these millions of individuals to be relocated? Can society benefit from this unfortunate situation and make the first tentative steps toward the reorganization of a machinist society? Can society imagine how these two million men will be grouped, agglomerated, and dispersed across the land under conditions that would guarantee their happiness, and not their misfortune? "I repeat it: there is a duty to bring them to a good port and not to involve them in an infernal circle."[21] Ever the knight in shining armor, he lays out his plan of rescue.

Le Corbusier assumes that the Jewish population is accustomed to living in ghettos, or at least in cities and suburbs, and therefore has suffered the problems of these hideous places. Modern urbanism offers them new benefits by grouping them in "unités d'habitation" that will guarantee the vitality of the collective yet offer to each family a cell in perfect isolation. These unités "are therefore a natural application to the problem of the installation of new Jewish masses in lands of transplantation, whether it is a matter, in small quantity, in the French countryside, in great quantity in British Guyana, Northern Rhodesia, Palestine, Tanganyika or British Columbia, etc."[22] These separate places of transplantation display a variety of climates: some are humid and hot, others dry and hot, others hot and cold; some have rainy seasons, some have snow three months of the year. Unités d'habitation, however, are equipped with air-conditioning and heating, and can accommodate a range of different climates. They group at least two thousand to three thousand inhabitants together, and thus overcome the isolation of garden cities and offer sociability; they eradicate all the boredoms of dispersion and provide "essential joys."

Yet one important aspect remains to be solved: what will the transplanted Jewish masses do for work? Le Corbusier claims that they will find work in agricultural exploitation, both to feed themselves and for export.[23]

He concludes: the Jewish population's plight has opened the era of great migrations, which will eventually extend to all countries. A rational and productive reoccupation of territory begins, and eventually the happiness of entire masses will be secured.

II. THE POET AND THE AUTHORITIES

Throughout the troubled 1930s, Le Corbusier aligned himself with contradictory political positions. At the end of the decade and the beginning of the war, he wrote that he was a technician, not an administrator, and knew nothing about the strategies and tactics of implementing a plan. Yet a technician, he argued, is subtle, flexible, and even resourceful,

> Moving his rifle from one shoulder to the other as easily as he changes his shirt, capable of forging to the right so as not to get blocked on the left; he is like water, fluid, but impossible to stem, he will always find a way, always arrive where he wishes to go. He is ingenuity incarnate. And he is open to wise suggestions. But the pencil must be left in his hand.[24]

At the end of the war he would publicly declare, "I am an ingénu. An ingénu because I have never been crafty with society."[25] And he would never apologize for his collaboration with the Vichy government. Even after the war he continued to advocate the "spirit of the thirties," neither left nor right, and to portray himself as a disinterested or nonpartisan technician, a mere architect-planner who remained outside the realm of politics, without influence in places of authority, concerned only with how to alleviate problems of housing and urban growth.

Yet the majority of young apprentices working in Le Corbusier's atelier in the 1930s held political views far to the left of his position, and two of his closest associates, Charlotte Perriand and Pierre Jeanneret, had strong leftist leanings.[26] Was he a naive victim of his own idealistic fantasies, a willing opportunist who saw in Vichy the necessary authority to implement some of his lifelong dreams, or a survivor who ignored the bad and stressed the good? The question arises: why did he stray so far to the right, make so many overt compromises, and pursue his urban course regardless of what bedfellows were required?

The political puzzle set by Le Corbusier is a fascinating one. He had been interested since the 1920s in the social experiments of the USSR, yet was basically anti-statist and involved with the politically reactionary neo-syndicalists, many of whose beliefs he held during all of the 1930s and early 1940s. In Russia, his adversaries treated him as a Fascist; in Algiers, he was almost imprisoned as a Bolshevik and had to quickly exit the country in May 1942 to evade arrest.[27] He maintained an anti-capitalist stance when it came to the provision of housing or the reformulation of private property; he denounced the lust for money and was critical of America's rampant materialism, attributing the Depression to its financial recklessness. Yet he was full of praise for the manufacturing genius of Ford, the assembly-line mass production of affordable automobiles based on the standardization of parts, and the efficiency studies of Taylor.

He was intrigued by Mussolini, and when invited to Rome to give two lectures in May 1934, planned to meet him personally. Yet Mussolini was called to Venice to meet with Hitler instead. Le Corbusier wrote in a Fascist review in August 1934 that the "present spectacle of Italy, the state of her spiritual powers, announces the imminent dawn of the modern spirit. Her radiance, by its purity and force, illuminates the paths that have been obscured by the cowardly and the profiteers."[28] In 1947, he maintained he had quickly understood that Mussolini had been gripped by a madness of grandeur; yet even after Italy invaded Ethiopia in 1935–36, he sent plans for Addis Ababa to the Office of Foreign Affairs in Rome. And in November of 1939, after Germany and Italy had signed a pact of alliance, he solicited the commission in charge of the E42 (1942) Exposition in Rome for permission to build the French pavilion.[29]

Le Corbusier was sensitive to the position of the Popular Front after it came to power in the spring of 1936, supporting its platform to ameliorate the living conditions of workers and peasants; yet a few years later he could align himself with the reactionary regime of Vichy, whose policies were authoritarian, technocratic, anti-parliamentarian, and racist. War is an act of extreme coercion, emplacing absolute order, discipline, and hierarchy over society and requiring loyalty and devotion from each citizen; both Vichy and Le Corbusier believed in the merits of such discipline.[30]

To solve the riddle of Le Corbusier's political changes, it is helpful to review the outline of his projects just prior to and during the war. The last project that Le Corbusier undertook in the early months of 1940, before the war–during which he built nothing and never raised his pencil to design–was a commission from Raoul Dautry, the Minister of Armament, for a munitions factory to be located near Aubusson. He began at the same time to propose programs to industrialize housing and, with François de Pierrefeu, set up le Comité des études préparatoires d'urbanisme (CEPU, The Committee on Preparatory Studies of Urbanism) on November 29, 1939. It was presided over by Jean Giraudoux, the commissioner of information. This committee was supposed to inform the people about new housing designs, the industrial world about new methods to manufacture housing elements, and the authorities about urban plans and housing programs.[31] The committee, however, had no time to function before the German invasion.

Le Corbusier's armaments factory was never built, as Germany invaded and occupied northeastern France in May 1940. The French were demoralized and politically exhausted.[32] They had not yet recovered sufficiently from the disasters of World War I, the economic depression of the 1930s, or the divisive turmoil of the Popular Front, and they chose in the face of German occupation to adapt an attitude of "wait and see." Marshal Philippe Pétain, the hero of Verdun, was selected to head a new government and to negotiate for peace. Yet he compromised instead; after meeting with Hitler at Montoire on October 30, 1940, he even used the word "collaboration": "It is with honor and to maintain ten-century-old French unity in the framework of the constructive activity of the new European order that I embark today on a path of collaboration…Follow me. Keep your faith in *la France éternelle*."[33]

To the committee charged with drafting a new constitution for a government to be housed at Vichy in the unoccupied zones, Pétain gave instructions to define a regime "radically different" from its predecessor, discarding the idea of popular sovereignty. He envisioned a strong state that would be at all levels both hierarchical and authoritarian, a corporatist system based on the family and patriarchal discipline. Equality between men was an illusion; in its place, he would govern absolutely, expecting disciplined submission and unwavering compliance from those below.[34]

A few days before Germans troops entered Paris, on June 14, 1940, Le Corbusier closed his office, and with his wife and cousin, Pierre Jeanneret, retreated to the town of Ozon, a free zone at the foothills of the Pyrenees.[35] He stayed there three months before returning to Paris, preparing the manuscript of *Sur les Quatres Routes* (*The Four Routes*, 1941). In the early years of the war he was also busy writing two other books, *Destin de Paris* (*Destiny of Paris*, 1941) and *Les Constructions "Murondins"* (*"Murondins" Constructions*, 1942), the latter coauthored by Pierre Jeanneret.[36] After helping Le Corbusier develop schemes for *murondins*, jerry-built structures intended as temporary barracks for war refugees from Belgium and Holland, Pierre Jeanneret left for Grenoble in December 1940. Moving politically in the opposite direction, Le Corbusier was seeking during the summer and autumn of

1940 a position in the Vichy government through frequent visits to the town and through intermediaries. He was eager to see that his plans for Algiers be implemented and that his service to France in her hour of need be accepted.

Le Corbusier moves to Vichy in January of 1941, where he expects to find men of authority with sufficient power and will to impose his plans. He writes in *The Four Routes,*

> A man has won his spurs by the labor of a lifetime. His name now belongs to his country. Will the authorities of his country be failing in a sense of duty by allowing him an occasional chance...will they not rather be expressing a reasonable sense of gratitude?[37]

He has initial success: with François de Pierrefeu, he is assigned by the beginning of February to work with Robert Latournerie on the Comité d'Études du Batiment (Study Committee on Building) and charged with studying ways to revitalize the prostrate building industries. Things do not run smoothly, however, and by July 14, he receives notification that his collaboration with Vichy has been terminated, though the committee continues to function (renamed Comité d'Études de l'Habitation et de la Construction Immobilière [Study Committee on Housing and Construction]) until the end of 1941.[38]

Pierrefeu and Le Corbusier write *La Maison des hommes* (*The House of Man*, 1942) while remaining in Vichy, where Le Corbusier continues to try to secure another position. In the spring of 1941 he makes a quick visit to Algiers, still hoping to find reception for his *plan directeur.*[39] Throughout the following year he will develop these plans, visiting the city once again in April and May 1942. His Obus E scheme will be firmly rejected the following month. Throughout this year of waiting, Le Corbusier does not give up hope that he will eventually achieve a commission in the Vichy regime, no matter how dastardly their policies have become. He continues to work on plans for Paris, Ilôt 6, the Radiant Farm, and the Cooperative Village. Before leaving Vichy for good–on July 1, 1942–he is appointed to yet another committee, Comité d'Études de l'Habitation et de l'Urbanisme de Paris (Study Committee on Housing and Urbanism of Paris).[40]

Throughout the months of waiting for a commission, however, he slowly comes to the sad recognition that the men of Vichy do not want to collaborate with Le Corbusier; he finds they organize commissions on urbanism for the interior of France, for infrastructure, for the Paris region, and assign men to these study groups who know nothing about urbanism and are guided by traditional architectural styles. They reject modern technicians and new techniques, returning to the ways of old pastoral France, to the idealization of folklore and the peasant, but not to the modern ideas advocated by CIAM and the Charter of Athens.

His position with the Vichy government has been a matter of some controversy. In spite of being rejected as too revolutionary and idealistic, he nevertheless clearly sided with men of power and petitioned repetitively for commissions. While in Vichy, he began to revise the Charter of Athens, thinking it would be a useful platform for postwar reconstruction. He wrote Giedion that he saw a future in which the doctrine of CIAM would be triumphant, and requested material presented at CIAM IV for Brussels, Amsterdam, Warsaw, Gothenburg, Budapest, Helsinki, and Moscow–cities that might constitute a new European order receptive to modern ideals.[41]

Le Corbusier decides to bring together a group of architects, engineers, and other technicians under his direction as the Assemblée de Constructeurs pour une Renouvellement Architecturale (ASCORAL, Assembly of Constructors for Architectural Revolution–the word replaced by Renovation, and finally, Renewal). The group was formed on February 23, 1943, and began to meet discreetly in the spring, but lacking government support was necessarily restricted to research and publication.[42] ASCORAL proclaimed that its mission was to draw up plans to rebuild the regions of France devastated by war and reconstruct immense areas of the urban and rural domains crushed by dilapidation and delays in the provision of housing, factories, and services caused by diversion of materials for armaments. ASCORAL appealed to all those concerned with setting up "good relations" between man and his milieu: not just architects and engineers, but sociologists, economists, industrialists, doctors, biologists, intellectuals, and artists.[43] It proclaimed its intention to diffuse a doctrine of planning through publications and to intervene in reconstruction plans by offering proposals, information, and research. [FIGURE 12.1, p. 701]

ASCORAL was composed of eleven sections and half-sections, and met two times a month. Each section was charged with studying a specific theme, and its work was expected to culminate in the publication of a book. The work of the first section, "Idées générales et synthèse" ("General Ideas and Synthesis"), was published in *Manière de penser l'urbanisme* (*Looking at City Planning*, 1946). The other sections were devoted to education, housing (*savoir habiter*), health, work, folklore, finance, legislation, enterprise, ethics, aesthetics, the grilles of urbanism (CIAM's grid of four functions: to house, to work, to cultivate the body, to circulate), and the synthesis of the major arts. Le Corbusier coauthored a book with ASCORAL, *L'Urbanisme des Trois Établissements Humains* (*The Three Human Establishments*, 1945), in addition to writing a kind of question-and-answer book, entitled *Propos d'Urbanisme* (*Concerning Town Planning*, 1946).[44]

From 1943 to 1945, Le Corbusier and ASCORAL researched reconstruction plans for the cities of Saint-Dié, Nantes, Le Havre, Charleville-Mézières, and Montargis. Some time after the *Chartre d'Athènes* (*Athens Charter*) was published in 1943, he informed Raoul Dautry, head of the Ministry of Reconstruction and Urbanism—created by decree in November 1944 (a few months after France's liberation from the Nazis)—of the research group's existence and of the *Chartre*'s plans for reconstruction. At least 450,000 housing units had been destroyed in the war, displacing between one and two million inhabitants; 1,500 other localities had been largely destroyed, and 3,000 others damaged. The task of reconstruction was acute and colossal. ASCORAL remained one of the only entities in France that had a coherent program and policy toward managing the built domain, yet its ideas still found no reception among those responsible for reconstruction and postwar development.[45]

In the spring of 1945, Le Corbusier finally receives two commissions: he is named *architecte-conseil* for the reconstruction of Saint-Dié, a town destroyed by the Germans as they retreated in 1944, and for the rebuilding of the port of La Rochelle-La Pallice. In both cases, however, local authorities reject his plans.[46] Meanwhile, Dautry arranged on September 8, 1945, for Le Corbusier to be given a housing project as compensation for losing these larger commissions. This would be a demonstration project of one of his planned Unités d'habitation. Construction began in 1947. The site was Marseilles, which lay on the axis of Le Corbusier's linear city stretching from Le Havre to Algiers.

III. ELEMENTS OF A DOCTRINE

Every faith proclaims, or at least contains implicitly, a doctrine. Le Corbusier pointed out in 1948 that his own "*elements de doctrine*" were to be found mostly in his books written during World War II. A doctrine can be discovered, he explained, if the reader weaves together diverse texts and images from *Précisions* (1930), *Maison des Hommes* (1941), *L'Urbanisme des Trois Établissements Humains* (1945), *Propos d'urbanisme* (1946), and *Manière de penser l'urbanisme* (1946).[47] He does not mention *Sur les Quatres Routes* (1941) or *Destin de Paris* (1941), perhaps because he used these to secure a position within the Vichy government and does not want to recall that episode. Yet these two books, along with some shorter writings of the period, clearly belong on the list, and any attempt to abstract the elements of Le Corbusier's doctrine is incomplete without them.

Formally, these seven books are extremely repetitive, using the cumulative method first practiced in *The Radiant City*. One text is inserted into another text or a smaller book into a larger one; materials from different sources are re-edited and reused. Yet they are varied in format, if not in message: a wordy text addressed to the young, a picture book or short essay for governmental authorities, articles for journals expressing different political positions, a set of rhetorical questions and answers, lectures and drawings delivered orally then transcribed into texts.[48]

This group of essays, lectures, and books presents encounters with cities and designs promoting the Radiant City. They spell out Le Corbusier's determined belief that peace resides in the provision of unités d'habitation and the achievement of essential joys based on a politics of urban renewal according to Le Corbusian principles. This will miraculously "transmute" the negative politics of the 1930s and 1940s into something more radiant and peaceful. His arguments are repetitive and performative, intended to make a mark rather than prove a theorem. He claimed his doctrine was like a polar star, destined to guide heroic navigators called upon by the state to become the organizers of *plans directeurs* for cities and regions. As he displays the points of his doctrine, he consistently denies that he is being political, although he often seeks to convince municipal authorities, the governments of the Popular Front and Vichy, and the men in charge of reconstruction to implement his schemes. He was so convinced of his plans that he was willing to sacrifice essential democratic principles, including popular rule, in order to realize them.

In fact, in spite of his oft-repeated subterfuge of claiming that he was merely a technician, Le Corbusier's voice throughout the 1930s and early 1940s had become increasingly political: this was implicit in his choice to address himself directly to authorities who might have power to mandate implementation of his plans.

The discourse on reconstruction and Le Corbusier's *elements de doctrine* that these seven books contain expresses a will to knowledge, a *savoir habiter,* concerning housing and transportation, factors that in turn affect patterns of land use and the distribution of settlements. Le Corbusier's elements of a doctrine contain, he believes, a remedy for the oppression mankind suffered in cities and farmlands around the world. But first citizens, workers, peasants, the elite men of authority, and the young had to wake up and recognize this human predicament. Le Corbusier perceives a dualistic and arduous contest between good and bad forces, a battle against external forces of exploitation and deprivation as much as against feelings and emotions that inhibit men from acting. He was intent on founding what amounted to a system of secular salvation, a quasi-religion of urbanism.

The question I wish to focus on is not how misguided his fantasies were, or why his doctrine failed to gain worldwide acceptance, but what devices he deployed to promulgate this new faith. How did he spell out the elements of the doctrine to which he aspired? The short answer is that he tried any method that he could think of. He assembles evidence and establishes proofs; he tells stories of past achievements and failures; he draws icons; he accuses the false consciousness of the schools who divert the masses from salvation. Delays and obstacles are thrown in the path toward the temps nouveaux, but, he believes, the torrent of revolutionary ideas cannot be stopped. Victory, in a paradox common in revolutionary and salvationist discourse, is both inevitable and must be struggled for ceaselessly: he regales his audiences with tales of how he has heroically struggled for his humanistic cause across the many decades of his lifetime.

Le Corbusier's style of argument often proceeds by incoherent aphorisms and unusual combinations of stories. Yet it is the total situation, the entire dramatic picture of urban and rural malformation, that he seeks to transform. As early as 1935, he had called for an *urbanisme totale.*[49] At that time he declared it was no longer a matter of simply transforming furniture, changing the decorative form of objects of use, or constructing jolly suburbs and private villas. All these were backward binding gestures, mere details on the surface of deeper problems. Instead, it was a matter of discovering the directive line of society and persuading the entire country to follow the route leading toward a new "destiny," "to affirm that a page of human history has just been turned, and it is the first era of machinism (1830–1930) that has led us to an impasse from which we will leave only through a great decision."[50]

All the world is waiting for that event, for that decision to be made! They are waiting for a doctrine to guide them.

Like a religious faith, Le Corbusier's urbanism demands immersion, conversion, total commitment. It is not enough that the faith become part of the believer's world; the believer's world must be totally redefined in the terms of the faith. Urbanisme totale involves the entire country, all aspects of its existence: all of its inventors, thinkers, industries, and workers will be employed in a movement of renewal, the provision of equipment for a second machine civilization. Urbanisme totale implies a program to produce objects useful to man, at the service of man; it involves housing in cities, towns, and villages; and it aims at nothing less than a universal renewal and liberation of the spirit.[51] After fifteen years of study, Le Corbusier proclaims, he has developed a term for this new urbanization: he calls it *la Ville Radieuse*. A new program is born that completely overturns all architectural and urbanistic givens. The very term "la ville radieuse" is religious in its emotional resonance, almost a paraphrase of Biblical language about the New Jerusalem. By promising a new, salvific, renewed, and renewing city full of shining light, Le Corbusier is deploying archetypal religious imagery.[52]

In all of the books conveying his elements of doctrine, Le Corbusier feasts upon this theme of renewal, devoting many pages of testimony to support the claim that the first machine era (1830–1930) has ended, and the second machine era, the temps nouveaux, has begun. He musters historical anecdotes, technical conquests, and subtle twists of logic; he builds lists of the effects of scientific discoveries in order to convince the reader to adopt a new attitude toward life, to receive a new way of living, to understand that "transmutations" have revolutionized building techniques, the equipment of homes, and the entire habits and traditions of society.[53] The end, the means: "Knowing, accurate and magnificent interplay of shapes assembled in the light."[54]

Le Corbusier's discourse, the meeting points of his outpouring of words, was intended to initiate neophytes into a community of believers, that of CIAM–the force of his rhetoric eliciting courageous commitment to a new cause. A choice must be made if the facts are assessed, because there is nothing more important than to avoid the dire consequences of making a wrong choice. What he calls his "force-words" (*mots-force*) are always about expressing an action, making connections between thought and deed.[55] They are the stable signifying units imposed on his discourse, yet they also apply to a range of different situations and concerns.

Le Corbusier does not present a list of the elements that compose his doctrine; instead they are to be gleaned by extracting them from his many faceted texts. There is, however, a clear trajectory in his writings, a path of motion that leads away from the first machine era toward the second era of the temps nouveaux. There are obstacles to overcome on this path, and a dynamism to be experienced that is revelatory, allowing his daydreams to reach fulfillment and man to achieve redemption. As a précis, a series of force-words, master metaphors, and foundational texts allows a glimpse at some of the elements. "Radiant" and all of its variations is at the top of the list of force-words; it subsumes such concepts as "the force of light," "clarity," "sunlight," and "whiteness." "Nature" is another force-word, and this is linked to "landscape," "rocks," "trees," "flowerings," "the twenty-four hours of the day," and "built biology." "Unity," "harmony," and "solidarity" are other linked words, as are "destiny," "adventure," "game," "laboratory experiments," and "transmutations."

There are master metaphors such as "the joys of living," "a page has turned," "trinity of man-nature-cosmos," and "sun the dictator." Foundational texts, to which extended commentary is appended, are CIAM's advocacy of sun, space, and greenery, and the four functions of housing, work, leisure, and circulation, ensuring the "essential joys of living." And there is, as ever, constant reference to his voyage to the East in 1911, when he stood thunderstruck on the Acropolis and understood the moral responsibility of an architect to carry out his ideal of perfection. In pursuing this secular religion there are a variety of tools to use: housing, modes of transportation, and a variety of routes to carry forward his daydreams toward their fulfillment. And always there is a poetics to write, to convince and entertain the novices.

To decipher Le Corbusier's elements of doctrine, I begin with a series of six lectures that he delivered in Rio de Janeiro in August 1936.[56] On the first evening, he told the audience that everything he was about to explain to them was spoken as a "technician," a man who observes phenomena, analyzes, and makes a synthesis. A technician recognizes the laws of the world and discovers in them some new aspects concerning the permanent mobility and transformations of life. Then he folds this knowledge into works that are useful and submits these to the judgment of others. In spite of all the bad words that have been thrown at him by the academies in Paris or Moscow, in Berlin or Rome, he remains "imperturbable" and answers them all with the motto: "I make plans. These plans are for men."[57]

In the second lecture, Le Corbusier explains that since he travels so much and lectures continually, he must use expressions that are very concise. In order to save time, he has developed a series of force-words. Such terms allow the audience to reflect on the deeper meaning intended, knowing the ideas are based on a careful examination and judgment of facts.[58] It is these force-words, or so it is argued here, that form the basic elements of his doctrine.

In the third Rio lecture he claims that after his "study trip" six years earlier to South America, great ideas of urbanism came to him; his great urban preoccupations were born in South America. It was then that he decided to make architecture and cities "radiating" (*rayonnantes*), allowing his new thesis of urbanism to be animated by lyricism. He explains that the term Radiant City (*Ville Radieuse*) has touched the hearts of many. He has invited his adversaries to show that cities so planned are not radiant, but all of his enemies have failed to demonstrate their case and overturn his facts. Thus Le Corbusier announces triumphantly: he has won the battle![59]

But, apparently, he has not won so completely that he does not feel moved to explain why his detractors, those nonbelievers, are wrong. A year or two before, a book by Camille Mauclair appeared with the title *L'architecture va-t-elle mourir?* (*Architecture–Is It About to Die?*).[60] Le Corbusier explains yet again its venomous attack. It was paid for by the Chamber of Commerce in Paris, and made its appearance first as a series of articles in *Le Figaro*. Primarily concerned with the destiny of trades and handcrafts that utilize old-fashioned techniques on traditional materials such as stone and wood, the attack was intended to vanquish modern architecture. Tradesmen were paid millions to promote scandalous articles and to erect every barrier against those who were trying to create the temps nouveaux.

To explain himself further, he tells his audience he will examine the case of music and literature and make analogous arguments concerning architecture.

He begins with music, which critics say no longer exists. Le Corbusier, to the contrary, believes contemporary music is alive and well. We need only to listen with a new ear: the modern world is filled with all kinds of turbulent, strident, and quickly paced sounds. Noise and dissonance have become indispensable musical elements, Stravinsky being the first to acknowledge these sounds in his musical interpretations. And thanks to new technologies, music can currently be listened to everywhere: in restaurants and cinemas, on the radio, in circuses or dancing halls.

There is a parallel situation in literature, which Le Corbusier describes as the ability "to transcribe ideas through the means of syntax."[61] In the past forty years the entire world has experienced immense "gesticulations" and "events" affecting each individual. As a result, one reads other things besides novels, the latter requiring a good deal of time. Those who lead active lives are interested instead in reading travel accounts, records of technical inventions, or glancing at innumerable images in magazines: the everyday history of men.

Life, Le Corbusier concludes, transcribed into musical or literary form, and by extrapolation into architecture and urbanism, must be extricated from the clutches of critics who want to prevent the world from advancing toward the temps nouveaux, toward the creation of a "folklore of modern times."

What Le Corbusier is doing in these lectures, and will do again and again in his essays and books of subsequent years, is framing the issue, seeking to get his ideas across to a public already saturated with images and events.[62] His frames fit a certain imagistic logic, one fundamentally concerned with eschatology (the end of an old order and its replacement by a salvific and perfected one) and salvation: a force-word like "radiant" becomes a metaphoric bundle of different ideas that are "radiant," "rays of light," "radiating"; a concept like "unity," "solidarity," "adventure," or "destiny" associated with a multitude of others that on the surface appear to be a collage of disparate thoughts but are actually connected points in his doctrine. He repeats his ideas again and again, even complaining to his Rio audience that his arm is fatigued by drawing the same images over and over as he lectures; but he must, because these images are necessary to guarantee that his message strikes home.[63]

As the catastrophe of war came ever closer, finally curtailing his travels and lectures until after the war, Le Corbusier retreated to writing and rewriting his elements of doctrine, turning them into a system and experimenting with different formats in order to convince his followers that planning the provision of housing, infrastructure, settlements pattern of cities, even the geomorphic rearrangement of the countryside was a wise investment. A modern technician thinks ahead; men of the academies do not. His force-words push onwards, they contain revolutionary ideas that his adversaries can neither understand nor use. He is trying to attract a wide following, placing great hope in the young, who are more receptive to his ideas than older generations. He uses more frequently an ideogram of an open book to illustrate

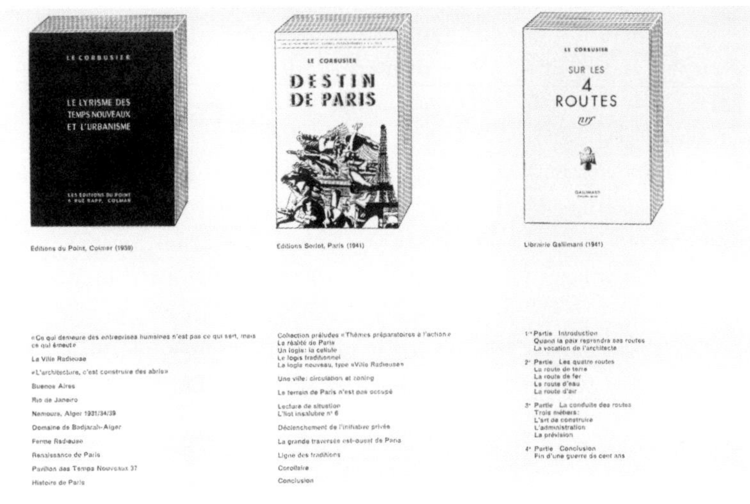

LE CORBUSIER

LE LYRISME DES TEMPS NOUVEAUX ET L'URBANISME

LES EDITIONS DU POINT
5 RUE RAPP, COLMAR

LE CORBUSIER

DESTIN DE PARIS

LE CORBUSIER

SUR LES 4 ROUTES

nrf

Editions du Point, Colmar (1939)

Editions Sorlot, Paris (1941)

Librairie Gallimard (1941)

«Ce qui demeure des entreprises humaines n'est pas ce qui sert, mais ce qui émeut»

La Ville Radieuse

«L'architecture, c'est construire des abris»

Buenos Aires

Rio de Janeiro

Nemours, Alger 1931/34/39

Domaine de Badjarah-Alger

Ferme Radieuse

Renaissance de Paris

Pavillon des Temps Nouveaux 37

Histoire de Paris

Collection préludes «Thèmes préparatoires à l'action»
La réalité de Paris
Un logis: la cellule
Le logis traditionnel
Le logis nouveau, type «Ville Radieuse»

Une ville: circulation et zoning

Le terrain de Paris n'est pas occupé

Lecture de situation
L'îlot insalubre n° 6

Déclenchement de l'initiative privée

La grande traversée est-ouest de Paris

Ligne des traditions

Corollaire

Conclusion

1re Partie Introduction
Quand la paix reprendra ses routes
La vocation de l'architecte

2e Partie Les quatre routes
La route de terre
La route de fer
La route d'eau
La route d'air

3e Partie La conduite des routes
Trois métiers:
L'art de construire
L'administration
La prévision

4e Partie Conclusion
Fin d'une guerre de cent ans

201

FIGURES 12.2, 12.3, AND 12.4: **These three pages illustrating covers of books written between 1938 and 1946 appear in volume 4 of Le Corbusier's *Oeuvre Complète*. They represent some of the books that compose his doctrine of urbanism.**

potential covers for his various books. This rapidly executed drawing, first appearing in the 1930s, reveals the left-hand page of a book lying flat on a table, the right half folded as if it has a flexible cover. It implies that his message is open, accessible, and clear–a *machine à lire* (machine for reading).

Paul Valéry spoke in 1926 of two properties of a book. First, a reader follows its argument from word to word, line to line, in a linear manner, creating in the wake of this movement a number of mental reactions and a combination of associated thoughts.[64] The second property of a book is to perceive it as a visual object, where the eyes scan over the surface in sheer delight, appropriating each page as graphic material in tones of black and white. This second manner of seeing is immediate and simultaneous. Valéry called these two aspects of the book, to read the text and to see the text, completely distinct but absolutely complementary in the best of books. There the text and image become a perfect *machine à lire*, both a work of art and a work that carries the precise marks of a particular thought. [FIGURES 12.2, 12.3, AND 12.4]

Le Corbusier mixes these two aspects of the book. He writes in a traditional linear manner, imparting information to the reader, proving points, using the tools of rhetoric to win his argument.

1941

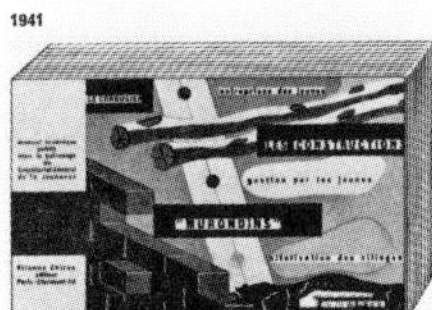

Edition Chiron, Paris (1941)

Ce livre Les Maisons «Murondins» est un petit cadeau à ses amis, les Jeunes de France, par Le Corbusier

(Résumé) Les grandes épreuves sont venues: l'exode de mai/juin 1940! On a senti, à ce moment, qu'on ne pourrait plus fabriquer à temps utile, en atelier, et transporter aux lieux prescrits, des abris nécessaires; et, devant cette situation sans espoir, d'un coup, la solution est apparue, comme l'œuf de Colomb: l'abri doit être construit sur place, par les usagers mêmes, avec des matériaux non ouvrés trouvés sur place: de la terre, du sable, des bois de forêt, des branches, des fagots, des mottes de gazon ...
Et notre abri s'est trouvé baptisé: «Murondins», c'est-à-dire: des murs et des rondins!

1942

Edition Plon (1942)

Le Corbusier et François de Pierrefeu
Les hommes sont mal logés
Une nouvelle société crée son foyer
La confusion est dans les esprits et l'erreur irréparable est en route
On s'ingénie à inventer des monstres à l'aspect séduisant:
cité-jardins
villes satellites
On oublie de regarder les traits du terrain, les traits de l'homme et les aspects du travail, sans quoi on inventerait ces trois réalisations «conformes»
La ville verte
La cité linéaire industrielle
Le village rural revitalisé
Voici comment se présente la juste occupation du sol, dans l'hexagone français
A la conquête des «joies essentielles»
Le pacte scellé avec la nature
La nature est inscrite dans le bail
Le maître-d'œuvre
Cent années de conquêtes scientifiques ont accompli la révolution architecturale. Un mot d'ordre, et elle entre dans les faits
L'unité architecturale est fille d'une «doctrine du domaine bâti» équilibrant:
la loi du nombre et
la loi du soleil
avec la topographie
L'ordonnateur
Modèle les villes
Fixe le type des «volumes bâtis»
Détermine le «statut du terrain»
Exploite les ressources du paysage
Vitalise la région, la province et le pays
Met en valeur le patrimoine d'art et d'histoire

1943

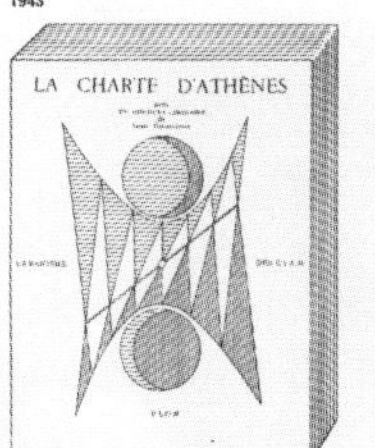

Edition Plon, Paris (1943)

Urbanisme des CIAM avec un discours liminaire de Jean Giraudoux

Loin d'un palais scandaleux

Vers un logis digne

Vers une forme nouvelle d'habitation

La maison des hommes

Pour la cité et pour la terre

Le groupe CIAM-France intervient

La charte:
La ville et sa région
Etat actuel critique des villes
Habitation
Loisirs
Travail
Circulation
Patrimoine historique
Points de doctrine

202

«Entretien avec les étudiants des écoles d'architecture»
Edition Denoël (1943)

I. Le désarroi (où en est l'architecture?)

II. Construire de logis

III. L'architecture
1 Le ciel domine
2 Le site est l'assiette de la composition architecturale
3 Une échelle s'attache
4 L'architecture se marche, se parcourt ...
5 La circulation
6 Palais des Soviets
7 Les initiatives
8 Loi du soleil
9 La proportion
10 Le logis digne
11 Folklores
12 Mes voyages
13 L'échelle
14 Le cubisme
15 Ma maison fût un Palais
16 Les couleurs

IV. Un Atelier de Recherches

Collection ASCORAL, Urbanisme des CIAM
Edition Denoël, Paris (1944)

1re Partie
Esquisse générale
Nourrir, Fabriquer, Echanger

2e Partie
Ethique du travail
I. Conditions morales (Travail, Lumière et Liberté)
II. Conditions matérielles (Habiter, Travailler, Cultiver le corps et l'esprit)

3e Partie
Les trois établissements humains
A. L'Unité d'Exploitation Agricole
1. Présentation de l'Unité d'Exploitation Agricole
2. Proposition des paysans: le Centre Coopératif
3. L'outil préparateur: l'Ecole Rurale
B. La Cité Linéaire Industrielle
1. Trois fonctions, deux rythmes
2. L'Usine Verte
3. A quatre kilomètres en travers
4. La qualification à cent kilomètres en long
C. Les Cités d'Echange

4e Partie
Réalités
I. De l'Océan à l'Oural
II. La vie ouvre elle-même les voies
III. Incidence sur Paris

Edition Bourrelier, Paris (1946)

1re Partie
Raccourci
Une civilisation de la production est née. Problème posé à l'aube de cette seconde ère machiniste: architecture et urbanisme

2e Partie
Coup d'œil sans préméditation jeté dans le passé
prouvant qu'en ces matières mille thèmes sont abordés parce qu'ils sont synchrones, l'urbanisme, «ordonnateur social par excellence», étant l'expression même des conditions matérielles et spirituelles d'une époque
Les villes: Strasbourg, le Capitole à Rome, Karlsruhe, Venise, etc.

3e Partie
On saisit l'occasion de répondre à une enquête
Dix-huit questions d'une «enquête sur la reconstruction»

203

To entice the reader, he also uses a journalistic approach, inserting contemporary issues, reaching back in time to illustrate how certain examples or values were formed, spinning off associative thoughts and stories, drawing a continuous path toward tomorrow. But Le Corbusier also envisions the world pictorially, and to record its diversity uses all manner of equations, diagrams, and images. Élie Faure likened reading *The Radiant City* to plunging into a bath of fresh water that was so clear it allowed him to see mosaics of very strange designs. It was not the form of the book, the logic of its message, or its readability that appeared to him so strangely wonderful, but the manner in which the illustrations drew the reader into the depths of the material: a complex of original photographs, aerial views, images of wheels and motors, stylish furniture, pipes, telephone exchanges, sketches drawn with charm and verve. Yet this assemblage of elements always underscored the rigor of Le Corbusier's linear argument.[65]

It appears that apart from using emotive words such as "radiant" or "unity," Le Corbusier's force-words are lacking in specific ideas–they are instead elements of an exhortative discourse. His slippage between words and icons reinforces his failure to lay down a list of specific prescriptions that can be articulated or enumerated as points of belief to affirm or dispute, i.e., points of doctrine. "Radiant" means essentially whatever Le Corbusier wants it to mean: it is indeed a "force-word," not an "idea-word," for it has no translatable content, contains no doctrinal concept. Likewise with other force-words and icons: the intent and effect is to cast a spell, an aura of light, not to construct a syllogism. They can be viewed as elements of a devotional poetics rather than points of a systematic doctrine. Le Corbusier is a technician, he is performing a set of laboratory experiments, he has years of experience, and he wants his words to be accepted as a matter of faith. He assures believers who follow him that "the adventure is designed with clarity: reason, good sense and with such powers of realization they will be the trampoline of art and the poetry of a new era."[66]

FOUNDATIONAL TEXTS

Le Corbusier's elements of doctrine remain implicit in his discourse on the reconstruction of the cities and countryside devastated by war or neglect. Discourse, as described by Michel Foucault, unfurls within a series of restrictions, controlling what can be said and who can speak with what authority and within what institutions.[67] Frames shape discourses, a common one being that commentary is limited to the discussion of certain primary texts. Constantly identifying with foundational statements prevents the production of unlimited and indefinite statements and marks the discourse with authority and coherence. Presenting the minimum amount of information, repetitive appeals to foundational texts are more like slogans than statements, whose purpose is to insure the transmission of orders to do this and think that.

In all the books that contain Le Corbusier's diffuse discourse on elements of doctrine, he refers to the statements proclaimed by CIAM in 1928 and elaborated into the Charter of Athens, a manifesto drawn from the fifty-nine proclamations made by CIAM IV in 1933 and expressly modeled after the ninety-nine theses of Martin Luther—another mark of kinship to reformist religious discourse.[68] They begin to specify some of his doctrinal elements. He states in *Destin de Paris* (1941) that CIAM IV made the first step by positing that urbanism consists of sun, space, trees, iron, and reinforced concrete. But this foundational statement has been transformed, and now includes large expanses of glass, soundproofing, site plans that enable the maximum amount of light to enter the house on December 21, plenty of green space and trees surrounding the house, spaces for recreation and sports at the foot of the house, and roof gardens on the top for flowers, health clubs, and swimming pools. These extensions embrace collective domestic services, dispensaries and hospitals, schools and kindergartens. They incorporate separate channels for pedestrians and automobiles, so these separate paths of movement never meet. Putting all these extensions together creates, Le Corbusier argues, "the Radiant City."[69] Thus Le Corbusier links the foundational texts to the position he advocates, weaving his separate points into a coherent commentary.

He refers to his foundational texts again in *The Four Routes* (1941), asserting that CIAM IV laid down a scheme for peace in the Charter of Athens that authorities must understand. If they apply its principles to real situations, the causes of unrest and war would be eliminated.[70] There are two kinds of planning: good and bad. The bad neglects an idea that stems from the time of World War I, an idea reiterated by the first meeting of CIAM in 1928 and repeated again in 1933: to battle against the existence of slums, to enlighten public opinion about the possibilities of "radiant" homes.[71]

In his first book coauthored with ASCORAL, *L'Urbanisme des Trois Établissements Humains* (1945), the texts of CIAM are again called on.[72] The Charter of Athens proclaims: "The materials of urbanism are sun, space, greenery." The conditions of nature, which have been abandoned, lost, and forgotten, must be reintroduced. CIAM reveals in a decisive manner how the march of machines has separated and denatured the three essential functions at the base of its proclamations: to live, to work, and to cultivate the body and mind.

In his second ASCORAL book, *Looking at City Planning* (1946), he refers again to the foundational texts, assembling what he calls an "atlas of the ways in which new ideas in architecture and city planning have been applied," beginning with Tony Garnier and his *La Cité Industrielle* (c. 1900), through Le Corbusier's own *A Contemporary City for Three Million Inhabitants* (1922), and on to the CIAM congresses of 1928 and 1933.

In *Concerning Town Planning* (1946), Le Corbusier responded to a question of whether towns destroyed by the war should be rebuilt on the same site and utilize the same transportation networks by reiterating his doctrinal themes and appealing to his foundational text:

> In 1928 at La Sarratz, Switzerland, a group of men came together and founded the CIAM (Congrès Internationaux d'Architecture Moderne); they tried to co-ordinate men's destinies with those of the house and town and land settlement.... [ASCORAL has made] a particular study of the places and conditions of work in a technical civilization, recognizing three natural establishments...1/ The unit of agricultural production. 2/ The linear industrial city (the manufacturing industries). 3/ The radio-concentric city of exchange (government, thought, art, commerce.). These establishments occupy space in a special way, each with its own function: food production, manufacture, distribution. Their destiny is conditioned by the routes that serve them (road, rail, and water). They may well be reshaped by the growing traffic in air.[73]

A FELLOWSHIP OF DISCOURSE

Discourse, as Foucault and others have pointed out, has a social origin: to communicate in order to foster cooperation. Thus a certain complicity with the world is called for: disciplinary discourse claims to be scientific and prescriptive, and unfurls a series of effects aimed at specific audiences. It defines a language that a group might speak. For example, when asked what part the arts would hold in the work of postwar reconstruction, Le Corbusier responded in part that

> We have still to learn the language that we have to speak. Gone are the metopes, pediments, tympana and even modern capitals. There will be different things, since the form of the sheltered domain is new. It is built otherwise than before and our technical civilization will express its own sensibilities. With what violence, with what eloquence and with what prodigious invention over a span of 40 years, has cubism already budded and flourished.[74]

Discourse is aimed at a specific audience, a closed community that comments on, renews, and updates the foundational texts. The discourse of Le Corbusier and CIAM is also concerned with making new converts to their system of belief–especially among the young, an oft-repeated theme for Le Corbusier, who has often told the story (and does so again in *The Four Routes*) of when he was a young man attending a meeting on the reconstruction of cities after World War I. A delegate, Le Corbusier says, spoke: "We will rebuild our villages and farms, stone upon stone, exactly as they were, the old dunghill in the same old place, the same stable, and the same door onto the road...nothing must be changed!" Le Corbusier approached the speaker after the meeting, thinking he was too young to interrupt him in public, but wanting to tell him that he was contemplating an "abominable crime," "the death of the country." The man answered: "Oh, voice of youth...how right you are: it is you who represent the fullness of life....what, oh, what have I said!"[75] Le Corbusier points out the moral: it is the young, the sap of a new spring, who will own and use the new world being prepared, and to whom Le Corbusier entrusts the will to reconstruct cities after the damage of World War II: "The awakening generation, [aware] that a new life must open up over the four routes."[76]

Repeatedly, persistently, Le Corbusier in *The Four Routes* drapes the idea of youth and its relationship to architecture with religious terminology and imagery: "One tie unites them, one faith: modern architecture."[77] They are the avant-garde of a new army, creating tomorrow, installing "a world-wide harmony of procedure," preparing a "new white flowering," because

> White denotes neither limitation nor austerity, but joy....Many medieval churches were white. Try to visualize their whiteness: luminous structures, cheerful with the lively and solid interplay of ribs and pillars, the great glass sections of the transept,

> transparent, made up of lively little diamonds set in lead, resembling some enchanting fish net.... And often stained-glass windows were brilliant rather than somber.... The dirt came later with the coal of the factories. With growing certainty, I see our cathedrals white.[78]

Nor, as we have already seen under the signs of Le Corbusier's attempt to recruit Vichy to his projects, will Le Corbusier's "one faith," modern architecture, flinch from invoking the secular arm: he is eager to revive the *compelle intrare* ("Compel them to come in," Luke 14:23). The government must, Le Corbusier argues one page after the passage just quoted, issue a circular, on one piece of paper, prohibiting the use of "styles." They must raise "the clenched fist of our national will power" and establish "*the rule.*"[79]

Having addressed himself extensively to youth and his concerns about its education, he turns to what he calls the only man capable of reconstructing the cities and farms of Europe: the engineer. This enterprising figure still holds pride of place in Le Corbusier's doctrine, although he has been subtly transformed from the engineer of 1922 into a builder.

> The term *builder* will group all those who, by means either of machine or hand, are called to re-equip our civilization: a magnificent wheel revealing in sequence its full gamut from mathematical calculation to imagination pure. Until now, the term *builder* only designated the members of building corporations, cabinet-makers, mechanics. But to-day everything can be used, everything which can drag the needed elements from the earth and transmute them; everything which can help to transport and lift as high as we wish in the air; to manufacture, carve, cut, assemble, screw, solder, model, mould, melt down, to finish off. Universality of the *builder.*[80]

Engineer-architects have already built marvelous structures: the Eiffel Tower, modeled after the bony fibers of a femur sawn lengthwise, the internationally renowned hangars at Orly airport, the marvelous ship hull of the *Normandie*. Though with reservations, one might read the engineer-architect class as the priesthood of Le Corbusier's "one faith," serving under a theocratic pyramid peak of right-thinking state authorities and served in turn by a still-larger, acolytic class of youth–all of it arranged, of course, for the salvation of the base of the pyramid, the people, the masses, who will dwell joyfully in the radiant city that is engineered for them according to "*the rule*."

WAR AND OTHER LABORATORY EXPERIMENTS

In the beginning, Le Corbusier believed World War II would end after a year or two, allowing the industrial machinery dedicated to war to be diverted to peacetime production. War was the apocalypse that clears the way for a New Jerusalem; death before resurrection, annihilation before new creation. It offered a great opportunity, as he argued in *The Four Routes*, "War has unleashed an era of movement, ousted stagnation, instituted works upon so vast a scale that into their framework the needs both of architecture and planning may now be fitted."[81] He drew a new ideogram: the two intertwining hands of architecture and of planning, together providing for the needs of peace.[82] These hands, activated by a modern conscience, would apply suitable methods to each of the four routes, the highway, railway, waterway, and airway.[83]

True, it wouldn't be easy:

> When at last the planes of war come down to a world at peace; when the fleets give up their sailors; when the rail roads and the land roads lead millions of soldiers back home, that day will be no picnic for the authorities.... By land, by water, by rail and in the air there will be a new call to arms.[84]

The fact that men were ill-housed, Le Corbusier idealistically assumed, was the root cause of their disquiet, the real reason for war (hence "architecture or revolution").[85] If one planned ahead, however, the storm of war and its upheavals could be met with equilibrating forces and foresight. [FIGURE 12.5] Le Corbusier lost no time in setting the tasks to be faced onto paper. He called his study of the four routes "a case history as precise and of the same nature as a laboratory test."[86] It was, he said, based on theoretical work and practical experience, carried out in a variety of latitudes around the world and supported with a series of planning experiments in Stockholm, Antwerp, Moscow, Paris, Buenos Aires, Algiers, and elsewhere. He believed that war as a "super-laboratory" opened the second era of the machine age, allowing France to travel the four routes toward a new world. In this new era all negative struggle would be transformed by positive willpower into constructive "adventures."[87]

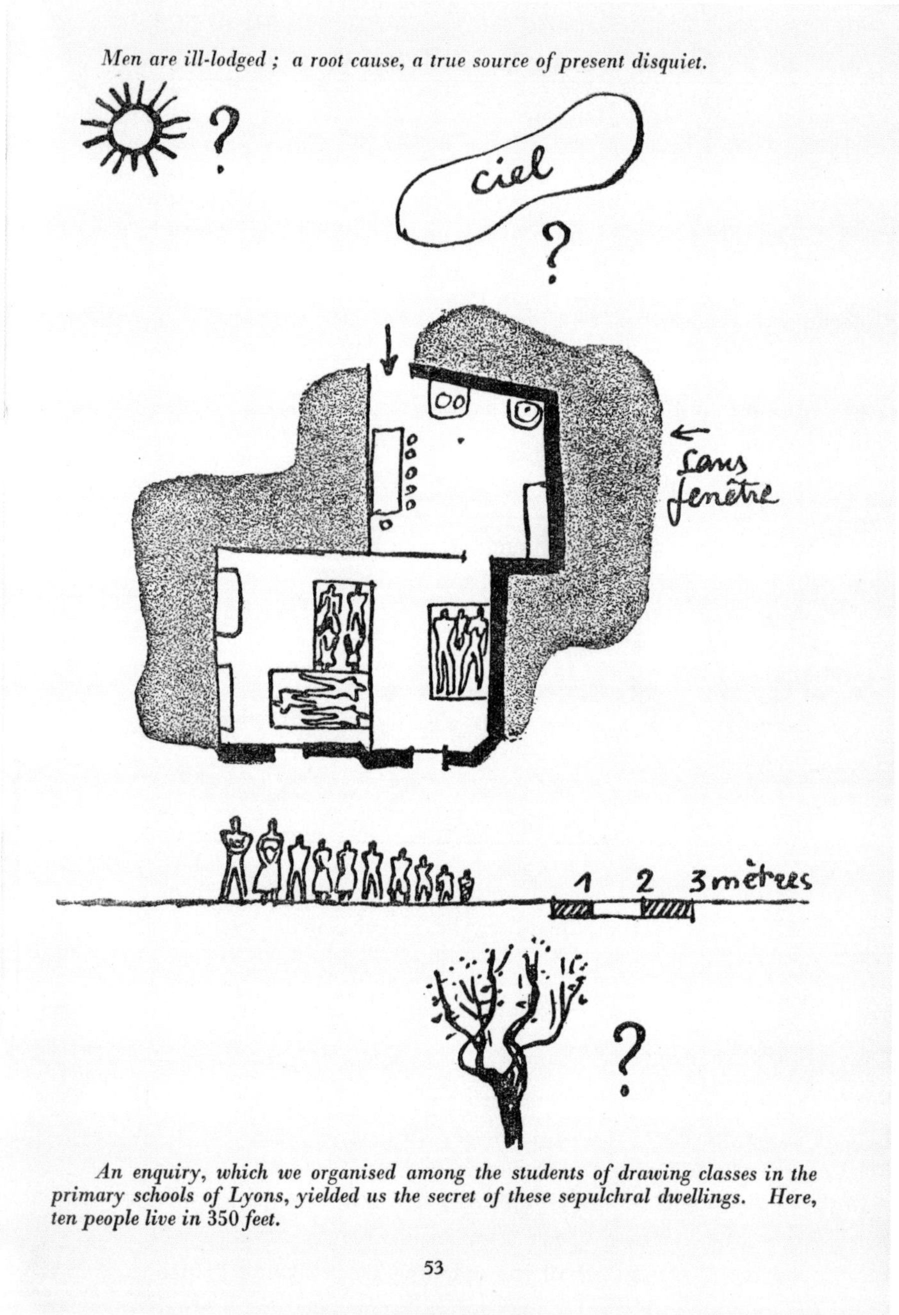

Men are ill-lodged ; a root cause, a true source of present disquiet.

An enquiry, which we organised among the students of drawing classes in the primary schools of Lyons, yielded us the secret of these sepulchral dwellings. Here, ten people live in 350 feet.

53

FIGURE 12.5: "Men are ill-lodged; a root cause, a true source of present disquiet."

Le Corbusier had often asserted during the 1930s, as he recalls in *The Four Routes*, the following arch-narrative: the first century of the first machine age (1830–1930) was over, the revolution in architecture accomplished, and now the second era of the temps nouveaux, the second machine age, could begin. Slowed down by the Depression, then World War II, and often blocked by the academies, conservative tradesmen, and money, the second era was nevertheless an inevitable "transmutation" touching all aspects of society and every nation. Man's entire muscular, technical, and intellectual energy could now be directed toward a new end: the reconstruction of the entire nation, both its cities and countryside. Such a great task asked the worker in his factory, the peasant on his land, the technician with his specialization, and the schoolmaster educating the young to dedicate themselves to the recreation of this second machine era, rebuilding a reason for "living."

Le Corbusier "admits" that once, long ago, he made "a knock-out statement": "the house is a machine for living"–a slogan that everyone misunderstood because what he meant by "living" was not merely meeting the material requirements of life, but the ability "to be able to think, or meditate, after the day's work." And thus he envisioned the home acquiring a new character, and in turn revolutionizing the entire layout of the city, the spatial arrangement of transportation networks, the concept of spatial relationships, and methods for constructing human habitation. This huge task of social transmutation–now a favorite word in Le Corbusier's vocabulary–demanded that all laboratory experiments be placed in the hands of engineers. He repeats his oft-stated refrain:

> If the methods now operative in the production of motor-cars were applied to the building industry, to town-planning, architecture and the equipment of the houses–contemporary society would possess the perfect home. And that home would be as delightful, as good to look at, as streamlined, as efficient, and as pleasing as a plane or a car.[88]

His concept of "living" also entailed a radical transmutation of work offset by creative leisure time.

> Leisure would offer an exit from the hell of that first machine age; would stand for happiness on every hearth. Leisure would wipe out the weary boredom of the hovel; must and will introduce a proper architecture and planning for our own time. And since leisure will require a man to spend more time in his room (Pascal's *desideratum*), a new concept of home will arise; an extension of the idea of home to take in the sun, all space and nature's green.[89]

IV. OBSTACLES

There are, however, many obstacles in the path of the necessary "transmutations," the triumph of the new "faith," the acceptance of the new "doctrine." Le Corbusier cites the early proposals of the Loucheur Law after World War I, which envisioned that a working man could draw up his own schemes for a house and engage his own architect.[90] In the beginning, Loucheur asked Le Corbusier to develop a type-house, and the Minister in charge proclaimed enthusiastically, "You will build them by the thousands." But Le Corbusier was wiser, and responded "never," because he knew there were obstacles to overcome. The working man of his own volition would never call on an atelier such as Le Corbusier's, and if he saw the plans proposed he would hate them, preferring a house in the suburbs, not a house produced as one in a series. The working class in addition held deeply rooted prejudices, believing that one's home must bear the marks of success, and hence be stuffed with all kinds of heavy cupboards and wardrobes.

There were other obstacles as well: the Loucheur Law left a loophole that big business cleverly exploited. Housing estates were built in the rotting suburbs and sold as a landlord's racket to the working class, producing an endless sea of leprous housing. Still more were raised by the building trades, who disliked prefabrication and spoke supposedly "in the name of Country, Beauty, and Intelligence." They advised turning back the clock to primitive virtues and resuming old, noble, and eternal traditions.

This fear of change, whether Le Corbusier is referring to the French defeat at the hands of the Germans in 1940, the country's "wait and see" attitude, or the refusal of authorities to adopt his proposals, raises one last obstacle against the nation's "destiny" and Le Corbusier's "adventures." At a slideshow Le Corbusier was asked to give on the Radiant City to a committee of inquiry into the condition of building production in France (probably the Vichy committee to which

Le Corbusier was assigned), a delegate from an official architectural society rose up and said: "You sir, have forgotten that the Frenchman is an individualist, and that such solutions as this are thus impossible in France."[91] Never mind, Le Corbusier replies, that cooperation built the four routes of France: a fleet of boats, the railway system, the network of highways, the system of air routes; never mind that cooperation might open the way to the second machine age and build radiant homes all over the country![92] This narrow concept of individualism is "stupid conservatism." The same men placing obstacles in his path have nevertheless accepted the radio as a substitute for thought, and the daily newspapers as a soporific for idle hours. They are responsible for horrible wallpapers; they force their families to live in bankrupt surroundings, under the shadow of a hired-purchase collector. They make sure there is no opportunity for reposeful white walls, no honest furniture indigenous to a real home, nothing to bring out individual personality. "And we have been accused of wishing to divorce Frenchmen from the virtues of individualism!"[93]

Le Corbusier knew the various obstacles standing in the way of his transmutations could only be overcome through a nationwide publicity campaign in the schools, cinema, newspapers, and magazines. Thus he dedicates himself to writing and describing the revolution of the temps nouveaux in order to educate men, especially the young, how to live in their new houses and cities–how to accept that a page of history had turned, a new civilization had been born.[94] "After a hundred years of struggle, of tumult and chaos, of shame, a second stage of mechanization commences; the era of harmony."[95] There had been revolutions before, and nothing had stopped their adventure, nothing kept them from fulfilling their destiny. The railway companies were not forbidden, even though they were a menace to the entire structure of society. Newspapers were not prohibited from being printed, yet they were instruments of political propaganda and helped to prepare the country for war. Nor were films banned, however much they revealed the baser instincts of man, and radios were allowed to invade the quiet and solitude of a woodsman's cabin, a settler's homestead, an overcrowded dwelling in the slums. Nothing was taboo. "As always, the phenomenon, stronger than all else, has pursued its irrevocable destiny."[96] So too with Le Corbusier's "adventure"–it should be given free rein to achieve its destiny even though he was not advocating preconceived ideas or traditional procedures.

> Nothing merits rejection in the name of custom; new organisms, corresponding to new functional requirements...must be allowed to come to life and develop.[97]

V. BUILT BIOLOGY

Le Corbusier's new "faith" is framed, as I have noted earlier, by a master narrative of universal fall and redemption. Its rhetoric is a blend of the lapsarian and biological, his basic claim being that humankind was plunged by the first machine era into a state of unnatural confusion or degradation, but may now emerge into a condition superior even to his unspoiled naive state, the temps nouveaux, a redeemed life in which "built biology"–biologically appropriate architecture–satisfies every emotional and intellectual need. It perpetuates the life of the Radiant City. Le Corbusier's tale of fall and redemption differs from Christianity's partly in that he claims biology, not deity, as his ultimate authority or standard of rightness. For numinous supernatural he substitutes impeccable and undeniable Nature.

This tale is retold with a particularly biological emphasis in *L'Urbanisme des Trois Établissements Humains* (1945) and *Concerning Town Planning* (1946). The first machine era, Le Corbusier says in the latter, erected on false postulates and confusion of thought, produced a legacy of irreparable mistakes. These faults plunged man, his home, and the city into one hundred years of disorder, a "fatal disarticulation" that was "homicidal." No poetry stirred behind the iron bars of houses, no streets of joy emerged in *tentaculaire* cities stretching out their fingers in default of a plan.[98] Man's ingenuity was misused by inventing seductive solutions: garden cities and satellite towns spread a philanthropic discourse, forcing a false category of social equilibrium. They were a "snare baited with the mirage of nature," and in turn had to be supported by a labyrinthine and costly communications network of roads and suburban railways, with consequent squandering of water, gas, electricity, and telephone utilities.[99]

The "family house" became an "old phrase" founded on the ideal of settled stability:

> A society seeking to defend an equilibrium which it has already lost, looks for means of tying down the nomadic elements of a society which is in need of a new and harmonious organization of its life....This so-called family house will never merit its title, but will drag society into the universal wasteland of garden cities. Universal, for the crisis is world-wide.[100]

As trade and industry developed, they located in cities, where manual methods were relinquished and precise industrial products emerged. Electricity eliminated the norm of night, turning cities into dazzling centers, seductively drawing into their confines the headlong rush of men exiting from the suffocating life of rural regions. The unity of the family was broken, traditional relationships ruptured, and violent contrasts flared up between different groups of workers. Nothing of the old yardstick remained to be used to evaluate the behavior of society wrenched away from its traditional forms. Unsuspected, a page of human history had turned.[101]

No one, then, can escape the fundamental fact that for the past one hundred years the machine has introduced a human existence that is neither pastoral nor warlike, but programmed for work.[102] In his naivety, Le Corbusier admits, he became interested in work, believing in the slogan "Man does not live by bread alone."[103] He saw everywhere intellectual hunger or boredom; all neglected the fact that after complete exhaustion from work, man must be restored by creative leisure and repose. Muscles, brain, and feeling are made to function; they are not for a vegetative life. Man is made to act in the light, the natural light, and his repose ought also to coincide with that of nature, with the hours when the sun has descended below the horizon.

For millennia, men came together to help, defend, or comfort each other, they lived in authentic harmony, maintaining intimacy with the human body and the mind. They did not disrupt with impunity the natural order of things–until cities began to molest men, starve them, falsify them, embitter them, crush them, even sterilize them.[104] The result: "Fever, the daily chaos, loss of freedom. The modern form of slavery."[105]

Work in modern times imposes a sedentary life, separating man from his natural environment, impoverishing and dangerously limiting his corporal activities, his capacity to adapt to his environment. A basically artificial environment is created, charged with nervous tension. Even the scientific organization of work is not without its negative reactions: mechanization of repeated gestures causes atrophy of motor thought.[106]

This rupture with nature caused the family to be broken. Physically and morally overwhelmed, the race became exhausted and depleted. No wonder that man became food for the cannons, that he abandoned himself to the violence of particular interests, that work became slavery, and that he struggled in vengeance against those who

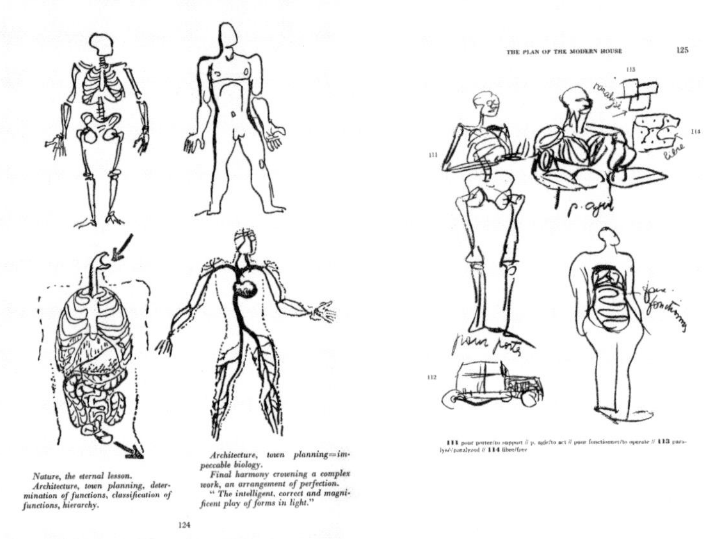

FIGURE 12.6: "Architecture, town planning = impeccable biology." Clockwise from top left are a skeleton, a body, a circulation system with heart, and a section of the digestive tract. FIGURE 12.7: The body and architecture are both constructed like an automobile, with a frame, a body, a motor, and organs of feeding and evacuation.

had conquered the machine.[107] No one realized that the limits of nature had been transcended, the envelope of the city separated from "cosmic forces" and the trinity "man-nature-cosmos" placed dangerously out of alignment.[108] Le Corbusier is simply stating, in secular terms, that man has fallen from a state of grace, the three pillars of his religion destroyed.

The effective cause of this brutal rupture in the framework of traditional life and of the destruction of human settlements living in harmony with geography, Le Corbusier argues, was speed. Nineteenth-century innovations led to the development of more rapid speeds, beyond the millennial pace of the foot of man, horse, donkey, or oxen: those of the automobile, the airplane, and the immeasurable rates of communication via the telegraph, telephone, and radio. As a consequence, goods and raw materials moved in a new circuit, and a new rhythm destroyed old habits and attitudes. Human measure was transgressed, nature forgotten or obliterated, everything for the last one hundred years.[109]

The aftermath is obvious: a congested jungle of places, a solar day of twenty-four hours that shows no tenderness toward the worker, forced to live artificially and dangerously out of touch with the natural conditions supportive of his life. The first hundred years of the machine era have completely disordered the pattern of human settlements, brought them to a point of crisis. They need to be organized into an authentic "built biology."[110] [FIGURES 12.6 AND 12.7]

Hence, Le Corbusier argues, "we go back directly to the very principles which constitute the human being and his environment. Man considered as a biological phenomenon–psycho-physiological value; the environment, its permanent essence, explored anew."[111] Life and the rules of biology are manifest in nature, where everything is involved in the cyclical processes of birth, growth, bloom, and decline. If architecture and planning lend themselves to an "impeccable biology," it is because they, too, make constant reference to "life" that animates each part of the organism and yet are constrained by a set of rules, a regime that maintains a healthy equilibrium.[112]

> Biology is a term eminently suited to architecture and city planning: biology, the qualities of living architecture, vivid city planning. Biology overseeing the plans and cross sections of the buildings, coordinating volumes, responding to functional needs making for flexible and harmonious circulation. Life develops outward from within and blossoms, open to light, offered to space.[113]

Le Corbusier utilizes the metaphor of the "tool" to explain "built biology." Tools perform specific functions efficiently; they are extensions of man's arms and legs; and the metaphor says the dwelling is a tool, the workshop a tool, the farm, and the route. Tools are also compared to organs of the body responsible for sustaining life, for making the body function efficiently. The stomach, the genitals, and the head are functional tools for nourishment, reproduction, and thought, respectively. Transposed to the level of the city, these organs become indispensable tools of planning in the form of architectural units. They are animated by principles of biology, provide for the cultivation of a sound and healthy body, offer an environment favorable to reproduction, and are joyful places for work and dwelling.[114] These *unités,* designed for "biological virtue," form a set of tools satisfying specific purposes.[115] Thus biology and the laws of nature are intertwined, and planning is charged with the purpose of balancing the binomial man-nature, bringing into a new, harmonious unity the trinity man-nature-cosmos.

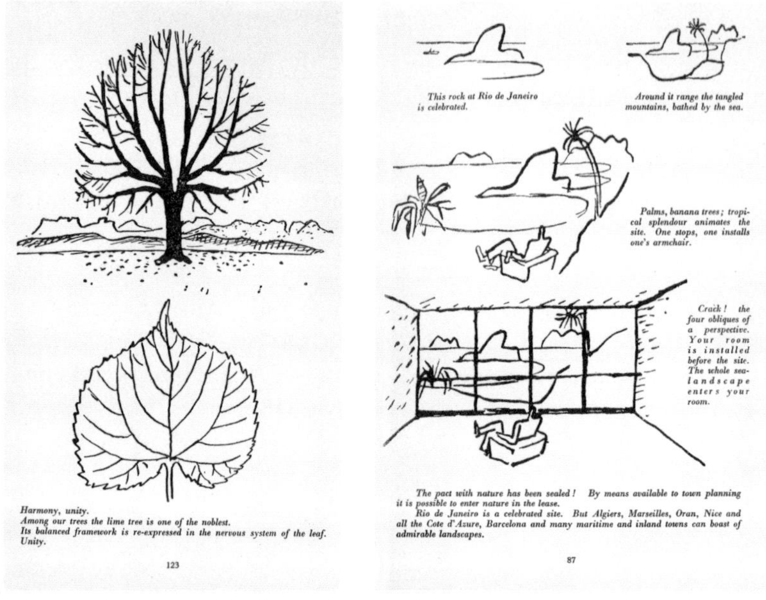

FIGURE 12.8: **Nature offers a lesson: unity in statue, purity of silhouette, graduated and diverse repetition of all the secondary elements.** FIGURE 12.9: **In modern architecture, a lease can be signed with nature, as in these sketches of Rio de Janeiro.**

Le Corbusier takes a rock in his hand, one recently retrieved by scientists from the depths of the sea. He draws a lesson from this millennium-old rock. Not the one that critics argue is linked by divine right to a house, being the stuff of its foundation and walls

> but, in much more eloquent terms, that these rocks which we find beautiful are a miracle of cellular composition, veritable microscopic limestone palaces cemented with silica. And that nature is organization in all things, from the infinitely large to the infinitely small.[116]

Nature lies in the expanse of a landscape, in the faraway horizon, beyond the balconies of the world that invite man to contemplate cosmic forces. [FIGURE 12.8]

In *The Home of Man,* Le Corbusier constantly repeats that "a pact can be made with nature. Nature can be entered into the lease"–if the planner is sensitized to these sites, and knows how to arrange them in a cinematographic manner.[117] [FIGURES 12.9 AND 12.10]

And the " essential joys " have entered the dwelling.
Nature is inscribed in the lease, a pact is signed with nature. Trees are present in the room of the dwelling.

97

FIGURE 12.10: Trees are companions of man; they enter into the lease as well.

In the heart of the business city where the skyscrapers raise their heads, the town still remains green. The trees are kings ; men, under their cover, live in the domain of proportion ; the link nature-man *is re-established.*

99

FIGURE 12.11: The Radiant City is a green city, and a pact is signed with nature.

> By means available to town planning it is possible to enter nature into the lease.[118]

> The town lies like a garment upon the body of the site. Architecture attains majesty and the citizens partake of the "essential joys."
> A pact is signed with nature.[119]

The tree holds a privileged position in the metaphorical system of Le Corbusier's elements of doctrine: a sensuous object connected with great depths of emotion, ranging from the lyrical to the rational, empathy to detachment. As we saw in Chapter 10, "the tree of life" is the ruling sign of *The Radiant City*, its master metaphor. [FIGURE 12.11]The tree, Le Corbusier writes, evokes pleasure, its foliage shimmering in the clear skies above the radiant city, its flowers and new buds returning to life each spring suggestive of the cycle of time where one era replaces another. As with other objects that move him, be they the desert, the stone, the sea, or the landscape, Le Corbusier gives the tree the power of expression–it speaks.

> Thick-set, bent, upright or slender, through the four seasons always speaking.
> A pact is signed between men and nature, between the houses and the gathered trees; nature is entered in the lease.[120]

Trees are friends of man, his constant companions throughout the year: in winter they offer an intelligent framework of trunks and branches, while in summer their heavy masses and volumes of leaves provide refreshing shade.[121] They come in an astounding number of forms: standing upright with houses, assembled into copses in woods. "Variety of species: play of forms and of colors, of denseness and heaviness, of lightness and of fineness."[122] Trees constitute one of the essential joys: screening the great blocks of dwellings from sight, creating a green dome out of the tangle of their branches and leaves until the entire town becomes "green"[123]:

> Trees, companions, friends of men. Bearers of shade and freshness inciting to poetry, sources of oxygen, retreats for the singing birds.
> The trees are entered in the lease.[124]

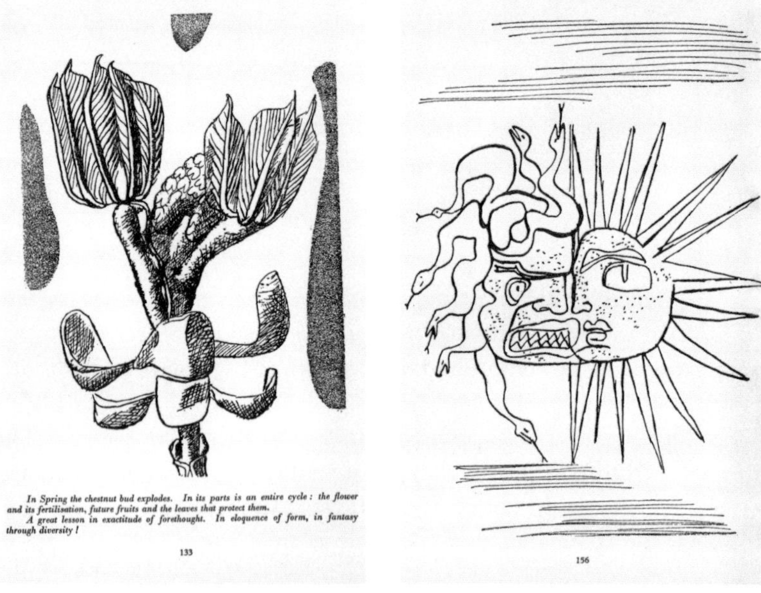

FIGURE 12.12: Nature teaches the architect many lessons: at the threshold of the house, it is installed as a vigilant guardian. FIGURE 12.13: This Janus-faced emblem combines the disaster of Medusa with the freedom of the sun. Faced with the issue of contemporary cities and the task of reconstruction, architect-planners must choose.

One more element must be considered in Le Corbusier's "built biology": the sun as dictator over climate, topography, and design. [FIGURES 12.12 AND 12.13] As we saw in Chapter 10, this symbol, too, is used as an ordering sign in *The Radiant City*: "It is the sun that governs us."[125] Though the tree is Le Corbusier's master metaphor, the sun is his metaphorical master. For in order to reestablish the home as the base of society, the sun must first be accepted as the master of all design and the measure of all human undertakings.[126] Referring to one of his foundational texts, Le Corbusier proclaims:

> Life is frightfully quotidian; it picks up its ritual at each rising of the sun. This ritual is made of simple actions, of standard acts of life. If the sun is in your home every day, it is also a little in your heart, perhaps more than you ever thought. *The Charter of Athens of CIAM* (1) proclaims:
>
> "The materials of urbanism are sun, space, greenery...." This manifests the will of CIAM to reintroduce, into the existence of human beings, the "conditions of nature" abandoned, lost, forgotten.[127] [FIGURE 12.14, p. 701]

The sun's course across the sky dictates the settlement patterns of the agricultural production unit, the layout of the linear industrial city, the extension of the radio-concentric city of exchange.[128] Our life, Le Corbusier maintains, is inseparable from this great solar cycle.

> It seems that antiquity understood this well: they adorned the facade of the Parthenon with such a wonderful allegory of day and of life. To the left, the chariot of the Sun rises above the waves; then occupying the empty center of the façade, the legend of the miraculous birth of Athena, whose spirit will guide the people–Pallas-Athena leaving all armed from the head of Jupiter. To the right, then, marking the end of the day, the chariot of the sun is buried in the sea.... Here, is evidence of the limits of the true life.[129]

And again: "The sun is the dictator; according to climates, according to seasons."[130] Hence the designer must understand how geography and topography, racial considerations and local customs, affect his plans.

> To take account of these factors is the chief concern of the architect, who is occupied with the creation of harmony. And if he attains harmony, there will be no risk of "uniformity throughout France"! Each site will demand its own adaptations, leading to variations on the standard theme, nuances which conduce–I agree a thousand times–to the joy of living.[131]

VI. THE FOUR ROUTES OF TRAVEL AND THE LAW OF HARMONY

Further development of his elements of doctrine enveloped Le Corbusier between 1935 and 1947. In *The Four Routes*, some of whose discursive methods have already been examined previously, he embarked on a new doctrinal discovery or extension of his architectural ideas to transportation: the "four routes," which he claimed would engender the country of tomorrow, reconstruct the face of the Earth into huge geomorphic structures, and reassemble the map of Europe, erasing political boundaries and the reasons for war.[132] But how did he arrive at this many-layered concept of the "route," and what do the layers all mean? How did the route itself become a lesson of life?

An important precursor to *The Four Routes* is an article on collective needs and the arts of space written for *L'Encyclopédie Française* in 1935. In it, Le Corbusier states that when asked to write the piece he quickly concluded that collective needs are those belonging to housing and transportation.[133] As for the arts of space, they too are affected by transportation, and he lists all the new installations encircling the earth, introducing new speeds, shrinking distances, condensing time: railroad, automobile, airplane, steamship, telegraph, telephone, and television. No one seemed to have planned these "events," indeed the world seemed out of breath merely trying to catch up to their speed and impact.

He first considers the railroad. It burst upon the scene more than one hundred years before, disrupting distances originally set by relays of horse and foot and deranging villages all along its route. Railroad stations became the new poles of attraction, eventually drawing people into cities and away from the countryside. Throughout the second half of the nineteenth century, marvelous structures were built to house locomotives, their workshops, and stations; they were prototypes of a new beauty and a new modern aesthetic appreciated only much later.

The railroad's technology was extended to steamships, and caused huge docks and warehouses to be built in order to store goods. Engineers pierced isthmuses for the Suez and Panama canals, encircling the earth with a continuous line of traffic. Like the trains, ships adapted themselves to the theories of aerodynamics, manifesting a new aesthetic and a new play of forms. Warships, steamships, or trawlers–all were essential contributors to an aesthetic of modern times. Since ships, ports, docks, canals, and locks have nothing in common with traditional uses, they escaped the limitations of formulas and routines. They have built a new architecture, utilizing new materials of cement and steel, applying unknown methods of construction. They offer a strong lesson: engineers occupied with serious needs and practical intentions have introduced the architecture of modern times.

They have also created the automobile and the airplane. The automobile has brought about a new civilization completely opposed to that of the railway. Its network of dispersion destroys the network of concentration brought by the railroad and brings life back to the rural areas, re-establishing contact with nature, setting up a harmonious relationship between town and country. France has a marvelous network of roads, a network able to absorb most of the new speeds the automobile presents. For the airplane, engineers have designed a splendid new architecture of hangars, and with the invention of vertical takeoffs and landings, soon airports will be located within the center of cities, saving travel time to airports on the edges of towns.

All of these new routes of circulation and tools of transport have greatly affected the layout of cities. Cities are congested with traffic, pedestrians have lost their freedom, and air pollution threatens them with death. Yet here as well, engineers have invented new means of transport: digging underground metros and linking these with huge metropolitan networks of buses, taxis, and automobiles.

The verdict is clear: engineers have worked for a century and delivered a decisive blow to a civilization conceived at the speed of one who walks. They have accomplished a revolution in transport that requires yet another revolution: that of urbanization.

Having dealt with transportation, Le Corbusier turns to what he calls the most important feature of cities: housing. Everything else, such as offices, factories, or places of entertainment, is only a corollary. Housing must be considered an extension of public services already delivered by engineers, such as sewers, gas, water, electricity, and the telephone. And it must overturn the narrowness of streets, the lack of open space, light, air, and greenery. Yet, though they have all necessary tools and techniques, engineers are not allowed to solve this problem and its corollaries. The elevator is the key to the solution of urban problems, as are the routes of circulation channeled by viaducts and highways. Engineers hold the key to modern times: their good sense, economy, and utility will bring about the birth of a new architecture, a new "unity."

Le Corbusier returns to these themes in *The Four Routes*, blaming the railroad for ushering in a first machine era full of chaos and turmoil, for which it must make amends.[134] The railway dirtied the city and disrupted the countryside. Yet after electricity is installed, the optimistic Le Corbusier foresees polished steel running on carpets of green, with flowers and trees planted along the rails right up to the central station.

Waxing poetical, he launches into the benefits of long-distance travel that the railroad still promises, complementing the qualities of the automobile:

> The highway, infinitely dispersed, is not designed for long-distance speed; it "irrigates" the countryside; distributes the living sap in the thinnest of trickles, and actually is still too slow, in spite of the motor-meteors, unable to keep in step with a modern

> time-table. The iron way, on the other hand, leaps over distance with a bland and steady speed. And nothing deters it: the darkness, the fog, the rain, excessive heat or cold; the guard's indigestion! Rigorously efficient, on a protected route it may run with closed eyes. It is cut out for the crossing of frontiers, to pierce the Continent's remotest points.[135]

Turning to the waterways, the third "route," Le Corbusier conjures up poetic dreams of ships on the oceans, of escapes into the unknown, of action and adventure.[136] "Why does it always move us? The whole sky above is reflected in the water. Pearly and azure shell. Feeling of space and the fluidity of matter."[137] Ships glide straight ahead into the open space, eliciting biological metaphors:

> The hull of these ships is well built: fruit of a sound hypothesis rooted in exactitude: water or air resistance: capacity of screw-propeller. A law is implicit in the working-plan for a hull, and if the harmony of that law were to fail, the ship would come to a standstill. As with the stance of the oak or the rose bush, the gazelle or the bull: there is a universal law of harmony.[138]

Le Corbusier recounts the thrill he received from mapping out on the counter of messieurs Cook and Company a long journey to start six months thence, fixing the itinerary of a trip to New York City, Buenos Aires, Chile, and Paris.

> And for this four months' journey you will carry a small booklet of detachable tickets in your waistcoat pocket.
>
> Poetry of efficiency, poetry to all who are attuned; a new ordering of time; a new use for that sense of order which the Greeks put into the grooves and entablatures of the Parthenon.[139]

The fourth "route" is air travel: rail, auto (land), ship, plane. All seek speed, and speed requires technical perfection, so the four routes show their best aspect to the world, with interesting consequences:

> And because of the emergence of a new spirit by which widened frontiers become the inevitable outcome of speed, because the very control once exercised (administration's *raison d'être*) was based on limitation, the administrator's world has crumbled.[140]

But more than the railway and the waterway, the highway and the automobile held the most fascination for Le Corbusier.[141] Once upon a time, the road was essential for the walking man and the man on horseback; it became a perfected system linking together points on the land. Then it was killed by the speed of the railway and its godlike power, carrying man long distances from home, linking one station with the next, widening the gap between city and land. Suddenly the automobile brings life back to the road.

> The country (the earth) opens up on all sides: she offers herself once more. There are no more derelict regions; no waste places. The earth is accessible as a whole [142]

The planner of roads must "create a pastoral symphony with the roads of France," laying out motor speedways at differing levels, allowing the natural curves of the landscape to be expressed.[143] Villages must be freed from the menace of the motorists and fiery accidents that pierce its heart. The road must glide around villages and pick up the main thread on the other side of town. Then a revival of communal life will return to main street, turning it once more into a public meeting-place, not a corridor of terror.[144]

At the end of the 1930s, as he goes on to relate in *The Four Routes*, Le Corbusier traveled from Paris to Nice over the Route Napoléon. He waxes poetic:

> This road is crystallization, a great poem of architectural landscape, although it was not built with that object in mind. The austerity of its design has brought about results which aesthetically move us. It does not merely offer works of art upon its surface; the road itself has become a work of art throughout its course. This road is the tangible expression of law and harmony, since every problem has been well solved.[145]

It took fifteen years to develop the whole system, with its careful treatment of bends and stupendous views allowing the route itself to control the car, easing it into endless twists and turns of the way.

> For the road has drawn the car into its bosom; the run is faultless, miraculous, over the stretched cord. Well played, engineers and labourers! These new craftsmen of the road caress with hand

> and tool curves which once upon a time another type of craftsmen (in cherrywood, walnut and oak) carved to make beautiful arm-chairs.[146]

> Here one finds certitude and comfort: the conviction that whatever germinates in the mind can and will become a reality: that nothing is too gigantic for the powers of man, nothing need remain merely visionary.... That harmony which we so passionately seek within the complex problem of town-planning, an ordered synthesis, unifying diversity, is already to be found on the road.[147]

Yet as this magnificent route enters the city it turns into streets. "Circulation is hell; torture of slowness, fines, accidents, waste of nervous energy, etc."[148] Thus, the "whole system of highways cries out for revolution."[149]

Le Corbusier, always enamored by the progress of design that automobiles achieved throughout the twentieth century, took them as his icon of power, speed. The automobile was a star performer in his toolbox for the temps nouveaux as it had been for the Esprit Nouveau. With Pierre Jeanneret, he designed a small automobile in 1928 called the "Voiture Maximum," selecting this name because the motor was located behind, not in front of, the driver in order to assure maximum comfort and visibility.[150] The passengers, Le Corbusier believed,

> ought to be in a free space disengaged as a belvedere (veranda or bow-window) that is in front of the automobile. Passengers ought not to be annoyed by the noise, smells (of gasoline and oil), heat and the direct vibrations of the motor, therefore: motor in the back.[151]

The car was given an aerodynamic form, with three seats in front and one behind, with the ability to transform the car into a couchette for the night. The two designers did not immediately propose their "revolutionary" scheme to any manufacturers. In 1936, however, when the Société des Ingénieurs de l'Automobile (Society of Automobile Engineers) held a competition for the design of a small automobile, Le Corbusier authorized the society to publicize their scheme.[152] At the same time he wrote to Fiat in Turin asking if they would like to collaborate on its production; their answer was no.[153]

VII. THE VIEW FROM ABOVE

After the war, the full force of Le Corbusier's enthusiasm turned to the newest of the "four routes," air travel. The airplane more than the automobile achieved pride of place as a major force-term in his doctrinal system. It was the newest "route," the form of modern transport most radically unlike any older form; its machinery was beautiful and improving with astonishing rapidity; it was by far the fastest and most obstacle-overleaping mode of transport; it was imbued with a mythology of heroic aviation; and above all (literally), it offered utterly new perspectives on the geometries of the Earth. It was mechanical, poetic, practical, mind-expanding, transformative. Thus, this last incarnation of Le Corbusier's elements of doctrine deserves to be fully examined, with all of its corollaries and extended meanings.

In 1947, in an article entitled "Urbanism and Aeronautics," he proclaimed that he was a great traveler by air, and that over the years he had observed the world as it was revealed by the bird's-eye view. The airplane, an astonishing tool, had greatly affected his ideas and thoughts.

Thirty years earlier, before World War I, he commented, one vomited in an airplane during a lengthy flight, and after landing vowed never to go up in the air again. The cabin was confining, without fresh air, the smell of oil and gas overwhelming. Nevertheless, though limited, the small airplane was a stimulating tool. Then war opened the door on an infinite number of experiments, and airplanes began to traverse the oceans. By 1947, airplanes such as the Constellation, carrying fifty passengers, had become places of rest, without noise or vibrations, with fresh air neither too cold nor too hot. Air France offered its passengers a restful, calm flight; you arrived at an impeccable station without any dust on your clothes and with the pleat of your pants intact. The mechanical adventure of Icarus with its impeccable rules challenges men to put other things and men in harmony, to render ordinary events amiable and natural.

Le Corbusier believes aviation opens the door on progress and on new spaces of inspiration and poetry. The airplane has placed the temps nouveaux at the sunrise of its architectural manifestation, of its architecture of constructors. Faced with this adventure of the air, the architecture of architects with diplomas, the schools that cultivate tradition and the application of established rules, will perish, and modern architecture will build new airports in concrete and steel. After traveling by air and witnessing the many geographical wonders of the earth, from the sea of clouds to icebergs in the ocean, from estuaries of immense oceans to the meander of rivers and more, one no longer has a taste for the columns and entablatures of a static architecture. The airplane has killed the third dimension of height. In order to trace out the places of its arrival on the world map, it is necessary to resort to an architecture of two dimensions: humble surfaces, wide expanses, and long, horizontal lines.

In his lectures in Bogotá that year (1947), Le Corbusier created two expressive neologisms: *horizontal aeronautiques* and *vertical aeronautiques*. Horizontal refers to the steamships of the air, which travel at an altitude of six thousand meters above oceans, savannahs, or the Andes range. The vertical signifies helicopters taking off and landing from places lacking airports, or from very small landing strips. Thus, in Bogotá, the airplane has opened all the doors on invention, adaptation, and imagination. It has placed the entire country in a state of fermentation. Since its land routes are mediocre, its water routes without importance, and its railroads nonexistent, only the air route is able to penetrate the country. It has tied Colombia to other Latin American countries, to the United States, to Paris, to Europe; it has enabled men of quality to establish contacts everywhere, and elite men of the professions to arrive in Colombia to see, to propose, and to consider.

Something extraordinary is taking place: Colombia's major port will no longer be on the sea, but in Bogotá, in its interior. In order to plan this new future of Bogotá, it is necessary to define the reasons for its existence, to project the relations it will have with the other parts of the country and the world that aviation now lays at its door. Thus urbanism once again affirms its reason for being: to describe and order territories, to manage the occupation of the land, and to place them in contact.[154]

The airplane and helicopter will complement the other three routes, which will leave between them vast zones of countryside, great natural reserves of agricultural land renewed and refreshed as radiant farms. The fourth route will thus aid in the revitalization of the countryside. It is only a problem of the displacement of people, of how to transport them into these new arrangements on the land.

A new geography of distances appears, no longer dominated by the kilometer but by flight time. Thus Paris–New York by plane will supplant Paris–Marseilles by railroad. New York–Paris and Moscow–Paris will become two extremities of a single world city, a single administrative surface.

He summarizes: the automobile has the advantage of going from door to door; it can transport man from his home directly to his destination. The railroad and the boat picked up the relay from railroad stations and ports, but introduced a rupture. The enemy of travel is waiting–anything that breaks the rhythm of motion. Before World War I, there were no police, customs duties, no money exchanges, nothing to interrupt the flow of travel. Hopefully the globe will once again ignore all these artificial boundaries and install a new global order, overcoming the friction of space and time.

Such is the outline of the new world order that Le Corbusier fantasizes of. But how did the airplane achieve such importance in his discourse? How did it engender a new map of Europe and arrange huge geomorphic structures on the land? To fill in the details, we return to the 1930s, when his love of travel by plane first became apparent.

AVIATION AND EQUIPMENT

In January of 1935, a London publishing house, The Studio, Ltd., sent Le Corbusier a letter inquiring whether he would be interested in collaborating on a series of books to be entitled *The New Vision*. The promoters explained that each book would be devoted to a unique event in industrial design, with specific attention paid to the designers, their aims, and the potential their designs held for social and human development. They would begin the series with a volume on the airplane. Le Corbusier was invited to write an introductory essay and captions to images they had already collected, and to offer a few suggestions for additional illustrations.[155] [FIGURES 12.15– 12.18]

He accepted the invitation. His reply, however, transformed the project. Instead of the word "airplane," he said, he preferred "aviation," by which he meant all the prodigious phenomena that were opening vast new horizons in space and influencing the future of "equipment" in the broadest sense of the word.[156] Already in *Précisions* (1930) he had written, "I replace the word 'urbanism' by the term 'equipment.' I have already replaced the term 'furniture' by that of 'equipment.'"[157] To his bag of equipment, Le Corbusier now adds "aviation," a tool of modern communication forging new modes of exchange and new links between nations.[158]

The material subsequently sent by the publishing house to Le Corbusier met with a lukewarm reception: he favored more lively documentation, such as of the views seen from an airplane as it flew over cities, vast open terrain, the sea, and the forests. And he wanted

FIGURE 12.15: Le Corbusier was invited in 1935 to provide captions for photographs provided primarily by The Studio, Ltd., publishing house for the book *Aircraft*.

1. CLEARNESS OF FUNCTION. THE WORLD'S MISERIES ARE DUE TO THE FACT THAT FUNCTIONS ARE NOWHERE DEFINED OR RESPECTED.

A STOCK OF OLD FUNCTIONS, ANACHRONISTIC OR CONFUSED—RESIDUE OF A CIVILISATION IN THE THROES—CLOGS THE WHEELS AND SLOWS DOWN THE JOYOUS AND PRODUCTIVE IMPULSE OF THE NEW MACHINE-CIVILISATION.

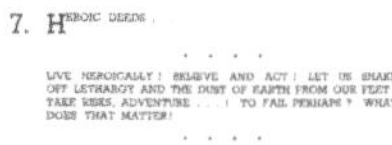

7. HEROIC DEEDS.

. . . .

LIVE HEROICALLY! BELIEVE AND ACT! LET US SHAKE OFF LETHARGY AND THE DUST OF EARTH FROM OUR FEET! TAKE RISKS, ADVENTURE . . . ! TO FAIL PERHAPS? WHAT DOES THAT MATTER!

. . . .

IT IS A VICTORY TO HAVE STARTED!

9. THE BIRD'S EYE VIEW.

. . . .

THE EYE NOW SEES IN SUBSTANCE WHAT THE MIND FORMERLY COULD ONLY SUBJECTIVELY CONCEIVE.

. . . .

IT IS A NEW FUNCTION ADDED TO OUR SENSES.
IT IS A NEW STANDARD OF MEASUREMENT.
IT IS A NEW BASIS OF SENSATION.

. . . .

MAN WILL MAKE USE OF IT TO CONCEIVE NEW AIMS.
CITIES WILL ARISE OUT OF THEIR ASHES.

FIGURE 12.16: The airplane flies straight from one point to another. This Fairey Long-Range Monoplane attained a record for straight-line flight without refueling in February 1933. FIGURE 12.17: The pleasures of daring, of breaking through present-day stupidities, are illustrated by this American glider in flight. FIGURE 12.18: The airplane indicts the cities; they are old, frightening, diseased, finished.

more narrative treatment of the lives of aviators, their psychological and social attitudes, and analysis of the great aerial routes being drawn between Europe and America, Africa and Asia. The publishing house was unable to fulfill Le Corbusier's expectations; they reminded him that their focus was limited to the *airplane*, and that they expected to receive all his material by May.[159]

What did Le Corbusier mean by "aviation" and the "epic of the air," a phrase he used in the preface of the subsequent book *Aircraft* (1935)? How did aviation, according to him, affect the perception of space and the process of reading the terrain as a two-dimensional map or a plan? And what did aviation have to do with "equipment"?

The rapid growth of aviation during the interwar period was mercurial, dramatically reshaping perception of the earth and of space: this fired Le Corbusier's enthusiasm. There were daring flights of aviators challenging oceans and deserts, the heights of Everest, the length of Africa, the uncharted terrain of the North and South Poles. Aerial photography recorded in precise detail the realistic shapes of landmasses, coastlines, seas, deserts, and mountains, perfecting the process of map-making and enriching the documentary archive of the world. But the airplane not only internationalized cartography; it was also a tool for exploring and controlling the colonies.

Aviation continually shrunk the effective size of the globe after the initial KLM flight between Amsterdam and Jakarta in 1924. It took fifty-five days to navigate the nine thousand miles; within five years the time had been reduced to a mere twelve days. A world map criss-crossed with national air routes came into being. In the 1930s, civil airlines began to offer passenger and mail service between London and the Middle East, then to India and Australia and between Toulouse and Dakar, and shorter flights between Paris and Brussels.[160]

Although the air was physically undivided, each nationality was intent on assuring that the aerial routes served their own national interests. To fly across Europe it was therefore necessary to change planes several times and zigzag through trunk routes to arrive at a destination. There was no direct aerial route between England and Egypt, for example, because various European nations forbade English planes to fly over their territory; passengers bound for the Middle East had to take a train to Geneva and then a hydrofoil to Alexandria.

By 1937, six different intercontinental routes crossed the Mediterranean. Germany, Belgium, France, England, Italy, and Holland all drew their own national lines across the sea–a mirror reflection of the anarchic state of international relations. Added to this global network was a comparatively invisible development: two thirds of all air routes until the late 1930s were developed in response to local needs for commercial exchange in remote areas such as Siberia, Canada, Central Africa, Brazil, Peru, Colombia, and Argentina.[161]

"Aviation," then, could plausibly be seen by Le Corbusier as destroying an old order while simultaneously giving birth to a temps nouveaux. Perhaps this is why he repeats a possibly apocryphal story in *Aircraft* and again in *The Four Routes* about an "aerial locomotion show" he says was organized in Juvisy by the Lathams and Voisins around 1910.[162] Le Corbusier left Paris at noon to travel by train the fifteen kilometers to Juvisy, but so did three hundred thousand other enthusiasts. The railroad company was not prepared for such a crush, and so they arrived in the pitch dark long after the air show had finished. Le Corbusier remembered they had amused themselves on the delayed journey by pelting returning trains with stones and smashing everything in sight, the furniture, the signal boxes, and even the station. Le Corbusier wondered:

> Was it a symbolic assault by the neophytes of the air against that black tyranny of the railroad? Or was it a demonstration by the forces of optimism who felt that in our country laziness was systematically blocking the way? Or was it anarchy?[163]

Le Corbusier's *Esprit Nouveau* articles in the 1920s on "eyes which do not see" (see Chapter 7) were intended to increase awareness about the prodigious new world that modern technology and science had created, as evidenced in the marvels of the steamship, the automobile, and the airplane; in the 1930s it was above all the "bird's-eye view" from the airplane and the third dimension it added to architecture that he wanted to explore.

The aerial view touched Le Corbusier profoundly, for he was a man who "lived to see." The view from the airplane enabled him to develop a new awareness of how the entire landscape in its natural setting was configured, of the negative effect man had on the land, and of the dependency of the Earth on its fragile biosphere. This reading engendered a new mode of thought about natural laws, visualizing these as organic chains of events. The sun became a "dictator" of temporal pattern, the meander of rivers a law reflected in cultural experience. Flying through the air, immersed in clouds, buffeted by the wind and noise, was an "ecstatic" experience for Le Corbusier. He said in *Précisions* that from "the plane I saw sights that one may call cosmic. What an invitation to meditation, what a reminder of the fundamental truths of our earth!"[164] What a call to believe in the temps nouveaux!

Le Corbusier first gained the synoptic aerial view when he flew to Moscow in 1928. It was reinforced by flights over South America the following year and over the desert of North Africa in 1933. The living tableau of the land seen from on high completely transformed his visual imagery, concepts of geography, and procedures of map-making. He witnessed not only the vast open terrain of space, but the mosaic pattern of land ownership and the curvature of the earth's horizon. The multidirectional flow of rivers, the freedom of the airplane's mobility through space, and the great speed of air travel transfigured his thought. Sitting in an airplane with sketchbook in hand, he forged a hybrid system of analysis, varying his angles of observation: the vast expanse of the landscape was read as a new planned text, its contours and masses reduced to so many lines traced out on a grid, while flows and meanders coursed through the space. Lyrical intuition fused with his bent for Cartesian rationality.

Le Corbusier said in *Aircraft* that while sketching Rio de Janeiro during a flight in 1929, "the conception of a vast programme of organic town-planning came like a revelation."[165] This double vision of reason and poetry, analysis and revelation, for the next two decades not only modeled his urban images but sustained their geopolitical after-image as well. The adventure of aviation seemed to Le Corbusier, as to so many other technologically oriented idealists before World War II (e.g., H. G. Wells), to destroy old concepts of spheres of influence and the balance of powers, and to conjure up instead a new world order and transnational organizations for peace. He was aware of Antoine de Saint-Exupéry, the writer of aviation novels, who proclaimed: "The aeroplane is not an end in itself: it is a tool, like a plough."[166] This tool enabled Le Corbusier to conceive of great geomorphic structures stretching across space, rendering obsolete the existing manner of partitioning land, cities, and regional and national boundaries. In the temps nouveaux, the era of the second industrial revolution, the concentric city of the first industrial age would be rejected in favor of new geopolitical alignments drawing the north and the south together.

HEROICS AND MYTH-MAKING

Le Corbusier was spiritually aroused by the feats of the aviator who was sent out to challenge uncharted realms, to fly over the Poles, oceans, deserts, and the highest mountain ranges. During the 1920s and 1930s, the figure of the aviator was laden with dreams of grandeur, soaring beyond mundane reality into the heavens beyond. And returning to earth, he was expected to be an exemplar and leader of men. Aviation, it was believed, provided new standards for worldly reform and spiritual regeneration: it enriched the world by the challenges it posed, the audacious bravery it required, and the elite leadership it demanded.[167] Nor was it forgotten that the aviator's feats relied on a network of ground support, including hangars, fuel stops, weather stations, and radio signals and flags.[168]

For Le Corbusier, "equipment" stood not only for the machinery of flight but for all of the new organizational methods that aviation engendered, especially the collapsing of space. He had already written in the pages of *The Radiant City* (1935) about a visit to the Amsterdam airport, where he thrilled over the vast mural map of Europe, Africa, and Asia marked with red and blue lines representing eight different routes, and how he shook with excitement as he realized that airplanes were at that very moment flying along those lines but at different times of the day! To arrive at such collective action, personal participation must be felt every step of the way, and the materiality of labor enlightened by a spirit of cooperation: all of this informed Le Corbusier's extended meaning of "equipment."[169]

During the 1930s, the aviator became increasingly free of his former reliance on the ground. His equipment enabled him to stay on course without having to recognize landmarks. Now he could fly through the day and the night, through sun or fog, keeping to a rigorous schedule and arriving on time. Le Corbusier exclaimed: "The flight of the airplane no longer pays attention to the millennial facts of the route on the lands; it passes above, across, no longer concerned with gradients determined by slopes or distances."[170]

The Americas, Europe, Asia, and Africa were no longer continents but direct trajectories of communication flowing between dots on the map. Already the Congress of French Aviation in 1945 had begun a planning initiative on this new basis in order to guide urbanists in their new task of postwar reconstruction. Le Corbusier offered the congress the schemes outlined in his *Trois Établissements* (1945), for certainly the airplane–or so he believed–would bring life or death to the radio-centric

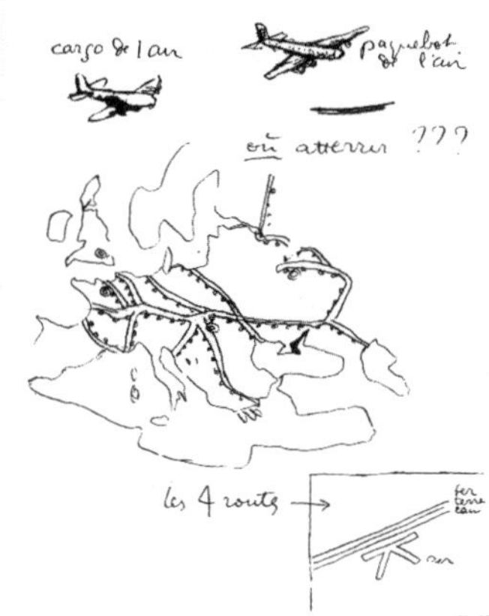

FIGURE 12.19: The fourth route—the route of the air—joins the existing pattern established by the three former routes of land, water, and rail.

city; some will be qualified while others will be disqualified, and in their place new linear industrial cities and radiant farms would develop instead.[171] [FIGURE 12.19]

As various pilots and astronauts have testified, the view from high altitudes can engender sensations of ultramundane transcendence: it seems to some such travelers (especially the earlier users of such technologies) that just being there, so far above the world, must be significant, transfigurative. It certainly seemed to Le Corbusier that the airplane changed everything. It made every place accessible, that no part of nature—not mountains, oceans, icecaps, or deserts—stood in its way.[172] It surveyed every nook and cranny, throwing a net of surveillance over the world. The aerial view appeared to make national boundaries obsolete: it was easier to understand the natural formation of regions, the unity of river valleys, the expanse of farmlands, and location of mineral deposits.

Aviation, with its stress on technical mastery, elite leadership, and organizational discipline offered a whole array of transformative geopolitical consequences. It seemed to prove that nature could be transcended, that a revolution of perception and visual interpretation was at hand, that a new world order was imminent.

But did the aviator's humility before nature's forces and his awareness of the cultural diversity of the world hold out the ideal of a new peaceful community of nations, as Saint-Exupéry and Le Corbusier hoped? There are no unmediated maps or views. In the 1930s, the neo-syndicalists projected their ideas of a new world order onto the map of France, Europe, and the colonial empire, forcing incompatibles together and overriding established boundaries–in their minds. It was not innocent or objective to write of the "white world of the west," of regionalism, ethnography, and race, of north-south axes: each statement drew boundaries and distinctions at the very moment when aviation was supposedly eradicating these markers of space. This is not surprising: as a rule, ideology has always managed to manufacture space faster than technology can eat it up. Neither the airplane, spacecraft, or the internet, despite early enthusiasm, has created or ever will create a postnational utopia. Yet it is precisely this otherworldly order that the neo-syndicalists and Le Corbusier's doctrine proclaim.

The neo-syndicalists sought to replace the political and economic chaos of the 1930s with a pictorial atlas of space arranged according to the transcendent schema achieved in an aerial view. As Le Corbusier wrote in 1937 in describing the Pavillon des temps nouveaux:

> The world is coming back to life! such is the phrase which appeared before the eyes of the visitor to the Pavilion at his exit from the demonstration of urbanism of the temps nouveaux. It is necessary to know how to extend contingent miseries, to be transported above local events, in order to acquire this special view–that bird's-eye view–from on high, *which grasps the DIRECTION of masses in movement.*[173]

THE AIRPLANE ACCUSES!

Every technological invention opens up new routes of discovery; such was also the case with the airplane. The polar opposite of the microscope (for the telescope does not show us our own world), the aerial view revealed spaces so vast they could not be comprehended in a single glance. From the air a new geometry was visible. One's image of the world was rearranged into new representational forms: boundaries of fields slashed zigzags across terrain, linear traces of canals, roads, and railways left sharp, clear marks, elevated plateaus and depressions stood out in relief, windswept deserts and ice fields appeared as serrated expanses, while mountains turned into heavily creased folds. From on high, Le Corbusier could see the evidence of our fall, the curse of the first, bungled machine age, writ plain in urban structure:

> Take an airplane. Fly over our nineteenth century cities, over those immense sites encrusted with row after row of houses without hearts, furrowed with their canyons of soulless streets.

> Look down and judge for yourself. I say that these things are the signs of a tragic denaturing of human labor. They are the proof that men, subjugated by the titanic growth of the machine, have succumbed to the machinations of a world powered by money. The architects of the past hundred years did not build for men: they built for money.[174]

Flying across the wild stretches of South America, on his way back to Buenos Aires in 1929, Le Corbusier observed settlers' farms, then hamlets, villages, small towns, and finally, the capital city.[175] All South American towns since the conquest, he saw, had developed according to a living unit, the *cuadra* (square) with sides 110 meters in length. It was a simple geometrical unit determined by the length of a man's stride and the distance he was able to see: well and good, so far as it went. But the aerial view revealed an appalling disease on the land: at the end of the journey appeared the immense scab of Buenos Aires, a skin disease spreading beyond all proportion. Where nature would have provided the requisite structure of viscera, lungs, bones, and limbs, human heedlessness had allowed an organic form of life to exceed the dimensions of its cellular structure.[176] The aerial view is above all, for Le Corbusier, revelatory: it reveals cause and effect to the eye at landscape scale. And what it reveals to him, more clearly than ever, is that very narrative of fallen man caused by industrialism of the first machine era that he has been preaching even before being transported to the heights. It offers proof!

In *Aircraft* (1935), sections of which he repeats word for word in *The Four Routes* (1941), he continues the theme: the airplane accuses! We can no longer escape its truth and ignore the horror of a city's physical dirt or the failure of moral integrity expressed by those responsible for such disorder. The airplane flight takes Le Corbusier to the mountaintop, to the wilderness, to the place apart and above from which both the moral and physical are laid out, their imperfections exposed: he descends to speak of his experience in a recognizably prophetic register, crying woe to the doomed city:

> The plane has enlightened us. The plane has seen. The plane had indicted.[177]

> And the plane observes, works quickly, sees quickly, never tires. In addition, the plane plunges deep into realism. Its implacable eye penetrates the misery of cities and brings back the

> photographic record for those who lack the courage to go and see for themselves–from the air.... The plane inaugurates in a superlative degree a new stage of consciousness, a modern conscience. The cities must be rescued from disaster; their rotten sections must be destroyed; new cities must be built.[178]

Returning to this theme in the 1940s, Le Corbusier claimed the aerial view enabled man to see what hitherto had only been an imaginary view. "The whole spirit of our plans will be illuminated and amplified by this new point of view."[179] The bird's-eye view has determined that plans "are no longer simply a game of the mind; henceforth they see themselves. And the mind proclaims their order and their grandeur."[180] The bird's-eye view, he continued, is an innovation of import, it enables the mind to see clearly and efficiently; it allows for the development of the third dimension of height. A great part of the confusion that exists in the reading of plans has come about because the eyes of man are only one meter and sixty centimeters above the ground. The aerial view resolves this confusion by allowing a different reflexive reading without ambiguity.[181]

THE CARTOGRAPHIC VIEW

Maps colonize space by extracting from the ground specific geographical facts while silencing others; they are surfaces on which selected facts are exhibited. As Michel de Certeau put it, they "form tables of *legible* results."[182] Yet maps also enable a spatial imaginary to play over their surface: one can trace routes to follow, dream about places to inhabit, or project specific visions onto the lay of the land.

During his trip to South America in 1929, Le Corbusier pored over the maps of Argentina, blending together regional facts with exotic adventures, a form of eroto-topography.

> I.... measured the lines of the rivers, the great stretches of plains and plateaus, the barrier of the Andes, studied the network of railroads that already irrigate your country. I knew for the first time that Argentina is immense, that it begins at the latitude of the Chaco whose Indians are naked and that it goes all the way to the icebergs, to the Tierra del Fuego.... I flew far over your country by plane. I saw that it was empty, that there was enormous room for a fantastic expansion.[183]

Returning to Buenos Aires, this time on a hydroplane, he saw the city from five hundred meters up. It was a bristling tumultuous city, a "sign of a prodigious vitality, but also of improvisation, of incoherence."[184] Over this painful sight his cartographic eye superimposed an ordered arrangement of glass skyscraper prisms on an enormous platform of reinforced concrete jutting out into the sea: the simple horizontal line where the pampas met the ocean would be punctuated with crystalline cubes lit up at night.[185]

Next he flew over Rio de Janeiro. When one has gone up in an airplane, he says, has glided like a bird over the bays and peaks of a city and torn away in a single glance all the secrets it hides from the man on the ground, then one understands the lay of the land. From a plane, everything becomes clear to the cartographic eye, and "you have felt ideas being born, you have entered into the body and the heart of the city, you have understood part of its destiny."[186] Ideas strike with revelatory breadth and force:

> When one has taken a long flight over the city like a bird gliding, ideas attack you.
>
> Ideas attack you when, for three months, one has been under pressure, when one has descended into the depths of architecture and planning, when one is on the way to deductions, when everywhere one envisages, one feels, one sees consequences.
>
> In the plane I had my sketchbook as everything became clear to me I sketched. I expressed the ideas of modern planning.[187]

In a sketch of Rio de Janeiro, Le Corbusier drew an immense expressway joining at mid-height the fingers of the promontories and connecting the city with the high hinterlands of its plateau.[188] This viaduct architecture had a highway on top and housing below, each apartment equipped with hanging gardens and window walls raised high above the ground. Out at sea, he took up his sketchbook again and drew the mountainous peaks and the great faultless horizontal beltline he had conceived suspended above the city.

> The whole site began to speak, on the water, on earth, in the air; it spoke of architecture. This discourse was a poem of human geometry and of immense natural fantasy. The eye saw

> something, two things: nature and the product of the work of men. The city announced itself by the only line that can harmonize with the vehement caprice of the mountains; the horizontal.[189]

Next he took a flight over São Paulo, where he commanded the pilot to fly low over the center of the city so he could see its outline, where rises occurred in the land, and where the business district pushed upwards toward the sky, an indisputable sign of disease. By automobile, he measured the time it took to travel from point to point over valleys, contours, and slopes. He grew, he says, to understand the general topography of hills and hollows and the inadequate network of streets that tried to go straight in a hilly terrain. And then, suddenly, he was seized with the solution: he drew a horizontal line forty-five kilometers in length from hill to hill, and then a second line at right angles. "These straight horizontals are the expressways coming into the city, in reality crossing it. You won't fly over the city with your autos, but you will drive over it. Do not build expensive arches to hold up your viaducts, but carry your viaducts on reinforced concrete structures that will make up offices in the center of the city and homes in the outskirts."[190] He called these horizontal expressways "earthscrapers," and wondered "is there anything more elegant than the pure line of a viaduct in an undulating site and more varied than its substructures sinking into the valleys to meet the ground?"[191]

From hindsight, Le Corbusier would write in 1935 of the grand lyrical exercises he planned for the cities of South America, the airplane flights over the pampas, savannahs, and virgin forests, along the great rivers where future cities of colonization began to appear, farms of the pioneers, towns on the bend of rivers, the immense and disarticulated cities on the delta. And suddenly he achieved an epiphany, realizing the Radiant City was born at that moment, a modern doctrine of urbanization replacing the unspeakable misery of existing conditions.[192] [FIGURE 12.20]

By the early 1940s, Le Corbusier's voice had become more commanding. He believed, under the authoritarian rule of the Vichy government, the hour had struck to put his plans into action. "The plane flying over forest, rivers, mountains, and seas reveals some fundamental laws, simple principles which prevail in nature, and as a result we may hope that dignity, strength, and a proper sense of values will become apparent in the aspect of our new cities."[193]

224

The Prefect of São Paulo had told me: "We're lost; we don't know how to remedy the chaos of our city."
Answer: here is order.

This American trip, with its stopovers and its cities, and that emptiness of mind which the inertia of an ocean voyage creates, was an astonishing stimulant, a detector. Clear and clean-cut, ideas burst out "above the roaring crowd," above the day-to-day dilemmas; energy-ideas, nourished and fertilized by an already lengthy meditation on the state of architecture and city planning.

In Buenos Aires: "Your city is choking? Give it its vital axes, of deep and distant origin, in the hinterlands and the provinces. You have no land left at the critical point of concentration? Then take the sea, build on the water: there's nothing to it, it's easy."

In Montevideo: "Your topography is against you? Your old town slides down steeply to the port? There's no room? Then why not build artificial sites? And that labyrinthine, treacherous slope of streets not made for automobiles – get rid of it, lay out your great horizontal boulevard at the summit of your artificial sites."

In São Paulo: "You're completely tangled up in your valleys and your hills. You can't get across the city any more! Drain off your traffic! But do it from above, from up high, in the air above your city, where you're free!"

Montevideo:
It would be so simple!
valorization,
efficiency,
architectural splendor!

222

FIGURE 12.20: A new synthesis is born from the aerial view: linear industrial cities, revitalized farmlands, and compact, concentric cities.

The airplane is the mark of a new age; it is the peak of a huge pyramid of mechanical progress that rushes forward into a new era on widespread wings.

> The aeroplane, in the sky, carries our hearts above the humdrum
> of daily living. The plane has given us a "bird's-eye" view.
> And when the eye sees clearly, the mind makes wise decisions.[194]

THE LAW OF THE MEANDER

One of the "fundamental truths" Le Corbusier said were revealed to him by the aerial view was the law of the meander, whose theory he developed in *The Radiant City*. This was not a physical law governing meander formation, of course, but a metaphorical law relating stagnation to progress. Flying over the great rivers of South America–the Parana, the Uruguay, and the Paraguay–it struck him that they followed the law of physics (as he put it) on the steepest gradient, but when they flowed across flat terrain, erosion caused a meander to appear. Something had disturbed the law of nature (i.e., the simple, visually obvious law that water flows directly downhill). He found there were parallels between this effect and the flow of creative thinking and human invention. "Following the outlines of a meander from above, I understood the difficulties met in human affairs, the dead ends in which they get stuck and the apparently miraculous solutions that suddenly resolve apparently inextricable situations."[195]

The law of the meander quickly became for Le Corbusier a personal symbol under which he introduced his propositions for reforms in architecture and urbanism. As the worldwide economic crisis of the 1930s deepened, and as Le Corbusier met constant opposition to his urbanism, he expanded on his law of the meander. He posited that water is a fluid, and thus mobile; it flows according to the law of gravity. From then on it is a matter of simple arithmetic: rivulets flow into each other and width is added to form a stream, streams flow into each other, and width is added to form a great river. The river flows toward the sea and reaches a delta, where its powerful flow is subdivided before flowing gently through the estuary and out into the open sea.[196] From the airplane, the eye can observe that where the flow of the water meets an obstacle, an abnormality forces the river to zigzag, a meander is formed. So, too, the grand works of urbanism are forced to zigzag when they meet the rock of opposition.

All the many city plans that Le Corbusier designed during the 1930s and 1940s came to naught, blocked by forces standing in the stream of their energetic flow. In 1945, he returned to the law of the meander, but with a new twist, for now he believed the aerial route had definitively surpassed all terrestrial routes, and that this had major consequences. He explained:

> The earth is born without political frontiers: it is round and continuous; the human species has multiplied across the four quarters of the world, following laws of climate, of water-shed, of winds.... Roads follow the shortest routes compatible with the slopes in their path. Obstacles assert their pressure on this tracery: rivers, mountains, and the routes establish themselves throughout millenniums.... The three routes embodied in the earth's surface, the roadway, the waterway, the iron way, all have their destinies fixed by the nature of the terrain: Geography. The new route of the air goes straight, cuts straight, goes everywhere, above all indifferent to geographical obstacles.[197]

As planning for reconstruction took on greater urgency during World War II, Le Corbusier decided "to play the game of the day" and "to scout out the pathways to tomorrow."[198]

> If a serious attempt to ponder the problems of aviation had been made fifty, or even just twenty or thirty years ago, couldn't it have guided a whole swarm of decisions which had, instead to be taken amidst the perilous improvisation of sentiment or interest or panic?[199]

But now the hour was striking, the time had arrived when the world must absolutely look ahead, when the cascade of elements accumulated in the meander's flow must eventually break free and flow forward in a straight line! Le Corbusier drew a wedge of territory containing the diversified features of a continent, suggestive of Europe, with a sea to the north and the south, an ocean to the west, a sea to the east. This territory, its slopes, valleys, and plains clearly depicted in an aerial view, created natural pathways for streams, brooks, and rivers that led man and things down to the sea.[200]

> The purpose of our exploration is to discern, from amidst the present confusion, the efficient, economic and elegant process governing the regular acts of a society extending over a territory. Efficiency considered, not in relation to money but in relation to man, man being installed in his environment, the environment specific to his action, his existence.
>
> What is actually involved is the occupation of the ground for various purposes: to produce and to trade in order to consume (feed, clothe and amuse).[201]

Architectural unity is the offspring of the doctrine of the "built domain," which establishes equilibrium between the law of number, the rule of the sun, and topography.[202]

A GLOBAL VIEW: THE COMPRESSION OF SPACE AND TIME

Le Corbusier perceived, as he traveled across South America, that any communication technology–locomotive, newspaper, photography, radio, cinema, or other–is a conquistador, crushing before its advance regional customs and habits. Through these new devices anyone could know, hear, and feel any other part of the world. All landscapes became familiar, all songs known. The archive of knowledge about the world had increased, but with its accumulation, a sense of mystery had disappeared. Now the last white spaces of the map were filled out: one had seen up close the ice blocks of the North Pole and the rippled sands of the desert. "And the locomotive has brought you the suits of London and the fashions of Paris," he exclaimed to the South Americans: "You are wearing bowlers!"[203] "Airplanes go everywhere; their eagle eyes have searched the deserts and penetrated the rain forest. Hastening interpenetration, the railway, the telephone unceasingly run the country into the city, the city into the country."[204]

The aerial view offered proof that the spherical mass of the earth was without borders. The state, a territorial unit with frontiers to be defended, depended on the notion of boundaries. Yet the telegraph, the airplane, and the camera eradicated these boundaries. The aerial view has given man a new understanding of geography, of the importance of the land, which has remained while many a civilization has passed with time. "Geography speaks, proclaiming certain fundamental truths."[205] Where men have made contact with each other, established a flow of information, and explored new territories, there the discourse of geography has penetrated as well.

> That is to say that the fruits of modern work are destined for everyone, implicating already a volume without comparison to that which has been up to now. So that the body of our civilization becomes work itself: the fact of "work" will be reconsidered, discussed; some new propositions submitted; some restraints imposed; some arrangement taken finally to equilibrate the forces of the world, to make circulate the sap, to expand life, to make regenerate, to make bloom the springtime of this second cycle of machine civilization.[206]

Le Corbusier turns to history to buttress this messianic claim. Ancient Rome was the center of its empire, in the heart of the Mediterranean. Caravans bearing rare and exotic products from faraway horizons traveled there. But for a long time now this empire has ceased to be; populations have spread over the entire surface of the Earth, along with their gigantic powers of production and means of circulation and transport.[207] When the world returns to peace, new places of production will be created where primary and secondary materials will be transformed into consumer products. In the first machine age, these places were dispersed, but in the second machine age they will be distributed according to the law of the "three establishments" (units of agricultural production, linear industrial cities, and radio-concentric social cities). [FIGURES 12.21 AND 12.22]

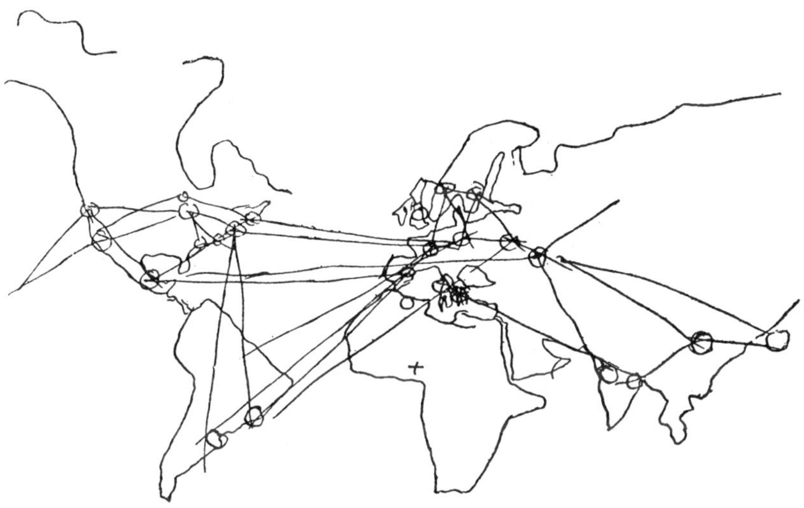

FIGURE 12.21: Techniques are no longer regional: books, reviews, and thoughts flash across the world. Materials are distributed by nature, and are, hence, regional. The architect must respect the dictates of climate, topography, and site. There is no risk of uniformity.

FIGURE 12.22: Le Corbusier wanted to erect new Unités d'Habitation along the crucial meridian of France, on a line stretching from Le Havre to Algiers.

AERIAL WARFARE

While considering plans for Moscow in 1930, Le Corbusier commented on a formidable menace threatening all urban existence: aerial warfare. Lieutenant Colonel Vauthier had just given Le Corbusier a copy of his book *The Aerial Danger and the Future of the Country.*[208] Now Le Corbusier understood, as he explained in *Précisions* (1930), that the air would be the new theater of military operations, and that threat of aerial warfare emanated not only from explosive projectiles that would destroy a city's built structures, but also from poison gas and chemical warfare that would asphyxiate its inhabitants, and from flammable liquids that would spread a firestorm beyond imagination. A city could be destroyed all at once. But it just so happened that, quite without realizing it, Le Corbusier had already provided a necessary defense against this new danger of aerial warfare in his studies for *Urbanisme* (1925) and in the book *Précisions.*

He had proposed the construction of housing in reinforced concrete, a fireproof material strong enough to withstand the impact of bombs. He had also proposed that these structures be isolated in great open spaces, that housing, commerce, and industry be located in separate zones, and that the entire built surface of the city be reduced. These were essential conditions needed to lessen the exposure of built structures to aerial attack and to contain the spread of any conflagration. To avoid the disaster of poisonous gas, his proposal for suppressing meager courtyards and narrow corridor streets, along with the provision of wide open spaces and housing raised on piloti, would allow sufficient wind and water from protected hydrants or large open-air swimming pools to cleanse the air. Le Corbusier stated that his housing and planning schemes had been offered as solutions for the problem of work and leisure in the first machine age, but recently, the French military, having studied different plans for the development of Paris, discovered that only Le Corbusier's earlier schemes provided adequate resistance to the dangers of aerial warfare.[209]

As World War II continued and Paris remained occupied by the Germans, questions were raised concerning the evacuation of the city in case of air raids and carpet-bombing. Le Corbusier knew what could be expected: bottlenecks at every street corner and road-jams along the routes of exodus. He wrote in *The Four Routes*,

> It would be a stampede, and, in case of machine-gunning, a massacre.... Noxious gases [would] pour into our trench-like streets

> and into those wells which our courtyards provide; one can't get rid of them; they achieve a maximum result: the population is asphyxiated.[210]

If only Le Corbusier's *The Radiant City* scheme could be built, it would dramatically reduce the vulnerability of the city. In collaboration with the Air Defense Staff, Le Corbusier's housing projects could be equipped with bomb-and torpedo-proof roofing, provided with both anti-explosion chambers and floor plates able to resist any projectiles not already exploded. Instead of underground shelters becoming the collective tomb of all who gathered there, bomb shelters could be located in the highest stories of apartment houses, where pure air provided by air conditioners would allow the residents to breathe in safety. Such defense measures, decreed for the safety of Parisians, would ensure the realization of rational town-planning schemes; "Or, vice versa, in rationalizing a plan for the city of Paris, to save her from the shameful chaos into which she is now plunged, we shall automatically satisfy the need for aerial defense."[211]

With aerial warfare, new considerations have replaced the old set of tools, and new urban forms, the linear radiant city, have been developed for the entire nation.

> At a time when aviation begins to reign over the inferno of war and could aspire to be the delight of our peacetime existence, then the idea that aviation should be banned from the sky above any city will be a priori, since a free and silent sky is a boon to all men.[212]

GEOMORPHIC STRUCTURES ON THE LAND

The basic elements to be included on the list of planning requirements for postwar reconstruction–at least on Le Corbusier's list–were the use of machines, new communication devices, information flows, and administrative requirements. These were the variables in the equation that would determine the form and location of future settlement patterns around the globe. Yet production–or work–was for Le Corbusier the activating force: it propelled men, materials, and goods over the four routes of the world, those established by the roads, sea, railroads, and air.[213] The first two had developed a rational network of roads and ship lanes, while the railroad, followed by the automobile, sowed disruption and chaos in their wake. Now the fourth route, or aviation, was a catalyst for great mutations taking place throughout the world. Having taken to the air, the destiny of man was truly revolutionary![214]

Le Corbusier designed three different settlement patterns to shelter this new aerial civilization: units of agricultural production (food), linear industrial cities (manufacturing), and radio-concentric social cities (government, knowledge, commerce, and distribution). Due to the airplane, populations could now be rationally redistributed, and land more efficiently utilized. After a general territorial stocktaking, areas beyond the reach of the four routes would be allowed to sink into an indeterminate state, or possibly extinction (economic). [FIGURES 12.23 AND 12.24]

Replying to a question addressed to him in 1945 concerning the mission and doctrine of contemporary architecture in reconstruction, he replied: "Let us read the vital currents which flow through our land."[215] Along the crucial meridian line that crosses the breadth of France, new unites d'habitations must be built from Le Havre to Algiers. The Allies understood that airlines were the lifeline of defense; their relentless precision bombing of the cities of Germany eventually won the war. They understand the same lifeline will be necessary when the war ends.

FIGURES 12.23 AND 12.24: Le Corbusier called the architectural concept of airports "two-dimensional architecture." No structure seemed reasonable if juxtaposed against the magnificent aircraft.

> For the time of peace, they are preparing vast aerial fleets, which will produce an unimagined upheaval in the transport of men and goods. We need not lose our heads. The skies of our towns will be full of the roar and the whistling of aircraft. And if one day the physicians and the mechanics succeed in annulling the racket, the skies of our towns will remain no less encumbered with engines, far and near, like the monstrous white mice that fill the skies of the fantastic paintings of Hieronymus Bosch.[216]

> The war has turned a new page, that of the aircraft, with its extraordinary speeds and its routes as straight as the trajectories of missiles. Enthusiasm and ingenuity join hands to prepare splendid berths for these machines: airports. Each town will claim one, according to its needs and rights.
>
> It is dangerous to prophesy so soon after the event [of war]. But at least we must try to see whether the three human establishments of our technical civilization, hitherto founded upon the three routes of earth, water, and iron, will find their futures foreclosed or fostered by the fourth route, that of the air.[217]

If civilization is so fostered, then the map of Europe will be rearranged: there will be a linear industrial city extending from the Atlantic coast to the Urals, another from the North Sea to the Mediterranean. Within this network, industries will be transformed; they will house all sorts of specialists and manufacture a range of useful goods. They will embrace the radio-concentric cities already established by geography.

> Measures must be taken within the geography of Europe, the effect of which will be to join and to unite, and not to multiply the gun-muzzles along frontiers that are ready for dissolution before the sap which is thrusting from the future.
>
> Our snail's shell has become too small, we are left without any real shelter. It is time to leave it and build another.[218]

CONCLUSION: EXPLODING INFORMATION, FEAR, AND HOPE

For thousands of years man lived within a ten- to twelve-mile radius of his shelter, but now, Le Corbusier said, man can read about or view the entire world in dramatic new atlases of aerial photographs or documentary films of infinite detail. The flow of information has exploded, revealing a variety of forms of nature, cultures, and climates. Sitting in his armchair, man has access to

> geography (sites, flora and fauna, harvest and industrial products)–human races, as tallied by the illustrated document, the documentary film. They are revealed to us in detail, their appearance, their customs, what they build–climates from one pole to the other, by way of the tropics and the equator, and from sea level to the highest altitudes. Such an abundance of information means so many inducements to greed, and also so much encouragement of self-centered withdrawal.[219]

The first reaction to any expansion of horizons, as it has been throughout the history of mankind, is anxiety, or fear of the new. To find some assurance, man retreats to investigate the past. "Archaeology [after World War I] was supreme, reigning over all teaching. It was an invitation to a refusal to create, to loss of the *taste for creating*–taste for, joy in the *risk* of, creating."[220]

Then specialized schools developed to train engineers in the new sciences. They experimented, followed their curiosity, made prodigious leaps forward in the applied sciences. They designed automobiles and airplanes that embodied new speeds; they invented radios that wrapped the Earth in countless waves, picked up and relayed by receiving sets. These became the new vehicles that spread every kind of thought or slogan around the globe, snowballing to gigantic proportions as they gathered momentum.[221] Man was overwhelmed, crushed under all these new discoveries; as a consequence, society divided into hostile classes, and individuals were bruised and restricted in their daily endeavors. The human viewpoint was lost, and the rightful place of machines was denied.

In conclusion, Le Corbusier resorts to his famous refrain, "the hour is striking." The time is favorable. Now we absolutely must look ahead and plan for a world in which the aerial route will lie supreme.[222]

In 1945, as the war was drawing to a close, Le Corbusier wrote of great human enterprises, great gestures of the machine civilization that poets must write about and builders must erect. Exultant poetry lies in these great gestures. He remembers when the Americans came to fight in France, by airplane, jeeps, and tanks, armed with strategies and typewriters and manned by former bank employees and workers from the stockyards of Chicago, professors and blacks, all soldiers wearing the uniforms of war.[223] They razed Hamburg and Cologne, blew up stations and bridges. In frightening fire storms they illuminated the nights with incendiary bombs: blazing red, green, yellow, locating the places of carnage. He calls on the poet to remember the German helmets, the hysteria of Hitler's speeches–to remember these, but to write instead about the joys of living. To remember the smiles of the Americans, the English, the Russians who added their strength to that of France–but to write the poetry of tomorrow. He asks rhetorically:

> Do you want to withdraw your head and horns into your shell like a snail? France, the famous, the celebrated, the inimitable? Your snail no longer has any radiant housing, no stimulating places of work! Friends, all is to be built with the head, the heart and the hands of all, freely consented to and in a radiantly constructive spirit.[224]

[FIGURE 12.25]

guerre!

Septembre 39

FIRST, there were to be eight months of "phony war." Then suddenly the hurricane! The exodus! Then four years of the slow dissolution of thought.

No longer were there meat, milk, wine–no more vitamins.

No longer were there canvases, nor colors to paint with.

There were those who did everything to save thought and spirit. . . .

The new world will be infinitely newer than is imagined.

City planning is a science disregarded by everyone.

Architecture is waking up in all parts of the world.

The synthesis of the major arts will be realized only in extremely new forms: the old molds have cracked!

103

FIGURE 12.25: **Once World War II was over, Le Corbusier predicted the synthesis of the major arts would be realized in entirely new forms.**

EPILOGUE: A BOOK = A BOX OF MIRACLES

I'm not joking. It is serious. The world must begin again at zero. An entirely new order is needed"

–FERNAND LÉGER, 1946

The new world will be infinitely newer than imagined... Architecture is waking up in all parts of the world. The synthesis of the major arts will be realized only in extremely new forms: the old molds have cracked.

–LE CORBUSIER, 1948

THE SYNTHESIS OF THE ARTS

From Cap Martin in the summer of 1951, Le Corbusier scribbles a note to his mother and brother, inserting a drawing at the bottom of his vacation retreat. He is thrilled over his open-air villa (*villa décapotable*), in which he works at his painting and writing: without a roof, window, or door, only a calm breeze, a table, and a stool. [FIGURE E.1, p. 702] This sketch is emblematic of Le Corbusier's love of the sun, the Mediterranean, nature, and the activities of painting and writing, as we have seen in the preceding chapters. It also points to the far more poetic and artistic treatment that his books after 1947 represent.[1] Having outlined the points of his doctrine, and aware they were being accepted and partially implemented around the world, he turns instead to another preoccupation that he had begun to outline in the 1930s: the "synthesis of the arts," drawing a tighter circle around painting and writing, his private and public personae.[2] The time for polemics and manifestos is over, he has lost faith in authorities to implement his dreams. Now it is up to international organizations–be they the United Nations or CIAM–to begin again at zero and create an entirely new order.

Le Corbusier was far from the only architect or artist interested in the unification of the arts in the 1940s. As a rallying cry during the occupation of France, André Rousseau writing in *Le Figaro* proclaimed, "It is when France speaks, or when she writes...that she shines on the world."[3] The book as an art form, a beautiful vehicle of French thought, was one of the ways to maintain the prestige of French civilization faced with the cataclysm of war and its aftermath. There was however skepticism that works of universal and eternal value, which writers and artists had patiently assembled and offered to posterity before the war, would continue to be so important after the war as life continued to be vulnerable, full of contingencies and instabilities. Still, it was hoped the role of the artist and writer as witness of their times would remain.[4]

José Luis Sert, Sigfried Giedion, and Fernand Léger expressed concern over the lack of interest among modern architects in the creation of monuments that moved the spectator emotionally. Presenting a lecture on "Nine Points of Monumentality" to the American Abstract Artists in 1943, they called for the collaboration of artists, architects, and urbanists to work together to provide monuments of lasting value. Society needed monuments that spoke directly to eternal human emotions, linking together the past, present, and future, establishing universal symbols all humanity understood.[5] The three continued their support for the synthesis of the arts, making sure that this was a theme taken up by postwar CIAM meetings in Bridgwater (1947), Bergamo (1949), and Hoddesdon (1951). They believed it was the responsibility of the architect to meet the artist and the common man in the civic core of the city. James Richards, editor of *Architectural Review* and host of the Bridgwater congress, joined Giedion and Hans Arp in the formulation of a questionnaire offered to CIAM participants, hopeful that this would "crystallize" the meaning of the arts for the postwar period and involve the artists in the creation of public works. Giedion and Arp refined their questions for the Bergamo CIAM–this time questioning whether "the synthesis of the major arts" was possible, searching to discover the obstacles that stood in the way.[6]

The call for all artists in all mediums to work together for the common good of the new world order became one of the building blocks on which peace would be built. It was clear to Giedion that in order to implement this synthesis of the arts, the education of architects and artists needed to be reformed. Gathering thirty-three signatures, among them Sert's, Le Corbusier's, and Gropius's, he sent a letter in 1947 to the Director-General of UNESCO requesting this newly formed organization establish a committee to formulate fundamental reforms in the training of artists, architects, and planners, because UNESCO was the only organization that could achieve such reforms on an international scale.[7]

The founders of UNESCO believed that the recovery of the world would be through the promotion of education and the engagement of intellectuals in world affairs.[8] Committed to the interests of the common man, not just the elite, UNESCO followed the lead of CIAM and set out to secure freedom of expression for all artists around the world. It formulated a questionnaire of its own in 1949 to ascertain what the obstacles were confronting artistic expression and cooperative endeavors throughout the world. If CIAM dropped its interest in the synthesis of the arts after 1951, picking up the development of a "charter of housing" in its place, then UNESCO appears to have carried on the torch for the unification of the arts. The first international gathering of artists under UNESCO's sponsorship took place in Venice in 1951. Jaime Torres Bodet, its new Director-General, extended the concept of monumentality to the written word, reminding the audience in his opening speech that the greatness of "monuments of stone, color, sounds, and words" is their endurance beyond empires and wars–they are artifacts handed on to posterity.[9]

Not everyone agreed about the "monuments of culture," or whether architects should lead the way in the synthesis of the arts–there were other more drastic conditions of redevelopment and reconstruction that major cities faced, and the question of housing was a crucial issue throughout the world. There was, as well, the problem of mass society. How would architects react to these crucial issues? One side argued that architecture was a formal art, and must remain an elite gesture kept aloof from social concerns. Another side argued that if avant-garde art and architecture were to survive in the new world order, they must compromise their autonomy, come down from their pedestal, and be receptive to mass interests and tastes. This latter group believed that architects must satisfy the man in the street's emotional and material needs and stimulate his spiritual growth. This "common man," a universal, timeless figure–or so it was assumed–spoke a natural, not an abstract, language, one that everyone understood.

Le Corbusier, expressed his delight in this side of the postwar argument, proclaiming before the 1947 CIAM audience: "Finally imagination enters into CIAM."[10] During the postwar discussions of CIAM, Le Corbusier alluded to his own proposals for a Pavilion for the Synthesis of the Major Arts, to be located at Porte Maillot in Paris. Conceived as a temporary "workshop" for experimentation in all of the arts, he believed "this center will become a manifestation of human poetry–a manifestation of the sole justification for our existence:

a center for which we must produce works that are noble and irrefutable witness of our age, and not works that are full of excuses for our failings."[11]

THE BOOK AS A WORK OF ART

The postwar years find Le Corbusier more willing to expose himself as an artist involved with architecture, urbanism, paintings, sculpture, murals, tapestries, and books. If he had achieved certain fame for his passionate advocacy of an architecture for the new times, if his machine for living had been adopted worldwide as a symbol of revolt, perhaps now this public acceptance and admiration might offer a platform on which his more artistic, poetical nature could stand public scrutiny. Could he invert the tables? Thus he writes in 1948 "If one accords some signification to my architectural work, it is to this secret labor that it is necessary to attribute a profound value"[12] And in the article "Unité," appearing the same year, he clarified, "The foundation of my research and intellectual production has its secret in the uninterrupted practice of my painting. It is there that one must find the source of my spiritual freedom, my disinterestedness, my independence, and the faithfulness and integrity of my work."[13] He labels his activity "secret work" because even though he continued to devote each morning to painting, he refused to exhibit any of his artwork from 1923 until 1947, with the exception of an exhibit in Zurich in 1938.[14]

With renewed energy and hope as the war ended, Le Corbusier was drawn to be "the" master of artistic expression, an architect who would lead the world in carrying out its new interest in the synthesis of the arts. Books were one place where all the arts came together, especially sumptuous books that were themselves works of art.[15] Encouraged in general by his greater willingness to present his own art to the public, Le Corbusier's postwar books of 1948–65 represent layers of metaphorical musings, more intimate and autobiographical than his prewar writings. He puts his entire creative output into these literary projects, carrying out Stéphane Mallarmé's claim to the letter: "Everything in the World exists to end up in a book."[16] Le Corbusier had been his own publicist, editor, archivist, and historian. He had published four volumes of his *Oeuvre Complète* by 1946 and numerous manifestos; now he turns to exploit a self-enclosed form of writing, one that turns reflexively back on itself, in service to his poetic research, searching for new means to arouse the emotions of humankind.

POEM OF THE RIGHT ANGLE

The most significant graphic project and personal account in Le Corbusier's postwar writings was the project that began in 1948, *Le Poème de l'angle droit* (*The Poem of the Right Angle*), published as a limited edition of 250 in 1955. [FIGURE E.2, p. 702] Each book, signed by the author, circulated from his hand to the hand of a buyer, whom he was responsible for finding. It was a handsomely illustrated book of twenty colored gouaches and seventy black-and-white lithographs published by E. Tériade in 1955.[17] The images were accompanied by a series of prose-poems, handwritten by the artist himself from notes compiled between August 1951 and March 1953. There was nothing more personal than this tactile and gestural act, improvisational traces left by the hand like footprints in the sand. In one blow they upset the *machine à ecrire* (typewriter) as an exemplary act of efficiency and order. The process of writing these poems–or so Le Corbusier claimed–was "intuitive, as if sprouting from a bottle that spontaneously has burst open...and suddenly achieves its architecture: the color designs were created in one month in 1948 and the text...in traveling journals, written in airplanes or hotel rooms, places quite removed, conducive to thought."[18] Before beginning to write, Le Corbusier arranged the images in an iconostasis on the left-hand side of a piece of paper and then made a diagram of the iconostasis on the right-hand side, and slowly over time in various places filled out the blocks with poetic words.[19]

The meanings of his prose-poems and illustrations are opaque. The text, failing to illustrate an image, resists readability. Le Corbusier claimed "the painting is non-, in-explicable. To explain is to profane. It is to hunt the sacred."[20] To underscore and to praise this obscurity, and the fact that his handwritten words enter the painting as objects in themselves, he proposed to place an explanatory text at the back of the book, noting that "these designs are by no means spontaneous. They are part of my life, the markings inscribed in my paintings, my notebooks and on pieces of paper."[21] Upon the appearance of *Le Poème de l'angle droit* in art galleries and museum exhibitions–demonstrating the value of each separate page as a work of art–Le Corbusier allowed that it was "an arrangement of thoughts that, because of everyday activities, are rarely externalized. These things are not only the root of my character but also of my architectural and painted oeuvre."[22]

By creating a personal synthesis of the arts, Le Corbusier simultaneously makes a retrospective unity of all his creative activity.

He draws a continuous line linking together earlier with contemporary projects, the roots of concepts such as "the right angle," "ineffable space," "the sun that rules," "the law of the meander," "the pact with nature," joined with new articulations.[23] Emblematic of a reformulated unity between man and nature is the image he redraws around 1948 of interlacing right and left hands, this time for *Le Poème de l'angle droit*, to which he later adds the following prose-poem under the chapter of "environment":

> I thought that two hands
> and their fingers intertwined
> might express the left and
> right pitilessly standing
> together and so necessarily
> to be reconciled.
> The sole possibility of survival
> that life had to offer. [24]

PLANS FOR PARIS

In his series of postwar books, Le Corbusier resumes and elaborates the practice of inserting already written texts into new arrangements, now paying specific attention to the page as a discrete unit itself, utilizing "zip-a-tone" blobs of color placed over images, new collage arrangements between handwritten inserts and blocks of print. He offers the reader intimate gestures or traces to his immediate thought, allowing his handwriting to remain full of grammatical errors and crossed-out words. Just as important as *Le Poème de l'angle droit* in expressing the synthesis of the arts and the continuous trace of his thoughts is the book *Les Plans Le Corbusier de Paris 1956–1922* (1956).[25] [FIGURE E.3, p. 702] The title announces that it is a repertoire, a stroll backward over thirty years of planning for Paris.[26] There is nothing original about the text–every page has appeared elsewhere and is now inserted into a new assemblage: 110 pages from various *Oeuvre Complète*, 33 pages from *The Radiant City*, 19 pages from *Canons*, 4 from *La Maison des hommes*, and 2 pages from *When the Cathedrals Were White*. Given the same size format Le Corbusier favored for his *Oeuvre Complète*, *The Radiant City*, and *Canons*, a working title had been *Trente Années de Silence* (*Thirty years of Silence*), because each one of the plans Le Corbusier made for Paris had been summarily rejected, causing the author to suffer in silence. More poignantly, it may also refer to his thirty years of "secret work" as a painter.

What Le Corbusier calls a *piste vert* (green trail) runs across the pages as a reader's guide; it appears in various blobs of green of different shapes and sizes, into which are inserted a handwritten text addressed to the reader. The green path appears at random places and pages; the handwritten notes are a rumination on thirty years of research and city plans. They make no explicit reference to the series of already published pages of photographs, sketches, plans, and texts forming the backdrop for his rambling thoughts.

The handwritten text, "the word of today" is addressed to the reader, who can follow the trail of tears and form his own judgment. He introduces a number of literary giants who rose to help him man the barricades in the battle for the new order of modern times, including Paul Valéry, who labeled his book *L'Art Décoratif d'aujourd'hui* (1925) "admirable" when everyone else was blaming Le Corbusier for assassinating the decorative arts.[27] Someone had mentioned to him that André Gide held him in high esteem in his search for a decent habitat for all mankind.[28] And he places on this trail of supporters and friends Sigfried Giedion, Antoine de Saint-Exupéry, and Paul Éluard. In spite of these accolades from literary giants, and even though Le Corbusier believes he has made serious, well-written books over thirty-five years of struggle–books that have been translated into English, Spanish, and German–still he complains they remain unknown to badly informed government officials who control the destinies of cities. He confesses:

> I wrote not for pleasure to make some phrases but because, in our trade the difficulties are vast. Animated by a certain passion, when I could not build, (depression of 1929, Hitler's rise 1933–39, the war until '44, after the war until '47, etc.) I painted and I sketched...city plans, solutions filling five volumes of *Oeuvre Complète*: 1912–1953.[29]

And when he was not painting or designing, he lectured in all continents of the world, for thirty years, always improvised talks in front of friendly and hostile audiences. And when he did not lecture, he put all of his ideas into books–about how to cure the sickness of cities. Still, all the world awaits great decisions from Paris, expecting something marvelous from France, a country of inventors and thinkers. Men are capable of such blindness, they cannot see, and as a result nothing happens.[30] "It is necessary to see, to know and to begin.

That is why this book of *Les Plans de Paris 1956–1922*. Paris 10th July, 1955."[31] He ends by inserting an image of himself writing and the list of books originally printed in the fourth volume of *Oeuvre Complète* (1946).

INEFFABLE SPACE

Increasingly in this postwar period, as part of his synthesis of the arts Le Corbusier turns his attention to *l'espace indicible* (ineffable space), still believing that emotional *rayonings*, or "invisible vectors," emanate radiantly from special works of art and affect the environment. Now he calls this "plastic acoustics" when the object and the milieu begin to resonate together, causing darting arrows to penetrate the body, the spirit, and the mind as if an explosion had occurred. He situates architecture at this juncture, at the point when the machine for living passes into the machine to move you emotionally.[32]

Here too Le Corbusier's interest in "plastic acoustics" follows a continuous trail back to his first emotional experiences on the Acropolis in 1911. This is when he first understood how the Parthenon, the flat rock on which it sat, created the landscape. The Parthenon was the "pearl" in the shell, an admirable spectacle exploding outward to shock and to move. In one sweep of the hand, Le Corbusier reaches backwards and forward, drawing a line of continuity from his first Purist paintings to the sculptural garden on the roof of the Unité d'Habitation, from lessons of Athens to those of Paris. In *The New World of Space* he repeats a message first delivered to CIAM members in 1933: "Remember the clear, clean, intense, economical, violent Parthenon–that cry hurled into a landscape made of grace and terror. That monument to strength and purity."[33]

In turn espace indicible draws parallels with Le Corbusier's interest in "spontaneous theaters" that people create, watch, and perform, and which he increasingly inserts into urban plans for the postwar core of the city. He draws his first example from Brazil in 1936, where he witnessed how the collisions, contacts, and violent differences of three different races turned the streets of the city into veritable theaters; and he thought also of the dreams that many in France had after Liberation, when battalions of workers, all coming together to form a new aggregate, wanted to rebuild as soon as possible the blitzed areas of the city. Providing places for the expression of the great acts of life, a spontaneous theater for liberating self-expression was sheer poetry. He explains in the report of CIAM 8, "In designing literature, as well as in designs for physical planning, plastic art, and melodious sounds: in all designs, the idea leads to a form of poetry."[34]

In this meeting place of the arts, the core of the city–or in the pages of a book–he is sure of the architect's role in providing what he now calls a *boîte à miracles* (box of miracles). He begins with a simple box provided by the architect, in the same manner in which he began to describe the "language of architecture" in 1925:

> He [the architect] can create a magic box enclosing all that your heart desires. Scenes and actors materialize the moment the magic box appears; the magic box is a cube; with it comes everything that is needful to perform: miracles, levitation, manipulation, distraction, etc.
>
> The interior of the cube is empty, but your inventive spirit will fill it with everything you dream of–in the manner of performances of the old Commedia dell'Arte.[35]

Throughout the postwar years until his death in 1965, Le Corbusier keeps following a deep train of thought, nurturing a seed that was planted a long time before, some fifty years earlier. In the introduction to the fifth volume of *Oeuvre Complète* (1957), he wrote:

> Recently on an airplane trip, I noted in my sketch book the titles for three works asked for by different publishers, the ideas for which occurred to me at different times. These titles are:
>
> 1. End of a World: Deliverance [Fin d'un Monde; Déliverance]
> 2. The Base of the Matter [Le Fond du Sac]
> 3. Indefinable Space [L'Espace indicible][36]

These unpublished manuscripts he calls "acrobatic feats"–the forming of an exact aim, a regular and consistent effort, with correct timing and so much more–which all lead, as they do with a trapeze artist, to the successful achievement of a jump. Having done everything in this manner, whether successful or not, rewarded or not, this magnificent effort provokes in Le Corbusier, now seventy years of age, an intense emotion, something "indefinable" (*indicible*)–"Born [he writes] from a seed which has germinated since the beginning (where, how, why?) proposing and imposing a line of conduct" in the pursuit of an inspiring dream.[37] Deep in his subconscious, leaving a trail that runs across all of his writings, is an image first expressed in a letter he wrote to William Ritter in 1911. He described his dream of a rational city drawn on a Cartesian checkerboard with the sun making its way across the sky, an image that gave him premonitions of a tragedy or a comedy, he knew not which.[38] This is the seed planted fifty years before. He had followed this trail across the decades, hoping his ideas, thoughts, and designs made along the way would lead forward, upward toward a better world for tomorrow, a world dedicated to a better life for all mankind. [FIGURE E.4]

FIGURE E.4: **The "Box of Miracles," sketched by Le Corbusier, published in "The Core as the Meeting Place of the Arts."**

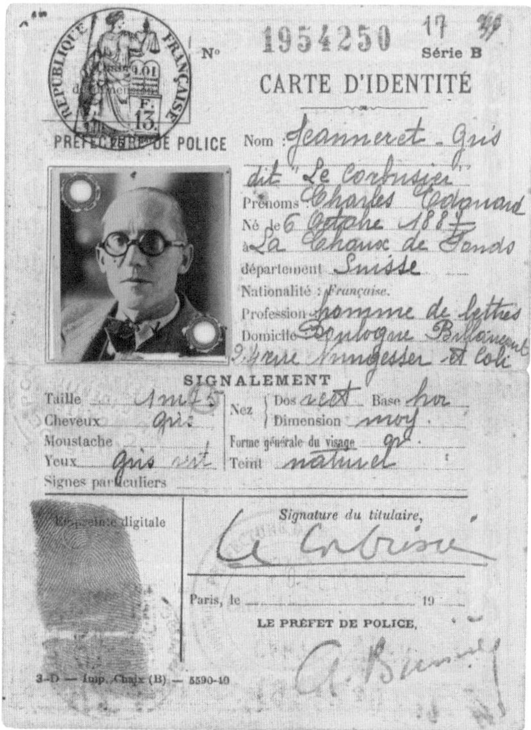

N° 1954250 17 Série B

CARTE D'IDENTITÉ

PRÉFECTURE DE POLICE

Nom : Jeanneret-Gris dit "Le Corbusier"

Prénoms : Charles Edouard

Né le 6 Octobre 1887

à La Chaux de Fonds

département Suisse

Nationalité : *Française.*

Profession homme de lettres

Domicile Boulogne Billancourt 24 rue Nungesser et Coli

SIGNALEMENT

Taille 1m75

Cheveux gris

Moustache

Yeux gris vert

Signes particuliers

Nez { Dos droit Base hor. Dimension moy.

Forme générale du visage ov.

Teint naturel

Empreinte digitale

Signature du titulaire,

Le Corbusier

Paris, le .... 19...

LE PRÉFET DE POLICE,

3-D — Imp. Chaix (B) — 5590-10

FIGURE I.2: Sketches from Jeanneret's 1908 stay in Paris reveal his desire to examine every aspect of Notre Dame and to fill every available space with drawings and words. FIGURE I.3: Note that when Le Corbusier became a naturalized French citizen in 1930, his identity card labeled his profession as "homme de lettres."

FIGURE I.4: By 1930, curvilinear forms and female figures became prevalent in Le Corbusier's drawings and paintings. This sketch of a nude reading a book was made during a trip to the Arcachon Basin, Le Piquey, in 1932.

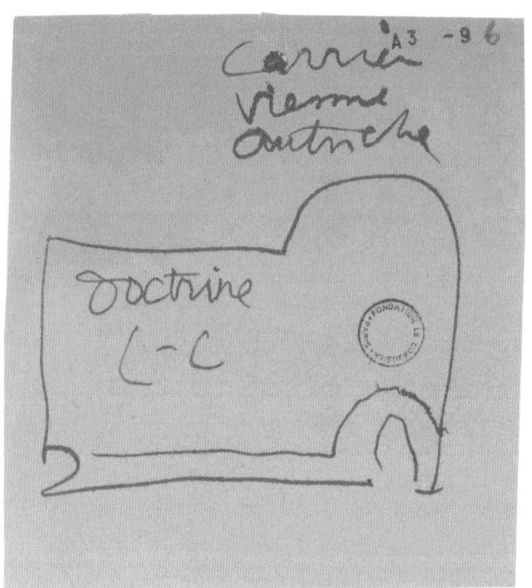

FIGURE I.11: This ideogram of a book opened to a page inscribed with "doctrine [of] L-C" was deployed to announce books that presented Le Corbusier's evolving doctrine of urbanism.

FIGURE I.14: In a letter written from Chandigarh in 1952 to Siegfried Giedion, Le Corbusier commented on those who called him a genius while he referred to himself as a donkey, and included this sketch. Beneath it he wrote, "Does the genius carry the donkey, or the donkey carry the genius?"

FIGURE 2.1: **Seven sketches by Charles-Édouard Jeanneret of details of the Cathedral of Pisa's facade.**

FIGURE 2.3 **Watercolor sketch by Charles-Édouard Jeanneret of the plan and section of the Moorish Rooms at the Museum of Decorative Arts, Vienna, from 1908.**

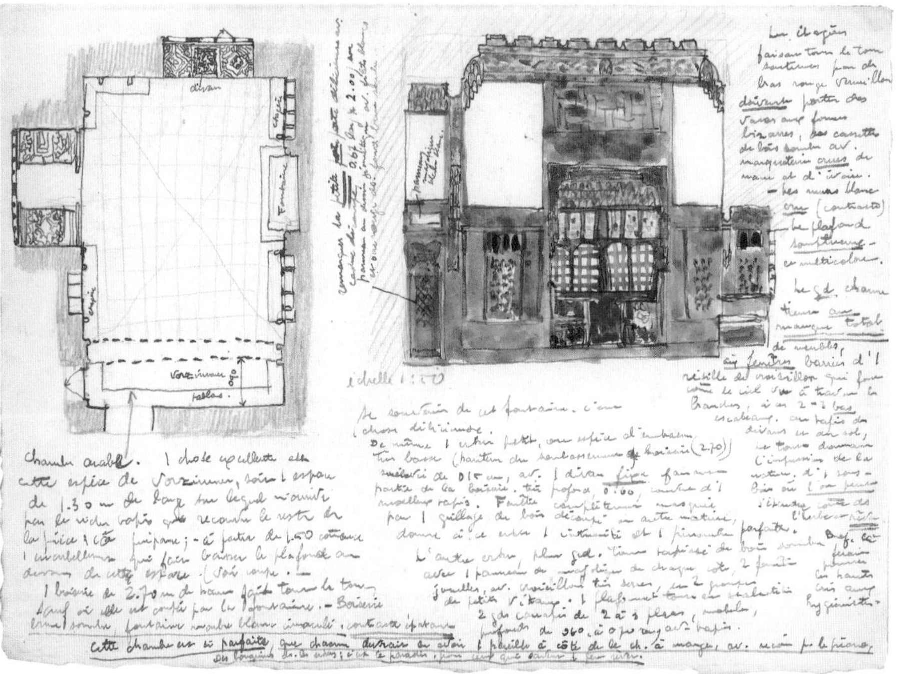

FIGURE 3.3: Illustration from a letter written by Charles-Édouard Jeanneret to William Ritter on May 2, 1911, while traveling down the Rhine from Mayence (Mainz) to Cologne. FIGURE 3.14: Colored pencil sketch by Charles-Édouard Jeanneret of the Parthenon, seen through a screen of columns

FIGURE 3.15: An undated crayon-and-watercolor sketch by Le Corbusier/Charles-Édouard Jeanneret of the Parthenon's stylobate and the distant horizon FIGURE 4.3: Drawing of the Villa Jeanneret-Perret by Charles-Édouard Jeanneret, designed for his parents in La Chaux-de-Fonds in 1912

FIGURE 4.5: *Persistantes souvenances du Bosphore*, drawn by Charles-Édouard Jeanneret in 1913 at La Chaux-de-Fonds
FIGURE 4.6: *Vin d'Athos*, a watercolor sketch by Charles-Édouard Jeanneret dated February 1913, while he was at La Chaux-de-Fonds

FIGURE 5.1: Charles-Édouard Jeanneret began to paint daily in 1918, and made numerous sketches, such as this one of nude prostitutes in Paris. FIGURE 5.4: The title of the book in this sketch by Charles-Édouard Jeanneret from around 1918 is *La Decadence de l'Art Sacre.*

FIGURE 5.7: Cover of the first issue of the journal *L'Esprit Nouveau* (1920), established by Amédée Ozenfant, Charles-Édouard Jeanneret, and Paul Dermée

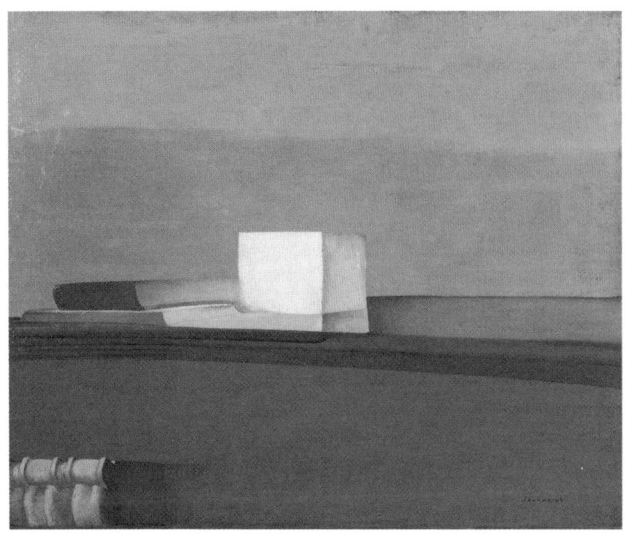

FIGURE 6.11: *La Cheminée* (1918) is one of the first of Charles-Édouard Jeanneret's oil paintings that he did not destroy. The book and cube on the mantel have the appearance of Purist architecture.

FIGURE 6.12: Purism was as much an art of the intellect as it was of the spirit, exemplified by the book and the reference to contemplative life in this painting by Charles-Édouard Jeanneret, *Still Life with Book, Glass and Pipe* (1918).

FIGURE 7.19: Advertisement for *L'Esprit Nouveau* book series, published by Georges Crès

FIGURE 8.1: Le Corbusier published *Une Maison–Un Palais* half in defense and half as a catalog for the controversial Palace of the League of Nations design. FIGURE 8.14: Le Corbusier delivers an outright attack on academicians who do not judge by themselves, never verify causes, and believe in absolute truths in his book *Croisade: ou Le Crépuscule des Académies.*

FIGURE 9.3: Lectures delivered by Le Corbusier during a trip to South America in 1929 were published in *Précisions sur un état présent de l'architecture et de l'urbanisme* (1930).

FIGURE 9.6: Le Corbusier, in search of peasant life and magnificent views, sketched the favela Ascencion in Rio de Janeiro when he visited it on October 24th, 1929.

FIGURE 9.7: Le Corbusier sketched the simple cubes of peasant architecture cascading down the hills of Rio de Janeiro in 1929.

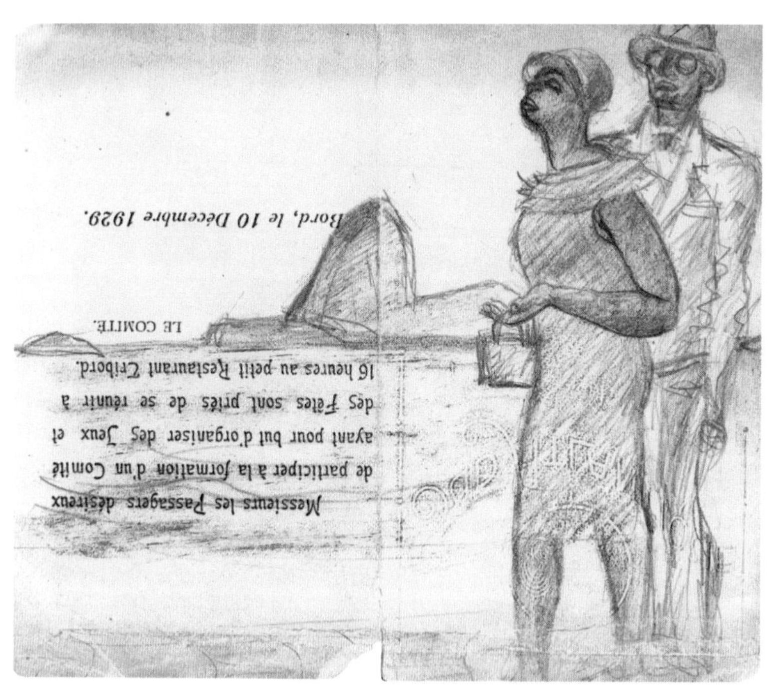

FIGURE 9.10: This self-portrait with Josephine Baker in front of Sugarloaf Mountain in Rio de Janeiro was sketched on the back of one of the ship *Giulio Cesare*'s announcements, dated December 10th, 1929.

FIGURE 9.11: Le Corbusier frequently sketched musical instruments, and music remained for him a source of secret and lyrical inspiration (1929).

FIGURE 9.12: Boats, the landscape, and new cities captured Le Corbusier's attention in this view of Montevideo, sketched on September 19, 1929.

FIGURE 9.13: Donkeys were a favorite subject for commentary and illustration throughout Le Corbusier's lifetime, as in this scene sketched in São Paulo (1929).

FIGURE 10.1: Part manifesto, part résumé of CIAM's work, and part catalog for the Pavillon des Temps Nouveaux, *Des Canons, Des Munitions? Merci! Des Logis...S. V. P.* was compiled in 1938.

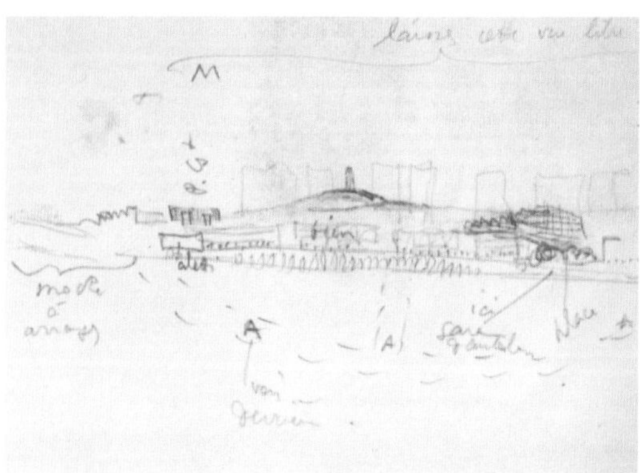

FIGURE 11.5: Le Corbusier's initial sketch of Algiers (1931) highlights important elements retained in all of his Obus plans for the city: a government palace, an obelisk on the hill, the seashore, and a Casbah.

FIGURE 11.6: A second sketch of Algiers announces the view from Fort l'Empereur, and states that the Casbah will remain untouched! (1931)

116 LA MAISON DES HOMMES

nom ou du chef d'un groupe social, de songer à lui confier le rôle de maître d'œuvre pour quelque tâche que ce soit, ni même, la partie la plus subalterne dans l'orchestre de la construction.

∴

Schéma du maître d'œuvre.

L'idée d'ensemble une fois exposée de ce que doit être un maître d'œuvre, les divers aspects de sa mission ressortiront plus clairement de la lecture d'un schéma synthétique qu'elle ne ferait d'une série de développements particuliers à chacun d'eux.

Le schéma en deux couleurs qui fait face à ces lignes figure *l'architecte* et *l'ingénieur* par deux cercles, situés, respectivement, au pôle supérieur et au pôle inférieur d'une bande centrale, laquelle représente, sous la forme d'un éventail déployé, les *tâches de la Construction*.

La couleur bleue signifie, sous le titre général de *connaissance de l'homme*, la prise en considération de toute la gamme des besoins de l'homme, savoir :

besoins spirituels,
» intellectuels,
» civiques,
» sociaux,
» familiaux,
» physiologiques,
» matériels.

La couleur rouge signifie, sous le titre général de *connaissance des lois physiques*, la prise de possession des éléments

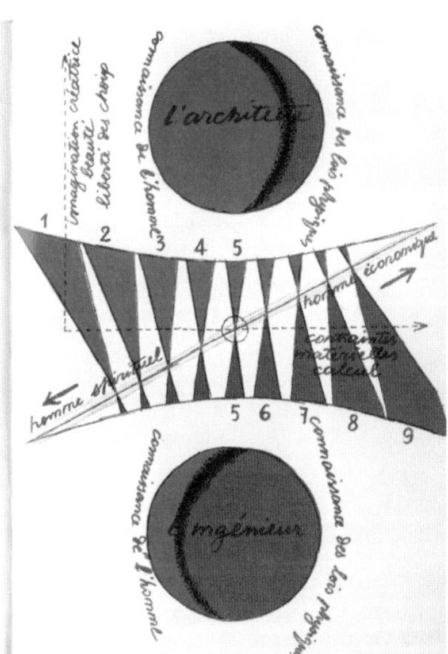

FIGURE 12.1: This emblem of ASCORAL entails the collaborative efforts between men of practicality and men of imagination, intertwining knowledge of physical laws with knowledge of man.

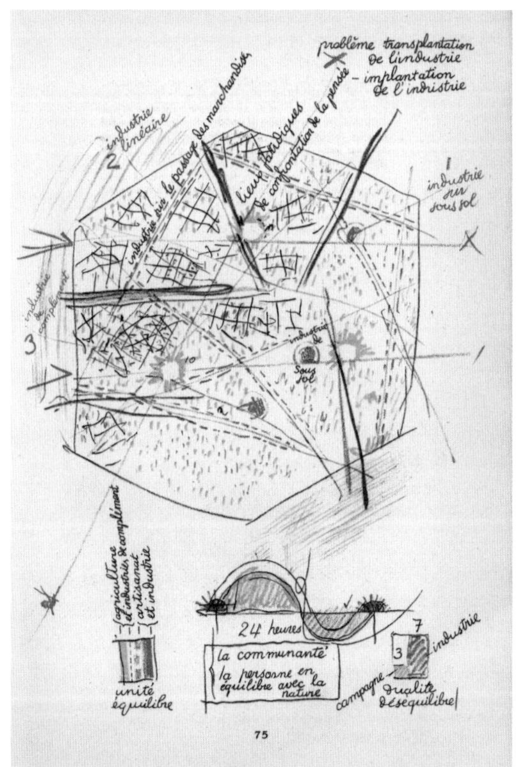

FIGURE 12.14: The cities of France will be reborn, the countryside reoccupied. The challenge before the architect-planner is to make hexagonal France blossom with greenery, and allow man to rediscover the conditions of nature.

FIGURE EPILOGUE.1: Le Corbusier required little for inspiration: a cell with an enclosed garden like a monk's "villa décapotable," open to the sky and the sun; an occasion for solitude and reverie, as sketched in this letter to his family in 1951.

FIGURE EPILOGUE.2: Le Corbusier made a portfolio of lithographs for *Le Poème de l'Angle Droit* between 1947 and 1953. This portfolio represents a synthesis of his artworks and his architecture. FIGURE EPILOGUE.3: Ever hopeful that the authorities would accept his plans for Paris, Le Corbusier compiled a personal dialogue with the reader, looking back over the many obstacles his hopes and plans for Paris confronted.

NOTES

CHAPTER 1

Epigraph Le Corbusier, *Almanach d'Architecture Moderne* (Paris: Les Éditions G. Crès et Cie, 1925), 5.

1 Fox Weber's biography is based primarily on letters Le Corbusier wrote to William Ritter, his family, his wife, and various lovers. It focuses on his private persona and completely ignores the public persona developed via his writings. Fox Weber circumvents how Le Corbusier's writings address his developing doctrine of architecture and urbanism. Nicholas Fox Weber, *Le Corbusier: A Life* (New York: Alfred A. Knopf, 2008).

2 A diploma was not required by French law until 1940. The title "architect" (or D.P.L.G. [Diplômé Par Le Gouvernement]) was an invention of the late nineteenth century, only recognized officially in 1914 and not obligatory until 1940. Until that point in time, the profession of architecture was an open affair. Marie-Jeanne Dumont, "Le Corbusier: L'élève et ses maîtres," *Le Visiteur* 9 (Fall 2002): 58, footnote 2.

3 Le Corbusier, *Les Plans Le Corbusier de Paris* (Paris: Les Éditions de Minuit, 1956), 85.

4 Ibid.

5 Arthus Rüegg, "Marcel Levaillant and 'La Question du Mobilier,'" in *Le Corbusier before Le Corbusier*, ed. Stanislaus von Moss and Arthur Rüegg (New Haven and London: Yale University Press, 2002), 109–32.

6 Le Corbusier, *Precisions on the Present State of Architecture and City Planning*, trans. Edith Schreiber Aujame (Cambridge: MIT Press, 1991); from p. 33 of French publication (1930).

7 Le Corbusier, "Mise au point" (1965), quoted and translated by Ivan Žaknić, *The Final Testament of Père Corbu* (New Haven: Yale University Press, 2007), 83.

8 Le Corbusier, *When the Cathedrals Were White*, trans. Francis E. Hyslop, Jr. (New York: McGraw-Hill Book Company, 1947), 30.

9 Ibid.

10 Mark Johnson, *The Meaning of the Body: Aesthetics of Human Understanding* (Chicago: University of Chicago Press, 2007), 19–32, 94–98.

11 Christophe Van Gerrewey, "Total Absence of Illusion, Unlimited Commitment," *OASES* 70 (2006): 8–36.

12 Le Corbusier, *The City of To-morrow and its Planning*, trans. Frederick Etchells (Cambridge: MIT Press, reprint 1971 [from the 8th edition of *Urbanisme*, 1929, original edition 1925]), 206.

13 Paul Valéry, *Leonardo Poe Mallarmé*, trans. Malcolm Cowley and James R. Lawler (Princeton: Princeton University Press, 1972), 20.

14 Ibid., 19.

15 Paul Valéry, "The physical aspects of a book" (1945) in *Aesthetics* (New York: Pantheon, 1964), 212, quoted by William Kluback, *Paul Valéry: The statesman of the intellect* (New York: Peter Lang Pub. Inc., 1999), 31.

16 Paul Valéry to Le Corbusier, republished in Le Corbusier, *The Decorative Arts of Today*, trans. James I. Dunnett (Cambridge: MIT Press, 1987), xii.

17 Romain Rolland to Le Corbusier, FLC T2-20-413 23, Nov. 1930.

18 "The Final Year," translated and quoted by Žaknić, *The Final Testament of Père Corbu*, 117.
19 For a lengthy discussion of how writing is tied to emotions, and to neurological centers of the brain, see Alice Flaherty, *The Midnight Disease: The Drive to Write, Writer's Block and the Creative Brain* (Boston: Houghton Mifflin Company, 2004).
20 This series of discussions took place between Karel Teige and Le Corbusier. Karel Teige, "Mundaneum," *Oppositions* 4 (Oct. 1974): 83–89; originally published in *Strava* (1929). Le Corbusier, "In Defense of Architecture," *Oppositions* 4 (Oct. 1974): 91–106; originally published in *Strava* (1929). Le Corbusier, "Defense de l'architecture," FLC D1-7-122-461, reprinted in *Architecture Aujourd'hui* (1933).
21 Camille Mauclair, *Les Couleurs du Maroc* (Paris: Bernard Grasset, 1933), 36.
22 Le Corbusier, "Les Temps Nouveaux et la Vocation de l'architecte" (lecture by Le Corbusier, Rio de Janeiro, 9 Dec. 1936, FLC C3-18-138–155).
23 Le Corbusier's criticism is repeated in Le Corbusier, *When the Cathedrals Were White*, and in Le Corbusier, *The Four Routes* (London: Dennis Dobston Ltd. Pub., 1947), trans. Dorothy Todd from *Sur les 4 Routes* (Paris: Gallimard, 1941).
24 Le Corbusier explains to Ritter that he made a grand voyage to South America for three and a half months as a kind of architectural ambassador and that he wrote another book, *Prècisions*, on his return voyage, to be published within a few months. No sooner was he back in Paris then he left for Moscow (three different times), commenting that something great was being elaborated there and it would be interesting to see its development. He had taken up painting again, committing every morning until one o'clock to this passion, and he sketched on trains and in hotels while traveling. "Life is short. Minute by minute I fill it with things almost all passionate. Thus pass the days and...ten intoxicating years." Le Corbusier to Ritter, FLC R3-19-423, Paris, 29 Mar. 1930.
25 Ibid.
26 Ritter to Le Corbusier, R3-20-37, 25 May 1930.
27 Le Corbusier, *The Modulor*, trans. Peter de Francia and Anna Bostock (London: Faber and Faber Ltd., 1954; French edition, 1951), 9.
28 Paul Valéry, "Les deux vertus d'un livre" (1926), *Arts et Métier Graphiques* 12 (14 Sept. 1927): 3–8.
29 Le Corbusier, "Sainte Alliance des Arts majeurs ou le Grand Art en Gésine," *La Bête Noire* (1 July 1935), FLC X1-12-91.
30 Tim Benton, *Le Corbusier Conférencier* (Paris: Editions Le Moniteur, 2007); Marie-Victoire de Vaubernier, "Le Corbusier, Editeur," in *Le Corbusier, Écritures Rencontres des 18 et 19 Juin, 1993* (Paris: Fondation le Corbusier, 1993), 37.
31 *Le Corbusier in America: Travels in the Land of the Timid*, trans. Madge Bacon (Cambridge: MIT Press, 2001), 60, also quoted in part by Tim Benton, *Le Corbusier Conférencier*, 13; also partially repeated in Žaknić "The Final Year," *The Final Testament of Père Corbu*, 113.
32 Le Corbusier, *Precisions*, 2, quotation 19.
33 Ibid., 25.
34 "Le livre sera fait avec *Propos d'urbanisme, Maison des Hommes, Précisions, Trois Etablissements, Manière de penser l'urbanisme* par *couture* de texte et d'images diverse." FLC A3-9-4, 21 May 1948. This is the order that Le Corbusier arranges the books as quoted by Catherine de Smet, "Le Livre comme synthèse des arts. Édition et design graphique chez Le Corbusier, 1945–1966" (Doctoral thesis, L'EHESS, 29 Oct. 2002): 255.
35 Marie-Brigitte Preteux, "Les Idées de Le Corbusier après la Second Guerre Mondial" (Unpublished thesis, Université de Paris, Sorbonne, Oct. 1995), FLC 03.21.
36 H. Allen Brooks, "Review of Jean Jenger (ed.), *Le Corbusier: Choix de lettres*," *JSAH* 62, no. 1 (Mar. 2003): 146–47.
37 Darlene Brady, *Le Corbusier: An Annotated Bibliography* (New York: Garland, 1985).
38 *Le Corbusier, une encyclopédie* (Paris: Centre National d'Art et de Culture Georges Pompidou, 1987), 482–89.
39 Preteux, "Les Idées de Le Corbusier," 165.
40 Catherine de Smet, "Le Livre comme synthèse des arts," 42–47.
41 Viveca Bosson, "Le Corbusier–the painter who became an architect," in *Le Corbusier Painter and Architect*, ed. Mogens Krustrup, Kataloget er Udgivet Med Stotte FRA (Denmark: Fonden Til Udgivelse Af Arkitekturtidsskrift, 1995), 17–58.
42 Ibid., 19–20.
43 Mogens Krustrup, "Persona," *Le Corbusier Painter and Architect*, 118–58.
44 H. Allen Brooks, *Le Corbusier's Formative Years* (Chicago: University of Chicago Press, 1997), 12.
45 Daniel Naegele, "Photographic illusionism and the 'New World of Space,'" *Le Corbusier Painter and Architect*, 83–117; and

Bosson, "Le Corbusier–the painter who became an architect."

46 Sigfried Giedion wrote, "Et come chez lui tout s'exprimait toujours de façon plastique, il m'envoya de Chandigarh une lettre accompagnée d'un dessin (fig. 339). Il y évoquait une conversation avec Ernesto N. Rogers architecte bien connu et éditeur de 'Casabella." Le Corbusier wrote, "Rogers prétendait que je suis un génie et moi je certifiais être un âne. J'ai alors représenté la question par ce croquis.' en dessous de son dessin, Le Corbuiser avait écrit 'Le génie porte-t'il l'âne, ou l'âne porte-t-il le génie?'" Siegfried Giedion, *Espace, Temps, Architecture* (Brussels: La Connaissance, 1968), 348, illustration 339. For information on this sketch see Bosson, "Le Corbusier–the painter who became an architect," 21.

47 Bosson, "Le Corbusier–the painter who became an architect," 21.

48 Catherine de Smet, "Le Livre comme synthèse des arts."

49 Mary Patricia Sekler, quoted by Krustrup, "Persona," *Le Corbusier Painter and Architect*, 119–20.

50 Le Corbusier introduces a text on piloti with this statement, quoted by Werner Oechslin, "5 Points d'une architecture nouvelle," in *Le Corbusier, une encyclopédie*, 94.

51 Journal of Le Corbusier, 9 Sept. 1920, cited by Petit, *Le Corbusier Lui-Même*, 53, quoted by Journel, "Le Corbusier: Un Architecte Ecrivain de la Modernité," 3.

52 Le Corbusier, "Calendrier d'Architecture," in *Almanach d'Architecture Moderne*, 6–7.

53 The five points were first manifested by Le Corbusier and Pierre Jeanneret during the design of their entry to the Weissemhof Exhibition in Stuttgart, 1927. Shortened into the style of a manifesto, the points begin to appear in such early writings as Le Corbusier, "Pour bâtir: Standardiser et Tayloriser," *Bulletin du Redressement Francais* (1 May 1928): 1–8.

54 Le Corbusier, "Déficit, Acquisition," FLC B2-16-97, not dated.

55 Ibid.

56 Le Corbusier, *Almanach d'Architecture Moderne*, 5.

57 Ibid., 74.

58 Le Corbusier, "L'Esprit Nouveau en Architecture," conference held 12 June 1924; Le Corbusier, *Almanach d'Architecture Moderne*, 17–40.

59 Ibid., 35.

60 Ibid., 36.

61 Ibid., 39.

62 Ibid., 39.

63 Le Corbusier, *Precisions*, 132–33, quotation on 133.

64 Le Corbusier, *Concerning Town Planning*, trans. Clive Entwistle (New Haven: Yale University Press, 1948); from the French *Propos d'Urbanisme* (Paris: Bourrelier, 1946).

65 Kenneth Silver, *Esprit de Corps* (Princeton: Princeton University Press, 1989), 46–47, 51–52.

66 Ibid., 53.

67 Françoise Ducros, "La Peinture Puriste et L'Esprit Nouveau" (Unpublished thesis, Paris, 26 Feb. 1986).

68 Susan L. Ball, *Ozenfant and Purism: The evolution of a Style 1915–1930* (Ann Arbor, Michigan: UMI Research Press, 1981), 15.

69 In spite of the avoidance of war topics, the cover of the first issue of *L'Élan*, designed by Ozenfant, displayed an image of Dame Victory, outlining on her forehead the French military front while her necklace represented the allied lines in France and Belgium. Silver, *Esprit de Corps*, 57. Among the contributors to this review were: Apollinaire, Sébastien Voirel, Auguste Perret, Pablo Picasso, André Lhote, André Derain, Raoul Dufy, Fernand Leger, Henri Matisse, and Ozenfant; Ball, *Ozenfant and Purism*, 14–24. See also Christopher Prochasson and Anne Rasmussen, *Au Nom de la Patrie* (Paris: Éditions La Dévouverte, 1996), 183.

70 Apollinaire created two short-lived journals: *Le Festin d'Ésope* (1903–4) and only one issue of *La Revue Immoralist* (Apr. 1915). Walter Adamson, "Apollinaire's Politics: Modernism, Nationalism and the Public Sphere in Avant-Garde Paris," *MODERNISM/Modernity* 6, no. 3 (Sept. 1999): 33–56, reference 41.

71 Margaret Davies, *Apollinaire* (Edinburgh and London: Oliver & Boyd, 1964), 283.

72 Contributors were Tristan Tzara, Philippe Soupault, Louis Aragon, Francis Picabia, and Paul Dermée. Prochasson and Rasmussen, *Au Nom de la Patrie*, 184.

73 Paul Dermée and Pierre Reverdy, *Nord-Sud* 1(Mar. 1917), quoted by Davies, *Apollinaire*, 284.

74 This magazine published contributions from Max Jacob, Vincent Huidobro, Andre Breton, Paul Dermée, Georges Braque, Tristan Tzara, and Fernand Leger. Between 1917 and 1923 there would be an outpouring in Paris of "little magazines" publishing experimental work and critical reviews. Johanna Drucker, *The Visible Word experimental typography and modern art, 1909–1923* (Chicago: University

of Chicago Press, 1994), 10; Prochasson and Rasmussen, *Au Nom de la Patrie*, 180–84.
75 Davies, *Apollinaire*, 287.
76 Fox Weber claims without revealing the source of his information that Le Corbusier attended *Parade* on 17 May 1917. Fox Weber, *Le Corbusier: A Life*, 136.
77 Apollinaire, quoted by Prochasson and Rasmussen, *Au Nom de la Patrie*, 131.
78 As early as 1911, the manifesto of a new review *L'Independence* declared that France had been able to transfer to the twentieth century classical heritage, whether Greek or Roman, because during several centuries French thinkers, artists and poets had kept from confusing disorder with liberty, originality with lack of taste. André Beaumier discussed the *esprit nouveau* by comparing the Renaissance to the New France in the early 1900s. "The Renaissance had been defined as 'a newness which is not new'; it resuscitated a magnificent past Antiquity. The novelty proclaimed in the two words 'New France' is not new either.... An ancient tradition is renewed...we are again on the beautiful and good path, broad and well lit by the sun of France." Quoted by Silver, *Esprit de Corps*, 93.
79 Guillaume Apollinaire, "The New Spirit and the Poets," in *Selected Writings of Guillaume Apollinaire*, trans. Roger Shattuck (New York: A New Directions Book, 1971), 227.
80 Davies, *Apollinaire*, 290.
81 "In the realm of inspiration, their liberty can not be less than that of a daily newspaper which on a single sheet treats the most diverse matters and ranges over the most distant countries. One wonders why the poet should not have at least an equal freedom, and should be restricted, in an era of telephone, the wireless, and aviation, to a great cautiousness in confronting space." Apollinaire, "The New Spirit and the Poets," 229.
82 Ibid., 237, quoted by K. R. Dutton, "Apollinaire and Communication," *Australian Journal of French Studies* 5, no. 3 (Sept.–Dec. 1968): 308–29, quotation on 326.
83 Davies, *Apollinaire*, 303.
84 David Berry, *The Creative Vision of Guillaume Apollinaire* (Saratoga, CA: Anma Libir, 1982), 153.
85 The phrase *retour à l'ordre* was first formulated at an exposition of Braque's work at La Galerie Moderne in March 1919. Prochasson and Rasmussen, *Au Nom de la Patrie*, 272.
86 Raymond Lefebvre, quoted by Prochasson and Rasmussen, *Au Nom de la Patrie*, 271.
87 In 1921, a retrospective of Ingres's paintings and drawings was organized as a benefit exhibition for facially wounded veterans of war. It received extreme praise in the press because it was believed that more than any other artist, Ingres instilled the Hellenistic spirit, teaching clarity and precision in his work. He epitomized the classical fervor for order and discipline. So it was argued by Arsène Alexandre "To understand Ingres is to understand Greece and France." Quoted by Silver, *Esprit de Corps*, 247.
88 Amédée Ozenfant and Charles-Édouard Jeanneret,"Le Purisme," *L'Esprit Nouveau* 4 (1921).
89 Amédée Ozenfant and Charles-Édouard Jeanneret, "Intégrer," *Création Revue d'Art* 2 (1921).
90 *L'Esprit Nouveau* 16 (May 1922).
91 "Domain de L'Esprit Nouveau" (signed "L'Esprit Nouveau"), *L'Esprit Nouveau* 1 (1920), no pagination.
92 "The Final Year," translated and quoted by Žaknić, *The Final Testament of Père Corbu*, 117.
93 The list of postwar books includes: Le Corbusier, *UN Headquarters* (1947); Le Corbusier, *New World of Space* (1948); Le Corbusier, *Poésie sur Alger* (1950); Le Corbusier, *Modulor* (1950); Le Corbusier, *L'Unité d'habitation de Marseille* (1950); Le Corbusier, *Une petite maison* (1954); Le Corbusier, *Poème de l'angle droit* (1955); Le Corbusier, *Modulor 2* (1955); Le Corbusier, *Les Plans Le Corbusier de Paris 1956–1922* (1956); Le Corbusier, *Ronchamp* (1957); Le Corbusier, *Les Plans de Paris* (1960); Le Corbusier, *Atelier de la recherché patiente* (1960).

CHAPTER 2

Epigraph Le Corbusier to L'Eplattenier, FLC E2-12-38, Paris, 22 Nov. 1908 and 25 Nov. 1908.
1 H. Allen Brooks states the date as September third, Nicholas Fox Weber that it was the first. H. Allen Brooks, *Le Corbusier's Formative Years* (Chicago: University of Chicago Press, 1997), 95; Nicholas Fox Weber, *Le Corbusier: A Life* (New York: Alfred A. Knopf, 2008), 40.
2 Charles L'Eplattenier (1874–1946).
3 Stanislaus von Moos, "Voyages en Zigzag," in *Le Corbusier before Le Corbusier*, ed. Stanislaus von Moss and Arthur R egg (New Haven and London: Yale University Press, 2002), 23–44, 283–85.

4 Charles Jencks, *Le Corbusier and the Continual Revolution in Architecture* (New York: The Monacelli Press, 2000), 37–41.
5 Jack Goody, *The Domestication of the Savage Mind* (Cambridge: Cambridge University Press, 1977), 74–111.
6 Le Corbusier to L'Eplattenier, FLC E2-12-6, Florence, 19 Sept. 1907.
7 Ibid.
8 William Ritter (1867–1955).
9 Both H. Allen Brooks and N. Fox Weber state that Jeanneret met Perrin in Florence on September 10. Jeanneret's letter of the nineteenth states that Perrin had waited two days for him in Pisa. Perhaps he left for Florence before Jeanneret's arrival. Brooks, *Le Corbusier's Formative Years*, 99; Fox Weber *Le Corbusier*, 43.
10 Le Corbusier to L'Eplattenier, 19 Sept. 1907.
11 Ibid.
12 Ibid.
13 Ibid., and Le Corbusier to family, FLC R1-4-14, Florence, 23 Sept. 1907.
14 Le Corbusier to L'Eplattenier, FLC E2-12-12, Venice, 1 Nov. 1907.
15 Brooks, *Le Corbusier's Formative Years*, 96, 101, 106. Quotation from Le Corbusier, *Modular* 2 (Basel: Birkhäuser, 1958), 296, quoted by Brooks, 101.
16 Jencks, *Le Corbusier and the Continual Revolution*, 38–39.
17 Le Corbusier to L'Eplattenier, 1 Nov. 1907.
18 Ibid.
19 Le Corbusier to L'Eplattenier, postcard, FLC E2-12-16-17, Vienna, 17 Nov. 1907.
20 Le Corbusier to L'Eplattenier, FLC E2-12-18, Vienna, 11 Dec. 1907.
21 Le Corbusier with Léon Perrin to L'Eplattenier, FLC E2-12-20-21, Vienna, 2 Jan. 1908.
22 Ibid.
23 Ibid.
24 Le Corbusier to L'Eplattenier, FLC E2-12-22, Vienna, 3 Jan. 1908.
25 Le Corbusier to L'Eplattenier, FLC E2-12-23, Vienna, 26 Feb. 1908.
26 The lack of a diploma haunted Le Corbusier throughout his lifetime. It might be that on his 1930 French identity card he listed his profession as *homme de lettres*, not architect, because he had no diploma. However, the title "architect" (or D.P.L.G., *Diplômé Par Le Gouvernement*) was an invention of the late nineteenth century, only recognized officially in 1914 and not obligatory until 1940. Until that time, the profession of architecture was an open affair. Marie-Jeanne Dumont, "Le Corbusier: L'élève et ses maîtres," *Le Visiteur* 9 (Fall 2002): 58, footnote 2.
27 Jeanneret's older brother Albert (1886–1973) passed his entrance examinations to the Conservatoire at Berlin in the spring of 1902 but in 1903 shifted to study with Henri Marteau in Geneva, moving there in 1906. He suffered from lack of self-confidence and began to experience cramps in his wrist as early as 1906. This ailment would lead him eventually to abandon the violin and focus on studying dancing and eurythmics with Jaques Dalcroze (Brooks, *Le Corbusier's Formative Years*, 15, 42–43).
28 Le Corbusier to L'Eplattenier, 26 Feb. 1908.
29 Le Corbusier to L'Eplattenier, FLC E22-12-26, Vienna, 29 Feb. 1908.
30 Ibid.
31 Le Corbusier to L'Eplattenier, FLC E2-12-28, Vienna, 2 Mar. 1908.
32 Ibid.
33 Le Corbusier to his parents, FLC R1-4-96, Vienna, 29 Feb. 1908.
34 Even though they notified their respective landlords on the first of March that they would be departing, still Jeanneret and Perrin wanted their mentor's approval, which they eventually got. Brooks *Le Corbusier's Formative Years*, 15, 147.
35 Le Corbusier to L'Eplattenier, FLC E2-12-32-33, Vienna, 2 Mar. 1908.
36 Ibid.
37 Le Corbusier to L'Eplattenier, FLC E2-12-34-36, Paris, undated 1908. Brooks says this letter is dated 3 July, 1908, but it may have been later because Jeanneret mentions having beside him Viollet-le-Duc. He purchased these books on August 1. This letter is reproduced in full along with the next Le Corbusier letter to L'Eplattenier, written on 22 Nov. 1908, and 25 Nov. 1908, in Jean Petit, *Le Corbusier Lui-Même* (Geneva: Editions Rousseau, 1970), 31–36; Le Corbusier to L'Eplattenier, FLC E2-12-38-50, Paris, 22 Nov. 1908, and 25 Nov. 1908.
38 Brooks, *Le Corbusier's Formative Years*, 15, 156.
39 Jeanneret would quit working for Perret November 2, 1909, to which he compares the fact that one year later he begins work with Behrens on November 1. See Le Corbusier to L'Eplattenier, postcard, FLC E2-12-78, Potsdam, 28 Oct. 1910.
40 Claudia Brodsky Lacour, *Lines of Thought: Discourse, Architectonics, and the Origin of*

Modern Philosophy (Durham and London: Duke University Press, 1996).

41 Le Corbusier to L'Eplattenier, FLC E2-12-34-36, Paris, undated 1908.

42 He purchased this set of books after receiving his first month's paycheck from Auguste Perret. In it he wrote, "I bought this work August 1, 1908 in order to *learn*, because, *knowing* I will then be able to create." Brooks, *Le Corbusier's Formative Years*, 15, 171.

43 Le Corbusier to L'Eplattenier, FLC E2-12-34-36, Paris, undated 1908. Brooks says the letter is dated 3 July, 1908.

44 Ibid.

45 Le Corbusier to L'Eplattenier, FLC E2-12-38, Paris, 22 Nov. 1908, and 25 Nov. 1908. This letter is translated in part by Brooks, *Le Corbusier's Formative Years*, 153–4; Geoffrey H. Baker, *Le Corbusier: The Creative Search* (New York, Van Nostrand Reinhold, 1996), 126–29; and Jencks, *Le Corbusier and the Continual Revolution*, 40–50.

46 Ibid.

47 Ibid.

48 Ibid.

49 Ibid.

50 Ibid.

51 Ibid.

52 Ibid.

53 Ibid.

54 Ibid.

55 Ibid.

56 Ibid.

57 Ibid. Brooks considers this letter to be "a remarkable letter," even "a marvelous letter." He states that it is not a forecast of the ideas the Jeanneret will espouse in the future with respect either to architecture or to L'Eplattenier's teachings; he admits that Jeanneret acquired in Paris a "philosophical approach based on logic and reason," but states that he would not hold to these ideas consistently and that they were probably based more on Ruskianian morality than on French rationalism. Brooks, *Le Corbusier's Formative Years*, 152–54, 159.

58 Le Corbusier to his parents, FLC R1-4-121-8, Paris, 2 May 1909.

59 Le Corbusier to his parents, FLC R1-4-137, Paris, 8 Nov. 1909.

60 Brooks, *Le Corbusier's Formative Years*, 196.

61 Baker, *Le Corbusier: The Creative Search*, 129–30; Brooks, *Le Corbursier's Formative Years*, 154.

62 Brooks, *Le Corbusier's Formative Years*, 216–7.

63 Ibid., 251–52.

64 Ibid., 251–53. Giuliano Gresleri, "The German Carnets: 'triomphe de l'ordre' and 'heureuse évolution,'" in Ch.-E. Jeanneret Le Corbusier, *Les voyages d'Allemagne Carnets* (New York and Paris: The Monacellli Press and the Fondation L.C., 1994), 9–22

65 Alice Flaherty argues that most researchers questioning the creative process converge on the assumption that it is the result of an interaction between divergent thinking which produces a number of solutions for a poorly defined problem "Divergent thinking is essential for the novelty of the creative product, whereas convegent thinking is essential for testing its appropriateness. Readers with Classical tastes may prefer to think of convergent thought as Appollonian and divergent thought as Dionysian." Alice Flaherty, *The Midnight Disease: The Drive to Write, Writer's Block and the Creative Brain* (Boston: Houghton Mifflin Company, 2004), 62.

66 Le Corbusier to L'Eplattenier, FLC E2-12-61, Munich, 16 Apr. 1910.; Le Corbusier to his parents, FLC F1-5-8-11, Munich, 18 Apr. 1910. He will utilize this motif of food in opening both his travel-writings on South America and the United States in 1929 and 1935, respectively.

67 Perhaps Jeanneret first met the art critic, painter, novelist and traveler William Ritter (1867–1955) during his winter sojourn in La Chaux-de-Fonds 1909–10, but he may have met him for the first time in Munich in the spring of 1910. William Ritter, a friend of L'Eplattenier, often spent time in the mountains of Les Brenets, the next town along the valley from La Chaux-de-Fonds, but resided most of the year in Munich. Twenty years Jeanneret's senior, Ritter nevertheless became a close confidant–a man whom Jeanneret trusted with his innermost doubts, thoughts, and emotions, to whom he demanded and expected honest truthful criticism and correction of his writing style and painting methods. William Ritter wrote art reviews in several journals: *La Gazette des Beaux Arts* (Paris), *L'Art et L'Artiste* (Paris), *Mercure de France* (Paris), *Feuilles d'Avis* (La Chaux-de-Fonds). He was also the writer of many novels. *L'Entêtement slovaque* (1910) particularly influenced Jeanneret. Baker, *Le Corbusier: The Creative Search*, 135–6. Brooks states that Jeanneret met Ritter at the end of May, 1910, in Munich. Brooks, *Le Corbusier's Formative Years*, 218; Le Corbusier to L'Eplattenier, FLC E2-12-61, Munich, 16 Apr. 1910.

68 "Je joins 1 feuilè qui résume 1 premier idée du petit ouvrage dont nous avions parlé: vous purriez me la retourner en y ajountant ds les marges les corrections et les compléments." Ibid.
69 Ibid.
70 Le Corbusier to L'Eplattenier, FLC E2-12-72, Munich, Apr. 1910. This letter at the FLC is out of order and appears just before a letter written on the first of October, 1910. Instead, it is written shortly after arriving in Munich in the middle of April, 1910.
71 Ibid.
72 "Or il me le faut ce bouqin et me voila le bec ds l'eau." Le Corbusier to L'Eplattenier, postcard, FLC E2-12-65, Munich, 19 May 1910.
73 To his parents, Jeanneret writes that he is working long hours in the library and has gathered very important and new information for his "métier." Le Corbusier to his parents, FLC F1-5-12-17, Munich, 16 May 1910.
74 "J'ai fini la plus gde partie de la brochure. J'ai l peine épouvantale à l'écrire en français. Mais la matière est dense et ce que j'aurai fait pourra intéresser peut-être polus que les architects de la Chaux-de-Fds." Le Corbusier to L'Eplattenier, postcard, FLC E2-12-66, Munich, 2 June 1910.
75 "Cette brochure est l heureuse affaire pour moi, elle me permit de m'orienter à l'abri de l'énervement et des attentes démoralisantes." Ibid.
76 Le Corbusier to L'Eplattenier, postcard, FLC E2-12-68, Munich, 7 July 1910.
77 Brooks, *Le Corbusier's Formative Years*, 219; Gresleri, "The German Carnets," 11.
78 While in Berlin, Jeanneret goes to the Rheingold restaurant designed by Bruno Schmitz (1906–7), with interior decoration by Franz Metzner. He visits different rooms, but finds them not overwhelming but unsettling in the use of heavy and strong materials. They offer at first an impression of beauty which becomes very tiring, and the scene in the end is more discomforting than pleasurable. He would return to the restaurant, on another visit to Berlin, and revise his opinion slightly: finding that while the main room was good, it left a cold, troubling impression. He knows only one café that appears to be successful in its decor: the Fledermaus café designed by Josef Hoffmann (1907) in Vienna. Ch.-E. Jeanneret Le Corbusier, *Les voyages d'Allemagne Carnets* (New York and Paris: The Monacellli Press and Fondation L.C., 1994). *Carnet* I: 53, 42–3. *Carnet* II: 132, 66.
79 Ch.-E. Jeanneret Le Corbusier, *Les voyages d'Allemagne Carnets*, 38–41.
80 "Figurez-vous que partout on ne veut pas me croire architecte, et que l'on m'attribue juste les vertus d'l peintre." Le Corbusier to L'Eplattenier, postcard, FLC E2-12-68, Munich, 27 June 1910.
81 Ibid.
82 "Cette étude, se terminé par l critique vigoureuse des moyens employés à La Chaux-de-Fonds et a pour but de les faire transformer du tou au tout. Cette étude sera publiée en l brochure, dont l'importance depasse mes prevision. Ce fut pour moi 1 passionnate question et j'espere bp en ses resultats directs. Elle sera signée de l'Ep et de moi et aura l interet pas eclusivement local." Le Corbusier to his parents, FLC F1-5-18-25, Munich, 29 June 1910.
83 "Autant dire ce qui est fait; ce qui est future n'appartient à personne, pas même à celui qui projette." Ibid.
84 "Ds l époque où tout est chaos, où tout ce qui est banal, est prone, où tout ce qui est force naissante est contesté, j'estime que ceux qui ne veulent pas suivre les sentiers battus, sont de bonnes têtes." Ibid.
85 August Klipstein (1885–1951).
86 Brooks, *Le Corbusier's Formative Years*, 226.
87 Le Corbusier to L'Eplattenier, postcard, FLC E2-12-69, Munich, 4 July 1910.
88 Le Corbusier to L'Eplattenier, postcard, FLC E2-12-70, Munich, 10 July 1910.
89 Brooks, *Le Corbusier's Formative Years*, 226, 228.
90 Le Corbusier to L'Eplattenier, FLC E2-12-74-77, Munich, 1 Oct. 1910.
91 "L'obélisque de Rome doit être stupide; *mais les 2 obélisques à Louqsor, durent être grandose.* Car c'était eux qui donnaient aux facades leurs surface, et les facades leur conféraient leur caractère d'obélisque." Ibid.
92 Ibid.
93 "Behhreus [*sic*] doit répondre 1 de ces jours. J'ai de l'anxiété: çà leur est si facile à ces Molochs-là de vous dire: 'repassez dans deux ans!' Vraiment je serai le bec dans l'eau et très contrarié, perplexe, et devrais m'attendre à trouver orte close partout, à cette saison où le travail d'hiver a repris son train." Ibid.
94 Ibid.
95 Le Corbusier to his parents, FLC F1-5-26-33, Munich, not dated (Sept. 1910).
96 "Si nous savions finir chaque journée en ecountant l'argent d'une vois profonde, alors chque matin nous nous leverions joyeu,

enjambant la journée brutale pour ouvrier le soir, l'oreille aux bruits bienfaisants." "Avant que de mourir, il faut jouir, et al Joie il faut la cueillir: elle est la, à gauche, une ame qui demande a être aimée–à droite, une fleur qui paqrle d'harmonie.... Tout est la: demeurer maître des circonstances et voir au-dessus de la realites, le reve, le reve dont insensement est pleine toute la nature et dont regarge le coeur." Ibid.

97 Brooks, *Le Corbusier's Formative Years*, 233, 235.

98 Actually he terminated employment with the Perrets on November 9, but symmetry of dates makes a better story. Le Corbusier to L'Eplattenier, postcard, FLC E2-12-78, Potsdam, 28 Oct. 1910.

99 "Octave, s'en alla rever à Bruges, et voila: 'au long des canaux de 'la ville morte... a la dérive, flottainet–des m–Epiloguant sur ceci, qu'en cette vie, la réalité n'est point soeur du reve. Octave finissait en distant: 'Non, Constantinople, Stamboul, je ne te verrai pas!'" Le Corbusier to L'Eplattenier, FLC E2-12-79, Neu Babelsberg, 8 Nov. 1910.

100 "Et nous aurons au milieu de nos 'hommes de la "vraie Vie,"'" Ibid.

101 "Pendant que d'autres s'ereintent et se font de la bile, il dit: 'Petit poisson dans l'eau, pigeon vole!'" Ibid.

102 "Dans sa cuisine fine et maladivement recherché, un morceau de bon pain d'affection." Ibid.

103 "William Ritter apppelle ca 'crétinisant' et après 15 ans séjour en pays allemand, il le parle horriblement mal." Ibid.

104 "Ependant je vous conseillerai encore la lecture d'un livre remarquable, écrit *pour vous*, 'ce qu'on a fait de mieux, dit M. William Ritter depuis Ruskin.' Inutile alors d'ajouter que le livre n'est aucun succes. Vous pardonnerez à l'auteur de ne point aimer votre premier timbre-poste: ses théories et ses gouts le portaient naturellement à critiquer cette oeuvre qui de vous, n'était pas définitif." Ibid.

105 He writes to his parents that after being his own master able to dispense his sorrows and joys as he will, it is difficult to work under such a strenuous task-master as Behrens. He is pleased to note, however, that of the thirteen young designers that Behrens employs not one of them has a "brevet" degree and not one of them tries to obtain one. Le Corbusier to his parents, FLC R1-5-34-37, Berlin/Neu-Babelsberg, 28 Oct. 1910. He describes Behrens as a "colossal," with a formidable build, a terrible autocrat who imposes a regime of terror on his workers. Evidently he believes in the affection of brutality–and Jeanneret admits that he admires the man in a masochistic manner. Le Corbusier to his parents, FLC R1-5-38-49 Berlin/Neu-Babelsberg, 11 Nov. 1910.

106 Quoted by Brooks, *Le Corbusier's Formative Years*, 237.

107 "Et je suis obsédé d'une vision: des belles lignes droites, mais des rapports sveltes et classiques; infiniment de clarté ds les harmonies, du soleil intense et des counchants d'une pureté à vous faire crever d'extase, une plaine aride et nue, mais des Apennins bleus. Et puis des cyprès./ Rome!" Le Corbusier to his parents, 11 Nov. 1910.

108 Le Corbusier to L'Eplattenier, FLC E2-12-54-59, Berlin, 16 Jan. 1910 (48 pages). This letter has been misdated at the FLC, and the year should be 1911, not 1910.

109 "La souvenir s'en va là où on lui offre un reposoir; l'affection là où on l'appelle." Ibid.

110 "S'en vient créer *les volumes qui jouent sous la lumière* en rythmes à base géométrique, joie de la forme enfin retrouvée pour le régal des yeux et que permit la bataille que gagna Rodin et qui finira pour luis par un Waterloo. [inserted: Phénix qui se brûle lui-même mais qui renait sous une nouvelle form] plus jeune et radieux." Ibid.

111 "La France sujugue l'Allemagne. Et l'Allemagne s'incline." Ibid.

112 Vassilis Lambropoulos, *The Rise of Eurocentrism: Anatomy of Interpretation* (Princeton: Princeton University Press, 2003), 83–84.

113 "Cet appétit scientifique des choses héllénique." Le Corbusier to L'Eplattenier, 16 Jan. 1910.

114 "Puis L'Europe dormit, hormis Paris qui travaillait Courbet Manet et leur suite furent les grands dévastateurs' tels des mineurs, ils rongèrent l'édifice lentement à sa base et provoquèrent la tempête actuelle." Ibid.

115 "C'est que la France n'opérant que par révolution ignore dans sa masse les beaux fruits qu'elle possède, et l'Allemagne plus ouverte de par son dévloppement indusgtriel à tout ce qu'est nouveauté, l'Allemagne *révèle à la France, que la France a des génies!"* Ibid.

116 "Car déjà en ces formes hystériques est le germe nouveau qui sera l'expression de demain." Ibid.

117 "Il ya deux choses à considérer: La *Révolte*;–puis l'Edification du Code Nouveau." Ibid.

118 "L'Allemagne fut sécessionniste comme un papier buvard mis en contact avec une flaque d'encre, finit par l'absorber." Ibid.

119 "Pensez-vous que l'esposition de Bruxelles et la manifestations münichoise au Salon d'Automne n'aient pas été giflés sous lesquelles, enfin, on se ribiffe? La France devra à l'Allemagne une fameuse chandelle." Ibid.

120 These Munich displays received much praise when the French saw them in Die Ausstellung Munich in 1908 and led to the invitation to exhibit at the Salon d'Automne of 1910. In Paris, the Munich display contained an ensemble of thirteen rooms, grouping each object so the whole suggested a lived in home of salons, boudoir, music room, dining room, library, bathroom, etc. While each interior contained an eclectic display of furniture and objects, their color schemes were coordinated with adjacent rooms giving the whole an appearance of a unit. There were other lessons that France must learn from her German rivals–not only must they pay attention to the international market, develop apprenticeships, and decentralized professional education but they must produced utilitarian items for every-day use, not merely objects of luxury and taste in which France had traditionally excelled. Nancy Troy, *Modernism and the Decorative Arts in France* (New Haven: Yale University Press, 1991), 52–67.

121 "Je me souviendrai toujours de ce matin plein de fleurs printannières de maronniers neigeux et de lilas nains, qui déploya devants mes yeux le spectacle colossal et inattendu de Versailles. Ce fut l'ècroulement de man mythologie enténébrée et alros rayonna la clarté classique." Le Corbusier to L'Eplattenier, 16 Jan. 1910.

122 "C'est là mon évolution. J'ai dans les yeux et je les regarde souvent une soixantaine d'intérieurs de Versailles de Compiègne, de Fontainebleau. Que de leçons à prendre! J'ai aussi un livre splendide de dorique, de ionien, de corynthien, de cet art romain fait de voûtes colossales et de grands murs pleins./ Et, depuis des mois, mes idées se fixent. Je n'irai point en Amérique, ni en Flandres. Mais je resterai ici jusqu'à ce que je sache la langue, abrégeant peut-être mon séjour chez Behrens pour aller à Dresde pour bâtir chez Tessenow l'institute Jacques Dalcroze, suivant la proposition qui m'a été faite. Puis je ferai mon voyage d'étude en Allemagne, et ensuite irai me recueuillir. Où? À Rome./ Alors, après, si vous me voulez encore–!" Ibid.

123 "Chez Behrens, le choc a été brutal. Figurez-vous, qu'ayant folâtré dans toutes sortes de clos fleuris, et les ayant explorés, j'en avais oublié un–énorme! J'ararivai chez Behrnes ne sachant presque pas ce qu'était un style, et ignorant totalement l'art des moullures et de leurs rapports. Je vous assure que ce n'est point facile. Et c'est pourtant de rapports que nait l'harmonieuse forme." Ibid.

124 "J'eus et j'ai encore une peine infinie. Ajoutez àcela, une main de fer, tyrannique, brutale, les exigences d'une boîte où tous les plus grands travaux se font, boîte peuplée de 23 nègres qui tremblent, ma foi, sous l'humeur grise de ce colosse." Ibid.

125 Ibid.

126 He finished writing the book in January 1912. Ch.E. Jeanneret, *Étude sur le mouvement d'art décoratif* (facsimile, New York: Da Capo Press, 1968).

127 Troy, *Modernism and the Decorative Arts*, 57–59.

128 During the period when he wrote this report, he was intimately involved not only with practical experience gained in the Ateliers d'Art Réunis created by L'Eplattenier, but in the Nouvelle Section of École d'Art where he began to teach in January of 1912. The Nouvelle Section claimed in its prospectus of 1912 that it intended to pursue collaborative efforts between Art and Industry.

129 Rupert Carabin, "Conseil Municipal de Paris" (1908), quoted by Troy, *Modernism and the Decorative Arts*, 61.

130 Ibid., 108.

131 "Ces faits posent bien les deux pays en face l'un de l'autre; l'Allemagne révolutionnée, la France évoluée. C'est un fait accidentel en Allemagne, qui conduit aqujourd'hui à une disproportion entre les racines trop minimes et la fleur démesurée." Ch.E. Jeanneret, *Étude sur le mouvement d'art décoratif*, 13.

132 Ibid., 13–14.

133 Ibid., 15–16.

134 "L'Allemagne demeure le grand chantier de production. Les expériences ont été faites là, les luttes y sont devenues effectives: la bâtisse est élevée et les salles, avec leurs murs historiés, racontent le triomphe de l'ordre et de la ténacité." Ibid., 74.

135 Ibid., 19–25.

136 Ibid., 25–28

137 Ibid., 30–35.

138 Ibid., 35–39.

139 "On sent là-bas des hommes capables d'affronter dorénavant n'importe quel problème. Berlin voulait être non seulement pratique, hygiénique, agréable, mais elle aussi et il y avait dans le décret de ce concours, qui dura quelques années, un peu de cette fierté florentine qui fit s'ériger la coupole de Ste-Marie des Fleurs." Ibid., 36.

140 Ibid.

141 Ibid., 37.

142 Ibid., 39.

143 Ibid., 41.

144 "Behrens est le génie puissant, profond, grave, foncièrement halluciné de domination, qui convenait à cette besogne et à cette époque, ainsi qu'à l'esprit allemand contemporain." Ibid., 44.

145 "C'est un art tout nouveau, jeune de quelques années. Il se développe avec une rapidité foudroyante." Ibid., 45.

146 Ibid., 44–47.

147 Ibid., 47–51.

148 "Ainsi le tout-Berlin des cités-jardins, par example, endosse cette défroque; la coupe n'est pas hideuse, l'étouffe n'est que moins bonne. Au demeurant cet effort est très louable et les résultats marquent un progrès." Ibid., 47.

149 Ibid., 48.

150 "Une vie saine, cossu, se développe autour de rues tracées pour le repos des yeux." Ibid.

151 "Et voyant autour de luis, il concevra ce qu'annoncent pour l'avenir ces premiers grand festivals où, dans *les cironstances les plus favorables, il est permis à un gé*nie de se révéler, à des artistes de faire oeuvre d'art presque intégrale: les cycles de musique, les cycles de théâtre…. / Est-ce que je rêve en disant cela? Ces chose, je les ai senties en toutes le cités-jardins, à Munisch, à Hagen, à Stuttgart, à Berlin. Je l'ai senti presque comme une réalité quelques mois plus tard à Hellerau près de Dresde./ C'était en effet plus étonnant que partout ailleurs." Ibid., 49.

152 Ibid., 49–50.

153 Ibid., 51–53.

154 "C'est là une sorte de propagande sans caquetage que devrait bien employer toute ville qui voit s'effondrer son patrimonine artistique sous la griffe des spéculateurs." Ibid., 53.

155 Ibid., 53–55.

156 "Pour autant paradoxal que cela puisse paraitre, on pourrait ajouter: 'plus le décor est riche, moins l'efet marque un progrès pour l'art.' Ce n'est pas là un fait d'ordre particulier, c'est un fait inhérent à l'art, inhérent à l'artiste." Ibid., 54.

157 "Concentrer les forces qui sont en état d'atteindre les résultats les plus parfaits avec les moyens les plus restreints." Ibid., 55.

158 Ibid., 59–70.

159 "Une école reste une école, et les travaux des élèves trahissent peu souvent autre chose qu'une imitation plus ou moins bien comprise de la pensée du maître. Tout revient donc à la valeur du maître et c'est ce qui fait l'intérêt des écoles allemandes d'aujourd'hui. Il est évident que des élèves soumis à l'influnce de Fischer, de Van de Velde, de Hoffmann, de Behrens, de Paul, de Kreis our de Pankok, sont aptes à devenir parfois des personnalités, en touc cas des bons ouvriers de l'heure." Ibid., 59.

CHAPTER 3

Epigraph Le Corbusier, *Voyage to the East*, trans. Ivan Žaknić (Cambridge, MA: MIT Press, 1989), 217.

1 Called the "'Reversed' Tour" by Giuliano Gresleri and repeated by Adolf Max Vogt, "Remarks on the 'Reversed' Grand Tour of Le Corbusier and Auguste Klipstein," *Assemblage* 4 (1987): 38–51.

2 Le Corbusier, *Voyage to the East*, 240.

3 Vogt, "Remarks on the 'Reversed' Grand Tour," 39.

4 Le Corbusier et Pierre Jeanneret, "Introduction," in *Oeuvre Complète* 1910–1929, Vol. 1 (Zurich: Les Éditions d'Architecture, 1964), 11.

5 H. Allen Brooks, *Le Corbusier's Formative Years* (Chicago: University of Chicago Press, 1997), 255–303.

6 Brooks, *Le Corbusier's Formative Years*, 210, 247.

7 Le Corbusier to L'Eplattenier, FLC E22-12-26, Vienna, 29 Feb. 1908; Le Corbusier to L'Eplattenier, FLC E2-12-54-59, Berlin, 16 Jan. 1910.

8 At least Germany taught him to not like schools of architecture or art, and helped him turn toward the modern. Le Corbusier to L'Eplattenier, FLC E2-12-92-94, Istanbul, 18 July 1911.

9 The translation by Ivan Žaknić of Le Corbusier's *Voyage to the East* conserves the order of Jeanneret's original manuscript of "Voyage en Orient" with the exception that material on the chapter on the disastrous fire in Stamboul appears to have been separated from the chapter on "Recollections and Regrets." Žaknić relies for his translation on a 1914 typewritten manuscript of parts 1 and 2, and two handwritten chapters on Athos and the Parthenon finished on the 24th of June, 1914.

10 The list of articles published in *La Feuille d'Avis de la Chaux-de-Fonds* and translated in their order of publication by Ivan Žaknić in Le Corbusier's *Voyage to the East* are the following: "A Few Impressions," *Voyage to the East*, 6–13 (written 6 June 1911, published 20 July in *La Feuille d'Avis*); "A Letter to Friends, at the 'Ateliers d'art' in La-Chaux-de-Fonds," *Voyage*, 14–24 (published 25 July, 3 and 8 Aug. in *La Feuille d'Avis*); "Vienna," *Voyage*, 25–31 (published 18 and 25 Aug. in *La Feuille d'Avis*); "Danube," *Voyage*, 32–49 (published 31 Aug., 4 and 13 Sept., and 13 Oct. in *La Feuille d'Avis*); "Bucharest," *Voyage*, 50–56 (published 18 Oct. in Aug. *La Feuille d'Avis*); "Tûrnovo," *Voyage*, 57–65 (published 24 and 25 Oct. in *La Feuille d'Avis*); "On Turkish Soil," *Voyage*, 66–82 (published 30 and 31 Oct. in *La Feuille d'Avis*); Constantinople," *Voyage*, 83–99 (published 14, 16, and 18 Nov. in *La Feuille d'Avis*); "The Mosques," *Voyage*, 100–119 (published 22 and 25 Nov. in *La Feuille d'Avis*), and excerpts also published as Le Corbusier, "Les Mosquées," and "Sur l'Acropole," in *Almanach D'Architecture Moderne* (Paris: Les Éditions G. Crès et Cie, 1925), 55–61.

11 The following are chapters translated by Ivan Žaknić in Le Corbusier's *Voyage to the East* that were not previously published. They were assembled into a manuscript by Jeanneret in 1914, with titles different than Žaknić's translation: "The Sepulchers," 120–27 (in manuscript Constantinople (Suite)/ Les Sépulcures); "She's and He's," 128–32 (in manuscript Constantinople (Suite)/ Elles et Eux); "A Café," 133–36 (in manuscript Constantinople (Suite)/ Un café); "The Sesame," 137–42 (in manuscript Constantinople (Suite)/ Sesame); "Two Fantasies, One Reality," 143–52 (in manuscript Constantinople (Suite)/ Deux féeries, une realité); "The Stamboul Disaster," 153–59 (in manuscript part of the chapter En Orient (Suite)/ Pêle-mêle, retours et…regrets); "A Jumble of Recollections and Regrets," 160–72 (in manuscript En Orient (Suite)/ Pêle-mêle, retours et…regrets); "In The West," 240–45 (in Manuscript "En Occident," 8–10 Oct. 1911).

12 "Reflections of Athos," 173–208 (handwritten Manuscript "Souvenirs l'Athos I, II, III," 24 June 1914); and "The Parthenon," 209–39 (handwritten Manuscript "Le Parthenon," approximately the same time as Athos, 24 June 1914). Extracts from this later work were published as Le Corbusier, "Sur l'Acropole" *Almanach D'Architecture Moderne* (Paris: Les Éditions G. Crès et Cie, 1925), 62–71.

13 Vogt, "Remarks on the 'Reversed' Grand Tour," 43.

14 FLC E2-12-54, 19 Jan. 1910 (probably written in 1911).

15 FLC E2-12-84, 8 May 1910 (probably written in 1911).

16 Ibid..

17 Le Corbusier's letters to L'Eplattenier from his voyage to the East are often about receiving or not receiving money or requesting letters of introduction. Le Corbusier to L'Eplattenier, postcard, FLC E2-12-91, Constantinople, 6 July 1911.

18 Le Corbusier to L'Eplattenier, postcard, FLC E2-12-87, Berlin, 16 May1911.

19 Ibid.

20 Jeanneret may have met William Ritter for the first time in Munich during the spring of 1910. Brooks, *Le Corbusier's Formative Years*, 218, 510; Giuliano Gresleri, "Ritter (William) (1867–1955)," *Le Corbusier, une encyclopédie* (Paris: Éditions du Centre Georges Pompidou, 1987), 349–50; Marie-Jeanne Dumont, "Le Corbusier: l'élève et ses maîtres," *le visiteur* 9 (Fall 2002):40–59.

21 Martin W. Lewis and Kären E. Wigen, *The Myth of Continents: A Critique of Metageography* (Berkeley: University of California Press, 1997).

22 Gresleri, "Klipstein (August) (1885–1951)," *Le Corbusier, une encyclopédie*, 216.

23 Le Corbusier to Ritter, FLC R3-18-59, New Babelsberg, 1 Mar. 1911. He is referring to Ernest Renan, "Prayer on the Acropolis," in *Recollections of My Youth* (New York: G. P. Putnam's Sons, 1883), 49–61.

24 Le Corbusier to Ritter, FLC R3-18-75-92, 8 May 1911.

25 Le Corbusier to Ritter, FLC R3-18-83, 8 May 1911.

26 Le Corbusier to Ritter, FLC R3-18-75, 8 May 1911.

27 Ibid.

28 Le Corbusier to L'Eplattenier, FLC E2-12-88-90, Belgrade, 9 June 1911; Le Corbusier to L'Eplattenier, postcard, FLC E2-12-91, Constantinople, 6 July 1911.

29 Le Corbusier to L'Eplattenier, FLC E2-12-92-93, Istanbul, 18 July 1911.

30 Le Corbusier to L'Eplattenier, postcard, FLC E2-12-94, Constantinople, 4 Aug. 1911.

31 Geoffrey H. Baker, *Le Corbusier: The Creative Search* (New York, Van Nostrand Reinhold, 1996), 19.

32 Le Corbusier, *Journey to the East*, 266.

33 Alice Flaherty, *The Midnight Disease: The Drive to Write, Writer's Block and the Creative Brain* (Boston: Houghton Mifflin Company, 2004), 24–25.

34 Ibid., 32, 43.
35 Le Corbusier to Ritter, FLC R3-18-12, Chaux de Fonds, 6 Oct. 1910.
36 Brooks, *Le Corbusier's Formative Years*, 237.
37 Gresleri, "The Rediscovered Sketchbooks," in *Voyage d'Orient* sketchbooks, by Charles-Édouard Jeanneret/Le Corbusier (New York: Electra Rizzoli, 1988), 8–22.
38 The description of Pierre Loti's "Orientalism" is developed in Dalia Kandiyoti, "Roland Barthes Abroad," in *Writing the Image After Roland Barthes*, ed. Jean-Michel Rabaté (Philadelphia: University of Pennsylvania, 1997), 228–42.
39 Christian Jacob, "Lieux de la cartes, espaces du savoir," in *Lieux ou Espaces de la Mémoire* (Paris: Les Cahiers de la Villa Gillet, 1996), 67–99.
40 Edward Said, *Orientalism* (New York: Pantheon Books, 1978), 1.
41 John Elsner, "From the pyramids to Pausanias and Piglet: monuments, travel and writing," in *Art and Text in Ancient Greek Culture*, ed. Simon Goldhill and Robin Osborne (Cambridge: Cambridge University Press, 1994), 226–29.
42 Sibel Bozdo an, "Journey to the East: Ways of Looking at the Orient and the Question Concerning Representation," *JAE* 42, no. 4 (Summer 1998): 38–45.
43 Gresleri, "The Rediscovered Sketchbooks," in *Le Corbusier, une encyclopédie*, 15.
44 Le Corbusier to L'Eplattenier, FLC E2-12-92-93, Istanbul, 18 July 1911, quotation: 92.
45 Le Corbusier to Ritter, FLC R3-18-87-92, undated, before reaching Belgrade, probably 30 May 1911, quotation: 90.
46 Le Corbusier to Ritter, FLC R3-18-93, Constantinople, undated probably mid-July, 1911.
47 Charles Blanc wrote in *Grammaire des arts du dessin* (1876): "The horizontals, which express, in nature, the calmness of the sea, the majesty of far-off horizons, the vegetal tranquility of the strong, resisting trees, the quietude of the globe, after the catastrophes that have upheaved it, motionless, eternal duration–the horizontals in painting express analogous sentiments, the same character of external repose, of peace, of duration. If such are the sentiments the painter wishes to stamp upon his work, the horizontal lines should dominate in it, and the contrast of the other lines, instead of attenuating the accent of horizontality will render it still more striking." Quoted in Albert Boime, *Art and the French Commune: Imagining Paris after War and Revolution* (Princeton: Princeton University Press, 1995), 142.
48 Adolf Max Vogt, *Le Corbusier, the Noble Savage Toward an Archaeology of Modernism*, trans. Radka Donnell (Cambridge: MIT Press, 1998), 13, 32–79. For Le Corbusier's "box of miracles," see Le Corbusier, "The Core as the Meeting Place of the Arts," in *The Heart of the City: toward the humanization of urban life*, ed. J. Tyrwhitt, J. L. Sert, E. N. Rogers (London: Lund Humphries & Co. Ltd., 1952), 52.
49 Le Corbusier, *Journey to the East*, 6.
50 Ibid., 8.
51 Le Corbusier to L'Eplattenier, FLC E2-12-88, Belgrade, 9 June 1911.
52 Le Corbusier, *Journey to the East*, 14.
53 Ibid., 15.
54 Ibid., 16.
55 Ibid.
56 Ibid., 18.
57 Ibid., 24.
58 Ibid., 20.
59 Ibid., 21.
60 Ibid., 42.
61 Jack Goody, *The Culture of Flowers* (New York: Cambridge University Press, 1993), 232–53.
62 Jeanneret is revealing other lessons that he drew from reading Henri Provensal's *L'Art de Demain* (1904). Provensal taught that architecture was an expression of thought, a three-dimensional demonstration based on pure cubic shapes arranged harmoniously in space. Eternal laws of equilibrium and cohesion governed all works of art, they revealed the ideals of harmony, numerical relations, unity and truth. In addition, Provensal considered the artist to be a member of the intellectual elite whose mission was to reform society. Brooks, *Le Corbusier's Formative Years*, 27, 57–58, 245.
63 Le Corbusier, *Journey to the East*, 23–24.
64 Ibid., 25.
65 Ibid., 26.
66 David Fromkin, *A Peace to End All Peace: The Fall of the Ottoman Empire and the Creation of the Modern Middle East* (New York: Avon Books, 1990), 23–50.
67 Le Corbusier, *Journey to the East*, 41.
68 Ibid., 35.
69 Ibid., 36.
70 Ibid., 39.
71 Ibid.
72 Ibid., 40.
73 Ibid.
74 Ibid., 42.
75 Ibid., 43.

76 Ibid., 45.
77 Ibid., 54–56.
78 "[Tûrnovo] is made up of thousands of houses; they are fastened onto the ridges of precipitous rocks and then piled up, rising one over the other all the way to the top of this tower like mountain. The walls are white and their frames black, and the roofing is like the bark of a tree. Seen from afar it is an arid stratification, some larger white spots signal the churches, not Byzantine but Baroque, and related to the exquisite architecture of the Bavarian and Tyrolese mountains." Le Corbusier, *Journey to the East*, 59, quotation in text: 57.
79 Ibid., 60.
80 Ibid., 70. Žaknić inserts the following note: Alexandre Gabriel Decamps (1803–1860) the French painter used Near Eastern subject matter in a belated romanticism of the French school. Ibid., note 2, 252
81 Ibid., 74.
82 Ibid., 76–77.
83 Ibid., 77.
84 Ibid., 85.
85 Le Corbusier to L'Eplattenier, postcard, FLC E2-12-91, Constantinople, 6 July 1911.
86 Le Corbusier, *Journey to the East*, 88.
87 Suzanne Lafont, *Suprêmes Clichés de Loti* (Toulouse: Presses Universitaires du Mirail, 1993); Alain Quella-Villéger, *La Politique Méditerranéene de la France 1870–1923: Un Témoin: Pierre Loti* (Paris: Éditions L'Harmattan, 1992); and Marie-Paule de Saint-Leger, *Pierre Loti l'Insaisissable* (Paris: L'Harmattan, 1996), 242.
88 Le Corbusier, *Journey to the East*, 83.
89 Ibid., 89.
90 Ibid., 90.
91 Ibid., 96.
92 Ibid., 123.
93 Le Corbusier to L'Eplattenier, FLC E2-12-92-93, Istanbul, 18 July 1911.
94 Le Corbusier to L'Eplattenier, FLC E2-12-92, Istanbul, 18 July 1911.
95 Ibid.
96 Ibid.
97 Le Corbusier, *Journey to the East*, 104.
98 Le Corbusier to L'Eplattenier, FLC E2-12-92, Istanbul, 18 July 1911.
99 Le Corbusier to L'Eplattenier, FLC E2-12-92-93, Istanbul, 18 July 1911.
100 Le Corbusier to L'Eplattenier, FLC E2-12-93, Istanbul, 18 July 1911. In the next letter Jeanneret comments about the visit to Istanbul made by August Perret, and how excited he is over the theater that Perret is designing in Paris. He comments he would be proud to return to work for the Perrets if he was not so attached to L'Eplattenier: "It is always sad to allow such an opportunity to learn to escape." Le Corbusier to L'Eplattenier, FLC E2-13-94, Istanbul, 4 Aug. 1911.
101 Ibid.
102 Le Corbusier, *Journey to the East*, 129–30.
103 Ibid., note 6, 257.
104 Ibid., 130.
105 Ibid., 130–31.
106 Ibid., 137–38.
107 Ibid., 143.
108 Ibid., 147.
109 Ibid., 152.
110 de Saint-Leger, *Pierre Loti*, 168–70.
111 Le Corbusier, *Journey to the East*, 156.
112 Ibid., 156–57.
113 Ibid., 157.
114 Ibid., 158.
115 Ibid., 160.
116 Ibid., 163–64.
117 Ibid., 164.
118 A footnote at the bottom of the page tires to clarify this presentiment. "It took me sixty years to locate the crucial point from which the knowledge of and the taste for contemporary art has spread. It seems to be the invention of offset printing which advanced the direct and integrative use of photography, in other words, automatic utilization without hand assistance, a true revolution!" Ibid., 171.
119 Le Corbusier to L'Eplattenier, postcard, FLC E2-12-95, Pise, 29 Oct. 1911.
120 Le Corbusier to L'Eplattenier, postcard, FLC E2-13-96, Rome, 15 Nov. 1911.
121 "Reflections of Athos," 173–208 (handwritten Manuscript "Souvenirs l'Athos I, II, III," 24 June 1914); and "The Parthenon," 209–39 (handwritten Manuscript "Le Parthenon," approximately the same time as Athos, 24 June 1914). Extracts from this later work were published as Le Corbusier, "Sur l'Acropole," *Almanach D'Architecture Moderne* (Paris: Les Éditions G. Crès et Cie, 1925), 62–71.
122 Le Corbusier, *Journey to the East*, 174.
123 Ibid., 176.
124 Ibid., 178.
125 Ibid., 179.
126 Ibid., 180.
127 Ibid., 181.
128 Ibid., 185.
129 Ibid., 189–90.
130 Ibid., 191.
131 Ibid., 197.
132 Ibid., 195.

133 Le Corbusier to Ritter, FLC R3-18-106-115, Athens, 10 Sept. 1911, quotation R3-18-108.
134 Ibid., quotation 109.
135 Le Corbusier to Ritter, FLC R3-18-112, Athens, 10 Sept. 1911.
136 Stanislaus von Moos, *Le Corbusier: Elements of a Synthesis* (Cambridge: MIT Press, 1979), 15.
137 Le Corbusier, *Journey to the East*, 209.
138 Ibid., 212.
139 Ibid., 214.
140 Ibid., 216.
141 Ibid.
142 Ibid., 236.
143 Ibid., footnote 5, 263.
144 Françoise Bradfer, "La mémoire écrite, la mémoire inscrite: Le Corbusier et le Parthénon," in *Pratiques du langage arts, architecture, littérature Cahiers thématiques* (Lille: Éditions de l'École d'architecture de Lille, Oct. 2003), 53–63.
145 Le Corbusier to Ritter, FLC R3-18-128-143, 1 Nov. 1911, quotation 128.
146 Le Corbusier to Ritter, FLC R3-18-130, 1 Nov. 1911.
147 This part of Le Corbusier's letter to Ritter is contained in Chapter 4.
148 Le Corbusier to Ritter, FLC R3-18-135-6, 1 Nov. 1911.

CHAPTER 4

Epigraph Attributed to William Ritter in Charles-Édouard Jeanneret/Le Corbusier, "La Construction des Villes" (unpublished manuscript), presentation and transcription by Marc E. Albert Emery (Paris: L'Age D'Homme, 1992): 163.
1 For complete analysis of these texts, see Jeanneret Le Corbusier, *La Construction des Villes*; and H. Allen Brooks, "Jeanneret and Sitte: Le Corbusier's Earliest Ideas on Urban Design," in *In Search of Modern Architecture: A tribute to Henry-Russell Hitchcock* (Cambridge: MIT Press, 1982), 278–97.
2 This level had slipped to 55 percent by 1914.
3 The crisis in watch-making is mentioned by Giuliano Gresleri, "The German Carnets; 'triomphe de l'ordre' and 'heureuse évolution,'" in Charles-Édouard Jeanneret Le Corbusier, *Les voyages d'Allemagne Carnets* (New York/Paris: The Monacelli Press/Fondation Le Corbusier, 1994), 14; and Adolf Max Vogt, *Le Corbusier, the Noble Savage: Toward an Archeology of Modernism* (Cambridge: MIT Press, 1998), 304–8.
4 M. Norton Wise, ed., "Introduction," in *The Values of Precision* (Princeton: Princeton University Press, 1995), 3–13.
5 Jeanneret Le Corbusier, *La Construction des Villes*, 17. H. Allen Brooks says L'Eplattenier read Sitte's 1902 publication with enthusiasm. H. Allen Brooks, *Le Corbusier's Formative Years* (Chicago: University of Chicago Press, 1997). See also Marc-Albert Emery, "Urbanisme: Premières réflexions: le manuscrit inédit de 'La construction des villes,'" in *Le Corbusier, une encyclopédie* (Paris: Centre Georges Pompidou, 1987), 432–35. Emery uses the date 1903 for Camille Martin's translation while Collins and Crasemann Collins use 1902. Camille Martin (1877–1928) was a Swiss architect and archeologist, and concerned, at the time of his translation of Sitte's work, with the restoration of medieval buildings. A city planner for Geneva, he also laid out the extension plan for La Chaux-de-Fonds. George Collins and Christiane Crasemann Collins, *Camillo Sitte: The Birth of Modern City Planning* (New York: Rizzoli, 1986), 73, 358.
6 Ibid., 41, 78–86.
7 Emery, "Urbanisme: Premières réflexions," 432.
8 Ibid.
9 Charles-Édouard Jeanneret, *Étude sur le mouvement d'art décoratif en Allemagne* (New York: Da Capo Press, 1968, originally published 1912), 5; see also Philippe Duboy, *Architecture de la Ville: Culture et Triomphe de l'Urbanisme: Ch. E. Jeanneret, "La Construction des Villes"* (Paris: Bibliothèque Nationale de Paris, 1915; reprinted Paris: CERNA, 1985) and Giuliano Gresleri, "The Rediscovered Sketchbooks," in Ch.-E. Jeanneret Le Corbusier, *Voyage d'Orient Sketchbooks* (New York: Electra/Rizzoli, 1988), 8–22.
10 Le Corbusier to L'Eplattenier, postcard, FLC E2-12-66, Munich, 2 June 1910.
11 Le Corbusier to L'Eplattenier, FLC E2-12-60, Munich, spring 1910. Probably this Le Corbusier letter was written at the end of May, because he mentions that he has just met William Ritter and Mr. Cadra for the first time. Emery writes that a four page outline had been sent to L'Eplattenier in April 16, 1910 and announces on May 19 that he has begun to write the introduction, and writes again on the 2nd, and June 7 that the work is almost finished, and on June 29 that he has 14 days to finish it. Emery, in Jeanneret Le Corbusier, *La Construction des Villes*, 10.

12 Brooks claims that Jeanneret met Ritter by the end of May, 1910. Brooks, *Le Corbusier's Formative Years*, 218. Geoffrey H. Baker thinks Jeanneret and William Ritter became friends in the winter of 1909. Geoffrey H. Baker, *Le Corbusier: The Creative Search* (New York, Van Nostrand Reinhold, 1996), 135. Marc E. Albert Emery suggests that it was the spring of 1910. Jeanneret Le Corbusier, "La Construction Des Villes," 10.

Le Corbusier to L'Eplattenier, postcard, FLC E2-12-87, Berlin, 16 May 1911.

13 Baker, *Le Corbusier: The Creative Search*, 385–86.

14 It is not clear when Jeanneret gave the various titled to his manuscripts of 1910 and 1915–16. "The Construction of Cities" ("La construction des villes") is the title he sometimes references in his letters to L'Eplattenier and his sketchbooks and is probably an attempt to translated the German word *Städtetbau*, the name of the journal Camillo Sitte and Thédor Goecke began to publish in 1904. And it also refers to Sitte's book published in 1889 under the title *Der Städtetbau nach seinen kunstlerisheen Grundsatzen*. Emery, "Une Question de Titre," in Jeanneret Le Corbusier, *La Construction des Villes*, 17–19.

15 Emery, "Une Question de Titre," in Jeanneret Le Corbusier, *La Construction des Villes*, 17–19.

16 Brooks, *Le Corbusier's Formative Years*, 106, 301; Baker, *Le Corbusier: The Creative Search*, 72.

17 Quoted by Emery, "Une Question de Titre," in Jeanneret Le Corbusier, *La Construction des Villes*, 19.

18 Le Corbusier, *The Modular*, trans. Peter de Francia and Anna Bostock (London: Editions Faber, Ltd., 1951), 27–28.

19 Charles-Édouard Jeanneret, "Art et Utilité publique," in "L'Abeille" (Chaux-de-Fonds, 15 May 1910); in Jeanneret Le Corbusier, *La Construction Des Villes*, 14–16

20 Ibid., 16.

21 Werner Oechslin, "Allemagne: Influences, confluences et reniement," *Le Corbusier, une encyclopédie* (Paris: Centre Georges Pompidou, 1987), 33–39.

22 Le Corbusier to Ritter, FLC R3-18-3, Berlin, 21 June 1910.

23 Le Corbusier to Ritter, FLC R3-18-12, Chaux-de-Fonds, 6 Oct. 1910.

24 Emery, "Évolution du Plan," in Jeanneret Le Corbusier, *La Construction des Villes*, 21–27.

25 Le Corbusier to Ritter, FLC R3-18-22, Berlin, 14 Oct. 1910.

26 Le Corbusier to Ritter, FLC R3-18-41, Berlin, 28 Oct. 1910

27 Le Corbusier to Ritter, FLC R3-18-28, Munich, undated (probably early- to mid-January 1911, because Jeanneret mentions he has been working for Behrens for two months).

28 Ibid.

29 Brooks, *Le Corbusier's Formative Years*, 233.

30 Ibid., 247.

31 Ibid., 245.

32 Le Corbusier to Ritter, FLC R3-18-106, Isle St. George, near Piraeus, 10 Sept. 1911.

33 Le Corbusier to Ritter, FLC R3-18-106–115, Isle St. George, near Piraeus, 10 Sept. 1911, quotation R3-18-106.

34 Le Corbusier to Ritter, FLC R3-18-110, Isle St. George, near Piraeus, 10 Sept. 1911.

35 Le Corbusier to Ritter, FLC R3-18-113, Isle St. George, near Piraeus, 10 Sept. 1911.

36 Le Corbusier to Ritter, FLC R3-18-128-143, voyage through Italy, 1 Nov. 1911, quotation R3-18-130.

37 Charles Jencks, *Le Corbusier and the Continual Revolution in Architecture* (New York: The Monacelli Press, 2000), 88.

38 Ibid., quotation R3-18-131-132. Jencks's translation of this letter does not agree with the letter at the FLC.

39 Ibid., quotation 132–33.

40 Ibid., quotation 131. Jencks's translation of this letter does not agree with the letter at the FLC.

41 Le Corbusier to Ritter, FLC R3-18-124, La Chaux-de-Fonds, fall 1911.

42 Le Corbusier to Ritter, FLC R3-18-126, La Chaux-de-Fonds, 12 Dec. 1911.

43 "Ces horizons sur le nez!" Le Corbusier to Ritter, FLC R3-18-144, La Chaux de Fonds, 15 Dec. 1911.

44 Ibid.

45 Le Corbusier to Ritter, FLC R3-18-161, La Chaux-de-Fonds, undated (January, 1912).

46 Baker, *Le Corbusier: The Creative Search*, 214; and Nancy Troy, *Modernism and the Decorative Arts in France: Art Nouveau to Le Corbusier* (New Haven: Yale University Press, 1991), 112–13.

47 Le Corbusier to Ritter, FLC R3-18-163, on train to Zurich, 3 May 1912.

48 Ibid.

49 Le Corbusier to Ritter, FLC R3-18-171, La Chaux-de-Fonds, 14 Apr. 1912; Le Corbusier to Ritter, FLC R3-18-186, La Chaux-de-Fonds, 27 May 1912; Le Corbusier to Ritter, FLC R3-18-163, La Chaux-de-Fonds, 24 June 1912.

50 Le Corbusier to Ritter, FLC R3-18-192, La Chaux-de-Fonds, 24 June 1912.
51 Ibid.
52 Le Corbusier to Ritter, FLC R3-18-197, La Chaux-de-Fonds, 24 Aug. 1912.
53 Ibid.
54 Le Corbusier's birthdate is October 1887. He was twenty-three at the time of his voyage to the East, although twenty-four when he returned to La Chaux-de-Fonds.
55 Le Corbusier to Ritter, FLC R3-18-197, La Chaux-de-Fonds, 24 Aug. 1912.
56 Le Corbusier to Ritter, FLC R3-18-208, La Chaux-de-Fonds, 14 Oct. 1912. For an account of Jeanneret's efforts to republish the work, see Troy, *Modernism and the Decorative Arts*, 107–8, 111–12.
57 Ibid., footnote 25, 249.
58 Ch.-E. Jeanneret, "En Allemagne," pts. 1–2, *L'Art de France* 2 (April–May, 1914): 347–95, 457–73. The letter to the editor Emmanuel de Thubert (29 May 1914) is quoted by Troy, *Modernism and the Decorative Arts*, 112.
59 Le Corbusier to Ritter, FLC R3-18-210, La Chaux-de-Fonds, 15 Oct. 1912.
60 Ibid.
61 Le Corbusier to Ritter, postcard, FLC R3-18-218, La Chaux-de-Fonds, 21 Oct. 1912.
62 Le Corbusier to Ritter, FLC R3-18-220-32, La Chaux-de-Fonds, 17 Nov. 1912.
63 Ibid.
64 Le Corbusier to Ritter, postcard, FLC R3-18-23332, La Chaux-de-Fonds, 26 Nov. 1912.
65 Le Corbusier to Ritter, postcard, FLC R3-18-241-42, La Chaux-de-Fonds, 2 Jan. 1913.
66 Le Corbusier to Ritter, FLC R3-18-243, La Chaux-de-Fonds, 16 Jan. 1913.
67 The following chronology surrounding the development of the Dom-ino idea is derived from Eleanor Gregh, "The Dom-ino Idea," *Oppositions* 15–16 (Spring 1979): 61–87. See also Vogt, *Le Corbusier, The Noble Savage*, 4–6.
68 Gregh, "The Dom-ino Idea," 66.
69 Le Corbusier to Ritter, FLC R3-18-252, La Chaux-de-Fonds, 10 Feb. 1913.
70 Le Corbusier to Ritter, FLC R3-18-257-59, La Chaux-de-Fonds, 6 Apr. 1913, quotation 257.
71 Ibid., quotation 258.
72 Le Corbusier to Ritter, FLC R3-18-260, La Chaux-de-Fonds, 6 Apr. 1913.
73 Le Corbusier, *The Decorative Arts of Today*, trans. James I. Dunnett (Cambridge: MIT Press, 1987), 207.
74 Ibid., 207.
75 Le Corbusier to Ritter, FLC R3-18-265, La Chaux-de-Fonds, 9 May 1913.
76 Le Corbusier to Ritter, FLC R3-18-274, Lausanne, 26 May 1913; Le Corbusier to Ritter, postcard, R3-18-288, Lausanne, 27 May 1913; Le Corbusier to Ritter, FLC R3-18-279, La Chaux-de-Fonds, 27 Sept. 1913.
77 Le Corbusier to Ritter, FKC R3-18-274, Lausanne, 26 May 1913.
78 Jodelet, "L'Inauguration du Théâtre des Champs-Elysées," *Gil Blas* (1 Apr. 1913): 1, quoted by Troy, *Modernism and the Decorative Arts*, footnote 70, 254–55.
79 Le Corbusier to Ritter, FLC R3-18-279, La Chaux-de-Fonds, 27 Sept. 1913; Brooks references this article as "La Maison Suisse," in *Etrennes Helvétiques, Almanach Illustré* (Paris, Dijon, La Chaux-De-Fonds, 1914), 33–39. Note that a drawing from Le Corbusier's favorite illustrator Rodolphe Topfferi, *Voyage en Zigzag*, leads off the article. Brooks, *Le Corbusier's Formative Years*, footnote 42, 355.
80 Le Corbusier to Ritter, FLC R3-18-279, La Chaux-de-Fonds, 27 Sept. 1913.
81 Le Corbusier to Ritter, FLC R3-18-301, La Chaux-de-Fonds, 23 Dec. 1913.
82 Charles-Édouard Jeanneret, "Le Renouveau dans l'Architecture," *L'Oeuvre 1, no. 2* (Berne, 1914): 33–37. Reprinted in Jeanneret Le Corbusier, *La Construction Des Villes*, 186–89.
83 Troy, *Modernism and the Decorative Arts*, 114–30.
84 He cut the pages of *Pury* and read the preface in September 1913. Le Corbusier to Ritter, FLC R3-18-279, La Chaux-de-Fonds, 27 Sept. 1913. Yet in December, 1913, he writes he read *Pury* in the library. Le Corbusier to Ritter, FLC R3-18-310, La Chaux-de-Fonds, 21 Jan. 1914. He may have lost his original copy, as the book at FLC is marked "Given to Jeanneret 27-01-1916." William Ritter, *Edmond de Pury*, illustrations by Frédéric Boissonnas (Geneva, 1913).
85 Le Corbusier to Ritter, FLC R3-18-279, La Chaux-de-Fonds, 27 Sept. 1913.
86 Le Corbusier to Ritter, FLC R3-18-292, La Chaux-de-Fonds, 3 Nov. 1913
87 Ibid.
88 Ibid.
89 Le Corbusier to Ritter, FLC R3-18-292, La Chaux-de-Fonds, 3 Nov. 1913.
90 Adolf Loos, "Architecture et le style modern," in *Les Cahiers d'Aujourd'hui* 2, trans. Marcel Ray (Dec. 1912): 82–92; Loos, "Ornement et crime," *Les Cahiers d'Aujourd'hui*

5, trans. Marcel Ray (June 1913): 247–56. Troy, *Modernism and the Decorative Arts*, 134, 255.

91 Ibid., 134–35.

92 Ritter had spoken about Palladio, or at least the Villa Rotonda, evoking Virgil. Jeanneret comments, "Ce sera un peintre pour *architecte* et le disant, j'accepte tout le paradoxal de ce dire." Le Corbusier to Ritter, FLC R3-18-292, La Chaux-de-Fonds, 3 Nov. 1913.

93 Le Corbusier to Ritter, FLC R3-18-301, La Chaux-de-Fonds, 23 Dec. 1913.

94 Ibid.

95 Ibid.

96 Ibid.

97 The material on Francis Jourdain follows Troy, *Modernism and the Decorative*, 134–42, 143, 144, 150, 154, 202.

98 Francis Jourdain, quoted by Troy, *Modernism and the Decorative*, 137–38.

99 Le Corbusier to Ritter, FLC R3-18-323, La Chaux-de-Fonds, 27 Jan. 1914.

100 Jeanneret, "Le Renouveau dans l'Architecture," in Jeanneret Le Corbusier, *La Construction Des Villes*, 186–89. He mentions this article in a letter to Max Du Bois on 29 Jan. 1914. See Gregh, "The Dom-ino Idea," 67.

101 Oechslin, "Allemagne: influences, confluences et reniement," 33–39.

102 Alan Colquhoun argues these are incompatible positions in Le Corbusier's "dualistic philosophy" in which he juxtaposes all sorts of -isms: rationalism, historicism, idealism, positivism, neo-platonism, classicism. Alan Colquhoun, "Architecture and Engineering: Le Corbusier and the Paradox of Reason," in *Modernity and the Classical Tradition* (Cambridge: MIT Press, 1989), 89–119. For the notion of polar opposition and the line of argumentation see Mark Turner, *Reading Minds: The Study of English in the Age of Cognitive Science* (Princeton: Princeton University Press, 1991), 65–95.

103 Adolf Loos, "Ornament and Crime," in *The Architecture of Adolf Loos* (London: Arts Council of Great Britain, 1987; originally published 1908), 100–103, quotation, 100.

104 The quotation is unattributed by Jeanneret, "Le Renouveau dans l'Architecture," 188.

105 Ibid., 189.

106 At the end of December, 1914, Jeanneret's parents were invited to an exposition of L'Eplattenier's pastel drawings and Jeanneret goes to the event as well. But L'Eplattenier was odious and turned his back on him. Although Jeanneret excused himself for appearing without an invitation, still he felt L'Eplattenier was the loser and to be pitied for hating one of his former students. Le Corbusier to Ritter, FLC R3-18-382, La Chaux-de-Fonds, 22 Dec. 1914. In early 1916, Jeanneret sent a postcard to Ritter exclaiming that L'Eplattenier had just visited his office, the first visit since May of 1914. The sound of his footstep in the stone corridor made Jeanneret turn cold and their handshake was at least 20 degrees below zero. He had the feeling that someone was looking at them obliquely. Le Corbusier to Ritter, postcard, FLC R3-19-6, La Chaux-de-Fonds, no date, but probably Jan. or Feb. 1916.

107 Le Corbusier to Ritter, FLC R3-18-329, La Chaux-de-Fonds, 24 Mar. 1914.

108 Ibid.

109 Ibid.

110 Le Corbusier to Ritter, postcard, FLC R3-18-339, La Chaux-de-Fonds, 11 Apr. 1914.

111 Le Corbusier to Emmanuel de Thubert, editor of *L'Art de France*, 30 Apr. 1914, quoted by Brooks, *Le Corbusier's Formative Years*, footnote 48, 357.

112 Brooks, *Le Corbusier's Formative Years*, 366–67; Troy, *Modernism and the Decorative Arts*, 113–14.

113 Jeanneret is referring to the work of the socialist Paul Graber to destroy the Nouvelle Section. Brooks thinks Jeanneret greatly overestimated the part played by the socialists. Brooks, *Le Corbusier's Formative Years*, 365.

114 Le Corbusier to Ritter, FLC R3-18-386, La Chaux de Fond, 1 May 1914.

115 Ibid.

116 Le Corbusier to Ritter, FLC R3-18-341, La Chaux de Fond, 7 June 1914.

117 Having accepted the invitation to review the German Werkbund that Thubert had offered him, he announces he plans to travel on June 27 to Cologne via Gurnewald, Strasbourg and Nancy and return via Geneva on July 6 and then Lyon on the 9th, reaching home by the 12th. Ibid.

118 Le Corbusier to Ritter, FLC R3-18-344, Nancy, 28 June 1914.

119 Ibid.

120 Le Corbusier to Mesdames Ritter, FLC R3-18-354, La Chaux-de-Fonds, 17 Sept. 1914.

121 Le Corbusier to Ritter, FLC R3-18-357, La Chaux-de-Fonds, 22 Sept. 1914; Le Corbusier to Ritter, FLC R3-18-368, La Chaux-de-Fonds, 9 Sept. 1914.

122 Le Corbusier to Ritter, La Chaux-de-Fonds, 22 Sept. 1914. A week later he writes news that his brother has received from Hellerau: the house of Jaques Dalcroze was ransacked and also of Dohrn, of Polish origin.

And six Russian students were imprisoned as spies. Le Corbusier to Ritter, FLC R3-18-366, La Chaux-de-Fonds, 30 Sept. 1914.
123 Le Corbusier to Ritter, FLC R3-18-368, La Chaux-de-Fonds, 9 Oct. 1914.
124 Le Corbusier to Ritter, FLC R3-18-376, La Chaux-de-Fonds, undated (probably Dec. 1910).
125 Brooks, *Le Corbusier's Formative Years*, 382–83. He wrote to Ritter on April 25, 1915 that he was very pleased, in fact enthusiastic, and finally satisfied over this competition work. He called it a beautiful bridge that was very Roman. Le Corbusier to Ritter, FLC R3-18-419, La Chaux-de-Fonds, 25 Apr. 1915. It also is one the three projects from his youth to be included in *Oeuvre Complète*.
126 Le Corbusier to Ritter, FLC R3-18-380, La Chaux-de-Fonds, 9 Dec. 1914.
127 Le Corbusier to Ritter, FLC R3-18-368, La Chaux-de-Fonds, 9 Jan. 1915.
128 Ibid.
129 Le Corbusier to Ritter, FLC R3-18-401-5, La Chaux-de-Fonds, 8 Feb. 1915.
130 Le Corbusier to Ritter, FLC R3-18-406-09, La Chaux-de-Fonds, 13 Mar. 1915.
131 Le Corbusier to Ritter, FLC R3-18-410, La Chaux-de-Fonds, 9 Apr. 1915.
132 Le Corbusier to Ritter, FLC R3-18-412, La Chaux-de-Fonds, 9 Apr. 1915.
133 Le Corbusier to Ritter, FLC R3-18-410-418, La Chaux-de-Fonds, 9 Apr. 1915.
134 Le Corbusier to Ritter, FLC R3-18-419, La Chaux-de-Fonds, 25 Apr. 1915.
135 Le Corbusier to Ritter, FLC R3-18-422, La Chaux-de-Fonds, undated, spring 1915.
136 Le Corbusier to Ritter, FLC R3-18-426-30, La Chaux-de-Fonds, 8 June 1915.
137 Brooks only makes a brief mention of this thirty-page letter, noting merely that "Marseille, which thrilled him because of its vitality. This we learn from one of Jeanneret's writing exercises, a travel essay that he submitted to Ritter (June 9, 1915) for comment and correction. Its rich descriptive prose, embedded in extended sentences endeavors to emulate Ritter's style which he so admired." Brooks, *Le Corbusier's Formative Years*, 402–3. Le Corbusier to Ritter, FLC R3-18-431-49, La Chaux-de-Fonds, 9 June 1915.
138 Le Corbusier to Ritter, FLC R3-18-432, La Chaux-de-Fonds, 9 June 1915.
139 Le Corbusier to Ritter, FLC R3-18-433, La Chaux-de-Fonds, 9 June 1915.
140 Le Corbusier to Ritter, FLC R3-18-434, La Chaux-de-Fonds, 9 June 1915.
141 Ibid.
142 Le Corbusier to Ritter, FLC R3-18-437, La Chaux-de-Fonds, 9 June 1915.
143 Ibid.
144 Le Corbusier to Ritter, FLC R3-18-438, La Chaux-de-Fonds, 9 June 1915.
145 Le Corbusier to Ritter, FLC R3-18-439, La Chaux-de-Fonds, 9 June 1915.
146 Ibid.
147 Le Corbusier to Ritter, FLC R3-18-445, La Chaux-de-Fonds, 9 June 1915.
148 Le Corbusier to Ritter, FLC R3-18-446-7, La Chaux-de-Fonds, 9 June 1915.
149 Le Corbusier to Ritter, FLC R3-18-449, La Chaux-de-Fonds, 9 June 1915.
150 Ibid. Jeanneret continues to describe Perret: about teaching him to bicycle, about his best work–the theater of Champs-Elysées–about being the best architect for a long time, but one without a diploma, about his thoughts as strong as the reinforced concrete with which he works.
151 Le Corbusier to Ritter, FLC R3-18-450-1, La Chaux-de-Fonds, 9 June 1915.
152 Le Corbusier to Ritter, FLC R3-18-451, La Chaux-de-Fonds, 9 June 1915.
153 Ibid.
154 Le Corbusier to Ritter, FLC R3-18-451-4, La Chaux-de-Fonds, 9 June 1915.
155 Le Corbusier to Ritter, FLC R3-18-454, La Chaux-de-Fonds, 9 June 1915.
156 Le Corbusier to Ritter, FLC R3-18-456, La Chaux-de-Fonds, 9 June 1915.
157 Ibid.
158 Le Corbusier to Max Du Bois, 9 June 1915, quoted by Brooks, *Le Corbusier's Formative Years*, 403.
159 Le Corbusier to Ritter, postcard, FLC R3-18-463 La Chaux-de-Fonds, 25 July 1915; Le Corbusier to Ritter, postcard, FLC R3-18-468, La Chaux-de-Fonds, 25 July 1915.
160 Le Corbusier to Ritter, postcard, FLC R3-18-408, 17 July 1915.
161 Brooks notes that Jeanneret sent only three postcards from Paris to Ritter, and no letters to his parents have been found. So it is difficult to discern exactly what he did during those six weeks. He did, however, visit Aristide Maillot at his home August 2 and 3, and was so thrilled with meeting him that he wrote a long report to Ritter, although he did not mail it until January 13, 1917 and called it "Grandeur et Serviture....Un jour et une nuit dans la maison d'Aristide Maillot, à Marly-le-Roy." Brooks, *Le Corbusier's Formative Years*, 403. See also Le Corbusier to Ritter, FLC R3-19-101-112, Paris, 13 Jan. 1917.

162 Le Corbusier to Ritter, postcard, FLC R3-18-476, Paris, 20/24 Aug. 1915.
163 The following account draws on material presented by Nancy Troy, *Modernism and the Decorative Arts in France: Art Nouveau to Le Corbusier* (New Haven: Yale University Press, 1991), 149–55. Troy quotes sources from FLC under the old numbering system Box B1 (20).
164 Troy, *Modernism and the Decorative Arts*, 157.
165 Sketchbook A2 (1915), in *Le Corbusier Sketchbooks, Vol. 1: 1914–1948* (New York: The Architectural History Foundation, 1981), quoted by Troy, *Modernism and the Decorative Arts*, 150.
166 Quoted by Troy, *Modernism and the Decorative Arts*, 153
167 No publisher was ever found, nor book ever produced, although some of the ideas may have found their way into an aggressive attack on "Allemagne" written by Paul Boulard [alias Jeanneret] in *L'Esprit Nouveau* no. 27. In *L'Esprit Nouveau* no 9, Jeanneret would write "Curiorisité–non, anomalie!" where he accused all modern German architecture of violence, finding it to be one of the most aggressive arms of a pan-Germanic front. Oechslin, "Allemagne: Influences, confluences et reniement," 33–39.
168 Philippe Duboy, *Architecture de la Ville: Culture et Triomphe de l'Urbanisme*; and Charles-Édouard Jeanneret, *La Construction des Villes* (1915; repr., Paris: ERNA, 1985).
169 Jeanneret, "Brochure" for "La Construction des Villes" in Jeanneret Le Corbusier, *La Construction des Villes*, 161–75.
170 Ibid., 163.
171 Ibid.
172 Ibid., 163–64.
173 Le Corbusier to Ritter, FLC R3-19-3, La Chaux-de-Fonds, 19 Feb. 1916.
174 Marc E. Albert Emery, the transcriber of the various components of Jeanneret's "La Construction des Villes," written between 1910–15, thinks the rupture with L'Eplattenier, which began in mid-1912 and culminated in May of 1914, was the major reason why Jeanneret found the project of 1910 to be misguided in 1915. Emery, "Evolution de l'Ecriture," in Jeanneret Le Corbusier, "La Construction des Villes," 177–85.
175 Emery, "Urbanisme: Premières réflexions: le manuscrit inédit de 'La Construction des Villes,'" in *Le Corbusier, une encyclopédie*, 434.
176 Brooks writes that the major rupture with L'Eplattenier in mid-1912 was probably caused by criticism over Jeanneret's teaching method. Brooks, *Le Corbusier's Formative Years*, 366
177 Le Corbusier to Ritter, FLC R3-18-220-232, La Chaux-de-fonds, 7 Nov. 1912.
178 See table of contents for the various manuscripts 1910, 1915. Jeanneret Le Corbusier, *La Construction des Villes*, 28–29.
179 Jeanneret, *La Construction des Villes.*
180 Ibid., "Textes de 1910 conserves en 1915."
181 Ibid., "Considérations générales," 69–72; "Des éléments constitutifs de la Ville," 72–137; and "Des moyens possibles," 138–60.
182 Ibid., "Principes généraux," 71–72.
183 Ibid., 72.
184 Ibid., 72–137.
185 Ibid., 72–76.
186 Ibid., 72–137.
187 Ibid., 76–80.
188 Ibid., 81–99.
189 Ibid., 81.
190 Ibid., 82.
191 Ibid., 83–4.
192 Ibid., 86.
193 Ibid., 87.
194 Ibid., 97.
195 Marc-Antoine Laugier, *An Essay on Architecture*, trans. Wolfgang and Anni Herrmann (Los Angeles: Hennessey & Ingalls, Inc., 1977), 129.
196 Jeanneret Le Corbusier, *La Construction des Villes*, 97.
197 Ibid., 98.
198 Ibid.
199 Ibid., 99.
200 Ibid., 99–135.
201 Ibid., 100.
202 Ibid., 103.
203 Ibid., 104.
204 Ibid., 105.
205 Ibid., 109–10.
206 Ibid., 111–13.
207 Ibid., 115–19.
208 Ibid., 119–27.
209 Ibid., 121.
210 Ibid., 125–26.
211 Ibid., 127–32.
212 Ibid., 135–37.
213 Ibid., 135.
214 Ibid., 137.
215 Ibid., 138–60.
216 Ibid., 139.
217 Ibid., 140.
218 Ibid., 142–43.
219 Ibid., 157–58.
220 Ibid., 158.
221 Although aware of Tony Garnier's architectural works, Jeanneret did not read *Cité Industrielle* until 1919.

222 M. Christine Boyer, *The City of Collective Memory* (Cambridge: The MIT Press, 1993).
223 Duboy, *Architecture de la Ville* and Jeanneret, *La Construction des Villes*, 9–12.
224 Gregh, "The Dom-ino Idea."
225 Paul Rabinow, *French Modern: Norms and Forms of the Social Environment* (Cambridge: The MIT Press, 1989), 254–57, 259–60, 267–77.
226 For a full discussion of the evolution of the Dom-ino project see Gregh, "The Dom-ino Idea."
227 Gregh, "The Dom-ino Idea," 82, footnote 33. For the sketchbooks, see Le Corbusier, *Sketchbooks: 1914–1918* (Cambridge: The MIT Press, 1981), 6.
228 Le Corbusier to Ritter, postcard, FLC R3-18-488, Le Chaux-de-Fonds, undated (probably the autumn of 1915).
229 Du Bois would be an influential but unacknowledged help, enabling Jeanneret to make many contacts in Paris–for example, introducing him to Raoul La Roche–and even offering financial backing for *L'Esprit Nouveau*. In 1919, Le Corbusier patented another system of housing, the barrel-vaulted Monol scheme, to be built like the Dom-ino in series. And in 1921 he designed his famous Citrohan housing. His interest in the construction of workers' housing would continue until 1923. Brooks, *Le Corbusier's Formative Years*, 472, 494.
230 Le Corbusier to Ritter, FLC R3-18-491-99, La Chaux-de-Fonds, 13 Oct. 1915.
231 Gregh, "The Dom-ino Idea," 70.
232 Le Corbusier to Ritter, FLC R3-18-501-13, La Chaux-de-Fonds, 2 Nov. 1915.
233 Ibid.
234 Ibid.
235 Ibid.
236 Le Corbusier to Ritter, FLC R3-18-517-8, La Chaux-de-Fonds, 8 Dec. 1915.
237 Le Corbusier to Du Bois, undated, probably mid-to-late October, 1915, quoted by Gregh"The Dom-ino Idea," 70.
238 Ibid.
239 Le Corbusier to Ritter, FLC R3-19-3-10-12, La Chaux-de-Fonds, 16 Feb.1916.
240 Le Corbusier to Ritter, FLC R3-19-15-17, La Chaux-de-Fonds, 21 Mar. 1916.
241 Le Corbusier to Ritter, FLC R3-19-18-21, La Chaux-de-Fonds, 22 Mar. 1916.
242 Le Corbusier to Ritter, FLC R3-19-32-6, La Chaux-de-Fonds, 22 May 1916.
243 Le Corbusier to Ritter, FLC R3-19-46, La Chaux-de-Fonds, 4 July 1916.
244 Le Corbusier to Ritter, FLC R3-19-50, La Chaux-de-Fonds, undated.
245 Le Corbusier to Ritter, FLC R3-19-57-59, La Chaux-de-Fonds, undated.
246 Le Corbusier to Ritter, FLC R3-19-60-62, La Chaux-de-Fonds, 17 Sept. 1916.
247 The date when Jeanneret met Ozenfant, his final mentor, is a matter of some confusion, and the context surrounding the place–a meeting of the group called Art et Liberté–is seldom explored. Troy, *Modernism and the Decorative Arts in France*, 155–58.
248 "The review will be responsible for printing and publishing at moderate prices, yet with artistic taste, books, brochures, prints, catalogues and in general all works of TYPOGRAPHIC ART." *L'Elan* 8 (1 Jan. 1916), quoted by Troy, *Modernism and the Decorative Arts*, 157.
249 Le Corbusier to Ritter, FLC R3-19-63-8, Paris, 14 Oct. 1916.
250 Ibid.
251 Le Corbusier to Ritter, FLC R3-19-69-71, Paris, Oct. 1916.
252 Ibid.
253 Ibid.
254 Le Corbusier to Ritter, FLC R3-19-113-6, Paris, 26 Jan. 1917.
255 Le Corbusier to Ritter, FLC R3-19-117-8, Paris, 8 Feb. 1917.
256 Le Corbusier to Ritter, FLC R3-19-119-21, Paris, 9 Feb. 1917.

CHAPTER 5

Epigraph 1 Le Corbusier to Ritter, entry 27 June 1918, FLC R3-19-268-283, Paris, 2 Aug. 1918.
Epigraph 2 Le Corbusier to Ritter, FLC R3-19-145-50, Paris, 3 May 1917.
1 Is one 1 year old at birth, or 1 at one's first birthday? Ivan Žaknić counts that Jeanneret was thirty when he moved to Paris in early 1917; Americans would count that Jeanneret was thirty on October 1917, nearly ten months after arriving in Paris. Ivan Žaknić in Le Corbusier, *The Final Testament of Père Corbu* (New Haven: Yale University Press, 2007), 134. Jeanneret in a Le Corbusier letter to Ritter written on October 4, 1917, stated "Tomorrow I will be 30 years old." Le Corbusier to Ritter, FLC R3-19-181-4, Paris, 4 Oct. 1917. Jeanneret's/Le Corbusier's own counting is often incorrect, as are dates of specific of events.
2 H. Allen Brooks, *Le Corbusier's Formative Years* (Chicago: University of Chicago Press, 1997), 480. See also François Ducros, *La Peinture Puriste et l'Esprit Nouveau* (Paris: Thèse

de troisième cycle soutenue le 26 Février 1986 à Paris IV).
3 Le Corbusier to Ritter, FLC R3-19-385-6, Paris, 30 July1921.
4 Ibid.
5 Alice Flaherty, *The Midnight Disease: The Drive to Write, Writer's Block and the Creative Brain* (Boston: Houghton Mifflin Company, 2004), 214–17.
6 Le Corbusier to Ritter, FLC R3-19-122-131, Paris, 19 Feb. 1917.
7 Le Corbusier to Ritter, postcard, FLC R3-19-143-4, Chartres, 30 Apr. 1917.
8 Le Corbusier to Ritter, FLC R3-19-145-50, Paris, 3 May 1917.
9 Ibid.
10 Ibid.
11 Ibid.
12 Ibid.
13 Le Corbusier to Ritter, FLC R3-19-153-9, Paris, 1 July 1917.
14 Ibid.
15 Ibid.
16 Ibid.
17 Ibid.
18 Le Corbusier to L'Eplattenier, FLC E22-12-22, Vienna, 29 Feb. 1908.
19 Le Corbusier to Ritter, FLC R3-19-166-171, Paris, 27 July 1917.
20 Le Corbusier to Ritter, FLC R3-19-179-84, Paris, 4 Oct. 1917.
21 Le Corbusier to Ritter, FLC R3-19-194-213, Paris, 27 Jan. 1918.
22 Ibid., entry 18 Nov. 1917.
23 Ibid., entry 2 Dec. 1917.
24 Ibid., entry 6 Dec. 1917.
25 Ibid., entry 29 Dec. 1917.
26 Jeanneret had been reading the 1912 French translation of the American industrial organizer F. W. Taylor's *The Principles of Scientific Management* (1911). He applied some of the efficiency techniques that Taylor recommended to the plan of the slaughterhouse.
27 Le Corbusier to Ritter, FLC R3-19-194-213, Paris, 27 Jan. 1918, entry 29 Dec. 1917.
28 Ibid.
29 Ibid., entries 31 Dec. 1917 and 3 Jan. 1918.
30 Ibid., entry 24 Jan. 1918.
31 Ducros, *La Peinture Puriste et l'Esprit Nouveau*, 13. In 1910, Ozenfant married a Russian art student, Zina de Klingberg. He made several trips to Russia before settling permanently in Paris. He and de Klingberg divorced in 1919.
32 Nancy Troy, *Modernism and the Decorative Arts in France* (New Haven: Yale University Press, 1991), 155–58.
33 Le Corbusier to Ritter, FLC R3-19-214-19, Paris, undated 1918, journal entry 31 Jan. 1918.
34 Ibid.
35 Ibid.
36 Ibid.
37 Ibid., entry 4 Mar. 1918.
38 Ibid., entry 14 Mar. 1918.
39 Ibid.
40 Ibid.
41 Ibid.
42 Le Corbusier to Ritter, FLC R3-19-222-230, Paris, 23 Mar. 1918.
43 Ibid.
44 Ibid.
45 Le Corbusier to Ritter, FLC R3-19-249-267, Paris, 18 June 1918, entry 12 May 1918.
46 Ibid.
47 Ibid., entry 22 May 1918.
48 Ibid.
49 Le Corbusier to Ritter, FLC R3-19-249-267, Paris, 18-06-1918, entry June 1918.
50 Le Corbusier to Ritter, FLC R3-19-268-283, Paris, 2 Aug. 1918.
51 Ibid., entry 27 June 1918.
52 Ibid.
53 Le Corbusier to Ritter, FLC R3-19-268-283, Paris, 2 Aug. 1918.
54 Ibid., entry 4 July 1918.
55 Ibid.
56 Ibid.
57 Ibid., entry 8 July 1918.
58 Ibid., entries 22 July 1918 and 26 July 1918.
59 Ibid., entry 26 July 1918.
60 Le Corbusier to Ritter, FLC R3-19-285, Paris, 3 Sept. 1918.
61 Le Corbusier to Ritter, postcard, FLC R3-19-286, Bordeaux, 17 Aug. 1918.
62 Le Corbusier to Ritter, FLC R3-19-288-91, Paris, 1 Oct. 1918; FLC F1-4-2, contract dated 16 Jan. 1917.
63 Le Corbusier to Ritter, FLC R3-19-288-91, Paris, 1 Oct. 1918.
64 Ibid.
65 Ibid.
66 Ibid.
67 Ibid.
68 Ibid.
69 Le Corbusier to Ritter, FLC R3-19-294-311, Paris, 4 Oct. 1918.
70 Ibid., entry 7 Aug. 1918.
71 Ibid., entry 8 Aug. 1918.
72 Ibid.
73 Ibid., entry 21 Aug. 1918.

74 Ibid.
75 Ibid., entry 22 Aug. 1918.
76 Ibid.
77 Ibid., entry 2 Sept. 1918
78 Ibid.
79 Troy, *Modernism and the Decorative Arts in France*, 161–62.
80 Le Corbusier to Ritter, FLC R3-19-294-311, Paris, 4 Oct. 1918, entry 2 Sept. 1918.
81 Ibid., entry 5 Sept. 1918.
82 Le Corbusier to Ritter, FLC R3-19-312-4, Paris, 20 Nov. 1918.
83 Ibid.
84 Ibid.
85 Le Corbusier to Ritter, FLC R3-19-315-7, S. Lazaire, 19 Dec. 1918.
86 There was at this time a renewed interest among Parisian artists in the painter Jean Ingres (1780–1867).
87 Le Corbusier to Ritter, FLC R3-19-315-7, S. Lazaire, 19 Dec. 1918.
88 Ibid.
89 Invitation to the exposition at the Galerie Thomas, FLC R3-19-318.
90 Ibid.
91 Ibid.
92 Ibid.
93 Le Corbusier to Ritter, FLC R3-19-343, Paris, 20 Jan. 1919.
94 Le Corbusier to Ritter, FLC R3-19-343, Paris, entry 20 Oct. 1919.
95 Le Corbusier to Ritter, FLC R3-19-343, Paris, 20 Jan. 1919, entry 21 Oct. 1918.
96 Ibid.
97 Ibid., entry 23 Oct. 1918
98 Jeanneret must have been referring to the armistice with Austria, signed November 3rd, not the armistice with Germany, signed November 11th.
99 Le Corbusier to Ritter, FLC R3-19-343, Paris, 20 Jan. 1919, entry 7 Nov. 1918
100 Ibid., entry 10 Nov. 1918
101 Ibid., entry 12 Nov. 1918
102 Ibid., entry 1 Jan. 1919
103 Le Corbusier to Ritter, FLC R3-19-335-39, Paris, 10 Apr. 1919.
104 Ibid.
105 Ibid.
106 Ibid., entry 29 Dec. 1918
107 Le Corbusier to Ritter, FLC R3-19-340-3, Paris, 1 June 1919.
108 Le Corbusier to Ritter, FLC R3-19-344-5, 8 July 1919; FLC R3-19-346-7, Toulouse.
109 Le Corbusier to Ritter, FLC R3-19-348-49, La Chaux-de-Fonds, 20 Aug. 1919
110 Le Corbusier to Ritter, FLC R3-19-350-1, Paris, 8 Sept. 1919.
111 Ibid.
112 Le Corbusier to Ritter, FLC R3-19-352-4, Paris, 13 Oct. 1919.
113 Ibid.
114 Le Corbusier to Ritter, FLC R3-19-355-8, La Rochelle, 09 Dec. 1919.
115 Ibid.
116 Viveca Bosson, "Le Corbusier–the painter who became an architect," in *Le Corbusier Painter and Architect*, ed. Mogens Krustrup, Kataloget er Udgivet Med Stotte FRA (Denmark: Fonden Til Udgivelse Af Arkitekturtidsskrift, 1995), 17–58; Brooks, *Le Corbusier's Formative Years*, 100.
117 Le Corbusier, *Modulor 2* (Basel: Birkhäuser, 1958), 296.
118 Le Corbusier to Ritter, FLC R3-19-355-8, La Rochelle, 9 Dec. 1919.
119 Ibid.
120 Ibid.
121 Le Corbusier to Ritter, FLC R3-19-35359-62, Paris, 14 Mar. 1920.
122 Le Corbusier to Ritter, FLC R3-19-365-67, Paris, 19 June 1920.
123 Ibid.
124 Le Corbusier to Ritter, FLC R3-19-368, Paris, 1 July 1920. His letter seems to imply that this mountain hut is relocatable and that they will find a park to place it outside of Paris.
125 Brooks dates the exhibition at the Galerie Druet to be Jan. 22–Feb. 5, 1921. Brooks, *Le Corbusier's Formative Years*, 503.
126 Le Corbusier to Ritter, FLC R3-19-371-4, Paris, 30 Jan. 1921.
127 Ibid.
128 Ibid.
129 Ibid.
130 Ibid.
131 Ibid.
132 Le Corbusier to Ritter, FLC R3-19-385-6, Paris, 30 July 1921.
133 Le Corbusier to Ritter, FLC R3-19-375-8, Paris, 11 Mar. 1921.
134 Ibid.
135 Ibid.
136 Ibid.
137 Le Corbusier to Ritter, FLC R3-19-379-80, Paris, 20 Mar. 1921.
138 Ibid.
139 Le Corbusier to Ritter, FLC R3-19-385-6, Paris, 30 July 1921.
140 Ibid.
141 Le Corbusier to Ritter, FLC R3-19-389-92, Paris, 7 April 1922.
142 Christopher Prochasson and Anne Rasmussen, *Au Nom de la Patrie* (Paris: Éditions la Découverte, 1996), 271.

143 Le Corbusier to Ritter, FLC R3-19-389-392, Paris, 07 Apr. 1922.
144 Ibid.
145 Mary Patricia Sekler, *Le Corbusier Painter and Architect* (Denmark: Fonden Til Udgivelse Af Arkitekturtidsskrift, 1995), 119–20, quoted in Mogens Krustrup, "Persona," in *Le Corbusier Painter and Architect*, 119–20.
146 Le Corbusier to Ritter, FLC R3-19-389-92, Paris, 7 Apr. 1922.
147 Le Corbusier to Ritter, FLC R3-19-395-6, Paris, 21 June 1922.
148 Ibid.
149 Le Corbusier to Ritter, FLC R3-19-405-7, Paris, 24 Feb. 1925.
150 Ibid.
151 Ibid.
152 Ibid.

CHAPTER 6

Epigraph Paul Valéry, "Descartes" (1937), in *Paul Valéry Masters and Friends*, Bollingen Series vol. 45, no. 9, trans. Martin Turnell (Princeton: Princeton University Press, 1968), 18, quotation translated by Suzanne Guerlac, *Literary Polemics: Bataille, Sartre, Valéry, Breton* (Stanford, CA: Stanford University Press, 1997), 112.
1 Amédée Ozenfant, "Notes sur le Cubisme," *L'Élan* 10 (Dec. 1916). See "Notes sur le Cubisme" in Appendix A in Susan L. Ball, *Ozenfant and Purism: The Evolution of a Style 1915–1930* (Ann Arbor, MI: UMI Research Press, 1981), 191–94.
2 Amédée Ozenfant, *Foundations of Modern Art* (1928; repr., New York: Dover Publications, Inc., 1952), 330.
3 Ozenfant, "Notes sur le Cubisme," 192; addendum to Ozenfant, *Foundations of Modern Art*, 324. For Mallarmé's poetry of perfection see Suzanne Guerlac, *Literary Polemics: Bataille, Sartre, Valéry, Breton*, 97–101.
4 Ozenfant, *Foundations of Modern Art*, 325. Ozenfant reminisced: "Between 1918 and 1925 everything we wrote was signed by both of us; all deserved to be, for each of us gave the best of himself."
5 Henri Poincaré, *Science and Method*, trans. Francis Maitland (1908; repr., New York: Dover Publications, Inc., 1952), 129
6 Ibid., 23.
7 Ibid.
8 Ibid., 17, 27, 34.
9 Ibid., 23–24.
10 Paul Valéry, "La crise de l'esprit," *L'Atheneum* (Apr.–May 1919); Paul Valéry, "Architecture et Musique," in *Paul Valéry et les Arts exposition catalogue* (Paris: Actes Sud, 1995), 115–17.
11 *Eupalinos*, was initially published as a luxury artist's album, the first of a series entitled *Architectures* published by Gaston Gallimard and designed for an elite audience by the decorators Louis Süe and André Marc. These two had already established a promotional base for their interior design work in the *Compagnie des Arts Française* in 1919. Süe would continue to solidify this base in books he published with Léandre Vaillat under the title *Rythme de l'architecture*. Gérard Monnier, "Un Retour à l'Ordre: Architecture, Géométrie, Société," in *Le Retour à l'Ordre dans les arts plastiques et l'architecture, 1919–1925* (Paris: Spaden, 1974), 45–64. Université de Saint-Etienne, Centre Interdiscipline d'Ëtudes et des Recherche su l'Expression, *Contemporaire* 8 (1974): 45–54; Claude Bouret, "Paul Valéry et l'architecture," *Gazette des Beaux-Arts*, September 1970, 185–208. Le Corbusier makes direct references to *Eupalinos* in "L'Esprit nouveau et l'architecture," *Bulletin de l'Order de l'Etoile d'Orient*, Janvier 1935, 35. This is a reprint of a speech he gave to a group of Parisian masons on November 10, 1924. See Luisa-Martina Colli, "Musique," in *Le Corbusier, une Encyclopédie* (Paris: Centre Georges Pompidou, 1987), 271 n. 22. Although Valéry remained aloof from contemporary architectural debates, nevertheless architects of various positions looking for support and inspiration quickly took up his ideas. For example, *L'Architecture Vivante*, no. 1 (1923) unfurled under the double patronage of Valéry and Auguste Perret. Bruno Foucart, "Paul Valéry devant l'architecture de son temps, d'Eupalinos à Auguste Perret," in *Parcours d'une expositionaire* (Paris: Actes Sud, 1995), 37–50.
12 Paul Valéry, *Leonardo Poe Mallarmé*, trans. Malcome Cowley and James R. Lawler (Princeton: Princeton University Press, 1972), 19.
13 Valéry, *Leonardo Poe Mallarmé*, 20.
14 Gérard Monnier, "Un Retour à l'Ordre," 52.
15 Invitation to Exposition sent to Ritter FLC R3-19-318. The date November 10 is crossed out and rewritten as December 21; see also *L'Esprit Nouveau* 5 (Feb. 1920): 568, quoted in Gladys C. Fabre, "The Modern Spirit in Figurative Painting from Modernist Iconography to a Modernist Conception of Plastic Art," in *Léger et l'esprit moderne: Une*

alternative d'avant-garde a l'art non-objectif (1918–31) (Paris: Musée d'Art Moderne de la ville de Paris, 1982), 167; H. Allen Brooks, *Le Corbusier's Formative Years* (Chicago: University of Chicago Press, 1997), 495. Brooks states the show was scheduled for November 15 but rescheduled for December 22nd; Françoise Ducros, "Amédée Ozenfant, 'Purist Brother,'" in Carol S. Eliel, ed., *L'Esprit Nouveau: Purism in Paris: 1918–1925* (Los Angeles: Los Angeles County Museum of Art; New York: Harry N. Abrams, Inc. Publishers, 2001), 80. Françoise Ducros states the date was December 22, 1918–January 11, 1919, the date was given as 15th–28th December in Françoise Ducros "La Peinture Puriste et l'Esprit Nouveau" (Thèse de troisième cycle soutenue le 26 février 1986 à Paris IV), 71.

16 Amédée Ozenfant and Charles-Édouard Jeanneret, *Après le Cubisme*, trans. John Goodman, quoted in Carol S. Eliel, ed., *L'Esprit Nouveau: Purism in Paris: 1918–1925.* (Los Angeles: Los Angeles County Museum of Art; New York: Harry N. Abrams, Inc. Publishers, 2001), 132. All quotations are taken from this translation.

17 Ozenfant and Jeanneret, *Après le Cubisme*, 152.

18 Ibid., 147.

19 George Lakoff and Rafael Núñez, "The Metaphorical Structure of Mathematics: Sketching Out Cognitive Foundations for a Mind-Based Mathematics," in *Mathematical Reasoning. Analogies, Metaphors, and Images*, ed. Lyn D. English (Mahwah, NJ: Lawrence Erlbaum Associates, Publishers, 1997), 25–27.

20 Ozenfant and Jeanneret, *Après le Cubisme*, 161.

21 Ibid., 133. The same quotation, translated by Kenneth Silver, gives "lucid" instead of "crisp." Kenneth Silver, *Esprit de Corps* (Princeton: Princeton University Press, 1989), 230. Le Corbusier's preferred word is 'lucid'.

22 François Ducros, *La Peinture Puriste et l'Esprit Nouveau*, 73.

23 Ozenfant and Jeanneret, *Après le Cubisme*, 145.

24 Ibid., 161.

25 Marie-Odile Briot, "L'Esprit Nouveau: Its View of Science," in *Léger et l'esprit moderne*, 62; and Jean-Paul Robert, "Pseudonymes" in *Le Corbusier, une encyclopédie* (Paris: Centre Georges Pompidou, 1987), 316–17.

26 While it is argued here that both the spirit of Apollinaire and Valèry guided the formation of Purism and aided the direction of *L'Esprit Nouveau*, it is only Apollinaire who was given explicit credit. Fearful that his legacy was diminishing with time, however, an entire issue, no. 26 (Oct. 1924), was dedicated to the memory of this magnanimous poet. Those who had formed the young avant-garde in 1916 paid tribute to his memory. The list and their tributes to Apollinaire includes Roche Grey, "Guillaume Apollinaire," André Salmon, "Vie Ancienne," Paul Dermée, "Guillaume Apollinaire," Henri Hertz, "Singulier Pluriel," and Alberto Savinio, "In Poetae Memoriam." On the other hand, Valéry's direct recognition in the pages of *L'Esprit Nouveau* is slight; he is praised by Paul Dermée in *L'Esprit Nouveau* 9 (Dec. 1923), for being both a geometer and poet. Like Plato, he was a called the master of an elliptical dance of ideas and a great intellectual poet.

27 Organisation du travail. FLC A1-15-437.

28 Stanislaus von Moos, "Industrie: Standard et élite: Le syndrome Citrohan," in *Le Corbusier, une encyclopédie* (Paris: Centre Georges Pompidou, 1987), 190–99. Documents examined in FLC do not contain industrialist as Jeanneret's profession. The secret treaty mentions only the profession of Dermée as *homme de letters* and does not assign professions to Ozenfant or Jeanneret. Traité secret entre MM. Dermée, Jeanneret et Ozenfant et Contract. FLC A1-19-1-3 25-02-1920. In a statute the following November, the professions assigned to Jeanneret is *architecte* and to Ozenfant, *artiste peintre*. Etude des Statues de la Sociétè, FLC A1-15-4-19 19-11-1920

29 Francoise Ducros, "Amédée Ozenfant, 'Purist Brother,'" 83.

30 van Doesburg to Dermée, FLC A1-10-32, 5 May 1920.

31 Dermée to van Doesburg, FLC A1-10-34, 11 Aug. 1920.

32 "Plan d'un numéro," FLC A1-15-424-31, 10 Sept. 1920.

33 *L'Esprit Nouveau* 1 (Oct. 1920). Seurat paintings directly influenced Leger's "La Ville," painted in 1919. The latter captures the state of mind a pedestrian of modern city streets might experience–depth is missing, while abstract bits of letters and a cheerful cacophony of forms fling themselves at the viewer. Silver, *Esprit de Corps*, 339–40.

34 "L'esthétique Mécanique," *L'Esprit Nouveau* 1 (Oct. 1920).

35 Le Corbusier, *L'Almanach d'architecture moderne* (Paris: Les Éditions G. Crès et Cie, 1925).

36 Silver, *Esprit de Corps*, 380.

37 These include the following articles written by Ozenfant and Jeanneret: "L'Esprit Nouveau," *L'Esprit Nouveau* 1 (Oct. 1920), 3–4; "L'Art et L'Esprit Nouveau," *Revue Internationale d'Economique* 1 (Jan. 1921); "Le Purisme," *L'Esprit Nouveau* 4 (Jan. 1921): 369–86; "Ce que nous avons fait. Ce que nous ferons," *L'Esprit Nouveau* 11/12 (Nov. 1921): 1211–14; and "Esthétique et le Purisme," *L'Esprit Nouveau* 15 (Feb. 1922): 1704–8.

38 During those four years Le Corbusier wrote 10,000 words a month–or so it has been claimed by Charles Jencks, *Le Corbusier and the Tragic View of Architecture* (Cambridge, MA: Harvard University Press, 1973), 63. For information about the conflicts between Jeanneret and Ozenfant see Ducros, "Amédée Ozenfant, 'Purist Brother,'" 71–99.

39 For the listing of dates of the three periods of *L'Esprit Nouveau* see Susan Ball, "Appendix," in *Ozenfant and Purism: The Evolution of a Style 1913–1930* (Ann Arbor: UMI Research Press, 1981), 197.

40 "Les Usines Fiat du Lingotto à Turin," *L'Esprit Nouveau* 19 (Dec. 1923).

41 Ozenfant and Jeanneret, "Formation de l'Optique Moderne," *L'Esprit Nouveau* 21 (March 1924). See *L'Esprit Nouveau* 18 (Nov. 1923) for a blueprint plan of a Voisin chassis.

42 The articles that comprise *La Peinture Moderne* written jointly by Ozenfant and Jeanneret have not been translated into English. They include "De la Peinture des Cavernes à la Peinture d'Aujourd'hui," *L'Esprit Nouveau* 15 (Feb. 1922): 1795–1803; "L'Angle Droite," *L'Esprit Nouveau* 18 (Nov. 1923): unpaginated; "Nature et Création," *L'Esprit Nouveau* 19 (Dec. 1923): unpaginated; "Destinées de la Peinture," *L'Esprit Nouveau* 20 (Jan./Feb. 1924): unpaginated; "Formation de l'Optique Moderne," *L'Esprit Nouveau* 21 (March 1924): unpaginated; "Le Cubisme, Première Epoque," *L'Esprit Nouveau* 23 (May 1924): unpaginated; "Le Cubisme, Deuxième Epoque," *L'Esprit Nouveau* 24 (June 1924): unpaginated; "Vers le cristal," *L'Esprit Nouveau* 25 (July 1924): unpaginated; and "Idées Personnelles," *L'Esprit Nouveau* 27 (Nov. 1924): unpaginated.

43 Ducros, "La Peinture Puriste et l'Esprit Nouveau."

44 Jeanneret to Ozenfant, 8 August 1924, quoted and translated by Ducros, "Amèdée Ozenfant, 'Purist Brother,'" 93.

45 Ozenfant to Jeanneret, 13 Aug. 1924, quoted and translated by Ducros, "Amèdée Ozenfant, 'Purist Brother,'" 93.

46 FLC A1-18-317, 25 July 1925.

47 FLC A1-18-318, 29 July 1925.

48 Caralo Olmo, "Revues: La Perception du Changement" in *Encycopédie*, 344–49. For the development of a planning mentality in American cities from 1893–1945, see M. Christine Boyer, *Dreaming the Rational City: The myth of American city planning* (Cambridge: MIT Press, 1983). From time to time, *L'Esprit Nouveau* would include articles on political affairs, such as R. Chennevier, "Wilson et l'humanisme français," *L'Esprit Nouveau* 11/12 (Nov. 1921): 1223–31; Henri Hertz, "L'Acheminement vers les grands Conseils Internationaux," *L'Esprit Nouveau* 15 (Feb. 1922): 1727–40; Paul Lafitte, "A propos de la Grande Crise," *L'Esprit Nouveau* 16 (May 1922): 1889–97; Henri Hertz, "Balbutiements de l'Esprit Politique," pt. 1, *L'Esprit Nouveau* 21 (Mar. 1924); Henri Hertz, "Balbutiements de l'Esprit Politique," pt. 2, *L'Esprit Nouveau* 22 (Apr. 1924); Henri Hertz, "Balbutiements de l'Esprit Politique," pt. 3, *L'Esprit Nouveau* 24 (June 1924).

49 Fabre, "The Modern Spirit in Figurative Painting," 166; Olmo, "La Perception du Changement," 344.

50 Olmo, "La Perception du Changement," 344–49.

51 Ozenfant et Jeanneret, "Ce Que Nous Avons Fait Ce Que Nous Ferons," *L'Esprit Nouveau* 11–12 (Nov.1921): 1211–14.

52 Le Corbusier, "L'Esprit Nouveau," FLC A2-5-1.

53 Ibid.

54 Ibid.

55 Ibid.

56 Ozenfant et Jeanneret, "Ce Que Nous Avons Fait Ce Que Nous Ferons," 1211–14.

57 *L'Esprit Nouveau* 4 (Jan. 1922). Ozenfant and Jeanneret praised the typewriter, placing a handwritten letter on one page opposite a typewritten text with its liberated blank spaces on the other. In Purism, bright colors were abhorred, they appealed to the senses not to the spirit. Natural colors were preferred like those found in ancient frescoes: yellow ocher, red, earth color, white, black, ultramarine. These colors kept their subordinate place in a painting, helping to order the elements into a unified structure. In architecture, whitewashed walls would suffice. As they explained: "Let us leave the sensory jubilation of the tube of color to the man who dyes clothes." Quoted in Fabre, "The Modern Spirit in Figurative Painting," 166.

58 Stanislaus von Moos, *Le Corbusier Elements of a Synthesis* (Cambridge, MA: MIT Press, 1979), 37–67; Beatriz Colomina, *Privacy and Publicity Modern Architecture as Mass Media* (Cambridge, MA: MIT Press, 1994), 140–95.
59 Fabre, "The Modern Spirit in Figurative Painting," 156.
60 Gaston Bachelard, *Poetics of Space*, trans. Maria Jolas (Boston: Beacon Press, 1969), 75. "Concepts are drawers which may be used to classify knowledge, concepts are ready-made clothes which de-individualize personal experience." Quoted in Briot, *Léger et l'esprit moderne*, 157.
61 Nancy Troy, *Modernism and the Decorative Arts in France* (New Haven: Yale University Press, 1991), 216.
62 "Publicité pour Innovation" to appear in *L'Esprit Nouveau* 22 (Apr. 1924), FLC A1-17-18.
63 In another copy he wrote: "We have spent some years of work establishing some models of the organization of interiors destined to transform the domestic exploitation of apartments; we want to simplify domestic work through classification, and order. / But we find ourselves still each day faced with apartments of which the plans inspired by ancient traditions make an obstacle in our support. We would like to make it understood to the inhabitants of the city of the twentieth century that the plan of the apartment ought to be remodeled and we would like to draw this to the attention of... architects." Publicité pour Innovation, FLC A1-17-4.
64 Fabre, "The Modern Spirit in Figurative Painting," 164.
65 In its first issue, *L'Esprit Nouveau* printed Henri-Pierre Roche's novel black and white photographs of American industrial architecture.
66 Fabre, "The Modern Spirit in Figurative Painting," 156; Christopher Green, *Cubism and its Enemies: Modern Movements and Reaction in French Art, 1916–1928* (New Haven: Yale University Press, 1987), 98.
67 *L'Esprit Nouveau* 21 (Mar. 1924), quoted in Green, *Cubism and its Enemies*, 211.
68 Troy, *Modernism and the Decorative Arts*, 208–9. Nancy Troy describes some of the conventional art journals that displayed the same images as *L'Esprit Nouveau*. She argues that the use of such images was not unique to *L'Esprit Nouveau*, but the manner they were manipulated was. For example, an article by André Fréchet entitled "L'Art de la caroisserie et l'automobile de luxe" appeared in 1921 in *Art et Décoration*. Parallel to Le Corbusier's "Eyes which do not See," Fréchet also illustrated the chassis of five horse-drawn carriages followed by two images of automobile chassis in order to argue the evolution of design. He wrote, "The automobile will not become a useful vehicle until the day when, thanks to the contribution of the carriage builders, the better thought-out mechanical chassis will be furnished with a solid, comfortable and elegant body. This is to say, in other words, that the establishment of an automobile vehicle requires the collaboration of the engineer and the artisan. While the former uses and adapts the latest discoveries of modern science, the latter contributes the acquired knowledge that he owes to a *métier* whose traditions are the fruit of several centuries of studies and experiment." Troy, *Modernism and the Decorative Arts*, 203. In addition, Troy notes that Guillaume Janneau published "Le mouvement moderne: l'esthétique de l'automobile," in *La Renaissance de l'Art Francais et des industries de Luxe* 4 (Nov. 1921, pp. 558–63) in 1921, and that he too gave credit to the engineers for perfecting the silhouette of the automobile without the aid of artists, finding that necessity seemed to have dictated a generalized [universal] form. Troy, *Modernism and the Decorative Arts*, 207.
69 Ozenfant and Jeanneret, "Purism," *L'Esprit Nouveau* 4 (Nov. 1920): 369–86; Robert L. Herbert, trans., "Purism," in *Modern Artists on Art: Ten Unabridged Essays*, ed. Robert L. Herbert (Englewood Cliffs, NJ: Prentice-Hall Inc., 1964), 73.
70 *L'Esprit Nouveau* 17 (June 1922), quoted in Fabre, "The Modern Spirit in Figurative Painting," 167.
71 Amédée Ozenfant, *Memoires 1886–1962* (Paris: Seghors, 1968), 93, quoted in Fabre, "The Modern Spirit and the Problem of Abstraction for Léger, his Friends and his students at the Academie moderne," in Briot, *Léger et l'esprit moderne*, 355–431; quotation: 425.
72 Ozenfant and Jeanneret, "Purism," 369–86; Ozenfant and Jeanneret, "Purism," in Herbert, *Modern Artists on Art*, 60.
73 Ozenfant and Jeanneret, *Après le Cubisme*, 135, 137, 138, 139.
74 Ibid., 138.
75 Ozenfant et Jeanneret, "Esthétique et Purism," *L'Esprit Nouveau* 15 (Feb. 1922): 1704–8; Ozenfant et Jeanneret, "Sur la Plastique," *L'Esprit Nouveau* 1 (Oct. 1920): 38–48; Ozenfant et Jeanneret, "Le Purisme," *L'Esprit Nouveau* 4 (Jan. 1921): 369–86.

76 Maurice Raynal, "Ozenfant et Jeanneret," *L'Esprit Nouveau* 7 (Apr. 1921): 807–32.
77 Ozenfant et Jeanneret, "Esthétique et Purism," 1706.
78 Ozenfant et Jeanneret, "Sur la Plastique," 38–48.
79 Ibid.
80 Ibid.
81 Ibid.
82 Ozenfant et Jeanneret, "L'Angle Droit," unpaginated.
83 Ibid.
84 Ibid.
85 Ibid. Searching for a term that described the state of knowledge and self-awareness acquired after a long period of research, Ozenfant and Jeanneret selected the term *hieratisme*. It designated the moment when man selected from among different technical means the one that best satisfied the spiritual needs of his newly gained intellectual state.
86 Ozenfant et Jeanneret, "Nature et Crèation," *L'Esprit Nouveau* 19 (Dec. 1923): unpaginated.
87 Ibid.
88 Ibid.
89 Ozenfant et Jeanneret, "Destinée de la peinture," *L'Esprit Nouveau* 20 (Jan./Feb. 1924): unpaginated.
90 Ozenfant et Jeanneret, "Formation du Optique Moderne," *L'Esprit Nouveau* 21 (Mar. 1924): unpaginated.
91 Valéry was actually inspired by Viollet-le-Duc's history of a house and became one of the protectors of a nationalistic regionalism, as an alternative to architecture called modern and international.
92 "Nous avons conclu à la necessité de la peinture architecturée." Ozenfant et Jeanneret, "Le Purisme," *L'Esprit Nouveau* 4.
93 Ibid.
94 Le Corbusier, *Le Corbusier, L'Atelier de la recherche patiente* (Paris: Vincent et Fréal, 1960), unpaginated. Translated by James Palmes as *Creation is a Patient Search,* (New York: Frederick A. Praeger, 1960).
95 Ibid.
96 Brooks, *Le Corbusier's Formative Years*, 493. Brooks thinks he exhibited "La Chiminée" while Silver thinks it was "Still-life with Book, Glass and Pipe"; Silver, *Esprit de Corps*, 232–33.
97 Viveca Bosson, "Le Corbusier–the painter who became an architect," in *Le Corbusier Painter and Architect* (Denmark: Fonden Til Udgivelse Af Arkitekturtidsskrift, 1995), 38. See also Danièle Pauly, "Dessin et Peinture: recerche et évolution d'un langage: 1918–1925," in *Le Corbusier, une encyclopédie* (Paris: Centre Georges Pompidou, 1987), 320–29.
98 *L'Esprit Nouveau* 5 (Feb. 1920): 568, quoted in Fabre, "The Modern Spirit in Figurative Painting," 167.
99 Raynal, "Ozenfant et Jeanneret," 807–32.
100 Olmo, "La Perception du Changement," 345.
101 Poincaré, *Science and Method*, 28–29.

CHAPTER 7

Epigraph Journal of Le Corbusier, 9 Sept. 1920, cited by Jean Petit, *Le Corbusier Lui-Même* (Geneva: Éditions Rousseau, 1970), 53, quoted by Guillemette Morel Journel, "Le Corbusier: Un Architecte Écrivain de la Modernité:... Rhétorique de le Corbusier," (unpublished Diplôme d'architecte DPLG, Université Paris I, June 1984): 3.
1 Evidently the English critic I. A. Richards said in 1925 that "A book is a machine to think with" (*Principles of Literary Criticism*, first sentence of Preface), but it is not known if Richards's analogy influenced Valèry.
2 Le Corbusier, *Towards a New Architecture*, trans. Frederick Etchells (New York: Praeger Publishers, 1960; facsimile of 1927 version [London: Architectural Press Publication]), 11. Etchells's 1927 translation was from the thirteenth edition of *Vers Une Architecture* (1923).
3 The chapters of *Vers une Architecture* open with "The Engineer's Aesthetic," published in *L'Esprit Nouveau* 11–12 (Nov. 1921). This is followed by the section "Three Reminders to Architects": "Mass," *L'Esprit Nouveau* 2 (Nov. 1920); "Surface," *L'Esprit Nouveau* 1 (Oct. 1920); and "Plan," *L'Esprit Nouveau* 4 (Jan. 1921). This is followed by a chapter standing alone: "Regulating Lines," *L'Esprit Nouveau* 5 (Feb. 1921). The next sections includes the three chapters of "Eyes which do not See": "Liners," *L'Esprit Nouveau* 8 (May 1921); "Airplanes," *L'Esprit Nouveau* 9 (June 1921); and "Automobiles," *L'Esprit Nouveau* 10 (July 1921). The three chapters in the section on "Architecture" are next: "The lesson of Rome," *L'Esprit Nouveau* 14 (Jan. 1922); "The Illusion of Plans," *L'Esprit Nouveau* 15 (Feb. 1922); and "Pure Creation of the Mind," *L'Esprit Nouveau* 16 (May 1922). The book is then concluded with "Mass Produced Houses," *L'Esprit Nouveau* 13 (December 1921) and the newly written chapter "Architecture or Revolution" (1923).

4 Françoise Ducros, "Amédée Ozenfant, 'Purist Brother,'" in *L'Esprit Nouveau: Purism in Paris, 1918–1925*, ed. Carol S. Eliel (Los Angeles: MoCA and Harry N. Abrams, Inc., 2001), 84.
5 Maria Lucia Cannarozzo, "Corbu et la Métaphore," *Le Corbusier, Ecritures Rencontres de 18 et 19 Juin, 1993* (Paris: Fondation le Corbusier, 1993), 89–109.
6 Cannarozzo argues that just as Valéry creates a metaphor in saying "The body is a machine for living," so Le Corbusier draws together his concept of the Taylorized efficiency machine and biological forms to establish a new synergy.
7 Cannarozzo, "Corbu et la Métaphore," 89–109.
8 Henri Poincaré, *Science and Method*, trans. Francis Maitland (1908; repr., New York: Dover Publications, Inc., 1952), 30.
9 Ibid., 34.
10 Le Corbusier, "The Engineer's Aesthetic," in *Towards a New Architecture*, 7–25.
11 Le Corbusier, "Three Reminders to Architects," in *Towards a New Architecture*, 26–63.
12 Le Corbusier, "Regulating Lines," in *Towards a New Architecture*, 64–79.
13 Le Corbusier, "Eyes which do not See," in *Towards a New Architecture*, 82–114, 122–38.
14 Le Corbusier, *Towards a New Architecture*, 18.
15 Ibid.
16 Ibid., 19.
17 Ibid., 20.
18 Ibid., 21.
19 Ibid., 23.
20 Ibid., 27.
21 Ibid.
22 Ibid., 28; repeated 45.
23 One can generalize and say that all forms are a projection of another form, that *n* dimensional space projects or engenders *n* + 1 dimensional form. See Henri Poincaré, *Science and Hypothesis* (London: Walter Scott Publishing, 1905), translated from the French *La Science et L'Hypothèse* (1902), especially Ch. 4, "Space and Geometry."
24 Le Corbusier, *Towards a New Architecture*, 31.
25 Ibid.
26 Ibid., 33.
27 Ibid.
28 Ibid., 41.
29 Ibid., 8; repeated 36.
30 Ibid., 44.
31 Ibid., 45.
32 Ibid., 46–7.
33 Ibid., 61–2.
34 Ibid., 68.
35 Ibid., 69–70.
36 Ibid., 83.
37 Ibid., 84.
38 Ibid., 86.
39 Ibid., 89.
40 Ibid.
41 Ibid., 96.
42 Ibid., 96–7.
43 Ibid., 97.
44 Ibid., 100.
45 Ibid., 101.
46 Le Corbusier slightly mischaracterizes Clement Ader's Avion III, the "Bat," 1897. This was a failed attempt at propeller-driven flight using steam for power and uncambered fixed wings modeled closely after those of a bat, only far larger. The machine was not an ornithopter (wing-flapping flying machine) and so did not exactly attempt to fly "like a bird"–at least, no more than other fixed-wing aircraft.
47 Le Corbusier, *Towards a New Architecture*, 105.
48 Ibid., 109–14.
49 Ibid., 114–9.
50 Ibid., 10 and 122.
51 Even in the 1920s, a projected hood with the engine beneath–and a compartment for driver (and possibly passengers) behind it–had become standard in both racing and "touring" cars. Perhaps Le Corbusier is working out ideas to be embedded in his future design for a touring car that would place the motor behind and allow the spectator a panoramic vision from the front. Le Corbusier, "Note: Établissement du Plan d'une Voiture Automobile," FLC T2 (16), 53–55. Paris, 2 Apr. 1936; Le Corbusier, "Voiture, projet non-réalisé," 1 Proposition, no. 102. FLC T2 (16), 56.
52 Le Corbusier, *Towards a New Architecture*, 129–31.
53 Ibid., 133.
54 Ibid.
55 Ibid., 138.
56 Ibid., 10; repeated 140.
57 Ibid., 141, 164.
58 Le Corbusier, "The Lesson of Rome 1–4," in *Towards a New Architecture*, 163–84.
59 For Loos's statements on antiquity and modernity, see Janet Stewart, *Fashioning Vienna: Adolf Loos's Cultural Criticism* (London and New York: Routledge, 2000), 56–8.
60 Victor Emmanuel III, King of Italy from 1900 to 1946.

61 Le Corbusier, *Towards a New Architecture*, 146.
62 Ibid., 149.
63 Ibid., 150–1.
64 Ibid., 151.
65 Ibid., 161.
66 Le Corbusier, "The Illusion of Plans," in *Towards a New Architecture*, 142–62.
67 Ibid., 166.
68 Ibid., 165.
69 Ibid., 166.
70 Ibid.
71 Ibid.
72 Ibid., 167.
73 Ibid., 168.
74 Ibid., 169.
75 Ibid.
76 Ibid., 172.
77 Ibid., 173.
78 Ibid.
79 Ibid., 175.
80 Ibid., 177–80.
81 Ibid., 179.
82 Ibid., 181–4.
83 Le Corbusier considers the plan of Karlsruhe a failure because from any point along its radiating streets a spectator can never see more than three windows of the castle, always the same three windows. A humble house would produce the same effect. Similarly from any window in the castle, one never looks down more than a single street at a time, the same effect produced by any small market town. It must be remembered: it is the human eye that judges the results of any plan drawn on paper.
84 Le Corbusier, "Pure Creation of the Mind," in *Towards a New Architecture*: 185–207.
85 Marie-Vicitoire de Vaubernier, "Le Corbusier, Editeur," *Le Corbusier, Ecritures Reconctres de 18 et 19 Juin, 1993* (Paris: Foundation le Corbusier, 1993), 31–45; Daniel Naegele, "Photographic illusionism and the 'new world of space,'" in *Le Corbusier Painter* and Architect, Kataloget er Udgivet Med Stotte FRA (Denmark: Fonden Til Udgivelse Af Arkitekturtidsskrift, 1995), 83–117.
86 Le Corbusier, *Towards a New Architecture*, 188.
87 Ibid.
88 Ibid., 190.
89 Ibid., 197–8.
90 Ibid., 198.
91 Ibid., 202.
92 Ibid., 204.
93 Ibid., 13, 210.
94 Ibid., 211–7.
95 Ibid., 217–8.
96 Ibid., 219, 245.
97 Ibid., 247.
98 Ibid., 251.
99 Ibid., 253.
100 Ibid., 254–5.
101 Ibid., 256.
102 Ibid., 259.
103 Ibid., 261.
104 Ibid., 266.
105 Ibid.
106 Ibid., 268–9.
107 Reyner Banham, *Theory and Design in the First Machine Age* (Cambridge: MIT Press, 1980), 220.
108 Ibid., 245–6.
109 Geoffrey H. Baker, *Le Corbusier: The Creative Search* (New York, Van Nostrand Reinhold, 1996), 280.
110 Baker, *Le Corbusier: The Creative Search*, 276; quotation, 273.
111 Guillemette Morel-Journel, "Le Corbusier: Structure Rhétorique et Volonté Littéraire," in *Le Corbusier, Ecritures Rencontres des 18 et 19 Juin, 1993* (Paris: Fondation le Corbusier, 1993), 17–29.
112 Le Corbusier, *Towards a New Architecture*, 269.
113 Le Corbusier, *Urbanisme*, quoted by Guillemette Morel Journel, "Le Corbusier's Binary Figures," *Daidalos* 64 (June 1997): 27. Journel points out that the English translation of this sentence ignores the rhetorical play on words and denies the ramifying effects the word "revolution" sets in motion. The English reads: "Things are not revolutionized by making revolutions. The real revolution lies in the solution of existing problems." The original French offers a play on words: "On ne révolutionne pas en révolutionnant. On révo lutionnne [*sic*] en révolutionnant." Journel, "Le Corbusier's Binary Figures," 28.
114 Le Corbusier, *The City of To-morrow and its planning*, trans. Frederick Etchells, from the 8th French edition of *Urbanisme* (Cambridge: MIT Press, 1971, original translation 1929). All citations are from Etchells's translation.
115 Le Corbusier, "Part I: General Considerations," *The City of To-morrow*, 9–156; Ch. I: "The Pack-Donkey's Way and Man's Way," 11–18, originally published as Le Corbusier, "Le Chemin des Anes, Le Chemin des Hommes," *L'Esprit Nouveau* 17 (June 1922); Ch. II: "Order," 21–32, originally published as Le Corbusier–Saugnier, "Ordre," *L'Esprit Nouveau* 18 (Nov. 1923); Ch. III: "Sensibility Comes into Play," 35–46,

originally published as Le Corbusier, "Le Sentiment déborde," *L'Esprit Nouveau* 19 (Dec. 1923); Chap. IV: "Permanence," 49–59, originally published as Le Corbusier, "Péréanité," *L'Esprit Nouveau* 20 (Jan./Feb. 1924); Ch. V: "Classification and Choice (A Survey)," 61–69, originally published as Le Corbusier, "Classement et choix," *L'Esprit Nouveau* 21 (Mar. 1924); Ch, VI: "Classification and Choice (Timely Decisions)," 71–82, originally published as Le Corbusier, "Classement et choix II," *L'Esprit Nouveau* 22 (Apr. 1924); Ch. VII: "The Great City," 86–105, originally published as Le Corbusier, "La Grande Ville," *L'Esprit Nouveau* 23 (May 1924); Ch. VIII: "Statistics," 107–26, originally published as Le Corbusier, "Statistique," *L'Esprit Nouveau* 24 (June 1924); Ch. IX: "Newspaper Cuttings and Catchwords," 129–37, originally published as Le Corbusier, "Coupures de Journaux," *L'Esprit Nouveau* 25 (July 1924); Ch. X, "Our Technical Equipment," 139–56, originally published as Le Corbusier, "Nos Moyens," *L'Esprit Nouveau* 27 (Nov. 1924).

116 Le Corbusier, Part II: "Laboratory Work: An Inquiry into Theory," in *The City of To-morrow*, 159–247; Ch. XI: "A Contemporary City," 159–78, originally published as Le Corbusier, "Une ville contemporaine," *L'Esprit Nouveau* 28 (Jan. 1925); Ch. XII, "The Working Day," 181–94; Ch. XIII: "The Hours of Repose," 197–244.

117 Le Corbusier, Part III: "A Concrete Case: The Centre of Paris," in *The City of To-morrow*, 250–301; Ch. XIV: "Physics or Surgery," 251–71; Ch. XV: "The Centre of Paris," 275–92; Ch. XVI: "Finance and Realization," 293–301.

118 Le Corbusier, "The Pack-Donkey's Way and Man's Way," in *The City of To-morrow*, 11–18.

119 Le Corbusier, *The City of To-morrow*, 11.

120 Ibid., 14.

121 Ibid., 16.

122 Ibid., 21–32.

123 Ibid., 28.

124 Ibid., 30–1.

125 Ibid., 35–46.

126 Ibid., 36.

127 Ibid., 40.

128 Ibid., 43.

129 Ibid., 49.

130 Ibid., 50.

131 Ibid., 51.

132 Ibid., 52.

133 Ibid., 52.

134 Ibid., 53–4.

135 Ibid., 59.

136 Le Corbusier, Ch. V: "Classification and Choice (A Survey)," *The City of To-morrow*, 61–9; Ch. VI: "Classification and Choice (Timely Decisions)," 71–82.

137 Ibid., 62–3.

138 Ibid., 64.

139 Ibid., 66.

140 Ibid., 69.

141 Ibid., 72.

142 Ibid.

143 Ibid., 73.

144 Ibid., 76.

145 Ibid., 77.

146 Ibid., 78.

147 Ibid., 80–2.

148 Ibid., 86.

149 Ibid., 87.

150 Ibid.

151 Ibid., 88.

152 Ibid., 89.

153 Ibid., 95.

154 Ibid., 96.

155 Ibid., 98.

156 Ibid.

157 Ibid., 107–26.

158 Ibid., 108.

159 Ibid., 110–11.

160 Ibid., 125.

161 Ibid., 129–37.

162 Ibid., 127.

163 Ibid., 129.

164 Ibid., 133–35.

165 Ibid., 138.

166 Ibid., 142–8.

167 Ibid., 144.

168 Ibid., 144–5.

169 Ibid., 146.

170 Ibid.

171 Ibid., 148.

172 Ibid.

173 Ibid., 152.

174 Ibid., 154.

175 Le Corbusier, Ch. 11: "The Contemporary City," in *The City of To-morrow*: 159–78; Ch. 12: "The Working Day," 181–94; Ch. 13: "Hours of Repose," 197–224.

176 Le Corbusier, *The City of To-morrow*, 161.

177 Ibid., 171.

178 Ibid., 176.

179 Ibid., 179.

180 Ibid., 184.

181 Ibid., 191.

182 Ibid., 208.

183 Ibid., 210.

184 Ibid., 212.

185 Ibid., 231.

186 Ibid., 237.

187 Ibid., 244.
188 Le Corbusier, Ch. 14: "Physic or Surgery," in *The City of To-morrow*, 251–71.
189 Le Corbusier, *The City of To-morrow*: 254–55.
190 Ibid., 261.
191 Ibid., 264.
192 Ibid., 275–301.
193 Ibid., 288.
194 Ibid., 280.
195 Ibid., 283.
196 Ibid., 287.
197 Ibid., 293–301.
198 Ibid., 296.
199 Ibid., 298.
200 Ibid.
201 Ibid., 301.
202 Le Corbusier, *The Decorative Arts of Today*, trans. James I. Dunnett (Cambridge: MIT Press, 1987). Ch 1: "Iconology. Iconolaters. Iconoclasts"(*L'Esprit Nouveau* 19); Ch. 2: "Other icons: the museums" (*L'Esprit Nouveau* 20); Ch. 3: "Plagiarism: folk culture"(*L'Esprit Nouveau* 21); Ch. 4: "Consequences of the crisis" (*L'Esprit Nouveau* 22); Ch. 5: "A hurricane"; Ch. 6: "Type-needs. Type-furniture" (*L'Esprit Nouveau* 23); Ch. 7: "The decorative art of today" (*L'Esprit Nouveau* 24); Ch. 8: "The Lesson of the Machine" (*L'Esprit Nouveau* 25); Ch. 9: "Respect for works of art" (*L'Esprit Nouveau* 26); Ch. 10: "The hour of architecture" (*L'Esprit Nouveau* 28); Ch. 11: "Milestones" (photographs); Ch. 12: "The Sense of Truth" (photographs); Ch. 13: "A coat of whitewash: The law of ripolin."
203 Ibid.
204 For an extended critique leveled by Le Corbusier at the feminization of modernity, Paris, and the 1925 Exposition, see Gronberg, "Making up the Modern City."
205 James Dunnett, "Introduction," in Le Corbusier, *The Decorative Arts of Today*, vii–xii. Banham, *Theory and Design,* vii.
206 The picturesque and bohemian Peter Altenberg was a poet and feuilletonist, best known for his short prose pieces. As an example of individualism carried to extreme, he became a cult figure influencing both Karl Kraus and Adolf Loos.
207 Adolf Loos, "L'Architecture et le style moderne," *Les Cahiers d'Aujourd'hui* 2, trans. Marcel Ray (Dec. 1912): 82–92; "Ornement et crime," *Les Cahiers d'Aujourd'hui* 5, trans. Marcel Ray (June 1913): 247–56; Noted in Nancy Troy, *Modernism and the Decorative Arts in France* (New Haven: Yale University Press, 1991), 134.
208 Adolf Loos, "Ornement et Crime," *L'Esprit Nouveau* 2 (Nov. 1920): 159–68.
209 Le Corbusier, *The Decorative Arts of Today*, 186.
210 Mark Anderson, *Kafka's Clothes* (Oxford and New York: Oxford University Press, 1992), 15.
211 Le Corbusier, *The Decorative Arts of Today*, 1.
212 Ibid., 7.
213 For an extension of this argument, see Gronberg, "Modernity on Display."
214 Le Corbusier, *The Decorative Arts of Today*, 55.
215 Ibid., xviii.
216 Ibid., 10–12.
217 Ibid., 13.
218 Ibid., 17.
219 Ibid., 22.
220 Ibid., 29.
221 Ibid., 33.
222 Ibid., 38.
223 Ibid., 42.
224 Ibid., 42–3.
225 Ibid., 47.
226 Ibid., 49.
227 Ibid., 54.
228 Ibid., 55.
229 Ibid., 57.
230 Ibid., 72.
231 Ibid., 76.
232 Ibid., 84.
233 Ibid., 85.
234 Ibid., 112.
235 Ibid., 117.
236 Ibid., 120.
237 Ibid., 126.
238 Ibid., 127.
239 Ibid., 166.
240 Ibid., 174.
241 Ibid., 180.
242 Ibid., 183.
243 Ibid., 189.
244 Ibid., 190.
245 Ibid., 192.
246 Le Corbusier, *Almanach d'Architecture Moderne* (Paris: Les Éditions G. Crès et Cie, 1925) contains the following chapter : "Les Architectures de L'Histoire"; "L'Esprit Nouveau en Architecture"; "Carnet de route, 1910: Les Mosquées"; "Sur L'Acropole"; "Un Tournant"; "Construire en Série"; "Un Standart meurt, Un Standart nait"; "Étude d'une Fenêtre moderne"; "Appel aux Industriels"; "Un Seul Corps de Métier"; "Modénature"; "L'Héritage de Charles Garnier"; "La Liberté par l'ordre";

"Inauguration du pavillon de l'Esprit Nouveau"; "Une Maison-Outil"; "Le Pavillon de L'Esprit Nouveau"; "Des Tapis Décoratifs"; "Une Ville Contemporaine de Trois Millions D'Habitants"; "Le Plan Voisin de Paris"; "Jury d'Urbanisme"; "Des Mots"; "Dates"(photographs); "Procèdes et Matériaux Nouveaux"; "Histoire Brève de nos Tribulations."

247 Naegele, "Photographic Illusionism and the 'New World of Space,'" 83–116.

248 Journel, "Le Corbusier's Binary Figures," 24–29.

249 Ozenfant and Jeanneret, "Sur la Plastique" *L'Esprit Nouveau* 1 (Oct. 1920): 38–48.

250 Ferdinand de Saussure gave his Geneva Lectures in 1907–11. His students would eventually turn this into *The General Course in Linguistics*. Roy Harris, *Saussure and his Interpreters* (New York: New York University Press, 2001); Roy Harris, *Rethinking Writing* (New York: Continuum, 2001, reprint of 2000 edition), 41.

251 Le Corbusier, "Almanach," in *Almanach d'Architecture Moderne*, 5.

252 Le Corbusier, "Un Tournant," in *Almanach d'Architecture Moderne*, 74.

253 Le Corbusier, "Exposé bref de nos tribulations: construction du Pavillon de l'Esprit Nouveau" (manuscript, FLC B2-16-22-52, 1929).

254 Le Corbusier, "Exposé bref de nos tribulations," (FLC B2-16-42-3).

255 Le Corbusier, "Au lecteur," in *Almanach d'Architecture Moderne*, 3–4

256 Le Corbusier, "Du Pavillon de L'Esprit Nouveau" in *Almanach d'Architecture Moderne*, 150.

257 Passage taken from *L'Architecte* (Sept. 1925), quoted by Le Corbusier, "Des Mots," in *Almanach d'Architecture Moderne*, 182.

258 Le Corbusier, *Almanach d'Architecture Moderne*, 184.

259 Le Corbusier, "L'Esprit Nouveau en Architecture," conference given at the Sorbonne 12 June 1924 and repeated to a group of the Order of the "l'Étoile d'Orient" 10 November 1924. *Almanach d'Architecture Moderne*, 17–54.

260 Le Corbusier, "L'Esprit Nouveau en Architecture," 20–21.

261 Ibid., 21–24.

262 Ibid., 24.

263 Ibid., 25.

264 Ibid.

265 Ibid., 26–7.

266 Ibid., 29.

267 Ibid., 31–36.

268 Ibid., 36–37.

269 Ibid., 40.

270 Le Corbusier, "Un Tournant" *Almanach d'Architecture Moderne* (Oct. 1924): 73–76.

271 Ibid., 75.

272 Ibid., 76.

273 Le Corbusier, "Construire en Série," in *Almanach d'Architecture Moderne*, 77–82.

274 Le Corbusier, "Un Standart Meurt un Standart Nait," in *Almanach d'Architecture Moderne*, 83–91.

275 Ibid., 91.

276 Le Corbusier, "Procédés et Matériaux Nouveaux," in *Almanach d'Architecture Moderne*, 190–96

277 The size of a large pocket watch when folded, the Swiss-made Mikiphone was patented by the Vadász Brothers in 1924. It was referred to as a travel phonograph.

278 Le Corbusier, "Innovation," in *Almanach d'Architecture Moderne*, 196–7.

279 Ozenfant and Jeanneret, "Intégrer," *Création Revue d'Art* 2 (1921).

280 Pierre Jeanneret and Le Corbusier, "Five Points of Architecture" (undated, FLC C3-16-111).

281 Journal of Le Corbusier, 9 Sept. 1920, cited by Petit, *Le Corbusier Lui-même*, 53, quoted by Journel, "Le Corbusier: Un Architecte Ecrivain de la Modernité," 3.

282 Le Corbusier, *Almanach d'Architecture Moderne*, 150.

283 Ibid., 149.

284 Christopher Eric Morgan Pearson, "Integrations of Art and Architecture in the work of Le Corbusier: Theory and Practice from Ornamentalism to the Synthesis of the Major Arts" (Unpublished Ph.D. dissertation, Stanford University, 1995): 203–32.

285 Paul Bonifas (Le Corbusier), "Réponse à l'article de M. A. De Senger, 'La Crise dans L'Architecture,'" *L'Œuvre* (Mar./Apr. 1928), FLC X1-6-46. Alexandre de Senger, "La Crise dans L'Architecture" *L'œuvre* (Feb. 1928): 5–9, FLC X1–6-29.

286 As reported by Jean Petit, Le Corbusier accomplished the following schedule of lectures between 1924 and 1939: 1924–Prague, Geneva; 1926–Brussels; 1927–Madrid, Barcelona; 1928–Moscow; 1929–Buenos Aires, Montevideo, Rio de Janeiro, São Paulo; 1930–Berne, Basel, Algiers; 1931–Amsterdam; 1932–Stockholm, Oslo, Gothenburg; 1933–Athens; 1934–Rome, Milan; 1935–New York, Chicago, Boston, Philadelphia; 1939–Smyrna, Istanbul. Petit, *Le Corbusier*

Lui-Même, 58. Tim Benton discusses many other lectures beginning with Le Corbusier's first, given in Strasbourg in 1923 on urbanism. Tim Benton, *Le Corbusier conférencier* (Paris: Éditions du Moniteur, 2007).
287 Catherine de Smet, "Le Livre comme synthèse des arts: Édition et design graphique chez Le Corbusier, 1945–1966" (Doctoral thesis, L'EHESS, 29 Oct. 2002).
288 Le Corbusier, *The Decorative Arts of Today*, 207.

CHAPTER 8

Epigraph Le Corbusier, "Introduction," in *Oeuvre Complète 1910–1929* (1935; repr., Zurich: Les Éditions d'Architecture, 1964), 11.
1 Le Corbusier, *Une Maison–Un Palais* (Paris: Les Éditions G. Crès et Cie, 1928), 172–73.
2 Christian Zervos, "Qui Bâtira le Palais des Nations?" *Cahiers d'Art* 9 (Nov. 1927). Reprinted in Le Corbusier, *Une Maison–Un Palais*, 216.
3 Le Corbusier, "La Voie de la S. D. N.," in *Une Maison–Un Palais*, 194–96; Richard Quincerto, "Le Champ de Bataille du Palais des Nations, 1923–1931," in *Le Corbusier à Genève 1922–1932* (Zurich: Editions Payot Lausanne, 1987), 35–48.
4 Le Corbusier, *Une Maison–Un Palais*, 1.
5 Ibid.
6 Ibid., 2.
7 Ibid.
8 Ibid., 3.
9 Ibid., 4.
10 Ibid., 5.
11 Ibid., 6.
12 Ibid., 46.
13 Ibid., 48.
14 Ibid.
15 Ibid., 50.
16 Ibid.
17 Ibid.
18 Ibid., 52.
19 Ibid.
20 Ibid.
21 Ibid., 53.
22 Ibid., 10.
23 Ibid., 12.
24 Ibid.
25 Ibid., 14.
26 Ibid.
27 Ibid.
28 Ibid., 16.
29 Ibid., 20.
30 Ibid., 22.
31 Ibid., 26.
32 Ibid., 28.
33 Ibid., 28, 30.
34 Ibid., 30.
35 Ibid.
36 Ibid., 32.
37 Ibid.
38 Ibid., 36.
39 Ibid.
40 Ibid., 38.
41 Ibid.
42 Ibid., 44.
43 Ibid., 53–54.
44 Ibid., 56–65.
45 Ibid., 78.
46 Ibid., 80.
47 Ibid., 80, 84.
48 Ibid., 84.
49 Ibid.
50 Ibid., 85–167.
51 Ibid., 95.
52 Ibid., 98.
53 Ibid., 107–19.
54 Ibid., 119–25.
55 Ibid., 125–45.
56 Le Corbusier, *Une Maison–Un Palais*, 147.
57 Ibid.
58 Ibid., 170.
59 Ibid.
60 Bruno Reichlin, "Utility is not Beautiful," *Daidalos* 64 (June 1997): 32–56; Karel Teige, "Mundaneum," trans. Ladislav Holovsky, Elizabeth Holovsky, and Lubamire Dolezel; Le Corbusier, "In Defense of Architecture," *Oppositions* 4, trans. Nancy Bray, André Lessard, Alan Levitt, and George Baird (Oct. 1974): 83–92, 93–108. All references are to the translations in *Oppositions*.
61 Teige to Le Corbusier, FLC B2-13-376, 30 Sept. 1929.
62 Le Corbusier and Jeanneret, *Oeuvre Complète 1910–1929*, 194.
63 Teige, "Mundaneum," 88.
64 Ibid., 89.
65 Ibid.
66 Ibid., 90.
67 Ibid.
68 Ibid., 91.
69 Le Corbusier, "In Defense of Architecture," 93.
70 Ibid., 94.
71 Ibid., 95.
72 Ibid.
73 Ibid., 95–96.
74 Ibid., 96.
75 Ibid.
76 Ibid., 98.
77 Ibid.

78 Ibid.
79 Ibid., 99.
80 Ibid., 101.
81 Ibid., 102.
82 Ibid.
83 Ibid.
84 Ibid., 104.
85 Ibid., 106.
86 Teige to Le Corbusier, FLC B2-13-376, 30 Sept. 1929; FLC B2-13-379, 10 Oct. 1929.
87 Le Corbusier and Pierre Jeanneret, *Oeuvre Complète 1929–1934,* vol. 2 (1935; repr., Zurich: Les Éditions d'Architecture, 1964), 16.
88 Ibid., 17.
89 Camille Mauclair, "Appalling Nudism," and "Houses without Soul," *Le Figaro* (1929), quoted in Deborah Dawson Hunt, "Rivalry and Representation: Regionalist Architecture and the Road to the 1937 Paris Exposition" (PhD diss., University of Virginia, 2005), 101–2.
90 Camille Mauclair, "Bolshevizing Architecture," *Le Figaro* 9 (Jan. 1933), quoted in Hunt, "Rivalry and Representation," 126.
91 Quoted in Romy Golan, *Modernity and Nostalgia: Art and Politics in France Between the Wars* (New Haven, CT: Yale University Press, 1995), 90.
92 Comments about Mauclair made by Le Corbusier, FLC U3-9-211-223, 1960s.
93 Golan, *Modernity and Nostalgia*, 89.
94 Gustave Umbdenstock, *Cours d'architecture École Polytechnique* (Paris: Gauthier-Villars et Cie., 1930).
95 Le Corbusier, *Croisade: ou le Crépuscule des Académies* (Paris: Les Éditions G. Crès et Cie, 1933).
96 Le Corbusier, *The Four Routes*, trans. Dorothy Todd (London: Dennis Dobston Ltd. Publishers, 1947), 183–85. Le Corbusier's reflection on this attack by "Money."
97 Le Corbusier, *Croisade*, footnote 1, 32–35. This response to Camille Mauclair's accusations appear as a mere footnote, but Le Corbusier mentioned his critiques so many times in so many other writings that it can be assumed he was greatly irritated by such attacks.
98 Ibid.
99 Ibid., 16.
100 Le Corbusier and Jeanneret, *Oeuvre Complète 1929–1934,* 16.
101 Le Corbusier, *Croisade*, 18.
102 Ibid., 8
103 Ibid., 13.
104 Ibid., 14–15.
105 Ibid., 16–17.
106 Ibid., 18.
107 Ibid., 19.
108 Ibid., 21.
109 Ibid., 22–23.
110 Ibid., 24–25.
111 Ibid., 27.
112 Ibid., 28.
113 Ibid., 32.
114 Ibid., 36–37.
115 Ibid., 37.
116 Ibid., 38.
117 Ibid., 48.
118 Ibid., 52–56.
119 Ibid., 56.
120 Ibid., 62–70.
121 Ibid., 71.
122 Ibid., 73.
123 Ibid., 75.
124 Ibid.
125 Ibid., 75–76.
126 Caralo Olmo, "La Perception du Changement," in *Le Corbusier, une encyclopédie* (Paris: Centre Georges Pompidou, 1987), 344–49.
127 Le Corbusier, *Almanach d'Architecture Moderne* (Paris: Les Éditions G. Crès et Cie, 1925), 5.
128 Le Corbusier, "Architecture d'Époque Machiniste," *Journal de Psychologie Normale et Pathologique* 23 (1926): 325–50.
129 Ibid., 325.
130 Ibid.
131 Ibid., 326–27.
132 Christopher Eric Morgan Pearson, "Integrations of Art and Architecture in the work of Le Corbusier: Theory and Practice from Ornamentalism to the Synthesis of the major arts" (PhD diss., Stanford University, 1995), 90. Christopher Pearson thinks that Le Corbusier, in utilizing the concept of "irradiation," is making an analogy to the therapeutic properties of radium. Pearson recounts that in the early part of the twentieth century the *curie thérapie*, or controlled exposure to the radiation of radium salts, was widely held to bring about improvement in general health. It was believed that these rays stimulated all forms of life and even prolonged human life. Pearson also draws a relationships between Le Corbusier's use of the verb *irradier* and Walter Benjamin's use of "aura."
133 Le Corbusier, *Almanach d'Architecture Moderne*, 146.
134 Ibid., 29.
135 Le Corbusier, "Architecture d'Époque Machiniste," 329.
136 Ibid.

137 Ibid., 331.
138 Ibid., 231.
139 Ibid., 345.
140 Ibid., 350.
141 Ibid.
142 Unpublished, untitled article, 1927, FLC A3-1-50-55.
143 Ibid.
144 Le Corbusier, "Tracés Régulateur," (typed manuscript, 1934), FLC U3-5-191-93.
145 FLC Le Corbusier, "Outillage Élémentaire," *Prélude* 15 (Dec. 1933).
146 Pearson, "Integrations of Art and Architecture."
147 Le Corbusier, "Les Arts dits Primitifs dans la Maison d'Aujourd'hui," FLC B1-15-332-333, 20 June 1935; "Dans La Maison de Verre...Exposition ouverte tous les jours...24, Rue Nungesser et coli." FLC C1-5-139-144, 20 June 1935.
148 Le Corbusier, "Les Arts Dits Primitifs."
149 FLC Doc. 8 (XVI), Le Corbusier, "Le Lyrisme des objets naturels" (Sept. 1935): 1.
150 Ibid., 1–2
151 Ibid., 2.
152 Ibid.
153 Le Corbusier, "Le 'Vrais', Seul Support de l'architecture," FLC A3-2-149 (seven pages), 17-06-1937.
154 Ibid., 149
155 Ibid.
156 Ibid.
157 Le Corbusier, "La Pierre, Amie de l'Homme," FLC B1-15-174-185, Paris, 23 Oct. 1937 (for a book about stone, to be published by Denoël).
158 Ibid., 177–78.
159 Ibid., 178.
160 Ibid., 179.
161 Ibid., 179.
162 Ibid., 181.
163 Ibid., 182.
164 Ibid., 185.
165 Le Corbusier, "La Maison Individuelle," FLC A3-1-233, Apr. 1939 (six pages).
166 Ibid., 233.
167 Ibid.
168 Raul Carter, *The Lie of the Land* (London: Faber and Faber, 1996), 129. Carter explains the treatment of rectilinear space versus poetic or curvilinear space.
169 Camille Mauclair, *Les Couleurs du Maroc* (Paris: Bernard Grasset, 1933), 36.
170 Le Corbusier, *The Radiant City: Elements of a doctrine of urbanism to be used as the basis of our machine-age civilization* (1935; repr., New York: The Orion Press, 1967), 230.
171 Ibid., 231.
172 Ibid., 232.
173 Le Corbusier, "Quatrième Entretien de Venise," FLC A3-2-247-250, 1935.
174 Part of his talk would be reprinted in Le Corbusier, *The Four Routes*, 153–64.
175 Le Corbusier, *The Four Routes*, 154.
176 Ibid., 155.
177 Ibid., 157.
178 Ibid., 158.
179 Ibid., 159
180 Le Corbusier, "Sainte Alliance des Arts majeurs ou le Grand Art en Gésine," *La Bête Noire* (1 July 1935).
181 Le Corbusier, "Sainte Alliance," 91.
182 Pearson, "Integrations of Art and Architecture." In June 1936, Le Corbusier becomes a founding member of the "Union pour l'art'" whose explicit aim was to foster collaboration between all creative artists and subsequently to present a strong united front in the upcoming Exposition of 1937.
183 Le Corbusier, "La querelle du réalisme," *Commune* (1936): 80–91, FLC X1-13-44.
184 Le Corbusier, "La querelle du réalisme," 86.
185 Le Corbusier, "Sainte Alliance," 91.
186 Le Corbusier, "L'Architecture et l'esprit mathématique," *Cahiers du sud* (4 Jan. 1946): 480–90, quote on page 480, FLC E2-8-160. For the English translation of this insertion see Le Corbusier, *New World of Space* (New York: Reynal & Hitchcock, 1948), 7–8, quotation on 7; Also see in French, Le Corbusier, "L'Espace Indicible," (typed manuscript, 1946), FLC B3-7-255-74.
187 Le Corbusier, "L'Architecture et l'esprit mathématique," 481.
188 Ibid.
189 Ibid., 483.
190 Ibid., 484.
191 Ibid., 486.
192 Catherine de Smet, "Le Livre comme synthèse des arts: Édition et design graphique chez Le Corbusier, 1945–1966" (Doctoral thesis, L'EHESS, 29 Oct. 2002), 92. In 1938, Le Corbusier had the first exhibition of his paintings since 1923 at Léonce Rosenberg in Zurich; Pearson "Integrations of Art and Architecture," 284. Pearson states that Sigfried Giedion organized this retrospective exhibition "Le Corbusier: l'oeuvre plastique 1919–1937" at the Zurich Kunsthaus Jan 15–Feb 6, 1938.
193 Le Corbusier to Ritter, journal entry 27 June 1918, FLC R3-19-268-283, Paris, 2 Aug. 1918.

194 Le Corbusier in a Catalogue of an exhibition of reproductions of his paintings, 1962, quoted in de Smet, "Le Livre comme synthèse des arts," 93.
195 Daphne Becket-Chary, "A study of the Le Corbusier's *Poème de l'angle droit*" (M.Phil Thesis in History and Philosophy of Architecture, Cambridge University, 1990).

CHAPTER 9
Epigraph Karl Krauss, "Introduction," in *Adolf Loos on Architecture*, trans. Michael Mitchell (Riverside, CA: Ariadne Press, 2002), 2.
1 For criticism of Le Corbusier as a Jacobean promoting the goddesses of Reason and the machine as well as the his mathematical approach, creating houses that lacked vitality, their empty interiors likened to a "caisse à suicide" or an extinct crater of the moon, see Alexandre de Senger, "La Crise dans L'architecture," *L'Oeuvre, (Suisse)* (Feb 1928), FLC X1-6-29-45.
2 François Fosca, "Pour l'art moderne contre Le Corbusier," *Revue de Genève, (Suisse)* (April 1929), 426–41, quotation: 434 FLC X1-8-71-87.
3 Ibid., 435.
4 Ibid., 437.
5 Ibid.
6 Teige to Le Corbusier, FLC B2-13-376, 30 Sept. 1929; Nicholas Fox Weber, *Le Corbusier: A Life* (New York: Alfred A. Knopf, 2008), 296. Weber notes Le Corbusier departed for the port of Bordeaux where he would board the *Massilia* on September 13th 1929.
7 MoMA's press release announced that Le Corbusier would take a lecture tour, with lectures as far away as Madison, Wisconsin, under the sponsorship of the Department of Architecture of MoMA. On the opening night of his exhibition at MoMA, Le Corbusier would lecture in French, and Chenal's motion picture "Architecture Aujourd'hui" would be shown. MoMA press release, 24 Oct. 1935, FLC Doc 4 (V).
8 Madge Bacon, *Le Corbusier in America: Travels in the Land of the Timid* (Cambridge: MIT Press, 2001), 60.
9 Le Corbusier, radio talk, Paris, 6 Apr. 1936.
10 "Résumé of the first conferences at MoMA," 24 Oct. 1935, FLC Doc 6 (VI).
11 Le Corbusier, *Précisions: sur un état présent de l'architecture et de l'urbanisme* (Paris: Les Éditions G. Crès et Cie, 1930), translated by Edith Schreiber Aujame as *Precisions: on the present state of architecture and city planning* (Cambridge: MIT Press, 1960); Jean-Louis Cohen, "De l'oral à l'écrit: Précisions et les Conférences Latino-Américaines de 1929," in *Le Corbusier, Ecritures Rencontres des 18 et 19 Juin, 1993* (Paris: Fondation le Corbusier, 1993), 47–53. Jean-Louis Cohen has argued that *Précisions* is different from the books that preceded it: containing neither didactic articles already written and published elsewhere nor polemical positions he clearly advocated. Instead, this book, together with *When the Cathedrals Were White* are travelogues condensing different viewpoints of the reporter, the moralist and the expert planner.
12 Le Corbusier, *Quand les Cathédrales étaient blanches: voyage aux pays de timides* (Paris: Librairie Plon, 1937), translated by Francis E. Hyslop, Jr. as *When the Cathedrals Were White: A Journey to the Country of Timid People* (New York: Reynal and Hitchcock, 1947).
13 Le Corbusier apparently felt free to engage in love affairs when he was not in Paris: thus his dalliance with Josephine Baker in South America and Marguerite Tjader Harris in New York. She was an excellent guide to the city: from skyscrapers heights to the depths of the subways, from Wall Street congestion to suburban sprawl. She introduced him to American popular culture: they went to Broadway theaters, jazz clubs, dance halls, and burlesque shows. Without these introductions, the narration of *Cathedrals* would not have been possible. They continued their secret affair throughout the 1940s. For details of his love affair with Marguerite Tjader Harris, see Bacon, *Le Corbusier in America*, 48–57, 350–52.
14 Mary Louise Pratt, *Imperial Eyes: Travel Writing and Transculturation* (New York: Routledge, 1992), 6–7.
15 Blaise Cendrars to Le Corbusier, FLC E1-13-11, 15 Nov. 1926; Le Corbusier, "Cendrars," *La Gazette de Lausanne* 207 (Sept. 1960), FLC U3-9-416-20, 14 Mar. 1960.
16 Le Corbusier, *Precisions*, 12.
17 Ibid., 12–13.
18 Ibid., 25.
19 Ibid., 33.
20 Ibid., 221–22.
21 Ibid., 225.
22 Ibid., 227.
23 Ibid., 38.
24 Le Corbusier, *When the Cathedrals Were White*, 103.
25 Louis Marin, *Food for Thought*, trans. Mette Hjort (Baltimore: The Johns Hopkins

Press, 1989); Philip Lewis, "Food for Sight: Perrault's 'Peau d'ane,'" *MLN* 106, no. 4 (Sept. 1991): 793–817.

26 Louis Marin, *Food for Thought.*

27 Isabelle Rieusset-Lemarié, "La Mémoire du goût sur le discernement de la saveur," *Champs Visuels* 5 (May 1997): 21–33; Geneviève Cornu, "Esthétique des images du goût," *Champs Visuels* 5 (May 1997): 72–81

28 Le Corbusier, *Precisions*, 21. Le Corbusier claimed he made three hundred yards of drawings, or six rolls of paper fifty yards in length, during his trip to the United States in 1935. He improvised, attacking the problem from different points of view. Le Corbusier, *When the Cathedrals Were White*, 137. He utilized the same technique in South America: improvising while he drew with charcoals and chalk, outlining "the frightening steps of logic." Le Corbusier, *Precisions*, 19.

29 Le Corbusier, *Precisions*, 5.

30 Ibid., 6.

31 Ibid., 7.

32 Ibid., 9.

33 Ibid., 9–10.

34 Ibid., 10.

35 Ibid.

36 Ibid.

37 Ibid., 11.

38 Ibid., 16.

39 Ibid.

40 Ibid., 16–17.

41 Ibid., 17.

42 Simon Goldhill, *Foucault's Virginity: Ancient Erotic Fiction and the History of Sexuality* (Cambridge, England: Cambridge University Press, 1995), 1–45.

43 Unknown reviewer, quoted in Andrea Stuart, "Looking at Josephine Baker," *Women: A Cultural Review* 5, no. 2 (1994): 139.

44 Le Corbusier, *Precisions*, 222–23.

45 Ibid., 13.

46 Darius Milhaud, "Les Ressources Nouvelles de la Musique," *L'Esprit Nouveau* 25 (July 1924).

47 Albert Jeanneret, "Musique," *L'Esprit Nouveau* 10–11 (Nov. 1921): 1294–97.

48 Albert Jeanneret, "La Rythmique," *L'Esprit Nouveau* 2 (Nov. 1920): 183–89. Albert Jeanneret continued to explain the Dalcroze method in "La Rythmique (fin)," *L'Esprit Nouveau* 3 (Dec. 1920): 331–38.

49 Le Corbusier, *When the Cathedrals Were White*, 158–59.

50 Ibid., 160.

51 Ibid.

52 Ibid., 161.

53 Ibid., 161–62.

54 Ibid., 162.

55 Ibid., 163.

56 Ibid., 93.

57 Ibid., 108.

58 Ibid., 109.

59 Mark Anderson, *Kafka's Clothes* (Oxford and New York: Oxford University Press, 1992), 1, 3.

60 Le Corbusier, *Precisions*, 33.

61 Ibid., 32.

62 Le Corbusier, *When the Cathedrals Were White*, 109–10; 155.

63 Ibid., 148.

64 Ibid., 157.

65 Ibid.

66 Wendy Martin, "'Remembering the Jungle' Josephine Baker and Modernist Parody," in *Prehistories of the Future: The Primitivist Project and the Culture of Modernism*, ed. Elazar Barkan and Ronald Bush (Stanford, CA: Stanford University Press, 1995), 310–25.

67 Le Corbusier, *Precisions*, 234.

68 Marie-Denise Shelton, "Primitive Self Colonial Impulses in Michel Leiris's 'L'Afrique fantôme,'" in *Prehistories of the Future*, 326–38.

69 Ronald Schleifer, *Rhetoric and Death: The Language of Modernism and Postmodern Discourse Theory* (Urbana-Champaign and Chicago: University of Illinois Press, 1990), 44.

70 Le Corbusier, *When the Cathedrals Were White*, 33–34.

71 Quoted in Schleifer, *Rhetoric and Death*, 48.

72 Ibid., 49.

73 Schleifer, *Rhetoric and Death*, 50.

74 Schleifer, *Rhetoric and Death*, 62.

75 Le Corbusier, *When the Cathedrals Were White*, xxi.

76 This preface was published in *Prélude* 16 (July/Aug. 1936): 1. See Bacon, *Le Corbusier in America*, 374 n. 5.

77 Le Corbusier, *When the Cathedrals Were White*, xxii.

78 Marin, *Food for Thought*, 118.

79 Jack Goody, *Domestication of the Savage Mind* (New York: Cambridge University Press, 1977), 144. Not surprisingly, Thoth, the archaic god of writing, was also the patron of physicians. He gave them skill to cure because he enabled medical recipes to be written down. Hence medical knowledge could be systematized, augmented, recorded and accumulated.

80 Le Corbusier, *When the Cathedrals Were White*, xxi.

81 Ibid., xxii.

82 Ibid.

83 Le Corbusier, *Precisions*, 245.
84 Le Corbusier, *When the Cathedrals Were White*, 65.
85 Ibid., 76.
86 Le Corbusier, *When the Cathedrals Were White*. The book is organized in two parts: a brief one entitled "Atmospheres" and the bulk of the book, "U.S.A." Le Corbusier has a tendency to create short two- or three-page sections, each with its own title, as in *Towards a New Architecture*. He attempts to mention a topic in a section that will be elaborated on in the next. However, the method is not necessary for the argument, and these sections appear as aperçus that could be inserted at any point in the text.
87 Le Corbusier, *When the Cathedrals Were White*, 3.
88 Ibid., 4.
89 Ibid.
90 Ibid., 5.
91 Ibid.
92 Ibid., 6.
93 Ibid.
94 Le Corbusier, "Decadence of the Spirit," in *When the Cathedrals Were White*, 10–24.
95 Le Corbusier, *When the Cathedrals Were White*, 26.
96 Le Corbusier, *When the Cathedrals Were White*, 27–217, quotation on 26. The remainder of the book, part two, is entitled "U.S.A." and consists of five chapters.
97 Le Corbusier, *When the Cathedrals Were White*, 29.
98 Ibid., 37.
99 Ibid., 38.
100 Ibid., 34.
101 Ibid.
102 Ibid.
103 Ibid., 92.
104 Ibid., 94.
105 Ibid., 108–15.
106 Ibid., 109.
107 Ibid., 111.
108 Ibid.
109 Ibid., 110–12.
110 Ibid., 112.
111 Ibid., 119–120.
112 Ibid., 130.
113 Ibid., 217.
114 Andrea Loselle, *History's Double: Cultural Tourism in Twentieth-Century Travel Writing* (New York: St. Martin's Press, 1997), 214 n. 14.
115 Fernand Léger, "New-York vu par F. Léger" *Cahiers d'Art* 6 nos. 9–10 (1931): 437–39. Reprinted in Fernand Léger, "New York," in *Functions of Painting*, trans. Alexandra Anderson (New York: The Viking Press, 1965), 84–90.
116 Léger, "New York," in *Functions of Painting*, 86.
117 Ibid., 88.
118 Le Corbusier, *When the Cathedrals Were White*, 59.
119 Ibid., 34.
120 Ibid., 109.
121 Ibid., 186–87.
122 Ibid., 36.
123 Ibid., 36–37.
124 Ibid., 83.
125 Ibid., 86.
126 Ibid., 87.
127 Hyslop has translated Le Corbusier's "territoire-type" as "type-area."
128 Le Corbusier, *When the Cathedrals Were White*, 87.
129 Ibid.
130 Le Corbusier, *When the Cathedrals Were White*, 88. Le Corbusier appears to be remarking on Thomas Adams, ed., *The Regional Plan of New York and its Environs* (New York: Russell Sage, 1929). The graphic edition has numerous sketches for the waterfront improvement, rendered in Beaux-Arts style.
131 Le Corbusier, *When the Cathedrals Were White*, 89.
132 Ibid., 90.
133 Ibid.
134 Ibid., 91.
135 Ibid., 42.
136 Ibid., 176.
137 Ibid., 80.
138 Ibid., 153.
139 Ibid., 154–55.
140 Ibid., 80–81.
141 Ibid., 106.
142 Ibid., 100–101.
143 Ibid., 101.
144 Ibid.
145 Ibid., 102.
146 Ibid., 72.
147 Ibid., 40.
148 Ibid., 43.
149 Ibid., 44.
150 Ibid., 114.
151 Ibid., 54.
152 Ibid., 65.
153 Ibid., 105.
154 Ibid., 123.
155 Ibid., 146.
156 Ibid., 145.
157 Ibid.
158 Ibid., 146.
159 Ibid., 149.

160 Ibid., 165.
161 Ibid.
162 Ibid., 166.
163 Bacon, *Le Corbusier in America*, xv, 6–14.
164 Bacon, *Le Corbusier in America*, 207.
165 Pierre Andreu, *Révoltes de l'Esprit Les revues des années 20* (Paris: Éditions Kimé, 1991); Michel Winock, *'Esprit': Des intellectuels dans la cité (1930–1950)* (Paris: Éditions du Seuile, 1996).
166 Jean Touchard, "L'esprit des années 1930: une tentative de renouvellement de la pensée politique française," in *Tendances Politiques dans la vie française depuis 1789* (Paris: Hachette: 1960), 89–118.
167 Le Corbusier, "L'autorité devant les tâches contemporaines," FLC B1-15-223 (six pages), 23 Aug. 1935.
168 Le Corbusier, "Une Goutte que vous n'avez jamais vue de votre vie," FLC A3-2-285-291 (handwritten 1929), 13 July 1935.
169 Ibid.
170 Le Corbusier, *Precisions*, 26.
171 Ibid., 27.
172 Nina Gorgus, *Le magicien des Vitrines*, trans. Marie-Anne Coadou (Paris: Éditions de la Maison des sciences de l'homme, 2003).
173 Le Corbusier to Docteur F. Rivet, FLC J3-1-2, 7 Oct. 1935.
174 F. Rivet to Le Corbusier, FLC J3-1-26, 13 Dec. 1935.
175 Le Corbusier, *Precisions*, 2.
176 Andrea Loselle, History's Double Cultural Tourism in Twentieth-Century French Writing (New York: St. Martin's Press, 1997), 1–16.
177 Le Corbusier, "Une maison est devenue une espèce de mythe," FLC, "Causerie du 6 Avril 1936 à Radio Paris," 4.
178 Ibid.
179 Le Corbusier, *Precisions*, 14, 17; Le Corbusier, *When the Cathedrals Were White*, 216–17.
180 Le Corbusier, *Precisions*, 17.

CHAPTER 10

Epigraph Paul Valéry, 1932, quoted in Shanny Peer, *France on Display: Peasants, Provincials and Folklore in the 1937 Paris World's Fair* (Albany, NY: SUNY Press, 1998), 16.
1 Jean Touchard, "L'esprit des années 1930: une tentative de renouvellement de la pensée politique française," in *Tendances Politiques dans la vie française depuis 1789* (Paris: Hachette, 1960), 89–118.
2 Denis de Rougement, "Cahiers de revendications," *Nouvelle Revue Française* 20 (1932): 51, quoted in Pierre Andreu, *Révoltes de l'esprit: Les revues des années 30* (Paris: Editions Kimé, 1991), 35, also quoted in François Dosse, *New History in France: The triumph of the* Annales (Urbana, IL: University of Illinois Press, 1994), 9, and in Touchard, "L'esprit des années 1930," 97.
3 Andreu, *Révoltes de l'esprit*, 16; Michel Winock, *"Esprit" des intellectuels dans la cité* (Paris: Éditions du Seuil, 1996), 108.
4 In March, 1930, the journal *Grand Route*, edited by Philippe Lamour and Reynaud de Jouvenal, published Le Corbusier and Pierre Jeanneret's "Analyse des éléments fondamentaux du problème de la Maison Minimum" ("Analysis of the fundamental elements of the problem of the Minimum House"), a talk delivered at CIAM 2. Its fifth and last issue contained "Corollaire Brésilien," an excerpt from Le Corbusier's book *Precisions*. Philippe Lamour had been Le Corbusier's and Jeanneret's lawyer during the League of Nations debacle. Mary McLeod, "Urbanism and Utopia: Le Corbusier from Regional Syndicalism to Vichy" (unpublished diss., Princeton University, 1985): 110.
5 The list of articles is published in *Le Corbusier, une encyclopédie* (Paris: Centre National d'Art et de Culture Georges Pompidou, 1987), 484–85. Thirteen of these articles will reappear in Le Corbusier, *The Radiant City: Elements of a doctrine of urbanism to be used as the basis of our machine-age civilization* (1935; repr., New York: The Orion Press, 1967). Lamour and the economist Lagardelle had both been members of the Fascistic party Le Faisceau. In addition, Lamour created his own party, Le Partie Fascist Révolutionnaire, in 1928. The medical doctor, Pierre Winter, friend and neighbor of Le Corbusier, whose articles appeared in *L'Esprit Nouveau* and *Plans,* also contributed to *Le Nouveau Siècle,* the official publication of Le Faisceau des Combattants et Producteurs, the political movement organized by George Valois, known popularly as the Blue Shirts. Lagardelle was a personal associate of Mussolini, and beginning in 1932 served as special counselor at the French embassy in Rome. Romy Golan, *Modernity and Nostalgia: Art and Politics in France Between the Wars* (New Haven: Yale University Press, 1995), 99–100; McLeod, "Urbanism and Utopia," 99, 110, 174–75 n. 43; Thierry Paquot, ed., "Le Parcours de l'Architecte," in *Les Passions Le Corbusier Penser*

l'Espace (Paris: Les Editions de la Villette, 1987), 11–34.
6 Jean Touchard, "L'esprit des années 1930," 95.
7 Le Corbusier developed plans for Moscow, Paris, and Algiers during the early 1930s. For Paris, see Le Corbusier, "Menace sur Paris," in *Plans* 2 (Feb. 1931): 49, reprinted in Le Corbusier, *The Radiant City*, 98–103; "Vivre!" *Plans* 3 (Mar. 1931), reprinted in *The Radiant City*, 33–48; and "Descartes est-il Américain?" *Plans* 7 (July 1931), reprinted in *The Radiant City*, 127–34.
8 McLeod, "Urbanism and Utopia," 108.
9 Ibid., 153.
10 Winock, *Esprit*, 108–38; Touchard, "L'esprit des années 1930," 107–8.
11 "La Ligne Générale," *Plans* 1 (Jan. 1931): 7–9; quotation: 7.
12 This retrospective view of the intentions of *Plans* is carried in "La Ligne Générale," *Plans* 7 (July 1931): 4–8.
13 Philippe Lamour, "Notions Claires pour une Civilisation Occidental," *Plans* 1 (Jan. 1931): 13–23.
14 "La Ligne Générale," *Plans* 7, 4–8.
15 Lamour, "Notions Claires," 23.
16 Le Corbusier, "Invite à l'Action," *Plans* 1 (Jan. 1931): 5–64, reprinted in Le Corbusier, "Invitation to Action," in *The Radiant City*, 92–97.
17 Le Corbusier, *The Radiant City*, 93.
18 Ibid., 96.
19 Ibid., 97.
20 "La Ligne Générale," *Plans* 2 (Feb. 1931): 5–9.
21 Le Corbusier, "Mieux vaut Construire," *Plans* 6 (June 1931): 59–67.
22 Ibid., 67.
23 Le Corbusier, *The Radiant City*, 342.
24 Ibid., 343.
25 Ibid., 344.
26 Ibid., 345.
27 Le Corbusier, "Préfères-tu faire la Guerre?" *Des Canons, Des Munitions? Merci! Des Logis... S. V. P.* (Paris: Collection de l'équipement de la civilisation machiniste, 1938), 8. Although intended as a catalogue of both the Pavillon des Temps Nouveaux and a résumé of various projects envisioned for the "radiant city," the publication date appears to be 1938, after the Exposition of 1937 had closed.
28 Le Corbusier, *Des Canons, Des Munitions*, 8.
29 Ibid.
30 Ibid.
31 Ibid., 66.
32 Auke van der Woud, ed., *CIAM, Housing, Town Planning* (Delft: Delft University Press, 1983), 74.
33 Le Corbusier, *The Radiant City*, 23.
34 FCL H2-14-165 referenced by Danilo Udovicki-Selb, "Le Corbusier and the Paris Exhibition of 1937" *JSAH* 56, no. 1 (Mar. 1997): 42–63. Philip H. Solomon, "Céline on the 1937 Paris Exposition Universelle as Jewish Conspiracy," in *Identity Papers Contested Nationhood in Twentieth-Century France*, by Steven Ungar and Tom Conley (Minneapolis: University of Minnesota Press, 1996), 66–87.
35 Le Corbusier to Dr. Pierre Winter, FLC A2-3-43, 19 Mar. 1932.
36 Ibid.
37 This manuscript has several penciled additions in Le Corbusier's handwriting. They are not always legible. Quotations are taken from the typescript. Le Corbusier, "Concevoir d'abord, Construire Ensuite," (Jan. 1933), FLC B3-5-92-101.
38 Ibid., FLC B3-5-93.
39 Ibid.
40 Ibid., FLC B3-5-94.
41 Ibid., FLC B3-5-97.
42 Ibid., FLC B3-5-98.
43 Ibid., FLC B3-5-100.
44 Ibid., FLC B3-5-101.
45 Le Corbusier to Costa, FLC A3-11-78-80, 22 Apr. 1930.
46 Le Corbusier to Costa, FLC A3-11-80, 12 July 1930.
47 Le Corbusier to Otlet, FLC A3-14-84, 30 Oct. 1930.
48 Le Corbusier, *The Radiant City*.
49 Le Corbusier writes to the administrator of Éditions Crès in May of 1934 that he has sent to the publisher all of the manuscript for *La Ville Radieuse* and illustrations will follow from the photographers in charge. The work is lengthy, the documents numerous and it has been a difficult task to assemble them. But he complains that the publisher keeps him in complete silence about the procedures to follow and that in the end is discouraging. Le Corbusier to Gas (administrator of Les Éditions G. Crès et Cie), FLC B2-7-3 03, May 1934. He writes to Philippe Lamour on the 30th of October that he is correcting the proofs for *Le Ville Radieuse*. Le Corbusier to Lamour, FLC B2-7-8, 30 Oct. 1934. In November and December he writes many letters of request for photographs: aerial view of suburbs around Paris, images from Venice, Rome, Barcelona, and illustrations already utilized in *Plans* and

Prelude. Le Corbusier, FLC B2-7-13, Nov.–Dec. 1934.
50 Le Corbusier, *The Radiant City*, 7.
51 Ibid., 6.
52 Ibid., 7.
53 Robert Dumas, *Traité de l'arbre: essai d'une philosophie occidentale* (Arles: Actes Sud, 2002). See also François Dagognet, Le *Catalogue du la vie* (Paris: PUF, 1970) and François Dagognet, *Une épistémologie de l'espace concrète* (Paris: Vrin, 1977).
54 Le Corbusier, *The Radiant City*, 5.
55 Le Corbusier, *Sur les 4 Routes* (Paris: Gallimard, 1941), 165, translated by Dorothy Todd as *The Four Routes* (London: Dennis Dobston Ltd. Publishers, 1947).
56 Le Corbusier, *When the Cathedrals Were White*, trans. Francis E. Hyslop Jr. (New York: McGraw-Hill Book Company, 1947), 71.
57 Le Corbusier, *The Radiant City*, 10.
58 Ibid., 11.
59 Ibid., 14.
60 Ibid., 16.
61 Ibid., 18.
62 Ibid.
63 Ibid., 29.
64 Ibid., 30.
65 Ibid.
66 Ibid., 33.
67 Ibid., 34–39.
68 Ibid., 51–55.
69 Ibid., 51.
70 Ibid.
71 Ibid., 52.
72 Ibid., 54–55.
73 Ibid., 53.
74 Ibid., 54.
75 Ibid., 57.
76 Ibid., 60–61.
77 Ibid., 61.
78 Le Corbusier, "Professors of Prediction," *Prélude* (Dec. 1932); reprinted in Le Corbusier, *The Radiant City*, 180–81.
79 Le Corbusier, *The Radiant City*, 180.
80 Le Corbusier, "The New Age," in *The Radiant City*, 63–88.
81 Le Corbusier, *The Radiant City*, 78.
82 Ibid.
83 Ibid., 79.
84 Ibid., 80.
85 Ibid., 81.
86 Ibid.
87 Ibid., 83.
88 Ibid.
89 Ibid., 77.
90 Le Corbusier, "The 'Radiant City,'" in *The Radiant City*, 89–173.
91 Le Corbusier, "To Live! (To Breathe)," *Plans* 3–4 (Mar.–Apr. 1931); reprinted in Le Corbusier, *The Radiant City*, 104–11.
92 Le Corbusier, *The Radiant City*, 109.
93 Ibid., 105.
94 Ibid., 106.
95 Ibid., 107.
96 Le Corbusier, "Prelude," in *The Radiant City*, 175–97.
97 Le Corbusier, "Bolshoi...or the Notion of Bigness," *Prélude* 4 (Apr. 1933); reprinted in Le Corbusier, *The Radiant City*, 182–85.
98 Le Corbusier, *The Radiant City*, 182–83.
99 Big Bertha was a large German artillery piece manufactured starting in 1914. It fired shells weighing 820 kilograms apiece and was used to destroy several large Allied fortifications.
100 Le Corbusier, *The Radiant City*, 183.
101 Ibid., 183–84.
102 Ibid., 184.
103 Ibid.
104 Ibid.
105 Ibid., 184–85.
106 Ibid., 185.
107 Ibid., 192–93.
108 Ibid., 193.
109 Ibid., 194.
110 Ibid.
111 Ibid., 91.
112 Ibid., 92.
113 Ibid., 147.
114 Ibid., 148.
115 Ibid.
116 Ibid.
117 Ibid., 149.
118 Ibid.
119 Ibid., 150.
120 Ibid., 153.
121 Ibid., 139.
122 Ibid., 176–80.
123 Le Corbusier, *The Radiant City*, 176.
124 Ibid. Le Corbusier, "Voyage d'Hiver Hollande," *Plans* 12 (Feb. 1932): 37–42.
125 In this account, Le Corbusier refers to the Van Ness tobacco factory, not the Van Nelle.
126 Le Corbusier, *The Radiant City*, 178–79.
127 Ibid., 179.
128 Ibid., 322–24.
129 Michael Curtis, *Verdict on Vichy: Power and Prejudice in the Vichy France Regime* (New York: Arcade Publishing, 2002), 51–52.
130 Le Corbusier, *The Radiant City*, 331.
131 Le Corbusier, "Rural Reorganization," in *The Radiant City*, 319–38.
132 Le Corbusier, "Reply to the Peasants," in *The Radiant City*, 331–39; quotation 331.

133 Le Corbusier, *The Radiant City*, 69.
134 Ibid., 192.
135 Norbert Bezard, a *Prélude* contributor, helped develop the Radiant Farm with Le Corbusier, who finished the drawings for Radiant Farm and Radiant Village in April 1934. The site selected was Sarthe, Bezard's native land, a diversified terrain of forests and pastureland in western France. McLeod, "Urbanism and Utopia," 289.
136 Le Corbusier, "The 'Radiant Farm,'" (written in 1931) in *The Radiant City*, 321–30; quotation: 321.
137 Le Corbusier, *The Radiant City*, 322.
138 Ibid.
139 Ibid., 323.
140 Ibid.
141 Ibid., 324.
142 Ibid., 325.
143 Ibid.
144 Ibid., 325–26.
145 Ibid., 328.
146 Ibid., 329.
147 Le Corbusier, "Truth from Diagrams," in *The Radiant City*, 190–95.
148 Le Corbusier, *The Radiant City*, 190.
149 Ibid., 190–91.
150 Le Corbusier, "To Live! (To Inhabit)," *Plans* 3 (Mar. 1931); reprinted in Le Corbusier, *The Radiant City*, 112–18.
151 Le Corbusier, *The Radiant City*, 112.
152 Thomas G. August, "Paris 1937: The Apotheosis of the Popular Front," *Contemporary French Civilization* 5, no. 1 (Fall 1980): 43–60.
153 Philip H. Solomon, "Céline on the 1937 Paris Exposition Universelle," in *Identity Papers: Contested Nationhood in Twentieth-Century France* (Minneapolis: University of Minnesota Press, 1996), 66–87.
154 August, "Paris 1937," 43–60.
155 Ibid.
156 Ibid.
157 Fascist atrocities against the Spanish Loyalists coincided with the jubilation at the Trocadero in 1937. The Spanish exhibition unveiled Picasso's *Guernica* and paid homage to poet Federico García Lorca, who had been shot dead by counterinsurgents in Grenada.
158 Le Corbusier, "Un Nouvel Ordre de Grandeur des Eléments Urbains une Nouvelle Unité d'Habitation," FLC B1-15-247-264, 18 Apr. 1934.
159 Le Corbusier, "Pour l'Architecture d'aujourd'hui," FLC A3-1-101-103; written for *Architecture d'Aujourd'hui*, 4 Apr. 1935.
160 Le Corbusier, "Urbanisme Totale," FLC U3-5-206-11, 18 Jan. 1935, unpublished manuscript
161 Le Corbusier, "L'Autorité devant les tâches contemporaines," FLC B1-15-223-28, 23 Aug. 1935; published in *Architecture d'Aujourd'hui* (Sept. 1935).
162 Le Corbusier, "L'Autorité devant les tâches contemporaines," FLC B1-15-228 23, Aug. 1935.
163 Le Corbusier, "Espoir de la Civilisation Machiniste: Le Logis," *Revue l'Europe* (Apr. 1938); reprinted in Le Corbusier, *Des Canons, Des Munitions*, 5–7.
164 Le Corbusier, *Des Canons, Des Munitions*, 5.
165 Ibid., 6.
166 The unification of heart and hand became a Fascist slogan, but it was also the message behind Fritz Lang's film *Metropolis* (1926–27).
167 In 1933 Aragon created "L'Association des Ecrivains et Artists Révolutionnaires," (AEAR) and they published in their journal *Commune* in June 1935 a series of articles composed under the title "Où va Peinture" ("Where is painting going?"). The AERA would be transformed in March 1935 into "Maison de la Culture" ("House of Culture").
168 Christopher Eric Morgan Pearson, "Integrations of Art and Architecture in the work of Le Corbusier: Theory and Practice from Ornamentalism to the Synthesis of the Major Arts" (PhD diss., Stanford University, 1995): 277–78. For a French edition of this talk, see Le Corbusier, "La querelle du réalisme," *Commune* (1936): 85, FLC X1-13-44. For English translations, see Le Corbusier, "Architecture and the Arts," *Transition* 25 (Fall 1936); see also J. Leslie Martin, Ben Nicholson, and Naum Gabo, *Circle: International Survey of Constructive Art* (London: Faber and Faber, 1937); see also Stamos Papadakis, ed., *Le Corbusier: Architect, Painter, Writer* (New York: Macmillan, 1948), 141–45; see also Gyorgy Kepes, ed., *The Visual Art of Today* (Middletown, CT: Wesleyan University, 1960), 46–51.
169 Le Corbusier, "Pavillon des Temps Modernes," FLC D2-(11)-Doc.3, 15 June 1936.
170 CIAM V, "Logis et Loisirs," was held at Maison de la Culture during the Exposition 1937. Anatole Kopp, *Quand le moderne n'était pas un style mais une cause* (Paris: École nationale supérieure des Beaux-arts, 1988), 162.

171 Le Corbusier, "The Biological Unit: The Cell," *Plans* 7 (July 1931); reprinted in Le Corbusier, *The Radiant City*, 143–46.
172 Le Corbusier, *The Radiant City*, 144.
173 Ibid., 144–45.
174 Ibid., 146.
175 Le Corbusier, "Le Thème d'une Exposition Internationale ou Universelle," *The March of Time* (30 June 1936), FLC A3-1-128-137. Danilo Udovicki-Selb argues that around February, 1936, Le Corbusier added the popular name "Pavillon des Temps Nouveaux" to the fragment "Musée d'Education Populaire" suggesting that 'pavillon' is a lesser exhibition than building a museum, and that 'temps nouveaux' was a more 'engaged' term. Udovicki-Selb, "Le Corbusier and the Paris Exhibition of 1937," 42–62. Throughout this June 1936 text cited above, the term "Pavillon des Temps Modernes " is utilized. However, throughout the 1930s Le Corbusier often slipped back and forth in the same text between "temps modernes" and "temps nouveaux," before finally settling on the latter. Therefore I give no particular significance to the change of names. The term "temps nouveaux" refers to the second machine age that Le Corbusier proclaimed began in 1930.
176 Nicoll, "Interview de Le Corbusier," in *1937, Notre Revue,* FLC A3-170-78 (June 1936). In *Des Canons, Des Munitions,* which appeared the following year, Le Corbusier writes that the he suggested the Exposition focus on housing and domestic equipment, and that the brochure produced was 32 pages in length. Le Corbusier, *Des Canons, Des Munitions*, 10.
177 Nicoll, "Interview de Le Corbusier," FLC A3-171.
178 Le Corbusier, *Des Canons, Des Munitions*, 11.
179 The Pavillon des Temps Nouveaux was designed and built by Charlotte Perriand, Jean Bossu, Chareau, Boyer, Barret, Beaugé, Clouzot, Laurens, Gischia, Effel, and so on. Ibid., 12.
180 Ibid., 24.
181 Nicoll, "Interview de Le Corbusier," FLC A3-177.
182 Le Corbusier, *Des Canons, Des Munitions*, 13.
183 Le Corbusier, "Un Contenant," in *Des Canons, Des Munitions*, 14–21.
184 Le Corbusier, "Les Tendances de l'architecture rationaliste en rapport avec la collaboration de la peinture et la sculpture (Communication à la Réunion Volta à Rome. Octobre 1936)"; reprinted in Françoise de Franclieu, *Le Corbusier–Savina* (Paris: Fondation Le Corbusier/Philippe Sers, 1984), 12–21, quotation: 21.
185 Le Corbusier, *Des Canons, Des Munitions*, 22. Just a year prior, Le Corbusier began his first painted murals in 1935, on the walls of the Vézelay house of Jean Badovici (editor of *L'Architecture Vivante)*. He will begin a series of murals in the Badovici-Grey house at Cap Martin a few years later in 1938–39. Christopher Eric Morgan Pearson, "Integrations of Art and Architecture in the work of Le Corbusier: Theory and Practice from Ornamentalism to the Synthesis of the Major Arts" (PhD diss., Stanford University, 1995).
186 Le Corbusier, "Polychromie = Joie," in *Des Canons, Des Munitions:*, 22–23.
187 Le Corbusier, *Des Canons, Des Munitions*, 28–29.
188 Ibid., 32.
189 Ibid., 36.
190 Ibid., 37.
191 Ibid., 40–41.
192 Ibid., 48–50.
193 Le Corbusier, "Volonté," *Revue Volonté* (Nov. 1937); reprinted in Le Corbusier, *Des Canons, Des Munitions*, 50–54.
194 Le Corbusier, *Des Canons, Des Munitions*, 52.
195 Le Corbusier, "Un Homme Chez Lui," *Revue Volonté* 4 (1938); reprinted in Le Corbusier, *Des Canons, Des Munitions*, 71–73.
196 Le Corbusier, *Des Canons, Des Munitions*, 71.
197 Ibid., 72.
198 Ibid., 72–73.
199 The mural on "habiter" was 14 meters by 6 meters. Ibid., 110.
200 The mural on "recréer" was 12 meters by 4 meters. Ibid., 111.
201 The mural on "travailler" was 14 meters by 4 meters. Ibid., 112.
202 Le Corbusier, "La Réforme Agraire," 113–117; "La Ferme Radieuse," 119–124; and "Le Village Coopératif," 125–135; in *Des Canons, Des Munitions.*
203 Le Corbusier, *Des Canons, Des Munitions*, 118.
204 Ibid., 137.
205 Ibid., 139.
206 Ibid., 143.

CHAPTER II

Epigraph Élie Faure, *The History of Art: The Spirit of the Forms*, trans. Walter Pach (1921; repr., New York: 1930), 202.

1 Le Corbusier, *When the Cathedrals Were White*, trans. Francis E. Hyslop, Jr. (New York: McGraw-Hill Book Company, 1947), 30. In 1930, Le Corbusier married Yvonne Gallis, a native of the Côte d'Azur whom he met in 1920 and for whom he constructed the Cabanon de Cap-Martin in 1952. Her spirit and temperament were meridianal.

2 Manfredo Tafuri, *Architecture and Utopia: Design and Capitalist Development*, trans. Barbara Luigia La Penta (Cambridge, MA: MIT Press, 1976), 127, 135. Manfredo Tafuri thought Le Corbusier's Obus schemes to be "unsurpassed from the point of view of both ideology and form." His failure to implement these schemes was due to the fact that he worked at the "intellectual" not "political" level, and thus transposed contradictions onto a strictly aesthetic plane.

3 For a description of cartographic discourse see Zbigniew Bialas, *Mapping Wild Gardens: the Symbolic Conquest of South Africa* (Essen: Verlag Die Blaue Eule, 1997).

4 David Henry Slavin, *Colonial Cinema and Imperial France, 1919–1939* (Baltimore: Johns Hopkins Press, 2001).

5 Pierre Sorlin, "The Fanciful Empire: French feature films and the Colonies in the 1930s," *French Cultural Studies* 2 (June 1991): 131–51.

6 Slavin, *Colonial Cinema and Imperial France*, 140–41.

7 Ibid., 61–63.

8 Ibid., 4.

9 John Reudy, *Modern Algeria: The Origins and Development of a Nation* (Bloomington, IN: Indiana University Press, 1992), 129–44.

10 F. Sherry McKay, "Le Corbusier, Negotiating Modernity: Representing Algiers, 1930–1942" (unpublished Ph.D. diss., The University of British Columbia, 1994), 31–34.

11 Although Le Corbusier writes about his plans for Algiers as "projectiles," by the time he publishes *The Radiant City* in 1935, the schemes are labeled "Obus."

12 "Cartes–Algérie à Egypte," FLC L5-3-1-94, a sample of Le Corbusier's collection of postcards.

13 Malek Alloula, *The Colonial Harem*, trans. Myrna Godzich and Wlad Godzich (Minneapolis: University of Minnesota Press, 1986), 5.

14 Samir Rafi, "Le Corbusier et les Femmes d'Alger," *Revue d'histoire et de civilisation du Maghreb* (Jan. 1968): 50–66; Stanislaus von Moos, "Le Corbusier as Painter," *Oppositions* 19–20 (Winter/Spring 1980): 89–107.

15 Deborah Dawson Hunt, "Rivalry and Representation: Regionalist Architecture and the Road to the 1937 Paris Exposition" (Ph.D. diss., University of Virginia, 2005).

16 Rafi, "Le Corbusier et les Femmes d'Alger," 51–52.

17 "Algiers drops out of sight, like a magnificent body, supple-hipped and full-breasted" (22 July 1934). Le Corbusier, *The Radiant City: Elements of a doctrine of urbanism to be used as the basis of our machine-age civilization* (1935; repr., New York: The Orion Press, 1967), 260.

18 McKay, "Le Corbusier, Negotiating Modernity," 74–75, 79.

19 Albert Sarrault quote in Jacques Marseille, L'Age d'Or de la France Coloniale, 5, quoted in Slavin, *Colonial Cinema and Imperial France*, 59.

20 Slavin, *Colonial Cinema and Imperial France*, 60.

21 Thomas August, *The Selling of the Empire: British and French Imperialist Propaganda 1890–1940* (Westport, CT: Greenwood Press, 1985), 54–66. Propaganda could as well help recruit for the empire already trained technicians, administrators, police, and lawyers and as well promote emigration.

22 Frederick Quinn, *The French Overseas Empire* (Westport, CT: Prager, 2000); Ruedy, *Modern Algeria*, 114–55.

23 Ruedy, *Modern Algeria*, 120–21.

24 Quinn, *The French Overseas Empire*, 193.

25 Paul Romain, "Le Corbusier à Lager: 'La Ville Radieuse,'" *Chantiers Nord Afrique* 5 (May 1931): 482, quoted in Jean-Pierre Giordani, "Le Corbusier et les Projets Pour la Ville d'Alger" (Thèses de 3eme cycle, Institute d'Urbanisme, Université de Paris VIII, Saint-Denis, 1987), 87.

26 Le Corbusier, "Louanges à l'Algérie," *Journal Général Travaux Publics et Bâtiments* 45 (25 and 27 June, 1931): 1.

27 Alain de Botton, *The Art of Travel* (New York: Vintage International, 2002).

28 Le Corbusier, "Louanges à l'Algérie," 1.

29 Ibid.

30 Ibid.

31 Ibid.

32 Ibid.

33 Ibid.

34 Ibid.

35 Ibid.

36 Ibid.

37 Le Corbusier, "Retour...ou L'enseignement du Voyage COUPE EN TRAVERS Espagne, Maroc, Algérie. Territoires du Sud." *Plans* 8 (Oct. 1931): 92–108.

38 Le Corbusier, "Retour," 92.
39 Ibid., 94.
40 Ibid., 97.
41 Ibid., 98.
42 Ibid.
43 Ibid.
44 Ibid.
45 Ibid., 99.
46 Ibid., 100.
47 Ibid., 100–1.
48 Ibid., 102.
49 Ibid.
50 Ibid., 103.
51 Ibid.
52 Ibid., 105.
53 Ibid., 106.
54 Ibid., 107.
55 Ibid.
56 Ibid., 108.
57 "Carnet B7 Sketch 643," *Le Corbusier Sketchbooks Volume 1, 1914–1948* (Paris: The Fondation Le Corbusier; New York: The Architectural History Foundation, 1981), 21. Giordani claims there were three sketches remaining from his first trip in the spring of 1931. The first is "Respect au site Algérois" ("Respect the site of Algiers), proclaims the topography of the city to be remarkable. "It allows a rational classification of the population, according to functions or tastes, into three clearly distinct zones: the great flat spaces of the littoral, the cliffs, and the slopes of the Sahel." Giordani, "Le Corbusier et les Projets Pour la Ville d'Alger," 87.
58 "Carnet B7 Sketch 644," *Le Corbusier Sketchbooks Volume 1, 1914–1948* (Paris: The Fondation Le Corbusier; New York: The Architectural History Foundation, 1981), 21. Giordani labels the second sketch, "Essai de classement" (Effort at Classification), which reveals his first ideas of very large buildings raised on piloti, forming a promontory perpendicular to the overall horizontality of the city. His third Algerian drawing, "Aménagement des boulevards et comblement des ravins " ("Plan for the boulevards and filling in of ravines"), implants housing blocks on the hill of Fort l'Empereur around the obelisk and locates the linear line of the auto route along the coastline. Giordani, "Le Corbusier et les Projets Pour la Ville d'Alger," 89.
59 Le Corbusier, "Death of the Street," *Chantiers Nord-Africans* (Dec. 1931), also printed in *Plans* 4 (Apr. 1931), and Le Corbusier, *The Radiant City*, 119–26. All quotations are from *The Radiant City*.
60 Obus A is described in Giordani, "Le Corbusier et les Projets Pour la Ville d'Alger," 114–214; McKay, "Le Corbusier, Negotiating Modernity," 159–64; and Mary McLeod, "Urbanism and Utopia: Le Corbusier from Regional Syndicalism to Vichy" (unpublished diss., Princeton University, 1985): 339–53.
61 Alex Gerber, "L'Algérie de le Corbusier: Les Voyages de 1931" (PhD diss., École Polytechnique Fédérale du Lausanne, 1992).
62 Le Corbusier to Ponsich, FLC I1-2-209, Paris, 2 Feb. 1932.
63 Le Corbusier to Ponsich, FLC I1-2-211, Paris, 12 Feb.1932. Pierre Chenal directed the film "Architecture Aujourd'hui" of Le Corbusier's villas and urban schemes in the summer of 1930; M. Christine Boyer, "Le Corbusier and Cinema: 'only film can make the new architecture intelligible'" (unpublished manuscript, 2004); Sigfried Giedion, *Frankreich Bauen* (1928), translated by J. Duncan Berry as *Building in France Building in Iron Building in Ferro-Concrete* (Santa Monica: The Getty Foundation, 1995), 168. Giedion claimed in 1928 "Only film can make the new architecture intelligible."
64 Le Corbusier to Ponsich, FLC I1-2-212, Paris, 21 Feb. 1932.
65 Le Corbusier to Ray, FLC B11 (2), Paris, 7 Mar. 1932, quoted in Giordani, "Le Corbusier et les Projets Pour la Ville d'Alger," 181–82.
66 Giordani, "Le Corbusier et les Projets Pour la Ville d'Alger," 57. Le Corbusier was aware of the 1930 urban plan for Algiers which zoned the city into five different areas, specified the creation of new residential districts, the management of roads and highways, the protection of green spaces, and the reconstruction of the Quartier of the Marine. He contested in his 1931–32 schemes many of these points.
67 Le Corbusier to Ponsich, FLC I1-2-213, Paris, 9 Mar. 1932.
68 Le Corbusier to Ponsich, FLC I1-2-216, Paris, 5 May 1932.
69 Le Corbusier, *The Radiant City*, 228.
70 Le Corbusier, "La querelle du réalisme," *Commune* (1936): 84. FLC X1-13-44.
71 Le Corbusier, *The Radiant City*, 228.
72 Ibid., 241.
73 Ibid., 233.
74 Giordani, "Le Corbusier et les Projets Pour la Ville d'Alger," 142.
75 Le Corbusier, *The Radiant City*, 244.
76 "Place en épingle de cravate devant la Cité," FLC B A3-2: 4–5. Le Corbusier, "Plan d'aménagement de la Ville d'Alger 1931–1932,"

quoted in Giordani "Le Corbusier et les Projets Pour la Ville d'Alger," 196.

77 Ibid., FLC B A3–2: 7.

78 Ibid., 131–35.

79 Le Corbusier, *The Radiant City*, 233.

80 Ibid., 247.

81 The final element of this first scheme for Algiers was the design of a "swimming club" at Hussein-Bey, the extreme southern limit of the city. At the point where the viaduct became an autoroute, Le Corbusier located a swimming pool, a protected basin, a small port for pleasure craft, and an ensemble of sports facilities.

82 Giordani, "Le Corbusier et les Projets Pour la Ville d'Alger," 218; McLeod, "Urbanism and Utopia," 339.

83 Giordani, "Le Corbusier et les Projets Pour la Ville d'Alger," 218.

84 McLeod, "Urbanism and Utopia," 68–72. McLeod writes that Ernest Mercier was managing director of the French utility company Est-Lumière in 1928, and later president of the Compagnie Français des Pétroles. He was the organizer of Redressement Français, in 1926, a group with whom Le Corbusier associated writing two pamphlets for the organization: "Vers le Paris de l'époque machiniste" and "Pour Bâtir: Standardization et Taylorism." Mercier represented an elite technician whom Le Corbusier admired as the new leaders of France, while Redressement sought to overhaul the government by installing expert leaders, to reform industry along technocratic lines, mass production, and efficiency techniques, and to provide for working class housing. Their slogan was "Enough politics. We want results."

85 Le Corbusier to Mercier, FLC B11 (2), Paris, 30 July 1932, quoted in Giordani, "Le Corbusier et les Projets Pour la Ville d'Alger," 218–19.

86 Obus B is described in Giordani, "Le Corbusier et les Projets Pour la Ville d'Alger," 215–57; McKay, "Le Corbusier, Negotiating Modernity," 189–213; and McCleod, "Urbanism and Utopia," 353–54.

87 FLC Questionnaire "A." There were four different questionnaires which merely repeated this question with slightly different emphasis. McKay, "Le Corbusier, Negotiating Modernity," 53, 53 n. 43.

88 Le Corbusier to Ponsich, FLC I1-2-225, Paris, 16 Nov. 1932; Le Corbusier to Ponsich, FLC I1-2-226, Paris, 26 Nov. 1932.

89 *Travaux Nord-Africains*, 1126 (17 Dec. 1932): 1. Referenced by Giordani, "Le Corbusier et les Projets Pour la Ville d'Alger," 234.

90 Le Corbusier to Brua, FLC B11(2), Paris, 22 Dec. 1932, quoted in Giordani, "Le Corbusier et les Projets Pour la Ville d'Alger," 236–37.

91 McKay, "Le Corbusier, Negotiating Modernity,"193–202.

92 Le Corbusier to Ponsich, FLC I1-2-232, Paris, 7 Feb. 1933. A letter to Ponsich explains that the model left Paris on February 7 and plans and photographs would follow the next day; Edmond Brua, "Quand Le Corbusier bombardait Alger du 'Projet-Obus,'" *Architecture Aujourd'hui* 45, no. 167 (May–June 1972): 72–75, quoted by Giordani, "Le Corbusier et les Projets Pour la Ville d'Alger," 253–54.

93 Gaston Martin, "URBANISME: La Ville Radieuse, Conférence de le Corbusier," *Alger-Etudiant* (1933): unpaginated.

94 Ibid.

95 Le Corbusier to Brua, FLC B11(2), Paris, 2 Dec. 1932, quoted in Giordani, "Le Corbusier et les Projets Pour la Ville d'Alger," 236–37.

96 Le Corbusier, *Aircraft* (London: The Studio, 1935; New York: Universe Books, 1988), 12–13; Le Corbusier, *The Four Routes* (London: Dennis Dobson Ltd. Publishers, 1947), originally published as *Sur les 4 Routes* (Paris: Gallimard, 1941), 109–10.

97 Alex Gerber, "L'Algérie de le Corbusier," 172–97.

98 Obus C is described in Giordani, "Le Corbusier et les Projets Pour la Ville d'Alger," 276–330; MacKay, "Le Corbusier, Negotiating Modernity," 230–44; McLeod, "Urbanism and Utopia," 354–60.

99 Le Corbusier to Brunel, FLC B I1 (2), Paris, 8 Mar. 1933, quoted in Giordani, "Le Corbusier et les Projets Pour la Ville d'Alger," 284–85.

100 Le Corbusier to Brunel, Maire d'Alger, FLC I1-2-235-236, Paris, 27 July 1933.

101 Ibid.

102 Le Corbusier, *The Radiant City*, 228.

103 Ibid.

104 "Un plan d'organisation Européen," *Prélude* 6 (June–July 1933): 1.

105 "La Féderation Latin," *Prélude* 7 (Aug.–Sept. 1933): 1.

106 Giordani, "Le Corbusier et les Projets Pour la Ville d'Alger," 300.

107 He expressed this opinion in a letter to his friend George Huisman, Referenced by Giordani, "Le Corbusier et les Projets Pour la Ville d'Alger," 301.

108 The first series of articles by Jean Cotereau–"Un nouveau bombardement," *Journal Général, Travaux Publics et Bâtiment Alger*–contained 10 articles from May 10 to July 3, 1934. Another series of articles appeared in *Travaux Nord-Africain* by Jean Pierre Faure, 6–21 Oct. 1934.
109 Le Corbusier, *The Radiant City*, 260.
110 Ruedy, *Modern Algeria*, 139–44; McKay, "Le Corbusier, Negotiating Modernity," 224–25.
111 Le Corbusier, "En Alger, des Logis Radieux," (1936), FLC A3-1-117.
112 Ibid.
113 Ibid.
114 Ibid.
115 Giordani, "Le Corbusier et les Projets Pour la Ville d'Alger," 310; McKay, "Le Corbusier, Negotiating Modernity," 273–300.
116 Giordani, "Le Corbusier et les Projets Pour la Ville d'Alger," 331.
117 Le Corbusier, "Palmes et Horizons sur Alger" (May 1942) FLC A3-404.
118 Ibid., FLC A3-404-6.
119 Ibid., FLC A3-405.
120 Ibid., FLC A3-409-10.
121 Ibid., FLC A3-411.
122 Ibid.
123 Ibid., FLC A3-412.
124 Le Corbusier, *When the Cathedrals Were White*, 30.
125 Anne Ruel, "L'Invention de la Méditerranée," *Vingtième Siècle. Revue d'Histoire* 32 (Oct.-Dec. 1991): 7–14.
126 Attributed to Élisée Reclus (source unattributed), quoted in Anne Dymond, "A Politicized Pastoral: Signac and the Cultural Geography of Mediterranean France," *Art Bulletin* 135, no. 2 (June 2003): 357–70; quotation: 358.
127 Ibid., 358; Béatrice Giblin, "Élisée Reclus: géographie, anarchisme," *Hérodote* 1 (Jan.-Mar. 1976): 30–49.
128 Ruel, "L'Invention de la Méditerranée," 11, 13.
129 Albert Camus, "La Culture Indigène La Nouvelle Culture Méditerranéenne," in *Essais* (Paris: Gallimard, 1965), 1321–27.
130 Ibid., 1321–22.
131 Ibid., 1323.
132 Albert Camus, "Présentation de la revue," *Rivages (Revue de culture Méditerranéenne)* (1938), reprinted in Camus, *Essais*, 1329–31.
133 Ibid., 1330.
134 Laszlo Mohly-Nagy filmed the voyage to Athens, including some of the side trips different groups made. The film is known as *Architects' Congress* (MoMA).
135 Jos Bosman, "Sur le Patris II de Marseille à Athènes," in *Le Corbusier et la Méditerranée* (Marseille: Éditions Parenthèses Musées de Marseille, 1987), 73–79.
136 For the manner in which Le Corbusier utilized the history of architecture, particularly the Acropolis, in support of modern architecture, see Yannis Tsiomis, "Sur Les Ailes Métalliques du Parthénon," in *Les Passions Le Corbusier Penser l'Espace*, ed. Thierry Paquot (Paris: Les Editions de la Villette, 1989), 105–16.
137 Le Corbusier, "Discours d'Athènes," in *Le Corbusier Lui-même*, ed. Jean Petit (Genève: Éditions Rousseau, 1970), 178.
138 Ibid.
139 Ibid.
140 Ibid., 178–79.
141 Ibid., 181.
142 Le Corbusier, in the company of Giedion, Moholy-Nagy, Ozenfant, Léger, and a few Greek associates, sailed around the Aegean on the small boat *Argos*: although the precise details of their trip remain unknown, evidently they did visit Delos, Mykonos, Santorini and Serifos. Other congress attendees visited Ossios Loucas, Delphi, and the islands of the Angossaronic. Georgios Simeoforidis and Georgios Tzirtzilakis, "Méditerreneité et Modernité: Le Dernier Voyage en Grèce," in *Le Corbusier et la Méditerranée* (Marseille: Éditions Parenthèses Musées de Marseille, 1987), 66.
143 Le Corbusier, *The Radiant City*, 52.
144 Simeofordidis and Tzirtzilakis, "Méditerreneité et Modernité," 66.
145 In November of 1932, Le Corbusier wrote an article about the Acropolis and the voice that emanates from its site, which he inserted into the conclusion of *Croisade* (1933). In order to grasp the complex sensations this rock outcropping emotes he resorted to a list of adjectives to describe its "pathetic discourse," "cry" or "clamor," labeling it "violent," "entire," "compact," "massive," "shrill," "sharp," "decisive." It is of course a discourse about Architecture for he also commented that after a house is finished, suddenly from the depths of its being, little by little a voice rises and reports, sings and describes things through which we suffer, we cry, we pray for or shout out our joy–the great, the gay, the sad, the soft, the strong, the tender, the brutal. Le Corbusier, *Croisade* (1933). See Chapter 8 for details.

146 Simeofordidis and Tzirtzilakis, "Méditerraneité et Modernité," 70.
147 Le Corbusier "Point du Départ," *Le Voyage en Grèce Cahiers Périodiques de Tourisme* (May–Sept. 1934): 4. FLC X1-12-10-11.
148 Ibid., 4.
149 Le Corbusier, "Théophilos," *Le Voyage en Grèce* (Spring 1936): 16. FLC X1-13-18.
150 Ibid.
151 Ibid.
152 Ibid.
153 Le Corbusier, "En Grèce, à l'Echelle Humain," Le *Voyage en Grèce* 11 (1939): 4–5. FLC X1-13-143.
154 Ibid.
155 Ibid.
156 Ibid.
157 Ibid.
158 Ibid.
159 Le Corbusier, "Rome," *Prélude* 4 (Apr. 1933): 8. Reprinted as "Rome" in Le Corbusier, *The Radiant City*, 185–86.
160 Le Corbusier, *The Radiant City*, 185.
161 Ibid.
162 Ibid.
163 Ibid., 186.
164 Ibid.
165 Le Corbusier, "Esprit Grec–Esprit Latin, Esprit Greco-Latin," *Prélude* 2 (Feb. 1933). FLC B3-5-243.
166 Ibid., FLC B3-5-244.
167 Ibid., FLC B3-5-247.
168 Ibid.
169 Ibid., FLC B3-5-247-8.
170 Ibid., FLC B3-5-249.
171 Ibid.,
172 Le Corbusier to Fiorini, FLC C3-5-150, Paris, 19 Mar. 1932.
173 Ibid.
174 Le Corbusier to Fiorini, FLC C3-5-154, Paris, 26 Aug. 1932.
175 Le Corbusier to Breuillot, FLC D1-5-10, Paris, 27 June 1934, quoted in Maria Luisa Cantelli, "Trois Lettres inédites" (Paris: Les Cahiers de la Recherche Architecturale, 1978), 36–38. FLC X2-17-240
176 Cantelli, "Trois Lettres."
177 Le Corbusier to Fiorini, FLC X2-17-240, Paris, 3 July 1934, quoted in Cantelli, "Trois Lettres."
178 Le Corbusier, *The Radiant City*, 329.
179 Le Corbusier to Magnelli, FLC X2-17-240, Paris, 13 July 1934, quoted in Cantelli, "Trois Lettres."
180 Le Corbusier to Bardi, FLC X2-17-240, 7 Aug. 1934, quoted in Cantelli, "Trois Lettres."
181 Ibid.
182 Ibid.
183 Le Corbusier to Fiorini, FLC C2-2-262, Paris, 23 Nov. 1934.
184 Letter from Sigfried Giedion, 22 October 1936, quoted in Ettore Janulardo, "Le Corbusier et Italie," http://lesmemoires.free.fr/LeCorbusier/LeCorbusier.html.
185 Le Corbusier, *The Radiant City*, 194.
186 McLeod, "Urbanism and Utopia," 309.
187 Le Corbusier, *The Four Routes*, 166.

CHAPTER 12

Epigraph Le Corbusier, "L'Urbanisme et le Lyrisme des Temps Nouveaux," *Le Point* (Jan. 1939), FLC B1-15-270-81.
1 Sigmund Freud, "The Relation of the Poet to Day-Dreaming," in *Character and Culture* (1908; repr., New York: Collier Books, 1963), 34–43.
2 Le Corbusier, "L'Urbanisme et le Lyrisme des Temps Nouveaux," *Le Point* (Jan. 1939), unpaginated, FLC B1-15-270-81.
3 Ibid., FLC B1-15-270-71.
4 Ibid., FLC B1-15-271.
5 Ibid.
6 Ibid.
7 Ibid., FLC B1-15-271-2.
8 Ibid., FLC B1-15-272.
9 Ibid., FLC B1-15-274.
10 Ibid., FLC B1-15-276-7.
11 Ibid., FLC B1-15-280.
12 Ibid., FLC B1-15-281.
13 Le Corbusier, "Untitled," *Atomes* 2 (Apr. 1946).
14 Ibid.
15 Anatole Kopp, Frédérique Boucher, and Danièle Pauly, *L'Architecture de la Reconstruction en France 1945–1953* (Paris: Moniteur, 1982), 22–23.
16 Ibid., 23.
17 Ibid., 41.
18 Brian W. Blouet, *Geopolitics and Globalization in the Twentieth Century* (London: Reaktion Books, 2001).
19 Le Corbusier, "Quelques sont des forms d'agregation d'une Nouvelle Societe Machiniste?" FLC A3-1-215-226, 3 Dec. 1938.
20 Ibid., FLC A3-1-215.
21 Ibid., FLC A3-1-222.
22 Ibid., FLC A3-1-223.
23 Ibid. Further considerations of employment opportunities have been eradicated from the record: although FLC's pagination is continuous, nevertheless page 11 is missing from the typed manuscript and has either been

censored by Le Corbusier or by someone in the archives, or lost in time.

24 Le Corbusier, *Sur les Quatre Routes* (Paris: Gallimard, 1941), translated by Dorothy Todd as *The Four Routes* (London: Dennis Dobston Ltd. Publishers, 1947); quotation from *The Four Routes*, 166.

25 Le Corbusier, "Un ingénu dans le siècle," *Caliban* 19 (1947): 29–33, quotation: 29, FLC X1-15-115.

26 Mary McLeod, "Urbanism and Utopia: Le Corbusier from Regional Syndicalism to Vichy" (unpublished diss., Princeton University, 1985): 98.

27 Le Corbusier, "Un ingénu dans le siècle," 31.

28 Le Corbusier, "L'Esprit romain et l'esthétique de la machine," *Stile Futuristica* 1, no. 2 (Aug. 1934): 13, quoted in McLeod, "Urbanism and Utopia," 308.

29 McLeod, "Urbanism and Utopia," 309.

30 Mary Kaldor, *New & Old Wars: Organized Violence in a Global Era* (Stanford, CA: Stanford University Press, 1999), 27.

31 Kopp, Boucher, and Pauly, *L'Architecture de la Reconstruction*, 71; Marie-Brigitte Preteux, "Les Idées de Le Corbusier après la Second Guerre Mondial: France? Europe? Monde? Quelle réalité dans l'application et la diffusion de ses idées de 1944 à 1965" (doctoral diss., Université de Paris, Oct. 1995).

32 Since most of the French adopted a policy of *attentisme* (wait and see), the Resistance formed a counter-community inside and outside of France. Planning for France's future was always a central activity of the Resistance: to plan for the future was to believe in the future. In a radio speech of June, 1940, Charles de Gaulle proclaimed that France had been overwhelmed by the weaponry of the enemy but defeat was not final. France would conquer in the future with the same brute force–the flame of resistance will never be extinguished. The French National Committee (FNC), the main group responsible for the French war effort, was based in London and later Algiers. It controlled the Resistance within France and focused not only on liberating France but cleansing it of all Fascist influence and rebuilding the country's shattered infrastructure. It began to plan for the postwar reconstruction in London after 1942. American troops liberated Algiers in 1942 in Operation Torch. Andrew Williams, "France and the New World Order, 1940–1947," *Modern & Contemporary France* 8, no. 2 (May 2000): 191–202.

33 Marshal Philippe Pétain, quoted in Michael Curtis, *Verdict on Vichy: Power and Prejudice in the Vichy France Regime* (New York: Arcade Publishing, 2002), 12.

34 Curtis, *Verdict on Vichy*, 89–96. Pétain proclaimed in November 1940, "This policy is mine. Ministers are only responsible to me. History will judge me alone." Marshal Pétain, speech from 10 Nov. 1940, quoted by Richard Vinen, *The Unfree French* (New Haven: Yale University Press, 2007), 53. On August 12th, 1941, he declared: "Authority no longer comes from below; it is what I propose or delegate." Marshal Philippe Pétain, quoted in Gregor Dallas, *1945: The War that Never Ended* (New Haven: Yale University Press, 2005), 66.

35 Rebecca A. Rabinow argues that Le Corbusier spent two years in Ozon on a farm painting and writing. The sale of some of his paintings and gouaches allowed him to survive during these tumultuous years. After the war his paintings were exhibited in Zurich, Amsterdam, and the United States. Amsterdam March 15, 1947, Paul Rosenberg Gallery May 5–22, 1948, a traveling exhibition organized by the ICA, Boston in 1948 going to Boston, Detroit, Cleveland, St Louis, San Francisco, Colorado Springs, Chicago, Los Angeles and then to Europe. Rebecca A. Rabinow, "The Legacy of la Rue Férou: *Livres d'Artiste* Created for Tériade by Rouault, Bonnard, Matisse, Léger, Le Corbuiser, Chagall, Giacometti, and Miró" (Doctoral diss., Institute of Fine Arts, NYU, Sept. 1995).

36 Le Corbusier, *Destin de Paris* (Paris: Clermont-Ferrand, 1941); Le Corbusier, *Sur les Quatre Routes* (Paris: Gallimard, 1941), translated by Dorothy Todd as *The Four Routes* (London: Dennis Dobston Ltd. Publishers, 1947); Le Corbusier with François de Pierrefeu, *La Maison des Hommes* (Paris: Plon, 1941), Le Corbusier's text translated by Clive Entwistle as *The House of Man* (London: The Architectural Press, 1948). Le Corbusier with Pierre Jeanneret, *Les Constructions "Murondins"* (Paris/Clermont-Ferrand: Chiron, 1942).

37 Le Corbusier, *The Four Routes*, 178.

38 For a detailed description of Le Corbusier's time in Vichy, see Nicholas Fox Weber, *Le Corbusier: A Life* (New York: Alfred A. Knopf, 2008), 413–55.

39 This trip was either around April 12th (Fox Weber, *Le Corbusier: A Life*, 438) or early June of 1941 (McLeod, "Urbanism and Utopia," 387, and Giordani, Jean-Pierre Giordani, "Le Corbusier et les Projets Pour la Ville d'Alger" [Thèses de 3ème cycle, Institute d'Urbanisme, Université de Paris VIII, Saint-Denis, 1987], 380).

40 F. Sherry McKay's "Le Corbusier : Negotiating Modernity" states that he was appointed by Vichy in February 1941 and dismissed July 14, 1941. Eric Mumford says Le Corbusier left Vichy in January, 1942, feeling the increasing hostility of the regime to his ideas. This would mean he left almost a full year after receiving an assignment. Eric Mumford, *The CIAM Discourse on Urbanism, 1928–1960*, (Cambridge, MA: MIT Press, 2000), 154. Robert Fishman claims, "He spent eighteen fruitless, farcical months as a minor official at Vichy, the regime's capital, convinced that he was destined to become the aged Marshal's advisor and the great dictator of French architecture." Robert Fishman, "From the Radiant City to Vichy: Le Corbusier's Plans and Politics, 1928–1941," in *The Open Hand: Essays on Le Corbusier*, ed. Russell Walden (Cambridge, MA: MIT Press, 1982), 245; Rémi Baudoui says that Le Corbusier was installed in Vichy on January 15, but left Vichy on the first of July, 1942 ("L'attitude de Le Corbusier pendant la guerre," *Le Corbusier, une encyclopédie* [Paris: Centre National d'Art et de Culture Georges Pompidou, 1987], 457), and McLeod claims he spent eighteen months in Vichy, finally rejecting it in November 1942 ("Urbanism and Utopia," 395, 400). Fox Weber claims he arrived in Vichy in mid-January, 1941, but left it for good on July 1st, 1942 (*Le Corbusier: A Life*, 432, 455).

41 Mumford, *The CIAM Discourse*, 154.

42 Ibid.

43 Creation of ASCORAL (Assemblée de Constructeurs pour une revolution architecturale), "ASCORAL 1939–45," D3(8) Doc 6. (II.86–87).

44 Le Corbusier and ASCORAL, *Les Trois Établissements* (Boulogne: Édition de l'Architecture d'Aujourd'hui, 1945); Le Corbusier and ASCORAL, *Manière de penser l'urbanisme* (Boulogne: Édition de l'Architecture d'Aujourd'hui, 1946), translated by Eleanor Levieux as *Looking At City Planning* (New York: Grossman, 1971). Le Corbusier, *Propos d'Urbanisme* (Paris: Courrelier, 1946), translated by Clive Entwistle as *Concerning Town Planning* (New Haven, CT: Yale University Press, 1948).

45 Mumford, *CIAM Discourse*, 156. Le Corbusier reopens his office with two employees; Gerhard Hanning and Jerzy Soltan.

46 In March, 1945, Le Corbusier received several letters from Association des sinistrés de la ville de Saint-Dié about being the architect-counsel for reconstruction of Saint-Dié. It was expected that his plan would turn the city into "une ville veritiblement humaine" (a truly humane city). Association des sinistrés de la ville de Saint-Dié to Le Corbusier, FLC H3-18-16, 26 Mar. 1945. He was informed one year later that, unfortunately, a plan that "accomodates the taste of the day" was chosen for reconstruction instead of his plan. Association des sinistrés de la ville de Saint-Dié to Le Corbusier, FLC H3-18-182, 1 Feb. 1946.

47 FLC A3-9-4, 21 May 1948. This is the order that Le Corbusier arranges the books as quoted by Catherine de Smet, "Le Livre comme synthèse des arts. Édition et design graphique chez Le Corbusier, 1945–1966" (Doctoral thesis, L'EHESS, 29 Oct. 2002): 255.

48 The English titles instead of the French are used in the text for those books that have been translated. Le Corbusier, *Sur les Quatre Routes* (Paris: Gallimard, 1941), translated by Dorothy Todd as *The Four Routes*, (London: Dennis Dobson Ltd. Publishers, 1947); Le Corbusier, *Destin de Paris* (Paris: Nouvelles Éditions Latine, 1941, reprinted 1987); Le Corbusier with François de Pierrefeu, *La Maison des Hommes* (Paris: Plon, 1941), translated by Clive Entwisle (for Le Corbusier) and Gordon Holt (for Pierrefeu) as *The House of Man*, (London: The Architectural Press, 1948); Le Corbusier and ASCORAL, *L'Urbanisme des Trois Établissements Humains* (Paris: Forces Vives aux Éditions de Minuit, 1945, reprinted in 1959); Le Corbusier and ASCORAL, *Manière de Penser l'Urbanisme* (Boulogne: Édition de l'Architecture d'Aujourd'hui, 1946), translated by Eleanor Levieux as *Looking At City Planning* (New York: Grossman, 1971); Le Corbusier, *Propos d'Urbanisme* (Paris: Courrelier, 1946), translated by Clive Entwistle as *Concerning Town Planning* (New Haven: Yale University Press, 1948).

49 Le Corbusier, "Urbanisme Totale," (unpublished manuscript, Jan. 1935), FLC U3-5-206-21.

50 Ibid.

51 Ibid.

52 See the twenty-first chapter of the book of Revelations: "And the nations of them which are saved shall walk in the light of it: and the kings of the earth do bring their glory and honour into it," King James version. See also John Bunyan's *Pilgrim's Progress*, where the Celestial City, the goal of the pilgrims, is indeed a Ville Radieuse, modeled on the New Jerusalem of the Bible of course: "So I saw that when they awoke, they addressed themselves to go up to the city; but, as I said, the reflection of the sun upon the city (for the city was pure gold) was so extremely glorious that they could not, as yet, with open face behold it."

53 Le Corbusier, *Concerning Town Planning*, 57.

54 Le Corbusier and ASCORAL, *Looking at City Planning*, 18.

55 Le Corbusier, "La dénaturalisation du phénomème urbain" (lecture, Instituto Nacional de Musica, Rio de Janeiro, FLC F2-17-66-85, 5 Aug. 1936).

56 Le Corbusier gave lectures in Rio de Janeiro at the Instituto Nacional de Musica on July 31, August 5, August 7, August 10, August 12, and August 14, 1936.

57 Le Corbusier, "Je fais des plans. Ces plans sont pour des hommes" (lecture, Instituto Nacional de Musica, Rio de Janeiro, 31 July 1936).

58 Le Corbusier, "La dénaturalisation du phénomème urbain."

59 Le Corbusier, "Les loisirs considérés comme occupation véritable de la civilisation machiniste" (lecture, Instituto Nacional de Musica, Rio de Janeiro, FLC F2-17-125-44, 7 Aug. 1936).

60 Le Corbusier,"Les Temps Nouveaux et la Vocation de l'architecte. Programme d'une faculté d'Architecture" (lecture, Instituto Nacional de Musica, Rio de Janeiro, FLC C3-18-138-155, 12 Aug. 1936).

61 Ibid.

62 George Lakoff, *Don't Think of an Elephant! Know Your values and Frame the Debate* (White River Junction, VT: Chelsea Green Publishing, 2004), 1–34.

63 Le Corbusier (lecture, Instituto Nacional de Musica, Rio de Janeiro, FLC F2-17-16-31, 31 July 1936).

64 Paul Valèry, "Les deux vertus d'un livre" (1926), in *Oeuvres* (Paris: Gallimard, 1960), 1246–50.

65 Élie Faure, "La VR," *L'Architecture Aujourd'hui* 11 (Nov. 1935): 1.

66 Le Corbusier, "Considerer L'Exagone-France," (unpublished manuscript, Aug. 1942), FLC U3-06-20.

67 Michel Foucault, "Appendix: The Discourse on Language," in *The Archaeology of Knowledge*, trans. A. M. Sheridan Smith (New York: Pantheon, 1972), 215–37. This discussion on discourse is inspired by, if not exactly following the letter of, Michel Foucault's "The Discourse on Language."

68 Le Corbusier, *The Radiant City: Elements of a doctrine of urbanism to be used as the basis of our machine-age civilization* (1935; repr., New York: The Orion Press, 1967), 19–25. Le Corbusier organized these fifty-nine points into a set of six different questions.

69 Le Corbusier, *Destin de Paris*, 13–23.

70 Le Corbusier, *The Four Routes*, 14.

71 Ibid., 114–15

72 Le Corbusier and ASCORAL, *Trois Établissements Humains*, 62–65.

73 Le Corbusier, *Concerning Town Planning*, 46, 48.

74 Ibid., 126.

75 Le Corbusier, *The Four Routes*, 186.

76 Ibid., 26.

77 Ibid., 131.

78 Ibid., 131–32.

79 Ibid., 138.

80 Ibid., 133.

81 Ibid., 14.

82 Ibid., 12.

83 Ibid., 22.

84 Ibid., 11.

85 Le Corbusier and de Pierrefeu, *The Home of Man*, 53.

86 Le Corbusier, *The Four Routes*, 7, 19; Le Corbusier, *The Radiant City*, 98. Le Corbusier had also called the materials assembled in *The Radiant City* a series of "laboratory studies."

87 Le Corbusier, *The Four Routes*, 17, 18.

88 Ibid., 162.

89 Ibid., 18.

90 Ibid., 179–81.

91 Ibid., 187.

92 Ibid., 188–89.

93 Ibid., 189.

94 Ibid., 183.

95 Le Corbusier, *Concerning Town Planning*, 11.

96 Le Corbusier, *The Four Routes*, 194–95.

97 Le Corbusier and ASCORAL, *Looking at City Planning*, 101.

98 Paul Chombart de Lauwe, ed., "La Vision Aérienne du Monde," in *La Découvert Aérienne du Monde* (Paris: Horizons de France, 1948), 54. Le Corbusier increasingly utilizes the word "tentacle," or *tentaculaire*, to describe the spread of cities into metropolitan regions. Although he never references him, circa 1900 the Belgian poet Verhaeren labeled the modern metropolis the tentacular city.

99 Le Corbusier, *Concerning Town Panning*, 68.

100 Le Corbusier, "Answer to Sixth Question," in *Concerning Town Planning*, 67–78; quotation: 68.

101 Le Corbusier and ASCORAL, *Looking at City Planning*, 14–15.
102 Le Corbusier and ASCORAL, *Trois Établissements Humains*, 58.
103 The chapter on "Conditions Morales" is re-edited by Hyacinthe Dubreuil, economist and sociologist. Le Corbusier and ASCORAL, *Trois Établissements Humains*, 59–61.
104 Le Corbusier, *Concerning Town Planning*, 11–13; Le Corbusier and de Pierrefeu, *The Home of Man*, 112.
105 Le Corbusier, *Concerning Town Planning*, 68.
106 Le Corbuiser and ASCORAL, *Trois Établissements Humains*, 62–65.
107 Ibid., 68–69.
108 Ibid., 70.
109 Le Corbusier and ASCORAL, *Looking at City Planning*, 18; Le Corbusier and ASCORAL, *Trois Établissements Humains*, 18–19.
110 Ibid., 72.
111 Le Corbusier and ASCORAL, *Looking at City Planning*, 28.
112 Le Corbusier and de Pierrefeu, *The Home of Man*, 124, 140; Le Corbusier, *Concerning Town Planning*, 13.
113 Le Corbusier and ASCORAL, *Looking at City Planning*, 28–29.
114 Ibid., 31.
115 Ibid., 44, 71.
116 Ibid., 7–8.
117 Le Corbusier and de Pierrefeu, *The Home of Man*, 86, 87, 89, 97.
118 Ibid., 87.
119 Ibid., 89.
120 Ibid., 96.
121 Ibid., 90.
122 Ibid., 95.
123 Ibid., 93.
124 Ibid., 94.
125 Le Corbusier, *The Radiant City*, 78.
126 Le Corbusier, *The Four Routes*, 132; Le Corbusier and de Pierrefeu, *The Home of Man*, 58.
127 Le Corbusier and ASCORAL, *Trois Établissements Humains*, 62.
128 Le Corbusier, *The Four Routes*, 63; Le Corbusier, *Concerning Town Planning*, 50–58.
129 Le Corbusier and ASCORAL, *Trois Établissements Humains*, 61.
130 Le Corbusier and de Pierrefeu, *The Home of Man*, 110.
131 Le Corbusier, *Concerning Town Planning*, 96.
132 Le Corbusier, *The Four Routes*, 139–40.
133 Le Corbusier, "Les besoins collectives et la génie civil," *L'Encyclopèdie Française* (Oct. 1935): 3–5, FLC X1-12-124.
134 Le Corbusier, *The Four Routes*, 81–85.
135 Ibid., 83.
136 Ibid., 86–96.
137 Ibid., 86.
138 Ibid.
139 Ibid., 30.
140 Ibid., 30–31.
141 Ibid., 29–80.
142 Ibid., 31.
143 Ibid., 32.
144 Ibid., 33.
145 Ibid., 34.
146 Ibid.
147 Ibid., 35.
148 Ibid., 37.
149 Ibid., 39.
150 The title "Voiture Maximum" might also be referring to a joint paper written by Pierre Jeanneret and Le Corbusier for CIAM III, "Minimum House."
151 Le Corbusier, "Voiture Le Corbusier, projet non-realizé," *Proposition* 1, no. 102, FLC T2 (16) 56.
152 Le Corbusier, "Note: Établissement du Plan d'une Voiture Automobile" (unpublished manuscript), FLC T2 (16) 53–55, Paris, 2 Apr. 1936.
153 Le Corbusier to M. Senateur Agnelli, Usines FIAT, FLC T2 (16) 112, Turin, 6 Oct. 1936.
154 In this article, Le Corbusier goes on to describe the foundation of ASCORAL and the reasons for its existence. It was formed in order to examine the management of the geographical environment, and planned to establish a coherent doctrine of land occupation, in particular the built domain and its extensions, and to respond to the four functions: to live, work, cultivate the body and spirit, and to circulate. Le Corbusier, "Urbanisme et Aeronautique" (unpublished manuscript), FLC U3-06-233-245, 9 Aug. 1947.
155 The Studio, Ltd. to Le Corbusier. FLC B3-14-1, London, ca. 16 Jan. 1935; The Studio, Ltd. to Le Corbusier, FLC B3-14-4, London, 31 Jan. 1935.
156 Le Corbusier to The Studio, Ltd., FLC B3-14-3, 22 Jan. 1935
157 Le Corbusier, *Précisions: sur un état présent de l'architecture et de l'urbanisme* (Paris: Les Éditions G. Crès et Cie, 1930), 143.
158 Note that in 1928 Le Corbusier participated in the design of a *table tube d'avion*, and

that the word *équipage* in French means the crew.
159 Le Corbusier to The Studio, Ltd., FLC B3-14-21, 7 May 1935; Le Corbusier to The Studio, Ltd., FLC B3-14-23, 9 May 1935.
160 Telecommunications were also on the rise: the BBC's Empire Services crackled over short-wave receivers for the first time in 1932.
161 Pierre Crochet-Damais, "L'Exploration Aérienne," in Paul Chombart de Lauwe, ed., *La Découvert Aérienne du Monde*, 57–96; Emmanuel de Martonne, *Géographie Aérienne* (Paris: Éditions Albin Michel: 1948), 67–101.
162 Le Corbusier, *Aircraft* (London: The Studio Publications, 1935), 7; Le Corbusier, *The Four Routes*, 97.
163 Le Corbusier, *The Four Routes*, 98–99.
164 Le Corbusier, *Précisions*, 4.
165 Le Corbusier, *Aircraft*, caption 112, unpaginated.
166 Pascal Ory, *The Legend of the Skies*, trans. Barry Tulett (Paris: Editions Hoëbeke, 2001), 13.
167 Peter Fritzsche, *A Nation of Fliers: German Aviation and the Popular Imagination* (Cambridge, MA: Harvard University Press, 1992), 59–101.
168 Ory, *The Legend of the Skies*, 58. The first successful aviation novel in France was Joseph Kessel's 1920s book *Équipage* (*The Crew*). It was adapted for the cinema three times within ten years.
169 Le Corbusier, *The Radiant City*, 179. Additional comments in Le Corbusier, *The Four Routes*, 102.
170 Le Corbusier and ASCORAL, *Trois Établissements Humains*, 138.
171 Ibid., 138–41.
172 Fritzsche, *A Nation of Fliers*, 172–75, 185.
173 Le Corbusier, "Préfères-tu faire la Guerre?" *Des Canons, Des Munitions? Merci! Des Logis… S. V. P.* (Paris: Collection de l'équipement de la civilisation machiniste, 1938), 137.
174 Le Corbusier, *The Radiant City*, 341.
175 Ibid., 81.
176 Ibid., 81.
177 Le Corbusier, *The Four Routes*, 108.
178 Ibid.
179 Le Corbusier and de Pierrefeu, *The Home of Man*, 125.
180 Ibid. 154.
181 Le Corbusier and ASCORAL, *Trois Établissements Humains*, 138–41
182 Michel de Certeau, *The Practice of Everyday Life* (Berkeley: University of California Press, 1984), 121.
183 Le Corbusier, *Précisions*, 202.
184 Ibid., 208.
185 Ibid., 205, 208.
186 Ibid., 235–36.
187 Ibid., 236.
188 Ibid., 242.
189 Ibid., 245.
190 Ibid., 241.
191 Ibid., 241–42.
192 Le Corbusier, "L'Urbanisme et le Lyrisme des Temps Nouveaux," unpaginated.
193 Le Corbusier, *The Four Routes*, 110.
194 Ibid., 111.
195 Le Corbusier, *Précisions*, 5.
196 Le Corbusier, *The Radiant City*, 79.
197 Le Corbusier, *Concerning Town Planning*, 45.
198 Le Corbusier and ASCORAL, *Looking at City Planning*, 77.
199 Ibid., 78.
200 Ibid., 78, 81.
201 Ibid., 83.
202 Le Corbusier and de Pierrefeu, *The Home of Man*, 52.
203 Le Corbusier, *Précisions*, 27.
204 Ibid., 26.
205 Le Corbusier and ASCORAL, *Trois Établissements Humains*, 132.
206 Ibid.
207 Ibid.
208 "Communication observations of Colonel Vauthier, 5th Congress CIAM," in Le Corbusier, *Précisions*, 192.
209 Le Corbusier, "Commentaires rélatifs à Moscow et à la 'Ville Verts'" (unpublished manuscript), FLC A3-1-65, 12 Mar. 1930.
210 Le Corbusier, *The Four Routes*, 44, 48.
211 Ibid., 51.
212 Le Corbusier and ASCORAL, *Looking at City Planning*, 43–44.
213 Le Corbusier, *Concerning Town Planning*, 11–12.
214 Note from Le Corbusier on Section 6 "Infrastructure Congrès National de l'Aviation Française…Realisation and Technique… signalisation and telecommunity." FLC C3-19-71-2.
215 Le Corbusier, *Concerning Town Planning*, 118.
216 Ibid., 118, 121.
217 Ibid., 121.
218 Ibid., 122.
219 Ibid., 12.
220 Ibid.
221 Ibid., 14.
222 Le Corbusier and ASCORAL, *Looking at City Planning*, 78.

223 Le Corbusier, "Les Nouvelles Épitres" (unpublished manuscript), FLC F3-1-93-5, 27 June 1945.
224 Ibid.

EPILOGUE

Epigraph 1 Fernand Léger to Le Corbusier, FLC E 2 8 68, Oct. 1946, quoted by Rebecca Rabinow, "The Legacy of la Rue Férou: Livres d'Artiste created for Tériade by Rouault, Bonnard, Matisse, Léger, Le Corbusier, Chagall, Giacometti and Miró" (Unpublished PhD diss., Institute of Fine Arts, NYU, Sept. 1995): 161.
Epigraph 2 Le Corbusier, *The New World of Space* (New York: Reynal & Hitchcock, 1948), 103.
1 The list of postwar books would include: Le Corbusier, *United Nations Headquarters* (New York: Reinhold, 1947); Le Corbusier, *New World of Space* (New York: Reinhold and Hitchcock, 1948); Le Corbusier, *Le Modulor* (Boulogne: Éditions de L'Architecture d'Aujourd'hui, 1950), translated into English as *The Modular* (London: Faber,1954); Le Corbusier, *L'Unité d'habitation de Marseille* (Mulhouse: Le Point, 1950), translated into English as *The Marseilles Block* (London: Harvill, 1953); Le Corbusier, *Poésie sur Alger* (Paris: Falaize, 1951); Le Corbusier, *Une petite maison* (Zurich: Ginsberger, 1954); Le Corbusier, *Poème de l'angle droit* (Paris: Verve, 1955); Le Corbusier, *Le Modulor 2* (Boulogne: Éditions de L'Architecture d'Aujourd'hui, 1955), translated into English as *The Modular 2* (London: Farber, 1958); Le Corbusier, *Les Plans Le Corbusier de Paris 1956–1922* (Paris: Éditions de Minuit, 1956); Le Corbusier, *Ronchamp* (Zurich: Ginsberger, 1957); Le Corbusier, *L'Atelier de la recherché patiente* (Paris: Vincent Fréal et Cie, 1960), translated into English as *Creation is a Patient Search* (New York: Praeger, 1990).
2 He had already moved toward this direction in his 1935 article "Sainte Alliance des arts majeurs or le grand art en gésine," published in E. Tériade's short-lived journal *La Bête Noir.* He believed in the 1930s that only an architect of genius like himself could effect this alliance, and thus urbanists, sculptors, and painters must succumb to his directives. It is always the architect who stands upright, he who establishes unity, balance and order and in the end forecloses collaborative efforts with all other artists.
3 André Rousseau, *Le Figaro* (3 May 1941): 4, quoted by Rebecca Rabinow, "The Legacy of la Rue Férou," 276.
4 Jean Schlumberger, "La Litterature Continue: A propos de deux manifestes," *Le Figaro Littéraire* (10 Aug. 1945): front page.
5 Sigfried Giedion, Jose Luis Sert, and Fernand Léger, "Nine Points of Monumentality" (1943) in Sigfried Giedion, *Architecture, You and Me: The Diary of Development* (Cambridge: Harvard University Press, 1958), 48–52.
6 Sigfried Giedion, "Bridgwater Questionnaire–1947" and "Bergamo Questionnaire–1948," in *A Decade of New Architecture* (Zurich: Ginsberger Press, 1951), 31–2, 38–9.
7 Giedion, *Architecture, You and Me,* 102. Ann Koll, "The Synthesis of the Arts in the Context of Post-WWII: A study of Le Corbusier's Ideas and his Porte Maillot Pavilion" (Unpublished PhD dissertation, CUNY, 1991): 138–84.
8 Ann Koll, "The Synthesis of the Arts in the Context of Post-WWII," 138–84.
9 Ibid., 151.
10 Le Corbusier, remarks at CIAM VI (held in 1947 in Bridgewater), in Sigfried Giedion, *Decade of New Architecture* (New York: Wittenborn, 1951), 36–7.
11 Le Corbusier, quoted by Giedion, *Architecture, You and Me*, 84. The "synthesis of the arts" was a personal project of André Bloc, the editor and publisher of the major architectural periodical in France, *Architecture d'Aujourd'hui.* In the fall of 1949, under the patronage of Bloc, "L' Association pour une Synthèse des Arts plastiques" was established following the recommendations of CIAM VI. Its aim was to assemble a large exhibition of collaborative efforts of artists and architects scheduled to take place in June 1950 at Porte Maillot in Paris. Matisse was appointed president, an honorary position, while Le Corbusier and Bloc shared the post of Vice-President. Such an exhibition, while reflecting the interests of both Bloc and Le Corbusier, also had an overtly political message. Even though New York was increasingly competitive with Paris over preeminence in artistic expression, this exhibition would remind the world that the French "synthesis of the arts" would be the wave of the future. Christopher Eric Morgan Pearson, "Integrations of Art and Architecture in the work of Le Corbusier: Theory and Practice form Ornamentalism to the Synthesis of the major art" (Unpublished

Ph.D. Dissertation, Stanford University, 1995), 354–7.

12 "Si l'on accorde quelque signification á mon œuvre d'architecte, c'est á ce labeur secret qu'il faut en attribuer la valeur profonde." Le Corbusier, *Architecture d'Aujourd'hui* (Apr. 1948): 39. This is a handwritten note inserted by Le Corbusier into a page of poetry about "Acrobat" in *Atelier de la recherche patiente* (Paris: Vincent et Fréal, 1960), 67.

13 Le Corbusier, "Unité" *L'Architecture d'aujourd'hui* 19 (special issue devoted to Le Corbusier, Apr. 1948): 11.

14 The 1938 exhibition was in the Kunsthaus of Zurich. Rebecca Rabinow gives the following list of exhibitions of Le Corbusier's paintings in 1947/48: Amsterdam (15 March 1947); Zurich (5–22 May 1948); and the United States (1948), an exhibition that traveled to Boston, Detroit, Cleveland, St. Louis, San Francisco, Colorado Springs, Chicago, and Los Angeles before returning to Europe. Rebecca A. Rabinow, "The Legacy of la Rue Férou: *Livres d'Artiste,*" 169

15 Book-art–or a book that is also an artistic expression–is different from a conventional book. It breaks with rectangular blocks of print and attempts via syntax, format, sizes and shapes of the paper and the quality of production to provide a different reading experience. The use of the term "book-art" is to avoid the debatable use of "artists' books" or the French equivalent *livres d'artistes*. Richard Kostelanetz, "On Book-Art" *Leonardo* 12, no. 1 (Winter, 1979): 43–4.

16 Stéphane Mallarmé, "Variations sur un sujet," (1895) in *Oeuvre Complète* (Paris: Gallimard, 1945), 343.

17 Born as Efstratios Eleftheriades in Lesbos (1889–1983), he arrived in Paris in 1915 as E. Tériade. He met Le Corbusier in the 1920s after he had been hired by Christian Zervos to be the artistic director of his new art journal *Cahiers d'Art* in the mid-1920s, a position he held until 1931. Meanwhile between 1928–33 he helped Maurice Raynal with the weekly arts page of *L'Intransigeant*; he joined Albert Skira in the publishing *Minotaure* between 1933–39; he acted as artistic director of *Le Voyage en Grèce periodiques de tourisme* published by Société Neptos; and he co-founded the short-lived broadside *La Bête Noire* in 1935. All of these publications carried articles by or interviews with Le Corbusier. Tériade established his own review, *Verve*, in 1937, and in one form or another it continued until 1960. It was planned as a sumptuous collector's item, setting the tone with its first issue. It displayed a cover by Henri Matisse and printed Dora Maar's now-famous photograph of *Guernica* in Picasso's studio. Tériade eventually turned to the publication of artists' books. Rebecca Rabinow, "The Legacy of la Rue Férou: *Livres d'Artiste,*" 7–12.

18 Le Corbusier, FLC F2 20 8, Chandigarh, 30 Mar. 1952, quoted by Rebecca Rabinow, "The Legacy of la Rue Férou: *Livres d'Artiste,*" 192.

19 Ibid., 173–4.

20 Le Corbusier, "Notes," FLC F2 18 104, 7 Nov. 1950, quoted by Rebecca Rabinow, "The Legacy of la Rue Férou," 174.

21 Le Corbusier to Tériade, 23 July 1955 (Paris, private collection), quoted by Rebecca Rabinow, "The Legacy of la Rue Férou: *Livres d'Artiste,*" 202.

22 Le Corbusier "Form letter and Subscription for *Poème de l'Angle Droit,*" FLC F2 20 292–354, 15 Jan. 1955, quoted by Rebecca Rabinow, "The Legacy of la Rue Férou: *Livres d'Artiste,*" 166.

23 Pearson, "Integrations of Art and Architecture in the work of Le Corbusier."

24 Le Corbusier, *Poème de l'Angle Droit* (Paris: Editions Verve, 1955), 48–9, quoted by Rebecca Rabinow, "The Legacy of la Rue Férou: *Livres d'Artiste,*" 178.

25 Le Corbusier, *Les Plans Le Corbusier de Paris* (Paris: Éditions de Minuit, 1956).

26 Catherine de Smet, "Le Livre comme synthèse des arts. Édition et design graphique chez Le Corbusier, 1945–1966" (Unpubished doctoral thesis, L'EHESS, 29 Sept. 2002): 227–42.

27 Le Corbusier, *Les Plans Le Corbusier de Paris*, 30, 36.

28 Ibid., 40, 47.

29 Ibid., 110, 112.

30 Ibid., 133–34, 150.

31 Ibid., 186.

32 He had written about this passage from usefulness to irradiation in 1926. Le Corbusier, "A ce passage d'un but à un autre, de la fonction *servite* à la fonction *irradier,* se situe l'architecture d'Époque Machiniste," *Journal de Psychologie Normale et Pathologique* (1926): 325–50, quotation 326.

33 Le Corbusier, *The New World of Space* (New York: Reynal & Hitchcock, 1948), 66.

34 Le Corbusier, "The Core as the Meeting Place of the Arts," in *The Heart of the City: toward the humanization of urban life*, ed. Jacqueline Tyrwhitt, Jose Luis Sert, and

Ernesto N. Rogers (London: Lund Humphries & Co. Ltd., 1952), 41–52, quotation, 48.

35 Le Corbusier, "The Core as the Meeting Place of the Arts," 52.

36 Le Corbusier, "Introduction," *Œuvre Complète 1952–1957*, vol. 6 (Zurich: Les Editions d'Architecture, 1957), 8. "Le Fond du Sac," FLC F2-10-410 (1948–60), is perhaps his most secret piece. I like to think they are leftover fragments at the bottom of a sack.

37 Le Corbusier, "Introduction," *Oeuvre Complète 1952–1957*, 9.

38 Le Corbusier to Ritter, R3-18-130-1, voyage through Italy, 1 Nov. 1911.

INDEX

Academy of Commerce, 57
Acropolis, 6, 10, 197, 211, 477, 603, 621, 749n145
    geometry and, 384
    Jeanneret's conversion to classicism and, 112
    language of architecture and, 307, 319–22, 366
    letters of confession and, 169, 173
    Parthenon and, 59, 70, 89, 109 (*see also* Parthenon)
    poetics and, 412–13, 421, 590–93
    Renan and, 117
    search for method and, 107, 296
    as theatrical spectacle, 149–52
    travel to, 145–53
AEG (Allegemeine Elektrizitäis Gesellschaft), 76, 92, 95, 99, 106–7, 156
Aerial Danger and the Future of the Country, The (Vauthier), 670
aesthetics
    American travels and, 433–34, 440, 478, 483
    Art Nouveau, 88
    Ateliers d'art réunis and, 68–69
    avant-garde, 40–44, 169, 178–79, 220, 227, 242–43, 246, 270, 277, 284, 609–10, 629, 679
    Cartesian, 297, 430, 468, 485, 607, 685
    center of gravity and, 319, 381
    city construction and, 156, 160–61, 198, 204
    Classical, 22, 41, 70, 88–92, 107, 114, 116, 119, 143–44, 168, 175, 187, 262, 272, 285, 303, 316, 326, 331, 406, 585, 591, 705n78, 706n87, 708n65
    comparison before judging and, 58
    constructivism and, 384–85
    Corinthian, 90, 114, 316
    Cours Supérieur and, 69
    Dom-ino scheme and, 21, 159, 190, 193–94, 199, 208–13, 234, 717n67
    Doric, 89–90, 107, 114, 316, 320, 386, 585, 590
    Eastern travels and, 112, 121, 126, 152
    equilibrium and, 37–40, 142, 155 (*see also* equilibrium)
    eternal balance and, 187
    five points of architecture and, 37–39, 276, 328, 360, 366, 371, 388, 402, 430, 704n53
    geometric form and, 39, 64, 70, 86, 128, 227, 264, 405, 593, 596 (*see also* geometry)
    German/French culture wars and, 91–95
    golden section and, 396–97
    Gothic, 60–61, 65–66, 73, 90, 107, 114, 174, 187, 222–23, 405–6, 416, 507, 509, 519
    higher goals for, 248–53
    humanism and, 160, 366, 413, 490–91, 619
    impressionism and, 54, 86–87, 244, 254, 268, 289, 588
    interior design and, 77, 100, 177, 184–85, 185, 195, 226
    interpreting, 51–53
    Ionian, 90, 114, 296
    knowledge of form and, 57
    language of architecture and, 303–4, 308, 326, 363, 366–69, 372
    Latin spirit and, 596–604
    Law of Ripolin and, 356–57
    letters of confession and, 182–83
    Mediterranean style, 593, 599
    method and, 53–54, 78, 87–93, 101,

262–76, 280–87, 298
minimalism and, 181
modeling methods and, 54–56, 64, 92
museums and, 53, 60, 68, 71, 74, 96, 100, 161, 291, 350–51, 354, 393, 483, 485, 543, 681
neoclassical, 180, 194, 533, 561, 590–92, 599
New Objectivity and, 392–96, 398, 413
obelisks and, 79–80
Orientalism and, 126
ornamentation and, 62, 105, 107, 168, 179, 181–83, 190, 275, 295, 349, 352–53, 401, 593
poetics and, 385, 391, 394, 398–400, 416
Purism and, 262–76, 280–87, 298
Renaissance and, 66, 316, 386, 406, 411, 416, 425, 509, 519, 705n78
retardataire, 182
Romanesque, 65, 237–38, 406, 510
secular faith and, 617, 646, 649
Sitte and, 71, 73–76, 80, 121, 156–57, 160–61, 164, 168, 197–206, 319, 330, 716nn5,14
spirit of the thirties and, 497–99
Suisse Romande, 83, 114, 176, 179, 190
synthesis of art and, 229, 252–54
utility and, 39, 105, 161, 166, 180–82, 197–98, 202–3, 207–9, 265, 351, 354, 361, 379–80, 386, 395, 413, 421–22, 430, 606–8, 647

"Aesthetics and Purism" (Jeanneret and Ozenfant), 286–87

Aircraft (Le Corbusier), 578, 655–57, 661

airplanes, 51
aviation and, 653–57
cartographic view from, 662–65
geomorphic land structures and, 671–73
law of the meander and, 665–67
machine age and, 645–73
myth-making and, 658–60
new routes of discovery from, 660–62
space-time compression and, 667–69
La Ville Radieuse and, 658, 664–65, 671
warfare and, 670–71

"Air-Sound-Light" (Le Corbusier), 500, 590

Albert-Birot, Pierre, 41

Algeria
assimilation and, 560
Charter of Demands of the Muslim Algerian People and, 584
emancipation and, 560
first trip to, 560–63
Foreign Legion and, 554
imaginary geography and, 558–59
mission civilatrice (civilizing mission) and, 554–56
Purism and, 556
rewriting of Algiers and, 553–60
second trip to, 563–70
technology of empire and, 559–60
third visit to, 577–79
La Ville Radieuse and, 561, 564, 572–73, 579–82, 593
white blind spots and, 554–58

Algiers, 46, 130
American travels and, 462, 478–79
Casbah and, 555, 558–63, 569–75, 579, 587
"Death of the Street" and, 570–75
final schemes for, 585–88
Fraternity and, 505–6, 511
Friends of Algiers and, 404, 560–61, 570–71, 577, 585
Mediterranean style and, 553–603
Obus A and, 570–75
Obus B and, 575–76
Obus C and, 579–85
Obus D and, 586
Obus E and, 586, 615
poetics and, 411, 424, 430
politics of denial and, 554–58
Regional Plan and, 572, 575–78, 583, 585–86
rewriting of, 553–60
secular faith and, 612, 615, 617, 631, 672
spirit of the thirties and, 498, 505–6, 511
La Ville Radieuse and, 505–6, 511

Allgemeine Städtbau Ausstellung, 161

Alloula, Malek, 556

Almanach d'Architecture Moderne (Le Corbusier), 38
Breton houses and, 368–69
"To Construct in Series" and, 367–68
Esprit Nouveau Pavilion and, 360
Exposition Internationale des Arts Décoratifs and, 360–61
folklore and, 367–69
houses and, 357, 361–69
innovation and, 369–70
language of architecture and, 357–70
"L'Esprit Nouveau in Architecture" and, 362–66
machines and, 414–15
"New Procedures and Materials" and, 370
Purism and, 358–59
"A Standard dies a Standard is born" and, 368–69
"A turning" and, 366–67
Voisin Plan and, 360–61

Altenberg, Peter, 347

American Architecture, The (journal), 468

American travels
blackness and, 449–54

clothing fashions and, 454–56
comparison to Eastern travels and, 436–37
folklore and, 479–85
food and, 439–50
happiness and, 457–59
jazz and, 449–54, 458, 468, 738n13
need for exoticism and, 433–34
neo-syndicalism and, 465, 479–85
Précisions and, 437–49
regionalism and, 479–85
sexuality and, 440, 449–50, 457, 473, 476–77
South America and, 437–38, 441, 444, 446, 449–50, 456–59, 483–84, 501–2
United States and, 435, 451, 455–58, 585
"Amis d'Alger, Les" (Friends of Algiers), 404, 560–61, 570–71, 577, 585
Annales, Les (newspaper), 378
apprentices, 52, 62, 93, 98–99, 106, 195, 429, 483, 558, 560, 612
Après le Cubisme (Le Corbusier and Ozenfant), 44
Purism and, 262, 264–68, 298
synthesis of art and, 236, 241–47, 250–54
World War I and, 265
Aragon, Louis, 538
Arc de Triomphe, 204, 398, 411
architectural lyricism, 396
Architectural Review journal, 678
architecture
artist as purist and, 296–98
center of gravity and, 319, 381
contemporary, 56, 367, 398, 413, 534, 672, 725n35
culinary art of, 439–49
defense of modern, 377–99
dictionary meanings of, 414–15
five points of, 37–39, 276, 328, 360, 366, 371, 388, 402, 430, 704n53
folk-lores and, 420–22
German/French culture wars and, 91–95, 112
golden section and, 396–97
intellectualism of, 198
interior design and, 77, 100, 177, 185, 195, 226
interpreting, 51–53
key in painting and, 55
knowledge of form and, 57
language of, 36–40, 166, 187, 296 (*see also* language of architecture)
machines and, 413–31 (*see also* machines)
man of letters and, 20–21, 24–29
materials that speak and, 420–22
as mirror of thought, 19
modeling methods and, 54–56, 64, 92
New Objectivity and, 392–96, 398, 413
as organism, 383–86
ornamentation and, 62, 105, 107, 168, 179, 181–83, 190, 275, 295, 349, 352–53, 401, 593
painting and, 179–80
Parthenon and, 70, 89, 109, 112–13 (*see also* Parthenon)
as plant, 380–83
poetics of, 413–31
popularization of art in public domain and, 103–5
prestressed concrete and, 72, 107, 219, 240, 363–64, 369, 382, 386–89, 401–3, 406–7, 411, 421, 430, 499–500, 562
Purism and, 44, 182, 220, 244, 248–49, 261–98, 302, 329, 336, 341, 358–59, 371, 392, 403, 430, 504, 556
reserves of, 387–92
skyscrapers and, 172, 199, 221, 272, 307, 342, 366, 430, 435, 453–54, 457–58, 461, 464, 466–76, 479, 573, 577, 586, 663
Suisse Romande, 83, 114, 176, 179, 190
town planning and, 24, 33, 76, 188, 208–9, 335, 341, 617, 628, 633, 636, 643, 650, 657, 671
Turbine Hall and, 77, 99
urbanism and, 71, 155–64 (*see also* urbanism)
visual perception and, 25
See also aesthetics
"Architecture" (Loos), 347
Architecture d'Aujourd'hui journal, 428–29, 534, 581
Architecture Vivante journal, 510, 575–76, 581
Aron, Robert, 489
Arp, Hans, 678
art, 45–46
aesthetics and, 53–54, 112, 121, 126 (*see also* aesthetics)
avant-garde, 40–44, 169, 178–79, 220, 227, 242–43, 246, 270, 277, 284, 609–10, 629, 679
books as, 680
commerce and, 98–103
contact with people and, 79–80
dictionary meanings of, 414–15
geometric form and, 39, 64, 70, 86, 128, 227, 264, 405, 593, 596
German utilitarian, 88
ineffable space and, 684–86
interpreting, 51–53
machines and, 155–56
ornamentation and, 62, 105, 107, 168, 179, 181–83, 190, 275, 295, 349, 352–53, 401, 593
poetics of machines and, 413–31 (*see also*

machines)
popularization of in public domain, 103–5
power of, 198
premature admiration and, 52
Purism and, 44 (*see also* Purism)
secessionist, 56, 89
in the service of commerce, 98–103
social, 161 (*see also* urbanism)
synthesis of, 220–25, 229–37, 241–59, 427–30, 677–79, 684–86
utility and, 39, 105, 161, 166 (*see also* utility)
Art et Liberté group, 229
"Art et Utilité Publique" ("Art and Public Utility") (Le Corbusier), 161
Art Nouveau, 88
Art of Building Cities, The (Sitte), 71, 73–75, 156, 203
"Arts des Primitifs, Les" ("The Arts of the Primitives") exhibition, 419
"Arts dits Primitifs dans La Maison d'Aujourd'hui, Les" ("The Arts Called Primitive in the House of Today") (Le Corbusier), 419
ASCORAL (Assemblée de Constructeurs pour une Renouvellement Architecturale), 616–17, 627–28
Association Generale des Hygienistes et Techniciens Municipaux, 43
Ateliers d'art réunis (workshops of combined art), 68–69, 186
avant-garde, 40–44, 220, 679
cubism and, 242–47 (*see also* cubism)
letters of confession and, 169, 178–79
method and, 270, 277, 284
Ozenfant and, 242–45
"La Parade" and, 227
secular faith and, 609–10, 629
Aziyadé (Loti), 142

Bacon, Madge, 478
Badovici, Jean, 510
Baedeker, 55
Baker, Geoffrey H., 5, 119, 327
Baker, Josephine, 449–51, 454, 468, 481–82
Balkan War, 111
ballet, 41, 227, 255, 352
Ballets Russes, 227
Ballie-Scott, 102
Baltard, 196
Banham, Reyner, 326–27
Bardi, Pietro Maria, 600–1
Basch, Victor, 284, 452
Basilica di Santa Maria della Salute, 55
Bastion Kellerman, 542
Bauen in Frankreich (Giedion), 392
Baugesellschaft-Hellerau, 102
Bauhaus, 497
bazaars, 100, 113, 140–41, 316–17
Behrens, Peter, 185, 214, 259, 707n39, 710n105
AEG and, 76, 92, 95, 99, 106–7, 156
as art director, 99
city construction and, 156, 163–64
classicism and, 112
Eastern travels and, 112, 116
industrial arts and, 97–98
letters of confession and, 168, 179
method and, 70–71, 76–77, 80–91, 95–101, 106
Neu-Babelsberg and, 82, 84–85, 163
Nouvelle Section at École d'Art and, 185
Turbine Hall and, 77, 99
Belgium, 88, 90, 158, 162, 189–90, 209, 614, 655
Benjamin, Walter, 25
Berbers, 559, 589
Bergson, Henri, 40, 282
Bertsch, 104
Bestelmeyer, 102–3
Bête Noir, La (journal), 427
Bêton Armê, Le (Du Bois), 174
Bézard, Norbert, 529–30
Bibliothèque Nationale, 159, 194, 196, 208, 225, 328
Blanc, Charles, 714n47
Blanche, Jacques-Emile, 227
Blum, Léon, 584
Bois de Vincennes, 542
Boissonnas, Frédéric, 320
Bonnier, Louis, 240–41
Bontempelli, 600
books, 30, 301, 680, 684–85
Bornand, 234, 240
Botticelli, 54
bouquets, 232–33
Brady, Darlene, 34
Broggi, Carlo, 377–78
Brooks, H. Allen, 5, 33, 111–12, 160, 164
Brua, Edmond, 575–76, 578
Brunel, Charles, 570, 575, 578–79, 581, 583
Brunelleschi's dome, 56
Brussels International Exhibition, 89
Budapest, 56, 130–31

Caesar, 237
Cahiers d'Aujourd'hui, Les (journal), 179–88, 378, 466
Camus, Albert, 589–90, 596
Cannarozzo, Maria Lucia, 303
Canons, Des Munitions? Merci! Des Logis...S. V.P., Des (Le Corbusier), 495, 536–37, 545, 548, 550, 682
Carabin, Rupert, 93–94, 196, 185
Caravaggio, 476

Carré, Louis, 419
Cartesian aesthetics, 297, 430, 468, 485, 607, 685
Cartesian geometric grid, 297
Cartesian logic, 22, 37, 47, 62, 319, 465, 607, 657
Carthusian monastery d'Ema (Chartreuse), 160–61, 197
Casa del Noce, 318
Casbah, 555–63, 569–75, 579, 587
Cathedral of Reims, 188
Cathedral of Strasbourg, 186–87
Cazamian, C., 466
C (culture) designation, 22, 152
Cendrars, Blaise, 437
center of gravity, 319, 381
Central Park, 474
Cezanne, 192, 225, 270
Champ de Mars, 345
Champs-Elysées, 176, 182, 194, 196, 198, 204, 345, 410–11
Chaplin, Charlie, 457
Charter of Athens, 616, 627, 644
Chartreuse d'Ema, la, 54
Chaux-de-Fonds, La, 6, 403, 406, 708n67
  Les Ateliers d'Art Réunis and, 169
  city construction and, 153–57, 161–62, 196, 199
  as "deep hole", 92
  Dom-ino scheme and, 210–15
  Du Bois and, 173–74
  Eastern travels and, 110–13, 118–20, 145, 153–54
  as leprous spot, 162
  letters of confession and, 165, 168–80
  man of letters and, 21, 33
  mechanization and, 155
  Mediterranean style and, 190–93
  method and, 51, 56–60, 68–69, 73–81, 87, 92
  primary industry of, 155–56
  reception in, 174
  synthesis of art and, 224, 226, 229–31, 248, 251
  urbanism studies and, 162
Cheminée, La (Le Corbusier), 296
Chenal, Pierre, 571
Choisy, 319
CIAM (Congrès Internationaux d'Architecture Moderne), 201, 392–93, 401, 404, 478, 497
  Acropolis and, 590
  Algeria and, 577, 579
  Charter of Athens and, 616, 627, 644
  elements of doctrine and, 620–21, 627–29
  Exposition Internationale des Arts et Techniques dans la Vie Moderne and, 533–36, 539–41, 545, 547, 551
  grid of four functions and, 617
  ineffable space and, 684
  minimum house and, 507
  modern techniques and, 507
  synthesis of art and, 677–79
  La Ville Radieuse and, 507–10
Cingria-Valneyre, Alexandre, 83–84, 112, 114, 116, 177, 179
Cité Industrielle, La (Le Corbusier and Garnier), 628
Cité Reconstituée exposition, 212
cities
  cellular units and, 160
  communal strengths and, 160
  condition of, 5
  La Construction des Villes and, 159–68, 175, 193–201, 208–11, 328, 342, 480
  construction of, 155–64
  Contemporary City for Three Million and, 160, 329, 341, 360, 389, 606–7, 628
  curved streets and, 342–43
  "Death of the Street" and, 570–75
  deurbanization and, 517, 540
  Dom-ino scheme and, 209–15
  Exposition of German City-Building and, 97, 101
  garden, 24, 76, 81–82, 92–94, 100–7, 160–68, 197, 199, 342–43, 366, 472, 500, 508, 511, 525, 566, 600, 611, 636
  International Town Planning Exhibition and, 188
  land division and, 201
  language of architecture and, 342–43 (*see also* language of architecture)
  monastery studies and, 160–61
  Obus plans and, 46, 570–75, 579–86, 615
  popularization of art in public domain in, 103–5
  progress and, 182–83
  Regional Plan and, 550, 572, 575–78, 583, 585–86
  Sitte and, 71, 73–76, 80, 121, 156–57, 160–61, 164, 168, 197–206, 203, 319, 330, 716nn5,14
  skyscrapers and, 172, 199, 221, 272, 307, 342, 366, 430, 435, 453–54, 457–58, 461, 464, 466–76, 479, 573, 577, 586, 663
  street layouts and, 201–4, 342–43, 570–75
  town planning and, 24, 33, 76, 188, 208–9, 335, 341, 617, 628, 633, 636, 643, 650, 657, 671
  urbanism and, 71 (*see also* urbanism)
  Urbanisme and, 329, 335–41
  Voisin Plan and, 46, 343–46, 360–61, 372
  See also specific city
Citrohan housing project, 275

Classical aesthetics, 187, 705n78, 706n87, 708n65
  Eastern travels and, 114, 116, 119, 143–44
  language of architecture and, 303, 316, 326, 331
  letters of confession and, 168, 175
  man of letters and, 22, 41
  Mediterranean style and, 585, 591
  method and, 70, 88–92, 107, 262, 272, 285
  poetics and, 406
Cocteau, Jean, 40–41, 227
Colonial Cinema and Imperial France, 1919–39 (Slavin), 554–55
Colonial Harem, The (Alloula), 556
color, 210
  American travels and, 458, 474, 481
  city construction and, 198, 200, 207
  Eastern travels and, 117, 120, 123–24, 128–38, 141–45, 150–52
  geometry and, 166
  Law of Ripolin and, 356–57
  letters of confession and, 166–67, 173–74
  Mediterranean style and, 191–93, 553, 583, 592–93
  method and, 100, 107, 267–68, 281, 286–87, 290–94
  painting and, 221, 231, 233, 239 (*see also* painting)
  poetics and, 417 (*see also* poetics)
  precise language for, 53–54
  secular faith and, 643
  spirit of the thirties and, 544–45, 550
  synthesis of art and, 221, 231, 233, 239, 250
  Werkbund and, 70
Colosseum, 183, 306
"Commentaries on Art and Modern Life" (Le Corbusier), 239
commerce, 98–103
Committee for the Preservation of Old Paris, 344
Commune journal, 538
communists, 401, 533, 538
Concerning Town Planning (Propos d'urbanisme) (Le Corbusier), 33, 628, 636
concrete blocks, 72
Constantinople, 38, 51, 82, 109, 213, 405, 468, 479
  bazaar and, 140–41
  beauty of, 215
  color and, 141–42
  La Construction des Villes and, 198–99
  disappointment with, 135–39
  Eastern travels and, 112–23, 134–43, 152
  language of architecture and, 330, 359
  letters of confession and, 168–72
  New York and, 468, 478
  return to, 173
  spectacles of, 135–43
  women of, 140
  World War I and, 189
Construction des Villes, La (Le Corbusier), 328, 342
  color and, 198
  Constantinople and, 198–99
  constitutive elements of the city and, 200–6
  division of land and, 201
  general considerations and, 199–200
  Germany and, 199
  L'Eplattenier and, 197–201
  letters of confession and, 165–68, 175
  means of implementation and, 207–9
  monument placement and, 206
  neo-syndicalism and, 480
  places and, 204–6
  poetics and, 159–63, 193–201, 208–11
  reworking of, 193–209
  Ritter and, 193–94, 197–99
  Sitte and, 197–206
  streets and, 201–4
  walls of enclosure and, 206–7
  World War I and, 199
Constructions "Murondins", Les ("Murondins" Constructions) (Le Corbusier), 614
constructivism, 384–85
Contamin, 196
"Contemporary City for 3 Million, A" (Le Corbusier), 160, 329, 341, 360, 389, 606–7, 628
Cooperative Village, 550, 615
Corinthian aesthetics, 90, 114, 316
Costa, Oswaldo, 501
Cotereau, Jean Pierre, 581
Couleurs du Maroc, Les (Mauclair), 424
Courbet, 88
Cours d'architecture professé à L'Ecole Polytechnique (Umbdenstock), 295, 401
Couszout, Henri, 346
Création Revue d'Art journal, 44–45, 370
Croisade: ou le Crépuscule des Académies (Crusade: or the Twilight of the Academies) (Le Corbusier), 401, 404–13
cubism, 192, 538, 629
  Après le Cubisme and, 44, 236, 241–47, 250–54, 261–98
  letters of confession and, 174, 177, 179
  method and, 262, 286
  poetics and, 430
  synthesis of art and, 227, 236, 241, 244–47, 250, 254
Cupido 80 camera, 122
Czeda, Janko, 222, 230, 253

Dadaism, 268

Daguerre, 192
Dalcroze, Émile Jaques, 35, 81, 84, 88, 90, 102, 107, 164, 707n27, 719n122
Dandieu, Arnaud, 489
D'Annunzio, Gabriel, 178
Danube, 113, 116–17, 123–31, 172, 213, 353, 494, 610
Darwinism, 335–36, 346
Daudet, Léon, 194
D'Autrefois (Ritter), 184, 186
"Death of the Street" (Le Corbusier), 570–75
Debat, F., 466
Decline of the West, The (Spengler), 459
"Défense de l'architecture" (Le Corbusier), 392–99
"Défense des métiers de main, La" ("Defense of handcrafts") (Umbdenstock), 404
Deiningers, 57
Delage Grand-Sport automobile, 313
Delft School of Design, 7
Derain, André, 270, 406
Dermée, Paul, 41, 44, 250, 268–70, 273, 277, 363
Desalle, Hugues, 26–27
Descartes, René, 52, 319
desert travels, 422–25
"Destin de la peinture" ("Destiny of Painting") (Le Corbusier), 538–39
Destin de Paris (Destiny of Paris) (Le Corbusier), 614, 618, 627
"Destinée de la Peinture" (Jeanneret and Ozenfant), 290–92
Deutsche Kunst journal, 74
Deutsche Werkstätte für Handwerkskunst, 102
Diaghilev, 41, 352
Dictionnaire raisonné de l'architecture français du XIe au XVe siècle, 63
Diogenes, 386, 391, 395, 602
Doge's Palace, 53, 55, 390
Dom-ino scheme, 21, 159, 190, 234, 717n67
  cement and, 210–11
  construction and, 193–94, 199
  development of, 209–15
  Du Bois and, 210–15
  Foville and, 209–10
  Musée Sociale and, 209–10
  Ozenfant and, 213–14
  Ritter and, 211–13
Doric aesthetics, 89–90, 107, 114, 316, 320, 386, 585, 590
Doué-La-Fontaine, 237–38
Dreaming the Rational City (Boyer), 5
Dresden, 56, 59–60
Dreyfus, Alfred, 24
Droz, Numa, 79–80, 83
Dubois, Georges, 115
Du Bois, Max, 158, 173–74, 188–89, 193, 210–15, 240, 721n229
Du Cerceau, Androuet, 519
Duhamel, G., 466
Durafour, Louis, 422, 578
Dutert, 196

E42 Exposition, 603
Eastern travels, 191
  Acropolis and, 145–52 (*see also* Acropolis)
  Adrianopolis and, 132
  architecture as organism and, 383–84
  Bibi-la-Douleur and, 171
  Budapest and, 130–31
  color and, 117, 120, 123–24, 128–38, 141–45, 150–52
  comparison to American travels, 436–37
  Constantinople and, 135–43, 173
  La Construction des Villes and, 198–99
  exotic sights of, 132–33
  food of, 133
  Golden Horn and, 116, 134–36, 139
  language of flowers and, 128–29
  learning narrative for, 119–22
  letters of confession and, 165–84
  letters to Ritter and, 116–19, 121, 123, 129, 131, 149, 153–55
  Loti and, 121, 124, 134–40, 142, 145
  Mount Athos and, 145–51, 173, 181, 184, 211
  music of, 133–34
  photography and, 122–24
  plans for, 115–19
  pure forms and, 166–67
  railroads and, 130
  return to La Chaux-de-Fonds, 153–54
  Sirocco and, 173
  travel writing on, 124–52
  Tûnovo and, 131–32
  Turkey and, 131–45
  urbanism and, 157
  Western civilization and, 172–73
  See also Mediterranean
École d'Art, 210, 711n128
  city construction and, 157–58
  letters of confession and, 168–69
  method and, 51–52, 68–69, 75
  war and, 184–85
École des Beaux-Arts, 465
  language of architecture and, 318
  method and, 295
  poetics and, 401, 404, 406, 409
  secular faith and, 609–10
  spirit of the thirties and, 535
École Polytechnique, 59–60, 295, 406, 535, 581, 590, 593
Edmond de Pury (Ritter), 177–78, 184
education
  American travels and, 433–85 (*see also*

American travels)
apprenticeship programs and, 52, 62, 93, 98–99, 106, 195, 429, 483, 558, 560, 612
art in the service of commerce and, 98–103
avant-garde and, 242–47
Behrens and, 70–71, 76–77, 80–91, 95–101, 106, 112, 116, 156, 163–64, 168, 179, 185, 214, 259, 707n39, 710n105
"burn what you have loved, and love what you have burned" motto and, 60, 66
Cartesian logic and, 22, 37, 47, 62, 319, 465, 607, 657
Cingria-Valneyre and, 83–84, 114, 116, 177, 179
color and, 117, 123–24
Constantinople and, 38, 51, 82, 109, 112–23, 134–43, 152, 168–72, 198, 215, 405, 468, 478–79
Cours Supérieur and, 69
Dalcroze and, 35, 81, 84, 88, 90, 102, 107, 164, 707n27, 719n122
of desire, 439–49
Eastern travels and, 191 (*see also* Eastern travels)
École d'Art and, 51, 68–69, 75, 157–58, 168–69, 184–85, 210, 711n128
French reforms in, 175
German sojourn and, 69–107
higher goals and, 248–53
learning to see and, 122–24
learning to write and, 119–22
letters of confession and, 165–74
Magne and, 65–66
mathematics and, 63 (*see also* mathematics)
museums and, 53, 60, 68, 71, 74, 96, 100, 161, 291, 350–51, 354, 393, 483, 485, 543, 681
Paris sojourn and, 62–69
self-invention and, 111–13
Sitte and, 71, 73–76, 80, 121, 156–57, 160–61, 164, 168, 197–206, 319, 330, 716nn5,14
solitude and, 63
urbanism and, 156–64 (*see also* urbanism)
use of lists and, 62–63
Viollet-le-Duc and, 63–64
Werkbund and, 29, 70, 76, 81, 92, 96, 98, 102–7, 156, 161, 176, 185–88, 224, 719n117
Eiffel Tower, 358, 411, 630
Eleftheriades, Eístratios (Tériade), 594
El Greco, 116–17, 123, 270
Éluard, Paul, 683
Emery, Pierre-André, 558
Emmanuel, Victor, 316
"En Alger, Des Logis Radieus" ("In Algiers, Radiant Housing") (Le Corbusier), 583
Entretiens de la Ville du Rouet, Les: essais dialogues sur les arts plastiques en Suisse romande (Cingria-Valneyre), 83–84, 114
equilibrium, 37–40, 272, 303, 714n62
American travels and, 435, 461, 469, 476, 480
city construction and, 155, 200, 207
Eastern travels and, 142
language of architecture and, 322, 331–33, 346, 351, 356
letters of confession and, 166, 177–78, 182
Mediterranean style and, 578, 589–93
poetics and, 381, 399, 403, 416, 428, 431
secular faith and, 636, 639, 667
spirit of the thirties and, 492, 507, 514, 534, 547
Erechtheum, 319
Erlwein, 104
Étoile, 345
Étude sur la construction des villes (Study of the Construction of Cities) (Le Corbusier), 480
city construction and, 159–64, 193–201, 208–9
Dom-ino scheme and, 209–11
language of architecture and, 328–29, 342
letters of confession and, 165–68, 172, 175
method and, 69, 71
Étude sur le mouvement d'art décoratif en Allemagne (Study of the Movement of the Decorative Arts in Germany) (Le Corbusier), 240, 278
city construction and, 157–60, 195
Eastern travels and, 112, 115, 120–21
letters of confession and, 166, 169, 171, 176
method and, 69, 71, 87, 91–95, 106
Étude sur l'urbanisation (Le Corbusier), 120–21, 158–59
Eucharist, 440
Eupalinos (Valéry), 264–65, 363–64, 725n11
Eurhythmic Society, 102–3
"Exposition de la Cité Reconstituée", 43–44
Exposition d'Urbanisme et d'Architecture, 576–78
Exposition Internationale de l'Esprit Nouveau, 276
Exposition Internationale des Arts Décoratifs, 240, 346, 350, 360–61, 419
Exposition Internationale des Arts et Techniques dans la Vie Moderne, 435
CIAM and, 533–36, 539–41, 545, 547, 551
Communist Party and, 533
Nazis and, 533
Palais de la Solidarité and, 532–34
photomurals and, 544–51
Popular Front and, 532–33, 538–39, 545

regionalism and, 543–44
symbolic importance of, 532
temps nouveaux and, 535–38, 542–48, 585
Unité d'Habitation and, 533–35, 542–43, 548
La Ville Radieuse and, 535–43, 548–50
Exposition of Germany City-Building, 97, 101
Exposition Universelle, 196
"Eyes which do not See" (Le Corbusier), 25

Faure, Élie, 626
Festival Hall, 84
Feu, Le (D'Annunzio), 178
Feuille d'Avis de La Chaux-de-Fonds, La (periodical), 110, 113, 115, 119, 181
F (folklore) designation, 22, 152
Fiat factory, 273, 275
Figaro, Le (newspaper), 28, 400, 403, 424, 622, 677
Fiorini, Guido, 599–601
"First Steps in a Dwelling" (Le Corbusier), 190
Fischer, Theodor, 72, 75, 101–2, 104, 161–62, 185
Flaherty, Alice, 708n65
Florence, 52–56, 160, 170, 202, 205–6
Fondation Le Corbusier, 6
Food for Thought (Marin), 440
Foreign Legion, 554
"Formation de L'Optique Moderne" (Jeanneret and Ozenfant), 292–94
Fort l'Empereur, 572–79, 587
Fosca, François, 28, 433–36
Foucault, Michel, 626
Foville, Alfred de, 209–10
France, 87
armistice with Germany and, 246
Art Nouveau and, 88
Bibliothèque Nationale and, 159, 194, 196, 208, 225, 328
boredom of wartime Paris and, 221–25
cultural war with Germany and, 91–95, 112
economic depression and, 489–90
educational reforms and, 175
Hommage à la République and, 75, 79
Latin movement and, 57–58
mission civilatrice (civilizing mission) and, 554–56
negrophilia and, 449–54
Paris sojourn and, 58–69
la patrie and, 404–6, 499
politics of denial and, 554–58
Popular Front and, 532–33, 538–39, 545, 584, 613–14, 618
Renaissance of, 386
riots in, 491, 498
spirit of the thirties and, 489–502
technology of empire and, 559–60
Vichy Regime and, 555, 586, 612–18, 630, 634, 664
France ou Allemagne (France or Germany) (Le Corbusier), 159, 194–95, 208–9, 213–14, 229
Frauenkirche, 205
Freud, Sigmund, 605–6

Galerie des Machines, 196
Galerie Druet, 250–52, 297
Galerie Grégoire, 235–36
Galerie Thomas, 296
Gallis, Yvonne, 33, 745n1
Ganivet, Pierre, 491
Gare d'Orsay, 406
Garnier, Tony, 188, 628
Garnissonkirche, 72
Gartenstadt-Hellerau, 102
Geddes, Norman Bel, 5
Geddes, Patrick, 208
geometry, 86, 131, 138, 468, 609, 660, 663
antithesis with nature and, 330–35
construction and, 203, 206
control and, 379–80
geometric form and, 39, 64, 70, 86, 128, 227, 264, 405, 593, 596
golden section and, 396–97
implacable order of, 383–84
language of architecture and, 306–8, 316–17, 322, 330–32, 336, 341–42, 354, 359, 363–69, 373
letters of confession and, 166–67, 175
Mediterranean style and, 567, 582, 596–97, 603
method and, 264, 266, 283, 285, 287, 290–95, 298
poetics and, 379, 383–87, 398, 414–16, 428
spirit of the thirties and, 516
George Washington Bridge, 461, 474
German modernity, 59, 92, 500
German movement, 57–58, 69
German Museum of Commercial and Industrial Art, 96–98
Germany
AEG and, 76, 92, 95, 99, 106–7, 156
apprentices and, 93, 98–99, 106, 195, 710n120
armistice with, 246
art in the service of commerce and, 98–103
balance between art and machines, 155–56
Behrens and, 70–71, 76–77, 80–91, 95–101, 106, 112, 116, 156, 163–64, 168, 179, 185, 214, 259, 707n39, 710n105
La Construction des Villes and, 199
cooperative spirit amongst artists in,

98–103
cultural war with France and, 91–95, 112
the Dome and, 94
economic progress of, 88, 94
education reform in, 106–7
Exposition of German City-Building and, 97, 101
first impressions of Munich and, 72–73
food quality of, 72
Garnissonkirche and, 72
graphic design and, 29–30
Hagen and, 83, 85, 102
Hellerau and, 81, 84, 90, 98, 102–3, 107, 160, 164
Historical Museum and, 74
importance of education in, 69–71
industrial arts and, 96–98
industrial cities of, 126
Jeanneret's sojourn in, 69–107
Klipstein and, 78–79
language of, 164
L'Eplattenier letters and, 69–92
modernity of, 59
Monument of Guillaume and, 94
Muthesius and, 77, 101–2
Nazis and, 409, 494, 497, 533, 586, 610, 613–14, 617, 675, 683
Neu-Babelsberg and, 82, 84–85, 163
painting and, 94
patriotism of, 88
popularization of art in public domain in, 103–5
protectionism and, 75
Reichstag and, 94
secessionist, 89
Sitte and, 71, 73–76, 80, 121, 156–57, 160–61, 164, 168, 197–206, 203, 319, 330, 716nn5,14
technology of, 76–77
Turbine Hall and, 77, 99
universal style and, 95
urbanism and, 69–72, 76–77, 92, 112, 156–57 (*see also* urbanism)
utilitarian arts and, 88
Victory Column and, 94
Wagner and, 57
Werkbund and, 29, 70, 76, 81, 92, 96, 98, 102–7, 156, 161, 176, 185–88, 224, 719n117
Ghyka, Matila, 416–17, 592
Gide, André, 683
Giedion, Sigfried, 35, 392, 616, 678
Gilman, Larry Clifford, 7
Giorini, Guido, 599
Giotto, 54
Giraudoux, Jean, 613
Gobineau, Arthur de, 87
Golden Horn, 116, 134–36, 139
golden section, 396–97
Gothas airplane, 229
Gothic style, 187
city construction and, 174
Eastern travels and, 114
method and, 60–61, 65–66, 73, 107
poetics and, 405–6, 416
spirit of the thirties and, 507, 509, 519
synthesis of art and, 222–23
Goujon, Jean, 386
Grand Palais, 406
Grand Revue journal, 211
Grands Travaux, 555
Grand Tour, 109–12
Grasset, Eugène, 66, 104, 185
Great Depression, 435, 478–79, 613, 633
Greece
Athens, 21, 38, 109, 112–13, 118, 145, 148–52, 181, 239, 359, 384, 404, 413, 421, 468, 547, 579, 590–91, 597–98, 616–17, 627, 644, 684
Parthenon and, 70, 89, 109 (*see also* Parthenon)
temps nouveaux and, 590–93
Théophilos and, 594–95
Green Mosque, 318
Gris, 270
Group of Six, 272, 491

Hadrian's Villa, 306
Hagen, 83, 85, 102
Halles Centrales, 196
Harris, Marguerite Tjader, 435
hashish, 123
Haussmann, 341, 344–45, 358, 378, 451
Hellerau, 81, 84, 90, 98, 102–3, 107, 160, 164
Hénard, Eugene, 208
Hennebique, François, 227
Hermès, 281
Hispano-Suiza sports car, 227
Hitler, Adolf, 409, 494, 497, 586, 610, 613–14, 675, 683
Hoffman, Joseph, 96
Hoffman, Ludwig, 104
Hoffmann-Darmstadt, Suzanne, 104
Holland Tunnel, 474
Hotel-de-Ville, 104
houses
Almanach d'Architecture Moderne and, 357, 361–69
as boxes, 334–35
Breton, 368–69
built to measure, 323
folklore and, 420–22
language of architecture and, 300–15, 319, 322–27, 330–35, 338, 341–44, 351–57,

361–69, 372
as machines, 25, 30, 39, 300–1, 303, 309–10, 377, 379–84, 387–89, 393–95, 405, 415–16
as plants, 380–83
revolution and, 322–26
Une Maison–Une Palais and, 377–99
Vers une Architecture manual and, 302–15
humanism, 160, 366, 413, 490–91, 619
Humber automobile, 313

I (industry) designation, 22, 152
impressionism, 54, 86–87, 244, 254, 268, 289, 588
ineffable space, 414, 427–31, 681, 684–86
Ingres, Jean, 243, 270, 272, 474
Innovation, 281
instantaneous visualization, 396
intellectualism
elitism and, 276–81
German/French cultural wars and, 91–95, 112
L'Esprit Nouveau and, 276–81
man of letters and, 20–21, 24–29
Paris literary scene and, 40–43
postwar environment and, 43–44
Purism and, 276–81 (*see also* Purism)
interior design, 77, 100, 177, 185, 191, 195, 226
International Town Planning Exhibition, 188
Invalides, the, 345
Ioannides, Héracles, 594
Ionian aesthetics, 90, 114, 296
Iribe, Paul, 40
Italian Renaissance, 66
Italy
Bargello and, 55
Brunelleschi's dome and, 56
Doge's Palace and, 53, 55
Florence, 54–56
Grand Tour and, 109
L'Eplattenier letters and, 51–56
Palazzo Vecchio and, 55
Piazza del Duomo and, 53–54
Saint Mark's Square and, 55
Venice, 55

Jansen, Hermann, 77
jazz, 246, 248, 272, 351, 449–54, 458, 468, 738n13
Jeanneret, Albert, 59, 81, 84, 252, 275, 284, 452
Jeanneret, Charles-Édouard
"burn what you have loved, and love what you have burned" motto and, 60, 66
Cartesian logic and, 52
commerce studies of, 98–103
Constantinople and, 38, 51, 82, 109, 112–23, 134–43, 152, 168–72, 198, 215, 405, 468, 478–79
Dom-ino scheme and, 21, 159, 190, 193–94, 199, 208–13, 234, 717n67
Eastern travels of, 6, 110–52
education and, 58–60 (*see also* education)
German/French cultural wars and, 91–96, 112
German industrial arts and, 96–98
German sojourn (1910–11) of, 69–91
higher goals of, 248–53
invention and, 111–13
Italian travels (1907) of, 51–56
learning to see and, 122–24
learning to write and, 119–22
L'Esprit Nouveau and, 253
letters of confession and, 165–84
master teacher appointment of, 118
meets Ozenfant, 111
modeling methods and, 54–56, 64, 92
moves to Paris, 220
museums and, 53, 60, 68, 71, 74, 96, 100, 161, 291, 350–51, 354, 393, 483, 485, 543, 681
new artistic directions and, 253–59
Nouvelle Section and, 184–85
painting and, 235–42 (*see also* painting)
Paris sojourn (1908–9) of, 58–59, 62–69
photography and, 122–24
popularization of arts in the public domain and, 103–5
precision and, 155–56
pseudonyms of, 34–36, 272, 329
Purism and, 262–98
real estate speculation and, 98–103
reversed Grand Tour of, 109–12
urbanism and, 155–64 (*see also* Urbanism)
Vienna sojourn (1907–8) of, 56–61
voyage of discovery of, 111–13
See also Le Corbusier
Jeanneret, Pierre, 563, 650, 704n53
method and, 275
poetics and, 377–78, 388–91
secular faith and, 612, 614
spirit of the thirties and, 507, 539
Jeanneret, Yvonne, 564
Jeanneret-Perret, Édouard, 155
Jencks, Charles, 52, 55
Jourdain, Francis, 66, 180–81
Journal Général Travaux Publics et Bâtiments, 561
Joyless Street, The (film), 537
Jura style, 84

Kabyles, 559, 563, 584, 587
Karlsruhe, 72, 320
Keaton, Buster, 457
Klipstein, August, 78–79, 113, 116–18, 123, 126, 130, 143

Kostrowitsky, Guillaume de (Apollinaire), 41–44, 46, 235–36, 246, 254, 265, 268, 298
Kraus, Karl, 347, 433
Kropotkin, 403

Labbé, Edmond, 535, 542
L'Abeille magazine, 161
Lagardelle, Hubert, 491
L'Almanach helvétique periodical, 177
Lalo, Charles, 284
Lamour, Philippe, 489–93
"L'Angle Droit" (Jeanneret and Ozenfant), 287–89
language of architecture, 6, 44, 124, 166, 187, 296, 685
- Acropolis and, 307, 319–22, 366
- aesthetics and, 303–4, 308, 326, 363, 366–69, 372
- airplanes and, 304–5, 309–12, 325–26, 345
- *Almanach d'Architecture Moderne* and, 357–70
- American engineers and, 306
- aphoristic style for, 299
- architecture of language and, 36–40, 300, 370
- automobiles and, 302, 309, 313–14, 326–27, 336
- Cartesian tropes and, 319
- center of gravity and, 319
- constructing a manual for housing and, 302–15
- decoration and, 305, 315, 318, 351–56, 362
- equilibrium and, 303, 322, 331–33, 346, 351, 356
- feminization and, 305, 346–57, 350
- houses and, 300–15, 319, 322–27, 330–35, 338, 341–44, 351–57, 361–69, 372
- *L'Art Décoratif d'aujord-hui* and, 346–57
- Law of Ripolin and, 356–57
- *L'Esprit Nouveau* and, 299–302, 309, 320, 323, 329, 347–48, 357–63, 373, 394
- Loos and, 301, 315–16, 323, 326, 347–56
- machines and, 300–4, 309–11, 314–15, 322, 325–26, 328, 332, 335–40, 343, 347–54, 358–72
- mass and, 306
- mathematics and, 302–8, 316–17, 321–22, 330–32, 336, 341–42, 354–55, 358–59, 363–69, 373
- Ozenfant and, 300, 302, 347, 357–59, 363, 370–71
- Parthenon and, 305–6, 313–15, 319–21, 326–27, 354, 367
- the Plan and, 307–8
- poetics and, 392–93, 399, 414–17
- Poincaré and, 303–6, 332, 337–38
- Purism and, 302, 329, 336, 341, 358–59, 371–72
- Rome and, 315–19, 330–31, 358, 366, 372
- Sitte and, 319, 330
- steamships and, 309–11, 326, 358, 362
- surface and, 306–7
- *Urbanisme* and, 328–46
- Valéry and, 300, 363
- *Vers une Architecture* and, 393
- Voisin Plan and, 343–46, 360–61, 372

"L'Architecture et le style moderne" (Loos), 183–84
L'architecture va-t-elle mourir? (Is Architecture going to die?) (Mauclair), 28–29, 400–1, 622
"L'Art Boche" ("German Art") (Daudet), 194
L'Art de Bâtir les villes (The Art of Building Cities) (Martin), 156
L'Art Decorative d'aujourd'hui (The Decorative Arts of Today) (Le Corbusier), 26, 275, 683
- folk culture and, 351–54
- "Iconology, Iconolaters and Iconoclasts" and, 348–51
- language of architecture and, 346–57
- Law of Ripolin and, 356–57
- Loos and, 347–56
- machines and, 347–54
- neo-syndicalism and, 480
- Purism and, 348–49
- revolution and, 348–57

L'Art de France journal, 171, 185
L'Atelier Ozenfant, 275
l'Ateliers Lipchitz and Mietschaninoff, 275–76
L'Atheneum (Valéry), 264
Latin movement, 57–58
Latin spirit, 596–604
Latournerie, Robert, 615
Laugier, Marc-Antoine, 203, 334
Laurel and Hardy, 457
Laurens, Henri, 419, 547
law of life, 23–24, 83
Law of Ripolin, 356–57
law of the meander, 665–67
League of Nations, 377–78, 388, 391–93, 400, 409, 496, 741n4
Le Corbu, 29, 34, 36
Le Corbusier
- Algeria and, 553–88
- *Après le Cubisme* and, 44, 236, 241–47, 250–54, 261–98
- bibliography of, 33–36
- commerce studies of, 98–103
- condition of cities and, 5
- confessional writing style of, 52
- death of, 23, 110
- destiny of, 24
- education reforms and, 106–7
- five points of architecture and, 37–39, 276,

328, 360, 366, 371, 388, 402, 430, 704n53
French identity card of, 20
German sojourn (1910–11) of, 69–91
as graphic designer, 29–33
ineffable space and, 414, 427–31, 681, 684
Italy travels of, 51–56
language of architecture and, 36–40, 299–373 (*see also* language of architecture)
lecturing style of, 30–31
as le père, 22
literary creativity of, 5, 19–24
literary milieu of Paris and, 40–43
as man of letters (*homme de lettres*), 20–21, 24–29, 40
meaning of name, 29, 34–35
mechanistic style of, 25
as naturalized citizen, 20
painting and, 33 (*see also* painting)
Paris sojourn (1908–9) of, 62–69
politics of, 612–16
popularization of art in public domain and, 103–5
raven-archer symbolism and, 34–35
real estate studies of, 98–103
reasons for name, 5
as romanticist, 22
secular faith of, 605–75 (*see also* secular faith)
spirit of the thirties and, 490–502
as student of history, 22–23
town planning and, 24, 33, 76, 188, 208–9, 335, 341, 617, 628, 633, 636, 643, 650, 657, 671
as traitor, 28
use of lists by, 62–63
Le Corbusier, une encyclopédie, 34
Le Corbusier: An Annotated Bibliography (Brady), 34
Le Corbusier's Formative Years (Brooks), 111
Le Corbusier: The Creative Search (Baker), 119
Lefebvre, Raymond, 44
Lefèvre, Camille, 377–78
Le Fresnaye, 270
Léger, Fernand, 179–88, 270, 419, 458, 466, 592, 677–78
L'Élan journal, 40–41, 213, 227, 237, 242, 261, 705n69
Lenin, 403
L'Entêtement Slovaque (Slavic Infatuation) (Ritter), 116, 162
L'Eplattenier, Charles, 6–7
boredom of wartime Paris and, 222, 224
La Construction des Villes and, 197–201
criticism of, 66–68, 85
Eastern travels and, 135
German sojourn and, 69–92, 112
Hommage à la République and, 75, 79
Italian travels and, 51–56
knowledge of form and, 57
letters of confession and, 165–66, 168, 170, 181
as mentor, 51–53
Nouvelle Section and, 185
Paris sojourn and, 62–69
rejection of Gothic and, 114
Sitte and, 198
urbanism and, 155–58, 161–64
Vienna sojourn and, 56–61
L'Eplattenier, Madame, 140
"L'Esprit Nouveau and Architecture" (Le Corbusier), 373
"L'Esprit nouveau et les poètes" ("The New Spirit and the Poets") (Apollinaire), 42
L'Esprit Nouveau magazine, 160, 401, 452, 480, 607
"Aesthetics and Purism" and, 286–87
airplanes and, 656
Almanach d'architecture moderne and, 271, 357–60
anonymous editorials of, 272–73
basic philosophy of, 271
context and, 295–96
criticism of, 295–96
Dermée and, 268–70, 273, 277
"Destinée de la Peinture" and, 290–92
dry rationalism of, 282
Editions de L'Esprit Nouveau, 269
financial backing of, 281–83
"Formation de L'Optique Moderne" and, 292–94
imagery in, 281–84
"L'Angle Droit" and, 287–89
language of architecture and, 299–302, 309, 320, 323, 329, 347–48, 357–63, 373, 394
machines and, 272–73, 277, 280–83, 286, 290–94, 298
man of letters and, 28, 34, 38, 44–45
maturing essays in, 299
method and, 262, 265, 268–86, 295–98
modern science and, 278–81
"Nature et Création" and, 289–90
neo-syndicalism and, 480
opening declaration of, 270–71
organizational elite and, 599
photography and, 283
poetics and, 607
Purism and, 265, 268–97
synthesis of art and, 252–57
three periods of, 272–75
uniqueness of, 271–72
use of pseudonyms in, 272
World War I and, 272

L'Esprit Nouveau Pavillion, 38, 160, 241, 271, 276, 359–62, 399–400
lesson of the gondola, 425–26
L'Esthetique des Proportions dans la Nature et dans les Arts (The Aesthetics of Proportions in Nature and in the Arts) (Ghyka), 416–17
"L'Ésthetique des villes" ("Aesthetics of Cities") (L'Eplattenier), 156
letters of confession
attraction of Mediterranean and, 174–75
depression and, 165–70, 173–74
Du Bois and, 173–74
education and, 165–74, 181
garden cities and, 167–68
good of others and, 169–70
horizons against nose and, 168
interior design and, 184–85
L'Eplattenier and, 165–66, 168, 170, 181
marriage and, 178–79
mathematics and, 167
modernity and, 170–71
parents and, 175–76
Ritter and, 165–81
"Letter to Friends" (Le Corbusier), 126–28
L'Exposition de la Cité Moderne (Exposition of the Modern City), 585
L'homme Réel: Revue du syndicalisme et de l'humanisme journal, 491
L'humour de New-York (Cazamian), 466
"Ligne Générale, La" ("The General Line") editorial, 491–93
Lipschitz, 270
Livre d'amour (Vildrac), 178–79
L'Oeuvre group, 176
L'Oeuvre magazine, 181
Looking at City Planning (Manière de penser l'urbanisme) (Le Corbusier), 33, 628
Loos, Adolf, 179–84, 198
language of architecture and, 301, 315–16, 323, 326, 347–56
proper attire and, 456
Lopez, Camille, 570, 575
Loti, Pierre, 121, 124, 134–40, 142, 145, 181
Louis XIII, 362
Louis XIV, 334, 340, 378, 604
Louis XV, 517, 548
Louis XVI, 548
L'Urbanisme des Trois Établissements Humains (Le Corbusier), 33, 618, 627, 636
"L'Urbanisme et le Lyrisme des Temps Nouveaux" ("Urbanism and the Poetry of the New Times"(Le Corbusier), 606–7
Lyautey, Marshal Hubert, 564, 566–67
"Lyrisme des objets naturels, Le" ("The Lyricism of Natural Objects") (Le Corbusier), 419–20

machines, 233
airplanes and, 645–75
Almanach d'Architecture Moderne and, 414–15
assembly-line production and, 156
books as, 30, 300–1
built biology and, 636–45
chairs as, 314–15
La Chaux-de-Fonds and, 155
craftsmanship and, 155–56
eclipse of humans by, 76–77
folklores and, 420–22
Great Depression and, 435
higher goals for, 248–53
houses as, 25, 30, 39, 300–1, 303, 309–10, 377, 379–84, 387–89, 393–95, 405, 415–16
language of architecture and, 300–4, 309–11, 314–15, 322, 325–26, 328, 332, 335–40, 343, 347–54, 358–72
L'Esprit Nouveau and, 272–73, 277, 280–83, 286, 290–94, 298
for living, 39
materials that speak and, 420–22
painting and, 300
photography and, 283
poetics of, 21, 413–31
Poincaré and, 303–6
Purism and, 261–62, 265–67, 272–73, 277, 280–83, 286, 290–94, 298
secular faith and, 620–21, 624, 628–39, 647, 651, 658, 660–61, 668–74
sense of order from, 310
spirit of the thirties and, 490–94, 498–502
temps nouveaux and, 426–27, 439, 462, 484, 490, 502 *(see also* temps nouveaux)
Une Maison–Une Palais and, 377, 379–84, 387–89, 393–95
verb and, 414–17
worship of, 433
Magne, Lucien, 65–66
Magnelli, 600–1
maître d'école (master teacher), 118
Maison de la Culture, 538–39
Maison des hommes, La (The House of Man) (Le Corbusier and Pierrefeu), 33, 615, 618, 640, 643, 682
"Maison Individuelle, La" ("The Individual House") (Le Corbusier), 422
Maisonseul, Jean de, 558
Mallarmé, Stéphane, 680
Manet, 88
"man from the Jura in Paris, a", 225–34
Manière de penser l'urbanisme (Le Corbusier), 618
man of letters (homme de lettres), 20–21, 24–29
March of Times, The (journal), 541
Marin, Louis, 440

Martin, Camille, 156, 161, 204
Martin, Gaston, 577–78
mathematics, 175, 232, 630, 737n1
American travels and, 443, 454, 457
animating law of nature and, 517–19
geometric form and, 39, 64, 70, 86, 128, 227, 264, 405, 593, 596 (*see also* geometry)
language of architecture and, 302–8, 316–17, 321–22, 330–32, 336, 341–42, 354–59, 363–69, 373
man of letters and, 35–37, 45
Mediterranean style and, 562, 567, 582, 591–94, 598
method and, 58, 62–63, 66, 263–67, 285–87, 294–98
Paris sojourn and, 62
poetics and, 379, 391, 394, 406–7, 414–17, 427–31
Poincaré and, 167, 303–6, 332, 337–38
Purism and, 262–67, 285–87, 294–98
spirit of the thirties and, 505, 516–18, 537
thrill of, 63
Matthey, Octave, 72–73, 78–80, 82, 85–86, 170
Mauclair, Camille, 28, 400–4, 424, 556, 591, 622
Mauss, Marcel, 483
Mawson, Theodore, 208
Maxence, Jean-Pierre, 489
McLeod, Mary, 5
Mediterranean, 568
Algeria and, 554 (*see also* Algeria)
Fez and, 567
folklore of, 564
food and, 568–69
geography lessons from, 588–603
imaginary aspect of, 588
inspiration of, 553, 588
Latin West and, 596–604
Medina and, 567
Morocco and, 117, 173, 424, 470, 554, 563–66, 585
neoclassical forms and, 561
Oasis of Laghouat and, 567–68
Pontinia and, 600–1
racial civilization in, 589
Rome and, 596–97 (*see also* Rome)
spirit of Greece and, 590–96
style of, 561, 585
union myth of, 566, 581
white blind spot and, 553
Mediterranean Federation, 555
Mercier, Ernest, 575
Mercure de France journal, 237, 245, 255
Meruon, Louis de, 193
Messel, 89
Metziner, 180
Meyer, 231
Michelangelo, 192, 225, 251, 317, 319
Mikiphone, 370
Milioutin, 540
minimalism, 181
Mise au Point (Bringing into Focus) (Le Corbusier), 23
modernity, 170, 510
constructive spirit of, 261–62
crisis in, 316
discontinuity and, 459
equipment of a house and, 275
French, 346, 350, 402
German, 59, 92, 500
icons of, 127
Le Corbusier's narrative and, 24–25
man of letters and, 20–21, 24–29
Mediterranean, 585
sense of impending death and, 458
tradition and, 183–84
Modulor, Le journal, 160, 266
monasteries, 54, 147, 160–61, 197
Monet, 225, 359
Montmollin, Jean Pierre de, 238
Monument of Guillaume, 94
Moos, Stanislaus von, 5
Morand, Paul, 466
Morris, William, 99
Mörsch, E., 173–74
Mot, Le journal, 40
Mounier, Emmanuel, 489
Mount Athos, 145–51, 173, 181, 184, 211
Mount Olympus, 149
mouvement d'art à La Chaux-de-Fonds, à propos de la Nouvelle Section de l'École d'art, Un (Le Corbusier), 184–85
Mukhina, Vera, 533
"Mundaneum" (Teige), 392–93, 396–98
Musée des Arts Décoratifs, 483
Musée d'Ethnographie, 483
Musée National des Beaux-Arts d'Alger, 558
Musée Sociale, 208–10
Museum of Art in Commerce and Industry, 96
Museum of Decorative Arts, 60, 291
Museum of Modern Art (MoMA), 435
Mussolini, 492, 598, 600, 613
Muthesius, Hermann, 77, 101–2
M'Zab, 422–25, 563, 578

Napoleon I, 89, 168, 225
Napoleon III, 204, 534
"Nature et Création" (Jeanneret and Ozenfant), 289–90
Nazis, 409, 494, 497, 533, 586, 610, 613–14, 617, 675, 683
negrophilia, 449–54
Nénot, Henri-Paul, 377–78, 394
neoclassical aesthetics, 180, 194, 533, 561,

590–92, 599
neo-syndicalism
American travels and, 465, 479–85
Mediterranean style and, 553, 555, 558, 564, 588, 590, 596
secular faith and, 612, 659–60
spirit of the thirties and, 494–502, 528
Nesvald, 606, 608
Neu-Babelsberg, 82, 84–85, 163
"Neue Sachlichkeit" ("New Objectivity"), 392–96, 398, 413
New World of Space, The (Le Corbusier), 684
New York, 478
as catastrophe, 469–77
Cathedrals and, 427–33, 466–68
Central Park, 474
Grand Central and, 473
great waste in, 427–34
inferiority complexes of, 476–77
love of, 466–68
Manhattan and, 470–77
Purism and, 471
New York (Morand), 466
New York flamboie (Renand), 466
New York: images mouvantes (Debat), 466
Nord-Sud journal, 41
Notre Dame, 60, 205, 345, 391
N.R.F. (La Nouvelle Revue Français) magazine, 255

obelisks, 79–80, 143, 573, 597
Obus plans, 46, 570–75, 579–86, 615
Oeuvre Complète (Le Corbusier), 22, 26, 29, 34, 111, 392, 400, 437, 601, 680, 682–85
Olbrich, 89
Olivetti Corporation, 600
Omega, 281
Omnia magazine, 227
Orcagna, 54
Orient. *See* Eastern travels
Orientalism (Said), 122
Orient Express, 129
Or'mo, 281
"Ornament and Crime" (Loos), 183, 347
Osthaus, Karl Ernst, 115, 161–62, 185
Ottoman Empire, 111
Ozenfant, Amédée, 6, 34, 41
Après le Cubisme and, 44, 236, 241–47, 250–54, 261–98
artistic compass of, 256
avant-garde and, 242–45
Ballets Russes and, 227
cubism and, 262
Dermée and, 250
Dom-ino scheme and, 213–14
L'Élan journal and, 40–41, 213, 227, 237, 242, 261, 705n69
Galerie Grégoire and, 235–36
Jeanneret's meeting of, 111, 227, 229
language of architecture and, 300, 302, 347, 357–59, 363, 370–71
L'Esprit Nouveau and, 253
as mentor, 175
painting and, 235–42, 300, 431
pseudonyms of, 272
Purism and, 220, 261–98
steel discipline of, 233
World War I and, 233, 261

Pabst, G. W., 537
painting, 22, 33–35, 117, 123, 211, 476, 538, 545, 594, 602, 677, 680–84
avant-garde and, 242–47 (*see also* avant-garde)
complete absorption of, 250–51
La Construction des Villes and, 193–95
controversy and, 392, 399, 415–19, 429, 431
cubism and, 236 (*see also* cubism)
Eastern travels and, 138, 143, 149
Galerie Druet and, 250–52
Galerie Grégoire and, 235–36
higher goals for, 248–53
impressionism and, 54, 86–87, 244, 254, 268, 289, 588
isms and, 230
key to architecture in, 55
language of architecture and, 44–45, 299–301, 313, 321, 327, 348, 357, 359, 371–73
letters of confession and, 168, 179–80
as machine for emotions, 300
man of letters and, 28
method and, 51, 54–57, 69, 86, 88, 92, 94, 100, 264–76, 284–99, 673
new artistic directions and, 253–59
Ozenfant and, 235–42
Purism and, 261, 264–76, 284–98
realism and, 538–39
Ritter letters and, 219–21, 224–27, 230–43, 246–61
self-image and, 36–37, 77
Théophilos and, 594–95
war and, 185–89
Palace of the League of Nations, 377–78, 387, 391, 393, 400
Palais des Soviets, 411
Palazzo Vecchio, 55
Palio in Sienna, 205
"Palms et Horizons sur Alger" ("Palms and Horizons of Algiers") (Le Corbusier), 586
Pantheon, 80, 331, 391
Paquet, 66
Parade, La (ballet), 41

"Parade, La" (benefit performance), 227
Paris, New York (Villani), 466
Parthenon, 171, 183–84, 468, 645, 648, 684
Acropolis travels and, 109, 112–13, 145, 149–52
language of architecture and, 305–6, 313–15, 319–21, 326–27, 354, 367
Mediterranean style and, 592, 594, 598
poetics and, 386–87, 396, 400, 409–10, 417, 422, 429
search for method and, 59, 70, 89, 286
synthesis of art and, 224, 249, 251
Parthénon, Le: histoire, l'architecture et la sculpture (Boissonnas), 320
patrie, la, 404–6, 499
Paul, Bruno, 77, 89, 95, 101
Peinture Moderne, La (Le Corbusier and Ozenfant), 357–58
Perret, Auguste, 307, 498, 562
Dom-ino scheme and, 193
letters of confession and, 178, 180, 182
personality of, 192
search for method and, 62, 65, 82
synthesis of art and, 208, 213–14, 224, 229, 241–42
Théâtre des Champs-Elysées and, 176, 182, 194, 196, 198
Perret, Gustave, 62, 65, 82
Perriand, Charlotte, 612
Perrin, Léon, 53, 56, 59–60, 75, 85, 706n9
Pessac, 24, 276, 540
Pétain, Philippe, 614
Petite Ville dans le Marais (Ritter), 213
Petit Trianon, 89
Peugeot, 281
Phèdre, 363–64
Piazza del Duomo, 53–54
Picasso, 41, 180, 227, 234, 270
Pierrefeu, François de, 491, 613, 615
Pisa, 53–54
Place de la Concorde, 79, 234, 345, 597
Plans de Paris, Les (Le Corbusier), 34, 683
Plans journal, 491–94, 498, 502, 518, 523, 555, 558, 564, 575
Plans Le Corbusier de Paris, Les (Le Corbusier), 682–83
Poème de l'angle droit (Poem of the Right Angle (Le Corbusier), 680–82
Poëte, Marcel, 208
poetics, 45, 206, 379, 393, 555–56, 621, 626
Apollinaire and, 41–44, 46, 235–36, 246, 254, 265, 268, 298
architecture of language and, 36–40
authorities and, 612–16
books and, 680
desert and, 422–25
law of life and, 23–24, 83
lesson of the gondola and, 425–26
machines and, 413–31 (*see also* machines)
method and, 262, 282, 298
new battles and, 609–11
Paris literary scene and, 40–43
poet as daydreamer and, 605–11
postwar environment and, 43–44
Purism and, 44, 182 (*see also* Purism)
raven-archer symbolism and, 34–35
right angle and, 680–82
romanticism and, 22
of space, 417–20
synthesis of the arts and, 427–30
temps nouveaux and, 606–7, 610
urbanist as poet and, 605–11
walls and, 206
world play and, 21
Poincaré, Henri, 167
language of architecture and, 303–6, 332, 337–38
machines and, 303–6
Purism and, 262–65, 272
Ponsich, Henri, 571, 576
Pont Alexandre III, 346
Pontinia, 600–1
Pont Neuf, 519
Popular Front
Exposition Internationale des Arts et Techniques dans la Vie Moderne and, 532–33, 538–39, 545
French politics and, 532–33, 538–39, 545, 584, 613–14, 618

Précisions sur un état présent de l'architecture et de l'urbanisme (Le Corbusier), 22–23, 26, 33, 392
adventure-tales and, 437–39
airplanes and, 653, 657, 670
American travels and, 435–41, 450, 455–56, 459–61, 478–82
analysis of, 478–85
Baker and, 450–51
clothing fashions and, 455–56
constraint of academies and, 456
culinary art of architecture and, 439–49
death and, 456
education of desire and, 439–49
elements of doctrine in, 618
folklore and, 479–85
food and, 439–49
jazz and, 452–54
neo-syndicalism and, 479–85
regionalism and, 479–85
secular faith and, 618, 653, 657, 670
United States and, 459–61
women's fashion and, 455–56
Prélude: organe mensuel de comité central d'action régionaliste et syndicaliste journal, 596–97

Algeria and, 555, 558, 575
spirit of the thirties and, 491–92, 502, 512, 519, 522, 525, 529, 547
La Ville Radieuse and, 502, 512, 519, 522, 525, 529
Principles of Scientific Management, The (Taylor), 278
Propos d'urbanisme (Le Corbusier), 618
Propp, Vladimir, 110
Propylaea, 320
Prost, Henri, 571, 576, 578, 583, 585
Proust, Marcel, 25
Pulaski Skyway, 474
Purism, 44, 182, 392, 403, 430, 556
aesthetics of, 262–76, 280–87, 298
Algeria and, 556
Almanach d'Architecture Moderne and, 358–59
Après le Cubisme and, 262, 264–68, 298
artist as purist and, 296–98
basic elements of, 266–67
coining of term, 261
elegance of, 263
elitism and, 276–81
folklores and, 420–22
food and, 443
higher goals and, 249
industrial techniques and, 261–62
Jeanneret and, 262–98
language of architecture and, 302, 329, 336, 341, 358–59, 371–72
L'Art Décoratif d'aujourd-hui and, 348–49
L'Esprit Nouveau and, 265, 268–98
machines and, 261–62, 265–67, 272–73, 277, 280–83, 286, 290–94, 298
mathematics and, 262–67, 285–87, 294–98
method and, 261–68, 271–72, 277, 281–87, 296–97
modern science and, 262–63, 278–81
New York and, 471
in outline, 261–62
Ozenfant and, 220, 261–98
painting and, 261, 264–76, 284–98
Poincaré and, 262–65, 272
Ritter and, 278, 296–97
roots of, 262–65
synthesis of art and, 220, 244, 248–49, 261
Valéry and, 261–65, 268, 272, 278, 295
van Doesburg and, 269–70
Vers une Architecture and, 327
La Ville Radieuse and, 504
"Purisme, Le" (Jeanneret and Ozenfant), 285–86
Pyramids, 306

Quadrante journal, 600–1
Quand les Cathédrales étaient blanches: voyage aux pays de timides (When the Cathedrals Were White: A Voyage to the Country of the Timid People) (Le Corbusier), 23, 118, 630, 682, 738n11
American travels and, 435, 439, 446, 452–66, 472, 478
analysis of, 478–85
clothing fashions and, 454–55
construction and, 204–5
Exposition Internationale des Arts et Techniques dans la Vie Moderne and, 537
folklore and, 479–85
food and, 439, 446, 449
jazz and, 452–53
language of architecture and, 331, 334
Mediterranean inspiration and, 552–53, 585, 588
neo-syndicalism and, 479–85
New York and, 427–33, 466–68
poetics and, 378, 410, 430
regionalism and, 479–85
spirit of the thirties and, 536–37, 552
synthesis of art and, 221–25
United States and, 459–62, 466–68
war and, 186, 188

Rabelais, 403
Radiant City, 411
American travels and, 464, 478
secular faith and, 618, 622, 627, 631, 634, 636
spirit of the thirties and, 502, 512, 517–21, 525, 536–43
Radiant Farm, 528–30, 536, 544, 550, 600–1, 615, 652, 659
Radiant Village, 531–32, 601
Raphael, 54
Raynal, Maurice, 284
real estate, 98–103
Reclus, Élisée, 589
regionalism, 479–85
Regional Plan, 572, 575–78, 583, 585–86
reinforced concrete, 66, 211
Dom-ino scheme and, 159
Fischer and, 161
Hennebique and, 227
language of architecture and, 343
method and, 279
Mörsch and, 173–74
Perret and, 182
Ritter letters and, 219–20, 227
SABA and, 173
secular faith and, 627, 663–65, 670
Renaissance aesthetics, 66, 316, 386, 406, 411, 416, 425, 509, 519, 705n78
Renan, Ernest, 117
Renand, J., 466
Renaud, Pierre, 586
"Renouveau dans l'Architecture, Le ("Renewal in

Architecture") (Le Corbusier), 181
"Renouveau de l'Art, Le" (L'Eplattenier), 181
Réponse à Moscou (Reply to Moscow) (Le Corbusier), 502
Reverdy, Pierre, 41
Revit, Paul, 483
"Révolution architecturale accomplie par les techniques modernes, La" ("Architectural Revolution accomplished through modern techniques") (Le Corbusier), 561
Rey, Rodolphe, 561, 571
Rhine, 117–18, 492, 532, 598
Richards, James, 678
Richelieu, 344
Riemerschmied, 102
Ritter, William, 6, 20–21, 29, 33–34, 158, 606, 685, 703nn1,24, 708n67
  Aix-en-Provence and, 255
  avant-garde and, 242–47
  classicism and, 112, 116
  La Construction des Villes and, 193–94, 197–99
  Czeda and, 222, 230, 253
  Dom-ino scheme and, 211–12
  Eastern travels and, 116–19, 121, 123, 129, 131, 149, 153–55
  Edmond de Pury and, 177–78, 184
  Galerie Grégoire and, 235–36
  higher goals and, 242–47
  letters of confession and, 165–81
  letters on synthesis of art and industry to, 220–25, 229–37, 241–59
  as mentor, 53, 158
  new artistic directions and, 253–59
  number of letters to, 33
  Oeuvre Complète and, 29
  Orient and, 116–18
  painting and, 235–42
  prose and, 112
  Purism and, 278, 296–97
  search for method and, 53, 73, 75–76, 78, 83, 93, 278, 296–97
  Slavic houses and, 116
  Switzerland and, 177
  urbanism and, 153–55, 158, 162–64
  World War I and, 187–90
Rivages: Revue de Culture Méditerranéene (Camus), 590
Rivière, Georges Henri, 483
Robert, Paul Théo, 193
Rockefeller Center, 461
Rodin, 359
Rodwin, Lloyd, 5
Rolland, Romain, 26
Roller, Alfred, 185
Romanesque aesthetics, 65, 237–38, 406, 510
Rome, 42, 79, 84, 90, 109, 462, 545, 613, 621, 668
  as a bazaar, 317
  construction and, 197, 206
  E42 Exposition and, 603
  Eastern travels and, 112–15, 118, 145
  Greeks and, 317
  language of architecture and, 315–19, 330–31, 358, 366, 372
  Latin spirit and, 596–604
  "The Lesson of Rome" and, 315–17
  letters of confession and, 180
  Mediterranean style and, 558, 563, 572, 580–81, 596–603
  Pantheon and, 80, 331, 391
  poetics and, 384
  rejection of Gothic and, 114
  Renaissance, 316
  synthesis of art and, 222, 225, 233, 255
  Volta Congress and, 602
"Rome" (Le Corbusier), 596–99
Roneo, 281
Rotival, Maurice, 576, 578, 583, 585
Rougement, Denis de, 489
Rousseau, André, 677
Rousseau, Jean-Jacques, 403
Royer, Jean, 610
Ruskin, 55, 83, 99, 205

SABA (Société d'Application de Béton Armé), 173, 210
Sahara, 450, 554, 556, 558, 564
Said, Edward, 122
"Sainte Alliance des Arts majeurs ou le Grand Art en Gésine" ("Holy Alliance of the major Arts of the Grand Art coming into Being") (Le Corbusier), 427–28
St. Maria's, 317
St. Mark's, 55, 57, 205
St. Peter's, 317, 319
St. Sophia, 116
Saint Sulpice, 222, 391
Salle Wagram, 401
Salon d'Automne, 89, 180–81, 341
Salon des Artistes Française, 378
San Michele, 57
Santa Sophia, 318
Sant'Ella, Antonio, 601
Sarraut, Albert, 559
Satie, Eric, 41, 272
Saugier, 591
Sauvage, 66
Scènes de la vie future (Duhamel), 466
Schinkel, Karl Friedrich, 88–89, 112
Schmitz, 89
Schumacher, Fritz, 104
Schwob, Anatole, 231
"Second Pilgrimage to the Tomb of Mahler,

The" (Ritter), 171
secular faith
airplanes and, 645–75
built biology and, 636–45
elements of doctrine and, 617–34, 645–75
a fellowship of discourse and, 628–31
foundational texts and, 626–28
four routes of travel and, 645–75
laboratory experiments and, 631–34
law of harmony and, 645–50
law of the meander and, 665–67
machines and, 620–21, 624, 628–39, 647, 651, 658–61, 668–74
obstacles to, 634–36
poetics and, 605–17
syntax and, 623
temps nouveaux and, 606–7, 610, 619–23, 633–36, 650, 656–60
war and, 631–34
SEIE (Société d'Enterprise Industrielle et d'Études) (Society of Industrial Enterprise and Studies), 219, 249, 254–55, 275, 278
Sekler, Mary Patricia, 36, 257
Senger, Alexandre de, 28, 433
Sert, José Luis, 678
Seurat, 270, 359
SIC (Sons, Idées, Couleurs) journal, 41
Signac, 117, 138
Signoria of Florence, 205
Sirocco, 173, 564
Sitte, Camillo
La Construction des Villes and, 197–99, 201, 203–6
language of architecture and, 319, 330
L'Eplattenier and, 198
Martin's interpretation of, 156–57, 161, 204
street layouts and, 201, 203
urbanism and, 71–75, 156–57, 168
Sketchbook (Le Corbusier), 76
slaughterhouse projects, 226, 230, 234, 239, 247–48, 278
Slavin, David, 554–55
Small Palais, 406
Smet, Catherine de, 34, 373
socialists, 175, 186, 497, 538
Société des Applications de l'Éverite (Society of Application of Everite), 239
Society for the Well-Being of the Working Classes, 161
Socrates, 264, 363–64
Speer, Albert, 533
Spellman, 231
Spengler, Oswald, 459
spirit of the thirties
Communism and, 490
construction and, 498–501
economic depression and, 489–90, 502
Exposition Internationale des Arts et Techniques dans la Vie Moderne and, 532–51
Fascism and, 490
humanism and, 490
intellectualism of, 489–502
machines and, 490–94, 498–502
neo-syndicalism and, 492–94, 502
peace, war and, 494–98
planning and, 494–98
temps nouveaux and, 490
time for action and, 501–2
La Ville Radieuse and, 502–32
Städtebau Ausstellung, 76
Städtebau journal, 203
Städtebau nach seinen künstlerischen Grundsätzens, Der (City Planning According to Artistic Principles) (Sitte), 156
Stavba journal, 392
Stemolak, Karl, 57
Stijl, de (magazine), 269–70
Still-Life with Book, Glass and Pipe (Le Corbusier), 296–97
Storet, M., 211
Stübben, Joseph, 208
Suisse Libérale, La (newspaper), 400
Suisse Romande aesthetics, 83, 114, 176, 179, 190
Sur les Quatres Routes (the Four Routes) (Le *Corbusier)*, 614–15, 618
airplanes and, 646–47, 651–75
automobiles and, 646–50
elements of doctrine and, 627–33
law of harmony and, 645–51
obstacles to, 635
railroads and, 646–49
ships and, 648–49
Switzerland, 118, 189, 193, 214, 334, 340, 628
decorative art reform and, 158
Dom-ino scheme and, 234
Eternit and, 240
letters of confession and, 176–77
poetics and, 400, 409
Suisse Romande aesthetics and, 83, 114, 176, 179, 190
Zurich, 60, 169, 173, 190, 269, 509, 511, 680

Taylor, F. W., 278, 500, 507
Teige, Karel, 392–99, 417, 433–34, 703n20
Temple of Luxor, 306
Temple of Paestum, 313
temps nouveaux, 25, 28, 46
elements of doctrine and, 621
Exposition Internationale des Arts et Techniques dans la Vie Moderne and,

535–38, 542–48, 585
poetics and, 606–7, 610
as second machine age, 426–27, 439, 462, 484, 490, 502
secular faith and, 606–7, 610, 619–23, 633–36, 650–51, 656–60
spirit of Greece and, 590–93
Tériade, E., 681
Tessenow, Heinrich, 84, 102–3
Théâtre des Champs-Elysées, 176, 182, 194, 196, 198
Théâtre du Vieux Colombier, 179
Théophilos, 594–95
Thought and Movement (Bergson), 282
Thubert, Emmanuel de, 185
Tilleuls, 104
timepieces, 155–56
Times Square, 275
Titian, 54
Treaty of Versailles, 610
Tuileries, the, 345
Tûnovo, 131–32
Turbine Hall, 76–77, 99
Turkey
bazaar and, 140–41
color and, 141–42
Constantinople and, 38, 51, 82, 109, 112–23, 134–43, 152, 168–72, 198–99, 213, 215, 330, 359, 405, 468, 478–79
Eastern travel letters and, 131–45
houses and, 334

Umbdenstock, Gustave, 295, 401–11, 556, 591
Une Maison–Une Palais (A House–A Palace) (Le Corbusier), 540–41
architecture as organism, 383–86
architecture as plant, 380–83
defense of modern architecture and, 377–99
dueling with academics and, 399–413
house as palace and, 380–83
League of Nations project and, 378
machines and, 377, 379–84, 387–89, 393–95
narrative style of, 378–79
reserves of architecture and, 387–92
UNESCO, 678–79
Unité d'Habitation, 37, 533–35, 542–43, 548, 684
United States, 585
blacks and, 449–54
Cathedrals and, 459–62, 466–68
clothing fashions and, 454–56
Great Depression and, 435, 478–79, 489
great waste in, 427–34
inferiority complexes of, 476–77
jazz and, 449–54, 458, 468, 738n13
Museum of Modern Art (MoMA) and, 435
neo-syndicalism and, 492
New York, 466–78
Précisions and, 459–61
radio broadcasts and, 458–59
as salvific catastrophe, 459–67
sexuality and, 473, 476–81
Universal Exposition, 358
Unwin, Raymond, 208
urbanism, 680, 703n1
American travels and, 440, 475–76, 484
Behrens and, 70–71, 76–77, 80–91, 95–101, 106, 112, 116, 156, 163–64, 168, 179, 185, 214, 259, 707n39, 710n105
Brooks and, 160, 164
Cartesian logic and, 22
cellular units and, 160
La Construction des Villes and, 159–68, 175, 193–201, 208–11, 328, 342, 480
construction of cities and, 155–64, 197–200, 208
defining, 71
deurbanization and, 517, 540
Dom-ino scheme and, 21, 159, 190, 193–94, 199, 208–15, 234, 717n67
Eastern travels and, 106, 112, 116, 157
elements of doctrine for, 617–34
evolving ideas on, 47
Exposition of German City-Building and, 97
first appearance of term in French, 155
Fischer and, 161
garden cities and, 24, 76, 81–82, 92–94, 100–7, 160, 162–68, 197, 199, 342–43, 366, 472, 500, 508, 511, 525, 566, 600, 611, 636
German, 69–72, 76–77, 91–97, 102–3, 107, 112
humanism and, 160, 366, 413, 490–91, 619
interior design and, 179–80
land division and, 201
language of architecture and, 39, 324, 328, 342–43, 346, 357–61, 366–67, 372–73
L'Eplattenier and, 155–58, 161–64
letters of confession and, 165–84
man of letters and, 19, 27, 31–39, 46–47
Martin's interpretation of, 156–57
Mediterranean style and, 575–78, 587, 591–93, 596, 599–601
monastery studies and, 160–61
new, 156, 292, 620, 671
new machine age and, 19
Osthaus and, 161–62
poetics and, 45, 206, 262, 282, 298,

379, 392–93, 410–14, 424–25, 431, 555–56, 605–11, 621, 626
popularization of art in public domain in, 103–5
progress and, 182–83
Ritter and, 153–55, 158, 162–64
search for method and, 51, 69–71, 76, 92, 275, 296
secular faith and, 606, 609–24, 627, 636, 644, 651–53, 660, 666, 670
Sitte and, 71–75, 156–57, 168
skyscrapers and, 172, 199, 221, 272, 307, 342, 366, 430, 435, 453–54, 457–58, 461, 464, 466–76, 479, 573, 577, 586, 663
spirit of the thirties and, 490, 494, 497–501, 505, 537–44, 547–50
street layouts and, 201–4
town planning and, 24, 33, 76, 188, 208–9, 335, 341, 617, 628, 633, 636, 643, 650, 657, 671
Voisin Plan and, 343–46, 360–61, 372
Werkbund and, 161–62
Urbanisme (The City of To-morrow) (Le Corbusier), 36, 160, 275, 324, 349, 357–59
airplanes and, 670
"The Centre of Paris" and, 345
"Classification and Choice" and, 333–35
"The Contemporary City of 3 million inhabitants" and, 341–43
"Finance and Realization" and, 345–46
"The Great City Today" and, 329, 335–41
"The Hours of Repose" and, 341–43
"Laboratory Work: An Inquiry into Theory" and, 341
language of architecture and, 328–46
"Newspaper Cuttings and Catchwords" and, 338
"Order" and, 330–31
"Our Technical Equipment" and, 338–41
"The Pack Donkey's Way and Man's Way" and, 329–30
"Permanence" and, 332
"Physic or Surgery" and, 344
resolution of antitheses and, 329–35
"Sensibility Comes into Play" and, 331–32
"The Working Day" and, 341–42
Voisin Plan and, 343–46, 360–61, 372
USSR, 409, 417, 492, 525, 602, 612
bolshoi and, 519–21
intellectualism and, 490
Moscow and, 28, 366, 392, 411, 462, 490, 501–2, 517, 519, 540, 572, 591, 598–99, 616, 621, 631, 652, 657, 670
Palais des Soviets and, 411
worldwide evolution and, 501
utility, 39, 105, 166, 647
construction of cities and, 161, 197–98, 202–3, 207–9
language of architecture and, 351, 354, 361
letters of confession and, 180–82
method and, 265
poetics and, 379–80, 386, 395, 413, 421–22, 430
secular faith and, 606–8

Vago, Giuseppe, 377–78
Valéry, Paul, 28, 30, 624, 725n35, 726n26, 728n91
books and, 25–26
dictum of, 25
on Jeanneret's writing style, 27, 683
language of architecture and, 300, 363
Purism and, 261–65, 268, 272, 278, 295
secular faith and, 624
spirit of the thirties and, 489
Vallette, Alfred, 237, 245
van de Velde, Henry, 77, 115
van Doesburg, Theo, 269–70
Van Gogh, 192
Van Nelle factory, 407
Vassar College, 476
Vauthier, 670
Venice, 55–56, 170, 197, 205–6, 248, 425–26, 599, 601, 613, 679
Verne, Jules, 214
Vers une Architecture (Towards a New Architecture) (Le Corbusier), 25, 272–73, 282, 301, 592
"Architecture" and, 315
"Architecture or Revolution" and, 322–28
constructing a manual for housing and, 302–15
critical assessment of, 326–28
"The Engineer's Aesthetic and Architecture" and, 303
"Eyes which do not See" and, 25, 304–5, 308–11, 313, 656, 728n68
heart of, 301–2
"The Illusion of Plans" and, 315, 317, 319
language of architecture and, 299–328, 393
"The Lessons of Rome" and, 315–17
"Mass Production Houses" and, 322
method of argumentation in, 301–2
"Pure Creation of the Mind" and, 315, 320–22
Purism and, 327
"Regulating Lines" and, 308
Vichy Regime, 555, 586, 612–18, 630, 634, 664
Victory Column, 94
Vienna, 56–62, 129
Vildrac, Charles, 178–80
Villa at d'Auteuil, 275

Villa Favre-Jacot, 169
Villa La Roche, 275
Villani, J., 466
Villa Savoye, 392
Villa Schwob, 234, 249
Villa Stotzer, 57
Ville Contemporaine, 275, 512
Ville Radieuse, La (The Radiant City) (Le Corbusier), 424, 682
airplanes and, 658, 664–65, 671
Algeria and, 505–6, 511, 561, 564, 572–73, 579–82, 593
battle of trees and, 519–23
bolshoi and, 519–21
built biology and, 636, 643–45
civic life and, 525–28
compilation of, 502
elements of doctrine and, 618, 622, 626–27, 631
Exposition Internationale des Arts et Techniques dans la Vie Moderne and, 535–43, 548–50
folklore and, 528–32
introductory chapter of, 502–4
life of a tree/man and, 517–19
limits of cities and, 523–25
Mediterranean style and, 564, 572, 579, 582, 593, 600
modern techniques and, 506–12
money civilization and, 528
"The New Age" and, 514–17
obstacles and, 634–35
peace, war and, 494
politics and, 494, 497–98
Pontinia and, 600
Prélude articles and, 491
Purism and, 504
"Rural Reorganization" and, 528–32
secular faith and, 618, 622, 626, 643–44
spirit of the thirties and, 491, 494, 497, 502, 504–12, 517, 522, 525, 528, 532
tree of knowledge and, 512–14
"tree of life" metaphor of, 504–5, 512, 514–17
USSR and, 520–22, 525
Viollet-le-Duc, 63–64
Voirol, Sebastien, 213
Voisin Plan, 46, 281, 343–46, 360–61, 372
Voltaire, 403
von Senger, M., 400
Voyage d'Orient (Journey to the East) (Le Corbusier), 6, 110–11, 113, 120, 122, 124, 129, 138–39
Voyage d'Orient (Žaknić), 6
Voyage en Grèce, Le (Le Corbusier), 594–96
Voyages d'Allemagne, Les (Le Corbusier), 71–72
Voyages Picturesques (illustrated travel accounts), 109
Voyage to the East (Le Corbusier), 113, 168, 211. *See also* Eastern travels

Wagner, Otto, 57
Walter, Jeanne, 491
watch industry, 155–56
Wells, H. G., 512, 657
Werkbund, 29, 156, 186–88, 224, 719n117
balance between art and machines, 156
education reform in, 106–7
founding of, 96
industrial arts and, 96–98
manifesto of, 176
Nouvelle Section and, 185
principles of, 102, 104
search for method and, 70, 76, 81, 92, 96, 98, 102–7
urbanism and, 161–62
white blind spots, 554–58
Winter, Pierre, 284, 491
World War I era, 44, 191, 209, 265
airplane bombings and, 229
américanisme and, 478
American travels and, 478, 484
Après le Cubisme and, 265
armistice and, 246
boredom of wartime Paris and, 221–25
Cathedral of Reims and, 188
Constantinople and, 189
La Construction des Villes and, 199
constructivism and, 384–85
Eastern travels and, 112, 145
language of architecture and, 311, 346
L'Esprit Nouveau and, 272
Ozenfant and, 233, 261
poetics and, 381, 384
Ritter and, 187–90, 229, 232
secular faith and, 614, 627, 629, 634, 651, 653, 674
spirit of thirties and, 490, 494, 496, 499, 538
World War II era, 5, 34, 40, 46
airplanes and, 657, 670–71
as Apocalypse, 631
laboratory experiments and, 631–34
secular faith and, 609–10, 617, 631, 633, 657, 667, 670–71
Wright, Frank Lloyd, 5

Žaknić, Ivan, 6
Zervos, Christian, 378, 592
Zurich, 60, 169, 173, 190, 269, 509, 511, 680